# ALL·IN·ONE

# A+
## Certification
### EXAM GUIDE
#### THIRD EDITION

## Michael Meyers

**Osborne / McGraw-Hill**
New York • Chicago • San Francisco • Lisbon
London • Madrid • Mexico City • Milan • New Delhi
San Juan • Seoul • Singapore • Sydney • Toronto

Osborne/**McGraw-Hill**
2600 Tenth Street
Berkeley, California 94710
U.S.A.

To arrange bulk purchase discounts for sales promotions, premiums, or fund-raisers, please contact Osborne/**McGraw-Hill** at the above address. For information on translations or book distributors outside the U.S.A., please see the International Contact Information page immediately following the index of this book.

### A+ All-in-One Certification Exam Guide, Third Edition

67890 DOC DOC 01987654321

Book p/n 0-07-212677-9 and CD p/n 0-07-212678-7
parts of

ISBN 0-07-212679-5

| | |
|---|---|
| **Publisher** | **Copy Editor** |
| Brandon A. Nordin | Jan Jue |
| | Claire Splan |
| **Vice President & Associate Publisher** | |
| Scott Rogers | **Proofreader** |
| | Stefany Otis |
| **Acquisitions Editor** | |
| Michael Sprague | **Compositor and Indexer** |
| | MacAllister Publishing Services, LLC |
| **Project Editor** | |
| Betsy Manini | **Graphic Artists** |
| | Michael Mueller |
| **Acquisitions Coordinator** | Beth Young |
| Paulina Pobocha | |
| | **Cover Design** |
| **Technical Editor** | Greg Scott |
| Scott Jernigan | |

# DEDICATION

This book is dedicated to everyone whose idea
of a red-hot Saturday night
is playing with PCs.

# ACKNOWLEDGMENTS

I like pain. That must be it. Suffering through the Second Edition wasn't enough, so here's the Third Edition of this book. Thanks to the following folks who helped make this one happen.

**To my good friend and in-house editor, Scott Jernigan**: May Lallace and Cantarius once again hunt Kodiaks in West Karanas—but next time please stay away from hill giants. You remain *Da Bomb*, but you're still buying the Guinness!

**To my friend and Osborne/McGraw-Hill acquisitions editor, Michael Sprague**: Thanks for the cattle prod and dog-training collar, but why did you give it to Scott instead of me? Seriously, thanks to you, Paulina Pobocha, and the rest of the New York crew for the fine job.

**To the team at Total Seminars Houston HQ—Dudley, Janelle, Cary, Roger, Dana, Amber, Martin, Richard, and of course Bambi**: I couldn't have done it without you!

**To Betsy Manini and her superb crews at Osborne/McGraw-Hill on the Left Coast and MacAllister Publishing Services, LLC in Indianapolis**: Thanks so much for the incredible work you folks did.

**To my Readers**: Keep the ideas, the complaints, and the compliments coming. I enjoy them all!

**And last, but first in my heart**: Thanks Alison and Emily for putting up with yet another insane book project.

Mike Meyers

# ABOUT THE AUTHOR

**Michael Meyers** is the industry's leading authority on A+ Certification. He is the president and founder of Total Seminars, LLC, a major provider of PC and network repair seminars for thousands of organizations throughout the world and a member of CompTIA.

# CONTENTS

## Chapter 2 Microprocessors        51

# Chapter 3 RAM      147

# Chapter 4 Motherboards and BIOS      193

# Chapter 5 Expansion Bus      259

# Chapter 17 Modems    1039

# Chapter 18 Portable PCs    1071

## Chapter 19  Printers                                                   1105

## Chapter 20  Networks                                                   1143

## Index                                                                  1219

## International Contact Information                                       1267

## About the CD                                                           1268

# INTRODUCTION

In this chapter, you will

- Understand the importance of A+ Certification
- Discover the structure and goals of the exam
- Get the *Where*, *When*, and *How Much* for the exams
- Plan a strategy to pass

## The Path to A+ Certification

Every profession requires specialized skills. If you want to *get* or *keep* a job that requires those specialized skills, you need some type of certification or license. If you want a job fixing automobiles, for example, you get the *Automotive Service Excellence* (ASE) Certification. If you want to prepare companies' taxes, you get your *Certified Public Accountant* (CPA) certification.

Nearly every profession has some method that enables you to show your competence and ability to perform at a certain level. You must pass some type of test to prove that you have the necessary skills to receive some piece of paper or pin or membership card that you can show to potential clients or employers. This certification gives those clients or employers at least a level of confidence that you can do what you say you can do for them. Without this certification, either you will not work in that profession, or nobody will trust you to do the work. Until recently, PC technicians have been the exception to this rule.

Since the inception of microcomputers in the late 1970s, PC technicians have had no common way to show clients or employers that they know what to do under the hood of a personal computer. Sure, there have been vendor-specific certifications, but the only way to get them was to get a job at an authorized warranty or repair facility first, and then get the certification. Not that there's anything wrong with vendor-specific training; it's just that no one manufacturer has taken enough market share to make IBM or Compaq training something that works for any job. (Then there is always that little detail of getting the job first before you can get certified!)

The software/networking side of our business does not suffer from the same lack of certifications. Due to the dominance of certain companies at one time or another (for example, Microsoft and Novell), the vendor-specific certifications have provided a great way to get and keep a job. For example, Microsoft's *Microsoft Certified Professional* (MCP) and *Microsoft Certified Systems Engineer* (MCSE), Novell's *Certified Novell Administrator* (CNA) and *Certified Novell Engineer* (CNE), as well as a few niche players like Cisco's *Cisco Certified Internetwork Expert* (CCIE) have opened the doors for many who have decided to pursue those certifications.

But what about the person who runs around all day replacing floppies, repartitioning hard drives, upgrading device drivers, and building systems? What about the PC hobbyists who decide to make the jump and want to get paid for their skills? What about the folks who, because they had the audacity to show that they knew the difference between a CMOS and a C: prompt, find themselves with a new title like "PC Support Technician" or "Electronic Services Specialist?" On the other hand, how about the worst title of them all: "The Person Who Doesn't Get a Nickel Extra but Who Fixes the Computers?"

For years, the *Information Technology* (IT) industry had no nationally recognized certification for PC technicians. Techs did not have a piece of paper to put on their wall or a pin to stick on their shirt to show they knew their stuff . . . until now. Welcome to **A+ Certification!**

## What Is A+ Certification?

A+ Certification is an industrywide, vendor-neutral certification program developed and sponsored by the *Computing Technology Industry Association* (CompTIA). The A+ Certification shows that you have a basic competence in supporting microcomputers. The test covers generally assumed knowledge held by a technician with six months of full-time PC support experience. You achieve this certification by taking two computer-based, multiple-choice examinations. A+ Certification enjoys wide recognition throughout the computer industry and significantly improves a technician's ability to secure and keep employment. To date, over 260,000 technicians have become A+ Certified, making it the most popular of all IT certifications.

## Who Is CompTIA?

CompTIA is a nonprofit, industry trade association based in Lombard, Illinois. It consists of over 8,000 computer resellers, *value-added resellers* (VARs), distributors, manufacturers, and training companies from all over the world.

CompTIA provides a forum for networking (as in meeting people), represents the interests of its members to the government, and provides certifications for many different aspects of the computer industry. CompTIA sponsors the A+, Network+, i-Net+, Server+, and other certifications. CompTIA works hard to watch the IT industry and constantly looks to provide new certifications to meet the ongoing demand from its membership. Check out the CompTIA Web site at **http://www.comptia.org** for details on the other certifications that you can obtain from CompTIA.

Virtually every company of consequence in the IT industry is a member of CompTIA. Here are a few of the biggies:

| | | | |
|---|---|---|---|
| 3Com | Adobe | AST | Digital |
| Black Box | Canon | Compaq | Hewlett-Packard |
| Epson | Fujitsu | Hayes | Lexmark |
| IBM | Intel | Iomega | Minolta |
| Lotus | Micro House | Microsoft | Novell |
| NEC | NETGEAR | Netscape | Peachtree |
| Oki Data | Oracle | Panasonic | Symantec |
| Rockwell | Sun Microsystems | Sybex | AT&T |
| Toshiba | Total Seminars, LLC (that's my company) | Plus about 8,000 more! | |

CompTIA began offering A+ Certification back in 1993. When it first debuted, the IT industry largely ignored A+ Certification. Over the course of the last few years, however, CompTIA has managed to position A+ Certification to the point where today it reigns as the *de facto* requirement for entrance into the PC industry. Many companies require A+ Certification for all of their PC support technicians, and the A+ Certification is becoming widely recognized both in the United States and internationally. Additionally, many other certifications recognize the A+ certification and use it as credit toward their certifications.

## The New A+ Certification Exams Release

CompTIA must occasionally update the A+ exams to reflect the change in the skills expected of a technician with six months experience. In January 2001, CompTIA released the current version of the A+ exams. **This book covers all you need to pass the new 2001 revisions of the A+ Certification exams.**

## How Do I Become A+ Certified?

Simple, you pass two computer-based, multiple-choice exams. No prerequisites are required for taking the A+ Certification exams. There is no required training course, and there are no training materials to buy. You *do* have to pay a testing fee and take the two exams. You will immediately know whether you have passed or failed. If you pass both exams, you are an "A+ Certified Service Technician." There are no requirements for professional experience. You do not have to go through an Authorized Training Center. There are no annual dues. There are no continuing education requirements. You pass, you are in. That's it. Now for the details.

The two exams are called *A+ Core Hardware* and *A+ Operating System Technologies*. The Core Hardware exam concentrates on the aspects of the PC that are not operating-system specific. This test is primarily a hardware identification and configuration exam. The Operating Systems exam concentrates on the organization, operation, function, and troubleshooting of Windows 9*x* and Windows 2000 systems with a significant understanding of the use of these operating systems at the command-prompt level. This exam also includes very basic network and Internet configuration questions.

## What Are the Tests Like and How Are They Structured?

Both of the exams are extremely practical with little or no interest in theory. All questions are multiple choice or "click on the right part of the picture" questions. You may take either test first. Although you may take the exams at separate times, most people schedule both exams in one session.

The A+ exams are presented in *Computerized Adaptive Testing* (called *CAT* or more commonly just *adaptive*) format. The adaptive exam format greatly shortens the testing but takes a little bit of explaining to understand.

**NOTE** CompTIA generally debuts new or revised exams as standard, non-adaptive multiple-choice exams. They switch to adaptive format when they have acquired sufficient statistical data. Check the CompTIA web site for current details before scheduling your exams.

From the viewpoint of the test taker, an adaptive exam looks exactly like a regular computerized exam. The questions still use a multiple choice or "click the right spot" format. The only significant difference lies in the fact that once you answer a question and move on to the next one, you may not go back to review any previous questions. Additionally, adaptive exams often seem quite short—usually only 15 to 20 questions.

Even though an adaptive exam looks much like a regular exam, it contains many important differences "under the hood." The main difference between a regular exam and an adaptive exam lies in the difficulty level of each question. Each question has a difficulty level (that is, easy, medium, or difficult). Answering a more difficult question scores more points than answering a simple question. CompTIA uses *Subject Matter Experts* (SMEs) to write the questions and even to determine what sort of questions the exams should ask. The SMEs determine the difficulty level of each question.

## Core Hardware Exam

The Core exam consists of 20 to 30 questions. The adaptive score scale ranges from 100 to 900. You need at least a 445 to pass. All of the Core exam questions fit into one of six areas or *domains*. The number of questions for each domain is based on the percentages shown next.

| | |
|---|---|
| Installation, Configuration, and Upgrading | 30% |
| Diagnosing and Troubleshooting | 30% |
| Preventive Maintenance | 5% |
| Motherboard/Processors/Memory | 15% |
| Printers | 10% |
| Basic Networking | 10% |

The Core Hardware exam tests you on your understanding of basic PC hardware. You should know how to recognize, clean, handle, install, diagnose, understand the function of, and know the different types of each of these components:

- CPUs
- RAM
- Motherboards
- Power supplies
- ROM/CMOS
- Expansion buses
- Floppy drives
- IDE drives
- SCSI devices
- CD-ROM drives
- Video cards
- Monitors
- Modems
- Printers
- Cables and connectors
- Laptops
- Network hubs and cabling

Basically, you should be able to install any device into a PC and completely assemble a standard PC. You should recognize every cable, every connector, and every plug used in a PC. The Core exam expects that you are comfortable with basic troubleshooting. You should be able to pick an obvious first step for a broad cross-section of symptoms linked to the previously mentioned hardware and software. You should be comfortable with the tools used for PC assembly/disassembly.

The Core Hardware exam tests your knowledge of I/O addressing, IRQs, and DMA. You need to know the I/O addresses and IRQs assigned to COM and LPT ports. Furthermore, the exams cover the default functions for all IRQs and DMA, as well as the most common I/O addresses. You must be able to look at a diagram for jumpers or switches and properly set them for all possible I/O address, IRQ, or DMA combinations. The exam assumes a good knowledge of basic binary, because many switches and jumpers use binary.

The network section covers a few basic issues, such as recognizing the different types of network cabling and their capacities/limits. You should know the different topologies and understand their benefits and weaknesses. The exam tests on the different protocols used and when to use one protocol over another. Finally, you should be able to diagnose basic network problems.

You should know how to use a *Volt-Ohm Meter* (VOM) to test power supplies. The A+ Core Hardware exam also requires you to be comfortable with the control of *electrostatic discharge* (ESD) and *electromagnetic interference* (EMI).

The following is an example of the type of questions you will see on the exam:

---

A dot-matrix printer is printing blank pages. Which item should you check first?

**A.** Printer drivers
**B.** Platen
**C.** Print head
**D.** Ribbon

The correct answer is D, the Ribbon. You can make an argument for any of the others, but common sense (and skill as a PC technician) tells you to check the simplest possibility first.

---

## Operating System Technologies Exam

The Operating System Technologies exam consists of 20 to 30 questions. The adaptive score scale ranges from 100 to 900. You need at least a 465 to pass. The Operating System Technologies exam follows on from the Core Hardware exam, assuming all of the same hardware and software knowledge that you need to pass the Core Hardware exam. However, the Operating System Technologies exam concentrates exclusively on the understanding of Windows 9*x* and Windows 2000. All of the Operating System Technologies exam questions fit into one of four domains. The number of questions for each domain is based on the following percentages:

| | |
|---|---|
| OS Fundamentals | 30% |
| Installation, Configuration, and Upgrading | 15% |
| Diagnosing and Troubleshooting | 40% |
| Networks | 15% |

From a hardware standpoint, you will be expected to know how to install and configure all of the hardware devices mentioned in the Core Hardware exam into a Windows 9*x* or Windows 2000. This includes non–*Plug and Play* (PnP) devices and resource conflicts in a PnP environment, so you must have a strong understanding of manual configuration of system resources. The test does not require DOS or Windows 3.*x* knowledge, but it does expect you to have strong command prompt skills. Furthermore, the exam tests your ability to work with older generation configuration files that both Windows 9*x* and Windows 2000 still support, such as CONFIG.SYS, AUTOEXEC.BAT, SYSTEM.INI, and WIN.INI. You must also possess a working knowledge of many command prompt commands. Last, the specter of DOS memory management still looms on the exam. Although that interest focuses on supporting DOS applications under Windows 9*x* and Windows 2000, you must still understand many DOS-centric terms such as conventional, extended, and expanded memory! To that end, I've added two chapters: Chapter 9, "DOS" and Chapter 12, "DOS Memory in a Windows World." Do not skip these chapters if you want to pass the A+ Operating System Technologies exam.

This exam tests your knowledge of system diagnosing and troubleshooting. You need to recognize and know how to fix a large number of boot errors in Windows 9*x* or Windows 2000. Also, you should know how to defragment and scan a drive for errors using standard Windows tools. Last, make sure you can diagnose *General Protection Faults* (GPFs), illegal operations, and system lockup issues.

Another major portion of the exam tests your ability to handle the installation and upgrading of Windows systems, including handling of problems that may take place during these processes. This includes a deep knowledge of all the pertinent boot files for Windows 9*x* and Windows 2000, handling PnP as well as non–PnP (legacy) devices, and the ability to make emergency repair disks/startup disks in all versions of Windows.

The Operating System Technologies exam asks a number of questions regarding system optimization. This includes DOS memory management, caching, and power management. You will be tested on your ability to configure hardware, CMOS, boot files, and TSRs to optimize a system properly.

**NOTE** CompTIA has and will make changes to the content and passing grade for the exams at any time—don't assume they'll wait for a major revision. Always check the CompTIA web site before scheduling your exams. Be prepared!

## How Do I Take the Tests?

Prometric/Thompson (formerly known as Sylvan Prometric) and *Virtual University Enterprises* (VUE) administer the actual A+ testing. There are thousands of Prometric and VUE testing centers across the United States and Canada as well as in over 75 other countries around the world. You may take the exam at any testing center. In the United States and Canada, call Prometric at 800-77MICRO or VUE at 877-551-7587 to schedule the exams and to locate the nearest testing center. International customers should go to CompTIA's Web site at **www.comptia.org** and go to "contact your test vendor" on the A+ Certification page. This page lists the contacts for each country by region.

You must pay for the exam when you call to schedule. Be prepared to sit on hold for a while. Have your social security number (or international equivalent) and a credit card ready when you call. Both Prometric and VUE will be glad to invoice you, but you won't be able to take the test until they receive full payment. Although both Prometric and VUE offer complete listings of all available testing centers online, only VUE offers you the ability to select the closest training center and schedule your exams online.

**www.prometric.com**
**www.vue.com**

If you require any special needs, both Prometric and VUE will be able to accommodate you, although your selection of testing locations may be a bit more limited.

## How Much Does the Test Cost?

The cost of the exam depends on whether you work for a CompTIA member or not. Also, there are discounts for taking both exams at once. At this writing, the cost for non-CompTIA members is $132 (U.S.) for one exam or $264 (U.S.) for two exams together. International prices vary; contact the CompTIA Web site for international pricing. Of course, the prices are subject to change without notice, so always check the CompTIA Web site for current pricing!

Very few people pay full price for the exam. Virtually every organization that provides A+ training and testing offers discount vouchers. Total Seminars (800-446-6004 or 281-922-4166) is one place to get discount vouchers. If you work for a CompTIA member, you can get discount vouchers at a very steep discount. No one should ever pay full price for A+ exams!

You must pass both exams within 90 days to be A+ Certified. You don't have to pass the Core Hardware exam before you can take the Operating System Technologies exam. If you pass one exam and fail another, you must repay and retake the other exam within 90 days. You must pay for every test you take, whether you pass or fail. If you fail to pass both exams within 90 days, you will have to pay for and retake *both* exams.

## How to Pass the A+ Exams

The single most important aspect to remember about the A+ Certification is that CompTIA designed the exams to test the knowledge of a technician with only six months experience—so keep it simple! The tests aren't interested in your ability to set CAS DRAM timings in CMOS manually or whether you can explain the difference between the Intel 430BX and i820 chipset. Don't bother with a lot of theory—the fact that you can do hex-to-binary conversions in your head won't help a bit. Think in terms of practical knowledge, read the book, take the practice tests on the CD in the back of the book, review any topics you miss, and you'll pass, no problem.

Is it safe to assume that it has probably been a while since you've had to take an exam? Along the same line, is it also safe to assume that it has been a while since you've had to *study* for an exam? If these statements are true, you are probably going to want to read the next sections. These show you a proven strategy to get you through and to pass the A+ exams. Try it. It works.

## Obligate Yourself

The very first step that you should take is to schedule yourself for the exam. Have you ever heard the old adage "Heat and pressure make diamonds?" Well, if you don't give yourself a little "heat," you'll end up procrastinating and unnecessarily delaying taking the exams. Even worse, you may not take the exams. Do yourself a favor. Determine the amount of time you need to study (see next), and then call Prometric or VUE and schedule the exams. When you know the tests are coming up, it makes it a lot easier to turn off the television and crack open the book. Keep in mind that Prometric and VUE let you schedule an exam up to only a few weeks in advance. If you schedule an exam and can't make it, you must reschedule at least a day in advance or you lose your money.

## Set Aside the Right Amount of Study Time

After helping thousands of techs get their A+ Certification, we at Total Seminars have developed a pretty good feel about the amount of study time needed to pass the A+ Certification exams. The following table quantifies the time to help you plan how much study you must commit to the A+ Certification exams. Keep in mind that these are averages. If you're not a great student or if you're a little on the nervous side, add another 10 percent. Equally, if you're the type who can learn an entire semester of geometry in one night, reduce the numbers by 10 percent. To use this table, just circle the values that are most accurate for you, and add them up to get the number of study hours.

**Table 1**   Study Hours Guide

| Amount of Experience | None | Once or Twice | Every Now and Then | Quite a Bit |
|---|---|---|---|---|
| Installing any type of card | 16 | 14 | 8 | 2 |
| Installing hard drives | 6 | 3 | 2 | 1 |
| Installing SCSI devices | 8 | 6 | 4 | 2 |
| Installing modems | 6 | 6 | 4 | 2 |
| Installing printers | 4 | 3 | 2 | 0 |
| Installing RAM | 8 | 6 | 4 | 2 |
| Installing CPUs | 6 | 6 | 4 | 3 |
| Fixing printers | 5 | 5 | 3 | 3 |
| Fixing monitors | 5 | 5 | 3 | 1 |
| Complete system builds | 12 | 10 | 8 | 4 |
| Using DOS | 8 | 8 | 6 | 2 |
| DOS memory management (EMM386, PIF files) | 10 | 10 | 6 | 4 |
| Using Windows 95, 98, or ME | 4 | 4 | 2 | 1 |
| Installing Windows 95 | 6 | 5 | 4 | 3 |
| Using Windows 2000 | 4 | 4 | 2 | 1 |
| Configuring a dial-up Internet connection | 4 | 4 | 2 | 0 |
| Installing a sound card | 2 | 2 | 1 | 0 |
| Installing a network card/network | 12 | 8 | 4 | 1 |
| Using a Volt-Ohm Meter | 4 | 3 | 2 | 1 |

To that value, add hours based on the number of months of direct, professional experience you have had supporting PCs:

| Months of Direct, Professional Experience… | To Your Study Time… |
| --- | --- |
| 0 | Add 50 hrs |
| Up to 6 | Add 20 hrs |
| 6 to 12 | Add 10 hrs |
| Over 12 | Add 0 hrs |

A total neophyte usually needs around 200 hours of study time. An experienced tech shouldn't need more than 40 hours.

Total hours for you to study is _____.

## Studying for the Test

Now that you have a feel as to how long it's going to take, you should have a strategy for study. The following strategy has proven itself to be an excellent game plan for getting the knowledge of the study materials into your head. Try it. It works!

This strategy has two paths. The first path is designed for highly experienced technicians who have a strong knowledge of PCs and want to concentrate on "just what is on the exam." Let's call this group the "Fast Track" group. The second path, and the one I'd strongly recommend, is geared toward the people like me—the ones who want to know why things work, who want to completely wrap their arms around a concept as opposed to just regurgitating answers to pass the A+ exams. Let's call this group the "Brainiacs."

To provide for both types of learners, I have broken down most of the chapters into three distinct parts:

- **Historical/Conceptual**   It's not on the A+ exams, but it's knowledge that will help you understand what is on the A+ exams more clearly.

- **Test Specific**   Topics that clearly fit under the A+ domains.

- **Beyond A+**   More advanced issues that probably will not be on the A+ exams.

The beginning of each of these areas is clearly marked with a large banner that looks like this:

## Historical/Conceptual

If you consider yourself a Fast Tracker, skip everything but the Test Specific areas in each chapter. After reading the Test Specific section, jump immediately to the end of chapter questions. All end of chapter questions concentrate on information in the Test Specific section. If you run into problems, review the Historical/Conceptual sections in that chapter. Be aware that you may need to skip back to previous chapters to get the Historical/Conceptual information you need for a later chapter.

 **NOTE** Not all chapters will have all three sections!

After going through every chapter as described, do the free practice exams on the CD-ROM that accompanies the book. First do them in Practice mode, and then switch to Adaptive. Once you start hitting in the 750 to 800 range, go take the test!

For the brainiacs, first read the book, *the whole book*. Read it as though you're reading a novel—start on page 1 and go all the way through. Don't skip around on the first read-through, even if you are a highly experienced tech. There are terms and concepts that build on each other—skipping around will make you confused, and you'll just end up closing the book and firing up your favorite PC game. Your goal on this first read is to understand concepts, to understand the "whys" and not just the "hows." It is very helpful to have a PC nearby as you read. You can stop and inspect the PC to see a piece of hardware or try a particular concept in the real world. As you read about floppy drives, for example, inspect the cables. Do they look like the book? Is there a variation? Why? It is imperative that you understand why you are doing something. Don't let yourself be limited to just knowing how to do it.

Second, read the Web chapter on "Essential Windows." The A+ Certification exams assume that you have basic user skills. The exams really try to trick you with questions on processes that you may do every day and not really think about. Here's a classic: "In order to move a file from the C:\WINDOWS folder to the A:\ using Windows Explorer, what key must you hold down while dragging the file?" The Web chapter covers the user-level skills in Windows, including the following:

- Recognizing all the components of the standard Windows Desktop
- Manipulating windows—resizing, moving, and so on
- Creating, deleting, renaming, moving, and copying files and folders
- Understanding file extensions and their relationship with program associations
- Using common keyboard shortcuts/hot-keys

You can find the "Essential Windows" Web chapter at the following addresses: **www.osborne.com** or **www.totalsem.com**. Don't miss this chapter!

Here's one of the greatest secrets in the computer business: "Everything old is new again." Sure, technology continues to get faster and data paths wider, but the underlying technology, the core of what makes your PC, your printer, and your modem operate, has changed very little since their inception 20 years ago. This leads to the last point on the initial read-through. You will notice a lot of historical data—Historical/Conceptual sections—that you may be tempted to skip. Don't skip it! By understanding how some of the older stuff worked, you can appreciate the need and the function of most components on your PC.

After you've completed the first read-through, go through the book again. This time try to knock out one chapter at a sitting. Concentrate on the Test Specific sections. Get a highlighter and mark the phrases and sentences that bring out major points. Take a hard look at the pictures and tables, noting how they elaborate the concepts.

Once you have read and studied the material in the book, check your knowledge with the practice exams included on the CD-ROM in the back of the book. The exams can be taken in practice mode, test mode, or adaptive mode. In practice mode, you are allowed to check references in the book (if you want) before you answer each question, and each question is graded immediately. In test mode, you answer all the questions and are given a test score. The adaptive mode precisely emulates a real adaptive exam. In each case there is a results summary that tells you what questions you missed, what the right answer is, and where to study.

**NOTE** The CD-ROM includes extra exams available for a nominal fee for those of you who like extra questions. You don't need them to pass the exam—but if you want some extra practice, they're a great deal!

Use the results of those exams to see where you need to bone up and try them again. Continue taking additional exams and reviewing the topics you miss until you are consistently scoring in the 750 to 800 range. When you get there, you are ready to pass that A+ exam!

If you have any problems, any questions, or if you just want to argue about something, feel free to send an e-mail to the author—**michaelm@totalsem.com**.

For any other information you might need, contact CompTIA directly at their Web site: **www.comptia.org**.

Good Luck!
Mike Meyers

# The Visible PC

In this chapter, you will

- See the major components of a PC
- Understand the different connectors in a PC
- Recognize the most common devices inside a PC
- Learn how to set jumpers and switches

Mastering the craft of the PC technician requires you to learn a lot of details about a zillion things. Even the most basic PC contains hundreds of discrete hardware components, each with its own set of characteristics, shapes, sizes, colors, connections, etc. By the end of this book, you will be able to discuss all of these components in detail.

In order to understand the details, you often need to understand the big picture first. This chapter should help you to recognize the main components of a typical PC and to understand their function. You will also see all the major connectors, plugs, and sockets, and learn to recognize a particular part simply by seeing what type of connector attaches to that part. Even if you are an expert, do not skip this chapter! It introduces a large number of terms that will be used throughout the rest of the book. Many of these terms you will know, but some you will not, so take some time and read it.

It is handy, although certainly not required, to have a PC that you can take the lid off and inspect as you progress. So get thee to a screwdriver, grab your PC, take off the lid, and see if you can recognize the various components as you read about them.

**CAUTION** If you decide to open a PC while reading this chapter, you must take proper steps to avoid the greatest killer of PCs—*electrostatic discharge* (ESD). ESD simply means the passage of a static electrical charge into your PC. Have you ever rubbed a balloon against your shirt, making the balloon stick to you? That's a classic example of static electricity. When that charge dissipates, you may not notice it happening—although on a cool, dry day, I've been shocked so hard by touching a doorknob that I could see a big, blue spark! If you decide to open a PC as you read this chapter, jump ahead to Chapter 6 on power supplies, and read up on ESD and how to prevent it—the life you save may be your PC's!

# CPU

The *central processing unit* (CPU), also called the *microprocessor,* performs all the calculations that take place inside a PC. CPUs come in a variety of shapes and sizes, as shown in Figure 1-1.

**Figure 1-1**
Typical CPUs

Modern CPUs generate a lot of heat and thus require a cooling fan or heat sink in order to run cool (Figure 1-2). You can usually remove this cooling device, although some CPU manufacturers sell the CPU with a fan permanently attached.

**Figure 1-2** Installed CPU under a fan

CPUs have a make and model, just like automobiles do. When talking about a particular car, for example, most people speak in terms of a Ford Taurus or a Toyota Camry. When they talk about CPUs, people say Intel Pentium III or AMD Athlon. Over the years, there have been only a few major CPU manufacturers, just as there are few auto manufacturers. The two most common makes of CPUs used in PCs are AMD and Intel, although other makers with names such as Cyrix and IDT have come and gone.

Although only a few manufacturers of CPUs have existed, those manufacturers have made hundreds of models of CPUs. Some of the more common models made over the years have names such as 8088, 286, 386, 486, Pentium, Pentium Pro, K5, K6, 6x86, Pentium II, Celeron, Athlon, and Pentium III (although most of these names are now obsolete). In the early years of CPUs, competing CPU manufacturers would sometimes make exactly the same model, so you could get an AMD 486 or an Intel 486 (Figure 1-3). This is no longer true, although some models function similarly, such as the Intel Pentium and the AMD K6.

CPUs measure potential performance with a *clock speed*, much like an automobile has a (theoretical) top speed listed on the speedometer. Manufacturers determine the clock speed—measured in *megahertz* (MHz)—at the factory. The first CPU used in PCs had a clock speed of approximately 4.77MHz. Today's CPUs have clock speeds of approxi-

**Figure 1-3** The AMD 486 and Intel 486—the same model—made by competing companies.

mately 1,000MHz. One thousand MHz equals 1 *gigahertz* (GHz), so the latest CPUs are mentioned often in terms of GHz. When talking about a CPU, people often cite the make, model, and clock speed, as in an 833MHz Intel Premium III or a 1.2GHz AMD Athlon.

Manufacturers produce CPUs of the same make and model with many different clock speeds (Figure 1-4). One particular make and model of CPU may come in five or six different speeds. The main reasons for picking one speed over another are the needs of your system and the thickness of your wallet.

**Figure 1-4** Two nearly identical Intel Celeron CPUs—300MHz on the left, and 333MHz on the right.

Finally, CPUs come in different packages. The most common packages are called *Pin Grid Array* (PGA) and *Single Edge Cartridge* (SEC). You cannot recognize a CPU solely by its package. Figure 1-5 shows two examples of the popular Celeron processor. Even though these two CPUs are virtually identical in terms of speed and power, they look quite different from each other.

**Figure 1-5**
Intel Celeron CPUs

# RAM

*Random-access memory* (RAM) stores programs and data currently being used by the CPU. RAM is measured in units called *bytes.* Modern PCs have many millions of bytes of RAM, so RAM is measured in units called *megabytes* (MB). An average PC will usually have from 32MB to 128MB of RAM, although you may see PCs with far more or far less RAM. RAM has been packaged in many different ways over the years. The most current package is called a 168-pin DIMM (Dual Inline Memory Module). An older type of RAM package—basically obsolete but added here for completeness—is called SIMM (Single Inline Memory Module). Figure 1-6 shows examples of a DIMM (top) and a SIMM (bottom).

**Figure I-6**
DIMM and SIMM
RAM packages

SIMMs and DIMMs come in several different physical packages. The two most common sizes of SIMMs are 30-pin and 72-pin, so-named for the number of metal contacts along one edge (Figure 1-7). It is easy to tell the difference between them, as the 72-pin SIMM is much larger than the 30-pin SIMM. 72-pin SIMMs are more modern and can hold more RAM than 30-pin SIMMs. 72-pin SIMMs can also transfer information to and from the CPU faster than 30-pin SIMMs can.

Three sizes of DIMMs are also available and used by PCs: a 168-pin DIMM and two sizes of *Small Outline* (SO) DIMMs—a 72-pin and a 144-pin version. Figure 1-8 shows a 168-pin DIMM (top) and a 72-pin SO DIMM (bottom). The SO DIMMs' small size makes them very popular in laptops. Most desktop PCs sold today use only the 168-pin DIMMs, although millions of older PCs sport SIMMs.

**Figure I-7**
SIMMs—30- and
72-pin

**Figure 1-8**
Examples of 168-pin
DIMM and 72-pin
SO DIMM

# Motherboard

You can compare a motherboard to the chassis of an automobile. In a car, everything connects to the chassis either directly or indirectly. In a PC, everything connects to the motherboard either directly or indirectly. A *motherboard* is a thin, flat piece of circuit board, usually green or gold colored, and often slightly larger than a typical piece of notebook paper (Figure 1-9).

**Figure I-9**   A bare motherboard

A motherboard contains a number of special sockets that accept various PC components. Motherboards provide sockets for the microprocessor (Figure 1-10); sockets for RAM (Figure 1-11); sockets to provide power (Figure 1-12); connectors for floppy drives and hard drives (Figure 1-13); and connectors for external devices, such as mice, printers, joysticks, and keyboards (Figure 1-14).

**Figure 1-10**
Socket for CPU

**Figure 1-11**
Sockets for RAM

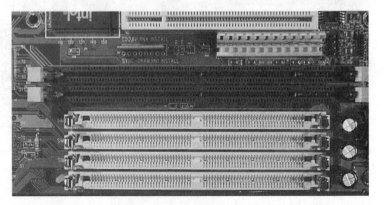

**Figure 1-12**
Sockets for
power plug

**Figure 1-13**   Floppy and hard drive connectors

Every motherboard has a few components soldered directly onto the motherboard (Figure 1-15).

Motherboards use tiny wires, called *traces,* to link together electrically the various components of the PC (Figure 1-16).

All  motherboards use multipurpose *expansion slots* that enable you to add optional components. Your PC accepts thousands of different types of optional devices, including scanners, modems, network cards, sound cards, and tape backups. The expansion slots create the connection that enables optional devices to communicate with the PC.

**Figure 1-14**
Various external
connectors

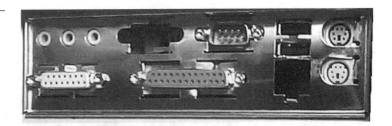

**Figure 1-15**
Soldered
components

**Figure 1-16**
Traces

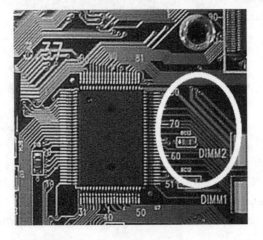

A device that connects to an expansion slot is generically called an "expansion card," or simply a "card." Different types of expansion slots exist for different types of cards (Figure 1-17).

The PC industry long ago standardized the position of the expansion slots and external components. The motherboard mounts inside the box or case, which is the part of the PC that you actually see (Figure 1-18).

**Figure 1-17**
Expansion slots—
one slot has a
card inserted

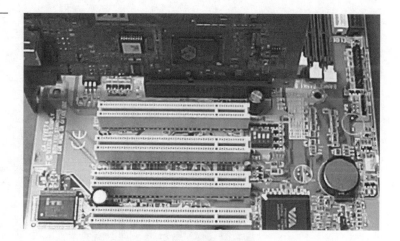

**Figure 1-18**   Motherboard in box

The case needs to have holes that enable devices to access the external connectors. Where the motherboard has a connector for a keyboard, for example, the case must have a hole through which you insert the keyboard plug. See Figure 1-19.

Equally important, if the expansion slots enable you to add cards to the PC, then the case must also provide slots that enable different devices to connect to their cards (Figure 1-20).

**Figure 1-19**
Keyboard socket visible through a hole in the box

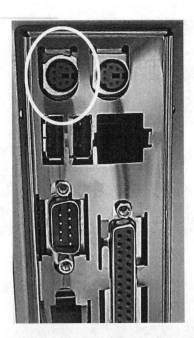

**Figure 1-20**
Inserted card from the back of the PC

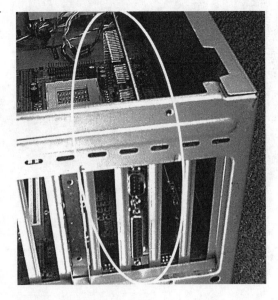

Certain types or layouts of motherboards require a case designed for that type. Fortunately, motherboards come in only a few layouts, requiring only a few types of cases. This will be discussed in more detail in Chapter 4, when motherboards are discussed.

# Power Supply

The *power supply*, as its name implies, provides the necessary electrical power to make the PC operate. The power supply takes standard (in the United States) 110-volt AC power and converts it into 12-volt, 5-volt, and 3.3-volt DC power. Most power supplies are about the size of a shoebox cut in half and are usually gray or metallic colored (Figure 1-21).

A number of connectors lead out of the power supply. Every power supply provides special connectors for the motherboard (Figure 1-22) and a number of other general-use connectors that provide power to any device that needs electricity (Figure 1-23).

**Figure 1-21**   Typical power supply

**Figure 1-22**   Power connectors for the motherboard

**Figure 1-23**   General-use power connectors

You can see the power supply if you look at the back of your PC. It has a connection for a power plug that in turn runs to an electrical outlet and also has a big fan inside. Every PC uses a fan or two to keep the interior of the PC cool (Figure 1-24). Check out both Chapter 4 and Chapter 6 for information detailing power supplies.

**Figure 1-24**
Power supply fan

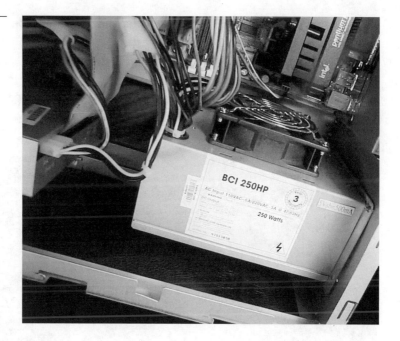

# Floppy Drive

The floppy drive enables you to access floppy disks (diskettes). Two types of floppy drives exist: the very common 3.5-inch floppy drive, which accepts diskettes 3.5 inches in diameter, and the rare 5.25-inch drive, which accepts 5.25-inch floppy disks (Figure 1-25). The 5.25-inch drive is obsolete, but you might still encounter one on older PCs.

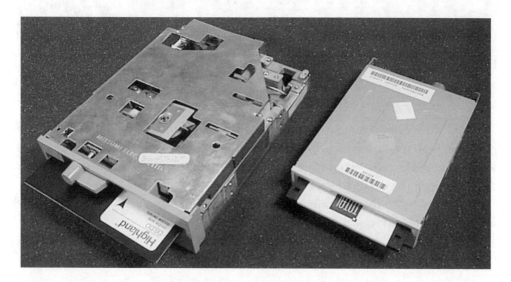

**Figure 1-25**    Floppy drives—5.25 inches and 3.5 inches

The floppy drive connects to the computer via a 34-pin *ribbon cable,* which in turn connects to the motherboard. The connection to the motherboard is known as the *floppy controller.* In early PCs, the floppy controller was a special card that inserted into an expansion slot, but today's PCs all have the floppy controller built into the mother-board (Figure 1-26). Though the floppy connection is no longer the controller, the name has stuck.

**Figure 1-26** Onboard floppy drive controller

Floppy drive ribbon cables (Figure 1-27) differ from other types of ribbon cable in two ways. First, they are the narrowest ribbon cable, only slightly more than 1.5 inches wide. Second, the cable has a twist in the middle, usually close to where the floppy drive cable connects to the floppy drive.

A PC can support up to two floppy drives. If it has two, both drives connect to the same ribbon cable (Figure 1-28).

Because floppy drives need power, a connector from the power supply must attach to the floppy drive (Figure 1-29).

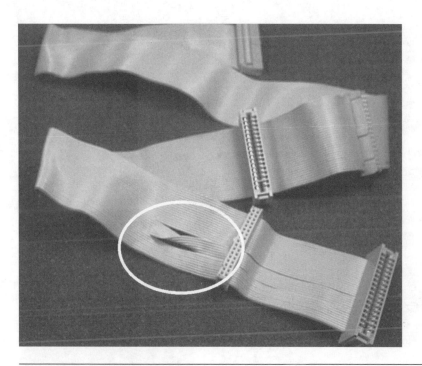

**Figure 1-27** Floppy drive cable

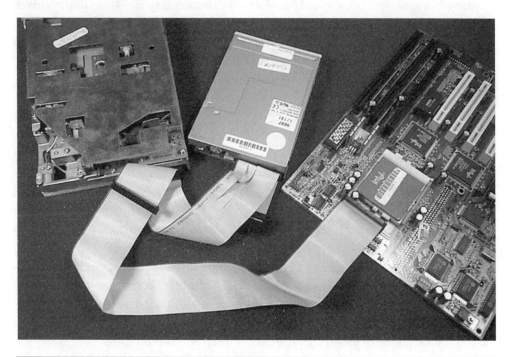

**Figure 1-28** Two floppy drives on one ribbon cable

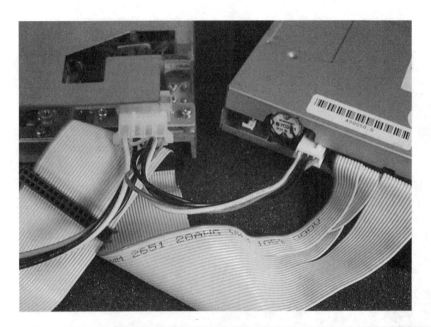

**Figure 1-29**   Floppy drive power connectors

Many PCs now also come with special drives that look very similar to floppy drives. They have names like the popular Iomega ZIP drives. These special drives look like floppies, but the PC sees them very differently. In Chapter 7, we will look at the different types of floppy drives—and we'll see a few of these special drives, too.

# Hard Drive

Hard drives store programs and data that are not currently being used by the CPU (Figure 1-30). As with RAM, hard drive capacity is measured in megabytes. Even though both hard drives and RAM use the same storage unit (the megabyte), a typical PC's hard drive stores much more data than a typical PC's RAM—usually thousands of megabytes. The capacity of a single hard drive in a typical PC can vary from as low as 500 megabytes (on very old systems) up to more than 75 gigabytes! (A *gigabyte* (GB) equals 1,024 megabytes.) A brand new system's hard drive usually stores over 10GB.

An average PC will have at least one hard drive, although almost every PC accepts up to four drives. Special PCs that need to store large amounts of data will contain many hard drives—eight to sixteen drives in some cases. Although the PC design allows for many hard drives, most generic desktop PCs only have one hard drive.

**Figure 1-30**
High-capacity hard
drive

As with so many other parts of the PC, industry standards define two common types of hard drives: EIDE and SCSI (Figure 1-31). Over 95 percent of all PCs use EIDE drives. SCSI drives show up in high-end PCs such as network servers or graphics workstations.

EIDE and SCSI drives can coexist in the same PC. Any PC might have an EIDE, SCSI, or both installed. SCSI and EIDE drives look quite similar. They are both about the same size as a floppy drive, but with wider ribbon cables. These cables have no twist. EIDE drives use a 2-inch-wide, 40-pin ribbon cable, whereas SCSI drives use a 2.5-inch-wide, 50-pin cable, or a densely packed, 68-pin cable that is nearly 2 inches wide.

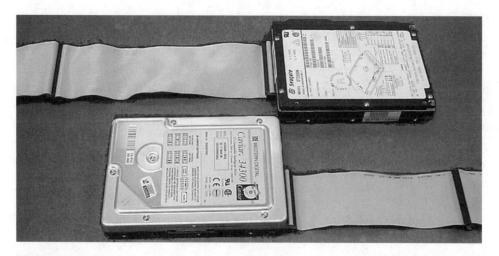

**Figure 1-31**    SCSI and EIDE hard drives with cables

The earliest PCs used a special card for a hard drive controller that snapped into an expansion slot. The early controller cards supported only two hard drives, although later cards supported up to four drives. Motherboard makers now build EIDE controllers directly into the motherboard (Figure 1-32).

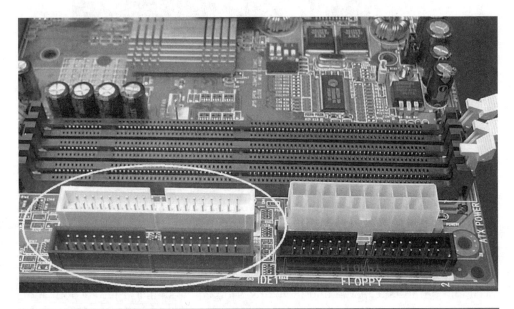

**Figure 1-32**   Onboard EIDE controllers

These controllers truly act only as connectors; however, the name "controller" has stuck, even though they only connect and don't actually control. Note that the motherboard shown in Figure 1-32 has two connectors. A special ribbon cable attaches to each connector. Each ribbon cable has two connectors for hard drives. With two controllers, each controlling two drives, a PC can support up to four EIDE drives.

SCSI drives might look like EIDE drives, but SCSI manifests in a PC very differently than EIDE does. First, very few motherboards have SCSI controllers. You usually need to buy a special SCSI controller card called a *SCSI host adapter*. Also, you can put more than two SCSI drives on the same ribbon. Additionally, SCSI supports many different types of devices other than hard drives. It is not at all uncommon to see CD-ROM drives, tape backups, and other devices connect to the same ribbon cable as the SCSI hard drive (Figure 1-33).

Both EIDE and SCSI need electricity. Every drive needs a power connector (Figure 1-34). Read the hard drive chapter (Chapter 8) and the SCSI chapter (Chapter 13) for all the details on hard drives.

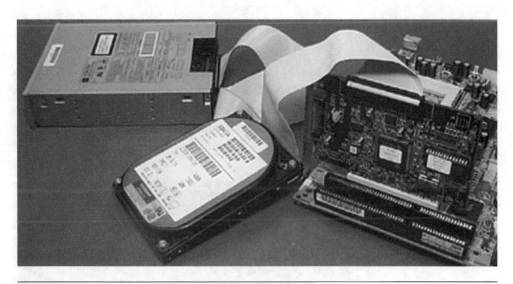

**Figure 1-33**   SCSI chain with multiple devices

**Figure 1-34**
Hard drive power
connector

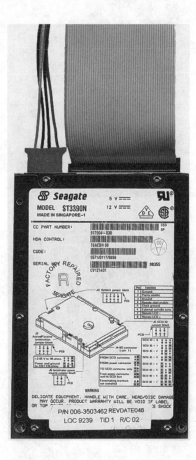

# CD-ROM Drive

CD-ROM drives enable the system to access CD-ROMs. CD-ROM drives are quite large, usually the single largest component inside the PC. With the front of the CD-ROM drive visible in the front of the PC, as well as its boxy shape and metallic appearance, you should easily recognize the CD-ROM drive (Figure 1-35). When CD-ROM drives were first developed, they had their own special controllers. Then, sound card makers began to add those special controllers to their sound cards (Figure 1-36).

**Figure 1-35**
Typical CD-ROM
drive

**Figure 1-36**
CD-ROM controlled
by sound card

These special controllers are now pretty much obsolete and have been replaced by CD-ROM drives that run on either EIDE or SCSI controllers, just like hard drives. So now, basically two types of CD-ROM drives exist: EIDE and SCSI. Most PCs have an EIDE hard drive and an EIDE CD-ROM drive on one controller (Figure 1-37).

SCSI CD-ROM drives go on the same ribbon cable as the SCSI hard drives. One beneficial aspect to SCSI is that since you can have up to seven devices on one ribbon cable, you can set up systems with a large number of CD-ROM drives. Of course, CD-ROM drives, like hard and floppy drives, also need power cables (Figure 1-38).

Many PCs now come with some type of recordable CD-ROM drive. For many years, the *Compact Disk-Recordable* (CD-R) was the only available form of recordable CD. CD-R drives enabled you to record onto special CD-R disks, but once the data was

**Figure I-37**
Hard drive and
CD-ROM

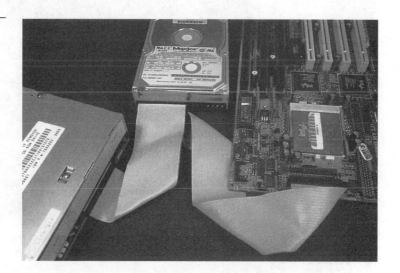

**Figure I-38**
CD-ROM power
connector

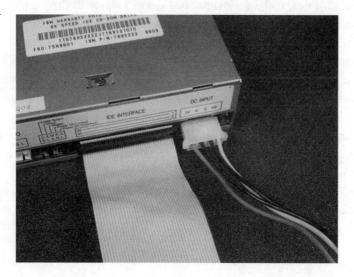

"burned" onto the CD-R, it could not be erased. Most regular CD-ROM drives as well as CD-R drives could read the CD-R disks.

Today, *Compact Disk-Rewritable* (CD-RW) drives have completely eclipsed the CD-R drives on PCs (Figure 1-39). CD-RW drives can write to special CD-RW disks, and then delete and rewrite to those disks numerous times. CD-RW drives can also write to CD-R disks. Further, CD-RW drives can read all three media (CD-ROM, CD-R, and CD-RW). Initially, only CD-RW drives could read CD-RW disks, but current CD-ROM drives can read them as well.

**Figure 1-39**
CD-R drive

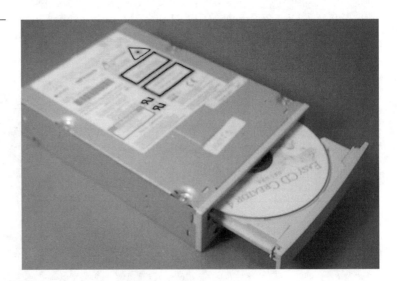

## Connectors

Up to this point, all of the described devices reside in the PC—you can't see how these devices connect unless you open the PC's case. The rest of the components that need to be discussed have some type of visible connection on the outside of the system case. So before diving into the realm of sound cards, modems, network cards, mice, etc., you need to understand the many types of connectors (often called *ports*) used by these different devices. All of these connectors have their own naming conventions that you should know. It's not acceptable to go around saying things like "that's a printer port" or "that's a 'little-type' keyboard connector." You need to be comfortable with the more commonly used naming conventions, so you can say "that's a male DB-25" or "that's a mini-DIN."

Although PCs use close to 50 different connectors, almost all connectors fit into one of seven major types: DB, DIN, Centronics, RJ, BNC, audio, and USB. Let's get acquainted with each type.

## DB Connectors

DB connectors have a slight "D" shape, which allows only one proper way to insert a plug into the socket. Each DB connector has groups of small pins and sockets (male/female) that insert as a group. DB connectors in the PC world can have from 9 to 37 pins, although you rarely see a DB connector with more than 25 pins. Sockets can be either male or female. Figure 1-40 shows some examples. DB type connectors are some of the oldest and most common connectors used in the back of PCs.

## DIN Connectors

Most PCs sport the European-designed DIN connectors. The round DIN connectors come in only two sizes: DIN and mini-DIN. The sockets are always female (Figure 1-41).

**Figure 1-40**
DB connectors

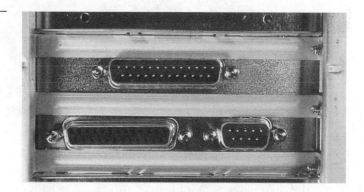

**Figure 1-41**
DIN and mini-DIN connectors

## Centronics Connectors

Similar to DB connectors, Centronics connectors have the same "D" shape to ensure proper insertion. Unlike DBs, however, Centronics connectors use one large central tab, covered with contacts instead of pins. Even though the Centronics connectors have flat contacts instead of pins, the word "pins" is still used to describe the number of contacts. For example, a Centronics connector with 36 contacts is still called a 36-pin connector. Centronics connectors are also distinctive in that the sockets have wire "wings" that lock the plug to the socket in order to reduce the chance of accidental removal. Sockets are always female. With the exception of some obsolete SCSI host adapters, Centronics sockets are rarely seen sticking out of the back of a PC. Almost every printer in existence, however, has a 36-pin Centronics socket (Figure 1-42).

**Figure 1-42**
Centronics port

## RJ Connectors

You have more than likely seen an RJ-type connector, whether or not you knew it by that name. The little plastic plug used to connect your telephone cord to the jack is a classic example of an RJ plug. Modern PCs use only two types of RJ jacks: the RJ-11 and the RJ-45. The phone jack is an RJ-11. It is used almost exclusively for modems. The slightly wider RJ-45 jack is used for one very popular type of network cabling. Most network cards have an RJ-45 socket. Figure 1-43 shows an RJ-45 jack (top) and RJ-11 jacks (bottom).

## BNC Connectors

BNC connectors, also (though incorrectly) known as coaxial or "coax" connectors, are beginning to fade from common PC use, but many PCs still have coax connectors hanging out the back (see Figure 1-44). The coax cable used with PCs looks exactly like the one that runs into the back of your TV. The connectors, however, are different in that they don't screw in the way the TV coax connectors do. The connectors use a twist-type connection. You insert the cable onto the BNC connector and twist to lock the cable

**Figure 1-43**
RJ jacks

**Figure 1-44**
BNC connector
on left

into place, similarly to how you connect a bayonet to a rifle. (This is why many techs assume BNC stands for "bayonet connector," although no one seems to have a definitive answer on the meaning of the initials.) Only one somewhat common type of network card, called a Thinnet card, still uses coax and a BNC connector.

Most new networks use RJ-45-based cabling, rather than BNC, and many of the older coax networks are being replaced with RJ-45 networks. While BNC slowly fades from the PC scene, screw-type coax connectors may show up in the back of a PC. You can purchase cards right now, for example, that enable your PC to act as a television. They have a screw-type coax connector for your TV cable! Hmm, Microsoft Word and MSNBC on the same screen at the same time. Could life be any better?

## Audio Connectors

Audio connectors are perhaps the simplest of all. Really only one type of connector sees popular use: the mini-audio connector. These small connectors have been around for years; they're just like the plug you use to insert headphones into a Sony Walkman or similar device. Audio connectors are used almost exclusively on sound cards (Figure 1-45).

**Figure 1-45**
Mini-audio
connectors

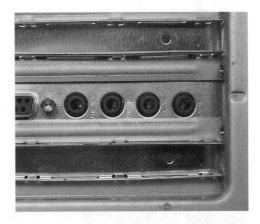

## USB Connectors

The newest type of connector seen on PCs is called *Universal Serial Bus* (USB). USB is the new general-purpose connection for PCs. You can find USB versions of many different devices, such as mice, keyboards, scanners, cameras, and even printers. A USB connector's distinctive rectangular shape makes it easily recognizable (Figure 1-46).

**Figure 1-46**   USB connector

USB has a number of features that make it particularly popular on PCs. First, USB devices are *hot swappable*—you can insert or remove them without restarting your system. Almost every other type of connector requires you to turn the system off, insert/remove the connector, and then turn the system back on. Hot swapping completely eliminates this process.

USB also enables you to *daisy-chain* USB devices. A USB *hub* links together USB devices, thus the term "daisy-chain" (Figure 1-47).

**Figure 1-47**
USB daisy-chained devices

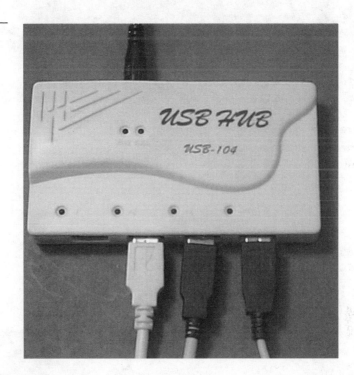

USB enables up to 127 USB devices to daisy-chain from one USB port. You can even put USB hubs into USB devices, enabling you to do interesting configurations such as plugging a USB mouse into a USB monitor, or plugging a USB keyboard into USB speakers (Figure 1-48).

## FireWire Connectors

One other connector worthy of mention is the amazing FireWire, also known as IEEE 1394. Although still rather rare, FireWire moves data at incredibly high speeds, making it the perfect connection for highly specialized devices such as streaming video. The chances of you seeing a FireWire connection (Figure 1-49) on your system are not very great, so we won't add it to our list of seven common connector types; however, do be aware that it exists.

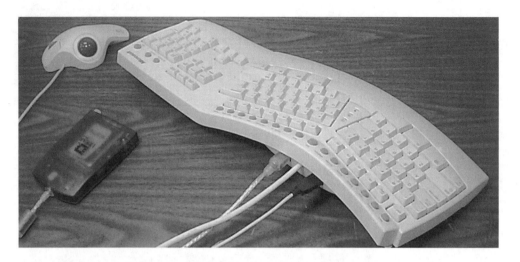

**Figure 1-48** USB hub with daisy-chained devices

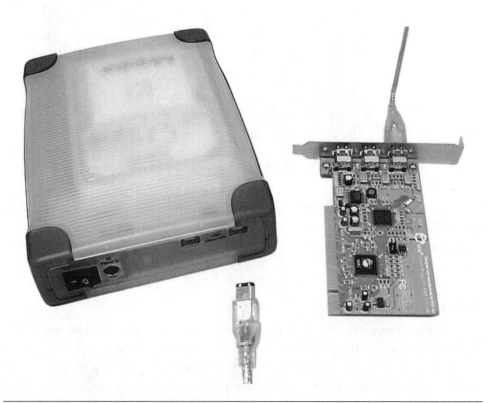

**Figure 1-49** IEEE 1394, FireWire drive, connection, and controller

# All Kinds of Connectors

Keep in mind that the variety of connectors is virtually endless. The preceding eight most common types of connectors cover the vast majority, but many others exist in the PC world. No law or standard requires device makers to use a particular connector, especially if they have no interest in making that device interchangeable with similar devices from other manufacturers.

Now that you have a sense of the connectors, let's turn to the devices common to almost every PC in order to learn which connectors go with which device.

# Sound Cards

Sound cards perform two functions. First, they take digital information and turn it into sound, outputting the sound through speakers. Second, they take sound that is input through a microphone and turn it into digital data. See Figure 1-50.

To play and record sounds, a sound card needs to connect to at least a set of speakers and a microphone. Virtually all sound cards have two miniature audio jacks for a microphone and a speaker. Many will also provide miniature audio jacks for "line in" and "line out." Most sound cards will also provide a female 15-pin DB socket that enables you to attach an electronic musical instrument or to add a joystick to your PC.

**Figure 1-50** Typical sound card connectors

The microphone and speaker sockets, as their names imply, connect a microphone and a set of speakers to the sound card. Line in enables a sound card to record from a stereo, tape recorder, or other audio source; line out enables the sound card to output to those same types of devices. Most systems use only the speaker and microphone sockets. And most PCs also have a small cable inside the case that runs between the sound card and the CD-ROM drive. This cable enables the CD-ROM drive to play audio CD-ROMs through the sound card, which in essence turns your PC into a stereo system (Figure 1-51).

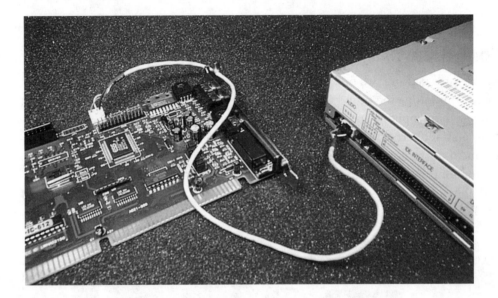

**Figure 1-51**   CD-ROM on sound card cable

# Video Cards

Of all the cards in a PC, the video card is by far the easiest to identify. Unless you use a PC made before roughly 1986, the video card uses a distinct, 15-pin female DB connector. And whereas most DB connectors only sport two rows of pins, the video card uses three rows of pins. There's nothing else like it in the back of a PC (Figure 1-52).

# Network Cards

Networks are groups of connected PCs that share information. The PCs most commonly connect via some type of cabling, usually an advanced type of phone cable or coax. *Network interface cards* (NICs) provide the interface between the network and the

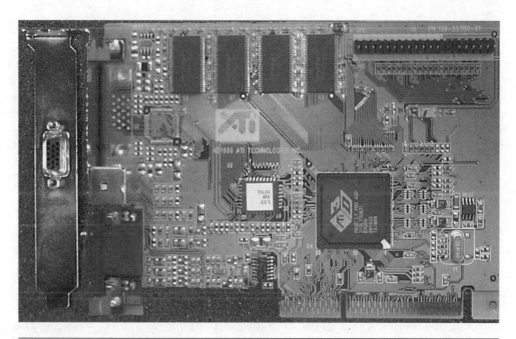

**Figure 1-52** Typical video card

PC. A NIC will have one or more of the following types of connectors: RJ-45, BNC, 15-pin two-row female DB, or 9-pin female DB. Figure 1-53 shows typical network cards with multiple connector types (9-pin not shown).

**Figure 1-53** Typical network card connectors

It is not uncommon to see NICs with more than one type of connector. Although a NIC may have any of these connectors, the networking industry has concentrated on networks that use the RJ-45 connection. Today, the most common NIC has a single RJ-45 connection (Figure 1-54).

# Keyboard

Today's keyboards come in many shapes and sizes. Although the keyboard itself may come in various shapes and sizes, basically only two types of keyboard connectors exist. All PCs have a keyboard port connected directly to the motherboard. The oldest, but still quite common type, is a special DIN-type connector popularly known as the AT style. The original IBM PC used the AT-style DIN, and most PCs until recently retained this style connector. The AT-style keyboard connector is quickly disappearing, however, being overshadowed by the smaller mini-DIN PS/2-style keyboard connector (Figure 1-55).

You can use an AT-style keyboard with a PS/2-style socket (or the other way around) by using a converter. Although the AT connector is unique in PCs (Figure 1-56), the PS/2-style mini-DIN is also used in more modern PCs for the mouse. Fortunately, most

**Figure 1-54**   Common network card with single RJ-45 connection

**Figure 1-55**
Mini-DIN keyboard
connector

**Figure 1-56**
AT-style keyboard
connector

PCs that use the mini-DIN for both the keyboard and mouse clearly mark each mini-DIN socket as to its correct use. Some new keyboards have a USB connection, but these are fairly rare compared to the PS/2-connection keyboards.

# Mouse

Before we talk about mice in general, we need a short discussion on something called *serial ports*. A better name for this section might be, "What's a serial port, what does it look like, and what does a mouse have to do with it?"

It's hard to believe, but there was a time, long ago and far away, when PCs worked just fine without mice. When IBM created the PC, mice were not part of the picture. But IBM did something very smart that enabled mice, as well as many other devices invented after the introduction of the PC, to become part of the PC quite easily.

IBM made the PC easily customizable by providing two ways to add components: expansion slots and standardized ports. IBM added many unused slots to which anyone (at least anyone with the technical know-how) could add special cards in order to add functions. The original PC had only two cards: the video card and the floppy drive controller. Hard drive controller cards, network cards, sound cards, modems, and a few thousand other devices were all created because IBM had the foresight to add expansion slots. This book devotes all of Chapter 5 to expansion slots.

Second, IBM included standardized ports on the PC that enabled people to add devices without opening the case. The first of these standardized ports was (and still is) called a serial port. Now please understand that IBM didn't invent serial ports. Serial ports had been around long before the PC was invented in 1980, but IBM made sure that every IBM PC came with two serial ports. Even today, every PC has at least one serial port. Isn't that fascinating? One of the oldest technologies in the computer world still soldiers on in the back of the most modern, powerful PCs!

A serial port does only one thing: It takes a stream of serial data (which runs on only one wire) and converts it into a format that the CPU can easily understand. Equally, a serial port takes data from the CPU and outputs it in serial format. Think of serial data as a telegraph wire sending Morse code, but instead of sending dots and dashes, it sends ones and zeros. Not only did IBM put serial ports in all its PCs, it told everyone how to write software that could talk to the serial port and manipulate the incoming or outgoing data. To top it all off, IBM standardized the serial connector, defining the size, shape, and number and function of all the pins. That way you knew if you invented a device that worked in one IBM PC, it would also work in all the others.

The super-standard IBM serial connector is either a 25- or a 9-pin male DB connector. No other connector in the back of a PC looks like these serial connectors. The 25-pin connector was the first of the two sizes, but over time it became obvious that most devices needed only about nine pins. As a result, very few systems still use the 25-pin serial port. Today, the 9-pin serial rules. You can get an adapter that enables you to convert 9 to 25 or 25 to 9. You would be hard-pressed to find a PC without at least one 9-pin serial port. Figures 1-57 and Figure 1-58, respectively, show 25-pin and 9-pin serial ports.

**Figure 1-57**
25-pin serial port

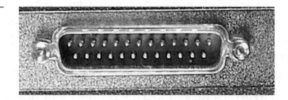

**Figure 1-58**
9-pin serial port

Most people reading this book have some PC experience. Somebody out there right now is reading this and asking the question: "Where do COM ports fit into this?" The answer is they don't. A COM port is not a physical thing. A COM port is comprised of two values, called the *I/O address* and the *IRQ*, assigned to a serial port by the system. If you don't know what an IRQ or I/O address is, don't worry. A later chapter covers them in detail. Calling a serial port a COM port is comparable to looking at the White House and saying "That's 1600 Pennsylvania Avenue." No, it's the White House. Its address is 1600 Pennsylvania Ave! Get the difference?

Now that you understand and can identify serial ports, we can turn our attention back to mice. For many years, a dedicated mouse port did not even exist. Mice simply connected via either 9-pin or 25-pin serial ports. The acceptance of the mouse as an integral part of the PC, however, created a demand for the mouse to have its own connector, just as the keyboard had its own connector. In the mid-1980s, a new type of mouse connection debuted with the introduction of the IBM PS/2 personal computer. Although still a serial port, the new PS/2-style dedicated mouse port used a mini-DIN connector (Figure 1-59).

In older days, serial ports were on a card, usually called an I/O card. Modern motherboards now have built-in serial ports. The serial ports usually connect directly to the back of the motherboard, although a few modern systems connect the serial port to the motherboard via a small ribbon cable. This bit of cable is rather ingloriously referred to as a *dongle* (Figure 1-60).

**Figure 1-59**
PS/2 mouse port

**Figure 1-60**
Typical dongle

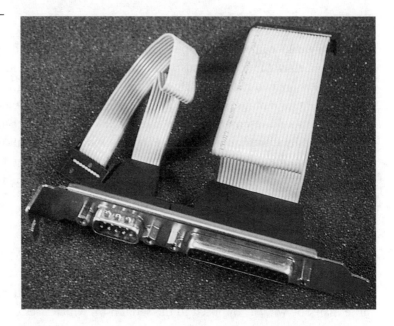

Many PC systems now use a USB port for the mouse. USB's daisy-chain feature often enables you to connect a USB mouse to the front of the system or into the keyboard, significantly reducing the amount of cable lying around your PC (Figure 1-61).

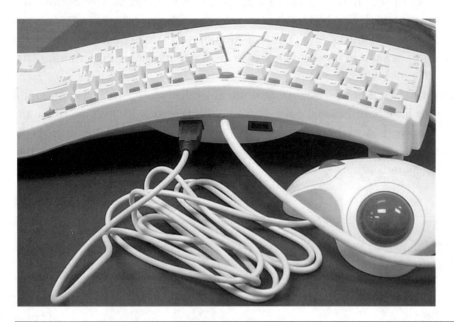

**Figure 1-61**    USB trackball connected to keyboard

## Modem

A modem works with your telephone line to translate analog telephone signals into digital serial data. Modems can also translate digital serial data into analog telephone signals. There are two types of modems: internal and external. An external modem sits outside the PC and plugs into a serial port. An internal modem is a card that snaps into an expansion slot. Internal modems carry their own onboard serial port. A modem is another easily identifiable device in PCs. All modems, internal or external, have two RJ-11 sockets. One connects the modem to the telephone jack on the wall, and the other is for an optional telephone so you can use the phone line when the modem is not in use (Figure 1-62).

## Printer

Most printers use a special connector called a *parallel port*. Parallel ports carry data on more than one wire, as opposed to the serial port, which uses only one wire. Parallel

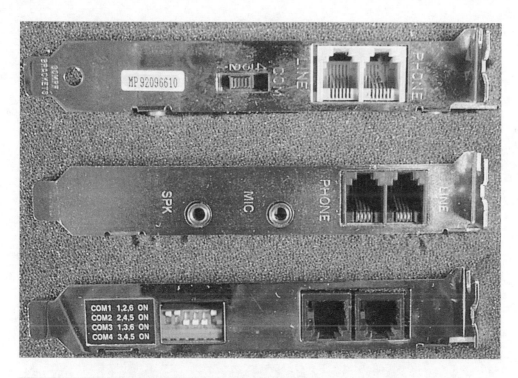

**Figure 1-62** Typical modem connections

**Figure 1-63**
Parallel port

ports use a 25-pin female DB connector (Figure 1-63). There are some SCSI host adapters with an identical 25-pin female DB connector, but these rarely appear in IBM-style PCs.

Like serial ports, parallel ports on earlier PCs mounted on a card, usually the same I/O card that contained the serial ports. Parallel ports today are directly supported by the motherboard through a direct connection or through a dongle (Figure 1-64).

Parallel ports used to be the exclusive domain of printers. Today, many other types of devices use a parallel port. Figure 1-65 shows an Iomega ZIP drive that uses the parallel port. Note that this drive has a second connector to enable you to daisy-chain another parallel device onto the ZIP drive. This parallel daisy-chaining has a number of problems that make it rather unstable unless very carefully configured. If you need to daisy-chain, get USB.

**Figure 1-64**
Parallel port
connected to
motherboard via
dongle

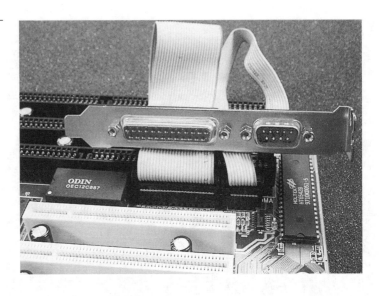

**Figure 1-65**   Daisy-chained parallel devices

# Joystick

Joysticks weren't supposed to be used just for games. When the folks at IBM added the 15-pin female DB joystick connector to PCs, they envisioned joysticks as hardworking input devices, just as the mouse is today (Figure 1-66). Except in the most rare circumstances, however, the only thing joysticks do today is enable you to turn your PC into a $1500+ game machine! But is there a more gratifying feeling than easing that joystick over, pressing the Fire button, and watching an enemy fighter jet get blasted by a well-placed Sidewinder missile? I think not.

**Figure 1-66**
Joystick port

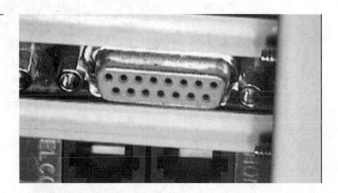

# Jumpers and Switches

Many motherboards and cards require configuration in one way or another. This book devotes entire chapters to the hows and whys of setting up these devices, but let's take a moment to look at the primary tools of hardware setup: jumpers and switches. Most motherboards and some cards have circuitry that must be turned on or off for various reasons. Jumpers and switches enable you to perform this turning on and off. This section teaches you how to recognize jumpers and switches and how to use them properly.

*Jumpers* are tiny pins, usually about half a centimeter long, closely grouped together in twos or threes. A tiny connector piece, called a *shunt*, slides down over two pins to create a circuit. Jumpers without a connected shunt are considered *open* or *off*, while jumpers with a shunt are considered *shorted, closed,* or *on* (Figure 1-67).

When the jumper setup uses two wires, off and on make a certain sense; but such may not be the case with a three-wire setup. With the latter, the documentation often describes settings such as "1-2" or "2-3," meaning you should place a jumper on the first and second (1-2) or second and third (2-3) pins. But which two of the three are the second and third pins? If you look closely at the board on which the jumpers are mounted, you should see a small number "1" on one side or the other, identifying the first pin. You would then short the other two pins.

**Figure 1-67**
Closed and open
jumpers

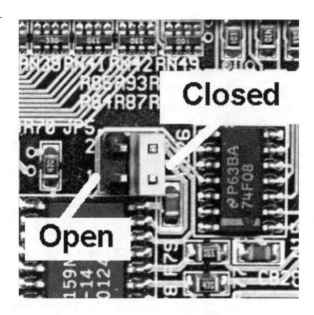

Each group of jumpers is identified by the nomenclature JP1, JP2, JP3, etc. Use this to identify the jumpers you want to set (Figure 1-68).

It is common to see a shunt on only one jumper pin, called a *parked* jumper (Figure 1-69). This is done to keep the shunt handy should you ever need to short that jumper later.

**Figure 1-68**
Jumper labeling

**Figure 1-69**
Parked jumper

Parked Jumpers

For the sake of simplicity, this book uses a specific diagram style to display jumper settings. For example, a set of jumpers that looks like Figure 1-70, with two pins shorted by a shunt, will be represented by a diagram that looks like Figure 1-71. If a jumper is shorted, the shunt will be represented by a black rectangle; otherwise, it will be considered open (Figure 1-72). Jumpers appear in numerous chapters of this book, so you should familiarize yourself with the diagram style in order to avoid confusion later.

*Switches*, more accurately called DIP switches, accomplish the same thing as jumpers, but you do not have to worry about losing those little shunts! Switches look like tiny, LEGO-sized blocks, usually brightly colored (although black is not uncommon), with a neat row of tiny rocker arm or slide switches across the top (Figure 1-73). You can turn a switch on or off by flipping the tiny switches.

The best way to flip these switches is by using a small screwdriver or a mechanical pencil with the lead removed (Figure 1-74). Do not use a pen or pencil, as they leave marks, making it harder to read next time. Worse, they leave ink or lead residue inside the PC, a potential problem if it gets in the wrong component. You can use your fingers or fingernails, of course, but might find it difficult if a lot of cards and cables are in the way.

**Figure 1-70** Jumpers

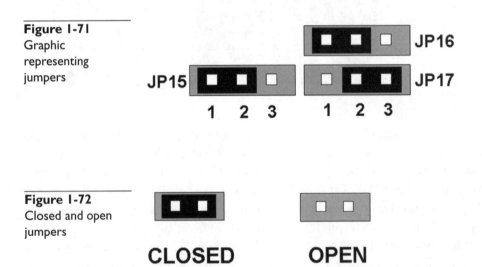

**Figure 1-71**
Graphic
representing
jumpers

**Figure 1-72**
Closed and open
jumpers

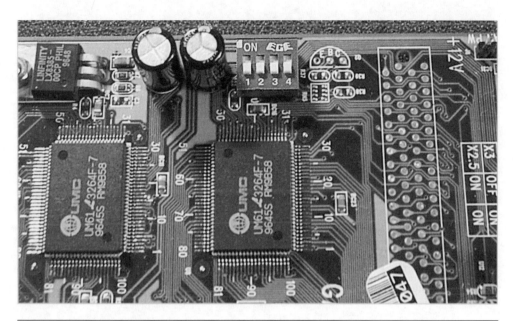

**Figure 1-73**   DIP switches

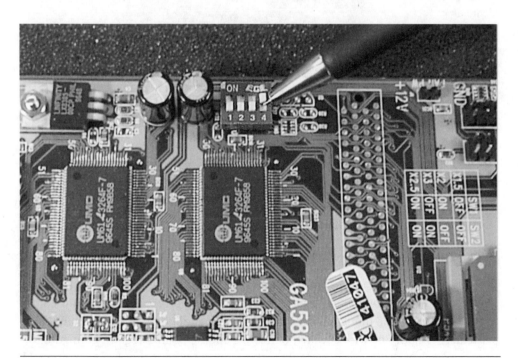

**Figure 1-74**   Flipping a DIP switch

You can usually determine how to set these switches by reading documentation that came with the device you want to configure. Unfortunately, the documentation does not always help you determine which set of switches you need to configure (many motherboards come with more than one) or even which way is on or off.

If you have more than one set of DIP switches, you need to read the numbers on the board next to the switches in order to figure out which switch you want. Switches always use the nomenclature S1, S2, etc., or SW1, SW2, etc., and manufacturers place that numbering directly onto the board. By looking for the "S" or "SW," you can identify one switch from another.

Determining on and off with a switch causes some confusion because the industry has not yet created standardized switches. DIP switch manufacturers use the terms "on," "closed," and "shorted" synonymously. Equally, "off" and "open" also mean the same thing. Most DIP switches have a word printed on the switch to give you a clue. If the switch does not have a word, look for a small dot. This dot points to the closed or on position, and should help you identify the state of the switch (Figure 1-75).

**Figure 1-75**
Switch state
identifier

## Documentation

Virtually every part of the PC comes with a small booklet that describes critical installation information about that device. Without this booklet, it is often difficult or impossible to install a modem, sound card, motherboard, or other component. This is particularly important with motherboards. All motherboards require configuration, using jumpers, switches, or other means. Every motherboard should also come with documentation, called the *motherboard book,* to tell you how to set them up. If you do not have that book, you are in for serious frustration and pain. Luckily, the Internet has alleviated that pain somewhat by making it relatively easy, if a bit time-consuming, to replace a lost or never-received motherboard book. Motherboard books are crucial, so store them in a safe place. Figure 1-76 shows a typical pile of documentation that comes with a new PC.

**Figure 1-76**   Typical documentation from a new PC

The importance of this chapter cannot be stressed enough! Decent technicians should be able to recognize the main parts of a PC. Anyone who wants to pass the A+ Certification exams should be able to name the different types of connectors and know what types of devices connect to those ports. You may not understand how these cards work yet, but make sure you know the differences between types of cards. Good technicians can tell the difference by simply running their fingers along the back of a PC, which sure beats pulling it out from under the desk!

## Review Questions

1. The CPU performs what function(s) in a personal computer?
   A. The central processing unit performs all the calculations that take place inside a PC.
   B. The central processing unit provides a central repository for system information.
   C. The central power unit provides DC electricity for the motherboard and devices inside a PC.
   D. The Celeron Pentium unit stores programs used by the microprocessor.

2. A mouse commonly plugs into which of the following ports?
   A. Parallel port
   B. Serial port
   C. DB-15 port
   D. FireWire port

3. A printer commonly plugs into which of the following ports?
   A. Parallel port
   B. Serial port
   C. DB-9 port
   D. DB-15 port

4. Which device(s) use the PS/2-style mini-DIN connector?
   A. Only keyboards
   B. Only mice
   C. Printers and mice
   D. Keyboards and mice

5. John finds an expansion card in a secondhand computer store with no descriptive tag. It has a cylindrical connector that looks suspiciously like a cable TV connector and a D-shaped, two-row, 15-pin female socket. Frida argues that the card is clearly a new video card, because it has a cable TV connector. Troy disagrees, saying that it must be a sound card because the 15-pin port is obviously a joystick port. Who is correct?
   A. Only Frida is correct.
   B. Only Troy is correct.
   C. Both Frida and Troy are correct. The card is a combination video/sound card for multimedia.
   D. Neither Frida nor Troy is correct. The card is a network interface card.

6. Modems commonly use which type of connector?
   A. RJ-11
   B. RJ-45
   C. DB-15
   D. BNC

7. Which of the following statements best describes the function of RAM in a personal computer?
   A. RAM provides permanent storage for programs and data.
   B. RAM provides temporary storage for programs and data currently being used by the CPU.
   C. RAM translates serial data to parallel data, and vice versa.
   D. RAM performs all the calculations that take place inside a personal computer.

8. Which of the following statements best describes the function of a hard drive in a personal computer?
   A. A hard drive provides permanent storage for programs and data.
   B. A hard drive provides temporary storage for programs and data currently being used by the CPU.
   C. A hard drive is the primary removable storage device in a PC.
   D. A hard drive enables the CPU to perform all the calculations that take place inside a personal computer.

9. What's an easy way to tell a current floppy drive ribbon cable from an EIDE cable?
   A. The floppy drive cable is round, whereas the EIDE cable is flat.
   B. The floppy drive cable is wider than the EIDE cable.
   C. The floppy drive cable has a twist in the wires near the end, whereas the EIDE cable runs straight.
   D. There is no difference!

10. Which of the following describes a two-wire jumper with a shunt covering the wires?
    A. Off
    B. Open
    C. Closed
    D. Parked

## Answers

1. **A.** The central processing unit handles all the mathematical calculations that make a personal computer function.

2. **B.** Mice use standard or dedicated serial ports.

3. **A.** Printers almost exclusively use parallel ports, although some USB printers have appeared on the scene.

4. **D.** Both keyboards and mice on current systems use mini-DIN connectors (although not the same one!).

5. **D.** The two-row, 15-pin connector coupled with a BNC (cable) connector clearly mark this as a network interface card.

6. **A.** Modems use RJ-11 jacks, just like a telephone.

7. **B.** RAM provides temporary storage for programs and data currently in use.

8. **A.** Hard drives provide permanent storage for programs and data.

9. **C.** The 34-pin floppy drive ribbon cables have a distinctive twist, whereas the 40-pin EIDE cables do not.

10. **C.** Putting a shunt over two jumper pins "closes" the circuit, making that circuit "on."

# Microprocessors

In this chapter, you will

- Learn about the concepts of buses, and the functions of the data bus and the address bus
- Understand the clock, clock speed, and the concept of clock doubling
- Learn about the relationship of RAM to the CPU and RAM caching
- See the different types of processors available in the past and today
- Learn how to install and upgrade processors

For all practical purposes, the terms *microprocessor* and *central processing unit* (CPU) mean the same thing: it's that big chip inside your computer that many people often describe as the brain of the system. From the previous chapter we know that CPU makers name their microprocessors in a fashion similar to the automobile industry: CPU names get a make and a model, such as Intel Pentium or AMD Duron. You probably already know what a CPU looks like—invariably covered by some huge fan or heat sink, a CPU stands out inside the case. See if you can spot the CPU in Figure 2-1.

## Historical/Conceptual

Although the computer might seem to act quite intelligently, comparing the CPU to a human brain hugely overstates its capabilities. A CPU functions more like a very powerful calculator than a brain—but, oh, what a calculator! Today's CPUs add, subtract, multiply, and divide millions of numbers per second. Processing that much information so quickly makes any CPU look quite intelligent. It's simply the speed of the CPU,

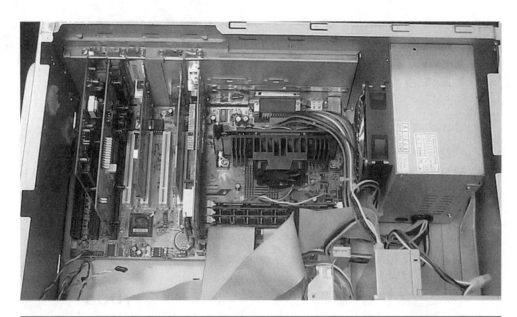

**Figure 2-1**  Spot the CPU

rather than actual intelligence, that enables computers to perform feats such as accessing the Internet, playing visually stunning games, or creating graphics.

A good PC technician needs to understand some basic CPU functions in order to support PCs well, so let's start with an analysis of how the CPU works. If you wanted to teach someone how an automobile engine works, you would use a relatively simple example engine, right? The same principle applies here. The CPU used in the following examples is the famous Intel 8088, invented in the late 1970s. Although this CPU first appeared over 20 years ago, it contains the same basic parts used in even the most advanced CPUs today. Stick with me, my friend. Prepare to enter that little bit of magic called the CPU.

Let's begin by visualizing the CPU as a man in a box (Figure 2-2). This is one clever guy in this box. He happily performs virtually any mathematical function, manipulates data, provides answers to questions, and he does it all very quickly.

You want to use this guy to get work done, but there's a catch. This man cannot see or hear anything outside the box. He cannot communicate with the outside world, and we cannot communicate with him. If we want to take advantage of this guy's skills, we need a way to talk to him (Figure 2-3).

## External Data Bus

Fortunately, this box comes with a communication device. Let's further imagine that this device consists of 16 light bulbs—8 inside the box and 8 outside the box. Each light bulb on the inside of the box connects to one on the outside, creating a pair of lights.

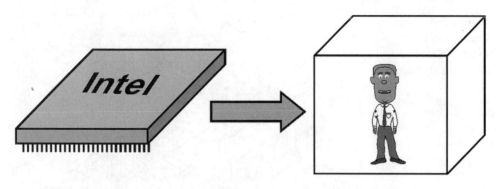

**Figure 2-2**    Imagine the CPU as a man in a box

**Figure 2-3**    How can we talk to the man in the box?

Each pair of lights must be either on or off. If a light bulb inside the box is on, the light bulb paired to that light outside the box is also on. If one is off, the other is off. Also, each connected pair of light bulbs has two switches, one switch on each side. This setup means that the man inside the box or someone outside the box can turn any one of the eight pairs of light bulbs on or off. We call this light bulb communication device the *external data bus.*

Figure 2-4 shows a cutaway view of the external data bus. Understand that if you flip a switch, both light bulbs go on and the switch on the other side also magically flips. If you turn a switch off, both light bulbs on each side turn off and the other switch turns off.

**Figure 2-4**
Cutaway of the
external data bus—
note one light is on

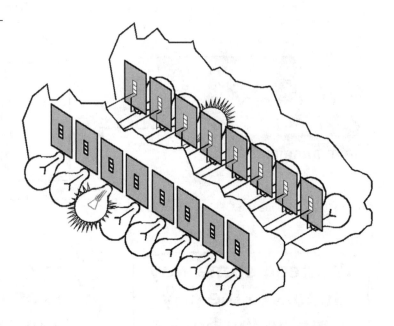

By creating different patterns of lights, you can communicate with the guy in the box. You must, however, come up with a sort of codebook so you can understand the patterns of lights. We'll come back to the external data bus in a moment. Now you can see what the CPU looks like from the outside (Figure 2-5).

**Figure 2-5**
The CPU from the
outside

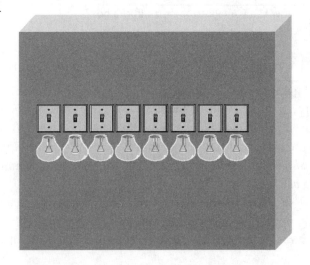

Before going any further, make sure you're clear on the fact that this is an analogy, not reality. There really is an external data bus, but you won't see any light bulbs or switches (Figure 2-6). You can, however, see little wires sticking out of the CPU. If you apply voltage to one of these wires, you in essence flip the switch. Get the idea? So if that wire had voltage, and if a tiny light bulb were attached to the wire, that light bulb would glow, would it not? By the same token, if the wire had no power, then the light bulb would not glow. That is why the switch-and-light-bulb analogy is used—to help you appreciate that these little wires flash on and off at a phenomenal rate.

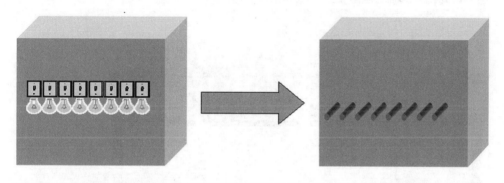

**Figure 2-6**   Analogy and reality—side-by-side

Computer technicians constantly discuss the state of many wires at any given moment. Rather than saying that one of the external data bus wires is on or off, the number 1 will be used to represent on and the number 0 to represent off (Figure 2-7). That way, instead of describing the state of the lights as "on-off-off-off-on-on-off-off," it can be described as "10001100."

In the world of computers, we constantly turn wires on and off. As a result, this "1 and 0" or *binary* system is used to describe the state of these wires at any given moment. This binary numbering system will be revisited in greater detail later in the book.

**Figure 2-7**
Here "1" means on,
"0" means off

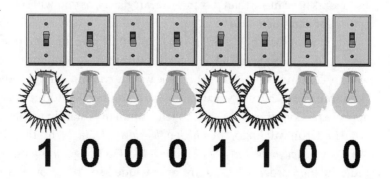

**1 0 0 0 1 1 0 0**

## Registers

Let's go inside the box for a moment and give the guy in the box four worktables to use. Don't think of these as tables in the classic sense; you can't eat a pizza or do your homework on them. They simply hold light bulbs. Each table holds 16 light bulbs with switches that the guy in the box turns on and off. This setup, however, is substantially different from the external data bus. Here the light bulbs are not in pairs; they're just 16 light bulbs straight across with one switch for each bulb, and *you* cannot access these light bulbs. Only the guy in the box manipulates them. These worktables are called *registers* (Figure 2-8).

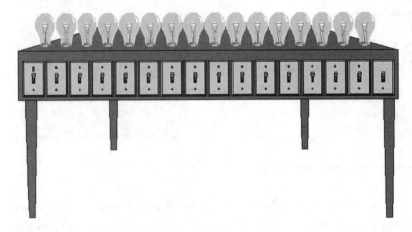

**Figure 2-8**  A register

Registers provide the man with a workplace for the problems you give him. You need to be able to identify each register, so let's give them names: AX, BX, CX, and DX (Figure 2-9). All CPUs contain more than just these four registers, but every CPU invented since IBM devised the term "PC" contains at least these four *general-purpose registers*. Processors have more than just these few registers, as you will see, but these four should suffice for demonstration.

Before you close the lid on the box, you must give the man one more tool. Remember the codebook we talked about earlier? Let's make one for the external data bus, so we can communicate. This codebook would contain information such as "10000111 (light bulbs 8-3-2-1 on) means move the number 7 into the AX register." Some rules apply here. Counting from right to left, commands start in the last four light bulbs 8-7-6-5 (in technical lingo, the *high-order bits*). Data is in the first four light bulbs 4-3-2-1 (the *low-order bits*). See Figure 2-10. (Do not get hung up on the concept of low order vs. high order—these terms are included so you know that various rules, rather than random chance, apply to the code.)

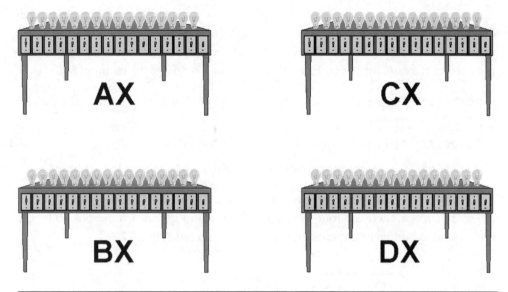

**Figure 2-9** The four data registers

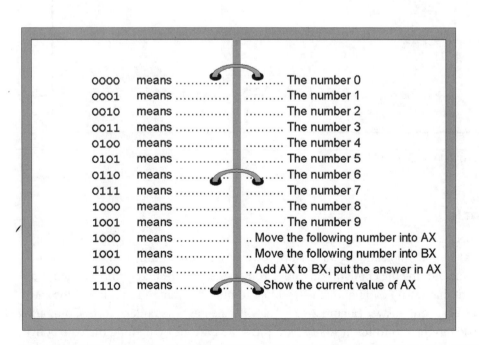

**Figure 2-10** The CPU's codebook

These commands are called the microprocessor's *machine language*. The commands described here are not actual commands; they've been simplified somewhat to clarify the concept. The 8088, however, had commands very similar to these—plus a few hundred more! Here are some examples of real machine language for the Intel 8088:

**10111010**  The next line of code is a number. Put that number into the DX register.

**01000001**  Add 1 to the number already in the CX register.

**00111100**  Compare the value in the AX register with the next line of code.

So here is our CPU so far: the guy can communicate with the outside world via the external data bus, there are four registers with him, and he has a codebook so he can understand the different patterns on the external data bus (Figure 2-11).

**Figure 2-11**   Our CPU so far

## Clock

Just because you switch the lights on and off doesn't mean the guy inside is going to look at his codebook and act on it. Have you ever seen an old-time manual calculator—the kind with the big crank on one side? You pressed the desired numbers, then the + key, but that wasn't good enough—you had to pull the crank on the side of the calculator to get your answer (Figure 2-12). The CPU also uses a crank of sorts. Comparing the CPU to the old-time calculator, you press the buttons by lighting the correct light

**Figure 2-12**
Old-style calculator

> **Nothing happens until you pull the crank!**

bulbs on the external data bus; now you need to pull the crank. The crank of the CPU is a special wire called the *clock* (most diagrams show the clock wire as CLK). Let's see how the clock functions.

To continue the analogy, let's put a buzzer inside the box with an activation button outside the box. Once you have the light bulbs on the external data bus set up, press the button to activate the buzzer, and the guy will act on the lights (Figure 2-13). Each time the CLK wire charges up is called a *clock cycle*. Once a command is placed on the external data bus, the clock wire must receive a given voltage—a clock cycle—in order for the CPU to process the command.

**Figure 2-13**  The CPU does nothing unless activated by the clock

The CPU needs at least two clock cycles to act on each command. Using the manual-calculator image, you need to pull the crank at least twice before anything happens. Some commands require hundreds of clock cycles to be processed (Figure 2-14).

Let's look at the old-time manual calculator one more time. If you tried to pull the crank too quickly, such as maybe 30 times per second, the calculator would break; it could not operate that quickly. CPUs have the same problem. If you place too many clock cycles on a CPU, it will overheat and stop working. The maximum number of clock cycles that your CPU can handle is called the *clock speed*. The CPU manufacturer sets a CPU's clock speed at the factory. The Intel 8088 processor had a clock speed of 4.77MHz (millions of cycles per second).

**Figure 2-14** The CPU needs more than one clock cycle to do anything

1 Hertz (1Hz) = 1 cycle per second

1 Megahertz (1MHz) = 1 million cycles per second

Understand that a CPU's clock speed is its *maximum* speed, not the speed at which it always runs. A CPU can run at any speed, as long as that speed does not exceed its clock speed (Figure 2-15).

The *system crystal* determines the speed at which a CPU and the rest of the PC operates. The system crystal is usually a quartz oscillator, very similar to the one in a wristwatch, soldered to the motherboard (Figure 2-16). As long as the PC is turned on, the quartz oscillator fires a charge on the CLK wire, in essence pushing the system along.

**Figure 2-15**
A CPU's clock speed is its top speed

**Figure 2-16**
One of many types of system crystals

It is crucial to understand the relationship of the system crystal to the clock speed of the CPU (Figure 2-17). It makes sense to visualize the system crystal as a metronome for the CPU. The first PCs had a fixed clock speed, but almost all of today's motherboards have methods that enable you to change the clock speed. (You'll see how to do this when we discuss Pentium processors later in this chapter.)

A CPU can be pushed by a crystal with a lower clock speed than its own, but the CPU will operate at the speed of the crystal (Figure 2-18). Don't try to run a CPU faster than its clock speed, or it will overheat and then lock up (Figure 2-19). *Underclocking* means to run a CPU *slower* than its rated clock speed. Similarly, *overclocking* means to run a CPU *faster* than its maximum clock speed. Underclocking does not take advantage of all the power of the CPU. If you overclock, the CPU won't work. We will go into more detail on overclocking in the section "Beyond A+," later in this chapter.

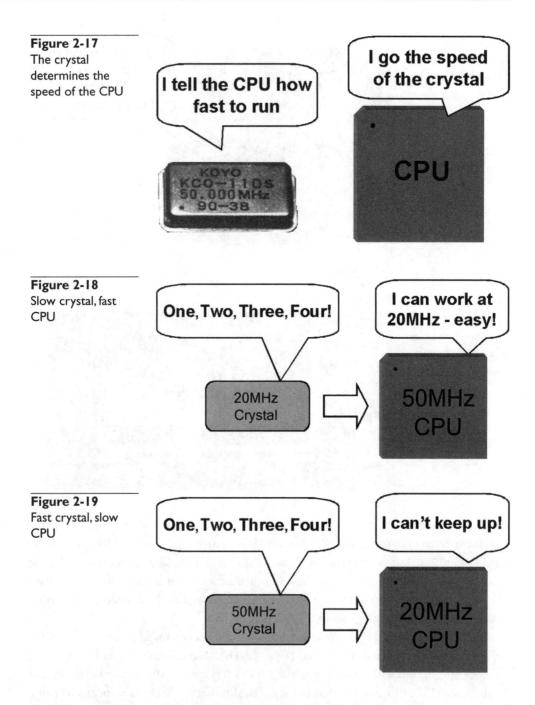

**Figure 2-17**
The crystal determines the speed of the CPU

**Figure 2-18**
Slow crystal, fast CPU

**Figure 2-19**
Fast crystal, slow CPU

## Back to the External Data Bus

Now that you have all the necessary components, let's watch how this setup enables a microprocessor to get work done. To do this, you are going to add 2 + 3 and receive an answer from the CPU. Keep sending commands to the microprocessor until you get the result. Let's refer back to the codebook to tell the guy in the box what to do (Figure 2-20). Using the codebook, here are the steps for 2 + 3:

1. Send the command 10000010 (move 2 into AX).

2. Send the command 10010011 (move 3 into BX).

3. Send the command 11000000 (add BX into AX).

4. Send the command 11100000 (show the value in AX).

This set of commands is known as a *program*, which is a series of commands sent to a CPU in a specific order for the CPU to perform work. Each discrete setting of the external data bus is a *line of code*. This program, therefore, has four lines of code.

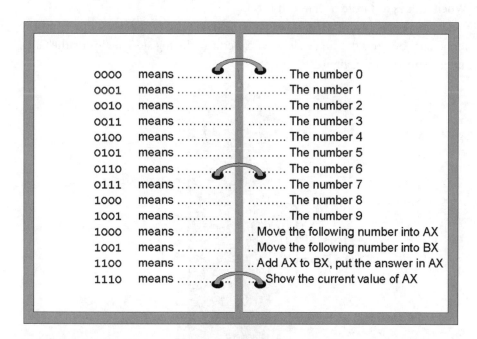

| | | |
|---|---|---|
| 0000 | means | The number 0 |
| 0001 | means | The number 1 |
| 0010 | means | The number 2 |
| 0011 | means | The number 3 |
| 0100 | means | The number 4 |
| 0101 | means | The number 5 |
| 0110 | means | The number 6 |
| 0111 | means | The number 7 |
| 1000 | means | The number 8 |
| 1001 | means | The number 9 |
| 1000 | means | Move the following number into AX |
| 1001 | means | Move the following number into BX |
| 1100 | means | Add AX to BX, put the answer in AX |
| 1110 | means | Show the current value of AX |

**Figure 2-20**   The CPU's codebook again (for reference on the following commands)

## Running the Program

Let's watch each step as the program executes:

1. Flip external data bus switches to 10000010.

2. Repeatedly add voltage to the CLK wire until the switches on the external data bus suddenly all turn off (that means the guy in the box has acted on the command).

3. Flip external data bus switches to 10010011.

4. Repeat step 2.

5. Flip external data bus switches to 11000000.

6. Repeat step 2.

7. Flip external data bus switches to 11100000.

8. Repeat step 2, except you will see the value 00000101 (5) suddenly appear on the external data bus.

Congratulations! You just added 2 + 3 and received the answer, 5. You are a programmer!

One more reality check—think about the registers again. Clearly, no tables or racks of light bulbs are present. The four registers store data temporarily for the CPU using microscopic semiconductor circuits (not light bulbs). When a circuit holds a charge, it is on. When it does not hold a charge, it is off.

Figure 2-21 is a diagram of a real 8088 CPU, showing the actual wires that compose the external data bus and the single clock wire. Because the registers are inside the CPU, they can't be shown in this figure.

**Figure 2-21**
Diagram of 8088
showing clock and
external data bus

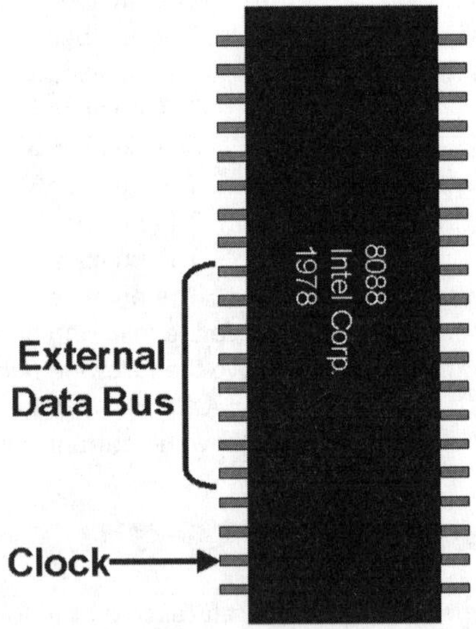

Memory

By using the program described in the previous section, you can add 2 + 3. I recently received a telephone call from a reader who actually took the time to wire up an old 8088 processor with some diodes and switches to do just this. He keeps promising me a photo and a schematic, but has not yet shown me the setup. Yet as interesting as doing this process may be, the reality is that the 8088 wants to run at a much higher speed than what you are capable of doing. Manually setting the voltages on the external data bus and clock wire is a very slow way to add 2 + 3. Keep in mind that the 8088 had a clock speed of 4.77MHz—meaning it could conceivably process several million lines of code every second. Modern CPUs can crank out over a billion lines every second. Clearly, the programs need to be stored on something that can feed each line of the program to the CPU at high speed. That way the processor reads the data as fast as it can process it, or at least much faster than you can flip switches.

What can you use to store programs? Because each line of code is nothing more than a pattern of eight 1's and 0's, any device that can store 1's and 0's eight across will do the trick. Devices that in any way hold 1's and 0's that the CPU accesses are known generically as *memory*.

At this point, you might be using words like "RAM" and "hard drive" to understand what I'm talking about. Stop that right now! Clear your mind. Pretend that only CPUs—and no other technology—exist. We must come up with some new technology that stores the 1's and 0's for the CPU to use. Let's take these ideas one at a time.

## Memory Storage Options

Why not store each line of code on a paper card? You could use one card for each line of code, stack the cards in the right order, and then run them through a card reader. The card reader would then feed the cards, sending the lines of code to the CPU at high speed. Sounds great, right? (Figure 2-22.)

**Figure 2-22**
Paper cards can
hold programs

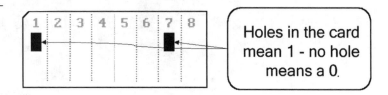

Paper cards were used in the early days of computing. Back when CPUs had clock speeds in the KHz (thousands of cycles per second) range, paper cards could feed programs into the CPU at sufficient speed to keep up with the processor. But today they would be horribly slow. Plus, a small problem exists: Programs generate data. When the CPU adds 2 + 3, it generates the answer of 5 on the external data bus. Cards store programs well, but what about data? You need some type of storage that accepts data from the CPU. When the CPU takes 1's and 0's from something, we call that *reading* data. The process of the CPU sending data to a storage place is called *writing* data. There's no way we can get a card to do this (Figure 2-23).

Okay, so paper cards cannot accept data. Some type of medium is needed that the CPU can both read from and write to in order to get work done. One early way of handling this problem was to place data on magnetic tape. Unlike paper cards, the CPU could write data on magnetic tape fairly easily. Magnetic tape, however, could not be randomly accessed (Figure 2-24). Every CPU has the ability to jump from one place in a program to another. If the CPU often has to jump to a new line of code, the tape would need to rewind and fast-forward constantly to get to the line of code the CPU needs.

**Figure 2-23**
The CPU can't write to a card

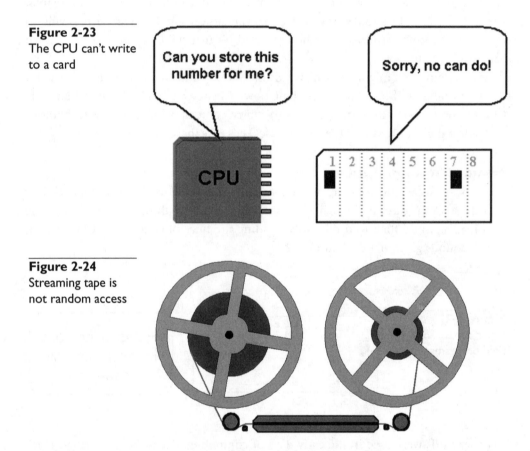

**Figure 2-24**
Streaming tape is not random access

## RAM: Random-Access Memory

Both paper cards and magnetic tape fail as storage media. A storage system is needed that stores not only programs, but also data. The CPU needs to be able to read and write to this storage medium. Additionally, this system must enable the CPU to jump to *any* line of code as easily as to any other line of code that it stores. All of this must be done at or at least near to the clock speed of the CPU. Fortunately, this magical device has existed for many years—*random-access memory* (RAM).

In the chapter of this book dedicated to RAM, the concept of RAM is developed in detail, but at this point let's look at RAM as an electronic spreadsheet, like one you can generate in Microsoft Excel or Lotus 1-2-3. Each cell in this spreadsheet can store only a one or a zero. Each cell is called a *bit*. Each row in the spreadsheet is eight bits across to match the external data bus of the 8088. Each row of eight bits is called a *byte*. In the PC world, RAM transfers and stores data to and from the CPU in byte-sized chunks. RAM is therefore arranged in byte-sized rows.

The number of rows of RAM varies from PC to PC. In the earlier PCs, from around 1980 to 1990, the typical system would have only a few hundred thousand rows of RAM. Today's systems often have tens, even hundreds of millions, of rows of RAM. For simplicity, just pretend we are back in the early 1980s and think in terms of thousands for now.

**Quick Terminology Chart**

Any individual 1 or 0 = a *bit*

4 bits = a *nibble*

8 bits = a *byte*

16 bits = a *word*

32 bits = a *double word*

64 bits = a *paragraph* or *quad word*

Let's stop here for a quick reality check. Electronically, RAM looks like a spreadsheet (Figure 2-25). Of course, RAM is not a spreadsheet. Physically, RAM is groups of semi-conductor chips on small cards that snap into your computer (Figure 2-26). Anyone caught confusing my clever analogy with reality will receive a merciless teasing from me!

**Figure 2-25**
To the CPU,
RAM looks like a
spreadsheet

**Figure 2-26**  Typical RAM (168-pin DIMM)

The CPU can access any one row of RAM as easily and as fast as any other row, which explains the "random access" part of RAM. Not only is RAM randomly accessible, it's also fast. By storing programs on RAM, the CPU can access and run programs very quickly. RAM also stores any data that the CPU actively uses.

Don't confuse RAM with mass storage devices like hard drives and floppy drives. You use hard drives and floppy drives to store programs and data permanently. Later chapters discuss permanent storage in intimate detail.

## Address Bus

So far, our entire PC consists of a CPU and RAM. We now need some connection between the CPU and the RAM so they can talk to each other. To do so, let's extend the external data bus (Figure 2-27).

**Figure 2-27**
Extending the
external data bus

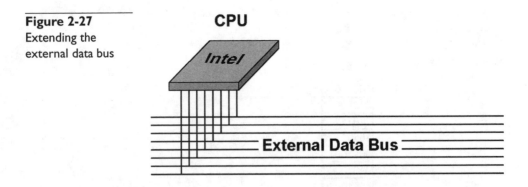

Wait a minute. How can you connect the RAM to the external data bus? (See Figure 2-28.) This is not a matter of just plugging it in. RAM is a spreadsheet with thousands and thousands of discrete rows, and you only need to look at the contents of one row of the spreadsheet at a time, right? What are you going to do?

We need a new device to facilitate the flow of data from RAM to CPU; plus, the CPU must have the ability to tell that new device precisely which row of RAM the CPU wants. The new "RAM-grabbing" device is called the *memory controller chip* (MCC). The

CPU also gains a second set of wires, the *address bus*, that enables it to communicate with the MCC.

The MCC has special circuitry that enables it to grab the contents of any single line of RAM and place that data or command on the external data bus. This in turn enables the CPU to act on that code (Figure 2-29).

Once the MCC is in place to grab any discrete byte of RAM, we need to give the CPU the ability to tell the MCC which line of code it needs (Figure 2-30).

**Figure 2-28**
How can we
connect RAM
to the CPU?

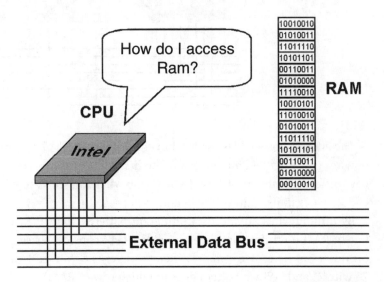

**Figure 2-29**
The MCC grabs a
byte of RAM

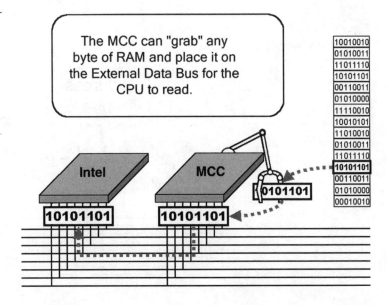

**Figure 2-30**
How can the CPU
control the MCC?

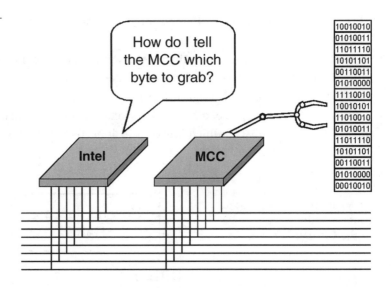

The address bus enables the CPU to control the MCC. The address bus is another set of wires (the external data bus being the first) that runs from the CPU. Different CPUs have different numbers of wires (which, you will soon see, is very significant). The 8088 had 20 wires in its address bus (Figure 2-31).

By turning wires on and off in different patterns, the CPU can tell the MCC which line of RAM it wants at any given moment. Let's consider these 20 wires. There are two big questions here: "How many different patterns of 'on' and 'off' wires can exist with 20 wires?" and "Which pattern goes to which row of RAM?"

**Figure 2-31**
The address bus

The answer to the first question can be reached fairly easily by using basic math. Each wire can be only on or off, so an individual wire exists in only one of two different states—on or off. If the address bus consisted of only one wire, that wire would be at any given moment either on or off. Mathematically, that gives us (pull out your old pre-algebra books) $2^1 = 2$ different combinations. If you have two address bus wires, the address bus wires create $2^2 = 4$ different combinations. If you have 20 wires, you would have $2^{20}$ (or 1,048,576) combinations. Because each pattern points to one line of code and each line of RAM is one byte, *if you know the number of wires in the address bus, you know the maximum amount of RAM that a particular CPU can handle.* Because the 8088 had a 20-wire address bus, the most RAM it could handle was $2^{20}$ or 1,048,576 bytes. The 8088, therefore, had an *address space* of 1,048,576 bytes.

Remember that everything in the CPU boils down to 1's and 0's. With the address bus, we care only about the maximum number of patterns it can generate (and therefore how much RAM the CPU can use). You know that the 8088 had 20 address wires and a total address space of 1,048,576 bytes. Although this is accurate, no one uses such an exact term to discuss the address space of the 8088. Instead you say that the 8088 had one *megabyte* (1MB) of address space.

 **NOTE** The base value used in computing is $2^{10}$ (or 1,024), which is called a *kilo* (K). Someone who speaks of having 1 kilobyte (1KB), really has 1,024 bytes. A *megabyte* is 1K × 1KB, or 1,024 × 1,024 bytes, which equals 1,048,576 bytes. So don't confuse one million (1,000,000) with 1 Meg (1,048,576), or one thousand (1,000) with 1K (1,024).

**Quick Terminology Chart**

1 kilobyte = $2^{10}$ = 1,024 bytes

1 megabyte = $2^{20}$ = 1,048,576 bytes

1 gigabyte = $2^{30}$ = 1,073,741,824 bytes

1K is *not* equal to 1,000 (one thousand)

1 Meg is *not* equal to 1,000,000 (one million)

1 Gig is *not* equal to 1,000,000,000 (one billion)

The second question is a little harder: "Which pattern goes to which line of RAM?" To understand this, let's take a moment to discuss binary counting. In binary, only two numbers exist, 0 and 1, which makes binary a handy way to work with wires that turn on and off. Let's try to count in binary: 0, 1, . . . what's next? It's not 2. The next number after 1 is 10! Now let's count in binary to 1000: 0, 1, 10, 11, 100, 101, 110, 111, 1000. Try counting to 10000. Don't worry, it hardly takes any time at all.

Super, you now count in binary like a math professor. Let's add to the concept. Stop thinking about binary and think about good old base 10 (regular numbers) for a moment. If you have the number 365, can you put zeros in front of the 365, like this: 000365? Sure you can—it doesn't change the value at all. Let's count again to 1000 in binary. In this case we will add enough zeros to make 20 places:

00000000000000000000

00000000000000000001

00000000000000000010

00000000000000000011

00000000000000000100

00000000000000000101

00000000000000000110

00000000000000000111

00000000000000001000

This would be a great way to represent each line of RAM on the address bus. The CPU can identify the first byte of RAM on the address bus as 00000000000000000000. The CPU identifies the last RAM row with 11111111111111111111. When the CPU turns off all the address bus wires, it wants the first line of RAM; when it turns on all of the wires, it wants the 1,048,576th line of RAM. Obviously, the address bus also addresses all of the other rows of RAM in between.

Now for another reality check. Figure 2-32 shows a diagram of an Intel 8088 microprocessor, with the location of the address wires. If you look back at the earlier diagram of the location of the 8088's external data bus wires (Figure 2-21), you'll notice that some of the external data bus and address bus wires overlap. That's okay—some of the wires do both. It's called *multiplexing*. Modern processors now have totally separate external data bus and address bus wires.

## Intel Still Defines the Standards

The original IBM PC used an Intel 8088 CPU, and Intel continues to dominate the microprocessor industry. Intel's presence from the beginning of the personal computer's development, combined with a fanatical determination to lead the CPU industry with faster, more powerful processors, gave them a virtual monopoly on the supply of CPUs for IBM-compatible PCs for many years. Although *Advanced Micro Devices* (AMD) now gives Intel some serious competition, Intel still sets the *de facto* standards that define what a CPU needs in order to be IBM compatible.

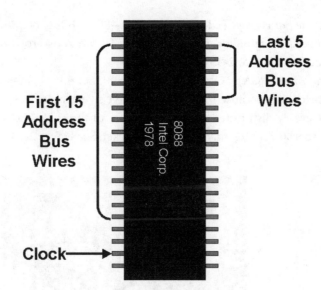

**Figure 2-32**
Location of
address bus wires
on an 8088

First 15
Address
Bus
Wires

Last 5
Address
Bus
Wires

8088
Intel Corp.
1978

Clock⟶

So far, this chapter has discussed the external data bus, the address bus, registers, and clock speed. As technology has progressed from the 8088 to the most current CPU, the sizes of the external data bus, address bus, and registers have grown dramatically. In addition, the clock speeds at which CPUs run have kept pace, getting faster and faster with each successive generation of processor. This progression from 8-bit technology to 16-bit, 32-bit, and finally 64-bit technology, combined with the radical increase in CPU speeds, has enabled systems to communicate and process more information faster and more efficiently.

Although Intel definitely has the largest share of the CPU market, a few other companies—in particular, Advanced Micro Devices—continue to grow in technology and sophistication. As the different CPUs are discussed, you will see that Intel dominated with the early processors. As we move forward, however, other brands of CPUs begin to appear. Today you have a choice in the brand of CPU to use in your PC.

Now that you have a basic understanding of registers, the external data bus, and the address bus, let's take a tour of the family of Intel processors, as well as some of its more famous competitors.

## CPU Packages

CPUs have come in a bewildering array of physical formats—or *packages*—over the years. Manufacturers continue to change them almost yearly to address more efficiently issues such as fragility, ease of installation, heat dissipation, and more. The following list runs through the most common CPU packages.

*Dual Inline Pin Package* (DIPP)   Obsolete—8088, 8086, 80286. DIPPs were the first generation of packaging for microprocessors. They had two rows of pins on either side of the processor (Figure 2-33).

*Pin Grid Array* (PGA)   Obsolete—80286, 80386, 486. PGAs were very popular for desktop machines, because their relatively large size enabled easy heat dissipation. The pins were evenly distributed along the bottom of the chip. PGA chips go into regular PGA or a special *Zero Insertion Force* (ZIF) socket. See Figure 2-34.

**Figure 2-33**
DIPP chip

**Figure 2-34**
PGA chip

*Staggered Pin Grid Array* (SPGA)   Pentium, Pentium Pro, K5, K6, 6×86. SPGAs have some or all of their pins organized in a diagonal pattern. This enables the CPU to have more closely packed pins, thereby keeping the overall package smaller. Like PGA chips, SPGA CPUs also have special ZIF sockets. See Figure 2-35.

**Figure 2-35**
SPGA chip

*Plastic/Ceramic Quad Flat Pack* (PQFP/CQFP)   Obsolete—80286, 80386, 486. Because of their small size, PQFPs were used primarily on laptop machines. They also had strong mounts, known as carrier rings, which made them difficult to jar loose. You could remove PQFPs easily, as long as you had a special tool. See Figure 2-36.

*Plastic/Ceramic Leaderless Chip Carrier* (PLCC/CLCC)   Obsolete—80286, 80386. PLCCs were popular for machines designed for upgradability, since they could be easily removed. They had no pins, which made them difficult to damage during removal or installation (Figure 2-37).

**Figure 2-36**
PQFP chip

**Figure 2-37**
PLCC chip

*Single Edge Contact Cartridge* (SECC)   Celeron, Pentium II, Pentium III, Athlon. Intel developed a new package for the Pentium II that wrapped the CPU in a plastic case and stood it on edge (Figure 2-38). The SEC cartridge takes up less space on the motherboard than earlier packages, and possibly enables better cooling of the CPU.

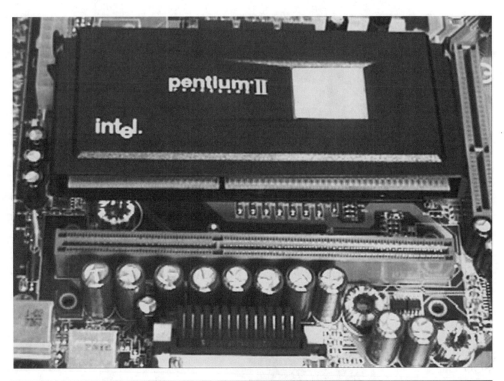

**Figure 2-38**   SEC cartridge

SEC cartridges come in a few package variations. The Pentium II uses the fully encased SECC, whereas the Pentium III comes in an SECC2 package, which simply uses less casing. The Celeron comes in a *Single Edge Processor Package* (SEPP), which throws away all the encasing. All three Intel SEC cartridge variations fit in the same socket, called Slot 1. Intel's SEC cartridges had the added benefit—at least from Intel's point of view—of being an Intel proprietary design, which stopped AMD from making pin-compatible CPUs (more on that later). So, AMD developed a variant SEC cartridge socket, called Slot A, for its first Athlon processors. Intel and AMD both plan to phase out the SEC-style CPU packages and are now producing processors in one of two new types of SPGA—PPGA and FC-PGA.

*Plastic Pin Grid Array* (PPGA)   Pentium, Celeron, Athlon, Duron. During the reign of the Pentium, advancements in CPU technology enabled manufacturers to redesign the classic ceramic SPGA package, using high-thermal plastics under the new name of PPGA (Figure 2-39).

*Flip-Chip Pin Grid Array* (FC-PGA)   Celeron, Pentium III. From the outside, FC-PGA looks basically the same as PPGA. This technology improves a few technical issues with the wiring process of the CPU (Figure 2-40).

**Figure 2-39**
Pentium PPGA

**Figure 2-40**
Celeron FC-PGA

*Ball-Grid Array* (BGA)   Numerous mobile processors. Visualize a PPGA CPU with tiny solder points that look like tiny balls replacing the typical pins. This is a BGA package. BGA processors are most common in laptops, where they are soldered to special *mobile modules,* making them more robust. Don't think that the soldering prevents CPU replacement/upgrade. Almost all laptops allow for upgrading by replacing the entire mobile module (Figure 2-41).

Don't bother memorizing all the different types of packages—simply appreciate that a wide variety is available and that each type of package requires its own unique socket or slot. Also appreciate the fact that these are simply generic types of packages. Each package has a number of very specific, very standardized versions, with names such as Slot A or Socket 370. We'll discuss these names when the chapter introduces the specific CPUs in more detail.

The A+ Certification Core Hardware exam expects you to identify and understand the function of CPUs, starting with the Pentium. It is far easier to understand modern CPUs, however, by first understanding how older CPUs functioned. Don't waste your time memorizing a bunch of facts about any CPUs before the Pentium. Do read about the earlier CPUs to make the understanding of the more modern CPUs much easier.

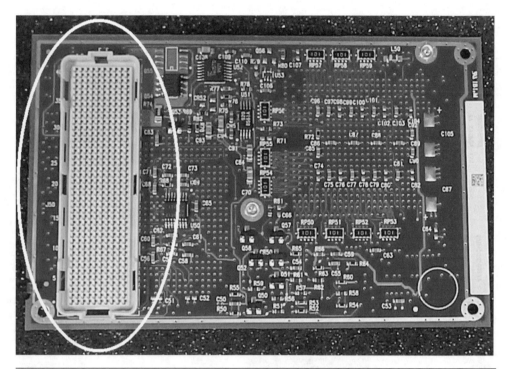

**Figure 2-41**    Ball-Grid Array on a mobile module

## The 8086 CPU Family

When IBM decided to enter the small-computer business, they settled on a CPU that matched five criteria. First, they decided that they would need a processor more powerful than the 8-bit microprocessors popular at the time. Second, IBM wanted a chip that would integrate easily into their systems. Third, they wanted a chip based on addressing concepts and machine language that programmers would easily understand. Fourth, they wanted a chip with flexibility and expandability. Fifth, it had to be priced competitively.

Intel invented an improved version of their popular 8080 processor, called the 8086, that nearly fit the bill on all five criteria (Figure 2-42). The 8086 CPU was a full 16-bit processor. Although some of Intel's competitors also produced 16-bit chips, the 8086 had the ability to address up to 1MB of memory, whereas all the competitors' CPUs could address only 64K of memory. Therefore, in terms of power and expandability, the 8086 beat the competition. Further, Intel achieved the dramatic increase in addressing capability without sacrificing compatibility with current 8-bit and 16-bit technology. Intel cleverly combined two 16-bit registers ($2^{16} = 64K$) into one 20-bit ($2^{20} = 1MB$) register. This addressing scheme sliced the one megabyte into 64K chunks, which made integrating programs written for earlier computers easier.

**Figure 2-42**
Intel 8086 chip

The 8086 had only one real problem: it was simply too powerful. The problem stemmed from the 8086's 16-bit external data bus. No contemporary devices could send or receive the 16-bit data to and from the 8086. To get an 8086 to speak to an 8-bit device, the 8086 had to chop its data into two pieces and send each piece separately. In order to fix this problem (and get their CPU picked for the IBM PC), Intel created a truncated 8086, called the 8088 processor (see Table 2-1). The 8088 was identical to the 8086, except it had only an 8-bit external data bus. IBM chose the 8088 to use in its first microcomputer, the IBM PC. The 8088 was also used in the upscale PC, the IBM XT. Compared to the 8088, the 8086 was rarely used.

**Table 2-1**    8086/8088 CPUs

| CHIP TYPE | CLOCK SPEED (MHz) | REGISTER SIZE | EXTERNAL DATA BUS | ADDRESS BUS |
|-----------|-------------------|---------------|-------------------|-------------|
| Intel 8088 | 4.77–10 | 16-bit | 8-bit | 20-bit |
| Intel 8086 | 4.77–10 | 16-bit | 16-bit | 20-bit |

## The 80286 CPU Family

In 1983, Intel introduced its next generation of chip, the 80286 (Table 2-2). (There was an interim chip, the 80186, which was little more than a slightly enhanced 8086. It died quickly with the appearance of the 80286.) The 80286, or as it was more popularly known, the 286, was a significant leap in technology from the 8086. The 286 first appeared in the IBM model *Advanced Technology* (AT) computer. See Figure 2-43.

**Table 2-2** 80286 CPUs

| CHIP TYPE | CLOCK SPEED (MHz) | REGISTER SIZE | EXTERNAL DATA BUS | ADDRESS BUS |
|---|---|---|---|---|
| Intel 80286 | 8–20 | 16-bit | 16-bit | 24-bit |

**Figure 2-43**
Intel 286 chip

## Modes

The 80286 had a number of major enhancements that made it far superior to the 8088/8086 chip. To take advantage of these functions, however, it needed programs that could use them. But what if all the programs were designed to run on the 8088? In this case, you wouldn't want the extra features of the 286; you'd simply want the 286 to run like an 8088. To handle this potential problem, Intel came up with a simple and elegant answer: starting with the 286 (and this is still true in today's CPUs), all CPUs would begin by acting like an 8088. To take advantage of the higher functions, you would then have to run special programs to "shift" the CPU into a higher mode. The 286 ran in two modes: *real mode*, which made it 8086 compatible; and *protected mode*, which enabled it to use advanced features.

## Protected Mode

When the 286 shifted into protected mode, it had the ability to use up to 16MB of memory and run more than one program at a time. This could happen only if you had an operating system designed to handle these advanced functions. MS-DOS (the most popular operating system of the day) was designed to run on an 8086, so if you ran DOS on a 286, you ran in real mode.

To take advantage of the 286 protected mode, you needed a special operating system. In protected mode, the computer could store multiple programs in memory. An operating system designed to run in protected mode could create a *focus*, running a few lines of one of the programs stored in memory. After some time, the operating system could then switch its focus to one of the other programs in memory. Technically speaking, this is not multitasking, but if the operating system could switch back and forth between the programs very rapidly, it would certainly look as though multitasking were taking place.

Did anyone write an operating system to take advantage of this power? Some people did. Certain flavors of UNIX were created to run on 286s. Novell NetWare 2.2 needed a 286, as did the first versions of OS/2. These were all very special situations. Also, once you switched into protected mode, the only way to go back to 8086 mode was to reboot the computer. For the most part, everyone ran DOS on 286s in those days, which meant that the 286 computers were little more than fast 8086s.

## The 80386 CPU: The 386DX Family

In 1985, Intel unveiled its next-generation chip, the 80386, or 386 for short (Figure 2-44). The 386 was Intel's first true 32-bit chip; the registers, address bus, and external data bus were all 32-bits wide (Table 2-3). The 386 also included a number of new registers for debugging and memory management. The 386 could run in three different modes: real mode, 286 protected mode, and its own very powerful 386 protected mode. Once the 386 switched to 386 protected mode, it had two functions that set it apart from earlier CPUs: *virtual memory* and a mode called *virtual 8086*.

**Figure 2-44**  Intel
386DX-33

**Table 2-3**  80386DX Family

| CHIP TYPE | CLK SPEED (MHz) | REGISTER SIZE | EXTERNAL DATA BUS | ADDRESS BUS | INTERNAL CACHE |
|---|---|---|---|---|---|
| Intel 80386DX | 16–33 | 32-bit | 32-bit | 32-bit | None |
| AMD AM386DX | 20–40 | 32-bit | 32-bit | 32-bit | None |
| AMD AM386DXL | 20–33 | 32-bit | 32-bit | 32-bit | None |
| AMD AM386DXLV | 25–33 | 32-bit | 32-bit | 32-bit | 8K |

## Virtual Memory

The 386's 32-bit address bus enabled it to address up to 4GB of memory, far more than even current PCs need ($2^{32}$ = 4,294,967,296 = 4GB). On the other hand, today's PCs can often use more RAM than they have installed. Programs run in RAM. If you try to load more programs than your RAM can store, you will get some kind of "out of memory" error. With the right operating system, the 386 chip can create "pretend RAM," better known as virtual memory, by electronically changing a part of permanent storage—in particular hard drives—into memory. This virtual memory looks like regular RAM to the operating system. The part of your hard drive that acts like virtual memory is called a *swap file*. Every current operating system uses a swap file. Virtual memory started with the 80386, and every subsequent CPU supports it.

## Virtual 8086

386s also had a more advanced protected mode known as virtual 8086. In 286 protected mode, it was impossible to run 8086-mode DOS programs. With virtual 8086, the operating system created virtual 8086 *bubbles*—memory areas completely separated and virtually addressed within the 1MB 8086 limit. In other words, a DOS program could run within an 8086 bubble while the CPU stayed in protected mode. The operating system created *virtual registers* whenever the program wanted to use them. The operating system would then inspect what the program was trying to do and verify that it wasn't trying to do something dangerous. Just as with virtual memory, every CPU generation since the 80386 supports virtual 8086.

## The 80386SX CPU Family

To increase the popularity of the 386 chip, Intel recognized the need for a 386 processor that could operate easily on 16-bit motherboards. Intel fulfilled this need with the 80386SX (Figure 2-45).

The 386SX differed from the standard 386 (now known as the 386DX) in two ways. First, Intel reduced the external data bus size from 32-bit to 16-bit to match the 286's external data bus. Second, the address bus was reduced to 24 bits, again matching the 286 specifications (Table 2-4). This limited the address range of the 386SX to 16MB ($2^{24}$ = 16MB).

Although the 386SX looked like a 286 on the outside, it was a full 386DX on the inside. The 386SX could handle all of the modes and functions of the DX—386 protected mode, virtual memory, and virtual 8086. Many people believe that the "SX" stood for "Single Channel" and the "DX" stood for "Dual Channel." There is no proof of this, and Intel has never made any statement to that effect. "SX" and "DX" are not abbreviations.

**Figure 2-45**
AMD 386SX

**Table 2-4**   80386SX Family

| CHIP TYPE | CLK (MHz) | REGISTER SIZE | EXTERNAL DATA BUS | ADDRESS BUS | CACHE | VOLTAGE | SMM |
|---|---|---|---|---|---|---|---|
| Intel 80386SX | 16–25 | 32-bit | 16-bit | 24-bit | None | 5 V | No |
| Intel 80386SL | 16–25 | 32-bit | 16-bit | 24-bit | None | 3.3 V | Yes |
| AMD AM386SX | 20–40 | 32-bit | 16-bit | 24-bit | None | 5 V | No |
| AMD AM386SXL | 16–40 | 32-bit | 16-bit | 24-bit | None | 5 V | Yes |
| AMD AM386SXLV | 33 | 32-bit | 16-bit | 24-bit | 8K | 3.3 V | Yes |
| IBM 386SLC | 20 | 32-bit | 16-bit | 24-bit | 8K | 3.3 V | Yes |

## Early Power-Saving Strategies— 386s and 486s

CPUs, like all other electrical components, need electricity. Also like all other electrical devices, CPUs require a certain voltage of electricity. During the time of the 8086s, 80286s, and 80386s, all CPUs needed 5 *volts* (V) to operate. During the time of the 80386s, however, a new type of PC started to become popular: the laptop. There were 80286 laptops, but it wasn't until the 386s that they became truly common. Earlier portable computers derived their power from AC outlets. You turned off the portable PC, unplugged it, moved it to another location, and then plugged it in again. Laptops were designed from the start to derive their power from built-in batteries. As we all can attest, batteries work for only a relatively short time. The first laptops had batteries that lasted less than half an hour—hardly acceptable for any serious work.

It quickly became obvious that if laptops were to become a mainstream product, they would have to have battery lives in the multiple-hour range. To do that, either battery technology would have to improve or the laptops would have to use less power. On the better-battery side, battery makers began to develop longer-lasting battery technologies with names like Nickel-Cadmium and Lithium-Ion. Intel decided to attack the power problem by making CPUs that required less power. Additionally, Intel introduced a new function for CPUs, called *System Management Mode* (SMM), which could shut down unused, power-draining peripherals.

### Lower Voltage

Intel introduced the first mainstream low-voltage CPU with the 386SL, a special 386SX-based chip that ran at only 3.3 volts, rather than the 5 volts all previous CPUs needed. By reducing the voltage usage from 5 to 3.3 volts, the 386SL used roughly half the power of an equivalent 386SX. Intel also reduced the voltage for all of the support chips in the laptop (down to 3.3 volts), which resulted in a laptop that would use far less power.

Lower voltages have taken over the PC world. Although many 486s and even a few of the first Pentium CPUs used 5 volts, all current CPUs, whether they are in a laptop or on your desk, use 3.3 or even lower voltage. Most modern CPUs use only slightly more than 2 volts.

A few late-generation 386 systems and all 486 systems had two voltage issues that technicians needed to address. First, you had to determine the voltage of the CPU. Second, you needed to make sure that the motherboard supplied the proper voltage to the CPU. Putting a low-voltage CPU on a motherboard set up for 5 volts, for example, would naturally be a bad idea. Today's systems, with a few exceptions, do all of this automatically.

During the reign of the 486 CPUs, CPUs began to have a high degree of interchangeability. This is discussed in more detail in the section, "The 486 CPU Family," but the bottom line is that a tremendous demand existed for single motherboards that could support both 5-volt and 3.3-volt CPUs. Fortunately, the answer was both simple and inexpensive and is still in use today.

### Voltage Regulators to the Rescue

A wonderful, cheap, little electric component called a *voltage regulator* does one thing well—it can convert one voltage of electricity into a lower voltage. Voltage regulators were not invented for the PC industry. They've been around for a long time and have millions of applications in our world. They come in a myriad of shapes and sizes, but the ones used in PCs are relatively common in appearance. They are roughly 3/4 to 1 inch long and have three wires (electricians call them *leads*) that are soldered to the motherboard. These devices tend to generate a lot of heat, so they are almost always mounted on some type of cooling fins. Figure 2-46 shows an example. By adding a voltage regulator to the motherboard, manufacturers could make systems that supported either a 3.3-volt or a 5-volt CPU.

This switchable 3.3-volt or 5-volt motherboard was very common in the days of the 486, so techs had to make sure to set the jumper properly for the type of CPU installed. Once you knew the correct voltage for the CPU, you then had to find the jumper(s) or switch(es) to flip for the correct voltage. It was usually easy to set this type of motherboard for either 3.3- or 5-volt operation, but not always. Figure 2-47 shows the jumper layout of a particularly difficult 486 system.

**Figure 2-46**
Typical PC voltage
regulator

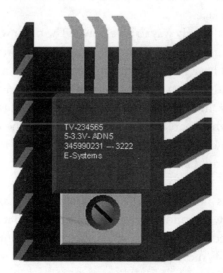

**Figure 2-47**   Typically complex set of jumpers on 486 system

On this particular motherboard, how could you know which set of jumpers changed voltage settings and what the function was of all the other jumpers? It was always a good thing to have your motherboard book. A 486 system could be configured for 3.3 or 5 volts in many different ways. Successful techs always verified their voltages.

As you might imagine, improper voltage settings could cause some serious problems, including destroying CPUs. Setting the proper voltage, along with other issues such as CPU speed, motivated Intel to create a new function called CPUID. CPUID gave the CPU the ability to inform the system of all the details about its required voltage, speed, and a host of other bits of important information. The system then automatically adjusts itself for everything the CPU needs. Except in very rare situations, we no longer concern ourselves with voltages.

Reducing voltage is not the only way to save power. The other way to save power is to turn off devices not being used by the system. For example, if you walk away from your PC, wouldn't it be nice to have the monitor turn itself off after a set amount of time? How about telling the hard drive to stop spinning if it hasn't been accessed after a few minutes? To perform this, Intel created *System Management Mode* (SMM). SMM is a hardware-based function that enables the CPU to shut down the monitor, hard drives, and any other peripheral not in use in order to save power.

Special programming would be run to tell the CPU to turn off the hard drive, monitor, and other devices after a certain number of minutes of inactivity. In the days of the 386s and 486s, SMM was nothing short of a disaster. The main problem was that programs didn't know how to handle accessing a peripheral that had been turned off. Persons using a DOS-based 386 laptop to write a letter, for example, would find after taking a short break that the moment they started typing again, the system would lock up. SMM didn't really hit its stride until Windows 95. Windows 95 understood SMM, and Microsoft created software standards with names like *Advanced Power Management* (APM) that were designed to work with SMM-capable CPUs.

Understanding SMM requires a lot more background information. For that reason, modern power management is discussed in Chapter 17. Here we continue to discuss CPU voltages, but Chapter 17 contains more details of modern power management.

## The 486 CPU Family

In 1989, Intel released the i486 (Figure 2-48). The i486 had 32-bit registers, a 32-bit external data bus, and a 32-bit memory address bus, exactly like the 386DX (Table 2-5). However, the i486 did far more than the 386DX. It actually combined a slightly improved 386DX, a built-in (and also improved) 387 math coprocessor, and most importantly, a built-in 8K write-through cache, all on the same chip.

**Figure 2-48**
Intel 486DX-50

## No New Modes!

The 486 ran in the same modes as an 80386. None of the new features of a 486 (math coprocessor and cache) were tied to a specific 486 mode. The most advanced mode the 486 could run was 80386 protected mode, with virtual memory and virtual 8086, just like an 80386. From a program's point of view, no difference existed between an 80386 with a math coprocessor and a 486.

## Improved Instruction Set

The 486's instruction set included new functions for optimizing the 486's ability to work in multitasking environments, as well as enabling control over new cache functions. Also, some of the 486's machine-language commands acted as *Reduced Instruction Set Computing* (RISC) instructions. This meant that machine-language commands did not have to be decoded inside the chip. The computer could see and immediately execute about 20 percent of the 486's most common commands. The other commands still had to be decoded. Because decoding took at least one clock cycle, removing decoding from the processor's functions, whenever possible, was a tremendous asset.

**NOTE**  The 486 was not a RISC chip. It was considered a *Complex Instruction Set Computing* (CISC) chip with a few RISC functions.

## Math Coprocessor

All CPUs, from the 8088 through the 386, could perform basic arithmetic commands such as add, subtract, multiply, and divide. But what if you wanted to perform a more complex mathematical function such as determining the cosine of a number? No built-in commands were available to perform higher math functions such as trigonometric (sine, cosine, tangent), logarithmic ($e^x$, log10x, ln x), or large floating-point numbers

**Table 2-5** 486 CPU Family

| CHIP TYPE | CPU SPEED (MHz) | CLK MULTIPLE | EXTERNAL DATA BUS | INTERNAL CACHE | MATH UNIT | VOLTAGE | SMM |
|---|---|---|---|---|---|---|---|
| Intel 80486DX | 25, 33, 50 | 1× | 32-bit | 8KB | Yes | 3.3/5 V | Yes |
| Intel 80486DX/2 | 25/50 33/66 | 2× | 32-bit | 8KB | Yes | 3.3/5 V | Yes |
| Intel 80486DX/4 | 25/75 33/100 | 3× | 32-bit | 16KB | Yes | 5 V | Yes |
| Intel 80486SX | 16, 20, 25 | 1× | 32-bit | 8KB | None | 5 V | Yes |
| Intel 80486SL | 16, 20, 25 | 1× | 32-bit | 8KB | None | 3.3 V | Yes |
| AMD AM486DX | 33, 40 | 1× | 32-bit | 8KB | Yes | 5 V | No |
| AMD AM486DXLV | 33 | 1× | 32-bit | 8KB | Yes | 3.3 V | Yes |
| AMD AM486DX2 | 25/50 40/80 | 2× | 32-bit | 8KB | Yes | 3.3/5 V | No |
| AMD AM486DX4 | 33/100 40/120 | 3× | 32-bit | 8KB | Yes | 3.3 V | Yes |
| AMD AM486DX4 "Enhanced" | 40/120 33/133 | 3× 4× | 32-bit | 16KB WB | Yes | 3.3 V | Yes |
| AMD AM486DXL2 | 25/50 40/80 | 2× | 32-bit | 8KB | Yes | 5 V | No |

**Table 2-5** 486 CPU Family (continued)

| CHIP TYPE | CPU SPEED (MHz) | CLK MULTIPLE | EXTERNAL DATA BUS | INTERNAL CACHE | MATH UNIT | VOLTAGE | SMM |
|---|---|---|---|---|---|---|---|
| AMD AM486SX. | 33, 40 | 1 × | 32-bit | 8KB | None | 5V | No |
| AMD AM486SXLV | 33 | 1 × | 32-bit | 8KB | None | 3.3V | Yes |
| AMD AM486SX2 | 25/50 | 2 × | 32-bit | 8KB | None | 5V | No |
| CYRIX CX486DX | 33 | 1 × | 32-bit | 8KB WB | Yes | 3.3/5V | Yes |
| CYRIX CX486DX2 | 25/50 40/80 | 2 × | 32-bit | 8KB WB | Yes | 3.3/5V | Yes |
| CYRIX CX486DLC | 33–40 | 1 × | 32-bit | 1KB WT | Yes | 5V | Yes |
| CYRIX CX486SLC | 20–33 | 1 × | 16-bit | 1KB WT | No | 3.3/5V | Yes |
| CYRIX CX486SLC2 | 25/50 | 2 × | 32-bit | 1KB WT | No | 3.3/5V | Yes |

$(3.027 \times 10^{24})$. To perform high math functions like these, programmers had to write code using approximation formulas. These took hundreds, maybe thousands, of lines of code to get an answer for something like a log (34.2321).

When Intel designed the 8088, it sold a supplementary CPU called the 8087 that could perform these calculations. Why not design the 8088 with all these functions built in? They could have, but it would have increased the cost of the 8088 by at least a factor of two. Plus, very few people needed these extra functions unless they were doing math-intensive calculations. So Intel felt that if you wanted to do extra calculations, you would be willing to pay more. The IBM PC had an extra socket on the motherboard designed for the optional *math coprocessor*. When the 80286 was created, an improved 8087, called the 80287, was developed. The IBM 286 AT had an optional 80287 slot, and similarly, the 80386 had the 80387 slot. Figure 2-49 shows an ancient 286 system's math coprocessor slot. Note the "80287" printed on the motherboard.

**Figure 2-49** 80287 math coprocessor socket

The 486 had a 387 math coprocessor built into the CPU. The built-in 387 math coprocessor was substantially more powerful than its external 80387 brother. Because it was on the CPU, it depended much less on clock cycles. Also, the internal math coprocessor was able to take advantage of the cache, as needed, to store data and code. Lastly, two different 32-bit pathways led to the math unit that worked at the same time, effectively providing a 64-bit program and data path between the math unit and the rest of the 486.

All CPUs since the 486 now have a built-in math coprocessor. Many people refer to the built-in math coprocessor as the *floating-point unit*.

## Onboard Cache

The 8K onboard write-through RAM cache enabled the 486 to store upcoming lines of instructions as well as data. Although an 8K cache seems small, it provided tremendous speed improvements. Let's see how caching works.

Webster's defines *cache* as follows: "to set something aside, or to store nearby for anticipated use." The word *cache* first became popular in the 18th century when French trappers would bury food and supplies in strategic areas in case they were ever stranded by the weather. In the computer world, *cache* means to set aside data used in the past in a special, fast storage area. Then if the CPU needs the data again, it can more easily (and much more quickly) access that data.

To understand caching, you need to understand that speed is everything in the PC world. Programs and data usually reside on some sort of mass storage device, such as a floppy disk, hard drive, or CD-ROM disk. When you access that data or application, the system must go first to the mass storage and then copy all the relevant files into RAM. Then the CPU can work with that information. The data returns through the same process—the CPU writes to RAM, and RAM writes to mass storage (Figure 2-50).

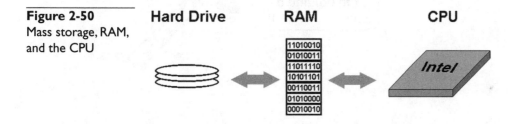

**Figure 2-50**
Mass storage, RAM, and the CPU

**Hard Drive**   **RAM**   **CPU**

This process runs into two major bottlenecks; mass storage is much slower than RAM, and RAM is much slower than the CPU. Caching enables you to speed up the system by creating special storage areas for data that is being moved from the hard drive, RAM, and CPU. Based on the diagram in Figure 2-51, you can see that there are two distinct types of caches: one for mass storage and another for RAM. At this point, let's concentrate on the RAM cache. For an in-depth discussion of hard drive caches, see Chapter 10 on Windows 9x.

### DRAM and Why It Is Cached

*Dynamic RAM* (DRAM) is the RAM of choice for the PC world. DRAM is cheap, small, and relatively fast, although not as fast as today's CPUs. DRAM works by making each storage bit a microscopic capacitor and transistor. A charged capacitor is a "1" and a discharged capacitor is a "0" (Figure 2-52).

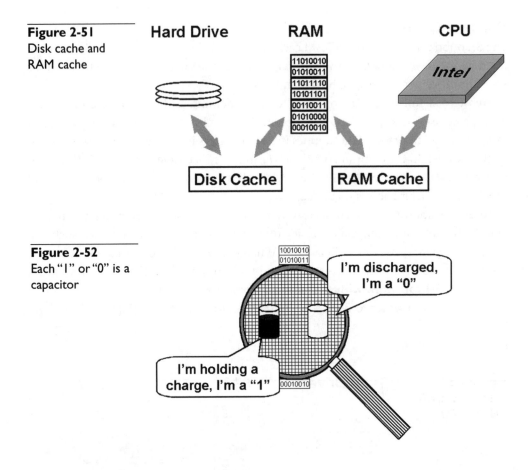

**Figure 2-51**
Disk cache and
RAM cache

**Figure 2-52**
Each "1" or "0" is a
capacitor

DRAM, however, has a small problem: the capacitors. A *capacitor* resembles a battery in that it holds a charge and then discharges it. Unlike a battery that holds a charge for months, the tiny capacitors in the DRAM hold their charges for about 16 milliseconds. Therefore, the DRAM needs an entire set of circuitry to keep the capacitors charged. The process of recharging these capacitors is called *refresh*. Without refresh, data added to RAM would disappear after 16 milliseconds, which is why DRAM is considered volatile RAM. Imagine the refresh circuitry as the MCC using an electronic garden hose to spray a refreshing charge of electricity on the DRAM (Figure 2-53).

The memory-controller chip tells the refresh circuitry on the DRAM chip when to refresh. Every few milliseconds, the MCC sends a refresh signal to the RAM, and the RAM chips begin their refresh. Unfortunately, if the CPU decides to access the RAM at this point, the MCC creates a *wait state* (Figure 2-54). The other problem with DRAM is that it is not as fast as the CPU. The CPU often has wait states, not because the RAM is refreshing, but simply because it has to wait for the DRAM to get the values it needs.

**Figure 2-53**
MCC refreshing
DRAM

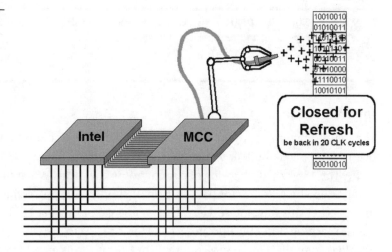

**Figure 2-54**
MCC forcing a
wait state

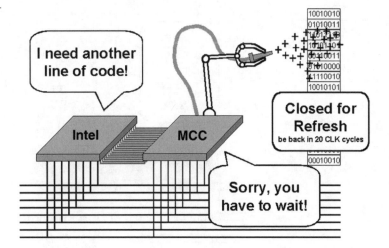

## SRAM

Wait states cause the computer to slow down. By getting around wait states, you could significantly increase computer speed. You can do this by adding special *Static RAM* (SRAM) chips to the computer. SRAM is another type of RAM that does not use tiny capacitors to store 1's and 0's. Instead, SRAM uses a special circuit called a *flip-flop*. Using flip-flops instead of capacitors means that SRAM does not have to be refreshed. SRAM is almost as fast as the fastest CPU.

Now that you have SRAM, how do you use it? Why not get rid of the DRAM and replace it with SRAM? Because SRAM is at least ten times more expensive than DRAM. However, you can afford a small amount of SRAM as a *RAM cache*.

**EXAM TIP** DRAM is fast, cheap, and must be refreshed; SRAM is very fast, very expensive, and requires no refresh.

## Internal Cache

The main difference between a 486 and 386 chip was that a 486 had a small (8,192-byte) SRAM cache built into the chip. All commands for the 486 went through the cache. The 486 stored a backlog of commands in the cache. When the CPU encountered a wait state, the 486 did not have to stop; it simply kept processing commands stored in the cache. This was, and still is, called an *internal* or *level-one* (L1) cache (Figure 2-55).

RAM caching stores the upcoming code for the CPU to use when it (the CPU) is ready. All CPUs from the 486 on have internal (or L1, the terms are interchangeable) caches.

**Figure 2-55**
MCC using cache

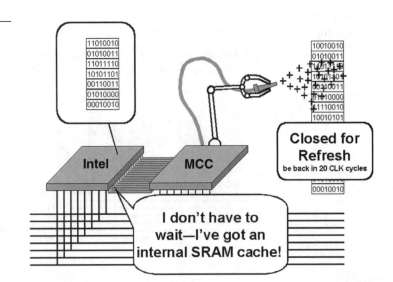

## External Cache

Although an internal cache on the CPU is very helpful, a CPU will happily use all the cache it can get. Therefore, almost all the 486 and Pentium MCCs could work with an *external* or *L2* cache. The first L2 caches manifested themselves with special SRAM chips that sat on the motherboard. An L2 cache was usually around 64K to 1MB, depending mainly on the size of your wallet. In 486s, the SRAM was DIPP style, snapped into special sockets, but by the time of the Pentiums, most motherboards had an L2 cache soldered permanently to the motherboard (Figure 2-56). Starting with the Pentium II, all CPUs now incorporate both the L1 and the L2 cache on the CPU itself—a modern motherboard with SRAM chips soldered on it is a rare sight.

**Figure 2-56**
Pentium-era
external cache
(L2) chips

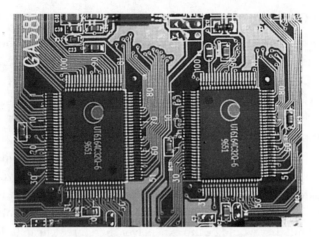

## Write-Back vs. Write-Through

Everything discussed so far is based only on reading from the RAM chips to the CPU. What would happen if you wrote data to the RAM? What should the cache do with this data? Some caches immediately send all data writes directly to RAM, even if it means hitting a wait state. This is called *write-through* (WT). However, some caches store the write data in the cache and write it to RAM later. These caches are called *write-back* (WB). Write-back caches are harder to implement, but are much more powerful than write-through caches. Write-through caches are cheaper to use, but not as powerful. See Figure 2-57.

**Figure 2-57**
Write-through vs.
write-back

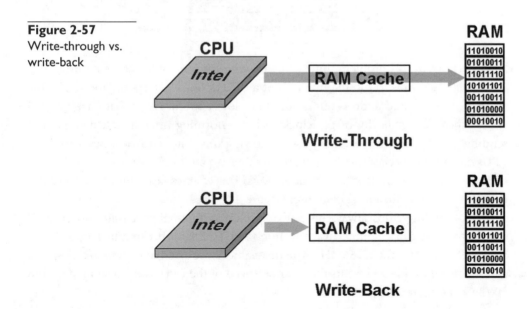

### Different Caches for Different Chips

Different makers of 486s had different ways of caching. Check the tables in this chapter to see the differences among chipmakers as to the size of caches and *write-through* vs. *write-back*. Cyrix, AMD, and Intel were constantly one-upping each other, touting their respective caches and sizes.

## Clock Doubling

Once 486s got up to a 33MHz clock speed, the PC industry found itself with a bit of a problem. CPU makers wanted to increase their CPU speeds beyond 33MHz, but the motherboards at the time couldn't go faster than 33MHz. This was due to *radio frequency interference* (RFI), among other problems. Oh sure, you could get a motherboard to go faster, but they would be too expensive. Therefore, "cheap technology" was locked at 33MHz. See Figure 2-58.

**Figure 2-58**
CPUs but not
motherboards
could be made
to break 33MHz

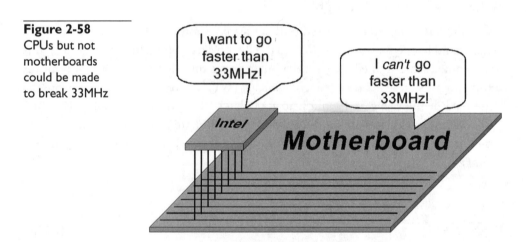

To circumvent this problem, Intel came up with the idea of a clock-doubling CPU. *Clock doubling* means to run the internals of a CPU at one clock speed, and to run the external data bus and address bus at another, slower speed. CPUs that have internal caches spend the majority of the clock cycles performing internal calculations, not sending any data on the external buses. Knowing this, Intel created a new family of CPUs containing special circuitry that enables them to multiply the system clock for the time when they run these internal calculations. This enables faster processing without having to speed up the entire computer (Figure 2-59).

Clock-doubling chips always have two speeds: an internal speed and an external speed. The first clock doubler was the Intel 486DX/2, and it came in two different speeds: 25/50MHz and 33/66MHz. The first value is the external or system bus speed, and the second value represents the internal speed of the CPU. AMD also made a 486 DX/2 CPU (Figure 2-60).

**Figure 2-59**
Relation of
clock doubling
between CPU and
motherboard

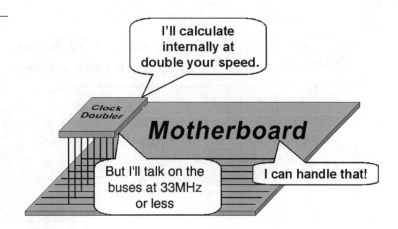

**Figure 2-60**
A clock-doubling
486—the AMD
486DX/2

In the 486 world, the circuitry that doubled the speed, called the *multiplier,* could not be changed. For example, the 486DX/2 multiplied the system crystal's clock by two. So if you had a 486DX/2 33/66 being pushed by a 33MHz crystal, it ran at an internal speed of 66MHz. But remember that the clock speed is a *maximum* speed; you could (and still can) run a CPU slower than its clock speed by pushing it with a slower crystal. If you decided to run the 486DX/2 33/66 with a 25MHz crystal, the 486DX/2 33/66 would run internally at only 50MHz (Figure 2-61).

The large number of multipliers available in 486s quickly changed the meaning of clock doubling to mean *any* multiplier. For example, the 486DX/4 actually tripled the clock speed, but it was still called the doubler. Just because some were called "doubler," you could not assume "times two."

Since the 486s, all CPUs now use multipliers. The clock doubling on all CPUs since the Pentium, however, uses *variable* multipliers. See the "Pentium Clock Doubling" section later in this chapter for details.

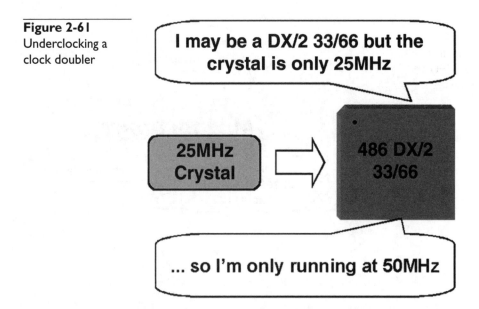

**Figure 2-61**
Underclocking a
clock doubler

## Upgrading 486 CPUs

A CPU is useless until you place it in a motherboard. The device into which you insert the CPU is classically called a *socket*. During the reign of the 8088s, 286s, and 386s, there was little interest in sockets, as the concept of upgrading a CPU was an extremely rare occurrence. Toward the end of the 386s, however, a number of standards, driven by customer demand, created the desire and the ability to upgrade CPUs.

The first technology change that made upgrading practical was motherboards that had more than one clock speed. Remember that the system crystal is on the motherboard. If you remove a 25MHz CPU and insert a 33MHz CPU, the 33MHz CPU would still run at only the speed of the system crystal—25MHz. Starting with a few 386 motherboards and becoming mainstream in the 486 motherboards, we began to see the ability to change the system crystal speed via jumpers on the motherboard (Figure 2-62).

**Figure 2-62**
Jumpers to adjust
motherboard speed

The second technology change that spurred upgrading was the strong adoption of the PGA-type CPU package. There were (and still are) many types of CPU packages, but by the time of the 486s, the vast majority of CPUs made were in the PGA package. Intel standardized the pin layouts on the PGA CPUs, creating subtypes called Socket *X*, where *X* indicated a particular number that defined the CPU package as well as the socket to which it was installed. Terms such as Socket 3 or Socket 6 were used to define the type of PGA package a particular chip used (Figure 2-63). This made CPUs highly interchangeable. As long as the motherboard had adjustable voltage and motherboard speed, you could easily change the CPU in the system.

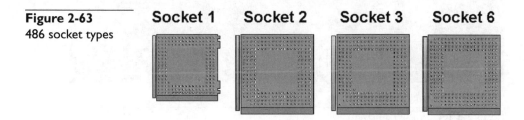

**Figure 2-63**
486 socket types

**Socket 1**  **Socket 2**  **Socket 3**  **Socket 6**

The third technology change that made upgrading easier was the *Zero Insertion Force* (ZIF) socket. ZIF sockets have a lever arm that enables simple removal and installation of CPUs. Before ZIF sockets came along, you had to use a special removal tool to take the CPU off the motherboard (Figure 2-64). ZIF sockets made removal much easier and safer (Figure 2-65). Many types of ZIF sockets exist; Figure 2-63 shows the different types of 486 ZIF sockets.

## Overdrive CPUs for 486s

When the 486 chip was first released, a number of computer manufacturers began to make upgradable systems. These had proprietary CPU cards, often called *daughter cards*, that could be removed and replaced with a daughter card that had a more powerful CPU. As more powerful 486s came into the market, Intel realized that first-generation 486s running at 25MHz would be good candidates for upgrading. Intel unveiled the 486 overdrive chips to take advantage of this anticipated market. The 486 overdrive chips were nothing more than a 486DX/2 or DX/4 with an extra pin. To take advantage of an overdrive processor, you normally needed a special, 169-pin PGA/ZIF socket designed especially for the overdrive chip.

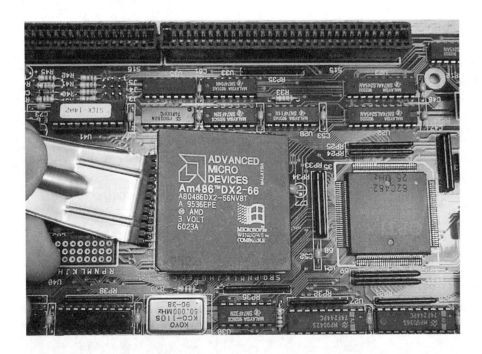

**Figure 2-64**   CPU removal tool

**Figure 2-65**
ZIF socket

Although overdrives were a simple, effective upgrade for systems that were prepared for their use, they did have some major downsides. First, if you plugged in an overdrive CPU, the old processor was disabled—*but you could not remove it.* This was frustrating considering that you could have sold your old 486SX or DX. Second, most 486 motherboards could accept multiple types of regular processors, which negated the need for an overdrive chip. If you already had an overdrive-ready motherboard, however, it was often a cost-effective option. Table 2-6 lists Intel 486 overdrive processors.

**Table 2-6**   486 Overdrive Processors

| CHIP | SPEED (MHz) | RECOMMENDED UPGRADES |
|------|-------------|----------------------|
| 486DX/2 | 25/50 | 486SX-25, 486DX-25 |
| 486DX/2 | 33/66 | 486SX-33, 486DX-33 |
| 486DX/4 | 25/75 | 486SX-25, 486DX-25, 486DX/2 25/50 |
| 486DX/4 | 33/100 | 486SX-33, 486DX-33, 486DX/2 33/66 |

The term *overdrive* was extended by Intel to describe a broad family of replacement processors, not only for 486 systems, but also for older Pentium systems. These 486-to-Pentium and old-Pentium-to-newer-Pentium overdrive CPUs are discussed in their own sections, later in this chapter. Intel no longer produces overdrive processors.

## Test Specific

### The Pentium CPU: The Early Years

Intel provided a major technological leap forward when they introduced the Pentium processor in 1993 (Figure 2-66). The Pentium had a 64-bit external data bus that split internally as two dual-pipelined 32-bit data buses. These data buses enabled the CPU to process two separate lines of code simultaneously. The Pentium also sported an 8K write-back cache for data and an 8K write-through cache for programs. The program cache was capable of *branch prediction,* where the program cache attempted to anticipate program branches before they got to the CPU itself. An IF statement provides a nice example of this: "If the value in the AX register = 5, then stop running this code and jump to another memory location." Such a jump would make all of the data in the cache useless. The internal cache in the Pentium could recognize a branch statement and would take code from both sides of the branch (it wasn't smart enough to know which way it was going to go) so that no matter which way the code went, the cache would have good data. Table 2-7 lists the early Pentium-class processors.

**Table 2-7**  Early Pentium CPUs

| CPU | MAKER | CORE SPEED (MHz) | EXT SPEED (MHz) | CLK MULT. | CACHE (KB) | VOLTAGE | PACKAGE[2] |
|---|---|---|---|---|---|---|---|
| Pentium P5 | Intel | 60 | 60 | 1 × | 8WT/8WB | 5 V | Socket 5 |
| Pentium P5 | Intel | 66 | 66 | 1 × | 8WT/8WB | 5 V | Socket 5 |
| Pentium P54C | Intel | 75 | 50 | 1.5 × | 8WT/8WB | 3.3 V | Socket 7 |
| Pentium P54C | Intel | 90 | 60 | 1.5 × | 8WT/8WB | 3.3 V | Socket 7 |
| Pentium P54C | Intel | 100 | 66 | 1.5 × | 8WT/8WB | 3.3 V | Socket 7 |
| Pentium P54C | Intel | 120 | 60 | 2 × | 8WT/8WB | 3.3 V | Socket 7 |
| Pentium P54C | Intel | 133 | 66 | 2 × | 8WT/8WB | 3.3 V | Socket 7 |
| Pentium P54C | Intel | 150 | 60 | 2.5 × | 8WT/8WB | 3.3 V | Socket 7 |
| Pentium P54C | Intel | 166 | 66 | 2.5 × | 8WT/8WB | 3.3 V | Socket 7 |
| Pentium P54C | Intel | 200 | 66 | 3 × | 8WT/8WB | 3.3 V | Socket 7 |
| K5 PR75[1] | AMD | 75 | 50 | 1.5 × | 8WT/8WB | 3.3 V | Socket 7 |
| K5 PR90[1] | AMD | 90 | 60 | 1.5 × | 8WT/8WB | 3.3 V | Socket 7 |

(continues)

**Table 2-7**   Early Pentium CPUs (continued)

| CPU | MAKER | CORE SPEED (MHz) | EXT SPEED (MHz) | CLK MULT. | CACHE (KB) | VOLTAGE | PACKAGE[2] |
|---|---|---|---|---|---|---|---|
| K5 PR100[1] | AMD | 100 | 66 | 1.5 × | 8WT/8WB | 3.3 V | Socket 7 |
| K5 PR120[1] | AMD | 90 | 60 | 1.5 × | 8WT/8WB | 3.3 V | Socket 7 |
| K5 PR133[1] | AMD | 100 | 66 | 1.5 × | 8WT/8WB | 3.3 V | Socket 7 |
| K5 PR166[1] | AMD | 116 | 66 | 1.75 × | 8WT/8WB | 3.3 V | Socket 7 |
| 6×86/6×86L P120[1] | Cyrix | 100 | 50 | 2 × | 8WT/8WB | 3.3 V[3] | Socket 7 |
| 6×86/6×86L P133[1] | Cyrix | 110 | 55 | 2 × | 8WT/8WB | 3.3 V[3] | Socket 7 |
| 6×86/6×86L P150[1] | Cyrix | 120 | 60 | 2 × | 8WT/8WB | 3.3 V[3] | Socket 7 |
| 6×86/6×86L P166[1] | Cyrix | 133 | 66 | 2 × | 8WT/8WB | 3.3 V[3] | Socket 7 |
| 6×86/6×86L P200[1] | Cyrix | 150 | 75 | 2 × | 8WT/8WB | 3.3 V[3] | Socket 7 |

[1]See P-rating.
[2]See Pentium Socket Types.
[3]The 6×86L used 2.9 volts.

**Figure 2-66**
Early Pentium

## Dual Pipeline

All CPUs have a pipeline. Think of a pipeline as the series of steps the CPU needs to process a command. Remember how we discussed the fact that you have to hit the clock wire a number of times before the answer appeared when we added 2 + 3? That is a perfect example of the CPU's pipeline processing the command. Each clock cycle moves the command one step along the pipeline. Different CPUs have different pipelines, but they all have the same basic steps. Figure 2-67 illustrates the pipeline for a 486.

**Figure 2-67**
Simplified CPU
pipeline

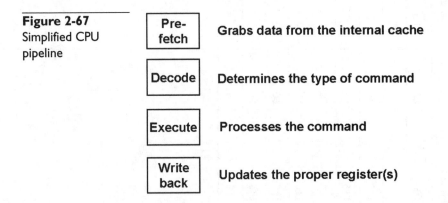

The problem with a typical CPU pipeline comes in the execution stage. Different sets of circuitry inside the CPU handle different commands (Figure 2-68), so a command passes through some or all of these circuits as it is processed (Figure 2-69). All commands, simple or complex, run through the same linear pipeline.

Think of pipelining as doing laundry. You don't sort, wash, dry, fold, and iron one load at a time. You get it all sorted, then you start one load in the washer. After that load is finished, you put it in the dryer and start another load in the washer so the washer and dryer are running at the same time. You keep this up until you are washing, drying, folding, and maybe even ironing at the same time. This is far more efficient. See Figure 2-70.

**Figure 2-68**
Four main processes
in a CPU

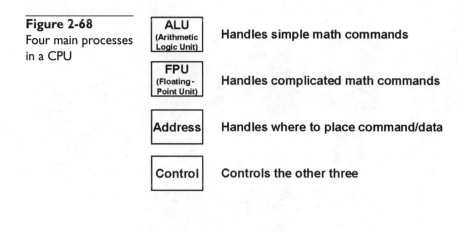

ALU (Arithmetic Logic Unit)    **Handles simple math commands**

FPU (Floating-Point Unit)    **Handles complicated math commands**

Address    **Handles where to place command/data**

Control    **Controls the other three**

**Figure 2-69**
Possible pipeline

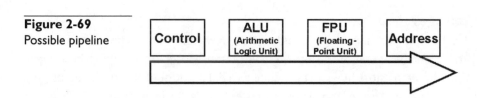

**Figure 2-70**
Pipelining is like
doing laundry.

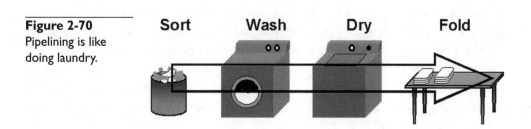

Having an extra washing machine and an extra dryer would certainly speed up the process, wouldn't it? Sure, you would sometimes have to wait on some of the other steps in the pipeline, but it would help (Figure 2-71). Well, a Pentium has a second, separate set of circuitry that enables more than one command (of certain types) to be processed at a time. This is called *dual pipelining*.

The names of the pipelines are U and V. The U pipeline is the main one, which can do anything; the V pipeline can handle only simple commands, such as integer addition.

**Figure 2-71**
Using dual pipelines
is comparable
to having extra
equipment.

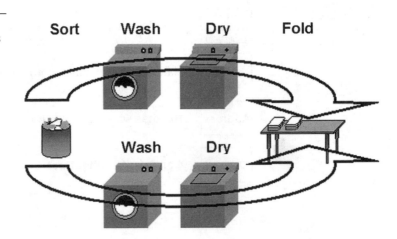

## CPU Voltages

A CPU is little more than a huge conglomeration of millions of tiny transistors. All transistors create heat, and the faster you make a transistor work, the more heat it generates. The tiny transistors in a CPU generate a trivial amount of heat individually, but as you add more and more transistors to faster and faster generations of CPUs, the amount of heat becomes significant. If a CPU gets too hot, it locks up and does not operate.

When you look at a CPU, you actually see the plastic or ceramic outer case. The electronics of the CPU are much smaller than the case (Figure 2-72). Why? The case helps dissipate the heat generated by the CPU. The heat from 8088, 286, and 386 systems was relatively low due to the relatively low speeds and low number of transistors. The outer case could easily handle the necessary dissipation. By the time of the 486, however, plastic cases were no longer acceptable, and ceramic cases became standard. Recent advances in plastics with high thermal tolerances have made plastic an acceptable CPU package material again.

Heat first became a serious problem in late-generation 486 CPUs. This was easily resolved for the most part by using cooling fans that could be attached to the CPU. However, the Pentium created some serious heat problems that simply adding a fan could not repair. The first two Pentium CPUs, the 60MHz and 66MHz, needed 5 volts for operation and subsequently ran very hot.

If you can make a CPU that will run at a lower voltage, usually by making the tiny transistors even tinier, the CPU will generate much less heat. So why didn't Intel make the first Pentiums 3.3 volts instead of 5 volts? Intel simply didn't have the technology at the time to make a 3.3 V CPU with that many transistors. Consequently, the original 5 V Pentiums had much larger cases than the later 3.3 V versions (Figure 2-73). As Intel developed the technology to make lower-power CPUs, the Pentium shrank to the smaller size.

**Figure 2-72**
Relative size of CPU
case to electronics

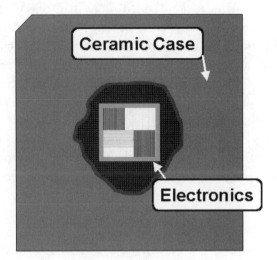

Ceramic Case

Electronics

**Figure 2-73**
Relative size
comparison of 5 V
vs. 3.3 V Pentiums

Pentium
60, 66

All other
Pentiums

## Low-Voltage CPUs in the Early Pentiums

CPU voltage in the early Pentium world was relatively simple. With the exception of the Pentium 60 and 66, which operated at 5 volts, the early Pentiums ran at 3.3 volts.

## What Voltage is Your Motherboard?

Even as 3.3 V CPUs began to dominate the early Pentiums, there was talk of lower-voltage CPUs. The potential introduction of even lower-voltage CPUs probably made it hard for motherboard makers to sleep at night. How could they make a motherboard that supported both 3.3 and lower voltages? How could they keep their new motherboards from becoming obsolete tomorrow? People don't want to buy computer parts, especially hard-to-replace motherboards that have a high potential of being obsolesced too quickly. Two industry changes (neither of which dealt with counting sheep) enabled multiple-voltage, upgradable motherboards (and let motherboard makers sleep peacefully).

First, motherboard manufacturers added more than one voltage regulator to the motherboard to support lower-voltage CPUs. The motherboard makers knew that the lower voltage was going to be in the range of 2.9 volts. Taking a chance, many motherboard makers simply added a second voltage regulator that dropped the voltage from 5 to 2.9 volts. Figure 2-74 is an example of a motherboard with two voltage regulators. You could activate the proper voltage regulator by moving the four jumpers located directly above the voltage regulators.

The second change, proposed by Intel, was to have CPUs come with their own standardized voltage regulators. Whatever voltage regulator was needed was soldered to a small card, called a *voltage regulator module* (VRM). The VRM would fit into a special VRM slot next to the CPU.

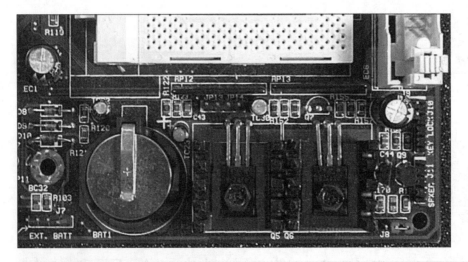

**Figure 2-74** Two voltage regulators

The example in Figure 2-75 has both a VRM and soldered voltage regulators. The jumpers inside the VRM slot control the voltage regulators. To install a VRM, you first removed the jumpers. This disabled the voltage regulators and gave the VRM control of the voltage. Advanced voltage regulators, containing special circuitry that gives the regulator the ability to switch quickly to a number of voltages, combined with the CPUID functions in the CPU, have made VRMs obsolete. Except in very rare circumstances, voltage is no longer an issue when CPUs are installed.

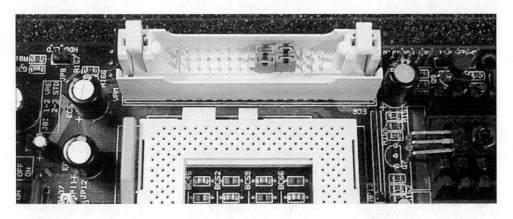

**Figure 2-75**   VRM slot

## Pentium Clock Doubling

Remember the 33MHz motherboard speed limit in the 486 world? Well, the Pentium systems soundly crashed through this limit. With the small exception of the very first 5 V Pentiums, all early Pentium motherboards ran at speeds up to at least 60 to 66MHz. However, early Pentium CPUs had clock speeds up to 200MHz. How could they do that on motherboards that ran only at 60 or 66MHz? Simple—they were all clock doublers (Figure 2-76). Plus, Pentium clock doubling, better known as the "multiplier" in the modern vernacular, isn't limited to whole numbers like 2 or 3 times the motherboard speed. An early Pentium could have multipliers of 1 ×, 1.5 ×, 2 ×, 2.5 ×, and 3 ×.

**Figure 2-76**
Pentiums are
multipliers

Equally interesting is the fact that you had to configure the multiplier on the early Pentiums. With 486s, if you bought, say, a 33/66 486DX/2, the multiplier was 2 and could not be changed. Sure, you could use different-speed motherboards, but you couldn't change the multiplier from times two to times three for example. The 486 multiplier was built in by the CPU manufacturer.

Pentium CPUs don't have a built-in multiplier. Of course, Intel would specify a particular motherboard speed and multiplier for a CPU, but it was up to you to configure the motherboard properly. All Pentium motherboards come with a set of jumpers or switches that enable you to set the proper multiplier. So when you install a Pentium, not only do you have to set the motherboard speed, but you also need to set the multiplier. Figure 2-77 is a graphic of a typical Pentium motherboard that shows both the multiplier jumpers and the motherboard speed. On some Pentium motherboards, the clock speed and multiplier could be adjusted via the CMOS Setup program. (See Chapter 4 for more information on CMOS.)

**Figure 2-77**
Pentium multiplier jumpers and motherboard clock

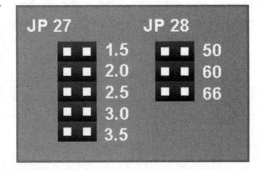

So how do you know the correct clock speed and multiplier? Simple—the manufacturer (Intel or AMD) tells you, and you do what they say. For example, if you bought a Pentium 200, you set the clock speed to 66 and the multiplier to 3 ×. When you bought a Pentium, the first question you had to ask the salesperson was, "What is the clock speed and multiplier?" If the supplier couldn't give you a quick answer, you ran away. The need to know the correct clock speed and multiplier certainly holds true for all CPUs today.

## Early Pentium Competitors

Because "Pentium" is a copyrighted product name, competitors chose to call their Pentium-equivalent chips by a variety of names, each intended to imply compatibility with the Intel ×86 family of processors. Unlike some of their later CPUs, early Pentium competitors had little success against the true Intel Pentium.

## AMD K5

The AMD K5 was pin-compatible to the Pentium, but it was a different animal on the inside. It was basically a *Reduced Instruction Set Computing* (RISC) CPU designed to be compatible with the Pentium (Figure 2-78). AMD sold them cheap and they made some serious sales in the low-end area. Other CPUs quickly eclipsed the K5.

**Figure 2-78**
AMD K5

## Cyrix 6×86/6×86L

The Cyrix 6×86 (Figure 2-79) delivered true Pentium-level performance at a very low price. Early in this chapter you saw how the 486 offered improved performance over the 386 by streamlining the operating instructions within the processor. Because Cyrix made similar improvements within the architecture of the 6×86, the CPU could process instructions as quickly as a Pentium that ran at a higher clock rate. The 6×86 CPU ran at a clock rate substantially slower than the Pentium chip it was designed to replace, yet delivered comparable performance. Unfortunately, the first 6×86 CPUs were very hot and had a few small bugs. The 6×86L eliminated these early problems and was a powerful, inexpensive CPU.

**Figure 2-79**
IBM/Cyrix 6×86

### P-Rating

Intel's competitors had a problem—they couldn't compare apples and oranges. For example, Cyrix made the 6×86, which ran at 100MHz. Cyrix knew that their 100MHz 6×86 could handle more calculations per second than an Intel 100MHz Pentium due to improvements in caching, pipelining, and program execution. In fact, the 100MHz 6×86 ran as fast as a 120MHz Pentium. How could they describe this to customers? To show this improvement, Cyrix, IBM Microelectronics, SGS-Thomson, and AMD developed the *P-rating*, which enabled you to compare quickly a Cyrix or AMD CPU against Intel chips.

P-ratings often caused confusion among consumers and technicians alike. When a person bought a Cyrix P-120, for example, he or she actually received a CPU that ran at 100MHz. When dealing with non-Intel CPUs, therefore, techs had to be prepared to install the CPU using different values than the ones printed on the CPU.

Although P-ratings have gone out of fashion, nothing inherently is wrong with them. In fact, they provided an excellent way to make rough comparisons between the potential performance of Intel CPUs and competitors' processors.

### Pentium Socket Types

The Pentium CPU had significantly more pins and therefore needed a larger case than the 486. The original Pentium 60 and 66 simply used a larger PGA-type package called Socket 4. All other Pentiums used a totally different type of package, called a *Staggered Pin Grid Array* (SPGA). The SPGA, as its name describes, staggers the pins, enabling a higher pin density and a smaller case. The two standard sockets for the lower-powered Pentiums were known as Socket 5 and Socket 7. The Socket 7 SPGA package continues to be the most popular package for most Pentium-class CPUs. See Figure 2-80.

**Figure 2-80**
Early Pentium socket types (graphic courtesy Intel)

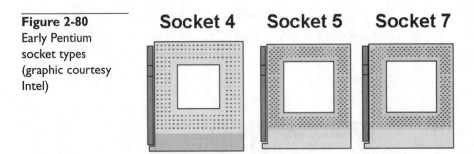

Socket 4     Socket 5     Socket 7

### Pentium Overdrive CPUs for 486 Systems

Known as the P24T before its release in early 1995, the Pentium overdrive was touted as a plug-in upgrade for 486 systems (Table 2-8). The Pentium overdrive was a Pentium with a 32-bit external data bus and two 16K caches instead of two 8K caches. A more realistic name for the Pentium overdrive might have been something like "Pentium SX." Intel specified a special 238-pin PGA *Zero Insertion Force* (ZIF) socket for Pentium overdrive that most motherboard manufacturers integrated into their 486 boards. However, the price of true Pentium motherboards had dropped so dramatically by the time the Pentium overdrive appeared that demand was low for the Pentium overdrive. You could simply purchase a real Pentium processor with a superior motherboard tuned to run a true Pentium 64-bit expansion bus for little more than the price of the Pentium overdrive. Nevertheless, the Pentium overdrive was a convenient and easy upgrade that many end users found attractive.

The AMD 5×86 was another popular overdrive-type processor for 486s. Despite the eye-catching name, this processor is simply a pin-compatible 486 that ran at a clock-quadrupled 133MHz (Figure 2-81). At this clock speed, it offered performance comparable to a 75MHz Pentium. As with all overdrive processors, time has obsolesced the AMD 5×86.

**Table 2-8**   486-to-Pentium Overdrive Processors

| CHIP | SPEED (MHz) | RECOMMENDED UPGRADES |
|------|-------------|----------------------|
| Pentium | 25/63 | 486SX-25, 486DX-25, 486DX/2 25/50, 486DX/4 25/75 |
| Pentium | 33/83 | 486SX-33, 486DX-33, 486DX/2 33/66, 486DX/4 33/100 |

**Figure 2-81**
AMD 5×86

## Pentium Overdrive CPUs for Pentium Systems

Intel no longer produces the Pentium overdrives for Pentium systems. As with their earlier overdrive brothers, the price of these CPUs made them a little too pricey for most pocketbooks, although many motherboards could only be upgraded with these chips. Table 2-9 shows the Pentium-to-Pentium overdrive processors.

**Table 2-9**   Pentium-to-Pentium Overdrive Processors

| CHIP | SPEED (MHz) | RECOMMENDED UPGRADES |
|------|-------------|----------------------|
| Pentium | 180 | Pentium 75 to 150 |
| Pentium | 200 | Pentium 100 to 166 |

## Pentium Pro

In 1995, Intel released the next generation of CPU, the Pentium Pro, often called the P6 (Table 2-10). The P6 had the same bus and register sizes as the Pentium. Three new items made the P6 more powerful than its predecessor: quad pipelining, dynamic processing, and an on-chip L2 cache. On the other hand, Intel optimized the P6 for true 32-bit code, which made the Pentium Pro often slower than a Pentium when running 16-bit code (DOS and Windows 3.*x*). The Pentium Pro had a distinctive, rectangular SPGA package (Figure 2-82).

**Table 2-10** Pentium Pro CPUs

| CHIP TYPE | CPU SPEED (MHz) | CLK MULTIPLE | EXTERNAL DATA BUS | L2 CACHE |
|---|---|---|---|---|
| PENTIUM PRO | 166 | 2.5 × | 64-bit | 512KB |
| PENTIUM PRO | 180 | 3 × | 64-bit | 256KB |
| PENTIUM PRO | 200 | 3 × | 64-bit | 256KB, 512KB, 1MB |

**Figure 2-82**
Pentium Pro

### Quad Pipelining

The Pentium was a dual-pipelined CPU, but the P6 could handle four separate pipelines simultaneously. On average, this enabled the equivalent of three simultaneous processes.

### Dynamic Processing

From time to time, a CPU must go to DRAM to access code, no matter how good its cache. When a RAM access takes place, the CPU must wait a few clock cycles before processing. Sometimes the wait can be 10 or 20 clock cycles. When the P6 was forced into wait states, it took advantage of the wait to look at the code in the pipeline to see if any commands could be run while the wait states were active. If it found commands it could process that were not dependent on the data being fetched from DRAM, it would run these commands *out of order*. After the DRAM returned with the code, it rearranged the commands and continued processing.

## On-Chip L2 Cache

The P6 had both an L1 and an L2 cache on the CPU. Because the L2 cache was on the chip, it ran almost as fast as the L1 cache (Figure 2-83).

The inclusion of the L2 cache on the chip gave rise to some new terms to describe the connections between the CPU, MCC, RAM, and L2 cache. The address bus and external data bus are now lumped between the CPU, MCC, and RAM into a single term called the *frontside bus* and the connection between the CPU and the L2 cache into the term *backside bus.* In Chapter 4, we will see that the MCC chip on modern systems has evolved into a multipurpose *chipset* that does far more than just handle memory requests. The modern chipset now acts more like the CPU's assistant and provides the primary interface between the CPU and RAM, and every other part of the PC.

**Figure 2-83**
Open sample
Pentium Pro
showing CPU
and L2 cache

So, even though the external data bus still exists, we rarely use that term anymore. Instead, the connection between the CPU and the L2 cache is referred to as "backside bus," and the connection between the CPU, MCC, and RAM, as "frontside bus." Figure 2-84 shows a more modern configuration, labeling the important buses. Note that the external data bus and address bus are there, but the chipset provides separate address buses and external data buses—one set just for the CPU and another set for the rest of the devices in the PC. No official name has been given to the interface between the RAM and the chipset. On the rare occasions when it is discussed, most techs simply call it the "RAM interface."

The Pentium Pro had a unique SPGA case that fit into a special socket, called Socket 8. No other CPU used this type of socket (Figure 2-85). The Pentium Pro made strong inroads in the high-end server market, but its poor performance running DOS and Windows 3.*x* programs, combined with its high cost, made it unacceptable as most people's desktop computer.

**Figure 2-84**
Frontside and
backside buses

Frontside Bus

Backside Bus

Separate
Address
Buses

CPU

L2
Cache

Chipset
(ex-MCC)

Separate
External Data
Buses

Video, Keyboard, Mouse,
Floppy Drive, Hard Drive,
Sound Card...

10010010
01010011
11011110
10101101
00110011
01010000
11110010
10010101
11010010
01010011
11011110
10101101
00110011
01010000
00010010

**Figure 2-85**
Socket 8, used by
the Pentium Pro

# Socket 8

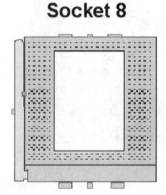

Although the Pentium Pro never saw a large volume of sales compared with the Pentium or Pentium II, many people in the industry consider it to be the most important chip ever created by Intel. The feature set of the Pentium Pro was the prototype for all CPUs designed ever since.

## Later Pentium-Class CPUs

Intel's usual game plan in the rough and tumble business of chip making is to introduce a new CPU and simultaneously declare all previous CPUs obsolete. This did not happen with the Pentium Pro, however, because Intel never really developed the P6 for most users. It was to be the CPU for powerful, higher-end systems. This kept the Pentium as the CPU of choice for all but the most power-hungry systems.

While the Pentium Pro languished on the high end for several years, Intel, AMD, and Cyrix developed new Pentium-class CPUs that incorporated a series of powerful improvements, some of which were taken from the Pentium Pro. These improvements require that they be regarded as a new family of CPUs, which I call the "later Pentium-class CPUs" (Table 2-11). Although certainly some profound differences exist between these CPUs, they all have four groups of similar improvements: MMX, split voltage, increased multipliers/clocks, and improved processing.

The introduction of the later Pentium-class processors marked a major shift in Intel's control of the CPU market. From that point to today, the CPU business has been nothing short of a knife fight among CPU makers. Both AMD and Cyrix produced CPUs that many considered superior to Intel's Pentium. In this case, the loser was Cyrix. After hitting upon financial hardships, Cyrix was sold to a few companies, eventually being bought by VIA Technologies, a major manufacturer of chipsets. Although VIA makes advanced processors under the Cyrix label (such as the MII and VIA Cyrix III processors), Cyrix is considered an extremely minor player in the CPU business. Of course, this may change in the future. If nothing else, the CPU industry is certainly interesting to watch.

## MMX

In 1996, Intel added a new enhancement to its Pentium CPU, called *multimedia extensions* (MMX). MMX manifests as four new registers and 57 new commands added to the Pentium codebook. These commands can be used to move and manipulate large chunks of data. This ability is particularly helpful (and was designed) for graphical applications such as games. Both Cyrix and AMD copied the MMX extensions in their CPUs. The downside to MMX is that applications need to be written to take advantage of MMX. Although a few such applications have been written, more advanced functions have been added to CPUs that have somewhat eclipsed MMX.

MMX is kind of like the built-in math coprocessor. You get it whether you need it or not. All new CPUs from all manufacturers are MMX enabled. You can't save money by trying to buy a non-MMX CPU.

## Split Voltage

Improvements in CPU manufacturing continued, resulting in Pentium-class CPUs that ran at voltages even lower than 3.3 volts. Yet these CPUs still needed 3.3 volts in order to communicate with other chips on the motherboard. To fulfill both needs, all later Pentium-class processors have *split voltage*. They need two different voltages to operate properly. Although later Pentium-class processors use the same Socket 7 used by most earlier Pentiums, you can't install a later Pentium-class CPU into these motherboards because the boards can't provide the proper voltage.

**Table 2-11** Later Pentium CPUs

| CPU | MAKE | INTERNAL SPEED (MHz) | EXTERNAL SPEED (MHz) | CLK MULT. | L1 CACHE (KB) | EXT. VOLTAGE | CORE VOLTAGE | PACKAGE |
|---|---|---|---|---|---|---|---|---|
| Pentium P55C | Intel | 166 | 66 | 2.5 × | 16WT/16WB | 3.3 V | 2.8 V | Socket 7 |
| Pentium P55C | Intel | 200 | 66 | 3 × | 16WT/16WB | 3.3 V | 2.8 V | Socket 7 |
| Pentium P55C | Intel | 233 | 66 | 3.5 × | 16WT/16WB | 3.3 V | 2.8 V | Socket 7 |
| Pentium P55C | Intel | 266 | 66 | 4 × | 16WT/16WB | 3.3 V | 2.8 V | Socket 7 |
| Pentium P55C | Intel | 300 | 66 | 4.5 × | 16WT/16WB | 3.3 V | 2.8 V | Socket 7 |
| Pentium P55C | Intel | 333 | 75 | 4.5 × | 16WT/16WB | 3.3 V | 2.8 V | Socket 7 |
| K6 | AMD | 166 | 66 | 2.5 | 32WT/32WB | 3.3 V | 2.9 V | Socket 7 |
| K6 | AMD | 200 | 66 | 3 × | 32WT/32WB | 3.3 V | 2.9 V | Socket 7 |
| K6 | AMD | 233 | 66 | 3.5 × | 32WT/32WB | 3.3 V | 3.2 V | Socket 7 |
| K6 | AMD | 266 | 66 | 4 × | 32WT/32WB | 4.3 V | 3.2 V | Socket 7 |
| 6×86MX PR166 | Cyrix | 133 | 66 | 2 × | 64WB | 3.3 V | 2.9 V | Socket 7 |
| 6×86MX PR166 | Cyrix | 150 | 60 | 2.5 × | 64WB | 3.3 V | 2.9 V | Socket 7 |
| 6×86MX PR200 | Cyrix | 150 | 75 | 2 × | 64WB | 3.3 V | 2.9 V | Socket 7 |
| 6×86MX PR200 | Cyrix | 166 | 66 | 2.5 × | 64WB | 3.3 V | 2.9 V | Socket 7 |
| 6×86MX PR233 | Cyrix | 188 | 75 | 2.5 × | 64WB | 3.3 V | 2.9 V | Socket 7 |

Manufacturers have produced a whole new family of motherboards to support split-voltage CPUs. This new type of motherboard, Super Socket 7, can support any Socket 7 CPU, from the early Pentiums to the last of the powerful AMD K6 series. The actual socket on a Super Socket 7 motherboard is absolutely identical to a regular Socket 7—the difference is in the broad selection of voltages, motherboard speeds, and multipliers provided by the Super Socket 7 motherboard. Figure 2-86 shows a clip from the web site of Tyan Computer Corporation, a major manufacturer of motherboards. Note the clear indication of Super Socket 7.

**Figure 2-86**
Typical catalog listing of Super Socket 7

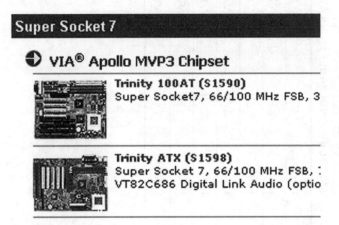

**Super Socket 7**

⟶ **VIA® Apollo MVP3 Chipset**

**Trinity 100AT (S1590)**
Super Socket7, 66/100 MHz FSB, 3

**Trinity ATX (S1598)**
Super Socket 7, 66/100 MHz FSB, :
VT82C686 Digital Link Audio (optio

## Increased Clocks and Multipliers

Later Pentiums all have vastly increased multipliers, resulting in higher speeds. Most early Pentiums used 2.5 × multipliers at best, but later Pentium-class processors had up to 4.5 × multipliers.

## Improved Processing

All later Pentium-class processors have some improvement in plain old Pentium branch prediction. The Intel Pentium has made a slight improvement by making the branch prediction a little smarter, giving it a better chance of getting the correct code. The Cyrix 6×86MX and the AMD K6 have incorporated the Pentium Pro features of speculative execution and out-of-order execution, making them more like the Pentium Pro and Pentium II (see next section) than the Pentium.

## Pentium II

Intel's next major CPU was the Pentium II (Table 2-12). In reality, the Pentium II is little more than a faster Pentium Pro with MMX and a refined instruction set. The introduction of the Pentium II merged Intel's two primary CPU lines. The Pentium II comes

**Table 2-12** Pentium II CPUs

| CHIP TYPE | INTERNAL SPEED (MHz) | EXTERNAL SPEED (MHz) | CLK MULT. | EXT. VOLTAGE | CORE VOLTAGE | L1 CACHE (KB) | L2 CACHE (KB) |
|---|---|---|---|---|---|---|---|
| Pentium II | 233 | 66 | 3.5 × | 3.3 V | 2.8 V | 16WT/16WB | 512 |
| Pentium II | 266 | 66 | 4 × | 3.3 V | 2.8 V | 16WT/16WB | 512 |
| Pentium II | 300 | 66 | 4.5 × | 3.3 V | 2.8 V | 16WT/16WB | 512 |
| Pentium II | 333 | 66 | 5.0 × | 3.3 V | 2.8 V | 16WT/16WB | 512 |
| Pentium II | 350 | 100 | 3.5 × | 3.3 V | 2.8 V | 16WT/16WB | 512 |
| Pentium II | 400 | 100 | 4.0 × | 3.3 V | 2.8 V | 16WT/16WB | 512 |
| Pentium II | 450 | 100 | 4.5 × | 3.3 V | 2.9 V | 16WT/16WB | 512 |

in a distinctive SEC cartridge, replacing the older-style SPGA socket of the Pentium Pro and freeing up more room on the motherboard (Figure 2-87).

The Pentium II initially achieved the higher clock speeds by using high multiples of a 66MHz motherboard. During this time, Intel competitors began to sell CPUs designed to run on 100MHz motherboards. Although the final Pentium II models most certainly also run on 100MHz motherboards, Intel's slow adoption of 100MHz lost market share for Intel.

**Figure 2-87**
Pentium II (photo
courtesy Intel)

The SEC cartridge also creates a problem because Intel licenses it. This prevents other CPU manufacturers from making CPUs that fit in the SEC's special Slot 1 connection. Although this might have been seen by Intel as a big opportunity to take even more market share, it virtually guaranteed that many systems would continue to use the older SPGA-type Socket 7 and, as in the case of AMD, would create their own SEC and PGA packages that are incompatible with Intel's.

## AMD K6 Series

From 1997 to 2000, AMD produced a series of Super Socket 7 processors called the K6 that matched, and in many people's view, surpassed, the Pentium II, propelling AMD into serious competition with Intel (Figure 2-88). Four models were included in the K6 series: the K6, K6-2, K6-2+, and the K6-III, each incorporating more advanced features than the previous model. The K6 processors incorporated a number of improvements, including 64KB L1 cache (32K for programs, 32K for data), extremely advanced pipelining, and support for motherboard speeds of 100MHz (on later models). The K6-2 added AMD's proprietary 3Dnow!™ instruction set—a significant advancement in graphics handling capabilities—and increased clock speeds. The K6-III included even more advancements in pipelining and added a 256K L2 cache, all on a standard Socket 7 PGA package. All K6s required a Super Socket 7 motherboard. Table 2-13 lists the K6 family of processors.

**Table 2-13**  K6 Family

| CHIP TYPE | CLK MULT. | BUS SPEED (MHz) | CORE VOLTAGE | EXT. VOLTAGE | L1 CACHE |
|---|---|---|---|---|---|
| K6 200 | 3 × | 66 | 2.9 V | 3.3 V | 32T[1]/32B[2] |
| K6 233 | 3.5 × | 66 | 3.2 V | 3.3 V | 32T/32B |
| K6 266 | 4 × | 66 | 2.2 V | 3.3 V | 32T/32B |
| K6 300 | 4.5 × | 66 | 2.2 V | 3.45 V | 32T/32B |
| K6-2 266 | 4 × | 66 | 2.2 V | 3.3 V | 32T/32B |
| K6-2 300 | 3 × | 100 | 2.2 V | 3.3 V | 32T/32B |
| K6-2 300 | 4.5 × | 66 | 2.2 V | 3.3 V | 32T/32B |
| K6-2 333 | 3.5 × | 95 | 2.2 V | 3.3 V | 32T/32B |
| K6-2 333 | 5 × | 66 | 2.2 V | 3.3 V | 32T/32B |
| K6-2 350 | 3.5 × | 100 | 2.2 V | 3.3 V | 32T/32B |
| K6-2 366 | 5.5 × | 66 | 2.2 V | 3.3 V | 32T/32B |
| K6-2 380 | 4 × | 95 | 2.2 V | 3.3 V | 32T/32B |
| K6-2 400 | 4 × | 100 | 2.2 V | 3.3 V | 32T/32B |
| K6-2 450 | 4.5 × | 100 | 2.2 V | 3.3 V | 32T/32B |
| K6-2 450 | 4.5 × | 100 | 2.4 V | 3.3 V | 32T/32B |
| K6-2 475 | 5 × | 95 | 2.2 V | 3.3 V | 32T/32B |
| K6-2 475 | 5 × | 95 | 2.4 V | 3.3 V | 32T/32B |
| K6-2 500 | 5 × | 100 | 2.2 V | 3.3 V | 32T/32B |
| K6-2 533 | 5.5 × | 97 | 2.2 V | 3.3 V | 32T/32B |
| K6-2 550 | 5.5 × | 100 | 2.3 V | 3.3 V | 32T/32B |
| K6III 400 | 4 × | 100 | 2.4 V | 3.3 V | 32T/32B |
| K6III 450 | 4.5 × | 100 | 2.4 V | 3.3 V | 32T/32B |

[1]KBs of write-through
[2]KBs of write-back

**Figure 2-88**
AMD K6 (Picture
courtesy of AMD)

## Celeron

In an attempt to capture more market share of low-end PCs, Intel developed an off-shoot of the Pentium II called the Celeron (Figure 2-89). The first Celerons were SEC but lacked any protective covering, making them distinct from a Pentium II. Intel calls this the *Single Edge Processor* (SEP) package. The first two versions, running at 266 and 300MHz, also lacked any L2 cache, making them very poor performers; as a result, they were rather unpopular. Intel quickly added a 128K cache, starting with the Celeron 300 (the improved 300s were called the 300A to distinguish them from the 300 without the L2 cache). Although touted by Intel as a low-end solution and limited to only a 66MHz bus speed, the Celeron CPU's cheap price has made it a huge success in a broad cross-section of systems.

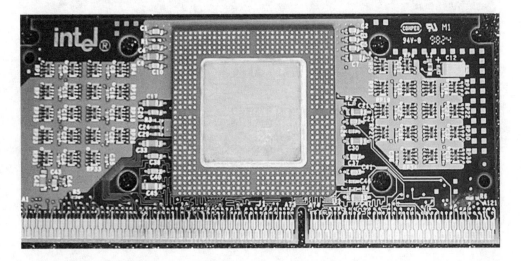

**Figure 2-89**   Celeron SEP

A new type of Celeron, based on the Pentium III and unofficially called the Celeron II, is now available. It is distinguished from the earlier Celerons by its PPGA or FC-PGA package (Figure 2-90). These PGA processors fit into a socket called Socket 370 (Figure 2-91). Table 2-14 lists the Celeron processors.

**Figure 2-90**
Celeron II PPGA
(White label is from
the wholesaler.)

**Figure 2-91**    Socket 370

**Table 2-14**   Celeron Family

| CHIP TYPE | CLK MULT. | BUS SPEED (MHz) | CORE VOLTAGE | L1 CACHE (KB) | L2 CACHE (KB) | PACKAGE |
|---|---|---|---|---|---|---|
| Celeron 266 | 4 × | 66 | 2V[3] | 16T[1]/16B[2] | None | SEPP |
| Celeron 300 | 4.5 × | 66 | 2V | 16T/16B | None | SEPP |
| Celeron 300A | 4.5 × | 66 | 2V | 16T/16B | 128 | Both |
| Celeron 333 | 5 × | 66 | 2V | 16T/16B | 128 | Both |
| Celeron 366 | 5.5 × | 66 | 2V | 16T/16B | 128 | Both |
| Celeron 400 | 6 × | 66 | 2V | 16T/16B | 128 | Both |
| Celeron 433 | 6.5 × | 66 | 2V | 16T/16B | 128 | Both |
| Celeron 500 | 7.5 × | 66 | 2V | 16T/16B | 128 | PGA[4] |
| Celeron 533 | 8 × | 66 | 2V | 16T/16B | 128 | PGA |
| Celeron 533A | 8 × | 66 | 1.7V | 16T/16B | 128 | PGA |
| Celeron 566 | 8.5 × | 66 | 1.7V | 16T/16B | 128 | PGA |
| Celeron 600 | 9 | 66 | 1.7V | 16T/16B | 128 | PGA |
| Celeron 633 | 9.5 × | 66 | 1.7V | 16T/16B | 128 | PGA |
| Celeron 667 | 10 × | 66 | 1.7V | 16T/16B | 128 | PGA |
| Celeron 700 | 10.5 × | 66 | 1.7V | 16T/16B | 128 | PGA |

[1]KBs of write-through
[2]KBs of write-back
[3]All Celeron packages require a number of unique voltage inputs. Use only as an approximate value.
[4]All PGA Celerons come in both PPGA and FC-PGA packages.

## Pentium III

The Pentium III improves on the Pentium II by incorporating *Streaming SIMD Extensions* (SSE), Intel's direct competitor to AMD's 3DNow!™, a number of internal processing/pipelining improvements, full support for 100MHz and 133MHz motherboard speeds, and high-speed L2 caches. This combination of improvements makes the Pentium III an incredibly powerful and popular processor. The Pentium III was first produced in a derivative of the SEC package called SECC-2 (Figure 2-92), but improvements in die technology now enable the Pentium III to use the PPGA or FC-PGA package. Intel can produce these packages more cheaply than the SEC-style packages, and they take up much less real estate inside the PC. Table 2-15 lists the Pentium III processors.

**Table 2-15** Pentium III Family

| CHIP TYPE | CLK MULT | BUS SPEED (MHz) | CORE VOLTAGE | L1 CACHE (KB) | L2 CACHE (KB) | PACKAGE |
|---|---|---|---|---|---|---|
| Pentium III 450 | 4.5 × | 100 | 2V[3] | 16T[1]/16B[2] | 512 | SECC-2 |
| Pentium III 500 | 5 × | 100 | 2V | 16T/16B | 512 | SECC-2 |
| Pentium III 500E | 5 × | 100 | 2V | 16T/16B | 256 | FCPGA |
| Pentium III 533B | 4 × | 133 | 2V | 16T/16B | 512 | SECC-2 |
| Pentium III 533EB | 4 × | 133 | 1.7V | 16T/16B | 256 | Both |
| Pentium III 550 | 5.5 × | 100 | 2V | 16T/16B | 512 | SECC-2 |
| Pentium III 550E | 5.5 × | 100 | 1.7V | 16T/16B | 256 | Both |
| Pentium III 600 | 6 × | 100 | 2V | 16T/16B | 512 | SECC-2 |
| Pentium III 600B | 4.5 × | 133 | 2V | 16T/16B | 512 | SECC-2 |
| Pentium III 600E | 6 × | 100 | 1.7V | 16T/16B | 512/256 | Both |
| Pentium III 600EB | 4.4 × | 133 | 1.7V | 16T/16B | 512/256 | Both |
| Pentium III 650 | 6.5 × | 100 | 1.7V | 16T/16B | 256 | Both |
| Pentium III 667 | 6.5 × | 133 | 1.7V | 16T/16B | 256 | Both |
| Pentium III 700 | 7 × | 100 | 1.7V | 16T/16B | 256 | Both |
| Pentium III 733 | 5.5 × | 133 | 1.7V | 16T/16B | 256 | Both |
| Pentium III 750 | 7.5 × | 100 | 1.7V | 16T/16B | 256 | Both |
| Pentium III 800 | 8 × | 100 | 1.7V | 16T/16B | 256 | Both |
| Pentium III 800EB | 6 × | 133 | 1.7V | 16T/16B | 256 | Both |
| Pentium III 850 | 8.5 × | 100 | 1.7V | 16T/16B | 256 | Both |
| Pentium III 866 | 6.5 × | 133 | 1.7V | 16T/16B | 256 | Both |
| Pentium III 933 | 7 × | 133 | 1.7V | 16T/16B | 256 | Both |
| Pentium III 1000 | 10 × | 100 | 1.7V | 16T/16B | 256 | SECC-2 |
| Pentium III 1000B | 7.5 × | 133 | 1.7V | 16T/16B | 256 | Both |
| Pentium III 1133 | 10 × | 133 | 1.8V | 16T/16B | 256 | SECC-2 |

[1]KBs of write-through
[2]KBs of write-back
[3]Both Pentium III packages require a number of unique voltage inputs. Use only as an approximate value.

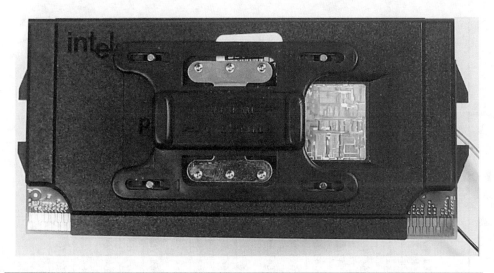

**Figure 2-92**  Pentium III SECC-2 (fan mount attached)

## Athlon

Often referred to as "the CPU that keeps Intel awake at night," the Athlon CPU was AMD's first product to drop any attempt at pin compatibility with Intel chips. The first Athlon CPUs used an SEC package called Slot A that was mechanically compatible but *not* pin compatible with Slot 1 (Figure 2-93). In other words, you could snap an Athlon into a Slot 1 motherboard, but it wouldn't work. If you want an Athlon, you must buy a motherboard with Slot A, not Slot 1. Table 2-16 lists the Athlon processors.

**Figure 2-93**  Early Athlon

**Table 2-16**  Athlon Family

| CHIP TYPE | CLK MULT | MOTHER-BOARD BUS SPEED (MHz) | SYSTEM BUS SPEED (MHz) | CORE VOLTAGE | L1 CACHE (KB) | L2 CACHE (KB) | PACKAGE |
|---|---|---|---|---|---|---|---|
| Athlon 500 | 5 × | 100 | 200 | 1.75 V | 64T[1]/64B[2] | 512 | SEC |
| Athlon 550 | 5.5 × | 100 | 200 | 1.75 V | 64T/64B | 512 | SEC |
| Athlon 600 | 6 × | 100 | 200 | 1.75 V | 64T/64B | 512 | SEC |
| Athlon 650 | 6.5 × | 100 | 200 | 1.75 V | 64T/64B | 512/256[3] | Both |
| Athlon 700 | 7 × | 100 | 200 | 1.75 V | 64T/64B | 512/256 | Both |
| Athlon 750 | 7.5 × | 100 | 200 | 1.75 V | 64T/64B | 512/256 | Both |
| Athlon 800 | 8 × | 100 | 200 | 1.75 V | 64T/64B | 512/256 | Both |
| Athlon 850 | 8.5 × | 100 | 200 | 1.75 V | 64T/64B | 512/256 | Both |
| Athlon 900 | 9 × | 100 | 200 | 1.75 V | 64T/64B | 512/256 | Both |
| Athlon 950 | 9.5 × | 100 | 200 | 1.75 V | 64T/64B | 512/256 | Both |
| Athlon 1000 | 10 × | 100 | 200 | 1.75 V | 64T/64B | 512/256 | Both |
| Athlon 1100 | 10.5 × | 100 | 200 | 1.75 V | 64T/64B | 256 | CPGA |
| Athlon 1000 | 7.5 × | 133 | 266 | 1.75 V | 64T/64B | 256 | CPGA |
| Athlon 1133 | 8.5 × | 133 | 266 | 1.75 V | 64T/64B | 256 | CPGA |
| Athlon 1200 | 9 × | 133 | 266 | 1.75 V | 64T/64B | 256 | CPGA |

[1]KBs of write-through
[2]KBs of write-back
[3]SEC type Athlons use 512KB of L2; CPGAs use 256KB.

The Athlon contains a number of amazing technologies, including a whopping nine pipelines and very advanced dynamic branch prediction, but the most talked about aspect of the Athlon stems from its use of either a 200MHz or 266MHz *system* bus. This gets a little confusing. What AMD calls the system bus, we would call "most of the frontside bus." These are the wires leading between the CPU and the chipset. To make it a tad more confusing, the bus still runs at just 100MHz or 133MHz, but the CPU and the chipset perform two calculations on every clock cycle. The data truly does move at double the motherboard speed so you can enjoy much faster processing. (Figure 2-94).

**Figure 2-94**
Athlon 200MHz bus

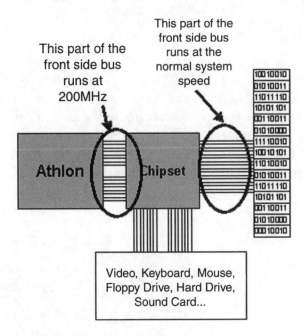

This doubling effect makes the Athlon CPU a natural fit for the popular DDR SDRAM technology because they both work on the "one click of the clock gets two jobs done" idea. Already a number of chipsets support both the Athlon and DDR SDRAM. (See Chapter 3 for a discussion of DDR SDRAM.)

AMD has produced an SPGA version of the Athlon. This unique ceramic SPGA package, called Socket A, is proprietary to AMD and is not compatible with the Socket 370 (Figure 2-95).

When the Athlon first came out, concern was prompted by the possibility that the lack of compatibility would prevent the Athlon from being successful. Instead, the power and reliability of the Athlon, combined with a strong marketing effort on the part of AMD, has made it a popular CPU with solid support from almost every major manufacturer of motherboards.

**Figure 2-95**
Athlon Socket A
(Graphic courtesy
of AMD)

## Duron

The Duron is AMD's direct competitor to the Intel Celeron. Basically a cut-down Athlon, the Duron supports a 200MHz frontside bus, giving it a slight edge over the Celeron. The Duron enjoys a sizable market on lower-end PCs, although the Celeron continues to dominate. The Duron comes in the same Socket A package as the later Athlons (Figure 2-96). Table 2-17 lists the Duron processors.

**Figure 2-96**
AMD Duron
(Graphic courtesy
of AMD)

## Mobile Processors

The inside of a laptop PC is a cramped, hot environment, where no self-respecting CPU should ever need to operate. Ever since the days of the 386SL, CPU manufacturers have endeavored to make specialized versions of their processors to function in the rugged world of laptops. Over the years, a number of CPU laptop solutions have appeared.

**Table 2-17**   Duron Family

| CHIP TYPE | CLK MULT. | BUS SPEED (MHz) | CORE VOLTAGE | L1 CACHE (KB) | L2 CACHE (KB) | PACKAGE |
|-----------|-----------|-----------------|--------------|---------------|---------------|---------|
| Duron 600 | 6 × | 100 | 1.6 V | 64T[1]/64B[2] | 64 | CPGA |
| Duron 650 | 65 × | 100 | 1.6 V | 64T/64B | 64 | CPGA |
| Duron 700 | 7 × | 100 | 1.6 V | 64T/64B | 64 | CPGA |
| Duron 750 | 7.5 × | 100 | 1.6 V | 64T/64B | 64 | CPGA |
| Duron 800 | 8 × | 100 | 1.6 V | 64T/64B | 64 | CPGA |

[1]KBs of write-through
[2]KBs of write-back

An early solution was simply to use regular CPUs. Every desktop CPU has relatively low voltage and has some form of power management. The biggest problems are heat and lack of space. During the 486 and Pentium days, it was quite common to see regular desktop CPUs installed inside laptops. Many laptop makers demanded, and got, CPUs with thinner packages and lower MHz (and thus less heat). The CPU makers realized that they had a market for specialized "mobile" CPUs.

One of the first manifestations of mobile CPUs was the *Tape Carrier Package* (TCP). These are nothing more than the CPU without the packaging. Some notebook makers take the TCP and solder it directly to the motherboard, giving the motherboard the responsibility for heat dissipation. TCPs, although still used, have lost ground to other mobile packages (Figure 2-97).

**Figure 2-97**
Tape Carrier
Package

Pentium II processors presented a serious problem for Intel, as their huge size made them impractical for laptops. To make the Pentium II attractive to the laptop market, Intel unveiled the mobile module. The mobile module is virtually an entire PC on a small card. The mobile module includes the processor and primary support chips on a standardized, replaceable package. Intel's mobile modules are very popular on today's laptops and are a major contributor to Intel's dominance of the mobile market (Figure 2-98).

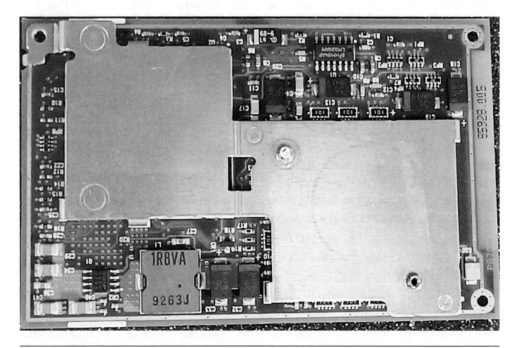

**Figure 2-98**   Intel mobile module (chips covered by heat sink)

Because the mobile module is a proprietary design of Intel, AMD simply chooses to make Super Socket 7 CPUs with very low voltage.

## Inserting a PGA-Type CPU

Inserting and removing PGA CPUs is a relatively simple process; just *don't touch the pins,* or you might destroy the CPU. Figure 2-99 shows a technician installing a Celeron PPGA into Socket 370. Note the notch and dot printed on the corners of the CPU. These *orientation markers* or *index corners* are designed to help you align the CPU correctly. It must line up with the notch(es) on the socket. Although the orientation marks make it very difficult to install a CPU improperly, incorrectly installing your CPU will almost certainly destroy the CPU or the motherboard, or both!

**Figure 2-99**
Close-up of CPU
and socket showing
orientation marks
and notches

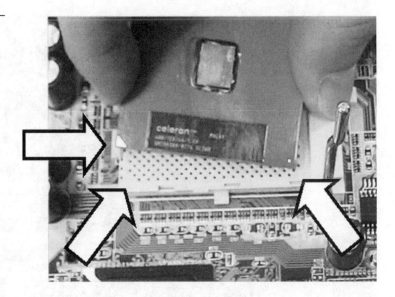

 **CAUTION** Before attempting to do anything inside the CPU, make sure you have adequate ESD protection. Make sure the power is off and the system is unplugged. Laptop CPUs require extra care—refer to Chapter 18, the laptop chapter, for details.

Installing a CPU into a ZIF socket is as simple as making sure that the orientation notches line up on the CPU and ZIF socket. Lift the ZIF arm, align the CPU, and it should drop right in (Figure 2-100). If it doesn't, verify your alignment and check for bent pins on the CPU. If I encounter a slightly bent pin, I often use a mechanical pencil that takes thick (0.9mm) lead. I take the lead out of the mechanical pencil, slide the pencil tip over the bent pin, and straighten it out. Be careful, a broken CPU pin ruins the CPU. Make sure the CPU is all the way in (no visible pins), and snap down the ZIF arm.

All PGA-type CPUs, with the exception of *very* old (pre-486) CPUs, need some form of heat dissipation. Today's CPUs require large heat sinks and powerful fans. Some PGA-type CPUs come with permanently attached fans, but most require you to install a fan after the CPU has been inserted into the socket.

Before inserting the fan, you need to add a small amount of heat sink compound. This paste, usually white, helps transfer heat from the CPU to the heat sink/fan. Any electronics store sells heat sink compound. Many fans come with heat sink compound already on them; the heat sink compound on these pre-doped fans is covered by a small square of tape—be sure to take it off before you snap down the fan. See Figure 2-101.

**Figure 2-100**
Inserting a
PGA-type CPU

**Figure 2-101**
Heat sink/fan
assembly removed
from CPU to
show heat sink
compound

Securing fans makes even the most jaded PC technician a little nervous. Figure 2-102 shows a more common type of fan that snaps into notches on the socket. In most cases, you must apply a fairly strong amount of force to snap the fan into place—far more than you might think you should. Also, make certain that the fan you install can work with your CPU package. Some Socket 370-specific fans, for example, will crack the ceramic casing on Socket A Duron CPUs, and vice versa.

Most fans require power. Look for a power connection on the motherboard, and snap it into place. Most motherboards clearly mark this connector (Figure 2-103).

**Figure 2-102**
Snapping down the fan

**Figure 2-103**
Inserting the CPU fan power— note the identical connector for a secondary fan

## Inserting a Slot 1/Slot A CPU

Because Slot 1 and Slot A are mechanically identical, we can lump them together. First, you need to install the *CPU mount*. This keeps the CPU secure. Many different types of mounts exist. Most mounts require the motherboard to be out of the case to install them. Figure 2-104 shows one of the more common types of mounts.

All SEC CPUs must have a fan. Like CPU mounts, fans come in a bewildering variety of shapes and sizes. Be sure to add a *small* amount of heat sink compound before you mount the fan (Figure 2-105).

**Figure 2-104**   Typical slot mount

**Figure 2-105**
Adding heat
compound

To install the CPU, just slide it straight down into the slot (Figure 2-106). Special notches in the slot make it impossible to install them incorrectly. So remember, if it does not go in easily, it is probably not correct. Be sure to plug in the CPU fan's power.

**Figure 2-106**
Snapping down
the CPU

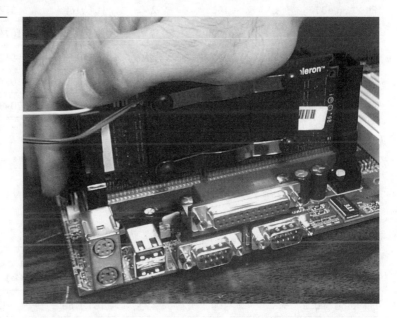

## Know Your CPUs

In this chapter, you have seen the basic components and functions of a PC's CPU. A historical view has been provided to help you better understand the amazing evolution of CPUs in the less than 20-year life span of the personal computer.

The information in this chapter will be referred to again and again throughout the book. Take the time to memorize certain facts, such as the size of the L1 and L2 caches, CPU speeds, and clock-doubling features. These are things that good technicians can spout off without having to refer to a book.

# Beyond A+

## Xeon Processors

Intel has manufactured a series of powerful Slot 1 CPUs called Xeon. Based originally on the Pentium II and now the Pentium III, Xeon CPUs build on the Pentium II and III core processors via the addition of massive L2 caches and strong multiprocessor support (Figure 2-107). Xeon processors enjoy broad popularity in the high-horsepower world of server systems. (See Tables 2-18 and 2-19.)

**Table 2-18**  Pentium II Xeon Family

| CHIP TYPE | CLK MULT. | BUS SPEED (MHz) | CORE VOLTAGE | L1 CACHE (KB) | L2 CACHE (KB) | PACKAGE |
|---|---|---|---|---|---|---|
| PII Xeon 400 | 4 × | 100 | 2V[3] | 16T[1]/16B[2] | 512 | SEC |
| PII Xeon 400 | 4 × | 100 | 2V | 16T/16B | 1024 | SEC |
| PII Xeon 450 | 4.5 × | 100 | 2V | 16T/16B | 512 | SEC |
| PII Xeon 450 | 4.5 × | 100 | 2V | 16T/16B | 1024 | SEC |
| PII Xeon 450 | 4.5 × | 100 | 2V | 16T/16B | 2048 | SEC |

[1]KBs of write-through
[2]KBs of write-back
[3]Pentium Xeons require a number of unique voltage inputs. Use only as an approximate value.

**Table 2-19**  Pentium III Xeon Family

| CHIP TYPE | CLK MULT. | BUS SPEED (MHz) | CORE VOLTAGE | L1 CACHE (KB) | L2 CACHE (KB) | PACKAGE |
|---|---|---|---|---|---|---|
| PIII Xeon 500 | 5 × | 100 | 2V[3] | 16T[1]/16B[2] | 512 | SEC |
| PIII Xeon 500 | 5 × | 100 | 2V | 16T/16B | 1024 | SEC |
| PIII Xeon 500 | 5 × | 100 | 2V | 16T/16B | 2048 | SEC |
| PIII Xeon 550 | 5.5 × | 100 | 2V | 16T/16B | 512 | SEC |
| PIII Xeon 550 | 5.5 × | 100 | 2V | 16T/16B | 1024 | SEC |
| PIII Xeon 550 | 5.5 × | 100 | 2V | 16T/16B | 2048 | SEC |
| PIII Xeon 600 | 4.5 × | 133 | 2V | 16T/16B | 256 | SEC |
| PIII Xeon 667 | 5 × | 133 | 2V | 16T/16B | 256 | SEC |
| PIII Xeon 733 | 5.5 × | 133 | 2V | 16T/16B | 256 | SEC |
| PIII Xeon 800 | 6 × | 133 | 2V | 16T/16B | 256 | SEC |
| PIII Xeon 866 | 6.5 × | 133 | 2V | 16T/16B | 256 | SEC |
| PIII Xeon 933 | 7 × | 133 | 2V | 16T/16B | 256 | SEC |
| PIII Xeon 1000 | 7.5 × | 133 | 2V | 16T/16B | 256 | SEC |

[1]KBs of write-through
[2]KBs of write-back
[3]Pentium Xeons require a number of unique voltage inputs. Use only as an approximate value.

**Figure 2-107**
Pentium III Xeon

## Pentium 4

If we refer to the Athlon as "the CPU that keeps Intel awake at night," then we should call the Intel Pentium 4 "the CPU that reminds AMD who's in charge around here!"

For all the improvements in speed and caching, all Intel Pentium II and III CPUs are based on the powerful, but now aging, Pentium Pro technology. The Pentium 4 breaks that tradition with a totally new, dramatically more powerful core processing function that includes an incredible 20-step pipeline and an amazing array of new hyper-intelligent features. The Pentium 4 includes a number of enhancements for graphics, which undoubtedly will make it very popular for the high-end workstation market. The P4 takes the Athlon's 200MHz system bus and doubles it to an amazing 400MHz on a 100MHz bus by utilizing four data transfers per clock cycle. This makes the Pentium 4 a natural fit for RDRAM as opposed to DDR-SDRAM in the Athlon. (See Chapter 3 for a discussion of RDRAM.) Table 2-20 lists the Pentium 4 processors.

**Table 2-20**   Pentium 4 Family

| CHIP TYPE | CLK MULT | MOTHER-BOARD BUS SPEED (MHz) | SYSTEM BUS SPEED (MHz) | CORE VOLTAGE | L1 CACHE (KB) | L2 CACHE (KB) | PACKAGE |
|---|---|---|---|---|---|---|---|
| Pentium 4 1400 | 5 × | 100 | 400 | 1.7V | 8K | 256K | FCPGA |
| Pentium 4 1500 | 5 × | 100 | 400 | 1.7V | 8K | 256K | FCPGA |

## Slockets

Intel's move from Slot 1 to Socket 370 FC-PGA packages created the demand for special converters to enable you to run an Intel Socket 370 CPU in a Slot 1 motherboard. These nifty devices are known variously as *slockets* or *slotkets*. Figure 2-108 shows a typical slocket. AMD only adopted the Slot A format for a short time. As a result, no one has made a Slot A to Socket A slocket—at least as of this writing.

Slockets should enjoy quite a bit of popularity for the next few years as we upgrade our existing Slot 1 CPUs to take Socket 370 and possibly even newer socket-type processors as they appear.

**Figure 2-108**   Typical slocket

## Overclocking

If you remember from the beginning of this chapter, the concept that the CPU is pushed by the system clock on the motherboard was discussed in detail. Jumpers or software are used to set the motherboard speed, multiplier, and voltage—or as is the case in many systems, we count on the motherboard to use CPUID functions to set this automatically.

The fact that a CPU must run at its designed speed was also discussed. For example, if I have a Celeron 566, Intel tells me that it should run at 66MHz motherboard speed with a ×8.5 multiplier. However, starting way back in the days of the 486, people began to run their systems intentionally at clock speeds higher than the CPU was rated, and they worked. Well, *sometimes* the systems worked, and sometimes they didn't. Intel has a reason for marking a CPU at a particular clock speed—that's the highest speed that Intel will guarantee that it will work. If you intentionally run a CPU at a speed higher than its rated clock speed, you are *overclocking* the CPU.

Before I say anything else, I must warn you that intentional overclocking of a CPU immediately voids any warranty. Overclocking has been known to destroy CPUs. Overclocking might also make your system unstable—prone to lockups and reboots. I neither applaud nor do I decry the practice of overclocking. My goal here is to simply inform you of the practice. You make your own decisions.

CPU makers hate it when you overclock. Why would you pay more for a faster processor when you can take a cheaper, slower CPU and just make it run faster? To that end, CPU makers, especially Intel, have gone to great lengths to discourage the practice. For example, Intel now makes CPUs with locked multipliers and special overspeed electronics to deter the practice.

I don't think Intel really cares too much what end users do with their CPUs—you own it, you take the risks. A number of criminals, however, have learned to make a good business of remarking CPUs with higher than rated speeds and selling them as legitimate CPUs. These counterfeit CPUs have created a nightmare where unsuspecting retailers and end users have been given overclocked CPUs. When they run into trouble, they innocently ask for warranty support, only to discover that their CPU is counterfeit and the warranty is void.

Intel provides a handy free utility to tell you exactly what type of CPU you have, the rated clock speed and multiplier, and the clock and multiplier that the CPU is currently running. They call this tool the clever name of Intel Processor Frequency ID Utility. This tool runs under DOS, Windows 9*x*, and Windows 2000. You can download the utility at **http://support.intel.com/support/processors/tools/frequencyid/ freqid.htm**.

Of course, Intel is notorious for changing their web site. If this link becomes invalid, simply go to **http://support.intel.com** and search for the utility. Figure 2-109 shows a detail of the utility in action, displaying a Celeron 566 that has been intentionally overclocked to 850MHz.

## 64-Bit Processing

Before this revision of the book goes out of print, we will begin to see the first true 64-bit processors appear on the market. The term "64-bit" is a little misleading—we already have CPUs with 64-bit external data buses and registers. This new class of processors will expand the only item left on a CPU that is still at 32-bit: the address bus. With a 64-bit address bus, we will see CPUs that can address $2^{64}$ bytes of memory, or more precisely, 18,446,744,073,709,551,616 bytes of memory.

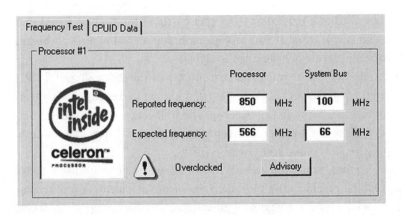

**Figure 2-109**   A Celeron 566 that has been intentionally overclocked to 850MHz

For the first time since 1986, we will see a new operating mode. Further, new operating systems must be designed to take advantage of these new processors. Running Windows 2000 on a system with a 64-bit CPU will be akin to running DOS on a Pentium III system; the current 32-bit operating systems are designed to use only 4GB of RAM.

Both AMD and Intel are racing ahead with competing 64-bit processors. We will see compatibility issues, problems, and delays—the likes of which haven't been seen since 1986. Imagine a world where we need a "Virtual Pentium" on a 64-bit CPU just as we saw the "virtual 8086" when the first 32-bit 80386s came out. In later chapters, we will discover the rather confusing world of DOS memory management and see how Windows 9*x* and Windows 2000 take advantage of virtual 8086 to provide support for DOS applications. Imagine a new world where a 64-bit operating system must go through a dramatically more complex configuration to support 32-bit applications. Will this happen? I don't know. The next few years should prove to be quite interesting indeed.

## Review Questions

1. What do registers provide for the CPU?
   A. Registers determine the clock speed.
   B. The CPU uses registers for temporary storage of internal commands and data.
   C. Registers enable the CPU to address RAM.
   D. Registers enable the CPU to control the address bus.

2. What function does the external data bus have in the PC?
   A. The external data bus determines the clock speed for the CPU.
   B. The CPU uses the external data bus to address RAM.
   C. The external data bus provides a channel for the flow of data and commands between the CPU and RAM.
   D. The CPU uses the external data bus to access registers.

3. What is the function of the address bus in the PC?
   A. The address bus enables the CPU to communicate with the chipset.
   B. The address bus enables the memory controller chip to communicate with the RAM.
   C. The address bus provides a channel for the flow of data and commands between the CPU and RAM.
   D. The address bus enables the CPU to access registers.

4. What is the size of the data bus and address bus on a Pentium II CPU?
   A. 16-bit data bus, 24-bit address bus
   B. 32-bit data bus, 32-bit address bus
   C. 64-bit data bus, 32-bit address bus
   D. 64-bit data bus, 64-bit address bus

5. The Pentium III can run in which of the following modes? (Choose the best answer.)
   A. Real mode
   B. Real mode, 286 protected mode, 386 protected mode
   C. Real mode, 286 protected mode, 386 protected mode, Pentium protected mode
   D. Pentium protected mode, Pentium III protected mode

6. When a tech adds a new Pentium III processor to a motherboard, which of the following should he or she check? (Choose the best answer.)
   A. Clock speed of the CPU, clock multiple for the CPU
   B. Clock speed of the CPU, clock multiple for the CPU, voltage settings on the motherboard
   C. Clock speed of the CPU, clock multiple for the CPU, voltage settings on the motherboard, system clock speed
   D. Voltage settings on the motherboard, system clock speed

7. The Pentium II has which of the following advantages over the Pentium?
   A. Level 1 cache
   B. 64-bit data bus
   C. Dual pipelining
   D. Quad pipelining

8. The Pentium III processor has 32K of Level 1 cache, whereas the Athlon has 128K of Level 1 cache. What does the cache provide for the processor(s)?
   A. Cache enables the CPU to continue working during system RAM refreshes.
   B. Cache enables the CPU to continue working during hard drive refreshes.
   C. Cache enables the CPU to access RAM.
   D. Cache enables the CPU to access the chipset memory controller.

9. Jane, the hardware technician for a nonprofit corporation, has 10 systems that she needs to upgrade with new microprocessors. Each system currently has an ATX motherboard with a Slot 1 Intel Pentium II 266MHz installed. The motherboards can operate at voltages from 2.0 to 2.9 volts. To keep the upgrade costs low, her boss has told her to use the existing motherboards if possible.

   **Primary objective:** Upgrade the systems with faster CPUs.

   **Optional objectives:** Use existing motherboards and avoid adding any hardware aside from the CPU.

   **Proposed solution:** Jane places an order for 10 PPGA Celeron 533 processors and 10 slockets for PGA to Slot 1 conversion.

   **The proposed solution:**
   A. Meets only the primary objective.
   B. Meets the primary objective and one of the optional objectives.
   C. Meets the primary objective and both of the optional objectives.
   D. Meets only the optional objectives.

10. A donor gives five SEC-style Athlon 800MHz processors to the nonprofit corporation for which Jane works as a technician. She has several systems with ATX motherboards and Slot 1 Intel Pentium III 800MHz CPUs installed. Her boss wants her to upgrade five systems with the new processors but to keep the upgrade costs low if possible by using the existing motherboards.

    **Primary objective:** Upgrade the systems with faster CPUs.

    **Optional objective:** Use existing motherboards.

    **Proposed solution:** Remove the Pentium III CPUs on five systems and replace them with the new Athlon CPUs.

    **The proposed solution:**
    A. Meets only the primary objective.
    B. Meets only the optional objective.
    C. Meets the primary and optional objectives.
    D. Meets neither objective.

## Answers

1. **B.** The CPU uses registers for temporary storage of internal commands and data.

2. **C.** The external data bus provides a channel for the flow of data and commands between the CPU and RAM.

3. **A.** The address bus enables the CPU to communicate with the chipset.

4. **C.** All Pentium and later processors have a 64-bit data bus and a 32-bit address bus.

5. **B.** All CPUs from the 80386 to the present can run in only three modes: real mode, 286 protected mode, and 386 protected mode.

6. **C.** Even with the current CPUID built into the Pentium III CPUs, a good tech should check the motherboard settings for speed, clock multiple, and voltage. He or she also should definitely know the speed of the CPU.

7. **D.** The Pentium II shares certain characteristics with the Pentium, including 32K L1 cache and a 64-bit data bus, but is quad pipelined rather than merely dual pipelined.

8. **A.** Cache enables the CPU to continue working during system RAM refreshes.

9. **B.** The Celeron CPUs can easily use the earlier Slot 1 motherboards, so the proposed solution addresses both the primary and one optional objective. She needs the additional slotket converters because the specific Celerons purchased were PPGA (for Socket 370) rather than SEC (for Slot 1).

10. **D.** Although Athlon CPUs can fit into the Pentium III slot (and vice versa), they definitely would not work. Athlons require their own type of motherboard. Further, although some might argue that an Athlon might edge out a clock speed-comparable Pentium III slightly in benchmarks, no one would suggest that any appreciable difference exists in real-world applications.

# RAM

In this chapter, you will

- See the different types of RAM packaging
- Understand RAM banking
- Learn about different types of DRAM
- See how to install RAM properly
- Understand RAM access speed

## Historical/Conceptual

*Random-access memory* (RAM) is the working memory of your PC. Although we touched on this in Chapter 1, let's review the function of RAM in the PC. When not in use, programs are held in mass storage, which usually means a hard drive, but could also mean floppy disks, a CD-ROM disk, or some other device that can hold values when the computer is turned off (Figure 3-1). When you load a program by clicking an icon in Windows, the program is copied from the mass storage device to RAM and then run (Figure 3-2).

Any device that can hold data is memory. "Random access" means that any part of the memory can be accessed with equal ease. Don't limit your thinking on this topic just to electronic components. A sheet of paper with a list of names could be called random access because you see any one name as easily as another one. A cassette tape would not be random access because you would have to rewind or fast-forward the tape to access a particular piece of information. The term "random-access memory" in the PC world, however, refers to a specific type of electronic storage device known as *dynamic random-access memory* (DRAM).

**Figure 3-1**
Mass storage holds
unused programs.

**Figure 3-2**
Programs run
in RAM.

## DRAM

DRAM is the most popular type of electronic memory in the PC world. As mentioned in Chapter 2, DRAM is a special type of semiconductor that stores individual 1's and 0's using microscopic capacitors and transistors (Figure 3-3). DRAM usually manifests itself as a number of chips soldered onto a card of some type (Figure 3-4).

**Figure 3-3**
Schematic of a one-
bit DRAM storage
chip

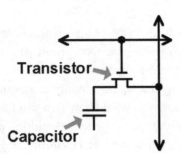

**Figure 3-4**   A typical DRAM card

I will talk about the different DRAM cards later in the chapter, but for the moment, I'm going to concentrate on the individual chips on the cards (Figure 3-5). Once you understand how the individual chips are organized, I will return to the cards and describe how the individual chips work together on the cards.

**Figure 3-5**   Close-up of DRAM chip

## Organizing DRAM

Due to its low cost, high speed, and ability to contain a lot of data in a relatively small package, DRAM is the standard RAM used in all computers today. Even Macintoshes and mainframes use DRAM. In fact, DRAM can be found in just about everything today, from automobiles to automatic bread makers (Figure 3-6).

**Figure 3-6**   Lots of things need DRAM.

What kind of DRAM do you need for PCs? Well, what does RAM do in a PC? It stores programs and data. So in what format should we store the programs and data? Let's consider what the CPU needs. Remember that the original 8088 processor had an 8-bit external data bus. All the commands given to an 8088 processor were in discrete, 8-bit chunks. (Refer back to Chapter 2 if this is not clear.) Therefore, you need RAM that can store data in 8-bit chunks. Even today's latest and greatest CPUs still run all of the original 8088 commands (along with all of their own more advanced commands) for backward compatibility, so the necessary RAM "width" is still eight bits. When people talk about PC memory, they say things like "32 megabytes," "128 megabytes," or, if your computer is really old, "640 kilobytes." You'd never say something like "16 megawords" or "32 megabits." That's because your CPU needs memory that stores programs and data in 8-bit (1-byte) chunks. So when discussing memory in PCs, we always talk about *byte-wide* memory (Figure 3-7).

But DRAM is not manufactured just for the PC industry. Many devices that use DRAM don't use byte-wide memory, so DRAM manufacturers sell their chips in a broad range of sizes that wouldn't be familiar to PC people (Figure 3-8).

Let's take some time to understand how DRAM manufacturers sell chips, and then we'll fit that into the byte-wide PC world. When referring to individual DRAM chips,

**Figure 3-7**
PCs need byte-wide
DRAM

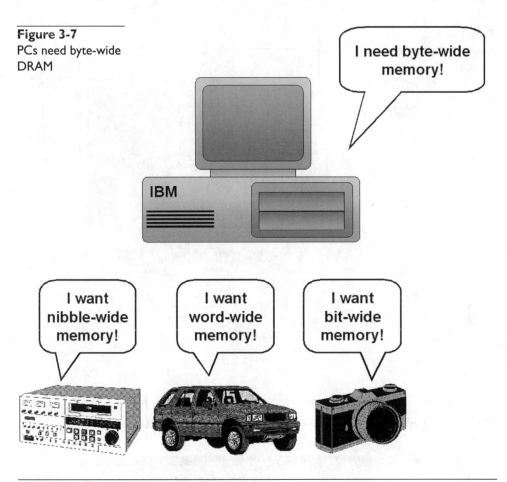

Figure 3-8    Many widths of DRAM are needed.

you primarily will be interested in two values: the *depth* and the *width*. To explain this, I'll use a couple of analogies. Have you ever taken film in to be developed? You can usually select how large you want the photographs to be, right? In the United States, you usually get them in either 3×5-inch or 4×6-inch format. If you're willing to pay more, you can even get them in the 6×8 size (Figure 3-9).

When you say "5," what does that mean? Of course, it means three inches high by five inches wide. You do the same thing when discussing lumber, saying things like "2×4" or "1×12" (Figure 3-10).

DRAM works exactly the same way. DRAM has a depth and a width that are measured in units of bits. Some common depths are 256Kb, 1Mb, 4Mb, 16Mb, and 64Mb, and some common widths are 1 bit, 4 bits, 8 bits, and 16 bits. When you combine the

**Figure 3-9**
Height and width of photos

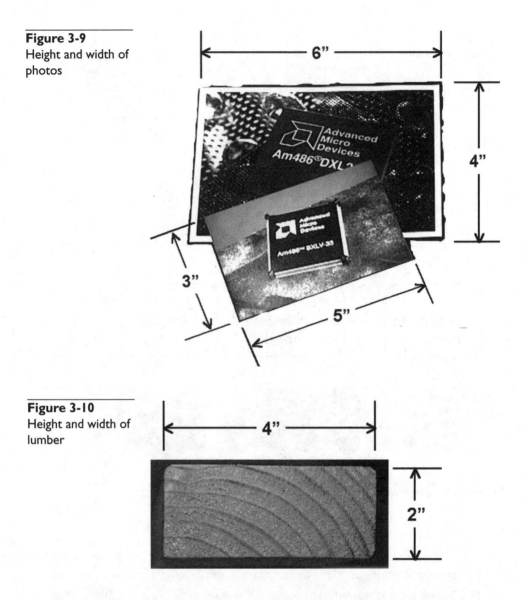

**Figure 3-10**
Height and width of lumber

depth and the width, you get the size of the DRAM chip. When talking about individual DRAM chips, then, you'd say something like 1 Meg × 4 or 256Kb × 1 (Figure 3-11).

Suppose someone were to hold up a 3 × 5 photo and ask you, "How large a photo am I holding?" You could probably eyeball it and say: "That's a 3 × 5 photo." Unfortunately, it is virtually impossible to do that with DRAM. Two chips that look identical can be very different on the inside. The only way you can tell one DRAM from another is by reading the information printed on the chip itself. (By the way, don't bother to try to read that indecipherable nonsense on the chips—the only people who can make

**Figure 3-11**
Height and width
of DRAM

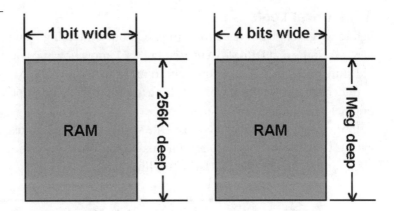

sense of that gibberish are the manufacturers.) No direct correlation exists between physical size and the internal organization of the chip (Figure 3-12).

**NOTE** Remember that 1KB = 1,024 bytes and 1MB = 1,048,576 bytes. In the DRAM world, we often use K and Meg to define the depth of a chip, dropping the word "bits." For example, 256K (bits) × 1 (bit) is shortened simply to 256K × 1.

So if you were to go up to a DRAM salesman and say: "I'd like 32 megabytes of RAM, please," he would look at you a bit strangely. DRAM makers don't think in terms of bytes. DRAM is sold in depth-by-width units such as 256K × 4. Now we need to put the DRAM world into the PC world and understand how the two work together.

**Figure 3-12**
Different DRAM
may look identical.

## A Historical Look

Before we get started, I need to warn you about something. You're going back in time here, when the first DRAMs were used in PCs. I know how most folks hate to talk about old stuff—I do, too—but if you want to understand how DRAM works now, you have to understand how DRAM worked a long time ago. You'd be surprised how much of the original technology is still used today.

In the original IBM PC, the most DRAM that the PC could use was 640K (655,360 bytes). Later in the book, I'll explain this limitation—but for now I need you to trust me. I promise to completely clarify this limit later.

**NOTE** The single greatest truism of the PC business is "Everything old is new again!"

PCs need byte-wide RAM. Although today's DRAM chips can have widths of greater than 1 bit, back in the old days all DRAMS were 1 bit wide. That means you only had sizes like 64K × 1 or 256K × 1—always 1 bit wide. So how was 1-bit-wide DRAM turned into 8-bit-wide memory? To help you understand what was done, visualize RAM as an electronic spreadsheet. You've probably used a spreadsheet such as Microsoft Excel or Lotus 1-2-3. Imagine a spreadsheet where the only values you can enter are 0 and 1. The number of columns is the width, and the number of rows is the depth. This spreadsheet concept is exactly how the CPU sees RAM, so 640K of RAM would look like Figure 3-13 to the CPU.

**Figure 3-13**
RAM spreadsheet

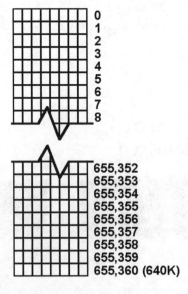

So how do we take a bunch of 1-bit-wide DRAM chips and turn them into 8-bit-wide RAM (Figure 3-14)? The answer is quite simple: just take eight 1-bit-wide chips and electronically organize them with the memory controller chip. First, put eight 1-bit-wide chips in a row on the motherboard (Figure 3-15), and then wire up this row of DRAM chips to the memory controller chip (which has to be designed to handle this) to make byte-wide memory (Figure 3-16). You just made eight 1-bit-wide DRAMs look like one 8-bit-wide DRAM (Figure 3-17). This row of chips has to add up to eight bits, and each chip has to be the same depth. You couldn't use seven 256K × 1 chips and one 64K × 1 chip; it wouldn't add up to 256 kilobytes (Figure 3-18).

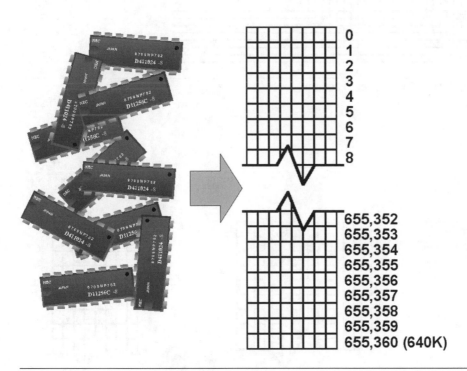

**Figure 3-14**   How do we turn chips into a spreadsheet?

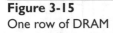
**Figure 3-15**
One row of DRAM

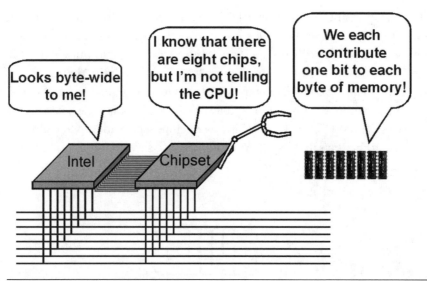

**Figure 3-16** The chipset in action

**Figure 3-17**
Eight one-wide
make one eight-
wide.

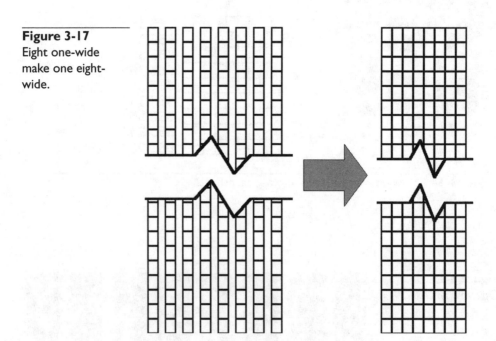

**Figure 3-18**
All DRAM in a row
must be the same
depth.

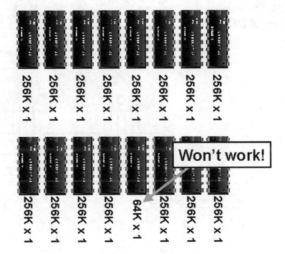

## Multiple Rows

You can use multiple DRAMs to create byte-wide memory, but there's a little problem. Back in the days of the 8088 processor, the biggest DRAM chip you could get was 256K × 1. With eight of these, the biggest row you could have was 256 kilobytes, but computers needed more than 256 kilobytes of RAM. Because the biggest row was 256 kilobytes, the only way to get more RAM was to add more rows. Adding more rows required an improved memory controller chip that could control more than one row of chips, so new types of chipsets were created that could handle two or more rows of RAM (Figure 3-19).

When the CPU needs a certain byte of memory, the CPU requests that byte via the address bus. The CPU has no idea where the byte of RAM is physically located. The chipset keeps track of this and just gives the CPU whatever byte it requests (Figure 3-20). Back in the old days, it was easy to determine if your CPU could handle more than one row of RAM. All you had to do was look at the motherboard. You could see rows of sockets ready for you to add RAM (Figure 3-21). You didn't have to use all the rows, but if you used a row, it had to be completely filled with chips of the same depth.

**NOTE** *Populated* means a row with DRAM inserted; *unpopulated* means a row that has no DRAM.

**Figure 3-19**
Chipset with two
rows of DRAM

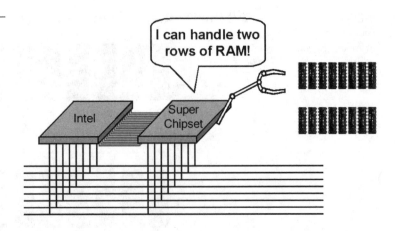

**Figure 3-20**
The chipset knows
the real location of
the DRAM.

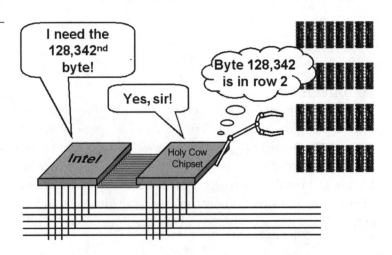

**Figure 3-21**
Empty rows, ready
for DRAM to be
added

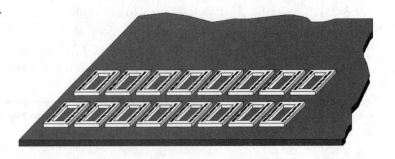

These rules of rows are still true today. You can have different sizes of DRAM in different rows (Figure 3-22); just remember that the DRAM chips in the same row have to be the same size (Figure 3-23). The total amount of RAM is the sum of all the rows (Figure 3-24).

**Figure 3-22**
One populated and one unpopulated row

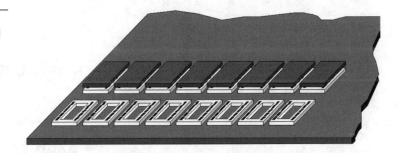

## Chips in different rows can have different depths!

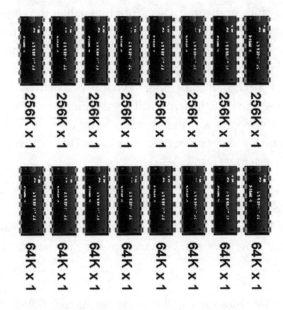

256K × 1  256K × 1  256K × 1  256K × 1  256K × 1  256K × 1  256K × 1  256K × 1

64K × 1  64K × 1  64K × 1  64K × 1  64K × 1  64K × 1  64K × 1  64K × 1

**Figure 3-23**  Different rows can have different depths.

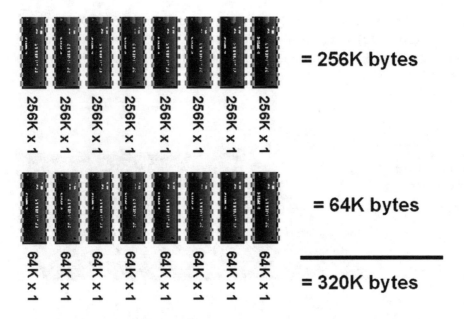

Figure 3-24   All DRAM is cumulative.

## Parity

Parity is for error detection. Parity manifests through an extra chip that is 1 bit wide and as deep as all the other chips in the row. This ninth bit enables the chipset to compare the number of 1's stored in a byte with the number of 1's found when the byte is accessed. For parity to work, you must have a chipset designed to use the parity chip.

Every time data is placed in RAM, the parity bit is set. Every time you access that byte of RAM, the parity bit is checked. If something has happened between data storage and retrieval to change one of the bits, then you will get the infamous "Parity error, system halted" message. Parity checking was useful in the early days of desktop computers when DRAM had a relatively high failure rate, but today's DRAM is so dependable that very few PCs still support parity (Figure 3-25).

## RAM Packaging, Part I

Many popular types of RAM packages have been developed over the years. This section takes a quick look at the more common ones used in the early part of the PC industry.

## DIPPs

The first-generation DRAM chips used a *Dual Inline Pin Package* (DIPP). These types of chips are distinguished by two rows of pins extending from either side of the package (Figure 3-26). Installing DIPPs was, at best, a hassle. It was easy to break a pin or to

**Figure 3-25** Here's a close-up of older-style DIPP DRAM. The nine chips show it is parity.

**Figure 3-26**
Classic DIPP
package

improperly insert the DRAM into its socket. Plus, as RAM chips began to drop in price during the late 1980s and early 1990s, it became obvious that when dealing with DRAM, you were dealing more with complete rows than with individual chips. Think about it. When you want to add RAM, you have to populate an entire row, right? If you want to remove RAM, again you must remove an entire row. So why mess with individual chips when 99 percent of the time you have to deal with entire rows?

This demand created a new type of DRAM package. Instead of individual chips inserted into individual sockets, the RAM was soldered to a small board that could be inserted into the motherboard. This type of package was called a *Single Inline Pin Package* (SIPP).

## 30-Pin SIPPs

The SIPP used a standardized set of pins that mounted into the motherboard, which eliminated the need for individual mounts for each DRAM. The SIPP revolutionized the way DRAM was used in a PC. For example, by the time SIPPs had been invented, new DRAM chips were available that were more than 1 bit wide—so you could find

256K × 4 chips. The rule is that each row must equal eight bits, which used to mean that you had to use eight 1-bit chips. But now you could use two 4-bit chips to do the same thing. With DIPPs, you had to use whatever chips were designed to use the sockets soldered to the motherboard. If you had eight little sockets on the motherboard, that was what you had to use. But with a SIPP, the 30-pin connector was independent of the type of chips soldered onto it. So you could take out a 30-pin SIPP with eight 256K × 1 chips, replace it with a 30-pin SIPP with two 256K × 4 chips, and the system wouldn't know the difference. SIPPs made installing and removing RAM much simpler (Figure 3-27).

**Figure 3-27**   Thirty-pin SIPP

SIPPs plugged directly into the motherboard via their own special socket. They were relatively easy to install; all you had to do was push down. Unfortunately, SIPPs also had a rather nasty Achilles heel. The 30 pins that connected the package to the motherboard were just as delicate as the pins on the DIPP chips. Like the DIPP chips, it was just too easy to break off one of the pins accidentally—which made the whole SIPP garbage. So, although SIPPs were revolutionary, they were quickly replaced by their much more robust successor, the 30-pin SIMM.

## Thirty-Pin SIMMs

*Single Inline Memory Modules* (SIMMs) were the next rung on DRAM's evolutionary ladder. Physically, they looked very similar to SIPPs, with one exception: no pins. There was nothing to bend and no way to inflict serious bodily harm to you or the chips (Figure 3-28).

SIMMs were inserted into a special SIMM socket. It was virtually impossible to install SIMMs improperly due to the notch on one side of the card. Electronically, 30-pin SIMMs were identical to 30-pin SIPPs. You could even purchase a simple converter that enabled you to insert SIPPs into SIMM sockets and vice versa (Figure 3-29).

**Figure 3-28**  Thirty-pin SIMM

**Figure 3-29**  Eight rows for 30-pin SIMMs

In 30-pin SIMMs, each printed circuit card had 30 pins or contacts along the edge. The most important thing to remember about 30-pin SIMMs was that, although their depths varied, they were always 8 data bits (1 byte) wide. Although a SIMM chip was always 8 bits wide, the chips on the package could differ widely. Figure 3-30 shows some examples of different chip layouts for a 30-pin SIMM.

## Keeping Track of Your SIMMs

One unfortunate aspect of 30-pin SIMMs (you will see this is true for all DRAM) was that you couldn't tell how deep a SIMM chip was simply by looking at it. Figure 3-31 shows a 4 × 3 SIMM and a 1 × 3 SIMM. Notice that they look almost identical. The best way to know what depth SIMM you had was to label it when you bought it. Every SIMM I owned had a small label on it that told me its size—that way I never had to guess (Figure 3-32). You could, however, quite readily tell a parity from a nonparity 30-pin SIMM. All nonparity 30-pin SIMMs had an even number of chips. All parity 30-pin SIMMs had an odd number of chips.

**Figure 3-30**
Different chip layouts on SIMMs

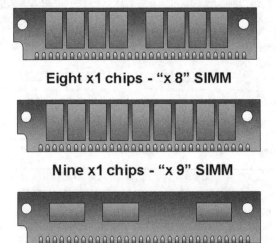

**Eight x1 chips - "x 8" SIMM**

**Nine x1 chips - "x 9" SIMM**

**Two x4 chips & one x1 - "x 3" SIMM**

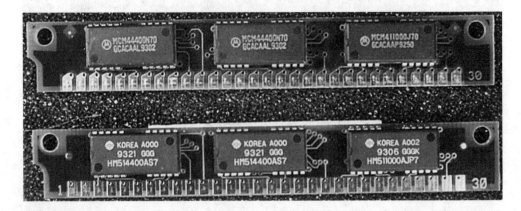

**Figure 3-31**
Identical looking but very different SIMMs

**Figure 3-32**  How to be sure of the size—a SIMM labeled "1 × 9"

## SIMM Chips and Parity

When purchasing SIMM chips, the question was, "Do I need parity or nonparity?" The type of motherboard you had always decided this question. The motherboard book would say whether your machine required parity or nonparity chips. If you did not have a motherboard book, you could sometimes get a clue by looking at the SIMMs currently in the PC. Did they have an odd (parity) or even (nonparity) number of chips?

Some PCs enabled you to turn off the parity. Figure 3-33 shows a screen from an older PC's advanced CMOS settings. (See Chapter 4, for a discussion of CMOS.) On these machines, you could mix parity with nonparity chips, as long as the parity was turned off.

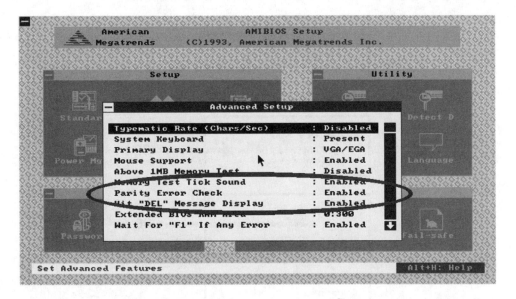

**Figure 3-33**  Parity option on older CMOS

## Access Speed

We know from Chapter 2 that the system clock controls the CPU speed. We know for example, exactly how many clock cycles the CPU needs to calculate 2 + 3. The DRAM used for the first ten years of the PC industry did not use a clock. The chipset simply talked to the DRAM and then had to wait until the DRAM came up with the information it requested. This early type of RAM was called *Fast Page Mode* (FPM) RAM. It took a certain amount of time for the FPM DRAM chip to supply the chipset with the requested data. This was called the *access speed,* and it was typically given in *nanoseconds* (nanoseconds). The faster the chip, the shorter the delay and the smaller the access-speed number. Therefore, a 100 nanosecond chip was slower than a 60 nanosecond chip.

**NOTE** **A lower access-speed number means faster access.**

Every chipset was designed to send a data request to FPM DRAM and then wait a certain number of clock cycles for the answer. As a result, each motherboard required a certain speed of FPM DRAM, so it was crucial for you to be able to eyeball a DRAM chip to determine its access speed. Access speeds ranged from as slow as 200 nanoseconds on ancient 8088s, up to 50 nanoseconds for the last of the FPM DRAMs. Figure 3-34 shows some examples of chips and how to determine their access speeds.

**Figure 3-34**
Determining access rates

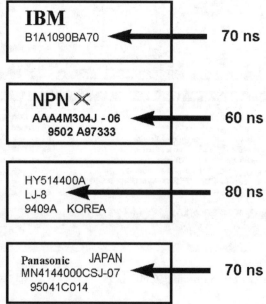

Although there were some exceptions, which you will visit later, the easiest guideline was to follow the motherboard book guidelines on the proper-speed FPM DRAM and thus make sure that every piece of DRAM was that speed.

Even as we march into the 21ˢᵗ century, manufacturers continue to make small amounts of 30-pin SIMMs for system replacement, although the days of the 30-pin SIMM in a new PC have long since passed.

## Talking the Talk with 30-Pin SIMMs

If you want to purchase SIMMs for whatever reason, you must speak the language of DRAM. Each individual SIMM is called a *stick*. So if you want four SIMM packages, for example, you would say: "Give me four sticks of RAM, (please)." Further, you never say "30-pin SIMM." Rather, use the numbers. If you say "by 3," by 8," or "by 9," for example, every dealer knows you want 30-pin SIMMs. Never ask for parity or nonparity. Only three widths of DRAM are available in 30-pin SIMMs: "× 8," which is by definition nonparity; "× 9," which is by definition parity; and "× 3," which is simply a "× 9" SIMM in a three-chip package and also parity. So by saying "× 8" or "× 9," you specify whether you want a nonparity or parity 30-pin SIMM.

Only three common sizes exist in 30-pin SIMMs: 256K, 1MB, and 4MB. These three sizes make up 95 percent of all 30-pin SIMMs, so when describing these sizes, you want to drop the unit values and just use the number. When talking about a 30-pin SIMM, therefore, you'd just say "4 × 8" or a "1 × 3."

Finally, when you specify an access speed, don't say "50 nanoseconds." Just say "fifties" or "eighties." If you buy just one stick, say "50" or "60." So if you order some 30-pin SIMMs, the conversation would go something like this: "I'd like 16 sticks of 1 × 8 sixties, and 4 sticks of 256 × 9 eighties, please."

## Banking

The 8088 processor inside the original IBM PC defined many of the rules still in force today as to how RAM is accessed, but RAM access functions have not stood still. The first major improvement to RAM access from the IBM PC was a concept known as banking. Simply put, *banking* means accessing more than one row of DRAM at a time. Every PC since the 286 performs this banking function. Let's see how banking came to be and how it is used today.

One concept that must be clarified is that not every command in the 8088 CPU's machine language was only one byte wide. Many commands were 16 or even 32 bits wide. So how could the 8088, with only an 8-bit external data bus, handle commands that were more than one byte wide? The answer was simple; it chopped the commands into one-byte chunks.

So every time the 8088 CPU ran into commands like these, it would have to access RAM at least twice before it could act on the command, due to its 8-bit external data bus. When the 286 CPUs arrived, an opportunity arose. Do you remember from Chapter 2 that a 286 had a 16-bit external data bus? With the right chipset, a 286 could access 16 bits every time memory was accessed. It would be much faster to access two bytes every time you went to RAM instead of just one (Figure 3-35). The only problem with this was that one row (or one SIMM) could give only one byte each time it was accessed, because that's all it was designed to do (Figure 3-36). A new type of 16-bit wide DRAM would have to be invented (which nobody wanted to do back then), or you could just install DRAM in pairs that worked together as a team (Figure 3-37).

**Figure 3-35**
Most chipsets can send more than eight bits at a time.

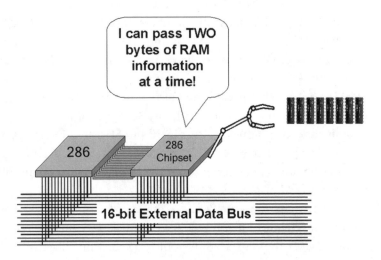

**Figure 3-36**
One 8-bit row can only send one byte.

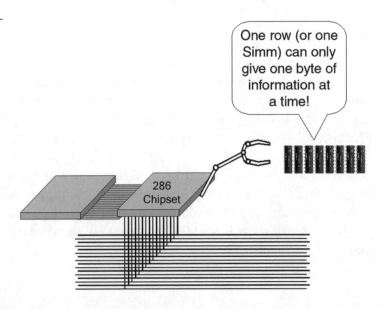

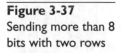

**Figure 3-37**
Sending more than 8
bits with two rows

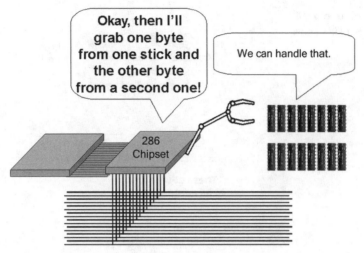

When the 386s and 486s with their 32-bit external data buses came out, two more rows or two more SIMMs were simply added to the two existing ones to make four 8-bit rows. The RAM had to be wide enough to match the size of the external data bus. Combining the widths of DRAM to match the width of the external data bus is called *banking*. The number of SIMMs that make up a bank depends on the chipset, which in turn depends on the CPU's external data bus size.

**NOTE**   The number of rows of SIMMs that can be simultaneously accessed by the chipset is a *bank*.

Figure 3-38 lists some rules for banking with 30-pin SIMMs. The most important rule of banking is that all SIMMs in the same bank must be identical. For example, if you have a 486 (32-bit external data bus) and 30-pin SIMMs (8 bits wide), you must have four identical 30-pin SIMMs to make a bank. You can have four $1 \times 8$s, four $4 \times 3$s, or four $256 \times 9$s—it doesn't matter, as long as they are identical to each other. They also should be the same speed. See Figure 3-39.

To determine the total capacity of RAM, simply add up the amount of RAM in each bank. Using the earlier example of a 486, if you have four $1 \times 8$ SIMMs, you have four times one megabyte, or four megabytes of RAM. If you have a 286 with two $256 \times 9$ SIMMs, you have 512K of RAM. Almost all PCs have more than one bank. Figure 3-40 shows an old 486 system with connectors for up to eight rows of 30-pin SIMMs.

**Figure 3-38**
Banking rules

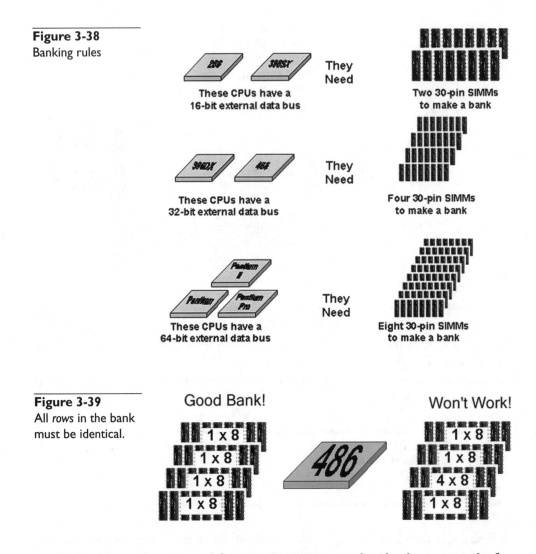

These CPUs have a
16-bit external data bus

They
Need

Two 30-pin SIMMs
to make a bank

These CPUs have a
32-bit external data bus

They
Need

Four 30-pin SIMMs
to make a bank

These CPUs have a
64-bit external data bus

They
Need

Eight 30-pin SIMMs
to make a bank

**Figure 3-39**
All *rows* in the bank
must be identical.

Good Bank!

1 x 8
1 x 8
1 x 8
1 x 8

486

Won't Work!

1 x 8
1 x 8
4 x 8
1 x 8

Since you know that you need four 30-pin SIMMs to make a bank on a 486, the fact that this motherboard has eight slots tells you that it is designed for two banks. Having more than one bank on a motherboard gives flexibility in the amount of RAM in your system. You can have different size SIMMs in different banks. For example, assuming you have a 486 system with two banks, you can install 4 × 8 SIMMs in one bank (16MB) and 1 × 8 SIMMs in another (4MB), for a total RAM of 20MB (Figure 3-41). Imagine how limited RAM installation would be if you didn't have multiple banks! Today, all systems have multiple banks for RAM.

The connectors where you install a bank are also collectively called a *bank*. A bank without any SIMMs is called an *unpopulated* bank, and a bank filled with SIMMs is called a *populated* bank.

**Figure 3-40**   Eight 30-pin SIMM slots in a 486 make two banks.

**Figure 3-41**
Banks are
cumulative.

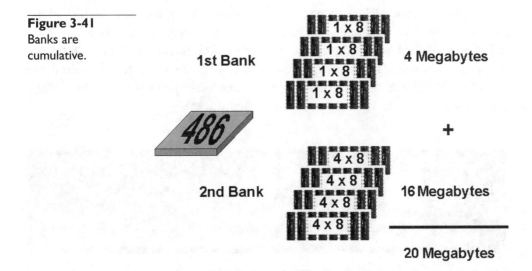

A bank must be either completely populated or completely unpopulated. This is fairly obvious, but I want to be completely clear. Let's say you have a 486 system that needs four sticks to make a bank. You have two banks. You will have either four or eight sticks in the system—not two, three, five, or six—because that's the only way to fill four-stick banks properly.

## Test Specific

### RAM Packaging, Part 2

Now that you have a basic understanding of the different types of earlier DRAM packages, you can move forward into the more modern types of DRAM with the necessary conceptual tools to appreciate why they're used in today's machines.

### 72-Pin SIMMs

Most of the examples in the previous section used 486 CPUs. Why didn't I use a more modern CPU such as a Pentium III? Modern CPUs (everything since the 486) have 64-bit external data buses, and newer motherboards don't use 30-pin SIMMs—for a very good reason. You would need eight 30-pin SIMMs ($8 \times 8 = 64$) to make a bank to match the 64-bit external data bus of the latest CPUs. Although this is not a problem electronically, it takes up a massive amount of physical space on the motherboard. You would need 16 slots just to create two banks! We needed a new type of DRAM packaging that was more than eight bits wide.

Enter the 72-pin SIMM. Like its little brother, the 72-pin SIMM had the same number of pins on each stick as its name would imply—72, in this case. Unlike 30-pin SIMMs, however, each 72-pin SIMM was 32 bits wide. This meant that for a 386 DX or a 486 motherboard, you could replace four 30-pin SIMMs with one 72-pin SIMM. For a Pentium, you would need only two 72-pin SIMMs (Figure 3-42). Although similar to the 30-pin SIMM, the 72-pin SIMM is about an inch longer and has a notch in the middle of the pins to assist in inserting the stick (Figure 3-43).

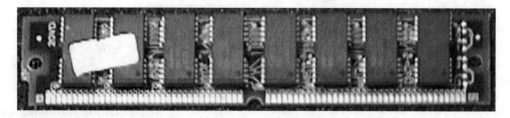

**Figure 3-42**   A 72-pin SIMM

**Figure 3-43**   Four 72-pin SIMM slots

Because 72-pin SIMMs were 32 bits wide, the term "× 32" described a nonparity SIMM and "× 36" described a parity SIMM. Don't let the numbers confuse you. You might be inclined to think a "1 × 32 SIMM" referred to a 1MB-capacity RAM stick, but that is incorrect. A 1 × 32 SIMM has 1MB of 32 bits, which is equal to 4MB of 8 bits, which means that the SIMM could hold 4MB of RAM (1,048,576 × 32 = 4MB). Here are some common 72-pin SIMMs and their sizes:

1 × 32 = 4MB, no parity

1 × 36 = 4MB, parity

2 × 32 = 8MB, no parity

2 × 36 = 8MB, parity

4 × 32 = 16MB, no parity

4 × 36 = 16MB, parity

8 × 32 = 32MB, no parity

8 × 36 = 32MB, parity

16 × 32 = 64MB, no parity

16 × 36 = 64MB, parity

Another benefit to the 32-bit-wide 72-pin SIMMs was that you needed only one 72-pin SIMM to make a bank in a 386 or 486. You needed two 72-pin SIMMs to make a bank on a Pentium or Pentium Pro.

Other than the width, 72-pin SIMMs were just like the older 30-pin SIMMs. They were FPM DRAM, they had an access speed, you could choose parity or nonparity, and they followed the banking rules. Like 30-pin SIMMs, a small notch on one end made it virtually impossible to install a 72-pin SIMM incorrectly.

Unlike the 30-pin SIMMs, there was no definite way to tell a parity 72-pin SIMM from a nonparity 72-pin SIMM. You just made sure you wrote the type of SIMM on the back of the stick, and you never had a problem. In fact, many DRAM makers and distributors around this time began to print this information right on the SIMM, as shown in Figure 3-44. (They were not being nice, necessarily; they just didn't want you to bother them with silly questions.)

Interestingly, two types of parity SIMMs were available: true and TTL parity. *True* parity was just as it sounds: a real parity chip for every eight data bits. *TTL* parity emulates parity and costs less. The few systems that used parity told you which one to use.

**Figure 3-44**  Labeling is the secret to identification.

## Talking the Talk with 72-Pin SIMMs

Although the size of a 30-pin SIMM was fairly easy to understand, 72-pin SIMMs confused many people. People had a hard time understanding that a 1MB × 4-byte-wide RAM (1 × 32) was not 1 megabyte, but 4 megabytes in capacity. Additionally, you could purchase RAM at your local computer store for a fairly good price. As a result, many RAM makers began to cave in to less knowledgeable purchasers. We started to see less use of the correct (but confusing) naming terminology; instead you'd see  1 × 32, 72-pin SIMM called a "4-megabyte, nonparity, 72-pin SIMM." But those in the know still use proper naming conventions. If you say "× 32," you want nonparity (or "× 36" for parity) 72-pin SIMMs. The term *stick* is still used to define an individual SIMM.

All the access speed terminology we learned for 30-pin SIMMs still holds true. When you specify an access speed, don't say "50 nanoseconds;" instead, say "fifties" or "eighties." If you buy just one stick, say "50" or "60." So if you ordered some 72-pin SIMMs, the conversation would go something like this: "I'd like 4 sticks of 4 × 32 fifties and 2 sticks of 4 × 36 sixties, please."

# DIMM

The most popular DRAM package in use today is the *Dual Inline Memory Module* (DIMM). DIMMs come in a wide variety of pin sizes, but the 168-pin DIMM currently dominates in modern systems. A DIMM is more than just a bigger, wider SIMM. The "dual" in DIMM comes from the fact that each side of each pin has a separate function, whereas each side of each pin is the same on a SIMM. DIMMs have the extra pins necessary to enable rather interesting options, such as buffering and ECC. DIMMs can also handle the new types of RAM, such as SDRAM, DDR SDRAM, and Rambus, which we cover later in this chapter. A 168-pin DIMM stick is 64 bits wide, which means you need only one to create a bank in a Pentium class or later motherboard (Figure 3-45).

Another type of DIMM is most commonly used in laptops: the *Small Outline* (SO-) DIMM. SO-DIMMs are much shorter than 168-pin DIMMs. They come in two sizes: a 72-pin version with a 32-bit data path and a 144-pin version with a 64-bit-wide data path (Figure 3-46). Their convenient size has made them extremely popular for use with laptops.

**Figure 3-45**   A 168-pin DIMM

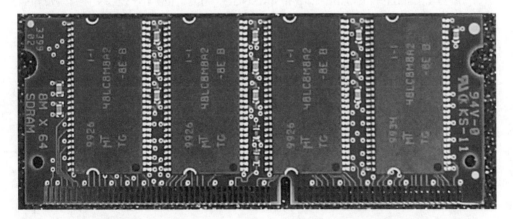

**Figure 3-46**   A 144-pin SO-DIMM

Because a 168-pin DIMM is 64 bits wide, a $1 \times 64$ DIMM is 1MB of 64 bits wide, or 8 megabytes. Here are some common 168-pin DIMMs and their sizes:

$2 \times 64 = 16MB$

$4 \times 64 = 32MB$

$8 \times 64 = 64MB$

$16 \times 64 = 128MB$

$32 \times 64 = 256MB$

Although 168-pin DIMMs are officially "$\times 64$" wide chips, many technicians just say "16-megabyte 168-pin DIMMs." Be ready to "talk the talk" either way.

## The Magic Banking Formula

With 30-pin SIMMs, 72-pin SIMMs, SO-DIMMs, and 168-pin DIMMs, it can get a little challenging to remember how many sticks of each type of DRAM are needed to make a bank on different systems. Don't bother trying to memorize them; the powers that be are just going to come out with wider SIMMs/DIMMs and wider external data buses, and you'll be right back where you started. Instead, I have a formula you can use to determine the number of SIMM/DIMM sticks needed to make one bank; I call it my "magic banking formula:"

One bank = Width of the CPU's external data bus/Width of the SIMM or DIMM

Let's try this a few times:

**How many 30-pin SIMMs are needed to make a bank on a 486?** A 486 has a 32-bit external data bus, and 30-pin SIMMs are 8 bits wide, so: $32 \div 8 = 4$. We need four 30-pin SIMMs per bank for a 486.

**How many 168-pin DIMMs are needed to make a bank on a Pentium III?** A Pentium III has a 64-bit external data bus, and 168-pin DIMMs are 64 bits wide, so: $64 \div 64 = 1$. We need one 168-pin DIMM per bank for a Pentium III.

Stick with this formula, no matter what they throw at you in the future. It will always tell you the number of sticks needed to make a bank.

For years, banking was a critical issue when dealing with RAM. The external data bus on all CPUs, however, has never gone beyond 64 bits since the days of the original Pentium. This, combined with the overwhelming dominance of 168-pin DIMMs, has made banking virtually a non-issue in today's systems. Don't let this make you too complacent! Be aware that Intel and AMD are already planning new CPUs with 128-bit external data buses. These systems will need two 168-DIMMs per bank. Remember, you heard it here first!

## Improvements in DRAM

As we look at RAM, you need to understand some of the improvements on the classic FPM DRAM of the original 8088 days. When I say improvements, I'm talking about functional technology improvements, not just widening the RAM via a new type of stick, as you saw in the previous sections. My goal here is not to go into great depth on these improvements, but rather to enable you to recognize these improvements and take advantage of them when they are available.

### EDO

As described in Chapter 2, all DRAM needs to be refreshed to keep the data and programs it stores valid. The process of refresh creates a big bottleneck in RAM access. Of course, things like SRAM caches certainly reduce the impact, but any way to minimize the frequency of refresh will improve the overall speed of the computer—thus, the creation of *Extended Data Out* (EDO) DRAM back in the early 1990s. EDO DRAM was nothing more than a moderate improvement on old-style FPM DRAM. EDO needed to be refreshed much less often, thereby providing an extended period where data could be taken out of RAM. EDO DRAM enabled a system to access data more quickly than a comparably equipped system with FPM RAM. EDO RAM was on either a 72-pin SIMM or a DIMM (168 or SO), and looked exactly like regular DRAM. There was no standard way to tell EDO from FPM DRAM, so again we were always careful to label our EDO RAM as such (Figure 3-47).

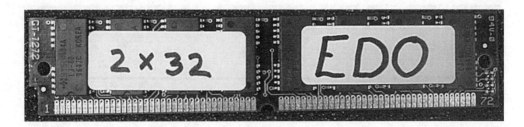

**Figure 3-47**   How to tell EDO from FPM—another label

You wanted to use EDO whenever possible. Unfortunately, you couldn't just put EDO RAM in any computer. To take advantage of EDO, you needed a chipset designed to handle EDO. The majority of the early Pentium systems used EDO RAM, but that was not true of the 486s with 72-pin SIMM slots. You had to refer to your motherboard book to see if your system could use EDO RAM. EDO RAM enjoyed wide acceptance through most of the 1990s until the advent of a new, extremely powerful type of DRAM called SDRAM. FPM and EDO RAM are now considered obsolete.

## SDRAM

The DRAM that everyone uses today is called *Synchronous Dynamic Random-Access Memory* (SDRAM). SDRAM is still DRAM, but it is synchronous—tied to the system clock. Let me explain. As mentioned earlier, regular DRAM (EDO or FPM) was not tied to any clock. If the CPU wanted some data from RAM, the chipset sent the necessary signals to the DRAM, waited a certain number of clock ticks, and then accessed the RAM again to get the data. The number of clicks of the clock was either set through CMOS or determined by the chipset every time the system booted up. The number of clicks was not exact, but rather rounded up to ensure that the chipset wouldn't access DRAM before the necessary data was ready. This rounding up wasted system time, but until recently DRAM was too slow to be handled any other way.

SDRAM is tied to the system clock, just like the CPU and chipset, so the chipset knows when data is ready to be grabbed from SDRAM, resulting in little wasted time. Plus, SDRAM is quite a bit faster than DRAM. Further, SDRAM pipelines instructions from the chipset that enable commands to be ready as soon as the previous one is taken by the chipset. Collectively, these improvements make SDRAM four to six times faster than regular DRAM.

Currently, SDRAM is available only on DIMMs, so many people think that every time they see a DIMM it must be SDRAM. This is wrong. A 168-pin DIMM can also be regular FPM or EDO DRAM, although that is pretty rare. If you see a DIMM today, you can be pretty sure you are looking at SDRAM.

---

 **EXAM TIP**   SDRAM is always a DIMM, but a DIMM isn't always SDRAM.

---

To take advantage of SDRAM, you must have a system that is designed to use it. Chances are that if you have a system with slots for 168-pin DIMMs, your system can handle SDRAM. Because SDRAM ties to the system clock, it doesn't have an access speed; it has a clock speed just like a CPU. Five clock speeds are commonly used today: 66, 75, 83, 100, and 133 MHz. Manufacturers mark these speeds on the DIMM. You need to get a clock speed that is faster than or equal to the motherboard speed. If you have a Celeron 500, for example, 66 MHz SDRAM would suffice because the Celeron talks to the motherboard at 66 MHz. A Pentium III that uses a 133 MHz front-side bus, in contrast, would obviously need SDRAM that could run at 133 MHz.

## PC100/133 Standards

As Pentium II systems using 168-pin SDRAM DIMMs began to replace Pentium systems that used 72-pin SIMMs, most motherboards still ran at 66 MHz. In the last few years,

motherboard speeds have increased to 100 MHz and even 133 MHz. The first generation of 100 MHz SDRAM DIMMs ran into some compatibility problems. Intel recognized this issue and created the famous "PC100" and later the "PC133" specifications
that define the construction of high-speed DRAM. These standards require the use of
DIMMs or SO-DIMMs and a unique little chip called a *serial presence detect* (SPD) chip
installed on every DIMM stick. The SPD provides the system with all of the details
about the DIMM, including its size, speed, and a number of other more technical bits
of information. Most motherboards require the use of PC100 or PC133 DIMMs. People who sell DIMMs will clearly advertise which DIMMs are PC100 or PC133, and
which are not.

I always get the fastest SDRAM I can afford, even if the motherboard doesn't require
it. For example, if I build a Celeron system, I could get away with 66 MHz DIMMs. I
would buy at least PC100 DIMMs, however, because I want RAM that will last for a
while. Who knows when I'm going to upgrade to a faster motherboard?

## ECC

Many higher-end systems use a special type of RAM called *error correction code* (*ECC*)
DRAM. ECC is a major advance in error checking on DRAM. As mentioned earlier,
DRAM rarely goes bad anymore, but it can still have the occasional hiccup that can
cause data loss. (These hiccups do not have any lasting effect on the hardware.) Parity
is virtually useless for these types of occasional problems, but ECC detects problems in
RAM quite well and can fix most of them on the fly. Any size RAM stick can use ECC
DRAM, but it is most common as 168-pin DIMMs. To take advantage of ECC RAM, you
need a motherboard that is designed to use ECC. Check your motherboard book. You
rarely see ECC RAM in the standard home or office system.

## Battle of the RAM Titans

A fierce battle is taking place in the RAM industry. A few years ago, Intel announced
plans to replace SDRAM with a very fast new type of RAM called *Rambus DRAM* or simply RDRAM (Figure 3-48). Hailed by Intel as the next great leap in DRAM technology,
RDRAM can handle speeds up to 800 MHz. Like older kinds of RAM, RDRAM comes
on sticks, called *RIMMs*. In this case, however, the letters don't actually stand for anything, they just rhyme: SIMMs, DIMMs, and now RIMMs, get it?

Rambus was greatly anticipated by the industry for years, but industry support for
RDRAM has been less than enthusiastic, due to significant delays in development plus
a price that is over six times that of SDRAM. Despite this grudging support, almost all
major PC makers sell systems—usually very high-end workstations and servers—that
use RDRAM.

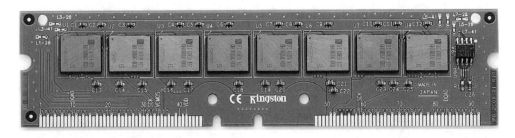

**Figure 3-48**  RDRAM (RIMM)

From a tech's standpoint, RDRAM shares almost all of the characteristics of SDRAM. RDRAM RIMMs come in two sizes: a 184-pin for desktops and a 160-pin SO-RIMM for laptops. Individual RDRAM chips have a capacity, with 64, 128, and 256MB as the most common, and a speed rating, with 600, 700, and 800 MHz as the most common.

RIMMs have a couple of quirks that deal with heat and termination. RIMMs need a special heat dissipation device, rather logically called a *heat spreader*. Also, RDRAM requires that all slots be populated. Unused slots must have a passive device called a *Continuity RIMM* (CRIMM) to enable the RDRAM system to terminate properly.

The jury is still out on RDRAM. Although no one doubts the tremendous power of Rambus technology, the outrageous cost must come down before it can gain anything but a tiny margin of the PC DRAM market. In addition, a newer, cheaper, nearly as powerful type of DRAM, called *Double Data Rate SDRAM* (DDR SDRAM), has entered the market and now poses a serious threat to Rambus DRAM.

DDR SDRAM, as the name implies, simply doubles the throughput of SDRAM. In essence, DDR SDRAM makes two processes for every clock cycle. DDR SDRAM comes in 184-pin DIMMs, which match the 168-pin DIMMs of regular SDRAM in physical size, but not in pin compatibility. The slots for the two types of RAM appear similar as well, but have different guide notches, making it impossible to insert either type of RAM into the other's slot.

DDR SDRAM runs at 200 MHz or 266 MHz (two times 100 MHz and 133 MHz), a crawl compared with the 800 MHz offered by RDRAM. Although DDR SDRAM clearly runs much more slowly than Rambus DRAM, it costs only slightly more than regular SDRAM. AMD and many major system and memory makers have thrown their support behind DDR SDRAM.

So which type of RAM will prevail? The most probable answer, at least for the next few years, is both. Despite the new technology, all of the rules we have learned will still hold true. As long as we can snap it in and make it work, our interest in RAM technology is little more than in ensuring that the right type of RAM goes into the systems under our care.

## Working with RAM

All DRAM chips are extremely sensitive to static, so use extreme caution when working with DRAM. When I install DRAM, I always use an antistatic wrist pad, available at any electronics store. Always handle SIMMs and DIMMs like a piece of film, keeping your fingers on the edges. Few tech moments feel quite as awful as destroying a 128MB DIMM because of static discharge.

## Mixing DRAM Packages

When new types of RAM packages start to become popular, motherboard manufacturers invariably start producing specially designed motherboards with slots for more than one type of DRAM. This adds more flexibility to motherboards and enables you to move from an older type of DRAM to a newer type without losing your investment in the older type of DRAM. Figure 3-49 shows an old 486 motherboard that can handle both 30-pin and 72-pin SIMMs.

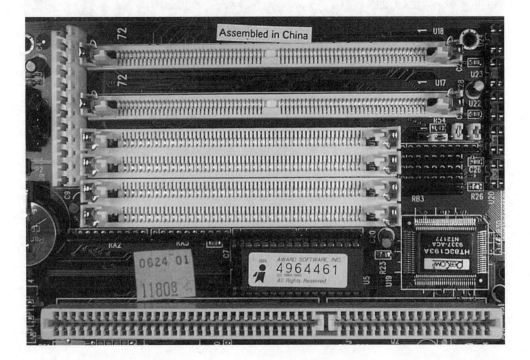

**Figure 3-49** SIMM slots for 30-pin and 72-pin SIMMs

Most of these transitional motherboards work great, but some have a few quirks. You might have to move a jumper or two around to get them to work, for example. Also be aware that some types of SIMMs take precedence over others. On the motherboard in Figure 3-49, for example, if you populate both of the 72-pin banks and the 30-pin bank, the system will ignore one of the 72-pin banks—I have no idea why. Figure 3-50 shows a motherboard that takes both 72-pin SIMMs and 168-pin DIMMs. In this case, you can install either SIMMs or DIMMs, but not some of each. I have another virtually identical motherboard that enables them to work together; go figure! Most current motherboards have only DIMM slots.

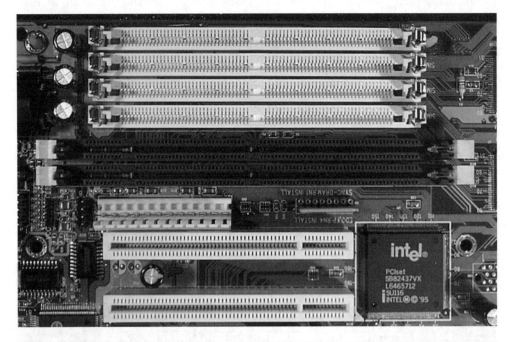

**Figure 3-50**   SIMM and DIMM slots

With the current hot new Rambus DRAM and DDR SDRAM technologies popping up on systems, you might expect the appearance of new transitional motherboards, but that has not been the case. As of this writing, we have yet to see any motherboards that support both SDRAM and the newer DRAM technologies. Intel has created devices to enable some RDRAM-based motherboards to use SDRAM, but overall it seems that the day of the transitional motherboard may have passed.

## A Few Words on Speed

Whether working with an old 486 with 72-pin 60 nanoseconds SIMMs, or a new system sporting PC133 SDRAM (or better), you may often find yourself tempted to mix speeds of DRAM in the same system. Although in some situations you might be able to get away with mixing speeds on a system, the safest, easiest rule to follow is: Always use the speed of DRAM specified in the motherboard book, and make sure that every piece of DRAM runs at that speed. In a worst-case scenario, mixing DRAM speeds can cause the system to lock up every few seconds or every few minutes. You might also get some data corruption. Mixing speeds sometimes works fine, but don't do your income tax on a machine with mixed DRAM speeds until the system has proven to be stable for a few days. The important thing to note here is that you won't break anything, other than possibly data, by experimenting.

Okay, enough disclaimers have been mentioned. Modern motherboards provide some flexibility regarding RAM speeds and mixing. First, you can use RAM that is faster than what the motherboard specifies. For example, if the system needs 100 MHz SDRAM, you can put in 133 MHz SDRAM and it will work fine. Faster DRAM is not going to make the systems run any faster, however, so don't look for any system improvement.

Second, you can usually get away with putting one speed of DRAM in one bank and another speed in another bank, as long as all the speeds are as fast or faster than the speed specified by the motherboard. Don't bother trying to put different-speed DRAMs in the same bank. Yes, it works once in a while, but it's too chancy. I avoid it.

## A Few Words on Banks

Although banks are generally straightforward and rarely cause problems, you need to be aware of a few situations that might cause trouble. All systems number their banks, usually starting with the number 0. Some systems require you to populate bank 0 before you populate any other bank. Most systems don't care. So if you install some RAM and the system doesn't boot up, always try the RAM in another bank to be sure that your system isn't bank sensitive. Inserting RAM into an incorrect bank—with some motherboards—presents no danger. The system simply won't see the RAM when you boot up.

Not all banks take all sizes of DRAM. I have some older Pentium II motherboards that take 168-pin DIMMs, for example, but that cannot handle any DIMMs bigger than 64MB. There's no way around it.

## Installing SIMMs

All SIMMs have a notch on one side that prevents you from installing them improperly. When installing SIMMs, insert the SIMMs at the angle shown in Figure 3-51. When I install SIMMs, I visualize the same motion as a chip shot in golf. If you're not a golfer, visualize scooping ice cream out of a container.

**Figure 3-51**
Inserting a SIMM

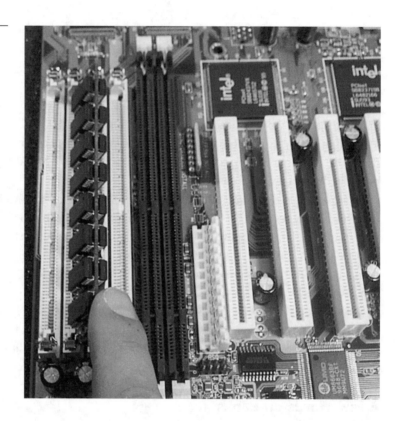

After the SIMM is securely seated in the slot, push it upright until the holding clamps on either side are secured. Make sure that the holes on either end show the small retaining pegs coming through (Figure 3-52). If the SIMM does not insert relatively easily, it's probably backwards. Also, most SIMMs will stand up vertically when properly installed, so if it isn't vertical, it's probably backwards.

Take advantage of installing more than one SIMM to see how they line up across their tops. An improperly installed SIMM will almost always give itself away by not having a nice uniform appearance across the top, as compared with the other SIMMs (Figure 3-53).

## Installing DIMMs and RIMMs

DIMMs and RIMMs are far easier to install than SIMMs. First, swing the side tabs on the RAM slots down from the upright position. Then a good hard push down is usually all you need to ensure a solid connection. Make sure that the DIMM snaps into position to show it is completely seated. You will also notice that the two side tabs will move in to reflect a tight connection (Figure 3-54).

**Figure 3-52**
SIMMs need to be
pushed upright and
snapped into place.

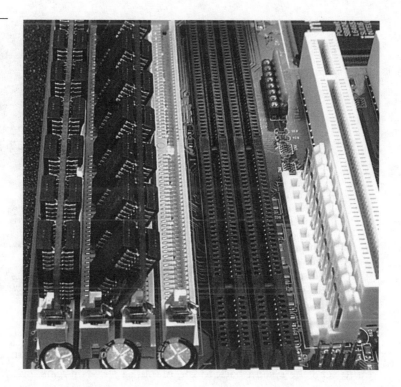

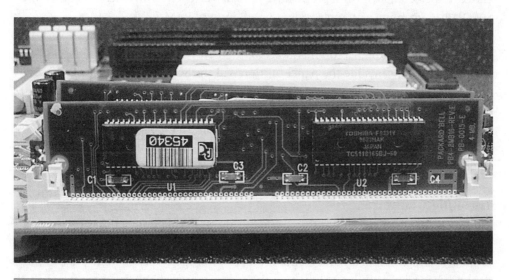

**Figure 3-53**   An improperly inserted SIMM

**Figure 3-54**
Inserting a DIMM

## Installing SO-DIMMs in Laptops

It wasn't that long ago that adding RAM to a laptop was either impossible or required you to send the system back to the manufacturer. For years, every laptop maker had custom-made, proprietary RAM packages that were difficult to handle and staggeringly expensive. The wide acceptance of SO-DIMMs over the last few years has virtually erased these problems. All laptops now provide relatively convenient access to their SO-DIMMs, enabling easy replacement or addition of RAM.

Access to RAM usually requires removing a panel or lifting up the keyboard—the procedure varies among laptop manufacturers. Figure 3-55 shows a typical laptop RAM access panel. You can slide the panel off to reveal the SO-DIMMs. SO-DIMMs usually insert exactly like the old SIMMs—slide the pins into position, and snap the SO-DIMM down into the retaining clips (Figure 3-56).

Remember that before doing any work on a laptop, you must make sure that the system is off, that no AC connection exists, and that all batteries are removed. Use an anti-static wrist strap, as laptops are far more susceptible to ESD than desktop PCs.

## The RAM Count

After installing the new RAM, turn on the PC. If you installed the DRAM correctly, the RAM count on the PC will reflect the new value. If the RAM value stays the same, you probably have a disabled bank or the RAM is not properly installed. If the computer does not boot and nothing is shown on the screen, you probably have not installed all the RAM sticks correctly. Usually a good second look is all you need to determine the problem (Figure 3-57 and Figure 3-58).

**Figure 3-55** A RAM access panel on a laptop

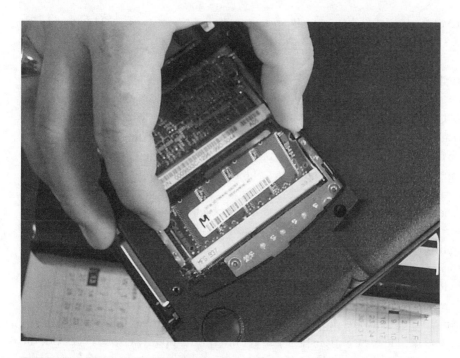

**Figure 3-56** Snapping in an SO-DIMM

```
PhoenixBIOS 4.0 Release 6.0
Copyright 1985-1998 Phoenix Technologies Ltd.
All Rights Reserved

DELL Inspiron 7500 C400LT BIOS Rev A13      (037A)

CPU = Pentium III  600 MHz
```

**Figure 3-57**  Hey, where's my RAM?!

```
PhoenixBIOS 4.0 Release 6.0
Copyright 1985-1998 Phoenix Technologies Ltd.
All Rights Reserved

DELL Inspiron 7500 C400LT BIOS Rev A13      (037A)

CPU = Pentium III  600 MHz
0640K System RAM Passed
0127M Extended RAM Passed
0512K Cache SRAM Passed
Mouse initialized
Fixed Disk 0: FUJITSU MHG2102AT
DVD-ROM: TORiSAN DVD-ROM DRD-U624
```

**Figure 3-58**  RAM count after proper insertion of DIMMs.

All RAM counts listed when your PC boots are based on units of 1,024 bytes (1KB). So 16MB shows up as 16384, 32MB shows 32768, and so on.

## Troubleshooting RAM

"Memory" errors show up in a variety of ways on modern systems, including parity errors, ECC error messages, system lockups, and page faults in Windows. These errors can indicate bad RAM, but often point to something completely unrelated to RAM. The challenge for techs is to determine which part of the system caused the "memory" error.

You can get two radically different types of parity errors: real and phantom. Real parity errors are simply errors that the chipset detects from the parity chips (if you have them). The operating system then reports the problem in an error message, such as "Parity error at *xxxx:xxxxxxxx*," where *xxxx:xxxxxxxx* is a hexadecimal value. If you get an error like this, write down the value. A real parity error will show up at the same place in memory each time and almost always indicates that you have a bad RAM stick.

If Windows generates "parity" errors with different addresses, then you most likely do *not* have a problem with RAM. These phantom errors can occur for a variety of reasons, including software problems, heat or dust, solar flares, fluctuations in the Force . . . you get the idea. Seriously, if you get intermittent parity errors, check out the power supply. Often, these phantom errors show up even when you don't have parity RAM in your system.

Modern systems running the solidly dependable ECC DRAM have a completely different level of error detection. ECC DRAM can report bad RAM sections at boot and then redirect those memory addresses to good sections of RAM. This manifests as a brief message to that effect.

System lockups and page faults (they often go hand in hand) in Windows can indicate a problem with RAM. Certainly page faults *look* like RAM issues, because Windows generates frightening error messages filled with long strings of hexadecimal digits, such as "KRNL386 caused a page fault at 03F2:25A003BC." Just because the error message contains a memory address, however, does not mean that you have a problem with your RAM. Write down the address. If it repeats in later error messages, you probably have a bad RAM stick. If Windows displays different memory locations, then you need to look elsewhere for the culprit.

Finally, intermittent memory errors can come from a variety of sources, including a dying power supply, electrical interference, buggy applications, buggy hardware, and so on. These errors show up as lockups, general protection faults, page faults, and parity errors, but never have the same address or happen with the same applications. Try the power supply first with non-application-specific intermittent errors of any sort.

### Testing RAM

Once you discover that you may have a RAM problem, you have a couple of options. First, several companies manufacture hardware RAM testing devices, but unless you have a lot of disposable income, they're probably priced way too high for the average tech (US$1000+). Second, you can use the method I use—"replace and pray." Open the system case and replace each stick, one at a time, with a known good replacement stick. (You have one of those lying around, don't you?) This method, although potentially time-consuming, certainly works. With PC prices as low as they are now, you could simply replace the whole system for less than the price of a dedicated RAM tester.

## Review Questions

1. Joey has a Pentium motherboard with four 72-pin SIMM slots and two 168-pin DIMM slots. How many 72-pin SIMMs does he need to install to fill a bank of RAM?

   A. 1

   B. 2

   C. 4

   D. 4, plus fill one of the DIMM slots

2. What does ECC DRAM provide that regular DRAM does not?

    A. ECC DRAM has a much lower response time than other forms of DRAM.

    B. ECC DRAM runs at much lower temperatures than other forms of DRAM.

    C. ECC DRAM enables error checking and correcting.

    D. ECC DRAM enables synchronous data transfers.

3. Steve adds a second 128-megabyte 168-pin DIMM to his PC, which should bring the total RAM in the system up to 256MB. The PC has a Pentium III 600 MHz processor and three 168-pin DIMM slots on the motherboard. When he turns on the PC, however, only 128 megabytes of RAM show up during the RAM count. Which of the following is most likely to be the problem?

    A. Steve failed to seat the RAM properly.

    B. Steve put DDR SDRAM in a standard SDRAM slot.

    C. The CPU cannot handle 256 megabytes of RAM.

    D. The motherboard can use only one RAM slot at a time.

4. Of the following choices, which is the fastest RAM you could put on a motherboard running at 133 MHz?

    A. FPM RAM

    B. EDO RAM

    C. ECC RAM

    D. SDRAM

5. What are the standard pin sizes for SO-DIMMs?

    A. 30-pin, 72-pin

    B. 72-pin, 80-pin

    C. 72-pin, 144-pin

    D. 72-pin, 168-pin

6. SDRAM commonly comes in which of the following RAM packages?

    A. 72-pin SIMM

    B. 148-pin DIMM

    C. 168-pin DIMM

    D. 184-pin RIMM

7. Fred has a Pentium motherboard with two 72-pin SIMM slots and two 168-pin DIMM slots. How many DIMMs does it take to fill a single bank of RAM on this motherboard?

    A. One

    B. Two

C. One plus one of the SIMMs

D. Two plus two of the SIMMs

8. Zelda has a motherboard with two 168-pin DIMM slots. One slot is filled with a 64-megabyte DIMM, but the other is empty. When she tries to install a second 168-pin DIMM, she finds that it will not snap into place, due to a raised bump in the DIMM socket. Bill argues that the bump is a defect in the socket and Zelda should file it down. Andrew argues, in contrast, that she probably has a defective DIMM with the notch cut in the wrong spot. Who is most likely correct?

A. Only Bill is correct.

B. Only Andrew is correct.

C. Both Bill and Andrew are correct.

D. Neither Bill nor Andrew is correct.

9. Which of the following SDRAM speeds would *not* work on a 66 MHz mother-board?

A. 60 MHz

B. 66 MHz

C. 100 MHz

D. 133 MHz

10. Scott wants to add 512MB of PC100 SDRAM to his desktop system. His system has a 100 MHz motherboard and currently has 64MB of non-ECC SDRAM in the system. What else does he need to know before installing?

A. What speed of RAM does he need?

B. What type of RAM does he need?

C. How many pins does the RAM have?

D. Can his system handle that much RAM?

## Answers

1. **B.** The 64-bit data bus of the Pentium requires 64-bit-wide RAM. Each 72-pin SIMM can only provide 32 bits of data at a time, so the motherboard requires two to make a bank.

2. **C.** ECC DRAM enables error checking and correcting.

3. **A.** Steve failed to seat the RAM properly.

4. **D.** Of the choices provided, SDRAM is the fastest.

5. **C.** SO-DIMMs come in two common sizes, 72-pin and 144-pin.

6. **C.** SDRAM comes in 168-pin DIMMs.

7. **A.** One 64-bit-wide DIMM fills the bank of a 64-bit-wide Pentium.

8. **D.** She probably has the DIMM reversed.

9. **A.** RAM must be able to run at least as fast as the motherboard clock speed.

10. **D.** That's a huge amount of RAM. He should check the motherboard manual before trying to install.

# Motherboards and BIOS

In this chapter, you will

- Understand the function of BIOS
- See different types of BIOS
- Examine various CMOS setups
- Learn to configure and maintain CMOS properly
- Understand different motherboard form factors

## Historical/Conceptual

In Chapter 2, "Microprocessors," you saw how the address bus and external data bus connect RAM to the CPU via the chipset in order to run programs and transfer data. However, the computer needs more than just a CPU, chipset, and RAM. It needs devices such as keyboards and mice to accept input from users. The computer needs output devices like monitors and sound cards to display the current state of the programs being run. A computer also needs permanent storage devices, such as floppy drives and hard drives, in which to store programs and data when you turn off the computer. The external data bus joins together all of these parts of the computer (Figure 4-1).

The external data bus is not the only bus that connects all the parts of the PC. The address bus also connects to the different parts of the PC (Figure 4-2).

Hey, wait a minute! What happened to the chipset? Let's take a moment here to clarify a few "bus" items. I don't want you confusing address bus and external data bus with the front-side bus discussed in Chapter 2. Look at Figure 4-3. Seem familiar? It should—this is a slightly different representation of the illustration shown in Chapter 2. Note that it shows two address buses: one between the CPU and the chipset, and

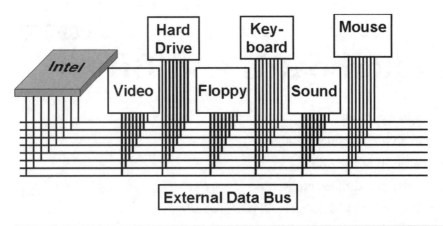

**Figure 4-1**   Everything is connected to the external data bus.

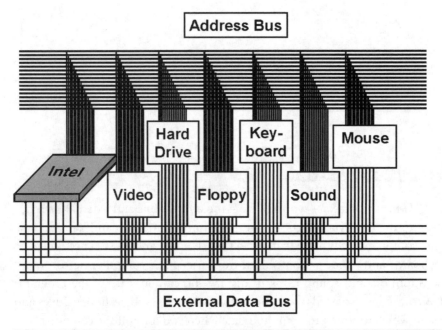

**Figure 4-2**   Everything is also connected to the address bus.

another between the chipset and the rest of the PC. It also shows two external data buses: one between the CPU and the chipset, and another between the chipset and the rest of the PC. In Chapter 2, the buses from the chipset to the rest of the PC were ignored because our interest was primarily the communication between the CPU and RAM. Now we are no longer only interested in the CPU talking to RAM—we want to know how the CPU talks to *everything else* in the system. That's where these other buses become important.

**Figure 4-3**
Frontside bus
diagram

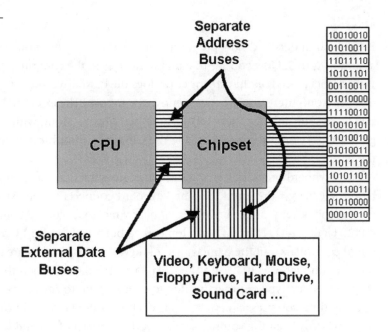

Notice in Figure 4-2 that we didn't show the chipset—we simply represented the CPU as though it connected directly to the same external data bus and address bus as the rest of the devices in the PC. Now, you know this is not reality! The chipset is still there, happily doing its job. When the CPU needs to communicate with other devices, however, the chipset does almost nothing. It simply moves information back and forth from the "inside" external data bus and address bus to the "outside" external data bus and address bus. Because the chipset has no real function in this situation, the system basically acts as though the chipset does not exist. So, for the sake of simplicity, I have removed the chipset for a bit so that you can appreciate the processes that take place to enable the CPU to communicate with the other devices inside the PC.

So, please raise your right hand, place your left hand on this book, and repeat the following statement out loud:

"I understand that Mike has taken the chipset out of the next few graphics for the sake of simplifying a concept. I affirm that even though Mike did not show the chipset, it is, in realty, involved in this process, although in only a very marginal way."

Having acknowledged this, one big question comes to mind: "How do these two buses enable communication between the CPU and the different components of the PC?" This question will be answered in this chapter through an examination of something called BIOS.

## BIOS

So far, you understand how programs can be written to accomplish simple work such as adding 2 to 3. Now you see that all the devices in the computer connect to the CPU. How is data placed on the screen? How does the hard drive know to retrieve a file? How does the computer know when you move the mouse? The external data bus and address bus are responsible for these jobs! These two buses—along with special support programming—work together to enable the CPU to communicate with all the devices in the PC.

The keyboard provides a great example of how the buses and support programming help the CPU get the job done. The keyboard connects to the external data bus via a special chip known as the *keyboard controller*. An early keyboard controller was the Intel 8042 (Figure 4-4). The 8042 has long since been obsolesced by more advanced keyboard controllers, but the name stuck. All keyboard controllers are generally called "an 8042." Although the 8042 and the CPU exchange data through the external data bus, they need some type of programming to enable them to speak to each other.

Every time you press a key, a scanning chip in the keyboard notices which key has been pressed. Then the scanner sends a coded pattern of 1's and 0's to the 8042 chip, called the *scan code*. Every key on your keyboard has a unique scan code. The 8042 chip stores the scan code in its own memory registers.

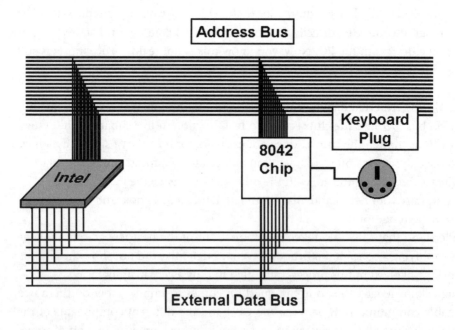

**Figure 4-4** The 8042 chip

How does the CPU get the scan code out of the 8042? (See Figure 4-5.) The 8042 chip accepts commands exactly like the 8088 CPU. Remember when you added 2 to 3 with the 8088? You had to use specific commands from the 8088's codebook to tell the CPU to do the addition and then place the answer on the external data bus. The 8042 has its own codebook—one much simpler than the CPU but conceptually the same. To determine the scan code stored inside the 8042, you need to know the command (or series of commands) to make the 8042 put the scan code of the letter on the external data bus so the CPU can read it.

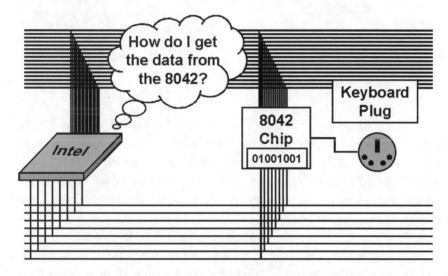

**Figure 4-5** How does the CPU communicate with the 8042?

You need a program to enable the CPU to talk to the 8042, which creates two major issues. First, the problem of different 8042 chips arises (Figure 4-6). You see, the original 8042 chip, designed in 1978, has been redesigned and improved upon many times over the years, and with each redesign the codebook of the 8042 has been expanded or changed. Second, where is this program stored? You can't store the program on a hard or floppy drive. As you will see later in this chapter, the keyboard needs to be installed and working before you can install a storage device.

So how do you handle these issues? Many different 8042 chips are available, but your motherboard will have a particular 8042 chip soldered on it. You're not going to be changing the 8042 chip, so you need to put the program that knows how to talk to the specific 8042 chip on the motherboard. Now, where is this program stored? On DRAM? No, it would be erased every time the computer was turned off. You need some type of permanent program storage device that does not depend on other peripherals in order to work.

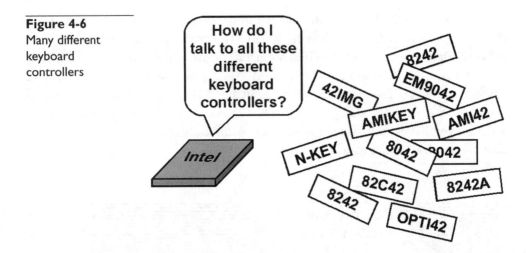

**Figure 4-6**
Many different keyboard controllers

The program is stored on a special type of device called a *read-only memory* (ROM) *chip*. ROM chips can store programs exactly like RAM chips, with two major differences. First, ROM chips are nonvolatile, meaning that the program(s) stored on ROM aren't erased, even when the computer is turned off. Second, ROM chips are read-only, meaning that once the program(s) are stored, they can't be changed. Figure 4-7 shows a typical ROM chip on your motherboard.

When the CPU wants to talk to the 8042, it goes to the ROM chip to access the proper program. Understand that many programs exist on the ROM chip. The ROM chip stores a number of programs just to talk to the 8042, with each program tackling a specific job (Figure 4-8).

One program accesses the scan code, for example, but other programs on the ROM chip tell the keyboard to change the typematic buffer rate (when you hold down a key and the letter repeats) or turn the NumLock light on/off, as well as a few other jobs the keyboard needs to do for the system.

The keyboard controller programs are not alone on the ROM. The ROM chip also stores programs to talk to the floppy drive(s), the hard drive(s), the monitor, and a few other basic devices on your computer. Clearly, not just one program exists on that ROM chip! Each different device needs a number of programs, and many basic devices store their communication programs on the ROM chip. To talk to all of that hardware requires hundreds of little programs (2 to 30 lines of code each). These hundreds of little programs stored on the ROM chip are called, collectively, the *basic input/output services* (BIOS). Each tiny program is called a *service*. See Figure 4-9.

The BIOS are hundreds of little programs designed to talk to the most basic parts of your computer. Programs stored on ROM chips are known collectively as *firmware*, as

**Figure 4-7** Typical ROM BIOS

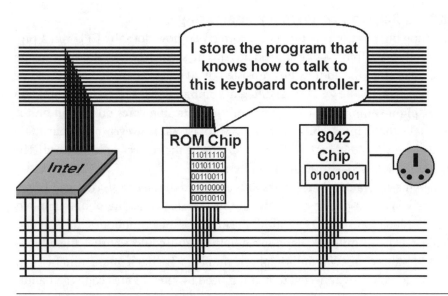

**Figure 4-8** Function of the ROM chip

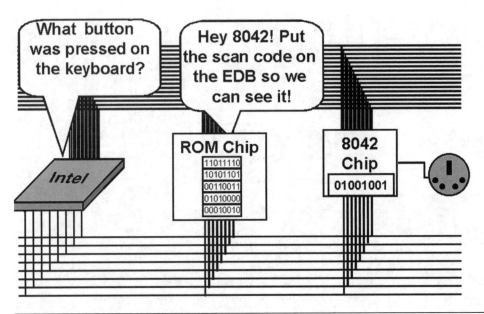

**Figure 4-9**  CPU running BIOS routine

opposed to programs stored on erasable media that are collectively called *software*. Motherboard manufacturers use a ROM chip to store essential BIOS because the ROM chip can hold the programs even when you turn off the computer. Although some variance exists, most ROM chips store around 65,536 lines of BIOS programming.

## BIOS and Its Relation to Memory Addressing

BIOS is nothing but a set of tiny programs, correct? So how does the CPU run a program? If the software is in RAM, the address bus specifies which byte of RAM to run. On the original 8088 chip, the address bus consisted of 20 wires. These 20 wires could be turned on and off in 1,048,576 (1Meg) different combinations, and each combination was like the "phone number" for every byte of RAM. Turning wires on and off on the address bus tells the chipset which byte of RAM to access. However, now your ROM chip is loaded with 65,536 bytes of BIOS code. How is the correct code accessed? The same way RAM is accessed—through the address bus.

All the patterns generated by the address bus are called the *address space*. A good analogy would be your local phone company. In the 713 area code, the phone numbers from 713-000-0000 to 713-999-9999 are all the numbers that our phones can generate, right? That's exactly 10 million telephone numbers. You could say that the address space of the 713 area code is 10 million phone numbers. Each telephone number may not actually have a phone connected to it, but if need be, the 713 area code can handle 10 million telephone numbers. The address space for an 8088 processor is 1,048,576 bytes or *1 megabyte* (1MB). That does not mean that every 8088 system has one *megabyte* (MB) of RAM, but the CPU could theoretically handle that much!

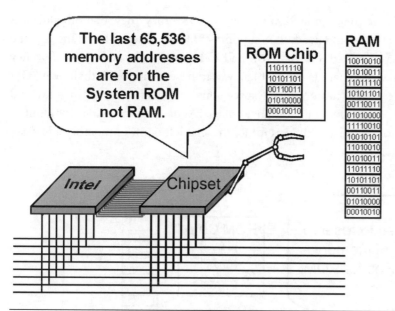

**Figure 4-10**   Reserving address space for ROM

When IBM invented the IBM PC, they declared that the last 65,536 addresses on the address bus would be "reserved" for the BIOS on the ROM chip (Figure 4-10), which means that you could not add 1MB of RAM to a computer with an 8088 chip. At this point, the maximum amount of RAM you could add was about 1MB minus 65,536 bytes. Using the telephone analogy, it would be similar to the phone company keeping all the phone numbers from 888-8888 up to 999-9999 for its own use. When the chipset sees the CPU "dial up" one of these reserved addresses, it knows to talk directly to the ROM BIOS.

The CPU needs the ability to communicate with every piece of hardware in your computer. You have to be able to tell the sound card to play a song, or tell the video card to put graphics on the monitor. The CPU has no built-in commands that know how to talk to any of the hardware on your PC. It must rely on a program to tell it how to talk to any particular device, yet the ROM BIOS only contains programming for certain basic hardware. Therefore, some kind of separate, unique program (or set of programs) must be provided for every device on your PC. In essence, the PC must provide a method for you to add more BIOS to the PC whenever you add a new piece of hardware not supported by the BIOS on the ROM chip.

The BIOS stored on the ROM chip attached to the motherboard is officially known as the *system BIOS*. The reason the onboard BIOS is called the system BIOS is to differentiate it from other forms of BIOS that might be on the computer. That's right, your PC may contain many sets of BIOS! The ROM chip that stores the system BIOS is called the *system ROM*.

When IBM designed the original IBM PC back in 1981, they knew that other devices would be invented that would need BIOS support. IBM did not want to get into a game where every time you added a device, you had to replace the system ROM. So, they decided the easiest way to handle the problem was to have devices with their own ROM chip. More ROMs means more address space must be taken away from RAM and reserved for ROM. Therefore, in the original 8088, IBM decided to reserve 384K out of the 1024K (1MB) of memory addresses for ROM. That left 640K of memory addresses for RAM (Figure 4-11).

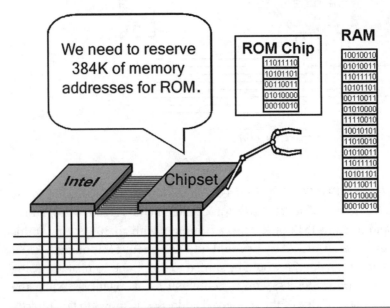

**Figure 4-11**   Reserving memory addresses for ROM

What if you have a modern CPU like a Pentium III? A Pentium III has much larger address buses, 32 wires, which means it has an address space of over 4 *billion* bytes! However, every PC must still reserve the last 384K of the first megabyte of memory space for BIOS to provide backward compatibility with the 8088. This concept will be discussed in more detail later in the book. For now, let's simply appreciate that every piece of hardware needs BIOS and see the different ways BIOS exists on yesterday's and today's PCs.

## The Many Faces of BIOS

A computer's hardware breaks down into three groups. The first group is hardware that is common, necessary, and never changes. The system BIOS ROM chip stores the BIOS for these devices. The keyboard is a great example of this type of device. For our purposes, this first group of hardware is referred to as the *core group*. The second group is hardware that is also common and necessary, but that might change from time to time. This group includes RAM (you can add RAM), hard drives (you can replace your hard drive with a larger drive or add a second hard drive), and floppy drives (you can add another floppy drive). The BIOS for these devices is also stored on the system BIOS chip. This second group of hardware requires BIOS information that you can change, so critical information that describes these devices must be stored on a separate, special RAM chip called a *complementary metal-oxide semiconductor* (CMOS) chip. This group of devices will be referred to as the *CMOS group.* The last group is composed of non-core devices such as mice, sound cards, tape backup units, and CD-ROM drives, and will be called the *everything else group.* Let's look at all three groups in detail to see how they store their BIOS.

## Test Specific

### Core Group: The System ROM

You have seen an example of a core device with the keyboard/8042 chip. Other examples of core devices are as follows:

- Chipset
- Speaker
- Support chips

Look at the system ROM chip a little more closely. The system ROM chip, which stores the system BIOS, resides on the motherboard. ROM chips usually come in DIPP packages and almost always have a shiny label. Figure 4-12 shows a pair of typical system ROMs.

Although you can buy ROM chips that can store megabytes of programming, the ROM chips on the majority of IBM-compatible PCs store around 64K of programming. Because they are nonvolatile, ROM chips are the best way to store BIOS. "Nonvolatile" means that the chip does not need electricity to store programs. You can turn off the computer on Friday and turn it back on the following Monday, and the BIOS programs will still be there. It is easy to see the importance of nonvolatility. The downside to ROM is that you cannot change the BIOS routines once they are stored on the chip. Additionally, ROM is very slow compared with other types of memory such as DRAM.

Fortunately, the majority of technicians rarely deal with the system BIOS. Like a good hot-water heater, the system BIOS almost never fails. It works year after year, quietly and efficiently doing its work in the background. However, like a good hot-water heater, on those rare occasions when it does break, the result can be catastrophic. The failure of system BIOS will be discussed later in this chapter.

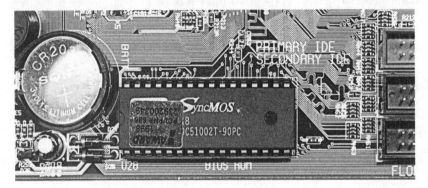

**Figure 4-12** Typical system ROMs

Once again—do not confuse ROM and BIOS! BIOS is a group of *programs*. ROM is a hardware *chip* that's often used to store BIOS. Software stored on ROM chips is often also known as "firmware." Don't be surprised to hear a fellow tech use the term firmware instead of BIOS.

### CMOS Group: The Changeable Ones

Some BIOS routines talk to other common devices that are more likely to change. These changeable hardware devices include things such as

- RAM
- Hard drives
- Floppy drives
- Serial and parallel ports

The BIOS routines for these devices are also stored on the system ROM chip. If you change one of these items, however, such as upgrading a hard drive or adding a second hard drive, you must also change certain parameters to reflect the modifications to the hardware. You cannot change the BIOS routines on the ROM, so you need another type of storage chip that can be modified to reflect these changes. This changeable chip is called the CMOS chip. CMOS chips do not store programs; they store only data that is read by BIOS to complete the programs needed to talk to changeable hardware. The CMOS chip also acts as a clock to keep the date and time.

At this point, don't worry about what parameters are stored on the CMOS chip; these parameters will be discussed in detail when the different types of hardware are described. For now, simply appreciate that a system ROM chip and a CMOS chip are present in your computer (Figure 4-13).

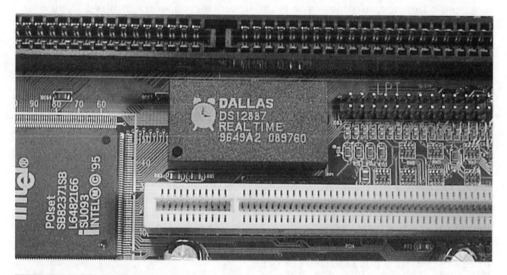

**Figure 4-13** Typical CMOS chip

Although CMOS chips usually store around 64K of data, the PC usually needs only a very small amount—about 128 bytes—to store all the necessary information on the changeable hardware. Don't let the tiny size fool you. The PC critically needs the information stored in CMOS!

If the data referencing a particular piece of hardware stored on the CMOS is different from the actual hardware, the computer will not be able to access that particular piece of hardware. It is crucial that this information be correct. If you change any of the previously mentioned hardware, you must update the CMOS to reflect those changes. You need to know, therefore, how to change the data on the CMOS chip.

### Updating CMOS: The Setup Program

Almost every PC ships with a program built into the system ROM, called the *CMOS setup program*, which enables you to access and update the data on the CMOS chip. The CMOS setup program can be started in many different ways, depending on the brand of BIOS you have on your computer. When you fire up your computer in the morning, the first thing you will likely see is the BIOS information. It might look like the example in Figure 4-14, or perhaps something like Figure 4-15.

Who or what is Award Software, and who or what is Phoenix Technologies? These are brand names of BIOS companies. They write BIOS programs and sell them to computer manufacturers. In the bad old days, the days of XTs and 286s, when a company made a motherboard, they usually hired a few programmers to write the BIOS. In today's world, almost nobody writes his or her own BIOS. Instead, they buy their BIOS from third-party BIOS makers such as Award Software and Phoenix Technologies. Although about ten different companies write BIOS, three big companies control 99 percent of the BIOS business: *American Megatrends* (AMI), Award Software, and Phoenix Technologies. A few years ago, Award merged with Phoenix, but the new company (Phoenix) still sells each brand name of BIOS as separate products. AMI, Award, and Phoenix pretty much control the entire BIOS market these days, and they have different ways to access the CMOS setup program.

```
PhoenixBIOS 4.0 Release 6.0
Copyright 1985-1998 Phoenix Technologies Ltd.
All Rights Reserved

DELL Inspiron 7500 C400LT BIOS Rev A13      (037A)

CPU = Pentium III  600 MHz
0640K System RAM Passed
0127M Extended RAM Passed
0512K Cache SRAM Passed
Mouse initialized
Fixed Disk 0: FUJITSU MHG2102AT
DVD-ROM: TORiSAN DVD-ROM DRD-U624
```

**Figure 4-14**  Phoenix BIOS

```
   Award Modular BIOS v6.00PG, An Energy Star Ally
   Copyright (C) 1984-2000, Award Software, Inc.

GREEN AGP/PCI/ISA SYSTEM

Main Processor : Pentium III 850MHz(100x8.5)
Memory Testing : 114688K

Award Plug and Play BIOS Extension v1.0A
Copyright (C) 2000 Award Software, Inc.

  Primary Master  : WDC WD1020AA, 80.10A80
  Primary Slave   : None
Secondary Master  : ATAPI CD-ROM DRIVE 40X
Secondary Slave   : None
```

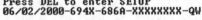

```
Press DEL to enter SETUP
06/02/2000-694X-686A-XXXXXXXX-QW
```

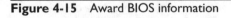

**Figure 4-15**  Award BIOS information

You access a system's CMOS setup at boot. The tough question is: *How* do I access the CMOS setup at boot? No single correct way exists to access every CMOS setup program. As a general rule, for AMI and Award, press the DEL key when the machine first begins to boot. For Phoenix, press CTRL-ALT-ESC or F2. Most BIOS manufacturers will tell you how to access the CMOS setup right on the screen as your computer boots up. Look at Figure 4-16 for an example.

Note that you simply press the F2 key in the pictured example to access the CMOS setup. Keep in mind that this is only one possible example! Motherboard manufacturers can change the key combinations to access the CMOS setup. You can even set up the computer so the message does not show—a smart idea for keeping nosy people out of your CMOS setup! If you don't see an "enter setup" type of message, wait until the RAM count starts and then press one of these keys or key combinations: DEL, CTRL-ALT-INS, CTRL-A, CTRL-S, CTRL-F1, F2, or F10. It may take a few tries, but you will eventually find the right key or key combination!

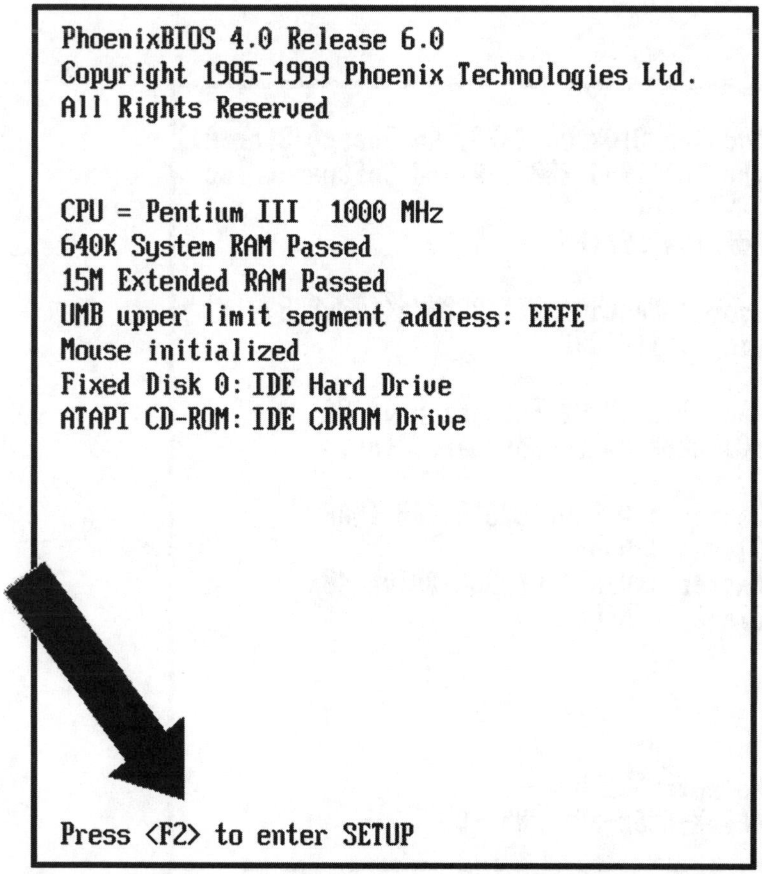

```
PhoenixBIOS 4.0 Release 6.0
Copyright 1985-1999 Phoenix Technologies Ltd.
All Rights Reserved


CPU = Pentium III  1000 MHz
640K System RAM Passed
15M Extended RAM Passed
UMB upper limit segment address: EEFE
Mouse initialized
Fixed Disk 0: IDE Hard Drive
ATAPI CD-ROM: IDE CDROM Drive










Press <F2> to enter SETUP
```

**Figure 4-16** Press F2 to enter SETUP.

AMI, Award, and Phoenix are not the only BIOS makers in the world. Watch your computer when it boots to determine your manufacturer. You can also take the cover off your PC and see whose name is on the system ROM chip. Read your motherboard book to determine the process to access the CMOS setup program.

### A Quick Tour Through a Typical CMOS Setup

Every maker of BIOS has a different CMOS setup program, but don't let the different screens confuse you! They all say basically the same thing; you just have to be comfortable "poking around." To avoid doing something foolish, do not save anything unless you have it set correctly. When you boot a machine with Award BIOS, you will see something similar to Figure 4-17 at the bottom of the screen.

Press DEL and the screen in Figure 4-18 will appear. You are now in the Main menu of the Award CMOS setup program! This program is stored on the ROM chip, but it solely edits the data on the CMOS chip. Select Standard CMOS Features, and the standard CMOS screen will appear (see Figure 4-19).

```
Award Modular BIOS v6.00PG, An Energy Star All
Copyright (C) 1984-2000, Award Software, Inc.

GREEN AGP/PCI/ISA SYSTEM

Main Processor : Pentium III 850MHz(100x8.5)
Memory Testing : 114688K

Award Plug and Play BIOS Extension v1.0A
Copyright (C) 2000 Award Software, Inc.

   Primary Master : WDC WD1020AA, 80.10A80
   Primary Slave  : None
   ondary Master : ATAPI CD-ROM DRIVE 40X
   ndary Slave   : None




Press DEL to enter SETUP
06/02/2000-694X-686A-XXXXXXXX-QW
```

**Figure 4-17**  Press DEL to enter SETUP.

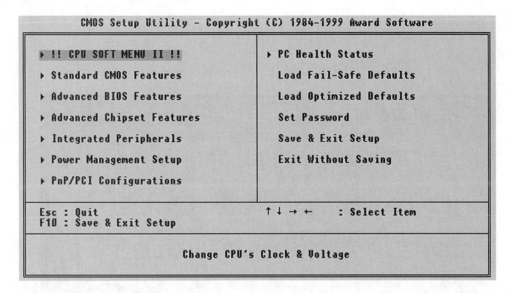

**Figure 4-18** Main menu

**Figure 4-19** Standard CMOS features screen

On the Standard CMOS Features screen you can change floppy drive, hard drive, and date/time settings. You will learn how to set up the CMOS for these devices in later chapters. At this point, the only goal is to introduce you to CMOS and to make sure you can access the CMOS setup on your PC. If you have a system that you are allowed to reboot, try accessing the CMOS setup now. Does it look anything like these examples? If not, can you find the screen that enables you to change the floppy and hard drives?

Trust me, the CMOS setup on that system has that screen somewhere! Just for another view, Figure 4-20 shows the same standard CMOS screen with a Phoenix BIOS. Note that Phoenix calls it "Main."

```
                         PhoenixBIOS Setup Utility
     Main     Advanced     Security     Power     Boot     Exit

                                                  Item Specific Help

     System Time:          [07:55:31]
     System Date:          [05/23/2001]
                                                  <Tab>, <Shift-Tab>, or
     Legacy Diskette A:    [1.44/1.25 MB  3½"]    <Enter> selects field.
     Legacy Diskette B:    [Disabled]

   ▶ Primary Master       [105MB]
   ▶ Primary Slave        [None]
   ▶ Secondary Master     [CD-ROM]
   ▶ Secondary Slave      [None]

   ▶ Keyboard Features

     System Memory:        640 KB
     Extended Memory:      15360 KB
     Language:             [English  (US)]


   F1   Help    ↑↓  Select Item   -/+    Change Values      F9   Setup Defaults
   Esc  Exit    ←   Select Menu   Enter  Select ▶ Sub-Menu  F10  Save and Exit
```

**Figure 4-20** Phoenix BIOS Main screen

The first BIOS was nothing more than a standard CMOS setup. Today, virtually all computers have many extra CMOS settings. They control items such as memory management, password and booting options, diagnostic and error handling, and power management. The following section takes a quick tour of a fairly typical Award CMOS setup program. Remember that your CMOS setup will almost certainly look at least a little different from mine, unless you happen to have the *same* BIOS. The chances of that happening are quite slim!

**NOTE** All of these screens tend to overwhelm new techs when they first encounter the many options. The techs feel they need to know every option on every screen in order to configure CMOS properly. They are wrong. Nobody knows what all these settings do for the system! Every new motherboard comes with settings that befuddle even the most experienced techs! Here's a good gauge: If we don't talk about a particular CMOS setting somewhere in this book, it's probably not important, either to the A+ exam or to a real tech.

Award has virtually cornered the desktop PC BIOS market with its Award Modular BIOS. Motherboard makers buy a basic BIOS from Award and can add or remove options (Award calls them "modules") based on the needs of the motherboard. This can cause problems, as seemingly identical CMOS setups can be extremely different. Options that show up on one computer might be missing from another. Compare the older Award screen in Figure 4-21 with the figure of the more modern main Award CMOS screen in Figure 4-18. This one looks different—and it should—as this much older system simply doesn't need the extra options shown on the newer system!

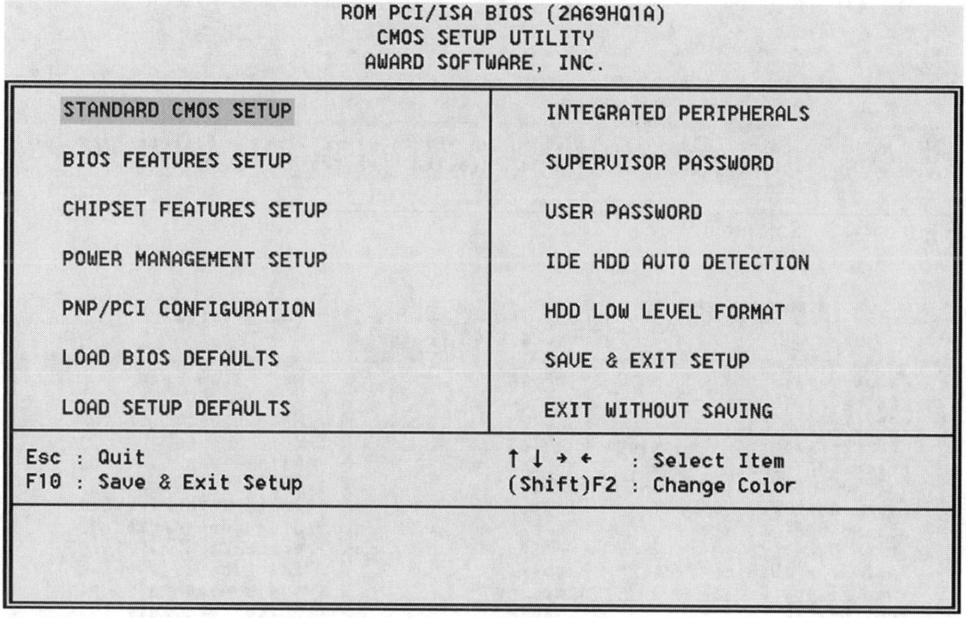

```
                    ROM PCI/ISA BIOS (2A69HQ1A)
                        CMOS SETUP UTILITY
                      AWARD SOFTWARE, INC.

    STANDARD CMOS SETUP              INTEGRATED PERIPHERALS

    BIOS FEATURES SETUP             SUPERVISOR PASSWORD

    CHIPSET FEATURES SETUP          USER PASSWORD

    POWER MANAGEMENT SETUP          IDE HDD AUTO DETECTION

    PNP/PCI CONFIGURATION           HDD LOW LEVEL FORMAT

    LOAD BIOS DEFAULTS              SAVE & EXIT SETUP

    LOAD SETUP DEFAULTS             EXIT WITHOUT SAVING

    Esc : Quit                  ↑ ↓ → ←    : Select Item
    F10 : Save & Exit Setup     (Shift)F2 : Change Color
```

**Figure 4-21**   Older Award Setup screen

## CPU Soft Menu

The CPU Soft menu enables you to set the voltage and multiplier settings on the motherboard for the CPU. "Jumperless" motherboards and motherboards that cater to overclockers tend to have this option. We usually just set this to "AUTO" and stay away from this screen (Figure 4-22)!

## Advanced BIOS Features

Advanced BIOS Features is the dumping ground for all the settings that aren't covered in the Standard menu but don't fit nicely under any other screen. This screen varies wildly from one system to the next. We use this screen most often to select the boot options (Figure 4-23).

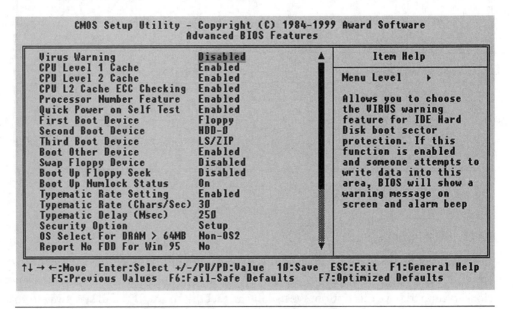

```
        CMOS Setup Utility - Copyright (C) 1984-1999 Award Software
                          !! CPU SOFT MENU II !!

  CPU Name is                Intel Pentium III MMX          Item Help

  CPU Operating Speed        User Define             Menu Level    ▶
  - Ext. Clock (PCI)         100MHz(1/3)
  - Multiplier Factor        x8
  - Speed Error Hold         Disabled

  CPU Power Supply           User Define
  - Core Voltage             1.00v

  Spread Spectrum            Disabled


↑↓ → ← :Move   Enter:Select +/-/PU/PD:Value  F10:Save  ESC:Exit  F1:General Help
     F5:Previous Values  F6:Fail-Safe Defaults    F7:Optimized Defaults
```

**Figure 4-22**   Soft menu

```
        CMOS Setup Utility - Copyright (C) 1984-1999 Award Software
                          Advanced BIOS Features

  Virus Warning              Disabled          ▲         Item Help
  CPU Level 1 Cache          Enabled
  CPU Level 2 Cache          Enabled                 Menu Level    ▶
  CPU L2 Cache ECC Checking  Enabled
  Processor Number Feature   Enabled                 Allows you to choose
  Quick Power on Self Test   Enabled                 the VIRUS warning
  First Boot Device          Floppy                  feature for IDE Hard
  Second Boot Device         HDD-0                   Disk boot sector
  Third Boot Device          LS/ZIP                  protection. If this
  Boot Other Device          Enabled                 function is enabled
  Swap Floppy Device         Disabled                and someone attempts to
  Boot Up Floppy Seek        Disabled                write data into this
  Boot Up Numlock Status     On                      area, BIOS will show a
  Typematic Rate Setting     Enabled                 warning message on
  Typematic Rate (Chars/Sec) 30                      screen and alarm beep
  Typematic Delay (Msec)     250
  Security Option            Setup
  OS Select For DRAM > 64MB  Non-OS2
  Report No FDD For Win 95   No                ▼

↑↓ → ← :Move   Enter:Select +/-/PU/PD:Value  10:Save  ESC:Exit  F1:General Help
     F5:Previous Values  F6:Fail-Safe Defaults    F7:Optimized Defaults
```

**Figure 4-23**   Advanced BIOS

## Advanced Chipset Features

This screen strikes fear into everyone because it deals with extremely low-level chipset functions. Avoid this screen unless a high-level tech (like a motherboard maker's tech support) explicitly tells you to do something in here (Figure 4-24).

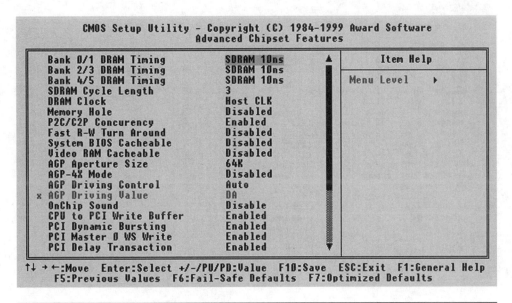

```
        CMOS Setup Utility - Copyright (C) 1984-1999 Award Software
                      Advanced Chipset Features
 ┌─────────────────────────────────────────────┬──────────────────────┐
 │  Bank 0/1 DRAM Timing      SDRAM 10ns    ▲   │      Item Help       │
 │  Bank 2/3 DRAM Timing      SDRAM 10ns        │                      │
 │  Bank 4/5 DRAM Timing      SDRAM 10ns        │  Menu Level      ▶   │
 │  SDRAM Cycle Length        3                 │                      │
 │  DRAM Clock                Host CLK          │                      │
 │  Memory Hole               Disabled          │                      │
 │  P2C/C2P Concurency        Enabled           │                      │
 │  Fast R-W Turn Around      Disabled          │                      │
 │  System BIOS Cacheable     Disabled          │                      │
 │  Video RAM Cacheable       Disabled          │                      │
 │  AGP Aperture Size         64K               │                      │
 │  AGP-4X Mode               Disabled          │                      │
 │  AGP Driving Control       Auto              │                      │
 │ x AGP Driving Value        DA                │                      │
 │  OnChip Sound              Disable           │                      │
 │  CPU to PCI Write Buffer   Enabled           │                      │
 │  PCI Dynamic Bursting      Enabled           │                      │
 │  PCI Master 0 WS Write     Enabled           │                      │
 │  PCI Delay Transaction     Enabled       ▼   │                      │
 └─────────────────────────────────────────────┴──────────────────────┘
 ↑↓ → ←:Move   Enter:Select +/-/PU/PD:Value  F10:Save  ESC:Exit  F1:General Help
      F5:Previous Values  F6:Fail-Safe Defaults  F7:Optimized Defaults
```

**Figure 4-24**  Advanced chipset

## Integrated Peripherals

You will use this screen quite often. This screen enables you to configure, enable, or disable the onboard ports, such as the serial and parallel ports. As these ports are discussed in more detail in later chapters, we will use this screen to get a lot of important work done (Figure 4-25).

## Power Management Setup

As the name implies, we use this screen to set up the power management settings for the system. These settings work in concert (sometimes in conflict) with Windows' power management settings to control how and when devices turn off and back on to conserve power (Figure 4-26).

## PnP/PCI Configurations

Anyone who deals with Plug and Play devices will surely see this screen from time to time. We most commonly use the PnP/PCI Configurations screen to set aside certain resources called "IRQs" to prevent the system from taking that resource away from a device that needs it (Figure 4-27). We will go into gritty detail about these resources in Chapter 5.

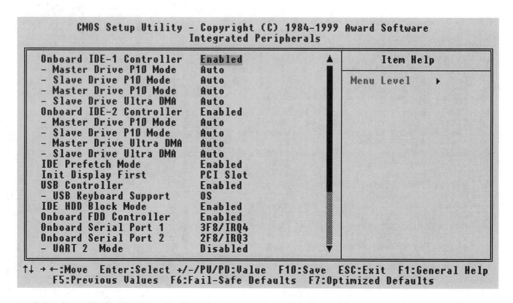

```
      CMOS Setup Utility - Copyright (C) 1984-1999 Award Software
                        Integrated Peripherals

  Onboard IDE-1 Controller    Enabled           ▲        Item Help
  - Master Drive PIO Mode      Auto
  - Slave Drive PIO Mode       Auto               Menu Level    ▶
  - Master Drive PIO Mode      Auto
  - Slave Drive Ultra DMA      Auto
  Onboard IDE-2 Controller    Enabled
  - Master Drive PIO Mode      Auto
  - Slave Drive PIO Mode       Auto
  - Master Drive Ultra DMA     Auto
  - Slave Drive Ultra DMA      Auto
  IDE Prefetch Mode           Enabled
  Init Display First          PCI Slot
  USB Controller              Enabled
  - USB Keyboard Support       OS
  IDE HDD Block Mode          Enabled
  Onboard FDD Controller      Enabled
  Onboard Serial Port 1       3F8/IRQ4
  Onboard Serial Port 2       2F8/IRQ3
  - UART 2 Mode               Disabled          ▼

 ↑↓ → ←:Move  Enter:Select +/-/PU/PD:Value  F10:Save  ESC:Exit  F1:General Help
    F5:Previous Values  F6:Fail-Safe Defaults  F7:Optimized Defaults
```

**Figure 4-25**  Integrated peripherals

```
      CMOS Setup Utility - Copyright (C) 1984-1999 Award Software
                        Power Management Setup

  ▶ Power Management           Press Enter               Item Help
    ACPI Suspend Type          S1(POS)
    PM Control by APM          Yes             Menu Level    ▶
    Video Off Option           Suspend -> Off
    Video Off Method           V/H SYNC+Blank
    MODEM Use IRQ              NA
    Soft-Off by PWRBTN         Instant-Off
  ▶ Wake Up Events             Press Enter




 ↑↓ → ←:Move  Enter:Select +/-/PU/PD:Value  F10:Save  ESC:Exit  F1:General Help
    F5:Previous Values  F6:Fail-Safe Defaults  F7:Optimized Defaults
```

**Figure 4-26**  Power management

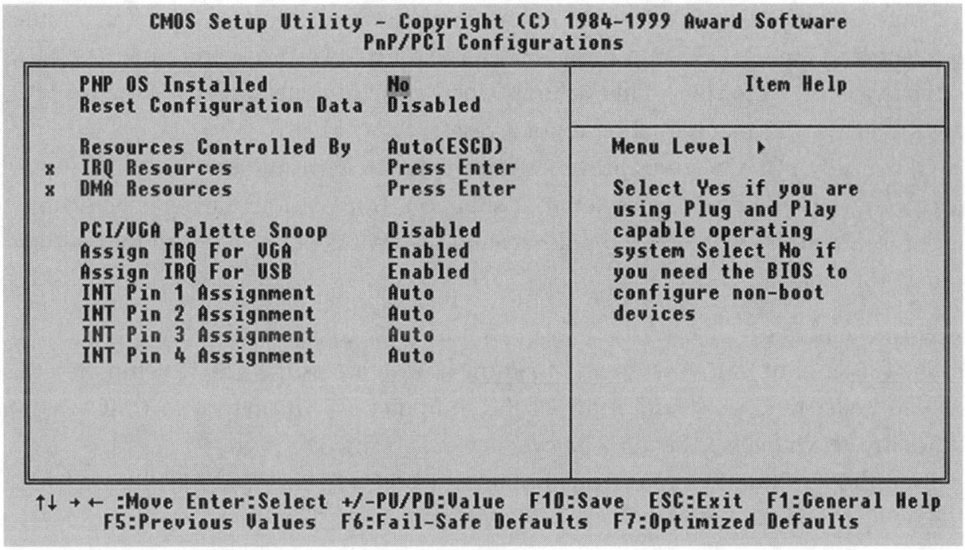

```
             CMOS Setup Utility - Copyright (C) 1984-1999 Award Software
                              PnP/PCI Configurations
    ┌───────────────────────────────────────────┬───────────────────────────┐
    │  PNP OS Installed          No              │         Item Help         │
    │  Reset Configuration Data  Disabled        │                           │
    │                                            ├───────────────────────────┤
    │  Resources Controlled By   Auto(ESCD)      │ Menu Level  ▶             │
    │ x IRQ Resources            Press Enter     │                           │
    │ x DMA Resources            Press Enter     │ Select Yes if you are     │
    │                                            │ using Plug and Play       │
    │  PCI/VGA Palette Snoop      Disabled       │ capable operating         │
    │  Assign IRQ For VGA         Enabled        │ system Select No if       │
    │  Assign IRQ For USB         Enabled        │ you need the BIOS to      │
    │  INT Pin 1 Assignment       Auto           │ configure non-boot        │
    │  INT Pin 2 Assignment       Auto           │ devices                   │
    │  INT Pin 3 Assignment       Auto           │                           │
    │  INT Pin 4 Assignment       Auto           │                           │
    │                                            │                           │
    │                                            │                           │
    │                                            │                           │
    ├────────────────────────────────────────────────────────────────────────┤
    │ ↑↓ →← :Move  Enter:Select  +/-PU/PD:Value  F10:Save  ESC:Exit  F1:General Help │
    │     F5:Previous Values  F6:Fail-Safe Defaults  F7:Optimized Defaults    │
    └────────────────────────────────────────────────────────────────────────┘
```

**Figure 4-27**   PnP/PCI configurations

## And the Rest of the CMOS Settings . . .

The other options on the main menu of our Award CMOS do not have their own screens. Rather, these simply have small dialog boxes that pop up, usually with "are you sure?"-type messages.

Load Fail-Safe/Optimized defaults keeps us from having to memorize all of those weird settings we never touch. Fail-Safe sets everything to very simple settings—we occasionally use this setting when very low-level problems like freeze ups occur, and we have checked more obvious areas first. Optimized sets the CMOS to the best possible speed/stability for our system. We often use this one when we have tampered with the CMOS too much and need to "put it back like it was!"

Many CMOS setup programs enable you to set a password in CMOS to force the user to enter a password every time the system boots. Don't confuse this with the Windows logon password! This CMOS password shows up at boot, long before Windows even starts to load. Figure 4-28 shows a typical CMOS password prompt.

**Figure 4-28**
CMOS password
prompt

```
┌──────────────────────────────┐
│  Enter Password:             │
└──────────────────────────────┘
```

Some CMOS setups enable you to create two passwords: one for boot and another for accessing the CMOS setup program. This extra password just for entering CMOS setup is a godsend for places like schools where nosy students tend to wreak havoc in areas (like CMOS) that they should not access!

Of course, all CMOS setups provide some method to Save and Exit and to Exit *Without* Saving. Use these as needed for your situation. Exit Without Saving is particularly nice for those folks who want to poke around the CMOS but don't want to mess anything up. Use it!

*A Time and Place for Everything*    At this point, the goal is only for you to be aware of the existence of CMOS setup and to know how to access the CMOS setup on a PC. As you understand more and more of the computer, we will return to CMOS many times in later chapters to set up whatever device is being discussed.

Even though Award enjoys strong popularity, both Phoenix and AMI have a broad following in today's systems.

*Phoenix BIOS*    Phoenix BIOS is the "Mercedes Benz" of BIOS programs. Phoenix creates a custom BIOS for optimal use in the machine for which it is designed. As a result, Phoenix BIOS programs have fewer, more unique options (Figure 4-29). You will usually see Phoenix BIOS programs in machines with proprietary motherboards, such as laptops.

*AMI BIOS*    American Megatrends competes directly with Award, providing highly flexible BIOS programs (Figure 4-30). AMI was the most-used BIOS for many years until Award gained market share, starting around 1994/1995. Although AMI no longer holds the virtual monopoly it once had in BIOS software, it is still quite popular.

*Care and Feeding of Your CMOS*    Losing CMOS information is a common problem. If some mishap suddenly erases the information on the CMOS chip, the computer will not boot up or you will get nasty-looking errors. Unfortunately, it is easy to lose CMOS information. Some of the more common reasons for losing CMOS data are as follows:

- Onboard battery runs out
- Pulling and inserting cards
- Touching the motherboard
- Dropping something on the motherboard
- Dirt on the motherboard
- Faulty power supplies
- Electrical surges

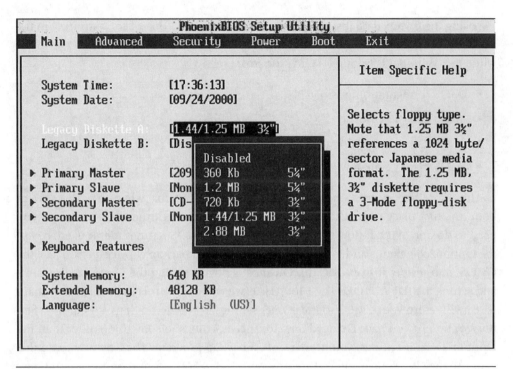

**Figure 4-29** Phoenix BIOS

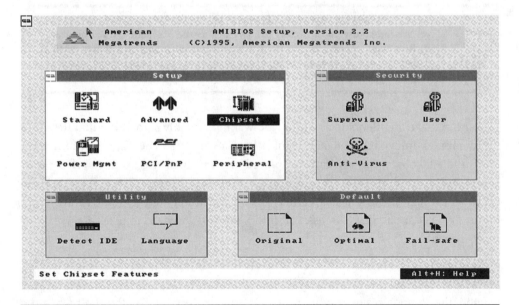

**Figure 4-30**

Losing the CMOS data just happens and is accepted as "one of those things" in the world of computing. The errors that point to lost CMOS information usually take place while the computer is booting. Watch for errors such as

- CMOS configuration mismatch
- CMOS date/time not set
- No boot device available
- CMOS battery state low

Although these errors sometimes point to other problems, when they show up at boot, the first place to check is the CMOS settings. To check the CMOS settings, you need to do one of the following: a) have all of your CMOS settings memorized; b) use the Optimized defaults and hope it works; or c) make a backup copy *before* you lose the CMOS, and restore it from backup. On most systems, setting the Optimized defaults and setting the IDE AUTODETECT to AUTO (we will discuss this in detail in the Chapter 8) will return your CMOS to the proper settings. If you do not have an Optimal Settings option or you have changed any Advanced Settings to something other than the Optimal Default settings, you need a CMOS backup program. The best way to do this is to use the CMOS save and restore program, CMOSSAVE, found on the accompanying CD-ROM.

**NOTE**  CMOSSAVE is stored in ZIP format on the CD-ROM as CMOS1.ZIP, so you'll need to use an unzipping utility (such as the excellent WinZip program by Nico Mak) in order to run the software. After unzipping to a folder (such as C:\CMOS), open a comman prompt and navigate to that folder. Then, insert a blank floppy disk, and type the following command: CMOSSAVE A:*filename*.

You can make the filename anything you want, preferably something that describes the computer for which you are saving the CMOS data. The CMOS information for hundreds of computers can be placed on one diskette. You can lose your CMOS information in many ways, as noted earlier. Back up your CMOS settings, especially with older (Pentium and earlier) systems. Current motherboards have more robust CMOS data storage (discussed shortly), but still you need to take care with your motherboards.

*The Battery*  The beauty of CMOS chips is that you can change the data stored on them. The trade-off for this ability is that the CMOS chip needs a trickle voltage whether the computer is turned on or not. To provide the CMOS with power when the computer is turned off, all motherboards come with a battery (see Figure 4-31). These batteries mount to the motherboard in one of three ways: the obsolete external battery, the most common onboard battery, and the increasingly common built-in battery.

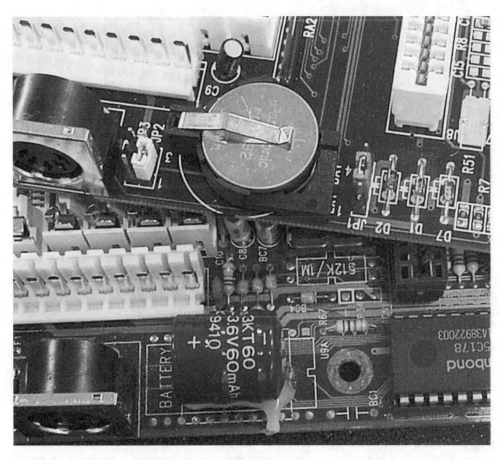

**Figure 4-31**   Onboard battery

Onboard batteries are mounted directly to the motherboard; external batteries are connected to the motherboard with wires. Many PCs today no longer need a removable battery because the CMOS chip itself has enough battery power to keep it running. These are called built-in batteries.

The voltage for this battery is approximately 3.6 or 6 volts, depending on whether you have a more modern (3.3 volts) or older (5 volts) motherboard. You should always check the motherboard documentation to verify the correct voltage. Onboard batteries are usually a rechargeable *nickel-cadmium alloy* (NiCd) or *lithium coin cells,* and will last for an average of five to seven years. External batteries (Figure 4-32) are usually non-rechargeable alkaline batteries and tend to last for two to four years.

You usually discover you have a built-in battery when you look at a motherboard and say, "Hey, I don't have a battery!" Don't worry, you do have a battery—it's just built into the CMOS chip. Built-in batteries last for years, but when they die, you need to get a new motherboard or hope that the motherboard has a connector to add an external battery—a very rare thing on modern motherboards.

**Figure 4-32**   External battery

It's usually pretty clear when the battery needs to be replaced. The first clue is that the CMOS clock begins to slow down. If you notice that your clock in Windows begins to lose time, then you probably need to change the battery. A second and much more obvious clue is when your system keeps losing CMOS data overnight or on Monday morning. The scenario goes something like this: You get CMOS errors that mention failed drives or one of the other common errors, so you reconfigure the CMOS settings. The system runs great all week long, and you dutifully power it down on Friday afternoon. Monday morning, you walk into the office, hit the power button, and bam! The errors have returned! It's definitely time to change the battery.

The CMOS chip contains a capacitor (or a battery) to enable you to replace the battery without losing data, as long as you move quickly. Definitely back up your CMOS settings before switching! For motherboards with soldered or glued-down batteries, a connection is usually provided to add an external battery to replace a worn-out onboard one. Remember that the external battery must have the same voltage as the onboard battery you are replacing.

If you have a motherboard that doesn't have a battery, you're in luck. The latest motherboards, as mentioned earlier, have CMOS chips with very long-lasting batteries built in. These batteries virtually never go out. Unfortunately, the machines almost never have an external battery connector. I've had only one go on me, and I just replaced the motherboard.

*Flash ROM*  Using ROM chips for the BIOS has a huge shortcoming. The problem is that you can't change the BIOS without physically replacing the ROM. A few years ago, Intel developed a new type of ROM chip, called *flash ROM*, and it has now become the primary type of system ROM used in PCs. Flash ROMs look exactly like regular ROM chips; you can't tell whether you have a flash just by looking at the system ROM chip. See Figure 4-33.

**Figure 4-33**  Flash ROM and clock

The major difference in flash ROM as compared with the old CMOS chip is that you can reprogram it without removing the chip! This is a tremendous advantage for today's systems, because every time some new type of technology comes out, invariably you need to update the BIOS to take advantage of this technology. Let's use a CPU upgrade as an example. You have an older Pentium II system and would like to upgrade to a Celeron. Unfortunately, your motherboard doesn't have the necessary multiplier to handle the new CPU. You won't be able to take full advantage of the Celeron unless your BIOS can be updated to handle the higher multipliers the Celeron needs to run at full speed. If you have a regular ROM, you might find a replacement ROM and physically yank out the old ROM chip and install the new one. You could also simply buy a new motherboard. This can get a little expensive—and difficult. But with flash ROM, you merely run a small command-line program combined with an update file to change your BIOS. Although the exact process varies from one BIOS maker to another, it usually entails booting off a floppy diskette and running a command such as

**AW P55T2.BIN**

It's really that simple! Most of these utilities enable you to make a backup of your BIOS in case the update causes trouble, so always make the backup! If for some reason a flash update messes up your computer, you might end up throwing the motherboard away without a good backup.

As a rule, don't update your BIOS unless you have a compelling reason to do so. As we so love to say in the PC business: "If it ain't broke, don't fix it!"

### Goodbye, CMOS

In reality, CMOS no longer exists. Flash ROMs now hold both the system BIOS and the CMOS settings. Although the CMOS chip may have gone away, its legacy lives in even the most modern systems. All techs still call the setup program the CMOS setup program, even though we know the data is now stored on flash ROM. Many BIOS still say the word "CMOS" at the top of the screens, even though CMOS is long gone. Most systems still use a battery, although its job is relegated to nothing more than keeping the clock running when you turn off the PC. You might still catch a glimpse of a real CMOS chip, but in all probability, it does little more than provide the clock and battery to keep time. CMOS may be gone, but the function—and the name—lives on.

Because of the robust flash ROM storage of precious CMOS data in modern systems, most of the nightmarish scenarios of complete system failures, lost hard drives, and so on, have disappeared. When working with new systems, you simply make the correct settings once for your hardware and get on with life!

## "Everything Else" Group

The last group of hardware contains "everything else." IBM could not possibly add all the necessary BIOS routines for every conceivable piece of hardware. When programmers wrote the first BIOS, for example, network cards, mice, and sound cards did not exist. Early PC designers at IBM understood that they could not anticipate every new type of hardware, so they gave us a few ways to BYOB (bring your own BIOS).

### Option ROM

The first way to BYOB is to put the BIOS on the hardware device itself. Look at the close-up of a popular card, an Adaptec 2940 SCSI host adapter, displayed in Figure 4-34. (We dedicate all of Chapter 13 to SCSI later in the book.) The card has a chip that looks very similar to the ROM chip on a motherboard, because it *is* a ROM chip, and that ROM chip stores BIOS! The system BIOS does not have a clue about how to talk to this card, so the card has to bring its own BIOS.

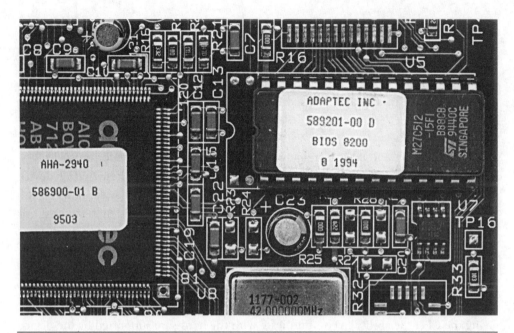

**Figure 4-34**   ROM on Adaptec 2940 host adapter

Most BIOS that come on option ROMs advertise that they exist by displaying information when you boot the system. My system has a SCSI host adapter with BIOS (some SCSI devices have option ROM BIOS) that makes this pretty screen at boot (Figure 4-35).

In the early days of the PC, you could find all sorts of devices with BIOS on option ROM. Today, option ROMs have been replaced by more flexible BYOB methods such as device drivers (see "Device Drivers," next section). One type of device makes a major exception: video cards. Every video card made today contains its own BIOS for internal functions.

```
     TEXRAM DC-390 PCI-SCSI Controller
     BIOS V2.02        Date : 1997-11-14


Installed at IOPORT = EC00h, IRQ = 11 - Level triggered
BIOS ROM mapped at C800h
◄◄◄ Press F2 or F6 to Enter Configuration Menu ►►►

ID-LUN:0-0 IOMEGA ZIP 100              E.08 Removable
        Xfer Rate=Asynchronous

No BIOS disk found ! SCSI BIOS not installed !
```

**Figure 4-35**   BIOS showing SCSI host adapter

*Internal function* is a key term here. Having a ROM BIOS on a device no longer exempts a device from using a device driver. Devices using onboard BIOS do so for internal needs—the BIOS services on the device are not used to talk to the CPU as was originally planned by IBM. Instead, everything relies on device drivers for BYOB. Let's take a moment to understand device drivers and how they are used in modern systems.

## Device Drivers

Installing BIOS on a ROM is extremely inflexible and is rarely done for most devices. Far more popular is adding special programs called *device drivers* to the system. A device driver is nothing more than a file stored on the PC's hard drive that contains all the BIOS commands necessary to talk to whatever device they were written to support. All operating systems employ a method of loading these device drivers into RAM every time the system boots. They know which device drivers to install because of some form of editable file or files that contain a "list" of which device drivers the system needs to load at boot time. All operating systems are designed to look at this list early on in the boot process and employ some method of copying this list of files into RAM, thereby giving the CPU the ability to communicate with the hardware supported by the device driver.

Device drivers come with the device when you buy it. When you buy a sound card, for example, it comes with a diskette or CD-ROM that holds all the necessary device drivers (and usually a bunch of extra goodies). We generically call these floppies and CD-ROMs the *installation disks*. Figure 4-36 shows some typical installation disks. All installation disks come with some form of installation process (usually a program or a special file) that automatically installs the necessary drivers and updates these special "list" files.

The list of device drivers comes in a variety of formats. This list can be one text file, many text files, or, in the case of Windows 95/98/2000, a special database. Without these special files, the system does not know which device drivers to load. As far as the PC is concerned, if a device driver does not load for a particular piece of hardware, that device simply does not exist. Clearly, these files that contain the list of device drivers are extremely important—you must know all of these files, their locations, and how to edit them if you intend to pass the A+ and, equally important, if you intend to do any serious work on a PC. Let's take a look at some of these files and see how they work!

 **NOTE** If you're uncomfortable with the concept of text files, directories (folders), or file extensions, jump ahead to Chapter 9 for clarification.

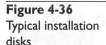

**Figure 4-36**
Typical installation
disks

*CONFIG.SYS*   DOS was the first popular operating system to take advantage of device drivers. DOS loaded device drivers through a special file called CONFIG.SYS, a text file in the root directory of the C: drive. Even though Microsoft no longer makes DOS, all versions of Windows 9*x* continue to run CONFIG.SYS if it exists in the root directory of the C: drive. (Windows can do many fun things with CONFIG.SYS, however, at this point, the only goal is to make you understand that while DOS may be dead, CONFIG.SYS is alive and well in many modern systems!) Figure 4-37 shows a typical CONFIG.SYS from the old DOS days—the file in this example is open in the old DOS text editor EDIT.COM.

You should learn how to use EDIT. Every version of Windows still comes with a copy of the EDIT program. EDIT will save you in situations where you need to boot a system from a floppy disk and you need to access CONFIG.SYS as well as a few other important files. When you're in Windows, use the SYSEDIT program (Figure 4-38) to edit CONFIG.SYS and other important text files. Just don't be surprised if you run SYSEDIT and find nothing in the CONFIG.SYS file—many modern systems no longer use CONFIG.SYS.

The main (but not the only) reason CONFIG.SYS exists is for you to load extra BIOS for hardware that your system BIOS does not support. DOS device drivers are stored on the hard drive. These files usually end with a .SYS or .EXE extension. Device driver files

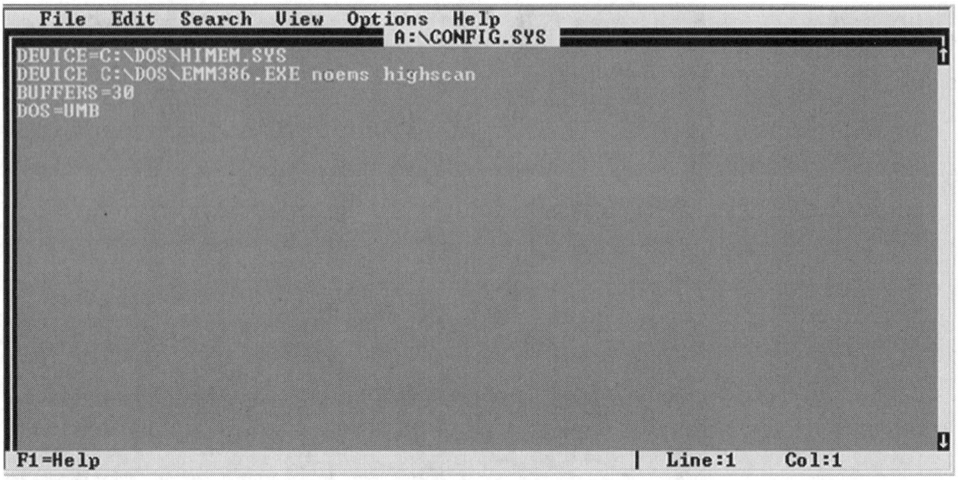

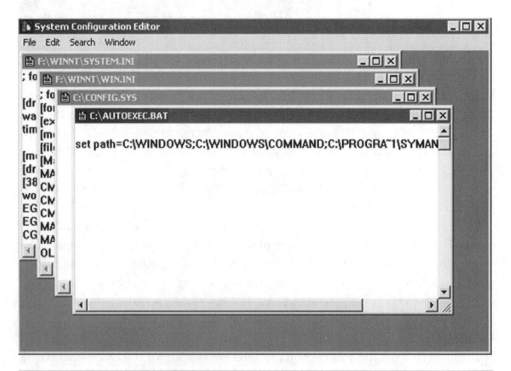

**Figure 4-37** Typical CONFIG.SYS file open in EDIT program

**Figure 4-38** SYSEDIT in action

can be easily identified in CONFIG.SYS. Any line that begins with DEVICE= or DEVICEHIGH= loads a device driver. Figure 4-39 shows the same CONFIG.SYS from the previous figure, identifying the device drivers.

When the computer boots up, the operating system reads the CONFIG.SYS file and loads the device drivers from the hard drive to RAM. We will see more of CONFIG.SYS throughout the book. Make sure you can open CONFIG.SYS for editing using both the EDIT program and SYSEDIT!

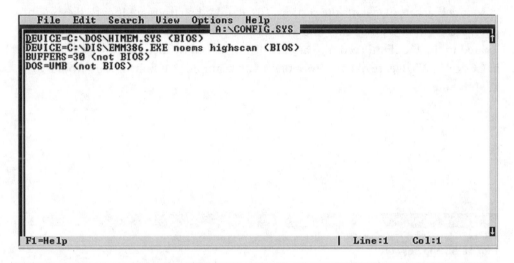

**Figure 4-39**    CONFIG.SYS identifying device drivers

*SYSTEM.INI*    Device drivers that run through CONFIG.SYS have certain limitations. Any device driver that runs in CONFIG.SYS must be designed to run under a DOS environment. Because DOS could use only 640K of RAM, and every device driver in your CONFIG.SYS takes up some of this precious 640K, the number of drivers that could load was limited.

Windows 3.x ran in protected mode, which Microsoft called "386 enhanced mode." Although Windows 3.x needed to use some device drivers from CONFIG.SYS, it was beneficial for it to use device drivers that could run in extended memory (addresses beyond one megabyte), saving the 640K of DOS memory for the programs that needed that memory. Enabling device drivers to load into extended memory also enabled larger and smarter device drivers. Therefore, Windows 3.x had its own set of drivers for accessing hardware in protected mode. Windows 3.x used a text file called SYSTEM.INI to know which protected-mode drivers to load when Windows started. The SYSTEM.INI file was located in the \Windows directory. Just like CONFIG.SYS under

DOS, even though Windows 3.*x* is no longer with us, every version of Windows continues to support SYSTEM.INI fully. Unlike CONFIG.SYS, every Windows system still has SYSTEM.INI. In fact, Windows 9*x* systems *must* have SYSTEM.INI or they will not boot! Windows 2000 does not require SYSTEM.INI, but does include it for backward compatibility with older Windows applications. You may delete the SYSTEM.INI that comes with Windows 2000, just don't go trying to run any old Windows 3.*x* programs! The result will be, quoting Microsoft, "unpredictable."

SYSTEM.INI is broken up into groups, and each group can be identified by the name in square brackets that starts the section. The standard sections are [boot], [keyboard], [boot description], [386Enh], and [drivers]. The majority of drivers that load are located in the [386Enh] section. They are distinguished by their device= line, just like in CONFIG.SYS. Figure 4-40 shows a part of an example [386Enh] section from a SYSTEM.INI file.

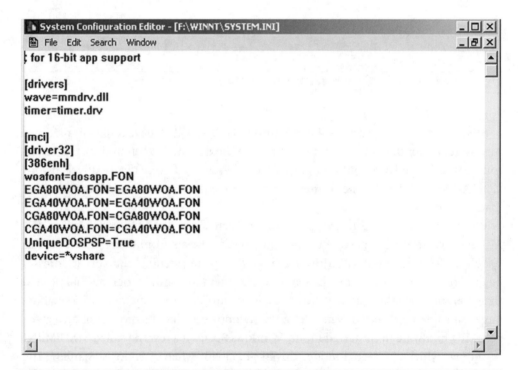

**Figure 4-40**   SYSTEM.INI file with [386Enh] section

*Registry*   One of the big problems of the DOS/Windows 3.*x* combination was that you could have device drivers installed in more than one location. Windows 95 consolidated the functions of CONFIG.SYS, SYSTEM.INI, as well as a number of other files you will eventually meet in this book, into a new type of configuration file collectively called the *Registry* (Figure 4-41). Every configuration setting in Windows 95 was stored in the Registry, including all device-driver information. Windows 98 and Windows 2000 also use the Registry to store all device driver information.

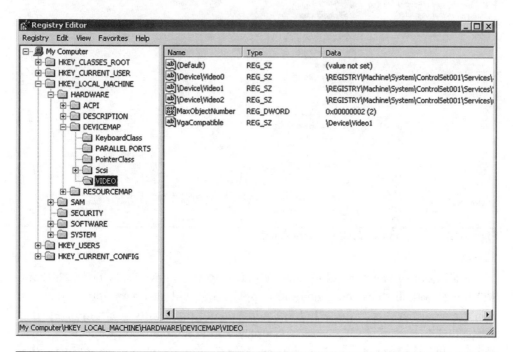

**Figure 4-41**   Registry

Unlike CONFIG.SYS and SYSTEM.INI, the Registry is not a text file. It is an incredibly complex binary file. We rarely access the Registry directly. In the overwhelming majority of situations, you use two programs, the Control Panel and Device Manager, to edit the Registry. These two programs provide a far more intuitive interface for configuring the system and hardware with the necessary drivers.

*Control Panel*   We access the Control Panel by clicking Start | Settings | Control Panel. The Control Panel (Figure 4-42) really has many *applets* that enable you to configure a broad range of system settings. Each applet provides a special tool for the configuring of one aspect of the Windows system.

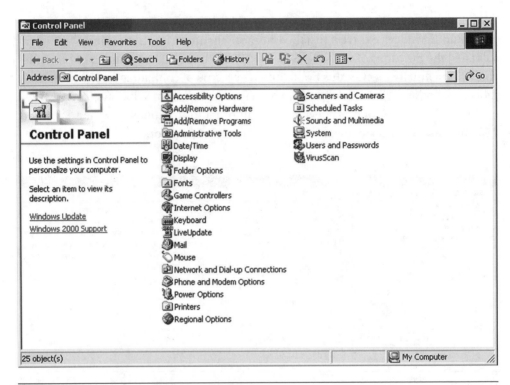

**Figure 4-42** Windows 2000 Control Panel

Not all Control Panels are the same. Windows 95, Windows 98, Windows NT, and Windows 2000 all share many common applets, but will also have applets that you won't see in other versions of Windows. Additionally, third-party applications such as Adobe QuickTime and Real Networks Realplayer add their own Control Panel applets. You should be comfortable seeing applets in one Control Panel that are not in another system's Control Panel. We will tour the important Control Panel applets in the appropriate chapters.

*Device Manager*  Windows provides the Device Manager (Figure 4-43) to change or remove the drivers for any particular device. We access the Device Manager differently in different versions of Windows. For Windows 95, 98, NT, or ME, access Device Manager from the System applet in the Control Panel, and select the Device Manager tab. If you use Windows 2000, you still open the System applet, but you must then select the Hardware tab and click the Device Manager button. Although different versions of Windows have different ways to get to Device Manager, once you open it, they all look basically the same.

We do not use Device Manager to install hardware—that's the job of the Add/Remove New Hardware Wizard in the Control Panel. Device Manager enables you

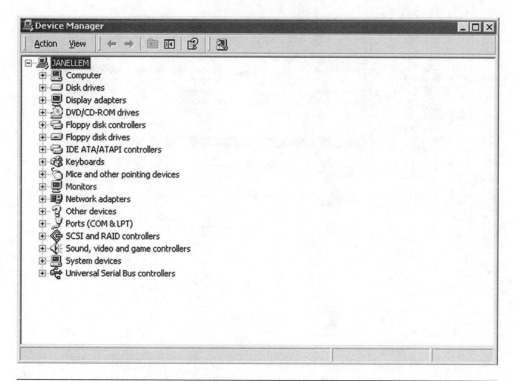

**Figure 4-43**    Device Manager

to see what devices the system uses and gives you a quick overview of the "health" of the system. We'll see a lot of Device Manager in the rest of the book. Make sure you can get to Device Manager in any version of Windows!

*REGEDIT and REGEDT32*    Microsoft provides one or two programs that enable you to access the Registry directly. If you use Windows 95, Windows 98, or Windows ME, you have a program called REGEDIT.EXE to enable you to edit the Registry (Figure 4-44). You run REGEDIT by using the Start | Run menu option, and then typing **REGEDIT**. Note the two sides of the REGEDIT screen—one side looks quite similar to Windows Explorer and shows the hierarchical configuration of the Registry.

Windows NT and Windows 2000 provide a second Registry Editor called REGEDT32.EXE. REGEDT32 has more powerful features needed by the more powerful operating systems. Interestingly, both NT and 2000 also provide a copy of good old REGEDIT, as they never bothered to put a "search" function in REGEDT32! NT and 2000 techs often run programs simultaneously—REGEDIT to find values and REGEDT32 to do the actual editing.

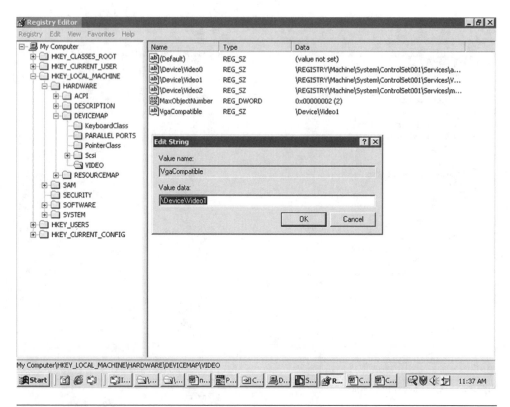

**Figure 4-44**    Making a change through the REGEDIT screen

---

 **NOTE**    The official name of both applications—REGEDIT and REGEDT32—is *Registry Editor*. We use the file names to avoid confusion.

---

Well, aren't you dangerous! Now that you know how to access the Registry, you have a license to kill any Windows system by messing around with the Registry settings. Again, we rarely use these tools, but the A+ exam expects you to know how to edit the Registry and understand its basic structure. We'll cover the registries of all the Windows operating systems in their respective chapters.

Windows 9*x*'s backward compatibility with SYSTEM.INI and CONFIG.SYS creates a bit of a problem. You can install some cards—a sound card, for example—into a Windows 9*x* system by using the DOS or Windows 3.*x* drivers, rather than loading the Windows 9*x* drivers. The installer loads the drivers onto your hard drive and SYSTEM.INI or CONFIG.SYS, and the sound card will work perfectly. Unfortunately, if you go into the Device Manager, you won't see any information about a sound card! Device Manager sees only the devices not controlled by CONFIG.SYS or SYSTEM.INI! This isn't good, as most new technicians only know to look in the Device Manager. If they don't see any information on the sound card, yet the sound card works, they immediately assume that some kind of witchcraft is going on inside the PC.

### BIOS, BIOS, Everywhere!

We now appreciate the fact that every piece of hardware on a system must have an accompanying program that provides the CPU with the code necessary to communicate with that particular device. This code may reside on the system ROM on the motherboard, on ROM on a card, or it may be in a file on the hard drive loaded into RAM at boot. BIOS is everywhere on your system, and you will need to deal with it occasionally. Make sure you know how to access the CMOS, CONFIG.SYS, SYSTEM.INI, and Registry on a given system.

In this section we learned that the system ROM stores two different sets of programs: the BIOS routines and the CMOS setup program. But the system ROM doesn't stop there! Let's take a look at the third and last aspect of the system ROM: the POST.

### Power-On Self Test (POST)

When the computer is turned on or reset, it initiates a special program, also stored on the ROM chip, called the *power-on self test* (POST). The POST program checks out the system every time the computer boots. To perform this check, the POST sends out a standard command that says to all the devices "check yourselves out!" All the devices in the computer then run their own internal diagnostic—the POST doesn't specify what to check. The quality of the diagnostic is up to the people who made that particular device.

Let's consider the POST for a moment. Some device, suppose the 8042 chip, runs its diagnostic and determines that it is not working properly. What will the POST do about it? Only one thing can be done—tell the human being in front of the PC! So how does the computer tell the human? The first thought is to put some information on the monitor. That's fine, but what if the video card is faulty? What if some really low-level device (many devices still have yet to be covered) isn't operational? All POSTs first test all the most basic devices. If anything goes wrong on this first group of devices, the computer will beep using its built-in speaker. But if the speaker doesn't work, trouble results. The POST assumes it always works. All PCs beep on startup to let the user know the speaker is working. Now you know why every computer always beeps when it first starts!

The POST can therefore be divided into two parts. First is the test of the most basic devices—up to and including the video. If anything goes wrong, the computer will beep. Second is a test of the rest of the devices. If anything goes wrong here, a text error message will appear on the screen.

## Before and During the Video Test: The Beep Codes

The computer tests the most basic parts of the computer first. If anything goes wrong, the computer will send a series of beeps. The meaning of these beeps varies from one BIOS manufacturer to another. Additionally, BIOS makers have changed the beep codes over time. Tables 4-1 and 4-2 show the beep codes for the most current versions of AMI and Phoenix BIOS. Award BIOS no longer uses beep codes except for when the video card fails—it gives one long beep followed by two short beeps. Check the accompanying CD for a recording of an Award BIOS reporting a failed video test under the \WAV directory.

Most systems make a rather strange noise when the RAM is missing or very seriously damaged. This tone makes you think you have a beep code. Sure, the speaker beeps, but this "sound of RAM death" is not really considered a beep code. Unlike beep codes, this code repeats until you shut off the system. I've included a recording of this sound on the CD under the \WAV directory.

Refer to your motherboard book for your POST's beep codes. If the motherboard book failed to include beep codes, go to these BIOS maker's Web sites for exhaustive listings:

| | |
|---|---|
| AMI BIOS | www.ami.com/support/doclib.cfm |
| Phoenix BIOS | www.phoenix.com/pcuser/BIOS/phoenix_home.htm |
| Award BIOS | www.phoenix.com/pcuser/BIOS/award_error_codes.htm |

Keep in mind that Web sites often change!

Table 4-3 lists the most common POST problems and how to deal with them. Watch out for false beep codes. Many computers with a bad power supply generate intermittent beep codes. The secret to determining if you have a bad power supply is to turn the computer on and off three or four times, and see if you generate the same beep code every time. If you get the same beep code, it's probably legitimate. If the beep codes change, if the machine stops working, or if the computer seems to heal itself, check the power supply.

**Table 4-1**   AMI Beep Codes

| BEEPS | AMI BIOS 4.5 POST ROUTINE DESCRIPTION |
|---|---|
| 1 | Refresh failure |
| 2 | Parity error |
| 3 | Base 64K memory failure |
| 4 | Timer not operational |
| 5 | Processor error |
| 6 | 8042—gate A20 failure |
| 7 | Processor exception interrupt error |
| 8 | Display memory read/write failure |
| 9 | ROM checksum error |
| 10 | CMOS shutdown register read/write error |
| 11 | Cache memory bad |

**Table 4-2**   Phoenix Beep Codes

| BEEPS | PHOENIX BIOS 4.0 RELEASE 6.x POST ROUTINE DESCRIPTION |
|---|---|
| 1-2-2-3 | BIOS ROM checksum |
| 1-3-1-1 | Test DRAM refresh |
| 1-3-1-3 | Test 8742 keyboard controller |
| 1-3-4-1 | RAM failure on address line *xxxx* |
| 1-3-4-3 | RAM failure on data bits *xxxx* of low byte of memory bus |
| 2-1-2-3 | Check ROM copyright notice |
| 2-2-3-1 | Test for unexpected interrupts |
| 1-2 | Search for option ROMs; one long, two short beeps on checksum failure |
| 1 | One short beep before boot |

**Table 4-3**  Common POST Beep Errors and Solutions

| PROBLEM | SOLUTION |
|---------|----------|
| RAM refresh failure<br>Parity error<br>RAM bit error<br>Base 64K error | (1) Reseat and clean the RAM chips.<br>(2) Replace individual chips until the problem is corrected. |
| 8042 error<br>Gate A20 error | (1) Reseat and clean keyboard chip.<br>(2) Replace keyboard.<br>(3) Replace motherboard. |
| BIOS checksum error | (1) Reseat and clean ROM chip.<br>(2) Replace BIOS chip. |
| Video errors | (1) Reseat video card.<br>(2) Replace video card. |
| Cache memory error | (1) Reseat and clean cache chips.<br>(2) Verify cache jumper settings are correct.<br>(3) Replace cache chips. |
| Everything else | (1) Clean motherboard.<br>(2) Replace motherboard. |

## After the Video Test: The Error Messages

Once the video has been tested, the POST displays any error messages on the screen. In "the old days" (as in pre-Pentium), most systems displayed a numeric code that you needed to decipher. Today's systems use text error messages that simply say where the problem lies in the system. Let's look at both.

### Numeric Error Codes

When an old computer's POST generated a numeric error code, the machine locked up and a numeric error code appeared in the upper-left corner of the screen. For example, the numeric error code in Figure 4-45 indicates that the keyboard is not responding. Hundreds of numeric error codes existed, and fortunately they have been replaced with simple text messages. However, you need to be aware of their existence. Table 4-4 lists the five most common numeric error codes and the probable causes of the problem.

**Figure 4-45**
Old style numeric
error code

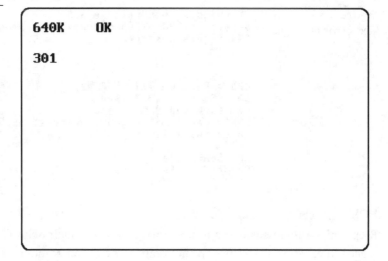

**640K      OK**

**301**

**Table 4-4**   Common Numeric Error Codes

| ERROR CODE | PROBLEM |
| --- | --- |
| 301 | The keyboard is broken or not plugged in. |
| 1701 | The hard drive controller is bad. |
| 7301 | Floppy drive controller is bad. |
| 161 | Dead battery. |
| 1101 | Bad serial card. |

## Text Error Codes

BIOS programs no longer use numeric error codes. After years of PC technicians trying to memorize a bunch of cryptic codes, AMI realized that the overwhelming majority of numeric error codes are never used. So AMI reduced the number of error codes to about 30 and substituted text that described the problem. Today, instead of mysterious numbers, you get text that is usually, but not always, self-explanatory (Figure 4-46).

Text errors are far more useful because you can simply read the screen to determine the bad device. I should add here that a few PC makers (read: IBM) still use numeric error codes in some models. But in these cases, they invariably also add a text code for clarity.

Don't bother memorizing any error codes! The exam wants you to know an error code when you encounter one, but will definitely not quiz you on "What does the error code 1701 mean" or "If your system gives eight beeps, what should you check?"

**Figure 4-46**

Text error messages

```
PhoenixBIOS 4.0 release 6.0
Copyright 1985-2000 Phoenix Technologies Ltd.
All Rights Reserved


CPU = Pentium III  500MHz
640K System RAM Passed
47M Extended RAM Passed
USB upper limit segment address:  EEFE
Mouse initialized

HDD Controller Failure
Press <F1> to resume
```

## POST Cards

Beep codes, numeric codes, and text error codes, although helpful, can sometimes be misleading. Worse than that, an inoperative device can sometimes disrupt the POST, forcing the machine into an endless loop. This causes the PC to act "dead"—no beeps and nothing on the screen. In this case, you need a device to monitor the POST and report which piece of hardware is causing the trouble. The devices designed for this are known as *POST cards*.

POST cards are simple cards that snap into an expansion slot on your system. All POST cards have a small, two-character LED readout that informs you what device the POST is currently testing (Figure 4-47). We use documentation that comes with the POST card to determine what the codes mean. BIOS makers also provide this information—use the same Web addresses you saw earlier to get that information for your BIOS.

Manufacturers make POST cards for all types of PCs. They will work with any BIOS, but you need to know the type of BIOS you have in order to interpret the read-out properly.

We usually only pull out the POST cards when the usual POST errors fail to appear. When a computer provides a beep or text error code that doesn't make sense, or if your machine keeps locking up, some device has stalled the POST. Because the POST card will tell you which device is being tested, the frozen system will stay at that point in the POST, and the error will stay on the POST card's readout. Many people sell POST cards today, with prices ranging from $50 up to $1,500. Spend the absolute least amount of money you can. The more expensive cards add bells and whistles that you do not need, like diagnostic software and voltmeters. Try JDR Microdevices (800-538-5000) for a good, cheap POST card. Mention Total Seminars, and they should sell it to you for less than $50. In addition, they have a JDR-PDI card, a combination POST card and IRQ/DMA tester card (I'll explain IRQ/DMA later), for about $100, which is an excellent value.

**Figure 4-47** POST card in action

Using a POST card is straightforward. Turn off the PC, install the POST card in any unused slot, and turn on the PC. As you watch the display, notice the different hexadecimal readouts and refer to them as your POST progresses. Notice how quickly they change. If you get an "FF" or "00," that means the POST is over and everything passed—time to check the operating system. If a device stalls the POST, however, the POST card will display an error code. That's the problem device! Good technicians will often memorize 10 to 20 different POST codes. Memorizing them is faster than looking them up in a book.

So you got a beep code, a text error code, or a POST error. Now what do you do with that knowledge? The important thing to remember is that a POST error does not fix the computer; it only tells you where to look. You then have to know how to deal with that bad or improperly configured component. If you use a POST card, for example, and it hangs at the "Initializing Floppy Drive" test, you better know how to work on a floppy drive!

Sometimes the error code itself confuses us. What device do you point at when you get a "CMOS shutdown register read/write error" beep code from your system? First of all, read the error carefully. Let's say on that same system you got an "8042—gate A20 failure" beep code. What will you do? Well, you know the 8042 stands for the keyboard, so a quick peek at the keyboard and the connection would be in order. But outside of that, a good general rule is: "If you don't know what the error means or the bad part won't come off, replace the motherboard!" Clearly, you will stumble across exceptions to this rule, but more often than not, the rule stands.

## The Last BIOS Duty—The Boot Process

All PCs need a process to begin their operations. Before PCs, most computers had a Power switch and a Run button. You powered up the computer, lined up a program to run, and then pressed the Run button to run the program. Those days are long gone. You never see a Run button on the front of the PC. Instead, IBM decided when they first developed the PC to create a process where the user simply flips the on/off switch and the computer runs. Once you feed power to the PC, the tight interrelation of hardware, firmware, and software enables the PC to start itself, to "pull itself up by the bootstraps" or "boot" itself. All PCs still follow the original boot process as described by IBM for the original IBM 286 AT computer.

The first electrical component to "wake up" when the computer is turned on is the CPU itself. As soon as the power supply provides the proper voltage, the CPU reads a special wire called *power good*. If this wire has a certain charge, the CPU knows the system has enough power coming in to begin the boot process. Every Intel and clone CPU has a built-in memory address that it immediately sends via its address bus the moment the power good wire wakes up the CPU. This special address is the same on every Intel and clone CPU, from the oldest 8086 to the most recent microprocessor. This address is the first line of the POST program on the system ROM! That's how the system starts the POST.

After the POST has finished, there must be a way for the computer to find the programs on the hard drive in order to start the operating system (usually Windows). The POST passes control to the last BIOS function: the *bootstrap loader*. The bootstrap loader is little more than a few dozen lines of BIOS code tacked to the end of the POST program that looks for the operating system. The bootstrap loader will first check to see if a diskette is in the floppy drive. If a floppy diskette is inserted, the PC assumes that the operating system is on the floppy disk. If a floppy disk is not inserted, the system then looks for an operating system on the hard drive. All floppy and hard disks have a very specific location on them called the *boot sector*. If the disk is bootable, it will contain special programming designed to tell the system where to locate the operating system. A disk that has a functional operating system is called a *bootable disk* or a *system disk*. If the bootstrap loader locates a good boot sector, it passes control to the operating system and removes itself from memory. Even though BIOS has left the RAM, the little BIOS programs (the "services"—did you forget about them?) stand ready to assist the CPU to talk to the hard drives, floppy drives, and so on.

## Boot Configuration

If the bootstrap loader cannot find a bootable disk, you will get the error shown in Figure 4-48.

This error is easy to re-create. Just reboot your computer with a blank floppy disk in the floppy drive! Many BIOS programs have CMOS settings that enable you to change the order in which the boot loader searches devices for an operating system. Figure 4-49 shows a typical CMOS search order screen. This screen enables you to choose the boot order from the floppy drive, hard drive, CD-ROM, LS-120/ZIP drive (see Chapter 7 for a discussion of floppy drives), and network boot (booting from a special type of network card). You may put these in any order. We commonly change the boot order to prevent a hacker from inserting a bootable floppy and accessing the system.

```
PCI device listing...
Bus No. Device No. Func No. Vendor ID Device ID Device Class            IRQ

     0       7         1       8086     7111     IDE Controller           14
     0       7         2       8086     7112     Serial Bus Controller    10
     0       9         0       1102     0002     Multimedia Device        11
     0       9         1       1102     7002     Input Device             NA
     0      10         0       9904     7178     Mass Storage Controller  12
     0      11         0       8086     1229     Network Controller        5
     0      13         0       104C     8019     Serial Bus Controller     5
     1       0         0       102B     0525     Display Controller       11
                                                 ACPI Controller           9


Verifying DMI Pool Data.......

Non-system disk or disk error
Replace and press any key when ready
```

**Figure 4-48**  Non-system disk or disk error—Replace and press any key when ready

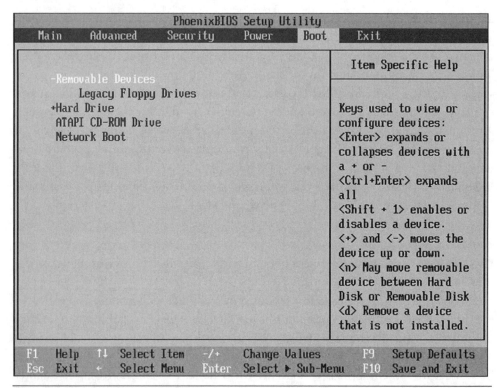

**Figure 4-49** CMOS changing boot sequence

The complex world of BIOS takes up a good part of any technician's day. Unless you never change hardware and have systems that never crash, you will spend a good deal of time accessing CMOS, installing device drivers, and editing critical files. Understanding the many faces of BIOS gives you the tools you need to pass the A+ exams and to become a good PC technician.

## Motherboard Layouts

All motherboards come in a basic rectangular shape, but they come in a dizzying variety of sizes. As you look at the many sizes, you begin to appreciate that the position of every motherboard's connectors seems to take about the same place on most every board. The expansion slots always seem to take roughly the same part of the motherboard. The particular way components are positioned on a motherboard is called the motherboard's *form factor*. The overwhelmingly most popular form factor is ATX, followed at a distant second by the old AT form factor. Although AT is basically obsolete, you still find AT motherboards for sale as the last of the AT form factor motherboard makers wind down and shift to ATX. Let's look at both of these form factors, plus a few others.

## AT Form Factor

Given the AT form factor's large installed base, the A+ exam expects you to know this form factor. Plus, learning about AT will help you appreciate ATX all the more. Let's look at the AT form factor motherboards.

The AT form factor, invented by IBM in the early 80s, was the predominant form factor for motherboards through the mid-1990s. The AT-type motherboard can be distinguished by the position of the keyboard plug and its power socket (Figure 4-50).

The AT motherboard has a few size variations (Figure 4-51). The original size of the AT motherboard was almost the same size as two pieces of 8.5×11-inch notebook paper laid side by side. It needed that massive size because the first PCs carried a lot of individual chips. As technology improved, the demand for a smaller (and less expensive to manufacture) AT motherboard increased. A smaller size was created and dubbed "baby AT." The original-size AT motherboard then became known variously as a "full AT," "regular AT," or sometimes just "AT."

Some variation in size even exists within baby ATs! One motherboard might be slightly larger or smaller than another, which is okay as long as the keyboard and expansion slots stick to the form-factor specifications (Figure 4-52).

**Figure 4-50** AT motherboard

**Figure 4-51** Different sizes of AT motherboards

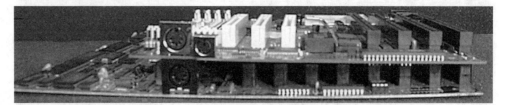

**Figure 4-52** Commonality between AT motherboards

During the dominant period of the AT form factor, a number of problems began to surface. The AT form factor lacked support for any connection other than the keyboard. Clearly, PCs have quite a few more cables hanging out their backs! When PCs were first invented, however, the only devices plugged into the average PC were a monitor and a keyboard. That's what the AT was designed to handle. The only dedicated connector on an AT motherboard is the keyboard plug. If you want to add connectors for anything else, you have to do it through the expansion slots.

## The Need for a New Form Factor

Over the years, the number of devices plugged into the back of the PC has grown tremendously. Your average PC today has a keyboard, a mouse, a printer, some speakers, a monitor, and a phone line connected to it. These added components have created a demand for a new type of form factor, one with more dedicated connectors for more devices. Many attempts were made to create a new standard form factor. Invariably, these new form factors integrated dedicated connectors for at least the mouse and printer, and many even added connectors for video, sound, and phone lines. Although motherboard manufacturers created many excellent designs, no single new form factor became very popular. One form factor that still enjoys a degree of success is the "slimline" form factor. The first slimline form factor was known as LPX (Figure 4-53). It was replaced by the NLX form factor.

**Figure 4-53**   LPX motherboard

The LPX and now the NLX form factor meet the demands of the slimline market by providing a central riser slot to enable the insertion of a special riser card. Expansion cards then fit into the riser card horizontally. Combining built-in connections with a riser card enables manufacturers to produce PCs shorter than 4 inches.

The main problem with form factors like LPX was their inflexibility. Certainly, no problem occurred with dedicated connections for devices like mice or printers, but the new form factors also added connectors for devices like video and sound-devices that were prone to obsolescence, making the motherboard useless the moment a new type of video or sound card came into popularity.

## Enter ATX

Yet there continued to be a tremendous demand for a new form factor—a form factor that had more standard connectors, but at the same time was flexible enough for possible changes in technology. This demand led to the creation of the ATX form factor in 1995 (Figure 4-54).

ATX got off to a slow start, but by around 1998 ATX overtook AT to become the most common form factor used today. ATX shares the same dimensions as a baby AT, but mounts 90 degrees relative to the computer's box. ATX is distinct from the AT in the lack of an AT keyboard port, replaced with a rear plate that enables access to all necessary ports (Figure 4-55). ATX also uses a P1 power connector instead of P8 and P9 (Figure 4-56).

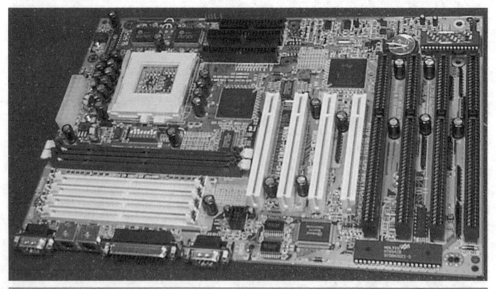

**Figure 4-54** ATX motherboard

**Figure 4-55**   ATX ports

**Figure 4-56**   P1 connector

The ATX form factor includes many improvements over AT. The position of the power supply enables better air movement. The CPU and RAM are placed to enable easier access.

Unlike AT power supplies, ATX uses a feature called "soft power." This means that it can use software to turn the PC on and off. The physical manifestation of soft power is the power switch. Instead of the thick power cord used in AT systems, an ATX power switch is little more than a pair of small wires leading to the motherboard. We will delve into this in more detail in Chapter 6.

Just as the original AT generated the baby AT, ATX has two smaller versions: the Micro ATX and the Flex ATX. Micro ATX (Figure 4-57) is about 30 percent smaller than standard ATX, yet still uses the standard ATX connections. A Micro ATX motherboard fits into a standard ATX case. Flex ATX is even smaller than Micro ATX. Although Flex ATX can use a standard ATX power supply, most Flex ATX systems use a special "Flex ATX only" power supply.

Keep in mind that each main type of form factor requires its own case. AT motherboards go into AT cases, NLX motherboards go into NLX cases, and ATX motherboards go into ATX cases. You cannot replace one form factor with another without purchasing a new case.

## Motherboard Installation and Replacement

To most techs, the concept of adding or replacing a motherboard can be extremely intimidating. It really shouldn't be; motherboard installation is a common and necessary part of PC repair. It is inexpensive and easy, although it can sometimes be a little tedious and messy due to the large number of parts involved. This section covers the process of installation/replacement and will show you some of the tricks that make this necessary process easy to handle.

## Choosing the Motherboard and Case

First, determine what motherboard you need. What CPU are you using? Will the motherboard work with that CPU? Because most of us buy the CPU and the motherboard at the same time, make the seller guarantee that the CPU will work with the motherboard. How much RAM do you intend to install? Are extra RAM sockets available for future upgrades? A number of excellent motherboard manufacturers are available today. Some of the more popular brands are Tyan, Asus, Shuttle, Supermicro, and Gigabyte. Your supplier may also have some lesser-known but perfectly acceptable brands of motherboards. As long as the supplier has an easy return policy, it's perfectly fine to try one of these.

**Figure 4-57**   Micro ATX motherboard

Second, do not worry about size. Virtually any motherboard will fit into any case made today. Usually a quick visual inspection will be sufficient to see if it will fit. Keep form factor with form factor—AT motherboards for AT boxes, and ATX motherboards with ATX boxes.

Third, all motherboards come with a technical manual, better known as the *motherboard book*. You must have this book! This book is your only source for all of the critical information about the motherboard. For example, if you have an onboard battery and that battery decides to die, where would you install a replacement external battery? Where do you plug in the speaker? Even if you let someone else install the motherboard, insist on the motherboard book; you will need it.

Fourth, pick your case carefully. Cases come in five basic sizes: slimline, desktop, mini-tower, mid-tower, and tower. The desktop and mini-tower cases are the most popular choices. Make sure you get a case that will fit your motherboard—most Micro and Flex ATX cases are too small for a regular ATX motherboard. A quick test fit before you buy saves a lot of return trips to the supplier. Cases come with many different options, but two more common options point to a better case. One option is a removable face (Figure 4-58)—many cheaper cases will screw the face into the metal frame using wood screws. A removable face makes disassembly much easier.

Another option is a detachable motherboard mount. Clearly, the motherboard will have to be attached to the case in some fashion. In better cases, this is handled by a removable tray or plate (Figure 4-59). This enables you to attach the motherboard to the case separately, saving you from the difficult chore of sticking your arms into the case to turn screws.

Power supplies come with the case. Watch out for "really good deal" cases because that invariably points to a cheap power supply. You also need to verify that the power supply has sufficient wattage. This issue is better handled in Chapter 6.

## Installing the Motherboard

If you're replacing a motherboard, first remove the old motherboard. Begin by removing all the cards. Also remove anything else that might impede removal or installation of the motherboard, such as hard or floppy drives. Keep track of your screws—the best idea is to return the screws to their mounting holes temporarily, at least until you can reinstall the parts. Sometimes even the power supply has to be removed temporarily to enable access to the motherboard. Document the position of the little wires for the speaker, turbo switch, turbo light, and reset button in case you need to reinstall them.

Unscrew the motherboard. *It will not simply lift out.* The motherboard mounts to the case via small connectors called *standouts* that slide into keyed slots or screw into the bottom of the case. Screws then go into the standouts to hold the motherboard in place. If the CPU or RAM has been removed, be sure to replace them before installing the new motherboard.

**Figure 4-58**   Removable face

**Figure 4-59**
Motherboard tray

When you insert the new motherboard, do not assume that you will put the screws and standouts in the same place as they were in your old motherboard. When it comes to the placement of screws and standouts, only one rule applies: "anywhere it fits." Do not be afraid to be a little tough here! Installing motherboards can be a wiggling, twisting, knuckle-scraping process.

Once you get the motherboard mounted in the case with the CPU and RAM properly installed, it's time to insert the power connections and test it. A POST card can be helpful with the system test because you won't have to add the speaker, a video card, monitor, and keyboard to verify that the system is booting. If you have a POST card, start the system, and watch to see if the POST takes place—you should see a number of POST codes before the POST stops. If you don't have a POST card, install a keyboard, video card, and monitor. Boot the system and see if the BIOS information shows up on the screen. If it does, you're probably okay. If it doesn't, it's time to refer to the motherboard book to see where a mistake was made.

**NOTE**  Refer to Chapter 6 for the quirks of working with AT and ATX power supplies, especially the latter's soft power feature. You can easily fry components by plugging them in with the power supply attached and supplied with electricity from the wall socket, even if the system is turned off! Also, brush up on the "joys" of electrostatic discharge in that same chapter.

## Wires, Wires, Wires

The last, and often the most frustrating, part of motherboard installation is connecting the lights andbuttons on the front of the box. These usually include the following:

- Soft power
- Turbo switch
- Turbo light
- Reset button
- Keylock
- Speaker
- Hard drive active light

These wires have specific pin connections to the motherboard. Although you can refer to the motherboard book for their location, usually a quick inspection of the motherboard will suffice for an experienced tech (Figure 4-60).

A few rules need to be followed when installing these wires. The first rule is "The lights are *light emitting diodes* (LEDs) not light bulbs—they have a positive and negative side. If they don't work one way, turn the connector around and try it the other." The second rule is "When in doubt, guess." Incorrect installation will not result in damage to the computer. The device that was incorrectly wired simply will not work. Refer to the motherboard book for the correct installation. The third and last rule is "With the exception of the soft power switch on an ATX system, you do not need any of these wires for the computer to run!" Many techs often simply ignore these wires; although, this would not be something I'd do to any system but my own!

No hard and fast rule exists for determining the function of each wire. Often the function of each wire is printed on the connector (Figure 4-61). If not, track each wire to the light or switch to determine its function.

## The Next Step

We have described the motherboard's function as providing easy access to the wires of the external data bus and the address bus for all of its devices. This chapter has described the devices (ROM chips, CMOS chips, keyboard controllers, and so on) that mount directly onto the motherboard. What if we want to add other devices? For other optional devices, an additional bridge is required: the expansion bus.

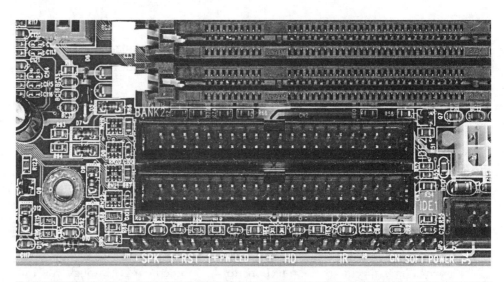

**Figure 4-60**   Motherboard wire connections labeled on the motherboard

**Figure 4-61**
Sample of case wires

# Review Questions

1. What does *Basic Input/Output Services* (BIOS) provide for the computer? (Choose the best answer.)

   A. BIOS provides the physical interface for various devices, such as the serial and parallel ports.

   B. BIOS provides the programming that enables the CPU to communicate with other hardware.

   C. BIOS provides memory space for applications to load into from the hard drive.

   D. BIOS provides a memory space for applications to load into from the main system RAM.

2. Bill and John are arguing near the water cooler about BIOS. Bill claims that BIOS always comes on ROM, thus the name "firmware." John disagrees, arguing that BIOS is always software. Who is correct?

   A. Only Bill is correct.

   B. Only John is correct.

   C. Both are correct.

   D. Neither is correct.

3. Ernie puts together a new system and seems to have everything in place. When he powers up the system, however, he hears a series of beeps (one long and two short) and then nothing else. The monitor stays blank and Windows does not load as far as he can tell. What is the most probable cause of the beeping and "dead" PC?

   A. Ernie forgot to plug the PC into the power.

   B. Ernie does not have the RAM seated properly.

   C. Ernie does not have the CPU seated properly.

   D. Ernie does not have the video card seated properly.

4. Jill boots up an older Pentium system that has been the cause of several user complaints at the office. The system powers up and starts to run through POST, but then stops. The screen displays a "CMOS configuration mismatch" error. Of the following list, what is the most likely cause of this error?

   A. Dying CMOS battery

   B. Bad CPU

   C. Bad RAM

   D. Corrupt system BIOS

5. Jill installs a new SCSI host adapter in a system. When she boots up the system, a new text message appears and seems to cause the system to halt for a minute. Then the system continues, and Windows loads normally. The host adapter appears in her Device Manager and seems to be working. What could be the cause of the odd text message and slowdown at boot?

   A. The SCSI host adapter must have buggy drivers.

   B. The SCSI host adapter must need drivers loaded.

   C. The SCSI host adapter has option ROM that loads BIOS for the card.

   D. The SCSI host adapter has option RAM that has to search the hard drive for drivers before it can load.

6. Which is the correct boot sequence for a PC?

   A. CPU, POST, Power Good, Boot Loader, Operating System

   B. POST, Power Good, CPU, Boot Loader, Operating System

   C. Power Good, Boot Loader, CPU, POST, Operating System

   D. CPU, Power Good, POST, Boot Loader, Operating System

7. Jill has a motherboard with a series of connectors on the back, including PS/2 mouse and keyboard ports, two serial ports, and a parallel port. When she attempts to install the motherboard in her old case, she finds several problems— the case does not have holes for the ports! Jack claims that she has to cut new holes in order for the motherboard to line up properly in the case. Motherboards and cases have no standardization, so this is fairly typical. Bill disagrees, arguing that she has the wrong case for her motherboard, or vice versa. Who is correct?

   A. Only Jack is correct.

   B. Only Bill is correct.

   C. Both Jack and Bill are correct.

   D. Neither Jack nor Bill is correct.

8. Which of the following is *not* a common form factor?

   A. AT

   B. ATI

   C. ATX

   D. Flex ATX

9. Which of the following most accurately describes the relationship between BIOS and hardware?

   A. All hardware needs BIOS.

   B. All hardware that attaches to the motherboard via ribbon cables needs BIOS.

   C. All hardware built into the motherboard needs BIOS.

   D. Some hardware devices need BIOS.

**10.** Jill takes care of a group of 25 PCs, all Pentium systems with AT keyboards attached directly to the AT keyboard connector on the motherboard. She wants to migrate ten of those systems to Pentium III CPUs on motherboards with built-in connectors for PS/2 keyboards and mice, and serial, parallel, and USB ports.

**The primary objective:** Upgrade ten systems to Pentium III systems.

**Optional objectives:** Upgrade to motherboards with lots of built-in ports and use the current cases.

**The proposed solution:** Purchase ten 933 MHz Pentium III CPUs and ten ATX motherboards. Install the new hardware into the existing cases if possible, but if not, purchase ten new cases.

A. Accomplishes only the primary objective.

B. Accomplishes the primary objective and one of the optional objectives.

C. Accomplishes the primary objective and both of the optional objectives.

D. Accomplishes neither the primary nor the optional objectives.

## Answers

1. **B.** BIOS provides the programming that enables the CPU to communicate with other hardware.

2. **D.** Neither is correct. BIOS comes in many forms, including software and firmware.

3. **D.** Ernie does not have the video card seated properly.

4. **A.** The CMOS battery is probably dying.

5. **C.** The SCSI host adapter has option ROM that loads BIOS for the card.

6. **D.** Here's the boot sequence: CPU, Power Good, POST, Boot Loader, Operating System.

7. **B.** Bill has the answer—she's trying to put an ATX motherboard into an AT case!

8. **B.** ATI is a video card company, not a form factor!

9. **A.** All hardware needs BIOS.

10. **B.** The new CPUs and motherboards clearly upgrade the systems, but you cannot put ATX motherboards into AT cases. She needs to upgrade the cases as well.

## CHAPTER 5

# Expansion Bus

In this chapter, you will

- Understand the function of an external data bus
- See how I/O addressing works
- See how IRQs and DMAs work
- Understand COM and LPT ports
- Look at some common installation issues
- Understand the different types of expansion buses

This chapter covers a broad but closely linked set of topics that I have decided to call the "expansion bus." A better title might be something like "How can I successfully add cards and other devices to an existing system?" But I might have a little trouble getting all that on the title page! Let's start with the expansion slots. Your PC's expansion slots give you tremendous flexibility in configuration when adding devices to your PC. Expansion slots provide a standardized interface for installing new devices.

In today's world of *Plug and Play* (PnP) devices, many might argue that this topic isn't very important, but that analysis misses a key point. Granted, the ability to snap in a new device and have it work automatically is wonderful, but it also does not work every time! As you will see, many PnP devices today have some rather nasty habits and don't work properly. Understanding how motherboards and the expansion slots soldered to them work together to enable a sound card or modem to run properly is absolutely vital. You need to understand the expansion bus and motherboard, so we'll start with something you already know—the external data bus and address bus.

## Historical/Conceptual

### It's the Crystals!

Every device in the computer—RAM, keyboard, network card, sound card, and so on—connects to the external data bus and the address bus. Whether a device is soldered to the motherboard or snapped into a socket makes no difference. Oh sure, we understand that the chipset sort of separates the address bus and external data bus into an inside part that we call the frontside bus and an outside part, which we really haven't yet given a name—although we are about to do so (Figure 5-1).

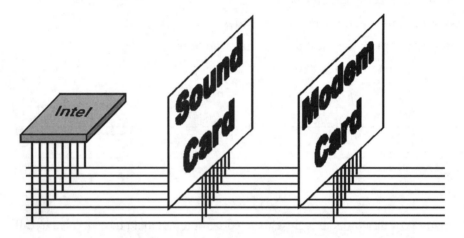

**Figure 5-1**    The CPU and two cards tied to the external data bus

We know from the CPU chapter that the CPU is "pushed" by a clock crystal. CPUs aren't alone in this; almost all integrated circuits must be regulated by a clock crystal. The crystal acts like a drill sergeant calling a cadence, setting the pace of activity in the computer. Every device soldered to the motherboard is designed to run at the speed of the system crystal. For example, a 133 MHz motherboard has a 133 MHz keyboard chip, a 133 MHz chipset, and 133 MHz everything else, all timed by a 133 MHz crystal (Figure 5-2).

Now consider what happens if you buy a device that did not come with your computer. Take a sound card as an example. Like almost every other electronic device, the chips on a sound card need to be pushed by a crystal. At what speed should these chips run? 66 MHz? 100 MHz? 133 MHz? If you used the system crystal to push that sound card, you would need to have sound cards for every possible computer speed. You would not be able to buy any available sound card. You would have to find one that ran at the same speed as your motherboard. You would have to buy a 100 MHz sound card for a 100 MHz system or a 133 MHz sound card for a 133 MHz system. That also means

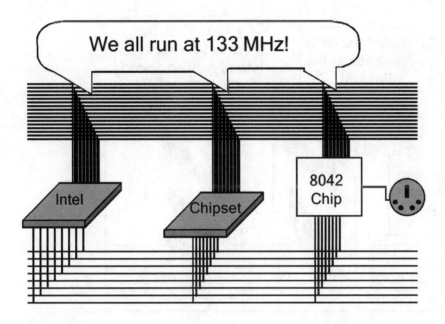

**Figure 5-2**   We all run at 133 MHz!

that if you make sound cards for a living, you would have to make them for every possible speed.

This is ridiculous, and IBM knew it when they designed the PC. They had to make an extension to the external data bus that *ran at its own standardized speed.* You would use this part of the external data bus to snap new devices into the PC. IBM achieved this goal by adding a different crystal that controlled the part of the external data bus connected to the expansion slots. We call this the *expansion bus crystal* (Figure 5-3).

On a typical PC, only the frontside bus runs at the motherboard speed. The expansion slots run at another, much slower speed. The chipset acts as the divider between the two buses, compensating for the speed difference with wait states and special buffering (storage) areas. This way, no matter what speed CPU you have, the expansion slots all run at a standard speed. In the original IBM PC, that speed was about 14.31818 MHz ÷ 2, or about 7.16 MHz (Figure 5-4).

So now you have, in essence, two different buses. The first bus is the frontside bus (a.k.a. "system bus") running at the speed of the system crystal. The second bus is the *expansion bus,* running at the speed of the expansion bus crystal.

The expansion bus, just like every other part of the PC, has grown dramatically in terms of speed and complexity over the years. Even today, new technologies continue to push the expansion bus to new performance heights. But for all these tremendous improvements, all but the very latest motherboards still provide for total backward support of the oldest expansion bus, requiring you to appreciate a host of complex

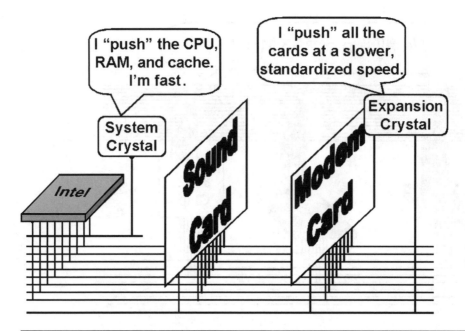

**Figure 5-3**   Function of system and expansion crystal

configuration issues that we lump together into the term "system resources." If you want to pass the A+ Certification exams and if you want to work competently on PCs, you need to understand the expansion bus.

## History of PC Expansion Buses: Part I

In this first section, we will see some of the oldest expansion slots that came with PCs and appreciate some of the issues that techs had to deal with manually to make devices work. While the PC handles most of these issues automatically via a magical function called "Plug and Play," CompTIA continues to demand that we understand how these functions work. So, as with most stories, the best place to start is at the beginning, with the original expansion bus on the first IBM PC.

## PC Bus

On first-generation IBM XTs, the 8088 processor had an 8-bit external data bus and ran at a top speed of 4.77 MHz. Therefore, IBM made the expansion slots on the XT with an 8-bit external bus connection. IBM wanted the bus to run at the speed of the CPU, and even way back then 4.77 MHz was an easy speed to achieve. IBM settled on a standard expansion bus speed of ~7 MHz. Seven MHz was plenty fast enough—at the time it was faster than the CPU! But IBM knew that Intel had new CPUs on the way and expected the expansion bus to keep up with the system bus. This expansion bus was

**Figure 5-4**  Typical expansion bus crystal

called the "PC Bus" or "XT Bus," and the slots looked like Figure 5-5. (The change to the term "ISA" is discussed shortly.)

Figure 5-6 shows the function of the individual pins on the PC bus. The connections that start with the letter "A" are the 20 address bus wires, and the connections that start with the letter "D" are the eight external data bus wires. I will discuss the function of most of the other connections as we progress through this chapter.

IBM did something no one had ever done. They enabled competitors to copy the PC bus without having to pay a licensing fee or royalty. They also enabled third parties to make cards that would snap into their PC bus. Remember that IBM invented the PC bus. It was (and still is) a patented product of IBM Corporation. By enabling everyone to copy the PC expansion bus technology, IBM established the industry standard and created the clone market. If IBM had not enabled this to happen, companies such as Compaq, Dell, and Gateway never would have existed. Component makers like Logitech, Hayes, and 3Com would never be the companies they are today without the help of IBM. Who knows, if IBM had not opened the PC bus to the world, this book and the A+ exams might have been based on Apple Computers!

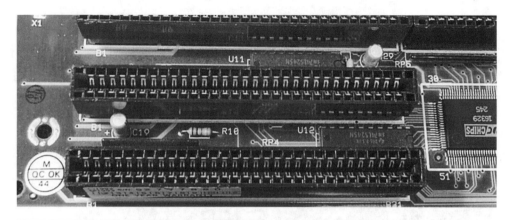

**Figure 5-5**  Eight-bit ISA or PC/XT slots

## Sixteen-Bit ISA

When Intel invented the 286, IBM wanted to create a new expansion bus that would take advantage of the 286's 16-bit external data bus yet still be backwardly compatible with older 8-bit cards. This was achieved by simply adding a set of connections to the end of the PC bus, creating a new 16-bit bus (Figure 5-7). We called this bus the "AT bus" after the first system to use these slots, the 286-based IBM AT (Advanced Technology) computer.

Notice that the connectors add eight more external data bus wires and four more address wires. This new 16-bit bus also ran at a top speed of 8.33 MHz, but just about every motherboard maker used the same ~7 MHz crystal as on the 8-bit ISA bus to ensure total compatibility. See Figure 5-8.

IBM, while retaining the patent rights, enabled third parties to copy their bus architecture, but they never released the complete specifications for these two types of expansion buses. A number of clone makers got together in the early 1980s and pooled their combined knowledge of the PC/XT and AT buses to create a book of standards called the "ISA Bus Standards." Today we call these buses *8-bit ISA* and *16-bit ISA*. Because the term "ISA" (Industry Standard Architecture) did not become official until 1990, many people still refer to these buses as the *PC/XT* or *AT* buses.

The first years of the PC industry saw only two types of standardized expansion slots: 8-bit ISA and 16-bit ISA. These slots were extensions of the external data bus, yet they ran at only around 7 MHz, regardless of the speed of the system. This is still true today. The ISA bus's best throughput is 16 bits wide at 7 MHz. This provides sufficient data transfers as long as the external data bus on the CPU is 16 bits or less (8088 and 80286). The 7-MHz speed is only slightly slower than the 12 MHz of the fastest 286.

**Figure 5-6**
Pinout for an 8-bit
ISA slot

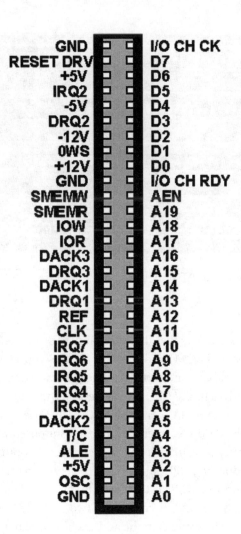

| | |
|---|---|
| GND | I/O CH CK |
| RESET DRV | D7 |
| +5V | D6 |
| IRQ2 | D5 |
| -5V | D4 |
| DRQ2 | D3 |
| -12V | D2 |
| 0WS | D1 |
| +12V | D0 |
| GND | I/O CH RDY |
| SMEMW | AEN |
| SMEMR | A19 |
| IOW | A18 |
| IOR | A17 |
| DACK3 | A16 |
| DRQ3 | A15 |
| DACK1 | A14 |
| DRQ1 | A13 |
| REF | A12 |
| CLK | A11 |
| IRQ7 | A10 |
| IRQ6 | A9 |
| IRQ5 | A8 |
| IRQ4 | A7 |
| IRQ3 | A6 |
| DACK2 | A5 |
| T/C | A4 |
| ALE | A3 |
| +5V | A2 |
| OSC | A1 |
| GND | A0 |

The 8-bit and 16-bit ISA buses were for many years the only serious option for PC users. The PC industry was built upon these expansion buses. Although other expansion buses now have made ISA nearly obsolete, I need to describe some generic features of card installation that use the ISA bus for the basics. Once you understand these concepts, you can move on to the more advanced expansion buses with a solid, clear understanding of their benefits.

The next few sections delve into the "big three" of card installation: I/O addresses, IRQs, and DMA. These three topics are together probably the single greatest headache confronting PC technicians. I will go over each of these in detail, starting with I/O addresses.

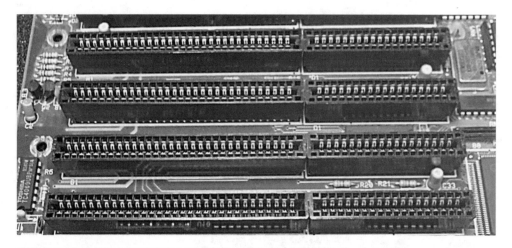

**Figure 5-7**   Sixteen-bit ISA or AT slots

## I/O Addresses

We know from previous chapters that the external data bus transfers lines of programs between memory (RAM and ROM) and the CPU via the chipset. The external data bus also enables data to travel back and forth from peripherals such as the keyboard, hard drives, and CD-ROM drives to the CPU. We understand that the CPU uses the address bus to access programs both in RAM and ROM. The CPU uses BIOS routines stored in ROM to tell peripherals to do whatever it is they are supposed to do. That leaves two related questions: "If everything in the computer connects to both the external data bus and address bus, how does the CPU know how to talk to a particular device, and how do particular devices know the CPU is talking to them?" See Figure 5-9.

Remember that the expansion bus consists of two separate buses: the external data bus and the address bus. The secret is in the address bus. We know that every device on the PC connects to both buses. When IBM first designed the PC, they assigned groups of unique patterns of 1's and 0's *on the address bus* for each device in the computer. But the address bus only enables the CPU to tell the chipset what line of program to get, correct? Not anymore. Now the address bus has a second, very different function. The 8086 CPU used an extra wire, called the *input/output or memory* (IO/MEM) wire to notify devices that the CPU was *not* using the address bus to specify an address in memory (Figure 5-10). Instead, it was being used to communicate with a particular device. The 8086 address bus had 20 wires, but when the IO/MEM wire had voltage, only the first 16 wires were monitored by the devices. This is still true today. You may have a Pentium 4 with a 32-bit address bus, but the moment the CPU places a voltage on the IO/MEM wire, the RAM takes a nap and every device watches the first 16 wires on the address bus, waiting to see if one of their patterns of 1's and 0's comes up.

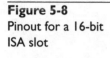

**Figure 5-8**
Pinout for a 16-bit
ISA slot

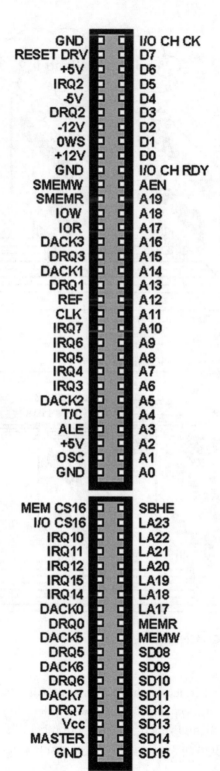

| | |
|---|---|
| GND | I/O CH CK |
| RESET DRV | D7 |
| +5V | D6 |
| IRQ2 | D5 |
| -5V | D4 |
| DRQ2 | D3 |
| -12V | D2 |
| 0WS | D1 |
| +12V | D0 |
| GND | I/O CH RDY |
| SMEMW | AEN |
| SMEMR | A19 |
| IOW | A18 |
| IOR | A17 |
| DACK3 | A16 |
| DRQ3 | A15 |
| DACK1 | A14 |
| DRQ1 | A13 |
| REF | A12 |
| CLK | A11 |
| IRQ7 | A10 |
| IRQ6 | A9 |
| IRQ5 | A8 |
| IRQ4 | A7 |
| IRQ3 | A6 |
| DACK2 | A5 |
| T/C | A4 |
| ALE | A3 |
| +5V | A2 |
| OSC | A1 |
| GND | A0 |
| | |
| MEM CS16 | SBHE |
| I/O CS16 | LA23 |
| IRQ10 | LA22 |
| IRQ11 | LA21 |
| IRQ12 | LA20 |
| IRQ15 | LA19 |
| IRQ14 | LA18 |
| DACK0 | LA17 |
| DRQ0 | MEMR |
| DACK5 | MEMW |
| DRQ5 | SD08 |
| DACK6 | SD09 |
| DRQ6 | SD10 |
| DACK7 | SD11 |
| DRQ7 | SD12 |
| Vcc | SD13 |
| MASTER | SD14 |
| GND | SD15 |

**Figure 5-9**   How can the CPU talk to only one device?

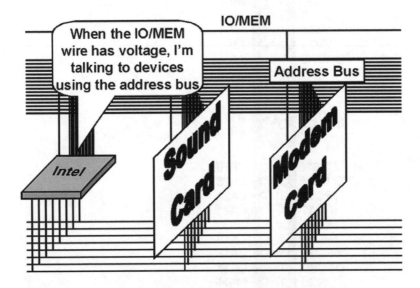

**Figure 5-10**   Function of IO/MEM wire

All devices, both those embedded on the motherboard (like the 8042 keyboard controller) and those inserted into expansion slots (like a video card), respond to special, unique patterns built into them. Every device gets a number of patterns—not just one pattern! Each different pattern of 16 1's and 0's is a unique command for that device.

For example, the keyboard controller has four unique patterns. The hard-drive controller responds to 16 unique commands, each telling the hard drive to perform a certain function. If the CPU lights up the IO/MEM wire and puts the pattern 0000000111110000 onto the address bus, the hard-drive controller will send back a message describing its error status. All the different patterns used by the CPU to talk to the devices inside your computer are known as the *I/O addresses* (Figure 5-11).

## Hexadecimal

Sorry, but before I go any further, we have to talk about hexadecimal numbers. I know that most of us hate the thought, but if you plan to fix computers, you have to know how to talk the dreaded hex!

This entire section is repeated, in a slightly different context, in the memory management chapter.

Don't panic. Hex is really almost trivial once you understand the secret. Hexadecimal, also known as base-16 mathematics, is a complete numbering system based on 16 instead of 10 digits. You can add, subtract, even do trigonometry with hex. Big deal! The only part of hex you need to know as an A+ Certified technician is how the PC world uses it. To help you understand hex, I will use the address bus. When the CPU turns the IO/MEM wire on, it can then use the first 16 address bus wires to talk to the devices in

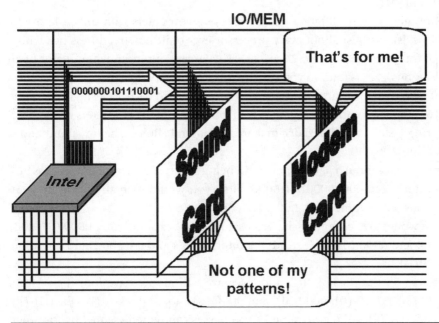

**Figure 5-11**   Sending an I/O address

the computer. These wires can have either voltage or no voltage on them. A wire with voltage is represented by 1, and a wire with no voltage is 0. With 16 wires, 65,536 different combinations of 1's and 0's are possible, from 0000000000000000 to 1111111111111111.

Each different combination of charged and uncharged wires represents one pattern that the CPU can send down the address bus to talk to some device. The problem here is that it is a real pain to say things like, "The command to tell the hard-drive controller to show its error status is 000000111110000." Think how difficult it would be to try to talk to someone about these different patterns of 1's and 0's! For example, try telling another person to write down the following series of 1's and 0's as you dictate them:

0010010001001001001001001001001001000010011111110101010101010000101011100

I guarantee that they will mess up somewhere as they try to write them down. Forget it! Although your computer is good at talking in 1's and 0's, human beings find it very difficult. We need some kind of shorthand, some way to talk about 1's and 0's so human beings can understand it. This is where hexadecimal becomes very useful. Hex is a shorthand description of the state of wires. In the PC world, hexadecimal is nothing more than a shorthand method of describing a series of binary values.

Pretend that you have a computer with a four-wire address bus. How many different patterns can you create? Look at all the possibilities of 1's and 0's you can make with four wires: 0000, 0001, 0010, 0011, 0100, 0101, 0110, 0111, 1000, 1001, 1010, 1011, 1100, 1101, 1110, and 1111.

Four wires give you 16 different possibilities. No computers with only a four-wire address bus exist, but just about every processor ever built has an address bus with a multiple of four wires (8, 16, 20, 24, or 32). The largest common denominator of all these address bus sizes is four, so you can use this four binary digit grouping to create a shorthand by representing any combination of four 1's and 0's with a single character. Because 16 different combinations are possible, the 16 unique characters of the base-16 numbering system called hexadecimal are the natural choice. The hex shorthand is shown in Table 5-1.

So when you talk about a particular pattern being sent to a device on the address bus, you would not specify 0000000111110000. First, you would mentally break these 16 digits into four sets of four: 0000, 0001, 1111, and 0000.

Then you would give each four-character set its own hex shorthand: 0000 (0), 0001 (1), 1111 (F), and 0000 (0). So instead of a bunch of 1's and 0's, you could say something like "01F0."

To represent all the possible I/O addresses, we will always have four digits, from all 0's—0000 (0), 0000 (0), 0000 (0), and 0000 (0)—to all ones—1111 (F), 1111 (F), 1111 (F), and 1111 (F). All the possible I/O addresses can be represented by four-digit hexadecimal values, starting at 0000 and ending at FFFF.

**Table 5-1** Possible Permutations for Four Wires

| BINARY NUMBER | | HEXADECIMAL VALUE |
|---|---|---|
| 0000 | All wires off | 0 |
| 0001 | Only 4th wire on | 1 |
| 0010 | Only 3rd wire on | 2 |
| 0011 | 3rd and 4th on | 3 |
| 0100 | Only 2nd wire on | 4 |
| 0101 | 2nd and 4th wire on | 5 |
| 0110 | 2nd and 3rd wire on | 6 |
| 0111 | Only 1st wire off | 7 |
| 1000 | Only 1st wire on | 8 |
| 1001 | 1st and 4th on | 9 |
| 1010 | 1st and 3rd on | A |
| 1011 | Only 2nd off | B |
| 1100 | 1st and 2nd on | C |
| 1101 | Only 3rd off | D |
| 1110 | Only 4th off | E |
| 1111 | All wires on | F |

This explanation of hexadecimal is heavily slanted to the concept of I/O addresses, but hex is used in many other areas of the PC. We'll revisit this entire concept during the discussion of memory management.

## The Rules of I/O Addresses

Three basic rules apply to I/O addresses: all devices have I/O addresses; all devices use more than one address; and two devices cannot have the same I/O address in a single system. Amazingly for the PC industry, these three rules apply universally.

### All Devices Must Have an I/O Address

This is how the CPU talks to everything in your computer and there is no exception. Every device in your computer either has a preset I/O address, or you must give it one. Basic devices in the computer have preset I/O addresses. For example, if you buy a hard-drive controller, it will have preset I/O addresses of 01F0 – 01FF. A sound card has to configure its own I/O address when you install it into a system.

### All Devices Use More than One I/O Address

All devices respond to more than one pattern of 1's and 0's. The CPU uses the different I/O addresses to give various commands to each device, and each device must also have one or more I/O addresses to respond to the CPU. For example, the hard drive's I/O address range is 01F0 – 01FF. If the CPU sends a 01F0 pattern, it asks the hard-drive controller if an error occurred anywhere. The command 01F1 is a totally separate command. No device has only one I/O address.

### Once a Device Has an I/O Address, No Other Device Can Use It

When you install an expansion card, such as a new sound card, in your system, you must know the I/O addresses currently taken. You then must make certain that the sound card uses I/O addresses that no other device uses. Every device in your computer has an I/O address. No two devices can share any I/O addresses; otherwise, the device(s) won't work.

So the big question here is "How do I know what I/O addresses are being used in my computer?" Fortunately, most of the I/O addresses were set up by IBM a long time ago. When IBM released the PC to the public domain, they provided a list of I/O addresses that manufacturers must use in order to make components and systems IBM compatible. This list, shown in Table 5-2, is still followed by every PC in the world today.

## Talking the Talk

Techs have a few quirks (go figure!) when discussing I/O addresses that you need to know in order to "talk the talk." Sixteen-bit I/O addresses, as you know from the preceding discussion, are always represented by four hexadecimal numbers, such as 01F0. When discussing I/O addresses, however, most techs drop the leading zeros. Techs refer to address 01F0, for example, as 1F0. Also, almost no one talks about the entire range of I/O addresses. We usually discuss only the first I/O address, which we call the *I/O base address*. If the hard drive uses the I/O addresses of 1F0-1FF, for example, the I/O base address is 1F0. Finally, when discussing any hex value, many people put a lowercase "h" on the end to show you it is a hex value. For example, some people will show the I/O base address for the floppy controller as 3F0h. Here are the talking rules in a nutshell:

- When talking about I/O addresses, always drop the leading zeros.
- All devices get a range of I/O addresses; the joystick, for example, uses I/O addresses 200 – 207.
- The I/O base address is the first I/O address for a device; the I/O base address for the joystick is 200.
- Many people put an "h" on the end of a hex value to show that it is hex; the I/O base address for the floppy is 3F0h.

**Table 5-2**   The Original IBM I/O Address List

| I/O ADDRESS RANGE | USAGE |
| --- | --- |
| 0000 – 000F | DMA controller |
| 0020 – 002F | Master IRQ controller |
| 0030 – 003F | Master IRQ controller |
| 0040 – 0043 | System timer |
| 0060 – 0063 | Keyboard |
| 0070 – 0071 | CMOS clock |
| 0080 – 008F | DMA page registers |
| 0090 – 009F | DMA page registers |
| 00A0 – 00AF | Slave IRQ controller |
| 00B0 – 00BF | Slave IRQ controller |
| 00C0 – 00CF | DMA controller |
| 00E0 – 00EF | Reserved |
| 00F0 – 00FF | Math coprocessor |
| 0170 – 0177 | Secondary hard drive controller |
| 01F0 – 01FF | Primary hard drive controller |
| 0200 – 0207 | Joystick |
| 0210 – 0217 | Reserved |
| 0278 – 027F | LPT2 |
| 02B0 – 02DF | Secondary EGA |
| 02E8 – 02EF | COM4 |
| 02F8 – 02FF | COM2 |
| 0378 – 037F | LPT1 |
| 03B0 – 03BF | Mono video |
| 03C0 – 03CF | Primary EGA |
| 03D0 – 03DF | CGA video |
| 03E8 – 03EF | COM3 |
| 03F0 – 03F7 | Floppy controller |
| 03F8 – 03FF | COM1 |

Armed with this knowledge, you can understand the I/O address map displayed in Table 5-3.

Take a close look at the I/O address map one more time. Notice that neither sound cards nor network cards have I/O addresses. In fact, IBM mapped out the I/O addresses for only the most common devices. So if you want to install a sound card, what I/O addresses are available? Look at I/O base address 210h, and then look at the next I/O base address—it's 278h, isn't it? All the I/O addresses between these two are open for use, so plenty of unused addresses are available! By the way, you'll notice that the last address is 3F8h, so couldn't you use all the addresses from 3F8 all the way to FFFF? Unfortunately, you can't, due to a limitation of both DOS and Windows. (Okay, there is a way, but bear with me for a moment and assume that you can't; I promise to explain later!)

I/O addresses provide a two-way communication pathway between peripherals and the CPU. If the CPU wants to talk to a device, it can run BIOS routines or device drivers (little programs, remember?) that can use I/O addresses to initiate conversations over the external data bus. Later in this chapter, this theory will be put into practice.

## Interrupts

The CPU can now communicate with all of the devices inside the computer, but a small problem still exists. I/O addressing enables two-way communication, but the CPU must start all that communication. A device such as a mouse can't send its own I/O address to the CPU to get the CPU's attention. So how does a device initiate a conversation with the CPU? For example, how does the mouse tell the CPU that it has moved? How does the keyboard tell the CPU that somebody just pressed the J key? The PC needs some kind of mechanism to tell the CPU to stop doing whatever it is doing and talk to a particular device (Figure 5-12).

This mechanism is called *interruption*. Every CPU in the PC world has an INT (interrupt) wire, shown in Figure 5-13. If this wire is charged, the CPU will stop what it is doing and deal with the device. Suppose you have a PC with only one peripheral, a keyboard. The CPU is running WordPerfect, and the user presses the J key. The keyboard is connected to the CPU's INT wire and charges the wire. The CPU temporarily stops running WordPerfect and runs the necessary BIOS routine to query the keyboard.

This would be fine if the computer had only one device. As we all know, however, PCs have many devices, and almost all of them will need to interrupt the CPU at some point. So the PC needs some kind of "traffic cop" chip to act as an intermediary between all the devices and the CPU's INT wire. The original IBM PC used a chip known as the 8259 to handle this function.

**Table 5-3**  Updated I/O Address Map

| I/O BASE ADDRESS | USAGE |
| --- | --- |
| 0h | DMA controller |
| 20h | Master IRQ controller |
| 30h | Master IRQ controller |
| 40h | System timer |
| 60h | Keyboard |
| 70h | CMOS clock |
| 80h | DMA page registers |
| 90h | DMA page registers |
| A0h | Slave IRQ controller |
| B0h | Slave IRQ controller |
| C0h | DMA controller |
| E0h | Reserved |
| F0h | Math coprocessor |
| 170h | Secondary hard drive controller |
| 1F0h | Primary hard drive controller |
| 200h | Joystick |
| 210h | Reserved |
| 278h | LPT2 |
| 2B0h | Secondary EGA |
| 2E8h | COM4 |
| 2F8h | COM2 |
| 378h | LPT1 |
| 3B0h | Mono video |
| 3C0h | Primary EGA |
| 3D0h | CGA video |
| 3E8h | COM3 |
| 3F0h | Floppy controller |
| 3F8h | COM1 |

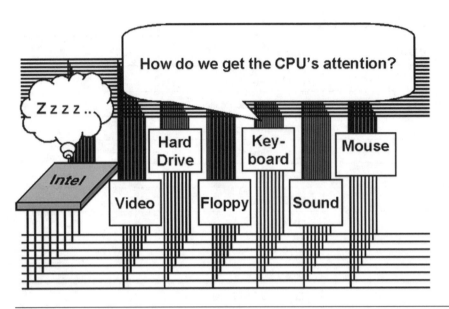

Figure 5-12   How do devices tell the CPU they need attention?

**Figure 5-13**
The INT wire

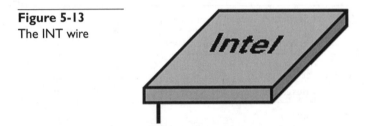

The 8259 hooked to the INT wire of the CPU on one side and had another eight wires called *interrupt requests* (IRQs) that extended out from the chip into the motherboard (Figure 5-14). Every device that needed to interrupt the CPU got an IRQ. If a device needed to interrupt the CPU, it lit its IRQ, and the 8259 then lit the INT wire on the CPU. Whenever the INT wire lit up, the CPU talked to the 8259 via its I/O addresses to determine which device had interrupted. The 8259 told the CPU which IRQ was lit, and this enabled the CPU to know which BIOS to run.

Most of the IRQ wires were dedicated to certain devices. IRQ0 went to a device called the system timer that told the RAM when to refresh. IRQ1 went to the keyboard, and the other six wires ran straight to the ISA expansion bus (Figure 5-15). So any ISA card could use IRQs 2 through 6. This system of IRQ usage, although developed way back in the early 1980s, is still used on today's PCs.

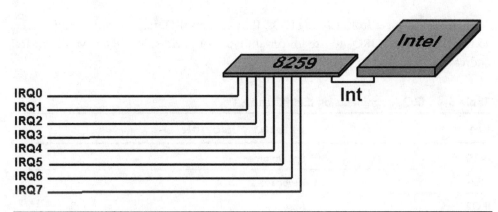

**Figure 5-14** The eight IRQs from the 8259

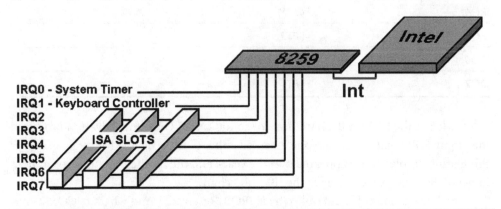

**Figure 5-15** IRQs for the system timer, keyboard controller, and ISA slots

## The Rules of IRQs

IRQ setup and use in a system follows a clear pair of rules. First, almost every device needs an IRQ. This includes devices built into the motherboard as well as devices that use the expansion bus slots. Second, under almost all circumstances, no two devices can share an IRQ. If one device uses IRQ3, for example, no other device can use that IRQ.

A few exceptions to rule one exist, most notably the joystick. A joystick doesn't use an IRQ. If you write a program to use a joystick, you have to write it to check the joystick constantly to see if a button has been pressed or if the stick has been moved.

Virtually every other device in a system, however, requires its own unique and individual IRQ. Technicians need to determine current IRQ usage and set up new devices to use available IRQs.

To prevent devices from sharing IRQs, IBM gave an IRQ map to card manufacturers so they knew which IRQs to use for certain types of devices, just like IBM did for I/O addresses (Table 5-4).

**Table 5-4**  IRQ Assignments on IBM PC and XT

| IRQ | DEFAULT FUNCTION |
| --- | --- |
| IRQ0 | System timer |
| IRQ1 | Keyboard |
| IRQ2 | Reserved |
| IRQ3 | COM2 |
| IRQ4 | COM1 |
| IRQ5 | LPT2 |
| IRQ6 | Floppy drive |
| IRQ7 | LPT1 |

So, where's the IRQ for the hard drive or sound cards? Unfortunately, IBM produced the original IRQ map before anyone invented either of these devices! Several "fixes" for this glaring problem have appeared over the years, and the next few sections cover them in detail. But first, look closely at the IBM IRQ chart.

Several things should stand out. Why is IRQ2 "reserved"? And what are COM2, and LPT1? Let's look at IRQ2 first. IBM didn't want anyone to use IRQ2; they were going to use it for something special, a mainframe card called the 3270. IBM thought that most PCs would hook up to mainframes, so they wanted to keep IRQ2 just for these 3270 cards.

The COM and LPT ports have caused tremendous confusion for techs over the years, so they warrant a more extensive explanation. Let's take a moment to discuss what they are and how they function in the PC.

## COM and LPT Ports

IRQs and I/O addresses were not invented for the IBM PC. Mainframes, minis, and pre-PC microcomputers all used IRQs and I/O addresses. When IBM designed the PC, they wanted to simplify the installation, programming, and operation of devices. Because virtually every peripheral needs both an IRQ and I/O address, IBM created standard preset combinations of IRQs and I/O addresses. For *serial* devices, the preset combinations are called COM ports. For *parallel* devices, they are called LPT ports. The word "port" is used to describe a "portal" or two-way access. Table 5-5 lists the preset combinations of I/O addresses and IRQs.

**Table 5-5**   COM and LPT Assignments

| PORT | I/O ADDRESS | IRQ |
|------|-------------|-----|
| COM1 | 3F8 | 4 |
| COM2 | 2F8 | 3 |
| LPT1 | 378 | 7 |
| LPT2 | 278 | 5 |

Ports do make installation easier. Consider modems; many do not have a setting for IRQs or I/O addresses. Instead, you set their COM port. Most people do not realize that when they select a COM port, they actually assign the IRQ and I/O address. If you set a modem to COM1, for example, you set that modem's IRQ to 4 and the modem's I/O address to 3F8 (Table 5-5).

**NOTE   COM and LPT ports are nothing more than preset combinations of IRQs and I/O addresses.**

Programmers also enjoy the benefits of ports. Support for all ports is built into the system BIOS, so programmers do not have to know the I/O address for a modem. They simply run the BIOS routine to output data or commands to the appropriate COM port, and the BIOS routine translates and sends the command or data to the correct I/O address. Even operating systems understand ports. Open an MS-DOS prompt in Windows 2000 and type **DIR > LPT1**. Windows knows which BIOS routine to activate so that the directory will output to the printer instead of the monitor.

### COM3 and COM4

Back in the original PCs, IBM dedicated two IRQs to serial ports: IRQ4 for COM1 and IRQ3 for COM2. Many systems needed more than two serial devices, however, and a lot of complaining erupted concerning the lack of COM ports. IBM then established two more COM port standards, COM3 and COM4, and assigned two previously unused sets of I/O addresses (3E8-3EF for COM3 and 2E8-2EF for COM4) to these ports (Table 5-6).

**Table 5-6**  COM Port Assignments

| COM PORT | IRQ | I/O BASE ADDRESS |
|----------|-----|------------------|
| COM1 | 4 | 3F8H |
| COM2 | 3 | 2F8H |
| COM3 | 4 | 3E8H |
| COM4 | 3 | 2E8H |

Remember, this was in the days when only one 8259 existed, so no extra IRQs were available. So IBM just doubled them up. COM3 used IRQ4, and COM4 used IRQ3. Hey, wait a minute! One of the most important rules for setting IRQs is that two devices should not share an IRQ. However, an exception to that rule is that two (or more) devices can share the same IRQ as long as they never talk at the same time!

Back in the old days, many devices could share IRQs. For example, you could have a dedicated fax card and a modem on the same IRQ. Neither device had a device driver (they used the BIOS for the COM port), and the fax would never run at the same time as the modem (this was before Windows). So these two devices could be set to COM1 and COM3. In today's computers, you can no longer set one device as COM1 and another device as COM3, or one device as COM2 and another as COM4. If you do, the computer will lock up.

If you accidentally have two devices sharing the same IRQ, the computer will eventually lock up. You won't destroy anything; just correct the problem and try again.

### LPT Ports

LPT port settings apply to parallel connections for devices such as printers. In the old days, in fact, only high-speed printers used parallel ports. When IBM standardized ports for parallel devices, they called them LPT ports—"LPT" being an abbreviation for line printer. Although IBM assigned both an I/O address and IRQ to the LPT ports, no devices at the time needed the IRQ. IBM therefore standardized the LPT ports so that they would not talk back. This meant IRQ7 for LPT1 and IRQ5 for LPT2 were never used by the LPT port, and other devices could "share" them.

Today, that picture has changed. Many devices other than simple line printers plug into the parallel port in the back of your PC. These devices (for example, tape backups and ZIP drives) use an interrupt. So, if you use IRQ7 for another device, do not plug anything other than your printer into LPT1. Even that might not work, however, because most new printers use the IRQ assigned to the port! If you need an extra parallel port, you can still purchase an LPT2 parallel port card.

## Physical vs. I/O Ports

Something needs to be clarified right away. A serial port is a physical item, a 9- or 15-pin male DB connector in the back of your PC, but a COM port is just the I/O address and IRQ assigned to it. A parallel port is a 25-pin female DB connector on the back of your PC, but an LPT is just the I/O address and IRQ assigned to it. Think of a telephone. If someone pointed to your phone and said, "that is a 555-1234," you would correct him or her: "No, that's a telephone. The number assigned to it is 555-1234." The same is true with serial and parallel ports. You would not look at a serial port and say, "That's COM1" (Figure 5-16).

**Figure 5-16**
Physical vs. I/O ports

## Back to the 8259

With the original PC, IBM discovered that six IRQs were not enough for most systems, so when they invented the 286 AT, IBM added another 8259. The 8259 was designed to run in a "cascade" (Figure 5-17), which means that you can hook another 8259 to the first 8259, but the INT connection on the second 8259 has to take one of the IRQs from the first 8259. IBM decided to take the INT wire from the second 8259 and hook it into the IRQ2 of the first. This created a problem, however, because many cards already used IRQ2. So IBM ran the IRQ9 wire over to the IRQ2 position on the ISA slot, enabling older cards to work. This cascading procedure added eight more IRQs, but took one away in the process. The eight new wires ran to the extension on the 16-bit ISA expansion slot (Table 5-7).

Table 5-7 lists the IRQ map as designed for the two 8259s in the original IBM AT computer. Again, notice that the cascade removes IRQ2. IRQ9 hooks to the old IRQ2 wire, so if a device is designed to run on IRQ2, it will run on IRQ9. In essence, IRQ2

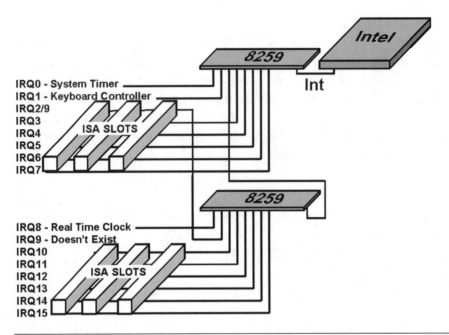

IRQ0 - System Timer
IRQ1 - Keyboard Controller
IRQ2/9
IRQ3
IRQ4
IRQ5
IRQ6
IRQ7

IRQ8 - Real Time Clock
IRQ9 - Doesn't Exist
IRQ10
IRQ11
IRQ12
IRQ13
IRQ14
IRQ15

**Figure 5-17**  Dual 8259 cascade

and IRQ9 are the same IRQ. Three IRQs are hard-wired (0, 1, and 8). Four IRQs have assignments so common that no PC or device maker dares change them for fear that their devices will not be compatible (6, 13, 14, and 15). Four IRQs default to specific types of devices, but are very changeable as long as the hardware device enables it (IRQ 3, 4, 5, and 7). The rest (IRQ2/9, 10, 11, and 12) are not specific and are open for use.

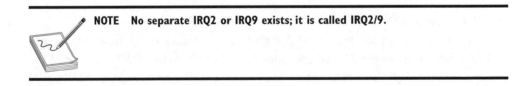

**NOTE**  No separate IRQ2 or IRQ9 exists; it is called IRQ2/9.

**Table 5-7**  IRQ Assignments with COM3 and COM4

| IRQ | DEFAULT FUNCTION |
|-----|------------------|
| IRQ0 | System timer |
| IRQ1 | Keyboard |
| IRQ2/9 | Open for use |

**Table 5-7** IRQ Assignments with COM3 and COM4 (*continued*)

| IRQ | DEFAULT FUNCTION |
| --- | --- |
| IRQ3 | Default COM2, COM4 |
| IRQ4 | Default COM1, COM3 |
| IRQ5 | LPT2 |
| IRQ6 | Floppy drive |
| IRQ7 | LPT1 |
| IRQ8 | Real-time clock |
| IRQ10 | Open for use |
| IRQ11 | Open for use |
| IRQ12 | Open for use |
| IRQ13 | Math coprocessor |
| IRQ14 | Primary hard drive controller |
| IRQ15 | Secondary hard drive controller |

These settings are somewhat flexible. If a device that uses a certain IRQ is not present, then another device can use that IRQ. For example, if you do not have a secondary hard-drive controller, you can use IRQ15 for another device.

## COM and LPT Ports Today

Confusion concerning COM and LPT ports still remains among techs today. But now that you understand what IBM originally set up, that confusion can be eliminated. First, even though IBM dictated a specific I/O address and IRQ for a particular COM or LPT port, you can change the IRQ as long as the device can handle it and the software that talks to that device knows about the change. So you can change, say, COM1's IRQ from 4 to 5 if the hardware and software enables it. Let's use my motherboard as an example. My computer, like most computers today, has two built-in serial ports. You can change the COM port settings by accessing the CMOS (Figure 5-18).

Note that serial port 1 is set to I/O address 3F8 and IRQ4. What COM port is that? It's COM1, but that serial port could be changed to any of the following settings:

- 3F8/IRQ4: standard COM1
- 2F8/IRQ3: standard COM2
- 3F8/IRQ5: COM1 I/O address combined with the nonstandard IRQ5
- 2F8/IRQ5: COM2 I/O address combined with the nonstandard IRQ5

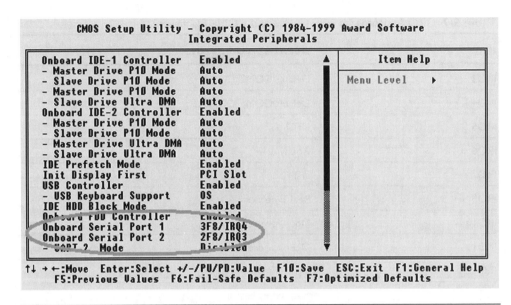

**Figure 5-18**  Port settings for an onboard serial port

In current usage, therefore, COM1, COM2, and so forth, often refer specifically to the I/O address (Table 5-8), but not necessarily to the IRQ. Many motherboards, for example, show the default serial port settings as "COM1/IRQ4" or "COM2/IRQ3." We know by definition that COM1 uses IRQ4 and COM2 uses IRQ3. Why do they do this? Why don't they simply show "COM1" and "COM2"? Why add the IRQs if any decent A+ Certified tech already knows this? In this day of COM ports that easily change to non-standard IRQs, the motherboard folks separate the COM port from the IRQ, ensuring that you won't accidentally create an unintentional conflict.

**Table 5-8**  Classic Open I/O Addresses

| 0170 – 0177 | **SECONDARY HARD DRIVE CONTROLLER** |
|---|---|
| **0178 – 01EF** | **Open for use** |
| 01F0 – 01FF | Primary hard drive controller |
| 0200 – 0207 | Joystick |
| 0210 – 0217 | Reserved |
| **0218 – 0277** | **Open for use, common sound card** |
| 0278 – 027F | LPT2 |

**Table 5-8** Classic Open I/O Addresses (*continued*)

| 0170 – 0177 | SECONDARY HARD DRIVE CONTROLLER |
|---|---|
| **0280 – 02AF** | **Open for use** |
| 02B0 – 02DF | Secondary EGA |
| 02E8 – 02EF | COM4 |
| 02F8 – 02FF | COM2 |
| **0300 – 0377** | **Open for use, common network, sound** |
| 0378 – 037F | LPT1 |
| 03B0 – 03BF | Mono video |

If a standard device does not use the IRQ assigned to it or if you don't have that device, the IRQ assigned to that device is open for use. The most common example of this is LPT2, which uses IRQ5. Most PCs today don't have a second parallel port, so various other devices often use IRQ5. Sound cards, for example, usually want to be set to IRQ5.

Don't forget that if you set a device to a COM or LPT port, you are using an IRQ. This is always a big problem for new technicians who don't understand IRQs and their relationship to COM and LPT ports. Most people have already heard that you don't let more than one device use an IRQ. But because they don't know that a COM or LPT port is by definition an I/O address and an IRQ combination, they get into trouble. If someone has a device set to COM1 and then tries to install some other device to IRQ4, the system will lock up. But they don't see the error, because they don't realize that part of COM1 is IRQ4!

The combination of I/O address and IRQ is the cornerstone of CPU-device communication. But one more aspect of this communication must be discussed—the badly misunderstood concept of DMA.

## Direct Memory Access (DMA)

CPUs do a lot of work. They run the BIOS, operating system, and applications. CPUs handle interrupts and access I/O addresses. CPUs also deal with one other item: data. CPUs constantly manipulate data. CPUs move data from one place in RAM to another. Peripherals (for example, a scanner or a laser printer) send data to RAM via the CPU, and the CPU sends data from RAM to peripherals.

Moving all this data is obviously necessary, but it is also very simple to do. Moving data wastes the CPU's power and time. Moreover, with all of the caches and such on today's CPUs, most of the time the system does nothing while the CPU handles some internal calculation (Figure 5-19).

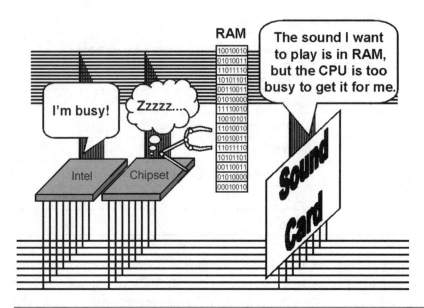

**Figure 5-19** The need for DMA

So, why not make devices that access memory directly, without involving the CPU (Figure 5-20)? The process of accessing memory without using the CPU is called *Direct Memory Access* (DMA).

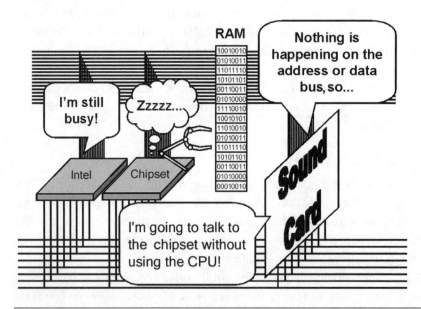

**Figure 5-20** Why not talk to the chipset directly?

DMA enables the system to run background applications without interfering with the CPU (Figure 5-21). This is excellent for creating background sounds in games, and for accessing floppy and hard drives.

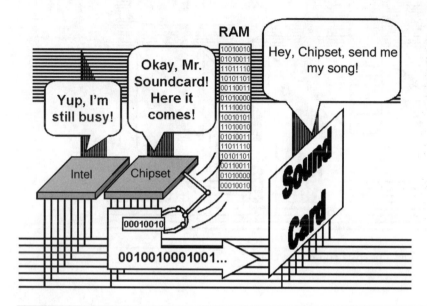

**Figure 5-21**   DMA in action

The concept of DMA as described here, however, has a problem. What if more than one device wants to use DMA? What keeps these devices from stomping on the external data bus at the same time? Plus, what if the CPU suddenly needs the data bus? How can you stop the device using DMA so the CPU, which should have priority, can access the bus (Figure 5-22)?

Knowing this, IBM installed another, very simple CPU called the 8237 chip to control all DMA functions (Figure 5-23). This primitive CPU can handle all the data passing from peripherals to RAM and vice versa. This takes necessary but simple work away from the CPU, so the CPU can spend time doing more productive work.

The DMA chip sends data along the external data bus when the CPU is busy and not using the external data bus. This is perfectly acceptable because the CPU accesses the external data bus only a small percentage of the time: 20 percent of the time on a 486, and 5 percent of the time on a Pentium or later CPU.

The 8237 chip links to the CPU via the HRQ wire. The 8237 uses the HRQ wire to inform the CPU when the external data bus is going to be busy. The 8237 has four wires, called *DMA requests* (DRQs), which lead to the DRAM refresh circuitry and ISA slots. DRQs were, and still are, more commonly known as *DMA channels*. If a device wants to perform a DMA data transfer, it must activate its assigned DMA channel (Figure 5-24).

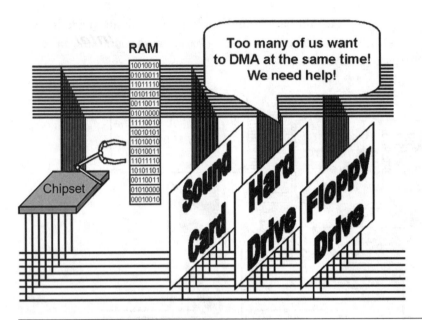

**Figure 5-22**   DMA needs a controlling chip

**Figure 5-23**
The 8237 controls
DMA transfers.

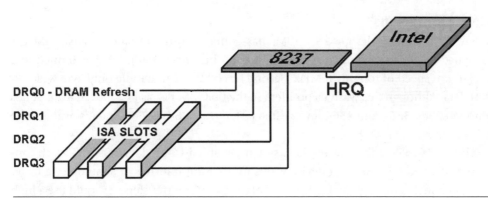

**Figure 5-24**   8237 in the original IBM PC

DRQs work exactly like IRQs, with all the same rules such as no two devices being able to share the same DMA channel. "DMA channel" and "DRQ" are identical terms. No two devices can share DRQs.

From the days of the 286 to the present, all systems have two cascaded DMA controller chips, for a total of seven DRQs; DRQ0, and DRQ4 are the same, just as IRQ2 and IRQ9 are the same (Figure 5-25). However, you never say DRQ04, just DRQ0.

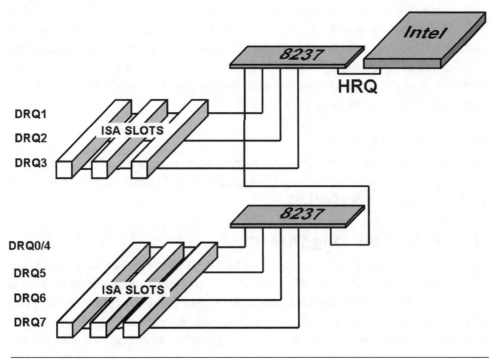

**Figure 5-25**   Cascaded 8237s

## DMA Limitations

DMA, as originally designed by IBM, has some serious limitations. First, DMA is designed to run from cards installed on the ISA bus. As a result, DMA is limited to a maximum speed of roughly 8 MHz. Second, each 8237 can handle only byte-wide (8-bit) data. Although this wasn't a problem in the first IBM PC, as PCs moved from 8088s through 286s, 386s, and 486s, it was often faster to skip 8-bit DMA and just wait for the CPU to move data.

The dual 8237s in the 286 and later systems enabled 16-bit data transfers—each controller handled one byte. If a device wants to use 8-bit transfers, it should use a lower DMA channel: 0 through 3. If a device wants to use 16-bit transfers, it should use a high DMA channel: 5 through 7. But even 16-bit data transfers ran at 8 MHz, which made them too slow for modern systems. This slowness relegated "Classic" DMA to low-speed, background jobs like floppy drive access, sound creation, and tape backup. A new process called *bus mastering*, however, has created a resurgence in the use of DMA in modern systems.

## Bus Mastering

Most devices today that use DMA do so without accessing the 8237s or the CPU. These devices are known as *bus masters*. Bus-mastering devices skip the 8237 altogether; they have circuitry that enables them to watch for other devices accessing the external data bus and can "get out of the way" on their own. Bus mastering has become extremely popular in hard drives. All of today's EIDE hard drives take advantage of bus mastering. Hard-drive bus mastering is hidden under terms such as "ULTRA DMA," and for the most part is totally automatic and invisible. See Chapter 8 for a detailed discussion of how hard drives use bus-mastering DMA.

## Who Uses Classic DMA?

Not very many devices use classic DMA. On most systems, only sound cards and floppy drives still use classic DMA. However, you may still find virtually any type of device designed to use DMA. See Table 5-9.

## Understand the "Big Three!"

Although it is important to understand the "whys" of I/O addresses, IRQs, and DMA, we also need to discuss the "hows" of installation, configuration, and troubleshooting these "big three." Today's PnP card installation makes problems more rare, but problems still occur often enough to warrant a good understanding of I/O addresses, IRQs, and DMA. The best way to do this is to give you a solid methodology to ensure that you can set up any device in any PC with a minimum of effort and a maximum of speed. Let's take a look at the more modern expansion buses available today and see how the "big three" fit into the picture of the modern PC.

**Table 5-9**   DMA Assignments

| DMA CHANNEL | TYPE | FUNCTION |
|:---:|---|---|
| 0 | 8-bit | None |
| 1 | 8-bit | Open for use |
| 2 | 8-bit | Floppy drive controller |
| 3 | 8-bit | Open for use |
| 5 | 16-bit | Open for use |
| 6 | 16-bit | Open for use |
| 7 | 16-bit | Open for use |

## A Better Bus

The first-generation expansion buses, 8-bit and 16-bit ISA, were both excellent buses for their time. In fact, the 16-bit ISA (which is often referred to as just "ISA") continues to soldier on in most PCs available today. Yet the ISA bus suffers from a couple of tremendous limitations. It is slow, running at up to only 8.33 MHz. It is also narrow and unable to handle the 32-bit and 64-bit external data buses of more modern processors. When Intel introduced the 386, there was tremendous demand to improve or even replace the ISA bus to correct these deficiencies. Let's look at this evolution of later-generation expansion buses in order to bring you up to date with the systems of today.

## History of PC Expansion Buses: Part 2

So far I have talked about only two types of expansion buses: 8-bit ISA and 16-bit ISA. The ISA buses run at a maximum of 8.33 MHz, although most run at around 7 MHz. The buses require users to configure I/O addresses, IRQs, and DMAs manually. The technology is free, however, because IBM released the design to the public domain.

## MCA

When the 386 CPU appeared in 1986, IBM decided to create a new type of expansion bus called *Microchannel Architecture* (MCA). Microchannel had a 32-bit bus to match the 386 (and later the 486) CPU's 32-bit external data bus. It was also faster than the ISA bus, running at about 12 MHz. What really made the MCA bus different was its ability to self-configure devices. When you bought a Microchannel device, it always came with a diskette called an options disk. You simply installed a new device in the microchannel computer, inserted the options disk when prompted, and the system automatically configured the IRQ, I/O addresses, and DMA channel! MCA was an excellent bus.

MCA had some major drawbacks. First, the slots were different, making MCA motherboards incompatible with ISA cards (Figure 5-26). Second, MCA was a licensed product of IBM, meaning that IBM did not release it to the public domain (which made MCA expensive).

MCA is now a dead technology. Virtually no manufacturers other than IBM made MCA computers, primarily because of licensing and manufacturing costs. Today, newer buses perform all the functions of MCA at a fraction of the cost.

**Figure 5-26**   Microchannel slots

## EISA

When MCA came out in the mid-1980s, it created quite a stir both for its technology and IBM's heavy-handedness. IBM tried not only to regain control of bus standards, but also to charge for licensing of that standard. As you might imagine, the rest of the industry did not like that! An industry group of clone makers created a competitor to MCA called *Enhanced ISA* (EISA—"EE-suh") in 1988. EISA did everything that MCA did: it was a faster, 32-bit, self-configuring expansion bus. EISA had two aspects that made it an attractive alternative to MCA. First, it was much cheaper than MCA, although not nearly as cheap as ISA. Second, EISA used a unique double-slot connector that was compatible with ISA devices (Figure 5-27). EISA was considered the high-end expansion bus for years and virtually eliminated MCA on its own. Like MCA, EISA is now considered a dead technology.

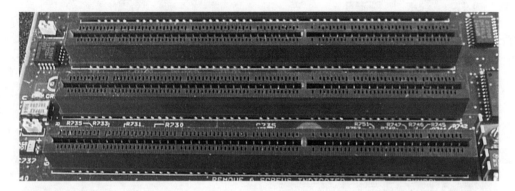

**Figure 5-27**   EISA slots

## VESA VL BUS

Although MCA and EISA offered attractive 32-bit solutions, most system manufacturers (and purchasers) continued to use ISA motherboards and expansion cards. Before Windows, the expansion bus speed of the ISA slots (7 MHz) sufficed for most tasks. As a result, virtually all 386 and early 486 systems had a strange combination of 32-bit external data and address buses running at the speed of the CPU, connected to a 7 MHz, 16-bit expansion bus. In essence, you had two data buses: a fast, wide local bus and a slow, narrow expansion bus (Figure 5-28).

Microsoft Windows changed that. The *graphical user interface* (GUI) of Windows put huge new demands on video. The 16-bit data path and 7-MHz top speed of the ISA video cards could not keep up with these new demands. To increase throughput, the *Video Electronics Standards Association* (VESA) created the *VESA local* (VL) bus. The VL bus solved both the speed and throughput problems by tapping into the "local" bus what we call the "frontside bus today (Figure 5-29).

By tapping directly into the local bus, VL-bus devices could use the full 32-bit data bus available on 386 and 486 machines. In addition, VL-bus devices could run at either the speed of the system bus (synchronously) or at the speed of a crystal on the VL bus itself (asynchronously). The VL bus had a top practical speed of 33 MHz.

VL- bus slots were parasitic slots (Figure 5-30). Each VL-bus slot was paired with another bus slot, usually a 16-bit ISA slot.

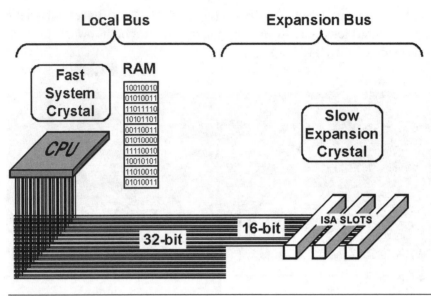

**Figure 5-28**   Local vs. expansion bus

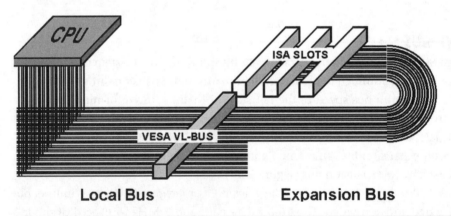

**Figure 5-29**   VESA VL bus

VL bus relied on the ISA slot for all basic control functions (I/O addressing, IRQs, DMA, and so on). The VL-bus slot controlled only the functions specific to VL-bus devices, including burst mode (the ability to "grab" control of the data bus for a few clicks of the clock), bus mastering, and 32-bit data transfers.

VL bus was a cheap, simple way to get a fast, wide data path. Except for the extra slot connection, installation of VL-bus devices was identical to the installation of any ISA device. You plugged in the VL-bus card, set the IRQ, I/O address, and DMA (if applicable), and you were ready to go.

**Figure 5-30**   VESA VL-bus slots

VL-bus systems provided an excellent upgrade solution for people with existing ISA expansion cards and a need for the speed and throughput to run Windows, but enjoyed only a short run on PC systems. The debut of the PCI bus architecture made VL bus obsolete, although the latter continued to run on many 486 systems.

## PCI

Intel introduced the *Peripheral Component Interconnect* (PCI) bus architecture (Figure 5-31) around the same time as it debuted the Pentium processor. Intel released PCI to the public domain, which certainly made PCI very attractive to manufacturers. The exceptional technology of the new bus, combined with the lack of a price tag, made manufacturers quickly adopt PCI and turn it into the standard for every motherboard today. PCI provides a stronger, faster, more flexible alternative to any other expansion bus.

Although the speed and bus-width of typical PCI systems differ little from those of VL-bus systems (most PCI boards run 32-bits at 33 MHz, just like VL-bus boards), the technology marks a radical departure in several ways. The flexible design enables PCI to coexist with other buses and scale up in speed and throughput. PCI devices are all self-configuring, and most can use fully bus-mastered DMA. Finally, PCI has a powerful burst mode feature that enables very efficient data transfers. All of these issues warrant further discussion, especially because you will work with lots of PCI motherboards and devices!

### Flexible Design

Intel built tremendous flexibility into the PCI specifications. Unlike many preceding expansion bus types, PCI functions independently of any type of CPU. Even Apple's Macintosh computers use PCI. We call PCI a "mezzanine" bus because it actually sits between the front-side (local) bus and any other expansion bus on the motherboard.

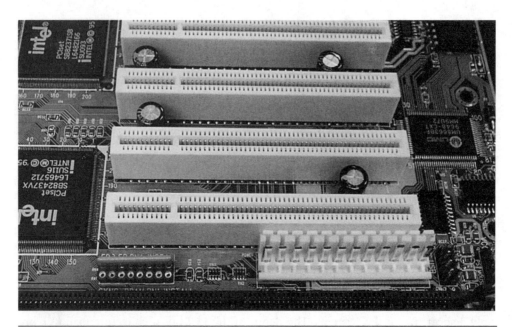

**Figure 5-31**    PCI expansion bus slots

In other words, PCI exists by itself on the motherboard, or it works with any other expansion bus. The only common combination is PCI with ISA (Figure 5-32).

The specifications also enable variation within PCI itself. Motherboard and expansion card manufacturers, for example, can produce 32-bit, 33-MHz components (the vast majority of PCs), or throw caution to the winds and produce 64-bit, 66-MHz components. They can even mix and match, creating 64-bit, 33-MHz components, and then put all three slots on the same motherboard!

Figure 5-33 shows a diagram of a classic PCI configuration. Note that it has two chips. PCI divides the chipset duties between two chips, the *northbridge* and the *southbridge*. The northbridge performs all of the classic chipset functions and controls the PCI bus. The southbridge acts as the intermediary between the PCI bus and whatever other bus you have on the motherboard (typically ISA—see the "Chipsets" section at the end of this chapter). Many terms exist for these two chips. Techs often refer to the northbridge as the PCI controller, for example, and the southbridge as the PCI to ISA bridge or just PCI bridge. Be ready to use these terms interchangeably!

### Self-Configuring

PCI enables completely self-configuring devices, which makes installation a breeze compared with ISA or VL-bus devices! Although PCI devices still need interrupts and I/O addresses, the PCI bus sets these resources. The *PCI Special Interest Group* (PCI SIG—the organization that defines the PCI standards) assumed that you will have

**Figure 5-32** PCI and ISA expansion bus slots

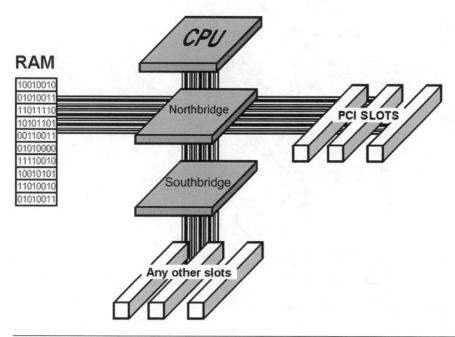

**Figure 5-33** PCI bus

a sound card, a network card, SCSI controller, and so on. In fact, they assumed that you might have multiple sound cards, network cards, SCSI controllers, etc. PCI SIG defined the I/O addresses and interrupts for multiple occurrences of virtually every device commonly in use today, as well as some not-yet-common devices. The intelligent PCI mezzanine bus interrogates PCI cards as they are installed and assigns them to preset I/O addresses and IRQs.

PCI supports I/O addresses past 3F8h—all the way up to FFFFh. PCI does not use IRQs; instead, it uses shareable "Interrupt Channels" labeled "INTA," "INTB," "INTC," and "INTD." The makers of the PCI devices configure these interrupt channels at manufacture, and only in the most rare of occasions do we need to change them.

### Bus Mastering

PCI implements bus-mastering DMA completely. Bus-mastering enables PCI devices to do things that ISA or VL-bus devices could never dream of doing. Two PCI devices can transfer data between themselves, for example, while the CPU uses the front-side bus, provided the CPU is not communicating with another PCI device (Figure 5-34). ISA devices, as you may recall, could only transfer data to and from RAM.

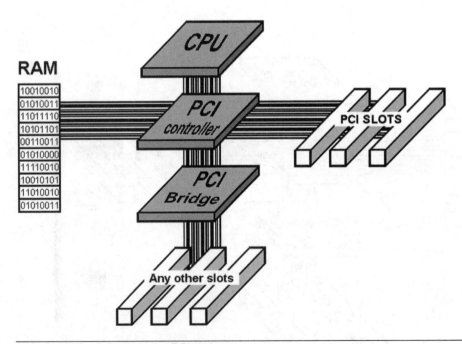

**Figure 5-34**   Bus mastering PCI style

## Burst Mode

Finally, the PCI bus uses a powerful "burst mode" that makes data transfers very efficient. The PCI bus recognizes when the reads or writes in its buffer have consecutive addresses. Instead of addressing each byte individually, the PCI bus groups them into packets and sends them to the PCI device as a single burst. The receiving unit assumes that consecutive bytes are to be written to consecutive addresses, eliminating the need to use up a clock cycle to relay addressing information. The PCI bus employs this burst mode independently of the CPU. Data sent by the CPU hits the PCI bus as individually addressed bytes, and the PCI bus converts them into bursts.

It is impossible to purchase a new motherboard today that is not PCI. The only real option you can get in expansion slots is PCI and ISA, or PCI alone. No doubt about it, PCI is king.

## AGP

If you have a modern motherboard, you will almost certainly notice a single connector that looks like a PCI slot, but is slightly shorter and usually brown (Figure 5-35). You also probably have a video card inserted into this strange little slot. This is an *Advanced Graphics Port* (AGP) slot. Only video cards use AGP, so the AGP discussion is saved for the video chapter.

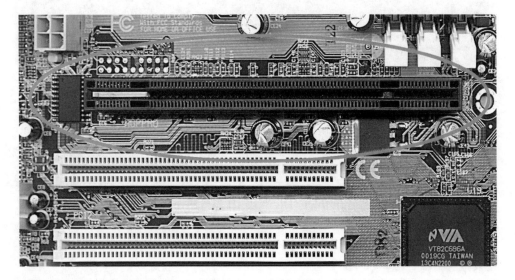

**Figure 5-35** AGP slot

## PC Cards

The PC card bus, once known as *Personal Computer Memory Card International Association* (PCMCIA), was designed to give laptop computers a measure of flexibility. The PC card bus manifests itself through the use of small, flat cards that are inserted into slots in the side of laptops (Figure 5-36). PC cards can be any type of device. Some of the more common PC card devices are modems, network cards, hard drives, and SCSI host adapters.

**Figure 5-36** PC card

PC cards are available in three standard thicknesses. The first, Type I, is 3.3 mm thick. These cards are rarely used today. The second, Type II, is slightly thicker than the Type I card at 5 mm. Manufacturers put an amazing variety of devices in Type II cards, which makes them the most common PC card in use today. The last standard thickness is Type III, which is 10.5 mm thick. The Type III card is used primarily for hard drives. We'll see more of PC cards in Chapter 18.

## Plug and Play (PnP)

Although PnP is not a type of expansion bus, I need to take a moment to explain the concept of PnP before moving into device installation. PnP consists of a series of standards designed to enable devices to self-configure. PnP is a broad standard, crossing over every type of expansion bus. PnP, in theory, makes device installation trivial. You simply install a device, and it automatically configures its I/O address, IRQ, and DMA with no user intervention. Unfortunately, given the amazing variety of devices currently used in PCs all over the world, PnP has yet to reach this worthy goal—but it's getting very close!

## Identifying Plug and Play

For PnP to work properly, the PC needs three items. First, you need a PnP BIOS. If you have a Pentium or later computer, you have a PnP BIOS. Sometimes you can verify this by watching the boot process, but to be sure, you must go into the CMOS utility. Figure 5-37 shows a typical PnP BIOS. Figure 5-38 shows the PnP/PCI Configurations screen.

Second, PnP also requires a PnP operating system such as Windows 95, Windows 98, or Windows 2000. Older operating systems, such as DOS and Windows 3.x, could only utilize PnP devices with the help of special device drivers and utility programs. Thankfully, the A+ exam isn't interested in these old operating systems.

Finally, you need a PnP device. How do you identify a PnP device? It's easy! No one makes non-PnP devices anymore! Every modem, every network card, every sound card, every everything fully supports PnP. Non-PnP devices belong in a museum. Unfortunately, although no one makes non-PnP devices any longer, the large installed base of non-PnP devices (we call non-PnP devices "legacy" devices) motivates CompTIA to test your skills installing them.

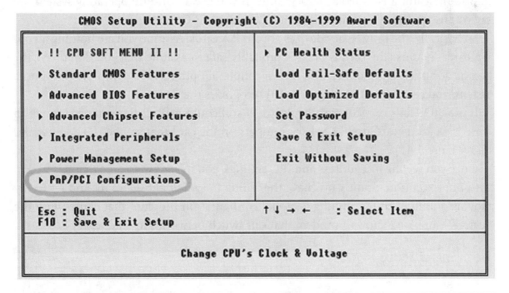

**Figure 5-37** PnP BIOS

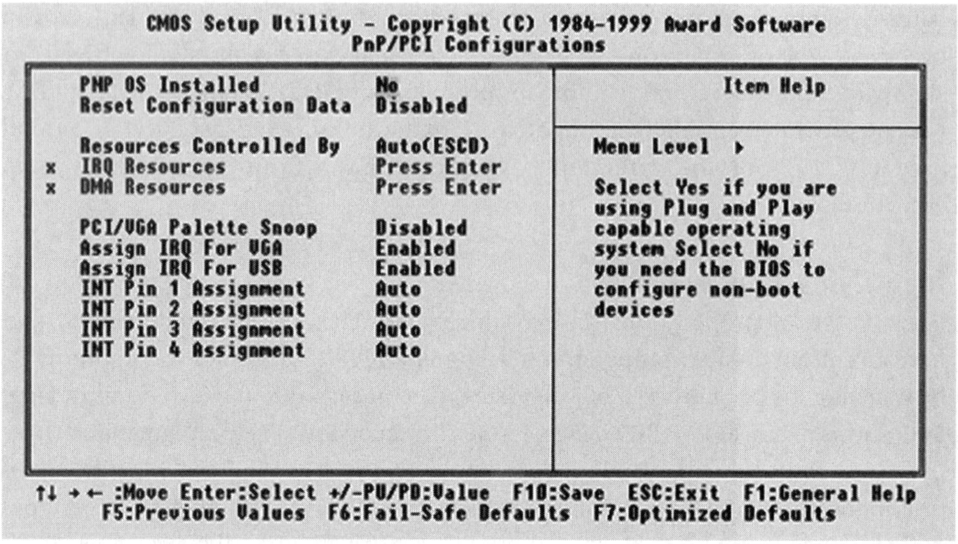

```
        CMOS Setup Utility - Copyright (C) 1984-1999 Award Software
                            PnP/PCI Configurations

    PNP OS Installed           No                       Item Help
    Reset Configuration Data   Disabled

    Resources Controlled By    Auto(ESCD)        Menu Level  ▶
  x IRQ Resources              Press Enter
  x DMA Resources              Press Enter       Select Yes if you are
                                                 using Plug and Play
    PCI/VGA Palette Snoop      Disabled          capable operating
    Assign IRQ For VGA         Enabled           system Select No if
    Assign IRQ For USB         Enabled           you need the BIOS to
    INT Pin 1 Assignment       Auto              configure non-boot
    INT Pin 2 Assignment       Auto              devices
    INT Pin 3 Assignment       Auto
    INT Pin 4 Assignment       Auto


  ↑↓ →← :Move Enter:Select +/-PU/PD:Value  F10:Save  ESC:Exit  F1:General Help
         F5:Previous Values  F6:Fail-Safe Defaults  F7:Optimized Defaults
```

**Figure 5-38**   Award BIOS PnP screen

So that leads us to the original question: How do you tell a PnP device from a legacy device? First of all, every PCI and AGP device is PnP. New ISA devices clearly advertise their PnP capabilities on the box as well as in the device's documentation (Figure 5-39).

The word "legacy" works for any non-PnP aspect of the system. For example, if you have a non-PnP motherboard, it is called a "legacy motherboard." If you have a non-PnP sound card, it is called a "legacy card." If you use a non-PnP operating system, we say you use a "legacy operating system." Get the idea? Good.

So basically, the only legacy devices are old ISA cards. Assume you are holding an old ISA card—because the card is old, it's probably safe to assume that you don't have the box or documentation either. You have a couple of options here. Drop the card into a system, and see if the BIOS (Figure 5-40) recognizes the device as PnP.

If the BIOS fails to recognize the device, it still could be PnP, but you need to take a close look at the card itself. Look for jumpers on the card that set the I/O address and IRQ (Figure 5-41).

Once you see the I/O address and IRQ settings, you may now assume that it is legacy, with one exception. Some cards have the ability to switch between PnP and legacy by moving a jumper or by running a special configuration program that comes with the device. Figure 5-42 shows a modem that can switch between PnP and legacy.

**Figure 5-39**   Device box with PnP noted

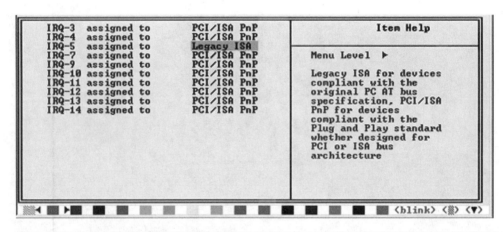

**Figure 5-40** Legacy device recognized in BIOS

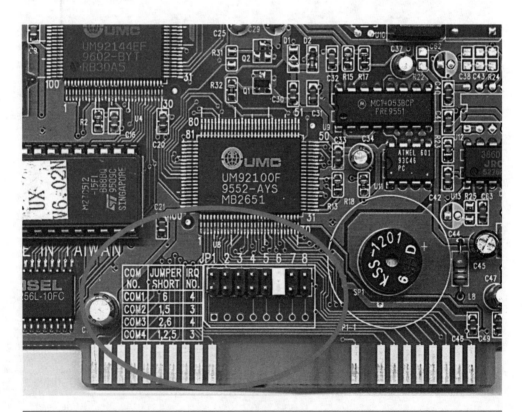

**Figure 5-41** ISA device with jumper markings to set I/O addresses and IRQs manually

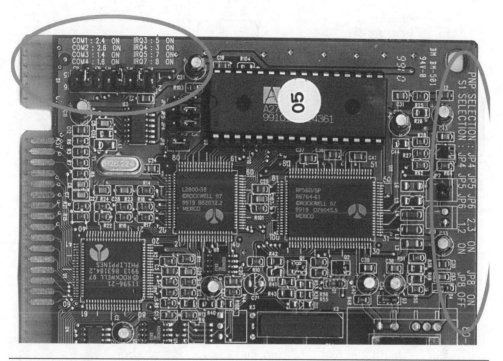

**Figure 5-42**   Modem with legacy or PnP option (jumpers open for PnP; jumpers closed for legacy)

## How Plug and Play Works

Consider a hypothetical scenario to learn how PnP works. To do this, assume that you have a machine with PnP BIOS, a PnP operating system (Windows 2000, for this example), and a mix of PnP and legacy devices. When you install a new PnP card, such as a fax/modem, PnP goes through a fairly standard process, the majority of which takes place during the boot process. During boot, watch the PnP BIOS, allocating system resources to devices in the system.

> **NOTE**   The PnP standard lumps I/O addresses, IRQs, and DMA together under the term "system resources." For example, the system resources for the floppy drive are I/O addresses 3F0-3F7, IRQ6, and DMA channel 2.

The PnP BIOS takes over immediately after the POST, first telling all PnP devices to "be quiet," so the BIOS can find any legacy ISA devices (Figure 5-43).

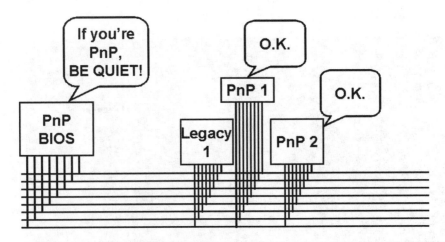

**Figure 5-43**   Initial PnP configuration—PnP devices go "quiet"

The PnP BIOS must then determine the resources used by legacy devices to see what's left over for the PnP devices. Basically, two ways are possible—the BIOS can try to find the ISA devices by querying a special list it keeps (more on this shortly), or you can tell the BIOS what system resources the legacy devices use and the BIOS will work around those resources. You can determine what the PnP BIOS will do by going into CMOS Setup and changing the PnP settings.

Figure 5-44 shows the PnP/PCI Configurations screen from a typical Award BIOS. The left side of the screen contains the PnP settings. Two items enable you to direct how BIOS will perform its resource search, the Resources Controlled By setting and the Reset Configuration Data option.

The Resources Controlled By setting enables you to select between Auto and Manual. If you set this to Auto, the BIOS will defer all system resource determination to the operating system. If you set it to Manual, you must manually set all the IRQ and DMA information to either PCI/ISA PnP or Legacy ISA.

Never use the manual setting unless your system contains legacy devices. If you do have legacy devices, I find the manual setting easier to use because I know what IRQs and DMAs the legacy devices use (because of jumper settings, and so on).

This brings to light a rather interesting point. It is relatively easy to write a BIOS routine to find what I/O addresses are being used by legacy devices, but it is impossible to write one that can reliably find the IRQs and DMAs on those same devices. As a result, most PnP BIOS will automatically find I/O addresses, but give you the choice of indi-

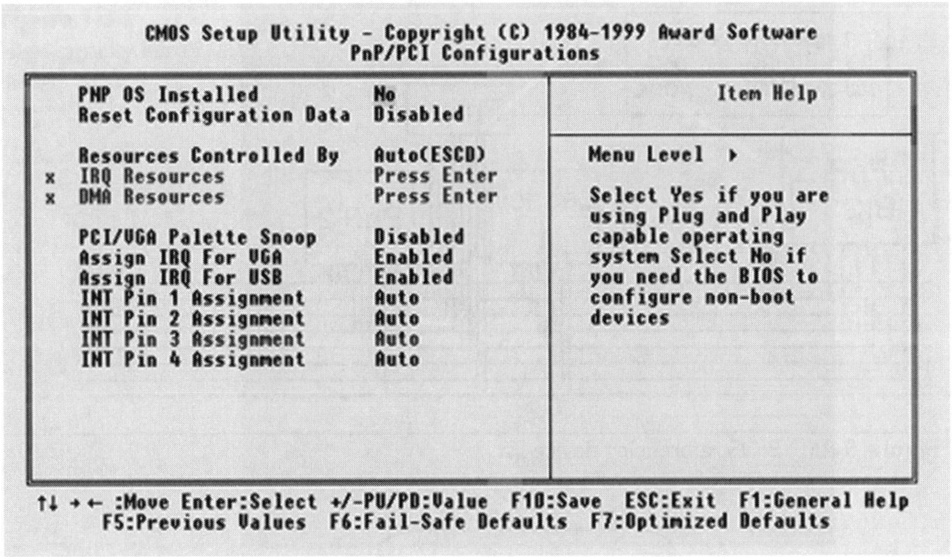

```
           CMOS Setup Utility - Copyright (C) 1984-1999 Award Software
                           PnP/PCI Configurations

     PHP OS Installed           No                    Item Help
     Reset Configuration Data   Disabled

     Resources Controlled By    Auto(ESCD)     Menu Level  ▶
   x IRQ Resources              Press Enter
   x DMA Resources              Press Enter     Select Yes if you are
                                                using Plug and Play
     PCI/VGA Palette Snoop      Disabled        capable operating
     Assign IRQ For VGA         Enabled         system Select No if
     Assign IRQ For USB         Enabled         you need the BIOS to
     INT Pin 1 Assignment       Auto            configure non-boot
     INT Pin 2 Assignment       Auto            devices
     INT Pin 3 Assignment       Auto
     INT Pin 4 Assignment       Auto



   ↑↓ →← :Move Enter:Select +/-PU/PD:Value  F10:Save  ESC:Exit  F1:General Help
        F5:Previous Values  F6:Fail-Safe Defaults  F7:Optimized Defaults
```

**Figure 5-44** Award BIOS PnP/PCI Configurations screen

cating which IRQs and DMAs are used—or they will pass off the responsibility of detecting legacy IRQs and DMAs to the operating system. The CMOS setup shows this rather clearly.

The second item in CMOS setup that concerns the BIOS search is the Reset Configuration Data option. To understand this option, you need to understand the function of what I call the "device list."

Every PnP BIOS keeps a list of all system resources used, usually on the CMOS or flash ROM. Interestingly, this storage area does not have an official name—although most folks call it the *Extended System Configuration Data* (ESCD) list. The PnP standard does not define the physical location of this data, but the standard strictly defines the PnP BIOS routines. In other words, the PnP standard doesn't care where the BIOS stores the information, just how the BIOS must respond when queried. I call this storage area simply the *device list* (Figure 5-45). In the example, assume that the IRQ and DMA resources are manually configured in CMOS. The PnP BIOS then refers to this list in order to determine which resources are already used.

Now that the BIOS knows which resources are available, it can "wake up" each PnP device, asking the device which system resources it needs (Figure 5-46). You can't give just any available system resource to a PnP device. Each PnP device has an internal list of acceptable system resources from which the BIOS must choose.

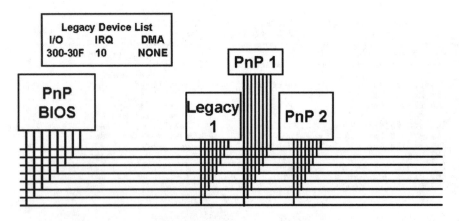

**Figure 5-45** BIOS referencing device list

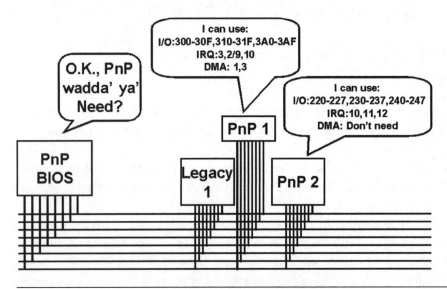

**Figure 5-46** BIOS querying PnP for system resources

If a device can use only IRQs 3, 5, or 7, for example, then the BIOS can't allocate IRQ10 to the device; it must choose from the device's list. As each PnP device calls for certain resources, the BIOS allocates those resources to the PnP device (Figure 5-47) and adds them to the device list (Figure 5-48).

Sometimes adding another piece of equipment can confuse the PnP settings. For example, if you have a PnP device that needs a resource already taken by another device, you need to make the system reallocate the resources. That's where the Reset Configuration Data option comes into play, by making the PnP BIOS reconfigure all

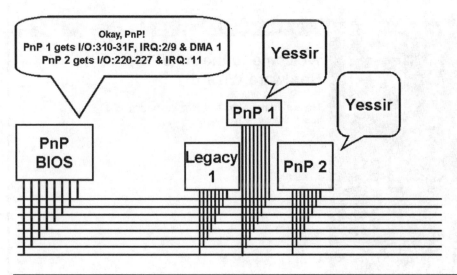

**Figure 5-47**   BIOS allocating system resources

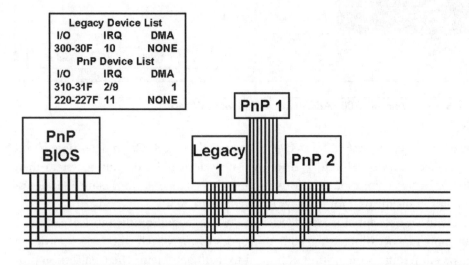

**Figure 5-48**   Updated device list

the devices. This is most often done when you install a device that doesn't seem to be recognized by the system.

The operating system can also update and edit the device list. Unlike the BIOS, Windows makes a strong attempt to find the IRQs and DMAs for legacy devices through its own system information program. This program runs automatically at boot and when the Add/Remove Hardware Wizard (Add New Hardware Wizard in Windows 9*x*) is run from the Control Panel (Figure 5-49).

**Figure 5-49**   Windows 2000 Add/Remove Hardware Wizard

Once the operating system takes over, it queries the PnP BIOS to determine if you have installed a device. Should it discover a new device, the operating system then updates its own system resource information, makes changes to the resources if necessary, and prompts the user for the device driver (Figure 5-50).

Even with an occasional legacy device, PnP works magnificently, most of the time. On the more rare occasions when something goes wrong, a tech who lacks knowledge about system resources might find it difficult to fix the problem. The next section provides you a methodology for device installation that gives you the tools you need to make every device installation successful.

## The Rules of Device Installation

We spend a substantial part of this book discussing device installation. For the most part, we cover the nuances of installing a particular device in that device's respective chapter. We already should know how to install CPUs and DRAM. In other chapters you will learn how to install hard drives, CD-ROM drives, sound cards, modems. From the book, you'll learn how to install just about everything you see in a PC.

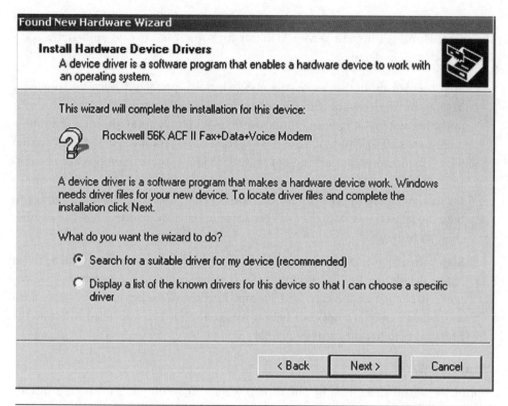

**Figure 5-50**   Windows 2000 prompts the user for new hardware device drivers.

Although going through all of these different devices definitely helps you pass the A+ exams, you must appreciate that many aspects of device installation are very generic—so generic that we can easily create a methodology for generic device installation, one that you will use again and again.

What do I mean by "generic device" installation? Basically, I mean any device outside of the most core devices: floppy drive, hard drive, RAM, and keyboard. If you can snap it into an expansion slot or plug it into the back of the PC, this methodology will work. I've used this for years and it will save you hours of frustration—just as it has for me!

Most technicians look at the concept of device installation from one of two extremes. On one side we see the techs who just drop a device in the PC and assume that it will work. I call this "Russian Roulette," and like the real Russian Roulette, it works great five out of six times! But, when things go wrong—disaster! Don't play Russian Roulette with your system!

The other extreme comes from the "fraidy cat" techs who, usually due to a bad past installation experience, insist on full system backups and about 20 other safeguards before they get anywhere near installing a device. We should strive for somewhere between these two extremes with a quick, efficient methodology that minimizes risk to your system.

I use a three-step system of device installation. First, know the device! Second, install the thing. Third, get thee to Device Manager for some final tweaks and checks. Let's look at each step in detail.

> **Step 1.** Learn about the device you wish to install—preferably *before* you purchase it! Does the device work with your operating system? Does it have drivers for your operating system? If you use Windows 98 or Windows 2000, the answer to these questions is almost always "yes." If you use an old operating system like Windows 95 or an uncommon operating system such as Linux, these questions become critical. Check the device's documentation and check the Web site for the device to see that you have the correct drivers. While you're checking, make sure that you have the latest driver. Most devices get driver updates more often than the weather changes in Texas.
>
> **Step 2.** Install the card. This step varies depending on whether you install a PnP or legacy device. For PnP, turn off the system, drop in the card, and reboot. The system will recognize the card and prompt for drivers. Legacy devices create a bit more hassle as you'll see, but before we go any further, you need to know the proper way to handle cards in general.

### Handling Cards

Optimally, a card should be in one of two places: in a computer or in an antistatic bag. When inserting or removing a card, be careful to hold the card only on its edges. Do not hold the card by the slot connectors or touch any components on the board (Figure 5-51).

Never insert or remove a card at an extreme angle. This may damage the card or wipe out the CMOS data. A slight angle is acceptable and even necessary for removing a card. Always screw the cards to the box with their connection screw. This keeps the cards

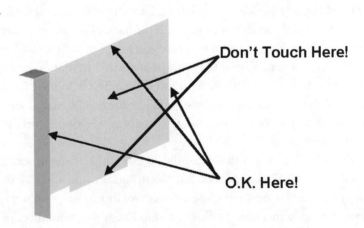

**Figure 5-51**
Where to handle
a card

Don't Touch Here!

O.K. Here!

from slipping out and potentially shorting against other cards. Also, many cards use the screw connection to ground the card to the box (Figure 5-52).

Many technicians have been told to clean the slot connectors if a particular card is not working. This is almost never necessary, and if done improperly, can cause damage. An installed card should never need the slots cleaned. You should only clean slot connectors if you have a card that's been on the shelf for a while and the slot connectors are obviously dull. *Never use a pencil eraser.* Pencil erasers leave behind bits of residue that

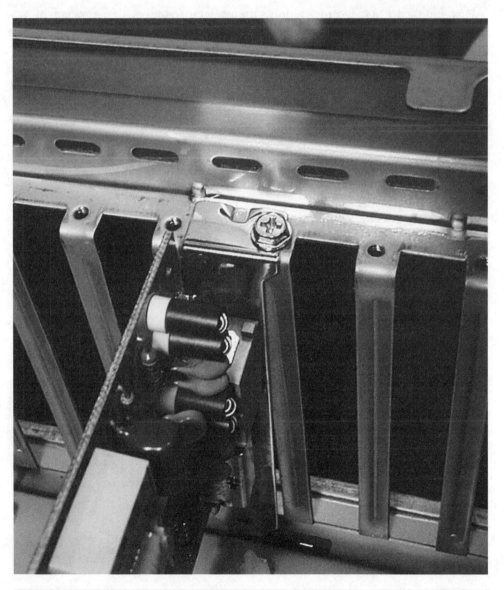

**Figure 5-52** Always screw down all cards.

wedge between the card and slot connector, preventing contact and causing the card to fail. Use a "Bright Boy" cleaning block. Bright Boy cleaning blocks look like large, gray pencil erasers and are perfect for polishing contacts. Be sure to rub lightly; otherwise, you'll rub the contact completely away! Look for a Bright Boy cleaning block at your local hobby shop.

Legacy devices add complexity to the installation process, requiring you to locate available resources, assign those resources, and then install the device! Let's go through these extra steps.

First, run Device Manager to determine the available resources for the system. All versions of Device Manager enable you to view the devices by resource. Figure 5-53 shows the Windows 2000 Device Manager sorting the devices by IRQ. Can you see any available IRQs?

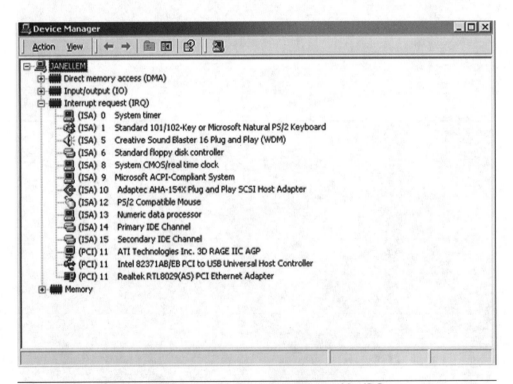

**Figure 5-53**   Windows 2000 Device Manager devices sorted by IRQ

Once you've determined the available resources, you must configure the device to use those resources. You may have to set jumpers, flip switches, or run a special setup program to do this. Figure 5-54 shows a typical legacy setup program.

After you configure the legacy device's system resources, you need to inform Windows of the legacy device by running the Add/Remove Hardware Wizard (Figure 5-55).

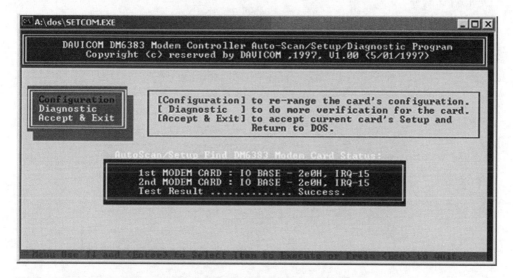

**Figure 5-54**   Typical legacy setup software program

**Figure 5-55**
Windows 2000
Add/Remove
Hardware Wizard

**Step 3.** Inspect the results of the installation and verify that the device works properly. Go into Device Manager and verify that the "device is working properly" (Figure 5-56).

**Figure 5-56**
Device Manager
shows the device
working properly.

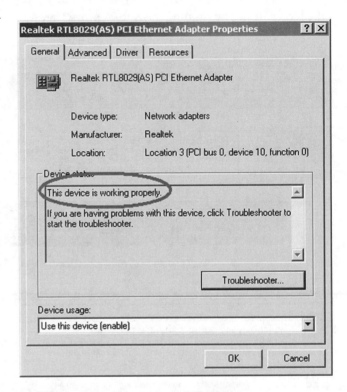

Assuming that Device Manager shows the device working properly, put the device to work by making it do whatever it is supposed to do. If you installed a printer, print something; if you installed a scanner, scan something. If it works, you're done!

Ah, if only it always worked this easily. Many times the Device Manager shows us a problem. First, it may not even show the new device. In that case, verify that you inserted the device properly and that the device has power, if necessary. Run the Add/Remove Hardware Wizard, and see if Windows recognizes the device. If the Device Manager doesn't recognize the device at this point, you have one of two problems: (a) the device is physically damaged and you must replace it; or (b) the device is legacy and you failed to properly configure its system resources.

The Device Manager rarely fails to see a device. More commonly, device problems manifest themselves in Device Manager via error symbols—a black "!", a red "X," a blue "I," or a green "?".

- A black "!" on a yellow circle indicates a device that is missing, that Windows does not recognize a device or a device driver problem. The device may still work with this error.

- A red "X" indicates a disabled device. This usually points to a system resource conflict or a damaged device. The device will not work with this error.

- A blue "I" on a white field indicates a PnP device on which someone has configured the system resources manually. This merely provides information and does not indicate an error with this device.

- A green "?" indicates that Windows does not have the correct driver but has successfully installed a compatible driver. The device works but may lack certain functions. This error symbol only appears with Windows ME.

The "!" symbol is the most common error symbol and usually the easiest to fix. First, double-check the device's connections. Second, try reinstalling the driver with the Update Driver button. To get to the Update Driver button, click the desired device and select Properties. In the Properties dialog box, select the Driver tab. On the Driver tab, click the Update Driver button (Figure 5-57).

**Figure 5-57**
Click on the Update Driver button.

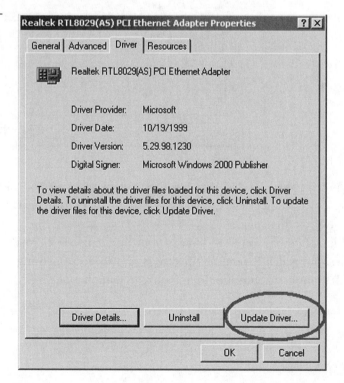

Red "X" errors strike fear into most technicians. First, check the Properties for the device to see if any resource conflict exists. Once a device installs, Windows Device Manager enables you to accept the installation as defined by accepting the default Use Automatic Settings option (Figure 5-58). If a resource conflict takes place, you can manually change the settings by clicking the Change Setting button (Figure 5-59).

**Figure 5-58**
Automatic Settings
option

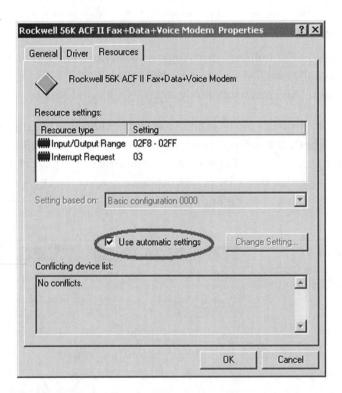

Windows then "locks" that resource out of the PnP and permanently dedicates the resource to that device, effectively making that resource no longer available (Figure 5-60).

Think of PnP as you would one of your children: love it, trust it, and let it do what it wishes, but watch it carefully in case it tries to do something irrational. PnP makes installations easier, but should not make us complacent.

**Figure 5-59**
Change Setting
button

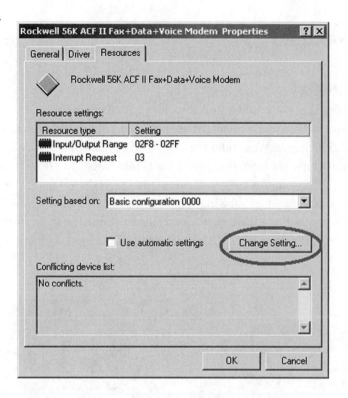

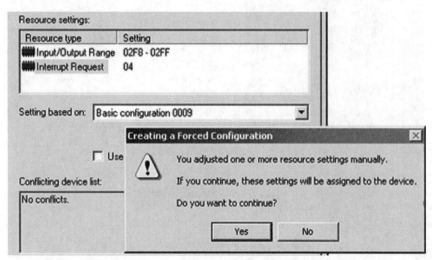

**Figure 5-60**    Manually setting a resource locks the resource out of the PnP

## Beyond A+

### Chipsets

"The time has come, the walrus said, to speak of many things . . . " If you look back over the past few chapters, you might imagine that a number of chips must populate the typical motherboard. We should see a CPU, RAM, the chipset (which we now define as two separate chips, the northbridge and the southbridge), the IRQ controller, the DMA controller, the System BIOS/CMOS chips, and the keyboard controller.

Take a look at the following modern motherboard. Note how very few chips populate the motherboard. We see the two chipset chips (the PCI controller has a large black heat sink), the flash ROM, CPU, and RAM, plus a few other small chips (Figure 5-61).

**Figure 5-61**　Modern motherboards have relatively few chips.

Hey! Where are the IRQ, DMA, or keyboard controllers? The chipset now handles all of these functions. Most chipsets divide the works as follows:

**Northbridge**

- Communicates to CPU
- Communicates to RAM (Memory controller)
- Communicates to AGP device
- Communicates to PCI devices

**Southbridge**

- Communicates to floppy drive
- Communicates to hard drives/CD-ROMs
- Communicates to ISA devices
- Communicates to parallel, serial, keyboard, and mouse ports

Before Intel introduced the Pentium, a number of companies made chipsets. You would see chipsets with names like SiS, VIA, Mr. BIOS, OPTi, and a host of other names. Intel introduced PCI and the Pentium at roughly the same time. They simultaneously introduced a chipset for these new technologies and virtually monopolized the chipset market for the next eight or nine years with a series of powerful chipsets. Table 5-10 shows the most common chipsets offered by Intel. To this day, Intel continues to dominate the chipset market with powerful, inexpensive chipsets.

Be careful reading this table. The chipset consists of both the northbridge and the southbridge. This combination of two chips receives a name from the chipset manufacturer. Don't confuse the name of the chipset with the names of the northbridge and the southbridge. The Intel 440BX chipset, for example, consists of the 82443BX northbridge and the 82371AB southbridge.

Take a look at the latest Intel chipsets. Note that most of the southbridge chips no longer support ISA! They *do* support ISA by adding another southbridge chip—in essence a "southbridge for the southbridge." If Intel has its way, ISA slots would no longer exist on motherboards.

The emergence of AMD as a serious player in the CPU market has opened up an entirely new world for chipsets, as you can bet that Intel refuses to make chipsets for AMD CPUs! VIA Technologies took advantage of AMD's growth and has established itself as a major force in chipset manufacturing, both for AMD and Intel CPUs. VIA's chipsets (Table 5-11) tend to edge out Intel chipsets in performance, but also tend to be a bit unstable unless carefully configured. Folks who like to "tweak and geek" with their systems tend to go for VIA; those who want to close up the systems and never open them migrate toward Intel.

**Table 5-10** Intel Chipsets

### INTEL CHIPSETS

| CHIPSET | NORTH-BRIDGE | CPU | MAX RAM TYPE | RAM | ECC | AGP | NUM CPUs | SOUTH-BRIDGE |
|---------|--------------|-----|--------------|-----|-----|-----|----------|--------------|
| 430FX | 82437FX | Pentium | EDO/FPM | 128MB | No | No | 1 | PIIX |
| 430VX | 82437VX | Pentium | PC66/EDO/FPM | 128MB | No | No | 1 | PIIX3 |
| 430TX | 82439TX | Pentium | PC66/EDO/FPM | 256MB | No | No | 1 | PIIX4 |
| 430HX | 82439HX | Pentium | EDO/FPM | 512MB | Yes | No | 2 | PIIX3 |
| 440LX | 82443LX | P II | PC66/EDO/FPM | 512MB | Yes | 1X | 2 | PIIX4E |
| 450NX | 82451NX | P II/III | PC100 | 256MB | No | No | 4 | PIIX4E |
| 440MX | 82443MX | Celeron | PC66 | 256MB | No | No | 1 | PIIX4E |
| 440MX-100 | 82443MX100 | P III/Celeron | PC100 | 256MB | No | No | 1 | PIIX4E |
| 440ZX-66 | 82443ZX66 | Celeron | PC66/EDO | 256MB | No | 2X | 1 | PIIX4E |
| 440ZX | 82443ZX | P II/III | PC100 | 8GB | Yes | 2X | 1 | PIIX4E |
| 440EX | 82443EX | Celeron | PC66/EDO | 256MB | No | 1X | 1 | PIIX4E |
| 440BX | 82443BX | P II/III | PC100 | 1GB | Yes | 2X | 2 | PIIX4 |
| 440GX | 82443GX | P II/III | PC100 | 2GB | Yes | 2X | 4 | PIIX4 |
| i810 | 82810 | P II/III | PC100 | 512MB | No | * | 1 | ICH |
| i810E | 82810 | P II/III | PC100 | 512MB | No | * | 1 | ICH |
| i815 | 82815 | P II/III | PC133 | 512MB | No | 4X | 1 | ICH |

*The Intel 810 series included an integrated i740 video processor.

**Table 5-10** Intel Chipsets (continued)

**INTEL CHIPSETS**

| CHIPSET | NORTH-BRIDGE | CPU | MAX RAM TYPE | RAM | ECC | AGP | NUM CPUs | SOUTH-BRIDGE |
|---------|-------------|-----|--------------|-----|-----|-----|----------|-------------|
| i820 | 82820 | P II/III | PC600-800 | 1GB | Yes | 4X | 2 | ICH |
| i820E | 82820 | P II/III | PC600-800 | 1GB | Yes | 4X | 2 | ICH2 |
| i840 | 82840 | P III | PC600-800 | 4GB | Yes | 4X | 2 | ICH |

**SOUTHBRIDGE TYPES**

| | IDE | USB | ISA |
|---|-----|-----|-----|
| PIIX | 82371FB | PIO Mode 4 | No | Yes |
| PIIX3 | 82371SB | PIO Mode 4 | 2 USB ports | Yes |
| PIIX4 | 82371AB | Ultra ATA 33 | 2 USB ports | Yes |
| PIIX4E | 82371EB | Major patch of the PIIX4—No new features | | |
| ICH | 82801AA | Ultra ATA 66 | 2 USB ports | No |
| ICH2 | 82801BA | Ultra ATA 100 | 4 USB ports | No |

**Table 5-11** VIA Chipsets

## VIA CHIPSETS

| CHIPSET | NORTH-BRIDGE | CPU | MAX BUS SPEED | RAM TYPE | MAX RAM | ECC | AGP | NUM CPUs | SOUTH-BRIDGE |
|---------|--------------|-----|---------------|----------|---------|-----|-----|----------|--------------|
| Apollo VP | VT82C580VP | Pentium | 66 MHz | PC66/EDO | 512MB | No | No | 1 | VT82C586 |
| Apollo VPX | VT82C580VPX | Pentium | 75 MHz | PC66/EDO | 512MB | No | No | 1 | VT82C586 |
| Apollo VP2 | VT82C595 | Pentium | 75 MHz | PC66/EDO | 512MB | Yes | No | 1 | VT82C586 |
| Apollo VP3 | VT82C597 | Pentium | 66 MHz | DDR/PC66/EDO | 512MB | Yes | 2× | 2 | VT82C586 |
| Apollo Pro | VT82C691 | P Pro/P II | 100 MHz | PC100/EDO | 1GB | Yes | 2× | 1 | VT82C596 |
| Apollo Pro Plus | VT82C693 | Slot 1/S 370 | 100 MHz | PC100/EDO | 1GB | Yes | 2× | 1 | VT82C596 |
| Apollo MVP3 | VT82C598AT | Super S 7 | 100 MHz | PC100/EDO | 768MB | Yes | 2× | 1 | VT82C686A |
| Apollo MVP4 | VT8501 | Super S 7 | 100 MHz | PC100/EDO | 768MB | Yes | * | 1 | VT82C686A |
| Apollo PM601 | VT8601 | Slot 1/S 370 | 133 MHz | PC133 | 1GB | Yes | * | 1 | VT82C686A |
| Apollo Pro 133 | VT82C693A | Slot 1/S 370 | 133 MHz | PC133 | 1.5GB | Yes | 2× | 1 | VT82C596B |
| Apollo Pro 133A | VT82C694X | Slot 1/S 370 | 133 MHz | PC133 | 1.5GB | Yes | 4× | 1 | VT82C596B |
| Apollo KX133 | VT8371 | Slot A | 200 MHz | PC133 | 2GB | Yes | 4× | 1 | VT82C686A |
| Apollo KT133 | VT8363 | Socket A | 200 MHz | PC133 | 2GB | ? | 4× | 1 | VT82C686A |
| Apollo Pro266 | VT8633 | Slot 1/S 370 | 133 MHz | DDR200/266 | 2GB | ? | 4× | 1 | VT8233 |

* Included integrated Trident Blade3D video

**Table 5-11**  VIA Chipsets (continued)

| | SOUTHBRIDGE TYPES | | | |
| --- | --- | --- | --- | --- |
| | IDE | USB | ISA | NOTES |
| VT82C586 | Ultra ATA 33 | 2 USB ports | Yes | Keyboard, PS/2 mouse support |
| VT82C586B | Ultra ATA 66 | 4 USB ports | Yes | Keyboard, PS/2 mouse support |
| VT82C596 | Ultra ATA 33 | 2 USB ports | Yes | Keyboard, PS/2 mouse support, Mobile |
| VT82C596A | Pin compatible to Intel PIIX4 | | | |
| VT82C596B | Ultra ATA 66 | 2 USB ports | Yes | Keyboard, PS/2 mouse support |
| VT82C686A | Ultra ATA 66 | 4 USB ports | Yes | Complete I/O solution, SoundBlaster |
| VT8233 | ATA 100 | 6 USB ports | ? | ? |

Even though the A+ has no interest in chipsets (as of this writing), any good tech should be able to spout off quickly the features of the most common chipsets. Besides, you don't want to stare blankly over your drink when your fellow techs debate the benefit of the latest Intel chipset vs. the latest VIA chipset, do you?!

## CNR

Even though the ATX form factor made a quantum leap past AT for standardizing connections, almost every PC system requires connectivity (network or modem) and sound. The ATX does not directly address these needs. To help manufacturers develop a standard connection for these devices, Intel forwarded the *Communications and Networking Riser* (CNR) specification in early 2000. The CNR provides a dedicated bus, free of electronic noise, to support network, modem, or sound devices—all of which tend to suffer from electronic noise to some degree.

**NOTE** You may run into a motherboard with an identical looking slot called an "AMR" slot. This was the short-lived predecessor to CNR.

Intel makes a strong point, saying: "CNR does not define an aftermarket standard I/O bus. Only system manufacturers and integrators should use CNR." In other words, don't bother going to the local computer store to find a card to snap into that CNR slot. You cannot find any CNR devices in the retail channel. CNR has a standard connection, but the pinouts vary from system to system. Even if you could get your hands on a CNR device, it probably would not work in your system (Figure 5-62). If you need to add something to your system, get PCI.

## Expansion Bus Forever!

It's a brave new world for expansion buses. The slow phase out of ISA, combined with mass integration of I/O into the chipsets, has created a whole new class of systems called "legacy-free" that remove all expansion slots as well as all of the common ports to make a cheap, virtually non-upgradable system. Legacy-free PCs do not have serial ports, parallel ports, PS/2 ports, or ISA slots. Legacy-free PCs rely exclusively on USB and IEEE-1394 (FireWire) ports. You may also see some "legacy-reduced" systems. Legacy-reduced PCs do not completely remove all of these items. For example, they may still have PS/2 ports for the keyboard and mouse. But as long as PC technology moves forward, the majority of systems will continue to provide expansion slots and require the skills of well-trained technicians for the foreseeable future.

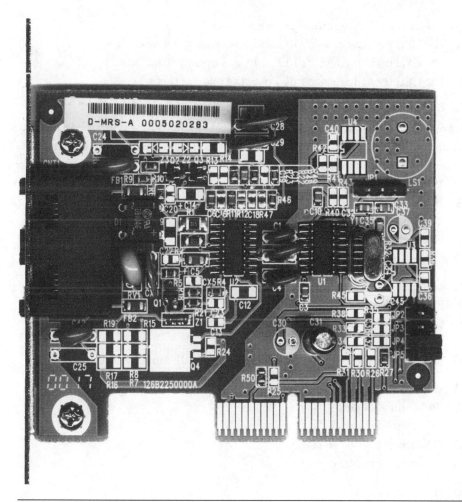

**Figure 5-62**   CNR device

## Review Questions

1. The *Industry Standard Architecture* (ISA) expansion slots came in two flavors. What were they?

   A.  4.77 MHz and 7.16 MHz

   B.  8-bit and 16-bit

   C.  16-bit and 24-bit

   D.  8 MHz and 16 MHz

2. How does the CPU communicate with a device?

A. The CPU uses the device's I/O addresses over the address bus.

B. The CPU uses the device's I/O addresses over the data bus.

C. The CPU uses the device's IRQ over the address bus.

D. The CPU uses the device's IRQ over the data bus

3. Steve adds two expansion cards to his system: a sound card and a network card. The sound card uses I/O addresses 300-330 and IRQ5. The network card uses I/O addresses 310-340 and IRQ2. When he boots the computer, it completely locks up. What is most likely the problem?

A. The network card cannot use IRQ2; it's a reserved IRQ.

B. A buggy device driver.

C. IRQ conflict between the sound card and the network card.

D. I/O address conflict between the sound card and the network card.

4. How does a device initiate a conversation with the CPU?

A. By using I/O addresses.

B. By using polling.

C. By using an IRQ.

D. The device has to wait for the CPU to initiate all conversations.

5. What is an "8259"?

A. IRQ controller chip

B. I/O controller chip

C. ISA expansion bus crystal

D. PCI expansion bus crystal

6. What is a COM port?

A. A serial port

B. A parallel port

C. A preset combination of I/O addresses and IRQ for a serial device

D. A preset combination of I/O addresses and IRQ for a parallel device

7. In Windows 2000, what is the best place to determine which devices get which system resources?

A. Right-click My Computer and select Properties. In System Properties, go to Hardware Profiles and double-click the Computer icon.

B. Double-click My Computer; then right-click the C drive and select Properties.

C. Right-click My Computer and select Properties. In System Properties, go to Device Manager and double-click the Computer icon.

D. Go to Start | Programs | Accessories | System Tools.

8. What is the difference between a Type II and a Type III PC card?
   A. Type II cards are 5 mm thick; Type III cards are 10.5 mm thick.
   B. Type II cards have a notch on one corner, but Type III cards do not.
   C. Type II cards can handle 2MB of RAM, but Type III cards can handle 3MB of RAM.
   D. Type II cards can be used only for RAM, whereas Type III cards can be used for any sort of device.

9. Carol has two external serial devices, a mouse and a modem, and two serial ports built into her motherboard. Ralph argues that she should set the serial ports to the traditional COM1 and COM2 and then plug in her devices. Sylvia argues that she should set up her serial ports as COM1 and COM3, but use IRQ5 for COM3. Which one offers advice that will enable Carol to set up the devices and avoid a resource conflict?
   A. Only Ralph is correct.
   B. Only Sylvia is correct.
   C. Both Ralph and Sylvia are correct.
   D. Neither Ralph nor Sylvia is correct.

10. Joan has a Pentium II system to which she wants to add several expansion cards. The system currently has only an AGP video card installed. She has a PCI sound card, a PCI network card, and an ISA modem that is not Plug and Play, but rather uses jumpers to allocate resources.
    **Primary objective:** Install the two PCI devices and avoid any resource conflict.
    **Optional objectives:** Install the ISA device and avoid any resource conflict. Avoid damaging any of the cards or the motherboard.
    **Proposed solution:** Install the cards one at a time, being careful to touch only the edges of the cards. When the BIOS detects each card and Windows loads and prompts for drivers, insert a driver disk. After each device installs, go to Device Manager and check the list to see if any conflicts exist. Then shut down and go through the installation scenario again.
    The **proposed solution:**
    A. Accomplishes the primary objective only
    B. Accomplishes the primary objective and one optional objective
    C. Accomplishes the primary objective and both optional objectives
    D. Accomplishes only the optional objectives

## Answers

1. **B.** The *Industry Standard Architecture* (ISA) expansion slots came in two flavors, 8-bit and 16-bit, although only 16-bit ISA lingers today.

2. **A.** The CPU uses the device's I/O addresses over the address bus to communicate with that device.

3. **D.** The I/O addresses assigned to the cards clearly overlap and cause the problem.

4. **C.** A device uses its IRQ to initiate a conversation with the CPU.

5. **A.** 8259 is the common name for an IRQ controller.

6. **C.** A COM port is a preset combination of I/O addresses and IRQ for a serial device.

7. **C.** Open Device Manager to check resource assignments.

8. **A.** Type II cards are 5 mm thick; Type III cards are 10.5 mm thick.

9. **C.** Either way will avoid a resource conflict between the two serial devices.

10. **C.** Joan clearly knows what she is doing!

# Power Supplies

In this chapter, we will

- Learn a few basic points about electrical power
- Be introduced to the standards of PC-compatible power supplies
- Inspect the different types of power connectors and their different functions
- Learn how to use a voltmeter to perform a basic test of a power supply
- See how to avoid electrostatic discharge
- Appreciate the need for surge suppressors and uninterruptible power supplies

## Historical/Conceptual

### Understanding Electricity

Before we can even begin to discuss power supplies, we need to know a few basics of electricity. Then we can turn to the more specific topics of how electricity works inside the PC and what techs need to do to keep a system electrically sound.

Electricity is simply a flow of negatively charged particles, called electrons, through matter. All matter enables the flow of electrons to some extent. Materials in which electrons move freely are called *conductors.* As you can probably guess, metallic wire is a very good conductor. The amount of electrons moving past a certain point on a wire is called the *current,* which is measured in units called *amperes* ("amps" or A). The "pressure" of the electrons through the wire is called *voltage* and is measured in units called *volts* (V).

Electricity comes in two flavors: *direct current* (DC), where the electrons flow in one direction around a continuous circuit, and *alternating current* (AC), where the flow of electrons alternates direction back and forth in a circuit (Figure 6-1).

**Figure 6-1**
Alternating current
(AC) vs. direct cur-
rent (DC)

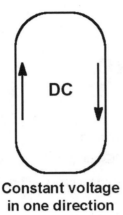
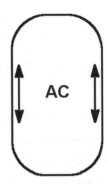

**DC**

**AC**

**Constant voltage
in one direction**

**Voltage in both directions,
constantly switching
back and forth**

Your PC uses DC voltage, but local power companies supply only AC voltage. Some conversion process must take place in order for the PC to function. The power supply in a computer converts high-voltage AC power to low-voltage DC.

**EXAM TIP** The A+ Core Hardware exam really shows its U.S. roots in the area of electrical power. For you folks outside the United States and Canada, watch out for power questions that are biased towards those countries' power standards—especially household current and outlet plug design.

## AC Power

AC power means that the flow of electrons "alternates" direction in the wires. It is a much more efficient way to transport power over long distances and is used in more types of electrical equipment than DC current. The frequency that the flow of electricity alternates in an AC power supply is measured in cycles per second, or *hertz* (Hz).

All standard electrical power in the United States is AC, approximately 115 volts and 60 Hz. The outlets (Figure 6-2) into which you plug toasters, TVs, and computers provide access to the power supplied by a power company.

Most household electrical outlets use three-prong connections. The smaller rectangular hole is called the *hot,* the larger rectangular hole is called the *neutral,* and the small round hole is called the *ground.* The combination of the hot and neutral wires supplies the path for the alternating current. They can be traced from the fuse box outside your house all the way back to the generator at the power station.

Four wires generally connect to the fuse box: A bare wire, that goes into some sort of "ground," and not to the power pole; a pair of 115-volt hot wires, always black, that

**Figure 6-2**
Household 115-volt
outlet

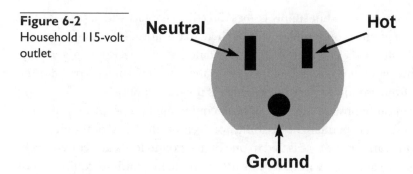

come from the pole to the fuse box; and a wire from the pole that can be black or sometimes striped, is the neutral wire.

Note that houses get 230 VAC from the pole, rather than 115 VAC; this enables
houses to run bigger appliances, such as water heaters, washing machines, dryers, dishwashers, air conditioners, and so on.

As the neutral returns to the power company, a series of safety connections called
*grounds* are placed at certain intervals. Grounds are simply connections between the
neutral and the earth. These connections are at your fuse box and every power pole.
They act as an emergency dump in case of a short circuit. In a short circuit, a large flow
(amps) of electricity discharges all at once. This short will burn out circuits unless it can
be "dumped" somewhere fast. See Figure 6-3.

So, if the neutral connects to grounds, what is the ground plug for? Imagine a short
circuit in your PC, where the current seeks the path of least resistance back to its volt-

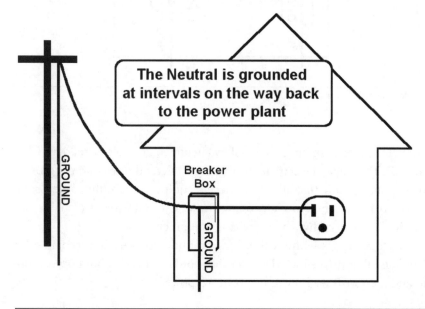

**Figure 6-3** Neutral's job

age source. For example, if the hot supply comes directly in contact with a case or cover that doesn't have a ground connected, it will sit there like a storm searching for something to hit. As a storm seeks a path of least resistance, so do electrons to a voltage source. If anything or anyone comes in contact with the case, it becomes a path for the current to travel from ground to the source, which is the hot supply.

This current can cause physical damage to both equipment and people. It can cause fires, component damage, permanent disability, or even death. The ground plug connects directly to the earth. If the case is tied to one of the ground leads, the current seeks the path of least resistance and will travel to earth without any harm to equipment or people in contact with it. See Figure 6-4.

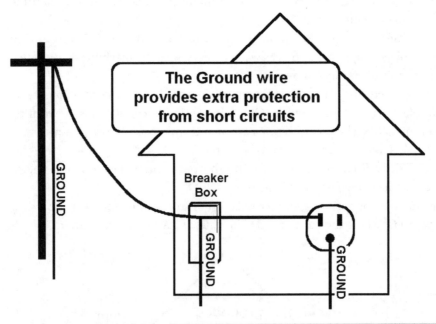

**Figure 6-4**  Safety ground

A ground, therefore, acts as an immediate safety circuit when an electrical device has a short (Figure 6-5). The surge of electricity from a short circuit dumps into the ground wire. Ground wires also ensure that all the connected equipment is at the same potential (0 V). This is very important, especially on networks. Ground wires also enable you to discharge static electricity easily when servicing equipment.

Nongrounded plugs—plugs without the third ground wire—are unacceptable for use in PCs! Don't use them! This includes extension cords! Let's talk about power supplies for a bit, and then we'll see how to test your AC power.

**Figure 6-5**
Electronic symbol
for ground

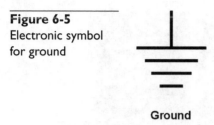

Ground

## Test Specific

### The Power Supply

The term "power supply" is a bit of a misnomer, as you have probably figured out by now. The power supply does not supply the power. After all, the electricity comes out of the wall socket, and ultimately from a power company. The power supply in a PC actually acts as a step-down transformer, converting high voltage alternating current (115 volts here in the United States) into 5, 12, and 3.3 volts direct current (DC). The PC uses the 12-volt current to power motors on devices like hard drives and CD-ROM drives, and uses the 5-volt/3.3-volt voltages for support of onboard electronics. Manufacturers may use these voltages any way they wish, however, and may deviate from these assumptions.

Two types of power supplies comprise over 99 percent of all power supplies installed in personal computers: AT (Figure 6-6) and ATX (Figure 6-7). AT is the older style and held sway from the early days of the PC. The ATX form factor motherboard, with its unique ATX power supply, dominates today's systems.

The AT form factor with its unique power supply has faded from the new PC market and will quickly disappear in the next few years. Even though AT form factor computers are fading away, their huge installed base requires you to recognize and understand the AT power supply. Most importantly, the A+ exam assumes that you have a solid understanding of both the AT and the ATX power supplies.

Whether AT or ATX, all power supplies share a number of common features:

- **Power connection**   Must plug into a power outlet
- **Motherboard power**   Some connection to provide power to the motherboard
- **Power switch**   Must have a way to turn the system on and off
- **Peripheral connections**   Connectors to provide power to internal devices
- **Fan**   Cools the inside of the power supply *and* provides air flow for the case

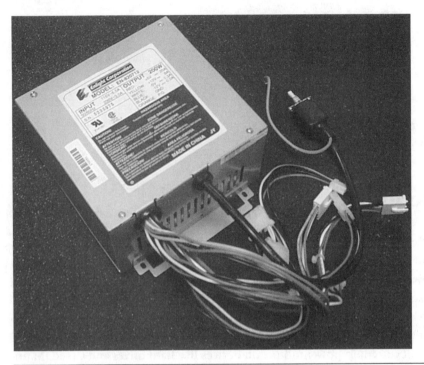

**Figure 6-6**   AT power supply

**Figure 6-7**   ATX power supply

Let's look at each aspect common to power supplies and, in the process, discuss issues important to A+ Certified techs—testing, installing, troubleshooting, and replacing.

## Power Connections

Every power supply must have standard AC power from the power company. The power supply connects to the power cord via a standard "IEC-320" connector. Take a look at the back of your PC to see that IEC-320 connector (Figure 6-8).

Some older power supplies include a special "IEC-320-2-2" connector (Figure 6-9). This enables the system to support another device, usually a monitor. The power needs of monitors make this connector useless on most occasions. Very few new systems still provide this outlet. Note that the previous power supply figure did not have this connector.

**Figure 6-8**
IEC-320 connection

## Testing Your AC Power

Before plugging anything in an AC outlet, take a moment to test the outlet first. Failure to test AC outlets properly can result in inoperable or destroyed equipment, as well as possible electrocution. When testing AC power, you want to check for three things: that the hot outputs approximately 115 V (or whatever your proper voltage for your part of the world), that the neutral connects to ground (0 V output), and that the ground connects to ground (again, 0 V). AC outlets are tested using a *multimeter* or with a device designed exclusively to test outlets.

**Figure 6-9**   IEC-320-2-2 connection

A multimeter—often also referred to as a *Volt-Ohm Meter* (VOM)—enables us to measure a number of different aspects of electrical current. Every multimeter provides at least four major measurements: AC voltage, DC voltage, continuity, and resistance. A multimeter consists of two probes, an analog or digital meter, and a dial to set the type of test you want to perform. Refer to Figure 6-10 to become familiar with the different components of the multimeter.

The concept of measuring AC and DC voltage is straightforward. Make sure the voltages read what they should read! (We'll look at how to do this in a moment.) Continuity and resistance, however, probably require a little explaining.

## Continuity

Continuity is simply whether or not a connection exists. In other words, if electricity can flow from one end of a wire to the other end, that wire has continuity. We use the setting on the multimeter to determine breaks in wires and components (Figure 6-11).

A multimeter will determine continuity by lights or beeps. If you don't have a continuity setting, use the resistance setting (explained in the next section). If the multimeter shows infinite resistance, then there is no continuity (see Figure 6-12); if the multimeter shows no resistance, then there is continuity.

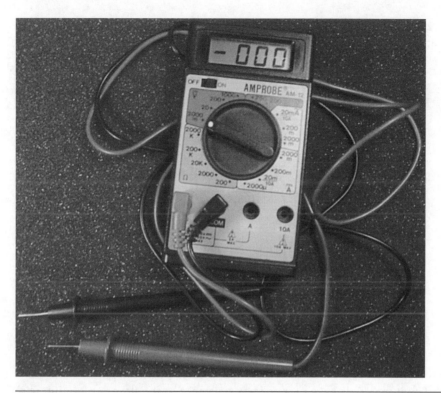

**Figure 6-10** Digital Volt-Ohm Meter / Multimeter

## This wire has CONTINUITY

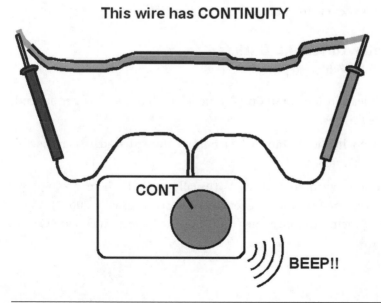

**Figure 6-11** Continuity

**Figure 6-12**
No continuity

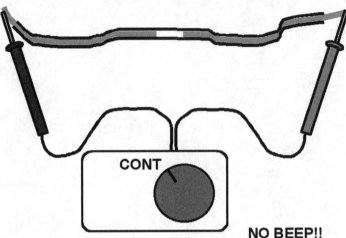

### Resistance

Resistance is the measurement of how much a wire or component resists the flow of current. Different materials have more or less resistance to the flow. A platinum wire, for example, has very little resistance, whereas a wooden desk has high resistance. Resistance is measured in units called *ohms,* and the symbol for an ohm is Ω.

Now that you have somewhat of an understanding of the functions available to test with a multimeter, let's use one to test an AC electrical outlet.

## Using a Multimeter to Test AC Outlets

To set up the meter, follow these steps:

1. Place the black lead in the common (-) hole. If the black lead is permanently attached, ignore this step.

2. Place the red lead in the V-Ohm-A (+) hole. If the red lead is permanently attached, ignore this step.

3. Move the selector switch to the AC V (usually red). If there are multiple selections, put it to the first scale higher than 120 volts (usually 200 V). "Auto-range" meters set their own range; they don't need any selection except AC volts. See Figure 6-13.

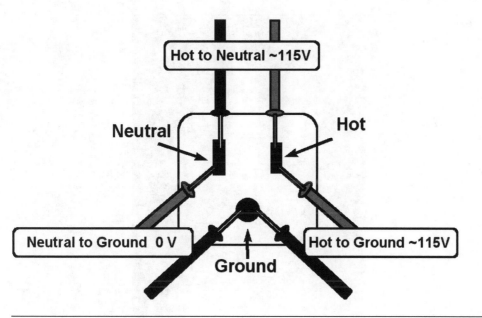

**Figure 6-13**   Outlet voltages

Now, to read the meter:

1.  Put either lead in hot, the other in neutral. You should read 110 to 120 volts AC.

2.  Put either lead in hot, the other in ground. You should read 110 to 120 volts AC.

3.  Put either lead in neutral, the other in ground. You should read 0 volts AC.

If any of these readings are different from what was described, it's time to call an electrician.

## Using Special Equipment to Test AC Voltage

A number of good AC-only testing devices are available. With these devices, you can test all voltages for an AC outlet, simply by inserting them into the outlet. Be sure to test all the outlets the computer system uses: power supply, external devices, and monitor. Although convenient, these devices aren't as accurate as a multimeter. My favorite tester is made by Radio Shack, catalog number 22-101 (Figure 6-14). This handy device provides three LEDs that describe everything that can go wrong with a plug.

**Figure 6-14**
Circuit tester

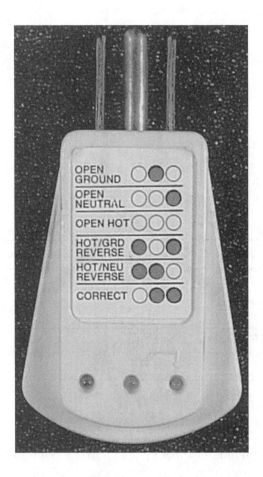

## Motherboard Power

Everything on your motherboard needs electrical power to run—CPUs, RAM, chipsets, and so on. Every power supply provides specialized connections to the motherboard to provide DC electricity in several voltages to feed the needs of the many devices. Just as we took a moment to understand AC power earlier, let's now take an equally brief moment to appreciate DC power before looking at the specific AT and ATX motherboard connections.

## DC Power

DC power is far simpler in concept than AC power. DC power comes out of your power supply ready to work, and it provides electricity for all the components in the PC. DC flows in one direction, making essentially big loops to each of the components—in, loop, and back around again. Batteries—such as the type that powers flashlights or radios—also provide DC power, and they might make the loop concept more real. Just like batteries, the PC power supply connectors have a distinct polarity—positive (+) and negative (-) wires—that points to the direction of the flow. (See Figure 6-15.)

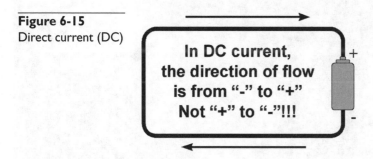

**Figure 6-15**
Direct current (DC)

In DC current, the direction of flow is from "-" to "+" Not "+" to "-"!!!

All PC power supplies provide both positive and negative voltages. Don't be too surprised to see a -5 V or -12 V on a power supply motherboard connection; the system needs these negative voltages as much as it needs the positive ones. Let's look at the connectors and then turn to testing DC power.

## AT Power Connectors

A pair of connectors, P8 and P9, link the AT power supply to the AT motherboard. These connectors have a row of teeth along one side and a small guide on the opposite side that help to hold the connection in place (see Figure 6-16). Figure 6-17 shows the plug on the motherboard.

You might find that installing P8 and P9 requires a little bit of work, because of facing, keying, and figuring out which one goes where. P8 and P9 are "faced" (that is, they have a front and a back), so you cannot install them backward. Sometimes the small keys on P8 and P9 require you to angle the connectors in before snapping them down all the way. Figure 6-18 shows a technician "angling in" the P8 and P9 connectors.

Although you cannot put P8 and P9 in backward, you certainly can reverse them by putting P8 where P9 should go, and vice versa. When connecting P8 and P9 to the motherboard, keep the black ground wires next to each other. All AT motherboards and power supplies follow this rule. Be careful; incorrectly inserting P8 and P9 can damage both the power supply and other components in the PC. Figure 6-19 shows properly inserted P8 and P9.

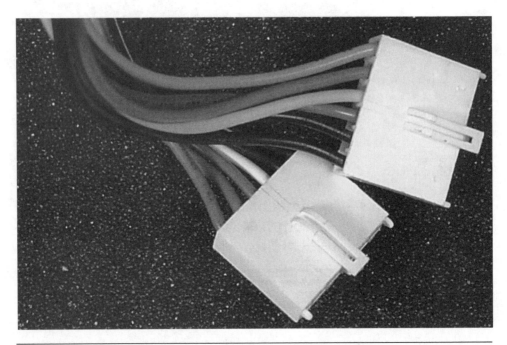

**Figure 6-16** P8 and P9 connectors

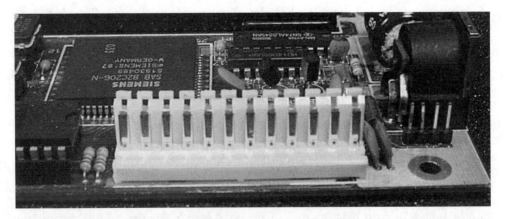

**Figure 6-17** A standard P8 and P9 connection

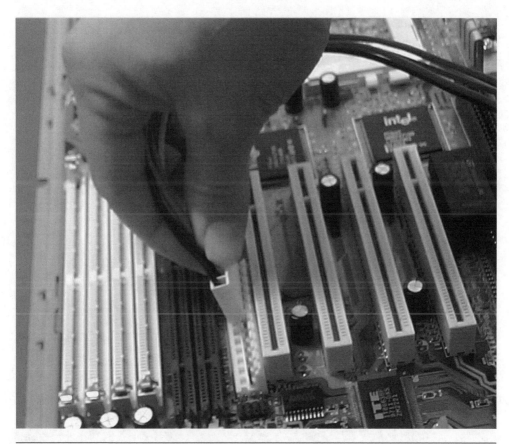

**Figure 6-18**   Technician installing P8 and P9 connections

## ATX Power Connector

ATX uses a single P1 power connector instead of the P8 and P9 commonly found on AT systems. The P1 connector requires its own special socket on the motherboard. P1 connectors include a 3.3-volt wire along with the standard 5-volt and 12-volt wires (Figure 6-20). The invariably white P1 socket stands out clearly on the motherboard (Figure 6-21). The P1 has a notched connector, only allowing you to insert it one way. You cannot install the P1 connector incorrectly. Figure 6-22 shows a properly inserted P1 connection.

**Figure 6-19**   Installed P8 and P9—note that the black grounds on each connector are together

## Testing DC

Probably a quarter of all PC problems can be traced either directly or indirectly to the power supply. A bad power supply causes intermittent lockups and reboots, as well as intermittent bootup difficulties. Bad power supplies erase CMOS information and sometimes even destroy data on mass storage devices. If you notice any of these symptoms, you need to perform a power supply test.

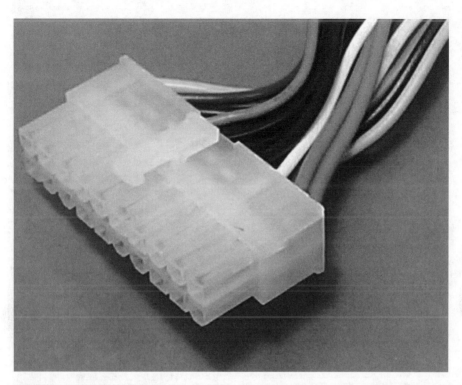

**Figure 6-20** P1 connector

**Figure 6-21** P1 socket

**Figure 6-22**   Properly installed PI connector

## Power Supply Test

The basic power supply test simply verifies voltages. Most slowly dying power supplies begin to show their age by a reduction in voltage. Although this voltage drop shows up in the 3.3-volt, 5-volt, and 12-volt outputs, the 12-volt output tends to have the most pronounced drop. Therefore, I concentrate most of my testing on a 12-volt output. Follow these steps to test for proper DC voltage using a multimeter:

1. Set the meter leads the same way as for AC testing. Turn the selector knob to DC-V, observing the scale if the multimeter doesn't auto-range. Most multimeters have a 15-volt DC range that works perfectly for PC voltages.

2. Test voltages at the motherboard connectors. As shown in Figure 6-23, put the multimeter's black (ground) lead onto any black wire connection, and the red (positive) lead onto a yellow +12-volt connection. Then read the voltages. A good voltage is between 11 and 13 volts; between 10.5 and 11, you need a new power supply; less than 10.5 volts, and you know why your PC won't boot!

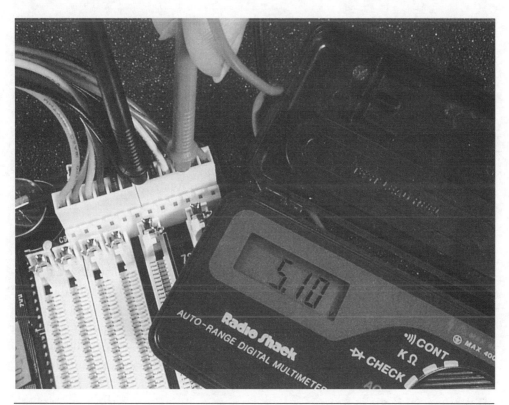

**Figure 6-23**　Testing voltage

3. When checking voltages with an analog meter, make sure that you reverse the leads when checking negative voltages. Because analog meters have only the one needle, you need to reverse the leads to show the negative voltage. The digital meter does not require switching the leads; it will show you a negative sign with the reading.

Make sure to isolate the problem when you can't detect a voltage. Hook up your meter leads as described earlier, turn off the AC power, disconnect all the power plugs from the devices (but not the motherboard), and turn the power back on. If you detect power on the motherboard, one of the devices has a problem and has caused the power supply to shut down. Now you have a simple matter of reconnecting each power plug until you find the guilty device. If you still fail to detect a voltage, turn the power back off and reconnect all power plugs, and then remove the motherboard connection(s). Turn the power back on and, if you now detect the proper voltage, you have a motherboard problem.

If the power supply stopped working when you added a new device, such as a CD-ROM drive, this might not be due to a dying power supply. The power supply simply might not have enough wattage to handle the demand. Most PCs today come equipped with a 230-watt-rated power supply, which is usually more than ample. But if you have an unusual setup, for instance two to three CD-ROM drives, four to five hard drives, or any device that draws more current than your power supply can deliver, you will have to replace the power supply with a larger one. A good guideline is, "Start with 200 watts. Then, for every two drives, increase your power supply by 50 watts." Following this guideline would mean you would need a 300-watt power supply, for example, for a system with two hard drives, a CD-ROM drive, and a CD-RW drive (for burning your own CDs).

## Power Switch

Every PC needs a power switch. Power switch utilization creates one of the major differences between AT and ATX power supplies. AT power switches simply turn the system on or off. ATX power supplies use a feature called *soft power,* which requires a little extra explanation to understand how the switch interacts with the power supply. Let's look at the AT power switch first, discuss some of the problems with AT—specifically its lack of support for current system needs such as power management—and then turn to ATX.

## AT Power Switches

AT power switches come in only two common types: *rocker* and *plunger.* Each of these switches has four tab connectors that attach to four color-coded wires leading from the power supply. These switches handle 120-volt current and are interchangeable. The type of computer box determines the type of switch used in a system (Figure 6-24).

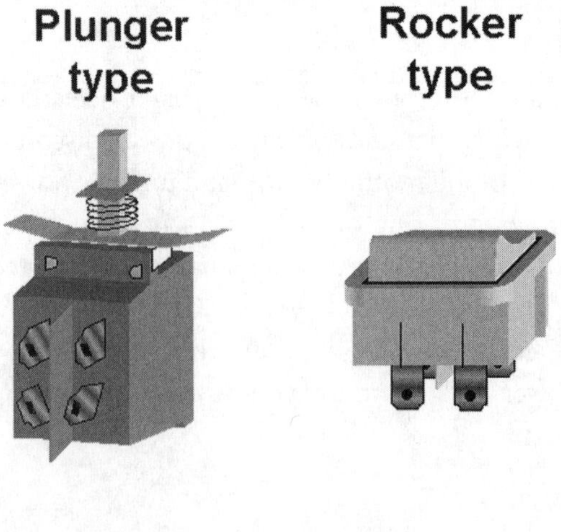

**Figure 6-24**
Types of switches

**Plunger type**

**Rocker type**

You can find inexpensive replacement switches readily at any electronics store, but you must use caution when wiring them. All power supplies must have these four colors properly matched or, when you turn on the power supply, you will be in the dark—literally, because you will blow a circuit breaker. Figure 6-25 shows the proper alignment for a plunger-type switch, with the brown and black wires on one side and the white and blue wires on the opposite side.

Rocker-type switches are a bit odder because they have no clear "left" or "right" sides. The picture below shows the proper orientation to follow. With the "on" position up, the blue and white wires go on one side (the "bottom") and the black and brown on the other.

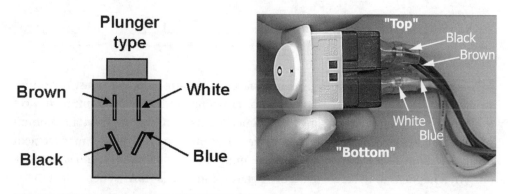

**Figure 6-25**   Correct wire placement

## The Problem with AT Power Management

The AT form factor and AT power supply do not mix well with any type of power management. Let's save the big discussion of power management for Chapter 18 with the discussion of portable PCs, but for now you should appreciate that most systems have the ability to shut down hardware not currently needed by the system. Most PCs enjoy the ability to go into a "hibernate" state where every device, including the CPU, either shuts down or goes into a frozen, hibernation-like state—thus the name "hibernate" or sometimes "sleep" mode. This powered-down mode presents a difficulty, because a system in hibernate mode looks exactly as though someone shut it down. But the system may still have open (and unsaved) files, and so on. So, what happens when a user walks up to a system in hibernate mode? He or she assumes the system is off and presses the on/off switch! In an AT system, if you hit that switch, the system turns off. If by any chance you don't know, turning off a Windows system without first performing a proper shutdown procedure makes several potentially bad things happen. You should never turn off a Windows system without performing a shutdown (Figure 6-26).

**Figure 6-26**
Windows 2000
shutting down

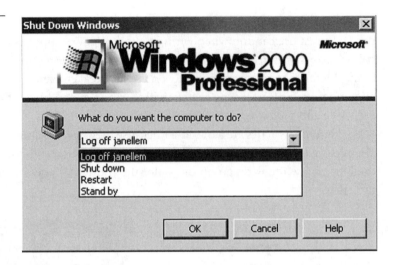

AT's poor compatibility with power management doesn't stop with just the on/off switch. Half of the process of going into power-saving modes involves putting devices to sleep, a fairly simple process involving timers designed to wait for a certain amount of inactivity before shutting down a device. The other half of power management involves waking devices back up. What determines that the monitor should come back on? What happens to make the hard drive start spinning again? AT systems do a pretty good job of waking up a system based on pressing a keyboard button or moving a mouse. But today's PC world revolves around remote access. We need servers running the popular Windows 2000 Remote Access Server to enable salespeople to dial in from a telephone line. Network administrators use powerful remote management tools to monitor and repair far-flung systems. What happens if the RAS server happens to kick into hibernate mode and the modem starts to receive an incoming call? How can network administrators access a user's system that decides to go to sleep at the moment they need to check it? We need systems smart enough to wake up when a modem detects an incoming call or if the *network interface card* (NIC) notices incoming traffic for the system. This is called "Wake on Modem" and "Wake on LAN." Although you may find an AT BIOS capable of these features, Intel designed ATX from the beginning with these functions in mind.

## ATX to the Rescue! Soft Power and CMOS

ATX motherboards and power supplies use a feature called *soft power* that handles all the power management issues quite nicely. ATX power supplies put a 5-volt charge on the motherboard at all times. In a way, as long as an ATX system has AC from the wall socket, an ATX system is "on." This gives ATX systems amazing features. When a phone call comes in, for example, the ATX system can power up the operating system and answer the call! (More on this topic shortly.)

All of the most important settings for ATX soft power reside in your CMOS setup. Start your CMOS and look for a Power Management section. Figure 6-27 shows a detail from a typical BIOS' Power Section. Note the "Wake Up On LAN/Ring." On some BIOS (not this one) you must also define the modem's IRQ. A quick check in Device Manager will give you that information.

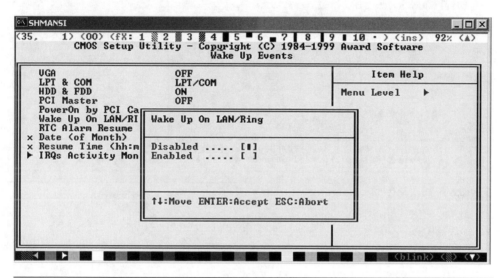

**Figure 6-27** BIOS settings for Wake Up On LAN/Ring

Take a look at the "Soft-Off by PWRBTN" option in Figure 6-28. This determines the function of the on/off switch. You may set this switch to work exactly like an AT switch (instant off), or you may set it to the more common "4 second delay." Many BIOS, most commonly laptop BIOS, give the option to kick the system into sleep mode with a quick press of the on/off button, or to go completely off if you hold down the button for a set number of seconds (usually 4-6 seconds).

## Handling Soft Power

Handling ATX power supplies requires special consideration. Understand that an ATX power supply **never turns off.** As long as that power supply stays connected to a power outlet, as mentioned previously, the power supply will continue to supply 5 volts to the motherboard, regardless of what power state the system is in currently. Always unplug an ATX system before you do any work! For years, techs constantly bickered about the merits of leaving a system plugged in or unplugged while you serviced a system. ATX settles this issue forever. Many ATX power supplies provide a real on/off switch on the back of the system (Figure 6-29). If you really need the system shut down with no power to the motherboard, use this switch.

```
          CMOS Setup Utility - Copyright (C) 1984-1999 Award Software
                            Power Management Setup

     ▶ Power Management          Press Enter                   Item Help
       ACPI Suspend Type         S1(POS)
       PM Control by APM         Yes                    Menu Level    ▶
       Video Off Option          Suspend -> Off
       Video Off Method          V/H SYNC+Blank
       MODEM Use IRQ             NA
       Soft-Off by PWRBTN        Instant-Off
     ▶ Wake Up Events            Press Enter




     ↑↓ → ←:Move  Enter:Select  +/-/PU/PD:Value  F10:Save  ESC:Exit  F1:General Help
          F5:Previous Values  F6:Fail-Safe Defaults  F7:Optimized Defaults
```

**Figure 6-28**   Soft-off options

**Figure 6-29**   On/off switch for ATX system

When working on a system, I often find using the power button inconvenient. Instead, I'll just use a set of car keys or a screwdriver to contact the two wires to start and stop the system. Just make sure to short only the two power jumpers (Figure 6-30).

**Figure 6-30**   Shorting the soft on/off jumpers

The power switch and soft power really show the most substantial differences between AT and ATX systems. Fortunately, the rest of the chapter issues are identical for both AT and ATX systems, starting with the connections to peripherals.

## Connections to Peripherals

Many different devices inside the PC require power. These include hard drives, floppy drives, CD-ROM drives, ZIP drives, and fans. Your power supply has two or possibly three different types of connectors that plug into your peripherals. Let's take a look at each of these power connections. Both AT and ATX share these same types of connectors.

## Molex Connectors

The first and most common type of connection is called the *Molex*. The Molex connector is primarily used for devices that need both 12 V and 5 V of power (Figure 6-31).

**Figure 6-31**
Standard Molex
connector

The Molex connector has *chamfers* (notches), which make for easy installation. These chamfers can be defeated if you push hard enough, so always inspect the Molex connection to ensure proper orientation before you install.

Installing a Molex backwards will almost certainly destroy the device into which the Molex is connected (Figure 6-32).

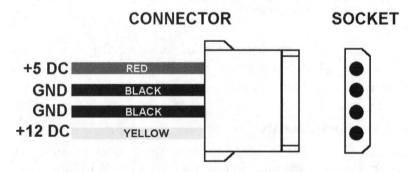

**Figure 6-32**   Diagram of Molex connector and socket

## Mini Connectors

Most systems also provide a *mini* connector. The mini is used primarily on 3.5-inch floppy drives, because floppy drive makers have adopted the mini connector for that use (Figure 6-33).

**Figure 6-33**
Standard
mini connector

Be careful about installing the mini connectors! Whereas Molex connectors are extremely difficult (but not impossible) to install incorrectly into a Molex socket, inserting a mini incorrectly takes very little effort. Installing a mini incorrectly will almost certainly destroy the device (Figure 6-34). Figure 6-35 depicts a correctly oriented mini connection.

## Splitters and Converters
You may occasionally find yourself not having enough connectors to power all of the devices inside your PC. In this case, you can purchase splitters to create more connections (Figure 6-36).

## Wattage
Power supplies are rated in watts. A PC requires sufficient wattage for the machine to run properly. The average desktop PC with two hard drives and a CD-ROM will need ~115 to ~130 watts while running and up to 200 watts when booting up. Play it safe and buy 230- to 250-watt power supplies. They are by far the most common wattages of power supplies and will give you plenty of extra power for bootup as well as for whatever you add to the system in the future.

## Sizes
Power supplies are available in a modest variety of shapes and sizes, usually tied to the form factor. Most desktop and mini-tower PCs use the standard ATX power supply.

**Figure 6-34**
Diagram of mini connector and socket

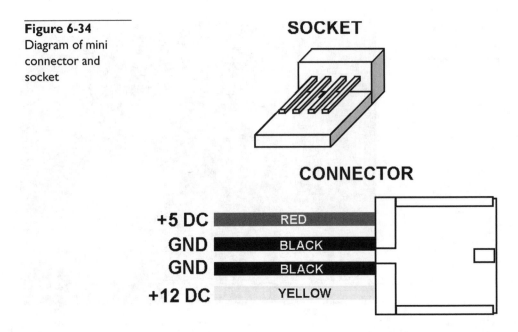

SOCKET

CONNECTOR

+5 DC RED
GND BLACK
GND BLACK
+12 DC YELLOW

When replacing a power supply, save time and repeat visits to your friendly neighborhood electronics parts shop. Remove the suspect power supply and take it in with you to guarantee you select the correct replacement.

## The Power Supply Fan

The power supply fan provides the basic cooling for the PC and, if it stops turning, can cause tremendous problems and equipment failure. If you turn the computer on and it boots up just fine but you notice the PC seems quiet, the power supply fan has died and needs to be replaced before running the PC again. Turn it off quickly! This fan not only keeps the voltage regulator circuits cool within the power supply, it also provides a constant flow of outside cool air through the computer's interior. Without this airflow, the CPU can quickly overheat and destroy itself.

Even a disruption (rather than a complete cessation) of the airflow can wreak havoc on computer components. Missing slot covers on the front or the back of the PC, for example, can change the airflow and cause devices to overheat. The CPU usually has its own fan and sits very near to the power supply so it will not overheat from a disruption. Peripherals such as expansion cards and hard drives, however, are not quite so lucky. Have you ever been in an air-conditioned car on a hot day when someone opened one of the windows just a bit? Whereas everyone was comfortable before, suddenly people

**Figure 6-35**   Correct orientation of a mini connector

**Figure 6-36**
Molex splitter

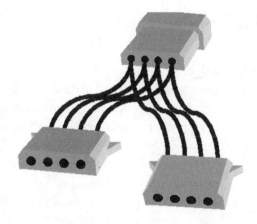

on one side of the car got hot; all the cold air runs out the open window. Leaving a slot cover off can cause a similar reaction inside the PC.

If the fan dies, simply replace it. (Yes, it voids the warranty to open a power supply, but still . . . ) Replacement fans are inexpensive and easy to come by at any Radio Shack or other electronics parts outlet. As you can see in Figure 6-37, only four easily removed screws hold the fan in the power supply. Note also the connector on the fan's power cord. It may be necessary to cut off the connector from the old fan and solder it onto the power leads of the replacement fan. Many power supplies now ship with an external fan, which you can remove/replace easily without opening the power supply.

**Figure 6-37**    Removing a power supply's fan

## When Power Supplies Die

Power supplies fail in two ways: "easy" and "hard." When they die "easy," the computer will not start and the fan in the power supply will not turn. In this case, verify that electricity is getting to the power supply before you do anything! Avoid the embarrassment of trying to repair a power supply when the only problem is a bad outlet or an extension cord that is not plugged in. Assuming that the system has electricity, the best way to absolutely verify that a power supply is working or not working is to check the voltages coming out of the power supply with a voltmeter (Figure 6-38).

Do not panic if your power supply puts out slightly more or less voltage than its nominal value. The voltages supplied by most PC power supplies can vary by as much as –10 percent to +8 percent of its stated value. This means that the 12-volt line

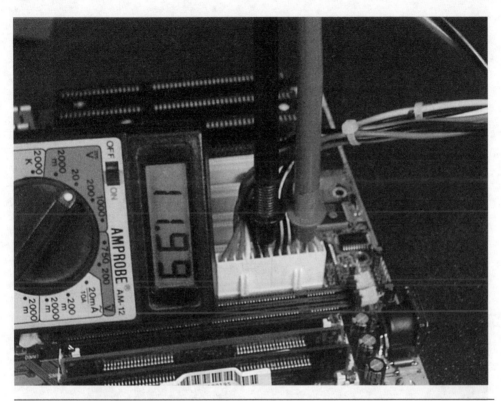

**Figure 6-38**   Testing one of the 12-volt DC connections (results look okay)

can vary from 10.8 to 12.9 volts without exceeding the tolerance of the various systems in the PC.

Be sure to test every connection on the power supply—that means every connection on P1 (P8 and P9 for AT systems) as well as every Molex and mini. Because all voltages are between –20 and +20 DC, simply set the voltmeter to the 20-volt DC range for everything. Figure 6-39 shows how I set my voltmeter.

If the power supply fails to provide power, throw it away and get a new one. If you know how to use a soldering iron and can tell a capacitor from a diode, you may want to open the power supply and see if any components failed. Otherwise, don't waste your or your company's time. The price of new power supplies makes replacement the obvious way to go!

## Switches

The power switch is behind the on/off button on every PC. It is usually secured to the front cover or inside front frame on your PC, making it a rather challenging part to access (Figure 6-40).

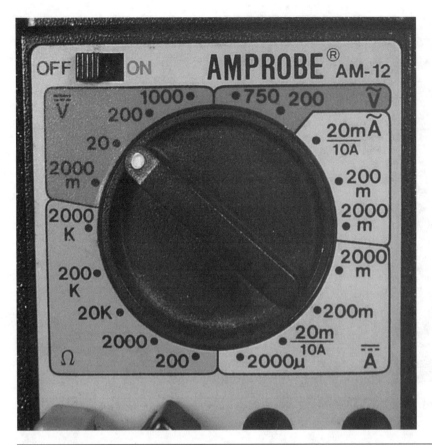

**Figure 6-39**   Voltmeter set to a 20-volt DC range

Broken power switches form a common source of problems for power supplies that fail to start. On an AT system, use a multimeter to check if the switch works properly. On an ATX system, try shorting the soft power jumpers with a key to start the system (Figure 6-41). If that works but the switch doesn't, you know you need a new switch! Any good electronics store stocks replacement switches for both AT and ATX.

## When Power Supplies Die Hard

If all power supplies died easy, this would be a much shorter chapter. Unfortunately, the majority of PC problems occur when power supplies die "hard." This means that one of the internal electronics of the power supply has begun to fail. The failures are *always* intermittent and tend to cause some of the most difficult to diagnose problems in PC

**Figure 6-40**
Typical location of
power switch

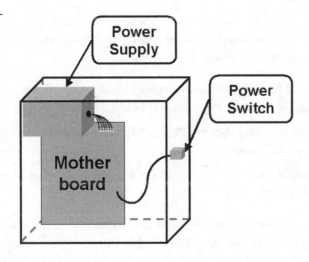

**Figure 6-41**   Shorting the soft on/off jumpers

repair. The secret to discovering that a power supply is dying lies in one word: intermittent. Whenever I have intermittent problems, my first guess is that the power supply is bad. Here are some other clues:

- "Whenever I start my computer in the morning, it starts to boot and then locks up. If I press CTRL-ALT-DEL two or three times, then it will boot up fine."

- "Sometimes when I start my PC, I get an error code. If I reboot it goes away. Sometimes I get different errors."

- "My computer will run fine for an hour or so. Then it locks up, sometimes once or twice an hour."

Sometimes something bad happens and sometimes it does not. That's the clue for replacing the power supply. And don't bother with the voltmeter; the voltages will show as within tolerances but only "once in a while" they will spike and sag, far more quickly than your voltmeter can measure and cause these "intermittent" errors. When in doubt, change the power supply. Power supplies break in computers more often than any other part of the PC except the floppy drives. I keep power supplies in stock for swapping and testing.

## Electrostatic Discharge (ESD)

In its purest term, static electricity is an "electrical charge at rest." If electricity is the continuing flow of electrons through a conductor, then static electricity is the build-up of electrons in a conductor (or insulator) waiting for a path to enable a flow of current. See Figure 6-42.

Friction along with a sudden separation of two dissimilar materials creates static electricity. Friction causes heat that excites the molecular particles. When the two materials separate, electrons from one material transfer to the other, causing an electrical charge, or *electrical potential*, to build up on both materials. One material becomes positive while the other becomes more negative. *Electrostatic discharge* (ESD) occurs when static electricity stops resting and moves toward a ground (Figure 6-43).

Lightning is perhaps the most common event displaying static discharge. Most people have experienced walking across carpeting and, upon touching a doorknob, receiving a shock. And everyone has occasionally experienced the "static cling" caused by the rubbing of different fabrics like wool and silk (Figure 6-44).

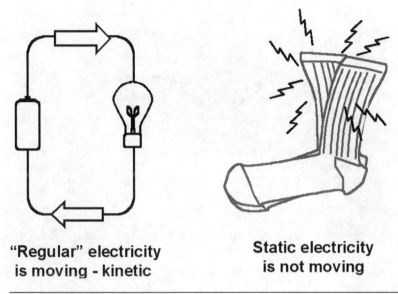

**"Regular" electricity is moving - kinetic**

**Static electricity is not moving**

**Figure 6-42**   Static electricity

**Figure 6-43**
ESD is charge
moving toward
ground

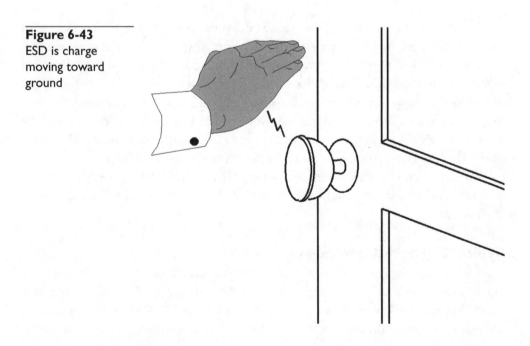

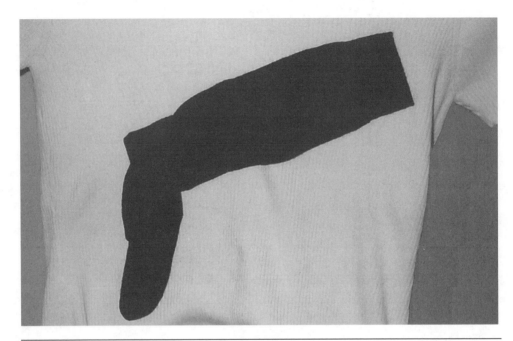

**Figure 6-44**   Static cling

The amount of static electricity generated depends on the materials in contact with each other, the amount of friction, the relative humidity, and the speed of separation. Common plastic will generally create the greatest static charge. Low humidity and buildings using dry heated air in the winter promote the generation of static charges. Materials that easily transfer charges between atoms are called *conductors* and have free electrons in their molecular construction. Good conductors are metals, carbon, and the human body's sweat layer. Materials that do not easily transfer charges are called *insulators*. The best known insulators are common plastics, glass, and air.

Both conductors and insulators can become charged with static potential. Conductors will discharge more rapidly than insulators, but insulators will discharge nonetheless.

## Typical Electrostatic Voltages

Humans can accumulate electrical potentials well over 25,000 volts. Although we might experience a shock or other sensation when the charge dissipates, it is a very quick, low-current flow that is not harmful. But as little as 30 volts can destroy some of today's more sophisticated integrated chips, so daily activities can generate static charges on your body that are potentially harmful to sensitive electronic components. Consider the following:

- Walking across carpet: 1,500 to 25,000 volts

- Walking over an untreated vinyl floor: 250 to 12,000 volts

- Picking up a common plastic bag: 1,200 to 20,000 volts

- Working at a bench: 700 to 6,000 volts

- Handling a vinyl envelope: 600 to 7,000 volts

## Costly Effects of ESD

An ESD must reach a minimum of 3,000 volts of electricity before most people notice the shock. Although most of us feel an ESD of 3,000 volts, we fail to feel smaller charges, and yet these charges still damage semiconductor devices. Many of the CMOS technology components can be destroyed by less than 1,000 volts.

Technology continues to advance, making smaller, more closely packed components. The microscopic spacing of insulators and circuits within chips is increasing the sensitivity to ESD. Proper ESD protection is a must!

Most of today's circuits are made using metal-oxide semiconductors. These very low-voltage devices microscopically space apart conductors and insulators. The closer the components, the less voltage required to run an otherwise equivalent device. Some of the latest CPUs, for example, now run on about 1.5 volts of power. The construction of these devices enables a relatively small footprint to contain millions of transistors, greatly enhancing the sensitivity to any voltage excesses.

## Types of ESD Damage

The damage caused by ESD takes on three forms: upset failures, latent catastrophic failures, and direct catastrophic failures.

*Upset* failures occur when a small ESD causes minor gate leakage. Upset failures are intermittent in nature. This type of damage might not be detected by quality control or end-user test programs, but it shows up as an unexplained loss of data. These ESD cause the most embarrassment to technicians because mishandling parts tends to create this type of error. The embarrassment manifests itself as repeated calls or, worst yet, installing a device such as extra RAM. The RAM takes an upset failure and displays random-memory errors during POST. Who was the last person to touch the system? You! "Everything was fine until *you* touched it!" Sound familiar?

*Latent catastrophic* failures occur when the ESD damage causes the transistor junction to weaken; we like to call these *zings*. This transistor might pass all tests, but over time will react with poorer system performance and eventual system lockups. Because latent failures show up well after installation, the cause of these lockups seems "unknown," and the cost to troubleshoot and repair usually makes system replacement worthwhile.

*Direct catastrophic* failures, known as *zaps,* usually occur with ESD shocks of more than 3,000 volts. The device that takes the shock fails completely, and you must replace the part. The obvious failure makes zaps the easiest to find, as diagnosis tends to point quickly to the failed device.

ESD frustrates the best of technicians. The subtle progress and difficulty of diagnosis motivates us to avoid ESD whenever possible. The secret is in your anti-ESD procedures. A good anti-ESD procedure makes the best defense for preventing ESD damage. Without a good ESD procedure in place, you will suffer from the challenge of continual ESD problems. Let's see how to implement good anti-ESD practices.

## Preventing ESD Events and ESD Damage

Once you understand that you can damage a semiconductor device just by handling it before you plug it in, you are well on your way to preventing ESD problems.

ESD problems happen anywhere, anytime. Have you ever watched jet planes as they refueled at an airport? First, they hook up a "static" strap to equalize the charges between the plane and the refueling truck. The truck then connects to a "ground" strap, which in turn connects to a ground rod in the concrete apron to dissipate any stray currents. Or, have you driven your car on a major toll road and seen a "static" wire just in front of the tollbooth to discharge the static from the car so the toll takers aren't shocked as you hand them the money? These two are just examples of how a "strap" is used to dissipate static to a safe place. PC technicians also use a wrist strap in the same manner.

Any good electronics store sells anti-ESD kits. Most contain an antistatic mat, wristband, static strap, and ground wire. Place the antistatic mat on the work surface next to the PC and connect the ground wire to the mat and frame of the PC. Connect the strap to the wristband and put the wristband on (Figure 6-45). Be sure the other end of the strap connects to the antistatic mat. By placing the removed components on the mat, you protect them from stray static stored in vinyl coverings, plastic boxes, and other unapproved surfaces.

Please be careful; AC voltage can kill. Never disconnect and remove boards from a PC with power applied. While you are connected to a "live" PC via the wrist strap, there is a 1-megaohm resistor in the strap to protect you in case of an accident.

 **CAUTION** Also *never, never, never* work on a monitor with the cabinet removed, power applied, and your wrist strap on. If you accidentally reach over the CRT assembly and the wrist strap comes in contact with the high-voltage wire (30,000 volts), you will most likely die.

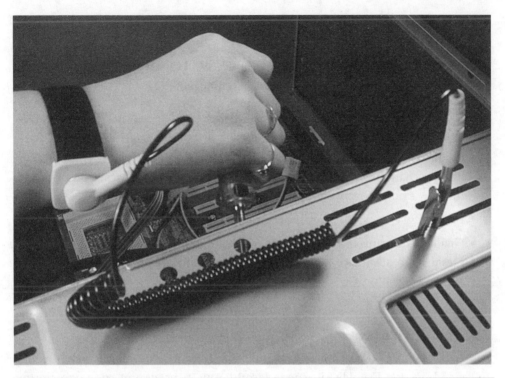

**Figure 6-45**   Proper use of wristband to prevent ESD

Get in the good habit of "grounding" yourself to the PC chassis, because sometimes it is neither practical nor convenient to put on a ground strap. As long as you touch a part of the metal chassis before removing devices and you do not move around a lot, it is okay to go without an antistatic strap occasionally. The following are guidelines:

- Do not be careless.
- Make sure you use good grounding practices.
- Do not place boards on metal or foil; they might have batteries installed.
- While working at a bench, wear the wristband.
- Try not to wear synthetic clothing when working on PCs.
- Store parts in antistatic bags. Styrofoam cups waved over a board can cause damage.

- Keep chips in protective foam while not in use, which keeps the pins straight and equal potential on all of them.

- Never place unprotected boards or components in plastic containers.

- Always touch the metal chassis before handling parts.

- Handle boards by the metal brackets.

- Use antistatic sprays for cleaning. Detergents can build up charges.

- Regular vacuum cleaners are bad! The crevice tool made of plastic will build up a massive charge from the dust it picks up. You can purchase special computer/electronics vacuums that avoid this problem.

- Do not use erasers. Not only are they abrasive, but the rubbing builds up static.

- Finally, make sure that everyone in your company knows about ESD, from the president to all novice PC users. Remember that prevention is the best defense against ESD failures.

## Surge Suppressors

In a perfect world, power companies would supply perfect AC voltage, free of voltage spikes and sags. We do not live in a perfect world. Your PC needs protection from the fluctuations in the power coming from the electric company despite their best efforts. We need devices that, at a minimum, protect from voltage spikes that, if allowed to pass into the system, will result in massive component destruction. We call this protection *surge suppression*. The power supply itself does a good job of surge suppression. Most power supplies handle spikes up to around 600 volts. But the power supply takes a lot of damage from this and will eventually fail. A surge suppressor needs to be inserted between the power supply and the outlet to protect the system from power surges (Figure 6-46).

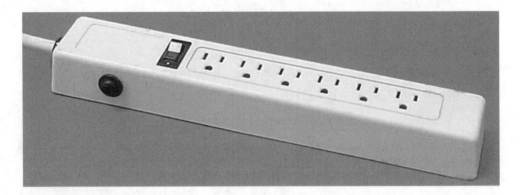

**Figure 6-46**   Surge suppressor

Most people tend to spend a lot of money on their PC and for some reason suddenly get real cheap on the surge suppressor. Don't do that! Make sure your surge suppressor has the "UL 1449 for 330V" rating to ensure substantial protection for your system. Additionally, check the joules rating before buying a new surge suppressor. A *joule* is a unit of electrical energy. Joules are used to describe how much energy a surge suppressor can support before it fails. Most authorities agree that your surge suppressor should rate at a minimum of 800 joules—the more joules, the better the protection! My surge suppressor rates out at 1,300 joules.

While you're protecting your system, make sure to get a surge suppressor with modem protection if you use a modem. Telephone lines produce spikes just as often as your power lines! Many manufacturers make surge suppressors with modem protection (Figure 6-47). Look for a UL 497A rating for the modem surge suppression.

No surge suppressor works forever. Make sure your surge suppressor has a test/reset button. Also, check the manufacturer's Web site for recommended replacement sched-

**Figure 6-47**   Surge suppressor with modem connections

ules. Many companies provide cash guarantees against system failure due to surges, but only if you follow their guidelines.

## Uninterruptible Power Supply (UPS)

An *uninterruptible power supply* (UPS) protects your computer (and, more importantly, your data) in the event of a power dip (brownout) or power outage (blackout). A UPS essentially contains a big battery that will provide AC power to your computer, regardless of the condition of the AC outlet. There are two basic types of UPS: *Online* (properly UPS) and *Stand-by* (SPS).

An Online UPS is a true uninterruptible power supply. A UPS converts AC power from the outlet and charges the battery. The battery in turn provides power for the computer. The UPS battery is always "online," protecting your data against accidental loss from power outages. An added benefit of the UPS is "power conditioning." The battery filters the AC power, thus giving your computer's power supply a very smooth AC current. Though not the budget choice, an Online UPS is clearly the best choice for the PC.

A Stand-by UPS removes the battery from the AC circuit until the AC power drops below ~80–90 volts. An SPS will then engage the battery and (hopefully) save your data. Although a less expensive solution than a true UPS, the SPS has two potential liabilities. Most obviously, removing the battery from the regular AC power also removes the AC conditioning. Data is not actually protected until the AC drops well below the standard 110–120 volts, and neither are the fragile electrical components of the computer. Second, if the battery dies at some point, you might not know until the SPS simply fails one day and your data is lost. An SPS provides fairly good protection from power outages at a reasonable price, but does not protect against poor or fluctuating AC from your electric company.

All uninterruptible power supplies are measured in watts, the amount of power they can supply in the event of a power outage. You can spend a lot of time and mental energy figuring precisely how much wattage your computer, monitor, drives, and so on, require to get the proper UPS for your system. A quicker method, however, is to look on the box provided by the manufacturer. Most manufacturers will list how many minutes the UPS will last with a certain voltage. Cut the number of minutes in half, and that will give you a good conservative estimate of that UPS' abilities.

Although a true or "Online" UPS provides far better protection than an SPS, almost all of the lower-priced "UPSs" sold today are actually SPSs. Regardless, any UPS will give protection for your data and for your equipment and should be considered a necessary part of a complete computer system today.

# Review Questions

1. Which of the following connectors would you *not* see on an AT-style power supply?

   A. P1

   B. P8

   C. P9

   D. Molex

2. Which of the following is least likely to cause a PC to overheat?

   A. Missing slot covers

   B. Broken room air conditioner

   C. Dead power supply fan

   D. Replacing a 250-watt power supply with a 300-watt power supply

3. What is an electrical spike?

   A. Unexpected reduction in power

   B. Steady, consistent increase in power

   C. Power alternating from AC to DC

   D. Short, unexpected, and sudden increase in power

4. What rule should you follow when inserting P8 and P9 into a motherboard?

   A. Orient the connectors so the black wires go to the center.

   B. Orient the connectors so the black wires go on the outside.

   C. Remember to "face" them correctly.

   D. Skip the center pin on the motherboard connection in order to provide proper grounding.

5. ATX power supplies provide all the following voltages, except:

   A. 2.0 volts

   B. 3.3 volts

   C. 5.0 volts

   D. 12 volts

6. Which of the following best describes "soft power?"

   A. Soft power enables AT systems to handle power management.

   B. Soft power enables ATX systems to handle power management.

   C. Soft power enables power supplies to deliver "smooth" DC voltage to the PC.

   D. Soft power enables techs to swap out components safely while the PC is on.

7. Every day at 2 P.M., Rico's computer at work spontaneously reboots. Jill says that his power supply must be dying and he should replace it. Jane disagrees, suggesting that Rico should get a UPS because his office AC, not DC, seems to be the problem. Who is most likely correct?

   A. Only Jill is correct.

   B. Only Jane is correct.

   C. Both Jill and Jane are correct.

   D. Neither Jill nor Jane is correct.

8. Farrah's company has a problem with electricity. Every day at various times, the lights flicker or dim and many of the personal computers reboot or hang. This is very frustrating because the problems do not occur at regular intervals. Thus, almost everybody loses data at some point during the day.

   **Primary Objective:** Stop the madness! Enable the PCs to run all day without spontaneous reboots.

   **Optional Objective:** Fix the problem as cost effectively as possible.

   **Proposed Solution:** Upgrade all the power supplies in the PCs to 300-watt power supplies; install stand-by uninterruptible power supplies (Stand-by UPSs) for each computer.

   **The Proposed Solution . . .**

   A. Meets the primary objective only

   B. Meets the primary and optional objective

   C. Meets the optional objective only

   D. Meets neither the primary nor optional objective

9. Joe reaches for a CPU he's installing in a client's computer and feels a sharp shock when he makes contact. What should he do?

   A. Nothing. Little shocks like that do nothing good or bad to computer components.

   B. Nothing. Little shocks like that actually help the CPU to function, like greasing a wheel.

   C. Test the CPU, and if it functions, button up the case and go on about his business.

   D. Test the CPU, but even if it functions, replace it in the client's PC. The CPU is undoubtedly damaged inside.

**10.** George turns on his PC and nothing happens. The drives do not spin, the LEDs on the case do not light up, and the fans do not turn. What should he do first?

A. Check the AC power source first to make sure the PC is plugged in.

B. Unplug all the power to devices except for the motherboard, and turn the PC on again to try to isolate the problem.

C. Unplug the motherboard power connector and turn the PC on again to try to isolate the problem.

D. Remove the power supply and check the internal fuse.

## Answers

1. **A.** ATX power supplies use a P1 connector.

2. **D.** Upgrading the power supply enables the system to support more devices, but has little to do with heat.

3. **D.** A spike is a short, unexpected, and sudden increase in power.

4. **A.** With P8 and P9, the rule is "black wires to black wires" or "ground to ground."

5. **A.** ATX power supplies do not supply 2.0 volts.

6. **B.** ATX systems use soft power for better power management.

7. **B.** Although you can make an argument for a dying power supply, the regularity of the problem suggests external factors. Dying power supplies usually cause intermittent problems.

8. **A.** Nothing in the question indicates a need for new power supplies, only for good UPS backup hardware.

9. **D.** Even if the CPU functions, it most likely has suffered serious internal damage and should be replaced.

10. **A.** Check the obvious thing first!

# Floppy Drives

In this chapter, you will

- Understand the different types of floppy drives
- See how to install a floppy drive
- Learn basic floppy-drive maintenance

## Historical/Conceptual

Floppy drives enjoy the unique distinction of being the only component of a modern PC to contain basically the same technology as the original IBM PC. Certainly, floppy disk capacities and types have grown tremendously, from the first 160KB, 5.25-inch, single-sided, single-density drives to the 1.44MB, 3.5-inch, dual-sided, dual-density drives in the latest systems. But a modern floppy drive still uses the same cabling, configuration, and BIOS routines used by the first floppy drives in the original IBM PC.

The first PCs predate hard drives. Hard to believe, but when the first PCs came out, the entire permanent storage system consisted of a single floppy drive! You booted the computer with a "bootable" floppy disk to get to an **A:** prompt. Once there, you removed your boot disk and inserted the program disk. If you wanted to save a file, you removed the program disk and inserted a data floppy. Messing with early PCs meant you were constantly swapping out floppy disks—but hey, we loved it! We were *computing!*

Some "high-end" systems used two floppy drives, reducing the amount of disk swapping considerably. If you had *two* floppy drives, you were the envy of the office (Figure 7-1)!

**Figure 7-1**
Ancient IBM PC*jr*
used dual floppy
drives

Let's clear up some terminology right now. The floppy *drive* resides inside the PC. Floppy *diskettes* are inserted into floppy drives. Be careful when using these terms because many techs (myself included) unintentionally interchange these terms or at least assume that you know one from the other. The floppy drive sits inside the system box. The floppy diskette stores the data.

## Why Floppies?

As you will see shortly, floppy disks hold at most only 1.44MB (megabytes) of data—a trivial, seemingly useless amount of data in a world where hard drive capacities store data in multiple gigabytes. Why do these tiny devices continue to survive in this high-capacity world? Surely you know of removable media diskettes, in particular the famous Iomega ZIP drives that store at least 100MB of data. You may even know of the "not-so-famous-but-trying-hard-to-be" LS-120 standard. LS-120 drives read both regular floppy diskettes *and* their own special 120MB diskettes! (We cover these drives in Chapter 8.) What makes the industry continue to use the ancient technology, tiny capacity floppy drives when these newer, faster, much higher capacity drives exist? The answer is fear. PC makers fear incompatibility more than anything else. To survive in the cutthroat hardware world, you must make a PC that works with any hardware or software designed for an "IBM Compatible" PC. As of this writing, no one has yet embraced a single standard for a floppy drive replacement that will ensure broad compatibility. If the entire PC industry—and that including the software makers, especially

Microsoft—could ever decide on a single standard, the venerable floppy drive would disappear overnight. But until that magic day—which, by the way, is nowhere in sight— we will continue to soldier on with an artifact from the Dark Ages of the PC world, the floppy drive.

## Understanding Floppy Drive Types

When floppy diskettes and floppy drives are discussed, the total *capacity* for a specific diskette is important, that is, how much data it can hold as well as the physical size of the drive. Diskettes have come in several different types over the years and in two different sizes. Combining a specific type of diskette with a specific size disk/drive gives you the working capacity of the diskette, although the reality is not quite that straightforward.

Describing a capacity for a floppy diskette creates a problem. Understand that many different devices use floppies. You find floppy drives in Apple Macintoshes, mainframe systems (yes, they still make them), UNIX workstations, and about one thousand other devices that have little or nothing to do with PCs. Each different device organizes—or "formats"—data differently on the floppy diskette, so the usable capacity of identical diskettes changes depending on the device.

The famous 3.5-inch floppy diskette provides a great example of this "flexible" capacity. On my PC, a 3.5-inch floppy formats to hold 1.44MB of data. Taking that same floppy disk and formatting it in my wife's *sewing machine*, however, gives a different story. A sewing machine with a floppy drive? It's true! My wife's sewing machine has a floppy drive. She buys complex embroidery patterns on a floppy disk, snaps it in the machine, and *voilà*! Out comes a "professional" embroidery job! The floppy diskette uses a totally different format. Don't even bother to try to put the disk into a PC; it will not know how to read the data.

So what do we do about this? To meet the broad demand of diskette formats, floppy disk makers use a separate terminology for floppy diskettes. When looking at a box of floppies, you see terms such as "double sided, double density" to describe the type of diskettes.

Most folks use floppy drives in PCs. Knowing this, floppy diskette makers usually preformat the floppy disks to a PC format so you *will* see capacities printed on the floppy disks—but only because they are preformatted (Figure 7-2).

## Types of Diskettes

Only three diskette types ever saw widespread use in PCs:

- Double sided, double density
- Double sided, high density
- Double sided, extra high density

**Figure 7-2**
Preformatted
1.44MB floppy disk

The first and the last are obsolete, leaving only the double-sided, high-density disks available today. Many of the double-density disks were sold in the early days, so you may still run into them. Note also that in order to read the different diskettes types, the drive has to support that type. All modern drives support both double-sided, double-density and double-sided, high-density diskette types.

Great! Now that we know the different types of diskettes, we can turn to the size of the drives and the diskettes that use them. Combining the type and size gives us the capacity of floppy disks formatted for PCs in bytes.

## Drive Size

The first PC floppy drives used a 5.25-inch format. The 5.25-inch figure actually described the drive, as you can see in Figure 7-3, but most users also called the diskettes for those drives 5.25-inch disks! In the 1970s and early 1980s, before PCs became predominant, you would occasionally see an 8-inch format floppy drive in pre-PC computers. Fortunately, these never saw any noticeable use in PCs. If you happen to run into an 8-inch drive or diskettes, keep them! Collectors of old computers pay big money for these old drives!

**NOTE** The term "floppy" comes from the fact that these older floppy disks were actually floppy! You could easily bend, crease, fold, or otherwise mutilate them. Newer floppy disks are rigid and therefore much more robust, but the term has stuck—we still call them floppies!

**Figure 7-3**
5.25-inch floppy
drive

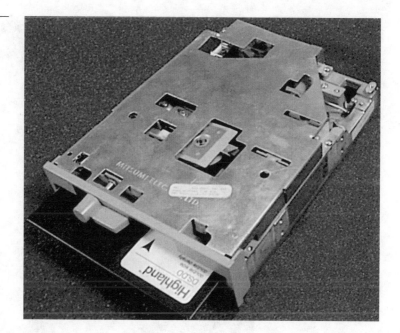

Around 1986, the 3.5-inch drives appeared, and within a few years came to dominate the floppy world completely (Figure 7-4). I'm keeping a few 5.25-inch drives and about a hundred 5.25-inch floppy disks—they may also start to appreciate in value soon!

Great! So we have two sizes of floppies and three capacities. If these are formatted for a PC, how much data will they store? Table 7-1 shows the different amounts.

Hey! What is that extra-high-density floppy disk? IBM tried to push a 2.88MB floppy drive on the industry years ago, but it never caught on. It is difficult to find anyone who still makes them (although someone probably does), but interestingly enough, most systems still support those drives. As mentioned earlier, PC makers fear incompatibility. Therefore when IBM introduced these drives, every BIOS maker added 2.88MB drive support, and most never dropped it.

**Table 7-1**    Floppy Drive Data Capacities

| MEDIA | 5.25 INCH | 3.5 INCH |
|---|---|---|
| Double sided, double density | 360KB | 720KB |
| Double sided, high density | 1.2MB | 1.44MB |
| Double sided, extra high density | None made | 2.88MB |

**Figure 7-4**
A 3.5-inch floppy
drive

We call this a "technology appendix." Similarly to the appendix in the human body, it had a use once, no longer is needed, but still exists. Many examples of technology appendices exist in the computing world. If you have Windows NT or Windows 2000, go to a command prompt and type **FORMAT /?** to bring up the FORMAT help information. Don't worry if you don't understand what FORMAT does; this will be explained later. Look way down at the bottom of the text, as shown in Figure 7-5. See the "20.8"? The FORMAT command supports a 20.8MB floppy disk that never got off the ground, but Microsoft designed the FORMAT command to work with it. Many technology appendices exist in the PC world!

## Test Specific

For all practical purposes, the only floppy drives found in PCs are the 1.44MB, 3.5-inch floppy drives. All of the other floppy drive types disappeared long ago. However, we still (barely) see enough of the 5.25-inch drives to make them interesting to us and to the A+ Certification exams. Fortunately, with the exception of a few connectors, the same procedures are used for the installation, configuration, and troubleshooting of these two types of floppy drives.

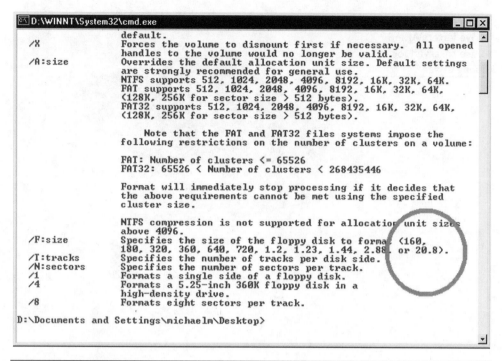

```
D:\WINNT\System32\cmd.exe                              _ □ ×
         default.
 /X      Forces the volume to dismount first if necessary.  All opened
         handles to the volume would no longer be valid.
 /A:size Overrides the default allocation unit size. Default settings
         are strongly recommended for general use.
         NTFS supports 512, 1024, 2048, 4096, 8192, 16K, 32K, 64K.
         FAT supports 512, 1024, 2048, 4096, 8192, 16K, 32K, 64K,
         (128K, 256K for sector size > 512 bytes).
         FAT32 supports 512, 1024, 2048, 4096, 8192, 16K, 32K, 64K,
         (128K, 256K for sector size > 512 bytes).

             Note that the FAT and FAT32 files systems impose the
         following restrictions on the number of clusters on a volume:

         FAT: Number of clusters <= 65526
         FAT32: 65526 < Number of clusters < 268435446

         Format will immediately stop processing if it decides that
         the above requirements cannot be met using the specified
         cluster size.

         NTFS compression is not supported for allocation unit sizes
         above 4096.
 /F:size Specifies the size of the floppy disk to format (160,
         180, 320, 360, 640, 720, 1.2, 1.23, 1.44, 2.88, or 20.8).
 /T:tracks Specifies the number of tracks per disk side.
 /N:sectors Specifies the number of sectors per track.
 /1      Formats a single side of a floppy disk.
 /4      Formats a 5.25-inch 360K floppy disk in a
         high-density drive.
 /8      Formats eight sectors per track.

D:\Documents and Settings\michaelm\Desktop>
```

**Figure 7-5**   FORMAT supports nonexistent and old technology

## Installing Floppy Drives

All Windows systems reserve the drive letters **A:** and **B:** for floppy drives. You cannot name them anything other than **A:** or **B:**, but you can configure a floppy to get either drive letter. In a moment, we will see how to configure a floppy for either **A:** or **B:**. However, convention dictates that if you have only one floppy drive, you should call it **A:**. The second floppy drive will then be called **B:** (See Figure 7-6).

Floppy drives connect to the computer via a 34-pin ribbon cable (Figure 7-7). If the cable supports two floppy drives, it will have a seven-wire twist used to differentiate electronically between the **A:** and **B:** drives. Given that the majority of users do not want two floppy drives, many system makers have dropped the twist and saved a couple of pennies on a simpler cable (Figure 7-8).

By default, almost all PCs will first look on the **A:** floppy drive and then the **C:** hard drive at boot, looking for an operating system. How many of you have seen someone (maybe you) turn on a PC and get the following famous error message:

```
Non-System disk or disk error
Replace and strike any key when ready
```

**Figure 7-6**
Drive letters A: and
B: are reserved for
floppy drives

# I can be A: or B: - that's it!

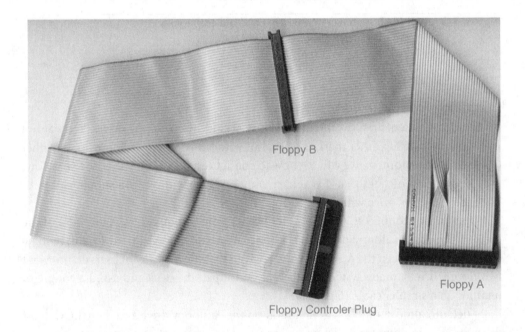

Floppy B

Floppy A

Floppy Controler Plug

**Figure 7-7**   Floppy cable that supports two drives

**Figure 7-8**   Floppy cable for only one drive

After a brief moment of panic, you notice that someone (definitely *not* you) had left a floppy disk in the drive when they turned it off. The system started up, saw the floppy disk, and tried to read the operating system! This process enables technicians to insert a floppy disk into a sick computer to run programs when the hard drives fail. It also allows for silly errors like the one just described, as well as enabling hackers to insert bootable floppy disks into servers and do bad things. Fortunately, most systems have special CMOS settings that enable you to change this. In just a moment, I'll show you how to change the boot order to something other than the default drive **A:** then **C:**.

## Inserting Ribbon Cables

Look again at the floppy cable in Figure 7-8. Notice the connector on the left side. This connector, identical to the other, plugs into the floppy controller on the motherboard, as shown in Figure 7-9. Make sure to orient the cable so that the colored stripe points to pin 1.

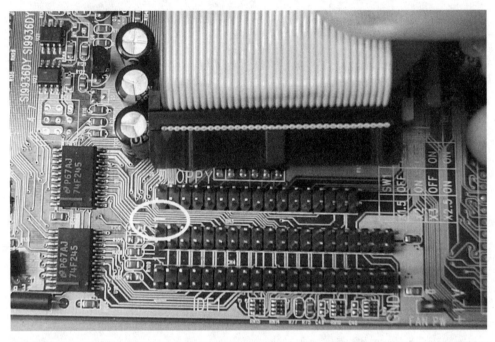

**Figure 7-9**  Plugging a floppy cable into a controller, pin 1 at left

Notice how clearly the motherboard has pin 1 marked in Figure 7-9. Not all motherboards are so clear. Here are a few tips on finding pin 1. By the way, these rules work for all ribbon cables, not just floppy cables! Ribbon cable connectors usually have a distinct orientation notch in the middle. If they have an orientation notch and the controller socket has a distinct slot in which the orientation notch will fit, you have pin 1 (Figure 7-10).

Unfortunately, not all connectors use the orientation notch, and many floppy drive controllers do not have slots, as Figure 7-9 demonstrated. Try looking in the motherboard book. All motherboard books provide a graphic of the motherboard, showing the proper orientation position (Figure 7-11).

**Figure 7-10**    Floppy controller with notch

## CN2 : FLOPPY PORT

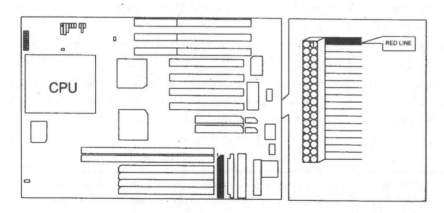

**Figure 7-11**    Motherboard books also show pin layout

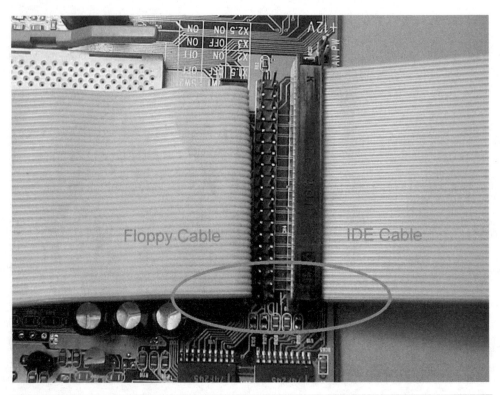

**Figure 7-12** Pin 1 placement is usually consistent on motherboards

Look at other ribbon cables on the motherboard. In almost all motherboards, all plugs orient the same way (Figure 7-12).

Last of all, just guess! You will not destroy anything by inserting the cable backwards. But when you boot up, the floppy drive will not work! This is not a big deal; turn off the system and try again!

After you insert the floppy ribbon cable into the floppy controller, you now need to insert the ribbon cable into the floppy drive. Watch out here! You still need to insert the cable into pin 1—all the rules of ribbon cable insertion work here, too. But before you plug in the floppy ribbon cable to the floppy drive, we need to appreciate which connector on the cable to use; it makes a big difference. The specific connector that you insert into the floppy drive determines its drive letter!

**EXAM TIP**  In the past, the A+ Exam has been very focused on the pins on cables! Know the number (34) and orientation (pin 1 to pin 1) for the pins.

## Determining Drive Letters

If the floppy drive is installed on the end connector, it is the **A:** drive; if the drive is installed on the middle connector, it is the **B:** drive (Figure 7-13). If you ever run into a situation with a two-floppy system where you want to turn the **A:** drive into the **B:** drive or vice versa, you can accomplish this easily by swapping the connectors. (Most systems enable you to do this through CMOS, as well. More on that shortly.)

**Figure 7-13**
Cable placement determines the drive letter

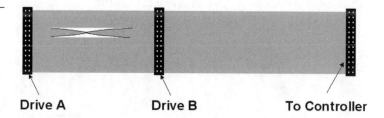

**Drive A**       **Drive B**       **To Controller**

A few floppy drives come with a special set of jumpers that enable you to change the floppy drive letter with a jumper. These jumpers usually say DS0, DS1, and Cable Select (Figure 7-14). (Don't count on this—floppy drive makers have wide marking variances, so no two makers do this the same way!) With this kind of drive you can set the jumper to DS0, forcing the drive to use the drive letter **A:**. Never do this! No one but you will

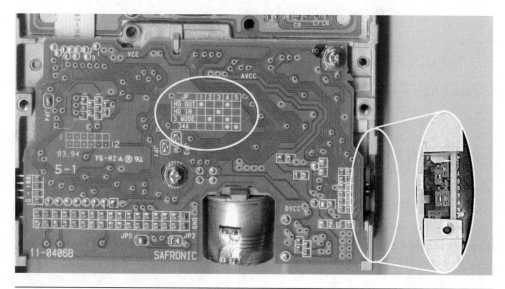

**Figure 7-14**   Floppy drive with jumpers

remember, and the next tech who looks at that floppy will invariably want to change it to B, won't understand why the stupid floppy won't go to B, and will throw it out.

Okay, so now you know that some floppy disk drives have jumpers. You also know to leave the jumpers alone!

## Connectors

All of the preceding cabling examples apply only to 3.5-inch drives. The 5.25-inch and 3.5-inch drives use different connectors. Figure 7-15 shows a 5.25-inch drive connector, and Figure 7-16 shows a 3.5-inch drive connector.

**Figure 7-15**   A 5.25-inch floppy cable connector

Most cables have only 3.5-inch connectors. A few cables have both types of connectors (Figure 7-17), giving less knowledgeable folks the idea that they can install more than two floppy drives. But look closely at Figure 7-17. Notice that one of each type of connector sits on either side of the twist. You can use either a 5.25-inch or 3.5-inch drive as the **A:** drive, but not both. The same applies for the **B:** drive; you can use one or the other, but not both.

**Figure 7-16**   A 3.5-inch floppy cable connection

**Figure 7-17**
Floppy cable with
5.25-inch and 3.5-
inch connections

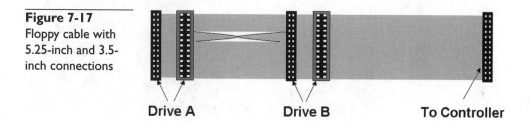

**Drive A**          **Drive B**          **To Controller**

Some really old floppy cables have connections only for the older 5.25-inch drives, but readily available converters exist that enable 3.5-inch drives to plug into them. Equally, stores sell converters to install 5.25-inch drives into 3.5-inch ribbon cable connectors. The controller connection never changes.

## Power

Floppy drives need electricity in order to work, just like every other device in the PC. The power connection will be either the large Molex-type connector for the 5.25-inch drives (Figure 7-18), or the smaller mini connector for the 3.5-inch drives (Figure 7-19).

**Figure 7-18**
5.25-inch floppy drive power connector (Molex)

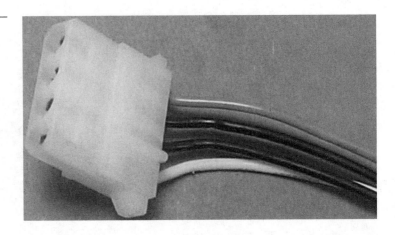

**Figure 7-19**
3.5-inch floppy drive power connector (mini)

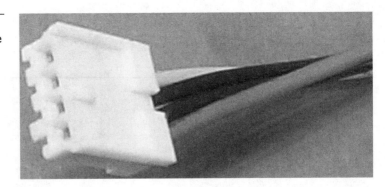

Incorrectly inserting a power connector will instantly destroy the floppy drive. Inspect the power connector carefully to ensure correct orientation before you plug it into the floppy drive! Inserting a Molex connector *correctly* often takes a lot of pushing and wiggling. Inserting a Molex incorrectly, on the other hand, requires more strength than I possess, but I have watched a few brawny techs do it!

Although incorrectly inserting a Molex rarely occurs, inserting a mini connector incorrectly takes little effort. Look at the following "from below" figure of a properly installed mini connector—note the chamfers beveled edges that show correct orientation (Figure 7-20). The problem lies in the plastic used to make the connector. The plastic connector easily bends, giving even the least brawny techs the ability to put the plug in a mini backwards or to hit only three of the four pins. Be careful inserting a mini connector!

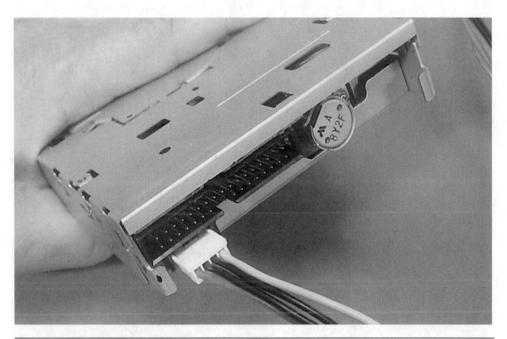

**Figure 7-20**    Properly installed mini connector

Great! You have installed a floppy drive! Compare your floppy drive connections with Figure 7-21. Do they look correct? Just for completeness, Figure 7-22 shows the installation of two floppy drives. Look at the connection to the ribbon cable to determine which one is **A:** and which one is **B:**. Once you have physically installed the floppy drive, it's time to go into CMOS.

## CMOS

After the floppy drive is installed, the next step is configuring the CMOS settings, which must correspond to the capacities of the drives. Look in your CMOS for something called "Standard CMOS Settings" or "Storage." Most CMOS setups have the **A:** drive configured by default for a 3.5-inch 1.44MB drive. You simply need to double-check the setting in CMOS and, if it's okay, get out without changing anything. Figure 7-23 shows a typical CMOS setting for floppy drives.

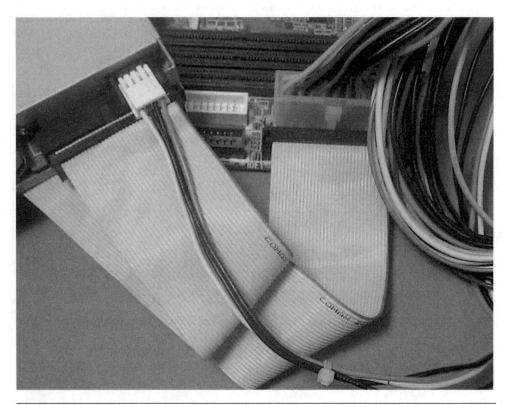

**Figure 7-21**    Floppy drive connections

On the rare occasion that you require a different setting from the typical 1.44MB 3.5-inch **A:** drive, simply select the drive (**A:** or **B:**) and enter the correct capacity. Figure 7-24 shows a CMOS with another 3.5-inch floppy drive on **B:**.

Do you notice the "Floppy 3 Mode Support" option? Look in the "Beyond A+" section, later in this chapter, for an explanation of this CMOS option!

You can find three other options on a current CMOS screen that interest techs: Swap Floppy Device, Boot Up Floppy Seek, and Boot Sequence. Each of these settings enables us to make useful, although not necessary, modifications.

The Swap Floppy Device setting enables you to change the **A:** and the **B:** drives without moving the cables. It may take some poking around to find it, and not every CMOS has the option (Figure 7-25). This is great in situations where you have a PC with two floppy drives but that won't boot to the **A:** drive. You can switch the cable connections, of course, but this CMOS setting does the switching electronically.

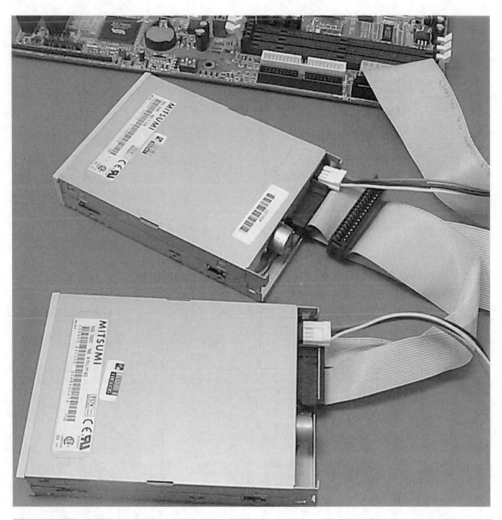

**Figure 7-22**   Installation of two floppy drives

Disabling the Boot Up Floppy Seek option tells the PC not to check the floppy disk during the POST, which isn't very handy except for speeding up the boot process. Please do not confuse this option with booting from the floppy! This option does not skip searching the floppy for an operating system after the POST (Figure 7-26). If you want to skip the floppy disk, read the next paragraph.

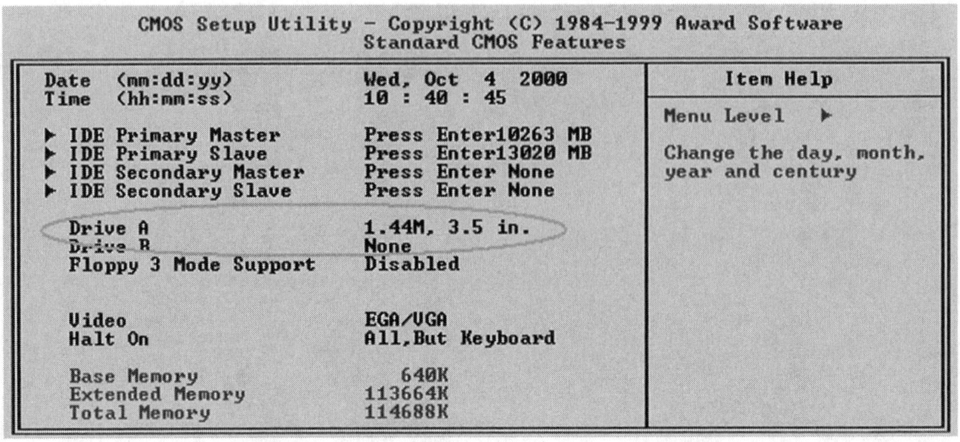

```
          CMOS Setup Utility - Copyright (C) 1984-1999 Award Software
                         Standard CMOS Features
 ┌─────────────────────────────────────────────────┬──────────────────────┐
 │ Date   (mm:dd:yy)          Wed, Oct  4  2000      │      Item Help       │
 │ Time   (hh:mm:ss)          10 : 40 : 45           │                      │
 │                                                   │ Menu Level   ▶       │
 │ ▶ IDE Primary Master       Press Enter10263 MB    │                      │
 │ ▶ IDE Primary Slave        Press Enter13020 MB    │ Change the day, month,│
 │ ▶ IDE Secondary Master     Press Enter None       │ year and century     │
 │ ▶ IDE Secondary Slave      Press Enter None       │                      │
 │                                                   │                      │
 │   Drive A                  1.44M, 3.5 in.         │                      │
 │   Drive B                  None                   │                      │
 │   Floppy 3 Mode Support    Disabled               │                      │
 │                                                   │                      │
 │   Video                    EGA/VGA                │                      │
 │   Halt On                  All,But Keyboard       │                      │
 │                                                   │                      │
 │   Base Memory                 640K                │                      │
 │   Extended Memory          113664K                │                      │
 │   Total Memory             114688K                │                      │
 └─────────────────────────────────────────────────┴──────────────────────┘
```

**Figure 7-23** CMOS with floppy drive selection

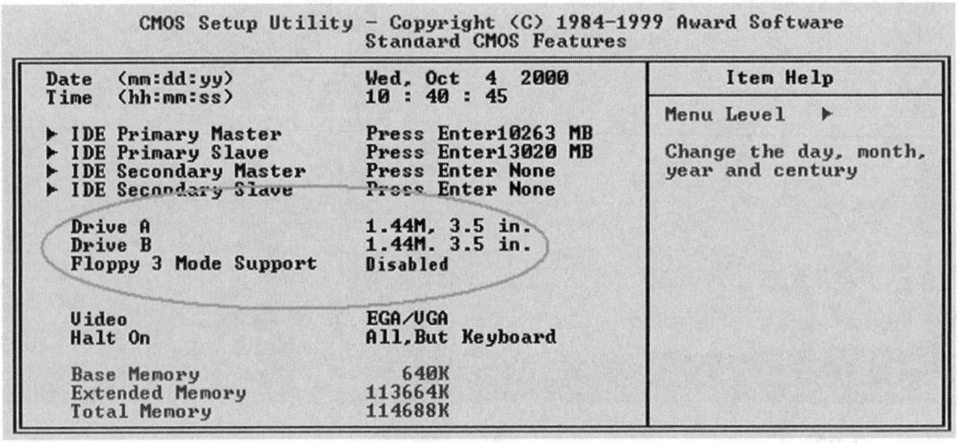

```
          CMOS Setup Utility - Copyright (C) 1984-1999 Award Software
                         Standard CMOS Features
 ┌─────────────────────────────────────────────────┬──────────────────────┐
 │ Date   (mm:dd:yy)          Wed, Oct  4  2000      │      Item Help       │
 │ Time   (hh:mm:ss)          10 : 40 : 45           │                      │
 │                                                   │ Menu Level   ▶       │
 │ ▶ IDE Primary Master       Press Enter10263 MB    │                      │
 │ ▶ IDE Primary Slave        Press Enter13020 MB    │ Change the day, month,│
 │ ▶ IDE Secondary Master     Press Enter None       │ year and century     │
 │ ▶ IDE Secondary Slave      Press Enter None       │                      │
 │                                                   │                      │
 │   Drive A                  1.44M, 3.5 in.         │                      │
 │   Drive B                  1.44M, 3.5 in.         │                      │
 │   Floppy 3 Mode Support    Disabled               │                      │
 │                                                   │                      │
 │   Video                    EGA/VGA                │                      │
 │   Halt On                  All,But Keyboard       │                      │
 │                                                   │                      │
 │   Base Memory                 640K                │                      │
 │   Extended Memory          113664K                │                      │
 │   Total Memory             114688K                │                      │
 └─────────────────────────────────────────────────┴──────────────────────┘
```

**Figure 7-24** CMOS setting for two different floppy drives

The third option techs often play with in CMOS is the Boot Sequence. Earlier, I mentioned that the default boot sequence for a PC is drive **A:** then drive **C:**. Although that statement certainly is true, almost every system provides at least three boot devices, usually A:, C:, and then the CD-ROM! Yes, most systems assume you may want to boot off of your CD-ROM drive. In fact, when we get to Windows 2000, you'll see that the Windows 2000 Install CD-ROM is bootable, motivating you to want to tell the system to

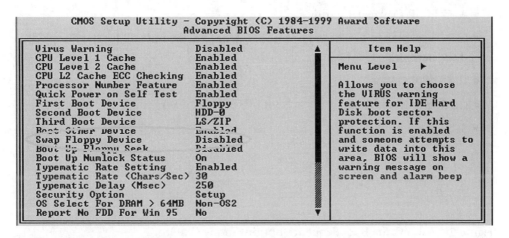

**Figure 7-25**   CMOS Swap Floppy Device option

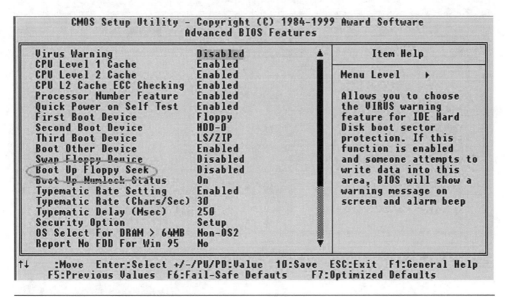

**Figure 7-26**   CMOS Boot Up Floppy Seek option

boot off of the CD-ROM. The Boot Sequence CMOS option enables you to change the boot sequence from the classic A then C to a broad selection of boot options. Here is a list of options from my CMOS. Remember, CMOS settings differ greatly between PCs—some systems may not even have this option!

- A, C, SCSI[1] (My usual setting)
- C, A, SCSI (When I want to boot from the hard drive, but still hit the floppy drive if the hard drive fails)
- C, CDROM, A
- CDROM, C, A (When I want to boot off the CD-ROM)
- SCSI, A, C
- SCSI, C, A
- C only (Super Safety option)
- LS/ZIP[2], C

Figure 7-27 shows the Boot Sequence options in my CMOS.

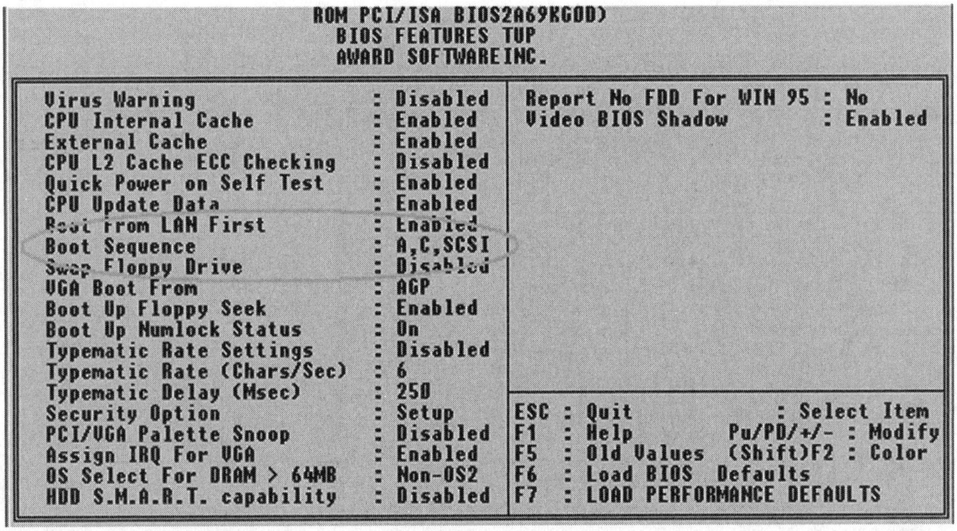

```
               ROM PCI/ISA BIOS2A69KGOD)
                   BIOS FEATURES TUP
                 AWARD SOFTWAREINC.

 Virus Warning              : Disabled   Report No FDD For WIN 95 : No
 CPU Internal Cache         : Enabled    Video BIOS Shadow        : Enabled
 External Cache             : Enabled
 CPU L2 Cache ECC Checking  : Disabled
 Quick Power on Self Test   : Enabled
 CPU Update Data            : Enabled
 Boot From LAN First        : Enabled
 Boot Sequence              : A,C,SCSI
 Swap Floppy Drive          : Disabled
 VGA Boot From              : AGP
 Boot Up Floppy Seek        : Enabled
 Boot Up Numlock Status     : On
 Typematic Rate Settings    : Disabled
 Typematic Rate (Chars/Sec) : 6
 Typematic Delay (Msec)     : 250
 Security Option            : Setup     ESC : Quit              : Select Item
 PCI/VGA Palette Snoop      : Disabled  F1  : Help        Pu/PD/+/- : Modify
 Assign IRQ For VGA         : Enabled   F5  : Old Values  (Shift)F2 : Color
 OS Select For DRAM > 64MB  : Non-OS2   F6  : Load BIOS  Defaults
 HDD S.M.A.R.T. capability  : Disabled  F7  : LOAD PERFORMANCE DEFAULTS
```

**Figure 7-27**   Boot Sequence options in CMOS

The Boot Sequence option gives us great flexibility in boot order. It gives us the ability to boot to CD-ROMs and other nonstandard boot devices, to load software for running diagnostics. Boot Sequence is also a powerful security tool, preventing would-be hackers from accessing a PC by loading a boot diskette.

---

[1] SCSI is a type of hard drive. See Chapter 13.

[2] LS/ZIP is an LS-120 or Iomega ZIP drive.

## Care and Feeding of Floppy Drives

No single component fails more often than the floppy drive. This is not really that surprising, because floppy drives have more exposure to the outside environment than anything but the keyboard. Only a small door (or in the case of 5.25-inch drives, not even a door) divides the read/write heads from dust and grime. Floppy drives are also exposed to the threat of mechanical damage. Many folks destroy floppy drives by accidentally inserting inverted disks, paper clips, and other foreign objects. Life is tough for floppy drives!

In the face of this abuse, the key preventative maintenance performed on floppy drives is cleaning. Above all, keep the floppy drive clean! All electronic stores sell excellent floppy drive cleaning kits. You should use them at least once a month to ensure the best possible performance from your floppy drives (Figure 7-28).

## Repairing Floppy Drives

When a floppy drive "dies," follow these steps to resolve the problem:

1. Blame the floppy disk.

2. Check for data errors on the disk.

3. Check the CMOS setting.

4. Blame the floppy controller.

5. Check the cable.

6. Replace the floppy drive.

## First, Blame the Floppy Disk

The vast majority of the time, when the floppy drive decides not to respond to reading the floppy disk, the bad guy is the floppy disk, not the floppy drive. When the floppy drive refuses to read a floppy disk, you usually get an error like the one shown in Figure 7-29.

Should you get this error, first try inserting another floppy disk. If a new diskette from a fresh box won't work, don't insert another one from the same box. Find another disk, preferably from another box or one just "lying around," to retest. If the floppy drive refuses to read two floppy disks, then start to consider the floppy drive as the problem. Otherwise, blame the disk!

## Second, Check for Data Errors on the Disk

If other floppy disks work in the drive, the floppy disk has a problem. If a floppy disk fails, you have three options. First, just throw it away. Second, reformat the floppy disk.

**Figure 7-28**
Floppy drive
cleaning kit

**Figure 7-29**
Floppy disk read
error

The only downside to these two options is that you lose the data on the floppy disk, and sometimes that is not an acceptable option. Third, run some sort of recovery/fixing software on the diskette.

Floppy disks come preformatted from the manufacturer. We reformat floppies for one of two reasons: either as a handy way to completely erase a floppy disk or as a last-ditch effort to try to fix a bad floppy. To reformat a floppy disk in any version of Windows, go to My Computer and alternate-click (right-click) the floppy icon. Select Format to see Figure 7-30.

Note the many format options. The capacity pull-down enables you to format the floppy as a 1.44MB or as an ancient 720KB. The Format Type radio button group enables you to choose between Quick (just erases data), Full (complete reformat), and Copy System Files Only (don't format the floppy, just make it bootable). You may

**Figure 7-30**
Formatting a floppy disk

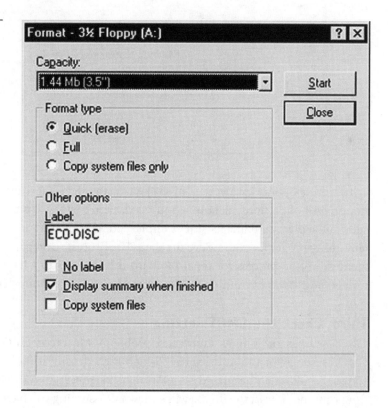

under "other options," add a "volume label," which simply enables you to place a small amount of text on the floppy to help describe the contents. Volume labels were quite popular in the DOS days but are almost never used today. "No Label" means what it says—no volume label. You may also select Display Summary When Finished (Figure 7-31) to see if the floppy drive has any bad "sectors"—512-byte storage areas used by floppy and hard drives. (See Chapter 8 for more details on sectors.) The last selection, Copy System Files, formats the floppy and makes it bootable. The default settings are almost always used.

**Figure 7-31**
Formatted floppy
disk with no errors

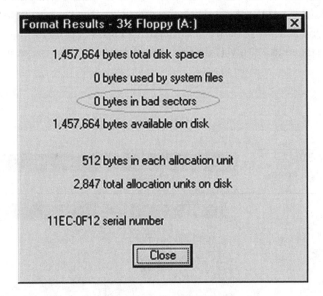

The third option (recovery software) saves the data—and maybe the disk! A bad floppy disk often holds data that you need. Don't panic! Unless the floppy disk has substantial physical damage—for example, your dog chewed on it for 20 minutes—certain utility programs can retrieve the data. The process for repairing floppy diskettes is identical to the process for repairing hard drives. Refer to Chapter 8 Hard Drives to review the process of running the "Scandisk/SpinRite" combination for data repair.

## Third, Check the CMOS Setting

CMOS settings for floppies rarely cause problems. Most recent BIOS makers default the CMOS settings for the A: drive to 3.5-inch high density if the CMOS is accidentally erased. So although an erased CMOS might keep everything else on your computer from running, at least the floppy will still work (assuming you have a 3.5-inch A: drive).

The rare instances of a problem with CMOS can be dangerous because technicians rarely look there. So double-check the CMOS. A quick peek can save a lot of time!

## Next, Blame the Floppy Controller

The floppy controller is extremely sensitive to static and trauma. It is common for floppy drives to fail after a move, after a few months in a high-static environment, or, most frustrating of all, when a new computer is first delivered. (I'm convinced delivery people use boxes with computer parts for their lunchtime volleyball games!)

If the data cable or power plug is loose, the POST will flag with either "FDD Controller Failure" or "Drive Not Ready" errors. At this point, open the machine and verify the connections. If the connections are good, remove and reseat the controller. If the same errors show up again, replace the controller.

Replacing the onboard controller requires two basic steps. First, we need to turn off the onboard controller. To turn off the controller, go into CMOS and find the Onboard FDD Controller option (or something like that) and disable it as shown in Figure 7-32.

Second, we must go to the computer store (Hooray!) and buy a new floppy-drive controller card. You will not find a floppy-drive controller card that is only a floppy-drive controller card. All floppy drive controllers come as part of I/O cards that invariably include some (and usually all) of the following:

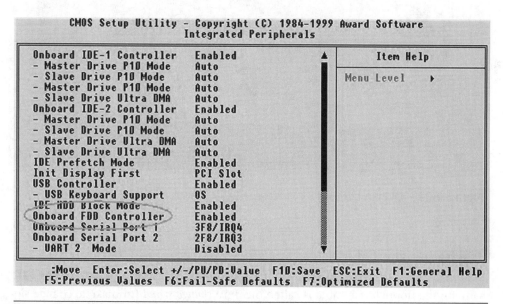

**Figure 7-32** Onboard FDD Controller option

- Hard-drive controllers
- Serial ports
- Parallel ports
- Joystick ports

Figure 7-33 shows a typical I/O card. Note that this one is an old ISA I/O card. These ancient cards sit in old computers, and as long as you have the documentation on how to turn off everything *but* the floppy controller, they work great. Beats paying money for a new one!

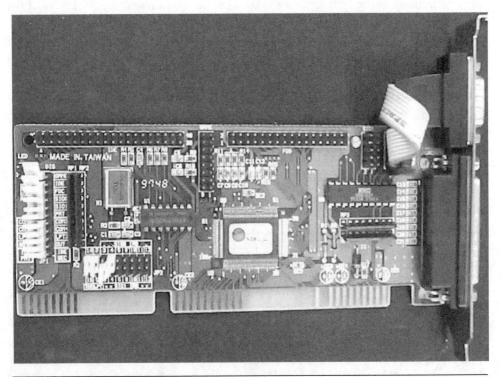

**Figure 7-33**   Old ISA I/O card

## Maybe It's the Cable . . .

If none of the other options work, you need to look at the cable as the culprit. The 34th wire on the floppy-drive cable is called the *drive change signal* (or diskette change signal). When a floppy drive is inserted or removed, this wire is active. When Windows first reads a floppy drive, it keeps a copy of the directory in RAM and will not update that information unless the floppy drive detects a drive removal and activates the drive change signal. This keeps the system from constantly rereading the very slow floppy drive unless Windows knows it needs rereading. However, if the drive change signal disconnects by a bent pin or bad cable, you will keep seeing the same directory, even if you change the diskette! This problem almost always traces back to a bad floppy cable, so replace it and retry.

Connectivity plays a big (and sometimes embarrassing) role in floppy drive "failure." One of the most common errors techs make installing floppy drives is reversing the ribbon cable on one or both ends.

If you reverse it on one end, invariably the LED on the drive (the "light") comes on the moment you turn on the system and stays on. Always check the light on the floppy drive when installing a new floppy!

If you reverse the cable on both ends, the LED will not come on at all—most of the time. Usually you will get an FDD error at POST, and the drive simply will not work. As mentioned earlier, current systems "key" the floppy drive connector and ribbon cable to minimize this issue, but no rule requires the floppy drive manufacturers to abide by this "standard!" Always check the cable!

### Last, Replace the Floppy Drive

At this point, if the floppy drive isn't working, the only recourse is to replace the drive. Replace the bad drive and throw it away. Keeping a bad floppy drive is a study in frustration because almost all bad floppy drives aren't "always bad"—just "sometimes bad." Technicians are often tempted to give a bad floppy drive "one more chance." They install the drive, and it works! They're convinced they made a mistake and declare the drive "good." If the drive is reinstalled somewhere else, however, it will soon die again. Throw it away.

Floppy drives fail more than any other part of a computer system. Given any five PCs, at least one floppy drive will need to be replaced in a year. So keep floppy drives in stock. Purchase them in quantity, at least five at a time, so you'll receive a discount. Buying floppy drives one at a time is expensive and a waste of time.

## Beyond A+

### Other CMOS Options

Many CMOS setup utilities now have an option called Floppy 3 Mode Support. Go way back to Figure 7-24 to see an example of a CMOS with this option. A Mode 3 floppy is a special 1.2MB format used outside of the United States, primarily in Japan. Unless you use Mode 3 floppy disks, clear this option.

"Report No FDD For Win 95" shows up in many CMOS setup utilities (Figure 7-34). This option will release IRQ6 (the floppy drive's IRQ) if the system does not have a floppy drive. You must also turn off the onboard floppy drive controller. It works. The problem with this setting is that very few PCs do not have floppy drives! If a PC does not have a floppy drive, it is probably such a simple system (a net PC or a legacy-free PC) that it doesn't need the extra IRQ. Last, very few Plug and Play devices will ever *try* to use IRQ6, even if it is available. I guess if you were desperate for one more IRQ and were willing to give up a floppy disk, it might be useful. I would leave it alone.

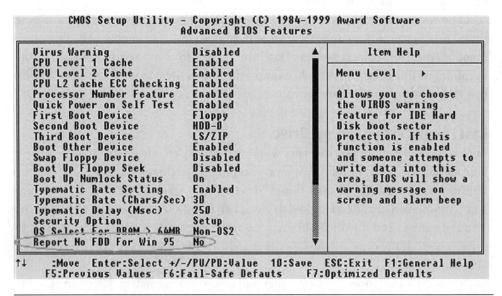

**Figure 7-34**   Report No FDD For Win95

## Fixing Floppy Drives

For years I have told techs to throw away bad floppy drives. But in reality, it is possible, even fairly easy, to fix floppy drives. Roughly 50 percent of all floppy drives fail due to misaligned read/write heads. Many manufacturers make special programs, combined with special testing disks, that enable you to readjust the read/write heads. Some of the programs require an oscilloscope. They are all very expensive, usually around $300 U.S. Unless you intend to repair 25 floppy drives or more a year, the time it takes to fix the floppy and the cost of the product do not make sense. But if you are a *big* operation, they do save you money in the long run.

## Review Questions

1. What is the standard type of floppy drive today?
   A. 1.2MB, 5.25-inch
   B. 720KB, 3.5-inch
   C. 1.44MB, 3.5-inch
   D. 2.88MB, 3.5-inch

2. Which statements are true about floppy drives? (Select all that apply.)
   A. You can only have a maximum of two floppy drives per system.
   B. Each floppy drive was a separate cable.
   C. If you have more than one floppy drive, they must be the same type.
   D. If you have more than one floppy drive, they must be two different types.

3. Rico complains that every floppy disk he inserts in the floppy disk drive reports the same contents, even though he knows for sure that each disk has different contents. What could be the problem?
   A. Pin 1 on the ribbon cable is broken.
   B. Pin 34 on the ribbon cable is broken.
   C. The floppy disk drive is bad.
   D. Rico's crazy. All the disks must have the same contents if that's the way they appear.

4. What is the purpose of the seven-wire twist in the floppy cable?
   A. To enable flexibility in the cable.
   B. The system doesn't use those wires, but it makes a floppy cable easier to identify.
   C. To differentiate between drive **A:** and drive **B:**.
   D. There is no twist in a floppy ribbon cable.

5. All Windows systems reserve the drive letters _____ and _____ for floppy drives.
   A. No letters are reserved. You can choose the ones you want.
   B. A and B
   C. C and D
   D. A and D

6. The floppy drive connects to the computer via a ____- pin ribbon cable.
   A. 68
   B. 40
   C. 36
   D. 34

7. Jill presses the power button on her computer and the system starts to boot up. Text appears on the screen as usual, but the boot-up stops before loading Windows and the following error message appears on the monitor screen:

   Non-System disk or disk error
   Replace and strike any key when ready

   Jill's computer was working great yesterday. What most likely caused Jill's system to get this error?
   A. There is no operating system on her computer.
   B. She messed up her CMOS settings.
   C. A floppy disk has been left in the floppy drive.
   D. Her hard drive died.

8. What determines the drive letter for a floppy drive?
   A. The placement of the floppy drive on the cable
   B. The operating system
   C. The floppy drive's capacity
   D. How the floppy controller connects to the motherboard

9. What power supply connector most commonly attaches to a 3.5-inch floppy drive?
   A. Molex
   B. Sub-mini
   C. Mini
   D. P1

10. George wants the boot sequence of his computer to be A, C, SCSI. Where does he go to change the boot sequence setting?
    A. BIOS
    B. He can't change it
    C. My Computer
    D. CMOS setup

## Answers

1. **C.** 1.44MB 3.5-inch floppy drives dominate the PC market.

2. **A.** You can have only two floppy drives in a system.

3. **B.** If pin 34 is damaged, the floppy drive does not notice when a new floppy disk has been inserted.

4. **C.** The twist in a floppy drive differentiates between the **A:** and **B:** drives.

5. **B.** In all Windows systems, the drive letters A and B are reserved for the floppy drives.

6. **D.** The floppy drive connects to the motherboard via a 34-pin ribbon cable.

7. **C.** Someone probably left a non-bootable floppy disk in the floppy drive.

8. **A.** The connection on the ribbon cable determines the drive letter used for the floppy drive.

9. **C.** The power supply connector to a 3.5-inch floppy drive is most commonly a mini connector.

10. **D.** Boot sequence is changed in CMOS setup.

# Hard Drives

In this chapter, you will

• Understand the concept of geometry

• See the different types of hard drives

• Learn how to install hard drives

• Understand partitioning and formatting

• Fix most common hard-drive problems

Of all the hardware on a PC, none gets more attention—or gives more anguish—than the hard drive. There's a good reason for this: If the hard drive breaks, you lose data. As we all know, when the data goes, you have to redo work or restore from backup—or worse. It's good to worry about the data, because the data runs the office, maintains the payrolls, and stores the e-mail. This level of concern is so strong that even the most neophyte PC user is exposed to terms such as "backup," "defragment," and "ScanDisk"—even if they don't put the terms into practice!

Most importantly, the goal of this chapter is to give you the tools necessary to ensure the safety of the data stored on hard drives. You must have a strong understanding of how they work, how to install them, and how to troubleshoot them. That way you won't have to worry about the bad things that could happen.

## Historical/Conceptual

IBM did not visualize a hard drive as part of the original IBM PC. When the first PC debuted in 1980, it boasted support for up to two floppy drives and support for an external cassette tape drive. It wasn't until the IBM AT computer in 1984 that we saw true hard-drive support in the form of a system BIOS that could talk to hard drives. Since then, many improvements have been made to hard drives. They are much faster and can hold thousands of times as much data as the first 5MB to 10MB drives. Hard drives today are much smaller and much more dependable. They are inarguably an integral part of a modern computer.

Let's start with a trip inside a typical hard drive to see how it works. Then we'll turn to other issues, such as installation, setup, and troubleshooting.

### Inside the Drive

All hard drives are alike in that each is composed of individual disks, or *platters*, with read/write heads on actuator arms controlled by a servo motor—all contained in a sealed case that prevents contamination by outside air (see Figure 8-1).

The platters are made of aluminum and are coated with a magnetic medium. Two tiny read/write heads service each platter, one to read the top and the other to read the bottom of the platter (see Figure 8-2).

**Figure 8-1**    Inside the hard drive

**Figure 8-2**   Top and bottom read/write heads and armatures

The coating on the platters is phenomenally smooth! It has to be as the read/write heads actually "float" on a cushion of air above the platters, which spin at speeds between 3,500 and 10,000 rpm. The distance (flying height) between the heads and the disk surface is less than the thickness of a fingerprint. The closer the read/write heads to the platter, the more densely the data packs onto the drive. These infinitesimal tolerances demand that the platters never expose themselves to outside air. Even a tiny dust particle on a platter would act like a mountain in the way of the read/write heads, and would cause catastrophic damage to the drive. To keep the air clean inside the drive, all hard drives use a tiny, heavily filtered aperture to keep the air pressure equalized between the interior and the exterior of the drive.

## Data Encoding

Although drives do store data in binary form on the hard drive, visualizing a magnetized spot representing a one and a non-magnetized spot representing a zero grossly over-simplifies the process. Hard drives store data in tiny magnetic fields—think of them as tiny magnets that can be placed in either direction on the platter as shown in Figure 8-3. Each tiny magnetic field is called a flux and can switch back and forth through a process called a *flux reversal* (see Figure 8-4).

The earliest hard drives used flux reversals as do the latest ones created today. In the most basic view, as the read/write head moves over a spot, the direction of the flux reversal defines a "1" or a "0." Look at Figure 8-5. As the read/write head passes from the left to the right, it recognizes fluxes in one direction as a "0" and the other direction as a "1." Hard drives read these flux reversals at a very high speed when accessing or writing data. Let's start with this idea and build to something more tangible as we learn a few more important concepts.

**Figure 8-3**   Data is stored in tiny magnetic fields.

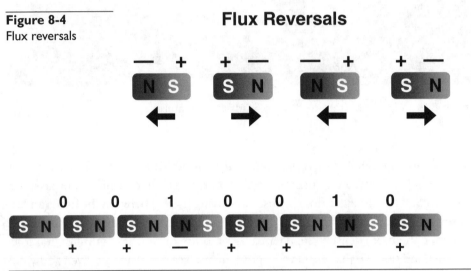

**Figure 8-4**
Flux reversals

**Figure 8-5**   Fluxes in one direction are read as "0" and the other direction as "1."

Certainly, the size required by each magnetic area on a hard drive has reduced considerably over the years, resulting in higher capacities; but the interesting point, and the place where great leaps in technology have taken place, is in how the hard drives use the flux reversals. This is called the "encoding method." Hard drive makers have changed methods for encoding several times over the years, resulting in dramatic increases in storage capacities.

Because hard drives constantly read flux reversals at outrageously fast rates, hard drives need a way to say "where the heck am I?" on the drive. The first encoding methods reserved some percentage of the fluxes to hold *timing bits*. Every timing bit on the drive reduced the amount of data fluxes, but for many years no other encoding method existed. The first method used on hard drives, called *frequency modulation* (FM), preceded every data flux with a timing bit, which took up significant (50 percent) disk space (see Figure 8-6). A substantial improvement to FM, called *modified frequency modulation* (MFM), quickly supplanted the older encoding technology in hard drives. MFM substantially reduced the number of timing bits by only placing them after two consecutive zeroes (see Figure 8-7). MFM stood as the predominant encoding method on hard drives for many years.

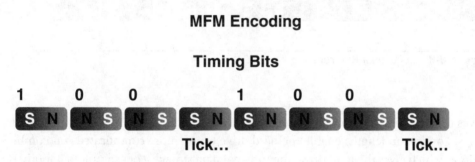

**FM Encoding**

**Timing Bits**

**Figure 8-6**   Frequency modulation

**MFM Encoding**

**Timing Bits**

**Figure 8-7**   Modified frequency modulation

Starting around 1991, hard drives began using a data encoding system known as *run length limited* (RLL). RLL stores data using "runs"—unique patterns of ones and zeros—to represent longer patterns of ones and zeros. For example, 110 in some versions of RLL represents 1000101. Whenever you see RLL, you also see two numbers: the minimum and the maximum run length, for example, "RLL 1,7" or "RLL 2,7." Using distinct "runs" enables RLL to eliminate the need for timing bits, and small combinations of RLL patterns can represent long strings of ones and zeros. Figure 8-8 shows two sequential RLL runs.

Today's drives use an extremely advanced method of RLL called *Partial Response Maximum Likelihood* (PRML) encoding. As hard drives pack more and more fluxes on the drive, the individual fluxes start to interact with each other, making it more and more difficult for the drive to verify where one flux stops and another starts. PRML uses powerful, intelligent circuitry to analyze each flux reversal and to make a "best guess" as to what type of flux reversal it just read. As a result, the maximum run length for PRML

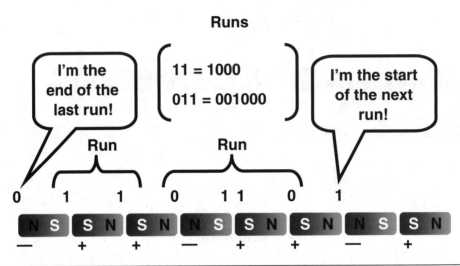

**Figure 8-8** Sequential RLL runs

drives reaches up to around 16-20 fluxes, far more than the seven or so we saw on RLL drives. Longer run lengths enable the hard drive to use more complicated run combinations, which gives the hard drive phenomenal data storage. For example, a hypothetical run of 1001010010101110 might equal:

100100100100101110100100010011100100100101011001001010101001010101001!

Virtually all hard drives use PRML (or a proprietary derivative) today. PRML is the unsung hero of increased drive capacities. Without PRML, hard drives could not pack the fluxes as closely as seen in today's hard drives.

For all this discussion and detail on data encoding, the day-to-day PC technician never really deals with encoding. This is important because so many questions come up on this topic and sometimes knowing what you don't need to know helps as much as knowing what you do need to know. Fortunately, data encoding is inherent to the hard drive and completely invisible to the system. You're never going to have to deal with data encoding! But you'll sure sound smart when talking to other PC techs if you know your MFM from your PRML!

## Moving the Arms

The read/write heads are moved across the platter on the ends of actuator arms. In the entire history of hard drives, manufacturers have used only two technologies: stepper motor and voice coil. Hard drives first used stepper motor technology but have long since moved to voice coil.

*Stepper motor* technology moved the arm in fixed increments or steps. This early technology had several limitations. Because the interface between motor and actuator arm required minimal slippage in order to ensure precise and reproducible movements, the positioning of the arms became less precise over time. This physical deterioration caused data transfer errors. Additionally, heat deformation wreaked havoc with stepper motor drives. Just as valve clearances in automobile engines change with operating temperature, the positioning accuracy changed as the PC operated and various hard drive components got warmer. Although very small, these changes caused problems. Accessing the data written on a cold hard drive, for example, became difficult after the disk warmed. In addition, the read/write heads could damage the disk surface if not "parked" (set in a nondata area) when not in use, requiring techs to use special "parking" programs before transporting a stepper motor drive.

All hard drives made today employ a linear motor to move the actuator arms. The linear motor, more popularly called a *voice coil* motor, uses a permanent magnet surrounding a coil on the actuator arm. When an electrical current passes, the coil generates a magnetic field that moves the actuator arm. The direction of the actuator arm's movement depends on the polarity of the electrical current through the coil. Because the voice coil and the actuator arm never touch, no degradation in positional accuracy takes place over time. Lastly, voice coil drives automatically park the heads when the drive loses power, making the old stepper motor park programs obsolete.

**NOTE** "Parking" a drive is meaningless in today's PCs.

Lacking the discrete "steps" of the stepper motor drive, a voice coil drive cannot accurately predict the movement of the heads across the disk. To make sure voice coil drives land exactly in the correct area, the drive reserves one side of one platter for navigational purposes. In essence, this area "maps" the exact location of the data on the drive. The voice coil moves the read/write head to its best guess about the correct position on the hard drive. The read/write head then uses this "map" to fine tune its true position and make any necessary adjustments.

Now that we have a basic understanding of how a drive physically stores data, let's turn to how the hard drive organizes that data in such a way as to enable us to use that drive.

## Geometry

Have you ever seen a cassette tape? If you look at the actual brown Mylar (a type of plastic) tape, you will not see anything to let you know if sound is recorded on that tape. Assuming the tape is not blank, however, you know *something* is on that cassette tape. The music on that tape is stored in distinct magnetized lines. You could say that the physical placement of those lines of magnetism is the tape's "geometry."

Geometry determines where the drive stores data on the hard drive. Just like the cassette tape if you opened up a hard drive, you would not see the geometry. But rest assured that the drive has geometry. Every model of hard drive uses a different geometry. We describe the geometry for a particular hard drive with a set of numbers that refer to five special values: the heads, cylinders, sectors per track, write precomp, and landing zone. The following sections describe what each value means.

### Heads

The number of heads for a specific hard drive describes, rather logically, the number of read/write heads used by the drive to store data. Every platter requires two heads. If a hard drive has four platters, for example, it would need eight heads (see Figure 8-9).

Based on this description of heads, you would think that hard drives would always have an even number of heads, right? Wrong! Most hard drives reserve a head or two for their own use. Therefore, a hard drive can have either an even or an odd number of heads.

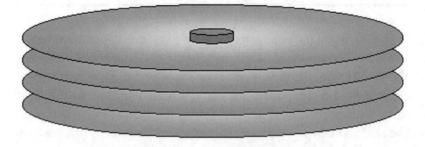

**Figure 8-9**   Heads

## Cylinders

To visualize cylinders, imagine taking a soup can and opening both ends of the can. Wash off the label and clean out the inside. Now look at the shape of the can; it is a geometric shape called a "cylinder." Now imagine taking that cylinder and sharpening one end so sharp that it easily cuts through the hardest metal. Visualize placing the ex-soup can over the hard drive and pushing it down through the drive. The can cuts into one side and out the other of each platter. Each circle transcribed by the can is where you store data on the drive, and is called a *track* (Figure 8-10).

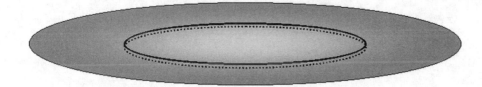

**Figure 8-10**　Track

Each side of each platter contains tens of thousands of tracks. Interestingly enough, the individual tracks themselves are not directly part of the drive geometry. Our interest lies in only the groups of tracks of the same diameter, going all of the way through the drive. Each group of tracks of the same diameter going completely through the drive is a called a *cylinder* (see Figure 8-11).

There's more than one cylinder! Go get yourself about a thousand more cans, each one a different diameter, and push them through the hard drive. A typical hard drive contains thousands of cylinders.

## All tracks of the same diameter are called a cylinder

**Figure 8-11** Cylinder

### Sectors per Track

Imagine cutting the hard drive like a birthday cake, slicing all the tracks into tens of thousands of small slivers. Each sliver is called a *sector*, and each sector stores 512 bytes of data (see Figure 8-12). Note that "sector" refers to the sliver when discussing the geometry, but refers to the specific spot on a single track within that sliver when discussing the data capacity.

The sector is the universal "atom" of all hard drives. You can't divide data into anything smaller than a sector. Although sectors are important, the number of sectors is not a geometry. The geometry value is called "sectors per track" (sectors/track). The sectors/track value is the number of "slices" in the hard drive, and it describes the number of sectors in each track (see Figure 8-13).

### The "Big Three"

Cylinders, heads, and sectors/track combine to define the hard drive's geometry. In most cases, these three critical values are referred to as *CHS*. The importance of these

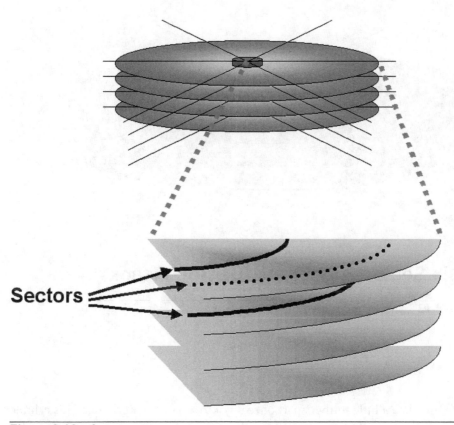

**Figure 8-12**   Sectors

three values lies in the fact that the PC's BIOS needs to know the drive's geometry in order to know how to talk to the drive. Back in "the old days," a technician needed to enter these values into CMOS manually. Today, every hard drive stores the CHS information in the drive itself in an electronic format that enables the BIOS to query the drive automatically in order to determine these values. We will see more of this later in the chapter.

If you recall, the geometry consists of five values, but so far only three have been introduced: cylinders, heads, and sectors/track. Two more values exist for the geometry. Unlike the CHS values, the last two—write precomp and landing zone—no longer have relevance in today's PCs; however, most CMOS setup utilities still support these two values—another classic example of a technology appendix! Let's see these two holdouts from another era so when you access CMOS, you won't say, "What the heck are these?"

## Write Precompensation Cylinder

Older hard drives had a real problem with the fact that sectors towards the inside of the drives were much smaller than sectors toward the outside. To handle this, an older drive

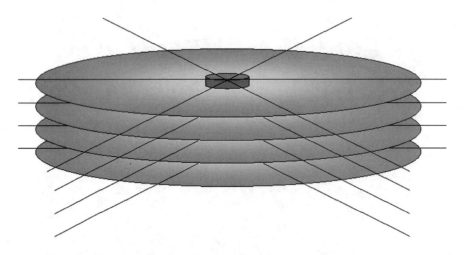

**Six Sectors per Track (Sectors/Track)**

**Figure 8-13** Sectors per track

would write data a little further apart once it got to a particular cylinder. This cylinder was called the Write Precompensation (write precomp) cylinder, and the PC had to know which cylinder began this wider spacing. Hard drives no longer have this problem, making the write precomp setting obsolete.

**NOTE** The write precomp is obsolete.

### Landing Zone

On older hard drives with stepper motors, the landing zone value designated an unused cylinder as a "parking place" for the read/write heads. As mentioned earlier, old stepper motor hard drives needed to have the read/write heads parked before being moved in order to avoid accidental damage. Today's voice coil drives park themselves whenever they're not accessing data, automatically placing the read/write heads on the landing zone. As a result, the BIOS no longer needs the landing zone geometry.

**NOTE**   The landing zone is obsolete.

## Talking the Talk

When discussing geometry on a hard drive, no one would say, "What are your cylinders, heads, and sectors/track?" You just say "What's the CHS?" or "What's the geometry?" Also watch for abbreviations. A geometry like landing zone can be shortened to Lzone, LZ, Park—just about anything. Use common sense and you'll be able to figure it out.

Now that we've covered the inside of the hard drive, go ahead and mentally "put the lid back on" the drive. Let's turn to one of the most interesting (and sometimes a little confusing) aspects of the hard drive—the interface to the PC.

## Hard Drive Interface to the PC

Over the years, many interfaces existed for hard drives with names like "ST-506" and "ESDI"—don't worry about what these abbreviations stood for; neither the A+ Certification exams nor the computer world at large has an interest in the "pre-historic" interfaces. Starting around 1990, a new interface called "IDE" appeared that has now virtually monopolized the hard drive market. Only one other type of interface, the moderately popular SCSI interface, has any consideration for hard drives. (An entire chapter is devoted to SCSI later in the book.) Let's understand the "king" of all hard drive interfaces—IDE and its progeny, EIDE.

## IDE/EIDE

When IBM unveiled the 80286-powered IBM PC AT in the early 1980s, it introduced the first PC to include BIOS support for hard drives. This BIOS supported up to two physical drives, and each drive could be up to 504MB—far larger than the 5MB and 10MB drives of the time. Although having built-in support for hard drives certainly improved the power of the PC, at that time, installing, configuring, and troubleshooting hard drives could at best be called "difficult." Earlier drive interfaces required a number of truly painful steps to get a new hard drive up and rolling. For example, back in those days, the hard drive controller was a separate card that snapped into an expansion slot. This was no big deal except that every time you installed one of these old interface drives into a hard drive controller you literally had to erase all the geometry. Not just the data; you literally wiped the drive clean and reinstalled the geometry with a new controller through a process called low-level formatting. The physical geometry didn't change on the drive; it always had the same CHS values; however, subtle differences in controllers meant that once a hard drive was installed, it either stayed with the controller or you did this "low-level" format thing, wiping out and reinstalling all the geometry whenever you moved the drive. Not only that, but early drive interfaces also required the tech literally to type the geometry into the CMOS. If you typed in even one number incorrectly, the drive wouldn't work! Additionally, the hard drive controller only supported hard drives. This last issue didn't bother anyone back in the early 1980s, as one had yet invented CD-ROM drives, Zip drives, or any of the other devices that today we happily snap into a hard drive controller without so much as a thought.

**NOTE** Don't confuse the low-level formatting discussed here with many of the "low-level format" utilities you see today; they have nothing in common but the name!

To address these problems, Western Digital and Compaq developed a new hard drive interface and placed this specification before the *American National Standards Institute* (ANSI) committees, which in turn put out the *AT Attachment* (ATA) interface in March of 1989. The ATA interface required a new 40-pin ribbon cable and a built-in controller card on the drive itself, instantly and forever removing the universally hated "low-level format."

**NOTE** More recent types of ATA drives, called ATA/66 and ATA/100, use an 80-pin cable. For now, just assume the 40-pin cable.

Most importantly, the ATA standard used the existing AT BIOS on a PC, which meant that you didn't have to replace the old system BIOS to make the drive work—a very important consideration for compatibility but one that would later haunt ATA drives. The official name for the standard, ATA, never made it into the common vernacular until recently. Everyone used the technically incorrect term of *Integrated Drive Electronics* (IDE) when referring to ATA drives. We still do so today.

In 1990, Western Digital forwarded a series of improvements to the IDE standard called *Enhanced IDE* (EIDE). EIDE included powerful new features such as higher capacities; support of non-hard drive storage devices; support for two more devices, for a maximum of four ATA devices; and substantially improved throughput. Regular IDE drives quickly disappeared, and by 1995, EIDE drives dominated the PC world. Figure 8-14 shows a typical EIDE drive. The terms "ATA," "IDE," and "EIDE" are used interchangeably to describe all ATA devices that subscribe to the EIDE improvements—and all ATA devices do!

**Figure 8-14**   EIDE drive

## Test Specific

### Physical Connections

EIDE drives connect to the computer via a 40-pin cable and a controller. Figure 8-15 shows the "business end" of an IDE drive, with the connectors for the controller and the power cable.

The controller is the support circuitry that acts as the intermediary between the hard drive and the external data bus. Electronically, the setup looks like Figure 8-16.

In reality, the EIDE drives have the controller built into the drive. What we call the EIDE controller is really no more than a device that provides connections to the rest of the PC system. When your BIOS talks to the hard drives, it actually talks to the onboard circuitry on the drive, not the connection on the motherboard. But, even though the *real* controller resides on the hard drive, the 40-pin connection on the motherboard is called the "controller." We sure have a lot of misnomers to live with in the ATA world!

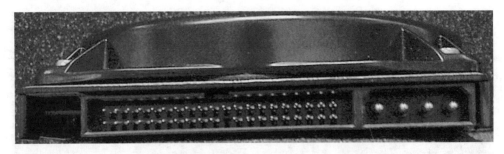

**Figure 8-15**  IDE drive connectors

**Figure 8-16**
Relation of drive,
controller, and bus

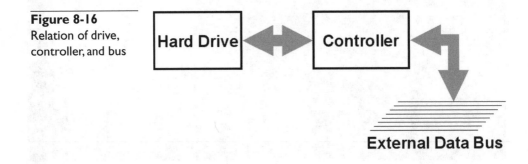

Almost all PCs provide two EIDE controllers. Each controller supports up to two ATA drives, giving PCs the ability to support up to four ATA devices. The controllers are usually on the motherboard (these are called *onboard controllers*) and manifest themselves as nothing more than two 40-pin male connectors. Much older machines might have the controllers on a card that snaps into the motherboard. Figure 8-17 shows some examples of EIDE controllers, both on cards and the vastly more common onboard controller.

Although each controller is equal in power and capability, the traditional-style AT BIOS only looks for one of the two when the system boots up. This is the primary controller. The other controller is the secondary controller. If you're going to use only one controller, it should be the primary controller, although most newer operating systems and BIOS no longer really care. When installing ATA devices it is important that you can distinguish the primary controller from the secondary controller. First, read the motherboard book to tell you which is which. Second, look on the motherboard to see if some printing actually identifies the ports. Figure 8-18 is a close-up of a typical motherboard, showing the primary marked as "IDE1" and the secondary marked as "IDE2."

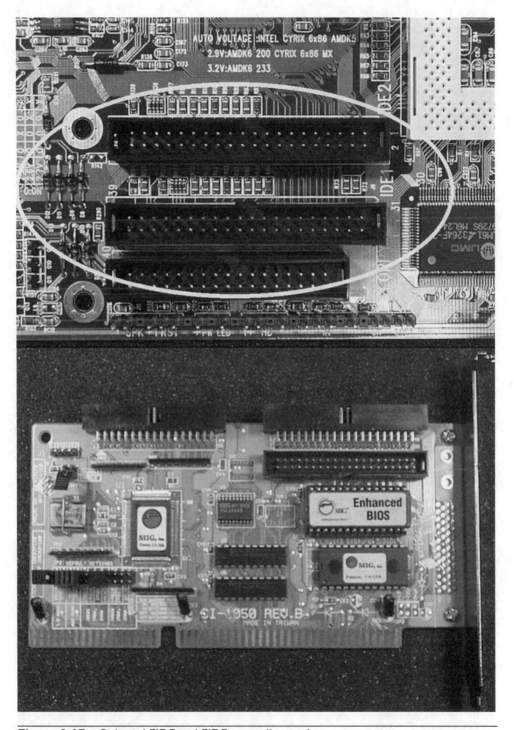

**Figure 8-17** Onboard EIDE and EIDE controller card

**Figure 8-18** Primary and secondary controllers labeled on a motherboard

## Cabling EIDE Drives

The EIDE drives connect to the controllers via a simple 40-pin cable. There are no twists, although you might occasionally see a cable that has a split. A single cable can connect up to two hard drives (see Figure 8-19).

 **EXAM TIP** The A+ exam traditionally focuses on the numbers of pins on ribbon cables of all types!

**To Hard Drives**     **To Controller**

**Figure 8-19** IDE cable

Because up to two drives can be connected to one controller via a single cable, you need to be able to identify each drive on the cable. The EIDE standard identifies the two different drives as "master" and "slave." The jumpers on each hard drive determine these settings. If you have only one hard drive, set the drive's jumpers to master. If you have two drives, set one to master and the other to slave. Figure 8-20 is a close-up of an EIDE hard drive showing the jumpers.

At first glance, you might notice that the jumpers aren't actually labeled "master" and "slave." So how do you know how to set them properly? The easiest way is to read the front of the drive; most drives have a nice diagram on the drive to explain how to set the jumpers properly. Figure 8-21 shows the front of one of these drives, so you can see how to set the drive to master or slave.

Hard disk drives can have other jumpers that may or may not concern you during installation. One common set of jumpers is used for diagnostics at the manufacturing plant or for special settings in other kinds of devices that use hard drives. Ignore them. They have no bearing in the PC world. Second, many drives provide a third setting called "single," which is used if only one drive connects to a controller. Often, master and single drive are the same setting on the hard drive, although some hard drives require separate settings. (Note that the name for the single drive setting varies among manufacturers. Some use single; others use 1 Drive or Standalone.)

**Figure 8-20**   Master/slave jumpers on a hard drive

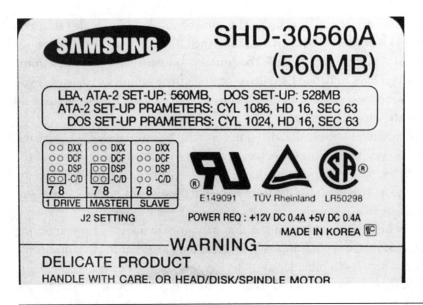

**Figure 8-21**    Drive label showing master/slave settings

## Getting Jumper Information

If you don't have a label on the drive that tells you how to set the jumpers, you have several options. First, look for the drive maker's Web site. Every drive manufacturer lists its drive jumper settings on the Web, although it might take a while to get the information you want. Second, try phoning the hard drive maker directly. Unlike many other PC parts manufacturers, hard drive producers tend to stay in business for a longer period of time and have great technical support.

## Plugging It In

It doesn't matter where the master or slave drive is installed on the cable; just make sure you have the jumpers set properly or the computer won't be able to access the drives. Hard-drive cables have a colored stripe that corresponds to the number-one pin on the connectors, just like on floppy drives. Failing to plug in the drive properly will also prevent the PC from recognizing the drive.

If you incorrectly set the master/slave jumpers or cable to the hard drives, you won't break anything; it just won't work. There are only three ways you can install a hard drive to one controller (see Figure 8-22).

## CMOS

After physically installing the hard drive, you must enter its geometry into the CMOS through the CMOS setup program. Without this information, the hard drive will not work. Before IDE drives, you used to have to take the numbers from the drive and type

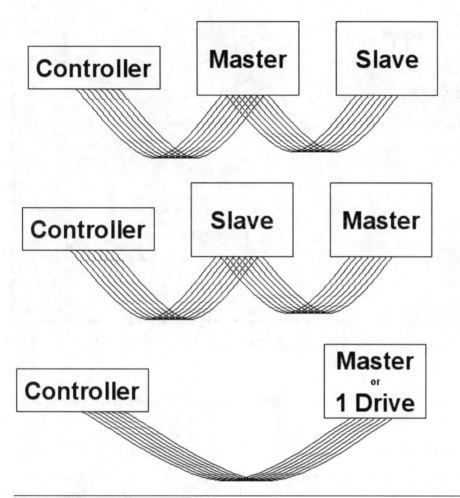

**Figure 8-22**    The three ways to connect to one controller

in each value for the cylinders, heads, sectors/track, landing zone, and write precomp. IDE/EIDE drives can be queried through software, and they will simply tell the CMOS the correct settings. Figure 8-23 shows the hard-drive configuration information in a typical CMOS—in this case, a CMOS from an older Award BIOS.

Note that settings exist for only two drives. In the days before EIDE, PCs could use only two drives. Why? Remember that the original CMOS in the first IBM 286 AT could store only 64 bytes of data. The original IBM engineers allocated just enough space for two sets of drive information, so the standard enabled only two drives. Besides, who would ever need more than two hard drives?

Today's EIDE CMOS setup utilities handle up to four ATA devices, and the days of typing in values are long gone. In fact, you can simply set the "type" to auto, and the system will set up the hard drive's CMOS settings for you. Setting up the drive in CMOS

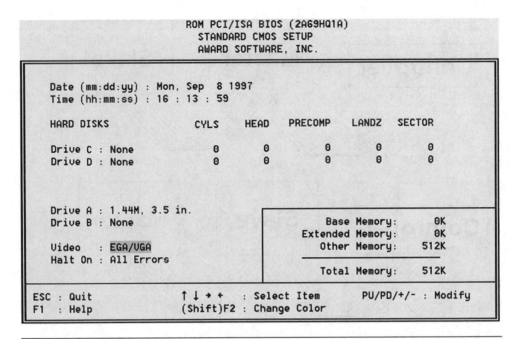

**Figure 8-23** Award CMOS hard drive configuration

is very easy with current PCs. Nevertheless, a few concepts need to be explained, starting with hard-drive types.

### Hard-Drive Types

The number of heads, cylinders, sectors/track, write precomp, and landing zone determine how the hard-drive controller accesses the physical hard drive. Each number must be correct if the hard drive is to function properly. When IBM created the first CMOS on the 286 AT, they believed that the five different geometry numbers would be too complicated for normal users to configure. For simplicity, IBM established 15 preset combinations of hard-drive geometries, called *hard-drive types* (see Table 8-1). So instead of worrying about five different variables, users could simply enter a hard-drive type into the CMOS. The concept of types did make configuring the hard drive geometry in CMOS much easier.

Initially, this worked well, but a problem arose. Note the capacities of the original 15 hard-drive types. They are small. If a manufacturer came up with a new, larger hard-drive type, the list would have to be expanded. At first, IBM did exactly that, eventually expanding the list to 37 different types (see Table 8-2.)

BIOS designers soon realized that adding to the list every time a manufacturer created a new hard-drive geometry was not practical, so IBM simply stopped using drives that required unique geometries and stopped adding drive types. The other BIOS makers continued to add types until they got to around 45 different types (see Table 8-3). At that time, AMI created a new "user" type. With this type, instead of selecting a special type, users could enter in the five geometry values manually. This provided more flexibility for hard-drive installation. Figure 8-24 shows an older Award BIOS with the CMOS set to user and the CHS values being entered manually.

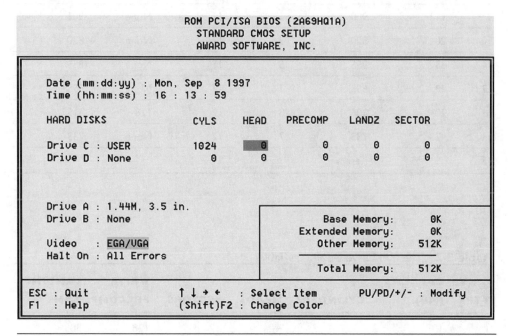

**Figure 8-24**   Award BIOS with CMOS set to user

**Table 8-1**   The Original Hard-Drive Table for the IBM AT

| DRIVE TYPE | CAPACITY (MB) | CYLINDERS | HEADS | SECTORS | WRITE PRECOMP | LANDING ZONE |
|---|---|---|---|---|---|---|
| 1 | 10 | 306 | 4 | 17 | 128 | 305 |
| 2 | 20 | 615 | 4 | 17 | 300 | 615 |
| 3 | 30 | 615 | 6 | 17 | 300 | 615 |
| 4 | 62 | 940 | 8 | 17 | 512 | 940 |
| 5 | 46 | 940 | 6 | 17 | 512 | 940 |
| 6 | 20 | 615 | 4 | 17 | None | 615 |

**Table 8-1**   The Original Hard-Drive Table for the IBM AT (continued)

| DRIVE TYPE | CAPACITY (MB) | CYLINDERS | HEADS | SECTORS | WRITE PRECOMP | LANDING ZONE |
|---|---|---|---|---|---|---|
| 7 | 30 | 462 | 8 | 17 | 256 | 511 |
| 8 | 30 | 733 | 5 | 17 | None | 733 |
| 9 | 112 | 900 | 15 | 17 | None | 901 |
| 10 | 20 | 820 | 3 | 17 | None | 820 |
| 11 | 35 | 855 | 5 | 17 | None | 855 |
| 12 | 49 | 855 | 7 | 17 | None | 855 |
| 13 | 20 | 306 | 8 | 17 | 128 | 319 |
| 14 | 42 | 733 | 7 | 17 | None | 733 |
| 15 | | Reserved | | | | |

**Table 8-2**   The IBM Drive Geometry Table

| DRIVE TYPE | CAPACITY (MB) | CYLINDERS | HEADS | SECTORS | WRITE PRECOMP | LANDING ZONE |
|---|---|---|---|---|---|---|
| 1 | 10 | 306 | 4 | 17 | 128 | 305 |
| 2 | 20 | 615 | 4 | 17 | 300 | 615 |
| 3 | 30 | 615 | 6 | 17 | 300 | 615 |
| 4 | 62 | 940 | 8 | 17 | 512 | 940 |
| 5 | 47 | 940 | 6 | 17 | 512 | 940 |
| 6 | 20 | 615 | 4 | 17 | None | 615 |
| 7 | 30 | 462 | 8 | 17 | 256 | 511 |
| 8 | 30 | 733 | 5 | 17 | None | 733 |
| 9 | 112 | 900 | 15 | 17 | None | 901 |
| 10 | 20 | 820 | 3 | 17 | None | 820 |
| 11 | 35 | 855 | 5 | 17 | None | 855 |

**Table 8-2**   The IBM Drive Geometry Table (continued)

| DRIVE TYPE | CAPACITY (MB) | CYLINDERS | HEADS | SECTORS | WRITE PRECOMP | LANDING ZONE |
|---|---|---|---|---|---|---|
| 12 | 50 | 855 | 7 | 17 | None | 855 |
| 13 | 20 | 306 | 8 | 17 | 128 | 319 |
| 14 | 42 | 733 | 7 | 17 | None | 733 |
| 15 | Reserved | | | | | |
| 16 | 20 | 612 | 4 | 17 | None | 633 |
| 17 | 40 | 977 | 5 | 17 | 300 | 977 |
| 18 | 57 | 977 | 7 | 17 | None | 977 |
| 19 | 60 | 1024 | 7 | 17 | 512 | 1023 |
| 20 | 30 | 733 | 5 | 17 | 300 | 732 |
| 21 | 42 | 733 | 7 | 17 | 300 | 732 |
| 22 | 30 | 733 | 5 | 17 | 300 | 733 |
| 23 | 10 | 306 | 4 | 17 | None | 336 |
| 24 | 20 | 612 | 4 | 17 | 305 | 663 |
| 25 | 10 | 306 | 4 | 17 | None | 340 |
| 26 | 20 | 612 | 4 | 17 | None | 670 |
| 27 | 40 | 698 | 7 | 17 | 300 | 732 |
| 28 | 40 | 976 | 5 | 17 | 488 | 977 |
| 29 | 10 | 306 | 4 | 17 | None | 340 |
| 30 | 20 | 611 | 4 | 17 | 306 | 663 |
| 31 | 42 | 732 | 7 | 17 | 300 | 732 |
| 32 | 42 | 1023 | 5 | 17 | None | 1023 |
| 33 | 30 | 614 | 4 | 25 | None | 663 |
| 34 | 20 | 775 | 2 | 27 | None | 900 |
| 35 | 30 | 921 | 2 | 33 | None | 1000 |
| 36 | 20 | 402 | 4 | 26 | None | 460 |
| 37 | 44 | 580 | 6 | 26 | None | 640 |

**Table 8-3**    The Final (AMI) Drive Geometry Table

| DRIVE TYPE | CAPACITY (MB) | CYLINDERS | HEADS | SECTORS | WRITE PRECOMP | LANDING ZONE |
|---|---|---|---|---|---|---|
| 1 | 10 | 306 | 4 | 17 | 128 | 305 |
| 2 | 20 | 615 | 4 | 17 | 300 | 615 |
| 3 | 31 | 615 | 6 | 17 | 300 | 615 |
| 4 | 62 | 940 | 8 | 17 | 512 | 940 |
| 5 | 47 | 940 | 6 | 17 | 512 | 940 |
| 6 | 20 | 615 | 4 | 17 | None | 615 |
| 7 | 31 | 462 | 8 | 17 | 256 | 511 |
| 8 | 30 | 733 | 5 | 17 | None | 733 |
| 9 | 112 | 900 | 15 | 17 | None | 901 |
| 10 | 20 | 820 | 3 | 17 | None | 820 |
| 11 | 36 | 855 | 5 | 17 | None | 855 |
| 12 | 50 | 855 | 7 | 17 | None | 855 |
| 13 | 20 | 306 | 8 | 17 | 128 | 319 |
| 14 | 43 | 733 | 7 | 17 | None | 733 |
| 15 | | | | | Reserved | |
| 16 | 20 | 612 | 4 | 17 | 0 | 663 |
| 17 | 41 | 977 | 5 | 17 | 300 | 977 |
| 18 | 29 | 697 | 5 | 17 | None | 697 |
| 19 | 60 | 1024 | 7 | 17 | 512 | 1023 |
| 20 | 40 | 965 | 5 | 17 | None | 965 |
| 21 | 80 | 965 | 10 | 17 | None | 965 |
| 22 | 65 | 733 | 7 | 26 | None | 733 |
| 23 | 101 | 845 | 7 | 35 | None | 845 |
| 24 | 31 | 612 | 4 | 26 | None | 612 |
| 25 | 104 | 1024 | 8 | 26 | None | 1024 |
| 26 | 65 | 1024 | 5 | 26 | None | 1024 |
| 27 | 42 | 1024 | 5 | 17 | None | 1024 |
| 28 | 102 | 855 | 7 | 35 | None | 855 |

**Table 8-3**  The Final (AMI) Drive Geometry Table (continued)

| DRIVE TYPE | CAPACITY (MB) | CYLINDERS | HEADS | SECTORS | WRITE PRECOMP | LANDING ZONE |
|---|---|---|---|---|---|---|
| 29 | 100 | 776 | 8 | 33 | None | 776 |
| 30 | 149 | 1250 | 7 | 35 | None | 1250 |
| 31 | 149 | 303 | 16 | 63 | None | 303 |
| 32 | 322 | 1224 | 15 | 36 | None | 1224 |
| 33 | 322 | 656 | 16 | 63 | None | 656 |
| 34 | 645 | 1632 | 15 | 54 | None | 1632 |
| 35 | 644 | 1309 | 16 | 63 | None | 1309 |
| 36 | 633 | 1632 | 15 | 53 | None | 1632 |
| 37 | 304 | 1224 | 15 | 34 | None | 1224 |
| 38 | 304 | 619 | 16 | 63 | None | 619 |
| 39 | 109 | 960 | 9 | 26 | None | 960 |
| 40 | 191 | 816 | 15 | 32 | None | 816 |
| 41 | 153 | 1249 | 7 | 36 | None | 1249 |
| 42 | 153 | 312 | 16 | 63 | None | 312 |
| 43 | 140 | 1024 | 8 | 35 | None | 1024 |
| 44 | 150 | 1224 | 7 | 36 | None | 1224 |
| 45 | 116 | 1314 | 7 | 26 | None | 1314 |
| 46 | 116 | 237 | 16 | 63 | None | 237 |
| 47 |  | User Type |  |  |  |  |

EIDE drives were very forgiving if you put incorrect information into the CMOS setup. If you installed a 1,020MB hard drive and set the CMOS to make it a 200MB hard drive, the 1,020MB would become a perfectly good 200MB hard drive! However, if you then reset the CMOS back to the proper settings to enable the drive to be 1,020MB again, you'd lose all the data on your drive! Autodetection (see following section) made the concept of hard-drive types obsolete, although many current CMOS setup utilities still provide drive types. On today's systems, just set the hard-drive type to Auto.

## Autodetection

Before roughly 1994, you had to use the hard-drive type to install a hard drive. This manual installation process was always a bit of a problem. You had to have the proper

CHS values, you had to be sure to type them in correctly, and you had to store these values in case your CMOS was accidentally erased. Today, all PCs can set the CMOS properly by using autodetection. All IDE/EIDE drives have their CHS values stored inside of them. Autodetection simply means that the CMOS asks the drive for those stored values and automatically updates the CMOS. There are two common ways to perform autodetection. First, most CMOS setup utilities have a hard-drive type called "Auto." By setting the hard-drive type to Auto, the CMOS automatically updates itself every time the computer is started. Figure 8-25 is a typical modern CMOS with the primary master and slave hard-drive types set to Auto.

The second, slightly older way to perform autodetection is through the IDE Autodetection option. This is a separate option, usually accessed from the main CMOS screen, as shown in Figure 8-26.

After selecting the Autodetection option, most CMOS setup utilities will look for any hard drive installed on the system. Figure 8-27 shows a typical autodetection.

Wait a minute! This CMOS has found a master drive on the primary controller (a primary master), but it shows you three different CHS settings. To explain what you're seeing, I'll have to take a detour into one big aspect of EIDE drives: *logical block addressing* (LBA) and *Enhanced CHS* (ECHS).

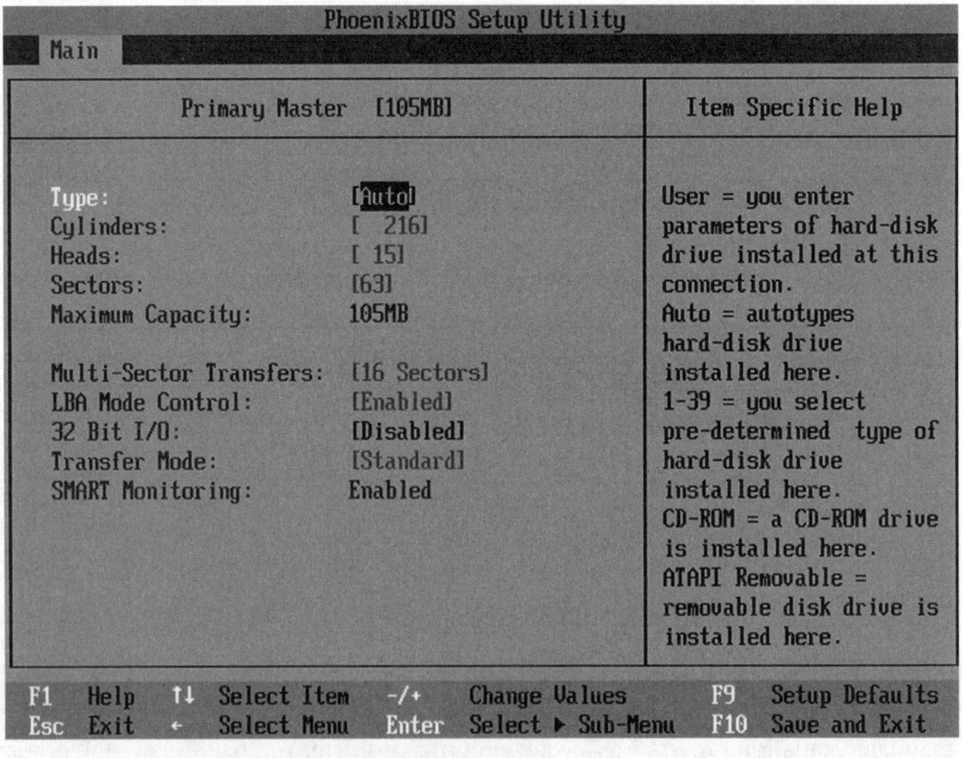

```
                    PhoenixBIOS Setup Utility
  Main

         Primary Master   [105MB]              Item Specific Help

   Type:                    [Auto]           User = you enter
   Cylinders:              [  216]           parameters of hard-disk
   Heads:                  [  15]            drive installed at this
   Sectors:                [63]              connection.
   Maximum Capacity:       105MB             Auto = autotypes
                                             hard-disk drive
   Multi-Sector Transfers: [16 Sectors]      installed here.
   LBA Mode Control:       [Enabled]         1-39 = you select
   32 Bit I/O:             [Disabled]        pre-determined  type of
   Transfer Mode:          [Standard]        hard-disk drive
   SMART Monitoring:       Enabled           installed here.
                                             CD-ROM = a CD-ROM drive
                                             is installed here.
                                             ATAPI Removable =
                                             removable disk drive is
                                             installed here.

   F1   Help   ↑↓  Select Item   -/+   Change Values    F9   Setup Defaults
   Esc  Exit   ←   Select Menu    Enter Select ▶ Sub-Menu  F10  Save and Exit
```

**Figure 8-25**   Modern CMOS set to Auto

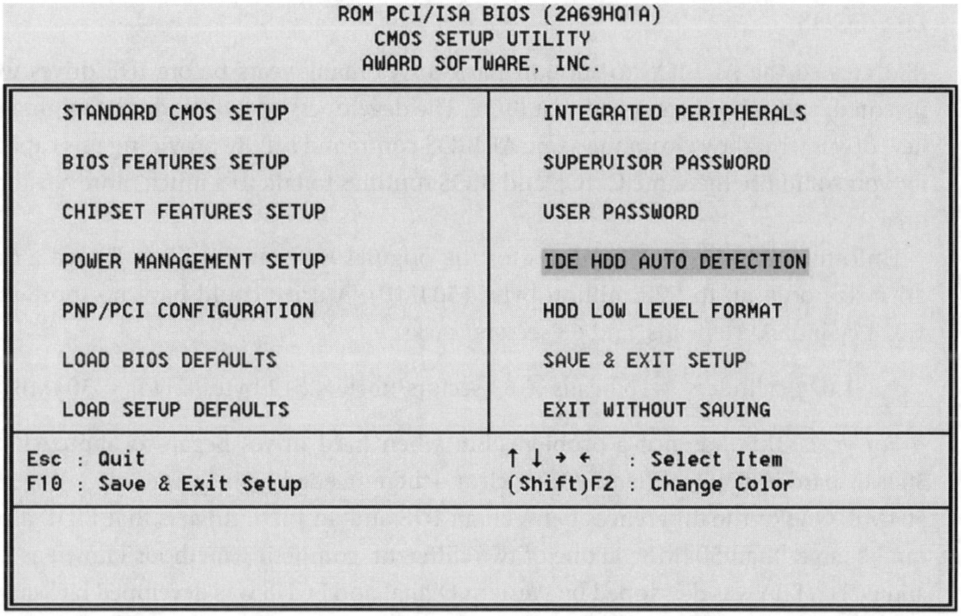

```
           ROM PCI/ISA BIOS (2A69HQ1A)
               CMOS SETUP UTILITY
             AWARD SOFTWARE, INC.

  STANDARD CMOS SETUP            INTEGRATED PERIPHERALS

  BIOS FEATURES SETUP            SUPERVISOR PASSWORD

  CHIPSET FEATURES SETUP         USER PASSWORD

  POWER MANAGEMENT SETUP         IDE HDD AUTO DETECTION

  PNP/PCI CONFIGURATION          HDD LOW LEVEL FORMAT

  LOAD BIOS DEFAULTS             SAVE & EXIT SETUP

  LOAD SETUP DEFAULTS            EXIT WITHOUT SAVING

 Esc : Quit                  ↑ ↓ → ←   : Select Item
 F10 : Save & Exit Setup     (Shift)F2 : Change Color
```

**Figure 8-26**   Award IDE HDD Auto Detection option

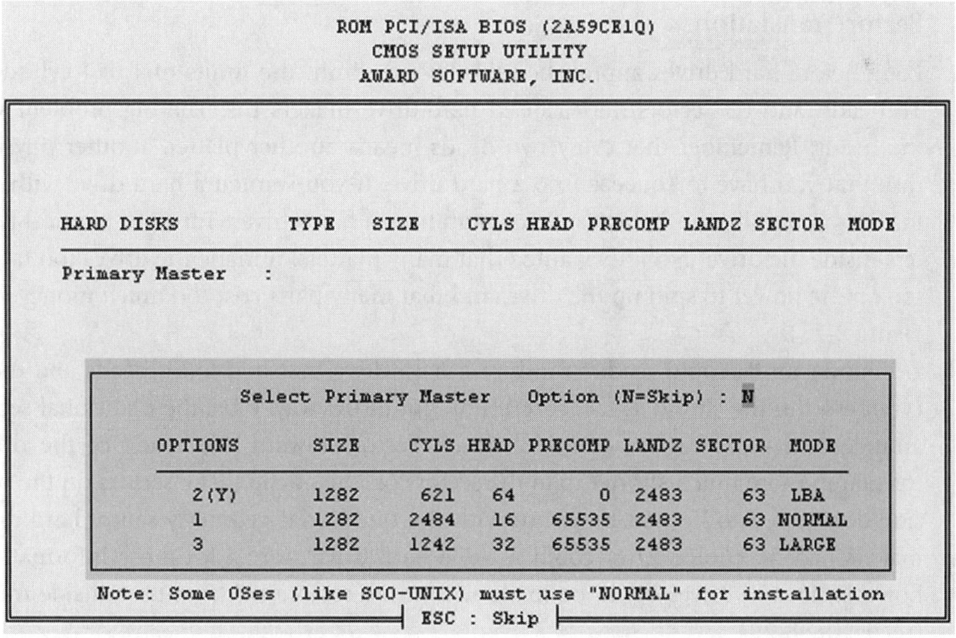

```
           ROM PCI/ISA BIOS (2A59CE1Q)
               CMOS SETUP UTILITY
             AWARD SOFTWARE, INC.


 HARD DISKS       TYPE   SIZE   CYLS HEAD PRECOMP LANDZ SECTOR  MODE

 Primary Master   :


       Select Primary Master    Option (N=Skip) : N

    OPTIONS     SIZE    CYLS HEAD PRECOMP LANDZ SECTOR  MODE

     2(Y)      1282     621   64      0   2483    63  LBA
       1       1282    2484   16  65535   2483    63  NORMAL
       3       1282    1242   32  65535   2483    63  LARGE

 Note: Some OSes (like SCO-UNIX) must use "NORMAL" for installation
                    ┤ ESC : Skip ├
```

**Figure 8-27**   Hard drive detected

## LBA/ECHS

IBM created the AT BIOS to support hard drives many years before IDE drives were invented, and every system had that BIOS. The developers of IDE made certain that the new drives would run from the same AT BIOS command set. By providing this capability, you could use the same CMOS and BIOS routines to talk to a much more advanced drive.

Unfortunately, the BIOS routines for the original AT command set allowed a hard drive size only up to 528 million bytes (504MB). A drive could have no more than 1,024 cylinders, 16 heads, and 63 sectors/track:

$$1{,}024 \text{ cylinders} \times 16 \text{ heads} \times 63 \text{ sectors/track} \times 512 \text{ bytes/sector} = 504\text{MB}$$

For years, this was not a problem. But when hard drives began to approach the 504MB barrier, the problem became clear—there needed to be a way of getting past 504MB. One of the differences between an IDE and an EIDE drive is that EIDE drives can be larger than 504MB via one of two different, competing methods known as LBA and ECHS. LBA was developed by Western Digital and ECHS was developed by Seagate. They accomplish virtually the same function in almost the same way (both will be discussed simultaneously). Basically, LBA/ECHS is the hard drive lying to the computer about its geometry, and is really nothing more than an advanced type of sector translation. Let's take a moment to understand sector translation, then come back to LBA/ECHS.

## Sector Translation

Long before hard drives approached the 504MB limit, the limits of 1,024 cylinders, 16 heads, and 63 sectors/track caused hard-drive makers fits. The big problem was the heads. Remember that every two heads means another platter, another physical disk that you have to squeeze into a hard drive. If you wanted a hard drive with the maximum number of 16 heads, you would have a hard drive with eight physical platters inside the drive! Nobody wanted that many platters: it made the drives too tall, it took more power to spin up the drive, and that many parts cost too much money (see Figure 8-28).

Manufacturers could readily produce a hard drive that had fewer heads and more cylinders, but the stupid 1,024/16/63 limit got in the way. Plus, the traditional sector arrangement wasted a lot of useful space. Sectors toward the inside of the drive, for example, are much shorter than the sectors on the outside. The sectors on the outside don't need to be that long, but with the traditional geometry setup, hard-drive makers had no choice. They could make a hard drive store a lot more information, however, if hard drives could be made with more sectors/track on the outside tracks (see Figure 8-29).

**Figure 8-28**
Too many heads

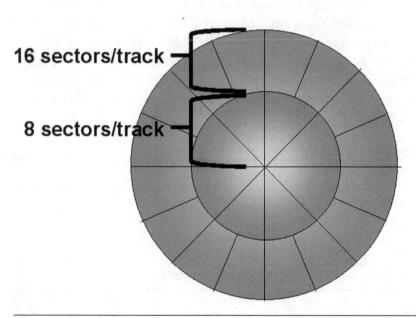

**Looks a little high!**

**Figure 8-29**  Multiple sectors/tracks

The IDE specification was designed to have two geometries. The *physical geometry* defined the real layout of the CHS inside the drive. The *logical geometry* described what the drive told the CMOS. In other words, the IDE drive lied to the CMOS, thus side-stepping the artificial limits of the BIOS. When data was being transferred to and from the drive, the onboard circuitry of the drive "translated" the logical geometry into the physical geometry. This function was, and still is, called *sector translation*.

Let's look at a couple of hypothetical examples in action. First, pretend that Seagate came out with a new, very cheap, very fast hard drive called the ST108. To get the ST108 drive fast and cheap, however, Seagate had to use a rather strange geometry, shown in Table 8-4.

**Table 8-4**   Seagate's ST108 Drive Geometry

| ST108 PHYSICAL | | BIOS LIMITS | |
| --- | --- | --- | --- |
| Cylinders | 2,048-*TOO BIG!* | Cylinders | 1,024 |
| Heads | 2 | Heads | 16 |
| Sectors/Track | 52 | Sectors/Track | 63 |
| Total Capacity | 108MB | | |

Notice that the cylinder number is greater than 1,024. To overcome this problem, the IDE drive performs a sector translation that reports a geometry to the BIOS that is totally different from the true geometry of the drive. Table 8-5 shows the actual geometry and the "logical" geometry of our mythical ST108 drive. Notice that the logical geometry is now within the acceptable parameters of the BIOS limitations. Sector translation never changes the capacity of the drive; it only changes the geometry to stay within the BIOS limits.

**Table 8-5**   Physical and Logical Geometry of the ST108 Drive

| PHYSICAL | | LOGICAL | |
| --- | --- | --- | --- |
| Cylinders | 2,048 | Cylinders | 512 |
| Heads | 2 | Heads | 8 |
| Sectors/Track | 52 | Sectors/Track | 52 |
| Total Capacity | 108MB | Total Capacity | 108MB |

## Back to LBA

Now let's watch how the advanced sector translation of LBA provides support for hard drives greater than 504MB. This time we have a Western Digital WD2160, a 2.1GB hard drive. Table 8-6 lists its physical and logical geometries. Note that, even with sector translation, the number of heads is greater than the allowed 16! So here's where the magic comes in. The WD2160 is capable of LBA. Now assuming that the BIOS is also capable of LBA, here's what happens. When the computer boots up, the BIOS asks the drives if they can perform LBA. If they say yes, the BIOS and the drive work together to change the way they talk to each other. They can do this without conflicting with the original AT BIOS commands by taking advantage of unused commands to use up to 256 heads. LBA enables support for a maximum of $1,024 \times 256 \times 63 \times 512$ bytes = 8.4GB hard drives.

**Table 8-6**  Western Digital WD2160's Physical and Logical Geometries

| PHYSICAL | | LOGICAL | |
|---|---|---|---|
| Cylinders | 16,384 | Cylinders | 1,024 |
| Heads | 4 | Heads | 64 |
| Sectors/Track | 63 | Sectors/Track | 63 |
| Total Capacity | 2.1GB | Total Capacity | 2.1GB |

ECHS is nothing more than a competitor to Western Digital's LBA. It works the same but comes up with different values than LBA. With LBA/ECHS, you can have 1,024 cylinders, 256 heads, and 63 sectors/track for a maximum size of 8.4GB. The ECHS option in CMOS setup utilities often shows up as "Large." ECHS has been completely eclipsed by LBA.

In order to have drives larger than 504MB, you must have a hard drive that has LBA/ECHS and a BIOS that supports LBA/ECHS. If you have an EIDE drive larger than 504MB, you can be sure the drive supports LBA and ECHS. All current BIOS support LBA and/or ECHS. Just run the autodetection utility.

### INT13 Extensions

You can always count on two things going up: taxes and hard-drive capacities. By the time LBA and ECHS became popular in the mid-1990s, it was painfully obvious that the 8.4GB maximum capacity was going to become a problem. In 1994, Phoenix Technologies (the BIOS manufacturer) came up with a new set of BIOS commands called *Interrupt 13* extensions (INT13). INT13 extensions break the 8.4GB barrier by completely ignoring the CHS values and instead feeding the LBA a stream of "addressable sectors." Sure, if you run Autodetect you'll see CHS values that equal the capacity of the drive, but the hard drive reports totally different values to the BIOS, avoiding the 8.4GB LBA limitation. A system with INT13 extensions can handle drives up to 137GB. Most systems made since 1998 have INT13 extension support. If you install a hard drive larger than 8.4GB and Autodetect doesn't detect more than 8.4GB, your system does not support INT13 extensions. See the "Single Drive, One Primary Partition" section, later in this chapter, for a quick discussion on how to upgrade your system to use INT13 extensions.

Be careful with INT13 extensions! Many systems require that you set the drive to Auto only. In fact, many CMOS setup utilities have dropped all options except for Auto or None—probably not a bad idea! Many systems work perfectly by using either the User or the Auto settings.

## Back to CMOS

Whew! That was a lot of information! But now you can go back to the IDE Autodetect screen and understand why three different choices are available: LBA, Normal, and Large (see Figure 8-30).

LBA, the most common CMOS setting for a drive, means the drive is capable of logical block addressing. The Normal setting tells the system to use the physical geometry, rather than the logical geometry for the drive. Normal is used only for operating systems that don't use the BIOS, such as Novell NetWare and certain types of UNIX. It is never used otherwise. (Worse, if you set a drive to Normal in a Windows environment, the size of the drive becomes no bigger than 504MB—no sector translation means it hits the ancient IDE limit!) Large shows that the drive is capable of ECHS. If you want, you can also set the drive to ECHS. (Windows 9x and Windows NT/2000 both use LBA and ECHS.)

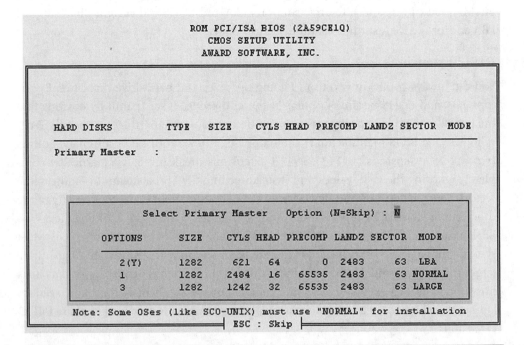

**Figure 8-30**  Autodetection revisited

I stay away from ECHS. It's not that there is anything wrong with it; it works perfectly. The problem is if I ever want to move the hard drive to another system, that other system also has to support ECHS. If it doesn't, I can install the drive under LBA but will lose all the data on the drive. Because even BIOS supports LBA, I never have to worry about this problem if I move the drive. Stick to LBA.

Autodetection has one other feature that makes it indispensable. When a drive doesn't work, the biggest question, especially during installation, is, "Did I plug it in correctly?" With autodetection, the answer is simple; if it doesn't see the drives, something is wrong with the hardware. Either a device has physically failed or, more likely, you didn't give the hard drive power, plugged a cable in backwards, or messed up some other connectivity issue.

## Transferring Data

ATA devices transfer data to and from the hard drive and memory via standardized protocols called *programmable input/output* (PIO) modes or by the far more popular DMA modes. PIO modes are older and far slower than DMA modes, but a number of slower, non-hard drive ATA devices still use PIO modes. This section looks at both of these modes and the settings available in CMOS.

### PIO Modes

Although the ATA drives could originally transfer data from the hard drive to RAM at a maximum rate of roughly 3.3 *megabytes per second* (MBps), drive makers quickly bumped up to 5.2MBps, and then 8.3MBps. The *Small Forms Factor* (SFF) standards committee defined these as PIO modes 0, 1, and 2. In the ATA world, all drives, as well as most non-drive ATA devices, can use all three modes. The SFF committee released a follow-up to the ATA standard that defined some new data throughput speeds. First, there were two new PIO speeds, called PIO 3 and PIO 4 (see Table 8-7). In order to get the best performance out of your hard drive, you must set the proper PIO mode for the drive.

Setting the PIO mode requires you to answer the following three questions:

- What is the fastest mode the hard drive supports?
- What is the fastest mode the controller supports?
- What is the fastest mode the BIOS or device driver supports?

The fastest PIO mode you can set is limited by the weakest link. For example, if you have a hard drive capable of PIO mode 4, a controller capable of mode 2, and a BIOS capable of mode 4, the best you will get is mode 2. You should never try to use a mode faster than what is recommended by the drive manufacturer. Although a faster mode will not damage your drive, it will most certainly damage your data.

**Table 8-7** PIO Speeds

| PIO MODE | CYCLE TIME (NS) | TRANSFER RATE (MBPS) |
|----------|-----------------|----------------------|
| 0 | 600 | 3.3 |
| I | 383 | 5.2 |
| 2 | 240 | 8.3 |
| 3 | 180 | 11.1 |
| 4 | 120 | 16.6 |

To make it simple, most modern PCs talk to the hard drive at boot and automatically set the proper PIO modes. It's easy to determine if the PC can perform this automatic negotiation. Go into the CMOS and look for something that says PIO, usually in the Advanced or Integrated Peripherals screens (see Figure 8-31).

If the system has an Auto option, take it. This setting will query the drive for its top PIO mode and automatically set it up for you. If a newly installed device generates read errors, you should try going back into CMOS and setting slower PIO modes until the errors disappear.

### DMA Modes

Newer hard drives ignore PIO modes and instead transfer data using *Direct Memory Access* (DMA) mode. DMA mode transfers bypass the CPU, sending data directly into memory, and thus leaving the CPU free to run programs. We first learned about DMA

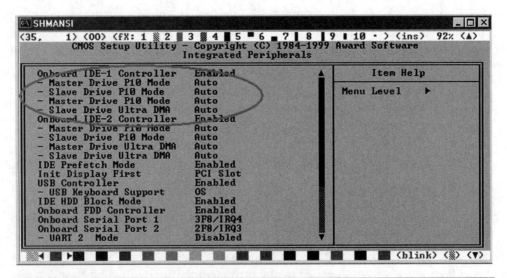

**Figure 8-31** PIO mode settings in CMOS with onboard controller

in Chapter 5. But that type of DMA required the device to request to use the expansion bus via the slow DMA controller (the 8237 chip). Modern drives use a bus-mastering controller that takes over the expansion bus and bypasses the built-in DMA controller. DMA data transfers can be either 16-bits (single word) or 32-bits (double word) wide. Virtually all systems now have PCI and will run at one of the very popular Ultra DMA mode speeds. See Table 8-8 for the transfer rates of the various DMA modes.

**Table 8-8**   DMA Speeds Including Ultra DMA Modes 3-5

| DMA MODE SINGLE WORD (16-BIT) | CYCLE TIME (ns) | TRANSFER RATE (MBps) |
| --- | --- | --- |
| 0 | 960 | 2.1 |
| 1 | 480 | 4.2 |
| 2 | 240 | 8.3 |

| DMA MODE DOUBLE WORD (32-BIT) | CYCLE TIME (ns) | TRANSFER RATE (MBps) |
| --- | --- | --- |
| 0 | 480 | 4.2 |
| 1 | 150 | 13.3 |
| 2 | 120 | 16.6 |
| 3 "Ultra DMA" | 60 | 33.3 |
| 4 "Ultra DMA" | 30 | 66 |
| 5 "Ultra DMA" | 20 | 100 |

**NOTE**   While the official terms for the more advanced DMA modes are Ultra DMA mode 4, mode 5, and so on, the term ATA/66 is used for mode 4 and ATA/100 for mode 5. For more details, see the section "ATA/66 and ATA/100" next in this chapter.

When DMA first became popular for hard drives in the mid-1990s, most systems did not have BIOS support for DMA, and thus required the use of third-party software drivers. Today, all BIOS have DMA, in particular Ultra DMA, support. Most CMOS setup utilities have an option to turn this on or off. This is almost always left on and forgotten, enabling users to enjoy the high speeds provided by Ultra DMA. Ultra DMA 3 (ATA/33), Ultra DMA 4 (ATA/66), and Ultra DMA 5 (ATA/100) now dominate the hard drive world.

## ATA/66 and ATA/100

The newer high-end drives use technology similar to all the drives that came before. The tech still sets master/slave jumpers, aligns pin 1 on the controller with pin 1 on the drive, and so on. The new drives completely eclipse the older ones in raw speed, however, giving data transfer rates of up to 100MBps! To achieve these higher speeds, the ATA/66 and ATA/100 drives require both a special controller and a fancy 80-pin ribbon cable.

### New Controllers, New Cables

In order to take advantage of the faster transfer rates, a drive has to connect to an appropriate controller. Current motherboards have ATA/66 or even ATA/100 controllers built into the motherboard. These controllers can do double duty, handling both old drives and new. Here's a picture of a fairly typical set of controllers on a motherboard (Figure 8-32). Although only the master IDE connector is blue (which denotes ATA/66 compatibility), both controllers can handle ATA/33 and ATA/66 drives. Be sure to plug the blue connector to the motherboard, the black to the master, and the gray to the slave if present!

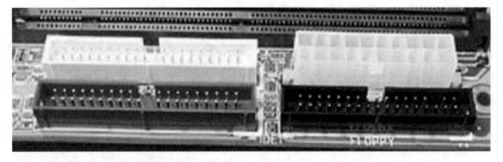

**Figure 8-32**  Typical ATA 66 hard drive controllers

Many current motherboards ship with four 40-pin controllers on the motherboards. Two handle "regular" EIDE drives (up to ATA/33), whereas the other two control ATA/66 or ATA/100 drives. With the four-controller motherboards, you can install up to eight EIDE devices in one system—very cool!

Just in case you were wondering, you won't see any CMOS settings for the Ultra ATA/66 or ATA/100 drives in these four-controller systems. The advanced motherboards come with extra System BIOS to detect these drives automatically.

Figure 8-33 shows the controllers on a typical motherboard. The primary IOE connector handles the faster ATA/66 or ATA/100 drives.

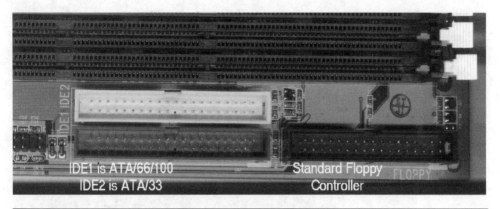

**Figure 8-33**   Multiple Controllers on a motherboard

If you do not have one of the fancy ATA/66 or ATA/100 connectors built into your motherboard, you can always get a controller on a PCI expansion card. These work great, although they do not support certain older technologies. Most have troubles with CD-ROM drives, for example, because of driver issues. One of the best expansion card controllers is the Promise FastTrack66. They sell for a nominal amount—somewhat less than $50 (U.S.)—and come with their own BIOS chip. In case you're curious, here's the Web address for Promise Technologies:

http://www.promise.com

## Compatibility

All the higher-end drives can run on lower-end controllers, and conversely, most controllers can handle lower-end drives. An ATA/66 controller can handle both ATA/66 and ATA/33 drives, for example, or even older PIO mode-based drives. The slower drives simply run at their slower speed. If you plug an ATA/100 drive into an ATA/33 controller, it will still work but will run as an ATA/33 drive!

"Hey, wait! You said the ATA/66 and ATA/100 drives use an 80-pin cable, not the standard IDE 40-pin. How can they possibly work?" The answer lies in the very funky and functional 80-pin cables.

## New Ribbon Cable

When manufacturers created drives that could break the 33MBps transfer rate limit, they ran into a serious problem with noise (EMI) on the traditional 40-pin cable. In order to run reliable transfers, they came up with a new 80-pin cable. The ends of the cable have 40 pins, so the connector is the same; the extra wires act as a sort of noise shield.

Figure 8-34 shows two cable snippets, with the 80-pin ATA/100 cable on top and the 40-pin ATA/33 cable on the bottom. Note that both connectors are the same size, but the ribbons differ radically.

ATA/66 and ATA/100 drives can use a 40-pin ribbon cable, but then operate as ATA/33 drives. This is great for those of us with older systems and a need for more storage space. You can buy a nice, big new drive and run it as an ATA/33 drive until you save up enough money for a motherboard or controller card purchase!

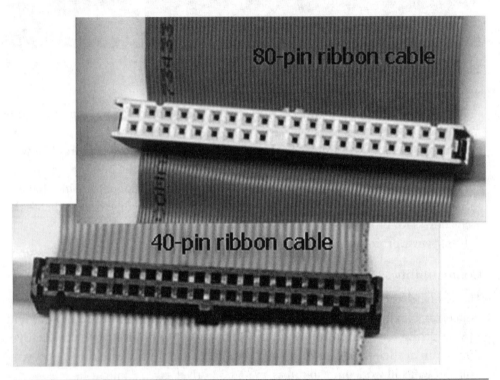

**Figure 8-34** 80-pin and 40-pin ribbon cables

## Physical Connections Are Easy

Let's review what it takes to get a drive physically installed. First, set the drive to master or slave, depending on where you decide to install the drive. If a drive is alone on the cable, set it to master or standalone. With two drives, one must be master and the other slave. Second, be sure to give the hard drive power. Most hard drives use a standard Molex connector. Third, boot the computer and go into CMOS. Use the Autodetect feature if available to see if the system recognizes the drive. If not, you may rest assured that one of the previous steps was done incorrectly. If the Autodetect does see the drive, pat yourself on the back. Use LBA and Auto if possible to ensure no compatibility problems, especially if you use ATA/66 or ATA/100 drives.

## Partitioning and Formatting

Once the hard drive has been successfully installed, you must perform two more steps to make the drive usable to the system: partition and format the drive. A partition is an electronic organization of the drive, turning the physical drive into one or more organizational groups. Each group typically is assigned a drive letter at this step, although with Windows 2000, you can turn a part of one hard drive into nothing more than a folder on another drive—a very powerful tool. After partitioning, you must "format" the drive. This step, sometimes still called "high-level format" to differentiate it from the earlier "low-level format," organizes each partition in such a way that the operating system can store files and folders on the drive.

## Partitioning

The process to partition and format a drive varies dramatically from one operating system to the next. The A+ Certification exams test your knowledge of *what* these processes do to make the drive work, as well as *how* to partition and format in both Windows 9*x* and Windows 2000. This section covers in detail the *what* part of the question, and sections in both Chapters 10 and 11 handle the *how* for each operating system.

---

 **NOTE** The next two sections will complete the process of setting up a new hard drive. Up to this point, everything has been done via hardware or CMOS. The next two steps, partitioning and high-level formatting, require special programs. The problem is that to complete these functions, you need a very important tool called a *bootable diskette*. Keep in mind that when you install a hard drive, you need to boot an operating system and have the necessary programs to set up the drive. Refer to Chapters 9, 10, and 11 for instructions on making bootable floppies.

---

Partitions are electronic, logical divisions of a hard drive that provide tremendous flexibility in the way we organize our hard drives. A computer might have only one physical hard drive, for example, but it could have anywhere from 1 to 24 logical drives, named C: to Z:.

Partitions exist for three reasons. First, when DOS was initially designed to use hard drives, the method used by DOS to store files limited the largest hard drive size to 32MB. Microsoft included partitioning in DOS 3.3 to enable PCs to use larger physical hard drives by creating multiple "logical" drives, up to 32MB each. Modern Windows systems support individual partitions up to 137GB (assuming you have INT13 extensions), but you still must partition a hard drive to use it. Secondly, partitions enable you to organize a drive in a way that suits your personal taste. For example, I partitioned my 30GB hard drive into a 25GB **C:** drive where I store Windows 2000 and all my programs, and a 5GB **D:** drive where I store all my personal data. This is a matter of personal choice—in my case, it makes backups simpler. Finally, partitioning enables a single hard drive to store more than one *operating system* (OS). One OS could be added to one partition and another OS could be added to another.

When the computer first boots to a hard drive, it looks for a special sector called the *boot sector*. The boot sector contains two critical pieces of information: the *master boot record* (MBR) and the *partition table*. The MBR takes control of the boot process from the system BIOS and begins to look for a partition with a valid operating system. It does so by looking in the partition table (Figure 8-35). The partition table defines all the partitions on the hard drive, because a hard drive may contain different partitions with different capabilities. Let's discuss the types of partitions and see how they work to appreciate the power of partitioning.

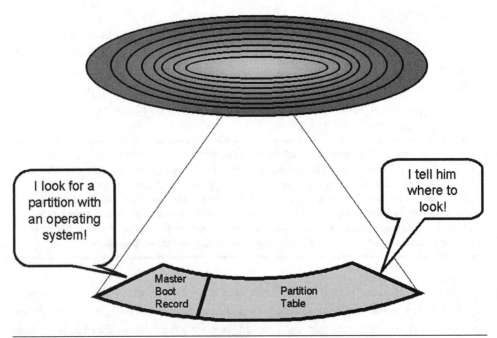

**Figure 8-35** Functions of the master boot record and partition table

## Partition Types

A hard drive may have up to four partitions. These partitions divide into one of two types: *primary* and *extended*. Each type of partition performs different functions and you create these partitions based on the needs of the particular PC system.

Some of you have seen hard drives chopped into more than four parts. Be careful here—the extended partition can have more than one drive letter associated with it. No matter how many drive letters you see, there are never more than four partitions per drive.

## Primary Partitions

Primary partitions store the OS(s). If you want to boot from a hard drive, it must have a primary partition. Therefore, the MBR must check the partition table for a primary partition (Figure 8-37). In Windows 9*x* and 2000, the primary partition is always C:, and you cannot change that (Figure 8-36).

A hard drive can have up to four primary partitions, but in the DOS/Windows 9*x* world, the built-in partitioning program, called FDISK, only enables one primary partition on the drive. I guess Microsoft, being a seller of operating systems, didn't want you to install other operating systems!

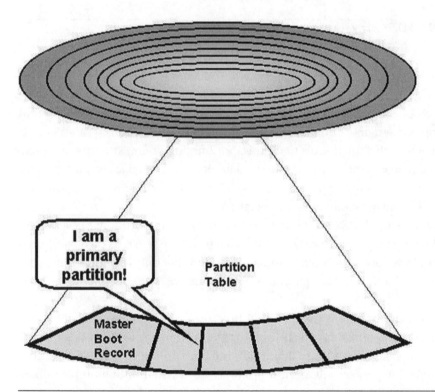

**Figure 8-36**   The master Boot Record checks the partition table to find a primary partition.

So even though hard drives support up to four primary partitions, we almost never see this in the Windows 9*x* world. Other operating systems, such as Windows 2000 and Linux, however, fully support multiple primary partitions on one drive. We use a number of terms for this function, but "dual-boot and "multi-boot" seem fairly common. As I constantly field questions regarding different operating systems, this is a very handy option for me to use. The system in my house, for example, uses four primary

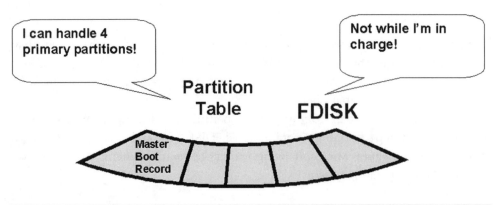

**Figure 8-37** FDISK can create only one primary partition.

partitions, each holding one operating system: Caldera Linux, Windows 2000, DOS 6.22, and Windows 98. In other words, I chopped my drive up into four chunks and installed each operating system. In order to do this, I used a third-party tool—in this case, the popular System Commander 2000—to set up the partitions. Windows 2000 and Linux come with similar tools to do this, but I find them messy to use and prefer System Commander. When my computer boots, System Commander yanks control from the MBR and asks me which OS I wish to boot. I select my OS and it appears! Figure 8-38 shows System Commander in operation.

Once I boot up, say, DOS 6.22, I don't see the other primary partitions. As far as DOS is concerned, only the **C:** drive exists. If I boot to Linux, it only sees its own partition. If I boot to Windows 2000, it sees other primary partitions but only because it is designed to read older DOS and Windows partitions. Even Windows 2000 doesn't see my Linux partition.

Multiple primary partitions may sound a little confusing, so let's make it simpler. Very few systems use more than one primary partition. You may work on PCs for years and never see a system with more than one primary partition. The A+ Certification exams certainly don't expect you to show how to create a system with multiple primary partitions, but they assume that you know you *can* add more than one primary partition to a hard drive if you so desire. For the rest of this book, we will assume that you only want one primary partition.

 **NOTE** Don't confuse a primary partition with the primary controller; they are totally different animals that just happen to share a similar name.

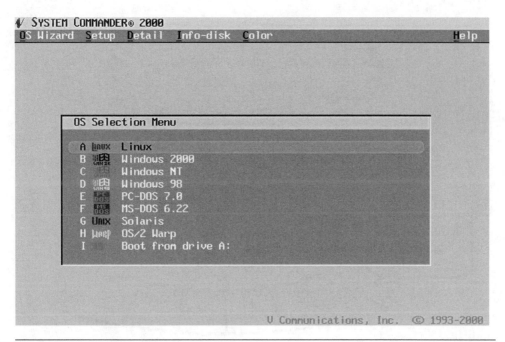

**Figure 8-38** System Commander

## Active Partition

If a hard drive stores multiple primary partitions, each with a valid operating system, how does the system know which one to boot? That's where the concept of *active partition* comes into play. For a primary partition to boot, you must set it as the active partition. Only one primary partition may be "active" at a time. Earlier I mentioned that the MBR looks for an operating system to boot. We may now define that a little more precisely. The MBR looks for a primary partition set to "active" (Figure 8-39).

When my System Commander boot screen comes up, it is really just asking me, "What primary partition do you want me to make active?" Well, that's fine for systems with many primary partitions, but what does active partitioning have to do with the system with only one primary partition? Well, when you create your single partition, you still must set that partition as "active" using your partitioning software. The system requires you to do this step, even though only one primary partition exists.

## Extended Partition

Your hard drive may or may not have the other partition type—an *extended partition*. Extended partitions are not bootable and one hard drive can only have one extended partition. If a hard drive has an extended partition, it takes up one of the areas in the partition map for the primary partitions. You may only have up to three primary

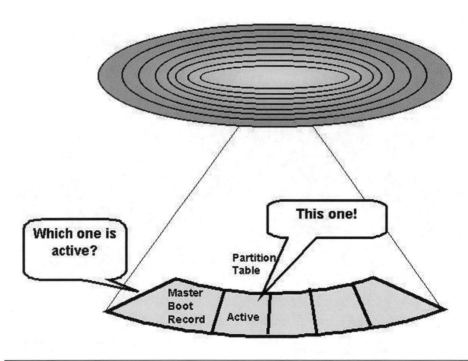

**Figure 8-39** Master boot record looks for an active, primary partition.

partitions on a drive with an extended partition. (This does not really matter considering that the vast majority of systems never use more then one primary partition anyway!)

Extended partitions are completely optional; you do not have to create an extended partition on a hard drive. So, if you can't boot to an extended partition and your hard drive doesn't need an extended partition, why would you want to create one? First of all, many systems do not use extended partitions. Some hard drives are partitioned as one big primary partition—nothing wrong with that. We use extended partitions when we find a situation where we want to chop a drive into multiple drive letters.

The beauty of an extended partition is in the way it handles drive letters. When you create a primary partition, it gets a drive letter and that's it. But when you create an extended partition, it does not automatically get a drive letter. Instead, you divide the extended partition into "logical drives." An extended partition may have as many logical drives as you wish, limited only by the letters of the alphabet for Windows 9x systems, enabling a maximum of 24 logical drives on one system (remember that A: and

**Figure 8-40**
You can have one
or many logical
drives in an
extended partition.

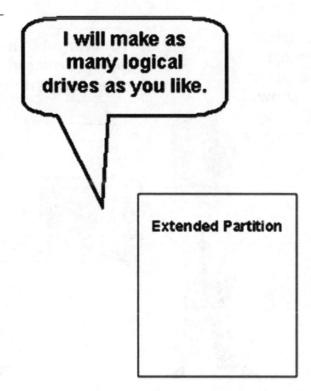

**Figure 8-40**
You can have one
or many logical
drives in an
extended partition.

**B:** are reserved for floppy drives). You may turn an extended partition into one logical drive or into multiple logical drives, whatever suits you (see Figure 8-40). You may set the size of each logical drive to any size you want.

All of this flexibility creates a little problem, especially for folks new to partitioning. Because a newly created extended partition doesn't yet have logical drives, working with extended partitions always requires two steps: first, make the extended partition, then create logical drives within that extended partition. This two-step process often confuses a new tech; they forget to create logical drives in the extended partition and wonder why they don't see any new drive letters in My Computer when they finish partitioning (see Figure 8-41).

Okay! We now know that you must partition a hard drive before the system may use it. We appreciate that a partition is not a physical thing; a partition is an electronic organization of the drive. In Windows 9*x*, we partition with a program called FDISK. Figure 8-42 shows the FDISK program. Windows 2000 uses a far more powerful, graphical Disk Management tool as displayed in Figure 8-43.

**Figure 8-41** Typical new tech error

```
                         Microsoft Winodws 98
                       Fixed Disk Setup Program
               (C)Copyright Microsoft Corp.  1983 - 1998

                          FDISK Options

     Current fixed disk drive: 1

     Choose one of the following:

     1. Create DOS partition or Logical DOS Drive
     2. Set active partition
     3. Delete partition or Logical DOS Drive
     4. Display partition information


     Enter choice: [1]



     Press ESC to exit FDISK
```

**Figure 8-42** FDISK

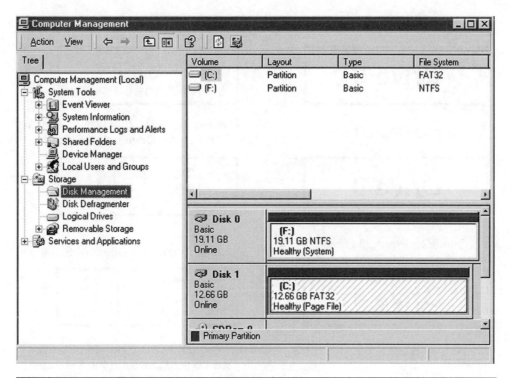

**Figure 8-43**  Windows 2000 Disk Management

This chapter uses the FDISK program to configure drives. We'll save the amazing Windows 2000 Disk Administrator for Chapter 11. But without even using these tools, you can probably guess some of their functions:

- Creating a primary partition
- Setting a primary partition as active
- Creating an extended partition
- Creating logical drive(s) in an extended partition
- Deleting partitions

## Partition Examples

Almost an infinite number of possible combinations for physical hard drives and partitions exist, but Figure 8-44 shows the most common.

Before going into the steps involved in partitioning, let's look at the final step in setting up a hard drive—the high-level format. After tackling the concepts in formatting, we'll come back and use both partitioning and formatting to set up a drive.

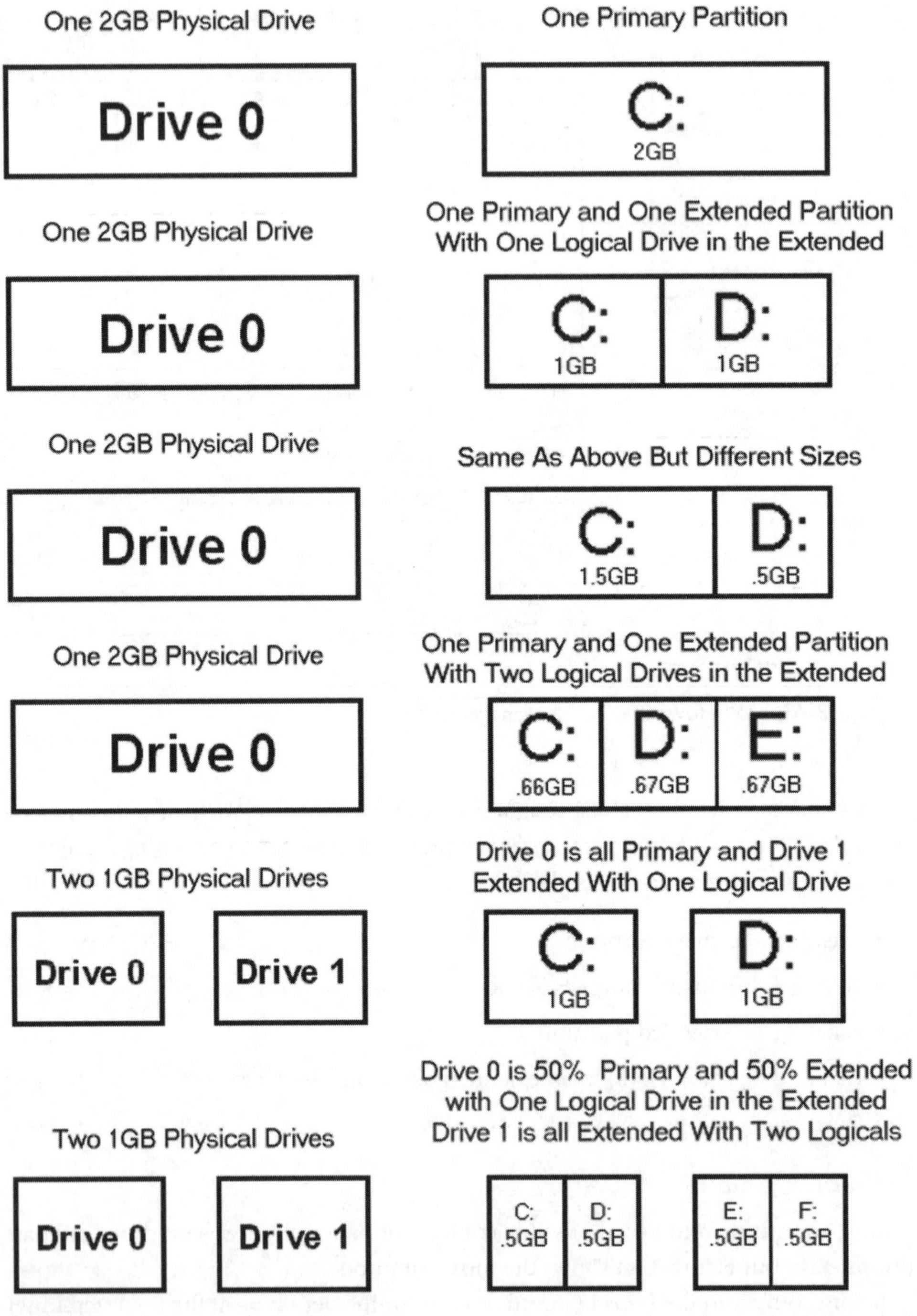

One 2GB Physical Drive

Drive 0

One Primary Partition

C:
2GB

One 2GB Physical Drive

Drive 0

One Primary and One Extended Partition
With One Logical Drive in the Extended

C:
1GB

D:
1GB

One 2GB Physical Drive

Drive 0

Same As Above But Different Sizes

C:
1.5GB

D:
.5GB

One 2GB Physical Drive

Drive 0

One Primary and One Extended Partition
With Two Logical Drives in the Extended

C:
.66GB

D:
.67GB

E:
.67GB

Two 1GB Physical Drives

Drive 0          Drive 1

Drive 0 is all Primary and Drive 1
Extended With One Logical Drive

C:
1GB

D:
1GB

Two 1GB Physical Drives

Drive 0          Drive 1

Drive 0 is 50% Primary and 50% Extended
with One Logical Drive in the Extended
Drive 1 is all Extended With Two Logicals

C:
.5GB

D:
.5GB

E:
.5GB

F:
.5GB

**Figure 8-44**   Examples of partitions

## High-Level Formatting

Each partition needs to be configured so that it may hold files and folders in a form suitable to the operating system. The official term for this last step is "high-level format," although most of us simply refer to it as "formatting." The high-level format actually performs two major functions: creating and configuring the *file allocation tables* (FATs), and creating the root directory. The root directory provides the foundation structure upon which the operating system builds files and folders. The FAT takes a little bit more explanation.

### File Allocation Table (FAT)

Every operating system has a FAT, although some of the more recent operating systems (e.g., Windows 2000) may use a different term. This section develops the idea of a "generic" FAT and then moves to specific file storage organizations.

### FAT in Concept

The base storage area for hard drives is a sector, with each sector storing up to 512 bytes of data. If an operating system stores a file smaller than 512 bytes in a sector, the rest of the sector goes to waste. We accept this waste because most files are far larger than 512 bytes. So what happens when an operating system stores a file larger than 512 bytes? The operating system needs a method to fill one sector, find another that's unused, and fill it, continuing to fill sectors until the file is completely stored. Once the operating system stores a file, it must remember which sectors hold that file, so that file can be retrieved later.

MS-DOS version 2.1 first supported hard drives using a special data structure to keep track of stored data on the hard drive, and Microsoft called this structure the FAT. Think of the FAT as nothing more than a card catalog that keeps track of which sectors store the various parts of a file. It's nice to call a FAT a *data structure* (the official jargon description), but it is more like a two-column spreadsheet.

The left column gives each sector a number, from 0000 to FFFF (in hex, of course). This means there are 65,536 (64K) sectors (see Figure 8-45).

Notice that the left-hand side contains 16 bits. (Four hex characters make 16 bits, remember?) We call this type of FAT a "16-bit FAT" or "FAT16." Not just hard drives have FATs. Floppy drives also use FATs, but their FATs are only 12 bits since they store so much less data.

The right-hand side of the FAT contains information on the status of sectors. All hard drives, even brand-new drives fresh from the factory, contain faulty sectors that cannot store data due to imperfections in the construction of the drive. The operating system must locate these bad sectors, mark them as unusable, and then prevent any files from

**Figure 8-45**
16-bit FAT

being written to them. This "mapping" of bad sectors is one of the functions of high-level formatting. After the format program creates the FAT, it then proceeds through the entire partition, writing and attempting to read from each sector sequentially. If it finds a bad sector, it places a special status code (FFF7) in the sector's FAT location, indicating that the sector is unavailable for use. Formatting also marks the good sectors as 0000.

Using the FAT to track sectors, however, creates a problem. The 16-bit FAT addresses a maximum of 64K ($2^{16}$) locations. Therefore, the size of a hard-drive partition should be limited to 64K × 512 bytes per sector, or 32MB. When Microsoft first unveiled FAT16, this 32MB limit presented no problem because most hard drives were only 5MB to 10MB. As hard drives grew in size, we used FDISK to break them up into multiple partitions. For example, we would break a 40MB hard drive into two partitions, each less than 32MB. But as hard drives started to become much larger, Microsoft realized that the 32MB limit for drives was unacceptable. We needed an improvement to the 16-bit FAT, a new and improved FAT16 that would enable larger drives while still maintaining backward compatibility with the old style 16-bit FAT. This need led to the development of a dramatic improvement in FAT16, called *clustering*, that enabled you to format partitions larger than 32MB (see Figure 8-46). This new FAT16 appeared way back in the DOS 4 days.

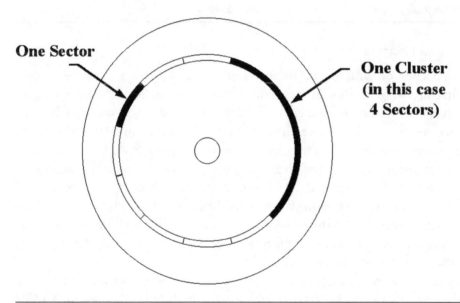

**One Sector**

**One Cluster (in this case 4 Sectors)**

**Figure 8-46**  Cluster vs. sector

Clustering simply means to combine a set of contiguous sectors and treat them as a single unit in the FAT. These units are called *file allocation units* or *clusters*. Each row of the FAT addressed a cluster instead of a sector. Unlike sectors, the size of a cluster is not fixed. This improved FAT16 still only contained 64K storage areas, so the formatting program had to determine the number of sectors in each cluster by the size of the partition in order to insure that we never went over 64K clusters. This kept clustering completely compatible with the 64K locations in the old 16-bit FAT. The new FAT16 could support partitions up to 2GB. (The old 16-bit FAT is so old that it doesn't really even have a name—if someone says FAT16, they mean the newer FAT16 that supports clustering). Table 8-9 shows the number of sectors per cluster for FAT16.

**Table 8-9**   Number of Sectors/Cluster by Partition Size for FAT16

| IF THE DISK MAKES A PARTITION THIS BIG | YOU'LL GET THIS MANY SECTORS/CLUSTER |
| --- | --- |
| 16 to 127.9 megabytes | 4 sectors/cluster |
| 128 to 255.9 megabytes | 8 sectors/cluster |
| 256 to 511.9 megabytes | 16 sectors/cluster |
| 512 to 1,023.9 megabytes | 32 sectors/cluster |
| 1,024 to 2,048 megabytes | 64 sectors/cluster |

### Sectors and Clusters

The introduction of clustering meant that a cluster, rather than a sector, became the basic unit of storage. Although this change enabled larger partition sizes—a good thing—it also increased the inherent wastefulness of FAT storage. With a sector-based FAT, when you saved a file of fewer than 512 bytes, the excess unused space in the sector went to waste. For example, saving a file of only 100 bytes left 412 bytes unused. We could accept this amount of waste because a typical file usually used a large number of sectors. For example, if you had a 15,000-byte file, you needed 30 sectors (15,000 bytes/512 bytes per sector) to store the entire file. The last sector was only about 30 percent full, wasting roughly 360 bytes. Big deal! Compared to the total amount of storage used by all of the sectors to store the file combined, this produced (360/15000 = .024), or less than a quarter of 1 percent waste.

This changed when clusters became the smallest storage area in a hard drive. Let's say that you stored that same 15,000-byte file on a 1,200MB (1.2GB) partition. A FAT16 partition of that size used 64 sectors/cluster (see Table 8-9), making each cluster $\cong$32,000 bytes. In this case, the 15,000-byte file took one 32,000-byte cluster, leaving 17,000 bytes wasted. Storing the same file in clusters created much greater waste due to the fact that clusters were so much larger.

To keep the waste as low as possible, we kept FAT16 partitions as small as possible, less than 1,023.9MB, or smaller if possible. A 1,023.9MB partition used 16K clusters, keeping the level of wasted storage at an acceptable level.

For all its shortcomings, every DOS, Windows 3.x, and the first Windows 95 systems all used FAT16. In fact, every version of Windows completely supports FAT16. You can, if you choose to do so, install Windows 2000 on a FAT16 partition (you would lose some neat features, but that's a discussion for another chapter). One nice aspect of

FAT16 lies in its relative simplicity. If you understand how FAT16 works, you'll gain a better understanding of more modern file systems and appreciate the need for many tools (like ScanDisk and Disk Defragmenter) that we use on today's systems. Let's watch FAT16 in action.

### FAT16 in Action

Assume we have a copy of Windows using FAT16. When an application such as Microsoft Word tells the operating system to save a file, Windows starts at the beginning of the FAT, looking for the first space marked "open for use" (0000), and begins to write to that cluster. If the entire file fits within that one cluster, Windows places the code "FFFF" (last cluster) into the cluster's status area in the FAT. Windows then goes to the folder storing the file and adds the filename and the cluster's number to the folder list. If the file takes more than one cluster, then Windows searches for the next open cluster and places the number of the next cluster in the status, filling and adding clusters until the file is saved. The last cluster then receives the end-of-file code (FFFF).

Let's do an example of this process, and start by selecting an arbitrary part of the FAT: from 3ABB to 3AC7. Assume you save a file, MOM.TXT. Before saving the file, the FAT looks like Figure 8-47.

| Cluster | Status |
|---------|--------|
| 3ABB | 0000 |
| 3ABC | 0000 |
| 3ABD | FFF7 |
| 3ABE | 0000 |
| 3ABF | 0000 |
| 3AC0 | 0000 |
| 3AC1 | 0000 |
| 3AC2 | 0000 |
| 3AC3 | 0000 |
| 3AC4 | 0000 |
| 3AC5 | 0000 |
| 3AC6 | 0000 |
| 3AC7 | 0000 |

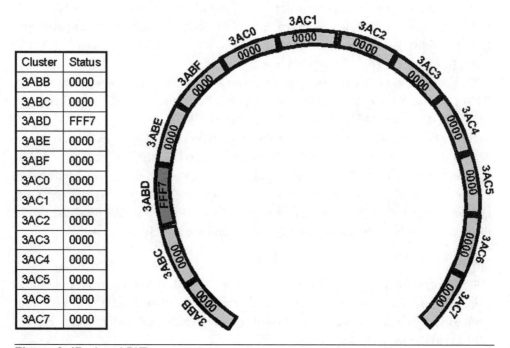

**Figure 8-47**   Initial FAT

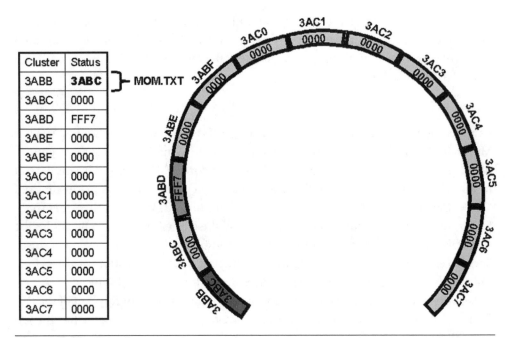

| Cluster | Status |
|---------|--------|
| 3ABB | **3ABC** |
| 3ABC | 0000 |
| 3ABD | FFF7 |
| 3ABE | 0000 |
| 3ABF | 0000 |
| 3AC0 | 0000 |
| 3AC1 | 0000 |
| 3AC2 | 0000 |
| 3AC3 | 0000 |
| 3AC4 | 0000 |
| 3AC5 | 0000 |
| 3AC6 | 0000 |
| 3AC7 | 0000 |

**Figure 8-48**   First cluster used

Windows finds the first open cluster, 3ABB, and fills it. But not all of the MOM.TXT fits into that cluster. Needing more space, it goes through the FAT to find the next open cluster. It finds cluster 3ABC. Before filling 3ABC, the value 3ABC is placed in 3ABB's status (see Figure 8-48).

Even after filling two clusters, more of the MOM.TXT file needs to be saved, so Windows must find one more cluster. The 3ABD has been marked FFF7 (bad cluster), so Windows skips over 3ABD, finding 3ABE (see Figure 8-49).

Before filling 3ABE, Windows enters the value 3ABE in 3ABC's status. Windows does not completely fill 3ABE, signifying that the entire MOM.TXT file has been stored. Windows enters the value FFFF in 3ABE's status, indicating the end of file (see Figure 8-50).

After saving all the clusters, Windows now locates the file's folder (yes, folders also get stored on clusters, but they get a different set of clusters, somewhere else on the disk) and records the filename, size, date/time, and starting cluster, as such:

MOM.TXT 19234 05-19-96 2:04p 3ABB

If a program requests that file, the process is reversed. Windows locates the folder containing the file to determine the starting cluster, and then pulls a copy of the file from each cluster until it sees the end-of-file cluster. Windows then hands the reassembled file to the requesting application.

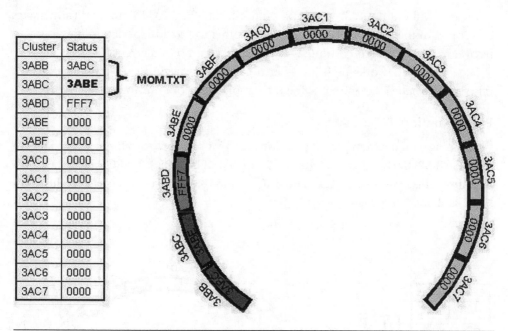

| Cluster | Status |
|---------|--------|
| 3ABB | 3ABC |
| 3ABC | **3ABE** |
| 3ABD | FFF7 |
| 3ABE | 0000 |
| 3ABF | 0000 |
| 3AC0 | 0000 |
| 3AC1 | 0000 |
| 3AC2 | 0000 |
| 3AC3 | 0000 |
| 3AC4 | 0000 |
| 3AC5 | 0000 |
| 3AC6 | 0000 |
| 3AC7 | 0000 |

**Figure 8-49**   Second cluster used

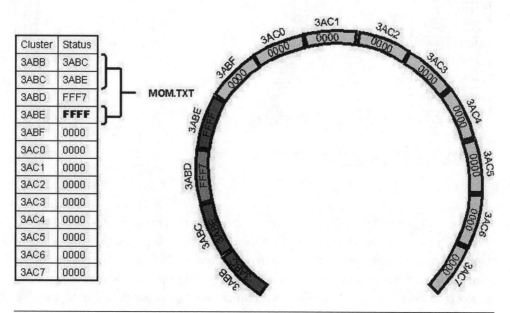

| Cluster | Status |
|---------|--------|
| 3ABB | 3ABC |
| 3ABC | 3ABE |
| 3ABD | FFF7 |
| 3ABE | **FFFF** |
| 3ABF | 0000 |
| 3AC0 | 0000 |
| 3AC1 | 0000 |
| 3AC2 | 0000 |
| 3AC3 | 0000 |
| 3AC4 | 0000 |
| 3AC5 | 0000 |
| 3AC6 | 0000 |
| 3AC7 | 0000 |

**Figure 8-50**   Final cluster used

Clearly, without the FAT, Windows cannot locate files. FAT16 automatically makes two copies of the FAT. One FAT backs up the other to provide special utilities a way to recover in case a FAT gets corrupted—a painfully common occurrence.

Even when FAT works perfectly, over time the files begin to separate in a process called *fragmentation*. Let me show fragmentation, using our previous description.

## Fragmentation

Continuing with the example, let's use Microsoft Word to save two more files: a letter to the IRS (IRSROB.DOC) and a letter to IBM (IBMHELP.DOC). IRSROB.DOC takes the next three clusters—3ABF, 3AC0, and 3AC1—and IBMHELP.DOC takes two clusters— 3AC2 and 3AC3 (see Figure 8-51).

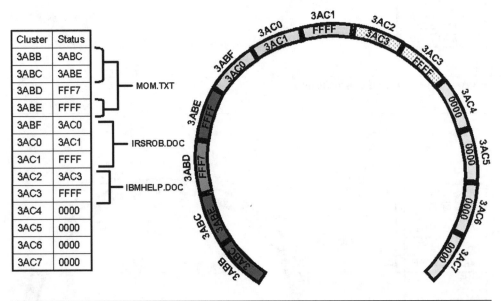

| Cluster | Status |
|---------|--------|
| 3ABB | 3ABC |
| 3ABC | 3ABE |
| 3ABD | FFF7 |
| 3ABE | FFFF |
| 3ABF | 3AC0 |
| 3AC0 | 3AC1 |
| 3AC1 | FFFF |
| 3AC2 | 3AC3 |
| 3AC3 | FFFF |
| 3AC4 | 0000 |
| 3AC5 | 0000 |
| 3AC6 | 0000 |
| 3AC7 | 0000 |

MOM.TXT — 3ABB, 3ABC, 3ABD, 3ABE
IRSROB.DOC — 3ABF, 3AC0, 3AC1
IBMHELP.DOC — 3AC2, 3AC3

**Figure 8-51** Three files saved

Now let's erase MOM.TXT. Windows does not delete the cluster entries for MOM.TXT when it erases a file. Windows only alters the information in the folder, simply changing the first letter of MOM.TXT to the Greek symbol σ. This causes the file to "disappear" as far as the operating system knows. It won't show up, for example, in Windows Explorer, even though the data still resides on the hard drive for the moment (see Figure 8-52).

Because all the data for MOM.TXT is intact, you could use some program to change the σ back into another letter, and thus get the document back. Programs such as the

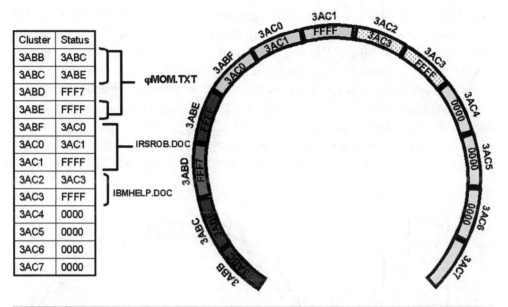

| Cluster | Status |
|---------|--------|
| 3ABB | 3ABC |
| 3ABC | 3ABE |
| 3ABD | FFF7 |
| 3ABE | FFFF |
| 3ABF | 3AC0 |
| 3AC0 | 3AC1 |
| 3AC1 | FFFF |
| 3AC2 | 3AC3 |
| 3AC3 | FFFF |
| 3AC4 | 0000 |
| 3AC5 | 0000 |
| 3AC6 | 0000 |
| 3AC7 | 0000 |

**Figure 8-52**   MOM.TXT erased

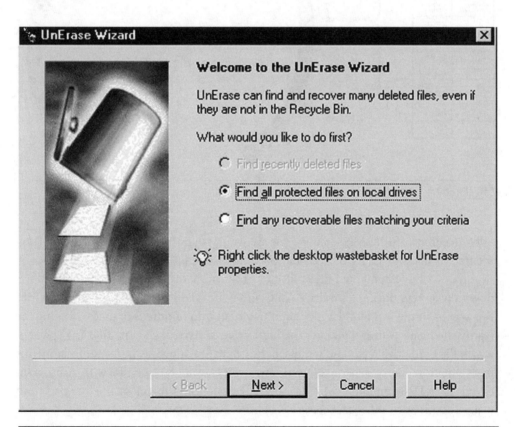

**Figure 8-53**   Norton Utilities' UnErase function

Recycle Bin work by temporarily protecting these files and remembering the first letter of the file's name until you enter the Empty Recycle Bin command. In fact, good utilities such as Norton Utilities' UnErase can still recover files after you dump the Recycle Bin, as long as no other file has yet overwritten it (Figure 8-53 on the previous page).

Let's say you just emptied your Recycle Bin, which removes the protection from all of your deleted files. You now save one more file, TAXREC.XLS, a big spreadsheet that will take six clusters, into the same folder that once held MOM.TXT. As Windows writes the file to the drive, it overwrites the space that MOM.TXT used, but it needs three more clusters. The next three available clusters are 3AC4, 3AC5, and 3AC6 (see Figure 8-54).

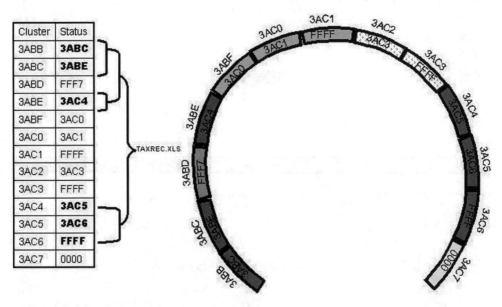

| Cluster | Status |
|---------|--------|
| 3ABB | **3ABC** |
| 3ABC | **3ABE** |
| 3ABD | FFF7 |
| 3ABE | **3AC4** |
| 3ABF | 3AC0 |
| 3AC0 | 3AC1 |
| 3AC1 | FFFF |
| 3AC2 | 3AC3 |
| 3AC3 | FFFF |
| 3AC4 | **3AC5** |
| 3AC5 | **3AC6** |
| 3AC6 | **FFFF** |
| 3AC7 | 0000 |

**Figure 8-54**   TAXREC.XLS fragmented

Notice that TAXREC.XLS is in two pieces; we say that the file is "fragmented." Fragmentation takes place all of the time on FAT16 systems. Although the system easily negotiates a tiny fragmented file split into only two parts, excess fragmentation slows down the system during hard drive reads and writes. This example is fragmented into two pieces; in the real world a file might fragment into hundreds of pieces, forcing the read/write heads to travel all over the hard drive to retrieve a single file. The speed at which the hard drive reads and writes can be improved dramatically by eliminating this fragmentation. Every version of Windows (aside from NT) comes with a program called "Disk Defragmenter," which is specially designed to rearrange the files back into neat contiguous chunks (see Figure 8-55).

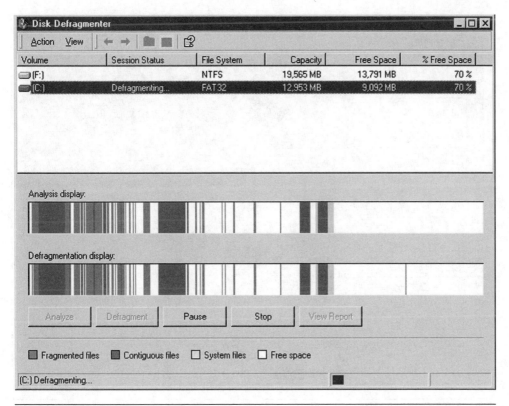

**Figure 8-55**  Windows Disk Defragmenter

Running a program to eliminate fragmentation is called *defragmenting* a drive. Although Microsoft's Disk Defragmenter does a fair job at defragmentation, third-party tools such as Norton Utilities' SpeedDisk (see Figure 8-56) give many more powerful options.

SpeedDisk supports different methods of defragmentation. Some examples are

- File reordering, in which only the files are defragmented
- Complete defragmentation, which also defragments folders
- Folder and/or file sorting

The last method simply puts the file and folder names in some order, usually alphabetical. This doesn't make file retrieval any faster, but it makes it easier to find a particular file or folder!

Defragmentation is crucial for ensuring the top performance of a hard drive. A good PC user performs a file reordering once a week and a full defragmentation at least once a month.

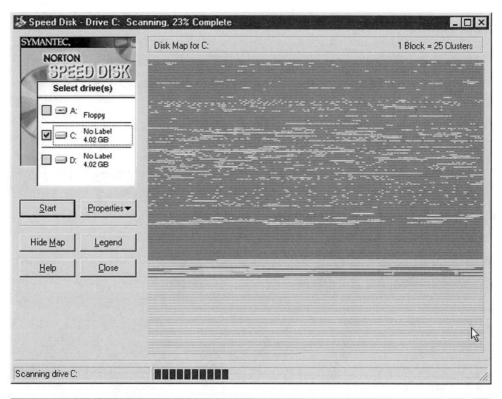

**Figure 8-56**   Norton's SpeedDisk

## Improved Formats

FAT16 continues to soldier on to this day. In fact, all versions of Windows, including Windows 2000, completely support FAT16 drives; however, two new format types, called FAT32 and NTFS now rule the Windows 9*x* (FAT32) and Windows 2000 (NTFS) landscape. Both offer many advantages over FAT16, including more efficient use of disk space, and, at least with NTFS, better security. In addition, Windows 95 introduced long file names for FAT partitions.

### Long File Names

Before Windows 95, FAT16 forced us to limit file names to eight letters/numbers (the filename), followed by a period, then three more letters/numbers (the extension). Windows 95 broke out of this "8.3" format by using unused space in folders to store long (up to 255 character) file names. Many folks think this is some new file format but in reality, long file names use simple FAT16 formatted partitions. The power of long file names lies with Windows, not FAT16. We will see more of long file names later in the book.

## FAT32

When Microsoft introduced Windows 95 OSR2, it also unveiled a totally new file format called FAT32 that brought a couple of dramatic improvements. First, FAT32 supports partitions up to 2 terabytes (more than 2 trillion bytes!). Second, as its name implies, FAT32 uses 32 bits to describe each cluster, which means clusters can drop to more reasonable sizes. FAT32's use of so many FAT entries gives it the power to use very small clusters, making the old "keep your partitions small" rule obsolete. However, FAT32 partitions still need defragmentation, just as often as FAT16 partitions. Always make sure that your defragmentation program supports FAT32 before you try to use it on a FAT32 partition. The results of using a FAT16 defragmenter on a FAT32 drive are not predictable! Table 8-10 shows cluster sizes for FAT32 partitions.

**Table 8-10**   FAT32 Cluster Sizes

| IF FDISK MAKES A PARTITION THIS BIG | YOU'LL GET THIS MANY SECTORS/CLUSTER |
| --- | --- |
| 512 to 8,191 megabytes | 8 sectors/cluster |
| 8192 to 16,383 megabytes | 16 sectors/cluster |
| 16,384 to 32,767 megabytes | 32 sectors/cluster |
| 32,768+ megabytes | 64 sectors/cluster |

## NTFS

Windows 2000 and its predecessor, Windows NT, use the vastly more powerful, more robust and flexible *NT File system* (NTFS). More discussion of NTFS will be found in Chapter 11, but for now let's just say that NTFS is virtually indestructible and provides ultra-high security for files, on-the-fly file and folder compression and encryption, and a wealth of other features. NTFS utilizes a "Super FAT" called the *Master File Table* (MFT) that builds substantially on the FAT concept. While NTFS is much less prone to fragmentation, Microsoft provides Disk Defragmenter with Windows 2000 for occasional defragmentation. Unlike FAT16 or FAT32, NTFS enables you to adjust the cluster sizes, although we rarely do so. Table 8-11 shows the default cluster sizes for NTFS.

By default, NTFS supports partitions up to 2 terabytes (2,199,023,255,552 bytes). By tweaking the cluster sizes, you can get NTFS to support partitions up to 16 exabytes, or 18,446,744,073,709,551,616 bytes! I think that might support any and all upcoming hard drive capacities for the next hundred years or so!

**Table 8-11** NTFS Cluster Sizes

| DRIVE SIZE | CLUSTER SIZE | NUMBER OF SECTORS |
|---|---|---|
| 512MB or less | 512 bytes | 1 |
| 513MB to 1,024MB (1GB) | 1,024 bytes (1KB) | 2 |
| 1,025MB to 2,048MB (2GB) | 2,048 bytes (2KB) | 4 |
| 2,049MB and larger | 4,096 bytes (4KB) | 8 |

### So Many File Formats!

With so many file formats, how do you know which one to use? In almost all cases, you want to use the best file format your operating system supports. If your system supports FAT32, use it. If you have Windows 2000, use NTFS.

Well, it has taken us a while to get to this point, but I think we are ready to partition and format a hard drive. Before we start, remember that partitioning and formatting wipe out all data on the hard drive. Don't run any of these programs on a drive with data you intend to keep!

## How to Partition and Format

For years, every operating system associated with the word "Microsoft" used the venerable FDISK program to partition a hard drive. DOS, Windows 3.*x*, Windows 95, Windows 98, and even Windows ME all use FDISK. The onset of Windows 2000 brings an entirely new dynamic to the table by completely eliminating FDISK in favor of the new Disk Administrator. Given the totally new method of partitioning presented by Windows 2000, we will save the Disk Administrator for Chapter 11. For now, let's meet FDISK and see a few examples of disk partitioning with FDISK. If you do not have access to a Windows 9*x* system, just read along. Do you have your Windows 95 or Windows 98 boot disk ready? If you don't have a hard drive to play with, you can still run FDISK and march through the screens, just don't change anything!

 **EXAM TIP** Don't be fooled by questions on the A+ exam that intentionally confuse Windows 2000 with Windows 9*x* functions! Know which programs and functions go with which operating systems!

### Single Drive, One Primary Partition

Let's start with the most common of all partitioning options, a single hard drive that we want to turn into one big C: drive. Clearly, we want to boot from this drive, so we need to make the entire drive a primary partition and then make it active. Assume that you have a 30GB hard drive properly installed and configured in CMOS and that you have a Windows 98 boot disk. Boot to the floppy, selecting No CD-ROM support when asked. If you have a Windows 95 boot disk, just boot normally. Eventually, you get to an A: prompt, although Windows 98 may complain that it can't find a C: drive—just ignore it! Type FDISK at the command prompt to start the program. When you run FDISK, you will see one of two things on your screen: a bunch of text or the main menu. Windows 95 version B and later FDISKs place a message on screen that starts with "Your computer has a disk larger than 512MB" and ends by requiring you to select yes (Y) or no (N) (see Figure 8-57).

```
Your computer has a disk larger than 512 MB.  This version of Windows
includes improved support for large disks, resulting in more efficient
use of disk space on large drives, and allowing disks over 2 GB to be
formatted as a single drive.

IMPORTANT: If you enable large disk support and create any new drives on this
disk, you will not be able to access the new drive(s) using other operating
systems, including some versions of Windows 95 and Windows NT, as well as
earlier versions of Windows and MS-DOS. In addition, disk utilities that
were not designed explicitly for the FAT32 file system will not be able
to work with this disk. If you need to access this disk with other operating
systems or older disk utilities, do not enable large drive support.

Do you wish to enable large disk support (Y/N) ...........? [ ]
```

**Figure 8-57**   Opening Windows 98 FDISK screen

> **NOTE**   If you get the error "No Fixed Disks Present," you can bet you forgot to tell the CMOS to look for the drive. Reboot, access CMOS, and try setting up the drive again.

This long-winded explanation is nothing more than Windows asking you whether you want to use FAT16 or FAT32. If you press "Y," everything you do will be FAT32; if you press "N" everything you do will be FAT16. For this example, we will select "Y" for yes. This brings us to the famous FDISK main menu (see Figure 8-58).

If you boot directly to the FDISK main menu without seeing the long paragraph about FAT32, you are using a Windows 95 or even a DOS FDISK. Nothing is wrong with those FDISKs, assuming that FAT16 is acceptable to you.

The FDISK main menu provides four choices. By choosing the first option, you can create a primary partition, an extended partition, or logical drives in an extended partition. The second option enables you to select the active partition. Option 3 enables you

```
                        Microsoft Winodws 98
                      Fixed Disk Setup Program
                (C)Copyright Microsoft Corp.  1983 - 1998
                           FDISK Options

      Current fixed disk drive: 1

      Choose one of the following:

      1. Create DOS partition or Logical DOS Drive
      2. Set active partition
      3. Delete partition or Logical DOS Drive
      4. Display partition information


      Enter choice: [1]


      Press ESC to exit FDISK
```

**Figure 8-58**   FDISK main menu

to delete partitions and logical drives. Option 4 displays current information. (Note that all versions of FDISK—from MS-DOS to Windows ME—call the partitions "DOS" partitions. Don't let that throw you!) Let's first select option 4 to verify that the drive is blank (see Figure 8-59).

If you see anything other than the screen shown in Figure 8-59, the drive has partitions. Jump down to the deleting partitions section to delete the partitions. (Remember, don't delete if you have *any* data on the drive that you want to keep!)

```
                    Dislay Partition Information

      Current fixed disk drive: 1




      No partitions defined

      Press Esc to continue
```

**Figure 8-59**   Nice, blank drive!

Nice, blank drive? Great! Press the ESC key to return to the main menu, just like it says at the bottom of the screen. We always use the ESC key to move back to the main menu in FDISK. Now select 1—Create DOS partition or Logical DOS Drive to open the Create Partition screen (Figure 8-60).

```
                    Create DOS Partition or Logical DOS Drive

Current fixed disk drive: 1

Choose one of the following:

1. Create Primary DOS Partition
2. Create Extended DOS Partition
3. Create Logical DOS Drive(s) in the Extended DOS Partition




Enter choice: [1]




Press ESC to return to FDISK Options
```

**Figure 8-60**    FDISK Create DOS Partition screen

Note the three options: Create Primary DOS Partition, Create Extended DOS Partition, and Create Logical DOS Drive(s) in the Extended DOS Partition. We need a primary partition, so select 1. The screen shown in Figure 8-61 displays.

If you get a "Primary partition already exists" error, you already have a primary partition. Remember Windows 9x only allows one primary partition per drive. See "Deleting Partitions" later in this chapter to learn how to delete it.

This screen asks you if you would like to make one big primary partition and make it active all in one shot. That's what we want to do, correct? If you select "Y" here, everything we need to do happens automatically. But that's way too easy! Let's do it the hard way! Press "N" to get the screen shown in Figure 8-62.

FDISK now wants you to choose the size of your primary partition. Notice that the prompt waits for me either to press ENTER to accept the entire drive or to type in a new value. If you only see approximately 8.4GB (remember, our example drive is 30GB), your BIOS does not have INT13 extensions. You will need to upgrade your BIOS or use an "overlay" program. Every hard drive maker gives away special programs to enable an older, non-INT13 system to accept hard drives larger than 8.4GB. Check the hard drive maker's Web site or ask for the program where you purchased the drive.

```
                 Create Primary DOS Partition

Current fixed disk drive: 1

Do you wish to use the maximum available size for a Primary DOS Partition
(Y/N)...............................................................? [N]




Press Esc to continue
```

**Figure 8-61**  FDISK's "Do it all in one shot?" screen

```
                 Create Primary DOS Partition

Current fixed disk drive: 1




Total disk space is   30000 Mbytes (1 Mbyte = 1048576 bytes)
Maximum space available for partition is 30000 Mbytes (100%)

Enter partition size in Mbytes or percent of disk space (%) to
create a Primary DOS Partition.............................: [ 30000]

No partitions defined




Press ESC to return to FDISK Options
```

**Figure 8-62**  Setting primary partition size

If you only see approximately 2.1GB, you are using FAT16. FAT16 only supports partitions up to 2.1GB. Upgrade the system so that it can use FAT32 or get ready to make an extended partition with a bunch of logical drives!

If we wanted to make the drive 50 percent **C:** and 50 percent **D:**, we could type in half the total or simply type in "50%". (Don't forget the % sign or you will get a 50MB primary partition!) To make the entire drive one big primary partition, just press ENTER. FDISK confirms the new primary partition with the screen shown in Figure 8-63. Press ESC to return to the main menu.

```
                  Create Primary DOS Partition

Current fixed disk drive: 1

Partition  Status    Type    Volume Label  Mbytes   System   Usage
   C: 1              PRI DOS                 30000   UNKNOWN   100%




Primary DOS Partition created

Press Esc to continue
```

**Figure 8-63**   The entire drive is one primary partition.

When you return to the main menu, you'll see an error message telling you there are no active partitions. What the heck? Remember, even though Windows does not do multiple primary partitions, FDISK still must have the primary partition set to active. This step is so easy I'll let you figure out how to do it yourself. Meet me back at the main screen. Do you want a clue? I'll give you two:

- READ THE SCREEN.

- The name of the drive you wish to set active is "1," not "C."

That's it! You have successfully partitioned the drive. Press ESC to exit FDISK and reboot, keeping the bootable floppy in the drive. You must reboot before the changes will take effect. Get to an **A:** prompt and type **FORMAT C:/S** and press ENTER. The screen shown in Figure 8-64 will appear.

When you format a drive, you wipe out all data on the drive and Windows just wants to be sure this is what you really want to do! Are you sure? Then press Y to start the formatting process. Most of the time, formatting is a slow, boring process. But sometimes the drive makes "bad sounds" and you start seeing errors like the one shown in Figure 8-65 at the bottom of the screen.

An allocation unit is FORMAT's term for a cluster. The drive has run across a bad cluster and is trying to fix it. For years, I've told techs that seeing this error a few (610) times doesn't mean anything; every drive comes with a few bad spots. This is no longer true. Modern EIDE drives actually hide a significant number of extra sectors that they use to replace bad sectors automatically. If a new drive gets a lot of "Trying to recover lost allocation unit" errors, you can bet that the drive is dying. Refer to the "How to Fix Hard Drives" section for ideas on troubleshooting.

Once the FORMAT C:/S command finishes, you may remove the floppy disk and reboot to your **C:** drive. In most cases, we rarely use the FORMAT program to format a

```
A:\>format C:/s

WARNING:  ALL DATA ON NON-REMOVABLE DISK
DRIVE C:  WILL BE LOST!
Proceed with Format  (Y/N)?y


Formatting  30709.65M
Format complete.
System transferred

Volume label (11 characters, ENTER for none)?

32,197,017,600 bytes total disk space
        262,144 bytes used by system
32,196,755,456 bytes available on disk

        491,520 bytes in each allocation unit.
        982,455 allocation units available on disk.


Volume Serial Number is 3166-11D9
```

**Figure 8-64**   Formatting

```
A:\>format C:/s

WARNING:  ALL DATA ON NON-REMOVABLE DISK
DRIVE C:  WILL BE LOST!
Proceed with Format  (Y/N)?y


Formatting  30709.65M

Trying to recover lost allocation unit 37,925
```

**Figure 8-65**   "Trying to recover lost allocation unit" error

primary partition. Instead, we rely on built-in formatting functions in the install programs of our operating systems. But for now, and for the A+ test, make sure you understand the concept of formatting. The FORMAT program will appear again in Chapter 9.

### Two Drives, Multiple Partitions

Well, that was fun! So much fun that I'd like to do this again! This time, let's imagine we have two hard drives. The first drive, the primary master, is the same 30GB drive, still containing the primary partition. For a second drive, let's install a 10GB drive as a primary slave. We want to divide the 30GB primary master into 50 percent C:, 25 percent D:, and 25 percent E:. We want to make the primary slave just one big extended partition called F:, as shown in Figure 8-66.

```
              Fixed Disk Drive Status

Disk    Drv    Mbytes    Free    Usage
  1             30000      0      100%
        C:      15000
        D:       7500
        E:       7500
  2             10000      0      100%
        F:      10000
```

**Figure 8-66**   Two drives, four partitions

## Dealing with Multiple Partitions

"But wait," I hear you say. "I thought you said a hard drive must have a primary parti-tion." No, I never said that—not exactly. I said that if you want to boot to a hard drive it must have a primary partition. I don't want to boot to the second drive, I only want to boot to the first drive. We *could* make the second drive primary. It wouldn't hurt a thing, but it would make for some strange drive letters. Here's an example. Say I had two identical 10GB hard drives. Each drive is partitioned identically, 50 percent primary and 50 percent extended with one logical drive in each extended partition. Look at Fig-ure 8-67 to see what I mean.

If I installed one of these drives into a PC, its primary partition would get **C**: and its logical drive in the extended partition would get **D**:. Primary partitions always get drive letters before extended partitions. If I installed these drives in the same system, the drive letters would look like the screen shown in Figure 8-68.

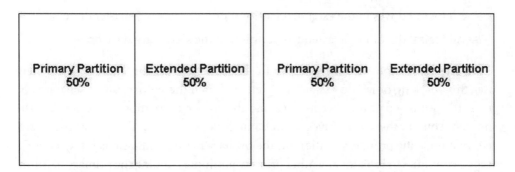

**Figure 8-67**   Identical drives each partitioned with 50 percent primary and 50 percent extended

```
                        Fixed Disk Drive Status

   Disk    Drv    Mbytes    Free    Usage
    1              10000      0      100%
           C:       5000
           E:       5000
    2              10000      0      100%
           D:       5000
           F:       5000




   (1 MByte = 1048576 bytes)

   A:/>
```

**Figure 8-68**  Messed up drive letters from two drives with primary partitions

Folks new to partitioning think that the drive letter gets "burned into the drive" when it is partitioned. This is untrue. The partitions receive their drive letters at every boot. Here's the order in which hard drives receive their letters:

1. Primary partition of the primary master drive

2. Primary partition of the primary slave drive

3. Primary partition of the secondary master drive

4. Primary partition of the secondary slave drive

5. All logical drives in the extended partition of the primary master drive

6. All logical drives in the extended partition of the primary slave drive

7. All logical drives in the extended partition of the secondary master drive

8. All logical drives in the extended partition of the secondary slave drive

So, let's look at our two drives again to see what's happening. At boot, the system uses this "pecking order" to assign drive letters. When these drives sit in separate systems, the primary partition becomes C: and the secondary partition becomes D:. The moment you put these two drives in the same system, however, this changes. The system first finds the primary partition on the primary master and assigns it the letter C:. It then continues to look for any other primary partitions, finding the primary partition on the primary slave and assigning that primary partition the letter D:. Not seeing any more primary partitions, it then goes back up to the primary master drive, now looking for logical drives in extended partitions. It finds one logical drive and assigns it the letter E:. If the system had found two logical drives on the primary master, they would receive the letters E: and F:. After giving the drive letter E: to the one logical drive in the extended partition, the system continues down the list, looking for more logical drives in more extended partitions. In this example, the system would find the other logical drive in the primary slave and assign it the letter F:.

## Deleting Partitions

Deleting partitions in FDISK follows a clear set of rules, but different configurations of drives and partitions require different steps. In a system where all drives have only primary partitions, the process is straightforward: boot to a floppy disk as we did previously and fire up FDISK. In a multiple-drive system, FDISK adds a fifth option to the main menu that enables you to choose the drive you wish to partition, as shown in Figure 8-69.

```
                    Microsoft Winodws 98
                  Fixed Disk Setup Program
              (C)Copyright Microsoft Corp.  1983 - 1998

                        FDISK Options

      Current fixed disk drive: 1

      Choose one of the following:

      1. Create DOS partition or Logical DOS Drive
      2. Set active partition
      3. Delete partition or Logical DOS Drive
      4. Display partition information
      5. Change current fixed disk drive


      Enter choice: [1]



      Press ESC to exit FDISK
```

**Figure 8-69**   FDISK main menu (five options)

If you choose option 5, you see a breakdown of all the drives that FDISK sees. Select the number corresponding to the drive. Be careful here! I don't even want to tell you how many times I meant to change partitions on one drive and accidentally wiped out the partition on another drive just because I didn't look carefully! Because the first drive has the primary partition we want to delete, we select 1 and return to the main menu. Now let's delete that primary partition. Select option 3—Delete partition or Logical DOS Drive to see the Delete Partition menu, as shown in Figure 8-70.

Select 1 to delete the primary partition. You will see a big warning screen. Most of this should be obvious except for the "Volume Label." *Volume labels* are names that you apply to partitions. They are rarely used anymore except in this one situation of delet-

```
          Delete DOS Partition or Logical DOS Drive

Current fixed disk drive: 1

Choose one of the following:

1. Delete Primary DOS Partition
2. Delete Extended DOS Partition
3. Delete Logical DOS Drive(s) in the Extended DOS Partition
4. Delete Non-DOS Partition


Enter choice: [1]



Press ESC to return to FDSIK options
```

**Figure 8-70**   FDISK's Delete Partition menu

ing partitions. Note that the area under the words "Volume Label" is blank. (You can see this in Figure 8-71.) This volume does not have a volume label—by far the most normal case. When the Delete menu asks for a volume label, simply enter what you see under the text "Volume Label" in the menu. In this case, the drive has no volume label so we just press ENTER, then Y when prompted, "Are you sure?" FDISK then deletes the primary partition. Press ESC to return to the main menu; do not return to the Delete menu.

Deleting extended partitions requires a two-step process. You first delete any logical drives in the extended partition, then delete the extended partition itself. If you try to delete an extended partition that still contains logical drives, you get the error shown in Figure 8-71. Note also that if you have a drive with both primary and logical drives, you must delete logical drives and the extended partition before you can delete the primary partition.

## Creating and Formatting Multiple Partitions

After deleting partitions, always return to the main menu and verify that neither drive contains any partitions. Although option 4—Display Partition Information provides the information you need, option 5—Change Current Fixed Disk Drive shows you both disks on a multiple-drive system at the same time, including any partitions on either drive. Figure 8-72 shows two nice, blank drives.

Time to start making some partitions! Let's start with the primary master drive we just erased. No law requires you to do so, but it will make your partitioning much smoother if you partition in the "pecking order" described earlier.

```
              Delete Extended DOS Partition
Current fixed disk drive: 1

Partition  Status    Type     Volume Label  Mbytes   System    Usage
  C: 1       A      PRI DOS                  15000    UNKNOWN    50%
     2               EXT DOS                 15000               50%


Total disk space is  30000 Mbytes (1Mbyte = 1048576 bytes)



Cannot delete extended DOS partitions while logical drives exist.
Press Esc to continue
```

**Figure 8-71**   You must delete logical drives first!

```
              Change Current Fixed Disk Drive

Disk    Drv    Mbytes    Free    Usage
  1             30000    30000    0%
  2             10000    10000    0%




(1 MByte = 1048576 bytes)
Enter Fixed Disk Drive Number (1-2).......................[ ]

Pres ESC to return to FDISK Options
```

**Figure 8-72**   Two blank drives in FDISK

First, make the primary partition. Follow the steps from the previous examples, except this time only, partition 50 percent of the drive as primary (Figure 8-73). Enter 50% into the partition size and press ENTER to see the screen shown in Figure 8-74. Then press ESC to return to the main menu. At this point, make the primary partition active (see Figure 8-75).

Now we need to make the extended partition. This step confuses folks unfamiliar with FDISK. Press 1—Create DOS Partition, then press 2—Create Extended DOS Partition to see the screen in Figure 8-76.

```
                    Create Primary DOS Partition

Current fixed disk drive: 1




Total disk space is   30000 Mbytes (1 Mbyte = 1048576 bytes)
Maximum space available for partition is 30000 Mbytes (100%)

Enter partition size in Mbytes or percent of disk space (%) to
create a Primary DOS Partition..............................: [ 50%]

No partitions defined



Press ESC to return to FDISK Options
```

**Figure 8-73**   Fifty percent of the primary master will be the primary partition.

```
                    Create Primary DOS Partition

Current fixed disk drive: 1

Partition  Status    Type      Volume Label  Mbytes    System    Usage
  C: 1               PRI DOS                  15000     UNKNOWN    50%




Primary DOS Partition created

Press Esc to continue
```

**Figure 8-74**   Creating the primary partition

You will never do anything other than press ENTER whenever you see this screen! Think about this. We've made 50 percent of the drive a primary partition. We now need to make two logical drives in an extended partition. The rest of the drive, the other 50 percent, must be the extended partition! Many people new to FDISK want to enter 25 percent here, thinking about the individual logical drives—don't do that! Make the rest

```
                      Set Active Partition

Current fixed disk drive: 1

Partition  Status    Type     Volume Label  Mbytes    System    Usage
   C: 1              PRI DOS                 15000    UNKNOWN    50%


Total disk space is  30000 Mbytes (1Mbyte = 1048576 bytes)



Enter the number of the partition you want to make active......: [ ]



Press Esc to return to FDISK Options
```

**Figure 8-75**   Making the partition active

```
                  Create Extended DOS Partition

Current fixed disk drive: 1

Partition  Status    Type     Volume Label  Mbytes    System    Usage
   C: 1              PRI DOS                 15000    UNKNOWN    50%

Total disk space is  15000 Mbytes (1Mbyte = 1048576 bytes)
Maximum space available for partition is 15000 Mbytes ( 50%)

Enter partition size in Mbytes or percent of disk space (%) to
create an Extended DOS Partition.............................: [15000]


Press Esc to return to FDISK Options
```

**Figure 8-76**   Creating an extended DOS partition

of the drive the extended partition *and then* go back and chop the extended partition into two logical drives. Just press ENTER here—no situation could occur where you would not make the rest of the drive the extended partition (unless you were intending to install another operating system, and we're not going down that path in the book). In fact, the moment you press ESC, instead of taking you back to the main screen, the system immediately prompts you to create the logical drives (see Figure 8-77).

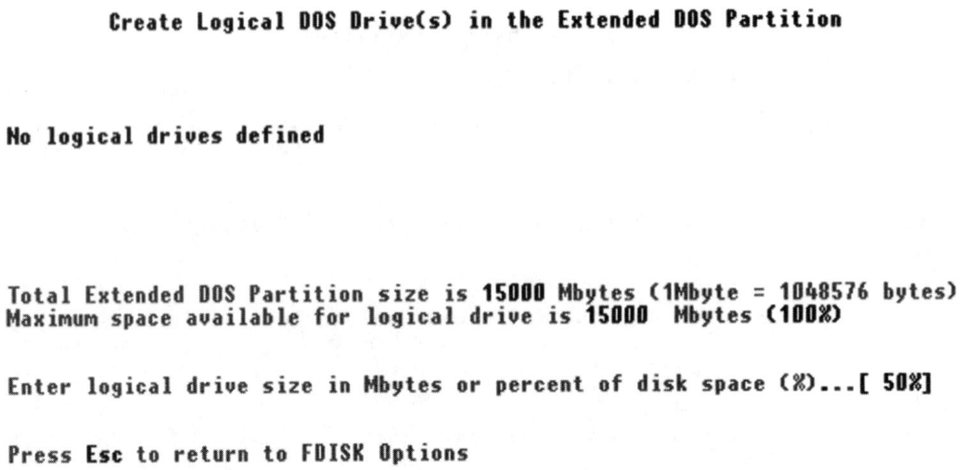

```
        Create Logical DOS Drive(s) in the Extended DOS Partition


No logical drives defined




Total Extended DOS Partition size is 15000 Mbytes (1Mbyte = 1048576 bytes)
Maximum space available for logical drive is 15000  Mbytes (100%)

Enter logical drive size in Mbytes or percent of disk space (%)...[ 50%]


Press Esc to return to FDISK Options
```

**Figure 8-77**   Creating the logical drives

We want to create two logical drives of the same size in the extended partition, each 7.5GB. Here, type in either **7,500** or **50%** (one-half of the extended partition). Try it and see what happens. It should look like Figure 8-78.

Notice that the new logical drive shows up at the top of the screen, while the bottom of the screen shows the remaining amount of unused extended partition. We want the next logical drive to use all the rest of the extended partition, so just press ENTER here to see the screen shown in Figure 8-79.

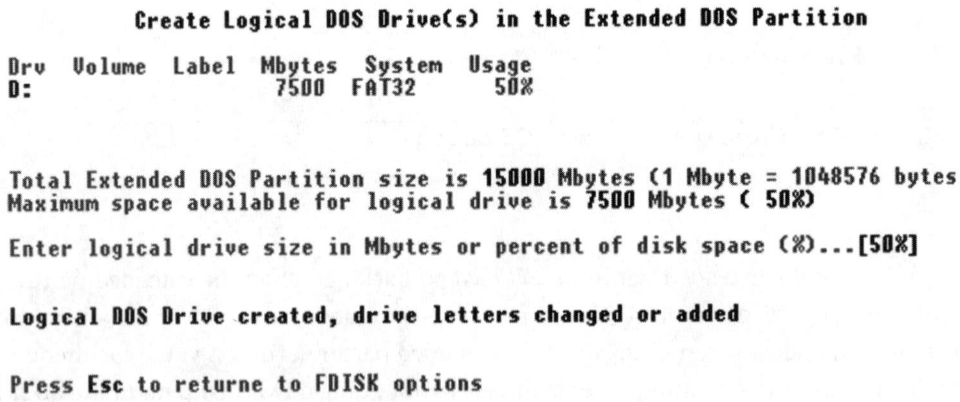

```
        Create Logical DOS Drive(s) in the Extended DOS Partition
Drv  Volume  Label  Mbytes  System  Usage
D:                   7500    FAT32    50%



Total Extended DOS Partition size is 15000 Mbytes (1 Mbyte = 1048576 bytes
Maximum space available for logical drive is 7500 Mbytes ( 50%)

Enter logical drive size in Mbytes or percent of disk space (%)...[50%]


Logical DOS Drive created, drive letters changed or added

Press Esc to returne to FDISK options
```

**Figure 8-78**   Creating the first logical drive

```
                Create Logical DOS Drive(s) in the Extended DOS Partition

Drv  Volume  Label  Mbytes  System  Usage
E:                    7500   FAT32    50%
```

```
All available space in the Extended DOS Partition
is assigned to logical drives.

Press Esc to continue
```

**Figure 8-79**   Creating the second logical drive

Press ESC to return to the main menu. One drive done, one to go. Use option 5 to move to the second drive. This time we just want to make the second hard drive one large extended partition. Press 1—Create DOS Partition, then press 2—Create Extended DOS Partition. This time, the Create Extended DOS Partition screen shows the entire drive (see Figure 8-80)

```
                        Create Extended DOS Partition

Current fixed disk drive: 2

Partition  Status   Type    Volume Label  Mbytes   System   Usage
  F: 1              PRI DOS                15000    UNKNOWN   50%


Total disk space is  10000 Mbytes (1Mbyte = 1048576 bytes)
Maximum space available for partition is 10000 Mbytes (100%)


Enter partition size in Mbytes or percent of disk space (%) to
create an Extended DOS Partition..............................: [10000]


Press Esc to return to FDISK Options
```

**Figure 8-80**   Creating one large extended partition

So once again, just press ENTER. At the next screen, press ESC. FDISK then will prompt you to make a logical drive. Since we only want one big logical partition, just press ENTER to make the entire extended partition one logical drive. The drive is done! Get back to the main menu and select option 5 to see your handiwork (see Figure 8-81).

Wow! We did it! Don't forget to reboot the system to see the changes. But before we poke around these new partitions, we still need to format all the partitions using the FORMAT program.

```
                    Change Current Fixed Disk Drive

    Disk    Drv    Mbytes    Free    Usage
      1             30000      0      100%
            C:      15000
            D:       7500
            E:       7500
      2             10000      0      100%
            F:      10000




    (1 MByte = 1048576 bytes)
    Enter Fixed Disk Drive Number (1-2).......................[ ]


    Press ESC to return to FDISK Options
```

**Figure 8-81**   Viewing drive partitions

Once again, type **FORMAT C:/S**. The /S puts a copy of the operating system on the drive. Once you format C:, type **FORMAT D:**. (We don't need a copy of the operating system on any drive but C:, so skip the /S option.) Repeat FORMAT for **E:** and **F:**

Congratulations! You just set up two drives!

### Partitioning and Formatting a Functional System

In all these examples, we started with blank hard drives (or immediately made them that way by deleting the partitions). The next step after partitioning and formatting with such systems is to install an OS. But many cases arise where you may need to partition and format drives on a perfectly configured PC. The classic example is when you add an extra drive to the system. Suppose your Windows 98 PC has one hard drive (a primary master) with only one big primary partition. After two years of good use, you managed to fill the drive almost completely. Even after careful cleaning out of unneeded files, the day has come when you say, "I need another hard drive." You run to the store and buy a new drive, install it as the primary slave, and set up CMOS. You reboot into Windows 98. Just because you are in a Windows environment, nothing changes in the process. From the Start | Run dialog box, type **FDISK**. Then it appears, just as before, except in a window (see Figure 8-82). It still works the same way. Partition the drive as you would like. Just be sure to restart Windows when you finish.

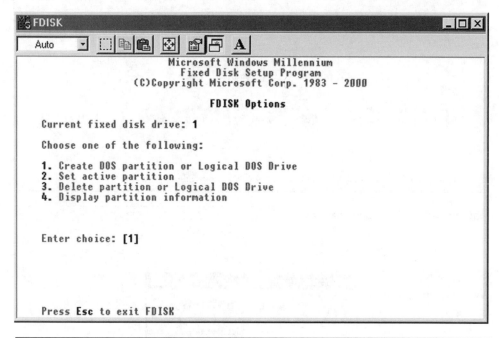

**Figure 8-82** FDISK in Windows

Figure 8-83 shows a new drive I just installed and partitioned in my Windows 98 system. One area that has changed is the FORMAT. If you would like, you may open a DOS box and run the FORMAT program, but Windows 9x provides an easier method. Open My Computer or Windows Explorer, alternate-click (right-click) on the icon of the drive (primary or logical) you wish to format and select Format. Windows 98 displays the screen shown in Figure 8-84. By the way, this also works in Windows 95 and Windows 2000, although the options vary a little in Windows 95 and vary considerably in Windows 2000.

Note how the hard drive format dialog box looks exactly like the floppy drive format dialog box shown in Chapter 7. All the rules are the same. Remember, you already have a bootable system (how could you be in Windows if you didn't?), so you do not need to copy system files. Let it format and your new drive is ready!

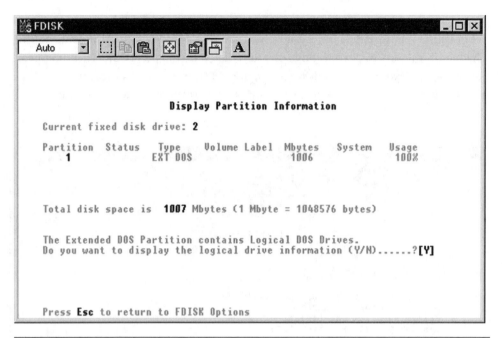

**Figure 8-83**  Partitioned hard drive

**Figure 8-84**
Windows 9x format
screen

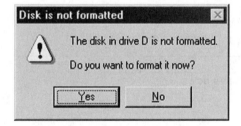

## A Final Warning

Please be careful using FDISK and FORMAT. In the wrong hands, these powerful tools can easily wipe out everything on a partition. Many organizations delete these files from working systems to keep untrained folks from accidentally erasing their hard drives! If you only want to see your partitions, use the System Information program. If you don't have Windows installed yet (often the case when building a new system) boot to a floppy disk, get to an **A:** prompt, and type **FDISK /STATUS**. This handy command tells FDISK just to report the current partition information (see Figure 8-85).

```
C:\>fdisk/status

                                    Fixed Disk Drive Status
    Disk    Drv    Mbytes    Free    Usage
      1                9590            100%
             C:       9590
```

```
     (1 MByte = 1048576 bytes)
C:\>
```

**Figure 8-85**   FDISK /STATUS

## The Finished Drive

Once you format any and all partitions you created, you may now use the drive for whatever reason you decided to install one. Let's review the steps to setting up a hard drive in a Windows 9x system:

1. Make the physical connection. Always use the primary controller first. There are two drives per chain, and every chain must have a master.

2. Set up CMOS. Use autodetection to verify the physical connection. If the drive isn't detected, it points to a hardware problem. Always use AUTO and LBA if your CMOS provides those settings.

3. Use FDISK to make the primary partition. Extended partitions are optional, unless your drive can't support the larger partitions.

4. Use the FORMAT program with the /S option, or the Format function in Windows to make it a bootable drive.

## The Capacity Issue

Before we talk about repairing hard drives, I'd like to take a moment to reflect back on maximum partition sizes for EIDE drives under Windows 9x. I get many calls from users who don't understand why they only get 2.1GB partitions on new INT13 systems or why CMOS reports a brand new 30GB hard drive as only 8.4GB. These problems all stem from capacity limits in either the type of BIOS or the type of file system. The largest partition you may have is the *smaller* of the maximum size supported by your BIOS file system. The following tables show the limits for BIOS and for file systems:

| BIOS | MAXIMUM SIZE DRIVE SUPPORTED |
|---|---|
| Pre-LBA/ECHS | 504MB |
| LBA/ECHS | 8.4GB |
| INT 13 | 137GB |

The current BIOS maximum for EIDE drives is 137GB.

| FILE SYSTEM | MAXIMUM PARTITION SIZE SUPPORTED |
|---|---|
| Pre-DOS 4 (old FAT16) | 32MB |
| FAT16 | 2.1GB |
| FAT32 | 2TB |
| NTFS | 2TB |

Using these tables you can answer drive size questions. If you have a 30GB hard drive under FAT16, you have a maximum partition size of 2.1GB. A 12GB hard drive using FAT32 will accept up to 137GB partitions. So, one day when you purchase a new 200GB hard drive and try to run it under a INT13 BIOS that only accepts 137GB, hope that by then a new type of BIOS has been invented; otherwise, you'll only get 137GB. Don't laugh, these capacities are right around the corner!

**NOTE**  Maximum "partition" size specifically refers to primary partition size or logical drive size. Extended partitions can grow to just about any size.

## How to Fix Hard Drives

The hard drive receives a bad reputation as the "problem child" of the computer. This may stem from the fact that many fixes for problems unrelated to the hard drive boil down to reinstalling software—maybe people just assume the hard drive caused the problem. Certainly, hard drives do fail a considerable amount of the time, but good maintenance and a few good repair tools will keep a hard drive running for many years.

Hard drives are cheap today; it's the data on the drive that's most important. Hard drive repair consists of two critical steps: good backups and a good process for fixing the drive. Although my repair process will fix most drives, including recovering the data, nothing beats a good backup.

## Backups

All computer users fit into one of two groups: those who back up their data and those who have not yet seen a hard drive spontaneously destroy itself and all of their data. Obviously, backing up your drive is critical, but unfortunately, no one seems to agree on what "backing up" means. The most primitive definition of backing up would be the process of creating extra copies of critical data to a secondary source. In other words, putting an extra copy of a term paper on a floppy disk is very much a backup. Yet backing up really goes much further. In its most advanced state, backing up implies using special cassette tape drives with powerful "backup" software to copy the entire contents of the hard drives to tape (see Figure 8-86).

In a perfect world, every system would come with a tape backup unit and users would remember to use it every half-hour. But we don't live in a perfect world. Instead, I assume that most PC users back up their critical data—Word documents, Excel spreadsheets, tax records, and so on—and that more "techie" types back up data and critical

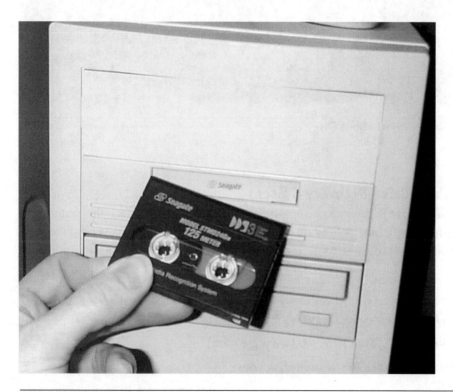

**Figure 8-86**   Tape backup unit

operating system files. The key here is determining precisely which files are "critical," which differs by the operating system. We'll discuss what to back up in each OS's respective chapter. I'll assume that if the drive needs replacing, all the data you need in order to return the system to a fairly recent state exists somewhere.

However, we can back up a few critical bits of information relatively easily. Use The Ultimate Boot Disk to make a copy of your boot sector and partition table. It automatically saves it to an Ultimate Boot Disk floppy (Figure 8-87).

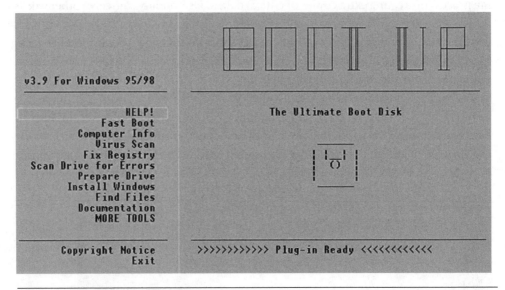

**Figure 8-87**   Ultimate Boot Disk

## Mike's Hard Drive Recovery System

"Mike's Hard-Drive Recovery System" works on all hard drives. In fact, this system also works with floppy disks! Follow these rules to repair drives and recover data as well. First, we need a few software tools. Here's what I recommend for a typical Windows 9*x* system:

- Windows Startup disk (I'll show you how to make one for each version of Windows in their respective chapters)

- SpinRite 5, by Gibson Research (**www.grc.com**)

- Ultimate Boot Disk (**www.smartdisk.com**)

- Self-Monitoring, Analysis, and Reporting Technology (S.M.A.R.T.) utility from the drive maker (I'll explain this in a moment)

For a Windows 2000 system, have these tools handy:

- Windows 2000 Emergency Rescue Disk

- The correct low-level format utility for the make and model of your drive

- Ultimate Boot Disk with Windows NT/2000 plug-in (**www.startdisk.com**)

- S.M.A.R.T. utility from the drive maker (I'll explain this in a moment)

The Ultimate Boot Disk takes your Windows Startup disk and turns it into a real powerhouse. Earlier we saw how to use it to back up our CMOS. Now let's make a backup of your boot sector! Many hard drive failure situations require a copy of the boot sector. The file is tiny and easily fits on the Ultimate Boot Disk. From the Ultimate Boot Disk main screen, select More Tools and then select Drive Medic to get to the screen shown in Figure 8-88.

OK, we're ready to start fixing drives!

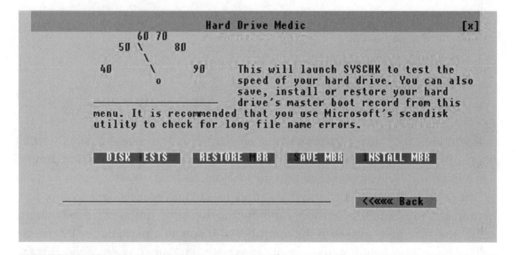

**Figure 8-88**   Boot sector backup

## When Good Drives Go Bad

All hard drive failures fit into one of four groups, listed from most to least common:

- Corrupted data on good sectors

- Corrupted data on physically bad sectors

- Installation errors

- Drives physically damaged beyond repair

With the first three groups, use the repair method outlined next to fix problems and save data. You can also use these methods to determine if a "dead" drive truly belongs in the last group. Let's look at installation errors first, and then look at the more common corrupted data groups.

## Installation Errors

Installing a drive and getting to the point where it can hold data requires four distinct steps: connectivity, CMOS, partitioning, and formatting. If you make a mistake at any point on any of these steps, the drive won't work. The beauty of this is that if you make an error, you can walk back through each step and check for problems.

### Connectivity

A Connectivity error means something isn't plugged in right or something has managed to unplug itself. These problems virtually always show themselves at boot time. Here are some classics:

- Hard-drive error
- No fixed disks present
- HDD controller failure
- No boot device available
- Drive not found

If you plug the cable in backwards for an IDE drive, the computer simply won't boot—it's a famous error and everyone who has ever installed a hard drive has done it. Just reinsert the cable properly and turn the machine back on.

You can usually conquer connectivity errors by carefully inspecting the entire connection system (including electricity) and finding the "silly" mistake (welcome to the club). Always remove and reseat the controller (if it's on an expansion card) if you get an HDD controller failure, as they are prone to static build-up. It is also a good idea to keep an extra controller around to verify if the controller is good. Cables can go bad, but it is very rare unless the cable is obviously ripped or pinched. If your BIOS has an IDE autodetection function, use it! It will not detect a drive unless everything is installed correctly. It's a great, quick connectivity verifier.

If you've just installed the drive, also check the jumper settings. You can't have two masters or two slaves on a single controller. And don't forget the 1 Drive or Standalone setting on some drives!

## CMOS

Modern systems rarely get CMOS errors, because the autodetection feature handles most drives. The errors that do occur generally fall into two groups: forgetting to run Autodetect and selecting the wrong sector translation in Autodetect. Two rules apply here: Always run Autodetect and *always* select LBA.

Older systems could lose CMOS data for a variety of reasons, including static electricity, inserting an expansion card, and blinking with too much force. It takes nothing to do a quick CMOS check to verify that the drive's geometry is correct using autodetection. Here are some of the more common errors that might point to CMOS problems:

- CMOS configuration mismatch
- No boot device available
- Drive not found
- Missing operating system

If Autodetect fails to see the drive in question, it's probably a connectivity problem. Grab a screwdriver and look inside the system!

## Partitions

Partitioning errors generally fall into two groups: failing to partition at all, and making the wrong size/type of partition. The first error invariably shows up when you try to access the non-partitioned drive. The operating system gives you a nice "Invalid Drive Specification" error, and you can't see the drive in anything but CMOS and FDISK. Simply add your partition of choice and go on.

The most common sizing issue comes from selecting less than the full remaining space when making an extended partition. This invariably shows up as a, "Hey! Why do I only have X megabytes of space? My drive is bigger than that!" Check the partitions in FDISK and redo them if necessary.

## Format

Failing to format a drive makes the drive unable to hold data. Accessing the drive in Windows will result in a drive "is not accessible" error, and from a C:\ prompt, you'll get the famous "Invalid Media Type" error. Format the drive unless you're certain that the drive has a format already. Check one of the sections on corrupted data later in this chapter for the fix.

## Mental Reinstall

Focus on the fact that all of these errors share a common thread—you just installed a drive! Installation errors don't show up on a system that has been running correctly for three weeks; they show up the moment you try to do something with the drive you just installed. If a newly installed drive fails to work, do a "mental reinstall." Does the drive show up in the CMOS Autodetect? No? Then recheck the cables, master/slave settings, and power! If it does show up, did you remember to partition and format the drive? Did it need to be set active? These are common-sense questions that come to mind as you march through your mental reinstall. Even though I've installed thousands of drives over the years, I'm amazed at how often I do things such as forget to plug in power to a drive, forget CMOS, or install a cable backwards. Do the mental reinstall—it really works!

## Corrupted Data on Good Sectors

All hard drives occasionally get corrupted data in individual sectors. Power surges, accidental shutdowns, corrupted install media, viruses, along with hundreds of other problems can cause this corruption. In most cases, this type of error shows up while Windows is running. Figure 8-89 shows a classic example of this type of error.

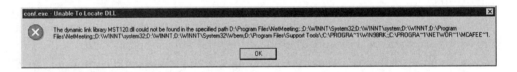

**Figure 8-89**   Corrupted data error

You may also see Windows error messages saying one of the following:

- "The following file is missing or corrupt"
- "The download location information is damaged"
- "Unable to load file"

If core boot files become corrupted, you may see text errors at boot, such as the following:

- "Cannot find COMMAND.COM"
- "Error loading operating system"
- "Invalid BOOT.INI"

On older programs you may see a command prompt open with errors such as this one:

```
Sector not found reading drive C: Abort, Retry, Fail?
```

These problems occur with such frequency that all versions of Windows provide a disk-checking utility. The most common way to access this tool is by alternate-clicking on the suspected drive and selecting Properties. Under the Tools tab, click the Check Now button to start the system-checking tool (see Figure 8-90).

**Figure 8-90**
Windows 2000 disk checker

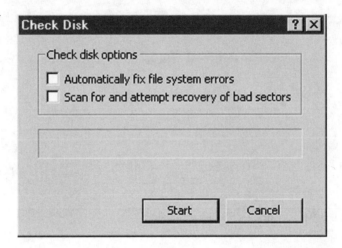

Although the "look and feel" of this tool varies between Windows 9*x* and Windows 2000, it performs the same function in both operating systems. The disk-checking program scans your drive, verifying proper drive structures; that is, it checks to see if the directories point to other directories and the filenames are valid. Then, it runs a disk scan to verify that the bad clusters are all marked in the FAT tables. If it finds any bad clusters, the disk-checking utility will mark those as bad. Before the program marks a cluster as bad, it attempts to move the data to a good cluster. This marking of bad clusters is where the disk-checking utility does its best work. This process usually works successfully and often recovers otherwise lost data. Figure 8-91 shows the disk error checker for Windows 98 at work. Note the word "ScanDisk" in the title bar, another common term for the disk checker retained from the old DOS days. Windows 2000 does not use that term.

Note some of the options available for Windows 98—the Thorough option checks the entire drive. Standard checks file and folders areas only. Note that both Windows 2000 and Windows 98 give the option to fix errors automatically. I don't like to use

**Figure 8-91**  Windows 98 disk checker

this—if errors begin to show, I want to see them. If I intend to run the program overnight however (it can take a long time), then the automatic fixing option works wonders! Just remember to turn off the screen saver!

### Extract/Expand

After marking a bad cluster, the disk-checking program might fail to move the data from that cluster to a new one, resulting in the same error. Although reinstalling the program that gives the error always works well, wouldn't it be nice just to grab that one file off of the install CD? Most Windows programs store all files in a compressed format called CAB (which is short for "cabinet file"). One CAB file contains many files, and most install disks have lots of CAB files (see Figure 8-92).

In order to replace a single corrupt file this way, you need to know two things: the location of the CAB file that contains the file you need and how to get the file out so you can copy it back to its original spot. Microsoft supplies the EXTRACT program (Windows 95/98) or the EXPAND program (Windows 2000) to enable you to get a new copy of the missing file from the CAB files on the installation CD-ROM disk. Also

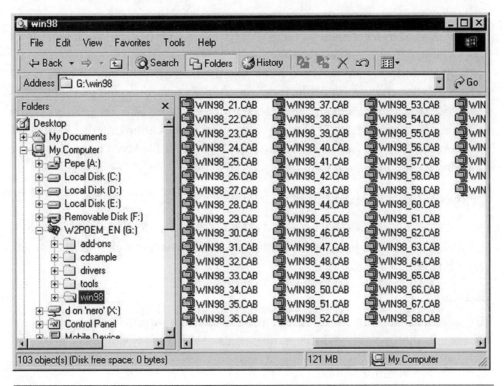

**Figure 8-92**  CAB files

notice how they are numbered—that's the secret to understanding these programs. Let's look first at EXTRACT.

> **NOTE**  This section assumes some comfort with the use of a command prompt. Some folks may want to read the next three chapters to get comfortable with command prompts first.

In most cases, all the CAB files for a program are piled into some folder, as shown in Figure 8-92. Let's say we need a file called OLEPRO32.DLL. I have no idea what this file does. I only know that Windows can't find it and I'm going to put it back! Get to a DOS prompt within Windows (Start | Programs | MS-DOS Prompt) and tell EXTRACT to check *all* the CAB files with this command

EXTRACT /Y /A WIN98_21.CAB OLEPRO32.DLL

EXTRACT goes through all the CAB files, starting with WIN98_21.CAB and finds the file. If you want to see details on the EXTRACT command, use the Windows Help or type **EXTRACT /?** at a command prompt.

EXPAND works equally well but has a slightly different command structure. Like EXTRACT, EXPAND runs at a command prompt. To get to a command prompt in Windows 2000, select Start | Run and type **CMD**. To access a file, type in the proper location and name, but use a special -**F:** switch. For example, to search the CAB files in the I386 folder on the CD-ROM (in this case, drive letter **X:\** ) for the file MWWDM.SYS, type the following at the command prompt:

EXPAND X:\I386\*.CAB -F:MWWDM.SYS C:\

EXPAND searches all CAB files in the X:\I386 folder, looking for the file MWWDM.SYS. When EXPAND locates the CAB file containing the desired file, it expands the file and places it in the **C:\** folder.

### Bad Boot Sector

Like any other part of a drive, your boot sector may occasionally get corrupted. Bad boot sectors show up as boot lockups, missing drive letters in My Computer, and errors such as the following:

- Invalid Partition
- Bad or Missing Command Interpreter

First, run an anti-virus program to insure that a virus has not attacked your boot sector. See the section on viruses in Chapter 9 to learn how to deal with a boot sector virus. Assuming no virus is present, you need to replace the boot sector. Hopefully, you made a backup of the boot sector with The Ultimate Boot Disk or with another utility. You simply boot off the disk and reinstall the MBR.

If you don't have an MBR, you will probably be repartitioning the hard drive and doing a complete reinstall. One last-ditch effort you should make is to boot to an **A:** prompt and enter the following command to reinstall the master boot record:

FDISK /MBR

It often works!

### Corrupted Data on Bad Sectors

If the same errors continue to appear after running the disk-checking utility described in the previous section, there's a chance that the drive has bad sectors.

Almost all drives today take advantage of built-in *error correction code* (ECC) that constantly checks the drive for bad sectors. If the ECC detects a bad sector, it marks the sector as bad in the drive's internal error map. Don't confuse this error map with a FAT. The partitioning program creates the FAT. The drive's internal error map was created at the factory on reserved drive heads and is invisible to the system. If the ECC finds a bad sector, you will get a corrupted data error as the computer attempts to read the bad sector. Disk checkers fix this problem most of the time.

Many times the ECC thinks a bad sector is good, however, and fails to update the internal error map. In this case, you need a program that goes back into the drive and marks the sectors as bad. That's where the powerful SpinRite utility from Gibson Research comes into play. SpinRite marks sectors as bad or good more accurately than ECC and does not disturb the data, enabling you to run SpinRite without fear of losing anything. And if it finds a bad sector with data in it, SpinRite has powerful algorithms that usually recover the data on all but the most badly damaged sectors (see Figure 8-93).

The power of SpinRite makes it required equipment in every tech's tool bag. Yet for all this power, SpinRite has an Achilles' heel—it does not work on NTFS partitions. Do me a favor, go to the Gibson Research Web site and tell Steve Gibson to update SpinRite for NTFS!

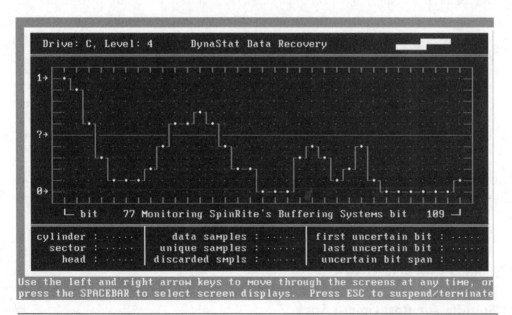

**Figure 8-93**  SpinRite

Without SpinRite, you must use a low-level format program supplied by the hard drive maker. These programs work like SpinRite in that they aggressively check the hard drive's sectors and update the internal error map. Unfortunately, all of them wipe out all data on the drive. At least the drive can be used, even if it means repartitioning, formatting, and reinstalling everything!

### Goodbye Drive!

Every hard drive reaches a failure point when it becomes time to throw it in the trash and replace it with a new one. The death signs for a hard drive are painfully obvious. The hard drive may not make any sound, telling you the motor has burned up. Powerful programs such as SpinRite lock up or report failures. The CMOS autodetection fails to see the drive, even though you have mentally reinstalled the drive five times. It is probably time to accept the fact that the hard drive has died.

## Beyond A+

Most hard drives have three-year warranties. Never throw a dead drive away! First, check the hard drive maker's Web site or call them to see if the drive is still under warranty. Ask for an *Return Material Authorization* (RMA). You'll be amazed how many times you get a newer, usually larger, hard drive for free! It never hurts to check!

### Going Deeper into Drive Technology

Modern hard drives have many other features worth knowing about, but that rarely impacts beginning techs. A couple of the more interesting ones are spindle speed and the S.M.A.R.T. feature that was mentioned earlier. Also, if you have a burning desire to dive into hard drives in all their glory, here are a couple of links to get you started.

Sharky Extreme (funny name, great site!) has an excellent hard drive guide that takes you through all the technology in detail. They have not updated at this writing to include ATA/100, but they discuss ATA/66 at length. Here's the URL:

**http://www.sharkyextreme.com/hardware/guides/harddrive/**

For specific drive reviews, you need not go any farther than the Storage Review, an excellent site dedicated solely to hard drives. Here's the link:

**http://www.storagereview.com**

### Spindle (or Rotational) Speed

Hard drives run at a set spindle speed, measured in *revolutions per minute* (RPM). Older drives run at the long-standard speed of 3,600RPM, but new drives are hitting

10,000RPM! The faster the spindle speed, the faster the controller can store and retrieve data. Here are the common speeds: 4,500, 5,400, 7,200, and 10,000RPM.

Faster drives mean better system performance, but they can also cause the computer to overheat. This is especially true in tight cases, such as mini-towers, and in cases containing many drives. Two 4,500RPM drives might run forever, snuggly tucked together in your old case. But slap a hot new 10,000RPM drive in that same case and watch your system start crashing right and left!

You can deal with these hotrod drives by adding drive bay fans between the drives or migrating to a more spacious case. Most enthusiasts end up doing both.

Drive bay fans sit at the front of a bay and blow air across the drive. They range in price from $10-100 (U.S.) and can lower the temperature of your drives dramatically. Figure 8-94 shows a picture of a higher-end triple-fan drive bay cooler, the IEC Cool-Venus.

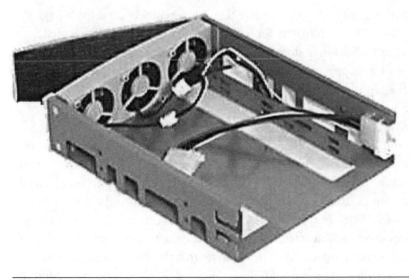

**Figure 8-94**   Triple-fan drive bay cooler (photo courtesy IEC)

Air flow in a case can make or break your system stability, especially when you add new drives that increase the ambient temperature. Hot systems get flaky and lock up at odd moments. Many things can impede the air flow—jumbled up ribbon cables, drives squished together in a tiny case, fans clogged by dust or animal hair, and so on.

Technicians need to be aware of the dangers when adding a new hard drive to an older system. Get into the habit of tying off ribbon cables, adding front fans to cases when systems lock up intermittently, and making sure the fan(s) run well. Finally, if a client wants a new drive and his system is a tiny mini-tower with only the power supply fan to cool it off, be gentle, but definitely steer him to one of the slower drives!

## S.M.A.R.T.

Most modern hard drives use a function called S.M.A.R.T. It provides a number of checks on the drive, watching for signs that it may be having problems. S.M.A.R.T. was developed to catch problems *before* the drive fails. As of this writing, no one has made a universal tool for desktop PCs using the S.M.A.R.T. technology. All hard drive makers provide free utilities that query the drive's S.M.A.R.T. functions. S.M.A.R.T. does not repair or pinpoint a problem, so these utilities just say if the drive is good or if it should be replaced.

## Zip and LS-120 Drives

For years, the small size of floppy disks made them unacceptable for most storage situations, and the only serious alternative for backups was tape drives. Folks wanted a new form of removable backup that stored a much larger amount of data while staying roughly the size of a floppy disk. This led to the creation of the now very popular Iomega Zip® drives in the mid-1990s. The original Zip disks held 100MB—just about the perfect size for data storage—and were roughly the same size as a floppy disk. Iomega's Zip drives weren't the only removable storage drives to appear at this time, but their low price and fairly high reliability, combined with cross platform support (you could use Zip drives with Macs or UNIX systems) slowly made Zip disks the *de facto* standard for removable media (Figure 8-95). Zip drives come in two common capacities: 100MB and 250MB. The 250MB drives read both the 250MB and the 100MB disks.

Iomega sells many different types of Zip drives: external drives that connect to a system's parallel port, internal and external drives that use the SCSI interface (see Chapter 13), and the most popular, internal ATAPI Zip drives that use the hard drive controllers. Figure 8-96 shows a typical external Zip drive. Figure 8-97 shows the classic internal ATAPI Zip drive.

When you install an ATAPI Zip drive, simply follow the same connectivity rules as for a hard drive. The Zip drive has a 40-pin connection, requires a Molex connector for power, and has master/slave jumpers. Unlike your EIDE drive, however, Zip drives do not use any CMOS settings and do require special drivers. Windows 98 and Windows 2000 have built-in driver support for Zip drives, although Iomega provides greatly enhanced drivers that enable a number of extra handy functions, such as password disk protection. Figure 8-98 shows a Zip drive on a Windows 2000 system with the enhanced drivers loaded.

**Figure 8-95**   Typical Zip disk

The only serious competitor to the Zip drive in the larger capacity removable disk business is the LS-120 drive. As the name implies, they use disks that hold 120MB of data. LS-120 and Zip drives use completely incompatible media. Unlike the proprietary Zip drive, LS-120 drives come from an industry consortium and have the added benefit of not only reading their own disks, but being fully backward compatible with 3.5-inch floppy disks. Almost all LS-120 drives are ATAPI and install exactly like their ATAPI competitors. Unfortunately, LS-120 drives never seemed to catch on like Zip drives, probably due to weak marketing and higher prices. But LS-120 drives and disks are still made and enjoy a modest degree of support (Figure 8-99).

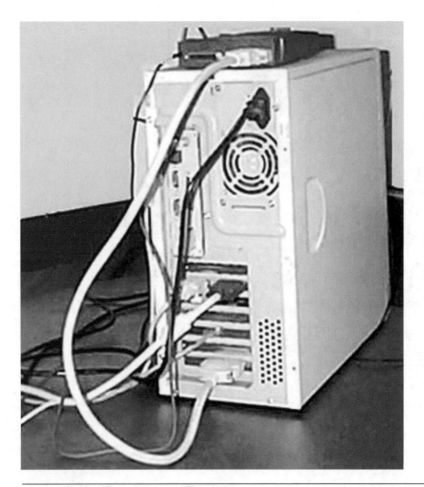

**Figure 8-96**    Typical external Zip drive

**Figure 8-97**
Typical internal
Zip drive

**Figure 8-98**
Enhanced Zip
settings

**Figure 8-99**
LS-120 drive

## Review Questions

1. John has two EIDE hard drives installed as master/slave on the primary IDE controller. How can he partition these drives? (Select all that apply.)

   A. The master drive must have a primary partition only. The slave can have a primary partition and an extended partition.

   B. The master drive can have both a primary partition and an extended partition. The slave can have both a primary partition and an extended partition.

   C. The master drive can have both a primary partition and an extended partition. The slave must have only an extended partition.

   D. The master drive must have a primary partition only. The slave must have only an extended partition.

2. Which three of the following are the most important geometries of hard drives?
   A. Cylinders
   B. Write precomp cylinder
   C. Heads
   D. Sectors per track

3. Which of the following is not true about IDE drives today?
   A. They are considered to be ATA, or AT attachment, drives.
   B. They need a 40-pin flat ribbon attachment to the IDE controller.
   C. They need to be "parked" before moving.
   D. Their volume is measured in megabytes or gigabytes.

4. How many IDE hard drives can you have on a system with two hard drive controllers?
   A. 1
   B. 2
   C. 3
   D. 4

5. How do you differentiate two IDE drives on the same cable?
   A. The flat ribbon cable has a seven-wire twist that determines which is which.
   B. By setting jumpers on the individual drives to determine which is master and which is slave.
   C. The IDE controller determines the hierarchy.
   D. Both drives are considered equal.

6. What happens if you cable an IDE hard drive incorrectly?
   A. You can destroy that hard drive.
   B. The data will be erased, but the hard drive will be OK.
   C. The system will not be able to communicate with that hard drive.
   D. Nothing. It doesn't matter how the cable is set up; it doesn't have the seven-wire twist.

7. What was the maximum size hard drive that the BIOS routines for an original AT command set enabled?
   A. 504 megabytes
   B. 504 million bytes
   C. 528 megabytes
   D. There was no limit.

8. When autodetecting an IDE hard drive, what are the three options that you can choose for setting up the drive?

   A. ECHS (enhanced, cylinders, heads, sectors)

   B. Normal

   C. EBA (enhanced block addressing)

   D. LBA (logical block addressing)

9. John has just purchased an ATA/66 capable hard drive for his ATA/66 capable system. However, he notices that he forgot to get the special 80-pin cable. If he installs the ATA/66 drive with a 40-pin EIDE cable, what will happen?

   A. The drive will work, but will not run at the ATA/66 speed.

   B. He might damage the motherboard.

   C. He won't be able to install the drive, because the cables are incompatible.

   D. He will not be able to run in ATA mode.

10. Susan needs to make her new C: partition bootable. What command should she use?

    A. FDISK C: /SYSTEM

    B. FDISK C: /S

    C. FORMAT C: /SYSTEM

    D. FORMAT C: /S

## Answers

1. **B.** How the drive connects to the motherboard has nothing to do with how it can be partitioned.

2. **A, C, D.** Cylinders, heads, and sectors/track define a hard drive's geometry.

3. **C.** Only early hard drives needed to be parked.

4. **D.** Each controller supports two drives.

5. **B.** Drives use master/slave jumpers to differentiate between the two drives.

6. **C.** Nothing will be damaged or lost—there just won't be any communication.

7. **A.** 504 megabytes (528 million bytes)

8. **A, B, D.** ECHS often appears as the "Large" option.

9. **A.** ATA/66 drives work fine with a 40-pin cable—they just won't run at ATA/66 speed.

10. **D.** The correct command is FORMAT C: /S.

# DOS

In this chapter, you will

- Uncover the secret knowledge behind the concept of an operating system
- Go back in time to relive the history of DOS
- See how DOS stores, manipulates, and retrieves data and programs
- Learn several DOS commands and functions

DOS? Why the heck does this book have a DOS chapter! Doesn't Mike know that the A+ Certification exams no longer cover DOS? Why leave it in?

OK, that's a fair set of questions, so let me answer them.

- Although A+ Certification has indeed dropped DOS from the examination domains, it still assumes you have a solid understanding of a large number of command-line prompt programs such as FDISK and FORMAT. The commands make more sense if you understand them in the context of DOS before you see them in Windows.

- The different processor modes discussed in Chapter 2, such as *386 protected mode* and *virtual 8086*, will make more sense if you understand how DOS works.

- A+ Certification tests you on DOS memory usage and configuring DOS programs in a Windows environment. Concepts like *conventional memory* or *extended memory* make more sense if you understand how DOS used them.

> *Those who fail to learn DOS are doomed never to understand Windows.*
> —Mike Meyers' corollary to the famous George Santayana quote

# Historical/Conceptual

Let me give you a little incentive to learn the old stuff. Every command you see in this chapter also works in every version of Windows and often offers a quicker way to accomplish a task than its graphical alternative. Furthermore, the A+ exam tests you on all of these commands. I'd rather explain these commands in a separate DOS section than wait for a related Windows chapter and have you scratching your head and wondering, "Why in the world is this command important?"

 **EXAM TIP** Every DOS command in this chapter is covered on the exam. I'll describe differences between versions of these commands where appropriate. Know the commands. Know them well.

So, let me put in another section header to make sure you appreciate the importance of this chapter:

# Test Specific

Let's get to work.

This section is easier to understand with a PC at hand. That way, you can follow along with the explanations and try exploring around your machine. Although this works best with true DOS, a computer running Windows also works acceptably. If your system runs Windows, use the MS-DOS Prompt if available (check under Start | Programs), or click Start, then Run. Type **COMMAND** (CMD in Windows 2000) and then click OK. You will be at a Windows equivalent of DOS. Just be aware that the Windows DOS is slightly different from true DOS. Even though all of the DOS commands discussed in this chapter will work in Windows DOS, many of the screens will look a little different. To make the experience even more realistic for Windows users, press ALT-ENTER to make the DOS window full screen. Press ALT-ENTER again to bring it back into a window.

Just as in Windows, most DOS commands can be executed several ways; however, showing you all those ways would take a huge amount of time and be counterproductive to the goals of this book. Therefore, only one method will be used for each command. This method might not be the fastest or easiest, but it will be the one that most clearly explains the command and the command's effect on the system.

## Every Computer Needs an Operating System

A computer exists only to perform one function—to run programs. The CPU inside your PC undoubtedly runs programs extremely well. Unfortunately, that CPU needs all the programs "fed" to it in a high-speed binary format. Even with a hard drive full of programs ready to run on that CPU, a number of functions must take place before, during, and after a CPU runs a program. Users need some way to "feed" the desired program to the CPU, for example, and then to deal with the data generated by that program. We all know that your PC stores programs and data on a hard, floppy, or CD-ROM disc, but how does the PC separate the hundreds of discrete pieces of programs and data it stores? How does the system organize these programs and data so you can select a program and then tell the CPU to run only that program? If a program runs many times and generates different data each time, what steps must users take to keep each piece of data separate? How is data organized so the users can later recall a certain piece of data? How can programs and data be moved, deleted, copied, and organized? All these functions, and many more, need to be in existence before a computer can do its job. In addition, these functions should be performed in such a way that they make sense to normal, nontechnical people.

## Enter the Operating System

The PC needs an *operating system* (OS) to handle all of these functions. An OS is a program that performs four basic functions. First, it must communicate, or at least provide a method for other programs to communicate, with the hardware of the PC. It's up to the OS to access the hard drives, respond to the keyboard, and output data to the monitor. Second, the OS must create a *user interface*—a visual representation of the computer on the monitor that makes sense to the people using the computer. The OS must also take advantage of standard input devices, such as mice and keyboards, to enable users to manipulate the user interface and thereby make changes to the computer. Third, the OS, via the user interface, must enable users to determine the available installed programs and run, use, and shut down the program of their choice. Fourth, the OS should enable users to add, move, and delete the installed programs and data.

## Operating System Traits

All operating systems have definite traits that set them apart from regular programs. First, an OS only works with a particular type of processor. The Intel and AMD "×86" line of CPUs heavily dominates today's PCs, but other platforms use different CPUs that are completely incompatible with the Intel and AMD lines. Two examples of the latter are the Compaq Alpha, used by many UNIX systems, and the Motorola Power PC, the CPU inside Macintosh computers. The OS must understand important aspects of the CPU, such as the amount of memory the CPU can handle, what modes of operation it is capable of performing, and the commands needed to perform any operation.

Certain OSs, such as Linux, run on more than one type of processor, but achieve this by having versions for each type of processor they support.

Second, an OS always starts running immediately after the PC has finished its POST, taking control of the PC. The OS continues running until you reboot or turn off the PC. You cannot turn off the OS unless you also turn off the PC.

Third, *application* programs, such as word processors, spreadsheets, and Web browsers, cannot run on a PC without an OS. Therefore, programmers write application programs to function under the control of a certain OS. You cannot write an application that works under different OSs. Whoever makes an OS always provides a "rule book" that tells programmers how to write programs for a particular OS. These rule books are known as *application programming interfaces* (APIs).

Last, an OS must have flexibility and provide some facility for using new software or hardware that might be installed. Refer to Table 9-1.

**Table 9-1**  Operating Systems and Applications

| PC OPERATING SYSTEMS | PC APPLICATIONS |
| --- | --- |
| DOS | Microsoft Word |
| Windows 95 | Lotus 1-2-3 |
| Windows 98 | Adobe Photoshop |
| Windows ME | Netscape Communicator |
| Windows NT | McAfee VirusScan |
| Windows 2000 | ICC ACT! |
| UNIX | Plus thousands more! |
| Linux | |
| BeOS | |

## Communicating with Hardware

In earlier chapters you learned that the system BIOS, stored on some type of non-volatile memory (ROM or Flash ROM) on the motherboard, stores programs that know how to talk to the most basic and important parts of the computer. These include the hard drives, floppy drives, keyboard, and basic video. The OS must work with the system BIOS to deal with these devices. If users want to access the hard drive to retrieve a program, the OS must take the request and pass it to the appropriate hard-drive BIOS instruction that tells the drive to send the program to RAM. Plus, if for some compelling reason the BIOS lacks the capability to perform its function, the OS should bypass the BIOS and talk to the piece of hardware directly. Most recent OSs, certainly including

Windows, skip BIOS and talk directly to almost every piece of hardware.

For the OS to take control of a new piece of hardware, it needs some method to communicate with that hardware. Therefore, the OS needs a method to add programming necessary to talk to that device. Because devices might be added or removed, the method of adding more programming must be simple and flexible. Most OSs use device drivers to add this necessary code. An OS maker (like Microsoft) tells hardware makers how to create these programs (and makes money selling the development tools), and also creates a method of adding the device driver to the OS code. Because makers of a particular hardware usually supply the device driver with the hardware, and because drivers act something like BIOS, it can be jokingly, although accurately, thought of as BYOB (bring your own BIOS).

Because the OS handles communicating with hardware, it should provide some type of error handling or at least error notification. If someone attempts to use a piece of hardware that isn't working properly, the OS should either try to fix the problem or at least attempt to communicate with the device a few more times. If the device continues to fail, the OS should provide an error screen to notify users of the problem.

## Creating a User Interface

Most users care about doing only a few simple functions with their PCs. First, they want to know about the available applications; second, they want easy access to those programs; and third, they want to save the results of an application (data) and label that discrete piece of data in such a way that they can find it later.

A shoe store makes a good analogy for a user interface. The front of the shoe store is filled with attractive displays of shoes, organized and grouped by gender (men and women), age (adult and children), function (dress or sports), and style. Shoe sellers do this to enable consumers to see everything that's available and to make it much easier to select the shoes they want to purchase. If a customer wants to buy a pair of shoes, what happens? The customer points out the shoes he or she wants to try on to the salesperson. The salesperson looks at the inside of the shoe and disappears through a small door. As the salesperson whisks away, the customer might wonder why the salesperson looked in the shoe. That salesperson was looking at the inventory code in the shoe.

Shoe manufacturers print an inventory code inside every shoe. Have you ever seen the back of a shoe store? It's scary. All the shoes are organized, not by style, color, gender, or age, but by inventory code. The salesperson reads the inventory code to know where to look for that shoe. Without understanding the code, no one would know where to search for a pair of shoes, but it's the best way to organize an inventory of 25,000 pairs of shoes. What a customer sees in the store is not all the shoes as they really are in the back, but a "user interface" of what's available. The front display in the store—the user interface—creates a pretty, easy to use, although entirely unrealistic display of the shoes in stock.

A computer's user interface performs the same function by providing to the user a display of the programs and data on the PC. The customers (users) look at the display (the user interface) and tell the salesperson (the OS) what they want, without ever really knowing how all the shoes (programs and data) are really organized.

Finishing the analogy, the shoe store's displays are not permanent. Salespeople can easily add shoes and replace old displays. They can change a rack of men's shoes into a rack of women's shoes, for example, relatively easily. Like the shoe store, a user interface should also be flexible and scalable, depending on the system in which it is installed.

## Accessing and Supporting Programs

An OS must enable users to start a program. This is a simple but important concept. When a program starts, the user interface must disappear and allow the application to take over the screen. If the OS is still visible, it must move away from the main part of the screen and set itself to the top, bottom, or sides. While the application runs, the OS must still provide access to hardware—changing the screen, saving data, printing— whatever the application needs. So, even though the OS disappears from the user inter- face, it continues to work. If a program loses control, the OS should have some way to stop the program, or at least to recognize what's happening and generate an error mes- sage. Last, the OS should instantly return to the user interface when the application shuts down so that users may then choose another application.

## Organizing and Manipulating Programs and Data

A PC stores data and programs primarily on floppies, hard drives, and CD-ROMs. One PC might store hundreds of programs and thousands of separate pieces of data. Simply making all the programs and data visible would be like taking all the shoes in the back of the shoe store and setting them neatly on the display room floor. Yes, you could locate shoes in this fashion, but it would be an overly complicated mess. A method of organizing the programs and data is needed.

This organization requires a few steps. First, the OS needs to give a label or name to each program and each individual piece of data, and this label or name must enable users to identify each item as either a program or data. If it's data, there must be some method of identifying what type of program uses that particular data.

Next, the OS must provide a naming system for all the drives. Each floppy, hard, and CD-ROM drive needs some sort of identifier. It can be as simple as a letter of the alpha- bet or as complex as a fully descriptive phrase. These drive names are usually deter- mined when the drive is first installed, and are rarely, if ever, changed.

Third, the user must be able to store data and programs in distinct groups on each drive, and the OS user interface must be able to interact with each of these groups individually. Users must be able to open and close these groups via the user interface. The users also need a method of copying, moving, and deleting programs and data. Last, the user interface must enable users to perform these functions easily and, especially in the case of deletions, ensure that actions are done only to the specified programs and data. Clearly, a good OS has a lot of work to do!

Operating systems existed long before PCs were invented. All of the functions just mentioned were performed on mainframes and minicomputers with a high degree of refinement. By the late 1970s, a few companies were already selling OSs for the first-generation microcomputer market. IBM began to search for a company that could provide them with an OS for a new computer they were developing called the IBM Personal Computer, better known as the PC. After being rebuffed by a company called Digital Research, they went to a tiny company that had invented a popular new programming language called BASIC. They asked the president if his company could create an OS for the IBM PC. Although his company had never actually written an OS, he brazenly said "Sure!" That man was Bill Gates, and the tiny company was Microsoft.

## In the Beginning, There Was DOS

After shaking hands with the IBM representatives, Bill Gates hurriedly began to search for an OS based on the Intel 8086 processor. He found a very primitive OS called *Quick-and-Dirty Operating System* (QDOS), written by a one-man shop, and purchased it for a few thousand dollars. After several minor changes, Microsoft released it as *Microsoft Disk Operating System* (MS-DOS), version 1.1. Although primitive by today's standards, MS-DOS 1.1 could provide all the functions needed for an OS. Over the years, MS-DOS went through version after version (see Table 9-2) until the last Microsoft version, MS-DOS 6.22, was released in 1994. Microsoft licensed MS-DOS to PC makers. They could add their own changes and then rename the program. IBM called their version PC-DOS. This chapter focuses on the last and most common of all the Microsoft DOS versions, MS-DOS 6.22.

**Table 9-2** Common DOS Versions

| DOS VERSION | CHARACTERISTICS |
| --- | --- |
| MS-DOS 1.0 | First version, very primitive |
| MS-DOS 1.1 | Supported 320KB floppy drives |
| MS-DOS 2.0 | Hard drive and subdirectory support |

**Table 9-2**  Common DOS Versions (*continued*)

| DOS VERSION | CHARACTERISTICS |
| --- | --- |
| MS-DOS 2.11 | International code page support |
| MS-DOS 3.0 | 1.2MB floppy support |
| MS-DOS 3.3 | 3.5-inch floppies; multiple partitions |
| MS-DOS 4.0 | 504MB partitions; very buggy |
| MS-DOS 4.01 | Patch to 4.0 |
| MS-DOS 5.0 | Memory management; improved utilities; EDIT, MEM, DOSSHELL; Help utility |
| MS-DOS 6.0 | MEMMAKER added |
| MS-DOS 6.2 | DoubleSpace disk compression; safer utilities |
| MS-DOS 6.21 | Disk compression removed |
| MS-DOS 6.22 | DriveSpace disk compression |

## DOS Concepts

Let's look at several major DOS concepts that are important to understand, especially for Windows users. First, Microsoft designed DOS to run on an 8086 processor. Microsoft never truly upgraded DOS to take advantage of the more advanced Intel processors' protected mode. DOS remains as it began, a *single-tasking* OS. Sure, DOS runs just fine on a Pentium 4, but DOS can't take advantage of any protected-mode functions on that advanced CPU. When you run DOS on a modern CPU, all you really have is an extremely fast 8086! Second, DOS is text based. Everything on the screen uses text, although individual applications may use graphical screens. All text is upper-case. If a lowercase letter is typed, it is automatically changed to uppercase. Third, DOS doesn't support mice, although it supports applications that use them.

Two subjects warrant more discussion: the ways that DOS uses files and directories. Techs who grew up in a Windows world might find DOS files, filenames, and directory structures a bit less than intuitive. Let's turn there now, and then delve much deeper into the OS later in the chapter.

 **NOTE**  **DOS is completely case insensitive.**

## Files

DOS manifests each program and piece of data as an individual *file*. Each file has a name, which is stored with the file on the drive. Names are broken down into two parts: the *filename* and the *extension*. The filename can be no longer than eight characters. The extension, which is optional, can be up to three characters long. No spaces or other illegal characters (/ \ [ ] | < > + = ; , * ?) can be used in the filename or extension. The filename and extension are separated by a period, or "dot." This naming system is known as the "eight dot three" (written as "8.3") system.

Here are some examples of acceptable DOS filenames:

FRED.EXE

SYSTEM.INI

FILE1.DOC

DRIVER3.SYS

JANET

CODE33.H

Here are some unacceptable DOS filenames:

FRED.EXEC

WAYTOOLONG.F

BAD>CHAR.BAT

.NO

Windows 9*x*/2000 do not suffer from the 8.3 filename limitation. These OSs allow filenames up to 255 characters. However, they keep complete backwards compatibility with DOS (Windows 2000 is an exception) by automatically creating 8.3 filenames for every file on the system. So a Windows 9*x* system has two names for every file, a long name and an 8.3 name.

The extension tells the computer the type or function of the file. Program files take the extensions EXE (for "executable") or COM (for "command"). Anything that is not a program is some form of data to support a program. Different programs use different types of data files. The extension is used to indicate which program uses that particular data file. For example, Microsoft Word for DOS (yes, there was a Microsoft Word for DOS) uses files with the extension DOC. Changing the extension of a data file does not affect its contents, but without the proper extension, it is difficult to know which program uses it.

Of course, all files are stored on the hard drive in binary format, but every program has its own way of reading and writing this binary data. Each unique method of binary organization is called a *file format*. One program cannot read another program's files unless it has the ability to convert the other program's format into its format. In the very early days of DOS, no programs were capable of performing this type of conversion, yet people wanted to exchange files. They wanted some type of common format that any program could read. The answer was a special format called *American Standard Code for Information Interchange* (ASCII). The ASCII standard defines 256 eight-bit characters. These characters include all the letters of the alphabet (uppercase and lowercase), numbers, punctuation, many foreign characters (such as accented vowels for French and Spanish—é, ì, ô—and other typical non-English characters), box-drawing characters, and a series of special characters for commands such as a carriage return, bell, and end of file (Figure 9-1). The ASCII standard, however, is for more than just files. For example, the keyboard sends the letters you press, in ASCII code, to the PC. Even the monitor outputs in ASCII when you are running DOS. ASCII files, more commonly known as *text files*, store all data in ASCII format.

| 000 | ⟨nul⟩ | 032 | sp | 064 | @ | 096 | ` | 128 | Ç | 160 | á | 192 | └ | 224 | α |
| 001 | ☺ ⟨soh⟩ | 033 | ! | 065 | A | 097 | a | 129 | ü | 161 | í | 193 | ┴ | 225 | β |
| 002 | ☻ ⟨stx⟩ | 034 | " | 066 | B | 098 | b | 130 | é | 162 | ó | 194 | ┬ | 226 | Γ |
| 003 | ♥ ⟨etx⟩ | 035 | # | 067 | C | 099 | c | 131 | â | 163 | ú | 195 | ├ | 227 | π |
| 004 | ♦ ⟨eot⟩ | 036 | $ | 068 | D | 100 | d | 132 | ä | 164 | ñ | 196 | ─ | 228 | Σ |
| 005 | ♣ ⟨enq⟩ | 037 | % | 069 | E | 101 | e | 133 | à | 165 | Ñ | 197 | ┼ | 229 | σ |
| 006 | ♠ ⟨ack⟩ | 038 | & | 070 | F | 102 | f | 134 | å | 166 | ª | 198 | ╞ | 230 | μ |
| 007 | • ⟨bel⟩ | 039 | ' | 071 | G | 103 | g | 135 | ç | 167 | º | 199 | ╟ | 231 | τ |
| 008 | ◘ ⟨bs⟩ | 040 | ( | 072 | H | 104 | h | 136 | ê | 168 | ¿ | 200 | ╚ | 232 | ō |
| 009 | ⟨tab⟩ | 041 | ) | 073 | I | 105 | i | 137 | ë | 169 | ⌐ | 201 | ╔ | 233 | θ |
| 010 | ⟨lf⟩ | 042 | * | 074 | J | 106 | j | 138 | è | 170 | ¬ | 202 | ╩ | 234 | Ω |
| 011 | ♂ ⟨vt⟩ | 043 | + | 075 | K | 107 | k | 139 | ï | 171 | ½ | 203 | ╦ | 235 | δ |
| 012 | ♀ ⟨np⟩ | 044 | , | 076 | L | 108 | l | 140 | î | 172 | ¼ | 204 | ╠ | 236 | ∞ |
| 013 | ⟨cr⟩ | 045 | - | 077 | M | 109 | m | 141 | ì | 173 | ¡ | 205 | ═ | 237 | ø |
| 014 | ♫ ⟨so⟩ | 046 | . | 078 | N | 110 | n | 142 | Ä | 174 | « | 206 | ╬ | 238 | ∈ |
| 015 | ☼ ⟨si⟩ | 047 | / | 079 | O | 111 | o | 143 | Å | 175 | » | 207 | ╧ | 239 | ∩ |
| 016 | ► ⟨dle⟩ | 048 | 0 | 080 | P | 112 | p | 144 | É | 176 | ▓ | 208 | ╨ | 240 | ≡ |
| 017 | ◄ ⟨dc1⟩ | 049 | 1 | 081 | Q | 113 | q | 145 | æ | 177 | ▒ | 209 | ╤ | 241 | ± |
| 018 | ↕ ⟨dc2⟩ | 050 | 2 | 082 | R | 114 | r | 146 | Æ | 178 | ▓ | 210 | ╥ | 242 | ≥ |
| 019 | ‼ ⟨dc3⟩ | 051 | 3 | 083 | S | 115 | s | 147 | ô | 179 | │ | 211 | ╙ | 243 | ≤ |
| 020 | ¶ ⟨dc4⟩ | 052 | 4 | 084 | T | 116 | t | 148 | ö | 180 | ┤ | 212 | ╘ | 244 | ⌠ |
| 021 | § ⟨nak⟩ | 053 | 5 | 085 | U | 117 | u | 149 | ò | 181 | ╡ | 213 | ╒ | 245 | ⌡ |
| 022 | ▬ ⟨syn⟩ | 054 | 6 | 086 | V | 118 | v | 150 | û | 182 | ╢ | 214 | ╓ | 246 | ÷ |
| 023 | ↨ ⟨etb⟩ | 055 | 7 | 087 | W | 119 | w | 151 | ù | 183 | ╖ | 215 | ╫ | 247 | ≈ |
| 024 | ↑ ⟨can⟩ | 056 | 8 | 088 | X | 120 | x | 152 | ÿ | 184 | ╕ | 216 | ╪ | 248 | ° |
| 025 | ↓ ⟨em⟩ | 057 | 9 | 089 | Y | 121 | y | 153 | Ö | 185 | ╣ | 217 | ┘ | 249 | · |
| 026 | ⟨eof⟩ | 058 | : | 090 | Z | 122 | z | 154 | Ü | 186 | ║ | 218 | ┌ | 250 | · |
| 027 | ← ⟨esc⟩ | 059 | ; | 091 | [ | 123 | { | 155 | ¢ | 187 | ╗ | 219 | █ | 251 | √ |
| 028 | ∟ ⟨fs⟩ | 060 | < | 092 | \ | 124 | | | 156 | £ | 188 | ╝ | 220 | ▄ | 252 | ⁿ |
| 029 | ↔ ⟨gs⟩ | 061 | = | 093 | ] | 125 | } | 157 | ¥ | 189 | ╜ | 221 | ▌ | 253 | ² |
| 030 | ▲ ⟨rs⟩ | 062 | > | 094 | ^ | 126 | ~ | 158 | ₧ | 190 | ╛ | 222 | ▐ | 254 | ■ |
| 031 | ▼ ⟨us⟩ | 063 | ? | 095 | _ | 127 | ⌂ | 159 | ƒ | 191 | ┐ | 223 | ▀ | 255 | |

**Figure 9-1**  ASCII characters

ASCII was the first universal file format. Virtually every type of program—word processors, spreadsheets, databases, presentation programs—can read and write text files. However, text files have severe limitations. A text file can't store important information such as shapes, colors, margins, or text attributes (bold, underline, font, and so on). Therefore, even though text files are fairly universal, they are also limited to only the 256 ASCII characters.

Even in the most basic text, there is a need to perform a number of actions beyond just printing simple characters. For example, how does the program reading the text file know when to start a new line? This is where the first 32 ASCII characters come into play. These first 32 characters are very special commands (actually, some of them are both commands and characters). For example, the ASCII value 7 can either be a large dot or a command to play a note (bell) on the PC speaker. ASCII value 9 is a Tab. ASCII value 27 is an Escape. How these first 32 values are treated depends on the program that reads them, but as a rule, DOS treats the first 32 ASCII values as commands.

DOS makes heavy use of text files for system configuration and optimization. A technician who uses DOS must be comfortable accessing and editing text files with a special program called a *text editor*. DOS comes with a text editor called EDIT that enables technicians to manipulate text files. You'll see more of EDIT later in this chapter.

## Drives and Directories

At boot, DOS assigns a drive letter to each hard drive partition and to each floppy or other disk drive. The first floppy drive is called *A:*, and the second, if installed, is called *B:*. DOS cannot support more than two floppy drives, because it supports the original IBM PC, which was designed for only two drives. Hard drives start with the letter *C:* and can continue to *Z:* if necessary. CD-ROM drives usually get the next available drive letter after the last hard drive. DOS defines these letters and will not let you change them.

Like almost every OS, DOS uses a *hierarchical directory tree* to organize the contents of these drives. All files are put into groups called *directories*. Windows also uses directories, but calls them *folders*. Any file not in a directory within the tree is said to be in the *root directory*. A system may have directories inside directories, which are called *subdirectories*. Any directory can have multiple subdirectories. Two or more files with the same name can exist in different directories on a PC, but two files in the same directory cannot have the same name. In the same way, no two subdirectories under the same directory can have the same name, but two subdirectories under different directories can have the same name.

When describing a drive, you use its letter. For example, the hard drive would be represented by "C:". To describe the root directory, put a backslash (\) after the "C:", as in "C:\". To describe a particular directory, add the name of the directory. For example, if a PC had a directory called TEST, it would be C:\TEST.

Subdirectories in a directory are displayed by adding backslashes and names. If the TEST directory had a subdirectory called SYSTEM, it would be shown like this: C:\TEST\SYSTEM. This naming convention provides for a complete description of the location and name of any file. If the C:\TEST\SYSTEM directory had a file called TEST2.TXT, it would be C:\TEST\SYSTEM\TEST2.TXT.

The exact location of a file is called its *path*. The path for the TEST2.TXT file is C:\TEST\SYSTEM. Here are some examples of possible paths:

```
C:\DOS
F:\FRUSCH3\CLEAR
A:\REPORTS
D:\
```

Directories are not required by any law of humans or nature—or DOS. A computer will work even if every file is dumped in the root directory. However, directories make the organization of files much easier. Generally, when you install a DOS program, the installing program gives the installed program its own directory. Unlike drive letters, however, directories are not permanent. Users can create and delete any directory, even one that holds files. It is common for users to create directories and subdirectories to store their own personal data files.

## DOS Structure: Three Main Files

The DOS operating system is composed of three main files, accompanied by roughly 80 support files. The three main files are IO.SYS, MSDOS.SYS, and COMMAND.COM. These files must be on the C: drive or the computer will not boot. IO.SYS handles talking to the BIOS and hardware; MSDOS.SYS is the primary DOS code, often called the *kernel*; and COMMAND.COM actually interprets commands typed into the computer and passes that information to MSDOS.SYS. COMMAND.COM is also called the *command interpreter*. The command interpreter stores a number of commands that you may enter to get work done. Commands that are built into COMMAND.COM are known as *internal commands*.

The core part of DOS is composed of these three files, but DOS also encompasses a large number of auxiliary files. These separate programs are usually stored in a directory called C:\DOS (the Windows 9x equivalents are stored in a directory called C:\WINDOWS\COMMAND). These very important *external programs* provide DOS with extra functions not built into COMMAND.COM. For example, FDISK.EXE and FORMAT.EXE are both external commands.

Files from different versions of DOS are for the most part not interchangeable. Let's say one PC runs MS-DOS 5.0 and another runs MS-DOS 6.2. Although they each have IO.SYS, MSDOS.SYS, and COMMAND.COM files, the 5.0 files would not function on the PC running 6.2, and vice versa. It is important to know the version of DOS for each machine you support. Later in this chapter you will learn how to determine the version of DOS on a particular PC.

## The DOS User Interface

The text-based DOS user interface might seem primitive when compared with the attractive, colorful, graphics-based Windows interface used by systems today, but it is actually quite fast and powerful. An experienced user can perform many equivalent jobs faster in DOS than in Windows 2000. But the interface is picky and unforgiving: One wrong keystroke can result in the loss of crucial data with no warning.

## The DOS Prompt

The DOS user interface is centered on the *prompt,* which is a path followed by a greater-than sign (>) and a flashing cursor. When you see the prompt, DOS is telling you, "I'm ready to take your commands!" See Figure 9-2.

**Figure 9-2**
The DOS prompt

DOS is always focused on some directory. The prompt shows you which directory currently has DOS' focus. This is important because any commands you issue are performed on the files in the directory on which DOS is focused. For example, if you see a prompt that looks like "C:\", you know that DOS is focused on the root directory of the C: drive. If you see a prompt that looks like "C:\DBASE\", then you know that DOS is focused on the DBASE directory of the C: drive. The trick to using DOS is remembering to first get DOS to focus on the drive and directory where you want to work. Let's put this idea to practice with the DIR command.

## DIR Command

The DIR command shows you the contents of the directory that currently has DOS' focus. DIR is used more often than any other command in DOS. Let's assume that DOS is focused on the root directory of C. You will know this because the prompt will look like "C:\". By typing in **DIR** and then pressing the ENTER key (you must always press ENTER after every command in DOS), you will see something like this:

```
C:\>DIR
 Volume in Drive C is
 Volume Serial Number is 1734-3234
 Directory of C:\
DOS              <DIR>          09-03-96      9:34a
COMMAND   COM            34222  04-01-94      4:33p
AUTOEXEC  BAT               14  04-03-00     11:55a
WINDOWS          <DIR>          11-07-99      1:34a
CONFIG    SYS               34  04-03-00      4:36p
MIKE             <DIR>          09-03-99      8:15a
JUNK      DOC            55677  05-13-99     10:03a
COMMAND   COM            23222  09-03-96      4:33p
9 file(s)          72233    bytes
                 18288834    bytes free
```

If you are following along on a PC, remember that different computers contain different files and different programs, so you will absolutely see something different from the preceding example! If a lot of text scrolls quickly down the screen, try typing **DIR/P** (pause) or **DIR/W** (wide). Don't forget to press ENTER!

---

 **NOTE** Extra text typed after a command, such as the "/W" or "/P" after DIR, is called a *switch*. Almost all switches can be used simultaneously to modify a command. For example, try typing **DIR/W/P**.

---

When you type a simple DIR command, you will see some of the entries look like this:

```
CONFIG    SYS      34      09-03-96       4:36p
```

All of these entries are files. The DIR command lists the filename, extension, file size in bytes, and creation date/time. The DIR/W command only shows you the names, but arranges them in five columns across your screen. Note how all of the filenames stay within the 8.3 limit.

Windows 9*x* and Windows 2000 support long filenames, making the DIR command look a little bit different than what you would see in DOS. Those of you using the DIR command at a command prompt in Windows 9*x* should see something similar to this (I removed the beginning of the DOS listing to concentrate on the filenames):

```
WEBSHOTS   INI          748   11-12-00   1:08p  webshots.ini
WEBSHO~1   EXE       28,672   03-09-00   3:56p  WebshotsUninstall.exe
SYSTEM     SYD        1,958   09-21-00   5:24p  SYSTEM.SYD
EMILY000   PWL          688   09-21-00   5:23p  EMILY000.PWL
EMILY001   PWL          688   09-21-00   5:52p  EMILY001.PWL
EXITTO~1   PIF          967   09-24-00   3:19p  Exit To DOS.pif
ST6UNST    EXE       73,216   10-15-00   4:54p  ST6UNST.EXE
DIRECTX    LOG       29,337   10-17-00   8:09p  Directx.log
EREG       DAT          501   10-17-00   8:09p  eReg.dat
NPSEXEC    EXE       33,792   04-02-99   4:37p  NPSExec.exe
          280 file(s)      89,898,614 bytes
           25 dir(s)    1,562,959,872 bytes free

C:\WINDOWS>
```

Look at the second file in the list. Windows shows both its DOS 8.3 name and its full Windows name, using a tilde (~) character and a number (in this case a "1") in the 8.3 name to replace the extra characters. As with the DOS DIR, the Windows DIR command separates the filenames from the extensions. Remember that the extensions enable you to distinguish the program files (for example, EXE) from the data files (for example, DAT). Notice that the Windows DIR listing displays slightly different information at the end than the DOS DIR listing. As other commands are reviewed, you will notice more examples of how, although DOS and Windows use the same commands, most of them show subtle differences.

Finally, type **HELP /?** to see the following:

```
C:\WINDOWS > dir /?
 [drive][path][filename]
                Specifies drive, directory, and/or files to list.
                (Could be enhanced file specification or multiple
                filespecs.)
    /P          Pauses after each screen of information.
    /W          Uses wide list format.
    /A          Displays files with specified attributes.
    attributes  D  Directories            R  Read-only files
                H  Hidden files           A  Files ready for
                                             archiving
                S  System files           -  Prefix meaning not
    /O          List by files in sorted order.
    sortorder   N  By name (alphabetic)   S  By size (smallest
                                             first)
                E  By extension (alphabetic)  D  By date & time
                                             (earliest first)
                G  Group directories first -  Prefix to reverse
                                             order
                A  By Last Access Date (earliest first)7
    /S          Displays files in specified directory and all
                subdirectories.
    /B          Uses bare format (no heading information or summary).
    /L          Uses lowercase.
    /V          Verbose mode.

    /4          Displays year with 4 digits (ignored if /V also
                given).
```

Switches may be preset in the DIRCMD environment variable. Override preset switches by prefixing any switch with a hyphen (-), for example, /-W. To see hidden files, try this special DIR command:

```
DIR /AH
```

Typing any command followed by a /? brings up a help screen for that particular command. Although these help screens can sometimes seem a little cryptic, they're helpful when you're not too familiar with a command or you can't figure out how to get a command to do something. Even though I have almost every command memorized, I still refer to these help screens—use them!

### Directories: The CD Command

Type **DIR** once again. This time ignore the file listings. See if you can find any entries that are followed by a "DIR." They may look like these samples from a Windows 2000 system:

```
07/30/2000   08:04p      <DIR>          Transcender
08/10/2000   07:23p      <DIR>          ts4.3
08/19/2000   10:47a      <DIR>          Office52
08/26/2000   12:23a      <DIR>          mgafold
11/10/2000   07:13a      <DIR>          BTMAGIC.PQ
11/10/2000   07:13a      <DIR>          WINNT
```

If you type **DIR/W**, these listings display differently. Instead of a "DIR" after the directory name, the name is enclosed in brackets. Do you see any listings that look like these when you type **DIR/W**?

```
[DOS]        [WINDOWS]        [QUAKE]        [OBIWAN]
```

These are *directories,* or *folders* as we say in the Windows world; the terms really are interchangeable.

The CD (or CHDIR) command enables you to change the focus of DOS to a different directory. To use the CD command, type **CD\** followed by the name of the directory on which you want DOS to focus. To go to the C:\OBIWAN directory, type CD\OBIWAN, and then press ENTER. If the system has an OBIWAN directory, DOS will change its focus to that directory, and the prompt will change to C:\OBIWAN. If there is no OBIWAN directory or if you accidentally typed something like OBIWAM, a DOS or Windows 9x system will report "Invalid directory." If you use Windows 2000, you get the error: "The system cannot find the path specified." If I only had a dollar for every time I've seen those errors! I usually get them due to typing too fast. If you get this error, check what you typed and try again.

**NOTE** Let's talk about errors in general for a moment, not just command prompt errors like "Invalid directory," but any error, including Windows errors like the one shown in Figure 9-3.

Many new computer users freeze in horror when they see an error message. Do not fear error messages. Error messages are good! Love them. Worship them. They will save you. Seriously, think how confusing it would be if the computer didn't tell you when you messed up! Error messages tell us what we did wrong in order to fix it.

You absolutely cannot hurt your PC in any way by typing the DIR or CD commands incorrectly. Take advantage of this knowledge and really experiment! Intentionally make mistakes to familiarize yourself with the error messages. Have fun! Learn from errors!

**Figure 9-3** Windows error message

To return to the root directory, just type **CD\** and press ENTER. You can use the CD command to point DOS to any directory. For example, you could type CD\FRED\BACKUP\TEST and the prompt would change to C:\FRED\BACKUP\TEST, assuming, of course, that your system *had* a directory called C:\FRED\BACKUP\TEST.

Once the prompt has changed, type **DIR** again. You should see a different list of files and directories. Every directory holds different files and subdirectories; as DOS points to different directories, the DIR command shows the contents of the directories.

One very important shortcut when using the CD command is the ability to use a space instead of a backslash. Go to the root directory by typing **CD\**. Then you could move the focus to the C:\WINDOWS directory by typing **CD WINDOWS**. You can use the CD space command to move one level at a time, like this:

```
C:\>CD FRED
C:\FRED\>CD BACKUP
C:\FRED\BACKUP>CD TEST
```

Or, you could jump multiple directory levels, like this:

```
C:\>CD FRED\BACKUP\TEST
```

Take some time to move the DOS focus around the directories of your PC using the CD and DIR commands. Use DIR to find a directory, and then use CD to move the focus to that directory. Remember, CD\ will always get you back to the root directory.

## Moving Between Drives

The CD command is *not* used to move between drives. To get DOS to "point" ("point" is DOS geek-speak for "switch its focus") to another drive, just type the drive letter and a colon. If DOS is pointing at the C:\DOS directory and you want to see what is on the floppy (A:) drive, just type **A:** and DOS will point to the floppy drive. You'll see the following on the screen:

```
C:\DOS>A:
A:\>
```

To return to the C: drive, just type **C:** and you'll see the following:

```
A:\>C:
C:\DOS>
```

Note that DOS returns you to the same directory you left. Just for fun, try typing in a drive letter that you know doesn't exist. I know that my system does not have a W: drive. If I type in a nonexistent drive on a DOS or Windows 9*x* system, I get the following error:

```
Invalid drive specification
```

In Windows 2000, I get the following error:

```
The system cannot find the drive specified.
```

Try inserting a floppy disk and using the CD command to point at its drive. Do the same with a CD-ROM disc. Type **DIR** to see the contents of the floppy or CD-ROM. Use the CD command to move the focus to any folders on the floppy or CD-ROM. Now return focus to the C: drive.

With the DIR, CD, and drive letter commands you can access any folder on any storage device on your system. Make sure you can use these commands comfortably to navigate inside your computer.

## Making Directories

So far, we have learned how to navigate in a command-prompt world. Now let's start making stuff, starting with a new directory.

To create (or make) a directory, use the MD (or MKDIR) command. To create a directory called QUAKE under the root directory of C:, for example, first ensure that you are in the root directory by typing **CD\**. You should see the prompt

```
C:\>
```

Now that DOS is pointing to the root directory, type the following:

```
MD QUAKE
```

DOS will not volunteer any information; you must use the DIR command to see that you have, in fact, created a new directory. Note that the QUAKE directory in this example is not listed last, as you might expect.

```
C:\>DIR
 Volume in Drive C is
 Volume Serial Number is 1734-3234
 Directory of C:\
DOS             <DIR>         09-03-96     9:34a
COMMAND  COM           34222   04-01-94     4:33p
AUTOEXEC BAT              14   04-03-00    11:55a
WINDOWS         <DIR>         11-07-99     1:34a
CONFIG   SYS              34   04-03-00     4:36p
MIKE            <DIR>         09-03-99     8:15a
QUAKE           <DIR>         09-22-01     8:15a
JUNK     DOC           55677   05-13-99    10:03a
COMMAND  COM           23222   09-03-96     4:33p
11 file(s)        72233    bytes
              18288834    bytes free
```

**NOTE** DOS almost never tells you that a command has been performed successfully. But be assured it will complain when you do something wrong! The old adage is: "DOS never pats you on the back, but it will slap you in the head!"

To create a FILES subdirectory in the QUAKE directory, first use the CD\ command to point DOS at the QUAKE directory:

```
CD\QUAKE
```

Then run the MD command to make the FILES directory:

```
MD FILES
```

Make sure that DOS points to the directory in which you want to make the new subdirectory before you execute the MD command. When you're done, type **DIR** to see the new FILES subdirectory. Just for fun, do the process again and add a GAMES directory under the QUAKE directory. Type **DIR** to verify success.

## Removing Directories

Removing subdirectories works exactly like making them. First, get to the directory that contains the subdirectory you want to delete, and then execute the RD (or RMDIR) command. In this example, let's delete the FILES subdirectory in the C:\QUAKE directory. First, get to where the FILES directory is located—C:\QUAKE—by typing **CD\QUAKE**. Then type **RD FILES**. If no response was received from DOS, you probably did it right! Type **DIR** to check that the FILES subdirectory is gone.

The RD command will not delete a directory if it contains files or subdirectories. If you want to delete a directory that contains files or subdirectories, you must first empty that directory using the DEL (for files) or RD (for subdirectories) command. You can also use the DELTREE command. DELTREE will delete the directory as well as all files and subdirectories. DELTREE is handy but dangerous, because it's easy to delete more than you want. When deleting, always follow the maxim "check twice and delete once." Let's delete the QUAKE and GAMES directories with DELTREE. Because the QUAKE directory is in the root directory, point DOS to the root directory with **CD\**. Now execute the DELTREE command: **DELTREE C:\QUAKE**. In a rare display of mercy, DOS will respond with the following:

```
Delete directory C:\QUAKE and all its subdirectories? [y/n]
```

Press the Y key and both C:\QUAKE and C:\QUAKE\GAMES will be eliminated.

## Running a Program

To run a DOS program, simply change DOS' focus to the directory where the program is, and then type the name of the program. To try this, go to the C:\DOS directory by using the CD command. If you're using Windows 9*x*, go to the C:\WINDOWS\COMMAND directory. Type **DIR/W** to see the files in wide format. You should see a file called MEM.EXE. As mentioned earlier, all files with the extensions EXE and COM are programs, so MEM.EXE is a program. To run the MEM.EXE program, just type the filename, in this case **MEM**, and press ENTER. Note that you do not have to type the .EXE extension, though you can. Congratulations, you have just run your first DOS program!

## Using Function Keys

You might find yourself repeatedly typing the same commands, or at least very similar commands, when working at a prompt. Microsoft provided a number of ways to access previously typed commands in DOS. Type in the DIR command at a command prompt. When you get back to a prompt, type F1, and the letter "D" will appear. Press F1 again. Now, the letter "I" appears after the "D." Do you see what is happening? The F1 key brings back the previous command one letter at a time. Pressing F3 brings back the entire command at once.

The DOSKEY command stores a large number of commands that you access by pressing the up arrow key. Just type DOSKEY at a prompt to activate it. F1 and F3 only help bring back the last command, whereas DOSKEY stores over a hundred commands. You may adjust how many commands it stores. Run DOSKEY /? to see how to change the number of stored commands. Once DOSKEY runs, it tracks the commands you input at the prompt. To access a command later, simply press the up arrow key repeatedly until you get the command you wish. DOSKEY comes with DOS and Windows 9*x*. Windows 2000 automatically starts DOSKEY whenever you access a prompt. DOSKEY will be discussed further, later in this chapter.

## Fun with Files

This section deals with basic file manipulation. You will learn how to look at, copy, move, and delete files. The examples in this section are based on a C: root directory with the following files and directories:

```
C:\>DIR
 Volume in Drive C is
 Volume Serial Number is 1734-3234
 Directory of C:\
DOS            <DIR>           09-03-96    9:34a
COMMAND   COM           34222   04-01-94    4:33p
AUTOEXEC  BAT           44      09-03-97    11:55a
```

```
WINDOWS          <DIR>              11-07-97    1:34a
OLD_DOS          <DIR>              09-03-97    11:55a
BACKUP           <DIR>              09-04-96    6:42p
SPINRITE  COM            144654     11-02-96    8:00a
CONFIG    BAK            34         02-03-98    4:36a
CONFIG    NU             32         11-07-97    3:30p
AUTOEXEC  OLD            31         09-02-97    12:04a
VIRUS     COM            81222      04-01-97    5:29p
AUTOEXEC  1ST            21         09-03-96    11:14a
CONFIG    SYS            34         02-03-98    4:36p
QUAKE            <DIR>              09-03-97    8:15a
JUNK      DOC            15677      04-03-98    10:03a
AUTOEXEC  NU             32         11-07-97    3:30p
18 file(s)       3542233      bytes
                 182888343    bytes free
```

Because you probably don't have a DOS system with these files and directories, follow the examples but use what's on your drive. In other words, create your own folders and copy files to them from various folders currently on your system.

## Attributes

All files have four special values, or *attributes*, which determine how the file will act in special situations. These attributes can be set through software. The first attribute is called *hidden*. If a file is hidden, it will not be displayed when the DIR command is performed. Next is the *read-only* attribute. A read-only file cannot be modified or deleted. Third is the *system* attribute, which is used only for system files such as IO.SYS and MSDOS.SYS. In reality, it does nothing more than provide an easy identifier for these files. Fourth is the *archive* attribute, which is used by backup software to identify files that have been changed since their last backup.

ATTRIB.EXE is an external DOS program that enables you to inspect and change file attributes. To inspect a file's attributes, type the **ATTRIB** command followed by the name of the file. To see the attributes of the file COMMAND.COM, type **ATTRIB COM-MAND.COM**. The result is

```
A       COMMAND.COM
```

The letter *A* stands for archive, the only attribute of COMMAND.COM. The letter *R* means read-only, *H* is hidden, and *S* is system.

Go to the C:\ directory and type ATTRIB by itself. If you're using DOS or Windows 9*x*, you'll see a result similar to the following:

```
A    H      C:\AUTOEXEC.BAT
A    H      C:\CONFIG.SYS
A    SHR    C:\IO.SYS
A    SHR    C:\MSDOS.SYS
A           C:\COMMAND.COM
```

Don't panic if you see a number of different files than the ones just listed. No two C:\ directories are ever the same. In most cases, you'll see many more files than just these five. Notice that MSDOS.SYS and IO.SYS both have the System, Hidden, and Read-Only attributes set. Microsoft does this to protect these important files.

The ATTRIB command is also used to change a file's attributes. To add an attribute to a file, type the attribute letter preceded by a plus sign (+), and then the filename. To delete an attribute, use a minus sign (-). For example, to add the read-only attribute to the file COMMAND.COM, type

```
ATTRIB +R COMMAND.COM
```

To remove the archive attribute, type

```
ATTRIB -A COMMAND.COM
```

Multiple attributes can be added or removed in one command. Here's an example of removing three attributes from the IO.SYS file:

```
ATTRIB -R -S -H MSDOS.SYS
```

## Wildcards

Visualize having 273 files in one directory. A few of these files have the extension DOC but the majority do not. You are looking only for files that end with the DOC extension. Wouldn't it be nice to type the DIR command so that only the .DOC files come up? You can! The answer is *wildcards.*

Wildcards are two special characters, asterisk (*) and question mark (?), that can be used in place of all or part of a filename to make a DOS command act on more than one file at a time. Wildcards work with all DOS commands that take filenames. A great example is the DIR command. When you execute a plain DIR command, it finds and displays all the files and folders in the specified directory; however, you can also narrow its search by adding a filename. For example, if you type the command **DIR COM-MAND.COM** while in your root (C:\) directory, you get the following result:

```
Volume in Drive C is
Volume Serial Number is 1734-3234
Directory of C:\
COMMAND   COM      34222      04-01-94    4:33p

1 file(s)     34222       bytes
            182888343     bytes free
```

If you just want to confirm the presence of a particular file in a particular place, this is very convenient. But suppose you wanted to see all files with the extension COM. In that case, you'd use the * wildcard, like this: DIR *.COM. A good way to think of the * wildcard is *"I don't care."* Replace the part of the filename that you don't care about with an asterisk (*). The result of DIR *.COM would be

```
Volume in Drive C is
Volume Serial Number is 1734-3234
Directory of C:\
COMMAND    COM      34222           04-01-94        4:33p
NDOS       COM      76248           04-01-95        6:13p
SPINRITE   COM     144654           11-02-96        8:00a
VIRUS      COM      81222           04-01-97        5:29p
4 file(s)         206338       bytes
                182888343       bytes free
```

Wildcards also substitute for extensions:

```
C:\>DIR CONFIG.*
 Volume in Drive C is
 Volume Serial Number is 1734-3234
 Directory of C:\
CONFIG    BAK    34      02-03-98        4:36a
CONFIG    NU     32      11-07-97        3:30p
CONFIG    SYS    34      02-03-98        4:36p
3 file(s)      100          bytes
             182888343     bytes free
```

Even better, they can substitute for parts of filenames. This DIR command will find every file that starts with the letter *C*.

```
C:\>DIR C*.*
 Volume in Drive C is
 Volume Serial Number is 1734-3234
 Directory of C:\
COMMAND   COM    34222    04-01-94      4:33p
CONFIG    BAK    34       02-03-98      4:36a
CONFIG    NU     32       11-07-97      4:30p
CONFIG    SYS    34       02-03-98      4:36p
4 file(s)      34322      bytes
             182888343    bytes free
```

The ? wildcard replaces any single character. This can be handy when you're looking for filenames with a specific number of characters. To find all files having four-character filenames and the extension COM, you would type

```
C:\>DIR ????.COM
 Volume in Drive C is
 Volume Serial Number is 1734-3234
 Directory of C:\
NDOS     COM      76248    04-01-95      6:13p
1 file(s)       76240      bytes
             182888343     bytes free
```

So far, we've only used wildcards with the DIR command, but virtually every command that deals with files will take wildcards. Let's examine the DEL command and see how it uses wildcards.

## Deleting Files

To delete files, you use the DEL or ERASE command. DEL and ERASE are identical commands and can be used interchangeably. Deleting files is very simple—maybe too simple. Windows' users enjoy the luxury of retrieving deleted files from the Recycle Bin on those "Oops, I didn't mean to delete that" occasions everyone encounters at one time or another. DOS, however, shows no such mercy to the careless user. It has no function equivalent to the Windows Recycle Bin. Once a file has been erased, it can only be recovered by using a special recovery utility such as Norton's UNERASE. Again, the rule here is to *check twice and delete once*.

To delete a single file, type the **DEL** command followed by the name of the file to delete. To delete the file AUTOEXEC.BAK, for example, type

```
DEL AUTOEXEC.BAK
```

Although nothing will appear on the screen to confirm it, the file is now gone. To confirm that the AUTOEXEC.BAK file is no longer listed, use the DIR command.

As with the DIR command, you can use wildcards with the DEL and ERASE commands to delete multiple files. For example, to delete all files with the extension COM in a directory, you would type

```
DEL *.COM
```

To delete all files with the filename CONFIG in a directory, type **DEL CONFIG.***. To delete all the files in a directory, you can use the popular *.* wildcard (often pronounced "star-dot-star"), like this

```
DEL *.*
```

This is one of the few DOS commands that will elicit a response from DOS. Upon receiving the DEL *.* command, DOS will respond with "Are you sure? (Y/N)," to which you respond with a Y or N. Pressing Y will erase every file in the directory, so be careful with *.*!

Don't confuse erasing files with erasing directories. DEL erases files, but it will not erase directories. Use RD or DELTREE to erase directories.

## Copying and Moving Files

The ability to copy and move files in DOS is crucial to all technicians. Due to its finicky nature and many options, the COPY command is also rather painful to learn, especially if you're used to simply dragging icons in Windows. The following tried-and-true, five-step process will make it easier, but the real secret is to get in front of a C: prompt and just copy and move files around until you're comfortable. Keep in mind that the only difference between copying and moving is whether the original is left behind (COPY) or not (MOVE). Once you've learned the COPY command, you've learned the MOVE command!

### Mike's Five-Step COPY/MOVE Process

I've been teaching folks how to copy and move files for years using this handy process. Keep in mind that hundreds of variations on this process exist. As you become more confident with these commands, try doing a COPY /? or MOVE /? at any handy prompt to see the real power of these commands. But at first, follow this process step-by-step.

1. Point DOS to the directory containing the files to be copied or moved.
2. Type **COPY** or **MOVE** and a space.
3. Type the name of the file(s) to be copied/moved (with or without wildcards) and a space.
4. Type the *path* of the new location for the files.
5. Press ENTER.

Let's try an example. The directory C:\QUAKE contains the file README.TXT. We'll copy this file to the floppy drive (A:).

1. Type **CD\QUAKE** to point DOS to the QUAKE directory.

   ```
   C:\>CD\QUAKE
   ```

2. Type **COPY** and a space.

   ```
   C:\QUAKE>COPY _
   ```

3. Type **README.TXT** and a space.

   ```
   C:\QUAKE>COPY README.TXT _
   ```

4. Type **A:\**.

   ```
   C:\QUAKE>COPY README.TXT A:\
   ```

5. Press ENTER.

The entire command and response would look like this:

```
C:\QUAKE>COPY README.TXT A:\
1 file(s) copied
```

If you point DOS to the A: drive and type **DIR**, the README.TXT file will be visible. Let's try another example. Suppose 100 files are in the C:\DOCS directory, 30 of which have the DOC extension, and suppose you want to move those files to the C:\QUAKE directory. Follow these steps:

1. Type **CD\DOCS** to point DOS to the DOCS directory.

   ```
   C:\>CD\DOCS
   ```

2. Type **MOVE** and a space.

   ```
   C:\DOCS>MOVE _
   ```

3. Type **\*.DOC** and a space.

   ```
   C:\DOCS>MOVE *.DOC _
   ```

4. Type **C:\ QUAKE**.

   ```
   C:\DOCS>MOVE *.DOC C:\QUAKE
   ```

5. Press ENTER.

   ```
   C:\DOCS>MOVE *.DOC C:\QUAKE
   30 file(s) copied
   ```

The power of the COPY/MOVE command makes it rather dangerous. The COPY/MOVE command not only lets you put a file in a new location, but it also lets you change the name of the file at the same time. Suppose you want to copy a file called AUTOEXEC.BAT from my C:\ folder to my floppy disk, for example, but you want the name of the copy on the floppy disk to be AUTO1.BAT. You can do both things with one COPY command, like this:

```
COPY C:\AUTOEXEC.BAT A:\AUTO1.BAT
```

Not only does the AUTOEXEC.BAT file get copied to my floppy disk, but the copy also gets the new name AUTO1.BAT. As another example, let's move all of the files with the extension DOC from the C:\DOCS directory to the C:\BACK directory and simultaneously change the DOC extension to .SAV. Here is the command:

```
MOVE C:\DOCS\*.DOC C:\BACK\*.SAV
```

This says, "Move all files that have the extension DOC from the directory C:\DOCS into the directory C:\BACK, and while you're at it change their file extensions to SAV." This is very handy, but very dangerous! Let's say for example that I made one tiny typo. Here I typed a semicolon instead of a colon after the second C.

```
MOVE C:\DOCS\*.DOC C;\BACK\*.SAV
```

DOS understands the semicolon to mean "end of command" and therefore ignores both the semicolon and anything you typed after it. As far as DOS is concerned, you typed

```
MOVE C:\DOCS\*.DOC C
```

This, unfortunately for you, means "take all the files with the extension DOC in the directory C:\DOCS and copy them back into that same directory, but squish them all together into a single file called C." If you run this command, DOS gives you only one clue something went wrong:

```
MOVE C:\DOCS\*.DOC C
1 file(s) copied
```

See "1 file(s) copied?" Feeling the chill hand of fate slide down your spine, you do a DIR of the directory, and you now see a single file called C where there used to be 30 files with the extension DOC. All of your DOC files are now gone, completely non-recoverable.

## XCOPY

The standard COPY/MOVE commands can only work on one directory at a time, making them a poor choice for copying or moving files in multiple directories. To help with these multi-directory jobs, Microsoft added the XCOPY command. (Note that there is no XMOVE, just XCOPY.)

XCOPY works similarly to COPY, but has extra switches that give XCOPY the power to work with multiple directories. Here's how it works. Let's say I have a directory on my C: drive called \DATA. The \DATA directory has three subdirectories: \JAN, \FEB, and \MAR. All of these directories, including the \DATA directory, contain about 50 files. If I wanted to copy all of these files to my D:\ drive in one command, I would use XCOPY in the following manner:

```
XCOPY C:\DATA D:\DATA /S
```

Because XCOPY works on directories, you don't have to use filenames as you would in COPY, although XCOPY certainly accepts filenames and wildcards. The /S switch, the most commonly used of all the many switches that come with XCOPY, tells XCOPY to copy all subdirectories except for empty ones. The /E switch tells XCOPY to copy empty subdirectories. When you have a lot of copying to do over many directories, XCOPY is the tool to use.

The power of XCOPY varies depending on the version of DOS (or Windows) you use. The XCOPY that comes with true DOS is fairly weak. Windows 9*x* comes with a second type of XCOPY called XCOPY32 that enables you to copy hidden, read-only, and system files. Windows 2000 no longer has XCOPY32 but has instead incorporated all the power of XCOPY and XCOPY32 into its version of XCOPY.

Their power and utility make the DEL, COPY/MOVE, and XCOPY commands indispensable for a PC technician, but that same power and utility can cause disaster. Only a trained Jedi, with the Force as his ally . . .well, wrong book, but the principle remains: beware of the quick and easy keystroke, for it may spell your doom. Think twice and execute the command once. The data you save may be yours!

## DOS in a Windows World

How does DOS manifest in a Windows world? It depends on the version of Windows. Both Windows 9*x* and Windows 2000 will give you a DOS prompt, but each does it a little differently. Let's start by looking at the one way they have in common—the DOS virtual machine.

### Virtual Machine

Before getting started, a very important term, *command prompt*, needs to be clarified. If you are staring at a C:\ prompt in Windows 9*x*, the proper term for what you see is *command prompt*. Officially, only genuine DOS has a *DOS prompt*. This term helps separate the concept of DOS from the idea of a prompt, letting everyone know that even though the system looks like DOS, it is really Windows. From now on, we will use the term command prompt.

 **NOTE** Many techs use the terms "DOS prompt" and "command prompt" interchangeably.

At the very beginning of the chapter, you were shown how to access the command prompt in Windows 9*x* and Windows 2000. If you think way back to the CPU chapter, you'll remember the discussion on the power of *virtual 8086 mode*. This special *protected mode* function creates a pretend 8086 that enables DOS programs to run in protected mode. When you select Start | Run and type **COMMAND.COM**, Windows instantly recognizes this as a DOS program and segregates some RAM for its use alone. As far as COMMAND.COM knows, it is running on a very fast 8086 computer. It has no idea the rest of the system is there. Windows "fakes" all of the BIOS commands exactly as if it were an original IBM PC (with a few improvements). The little windowed C: prompt, sometimes referred to as a *DOS box*, is Windows using the CPU's virtual 8086 function (Figure 9-4).

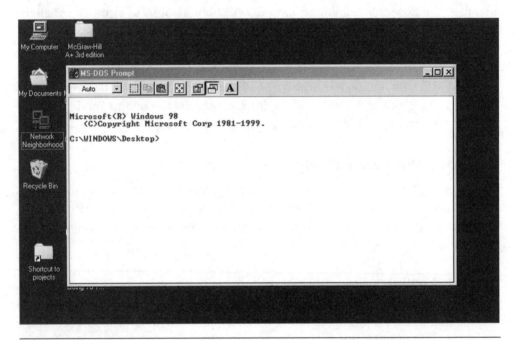

**Figure 9-4** DOS box

Windows 2000 still supports COMMAND.COM, but most techs needing a command prompt in Windows 2000 use CMD.EXE. You start CMD.EXE exactly as you start COMMAND.COM, just type in **CMD** at the Start | Run box. CMD.EXE is a much more advanced command processor that provides extra functions not available using plain COMMAND.COM. CMD.EXE will be discussed further in Chapter 11.

Although both Windows 9*x* and Windows 2000 share the concept of virtual 8086, they each have other methods of accessing a C: prompt that they do not share. All the methods manifest at the system boot up.

## Boot Modes in Windows 9x

Windows 9*x* gives you two ways to get to a true command prompt rather than a virtual machine. First, when a Windows 9*x* system boots, you will see

```
Starting Windows 9x...
```

for about two seconds before the pretty Windows startup screen appears. If you press the F8 key the moment that text appears, you get the Windows Startup menu (Figure 9-5). (Some systems don't show the "Starting . . . " text, in which case just hold down the F8 key at boot.)

```
Microsoft Windows 98 Startup Menu

  1. Normal
  2. Logged (\BOOTLOG.TXT)
  3. Safe mode
  4. Step-by-step confirmation
  5. Command prompt only
  6. Safe mode command prompt only

Enter a choice: 5




F5=Safe mode   Shift+F5=Command prompt   Shift+F8=Step-by-Step confirmation
```

**Figure 9-5**   Windows Startup menu

All of the Windows Startup menu options will be discussed in the next chapter, but for the moment, take note of the Command Prompt Only and Safe Mode Command Prompt Only options. In essence, these enable you to start Windows without the pretty graphical screen. One of these two options is often used when a Windows 9x system fails to boot normally.

The second option for booting to a command prompt in Windows 9x is to run a Shutdown and select "Restart in MS-DOS Mode" as shown in Figure 9-6. MS-DOS mode is similar to the Command Prompt Only option with one exception: When you type the command EXIT at the C:\ prompt, the system will automatically reboot itself and return to a normal Windows boot. You can also set particular DOS programs to boot into MS-DOS mode individually, which is explained in Chapter 12, "DOS Memory in a Windows World."

## Boot Mode in Windows 2000

Windows 2000 restricts access to the command prompt much more than Windows 9x. Windows 2000 does not have a true Command Prompt Only option. It does have a Safe Mode Command Prompt Only option, but this is actually just a typical Safe Mode with the CMD program running in its own Window, as shown in Figure 9-7.

**Figure 9-6**
Shutdown menu

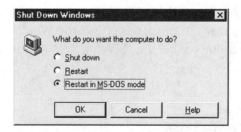

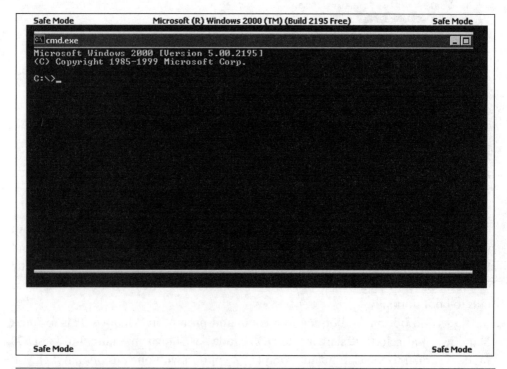

**Figure 9-7**  Windows 2000 Safe Mode command prompt only

This mode is rarely used in Windows 2000. Instead, we count on the powerful Recovery Console feature to work on Windows 2000 systems that refuse to boot (Figure 9-8).

Although the Windows 2000 Recovery Console looks somewhat like a command prompt, it has some significant limitations; but it has plenty of special tools to handle any boot problem Windows 2000 might encounter. The Recovery Console will appear again in Chapter 11.

```
Microsoft Windows 2000<TM> Recovery Console.

The Recovery Console provides system repair and recovery functionality.

Type EXIT to quit the Recovery Console and restart the computer.


1: C:\WINDOWS

Which Windows 2000 installation would you like to log onto
<To cancel, press ENTER>? 1
Type the Administrator password: ********
C:\WINDOWS>
```

**Figure 9-8** Recovery Console

## DOS Is DOS and Windows Is Windows

We will now return to the world of DOS, but before we do, take a moment to appreciate that every version of Windows still provides quick and easy access to a command prompt. Although we have yet to appreciate truly *why* this access to a command prompt exists (for a number of reasons, but that's the job of other chapters), make sure you remember that all versions of Windows *can* get you to a command prompt as needed. Trust me, if you work on Windows systems, you will need a command prompt from time to time!

## Communicating with Hardware

DOS can talk to a wide variety of PC hardware. The simplest way for DOS to talk to hardware is via the system BIOS. Every time the COPY command is run, for example, DOS talks to the PC's system BIOS, which in turn talks to the drives in order to copy data. These BIOS-level *calls* are completely built into DOS and are transparent to the user. DOS uses the system BIOS for all basic functions: hard drives, floppy drives, monitor, and keyboard. For these devices, you need only make sure that they are properly connected and, if necessary, configured in CMOS. DOS will automatically know they are there and respond to them.

When Microsoft invented DOS, they knew that new devices would be invented in the future. Because IBM had already invented the very flexible PC, DOS had to be equally flexible to access and use any future device. As you know from previous chapters, all hardware needs BIOS. If a new device is snapped into an expansion slot, how does it get BIOS? The system BIOS can't help, because it only knows how to talk to the most basic parts of the PC. Therefore, DOS must provide more programming to add extra BIOS for new devices.

DOS provides two special text files for adding control to new hardware: device drivers via CONFIG.SYS and TSRs via AUTOEXEC.BAT. Let's look at each of these important files in detail and understand what they are.

## Device Drivers and CONFIG.SYS

The most common way to add BIOS is through special files called *device drivers*. A device driver is little more than a file containing all the programming necessary to talk to a new device. Device drivers usually come from the same company that makes the hardware. If you buy a sound card or network card, it will come with a diskette or CD-ROM containing the necessary file(s). Most DOS device driver files use the extension SYS. Some examples of DOS device drivers are DRIVER.SYS, 3C509.SYS, and CLTV3.SYS.

As mentioned in Chapter 4, device drivers load through a special file called CONFIG.SYS, a text file that must be in the root directory of the C: drive. Although CONFIG.SYS has some secondary functions, the best way to describe it is as the "DOS BYOB (Bring Your Own BIOS) loader." The most common way to add device drivers in DOS is first to copy the device driver onto the C: drive from the floppy drive or CD-ROM (either manually using the COPY command, or automatically by running an installation program that does the copying for you). Either way, the result is a device driver on the C: drive, usually in its own directory. Once the device driver is copied to the C: drive, a line is added to the CONFIG.SYS file. This line starts with DEVICE= or DEVICEHIGH=, followed by the path/name of the device driver.

Windows 9*x* doesn't need a CONFIG.SYS file, but most PCs running Windows 9*x* have a CONFIG.SYS file anyway to support DOS programs and their device drivers. See if you have a CONFIG.SYS file in the root directory of your C: drive. If you do, you can see the contents of the CONFIG.SYS file by opening a command prompt, typing **CD\** to get to the root directory of C:, and then typing **TYPE CONFIG.SYS**.

Windows 2000 does not have a CONFIG.SYS file. Instead, it relies on the file CONFIG.NT to provide support for any DOS virtual machines. Even though the name is different, all the rules discussed here still apply.

Here are some typical device driver lines in CONFIG.SYS:

- `DEVICE5C:\DOS\ANSI.SYS` (DOS device driver)
- `DEVICE5D:\CR_ATAPI.SYS /D:MSCD000 /Q` (CD-ROM driver)
- `DEVICEHIGH=C:\VIBRA16\DRV\VIBRA16.SYS /BLASTER5A:220 I:5 D:1 H:5` (sound card driver)

Before going any further into CONFIG.SYS, you need to understand the following three rules.

First, you need a text editor to edit CONFIG.SYS. You can use DOS' built-in text editor, the EDIT program. EDIT works fine, but it takes a little practice to get comfortable with it, especially if you're used to Windows. Take the time to become familiar with opening and saving files, and exiting the EDIT program before you start messing around with anything important.

**NOTE** If you use Windows, try running the program SYSEDIT from the Start | Run box. This handy program opens CONFIG.SYS as well as other important startup files.

Second, don't make changes to CONFIG.SYS without first making a backup. The best way is to copy CONFIG.SYS to another directory. Make a directory called **\BACKUP** and copy CONFIG.SYS into it. This way, if you really mess it up, you can put a good copy back.

Finally, always do a "safe" delete. If you think a line is unnecessary, instead of deleting it from the file, *comment* it out. Just put a semicolon (;) at the beginning of the line, like this:

```
;DEVICE=C:\DOS\JUNK.SYS
```

The semicolon tells DOS to ignore the line. Then if you suddenly discover that you still need the line, simply remove the semicolon. If you comment out a line and the PC is still running properly after a couple of days, you can delete the line.

Having unfamiliar lines in your CONFIG.SYS file isn't necessarily bad. It's common simply to leave such lines alone, based on the theory, "if it ain't broke, don't fix it."

**NOTE** If you change CONFIG.SYS, the change will not be reflected by the system until the computer is rebooted.

The EDIT program automatically makes backup copies of CONFIG.SYS; they get the name CONFIG.BAK, then CONFIG.001, CONFIG.002, and so on. You may delete these backup files once you're sure they're not needed.

## DOS Device Drivers

DOS comes with many device drivers, most of which are so terribly obsolete that they weren't used even when DOS was the only game in town. Of the DOS drivers that are still useful, most are discussed later. A pair of device drivers warrant covering here: SETVER.EXE and ANSI.SYS.

### SETVER.EXE

A few DOS application programs, especially those for networks, were designed to run on a certain version of DOS. If you attempt to run one of these programs on a version of DOS other than the one for which it was designed, even if it's a more recent version, the program will return an error or lock up the computer. Using CONFIG.SYS, you can load the SETVER.EXE program as a device driver, and it will instruct DOS to claim to be whatever version of DOS you specify when you run the affected program. SETVER often looks something like this: DEVICE=C:\DOS\SETVER.EXE. Unless you are running some really old software, odds are good that you won't need this line.

### ANSI.SYS

The ANSI.SYS driver enables you to add color and features to the prompt. It also enables you to remap the keyboard. You don't need ANSI.SYS, but on a true DOS system, you want ANSI.SYS. ANSI.SYS wasn't always an optional item. Very early communications software programs would often require ANSI.SYS so DOS could emulate different terminals. The CONFIG.SYS line would look like this: DEVICE=C:\DOS\ANSI.SYS.

Many other device drivers come with DOS, but to understand their function, you must first have a stronger understanding of the hardware they support. Once you understand disk caching (later in this chapter) and memory management (Chapter 12), we'll return to CONFIG.SYS and the specialized drivers used by DOS to perform these functions.

## Configuration Commands in CONFIG.SYS

You can use CONFIG.SYS for much more than simply loading device drivers. DOS uses a large number of *configuration commands* to set up or optimize devices. This section covers the most common configuration commands. Although not an exhaustive list, these are the only ones used on a regular basis.

### BUFFERS

During disk I/O, DOS needs some memory, known as the *buffer space*, as an "assembly/disassembly area" for incoming and outgoing files. The BUFFERS statement defines the size of the space as follows: buffers=$nn,m$ where $nn$ is the number of buffers, with a range of 6−99, and $m$ is the number of buffers in the "look-ahead" buffer, with a range of 0−8 (optional). Here are some common BUFFERS= lines:

```
BUFFERS=20
BUFFERS=15,3
```

If you leave out the BUFFERS statement, you will get 15 buffers, which should be plenty. Leave out the BUFFERS statement unless you receive an error that contains the word "buffers." The look-ahead value is essentially a very early form of disk caching that is now obsolete.

## STACKS

A CPU uses its registers to run programs. Let's say you are running program X, so the registers inside your CPU are full of program X code. When a device like a mouse hits its IRQ, the CPU must run the mouse driver to act on the mouse IRQ. To run the mouse driver, the CPU must use the registers. But the CPU would like to return to program X when it's done with running the mouse driver. To do this, DOS sets aside some memory to store the register information temporarily. This memory is called the *stack*. The register values for program X are stored in the stack, the mouse driver is run, and then the register values for program X are restored to the registers.

The command's syntax is STACKS=*nn,mmm* where *nn* is the number of stacks, with a range of 0, 8–64, and *mmm* is the size of each stack (0, 32–512). Some common STACKS= lines are

```
STACKS=9,256
STACKS=32,128
```

The STACKS statement is rarely needed in CONFIG.SYS. By default, DOS sets STACKS=9,128. In the rare situation where you need a STACKS statement, you'll know because the machine will give you some nasty error such as "Stack Overflow." If you get an error like this, try increasing the size of each stack. If that doesn't help, reduce the stack size and increase the number of stacks. As a last resort, try increasing both. Stack errors are particularly likely where you have in-house programmers who write bad code. Resolve stack problems in this case by talking to the programmer, not by increasing the STACKS= statement.

## FILES

DOS needs to keep track of all files on the hard drive that are being used. A part of memory is set aside to store this information. The area of memory used to store the information for one file is called a *file handle*. The FILES= statement tells DOS how many file handles to use. Its syntax is FILES=*nnn*, where *nnn* is the number of files, with a range of 8–255. Here are a pair of common FILES= lines:

```
FILES=15
FILES=99
```

You need a FILES= statement. The default value of eight files is insufficient for most PCs. Set the files to FILES=20 for stand-alone PCs and FILES=99 for networked PCs. If you need more file handles, you'll get an error like "Insufficient file handles." Increase the value by tens until it goes away.

## SHELL

COMMAND.COM is known as the command interpreter because it interprets commands like DIR /W and then tells MSDOS.SYS that the user wants to see a directory in the wide format. However, COMMAND.COM also defines what DOS looks like. COMMAND.COM produces the C:\ prompt and the paths you see when you're working in DOS. In addition, it saves a small amount of memory for what are known as *environment variables*, which store information that is available to any program.

COMMAND.COM is therefore many things: a command interpreter, a holder of environment variables, and a "front end" that manifests the OS. Collectively, this is known as the *shell*. By default, the shell that you use in the root directory of the C: drive is COMMAND.COM. You don't have to use this COMMAND.COM, however; you can use another shell. The SHELL= statement defines the shell that DOS uses. The SHELL command's syntax is a bit complex:

```
SHELL=path_to_shell/P/E:nnnn location_of_transient_shell
```

The *path_to_shell* is the location of COMMAND.COM or another shell; /P is the *permanent* switch (you won't be able to exit this command interpreter); /E:*nnnn* is the size of environment space in bytes, with a range of 160<32768; and *location_of_transient_shell* tells where to find the transient shell if it's overwritten. Here are a pair of common SHELL= lines:

```
SHELL=C:\DOS\COMMAND.COM /P /E:512
SHELL=C:\COMMAND.COM /PC:\COMMAND.COM
```

You probably don't need the SHELL= statement. If you don't have one, the shell will be the COMMAND.COM in the root directory. The SHELL statement is usually needed for its options. For example, /E:*nnnn* increases the DOS environment (see AUTOEXEC.BAT and SET, later in this chapter). The DOS environment holds options like PATH, PROMPT, and TEMP. If you look in the AUTOEXEC.BAT, you will see options like:

```
SET TEMP=C:\WINDOWS\TEMP
SET BLASTER=A220 I7 D1
```

If you have more than 256 bytes of information in SET statements (including the PATH and PROMPT statement, which are really SET statements in disguise), you'll get the nasty error "Not Enough Environment Space," and your system will lock up. The /E:*nnnn* option adds environment space beyond the default 256 bytes to correct this error. Start with /E:512 and keep adding until the error goes away. The /P option prevents you from using the Exit command to stop the current COMMAND.COM. This option is usually only needed by programs like QEMM or Norton Utilities, which take control from or replace COMMAND.COM. If you don't use a SHELL= statement, the default is as though you had used one with a /P. Therefore, if you use a SHELL= statement, always add the /P option because that most closely mimics the DOS default.

The last option, *transient shell,* is a little weird, but you'll probably need it from time to time. COMMAND.COM is broken into two pieces: permanent and transient. The permanent part is loaded into conventional memory and is the part you see when you use the MEM /C/P command. This is also the part you can load into the HMA using the DOS=HIGH command. The transient part is loaded into the top of conventional memory and can be written over by programs that need the memory. If a program overwrites the transient part of COMMAND.COM, the transient part must be restored when the program ends. This setting specifies where to find the COMMAND.COM that has a copy of the transient area. The COMMAND.COM that has a copy of the transient area is invariably the main COMMAND.COM. The following example is a common way to do this:

```
SHELL=C:\DOS\COMMAND.COM /E:512 /P C:\DOS\COMMAND.COM
```

You don't add the transient portion to the SHELL statement unless a program won't return to the DOS prompt after it ends.

**NOTE   You might have to go to Chapter 12 to read up on DOS memory issues in order to make sense of the transient shell option.**

## TSRs and AUTOEXEC.BAT

The second way to add support for devices is through a *terminate and stay resident* (TSR) program. TSRs are less common than CONFIG.SYS device drivers, but they work equally well. You run a TSR like any other program, by typing its name at the prompt. Unlike other programs, however, a TSR will immediately return you to a DOS prompt (terminate), but will still be in RAM (stay resident). One of the most common DOS TSRs provides support for a mouse. Most mice come with a diskette that includes a TSR so you can use it in DOS. These TSR programs usually have a catchy name like MOUSE.COM. When you run the program, you'll see something like this:

```
C:\>MOUSE
Mouse driver version 8.20
Copyright (c) 1991-1993
All rights reserved
1993-11-09
Mouse driver installed
C:\>
```

It seems as though nothing has happened, but it has. The MOUSE program loaded into memory and will now support DOS programs that use a mouse. Try running the EDIT program and move your mouse. Tada! You have a mouse cursor! That's a classic use of a TSR.

Relatively few devices use TSRs in DOS; most use device drivers in CONFIG.SYS. However, DOS itself uses quite a few TSRs. Many have special functions that are covered in other sections of this book, but the following three should be discussed here:

### DOSKEY

One very popular TSR used in DOS and all versions of Windows is DOSKEY.COM, a handy program that keeps track of commands you have typed, creates keyboard *macros*, and adds extra power to the function keys for typing commands. The ability to store previously used commands is very helpful. Let's say you've been copying a bunch of files from different directories. It might be very handy to be able to bring back a command you typed two or three commands ago. If you have DOSKEY running, you can retrieve old commands just by pressing the UP ARROW key. You can also create a macro. In DOSKEY, a macro is a way to assign a series of keystrokes to one key combination such as CTRL-I. You can use DOSKEY for practical jokes, such as assigning the display "No directory today" to DIR. Try it. Type this command:

```
DOSKEY DIR=echo No directory today
```

The echo means to output to the screen, not to run a program. When you type **DIR**, you'll get

```
C:\>DIR
No directory today
```

Now type **DOSKEY DIR=** to erase the macro. Use your imagination for more practical examples. How about a macro that will automatically delete all files with the extension TMP from the C:\TEMP directory?

### MODE

The MODE.COM program is rarely used, but quite powerful. It can change the look of the monitor and enable you to redirect output from ports, as well as a number of other, less used features. Go to a prompt and type **MODE CO40**. You'll get wide letters (40 to a line). Type **MODE CO80** to put it back. When a screen mysteriously goes blank in DOS, MODE CO80 will often correct the problem. The MODE command is also handy for configuring and redirecting ports, although this is rarely done anymore. For example, to set COM1 to 9600 baud, eight data bits, no parity, and one stop bit, type **MODE COM1:9600,8,n,1**. This should be done only if an application tells you to do so. Another somewhat popular MODE command is MODE LPT1=COM1, which will redirect all data from the LPT1 port and output it to the COM1 port. Like the previous MODE command, this should be done only if an application tells you to.

## AUTOEXEC.BAT

Now let's say that you decide you like DOSKEY and you are going to use a mouse. Every time you reboot, you will have to enter DOSKEY.COM and MOUSE.COM before you start working. Wouldn't it be great if you could tell DOS to start certain TSRs automatically? That's the job of AUTOEXEC.BAT. AUTOEXEC.BAT is a text file that resides in the root directory of the C: drive, just like CONFIG.SYS. Using the EDIT program, you can create a text file with two lines:

```
DOSKEY
MOUSE
```

Save it with the name AUTOEXEC.BAT in the root directory of C:. Now, every time you boot the PC, DOSKEY.EXE and MOUSE.EXE will start automatically. Any command that you can type at the prompt you can add to the AUTOEXEC.BAT file. If you added CD\DOS

```
DOSKEY
MOUSE
CD\DOS
```

DOS would run DOSKEY and MOUSE, and then point to the C:\DOS directory every time it booted. A number of commands are available that you might like to run every time the PC boots. Let's take a look at these and see why.

## SET

The SET command creates environment variables, which are values that can be stored so any DOS program, including DOS itself, can read them. The SET command is commonly used with sound cards. A standard sound card creates a special environment variable to inform any DOS program that wants to use it that it is present and what it can do. Here's a common SET statement for a sound card:

```
SET BLASTER=A240 D3 I5 H5 T1 MIDI=D330 D1
```

All DOS programs that use sound cards look for an environment variable called BLASTER, which tells the program all the I/O information and the type of sound card. If you have DOS games that use sound cards, you'll want the BLASTER environment variable. Here are some other common SET statements:

```
SET TEMP=C:\WINDOWS\TEMP
SET CTCM=C:\CTCM
SET BACK=C:\BACKUP
```

Any program can make and use environment variables. Hundreds of different SET statements exist and they are quite common.

Two more environment variables that are created and used by DOS—PATH and PROMPT—are a little involved and warrant a more detailed inspection.

### PATH

The PATH environment variable specifies where to look for programs if they aren't in the current directory. Go to the C:\ directory, type **DIR**, and verify that the EDIT program is not there. Now type **EDIT**. The program runs! If you'll remember from an earlier discussion, you need to be in the directory where a program is located in order for it to work. Type **SET**. You'll see something like this:

```
PATH=C:\;C:\DOS;C:\WINDOWS;
PROMPT=$P$G
BLASTER= A240 D3 I5 H5 T1 MIDI=D330 D1
TEMP=C:\WINDOWS\TEMP
```

The SET statement shows all the environment variables. Look at the PATH= line. Do you see C:\DOS? That's why EDIT works! The PATH environment variable says, "If the program you're trying to run isn't in the current directory, look in these directories in the order listed." You can erase the PATH by typing **PATH=**. Now try running EDIT:

```
C:\>EDIT
Bad command or file name
C:\>
```

Replace the PATH using semicolons between each directory, by typing **PATH=C:\;C:\DOS;** and you should be able to run EDIT again. Clearly, the PATH is something you'll want to run every time the PC starts, so let's add it to the AUTOEXEC.BAT (make it the first line):

```
PATH=C:\;C:\DOS;C:\WINDOWS;
DOSKEY
MOUSE
CD\DOS
```

The very last versions of DOS automatically added C:\DOS to the PATH. You had to add anything else. The PATH line in AUTOEXEC.BAT can look different. It's really an environment variable, so it might look like SET PATH=C:\;C:\DOS; or it might not have the = sign, like this: SET PATH C:\;C:\ DOS;. They all work equally well.

## PROMPT

The PROMPT command defines how the prompt looks. Go to the C:\ prompt, type **PROMPT=\***, and watch what happens. Hmmm, where's the prompt? It's now an asterisk. Now type **CD\DOS**. The prompt is still just an asterisk, but in fact you are in the C:\DOS directory. If you type **DIR**, you will see the contents of that directory.

The PROMPT command takes some special *arguments* (extra things you add to the end of the command). Here's a partial list:

- $P = path
- $G = greater-than sign
- $D = date
- $T = time
- $$ = dollar sign
- $V = DOS version
- $L = less-than sign
- $E = escape

To change the prompt back to the way you're used to seeing it, type **PROMPT $P$G**. The prompt command can be used to make quite an impressive, colorful prompt if you have ANSI.SYS loaded. You need to use $E to do it. Try typing this (pay attention to which letters are upper- and lowercase):

```
C:\>PROMPT $E[1;34;40m$P$G$E[0;37;40m
```

My, what a pretty prompt! For the $E[X;Y;Zm part of the command, $X$ = brightness, $Y$ = foreground, and $Z$ = background. Replace the letters with the numbers for the colors and attributes (see Table 9-3). This command, for example, will make a red-on-white prompt:

```
PROMPT $E[0;31;47$p$g$E[0;37;40m
```

**Table 9-3**  Prompt Color Codes

| BRIGHTNESS | FOREGROUND | BACKGROUND |
|---|---|---|
| 0 for normal display | 30 black foreground | 40 black background |
| I bold on | 31 red foreground | 41 red background |
| 4 underline (mono only) | 32 green foreground | 42 green background |
| 5 blink on | 33 yellow foreground | 43 yellow background |
| 7 reverse video on | 34 blue foreground | 44 blue background |
| 8 invisible | 35 magenta foreground | 45 magenta background |
| | 36 cyan foreground | 46 cyan background |
| | 37 white foreground | 47 white background |

The PROMPT command goes way beyond even these settings. Check your DOS book for details on moving the cursor and remapping your keyboard. DOS defaults to PROMPT $P$G if no other prompt is specified. Now put all of this together in the AUTOEXEC.BAT file:

```
PATH=C:\;C:\DOS;C:\WINDOWS;
PROMPT $P$G
DOSKEY
MOUSE
```

## Startup Options

One of the big problems with CONFIG.SYS and AUTOEXEC.BAT is when they go wrong. Say you go to the local computer store and buy the new Acme GerbilMan 2000. This is an automated gerbil cage that automatically feeds, waters, and entertains your gerbil. It even cleans the cage for you! It comes with special software that enables you to schedule when and how to take care of your precious gerbil. The GerbilMan cage comes with an interface card that you install into an expansion slot. It also comes with a drivers disk. You snap the drivers disk into the A: drive, type A:, and then type **DIR**. You see the following:

```
A:\>DIR
 Volume in Drive A is
 Volume Serial Number is 1290-3331
 Directory of A:\

DOS             <DIR>           09-03-01      9:34a
READ     ME             34222   10-11-01      4:33p
WINDOWS31       <DIR>           09-03-01      9:34a
WIN9XME         <DIR>           09-03-01      9:34a
WINNT2K         <DIR>           09-03-01      9:34a
LINUX           <DIR>           09-03-01      9:34a
```

```
8 file(s)        34222    bytes
                128343    bytes free
```

As is typical for an install disk, note that it has drivers for many operating systems. Because we have a DOS system, type **CD\DOS** to access the directory containing the DOS install files. Type **DIR** in the A:\DOS directory to see the following:

```
Volume in Drive A is
Volume Serial Number is 1290-3331
Directory of A:\DOS

DOSREAD   ME          12222  10-11-01     4:33p
INSTALL   EXE          21434  10-11-01     4:33p
GBLDRV.SYS             43983  10-11-01     4:33p

5 file(s)        87639    bytes
                128343    bytes free
```

There's a program called INSTALL.EXE, so you run it. The INSTALL program creates a directory called C:\GERBIL and copies the application program. It then goes into your CONFIG.SYS and adds the following line:

```
DEVICE=C:\GERBIL\GBLDRV.SYS /FEED:YES /CLEAN:NO
```

You don't see any of this happening. All you see is a stupid "percent done" bar. Eventually, the installation stops and says

```
Installation Complete. To run GerbilMan, reboot and type GERBIL
from the C: Prompt.
```

Great! This is an easy installation. You reboot the PC, but unbeknownst to you, six weeks earlier an assembly-line worker at Acme software was in kind of a hurry while packing the box containing the GerbilMan you ended up buying. Instead of putting in the correct drivers disk (version 2.00.12/A), he threw in an old copy (version 2.00.06/F), the version for the GerbilMan 1998 card.

It just so happens that if you run driver version 2.00.06/F on a GerbilMan 2000 card, it will lock up like a stone the moment the device driver runs from CONFIG.SYS. This is clearly documented, as you would know if you had only read the READ.ME file, which would tell you to use the "ACME fax-back" service and request fax document G32342, or if you had taken the time to go to the http://www.acme.com/techsupp/gerbil/drivers/download/latest Web site, or if you had called the per-incident line and paid $35, or if you had read the tiny slip of paper labeled "Latest Developments" wedged between pages G-43 and G-44 of the User Manual.

**NOTE** You think I'm kidding here? There may be no such thing as a GerbilMan, but this type of thing happens every day in the world of a PC tech!

So, lucky you, the PC boots up, makes the usual noises, says "Starting MS-DOS," and then locks up like a stone. If the PC locks up at this point, the problem is in one of the DOS system files (IO.SYS, MSDOS.SYS, or COMMAND.COM) or in one of the startup files (CONFIG.SYS or AUTOEXEC.BAT). The only thing that has changed since the machine ran properly was updating CONFIG.SYS—but you can't look at CONFIG.SYS because the computer locks up every time you reboot.

This is a classic problem with DOS. To help, the later versions of DOS have two new uses for function keys F5 and F8: either completely overriding or stepping line by line through the CONFIG.SYS and AUTOEXEC.BAT files. When the computer shows

```
Starting MS-DOS
```

while booting, you have two seconds to press F5 or F8. If you press F5, you'll get

```
MS-DOS is bypassing your CONFIG.SYS and AUTOEXEC.BAT files.
C:\>
```

You have completely skipped both startup files and are sitting at the C:\ prompt. Good. Now you know the problem is in either CONFIG.SYS or AUTOEXEC.BAT. Reboot again, and this time press the F8 key. MS-DOS will prompt you to confirm each CONFIG.SYS command. Each line of the CONFIG.SYS will be displayed individually, with the option to run or not. Press Y to run the line and N to skip it:

```
DEVICE=C:\DOS\SETVER.EXE? [y/n] Y
DEVICE=C:\GERBIL\GBLDRV.SYS /FEED:YES /CLEAN:NO [y/n] Y
```

When you lock up, you've found the problem! Now I'll bet you'll start checking Web sites and reading documentation! You discover the clearly documented problem, download the correct driver, place it in the C:\GERBIL folder, and change the line in CONFIG.SYS to read

```
DEVICE=C:\GERBIL\GBLDRV2K.SYS /FEED:YES /CLEAN:NO
```

as specified in the clearly documented instructions that you now are reading. You fixed the problem!

## Batch Files

AUTOEXEC.BAT is a unique member of a type of files called *batch files*. Batch files enable you to automate any series of prompt commands, similarly to how

AUTOEXEC.BAT stores commands you want to start automatically every time you boot. With regular batch files, you use a text editor to list the series of commands you want to run, save the file with the extension BAT, and then type the name of the batch file from a command to activate. Try this—get to the C:\ prompt and type this command:

```
EDIT 1.BAT
```

You get a blank EDIT screen. Suppose you have a directory called C:\WINDOWS. Enter the line CD\WINDOWS into the EDIT screen. Save 1.BAT and exit the EDIT program. From the prompt, type **1**, press ENTER, and watch what happens. It should take you to the C:\WINDOWS directory, assuming you have one of course! Batch files work pretty much like any program—just type in the filename at a prompt and a batch file runs.

Batch files are extremely powerful. If you really want to be impressed, check out the batch files, including AUTOEXEC.BAT, on any Windows 98 Startup disk. Batch files are old, but we still use them frequently. Although the A+ Certification exams do not test your ability to create batch files, all accomplished techs can recognize and run batch files.

## Working with Drives

In the chapter on hard drives, I touched on using DOS to work with drives. I reviewed using FDISK and FORMAT to prepare drives for use. You saw how the PC boots and uses a bootable disk to set up a drive. In this section, you'll see some of the other programs that come with DOS that you can use to work with drives.

One of the most important items in your toolbox is a bootable floppy diskette. It has many uses, particularly booting up a system when the hard drive isn't working properly. You can make a bootable floppy from any properly operating PC. *Do not* wait to make one until you need it; you might not have a properly operating PC available! Make sure you have a bootable floppy for *every* version of DOS. To verify the version of DOS on a PC, type **VER** from any prompt. After you have verified the version, insert a blank floppy and use the SYS command to make it bootable. Then copy the following files onto the floppy:

FDISK.EXE or FDISK.COM (depends on the version of DOS)

FORMAT.EXE or FORMAT.COM (depends on the version of DOS)

SYS.COM

EDIT.COM (from Windows 95, but also works with old DOS)

HIMEM.SYS

EMM386.EXE

SMARTDRV.EXE

MSD.EXE or MSD.COM

MSCDEX.EXE

MEM.EXE

ATTRIB.EXE

DEFRAG.EXE

DELTREE.EXE

EXPAND.COM

LABEL.COM

SCANDISK.EXE

SHARE.EXE

These files just barely fit on a 3.5-inch floppy. Add or subtract from this list as you get more comfortable. Remember that many versions of DOS exist. Be prepared!

## VOL

Every drive has a volume label, which is roughly equivalent to a sign placed in front of a building. Like a sign, it tells the function of the drive. By contrast, the drive *letter* is likethe building's address. A volume label enables users to create more personal, more descriptive names for their drives. The volume label can be up to 11 characters and can include spaces. It is displayed every time you run the DIR command.

```
C:\>DIR C*.*

Volume in Drive C is Mike's PC
Volume Serial Number is 1734-3234
Directory of C:\

COMMAND COM     34222     04-01-94     4:33p
CONFIG  BAK     34        02-03-98     4:36a
CONFIG  NU      32        11-07-97     3:30p
CONFIG  SYS     34        02-03-98     4:36p

 4 file(s)     34322      bytes
              182888343   bytes free
```

You can also use the VOL command to see the volume label:

```
C:\>VOL
Volume in Drive C is Mike's PC
Volume Serial Number is 1734-3234
```

You can create or delete a volume label with the LABEL command:

```
C:\>label
Volume in drive C is Mikes PC
Volume Serial Number is 1734-3234
Volume label (ENTER for none)?
```

The volume label is not required, not used by any applications, and is considered obsolete. The only time you need to know the volume label is when you use the FDISK program to delete a primary partition—FDISK always asks you for the volume label. If you don't type in the correct volume label, you won't be able to delete the partition. Many technicians purposely add a volume label just to keep users from accidentally trashing a partition.

## SYS

The SYS command copies the three DOS system files to a partition, making it bootable. In the chapter on hard drives, you saw how to use the FORMAT command with the /S option to format a drive and copy the system files. Sometimes you don't want to reformat a drive; you just want to add or replace the system files. To do this, run the SYS command followed by the letter of the drive you want to make bootable. This command is very handy for making preformatted floppy diskettes bootable. The SYS command looks like this:

```
C:\>SYS A:
System transferred
```

The SYS command works equally well to replace a suspect system file on a hard drive. Whenever you lock up on boot after the POST, a quick SYS C: after booting to a bootable floppy disk is a handy way to verify that the system files are intact.

## LASTDRIVE

The LASTDRIVE= command enables you to allocate memory for the drive letters of storage devices other than local hard drives, such as CD-ROM, Zip, and network drives—anything that uses a drive letter but isn't a local hard drive. DOS allocates only enough space for two extra drive letters beyond C for these devices. For example, if you had a hard drive that was C:, then you could add only two CD-ROM drives before you would get the error "Not enough drive letters available."

To tell DOS to allocate more space for drive letters, add the command LASTDRIVE=$x$ to the CONFIG.SYS, where $x$ is the highest drive letter you'll need. LASTDRIVE= is almost always set to Z (LASTDRIVE=Z) to provide space for all the possible drive letters. LASTDRIVE is very commonly found in a DOS PC's CONFIG.SYS file.

## Checking Drives

The *D* in "DOS" stands for disk, because DOS was one of the first OSs that took a disk-centric approach to the PC. The greatest representation of this idea is the prompt itself, which always points to a drive and a directory. With DOS, you get the feeling of moving around inside of drives (CD) and looking around (DIR). This feeling is so prevalent that it is common for a person to say, "I'm in the FRED directory on my C: drive," or "Go to the FRED directory and delete all the files."

Clearly, a disk-centric OS like DOS is going to be interested in the general health and welfare of both hard and floppy drives. To help ensure that the drives are in good working order, DOS provides utilities to inspect, optimize, and repair drives. Some of these utilities were discussed earlier in the book, but now we'll look at them in more detail.

### CHKDSK

The CHKDSK program was the first disk utility to be included as a part of DOS. CHKDSK identifies and repairs lost cluster chains. It will also identify, but cannot repair, cross-linked files. In the chapter on hard drives, you learned that a lost cluster chain is a series of clusters that has no filename, whereas cross-linked files are two files trying to claim the same cluster. CHKDSK repairs a lost chain by giving it a filename called FILE*xxxx*.CHK, where *xxxx* starts with 0000 and increments for each lost chain CHKDSK locates. These files are then placed in the root directory of the drive that is being checked. For example, if you run CHKDSK and it finds three lost chains, it will give those chains the names FILE0000.CHK, FILE0001.CHK, and FILE0002.CHK. These files are usually just deleted, thereby recovering the disk space for use by other files. CHKDSK must be run with the /F option to repair lost chains; otherwise, it will simply report their existence without repairing them. If you use CHKDSK, use the /F option:

```
C:\>CHKDSK /F
Volume Serial Number is 306D-1CDA

2,111,537,152 bytes total disk space
    61,702,144 bytes in 113 hidden files
    11,272,192 bytes in 344 directories
   628,555,776 bytes in 6,256 user files
1,410,007,040 bytes available on disk

32,768 bytes in each allocation unit
64,439 total allocation units on disk
43,030 available allocation units on disk

655,360 total bytes memory
590,560 bytes free
```

Later versions of DOS come with the SCANDISK program. SCANDISK can reliably detect and fix a much wider range of disk problems than CHKDSK. If the version of DOS you are using comes with SCANDISK, there is no reason to use CHKDSK /F.

**NOTE** Windows 2000 has brought back CHKDSK as a valuable disk utility. DOS and Windows 9x don't need CHKDSK, but Windows 2000 does!

## SCANDISK

The SCANDISK program is a significant improvement over CHKDSK. SCANDISK is a highly flexible, relatively safe, and very powerful disk-repair utility (Figure 9-9). Where CHKDSK can fix only lost clusters, SCANDISK can repair not only lost clusters, but also cross-linked files, directory and file structures, *file allocation tables* (FATs), even volume labels. SCANDISK will also rescan all the clusters on a drive to verify their proper working order and FAT status. The best thing to say about SCANDISK is that there is so little to say. Its safety and ease of use make it the first line of defense in drive maintenance and troubleshooting.

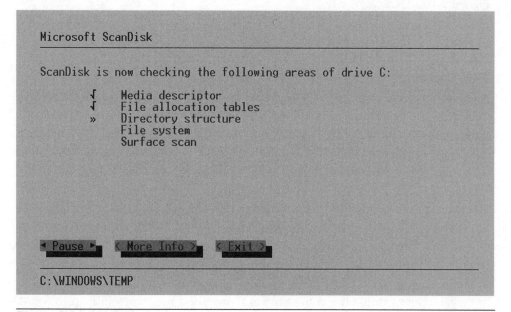

**Figure 9-9** ScanDisk

## DEFRAG

As discussed earlier in the book, hard drives need to be defragmented about once a week. DOS' DEFRAG program is a simple defragmentation program that does an admirable job of clearing up file fragmentation without any user intervention (Figure 9-10).

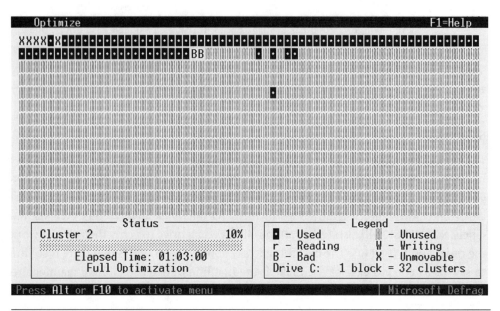

**Figure 9-10** DOS DEFRAG

## Disk Caching

Whenever someone asks, "What is the most important thing I can do to make my DOS PC faster?" the first answer should always be, "Make sure your disk cache is enabled!" A disk cache is crucial to the performance of your PC. I want to take a moment to explain the function of a disk cache, and then you can look at the venerable DOS disk cache *SmartDrive* (SMARTDRV) and learn some tweaks to ensure good PC performance.

Have you ever listened to your hard drive or watched your hard drive light while you're working on your PC? Have you noticed that quite a bit of activity occurs on the drives, even when you're doing work that has nothing to do with the drive? This is because the system constantly accesses the hard drive, not just when you start a program. When you start most DOS application programs, such as Microsoft Word for DOS, you aren't loading the entire program. Any good program will load into RAM only the part of its code necessary to do the business at hand. If you're not spell checking, why load the spell-checker code and data, thereby losing precious RAM that could be used for something else? Every program accesses many subroutines stored in files to perform different functions, like making margins, accessing menus, and importing graphics. These extra files are loaded on an as-needed basis (Figure 9-11) and are then unloaded from RAM when their work is done.

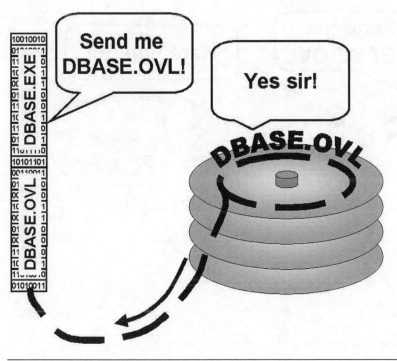

**Figure 9-11** Programs constantly access the hard drive

Not only do programs constantly access the hard drive, but they also constantly access the same files over and over again. As you know, accessing a hard drive is a very slow process compared with accessing RAM. To run efficiently, a PC needs some kind of fast storage area to place copies of files that the main program constantly needs to access. That way, when the program calls them, they're in something faster than the hard drive, ready to be used.

Special hardware devices and software programs set aside a part of RAM to be used as a disk cache, which is actually composed of two separate items: a RAM *holding pen* that stores data from the hard drive, and a program that monitors drive accesses. I'll call the monitoring program the *disk cache* and the RAM that holds the data the *holding pen*.

The disk cache monitors all access to the drive, keeping a copy of accessed data in its holding pen. Whenever a program needs to get something from RAM, the cache first checks its holding pen to see if the data is there. If the data is present, the cache passes the data to RAM, thus avoiding any need to access the relatively slow hard drive, and making the system run much faster (Figure 9-12).

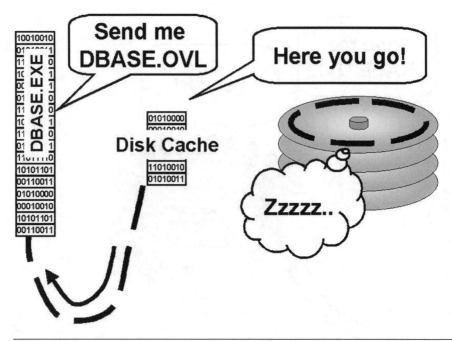

**Figure 9-12**   Cache at work

A disk cache can be made in several different ways. One way is to have special hard drive controller cards that are populated with RAM. These controllers store bits of hard drive data on RAM, on a sector-by-sector basis. When the computer asks for a particular sector, special programs on the controller search the onboard RAM to see if that sector is in the cache. If it is, the data is immediately sent to the system. If not, the sectors are taken off the drive, a copy is stored on the onboard RAM, and then it is sent to the system. If the system asks for that sector, the data is in the cache, ready to go. These are called *caching controllers.*

Hardware caching controllers are expensive and rare. Instead, most systems use a *software caching* method. Software caching is cheap, often free, and for most users it is just as good as a caching controller card. In software caching, a portion of the computer's DRAM is set aside electronically to be used as the cache, while the caching program resides in RAM.

Unlike hardware-based disk caches, software caches tend to look at the drive in clusters, but otherwise they work the same way. By far the most popular software disk cache in DOS computers is the famous SMARTDRV, which comes bundled free as a part of DOS.

## SMARTDRV

SMARTDRV is initiated from the AUTOEXEC.BAT file with a line like SMARTDRV.EXE. Simply adding this line provides an excellent disk cache. However, is it good enough? There are ways to measure the quality of the disk cache. The ultimate unit is called the *hit rate*, which is measured with the formula:

hit rate = (number of times data is in cache/number of times data is requested) $\times$ 100%

So the hit rate means "What percentage of all the times the system goes to the hard drive for data is the data already in the cache?" A good hit rate is in the area of 75 to 90 percent. That means a good disk cache will eliminate the need to use the slowest part of your computer, the hard drive, around 80 percent of the time. Measuring the hit rate is the tool you use to optimize the disk cache. You can determine the hit rate by typing **SMARTDRV /S** to see the following:

```
Microsoft SMARTDrive Disk Cache version 5.0
Copyright 1991,1993 Microsoft Corp.

Room for 16 elements of 8,192 bytes each
There have been 997 cache hits
and 291 cache misses
```

Once you have the numbers, use the formula mentioned previously to determine the hit rate. In this example, the hit rate = 997 hits/(291 misses + 997 hits) $\times$ 100% = 77%. This certainly could be better.

Although SMARTDRV will run if you add only the line SMARTDRV to the AUTOEXEC.BAT file, you can increase the hit rate substantially by tweaking the line. Here's a good SMARTDRV line:

```
SMARTDRV a- b- 1024 /B:32
```

The a- and b- tell SMARTDRV not to cache floppy drives. The whole idea behind caching is loading the cache with files that you're going to ask for again. Files on floppies aren't called repeatedly. Think about it. What is on a floppy? Usually, a floppy is used for something temporary that you work with and then dump. Don't waste cache space by loading files you won't call again. Turn off disk caching to the floppy drives.

The number, in this case 1,024, is the cache size. This is the size of the cache's holding pen. The rule for SMARTDRV's cache size is to make the cache one-quarter of the size of the total RAM, up to 2MB. Never make a SMARTDRV cache larger than 2MB. Please note that these limits apply only to SMARTDRV. The more advanced disk caches used by Windows 3.11 and Windows 9x are not subject to these limits.

The "/B:32" requires a little explaining. If you promise to defragment the hard drive, you can increase the look-ahead buffer. If enough room is available in the cache, SMARTDRV will grab extra clusters of data when it accesses the drive. The number of clusters to grab is set by the size of the look-ahead buffer. Without the /B option, SMARTDRV will set the look-ahead buffer to 16K by default. A well-defragmented drive will benefit from increasing the buffer to 32K.

SMARTDRV has many other options, but only *double buffering* has much relevance today. If you look in the CONFIG.SYS file, you might notice a line that looks like this:

```
DEVICE=C:\DOS\SMARTDRV.EXE /DOUBLE_BUFFER
```

This must be entered when bus-mastering controllers (drive controllers that do their own DMA transfers) are in the computer. Bus-mastering controllers conflict with SMARTDRV, and this line is necessary to make SMARTDRV run a special second buffer to prevent conflicts.

If you have a CD-ROM drive, you must load the MSCDEX driver (which gives the CD-ROM drive a drive letter) in AUTOEXEC.BAT before you load SMARTDRV. If you load MSCDEX after SMARTDRV, the disk cache won't know there is a CD-ROM drive to cache!

You won't use SMARTDRV with Windows 9*x* or Windows 2000. All versions of Windows use the much more powerful VCACHE disk cache. VCACHE is discussed in Chapter 10.

## RAM Drive

A RAM drive is RAM that thinks it's a hard drive. Unlike a disk cache, users have total control over what is stored in a RAM drive. A RAM drive actually has a drive letter assigned to it, and users can read, write, copy, and delete to and from a RAM drive just as if it were a hard drive. RAM drives can be handy on a DOS machine as a place to store files that are often called for by the system. RAM drives were particularly popular with DOS before SMARTDRV was introduced. Don't confuse a RAM drive with SMARTDRV!

DOS comes with the device driver necessary to create a RAM drive: RAMDRIVE.SYS. You can install a RAM drive by adding the following line to your CONFIG.SYS file:

```
DEVICE=C:\DOS\RAMDRIVE.SYS 1024
```

The number at the end is the amount of RAM (in KB) to set aside as a RAM drive. This RAM will no longer be used as regular RAM. Instead, it will be given the next available drive letter after the last real drive (See Figure 9-13). The onset of SMARTDRV made RAM drives virtually obsolete. Why create a fixed RAM drive for programs that are often called when the disk cache will probably have the same information?

**Figure 9-13**
RAM drive at work

NOTE   Windows 98/ME Startup disks load a RAM drive and then copy many useful tools to that drive. See Chapter 10 for more details on the resurrection of the RAM drive.

## The Computer Virus

Although computer viruses are not limited to DOS, this chapter provides a number of concepts that will help you to understand the function of computer viruses. Because these concepts are still fresh in your mind, this is a good point to learn about viruses and their prevention/removal.

The words, "I think your machine has a virus," can send shudders down the back of even the most competent PC technician. The thought of megabytes of critical data being wiped away by the work of some evil programmer is at best annoying and, at worst, a serious financial disaster.

So, where do viruses come from? Just like many human viruses, they live in host bodies, in this case computers. Your computer can only catch one if it interacts with other computers, or with programs or data from an infected computer. The problem is that these days almost everyone's computer (aside from folks like the CIA) is connected to the Internet, and thereby to many, many other computers. Also, many viruses are spread through the sharing of programs or information on floppy disks or CD-ROMs.

How do you know if you've caught a virus? You feel sluggish, start sneezing and coughing, want to sleep—or in this case, the computer equivalents of those symptoms: Your computer may seem unusually sluggish, generate strange error messages or other odd emissions, or possibly even lock up and refuse to function entirely. All these are classic symptoms, but you cannot assume your computer is virus free just because it seems fine. Some viruses do their work in secret, as you will discover here.

The secret to avoiding viruses is to understand how a virus works. A virus is a program that has two functions: *proliferate* (make more copies of itself) and *activate* (at some signal, count, date, and so on, do something—usually something bad like delete the boot sector). A virus does not have to do damage to be a virus. Some of the first viruses written were harmless and downright amusing. Without going into too much gritty detail, basically only four types of viruses exist: boot sector, executable, macro, and Trojan. A fifth type also exists that is really a combination of two others: bimodal/bipartite.

## Boot Sector

Boot sector viruses change the code in the *master boot record* (MBR) of the hard drive. Once the machine is booted, they reside in memory, attempting to infect the MBRs of other drives such as floppy drives, connected network machines, or removable media, and creating whatever havoc they are designed to do by the programmer.

## Executable

Executable viruses reside in executable files. They are literally extensions of executables and are unable to exist by themselves. Once the infected executable file is run, the virus loads into memory, adding copies of itself to other EXEs that are subsequently run, and again doing whatever evil that the virus was designed to do.

## Macro

Macro viruses are specially written application macros. Although they are not truly programs, they perform the same functions as regular viruses. These viruses will auto-start when the particular application is run and will then attempt to make more copies of themselves. Some will even try to find other copies of the same application across a network to propagate.

## Trojan

Trojans are true, freestanding programs that do something other than what the person who runs the program thinks they will do. An example of a Trojan would be a program that a person thinks is a game but that is actually a CMOS eraser. Some Trojans are quite sophisticated. It might be a game that works perfectly well, but when the user quits the game, it causes some type of damage.

### Bimodal/Bipartite

A bimodal or bipartite virus uses both boot-sector and executable functions.

## Antivirus Programs

The only way to protect your PC permanently from getting a virus is to disconnect from the Internet and never permit any potentially infected software to touch your precious computer. Because neither scenario is likely these days, you need to use a specialized antivirus program to help stave off the inevitable virus assaults.

An antivirus program protects your PC in two ways. It can be both sword and shield, working in an active "seek and destroy" mode and in a passive "sentry" mode. When ordered to seek and destroy, the program will scan the computer's boot sector and files for viruses, and if it finds any, presents you with the available options for removing or disabling them. Antivirus programs can also operate as virus shields that passively monitor your computer's activity, checking for viruses only when certain events occur, such as a program executing or a file being downloaded.

Antivirus programs use different techniques to combat different types of viruses. They detect boot sector viruses simply by comparing the drive's boot sector to a standard boot sector. This works because most boot sectors are basically the same. Some antivirus programs make a backup copy of the boot sector. If they detect a virus, the programs will use that backup copy to replace the infected boot sector. Executable viruses are a little more difficult to find because they can be on any file in the drive. To detect executable viruses, the antivirus program uses a library of *signatures*. A signature is a code pattern of a known virus. The antivirus program compares an executable file to its library of signatures. Instances have occurred where a perfectly clean program coincidentally held a virus signature. Usually the antivirus program's creator will provide a patch to prevent further alarms. Antivirus programs detect macro viruses through the presence of virus signatures or of certain macro commands that indicate a known macro virus. Now that we understand the types of viruses and how antivirus programs try to protect against them, let's review a few terms that are often used when describing certain traits of viruses.

### Polymorphics/Polymorphs

A polymorph virus attempts to change its signature to prevent detection by antivirus programs, usually by continually scrambling a bit of useless code. Fortunately, the scrambling code itself can be identified and used as the signature once the antivirus makers become aware of the virus. One technique that is sometimes used to combat unknown polymorphs is to have the antivirus program create a checksum on every file in the drive. A *checksum* in this context is a number generated by the software based on the contents of the file rather than the name, date, or size of that file. The algorithms for creating these checksums vary among different antivirus programs (they are also usually kept secret to help prevent virus makers from coming up with ways to beat them). Every time a program is run, the antivirus program calculates a new checksum and compares it with the earlier calculation. If the checksums are different, it is a sure sign of a virus.

## Stealth

The term "stealth" is more of a concept than an actual virus function. Most stealth virus programs are boot sector viruses that use various methods to hide from antivirus software. One popular stealth virus will hook on to a somewhat unknown, but often used, software interrupt, running only when that interrupt runs. Others make copies of innocent-looking files.

## Virus Prevention Tips

The secret to preventing damage from a virus attack is to keep from getting one in the first place. As discussed earlier, all good antivirus programs include a virus shield that will automatically scan floppies, downloads, and so on. Use it. It is also a good idea to scan a PC daily for possible virus attacks. Again, all antivirus programs include TSRs that will run every time the PC is booted. Last but not least, know where software has come from before you load it. Although the chance of commercial, shrink-wrapped software having a virus is virtually nil (a couple of well-publicized exceptions have occurred), that illegal copy of "Unreal Tournament" you borrowed from a local hacker should definitely be inspected with care.

Get into the habit of having an antivirus floppy disk—a bootable, copy-protected floppy with a copy of an antivirus program. If you suspect a virus, use the diskette, even if your antivirus program claims to have eliminated it. Turn off the PC and reboot it from the antivirus diskette. Run your antivirus program's most comprehensive virus scan. Then check all removable media that were exposed to the system and any other machine that may have received data from or is networked to the cleaned machine. A virus can often go for months before anyone knows of its presence.

## Why Mess with DOS?

This can be a tough chapter to get motivated to study, especially if you are a tried and true Windows user. What could possibly be the use of all of these DOS commands?

DOS is dead, right? Wrong. Although true DOS might be gone, *all* versions of Windows still need a command prompt and DOS commands. For example, Windows 98 makes a powerful, handy "Startup" disk, a special bootable floppy that lets you access a CD-ROM from an A: prompt and Install/Reinstall Windows or run special recovery software, as we will see in the next few chapters. The Windows 98 Startup disk uses CONFIG.SYS to load a CD-ROM driver, gives the CD-ROM a drive letter via AUTOEXEC.BAT, and creates a RAM drive into which all the critical external commands are copied. I love to watch new techs boot that has an unpartitioned hard drive to a new system and then try to figure out where the C: drive came from! RAMDRIVE takes the first available drive letter, so if you have no drive letters yet, as is the case on a new system with an unpartitioned hard drive, the RAMDRIVE takes the letter C. (Don't worry, as soon as you create the partition using FDISK, it gets out of the way.)

As we will see in the next two chapters, a number of utilities in Windows 9*x* and Windows 2000 need to run from a command prompt. This is especially true in Windows 2000. Additionally, as we will see in the networking chapter, most of the truly powerful networking utilities are run from a command prompt in both Windows 9*x* and Windows 2000. You simply cannot debug network problems without a command prompt.

The A+ Certification exams continue to stress the command prompt because every good PC tech needs to be as comfortable starting at the C: prompt as they are looking at My Computer. Understand the DOS commands shown in this chapter, not to prove you can use an obsolete operating system but so you can use today's most advanced operating systems. DOS may be dead, but the legacy of DOS lives on in every PC used today.

## Review Questions

1. What are the major functions of an operating system (OS)?
   A. An OS provides a method for other programs to communicate.
   B. An OS creates a user interface.
   C. An OS enables users to add, move, and delete installed programs and data.
   D. All of the above.

2. Which of the following shows a typical DOS prompt?
   A. A:\\
   B. D:/>
   C. C:\>
   D. C://

3. Which command(s) can DOS use to remove files from a drive? (Select all that apply.)

   A. REMOVE

   B. DEL

   C. DELTREE

   D. ERASE

4. Which of the following *best* describes the operating system's user interface?

   A. It enables the system to communicate with peripheral devices.

   B. It provides a display of the programs and data on a system to the user.

   C. It provides a display of the system hardware to the user.

   D. It provides error handling or notification displays when communicating with hardware.

5. To manipulate and organize data and programs, which of the following must the OS do? (Select all that apply.)

   A. Identify all the data and programs on the system and organize them in a binary-code format.

   B. Provide a method to identify data according to the type of program that uses that particular data.

   C. Provide a naming system for each drive.

   D. Give the user an interface to assign drive letters to drives.

6. Which of the following is true about DOS files?

   A. Names are broken down into filenames and extensions.

   B. Filenames can be no longer than eight alphanumeric characters.

   C. The optional extension defines the function of the file.

   D. All of the above.

7. DOS can support _____ floppy drives.

   A. 1

   B. 2

   C. 4

   D. unlimited

8. The three main files that make up DOS are

   A. MSDOS.SYS, CONFIG.SYS, and AUTOEXEC.BAT

   B. IO.SYS, MSDOS.SYS, and CONFIG.SYS

   C. IO.SYS, MSDOS.SYS, and COMMAND.COM

   D. COMMAND.COM, CONFIG.SYS, and AUTOEXEC.BAT

9. Which of the following statements accurately describe(s) CONFIG.SYS? (Select all that apply.)

    A. Your system can run fine without a CONFIG.SYS file.

    B. CONFIG.SYS is known as a BIOS loader.

    C. CONFIG.SYS is a static file. It cannot be modified.

    D. If the user notices an unfamiliar line in CONFIG.SYS, it is best to delete that line.

10. A computer virus can be categorized as which of the following? (Select all that apply.)

    A. Always destructive

    B. Self-replicating

    C. Self-activating

    D. Self-destructive

## Answers

1. **D.** All of the described functions are intrinsic to all operating systems.

2. **C.** C:\ is a typical DOS prompt.

3. **B, C and D.** All three of these are correct commands for removing files from a drive. DELTREE is the dangerous one because it will permanently delete files, directories, and subdirectories.

4. **B.** The user interface provides a display of the programs and data. A good interface will also provide error handling and notification, but this is not a requirement.

5. **B and C.** The user must have some method to know which data files are used by particular programs. Further, the OS must provide a naming system for every drive.

6. **D.** All of the statements are true for DOS files.

7. **B.** DOS only has support for A: and B: floppy disk drives.

8. **C.** IO.SYS, MSDOS.SYS, and COMMAND.COM

9. **A and B.** A DOS system can run fine without CONFIG.SYS, although it needs the file to load device drivers for all but the most basic hardware. Deleting lines in CONFIG.SYS without knowing what they do can lead to system errors or non-responsive hardware.

10. **B and C.** In order for a program to be considered a virus, it must be self-replicating and self-activating.

## CHAPTER 10

# Windows 9x

In this chapter, you will

- Understand the basic concepts behind Windows 9x
- Understand how to navigate in different Windows environments
- Learn how to maintain a healthy Windows 9x system
- Learn important troubleshooting procedures

## Chapter Prerequisites

Unlike any other chapter in this book, I need to assume (and so do the A+ Certification exams, for that matter) that you have basic *user* skills. Before you go any further in this chapter, make sure you can do the following:

- Recognize all the components of the standard Windows desktop
- Manipulate windows—resize, move, and so on
- Create, delete, rename, move, and copy files and folders
- Understand file extensions and their relationship with program associations
- Use common keyboard shortcuts/hotkeys

If any of this seems at all confusing to you or you're just not sure, don't panic! I have a special Web chapter just for you. Check out *Essential Windows*, online at either **www.osborne.com** or **www.totalsem.com**. In fact, even if you are sure you can do all user-level skills, the A+ Certification exams really try to trick you with questions on processes that you may do every day and not really think about. Here's a classic: "In order to move a file from the C:\WINDOWS folder to the A:\ using Windows Explorer, what key must you hold down while dragging the file?" Be safe and at least scan the Web chapter before you sit for the A+ exams! With that said, let's dive into Windows for techs.

### It All Started with Windows 3.*x*

At first glance, Microsoft Windows is a *graphical user interface* (GUI). Instead of using a character-based interface like DOS and memorizing a large number of commands to run programs and administer files, you *see* programs, files, and directory structures as tiny graphics called icons. You use a mouse to manipulate icons, start programs, and manipulate files.

Many people who use Windows assume that it is the computer's OS. A GUI, however, is not necessarily also an OS. It does nothing more than translate the manipulation of icons into commands that are understandable to an OS, which actually does the work. Application programs must be written for a GUI from the ground up in order to take advantage of the concept of GUI.

GUIs are implemented in many different ways. Some OSs, such as Apple's OS X, have GUIs built into them as integral parts of the OSs. In other words, a C:\ prompt is not an option on any Apple computer that uses OS X. No Macintosh user needs to understand the concept of a prompt everything, from starting programs to installing hard drives, is done from the built-in GUI. OS X is a completely graphical OS.

UNIX, OS/2, Windows 3.*x*, Windows 9*x*, and Windows 2000 are character-based OSs that come with an optional GUI to make life easier. The GUI is not required, but the OS installs it automatically and activates it on startup, giving the impression that the GUI is part of the OS, as with Macintosh OS X. It is not; however, most of these non-GUI OSs cannot perform all of their functions without the GUI. Some OSs, such as UNIX and Windows 2000, can perform most of their functions from a command prompt. Other OSs, like the Windows 9*x* series, are almost useless without the GUI.

## Historical/Conceptual

Very few people dispute that OS/2 was the first serious attempt at a GUI for the Intel platform. What few folks realize is that Microsoft was the primary developer of OS/2. In the mid-1980s, Microsoft and IBM were working hard on OS/2, and it was assumed that when they released OS/2, DOS would become obsolete. But all was not happy in those days. IBM kept adding extras to OS/2, such as built-in mainframe terminal emulators. These powerful programs were great if you wanted to link into an IBM mainframe, but they added extra cost and hardware requirements at a time when 8MB of RAM could easily set you back almost $500. Microsoft didn't like where OS/2 was heading, but they were legally bound not to create an OS that competed with OS/2. Thus it was that Microsoft Windows began life not as an OS but as a mere GUI add-on running on top of DOS. Microsoft took care *not* to advertise early versions of Windows as OSs (Figure 10-1).

**Figure 10-1**
Windows 3.0 GUI

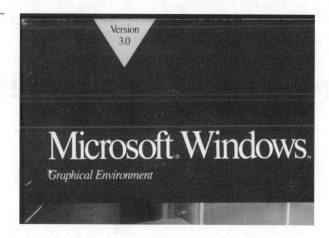

Microsoft used the first versions of Windows essentially as test beds for OS/2 GUI concepts. Although Windows version 1.0 amounted to little more than a primitive version of Windows Explorer, working with OS/2 gave Microsoft a good understanding of more advanced functions, such as how they could best use 386 protected mode, how to create a standard look and feel, and what key issues they needed to address when writing applications for the GUI environment. By incorporating these functions into their own software, Microsoft turned Windows into more than just a GUI that ran on top of DOS. Windows was now performing functions like an OS. Later versions of Windows took on more and more aspects of an OS. With the arrival of Windows version 3.11, almost all operating-system functions had been taken over by Windows.

The first popular generation of Microsoft Windows came in the following five versions:

- Windows 3.0
- Windows 3.1

- Windows for Workgroups 3.1

- Windows 3.11

- Windows for Workgroups 3.11

Versions of Windows existed before the 3.*x* line. They had names such as Windows 1.0, Windows 2.0, and Windows 386. However, these were very primitive and were virtually unknown in the real world. As a result, most people consider the first generation of Windows to be the Windows 3 versions, collectively called Windows 3.*x*.

Even though these later versions acted like OSs, they still needed DOS in order to run. After the computer booted to DOS, you started Windows 3.*x* by typing the command WIN. When Windows 3.*x* started, the user was confronted with the cornerstone of Windows 3.*x*—the Program Manager (Figure 10-2).

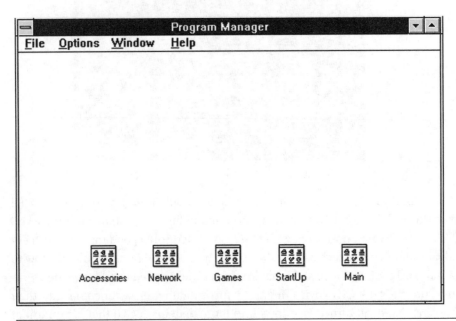

**Figure 10-2**  Windows 3.*x* Program Manager

Compared with a more advanced GUI such as the Desktop interface of Windows 9*x* or Windows 2000, the Program Manager was extremely limited. Windows 3.*x* had no Taskbar and no Start button with a handy listing of all installed programs. Instead, Windows 3.*x* users double-clicked special *Group* icons, which opened into windows containing icon pointers to related sets of programs. But at least Program Manager was graphical—much nicer than the DOS prompt!

## Structure

Although the Windows 3.*x* GUI left much to be desired, the inner workings of Windows 3.*x* created the cornerstone methodology and organization still used in Windows 9*x* (albeit greatly improved, as we will see later in this chapter). The Windows 3.*x* core consisted of three files: KRNL386.EXE, USER.EXE, and GDI.EXE. These three programs allocated and kept track of all system resources requested by applications. Each of these three files controlled a different set of resources. KRNL386.EXE controlled how programs used memory. USER.EXE handled user interface devices and determined how they affected the Windows system. GDI.EXE, the Graphics Device Interface, monitored and controlled the position of all the graphics on the screen. They used a number of special 64K storage areas of memory (called *heaps*) to keep track of which application used which resource.

Windows 3.*x* used a more primitive form of 386 protected mode multitasking called *cooperative multitasking*. Applications themselves were little more than requesters of resources. An application requested resources via very standardized subroutines, called the *application programming interface* (API). A program spoke to the Windows core directly or through a special file called a *dynamic link library* (DLL). A DLL acted as a storehouse of subroutines; some came pre-installed with Windows, some came with the compiler that created the application, and some were custom-made by the programmer. DLL files were distinctive in that they always ended with the extension DLL. In a cooperative multitasking environment, it was up to the applications themselves to ask for resources, run for a few milliseconds, and then stop running and let the next program run for a bit. The Windows core files could not control how long a program ran—what we call the *timeslice*. A programmer could easily write an application that did not release its timeslice, creating a number of problems for the system. The early history of Windows 3.*x* is filled with stories of ill-behaved programs that hogged the processor and never released their timeslices, resources, or both. Over time, programmers learned proper etiquette to make applications that worked well under the cooperative multitasking regime of Windows 3.*x*. It wasn't until Windows 95 that cooperative multitasking was replaced with something far better.

## Windows 3.x and DOS

It is absolutely imperative to understand that Windows 3.*x* needed DOS. This basic concept is often quite confusing to techs whose experience is limited to Windows 9*x*. To use Windows 3.*x*, you first bought a copy of DOS and installed it onto the PC. Then you installed Windows 3.*x*. Windows 3.*x* did not upgrade DOS. It did not erase or replace DOS. It ran, as we say, "on top of" DOS. DOS still booted the computer. CONFIG.SYS and AUTOEXEC.BAT still ran at boot. Windows 3.*x* did not start until the command

WIN was typed at the C: prompt. Many Windows 3.*x* systems put the WIN command in the AUTOEXEC.BAT, automatically starting Windows 3.*x* at boot and making the untrained person think that DOS was not part of the picture. Without a copy of DOS, Windows 3.*x* could not function.

Windows 3.*x* also used device drivers and *terminate and stay residents* (TSRs) loaded from CONFIG.SYS and AUTOEXEC.BAT. When Windows 3 came out, most hardware manufacturers were not willing to create special Windows 3 device drivers. Microsoft wanted people to be able to use their hardware even if the device used only DOS device drivers. When Windows 3.*x* loaded, it saw what DOS device drivers were loaded and used them. So, for example, if you wanted to use a CD-ROM drive in a Windows 3.*x* system, you still needed a CD-ROM driver in CONFIG.SYS and MSCDEX in AUTOEXEC.BAT (See Chapter 14 for CD-ROM device drivers and MSCDEX.) Granted, by the end of the Windows 3.*x* era we began to see special Windows device drivers, but they were rare. As a general rule, if you wanted to use a device in Windows 3.*x*, you needed DOS device drivers or TSRs.

### Disk Cache

While the early versions of Windows 3.*x* relied on SMARTDRV for disk caching, the last versions came out with a protected mode replacement to SMARTDRV called VCACHE. Windows 3.*x* required some manual configuration to make VCACHE run, but Windows 9*x* and Windows NT/2000 versions of VCACHE work automatically and invisibly. Because of VCACHE, no version of Windows 9*x* or Windows NT/2000 need SMART-DRV.

### Faster Drive Access

The last versions of Windows 3.*x* also overcame the final hurdle that prevented Windows from becoming a true OS-drive access. This took place through two different processes: 32-bit disk access (Fastdisk) and 32-bit file access (VFAT). Fastdisk is a protected mode method for skipping the system BIOS and enabling Windows to talk directly to the hard drive. VFAT is a 32-bit process that skips DOS for updating the FAT. Like VCACHE, both Fastdisk and VFAT are now standard equipment in all later versions of Windows.

### Swap Files

Because Windows 3.*x* ran in 386 protected mode, it took advantage of virtual memory. As explained in Chapter 2, virtual memory is an advanced function of 386 protected mode that enables the CPU to use mass storage devices (hard drives) as if they were RAM. When all of the real RAM had been used up by programs, the system could swap programs that it didn't need to this area of the hard drive, opening more space for programs currently active.

Virtual memory manifests itself through a special, hidden swap file. The swap file was very useful in Windows 3.*x*, due to the large amount of RAM used by the OS and applications and the very high price of DRAM in those days. Although Windows 3.*x* was the first Microsoft OS to use swap files, every later version of Windows uses them in basically the same fashion. Let's look at how a swap file works.

Let's assume you have a PC with 64MB of RAM. Figure 10-3 shows the system RAM as a thermometer with gradients from 0 to 64MB. As programs load, they take up RAM (Figure 10-4), and as more and more programs are loaded, more RAM is used (Figure 10-5).

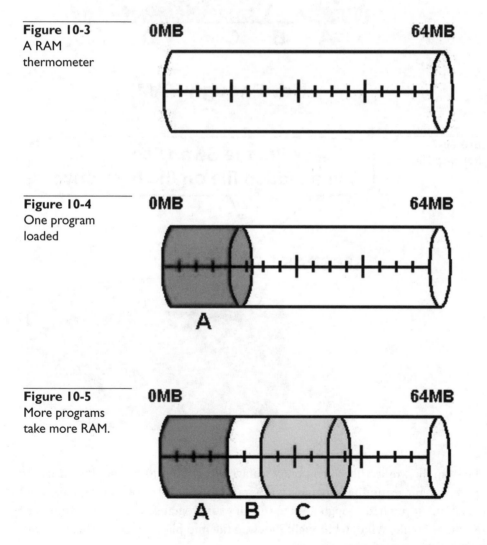

**Figure 10-3**
A RAM
thermometer

0MB      64MB

**Figure 10-4**
One program
loaded

0MB      64MB

A

**Figure 10-5**
More programs
take more RAM.

0MB      64MB

A   B   C

At a certain point, you won't have enough RAM to run any more programs (Figure 10-6). Sure, you could close one or more programs to make room for yet another program, but you can't keep all the programs running simultaneously. This is where Windows 3.*x* virtual memory came into play. Windows 3.*x* virtual memory created a swap file called 386SPART.PAR, which resided somewhere on your hard drive (see Figure 10-7).

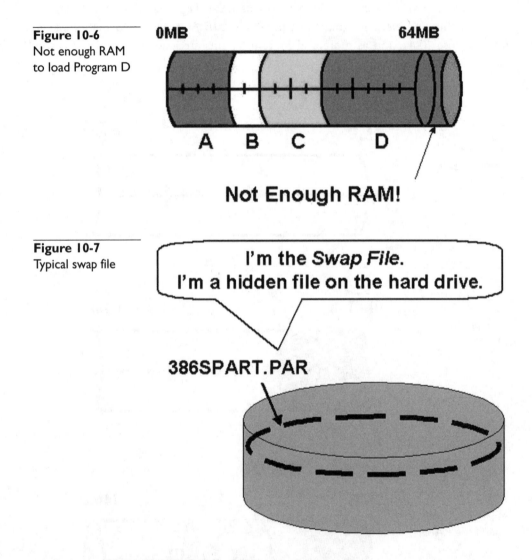

**Figure 10-6**
Not enough RAM
to load Program D

**Figure 10-7**
Typical swap file

The swap file worked like a temporary storage box (Figure 10-8). Windows used the swap file to remove running programs temporarily from RAM so other programs could load and run. If you had enough RAM to run all your programs, Windows did not need to use the swap file. Windows brought the swap file into play only when there was not enough RAM to run all open programs.

**Figure 10-8**
The swap file is like a storage box.

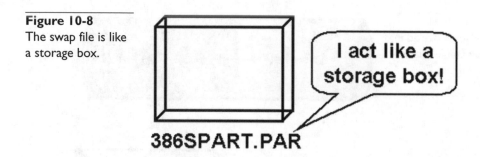

To load, Program D needs a certain amount of free RAM. Clearly, this requires that some other program (or programs) be unloaded from RAM without actually closing the program(s). Windows 3.*x* looks at all running programs, in this case A, B, and C, and decides which program is the least used. That program is then cut out of or swapped from RAM and copied into the swap file. In this case, Windows has chosen Program B (Figure 10-9). Unloading Program B from RAM provides enough RAM to load Program D (Figure 10-10).

**Figure 10-9**
Program B being unloaded from memory

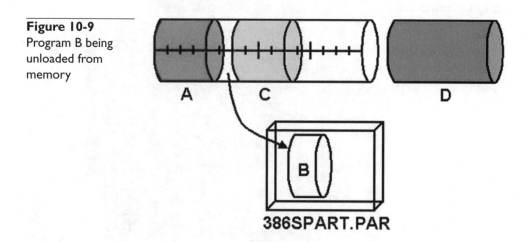

It is important to understand that none of this activity was visible on the screen! Program B's window was still visible along with those of all the other programs that were running. Nothing told the user that Program B was no longer in RAM (Figure 10-11).

So what happened if you clicked on Program B's window to bring it to the front? The program can't actually run from the swap file; it must be reloaded back into RAM. First, Windows decides which program must be removed from RAM, and this time Windows chooses Program C (Figure 10-12). Then it loads Program B into RAM (Figure 10-13).

**Figure 10-10**
Program B stored in the swap file—room for Program D

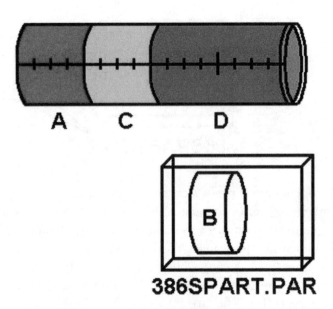

**Figure 10-11**
You can't tell if a program is swapped or not.

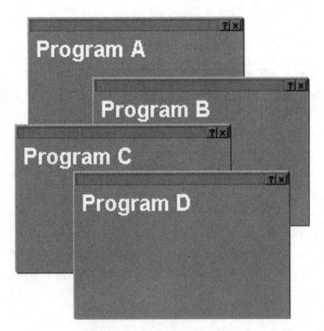

Swapping programs to and from the swap file and RAM takes time. Although no visual clues suggest that a swap is taking place, the machine will slow down quite noticeably as Windows performs the swaps. However, the alternative (Figure 10-14) is far less acceptable. Swap files were a crucial aspect of Windows 3.x operation and still

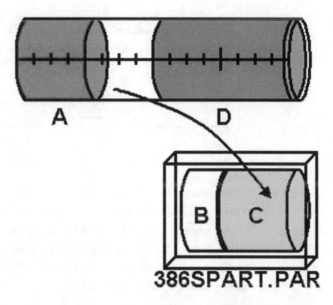

**Figure 10-12**
Program C is swapped to the swap file.

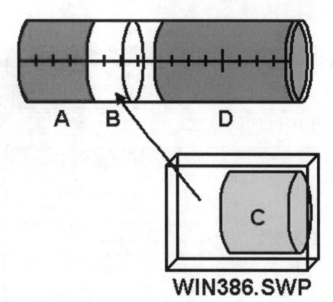

**Figure 10-13**
Program B is swapped back into RAM.

are important in the latest versions of Windows. Back in the Windows 3.x days, humans had to handle a number of issues with swap files that Windows 9x and Windows 2000 handle automatically, but a few hands-on issues still exist. Later in this chapter, you will see how to properly optimize a swap file for a Windows 9x system.

**Figure 10-14**
The alternative to
swap files

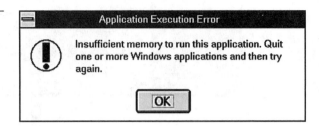

## INI Files

Windows 3.*x* used text files with the extension INI to initialize just about everything
from device drivers to applications to Windows itself. Any Windows 3.*x* computer had
at least three but usually dozens of these files stored in the \WINDOWS directory (Figure 10-15). Both Windows and Windows applications created initialization files.
Although Windows 9*x* and Windows 2000 rely much less on INI files, knowing how to
edit an INI file is crucial to repairing all Windows PCs.

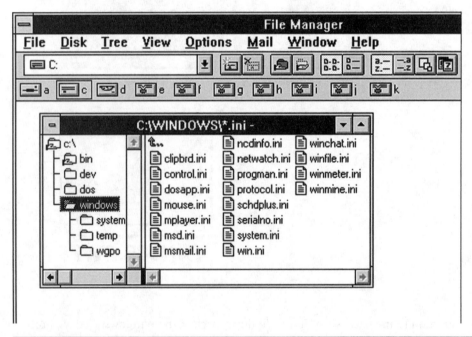

**Figure 10-15**   INI files in the Windows directory

All INI files are text files and thus can be edited with any text editor. You don't have to have Windows running; you can edit these files from a DOS prompt using EDIT or any other DOS-based word processor. All versions of Windows come with a handy GUI text editor called Notepad. Figure 10-16 shows Notepad displaying the contents of SERIALNO.INI, a typical INI file of the Windows 3.x days. SERIALNO.INI stored the registration information of the copy of Windows 3.x. Don't bother looking for this INI file on a Windows 9x or Windows 2000 system; it has been replaced by something else!

**Figure 10-16**
The contents of
SERIALNO.INI

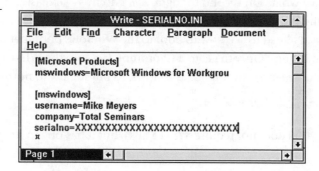

Note that all INI files are broken up into logical sections called *groups*. Each group starts with a word or words in square brackets, called a *group header*—for instance, [*mswindows*], as shown in Figure 10-16. Following each group header are the settings for that group. They are organized with the syntax *item=settings*. Although the typical Windows 3.x system used many INI files, two in particular require special consideration: SYSTEM.INI and WIN.INI.

## Test Specific

### SYSTEM.INI

SYSTEM.INI was the CONFIG.SYS of Windows. All the resources were initialized there, as well as a number of global settings that defined how resources were to be used. We often edited this file on Windows 3.x systems to tweak a large number of settings. The SYSTEM.INI file was absolutely required to run a Windows 3.x system. You still find SYSTEM.INI on all Windows systems today, including Windows 2000. Keeping the SYSTEM.INI file enables backward compatibility with older Windows 3.x applications that still look for a SYSTEM.INI file to load or determine critical settings. All Windows 9*x* systems still require SYSTEM.INI, even though the settings are no longer critical. If you don't believe me, rename the SYSTEM.INI file to YODA.INI on any version of Windows 9*x* and reboot the system. You'll get this nasty error:

```
Cannot find SYSTEM.INI.

You need to run Windows Setup again to install this file

Press any key to continue . . .
```

You know what? On second thought, *don't* do this—at least not until you learn how to access the Windows 9*x* boot menu later in the chapter! If by any chance you already did this, read ahead to see how to boot to the Windows boot menu. Boot to Safe Mode Command Prompt Only to get to a C: prompt. Get into the WINDOWS folder and type the REN (for *rename*) command, as follows, to put it back to normal:

```
REN YODA.INI SYSTEM.INI
```

Windows 2000 does not require SYSTEM.INI, but it has one to support older programs.

## WIN.INI

WIN.INI was the AUTOEXEC.BAT of Windows 3.*x*. It defined all the personalizations of Windows, such as fonts, screen savers, and display colors, and how resources interacted with applications. WIN.INI was also the dumping ground for settings that did not have a home anywhere else. This file was often manually edited. Windows 3.*x* didn't require WIN.INI to boot, but you lost a lot of functionality without it. Windows 9*x* and Windows 2000 rarely have a WIN.INI file unless an installed application makes one.

**TIP** Know how to edit SYSTEM.INI and WIN.INI on a Windows 9*x* and 2000 system. You can use EDIT.EXE, Notepad, or SYSEDIT to edit any text file, including AUTOEXEC.BAT, CONFIG.SYS, and INI files. Also, know why the INI files exist on Windows 3.*x* and Windows 9*x* systems and when they are needed!

### Dealing with SYSTEM.INI and WIN.INI

Windows 9*x* and Windows 2000 systems rarely need to bother with these two files, as all the sections in SYSTEM.INI and WIN.INI are properly created when Windows is installed and should never be changed. However, two situations warrant an occasional peek at these two files. First, we occasionally see an error in Windows 9*x* systems at boot that looks like this:

```
Cannot find a device file that may be needed to run Windows or a
Windows application.

The Windows Registry or SYSTEM.INI file refers to this device
file, but the device file no longer exists.

If you deleted this file on purpose, try uninstalling the associ-
ated application using its uninstall or setup program.

If you still want to use the application associated with this
device file, try reinstalling that application to replace the
missing file.

chimchim
Press a key to continue.
```

Notice the word "chimchim?" That's a line in the SYSTEM.INI file (probably) that needs correcting. Many applications and hardware install programs dump lines into the SYSTEM.INI that are in most cases useless. To edit the SYSTEM.INI file, use the handy SYSEDIT program (Figure 10-17). Note that the line in question is circled.

The [386Enh] section of SYSTEM.INI stores all the drivers for *386 enhanced mode*—Microsoft's term for the OS accessing the processor's 386 protected mode. Most of the problems associated with SYSTEM.INI on Windows 9x and 2000 systems can be attributed directly to drivers within this section. When I find these errors, I just add a semicolon (;) to the beginning of the offending line (turning it into a comment), and then reboot. These lines are rarely needed.

WIN.INI has two problem areas that can cause trouble on modern systems: LOAD= and RUN=. These lines automatically load programs when Windows starts, acting like a hidden Startup Group. If you find that a program keeps running but it isn't in a Startup Group, check here to see if one of these lines is starting the program.

Even though CompTIA claims it no longer covers Windows 3.x in the A+ Certification exams, don't think for a moment that legacy issues like INI files are not covered. By understanding Windows 3.x, you will find that many aspects of Windows 9x, and even to some extent Windows 2000, make a lot more sense. Like the spirits of Obi-wan, Anakin, and Yoda that Luke Skywalker sees in the final scene of *Return of the Jedi*, the spirits of Windows 3.x and DOS will be with us . . . always.

## Enter Windows 9x

The computing world rejoiced when Windows 95 arrived, thinking that all of the troubles that plagued PCs for years would be over. *Plug and Play* (PnP), 32-bit applications, the end of the command line . . . all promised something radically better than DOS and Windows 3.x. For the most part, Windows 95 delivered. For over five years, we have enjoyed Windows 95 and its many evolutions, including Windows 98 and Windows

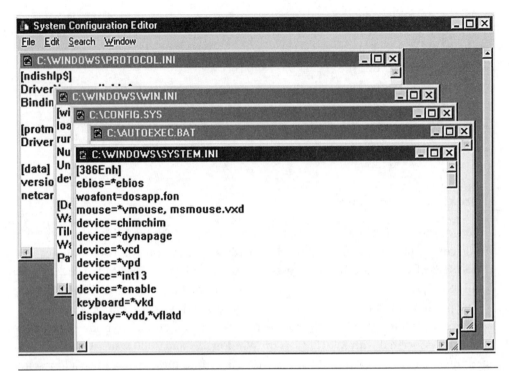

**Figure 10-17**  Editing the SYSTEM.INI file

ME—all of which we group together under the umbrella term of Windows 9x. Yet the great improvements provided by Windows 9x brought a host of new problems and issues that techs needed to handle. The A+ Certification exams test extensively on a number of issues related to Windows 9x systems: Windows installation, using Windows, version upgrading (patching), device installation, application install/uninstall, and general troubleshooting. You need to be up to speed on all these aspects of Windows 9x if you want to pass the tests.

## The Road to Windows 95

For years, Windows limped along as a series of patches to a program that started life as really no more than a test bed for Microsoft to experiment with new tools. The last versions of Windows 3.x had almost no commonality with the first versions of Windows, beyond the use of a graphical user interface. All of this patching and adding really showed in the large amount of technical support required to keep a Windows 3.x system running smoothly—I made a lot of money supporting Windows 3.x systems!

By 1993, Microsoft's vision of a real OS had shifted to a totally new OS called Windows NT (the latest version of NT, Windows 2000, is discussed in detail in Chapter 11). Although Windows NT had real power and avoided many of the problems inherent in the cobbled together Windows 3.*x*, it created its own problems as well. Windows NT lacked solid support for most applications written for DOS or for earlier versions of Windows, for example, and had massive hardware requirements that made it an unrealistic option for all but the most high-end systems. So how could Microsoft avoid creating two separate OS families, each requiring its own distinct set of applications? Microsoft knew that the huge installed base of applications running on the earlier systems would still have to be supported. They decided to create a series of interim OSs, adding more of the powerful NT features with each version, while still supporting older applications. These new OSs would have to require much lower-end hardware and substantially less technical support if they were to enjoy success in the market. This process began with Windows 95 (Figure 10-18).

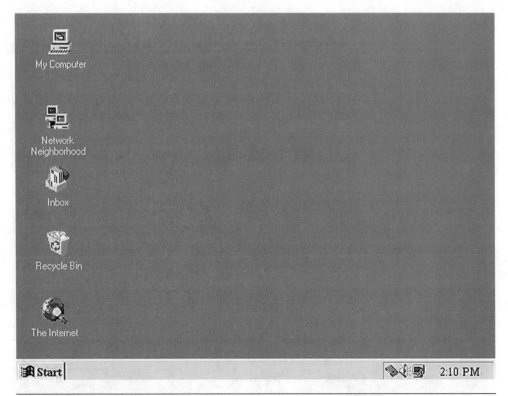

**Figure 10-18** Windows 95

Once you get past the pretty new interface, you'll see that in many ways Windows 95 (in fact every version of Windows 9*x*) is more evolutionary than revolutionary compared with Windows 3.*x*. Let's look under the hood of Windows 9*x* from the perspective of Windows 3.*x* and see how they compare.

## Windows 9x Still Needs DOS

One big difference touted between Windows 95 and Windows 3.*x* is that Windows 95 does not need DOS. This is really a matter of semantics. Windows 95 (and 98 and ME) still needs DOS, but instead of making you buy DOS separately, they come with a built-in copy. Both Windows 95 and Windows 98 still provide the ancient DOS utility called *Microsoft Diagnostics* (MSD) on the Windows installation CD-ROM. If you run the MSD that comes with Windows 95, it reports the OS as DOS 7, although the Windows 98 version of MSD reports the OS as Windows 4. See Figure 10-19.

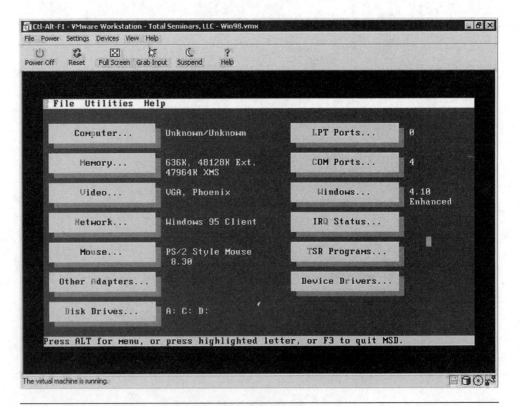

**Figure 10-19**   MSD shows the OS as Windows 4

While regular Windows users rarely see the DOS side of Windows 9x, as technicians we spend an inordinate amount of time staring at a C: prompt in Windows. Good thing you read the DOS chapter carefully, because I have no intention of repeating basic command prompt functions like creating folders (directories), moving around among folders, and performing basic file manipulations!

> **NOTE** Microsoft started calling directories "folders" in Windows 95, but most techs use the two terms interchangeably.

Windows still has MSDOS.SYS, IO.SYS, and COMMAND.COM, although you may not have COMMAND.COM in some circumstances. Although the names are the same, the functions have changed dramatically. We'll dive into these files in a moment.

## Core File Improvements

The big change from Windows 3.x to Windows 9x, and the one area that gets the least amount of attention, are the core files. Windows 9x still uses KRNL386.EXE, USER.EXE, and GDI.EXE as its core files, but it has turned them into real powerhouses. First, Windows 9x can perform true *preemptive multitasking*. "Preemptive" means that Windows 9x tells each application how much timeslice it receives and retains complete control of all system resources. The reason no one notices this is simply because it works so well. The nightmarish days of manually setting timeslices in Windows 3.x are no more than fading memories for a few old technicians like myself, and we don't miss those bad old days at all!

Additionally, the old 64K heap barrier that drove us batty (and created a whole industry of Windows 3.x optimization software) no longer plagues us in Windows 9x, which has more flexible and much bigger heaps—some heaps can grow to up to 2MB. The combination of preemptive multitasking and flexible heap size really makes Windows 9x far superior to the old Windows 3.x.

## Plug and Play

How could I dare list the improvements in Windows 9x without mentioning *Plug and Play* (PnP)? Compared with the old resource disasters of pre-PnP systems, PnP literally changed the job description of many PC technicians. Today's PnP world makes device installation so easy that it is more a user function than a tech job. The downside is that PnP has limitations and can sometimes create a real mess. PnP has turned device installation for PC technicians into a job where we don't really need to be there, but it's nice to have us around in case of problems! In this chapter, the entire device installation section really does little more than discuss those problems and how to fix them.

## Registry

Windows 3.*x*'s use of INI files created a bit of a problem in that you could have settings for a number of different aspects of the computer scattered among tens, possibly hundreds, of INI files across your computer. There was no standard format for INI files and no standard location, which made updates and uninstalling problematic at best. Realizing this, Microsoft created a new way to store system information for Windows 9*x*: the *registry*. The registry is composed of two binary files called SYSTEM.DAT and USER.DAT. These files reside in the \WINDOWS folder. The registry stores all the information about your PC, as well as information on all the hardware in the PC, network information, user preferences, file types, and virtually anything else you might run into with Windows 9*x*. Almost any form of configuration done to a Windows 9*x* system involves editing the registry. Fortunately, we rarely have to access these massive files directly. Instead, we rely on an entire set of relatively user-friendly applications to edit the registry for us.

## Safe Mode

Windows 3.*x* plagued us when a corrupted driver or simple misconfiguration prevented the PC from booting into Windows. Appreciating the many issues that prevented booting, Microsoft added the very handy Safe mode feature to all versions of Windows, including Windows 2000. Safe mode shuts down all of the advanced functions of Windows, such as the swap file, networking (optionally), and advanced video drivers. In most cases, Safe mode enables you to access Windows to make necessary adjustments or to reinstall drivers so that the system may then reboot normally.

## Built-in Driver Support

Windows 9*x* and Windows 2000 now include built-in driver support for a number of devices. Windows 9*x* automatically sees SCSI devices using the built-in Windows *Advanced SCSI Programming Interface* (ASPI) drivers (see Chapter 13 on SCSI) and CD-ROMs with built-in Windows *CD-ROM file system* (CDFS) drivers (see Chapter 14 on CD-ROM). Before Windows 9*x*, you had to add device drivers to access these devices. Windows 9*x* sees these devices as easily as DOS would see your floppy drive.

## Long Filenames

DOS and Windows 3.*x* both suffered from the ancient 8.3 naming convention. Windows 9*x* systems now allow filenames up to 255 characters while maintaining backward compatibility with the older 8.3 format. Additionally, Windows has extended the old 8-bit ASCII character set and created a new 16-bit Unicode character set. ASCII has only $2^8 = 256$ characters, but Unicode supports $2^{16} = 65,536$ characters. ASCII represents only Latin characters (a, A, b, B, c, D) and a few primitive drawing characters ($\uparrow$, $\llcorner$, =, $\leftrightarrow$), whereas Unicode supports virtually every text format known, including Cyrillic (Russian) and Kanji (Japanese) characters, as well as thousands of special drawing characters. The only trade-off with Unicode is that each character requires two bytes (16 bits) instead of 8 bits as in ASCII. Unicode fully supports the ASCII character set by making the first 256 characters identical to ASCII. So, the Greek symbol $\Sigma$ might be represented as 11100100 in ASCII, whereas in Unicode they just put eight 0's in the front to make 0000000011100100. All Windows applications now use Unicode. That's why you can add so many interesting symbols in Microsoft Word!

## FAT32

Later versions of Windows 95 and all versions of Windows 98, ME, and 2000 support the powerful FAT32 file format, enabling partitions up to 2 terabytes in size. Before FAT32, the old FAT16 format had a maximum partition size of only 2.1GB.

## And More

These only highlight some of the improvements in Windows 9x as compared with Windows 3.x. Many other improvements are more geared toward users and are of little interest to A+ Certification students, or are more advanced, requiring more discussion before we can bring them to light. But the improvements we've discussed, along with a rather large list we haven't mentioned, have made Windows 9x the single most popular OS available today.

## Windows 9x Version History

In its roughly six-year history, Windows 9x has seen more versions/revisions than any other previous Microsoft OS over an equivalent span of time. Every one of these versions has a unique version number. Simply trying to list the different version numbers of every variant of Windows 9x is rather difficult because Microsoft provided a large number of free improvements called *service packs* or *patches* over the years, which would then be incorporated into the next version of Windows. As a result, an earlier version of, say, Windows 95 with the service packs installed, could have nearly the same functionality as a later version. Free patches and service packs were (and still are) very nice, but Microsoft gives different version numbers for a version of Windows that you "patched" yourself versus a copy of Windows you purchase with the same patches. For the sake of simplicity, this listing includes only shrink-wrapped versions of Windows 9x—either versions that came with new systems or versions you could purchase in a store. We'll dive into the world of patches and service packs later in this chapter.

## Versions

You can determine the version number of any version of Windows, including Windows NT and Windows 2000, by double-clicking the System icon in the Control Panel and clicking the General tab. Figure 10-20 shows the location of the version number.

**Figure 10-20**
Determining the
Windows version

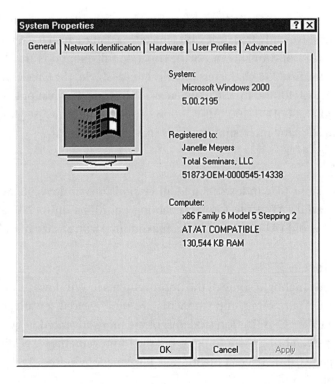

Table 10-1 lists all Windows 9x versions, the version number, and any noteworthy information. Remember, any version of Windows that has received a service pack or patch may show a version number not on this list. See the "Service Packs/Patches/Windows Update" section later in this chapter.

**Table 10-1** Common Windows 9x Versions

| VERSION | VERSION NUMBER | NOTES |
|---|---|---|
| Windows 95 Retail[1] | 4.00.950 | Original version |
| Windows 95 OEM[2] | 4.00.950 | Original version |
| Windows 95 Retail SP1[3] | 4.00.950A | Major bug fix |
| Windows 95 OEM SR2[4] | 4.00.1111 | Added FAT32, IE 3.0, NetMeeting 1.0, DirectX 2.0, bug fixes, other updates |
| Windows 95 OEM SR2.1 | 4.03.1212-1214 | Added USB support |
| Windows 95 OEM SR2.5 | 4.03.1214 | Added IE 4.01, Outlook Express, Internet Connection Wizard, DirectX 5.0, NetMeeting 2.1, Java VM, bug fixes |

**Table 10-1**   Common Windows 9x Versions (*continued*)

| VERSION | VERSION NUMBER | NOTES |
|---|---|---|
| Windows 98 Retail | 4.10.1998 | Original version |
| Windows 98 OEM | 4.10.1998 | Original version |
| Windows 98 SE | 4.10.2222A | Added IE 5, DirectX 6.1, NetMeeting 3.0, Media Player 6.2, bug fixes, other updates |
| Windows Millennium | 4.90.3000 | Original version |

[1]**Retail**   Available as retail product
[2]**OEM (original equipment manufacturer)**   Available only with a new PC
[3]**SP (Service Pack)**   General updates/enhancements
[4]**SR (Service Release)**   Replaced the term "Service Pack"

This table lists only *new* versions. Installing any of Microsoft's many free updates often changes the version number. We'll see these versions in the service pack section.

Okay! Now that we have a good overview of the Windows 9x family, let's really see how Windows 9x works. The best place to start is at the bottom, or in this case, at the *boot*. Let's look at the critical boot files of Windows 9x.

## Windows Boot Process

Windows 9x is really two products: a *DOS protected-mode interface* (DPMI) and a protected-mode GUI. The improved DOS part of Windows 9x looks and acts pretty much exactly like good old DOS. Windows 9x first starts the DOS aspect of Windows and then fires up the GUI. This means that you do not have to use the GUI to boot to Windows 9x!

> **NOTE**   Windows ME does not support a true DOS boot, but then again, it's not on the test!

This is important because many PC repair functions, particularly for the hard drive, are handled at a C: prompt. Do not confuse booting Windows 9x without the GUI with running a DOS window inside Windows 9x. They are completely different. For simplicity's sake (and to make Microsoft mad), I'll call this new and improved DPMI product DOS 7.

## DOS 7

Remember IO.SYS and MSDOS.SYS from older versions of DOS? They are still in Windows 9*x*, but all their functions have been combined into IO.SYS. MSDOS.SYS has been turned into a hidden, read-only text file in the root directory of the boot drive. MSDOS.SYS is used as a startup options file. COMMAND.COM is still there and still performs the same basic function as the old COMMAND.COM, providing the prompt. COMMAND.COM is no longer required if the system will always run in the GUI mode. But if a C:\ is ever needed, or if the system needs to use an AUTOEXEC.BAT file, COMMAND.COM must be present in the root directory. When the computer boots up and says "Starting Windows 95" or "Starting Windows 98," press the F8 key (for Windows 98, press the left CTRL key) and the Windows boot menu appears. We'll talk about this menu in a moment. For now, select Command Prompt Only. You will be at a DOS 7 prompt. Type **VER** and you'll see "Windows 95" or "Windows 98" as shown in Figure 10-21.

**Figure 10-21**
VER command at a
DOS prompt

```
C:\>ver

Windows 98  [version 4.10.2222]

C:\>
```

## Boot Menu

One of the many jobs of IO.SYS is to check to see if the F8 key (left CTRL key in Windows 98) has been pressed as Windows loads. If it has, the Windows boot menu loads. Let's take a look at the Windows boot menu.

The Windows boot menu provides a method for technicians to perform a number of boot methods "on the fly" to enable many different troubleshooting scenarios. Be warned that not all systems show the same boot options. Figure 10-22 shows a boot menu from a typical Windows 98 system.

**Figure 10-22**
Windows 98 boot
menu

```
Microsoft Windows 98 Startup Menu
=================================

   1. Normal
   2. Logged (\BOOTLOG.TXT)
   3. Safe mode
   4. Step-by-step confirmation
   5. Command prompt only
   6. Safe mode command prompt only

Enter a choice: 1
```

Although some of these options may seem obvious, others definitely need a bit of explaining. If you want to examine the boot menu for a bit, be sure to press the DOWN ARROW a few times, or the timer in the lower-right corner will boot the default option (usually the Normal option).

Some systems turn off the "Starting Windows 9x" text. In that case, just start pressing F8 at boot up. Don't hold down the key, press it about once a second until the boot menu shows up. If you miss, just restart the system and try again. Here's a list of the common boot menu options for Windows 9x:

- **Normal** This boots Windows normally.

- **Logged (\BOOTLOG.TXT)** This logs the boot process in a file called BOOT-LOG.TXT.

- **Safe mode** This boots Windows into Safe mode. (You can automatically boot into Safe mode by pressing the F5 key at boot.)

- **Safe mode with network support** This boots Safe mode but still loads the network drivers so you can access the network. This option only appears on networked systems—that does not include Dial-up Networking!

- **Step-by-step confirmation** Similar to the old DOS F8 step-by-step, this includes a number of auto-loading features that are normally invisible.

- **Command prompt only** This processes all startup files but does not start the GUI. You can type **WIN** from the C: prompt to start the GUI if desired.

- **Safe mode command prompt only** This skips all startup files to get to a C: prompt. You must reboot to start Windows.

- **Previous version of MS-DOS** If you installed Windows over a true DOS system, Windows keeps the original DOS boot files in the root directory with the extension DOS and shows this option. You may boot to them. Do not use this option if you do not have a previous version of DOS or if the version of Windows uses FAT32.

Take the time to make sure you can access the boot menu. We'll use this in some of the upcoming repair scenarios. Try all the options except for Previous Version Of MS-DOS. I especially suggest using the step-by-step option. You can see a number of very interesting options there!

## MSDOS.SYS

MSDOS.SYS is no longer the DOS kernel in DOS 7. It is now just a text file that replaces many of the AUTOEXEC.BAT and CONFIG.SYS functions that the system still needs before the GUI kicks in. A good Windows 9x tech should be comfortable editing an MSDOS.SYS file, so let's take a moment to see the contents of MSDOS.SYS. You may use any text editor to view or edit this file, but I prefer using the handy Notepad text editor. MSDOS.SYS has *hidden, system,* and *read-only* attributes by default, so you'll need to turn them off to see what's in this file. I don't use the ATTRIB command, although you certainly may if you want to make changing the attributes more of a challenge. I just boot to Windows, open the C: drive from My Computer, and make sure my Folder Options are set to show hidden and system files and that I can see the files' extensions.

In Windows 95, click the View | Options menu in the C: drive window and select the View tab. Select the "Show all files" radio button and make sure the "Hide MS-DOS file extensions for file types that are registered" check box is unselected.

In Windows 98, click the View | Folder Options menu in the C: drive window and select the View tab. Check the "Show all files" radio button and uncheck the "Hide file extensions for known file types" check box.

Click once on the MSDOS.SYS file to select it, and then alternate-click on the MSDOS.SYS file to show its properties. Uncheck the attributes as shown in Figure 10-23.

**Figure 10-23**
Changing file attributes

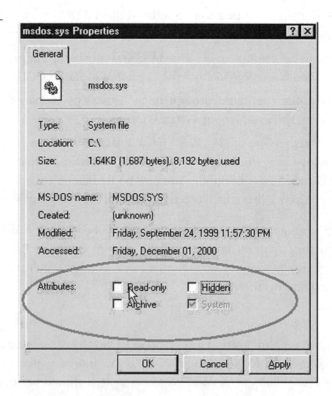

Now you can view the contents of MSDOS.SYS. Hold down the left SHIFT key and alternate-click on MSDOS.SYS again, but this time select the Open With option. (If you don't hold down the left SHIFT key, you won't see the Open With option.) Scroll through the list until you see Notepad, and make sure the "Always use this program to open this type of file" check box is unchecked. Click OK. Welcome to MSDOS.SYS. Do not make any changes! Just look! Click File | Exit when done.

Notice that MSDOS.SYS is organized just like an INI file with groups and options under each setting. The following options must be placed in the [Options] group. Each of the examples shows the default setting, but other settings are listed.

 **NOTE** I've added all the MSDOS.SYS settings I know of, but that certainly doesn't mean you'll use all of them! Most of these settings have default values that you do not want to change.

- **BootConfig**=1   This enables the computer to boot up a particular hardware configuration. For example, BootConfig=2 would start configuration 2.

- **DisableLog**=1   This enables the BOOTLOG.TXT file (0 = disable). See the "LOG Files" section later in this chapter.

- **SystemReg**=1   This loads the system registry (0 = don't load).

- **BootSafe**=0   This option does not force the machine to boot in Safe mode (1 = force Safe mode).

- **DRVSpace**=1 or **DBLSpace**=1   This loads DoubleSpace or DriveSpace drivers (0 = don't load). See disk compression in the FAT32 discussion later in this chapter.

- **BootWin**=1   This boots Windows (0 = DOS). This is a dangerous option and should never be used unless you installed a true DOS before you installed Windows and you only have FAT16 partitions.

- **BootWarn**=1   This shows the "You Are in Safe mode" warning message (0 = don't show). Why anyone would ever change this is beyond me!

- **BootKeys**=1   This specifies using the function keys (like F8) at boot (0 = no keys). Nice for keeping nosy users out of places they shouldn't go.

- **BootGUI**=1   This specifies booting the Windows 9x GUI (0 = DOS prompt only). I use this when I'm working on a system that I intend to reboot to a command prompt many times.

- **Network**=1 This shows boot in Safe mode, with a networking menu option available (0 = don't show). I use this option when I know I'm going to need to pull a driver off a server somewhere. Doesn't everyone keep all the drivers they use for every system on a server? You don't?

- **BootMenu**=0 This does not automatically load boot menu at boot (1 = show menu). I like to use this when I'm working on systems.

- **BootMenuDefault**=1 This shows the default boot menu option if you don't pick one:

  1 = Normal
  2 = Logged to Bootlog.txt
  3 = Safe mode
  4 = Safe mode with network support (if network settings are enabled)
  4 (if no networking) or 5 (if networking enabled) = Step-by-step
  5 (no networking) or 6 (networking) = Command prompt
  6 (no networking) or 7 (networking) = Safe mode command prompt
  7 (no networking) or 8 (networking) = Previous version of MS-DOS (if Boot-Multi=1)

I've never used this option.

- **DoubleBuffer**=1 This loads VFAT's double buffer (0 = don't load). Obsolete command for older SCSI drives.

- **BootMulti**=0 This is for dual-boot systems. If set to 0, the boot menu will not prompt for the previous version of MS-DOS in the boot menu. If set to 1, you will see the option "Previous version of MS-DOS." Don't mess with this option unless a) you installed on top of DOS and b) you did not use FAT32.

- **Logo**=1 This shows an animated logo (0 = don't show).

- **LoadTop**=1 This loads COMMAND.COM at the top of 640K (0 = load at the bottom). See Chapter 12 for explanation.

- **BootDelay**=X This specifies how long the computer waits, in seconds, after showing "Starting Windows 9*x*." Many techs set this to "0" to make booting faster.

- **AutoScan**=1 This option specifies whether ScanDisk runs automatically when you reboot after a crash. If you set this to 0, ScanDisk will not run. Set to 1 means the system will prompt you before running, and set to 2 means Windows will run ScanDisk without asking your approval (although it will prompt before making changes/fixes). This is only usable in OSR2 and later versions of Windows 9*x*.

The following options must be in the [Paths] group:

- **UninstallDir**=C:\   This specifies where to find the Windows 9*x* uninstall file.

- **WinDir**=C:\WINDOWS   This specifies the location of the Windows GUI files.

- **WinBootDir**=C:\WINDOWS   This specifies the location of the Windows files needed to boot. It is normally the same as the WinDir directory.

- **HostWinBootDrv**=C   This is always the C: drive.

Please don't kill yourself trying to memorize all these features. Do take the time to appreciate that MSDOS.SYS is now a text file. Make sure you know how to edit it if asked, and have a general idea of the types of options it provides. Take some time to appreciate what it does and does not do. Does it load device drivers or TSRs? No. Does it provide a number of boot options? Yes. Think about how some of these options might come in handy in a troubleshooting scenario.

## Safe Mode

When problems arise in Windows, we usually turn immediately to Safe mode as a first attempt at a fix. Safe mode turns off almost everything on your system. You can always tell you're in Safe mode by the distinct look at boot (Figure 10-24).

Among other items, Safe mode turns off any fancy video settings, so your icons will look strange. Don't worry, as soon as you reboot, they will return to normal. Safe mode turns off access to just about everything. You will not have access to the CD-ROM, printer, or many devices on the system. But you *do* have access to the tools you need to zero in on a malfunctioning device or software. If Windows fails to shut down properly, it instantly goes into Boot mode upon reboot, highlighting the Safe mode option. Let it go into Safe mode, and then restart the computer normally. Remember, you don't have to access the boot menu to access Safe mode, just press the F5 key at boot.

## Backwards Compatibility

Windows 9*x* holds complete backward compatibility to CONFIG.SYS, AUTOEXEC.BAT, SYSTEM.INI, and WIN.INI. In most cases, we enjoy the benefits of the backward support it provides to older hardware and software. On the bad side, if Windows detects a DOS or Windows 3.*x* driver, it won't bother loading its own, usually far superior driver. This may create problems when installing devices, as we will see.

## The Registry

The boot files start the system and the core files run the GUI, but the registry stores all the data that defines your system—from user names to hardware settings. Think of the

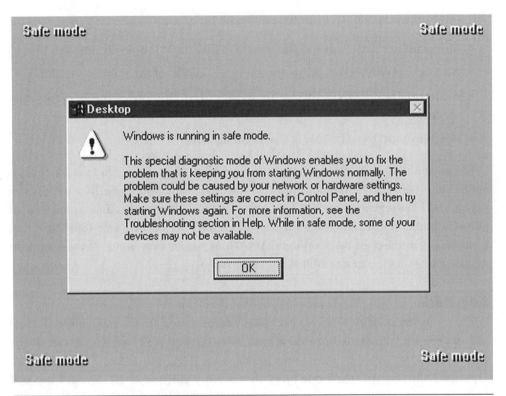

**Figure 10-24**  Windows 98 Safe mode

registry as the central repository of all configuration information for your system. Even applications store their configuration information there. In later sections, we discuss backing up and restoring the registry, but for now let's take a close look at this most critical component.

The idea of the registry is to have one common database for the entire PC. In a perfect world, the registry replaces CONFIG.SYS, AUTOEXEC.BAT, and every INI file. Windows 9x will, however, still read all INI files at boot time for backward compatibility with Windows 3.x programs that use them, and it will also read CONFIG.SYS and AUTOEXEC.BAT if they are present. Because of its critical importance, Windows creates backups of the two registry files, SYSTEM.DAT and USER.DAT, every time it starts. These backup copies are also stored in the \WINDOWS folder and have the extension DA0.

The registry is almost never accessed directly. It is meant to work in the background, quietly storing all necessary data for the system and being updated only by the actions of a few menus and installation programs. Unfortunately, the reality is that a technician will need to manipulate the registry from time to time. Therefore, let's take some time so you can become comfortable with accessing and changing the registry.

## Accessing the Registry

The main way to access the registry is through the Control Panel (Figure 10-25). You can get to the Control Panel in several ways. Double-click on the My Computer icon on your desktop, and select the Control Panel icon. Double-click and you're there. Alternately, go to Start | Settings | Control Panel. Notice all the applets in the Control Panel; their only function is to update the registry via fairly intuitive interfaces.

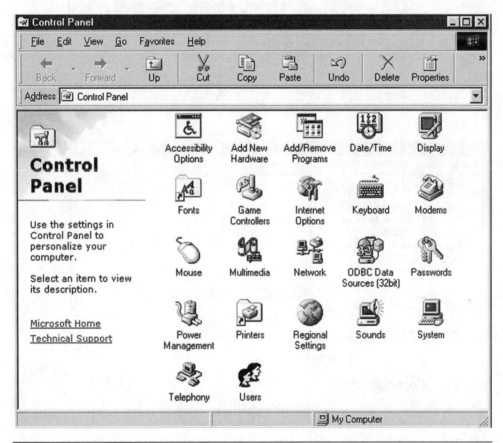

**Figure 10-25** Windows 98 Control Panel

In Windows 3.*x*, many necessary options were not available in the Control Panel, forcing you to open the SYSTEM.INI file directly to make changes. So far, this is basically untrue in Windows 9x. Everything necessary to configure the system so it works can be handled from the Control Panel, although the occasional tweak does comes along that requires direct registry access. When you want to access the registry directly, you must use the Registry Editor. To start the Registry Editor, go to Start | Run and type **REGEDIT** (Figure 10-26). This will start the Registry Editor (Figure 10-27). Remember that the registry files are binary. You cannot edit the registry with EDIT, Notepad, or any other text editor as you could with SYSTEM.INI. You must use REGEDIT.

**Figure 10-26**
Opening REGEDIT

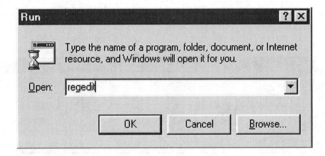

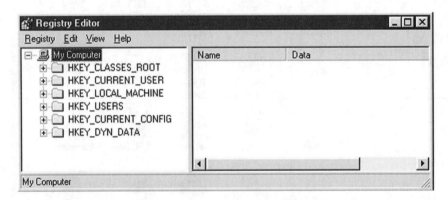

**Figure 10-27**   The Registry Editor

## Registry Components

The registry is organized in a tree structure similar to the folders in the PC. Once you open the Registry Editor, you see six main subgroups or *root keys*:

- HKEY_CLASSES_ROOT
- HKEY_CURRENT_USER
- HKEY_LOCAL_MACHINE
- HKEY_USERS
- HKEY_CURRENT_CONFIG
- HKEY_DYN_DATA

Try opening one of these root keys, and note that more subkeys are listed underneath them. A subkey also has other subkeys or *values*. Figure 10-28 shows an example of a subkey with some values. Notice that REGEDIT shows keys on the left and values on the right, just as Windows Explorer shows directories on the left and files on the right.

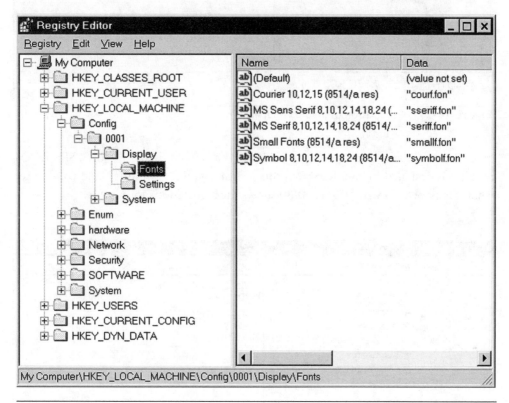

**Figure 10-28**   Typical keys and values

When writing about keys and values, I'll use the expression *key = value*. The secret to understanding the registry is to understand the function of the six root keys first. Each of these root keys has a specific function, so let's take a look at them individually.

### HKEY_CLASSES_ROOT

This root key defines the standard *class objects* used by Windows 9x. A class object is a named group of functions. Pretty much everything that has to do with files on the system is defined by a class object.

For example, a MIDI sound file is defined using two class objects. If you search the registry for the MID file extension, you will find the first class object, which associates the MID file extension with the name "midfile" (Figure 10-29).

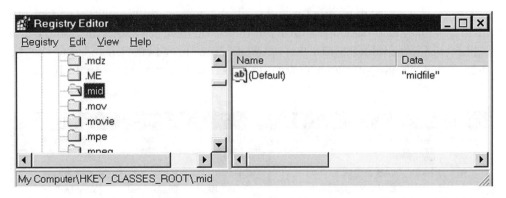

**Figure 10-29**   Association of .mid to midi files

Ah, but what are the properties of midfile? That's what the HKEY_CLASSES_ROOT root key is designed to handle. Search this section again for "midfile," and you can see what it is associated with. Figure 10-30 shows the associations for midfile.

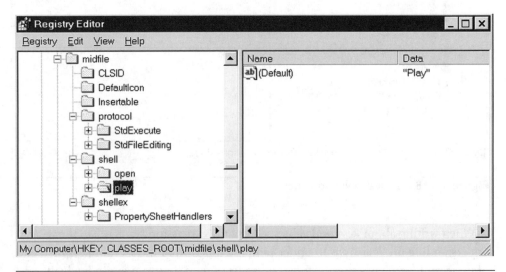

**Figure 10-30**   Midfile settings

As you can see, this subkey tells the system everything that needs to be known about a particular software item. It's here that the file associations are defined, icons are shown, and options are displayed when an item is alternate-clicked. Although it is possible to change these settings via REGEDIT, the normal way is to use the View | Options menu from Windows Explorer (Figure 10-31).

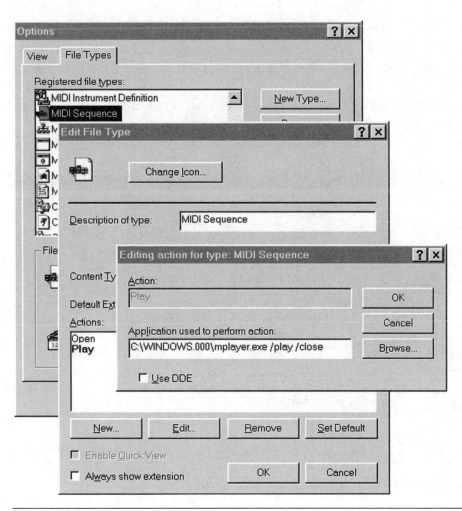

**Figure 10-31** Changing association options

## HKEY_USERS and HKEY_CURRENT_USER

Windows 9x can be configured to support more than one user on the same PC, storing personalized information such as colors, screen savers, and the contents of the Desktop. HKEY_USERS stores all of the personalization information for all users on a PC. HKEY_CURRENT_USER stores the current user settings, which makes it a good place to fix personalizations like fonts, icons, and colors on systems that are set up to support multiple users.

### HKEY_LOCAL_MACHINE

This root key contains all the data for a system's nonuser-specific configurations. This includes every device in your PC, including devices that you have removed. For example, Figure 10-32 shows the description of a SCSI Zip drive. You'll be seeing more of HKEY_LOCAL_MACHINE later in this chapter when we discuss configuration and repairing hardware in Windows 9x.

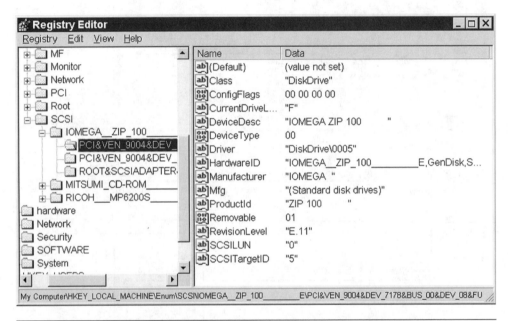

**Figure 10-32**   Registry information for a SCSI Zip drive

### HKEY_CURRENT_CONFIG

If values in HKEY_LOCAL_MACHINE have more than one option, such as two different monitors, this root key defines which one is currently being used. Because most people have only one type of monitor and similar equipment, this area is almost never touched.

### HKEY_DYN_DATA

This is registry data stored in RAM to speed up system configuration. A snapshot of all hardware in use is stored here. It is updated at boot and when any changes are made in the system configuration file.

**TIP** Make sure you know the six root keys of the registry.

## The Windows 9x GUI

The magic of Windows 9x starts when the GUI starts. Remember that it is a protected-mode overlay of the DOS 7 shell (Figure 10-33).

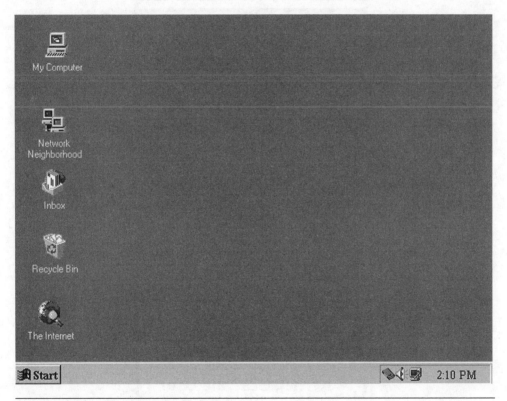

**Figure 10-33** The Windows 95 GUI shell

## The Windows 9x GUI

The GUI loads its own device drivers for everything. Assuming a Windows 9x device driver is available, you don't need CONFIG.SYS to load device drivers anymore. Windows 9x does everything CONFIG.SYS does. So again, assuming Windows 9x drivers are available, you do not need CONFIG.SYS. In addition, the GUI provides protected-mode mouse support for Windows 95, Windows 3.*x*, and DOS applications, so you probably don't need AUTOEXEC.BAT or WIN.INI either. Figure 10-34 shows how the GUI is organized.

**Figure 10-34**
GUI architecture

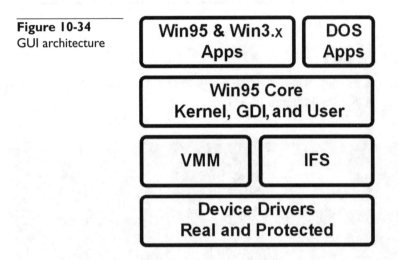

## Windows Structure

The lowest levels of Windows 9*x* are the device drivers—either real-mode drivers loaded at CONFIG.SYS or AUTOEXEC.BAT, or protected-mode drivers loaded with the GUI (Figure 10-35).

**Figure 10-35**
Device drivers

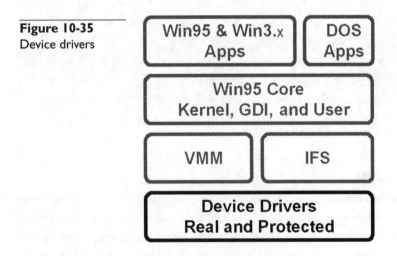

After the device drivers comes the *virtual memory manager* (VMM), which supports memory usage at both the DOS 7 and GUI levels. At the DOS 7 level, VMM does little more than load a simple DOS. When the GUI is loaded, VMM takes advantage of the power of 386 protected mode to create *virtual machines*, one for Windows 9x and one for each DOS program running in Windows 9x. At the same level as the VMM is the *installable file system* (IFS), which provides support for hard, CD-ROM, and network drives. The IFS also provides the support for long filenames. DOS 7, as well as the GUI, require the IFS. See Figure 10-36.

**Figure 10-36**
VMM and IFS

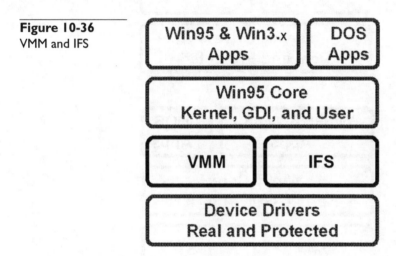

When the GUI is running, the main functions of Windows 9x are handled by the kernel, user, and *graphical device interface* (GDI) modules. These three modules perform the same basic functions that they did in Windows 3.x but provide much more power and flexibility. Most functions run in full 32-bit protected mode, whereas in Windows 3.x, most functions ran in 16-bit real mode, as shown in Figure 10-37.

At the top of the Windows 9x architecture is the user interface (Figure 10-38), which is what you actually *see* on the screen: the icons, windows, and toolbars. Windows 9x can use the default interface, the Windows 3.x interface, or even other shells. The GUI also enables the use of older Windows 3.x applications and DOS applications run within the GUI.

## Windows 9x Power

Okay, now, we're really getting some knowledge! We understand the structure of Windows 9x and have seen the boot sequence and the many boot options available. Most importantly, I hope you're starting to appreciate the power and the flexibility of the Windows 9x OS. Let's move now to how Windows accesses files.

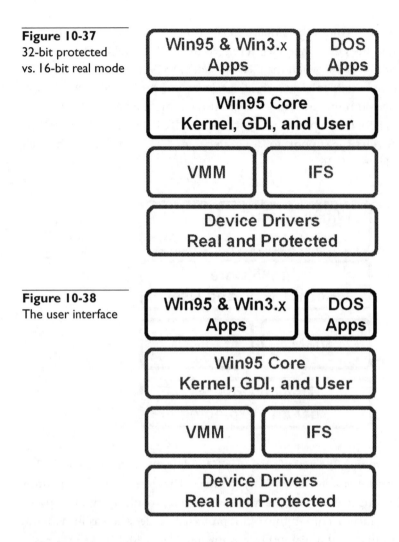

**Figure 10-37**
32-bit protected
vs. 16-bit real mode

**Figure 10-38**
The user interface

## Long Filenames

A major improvement in Windows 9x is *long filenames* (LFNs). LFNs remove the old 8.3 filename limitation of DOS. LFN support works whether you are using the DOS 7 or GUI shell. In the hard drive chapter, we showed how filenames are stored in special directory entries along with their date, byte size, attributes, and starting cluster, but we never really discussed how the directory structure works. In a regular DOS 8.3 directory, each file record in a directory requires 32 bytes. Table 10-2 shows the organization of a typical DOS file listing in a directory. (Remember, each ASCII character needs one byte.)

**Table 10-2**  Typical DOS 8.3 File Entry in a Directory

| SIZE IN BYTES | DESCRIPTION |
|---|---|
| 8 | Filename |
| 3 | Extension |
| 1 | Attributes (each attribute only needs one bit) |
| 10 | Reserved |
| 2 | Time |
| 2 | Date |
| 2 | Starting cluster number |
| 4 | File size |

LFNs exist on FAT partitions by creating an extra filename listing to store chunks of the LFN. Windows still uses one normal directory entry for the short name, but it reorganizes LFN directory entries as follows in Table 10-3.

**Table 10-3**  LFN Entry in a Directory

| SIZE IN BYTES | DESCRIPTION |
|---|---|
| 1 | LFN record sequence and flags byte |
| 10 | First part of long filename (Unicode) |
| 1 | Attributes |
| 1 | Reserved |
| 1 | Check sum for short filename |
| 12 | Second part of long filename (Unicode) |
| 2 | Always 00000000 |
| 4 | Third part of long filename (Unicode) |

Notice that each LFN entry uses 26 bytes, divided into three parts, to store the LFN characters. Because each character in Windows is Unicode, we can store a maximum of 13 characters in each LFN entry.

When an LFN is saved, the system first creates a short name by taking the first six characters that are not spaces, periods, or other illegal characters for the 8.3 standard, and adds a "~" and a number, starting with the number 1. If a large number of files are saved that share the same first six characters, Windows just contracts the next one to four characters and adds its own characters. Let's look at an example:

```
This is one heck of a long filename, don't you think.doc
```

Windows first saves a short name to an 8.3 filename (THISIS~1.DOC) and stores it in ASCII (not Unicode) in a regular directory entry like the one shown in Table 10-4. Notice that although Table 10-4 lists the values as text for readability, in real life they would be binary.

**Table 10-4**  Typical 8.3 Entry for Windows

| NAME | EXTENSION | ATTRIBUTES | RESERVED | TIME | DATE | STARTING CLUSTER | FILE SIZE |
|------|-----------|------------|----------|------|------|------------------|-----------|
| THISIS~1 | DOC | | | 7:30AM | 10/11/01 | 3ABC | 342834 |

Once Windows saves the short name, it begins chopping up the LFN into 13-character chunks and creates as many LFN entries as needed. These are placed directly behind the short name entry. Again, in Table 10-5 I've added text where, in reality, it would all be binary. Windows adds 40 in hex to the last LFN entry to signify the end of the long filename.

**Table 10-5**  LFN Entries for the File (don't forget, spaces are characters too!)

| RECORD NUMBER | 1ST PART 5 CHARS | ATTRIBUTES | RESERVED | CHECK SUM | 2ND PART 6 CHARS | ALWAYS ZEROS | 3RD PART 2 CHARS |
|---------------|------------------|------------|----------|-----------|------------------|--------------|------------------|
| 45 | k.doc | | | | | 00000000 | |
| 4 | on't | | | | you th | 00000000 | in |
| 3 | File | | | | name, | 00000000 | d |
| 2 | eck o | | | | f a lo | 00000000 | ng |
| 1 | This | | | | is one | 00000000 | h |

This is great, but it must be backwardly compatible with DOS programs and with DOS itself. To make LFNs compatible really means to make sure that DOS ignores the LFN entries in the directory structure. This is achieved by giving LFN entries the bizarre attribute combination of hidden, read-only, system, and volume label—the equivalent of 00001111. No instructions in DOS code deal with this combination of attributes, so DOS simply ignores them. Let's combine the two tables, leaving off the titles, to show a complete directory entry in Table 10-6.

**Table 10-6**  Complete Directory Entry for an LFN in Windows (don't forget, spaces are characters too!)

| NAME | EXTENSION | ATTRIBUTES | RESERVED | TIME | DATE | STARTING CLUSTER | FILE SIZE |
|------|-----------|------------|----------|------|------|-------------------|-----------|
| THISIS~1 | DOC | | | 7:30AM | 10/11/01 | 3ABC | 342834 |
| 45 | k.doc | 00001111 | | | | 00000000 | |
| 4 | on't | 00001111 | | | you th | 00000000 | in |
| 3 | file | 00001111 | | | name, | 00000000 | d |
| 2 | eck o | 00001111 | | | f a lo | 00000000 | ng |
| 1 | This | 00001111 | | | is one | 00000000 | h |

Unfortunately, old DOS disk utilities see LFN entries as errors and will erase them. It is crucial that you *never* run any old disk utility not specifically designed to support LFNs on a Windows 9x computer.

Windows 9x has also added some great new bits of file information, the best one being a "last accessed" date value that tells you when a particular file was last used. This includes executables, dynamic link libraries, and other non-user data files like font files. This is very handy for asking questions such as, "When was the last time you used Excel on this machine?"

All this extra information is stored with the file listing in the directory, of course! Remember the first table that showed a typical DOS directory file listing? Look at it again. See the 10 bytes of reserved area? Guess what Microsoft did? Yup, they now use it for storing the creation date and time as well as the last access date. Compare Table 10-7 with the earlier DOS table.

**Table 10-7**  Typical Windows 8.3 File Entry in a Directory

| SIZE IN BYTES | DESCRIPTION |
|---------------|-------------|
| 8 | Filename |
| 3 | Extension |
| 1 | Attributes (each attribute only needs one bit) |
| 1 | Case (converts all characters to uppercase—rarely used) |
| 1 | Creation time in milliseconds (rarely used) |
| 2 | Creation time |

**Table 10-7**  Typical Windows 8.3 File Entry in a Directory (*continued*)

| SIZE IN BYTES | DESCRIPTION |
|---|---|
| 2 | Creation date |
| 2 | Last access date |
| 2 | Reserved |
| 2 | Time |
| 2 | Date |
| 2 | Starting cluster number |
| 4 | File size |

Notice that we just used eight of the ten bytes of the reserved area. The problem now is what to do with the old date and time. Interestingly, these usually reflect the date that the file was last modified, as opposed to the date it was last accessed. Most modern programs update the access date and the old date and time simultaneously, so you really can't count on those old date and time values anymore.

## FAT32

When Windows 95 first came out, it introduced no new disk structures at all. Partitions and formats were good old DOS FAT16, identical to DOS with the exception of LFNs and creation/modified dates. You still needed FDISK and FORMAT to set up hard drives. A hard drive that was formatted with DOS was basically identical, well, at least as completely usable, as a drive formatted with Windows 95. This changed in 1996 with the introduction of a new format: FAT32.

Let me begin by saying FAT32 is optional on all versions of Windows. You don't have to use it if you don't want to, as FAT16 runs just fine with every version of Windows, including Windows 2000. But just because you *can* use FAT16 doesn't mean you should. FAT32 enhancements make it the formatting standard for all but the oldest Windows 95 systems. The only downside to FAT32, and this really isn't much of a downside, is that DOS, Windows NT, and the first versions of Windows 95 cannot read FAT32 formatted drives.

When it was first introduced, you could not buy Windows 95 with FAT32 off the shelf. It only came with new systems under Windows 95 version OSR2. Microsoft had a darn good reason to do this; they didn't want you to install Windows OSR2 onto a DOS system, upgrade the file format to FAT32, and then go into the boot menu and select "Previous version of MS-DOS." If you did, you seriously trashed the system, and Microsoft didn't want the support calls.

**NOTE** Windows 98 and Windows 2000 support FAT32 right out of the box. With Windows 95, however, only OSR2 supports FAT32.

FAT32 has some great advantages over FAT16. First is the reduced cluster size. As you'll remember from the chapter on hard drives, one of the big downsides to FAT16 is the way clusters are used by the system. A cluster is composed of sectors. Each sector is 512 bytes, and the size of each cluster is determined by the size of the partition. For example, if a partition is between 512MB and 1GB, there are 32 sectors/cluster. If a partition is between 1 and 2GB, there are 64 sectors/cluster. The cluster is the single smallest unit of storage on a hard drive, so if you create a 1-byte text file and save it in a 1.5GB partition, that 1-byte file will use one 64-sector cluster. That 64-sector cluster is 32KB, resulting in a dramatic loss of disk space. FAT32 clusters are only 4KB and seriously reduce the amount of wasted cluster space.

Secondly, FAT32 has no limit on the number of root directory entries. With FAT16, the root directory is a fixed structure and can contain no more than 255 entries. With FAT32, the root directory is treated like any other directory and can have an unlimited number of entries. Finally, FAT32 is more redundant. With FAT16, you have only one boot sector. If the boot sector is damaged, you can't boot up the system. FAT32 stores two copies of the boot sector, so if one boot sector is damaged, you can recover from the backup copy, assuming you have a good utility that knows how to use it.

FAT32 is completely compatible with all DOS and Windows applications, but you must never use any disk utilities unless they are designed for FAT32!

You set up and install FAT32 the same way you install FAT16—by using FDISK and FORMAT. When you run the FAT32-enabled OSR2 (or Windows 98/ME) FDISK, it asks you if you want "Support for large disks." If you answer yes, everything you do in FDISK will be FAT32. If you say no, everything will be FAT16. When you run OSR2 FORMAT, it reads what type of partition is made and formats accordingly—very simple.

FAT32 has only one potential problem: the FAT itself. Think about this for a second. With FAT16, we know that we have $2^{16}$ or 65,536 entries. Each entry stores 16 bits (2 bytes) of data. That means a FAT16 file allocation table will be exactly 2 bytes $\times$ 65,536 = 131,072 bytes. Big, but no big deal on today's multi-gigabyte hard drives. In fact, FAT16 stores two copies of the FAT. Who cares, even a 10MB hard drive can spare ~262,000 bytes for the FAT!

Now let's do this math one more time, except using FAT32. FAT32 handles $2^{32}$ or 4,294,967,296 entries in its FAT table. Each entry stores 32 bits (4 bytes) of data. So that means, unless we come up with an alternative, a FAT32 file allocation table will weigh in at 4 bytes $\times$ 4,294,967,296 = 17,179,869,184 bytes! That's 17GB just for the FAT!

Actually, Microsoft was aware of this long before they released FAT32, and they created a simple answer: They made the FAT only as big as was necessary for the drive. Let's say you have a 4GB drive that you want to make one big C: drive with FAT32. If you check back in Chapter 8, you know that FAT32 makes 4K (4,096 byte) clusters for a 4GB partition. So, that means we need 4GB = 4,000,000,000 / 4,096 = 976,563 entries to make a FAT big enough to store info on every cluster. 4 bytes $\times$ 976,563 = 3,906,252 or almost 4MB. Big, but bearable. To save space, FAT32 only makes one copy of the FAT.

Ah, great, so we can handle the larger FAT, but didn't you forget something? What does every file's directory entry store? The starting cluster! But now we have 32-bit cluster values, not just 16-bit. How do we store a 32-bit cluster value in our file's directory entry? Easy! Remember the two bytes (16 bits) left in the reserved area after we stole some of it for the creation and modification date/time? You got it! Microsoft used the last 2 bytes of the reserved area to store the extra cluster information. Table 10-8 shows a file's directory information in FAT32.

**Table 10-8**   Typical Windows FAT32 File Entry in a Directory

| SIZE IN BYTES | DESCRIPTION |
| --- | --- |
| 8 | Filename |
| 3 | Extension |
| 1 | Attributes (each attribute only needs one bit) |
| 1 | Case |
| 1 | Creation time in milliseconds (rarely used) |
| 2 | Creation time |
| 2 | Creation date |
| 2 | Last Access Date |
| 2 | **First part of starting cluster number** |
| 2 | Time |
| 2 | Date |
| 2 | **Last part of starting cluster number** |
| 4 | File size |

I'd say it's a safe bet that we won't be seeing any improvements made to FAT32; we've run out of unused space in our directory entries! But with the ability to support partitions up to 2 terabytes, I think we're okay, at least for the next year or so.

One other potential downside to FAT32 is that it does not support disk compression. Back in the DOS days when hard drives were small and cost a lot of money, a little company called Stac Electronics came up with a method of squishing the data on a FAT16 partition so that you could get, on average, about 50 percent more space on the drive. They sold a program called Stacker that performed this compression. Microsoft copied the idea, called their disk compression program DoubleSpace, and included it for free with DOS 6.2. Stac Electronics sued Microsoft and won. Microsoft paid the fine and came up with their own method that they called DriveSpace and gave it away with DOS 6.22.

With the big, cheap drives of today, compression has become much less of an issue, but Windows 9x still supports disk compression, even going so far as to provide a Windows-based compression program called DriveSpace 3 that you can access from Program files | Accessories | System Tools | DriveSpace 3. FAT32 has dropped support for disk compression, however, so don't bother looking for DriveSpace 3 if your system uses only FAT32 drives. Any version of Windows 9x that supports FAT32 won't even install the program unless you have a FAT16 partition. Watch out for trick questions on the A+ Certification exams that ask you how to make more space on a hard drive with only a FAT32 partition; they may toss in DriveSpace 3 as an option to try to trick you!

Just in case you were wondering, Windows 2000 supports FAT16, FAT32, and NTFS. Windows 9x systems capable of FAT32 cannot read NTFS, although they have FDISK programs that recognize them and let you delete them, which is nice when you need to turn a Windows 2000 system back to Windows 98. DOS and Windows 95 FAT16 systems see only FAT16 drives. If you run their FDISKs, they don't even see the FAT32 or NTFS partitions.

## Major Differences Between Windows 95 and 98

In my opinion, Windows 98 is no more than Windows 95 with a lot of new toys added to improve usability and to prevent or address system problems. Beyond the prettier interface, Windows 98 provides a set of extra features that are virtually a required update to Windows 95. Most of these features are available to Windows 95 via upgrades, but that's a rather tedious process, highly prone to messing up your system— far better just to upgrade. The following list details a few of the more outstanding features.

## A Great Startup Disk

Both Windows 95 and Windows 98 provide a method to create a startup disk. A *startup disk* is simply a special bootable floppy disk that contains a number of handy utilities to help you fix a system that won't boot Windows. Startup disks enable you to boot to an A: prompt and then run a few basic utilities. You cannot start Windows from a startup disk, so you can't run any graphical programs—but both Windows 95 and Windows 98 enable you to make a startup disk with enough tools that can run from an A: prompt to fix many common problems. One huge problem with the Windows 95 startup disk is that it does not support a CD-ROM. In many cases, we need to access the CD-ROM in order to install programs, so we have to go through a rather painful process to make the Windows 95 startup disk access the CD-ROM. I will show you how later in this chapter. The Windows 98 startup disk automatically supports almost every type of CD-ROM made. Why bother booting to an A: prompt if you can't access the CD-ROM to at least reinstall Windows? I love Windows 98 startup disks compared to the Windows 95 startup disks.

### Web-Based Windows

Windows 98 integrates HTML-enabled windows, providing seriously powerful and flexible customization. The power of Web-enabled windows is only now, many years after Windows 98 entered the market, becoming understood well enough for regular users to appreciate its potential.

### FAT32

This hardly needs any more discussion. FAT32 is the way to go!

### System Information Tool

The System Information tool provides a handy snapshot of your system in a fairly easy-to-read format. I think of the System Information tool as a "read-only Device Manager" in that you get to see all of the resource and driver information provided by Device Manager in a report format (Figure 10-39). Additionally, the System Information tool provides a launch point for almost every utility used by Windows 98. If you need to run a utility but you're not sure where to find it, look under the Tools menu for the System Information tool (Figure 10-40).

### Windows Update

Microsoft constantly provides free updates to its OSs. As we'll see later in the chapter, updating Windows 95 gave the best techs a bad case of the jitters because the updating order had to be carefully monitored. Windows 98 eliminates this problem completely with the Windows Update utility. This Web-based utility uses a special Web site to inspect your system and provides a simple method to update your system safely (Figure 10-41).

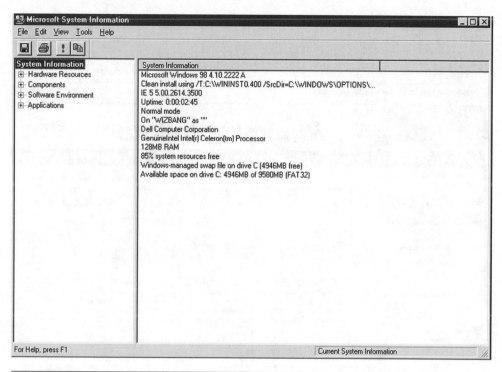

**Figure 10-39** System Information tool

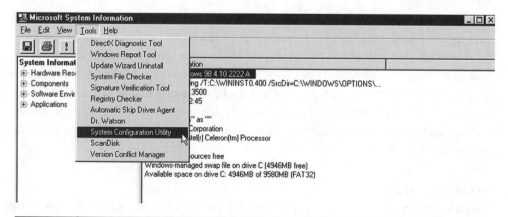

**Figure 10-40** System Information Tools menu

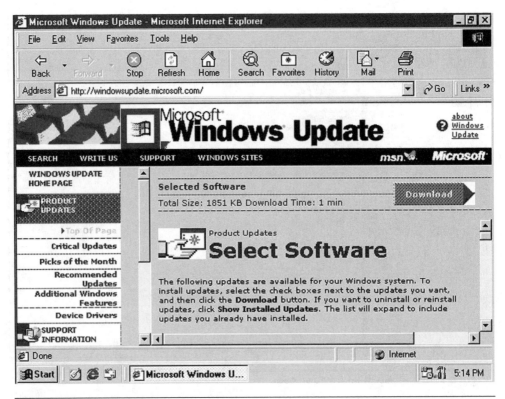

**Figure 10-41**  Windows 98 Update utility

## Disk Cleanup

Windows needs lots of unused disk space for swap files and temporary files generated by applications. In Windows 95, running out of disk space usually manifests itself as a "Not enough disk space" error at best. Usually lockups and general protection faults take place. Windows 98 has a Disk Cleanup utility that enables you to clean out unnecessary files (Figure 10-42). What makes this tool particularly handy is that it will automatically start when your drive reaches a certain minimum. Although third-party utilities such as Norton's CleanSweep do a better job, Disk Cleanup works perfectly well for most systems.

## Active Desktop

Windows 98 comes with a vastly improved version of Internet Explorer that includes the amazing Active Desktop, enabling the Desktop to load active Web pages directly. Why bother opening a browser when that often-accessed Web page sits on your Desktop, ready for instant viewing? New, even more powerful versions of Internet Explorer, have since been released.

**Figure 10-42**
Windows Disk
Cleanup

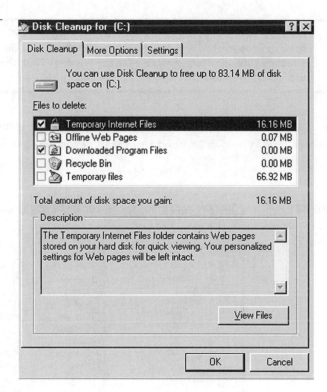

## But Underneath . . .

All of the extra functions in Windows 98 do not eliminate the fact that in nearly every aspect, Windows 98 is identical to Windows 95. The installation process, install functions, and troubleshooting procedures vary little between the two versions. Windows 98 warms the heart of the PC support person by making the job easier and faster as a result of these new functions.

## The Windows 9x Directory Structure

For this section, let's assume that you have installed Windows 9x on the C: drive in a folder called \WINDOWS—the default installation setting. Not all systems follow this; you can install Windows into any folder name. You can even install Windows into another drive letter! Don't get too excited. The Windows boot files, (IO.SYS, MSDOS.SYS, and COMMAND.COM) still must sit in the root folder of the C: drive. So even though it looks as if you installed Windows on the D: drive, you really just installed most of Windows there. Windows still must boot from the C: drive, just like DOS.

**NOTE** Windows 2000 varies dramatically from Windows 95 and Windows 98 in both its boot method and directory structure. We'll save the discussion of the Windows 2000 directory structure for the Windows 2000 chapter. This section only covers Windows 9x!

The best way to see this directory structure is graphically using the popular Windows Explorer. Find Windows Explorer from Start | Programs | Windows Explorer (Figure 10-43).

**Figure 10-43**
Windows Explorer
in Windows 95

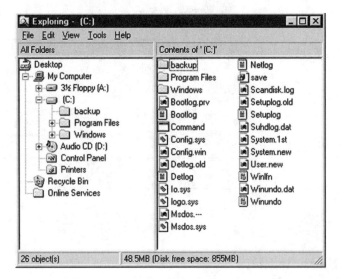

Windows Explorer might almost be thought of as a direct competitor to My Computer. Both of these tools enable you to navigate around the system quite easily. Each method has its benefits and downsides; in fact, pretty much all Windows people break down into the "We prefer Windows Explorer" and the "We prefer My Computer" camps. I've seen skinny-armed computer nerds literally come to blows over which tool is better! Personally, I like them both, but for this job, Windows Explorer's handy directory tree on the left-hand side makes it a far better way to see the Windows 9x directory structure.

When you first look at Windows Explorer, you notice that the top of the list shows the Desktop. Even though placing the Desktop at the top of the tree makes saving files and such handy, the real directory structure looks nothing like this. To see what the Windows directories really look like, first look at the C: drive. Notice the little minus (-) sign to the left? Click on that! You just 'collapsed' the C: drive folders. Now you should see a little plus (+) sign. Click on that to 'expand' the C: drive back to the way it looked when you first opened Windows Explorer.

On all Windows 9x systems, at least two folders exist: \Program Files and \Windows. By default, any application that you install gets a subfolder in \Program Files. Expand the \Program Files folder to see the installed applications (Figure 10-44). You may need to use the scroll bar to see all the folders. Try opening a subfolder—\Accessories is a good one. Try to find some real programs; look for the EXE extension. Do you see WORDPAD.EXE or maybe MSPAINT.EXE? Double-click on one to start the program. You don't have to start programs from the Programs menu, but most folks do. Close the program you just opened and collapse the \Program Files folder.

**Figure 10-44**
Installed
applications

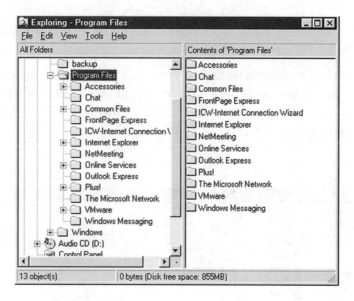

The real fun starts with the \Windows folder. If you are using Web view, Windows 98 systems require you to click a text link called Show Files in order to see any files. You will find tremendous variations in the contents of this folder even among different versions of Windows 9x, but they all share a number of important folders that you need to know about. I'll assume that you will find these folders with Windows Explorer, so I'll just list them and tell you what they do. Open each one to see what they contain.

**NOTE**  If you don't see any of these folders I list, click the **View | Options** menu and tell Windows Explorer to show all files.

• **C:\WINDOWS** This folder contains all the subfolders used by Windows. This is the general dumping ground for many different types of files. Notice all the INI files! You will see a number of programs, mostly simple ones like CALC.EXE (the Windows calculator program) and a few throwbacks from the Windows 3.*x* days such as WINFILE.EXE (the ancient Windows File Manager). You may also see graphics files with the BMP extension and lots of TXT files. These files contain wonderful information that most Windows techs never even bother to read. I read every one of these files (just double-click on them and they open in Notepad) whenever I get a new Windows version. You should also read them! Take a moment to locate the registry files, SYSTEM.DAT and USER.DAT. Finally, see if a file called WIN386.SWP resides in this folder. That's the Windows virtual memory swap file, which will be discussed later.

Take a moment now to click View . . . | Details to see more information on each file and folder. Do you see the column headers as shown in Figure 10-45? Click on each of these to sort by that value. Click them twice to see them in reverse order—very handy for helping you find files or folders!

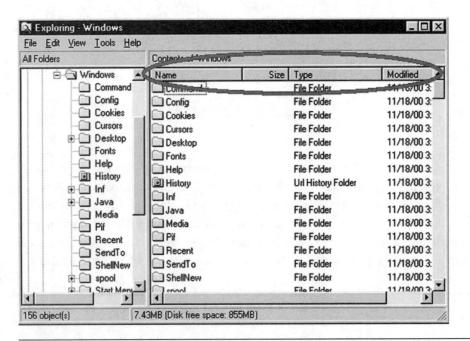

**Figure 10-45** Clicking headers

- **\WINDOWS\COMMAND** This folder stores all the DOS-equivalent command-line programs. You will see FDISK.EXE and FORMAT.COM, among others. Do you see EDIT.COM? Open that program; it looks just like the EDIT we saw in previous chapters! Close the EDIT program.

- **\WINDOWS\COOKIES** Here's where Windows stores cookies. The cookie folder is the only place that a Web site may place data. Cookies store usernames, personalization data—anything that a Web site may want to know about you, should you return to their Web site. The cookies folder gets pretty filled on most systems and is another good place to go when you want to delete excess files. Although the next time you go to your favorite Web site, you may find you have lost all your personal settings!

---

**CAUTION** Most cookies are fairly benign in intent, but certain vile individuals have created spyware, a form of cookie that sends data about your system or browsing habits without your knowledge or consent. Spyware (and other hostile cookies) fall well outside the scope of the A+ Certification exams, but you should be aware of their existence. For more information, visit our friends over at Gibson Research Corp.—http://grc.com/optout.htm.

---

- **\WINDOWS\CURSORS** Just like it sounds, here's where Windows stores the many different cursors you may use.

- **\WINDOWS\DESKTOP** The Windows Desktop in reality is just another subfolder under \Windows. If you save a file to your Desktop, you're really just saving it in this folder! Open it up. You should see some of the same icons you see on your Desktop. Notice that you do not see My Computer, the Recycle Bin, Network Neighborhood, and so on. Microsoft has some magical way of placing those icons on the Desktop. In a networking environment, users often share their desktops so they can easily transfer files among themselves. To share your Desktop, you need to know the location of this folder, and now you do!

- **\WINDOWS\FAVORITES** The \WINDOWS\FAVORITES folder stores all your saved Web sites. Internet Explorer calls them Favorites.

- **\WINDOWS\FONTS** Like the name suggests, Windows stores all fonts here. Note that fonts have one of two extensions: FON or TTF. FON files are old-style "screen" fonts. TTF files are the modern TrueType fonts. Try opening a font to see what it looks like.

- **\WINDOWS\HELP** This is the default location for all HLP (help) files. Open one to see what program uses it.

- **\WINDOWS\HISTORY** This is the Internet Explorer history list of Web sites you visited. It's a nice place to spy on what Web sites a person has visited. Most newer Web browsers have a History option that shows you the same information from within the browser.

- **\WINDOWS\INF** INF files make up the cornerstone of hardware installation. To install any device in Windows, that device must have an INF file. The INF file tells Windows what drivers to load, what updates to place into the registry, and what resources the device wants to use. All versions of Windows come with INF files for a broad cross-section of devices. Any new device loaded has the INF file copied here. We'll talk more on INF files when we discuss installation.

- **\WINDOWS\MEDIA** This is the default location for sounds and audio clips. Double-click a file with a WAV or MID extension to hear sounds.

- **\WINDOWS\PIF** Windows stores all Program Information Files here. PIF files are used to support DOS programs. We'll cover these in Chapter 12.

- **\WINDOWS\SPOOL\PRINTERS** When Windows prints to a printer, temporary files called spool files are stored here until they can be sent to the printer.

- **\WINDOWS\START MENU** Anything in this folder shows up on the Start menu.

- **\WINDOWS\START MENU\PROGRAMS** Anything in this folder shows up in the Programs menu, even submenus like Accessories. Do you see it?

- **\WINDOWS\START MENU\PROGRAMS\STARTUP** Any programs loaded here automatically start whenever you start Windows.

As you might imagine, we like to tinker around the \Start Menu folder and its sub-folders quite a bit. Microsoft thoughtfully provides you a way to access this folder quickly: Just alternate-click on the Start button, and select Explore to jump right to the \Start Menu folder (Figure 10-46).

**Figure 10-46**
Opening the \Start
Menu folder from
the Start button

- **\WINDOWS\SYSBCKUP**   This is definitely not on the test, but so many folks ask me about it that I thought I'd include it. This folder stores backup copies of critical DLL files. When Windows boots, if it detects any of these files as corrupt, it tries to take a copy from here to replace the corrupted file. Sometimes it works, sometimes it doesn't.

- **\WINDOWS\SYSTEM**   This is the real heart of Windows 9x. Here you see the core OS files: GDI.EXE, KRNL386.EXE, and USER.EXE. This folder also stores almost all of the DLL files used by Windows. Many Windows 9x systems also have the \WINDOWS\SYSTEM32 folder. This folder stores DLLs and other support files for programs designed to run under both Windows 9x and Windows NT/2000 systems.

- **\WINDOWS\Temp**   This is the default folder for temporary files. Many applications create temporary files for one reason or another. Windows dictates that they should always go in here, although we'll see that even some Microsoft programs ignore this rule. This folder really fills up with temporary files and folders, requiring us to clear it out periodically.

- **\WINDOWS\Temporary Internet Files**   This folder stores your browser's cache files, mostly graphics from Web pages you visited. This is another really great place to snoop into what folks have been browsing, even better than the \WINDOWS\HISTORY folder because users rarely think to clear this cache.

## Control Panel

The rest of this chapter dedicates itself to the issues most folks expect: installing, upgrading, and troubleshooting Windows 9x. But before we dive in, we need a quick tour of a very important part of Windows for techs: the Control Panel. The Control Panel handles most of the maintenance, upgrade, and configuration aspects of Windows. Click on Start | Settings | Control Panel to open the Control Panel (Figure 10-47).

A large number of programs, called applets, populate the Control Panel. The names and number of applets vary among versions of Windows and according to whether any installed programs added applets. But all versions of Windows share most of the same applets. Let's make sure we know the function of the common applets. I'll just give a quick description of most of these applets, as we go into much more detail on them in other chapters.

**NOTE**   Even these common applets may vary slightly between Windows versions. The A+ Certification exams do not test you on every little variance between the same applets in different versions—just know what each applet does!

**Figure 10-47**   Windows 9x Control Panel

The Control Panel applets enable you to do an amazing array of things to a Windows system. Each applet displays text that helps explain its functions. The Add New Hardware applet (Figure 10-48), for example, says quite clearly, "This wizard installs the software for a new hardware device." They are all like that. Take a look at Figure 10-49, the users applet. Can you tell its use? (If not, don't despair. We'll cover Users in Chapter 20.) Each Control Panel applet relevant to the A+ exams is discussed in detail in the relevant chapter, for example, the Modems applet in Chapter 17, Modems. If you need a handy reference, the Web chapter goes through all the applets in detail.

**Figure 10-48**
Add New
Hardware Wizard

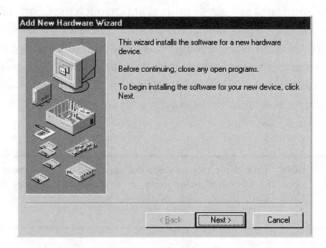

**Figure 10-49**
User Settings

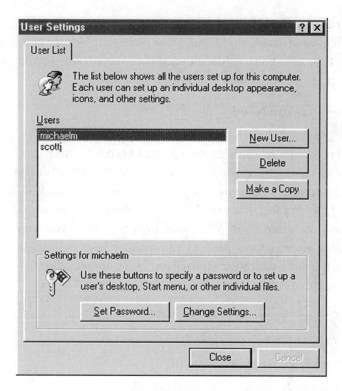

## Device Installation

Device installation, once the private domain of only the nerdiest of computer techs, has been completely transformed by the advent of PnP. Today almost anyone with the "do-it-yourself" spirit and enough sense to read instructions can easily succeed in installing most devices. Hard drives, CD-ROMs, motherboards, CPUs, and power supplies are, or at least should be, the few components that still require our skills. As long as the user does basic anti-ESD procedures, everything else is, literally, a snap to install. But for all the promise of PnP, we still see a number of problems still arise that require us to support device installation. Let's look at device installation first from the perfect scenario: a truly PnP device with full PnP support from both the OS—in this example, Windows 98-and a PnP BIOS.

Most PnP install problems start due to lack of basic procedure knowledge as to how to install a PnP device. Let me show you my process for purchasing and installing PnP devices.

## Before You Buy

Most hardware installation failures take place long before you put a screwdriver in your hand. They take place at the store or the Web site where you purchased the device. When purchasing a device, follow these basic rules:

### Know What You Need

Too many people buy the wrong hardware for their needs. Never walk into a store saying, "I need a sound card." Instead first ask yourself, "What do I want the sound card to do for me?" Make sure, whether you purchase the device for yourself or for a customer, that you have a solid understanding of the expectations. Will this sound card be for games? Do you just want to hear basic system sounds? Would you like to play CD-ROMs? How about DVD? What kind of speakers will you want? As you might anticipate, this often reduces itself to you making your best guess and spending a good amount of time educating yourself or the customer. When purchasing a device, you must juggle with four variables:

- What do I need this device to do?
- What are the expectations of the device?
- Can I or the customer afford it?
- How much do we care about this device?

Answering these questions takes time. I spend far more time researching my needs than I do actually getting the device. Every piece of PC technology changes so fast that I daily find myself confronted with a new term that I've never heard before. Never be afraid to ask questions. Remember, the most telling statement as to the quality and skill of a PC tech is his or her ability to say, "I don't know!" You need a lot of confidence to look a customer, boss, or spouse in the eye and say, "I don't know" on the one topic where everyone says you are the ultimate expert. I never trust techs with all the answers. No tech knows everything about PCs!

### Physical Compatibility

Once you think you know what you need—we're never completely positive, but we usually get to "pretty sure"—you then must make a determination as to how this will affect the system. The big question here is compatibility. First think about physical incompatibility. Where will this device plug into the system? The best PCI sound card in the world won't work in a system that has used all its PCI slots. That cool wireless mouse in your hand uses a serial port, and you need a PS/2 connection. That video card needs a secondary power input, and you're out of power connections.

## System Compatibility

Once you know, or at least feel comfortable that the device will install into your system, you must then consider the possibility of system incompatibility. Suppose you bought a Zip drive that plugs into your parallel port. You already have a printer on the parallel port, but the Zip drive has a pass-through connector that lets you plug the printer into the Zip drive. Will that work? Once I wanted to install a second video card into my Windows 2000 system so I could enjoy two monitors. Will this card support a two-monitor system?

Head over to the device maker's Web site and find the support area. Check the *frequently asked questions* (FAQ) lists. Send an e-mail to tech support. This will invariably answer your questions and usually shows you a thing or two you never considered!

The problem with these questions is that by this point you already know the device you want, and your mouse pointer is hovering over the Add To Cart button. System incompatibilities make for real frustration due to the fact that you probably must install the device to discover them. That's when you talk to the purchaser. Watch out for restocking charges or expensive return shipping costs. Never buy from a vendor who doesn't provide at least a seven-day return policy, ever.

After 15 years of PC support, I still find myself returning equipment roughly one out of every five purchases, and I buy some type of equipment twice a week!

### Driver Check

Always check the version of drivers that come with a device. Does the device you want have a driver for your OS? Most hardware comes with drivers for more mature OSs like Windows 98, but may not for older or more offbeat OSs. I always check before I walk out of the store.

Second, do you have the latest drivers? A large percentage of devices do not ship with the latest drivers. A quick check at the manufacturer's Web site always settles this issue quickly.

## Procedure Check

Okay, so now you are the proud owner of a new PnP device. Let's install that thing! Here are a few things to remember.

### Create a Startup Disk

All versions of Windows 9*x* provide the ability to create a startup disk. A startup disk is a bootable floppy disk that, in case of an emergency, enables you to boot to an A: prompt. We'll get into more detail later, but for now follow these steps:

1. Click on Start | Settings | Control Panel to open the Control Panel.

2. Locate the Add/Remove Programs icon and click it.

3. Click the Startup Disk tab.

4. Get a blank floppy disk, and insert it into the floppy drive.

5. Click Create Disk.

Windows will then create a startup disk. This disk contains just enough files to perform basic troubleshooting. On some systems, Windows prompts for the Windows installation CD-ROM, on others it will not. After Windows has created the startup disk, take it out of the floppy drive and set it aside for later. Hopefully, you won't need it.

One of the most important jobs for a startup disk is to enable you to gain access to your CD-ROM. Windows 95 startup disks lack the ability to provide access to the CD-ROM drive. You need to copy two files and edit two others so that a Windows 95 startup disk can access CD-ROMs. Windows 98 startup disks *do* provide CD-ROM access, so don't do this unless you still run Windows 95!

**NOTE**  Many techs, myself included, just use Windows 98 startup disks when working on Windows 95 systems—they work just fine!

To make a Windows 95 startup disk that supports a CD-ROM drive, follow these steps:

1. Download a special device driver called OAKCDROM.SYS. Over 100 Web sites provide this driver, but here's one: **http://www.computerhope.com/drivers/cdrom.htm.** Download the "Generic Driver." Remember, Web sites change, so if this link stops working, just do a little searching—you'll find it! Copy the OAKCDROM.SYS file to the Windows 95 Startup disk.

2. Locate a file called MSCDEX.EXE on your system. Most systems store this file in the \WINDOWS\COMMAND folder. Copy the MSCDEX file to the floppy disk. Once you've done this, you should see both files on the floppy disk, as shown in Figure 10-50.

**Figure 10-50**
OAKCDROM.SYS
and MSCDEX.EXE

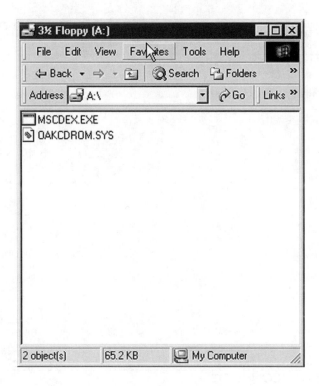

3. Go to the Run menu option in the Start menu, and type this command: **notepad a:\config.sys** to open the CONFIG.SYS file on the floppy disk for editing. Ignore any other text in the file; just add this line: **DEVICE=A:\CDROM.SYS /D:CDROM** to the end so it looks like Figure 10-51. Save and exit Notepad.

**NOTE** If you have multiple hard drives or hard drive partitions in a system, also add this line to the end of the **CONFIG.SYS** file: **LASTDRIVE=Z**.

4. Go to the Run menu option in the Start menu, and type this command: **notepad a:\autoexec.bat** to open the AUTOEXEC.BAT file on the floppy disk for editing. Ignore any other text in the file. Just add this line: **MSCDEX /D:CDROM** to the end so it looks like Figure 10-52. Save and exit Notepad.

The Windows 95 startup disk will now recognize the CD-ROM and give it a drive letter.

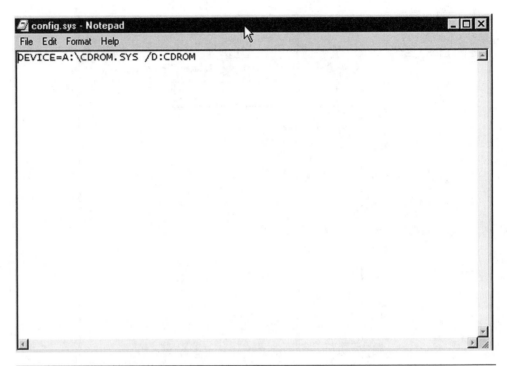

**Figure 10-51** CONFIG.SYS

## Backup

Let's list the five most important backup items before you install:

1. Back up the registry.
2. Back up the registry.
3. Back up the registry.
4. Back up the registry.
5. And . . . back up the registry.

When you install a new device, Windows changes the registry to reflect that new device. If you back up the registry and something goes wrong, you just restore the registry and try again. Failure to back up the registry means pain and heartache and an occasional complete system rebuild.

There are so many ways to back up the registry that listing them all here would take forever. Depending on the version, Windows 9x provides a number of methods to back up the registry, and many third-party vendors provide excellent backup tools. Both

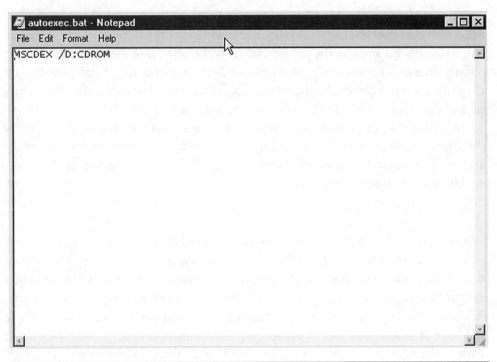

**Figure 10-52** AUTOEXEC.BAT

Windows and third-party programs contain many powerful extras and conveniences that make them very worthwhile. But you don't need them just to back up the registry. Try this:

(Use My Computer or Windows Explorer to perform these backup steps. If you really want to, you can do it from a DOS prompt, but why make life hard?)

1. Create a folder called C:\BACK.

2. Open the C:\WINDOWS\SYSTEM folder.

3. Make sure to set the View option to Show All Files.

4. Turn off all the file attributes on SYSTEM.DAT and USER.DAT. (Forgot how? Here's your clue: Properties!)

5. Copy SYSTEM.DAT and USER.DAT to the C:\BACK folder.

Congratulations. You just backed up the registry.

This method doesn't work with Windows 2000 because Windows 2000 uses different files for the registry. We'll save that for the next chapter.

You can also use the REGEDIT program to make a backup of the registry. Start REGEDIT and select the Export Registry File option from the Registry menu. Select the "All" radio button and give the location where you wish to save the backup copy of the registry. Your entire registry will be stored as a REG file. Be careful—a complete backup copy of the registry can easily surpass multiple megabytes! You can restore the registry by using the Import Registry File from the Registry menu in REGEDIT.

If anything doesn't go the way you want and you want to return the system to exactly the way it was before you tried installing that @#^%$ device, just restore the registry. To restore the registry, boot off of a startup floppy disk. When you get to an A: prompt, type the following command:

```
COPY C:\BACK\*.DAT C:\WINDOWS\SYSTEM
```

Although the A+ Certification exams always say to do a full system backup (completely back up everything) before you even look at a computer, I rarely do a system backup for basic device installs. The chances of messing up a drive by snapping in a card or plugging something into a port are very low. If I'm installing for someone else, however, I always give the same speech before I touch anything. I won't quote the whole routine, but it boils down to: "I am not responsible for your data." If they want me to back up their system, fine, but they get charged for my time. Have you ever taken a system into a shop for repair? That little piece of paper you sign invariably includes a "we're not responsible for your data" clause. Follow their lead and cover yourself, or at least have a boss you can hide behind if you wipe out all their data. Believe me, it can happen!

## Packaging

Remove the device carefully, try not to trash the packaging in case you ever need to return the device. Use proper anti-ESD procedures. Keep the packaging or tell the customer to keep the packaging. If possible, keep it until the warranty runs out.

## Read Me!

Read every scrap of documentation. Which disk holds the drivers? What procedure do I need to follow? I know you want to pop in your new toy, but first you need to sit down and read. Check for a file on the install CD-ROM or floppy disk called README.DOC or READ.ME or README.TXT. These files always provide critical information and notice of late-breaking issues.

Make sure you understand the setup process. I once bought a USB video camera that I couldn't get to work. The install instructions clearly said: "Do not insert the camera until after the drivers are installed!" Did I read that? No. Was I sorry? Yes!

Replacing one device with another invariably requires you to delete the old device from your Device Manager before you install a new one. Video cards almost always demand this procedure. If the documentation tells you to delete a driver, jump down to the "Device Manager" section to see how to delete old drivers.

## Physical Installation

Now, finally, we get to have some fun! Plug in that new device where it needs to go. Don't forget your antistatic procedures. Check, double-check, and then triple-check connections, power, and any switches or jumpers that the device needs. Fortunately, you read all the documentation and know all about any special issues—deal with those now. Boot the system and go to CMOS.

### CMOS Issues

Watch out for the myriad of little gotchas that may come into play here. If you're using a serial or parallel port, make sure to activate it and set it to any special COM or LPT settings your device needs. USB devices usually need an IRQ, so check to see that Assign IRQ to USB is active if you're dealing with USB.

Most PnP CMOS options are fine by default. Only make changes in here if something goes wrong or if you install legacy devices. Because this is the perfect PnP scenario, you shouldn't have to mess with the PnP settings unless you run into problems. Reboot the system.

### Driver Install

Driver installation in a PnP system is highly anticlimactic in most cases. You get to watch Windows discover the new device and show the famous "Windows has discovered new hardware" alert (Figure 10-53).

**Figure 10-53**
New hardware
screen

Windows 2000 no longer provides this prompt. With Windows 2000, you rarely see anything on the screen unless Windows needs your help. Windows either has the driver built-in, or it prompts you to provide the driver. Figure 10-54 shows the Found New Hardware Wizard in action.

**Figure 10-54**   Windows 2000 responding to a new device installed

Many systems give the "Windows has found unknown hardware and is installing software . . . " message. This usually comes from installing two devices at once, one depending on the other for connection to the system, like a new video card and monitor. This is fine; Windows will eventually find the unknown device, although it may take a few reboots, especially with Windows 95.

### Checking

Once the device installs, it's time to check it out. The first place we look to verify a good install is with the Device Manager.

## The Device Manager

The Device Manager is the primary tool for dealing with devices and device drivers in Windows. The Device Manager displays every device that Windows recognizes. Figure 10-55 shows a typical Device Manager screen with all installed devices in good order. If Windows detects a problem, it shows the device with a red "x" or a yellow exclamation point, as we'll see in the next section.

**Figure 10-55**
The Device Manager
detects a problem.

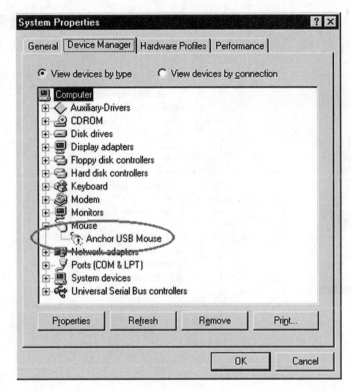

The Device Manager organizes devices in special groups called *types.* All devices of the same type are grouped under the same type heading. To see the devices of a particular type, you must open that type's group. Figure 10-56 shows the Ports type opened, revealing the COM and LPT ports on the system.

By double-clicking on a device (or by selecting the device and clicking the Properties button) and then clicking the Resources tab, we can see the resources used by that device.

## Applications

A new piece of hardware is useless without some application that uses it. Where the application comes from really depends on the device and the version of Windows. But we can break down applications into five groups-Built-in, Enhanced, Supplied Critical, Supplied Helpful, and Supplied Optional.

**Figure 10-56**
Installed COM and
LPT ports

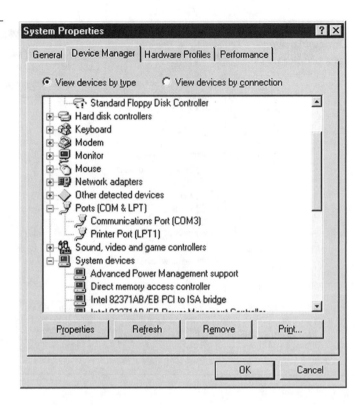

### Built-in

Windows comes with applications for many devices. Windows has complete support for a network card, for example via the Network Neighborhood, or for a CD-ROM via My Computer or Windows Explorer.

### Enhanced

Many new devices supported by Windows come with greatly enhanced applications. The best example of this is Zip drives. While most versions of Windows provide basic support for Zip drives, Iomega adds extra applications that provide password protection, better formatting, and other options that Windows alone cannot provide.

### Supplied Critical

Supplied critical applications come with the Install CD-ROM, and you must install them to make the hardware work. That new USB docking station for your Palm Pilot won't do a thing without the synchronization software. You must install these applications.

## Supplied Helpful

Supplied helpful applications come with the CD-ROM and may help but are not really required. My new USB camera came with this little utility that lets me do video captures. I don't plan to do video captures, but I may decide to install it just in case.

## Supplied Optional

Supplied optional really means "supplied but I doubt you'll want it." Your new modem might come with an America Online CD-ROM, but you already have an Internet service provider. Or your new sound card comes with a "Historical tour of Musical Instruments," but you bought the sound card to play online games. Don't fill your drive with applications you will never use.

## Plug and Play: Easier?

PnP certainly makes device installation easier, but even in the perfect world just described, we need to follow a number of steps to ensure a smooth installation. Of everything just discussed, remember the two Ds: documentation and drivers. Give those two your close consideration, and you'll eliminate most PnP install issues.

# Dealing with Plug and Play Problems

Time to jump out of fantasyland and move into the more unpleasant aspect of device installation: installation problems. Even in a perfect PnP world, I'd estimate that about one in every five installations creates unanticipated errors. Let's break these errors down and see how to deal with them.

## Windows Plug and Play Can't Find a Driver

Most techs feel that failure to find a correct device driver stands as the most common PnP install issue. Although we see some variance between Windows versions, basically every version of Windows always brings up the Add New Hardware Wizard and immediately moves to the "please tell me the location of the device" screen, as shown in Figure 10-57.

The issue boils down to the fact that Windows PnP queried the new device and knows that the device exists but cannot find the correct INF for that device. In most cases, we just click the Have Disk button and point the installer to the proper directory location. You know the correct directory location because you looked this up in the documentation. If you didn't look (like that would ever happen!), use the Browse feature to navigate around the install CD-ROM/floppy until the Add New Hardware Wizard finds an INF file (Figure 10-58).

**Figure 10-57**
Windows prompts the user for the device driver.

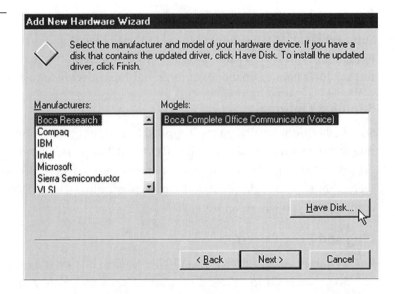

**Figure 10-58**
Browsing to find the INF file

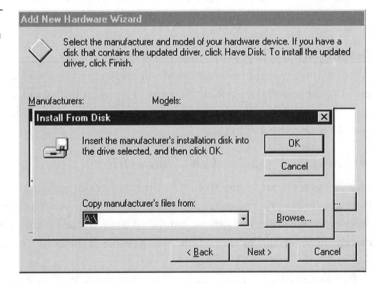

Use a little common sense here! If you have a Windows 98 system and the install floppy shows the following folders, guess where to look first:

- A:\LINUX
- A:\NETWARE4
- A:\NETWARE5
- A:\NT4

- A:\WIN2K

- A:\WIN95

- A:\WIN98

Please tell me you picked the A:\WIN98 folder!

Windows 2000 does a much nicer job than Windows 9x by providing an option to look in all removable drives for the proper INF file (Figure 10-59).

**Figure 10-59**
Windows 2000
browse option

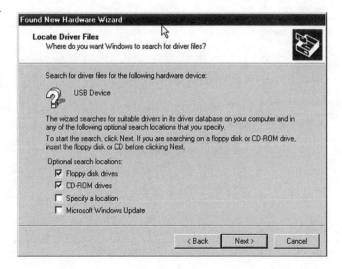

Make sure you insert the correct install disk, especially with Windows 9x, or you might install the wrong driver, requiring you to delete the device from the Device Manager and try again. In some cases, installing the wrong driver wreaks havoc: Windows copies the INF file to the \INF folder, so even if you delete the device from the Device Manager, Windows keeps reinstalling the wrong driver! To stop this action, you must first watch Windows as it installs. This happened to me recently (yes, I screw up every day!) and I documented it.

I purchased the Compaq iPAQ *Personal Digital Assistant* (PDA). It comes with a little USB cradle that enables you to "synch" your e-mail, Web sites, contacts, and so on, between a desktop system and the PDA. When I installed the cradle, I didn't bother reading the instructions, which clearly said to install the synch program before plugging in the device. I just plugged in the device and quickly installed the wrong driver. When I dropped the PDA into the cradle, the system locked up. After a quick scan of the documentation, I said, "Oops!" and promptly deleted the "Compaq Aero PDA" device from the Device Manager (Figure 10-60).

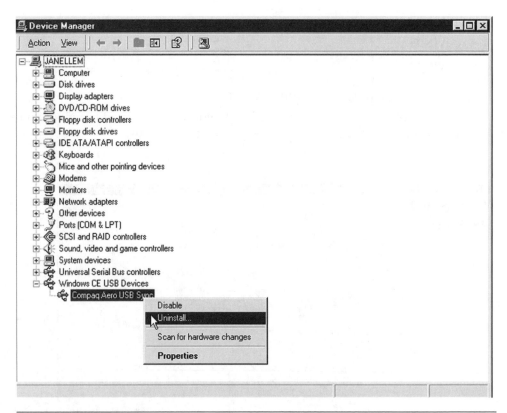

**Figure 10-60**   Removing a device in Device Manager

I rebooted and it immediately reinstalled itself. Ouch.

The fix to this problem required using the Search/Find menu to locate the INF file that contained the offending device. I knew that I needed to find the INF containing the text "Compaq Aero," so I just searched for it in the \INF folder and it appeared! See Figure 10-61.

Once I found it, I simply deleted it and did a complete uninstall/reinstall, this time according to the directions provided (and a phone call to Compaq tech support). I'll never neglect reading the documentation again—well, at least for another two weeks!

Many times hardware makers hide device drivers and INF files in a SETUP program. You must run the program to get all the files you need. In many cases, these SETUP programs don't really set up anything; they just uncompress themselves into a folder on the hard drive. Watch them as they unpack themselves; they always clearly show the destination folder. You can then rerun the Install Wizard and point it to the folder the SETUP program created (Figure 10-62).

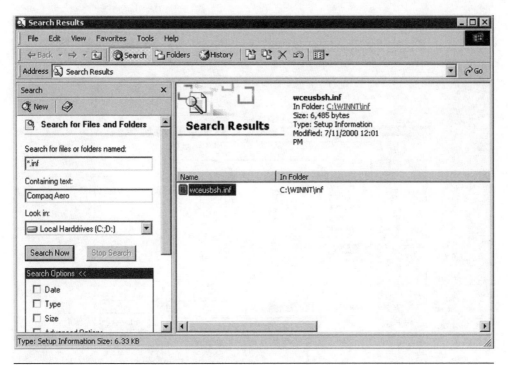

**Figure 10-61** INF file for Compaq Aero PDA

## Windows Plug and Play Doesn't See Device

The second most common install error occurs when PnP doesn't see the device you just installed. You know this happens when you install the device and nothing happens. Always check the Device Manager to see if the device installed! A fast Windows 9x system may display the install screens so quickly you miss them, and Windows 2000 doesn't even show screens! Let's assume you check the Device Manager, and you're positive the device is not there.

## Not Plug and Play

Make sure the device truly is PnP! No one makes legacy hardware anymore, but plenty of legacy devices still lurk at hardware swap meets, eBay, and other places. Look at the device to see if it uses any I/O addresses or IRQ jumpers, and check for jumpers or switches saying "PnP/jumperless." Many late-generation legacy devices used software

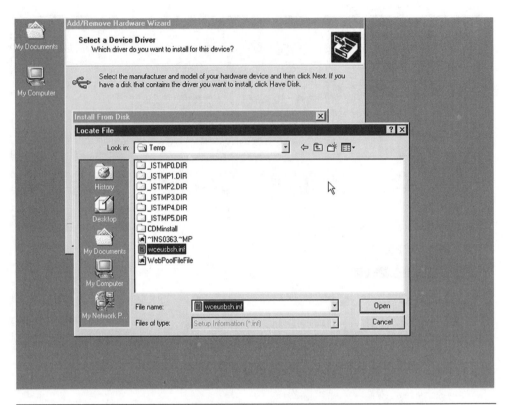

**Figure 10-62**   Choosing the setup files through the Install Wizard

installation (jumperless) configuration. If you don't have the software you need, check the device maker's Web site to see if they still support the legacy device. If they don't, throw the device in the trash!

### Try Again

Assuming you know you have a PnP device, shut off the system after a proper shutdown and remove the device. Reseat the device in the slot or connector and try again. PCI and AGP cards really need tight seating or they won't work. Verify all connections and make sure the device has power if it needs it. Reboot to see if Windows detects the device. Recheck the Device Manager.

### Resources

Windows may fail to see a PnP device if other devices are using all its available resources. This rarely happens in PnP systems; in most cases, the Windows PnP sees the device and lists it in the Device Manager but cannot configure it. Find the fix for resource conflict resolution later in the "Legacy Devices in a Plug and Play World" section of this chapter.

## Bad BIOS

The PnP standard has evolved over the years, and some system BIOS programs have grown too dated to support newer PnP hardware. Always verify that your system has the latest BIOS. Name-brand PC makers list BIOS updates by system model. Check the motherboard maker's Web site for BIOS updates for your motherboard. If your system is more than two years old, a BIOS update almost certainly exists.

## Chipset Anyone?

Chipsets need drivers just like any other device on the PC. OSs only contain drivers for chipsets as old as they are. If a new chipset comes out, they invariably fail to see it, causing other problems such as PnP failures. That's why so many motherboards come with a driver's CD-ROM—to support newer chipsets on older OSs. Take a look in the Device Manager under System to see if the system installed the proper chipsets for your system, as shown in Figure 10-63. If not, you need to get them!

**Figure 10-63**
Proper chipset driver

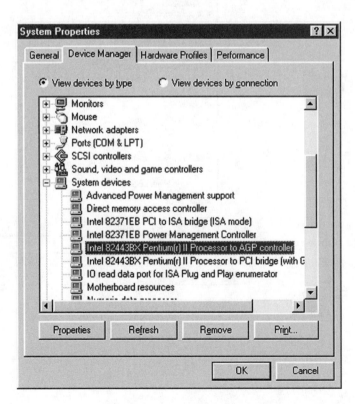

### Blame the Hardware?

When all else fails, blame the device. You may want to try inserting the device into another slot or port (if another one exists), but otherwise you need to point your finger at the device, return it from whence it came, and move on!

## Device Manager Errors

Windows often sees a PnP device and tries to install it, but for one reason or another fails to install the device properly. Unlike errors where the PnP simply fails to see the device, these devices show in the Device Manager, but they show one of two possible errors. If a device has a problem, it will show up with an exclamation point surrounded by a small yellow dot. A small red "x" on a device means the device has been disabled by Windows. Figure 10-64 shows an example of both problem icons.

**Figure 10-64**
Improperly installed device errors

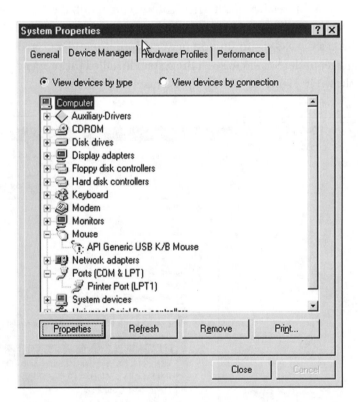

There's really no difference between the two errors in terms of how I deal with them. The bottom line is that the device "ain't working" and I need to fix it. Anyone reading the Microsoft Knowledge Base support documentation can see that probably 50 different types of problems cause these errors. In my experience, however, the vast majority of errors boil down to one of seven areas:

- Failure to follow install procedures
- Corruption/incompatibility with drivers or INF file
- Outdated support drivers
- Outdated BIOS
- Resource conflict
- Corrupted registry
- Bad device

## Failure to Follow Install Procedures

Failure to follow proper install procedure isn't really a Windows error; it's a human error that causes most of the Windows errors you're about to learn! All PnP devices require a very careful series of steps to ensure proper installation, particularly when you're replacing one device with a different one. You must read all documentation *carefully* before installing—have I harped on this enough yet?

Some of the more common install procedures include the following:

- Deleting the old driver first
- Running some SETUP program
- Checking for hardware incompatibilities
- Verifying the version of some Windows EXE, DLL, or driver

Every device maker provides this information through documentation, but the last item, version numbers, deserves a little extra attention. Every device driver, Windows EXE, and Windows DLL comes with a version number. You can verify the driver version of an installed device by checking the device's properties in Device Manager. Open the Driver tab (Figure 10-65).

You can check the version by clicking the Driver File Details button and then use the Update Driver button if needed. We'll discuss *when* to do this next; make sure you know where to find these options.

Many times some documentation asks you to verify the version of a certain Windows EXE or DLL before you install. Just use the Search/Find utility to locate the file and click the Version tab in the file's properties to find that information (Figure 10-66).

**Figure 10-65**
Driver tab for a
device driver

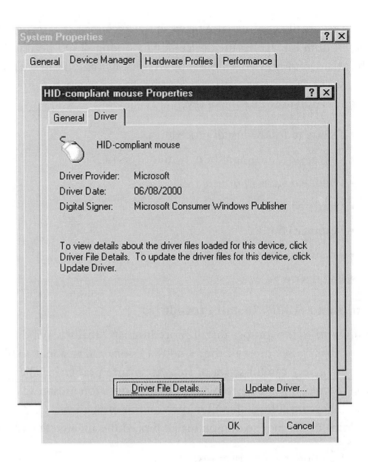

## A Word on Error Codes

One more item before we hit the fixes for device errors: error codes. When a device shows an error, you can use the General tab under the device's properties in Device Manager to get a clue as to where the problem lies. You will see some text with a code number (Figure 10-67). The Microsoft Knowledge Base lists all the code numbers under article number Q125174, if you want to look it up. The A+ Certification exams do not expect you to memorize them; just read the text and you'll know which of the following fixes to try first.

Okay, armed with this information, let's look at how I group Device Manager errors.

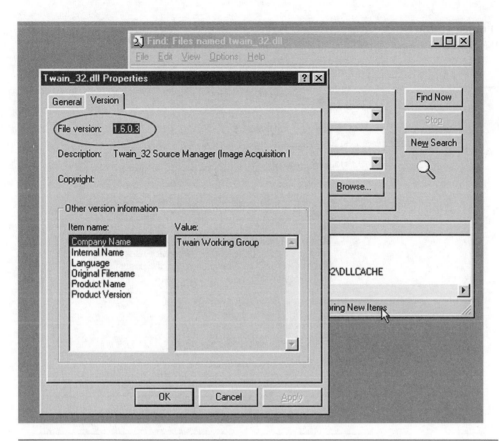

**Figure 10-66**  Verifying the file's version

## Corruption/Incompatibility with Drivers or INF File

Let's start with the first part: corruption. Files get corrupted all the time. An install CD-ROM may get a scratch at the location of a critical driver; Windows may decide to lock up for some reason halfway through copying an INF file; or maybe Windows will decide to copy files onto a hard drive sector that dies half a second after they get copied.

Whenever I see any error text complain about "not reading a driver," "couldn't find a driver," or "failing to load a driver," I immediately delete the driver, reboot, and try again. If that doesn't work, I download a driver from the device manufacturer's Web site. Still no good? I check the hard drive. That usually fixes it.

**Figure 10-67**
Error code example

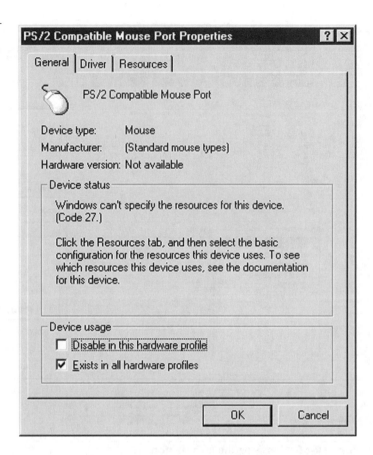

Incompatibilities tend to be more of a challenge. The Windows platform and hardware technologies evolve so quickly that incompatibilities show up constantly. The newer the technology, the more you see it. That's why I never like to be the "first kid on the block" with the newest, coolest device or latest OS—at least when it's a system I need to rely upon. That attitude of "gotta have the newest" invariably puts you on the "bleeding edge" of technology.

One of the most famous incompatibilities shows up as the always-amusing "Unknown Device" and "Unsupported Device" errors (Figure 10-68).

**Figure 10-68**
"Unknown Device"
error

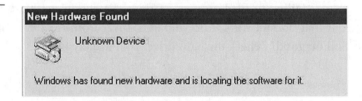

These errors crack me up! Basically, Windows knows that something is taking resources but has no idea *what*. If you see several device errors or unknown devices, incompatibility may be the culprit. After trying other options, I usually find myself on the phone with Microsoft and the device maker's tech support, trying to get one or the other to confess that the problem lies with them. The software folks love to point at the hardware folks, and the hardware folks love to point right back. Remember that Compaq iPAQ I mentioned earlier? I couldn't get the sync cradle to work on one system. Everyone pointed fingers at each other until I finally got two techs on a conference call (on my nickel), and they talked and yelled and made me do all kinds of evil things to my system until they eventually discovered that my chipset was too old to support USB!

 **NOTE** Good techs know when to try to fix something and when to call tech support! The better the techs, the faster they are at determining this point.

Bottom line was that I couldn't upgrade the BIOS, so I needed a new motherboard. The fix was easy, but finding the incompatibility took time.

Remember, no matter how far out into "bleeding-edge technology" you go, you're never alone. Five thousand other techs are staring at the same problem, all scratching their heads and trying to fix it. Wouldn't it be great if you could all work together? That's one of the main functions of Internet newsgroups! Every type of hardware and software has newsgroups. If you don't know where to start, go to **alt.certification.a-plus** first. A bunch of smart techs hang out there, and although our main focus is on the A+ Certification, we handle lots of tech support issues. Heck, if you hang around, you and I will get a chance to post to each other. Be sure to say hi!

## Outdated Support Drivers

If you visualize the CPU as the center of the computer, you'll notice that almost no devices connect directly to the CPU. There's always a chipset, a controller, or some other device between the CPU and the device you install. All these "middleman" devices also need device drivers. In many cases, that exclamation point or red "x" on the device you just installed in Device Manager points to a problem with another device that your new device plugs into. Most of the time these errors show up clearly because the support device *itself* shows an error, but sometimes it's not that easy.

Windows can provide rudimentary support for most chipsets, for example, but that doesn't always mean that the device support contains everything you need. Windows ME handles this nicely by putting a green question mark on devices that do not have optimal drivers, but that doesn't help us on 95, 98, or 2000—or the test. Windows 98 and 2000 do have a device error that says, "I'm not working because device X isn't working," but it's not foolproof. A clue that a support device isn't fully supported can be found in the description of the support devices under the System heading in the Device Manager. Well-supported devices always have very detailed names, whereas less-supported devices tend to get less-detailed names. Compare these two close-ups of the same Windows 95 system's System heading: first with Windows default support drivers, then after I used the CD-ROM that came with the motherboard to upgrade all the support devices—quite a difference! (See Figure 10-69.)

 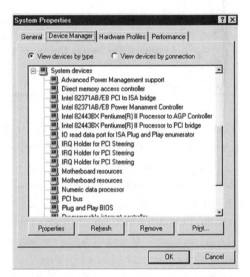

**Figure 10-69**   Proper device drivers vs. default device drivers

## Outdated BIOS

Hey, your BIOS can become dated just like everything else in your system. If you know you have all the latest drivers but you still get errors in Device Manager, see if the motherboard or system makers provide any BIOS updates. An outdated BIOS isn't too common, but certainly common enough to check!

## Resource Conflict

Resource conflicts are not as rare as you might think, even in a system with only PnP devices. An ISA PnP device does not have access to every resource; the manufacturer specifies a range of resources in the INF file. Open the INF file for an ISA PnP device and see for yourself (Figure 10-70).

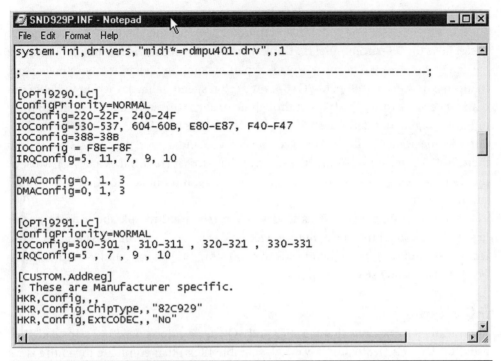

```
system.ini,drivers,"midi*=rdmpu401.drv",,1

;-----------------------------------------------------------;

[OPTi9290.LC]
ConfigPriority=NORMAL
IOConfig=220-22F, 240-24F
IOConfig=530-537, 604-60B, E80-E87, F40-F47
IOConfig=388-38B
IOConfig = F8E-F8F
IRQConfig=5, 11, 7, 9, 10

DMAConfig=0, 1, 3
DMAConfig=0, 1, 3


[OPTi9291.LC]
ConfigPriority=NORMAL
IOConfig=300-301 , 310-311 , 320-321 , 330-331
IRQConfig=5 , 7 , 9 , 10

[CUSTOM.AddReg]
; These are Manufacturer specific.
HKR,Config,,,
HKR,Config,ChipType,,"82C929"
HKR,Config,ExtCODEC,,"No"
```

**Figure 10-70**   IRQ settings in the INF file

Even if your system has only PCI and AGP devices, as long as your system uses ISA slots, resource conflicts might arise. Windows clearly reports resource conflicts in the error message, so you always know when they occur. Resource conflicts cover a lot of ground, so I've devoted the "Legacy Devices in a Plug and Play World" section to this topic.

### Corrupted Registry

In most cases, the device error will report this one very clearly: "Registry corrupted." No problem since you kept that backup copy, right? Right!

### Bad Device

After trying everything, you need to blame the device. Techs hate blaming hardware, primarily due to the fact that no tool exists that truly tests any single type of hardware (with a few exceptions), despite the fantastic claims by a number of vendors that I choose not to name. Unless the manufacturer provides a specialized command prompt-based tool (you must get the Windows GUI out of the way to inspect hardware directly) you cannot truly test a device. All Windows-based graphical "system information" or "diagnostic" programs count on Windows support, and if the device isn't working, Windows will not support it. With the few exceptions I mention in this book, don't waste your time trying to diagnose hardware, especially in the Windows GUI.

So how do you know a piece of hardware is bad? You can try installing the device in another system, assuming your job description allows for such luxuries, or you can just guess. I use the 75 percent rule: If I think there's a 75 percent chance that the hardware has failed, I replace it. The most expensive part of computer repair is labor, that is, *you*! It kills me to watch a well-paid PC support person spend half a day trying to figure out if a $30 network card is bad! It's as though he or she is driven by some unknown force to have to figure out definitively if a device is good or bad. Well, my little chickadees, don't let the academic fascination get between you and a good paycheck. If you think there is a 75 percent probability that a part is bad, toss it (return it, whatever). Most of the time you're right—once in a while you're wrong. But unlike the other techs, you'll still have a job.

Did I start ranting again? Back to device errors! I want to talk about dealing with legacy devices in a PnP world, but we need to cover two preliminary issues that cause techs to stumble or scratch their heads in confusion: IRQ steering and Windows memory. Let's tackle IRQ steering first.

## IRQ Steering

As we learned in previous chapters, PCI and AGP devices don't need IRQs. Instead, they use IRQ channels (really just advanced, sharable IRQs) that eliminate the entire issue of IRQ conflicts in these devices. The problem here stems from the fact that ISA devices still need IRQs. How can the PC control interrupts if the PCI devices ignore the ISA IRQ controller? The most modern Pentium 4 still only has one INT wire. What keeps the ISA interrupt controller from trying to interrupt the CPU when a PCI device is already sending an interrupt (Figure 10-71)?

**Figure 10-71**
ISA IRQ controller (in the south bridge chip) and the PCI controller (north bridge) trying to interrupt the CPU at the same time

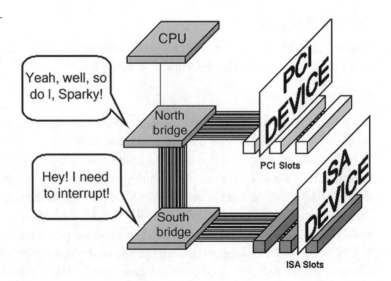

The first PnP standards handled this problem by assigning an IRQ to every PCI device at boot up. This data was stored in an area called the *IRQ Routing Table*. Not that the PCI device needed the IRQ, mind you, but it kept all the devices from trying to interrupt the CPU. If a PCI device did a normal interrupt, the PnP BIOS read the interrupt routing table to determine what IRQ was assigned to the PCI device and then sent that fake IRQ to the IRQ controller in the chipset. The IRQ controller thought it was receiving a normal ISA IRQ. With a little bit of simplification for clarity, it looked like Figure 10-72.

**Figure 10-72**
PnP BIOS sends
false information to
the IRQ controller.

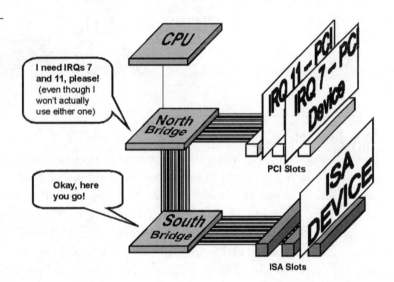

Although this system worked well, it wasted a ton of IRQs on devices that didn't need them. So, Microsoft and Intel worked together to come up with a clever little function called *IRQ steering*. The basic idea of IRQ steering is based on the premise, "Who cares what IRQ we give the IRQ controller, just as long as we give it one!" And thus, IRQ steering was born. With IRQ steering, PCI devices share one or more IRQs, depending on the chipset and on the function of the PCI device. When any PCI device fires an interrupt channel, the same IRQ gets sent to the ISA IRQ controller (Figure 10-73).

Because IRQ sharing depends so heavily on the chipset used, you cannot predict ahead of time what PCI device will share what IRQs. That's fine with us! As long as the PnP BIOS knows how to report this information, IRQ steering works perfectly and is completely transparent.

IRQ steering has one potentially nasty downside: Systems must have IRQ9 or IRQ11 available for IRQ steering. When I'm building a new system, I never install ISA cards until *after* I've installed Windows (9x or 2000). This enables me to see what IRQ the system wants to use for IRQ steering. I then make a point of leaving that IRQ alone when I'm installing ISA devices!

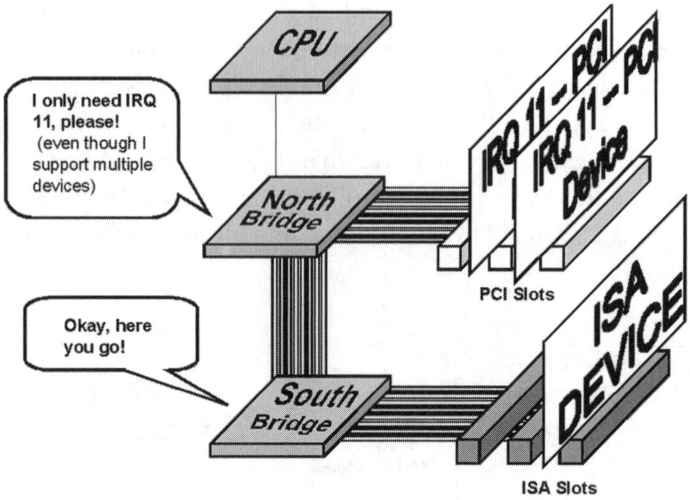

**Figure 10-73**
IRQ steering at work

## Windows Memory

In the next section, we'll understand the processes needed to configure system resources for a legacy device manually in the automatic world of PnP. Manypeople think this is a waste of time in our PnP world. Not so! Even though PnP makes device installation much easier, it comes with a price. The automation of PnP hides the reality of system resources. The gritty details of IRQs, I/O addresses, and DMAs disappear from the normal PC support person's view. So, when things go wrong (and they do), most PC techs lack the detailed skills necessary to get out of trouble. Hardly a waste of time!

The CompTIA members who define the skill sets for the A+ Certification exams respond to a very tough audience: themselves. CompTIA's membership list is comprised of the companies and the people who provide every level of the PC support structure. They know what you need to know to prove yourself as a successful tech in today's world. A good tech needs to understand resources—not so much because you'll use that knowledge every day (thankfully you won't), but more for those rare times when the beauty of PnP fails and you're faced with the daunting task of manual system resource configuration.

Earlier chapters already covered three system resources: I/O addresses, IRQs, and DMA; yet one more critical system resource exists, one so important that it gets its own entire chapter later in the book. But it's also one that we must bring to light—well, maybe just hold a match to it—so that we can take the big leap. We need to discuss the last critical resource: memory.

## Understanding Memory

From earlier chapters we know that every CPU has an address space: the total amount of memory the CPU can address. We know that the 8088/8086 with its 20-wire address bus could address up to $2^{20}$ or 1,048,576 bytes of memory. Hopefully, and I will harp on this again in Chapter 12, you understand that memory is not RAM. Think of memory as a giant list of all the different numbers that the address bus can generate. Each number points to one byte of something. Sure, most of those numbers on the list point to RAM, but we saw earlier that many other devices, ROMs in particular, need to provide a method for the CPU to run their programs. We set aside some of the numbers on the list for these other devices.

So memory is *not* RAM, memory is *not* ROM; memory is simply all of the permutations of 1's and 0's that the CPU's address bus can generate. This point is critical. So many good techs ask, "How much memory is on your PC?" when they really mean, "How much RAM is on your PC?" The former is technically incorrect, but we're not going to change this poor use of terminology—it's too late!

Many devices, even ultramodern PCI PnP devices, often come with an onboard ROM chip. That chip requires a bit of address space—a memory address. In the PCI world, memory addresses are so plentiful that this is simply not an issue. But in the ISA world, PnP or not, memory addressing still looms as an important issue. We'll save the *big* discussion of memory for Chapter 12, but given the fact that we're about to spend a disproportionate amount of time in Device Manager in this next section, I know you'll see the settings and wonder what they mean. This short discussion should suffice until we get hairy in Chapter 12.

## Hex and Memory

Because memory means all the permutations of 1's and 0's that the address bus can create, we find that using hexadecimal makes the discussion of memory addresses much easier. Although the ancient 8088/8086 used a 20-bit address bus, all modern CPUs use a 32-bit address bus. From the I/O address discussion in Chapter 5, you may recall that we can represent any four patterns of 1's and 0's with one hex character, so we can represent any permutation on a modern 32-bit address bus using eight hexadecimal characters. Devices that need memory use a range of memory addresses. These addresses are displayed using the format *XXXXXXXX-YYYYYYYY*. Figure 10-74 shows the resource usage for a typical PCI video card.

Note setting D8000000-D9FFFFFF. This denotes a memory address range used by the video card. See the IRQ and I/O addresses? From the standpoint of Windows, a memory address is just another resource. If I scroll up on the same screen, you see that this device uses multiple memory addresses as shown in Figure 10-75—a perfectly normal situation, just as some devices use multiple I/O addresses, IRQs, or DMAs.

**Figure 10-74**
Typical video card resources

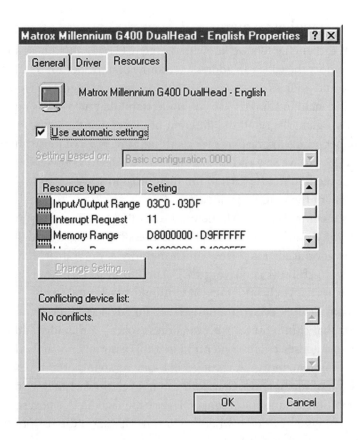

## Legacy Devices in a Plug and Play World

Now that we know all of the resources that a device may potentially use, I think it's time to start getting messy! In Chapter 5, we covered the tedious steps required to install legacy devices, but let's do a quick review. Installing devices before the advent of PnP required us to perform a number of careful steps to avoid resource conflicts.

1. We kept a paper inventory of used resources, in particular IRQs, because compared with DMA or I/O addresses, relatively few IRQs were available on a typical system.

2. Lacking a precise inventory, we ran system information tools that tried to discover all the devices on the system. These DOS-based tools varied considerably in accuracy, but the better ones could find most devices.

3. We then configured the device to use available system resources. This required setting jumpers or switches on the device, or in the case of later legacy devices, running a special configuration program to set the resources.

**Figure 10-75**
Multiple memory
addresses

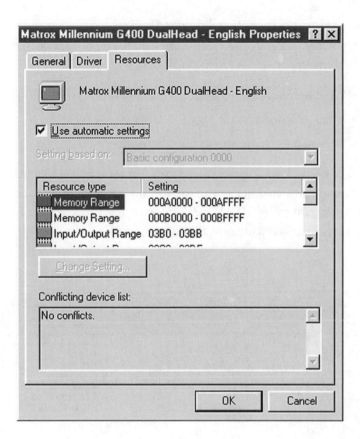

4. We then installed the device and started the system. In the DOS and Windows 3.*x*
   days, the OS did not handle resource configuration. Instead, the device drivers we
   installed into CONFIG.SYS or SYSTEM.INI required special resource settings so
   that the driver knew which resources to call on to locate the device.

5. We then installed the device's application and tested. If we had lockups, we
   assumed (usually correctly) that we had inadvertently created an IRQ or DMA
   conflict. If the device did not respond, we assumed we had an I/O address or
   memory address conflict.

Installing a legacy device in a PnP environment creates a unique challenge. PnP does
not eliminate the need to assess open resources, configure the device, or configure the
device driver, although the Device Manager does make the task of determining available resources trivial. We must create an environment that enables PnP devices to avoid
the fixed resources of the legacy device, and then set the resources and install and configure the driver for the legacy device.

## Preparing to Install a Legacy Device

Long before you grab a screwdriver to install a legacy device, you need to answer some critical questions:

- What resources are available on the system?
- What resources can the legacy device use?
- Do you have driver support for this device?

Let's say we have a legacy sound card that must have I/O addresses 0220-022F, IRQ5 or 9, and DMA channel 1. The sound card has no jumpers and instead uses a special DOS program called UTILITY.EXE to set its resources (Figure 10-76). Before installing the card, you need to answer all three questions.

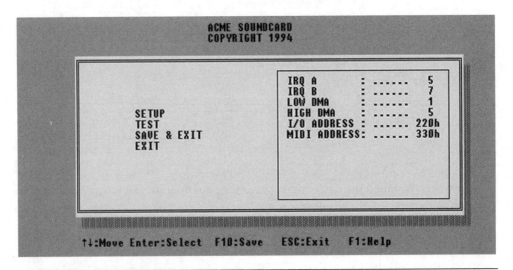

**Figure 10-76**  DOS install utility

### Determining Available Resources

The first step is by far the easiest. A quick trip to the Device Manager shows all available resources. In Windows 9x, click the Computer icon at the top of the Device Manager tree to see all resources used by devices. This special screen enables you to sort by any of the four resource types, making open resources obvious. Figure 10-77 shows the resources sorted by IRQ. I scrolled past some of the lower IRQs to reveal more available IRQs. From here you can see that IRQs 5 and 11 are open for use.

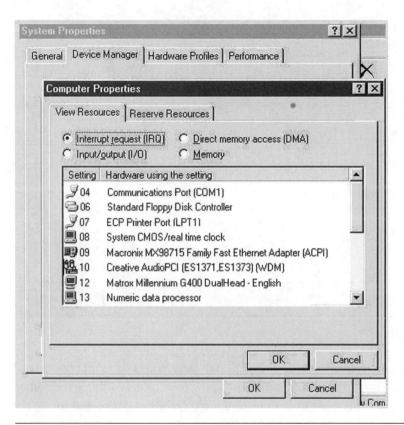

**Figure 10-77**   Resources sorted by IRQ

## Reserving Resources

Now we know what resources are available for the legacy device. That's great but we have no assurance that the legacy device can use any of these open resources. The makers of the legacy device and ISA PnP devices only provide so many resource options. IRQs create the only serious problem here because all other resources enjoy lots of unused areas. Referring to the previous figure, what happens when some old sound card cannot use IRQ5 or 11? In that case, you have to kick a PnP device off an IRQ that the sound card will use and onto some other resource. You can accomplish this by telling the PnP to reserve a particular IRQ for that device. We perform this operation in two areas: the CMOS and the Reserve Resources tab in the Computer properties.

## Reserving in Device Manager

Take one more peek at the previous figure—see that other tab? Click it to see Figure 10-78.

**Figure 10-78**
Reserve Resources
tab

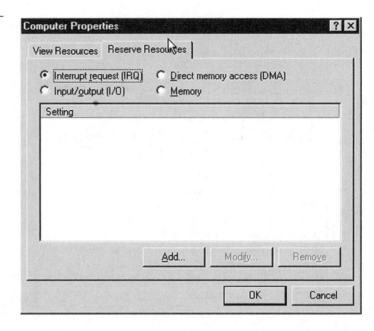

This screen enables us to tell Windows PnP to stay away from a particular resource(s) resources. Don't do anything in here now; just know how to get to this screen when needed. Before we do this, shut down the computer, get into CMOS, and locate the PnP/PCI option menu if available (Figure 10-79).

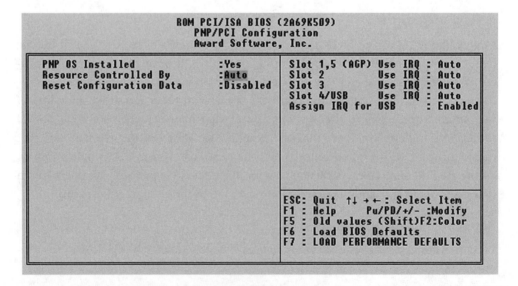

**Figure 10-79**  Award BIOS PnP/PCI Configuration menu

The options available for PnP in CMOS vary so wildly that brevity requires me to limit myself to a typical Award BIOS screen. Every CMOS will show at least one of the three main PnP settings:

- PNP OS Installed
- Reset Configuration Data
- Resources Controlled By

### PNP OS Installed

A PnP BIOS normally tries to initiate all PnP devices, including ISA PnP cards. If you set the PNP OS Installed option to Yes, the PnP BIOS only initializes ISA PnP devices required for boot, such as an ISA video card. Make sure to set this option to Yes.

Some newer systems that use *Advanced Configuration and Power Interface* (ACPI) require you to change this setting to "off." See Chapter 18 for details.

### Reset Configuration Data

This option makes the PnP reassign all resources for all devices. Set this option to Enabled after you install any ISA device, especially a legacy ISA device, to make the PnP avoid that device's resources. This option will always set itself back to Disabled at the next reboot.

### Resources Controlled By

This is the traditional place to reserve IRQs and, in some systems, DMA channels for legacy ISA devices. Set this option to manual to see the following (Figure 10-80).

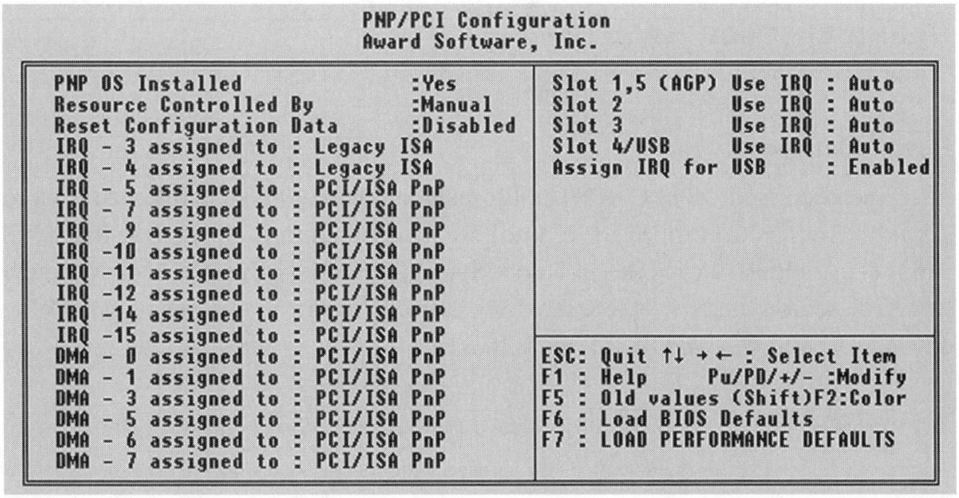

```
                    PNP/PCI Configuration
                    Award Software, Inc.

  PNP OS Installed            :Yes      Slot 1,5 (AGP) Use IRQ : Auto
  Resource Controlled By      :Manual   Slot 2         Use IRQ : Auto
  Reset Configuration Data    :Disabled Slot 3         Use IRQ : Auto
  IRQ -  3 assigned to : Legacy ISA     Slot 4/USB     Use IRQ : Auto
  IRQ -  4 assigned to : Legacy ISA     Assign IRQ for USB      : Enabled
  IRQ -  5 assigned to : PCI/ISA PnP
  IRQ -  7 assigned to : PCI/ISA PnP
  IRQ -  9 assigned to : PCI/ISA PnP
  IRQ -10 assigned to : PCI/ISA PnP
  IRQ -11 assigned to : PCI/ISA PnP
  IRQ -12 assigned to : PCI/ISA PnP
  IRQ -14 assigned to : PCI/ISA PnP
  IRQ -15 assigned to : PCI/ISA PnP
  DMA -  0 assigned to : PCI/ISA PnP
  DMA -  1 assigned to : PCI/ISA PnP    ESC: Quit  ↑↓ → ← : Select Item
  DMA -  3 assigned to : PCI/ISA PnP    F1 : Help      Pu/PD/+/- :Modify
  DMA -  5 assigned to : PCI/ISA PnP    F5 : Old values (Shift)F2:Color
  DMA -  6 assigned to : PCI/ISA PnP    F6 : Load BIOS Defaults
  DMA -  7 assigned to : PCI/ISA PnP    F7 : LOAD PERFORMANCE DEFAULTS
```

**Figure 10-80** Manual settings

Hey, wait a minute! Didn't we just see that the Device Manager enables us to reserve resources? Why do it here? Officially, you don't have to deal with this; if you just set it to Auto, the reserve settings in Windows will do all the reserving you need. I occasionally run across some systems where you reserve IRQs here, however, even though you have reserved the option in Device Manager. Many CMOS setup utilities have dropped this option and just count on you to handle reserving resources in Device Manager.

While you're still in CMOS, locate the Integrated Peripherals menu. Always turn off any unused serial ports, parallel ports, or USB ports, to open up those IRQs (Figure 10-81). You can free up a number of otherwise unavailable IRQs this way. Just remember to turn them back on if you decide to use them later!

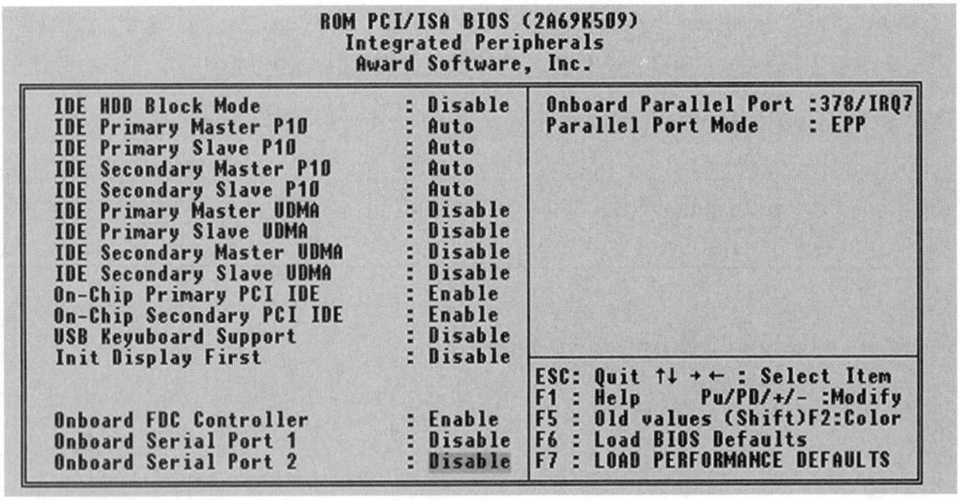

```
           ROM PCI/ISA BIOS (2A69K509)
              Integrated Peripherals
              Award Software, Inc.

 IDE HDD Block Mode          : Disable   Onboard Parallel Port :378/IRQ7
 IDE Primary Master P10      : Auto      Parallel Port Mode    : EPP
 IDE Primary Slave P10       : Auto
 IDE Secondary Master P10    : Auto
 IDE Secondary Slave P10     : Auto
 IDE Primary Master UDMA     : Disable
 IDE Primary Slave UDMA      : Disable
 IDE Secondary Master UDMA   : Disable
 IDE Secondary Slave UDMA    : Disable
 On-Chip Primary PCI IDE     : Enable
 On-Chip Secondary PCI IDE   : Enable
 USB Keyboard Support        : Disable
 Init Display First          : Disable
                                        ESC: Quit ↑↓ → ← : Select Item
                                        F1 : Help       Pu/PD/+/- :Modify
 Onboard FDC Controller      : Enable   F5 : Old values (Shift)F2:Color
 Onboard Serial Port 1       : Disable  F6 : Load BIOS Defaults
 Onboard Serial Port 2       : Disable  F7 : LOAD PERFORMANCE DEFAULTS
```

**Figure 10-81**  CMOS' Integrated Peripherals

### Device Manager

After reserving resources in CMOS (or just making sure that PNP OS Installed is set to Yes and Resources Controlled By to Auto), we need to return to the Reserve Resources tab under Computer Properties in Device Manager to reserve the resources. Although Reserve Resources enables us to reserve any resource, in my many years of using Windows 9x I've only reserved IRQs (Figure 10-82).

**Figure 10-82**
Reserved IRQs

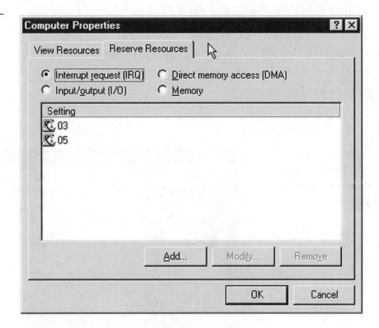

## Installing the Legacy Device

Once you have reserved all necessary resources, install the sound card and boot to a startup disk. Run the UTILITY.EXE program to set the resources for the card and then reboot the system normally into Windows.

Windows does not look for legacy devices at boot, so nothing "interesting" happens. We now need to run the Add New Hardware Wizard in the Control Panel to tell Windows to install the sound card (Figure 10-83).

**Figure 10-83**
Add New Hardware
Wizard opening

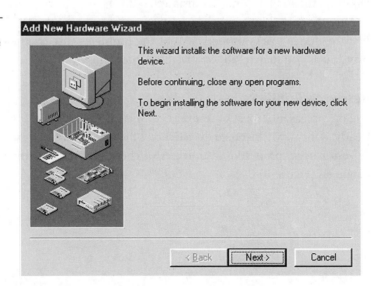

Windows comes with a powerful search function that finds most legacy devices. This confuses many techs into thinking their legacy card is PnP. Don't be fooled—it's just a neat aspect of Windows. In most cases, Windows will discover your card and will either install drivers if it recognizes the device (as shown in Figure 10-84), or in most cases, prompt you for a driver.

**Figure 10-84**
Windows ready to install recognized devices

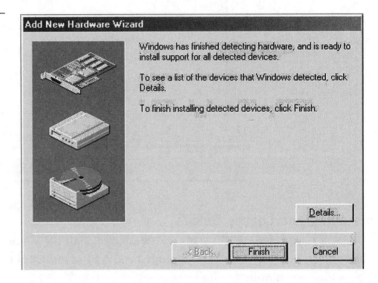

If Windows prompts for a driver, you must hope that the disk holding the UTILITY program also contains the proper drivers for your version of Windows. Click the Have Disk button, and let Windows install the drivers.

After the installation finishes, make a point to go to the Device Manager to verify that the device works properly. All of the problems discussed earlier may come into play, but as you may recall, we saved one problem for this section: resource conflicts.

## Resource Conflicts

The only pleasant aspect of resource conflicts is the way Windows reports them—very clearly. If the newly installed device shows the infamous black exclamation point or red "x" error in its properties, a quick error-check always confirms the resource conflict diagnosis (Figure 10-85).

**Figure 10-85**
Resource conflict
error

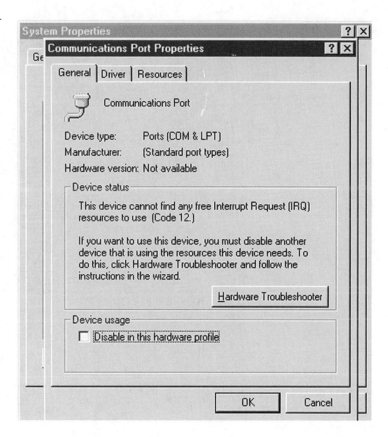

Note that this error shows both the conflict text warning and the device with which the legacy device conflicts. If you follow the preparation steps shown earlier, this error will not appear. I usually see this error when I dump in the legacy card without first reserving resources. If you failed to set the resources on the card, start over. But if you know the resources on the legacy device, you can manually configure them. Open the device's properties and go to the Resources tab (Figure 10-86).

The Resources tab differs wildly between different versions of Windows and various pieces of hardware, but almost all of them enable you to configure a device manually. To configure the device displayed in Figure 10-86, for example, you must click the Set Configuration Manually button and then on the subsequent dialog box (shown in Figure 10-87), uncheck the Use automatic settings check box. Always leave this checked—thus leaving the PnP manager in charge of resource allocation—unless you need to repair a resource conflict manually. Uncheck the box to activate the Setting based on pull-down menu. Click the pull-down menu to see the options (Figure 10-87).

**Figure 10-86**
Resources tab

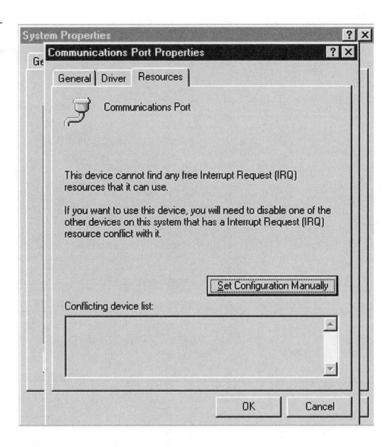

**Figure 10-86**
Resources tab

The Basic configurations are simply preset resource combinations used to set the device. If by some lucky chance one of these fits your resource needs, you may use it, however, most of the time, just scroll down and select the last Basic configuration option, which enables you to change individual resource settings (Figure 10-88).

Windows doesn't like it when you set resources manually and a big "Are you sure?" screen appears when complete. Just click OK and restart the system. The device now uses the manually configured resource.

**Figure 10-87**
Resource settings
pull-down menu

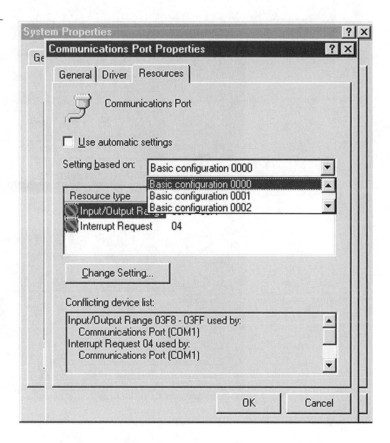

## Installing and Upgrading Windows 9x

Installing or upgrading Windows 9x is usually a surprisingly painless, roughly hour-long process. The combination of PnP with an amazingly intelligent installation program makes most installs a matter of typing in commands and trying to stay awake as files are copied and the system goes through a number of reboots. The A+ exam is very interested in your ability to install Windows 9x on a blank (unpartitioned) drive and to upgrade a Windows 95 to a Windows 98 system. This section covers both of these situations.

The upgrading or installing process always require three distinct areas:

1. Preparing to Upgrade or Install

2. Performing the Upgrade/Install

3. Debugging

This section will assume a stand-alone system without networking. We'll cover the networking installation steps and issues in Chapter 20.

**Figure 10-88**
Changing individual
resource settings

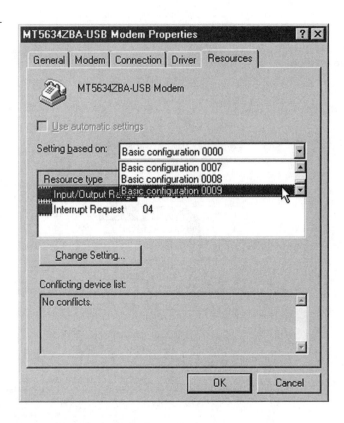

## Preparing to Upgrade/Install

Most Windows upgrades and installs fail for the simple reason that the tech fails to perform a few basic checks before installing/upgrading Windows 9*x*. Follow these few steps—they work.

## Minimum Requirements

Microsoft defines some fairly low hardware requirements for both Windows 95 and Windows 98. To make things more confusing, different types of Microsoft documentation give different values. After some serious research and a few phone calls to some "muckety mucks" I know over at Microsoft, here are the official minimum hardware requirements for Windows 9*x*:

- 486DX/66 CPU with 24MB of RAM

- Hard drive space up to 400MB—the average Windows install takes 200MB

- Video capable of 640 × 480 @ 16 colors

They also recommend a mouse, CD-ROM, and sound card. I find these requirements laughably low. Even Microsoft admits this, but it is possible to run (maybe a better term would be "walk") Windows 9*x* with this hardware.

## Hardware Compatibility

Assuming your system meets these requirements, you need to see how well Windows supports your hardware. Check the Microsoft hardware compatibility list at **http://www.microsoft.com/hcl/default.asp** for the definitive list. Don't panic if you don't see your device; many supported devices do not appear on that list. Check the floppies or CD-ROMs that come with your hardware for proper devices. Even when the HCL lists a piece of hardware, I still make a point to check the Web site for later drivers. Resist the temptation to use a Windows 95 driver on a Windows 98 system unless you simply have no choice.

## Antivirus and Backup

If you're upgrading, take a moment to run an antivirus utility on the system. An active virus during install will, at the very least, infect every file you place on the drive. In most cases, it simply destroys the installation process, requiring a complete "start from the top."

Also make a point to save any data when upgrading; Windows installations do fail occasionally. In some cases, they destroy everything on the drive.

## Setup Disk

Windows 9*x* installs only on a partitioned formatted drive. Many Windows installations come with a Setup disk (Figure 10-89) that will detect unpartitioned/unformatted drives. Then, they partition and format them for you automatically.

**Figure 10-89**
Windows 95 Setup
disk

Even when I have one of those Setup disks, I'm more comfortable doing it myself from a regular Windows startup disk. I like the flexibility of deciding how the drive will be partitioned. If you're not a control freak like me, those Setup disks work just fine. If you decide to use your own disk, make sure you have a Startup disk that can access the CD-ROM!

The other option is to boot directly from the CD-ROM. This assumes that your PC enables you to boot to a CD-ROM (check your CMOS) and that the Windows installation CD-ROM is bootable. Windows 98 installation CD-ROMs are bootable (so are Windows NT and Windows 2000), but Windows 95 installation CD-ROMs are not, requiring you to use some form of bootable floppy disk.

### Correct CD-ROM

Make sure you use the correct CD-ROM! Windows comes in both Upgrade and Full versions. Some systems require a special OEM version made just for that system, particularly laptops. Don't bother trying to use an upgrade version on a blank drive unless you also have a full earlier version of Windows.

### FAT16 or FAT32?

You need to decide ahead of time what type of partition you will want to use. Although you should almost always pick FAT32 for both clean installs and upgrades, three situations exist that might make you want to keep at least one FAT16 partition. First, consider if you might want to boot to the previous version of MS-DOS to support a DOS program that will not run in Windows, even in a DOS box. Second, you might have a version of Windows 95 that simply doesn't support FAT32. Third, you might want to set up some wild multiboot functions. Except in those rare cases, you should choose to use FAT32.

### Installing vs. Upgrading

The only real difference between installing and upgrading takes place at the very beginning. In an "upgrade from Windows 95 to Windows 98" scenario, you already have an OS and a number of nicely installed applications that you probably would prefer not to reinstall. In a clean install, you have a blank, unpartitioned drive with nothing on it. A clean install requires a few extra steps, because you must partition and format the drive before you can begin to install Windows 9x. To do a clean install, boot to the Startup disk and run FDISK to partition as you would like (here's your big chance to make a D: drive to store backups!), and then format the C: drive.

Many techs are aware of CVT.EXE (used at a command prompt) or the CVT1.EXE (Windows-based—select Programs | Accessories | System Tools | Drive Converter) utility that comes with Windows 98. These tools enable you to convert a FAT16 drive to FAT32 without losing data (Figure 10-90).

**Figure 10-90**
Drive conversion
tools

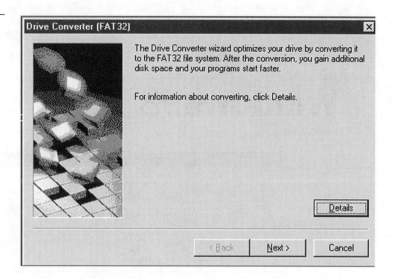

With such handy conversion tools, why bother worrying about using FAT16 or FAT32? Don't forget the 2GB partition size limitation of FAT16. A brand-new 30GB drive will need a lot of drive letters. Also, the convert tools have been known to fail disastrously, albeit rarely. Better to play it safe and decide ahead of time!

## The Install/Upgrade Process

Once the blank drive is formatted, the Install and the Upgrade processes become virtually identical. If you're upgrading, just boot normally into Windows 95 and toss in the upgrade disk to see the upgrade prompt (Figure 10-91).

If you're doing a clean install, run the SETUP.EXE program on the CD-ROM. If the setup software doesn't automatically show you a prompt, just manually start the SETUP.EXE program from the CD-ROM. (I hope your setup disk supports the CD-ROM, or you won't get a CD-ROM drive letter!)

A common installation trick is to copy the contents of the \WIN9x folder from the CD-ROM to a folder on your hard drive. Copying the installation files to your hard drive does two things. First, it makes the installation of Windows 9x faster, as CD-ROMs are very slow. Second, Windows 9x is notorious for needing the original CD-ROM virtually every time you make a change to the system's configuration. Windows will remember where it was installed from and will prompt for you to "Insert the Windows Installation CD-ROM." If you put the files in a folder on a local drive and then install from there, Windows will remember that and will immediately go straight to those files, saving you the hassle of trying to find the Install CD-ROM.

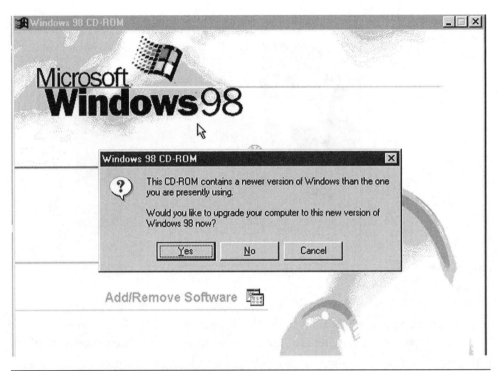

**Figure 10-91**   Windows 95 upgrade prompt

## DOS Part

Both Windows 95 and 98 clean installs always begin with a command prompt-level install process, which performs a quick ScanDisk and a quick check for video and mouse. Then the program loads a few critical files needed for installation, usually then initiating the first of many reboots (Figure 10-92).

## Graphical Install

After the initial command prompt install process, Windows shifts into a graphical install mode with the Install Setup Wizard. This wizard begins by installing a second set of critical installation files. It then uses these files first to verify that you have sufficient hard drive space, and then to prompt you for input on various Windows options. Let's look at the typical prompt screens.

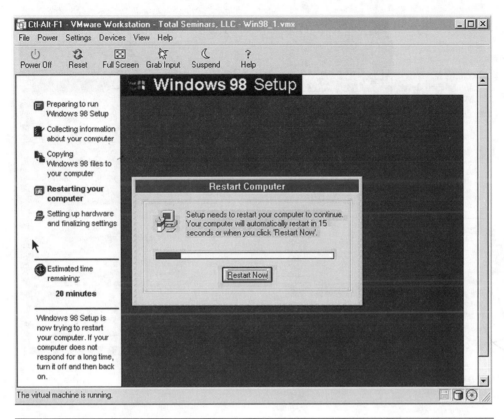

**Figure 10-92** Reboot?

## Prompt for Component Options

Windows 9*x* prompts for you to install with options that look like Figure 10-93. For most users, a Typical installation is the safest bet. Once they become familiar with the many options of the Windows 9*x* install, however, most folks prefer to use the Custom option. The Compact option is rarely used; it simply skips too many features that most users want. Never worry about this screen; you can always add or remove components after Windows installs by using the Add/Remove Software applet in the Control Panel.

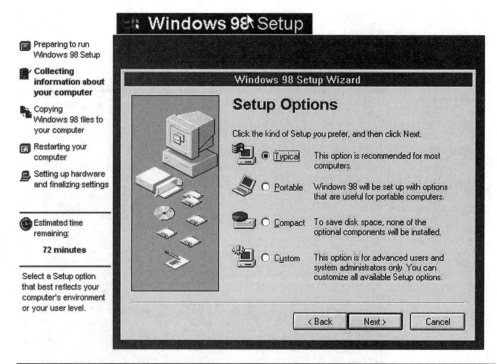

**Figure 10-93** Component options: Typical, Custom, and Compact

### Prompt for Product Key

Microsoft makes money by selling Windows, not by giving it away. Thus, the installation process prompts you to install the product key (as in Figure 10-94), which is invariably located on the CD-ROM container. Most techs learn the hard way that these covers tend to disappear when you need them most, and they write the product code directly on the CD-ROM itself (Figure 10-95). (Just don't use a ball-point pen; it'll scratch the surface of the disk.)

Windows 95 used to wait until near the end of the install process to ask for the product key, driving techs crazy when they realized they had spent 20 minutes installing just to discover that their key was missing. Windows 98 and 2000 both are kind enough to ask for the key early in the process, saving considerable inconvenience when you're juggling 23 different CD-ROMs all in the wrong cases, trying to punch in the correct product key.

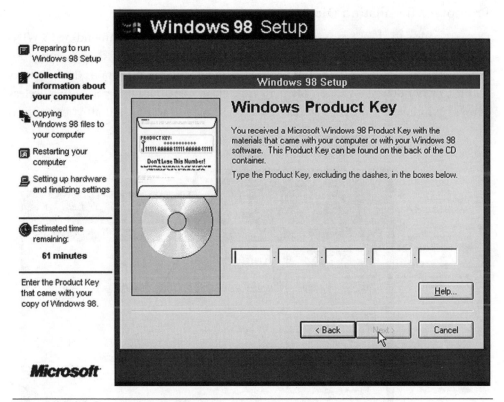

**Figure 10-94** Prompt for product key

**Figure 10-95**
Product key written
on the CD-ROM

### Prompt for Installation Directory

Clean installs will always prompt for an installation directory, recommending C:\WIN-DOWS (Figure 10-96). Use this default unless compelled not to. When upgrading from Windows 95 to Windows 98, you must use the same folder that contains the Windows 95 files, or Windows 98 will simply perform a clean install, leaving you with a useless copy of Windows 95 on your system, and requiring you to reinstall all your applications.

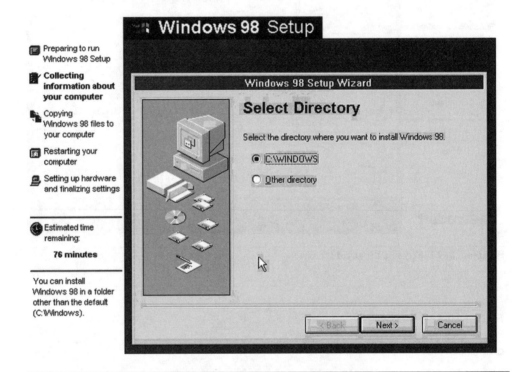

**Figure 10-96**    Prompt for installation directory

### Prompt for Startup Disk

You should already have a startup disk, but you can make another now if you would like. All startup disks for the same version of Windows are identical. If you choose not to make a startup disk, simply click Cancel when given the opportunity.

### Network Options

The Windows 95 Installation Wizard is kind of dumb here; it always prompts for networking information even if it does not detect a network card. Although our current installation example assumes a stand-alone system, we'll save this discussion for Chapter 20.

## Save System Files

When upgrading from Windows 95 to Windows 98, you are given the opportunity to save the Windows 95 system files. If you save these files, you may uninstall Windows 98 from the Add/Remove Programs | Windows Setup tab in the Control Panel.

## The Big Copy

No matter your version of Windows, the install process always gets to the point where Windows begins to install itself on the system. I call this "The Big Copy" and use this time to catch up on my reading, eat a sandwich, or count ceiling tiles.

## Hardware Detection

The point where the hardware detection phase begins varies between Windows 95 and Windows 98. They both work the same way, but Windows 98 is a bit more automated.

Windows follows the classic PnP search methodology described in Chapter 5. Windows first tries to find legacy devices (Windows 95 "cheats" by asking you if you have a sound card or a network card) and then kicks in the PnP hardware detection functions, searching for and configuring the detectable hardware on the system (Figure 10-97).

**Figure 10-97**
Hardware detection
and configuration

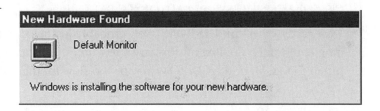

In a completely PnP environment, this is usually a matter of watching the installation process. As Windows detects devices, it will load the appropriate device drivers if it has them; if not, it will prompt you for a driver disk. This process is identical to the process described earlier of installing a device into an existing system.

## Installation Ain't So Tough!

Following these steps when installing or upgrading Windows 9x makes this process very simple in most cases. However, problems do occur during install that we need to take a moment to address.

## Install Problems

The term "install problem" is rather deceptive. The install process itself almost never fails. Usually, something else fails during the install process that makes us point at some intangible we call an "install failure." Let's look at some typical installation problems and how to correct them.

## DOS Level Errors

If I'm going to have an install problem, this is the place to get one. It's always better to have the error right off the bat, as opposed to when the installation is nearly complete. DOS errors only take place during clean installs and usually point to one of the following:

- **"No boot device present" when booting off the startup disk**   Either the startup disk is bad or the CMOS is not set to look to the floppy disk first.

- **"Windows has detected that drive C: does not contain a valid FAT partition"**   You forgot to partition the hard drive, or you're trying to install on a partition type that Windows doesn't understand.

- **"Windows Setup requires XXXX amount of available drive space"**   You forgot to format the C: drive, or there's a bunch of stuff on the drive already.

- **MSCDEX error "No CD-ROM detected"**   The CD-ROM settings are messed up. Check the CONFIG.SYS and AUTOEXEC.BAT settings.

- **"Not ready error" on CD-ROM**   You probably just need to give the CD-ROM a moment to catch up. Press **R** for retry a few times. You may also have a damaged Install CD-ROM, or the CD-ROM may be too slow for the system.

## Errors During Install

Once the install passes the DOS level and moves into the graphical portion, a whole new crop of problems may arise. These two are by far the most common:

- **Can't read CAB files**   This is probably the most common of all installation errors. Check the CD-ROM for scratches. Try copying all the files from the \WIN9x drive into a directory on your hard drive and running setup from there. Finally, try another CD-ROM drive.

- **This system already has an OS**   This is a common error when upgrading from 95 to 98. You're probably trying to use a full install CD-ROM for an upgrade. There's a perfectly legal way around this:

1. Exit setup.
2. Type **C:**.
3. Type **CD\SYSTEM**.
4. Type **ren setupx.dll setupx.ol1**.
5. Type **ren setupx.w95 setupx.ol2**.
6. Start Setup again.

## Lockups During Install

Lockups during install vary considerably depending on whether you install Windows 95 or 98. In Windows 95, lockups are fairly common; in Windows 98, they are rare.

### Safe Recovery

Most system lockups occur when Windows queries the hardware. If a system locks up once during an install, turn off the computer. Literally unplug the system. Do *not* press CTRL-ALT-DEL. Do *not* click Reset. Turn the system back on with the bootable floppy still inserted, and rerun the setup program. Windows will see the partial installation and prompt you for a "Safe Recovery" mode. This mode ignores all but the most critical hardware to complete the installation. Hopefully once you have installed Windows, you can then use the techniques we learned earlier in the chapter to focus on the problem component.

### CD-ROM/Hard Drive

Bad CD-ROM disks, CD-ROM drives, or hard drives may cause lockups. Check and replace the drive if necessary.

## Log Files

Windows 95 generates a number of special text files called log files that track the progress of certain processes. While Windows makes a number of different log files for different purposes, three files, all located in the root directory of your C: drive, most interest us:

- **SETUPLOG.TXT** tracks the complete installation process, logging the success or failure of file copying, registry updates, reboots, and so on.
- **DETLOG.TXT** is created during the hardware detection process. It tracks the detection, query, and installation of all devices.
- **BOOTLOG.TXT** tracks the boot process, logging as each device driver and program loads.

Honestly, the chances of you ever actually reading a log file, understanding it, and then getting something fixed as a result of that understanding, are pretty small. What makes log files handy is when you call Microsoft or a hardware manufacturer. They *love* to read these files and actually have people who understand them. Don't worry about trying to understand log files for either the A+ exam or for real life; just make sure you know the names of the log files and their location. Leave the details to the Ubergeeks.

## No Install Is Perfect

Even when the installation seems smooth, issues may slowly surface, especially in the case of upgrades. Be prepared to reinstall applications or deal with new functions absent in the previous OS. If things really fall apart, you can always go back to the previous OS.

## Optimizing and Maintaining Windows 9x

If you were looking forward to seeing the "Hot-Rodder's Guide to Windows 9x" in this section, you're in for a big disappointment. All versions of Windows 9x come pretty well optimized out of the box. There is very little you can do to make a Windows system run faster or better by "tweaking the system." Sure, I read the same Web sites and magazines you do that tout some bizarre registry setting that makes a Windows system better, but on the whole I've found them to be hardly worth the effort and certainly way outside the scope of the A+ exams! Instead, optimization of Windows 9x means little more than checking the status of a few settings, which in all probability are already set properly by Windows, and making sure a Windows system takes advantage of the latest updates.

Maintenance, as you might expect, focuses on running an occasional ScanDisk, Defrag, antivirus, system cleanup, and system backup. When installed properly, all of these functions work automatically, or nearly automatically, freeing us up for more interesting problems. Let's begin with the most important of all jobs: updating Windows with service packs and patches.

## Service Packs/Patches/Windows Update

Windows has gone through a number of evolutionary changes over the years. Since its inception, Windows 9x has received a number of patches and upgrades to correct or improve a broad cross-section of problems. There are three different ways to update Windows: patches, service packs, and new versions.

Patches are EXE files that you get from Microsoft to fix a specific problem. You run these programs, and they do whatever they're supposed to do—update DLLs, reconfigure registry settings, or whatever else they need to do to fix a particular problem. For example, Figure 10-98 is a patch to fix a problem Windows had with extended partitions on LBA drives.

What is a "TSD Virtual Device?" Who cares? What matters is that these patches are

**Figure 10-98**
Patch to fix partition problem

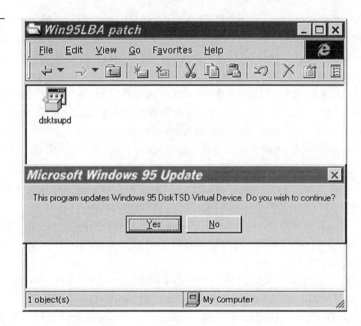

required to keep Windows running properly. This does not mean that Windows 9*x* requires every patch produced. Ignore the patches that have nothing to do with what you do or that fix a problem that you don't have. There are roughly 200 patches for Windows 95 and about 10 to 20 for Windows 98. The majority of them are important. I'll show you how to determine what you need in a moment.

Sometimes a patch might not totally fix a particular problem or might even cause other problems. In that case, you'll need a patch for the patch. Also, some patches need to be installed before another patch can be used. This creates a unique situation where the patch order is quite important.

 **NOTE   The order in which you install patches in Windows 95 can be crucial!**

The first Windows 95 release was followed by a long series of patches over the next few months, fixing everything from password problems to memory leaks. Microsoft packaged these together into a single EXE file that would perform the patches simultaneously. This grouping of patches is called a *service pack*. Currently, two Windows 95 service packs exist, predictably called Service Pack 1 and Service Pack 2 (assuming you have an original version of Windows 95).

Microsoft eventually sold Windows 95 with Service Pack 1 already installed. This version was called *OEM service release 1* (OSR 1). After OSR 1, more patches were created, and so roughly a year later, another set of patches was combined into OSR 2. A number of patches have been created since OSR 2.

As time goes by, Microsoft continues to redefine the names for patches. For example, a patch that fixes a security problem is now called a "security update." Don't let terminology prevent you from getting what you need!

Windows 98 only had one major update, which they call the Customer Service Pack. Windows 98 SE includes the Customer Service Pack, plus a number of other enhancements like new versions of Internet Explorer, Outlook Express, and other applications. A number of minor patches have also been released.

Okay, you're convinced of the need to update Windows. You now need to be able to answer the questions "What service packs/patches are on my system now, and what should I install?"

This is one area where the power of Windows 98 shines through. Just go to the Windows Update utility and let Microsoft tell you (Figure 10-99)!

The Windows Update utility queries your system and provides a list of the updates you require. Simply read about them and select the ones you want. Just know ahead of time that most of these updates are huge—a little tough to download on a 56K modem. Microsoft will gladly provide them on CD-ROM for a nominal fee.

Identifying patches in Windows 95 is tougher. The best way to determine the patches currently loaded on your Windows 95 system is to use Microsoft's QFECHECK (Figure 10-100).

QFECHECK can be downloaded from the Microsoft Web site and generates a detailed list of all patches performed on your machine. Note that the listed patches can be expanded to show the details of the files that were updated. In this case, a file called SHELL32.DLL was updated to version 4.0.0.1111.

Remember that service packs and OSRs are compilations of patches. When you install a service pack or purchase a machine with an OSR, QFECHECK will show *all* the patches performed by the service pack or OSR. In Figure 10-101, only Service Packs and a few other patches have been installed, but QFECHECK breaks down the Service Packs to show separate patches.

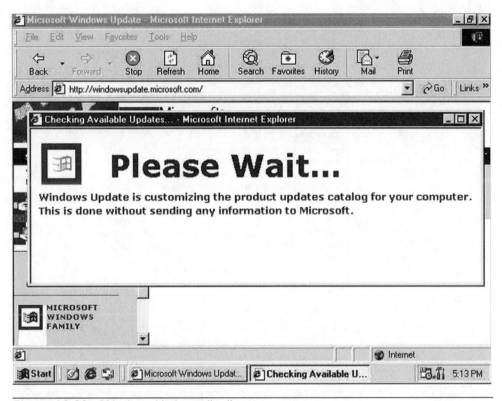

**Figure 10-99** Windows Update tells all . . .

## I Want it All . . . ?

Remember, you don't need every update Microsoft offers. Make sure you understand the needs of the system before you download the latest security update or service pack. When a new one comes out, let other folks test it for a few weeks, and then do a search on the Internet to see if any problems occur with that update. There's no worse feeling than installing a patch to improve a system, only to find you've made it worse!

## Drive Maintenance

Drive maintenance is one of the most boring, tedious, mind-numbing jobs that a PC support person must perform. It is also the single most important way to ensure the long-term health of a PC system. As you know from other chapters, the two most important functions are disk scanning and defragmentation. Windows adds one more important function: the occasional disk cleanup. Let's look at all three.

**Figure 10-100**
QFECHECK

**Figure 10-100**
QFECHECK

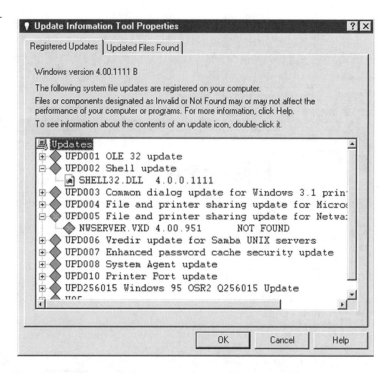

**Figure 10-101**
Service Packs contain many patches.

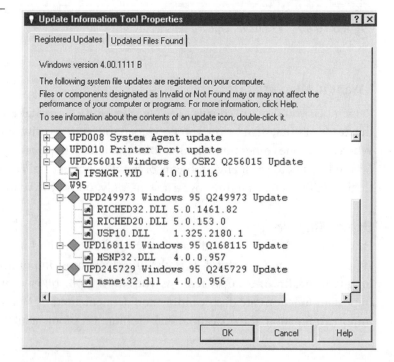

**Defragmentation**  All versions of Windows come with a disk defragmentation utility called Disk Defragmenter. Most techs still just refer to it as *Defrag*—the name of the old DOS disk defragmentation utility. You access Defrag from the Programs | Accessories | System Tools menu. Although the look of Defrag has changed over the Windows versions, it still does the same job. Use as directed in Chapter 8 (Figure 10-102).

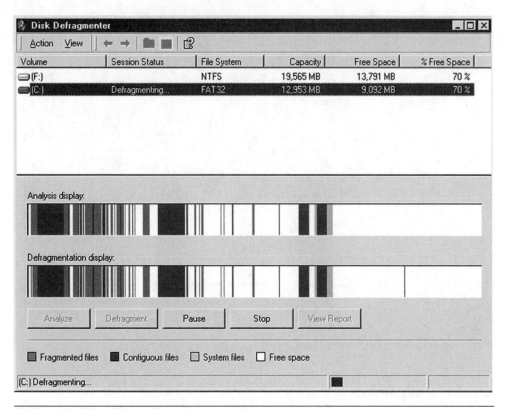

**Figure 10-102**  Disk defragmentation utility

**Disk Scanning**  Just as all versions of Windows come with a disk defragmentation utility, all versions also include a disk scanning program that checks for errors, just like the old ScanDisk utility used to do. As with the term *Defrag*, we still refer to any tool of this type as *ScanDisk*. In Windows 9x, you access ScanDisk from the Programs | Accessories | System Tools menu. Windows 2000 no longer supplies menu support for this tool, opting instead for the Tools tab when you display the properties of each drive (Figure 10-103). All versions of Windows provide access to both Defrag and ScanDisk this way—another example of Windows giving you a number of ways to do the same job.

**Figure 10-103**
Windows 2000
Properties Tools tab

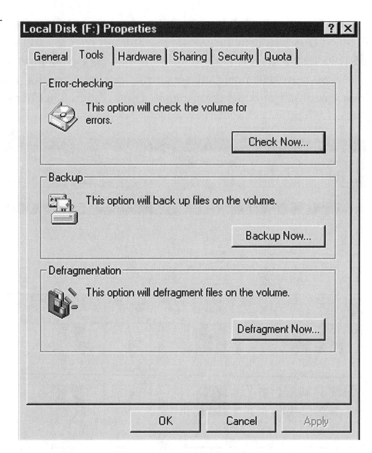

## Drive Cleanup Utilities

As mentioned earlier, Windows really puts a lot of junk files on the system. These junk files fall into one of six categories:

1. Application temporary files that failed to delete

2. Installation temporary files that failed to delete

3. Internet Browser cache files

4. Files in the Recycle Bin

5. Internet cookie files

6. Identical files in separate locations

These files can take up a large percentage of your hard drive. As long as you have lots of extra drive space, these files are unimportant. But as you begin to fill drives, you need to recover that space. Windows 95 brought this problem to light and created an industry of third-party cleanup programs that enabled you to eliminate these files selectively. Not all programs choose the six just listed; most delete fewer, and a couple of programs far more. Either way, disk cleanup has become a critical part of drive maintenance.

Starting with Windows 98, Microsoft introduced a built-in disk cleanup program called, cleverly enough, Disk Cleanup. Most third-party disk cleanup tools do a far better job than Disk Cleanup, but it's not a bad little program (Figure 10-104). I find that some of the better third-party utilities are more flexible. I want a tool, for example, that only deletes Internet cookies that haven't been accessed in the last 60 days. I hate typing in all my Amazon.com data over again!

**Figure 10-104**
Disk Cleanup utility

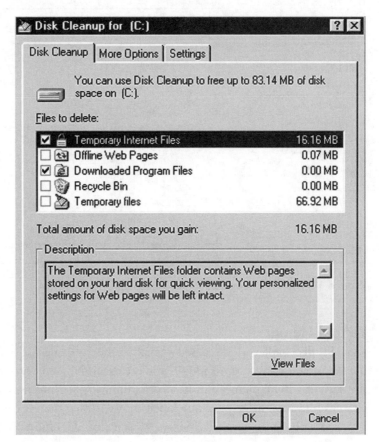

## Task Scheduling

Why bother running these programs manually when you can just tell the Windows Task Scheduler to run them at a certain time? Born from the same third-party utilities, handy task scheduling utilities now come with Windows 98 and Windows 2000. You can simply choose the program you wish to run, when and how often you want it to run, and disk maintenance no longer becomes a part of your job description. I particularly like the one that comes with Windows 2000 (Figure 10-105), although Windows 98's serves well enough.

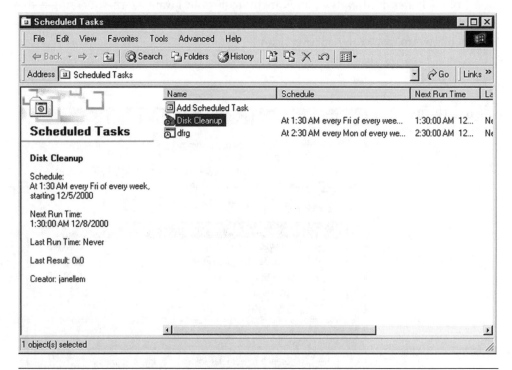

**Figure 10-105**   Windows 2000 task scheduling utility

## Virtual Memory

Early in this chapter we discussed virtual memory during the quick visit to Windows 3.*x*. All versions of Windows require the use of virtual memory—mapping a portion of the hard drive with memory addresses to mimic RAM. Windows creates a swap file that enables it to have more programs open on the screen than it could normally hold in real RAM. The swap file in Windows 9*x* is called WIN386.SWP, while the Windows

2000 swap file is called PAGEFILE.SYS. Windows sets the initial size of the swap file automatically according to the amount of free space available on the C: drive. Although this automatic setting works fairly well, you can easily optimize Windows' use of that swap file with a few judicious alterations. The Windows 9x swap file is configured in the Device Manager. Click the Virtual Memory button on the Performance tab (Figure 10-106).

**Figure 10-106**
Configure Windows
9x swap file

The Windows 2000 swap file settings can be found by alternate-clicking on the My Computer icon on your Desktop, selecting the Advanced tab, and then clicking the Performance Options button. The Performance Options window shows several radio buttons (we'll discuss those in the next chapter); clicking on the Change button opens the Virtual Memory dialog box (Figure 10-107).

**Figure 10-107**
Change Windows 2000 swap file settings.

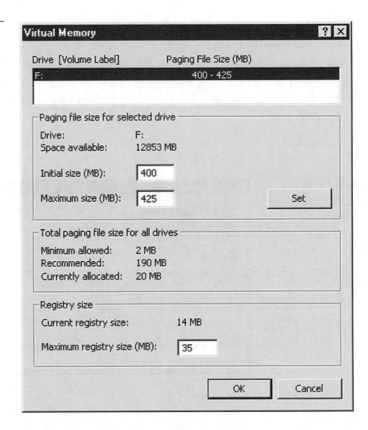

The most common reason for changing the default swap file is to move it to some drive other than C:. Many systems tend to fill up the C: drive, so little or no room is left for the swap file. The swap file can use only the free space on a drive. When the space is filled, the swap file can't get any larger, resulting in the nasty "Not Enough Memory" error. The solution is to move the swap file to another drive.

To move the file in Windows 9x, click on the Let me specify my own virtual memory settings radio button and select another drive (Figure 10-108). In Windows 2000, click the drive letter to which you wish to move the swap file, then click the Set button (Figure 10-109), and close back out of the various windows.

Notice the minimum and maximum swap-file sizes. Windows 9x sets the minimum to zero and the maximum to the size of the free space on the drive, whereas Windows 2000 sets a minimum and maximum by a fairly complex set of rules. Experimentation has shown that leaving these settings at their defaults creates enormous swap files, far larger than you really need. The current consensus is to reduce the swap-file size down to around two or three times the amount of RAM (Figure 10-110), meaning a system with 64MB of RAM is going to have its swap file set somewhere around 128 to 192MB. Set both the minimum and maximum to the same number.

**Figure 10-108**
Selecting a new drive for the Windows 9x swap file

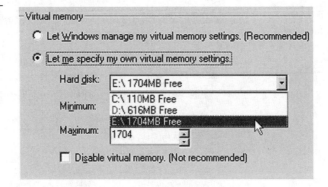

**Figure 10-109**
Setting a new drive for the Windows 2000 swap file

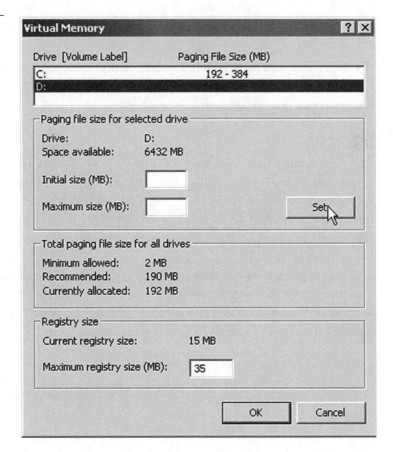

**Figure 10-110**
Set swap-file size
according to RAM.

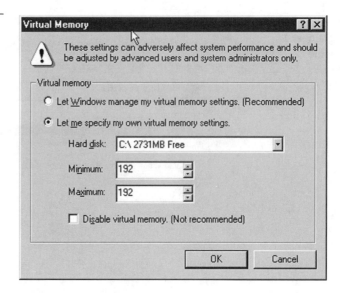

Certain programs demand large swap files. If you use programs like CorelDraw, you will find that the "two to three times" rule won't work. Gradually increase these settings until the "Not Enough Memory" errors go away.

## Disk Cache

The disk caching that comes with Windows installs automatically and is virtually maintenance-free. The size of the disk cache is roughly one-fourth the total size of the RAM. Windows automatically sets the size of the disk-cache holding pen based on settings that are given at setup. You can change these settings by accessing the System Properties | Performance tab | File System button, which opens the File System Properties (see Figure 10-111).

There are two settings for changing the disk cache, both found on the Hard Disk tab: Typical role of this computer and Read-ahead optimization. The Typical role setting determines how much RAM to set aside for the disk cache holding pen. Setting this to Network server can produce a moderate performance boost.

**Figure 10-111**
Change the disk
cache settings.

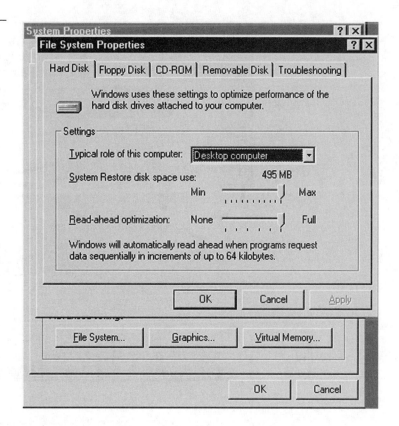

Read-ahead optimization determines how much to read ahead when the system goes
to the hard drive. Think about this for a minute. The disk cache doesn't think in terms
of files; it thinks in terms of clusters. When the hard drive asks for data, it's actually asking for a number of clusters, because files tend to span many clusters. So if the system
asks for one cluster, what are the chances that it will come back in a few milliseconds
and ask for the next cluster? Pretty good, it seems. So, why not have the disk cache grab
a few more clusters, on the assumption that the program will ask for them? This is
called the read-ahead (Figure 10-112). You can adjust the read-ahead using a sliding bar
(Figure 10-113). It should always be set to Full. This enables the disk cache to read
ahead 64K worth of clusters, or two to four clusters ahead on most systems.

**Figure 10-112**
Read-ahead
optimization

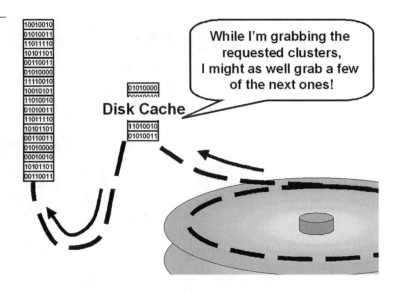

**Figure 10-113**
Sliding bar adjusts
read-ahead

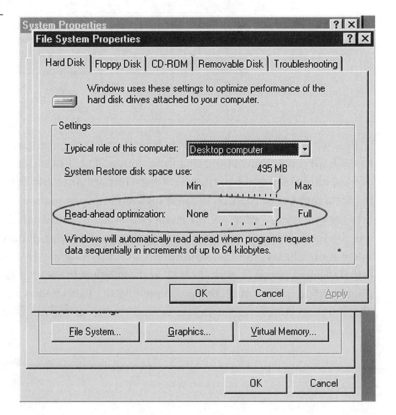

## Resource Tracking Tools

Even though default Windows installations come well optimized, many Windows systems experience substantial system degradation over time. Good disk maintenance and basic optimization take you only so far on systems before they begin to suffer slowdowns. Most of the trouble stems from software bloat—too many programs trying to run at the same time. Sure, we know that opening a number of applications at once eats memory, but the average system is stuffed with background programs that also consume memory. Before we begin to inspect the culprits, you need to know how to use the necessary tools to watch for these problems. These tools will also come into play for other problems.

### System Resources

One area that many techs look to for system resource information on a Windows 9x system is the System Resources percentage on the Performance tab of System Properties (Figure 10-114).

**Figure 10-114**
System Resources
percentage

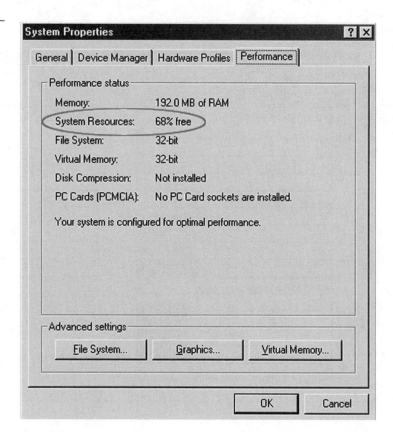

Even though the A+ Certification exams put great stock in this setting, I find it too incomplete to be much help. As we know from earlier in this chapter, Windows 9x uses a number of heaps to store many types of general housekeeping information. To calculate this value, Windows takes a snapshot of all resources' heap usage at boot time. It then monitors all heaps, dividing the current usage by the boot usage, and shows the lowest value for the System Resources usage. Many systems can run down into the low 20s with absolutely no ill effect.

### System Monitor

My favorite tool for checking system problems is the System Monitor. The System Monitor provides a graphic snapshot of a broad number of system processes. You can track free physical memory, CPU usage, network throughput—in fact, almost any process where you need to see what's happening on your PC (Figure 10-115).

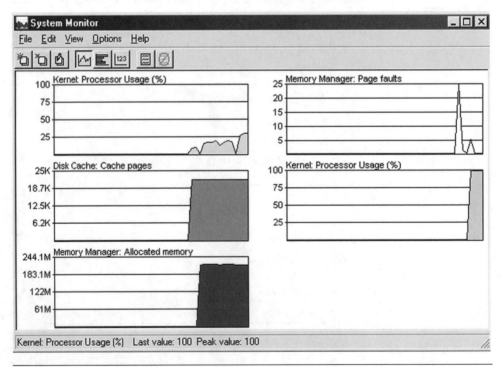

**Figure 10-115**   System Monitor

## System Resource Meter

Heaps are limited in size and are prone to filling up on some systems. While sometimes an overfilled heap will provide an error, as shown in Figure 10-116, other heap over-flows may lock up the system. One clear result of heap filling is substantial system slow-down. To keep an eye on your heaps, use the System Resource Meter (Figure 10-117).

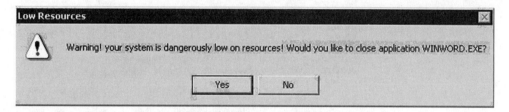

**Figure 10-116**   Overfilled heap error

**Figure 10-117**
System Resource
Meter watches
heaps.

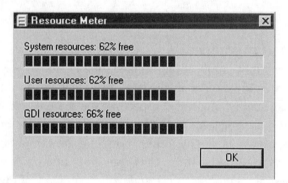

   This handy tool does a much better job of showing you where problems lie. I always load this when I notice a system slowdown—it runs quite nicely from the system tray. As I load applications, I see which ones are eating heap space. If I don't see any sub-stantial heap space usage, I usually head for the System Monitor to look for other prob-lems.

## Task Manager

You access the Task Manager by pressing CTRL-ALT-DEL. The Task Manager shows all run-ning programs, including hidden ones (Figure 10-118). I often use the Task Manager in concert with the System Resource Meter to close background programs that seem to defy closing anyplace else. Just remember never to close Explorer or Systray, as these two programs must run in order to keep Windows running. Actually, there is one rea-son to close the Explorer, which will be shown in a minute.

**Figure 10-118**
The Task Manager shows all programs.

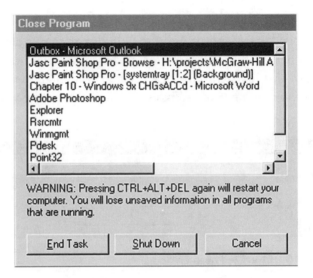

**Auto-Starting Programs**

It seems that every third application installed on a PC today uses some form of background program. In most cases, this is perfectly acceptable—I want my antivirus program to run constantly, invisibly inspecting the system for problems. Yet when someone brings me a sluggish system, my first step is to boot normally and check the processor usage, the available physical memory, and the amount of the swap file in use by using the System Monitor. If the CPU constantly runs at nearly 100 percent, or if most of the physical memory is in use and worse yet, if any of the swap file is in use, I know that I've got way too many auto-starting programs.

Windows has many interesting places for auto-starting programs. To disable or close a few and reclaim precious resources, first go to the System Tray and say to yourself, "Which of these can I live without?" You'll be amazed how many of these programs provide simple "Do you want me to start at next boot?" options that you can turn off. Don't go crazy here; keep the programs you need or want, but close or disable those you don't (Figure 10-119).

If you have Windows 98, fire up the System Information program, and then open the System Configuration Utility from the Tools menu. Go to the Startup tab and uncheck suspicious programs. Don't turn off the System Tray. While you're here, click the WIN.INI tab and open the Windows folder to make sure that no programs are starting under Run= or Load= (Figure 10-120).

**Figure 10-119**
Remove unneeded
programs from the
System Tray.

**Figure 10-120**
Check for programs
loading in WIN.INI.

Finally, see what's running under AUTOEXEC.BAT. The TSRs rarely have much effect on Windows memory, but it never hurts to check.

If you use Windows 95, locate the \WINDOWS\START MENU\PROGRAMS\ STARTUP folder to locate auto-starting programs. Then run SYSEDIT to check the SYSTEM.INI and WIN.INI files.

## Installing Software

Once you have a Windows 9*x* system up and running with the Task Scheduler set up to run maintenance programs such as ScanDisk and Defrag, you will invariably install application software. No matter how perfectly you have installed and optimized Windows, however, installing one poorly written application can completely trash the system. Part of proper system maintenance, therefore, requires you to get your system back to the way it was *before* you installed nasty Program X. There's really only one trick here: Get some kind of program that enables you to return the system to its previous state in case the installation has problems. My favorite is Q-Recovery from Hyper-Q (Figure 10-121).

Lacking a decent "go back to the way it was before" program, copy the registry files as described earlier in this chapter—not perfect, but better then nothing!

**Figure 10-121**
Q-Recovery

## Troubleshooting Windows 9x

We've spent quite a bit of this chapter discussing troubleshooting problems in Windows 9x systems for particular situations such as device installation. In this section, I want to focus on some of the more common problems that seem to arise magically "out of nowhere" on a system. All of these problems share one thing in common: fixing them usually requires you to restore a previously working system. Let's look at the fix first and then address the common problems.

## Be Prepared

In almost every case, we fix a broken or unstable Windows by restoring some kind of backup of some kind of data. You already know how to back up the registry, and you know about a class of programs that enable you to go back to a previous configuration as needed, but we need to discuss the concept of backup in a more generic sense.

## Backup

People get terribly confused by the word "backup." Simply put, backup means to take a copy of a file and place it somewhere else so it can be retrieved in the event of a problem with the original. To me, there are four different groups of files it may be advisable to back up (some of these overlap):

1. Personal data files (usually all the stuff in My Documents).

2. Personal data used by applications (for example, address book entries, favorites, or data files used by accounting programs like Quicken and Peachtree).

3. Current system state files—the registry.

4. The complete contents of the hard drive.

Every version of Windows comes with a Backup program, and although they vary in quality, they can all do any of the preceding jobs.

If I owned the world, I'd make sure every computer had an Iomega Zip® drive onto which users would carefully copy all of their personal files every day. Every memo made by a secretary, every spreadsheet made by an accountant, and every graphic made by an artist would carefully make its way to the Zip disk. Then every user would use the export features of their contact software, account programs, e-mail, and Web browsers to make a daily backup of all this data onto those same Zip disks. But that's not going to happen except in the best of circumstances. Instead, Windows provides us with the handy Backup program which, when combined with a good tape backup system, will save you from data disasters and application installation nightmares time and time again (Figure 10-122).

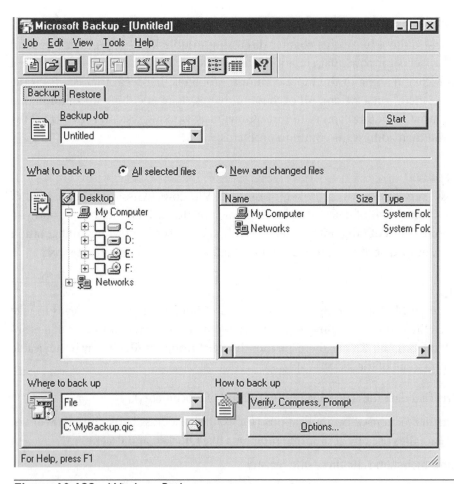

**Figure 10-122** Windows Backup program

Get a tape backup that can hold all your data—the popular DAT format disks are inexpensive and reliable. Figure 10-123 shows a typical tape for backing up a system. Schedule the backup to run at night since backups take a lot of time.

You can speed up the backup process by using a good backup program that enables you to perform different types of backups. Remember in the last chapter when we discussed the archive attribute? Now I can finally explain what it does. Backup programs use the archive bit to determine if a file has been changed since the last time it was backed up. Every time a file is accessed, Windows turns on the archive bit. Backup programs use this fact to reduce the amount of backup time. Why back up a file that's already been backed up and hasn't changed? Knowing this, we divide backups into four types: copy, full, incremental, and differential.

**Figure 10-123**
DAT tape

- **Copy**   Copies selected files and folders to the backup device without turning off the archive bit.

- **Full**   Backs up every file and folder and turns off the archive bit.

- **Incremental**   Backs up only files and folders with the archive bit turned on, and turns off the archive bit.

- **Differential**   Backs up only files and folders with the archive bit turned on, but does not turn off the archive bit.

Whoa! Copy and full make sense, but what's the deal with incremental and differential? You need to appreciate that most people do a full backup about once a week and then do only partial backups during the week. Let's assume that you set up your backup program to do a full backup automatically every Monday night at 10:00 PM. If the system performs a differential backup every other weeknight at 10:00 PM, here's what will happen:

1. Monday night—Full backup

2. Tuesday night—Back up of all files changed since last full backup

3. Wednesday night—Back up of all files changed since last full backup

4. Thursday night—Back up of all files changed since last full backup

5. Friday night—Back up of all files changed since last full backup

A differential backup really just makes you use two tapes: one for the full backup on Monday and another tape for all the other daily backups. This works well, but each differential backup can take longer and longer each evening because every file changed since Monday night keeps getting backed up.

An incremental backup, in contrast, gets only the files changed since the last backup, whether full or partial. Here's the same five-day setup with an incremental backup:

1. Monday night—Full backup

2. Tuesday night—Back up of all files changed since Monday

3. Wednesday night—Back up of all files changed since Tuesday

4. Thursday night—Back up of all files changed since Wednesday

5. Friday night—Back up of all files changed since Thursday

In this case you need a different tape each night because each backup stores only that day's changes. This makes for a fast backup. If you need to restore, however, you end up having to juggle a bunch of tapes. Which one should you use? It doesn't really matter—just make sure you understand how each one works and the benefits of each method. Now that you know the fix for many Windows problems, let's dive into some specific common problems.

## Windows Boot Problems

Many Windows troubleshooting issues deal with boot problems. In most cases, these are fairly simple fixes. Here are a few of the classics:

### No OS Found

This points to a corrupted or missing IO.SYS or MSDOS.SYS. Just pop in your startup disk and use the SYS program to put back the missing file. From the A: prompt, type the following command:

```
SYS C:
```

This automatically restores the IO.SYS, MSDOS.SYS, and COMMAND.COM files. If you edited the MSDOS.SYS file, you will have to restore any edits.

### Bad or Missing COMMAND.COM

This problem is an easy one to fix. Just use your startup disk to copy the COMMAND.COM file back onto the C: drive.

### Error in CONFIG.SYS (line XX)

This one rarely happens unless you've been working in the CONFIG.SYS file or installing some older device that tossed something into CONFIG.SYS. Edit the CONFIG.SYS file and count the line numbers until you get to the one in question. Look for typos. Because most Windows systems pretty much ignore the CONFIG.SYS file anyway, just put a semicolon (;) at the very beginning of the line. If everything runs fine for a few days, go back in and remove the line completely.

### Device Referenced in SYSTEM.INI Not Found

This is exactly the same scenario as described before for CONFIG.SYS, except this usually shows the device name in question. Look back to the section on "Dealing with SYSTEM.INI and WIN.INI" for details.

### HIMEM.SYS Not Loaded or MISSING
### or Corrupt HIMEM.SYS

Windows must load the HIMEM.SYS file at each boot. Because Windows does this automatically, this is rarely an issue. This error tends to result from a hard drive that needs some serious scandisking! As a quick fix, boot off the startup disk and add this line to the CONFIG.SYS file using EDIT:

```
DEVICE=C:\HIMEM.SYS
```

Then, copy the HIMEM.SYS file from the startup disk to the C: drive. Now boot normally and check that hard drive!

### Won't Boot to GUI

Have you ever booted a copy of Windows just to get stuck at the pretty Windows startup screen? Failure to boot into the GUI can have many causes. Let's look at these in order of most to least common.

The first thing to blame is a corrupted swap file. Boot into Safe mode and disable virtual memory. Restart the system when prompted by Windows. If the swap file was the culprit, the system will boot normally, although it may run rather slowly. Turn the swap file back on and reboot again.

 **CAUTION** On systems with small amounts of physical RAM (32MB or less), this might cause serious instability when you first boot. It will still solve the problem of a corrupted swap file. To open System Properties to turn virtual memory back on, however, you might have to boot into Safe mode.

The next thing to try is a step-by-step configuration from the boot menu. This will usually give you a good feel as to which of the following areas should be checked next.

You may need to restore the previous registry copy. Use whatever tool you have to restore a known good copy of the registry. If you don't have one, try replacing SYSTEM.DAT and USER.DAT with SYSTEM.DA0 and the USER.DA0. All of these files are hidden and read-only, so use the ATTRIB command from the startup disk to turn off the attributes. It would look something like this:

```
ATTRIB -r -s -h c:\WINDOWS\SYSTEM\*.dat
COPY c:\WINDOWS\SYSTEM\*.da0 C:\WINDOWS\SYSTEM\*.dat
```

If you have Windows 98, boot to the startup disk and run the Windows Registry Checker tool. From the A: prompt, type

```
C:\WINDOWS\COMMAND\SCANREG /fix
```

Try booting again. If the registry was the problem, you should now boot normally.

Resource conflicts can sometimes prevent the GUI from booting. A quick boot to Safe mode and a check of the Device Manager should confirm this. Fix resource conflicts as described previously.

A bad driver may cause problems. For this, use the *Automatic Skip Driver* (ASD) tool in Safe mode. You can find it under the Tools menu in the System Information tool, although I usually go to Start | Run and type in **ASD**. The ASD looks over your log files and prevents any drivers that failed previously from loading at the next boot. If this works, check for a driver update or remove the offending device.

## Lockups/Reboots

All system lockups fit into one of two groups. The first group is the lockups that take place immediately after you add a new program or device. These almost always point to resource conflicts or software version incompatibilities. Use the techniques described earlier to fix these problems.

The second group is the "lockups from nowhere." These invariably point either to a virus attack (see the big virus discussion in Chapter 9) or to a hardware problem, usually the power supply, RAM, or hard drive. Test/replace until the problem goes away.

Spontaneous reboots always point to bad hardware or a virus. The power supply is the first item to check, followed closely by the CPU. Overheated CPUs love to reboot spontaneously. Make sure the fan works. Most CMOS setup utilities have a screen that enables you to set overheat alarms to monitor the CPU (Figure 10-124).

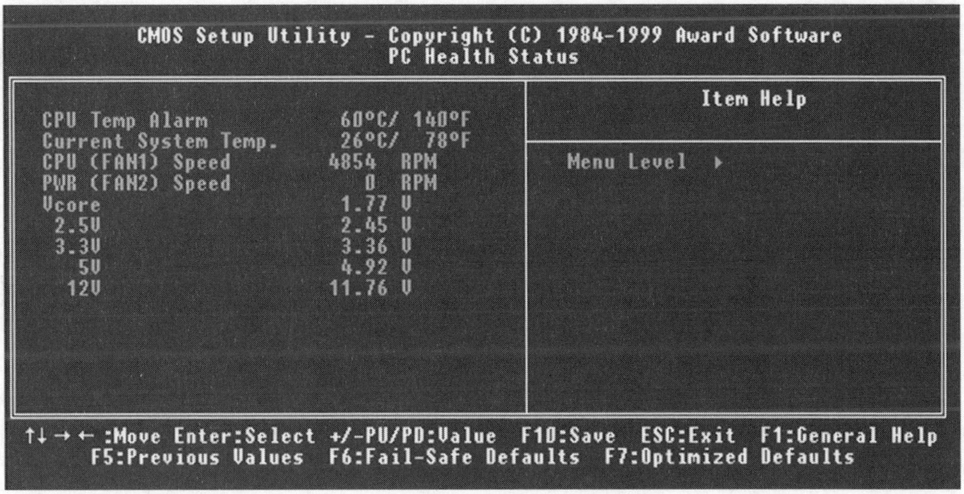

```
           CMOS Setup Utility - Copyright (C) 1984-1999 Award Software
                                PC Health Status

                                                              Item Help
     CPU Temp Alarm            60°C/ 140°F
     Current System Temp.      26°C/  78°F
     CPU (FAN1) Speed        4854   RPM          Menu Level  ▶
     PWR (FAN2) Speed           0   RPM
     Vcore                    1.77 V
      2.5V                    2.45 V
      3.3V                    3.36 V
       5V                     4.92 V
      12V                    11.76 V




     ↑↓ → ← :Move Enter:Select +/-PU/PD:Value  F10:Save  ESC:Exit  F1:General Help
            F5:Previous Values  F6:Fail-Safe Defaults  F7:Optimized Defaults
```

**Figure 10-124**  Set CPU overheat alarms in CMOS setup.

## General Protection Faults

*General protection faults* (GPFs) occur when one program tries to stomp on another program's memory area. If I get an occasional GPF (say, once every two weeks), I usually just ignore it; static and subtle incompatibilities just make GPFs something we live with in Windows. However, consistent GPFs that always point to the same filename as the culprit require attention. If the system has not been changed, the named file may be corrupt. Try reloading the file from the installation CD-ROM. Use the EXTRACT command to locate the file on the CD-ROM, and copy it to the same location as the potentially bad one. Use the search function to locate the bad file.

## Windows Protection Errors

Windows protection errors take place when a special type of driver file, called a *virtual device driver* (VxD) fails to load or unload. VxDs are used to support older Windows programs, and this error usually occurs when a device somehow gets a device driver in both CONFIG.SYS and SYSTEM.INI or the registry. Running SYSEDIT will show us any drivers in CONFIG.SYS. Put semicolons in front of DEVICE= lines until the problem goes away. If that doesn't fix it, check for resource conflicts in the Device Manager and then restore the registry.

## Fatal Exception Errors

Fatal exception errors are caused by software or hardware that sends a particular type of error that Windows is not designed to contain. If these arise from a new device or software, uninstall the offending beast and check the manufacturer's Web site and the Microsoft Knowledge Base for known issues related to that software or device.

## Dr. Watson Utility

In some cases, these problems simply defy the best of our repair attempts. At this point you'll probably need to call tech support. But before you call, run the Dr. Watson utility and re-create the error. Dr. Watson generates a detailed report on the status of the system at the time of the error, and although the information in that report goes way outside of the knowledge of most techs, it provides critical insight to very high-level techs.

## Shutdown Problems

I find it interesting that most shutdown problems are identical to startup issues. Bad drivers, a corrupted registry, and faulty page files all cause shutdown problems. Let's add a few other fixes that are unique to shutdown problems.

### Disable Fast Shutdown (Windows 98 Only)

Windows 98 normally "turns off" every device driver at shutdown. You can choose not to turn off device drivers, however, by using a tool called Fast Shutdown. Fast Shutdown works well on most systems but gives others fits. Make sure to disable Fast Shutdown. It's in the System Configuration Utility—click the Advanced button on the General tab. The Disable Fast Save check box is third from the bottom.

### Application Not Closing

Some applications refuse to close. Windows 98 does a good job of closing them anyway, but Windows 95 often needs you to close an application manually before it can shut down. Try to close the application normally, but if that fails, use the Task Manager to shut it down. If you click End Task and nothing happens, try again. I sometimes have to "End" Microsoft Word three or four times before it obeys.

### Sound File

If the Windows Shutdown sound file corrupts, the system will not shut down. Use the Sound applet in the Control Panel to turn off the shutdown sound.

## The End of Windows 9x?

From the first day Microsoft unveiled Windows NT, their goal has been to create one basic, scalable OS that will meet the needs of every PC, from home machines to Web servers. With the introduction of Windows 2000, along with the rapidly dropping cost of PC hardware, this dream may finally start to approach reality. Certainly, we will see a few more versions of 9x, hidden under silly marketing terms like Windows ME, but the future sits squarely in the hands of Windows 2000. Until that day when we upgrade our last 9x machine to whatever great uni-OS Microsoft creates, however, we must continue to have the skills to support this powerful, convenient platform. Windows 9x will stick around for a long time to come.

## Review Questions

1. Ian complains that his SYSTEM.DAT and USER.DAT files got corrupted. What is he talking about?
   A. These are the Windows files that replace IO.SYS and MSDOS.SYS.
   B. These are the Windows registry files.
   C. These are the DOS configuration files.
   D. He's talking techno babble to impress the coworkers.

2. What is the best way to access the Registry Editor in Windows 9x?
   A. Start | Programs | DOS prompt icon. Type EDIT.
   B. Start | Programs | Registry Editor.
   C. Start | Run | Type REGEDIT and click OK.
   D. Start | Run | Type REGEDT32 and click OK.

3. Which of the following boot menu options in Windows 9x enables the system to boot to the GUI for troubleshooting purposes, but without the advanced functions of Windows?
   A. Safe mode
   B. Safe mode Command Prompt only
   C. Command Prompt only
   D. Troubleshooting Mode

4. Which of the following actions would enable you to increase the disk cache settings for a Windows 9x system?
   A. Go to Control Panel | System | Device Manager tab and adjust the disk cache.
   B. Go to Control Panel | System | Performance tab | File System button | Hard Disk tab and change the "Typical role of this computer" from "Desktop computer" to "Network server."

C. Go to Control Panel | System | Performance tab | File System button | Hard Disk tab and change the "Read-ahead optimization" from "Full" to "None."

D. Go to Control Panel | System | Performance tab | File System button | Troubleshooting tab and select the option "Disable write-behind caching for all drives."

5. Julie mentions that she manually set the swap-file size and location on her Windows 9x system and asks what you think. How do you respond?

A. Impossible! You can't do that in Windows 9x, only Windows 3.x.

B. Great! Windows' default settings for the swap file are inefficient.

C. You should not have done that! Windows needs to set the size automatically.

D. You should have disabled it altogether. With enough real RAM, you don't need virtual memory.

6. Which of the following is *not* true about FAT32?

A. FAT32 stores two copies of the boot sector.

B. Compared to FAT16, FAT32 has a reduced cluster size.

C. FAT32 is not compatible with DOS and Windows applications.

D. FAT32 has no limit on the number of root directory entries.

7. Which of the following files does Windows 9x need in order to load?

A. Real mode drivers for hardware

B. CONFIG.SYS

C. AUTOEXEC.BAT

D. None of the above

8. Which of the following is *not* a registry root key in Windows 9x?

A. HKEY_CURRENT_MACHINE

B. HKEY_CLASSES_ROOT

C. HKEY_CURRENT_USER

D. HKEY_LOCAL_MACHINE

9. George is running Windows 98 on his system. He gets an error message:

**Cannot find SYSTEM.INI**

Now he can only access the command prompt, not the GUI. How can he correct this problem?

A. Ignore it. SYSTEM.INI is no longer an important file.

B. He needs to run Windows Setup again to install this file.

C. Go into SYSEDIT and re-create SYSTEM.INI.

D. Delete the error message.

**10.** How does the Windows 9*x* version of MSDOS.SYS differ from earlier versions? (Choose all that apply.)

    **A.** It is now a hidden, read-only binary file.

    **B.** It is now a hidden, read-only text file.

    **C.** It is no longer the DOS kernel, as it was before Windows 9*x*.

    **D.** It is now the only DOS kernel.

## Answers

1. **B.** SYSTEM.DAT and USER.DAT are the registry files.

2. **C.** EDIT is for text files, not binary files like the registry. REGEDT32 is for Windows 2000 not Windows 9*x*.

3. **A.** Safe mode is your first step to attempt a fix in Windows. Safe mode turns off access to just about everything, but you do have access to the tools you need to use on a malfunctioning device or software.

4. **B.** Changing the "Typical role of this computer" setting from "Desktop computer" to "Network server" increases the cache size and modestly enhances performance.

5. **B.** Although common sense says that with enough RAM you should not need a swap file, Windows and applications for Windows were designed to use virtual memory and real memory together.

6. **C.** FAT32 is completely compatible with all DOS and Windows applications, but you must never use any disk utilities unless they are designed for FAT32.

7. **D.** As a protected-mode overlay of the DOS shell, Windows loads internally all its own drivers. The DOS configuration files will work but are not necessary.

8. **A.** HKEY_CURRENT_MACHINE is not a registry root key.

9. **B.** Windows 9*x* systems still require SYSTEM.INI, even though the settings are no longer critical.

10. **B, C.** MSDOS.SYS in Windows 9*x* is a text file you can edit to change how Windows boots. It is not part of the Windows 9*x* kernel.

# Windows 2000

In this chapter, you will

- Understand the internal functions and structure of Windows NT and 2000
- See how Windows 2000 differs from Windows 9x
- Learn how to use the many new tools in Windows 2000
- Learn how to install/upgrade Windows 2000

Early in the life of Windows, way back when Windows 3.x still ruled the land, Microsoft began to develop a new, super-powerful version of Windows that sacrificed backward-compatibility for stability, scalability, and cross-platform support. Microsoft knew that the hardware and power of this new "Super Windows" would make it useful only for the most powerful user needs. They ended up with two *operating system* (OS) lines—what I call Regular and Super. *Regular* Windows is made up of the Windows 3.x, Windows 95, Windows 98, and Windows ME lines. The *Super* Windows line is called Windows *New Technology* (NT).

Windows NT first burst onto the scene in the early 1990s as version 3.1 to compete with the then quite popular Novell NetWare 3.1. Like regular Windows, NT went through many versions after the first: Windows NT 3.5, Windows NT 3.51, and Windows 4.0. The latest version of "Super Windows," Windows 2000, drops the "NT" but don't let that fool you! Although Windows 2000 boasts a number of powerful enhancements over the previous versions, the heart of NT still beats inside every Windows 2000 system.

## Historical/Conceptual

### Windows NT

To appreciate Windows 2000, you must first appreciate its direct predecessor, Windows NT version 4.0. NT 4.0 stills works hard for a living inside millions of systems all over the world. Windows 2000 and Windows NT share the vast majority of critical functions, files, and organization; understanding NT makes understanding Windows 2000 much easier. Everything discussed in this section is exactly the same in Windows 2000.

> **EXAM TIP** The A+ exams do not explicitly say you should know Windows NT, but they do allude to it. So, even though I've described this section as historical/conceptual, you should take the time to read through it.

From the outside, Windows NT 4.0 looks pretty much just like Windows 95 (Figure 11-1). For the most part, that's where the similarities end. Windows NT has so many features beyond Windows 9x that it takes a moment to decide where to start! Let's begin with the organization of the operating system.

**Figure 11-1** Twins?!

> **NOTE** Windows 2000 has the same basic organization as Windows NT.

## Operating System Organization

Three words best describe NT's organization: robust, scalable, and cross-platform. NT takes an object-oriented approach to the OS, separating the OS into three distinct parts: the drivers, the NT Executive, and the subsystems (Figure 11-2).

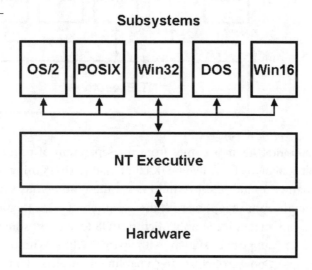

**Figure 11-2**
Windows NT
organization

**Subsystems**

NT was designed to support different CPU platforms beyond the x86, such as DEC Alpha, MIPS, and PowerPC. To achieve this, the NT Executive holds the *Hardware Abstraction Layer* (HAL) to separate the system-specific device drivers from the rest of the NT system (Figure 11-3). Although Windows 2000 shares this organization, Microsoft has chosen to drop support for all but Intel x86 systems in Windows 2000.

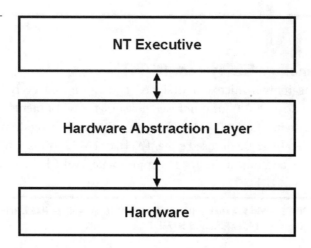

**Figure 11-3**
NT Executive and
the HAL

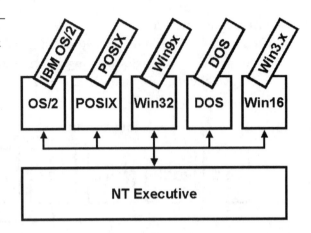

Figure 11-4
NT can handle a lot
of different
operating systems.

NT and 2000's robustness comes from the separation of running processes into a myriad of subsystems. NT is fully POSIX-compliant (a UNIX thing) and has support for OS/2, DOS, and 16- and 32-bit Windows via these numerous subsystems. Windows 2000 keeps all the same supports with the exception of OS/2 (Figure 11-4).

NT's scalability makes it the only Microsoft OS to support *symmetric multiprocessing* (SMP), providing support for systems with up to 32 CPUs. Windows 2000 goes beyond SMP by adding the power of clustering, enabling multiple systems to share redundant data for ultimate protection. If one system goes down, the other systems continue to run.

 **TIP** For those of you a little weak on networking, take a moment to read through Chapter 20 on networks. You need to understand basic networking to appreciate Windows NT/2000.

## New Technology File System (NTFS)

From the beginning, Microsoft designed and optimized every aspect of Windows NT (and Windows 2000) for multiuser, networked environments. This is most evident in the file system—how NT stores files on your hard drive(s). Whereas all previous Microsoft operating systems used either FAT16 or FAT32 formats, NT and 2000 use a far more powerful and robust file system, appropriately called, *NT File System* (NTFS).

 **NOTE** Windows NT fully supports FAT16 as well as NTFS. Windows 2000 supports FAT16, FAT32, and NTFS.

A fairly good description of NTFS was given in Chapter 8, but let's go into a bit more detail on this amazing file system. NTFS offers the following excellent features:

- Long filenames
- Redundancy
- Backward compatibility
- Recoverability
- Security

## Long Filenames

NTFS supported long filenames long before FAT32 even existed. Like LFNs, NTFS filenames can be up to 255 characters.

## Redundancy

NTFS has a very advanced FAT called the *Master File Table* (MFT). An NTFS partition keeps a backup copy of the most critical parts of the MFT in the middle of the disk, reducing the chance that a serious drive error can wipe out both the MFT and the MFT copy. Whenever you defrag an NTFS partition, you'll see a small, immovable "chunk" in the middle of the drive; that's the backup MFT.

## Backward Compatibility

For all its power, NTFS is amazingly backward compatible. You can copy DOS or Windows 9*x* programs to an NTFS partition. Windows even keeps the LFNs.

## Recoverability

Accidental system shutdowns, reboots, and lockups in the midst of a file save or retrieval wreak havoc on most systems. NTFS avoids this with *transaction logging*. Transaction logging determines incomplete file transactions and restores the file to the original format automatically and invisibly.

## Security

NTFS truly shines with its powerful security functions. When most people hear the term "security," they tend to think about networks. NTFS security works perfectly in a network environment, but for the moment, let's just pretend that only one Windows NT/2000 system exists in the entire world. Three different people use this computer. Each person has one personal folder that they don't want others to access. On a Windows 9*x* system, anyone who can get in front of the keyboard of a system can access any folder, the password only allows him or her on the network. This is not so with Windows NT/2000! Let's look at three major features of NTFS security: accounts, groups, and permissions.

**Accounts** To use a Windows NT/2000 system, you must have a valid account and password. Without that account, you cannot use the system (Figure 11-5).

Every Windows NT/2000 system has a "super" account called *administrator*. When you first install a Windows NT/2000 system, it prompts you for a password for the administrator account. As you might imagine, this account has access to everything—a dangerous thing in the wrong hands!

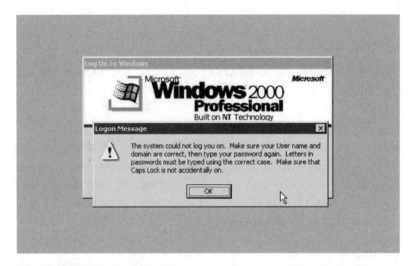

**Figure 11-5** Login failure

**Groups** The administrator creates user accounts with a special program called Users and Passwords in Windows 2000 (Figure 11-6). Note the account list has three columns: User Name, Domain, and Group. To understand domains requires extensive networking discussion, so we'll leave that for Chapter 20 and instead focus here on user names and groups. A *user name* defines an account for a person who has access to the PC. A *group* is simply a collection of accounts that share the same access abilities. A single account can be a member of multiple groups.

Groups make Windows administration much easier in two ways. First, we can assign a certain level of access for a file or folder to a group instead of an account. We can make a group called Accounting and put all the accounting user accounts in that group. If a person quits, we don't need to worry about deleting her account and then creating a new one for her replacement, including reassigning all the proper access levels. We just make a new account and add that new person to a group!

**Figure 11-6**
Users and
Passwords
dialog box

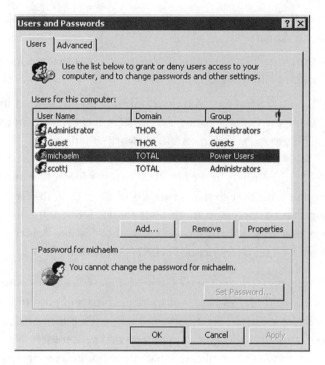

Secondly, Windows provides seven built-in groups: Administrators, Power Users, Users, Backup Operators, Replicator, Everyone, and Guests. These built-in groups have a number of preset abilities. You cannot delete these groups.

- **Administrators**   Any account that is a member of this group has complete administrator privileges. It is very common for the primary user of a Windows 2000 system to have his or her account in the Administrators group.

- **Power Users**   Power Users are almost as powerful as administrators, but they cannot install new devices or access other users' files or folders unless the file or folder specifically provides them access.

- **Users**   Users cannot edit the Registry or access critical system files. They can create groups, but can only manage the ones they create.

- **Backup Operators**   Backup operators have the same rights as users, but they can run backup programs that access any file or folder—for backup purposes only.

- **Replicator**   Members of the Replicator group can replicate files and folders in a domain.

- **Everyone**   This account applies to any user that can log onto the system. You cannot edit this group.

- **Guests**   Someone who does not have an account on the system can log on using the Guest account if the system has been set up to enable that feature. This group is used in certain network situations.

**NTFS Permissions**   In the NT/2000 world, every folder and file on an NTFS partition has a list that contains two sets of data. First, the list details every user and group that has access to that file or folder. Second, the list specifies the level of access that each user or group has to that file and folder. The level of access is defined by a set of restrictions called "permissions."

*Permissions*   These define exactly what a particular account can or cannot do to the file or folder and are thus quite detailed and powerful. You can make it possible, for example, for a person to edit a file but not delete it. You can create a folder and not allow other people to make subfolders. NTFS file and folder permissions are so complicated that entire books have been written on them! Fortunately for us, the A+ Certification exams only test your understanding of a few basic concepts of NTFS permissions: Ownership, Changing permissions, folder permissions, and File permissions.

*Ownership*   When you create a new file or folder on an NTFS partition, you become the *owner* of that file or folder. A newly created file or folder by default gives Full permission to Everyone to access, delete, and otherwise manipulate that file or folder. Owners can do anything they want to the files or folders they own, including changing the permissions to prevent anybody, even administrators, from accessing them.

One special permission, however, called Take Ownership, enables anyone with that permission to do just that—seize control of a file or folder. Administrator accounts have Take Ownership permission for everything. Note the difference here between owning a file and accessing a file. If you own a file you can prevent anyone from accessing that file. An administrator who you have blocked, however, can take that ownership away from you and *then* access that file! Get it?

*Change Permissions*   Another important permission for all NTFS files and folders is Change permissions. An account with this permission can give or take away permissions for other accounts.

*Folder Permissions*   Let's look at a typical folder in my Windows 2000 system to see how all this works. My D: drive is formatted as NTFS. On the D: drive I created a folder called D:\MIKE. In My Computer, it looks like Figure 11-7. I set the permissions for the folder by accessing the folder's properties and clicking on the Security tab (Figure 11-8).

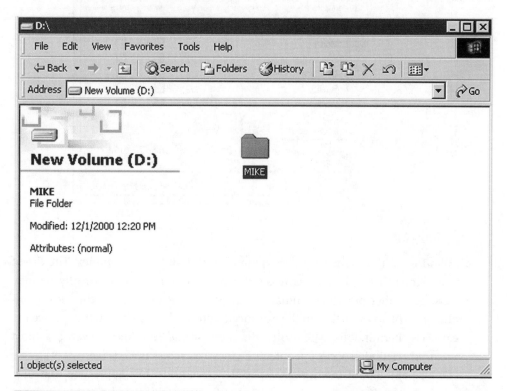

**Figure 11-7**   A typical folder—isn't it lovely?

In Windows NT/2000, just about everything in the computer has a security tab in its properties. Every security tab contains two main areas. The top area shows the list of accounts that have permissions for that resource. The lower area shows exactly what permissions have been assigned to that account.

**Figure 11-8**
Security tab

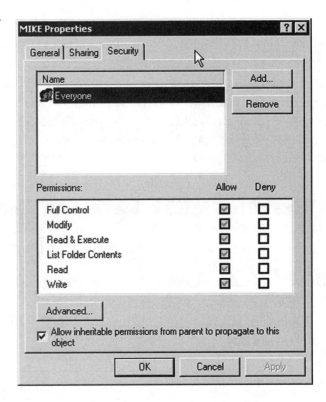

Windows NTFS permissions are quite powerful and quite complex. The list of permissions shown in the permission area, for example, are not really permissions, but rather pre-set combinations of permissions that cover the most common types of access. Click on the Advanced button, then click View/Edit to see the real NTFS permissions; Microsoft calls them *special permissions*. Even the most advanced NT/2000 support people rarely need to access these (Figure 11-9).

Don't panic about memorizing special permissions; just appreciate that they exist and that the permissions we see in the Security tab cover the vast majority of our needs. Here are the standard permissions for a folder:

- **Full Control**   Enables you to do anything you want!

- **Modify**   Enables you to do anything except delete files or subfolders.

- **Read & Execute**   Enables you to see the contents of the folder and any subfolders.

**Figure 11-9**
Special permissions

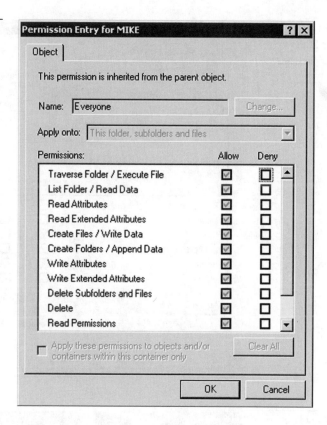

- **List Folder Contents** Enables you to see the contents of the folder and any subfolders. (This permission seems the same as the Read & Execute permission, but is only inherited by folders.)

- **Read** Enables you to read any files in the folder.

- **Write** Enables you to write to files and create new files and folders.

If you look at the bottom of the Security tab, you'll see a little check box that says: "Allow inheritable permission from parent to propagate to this object." In other words, any files or subfolders created in this folder get the same permissions for the same users/groups that the folder has.

This enables you to stop a user from getting a specific permission via inheritance. Windows 2000 (unlike NT) provides explicit "Deny" functions to each option (Figure 11-10).

*File Permissions* File permissions are quite similar to Folder permissions. Take a look at the Security tab on a typical file (Figure 11-11).

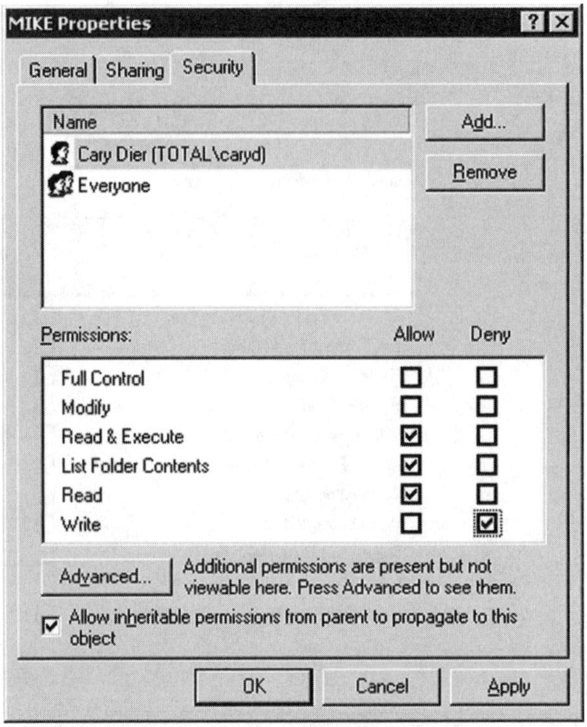

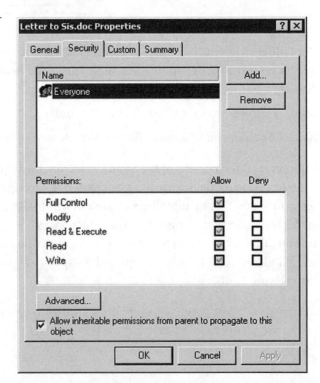

**Figure 11-10**
Windows 2000
folder permissions

**Figure 11-11**
Security tab

- **Full Control**   Enables you to do anything you want!

- **Modify**   Enables you to do anything except take ownership or change permissions on the file.

- **Read & Execute**   If the file is a program, you can run it.

- **Read**   If the file is data, you can read it.

- **Write**   Enables you to write to the file.

Take some time to think about these permissions. Why would Microsoft create them? Think of situations where you might want to give a group Modify permission. Also, you can assign more than one permission. In many situations, we like to give users both the Read as well as the Write permission.

Permissions are cumulative. If you have Full Control on a folder and only Read permission on the file, you get Full Control on the file.

**EXAM TIP**   Don't bother memorizing all of these NTFS permissions! Simply appreciate that NTFS enables NT and 2000 to provide a tremendous level of security. Windows 9x uses the far more primitive FAT16 or FAT32 file systems. These file systems provide almost no security. If you want powerful, flexible security, you need Windows NT/2000 with NTFS.

## Techs and Permissions

Techs, as a rule, hate NTFS permissions. You must have administrative privileges in order to do almost anything on a Windows NT or Windows 2000 machine. Most administrators hate giving out administrative permissions (for obvious reasons). If one does give you administrative permission for a PC and something goes wrong with that system while you're working on it, you immediately become the primary suspect! If you're working on an NT/2000 system administered by someone else, make sure he or she understands what you are doing and how long you think it will take. Have the administrator create a new account for you with administrator privileges. Never ask for the password for a permanent administrator account! That way, you won't be blamed if anything goes wrong on that system: "Well, I told Janet the password when she installed the new hard drive . . . maybe she did it!" When you have fixed the system, make sure that that the administrator deletes the account you used.

This "protect yourself from passwords" attitude transcends just Windows NT/2000. PC support folks get lots of passwords, scan cards, keys, and ID tags. Most newer techs tend to get an "I can go anywhere and access anything" attitude. This is a very dangerous attitude. I've seen many jobs lost and friendships ruined when a tape backup suddenly disappears or a critical file gets erased. Everybody points to the support tech in these situations. In physical security situations, make other people unlock doors for you. In some cases, I've literally made the administrator or system owner sit behind me reading a magazine, jumping up and punching in passwords as needed. What you don't have access to can't hurt you.

## Test Specific

### Booting Up vs. Going Graphical

Windows 9x and Windows 2000 share a surface resemblance; they are both graphical OS. Inside, however, they differ significantly in the level of integration between the graphical interface and text-based functions. Both versions of Windows make a strong distinction between booting the OS and "going graphical." Windows 2000 and Windows 9x have primary boot files that start the OS. Once these files have started the system, a completely different set of files starts the *graphical user interface* (GUI). The boot files are usually quite small in size and there are very few of them, compared to the size and the number of the GUI files. The distinction between text-based OS and GUI files is sharp in Windows 9x, but much muddier in Windows 2000.

In Windows 9x, a very clear distinction exists between the boot files and the GUI files. This can be easily shown by the many ways that you can skip the GUI completely, such as the Command Prompt Only option in the Startup Options menu that was discussed in Chapter 10.

Windows NT and Windows 2000 do not have a pure command prompt environment. Certainly, you can access a command prompt within NT/2000, but the Windows 9x separation of GUI from the command prompt is not valid in NT/2000.

In Windows 9x machines, the boot files must be installed onto the C: partition, but the GUI files can be installed onto any other drive letter. Of course, most installations place the GUI files in a directory called \WINDOWS on the C: drive, but this is not at all required. The boot files and the GUI files are totally separate issues in Windows 9x (Figure 11-12).

Windows NT and 2000 also separate the boot from the GUI files. Like Windows 9x, the boot files must be on the boot partition, and the GUI files can be anywhere else. Unlike Windows 9x, however, the boot and GUI files are closely linked. There is no way to boot NT to a command prompt only, as is possible in Windows 9x. The boot files only start the OS and pass control to the GUI. The only way to get to a command prompt in NT is after the GUI is started. Windows 2000 uses something that looks like Windows 9x's Safe Mode Command Prompt Only but in reality, is nothing more than a windowed command prompt—we'll see this shortly.

**Figure 11-12**
Boot and GUI files in Windows Explorer

BOOT files here

GUI files here

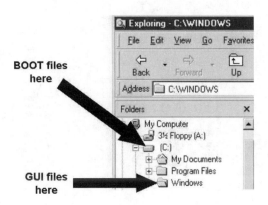

That is about where the comparisons between Windows 9*x* and NT/2000 end. Windows NT and 2000 share a vastly more complicated boot file structure and organization. Additionally, Microsoft uses some terms very differently than other authorities, requiring a little bit of unlearning and accepting the "Microsoft Way" of defining different aspects of the boot process. The best way to understand the NT/2000 boot process is to begin with an overview of the different files used in the boot process.

## The Boot Process

The Windows NT OS itself consists of NTOSKRNL.EXE (the Windows NT kernel), the \WINNT\SYSTEM32\CONFIG\SYSTEM file (which controls the loading of device drivers), and the device drivers themselves. Even though these files are the core of the Windows NT OS, they are not capable of booting the system. They can reside on any partition in the system. So how does a computer find those files so that they can be run to start the OS? The answer is that Windows NT needs boot files that can "point" to these critical files (Figure 11-13).

It's time for a little Microsoft terminology. The NTOSKRNL.EXE, SYSTEM, and device driver files that make up the OS are stored on the boot partition. The files that will help us find the OS when the system boots up are stored on the system partition. That is not a typo. In Microsoft's terminology, the partition that you boot from, the bootable partition, is the system partition; the partition that holds the actual NT or 2000 OS is called the *boot partition*. It's completely backwards from what we would expect; everyone knows that it's backwards, and it's too late to change it. In an NT/2000 system, there will be only one system partition and one boot partition. If you have the system and boot files on the same partition, of course, then that one partition serves as both.

**Figure 11-13**
Pointers

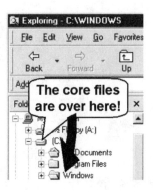

In the NT days, we would often make a small (<50MB) FAT16 primary partition and make a huge extended partition with one logical drive formatted as NTFS. This process enabled us to boot the system in case we had a problem with NT. Windows 2000 comes with a new tool called the Recovery Console that eliminates the need for a FAT16 partition. We'll see how to access the Recovery Console in a bit.

NT can coexist with Windows 9x on the same boot partition, as long as the partition is FAT16 (Windows 2000 also coexists with FAT32). Although you *could* do this, your inability to use NTFS makes this idea ludicrous. The best method for dual booting Windows 9x and Windows 2000 is to make a primary partition formatted FAT32 and install Windows 9x on the drive. Then install Windows 2000 on the unused portion of the drive. Both Windows NT and Windows 2000 have nice setup programs that can create a dual-boot system with ease. Many systems (including the one used to write this book) have Windows 2000/Windows 9x dual-boot capabilities (Figure 11-14).

**Figure 11-14**
Mike's dual-boot
setup

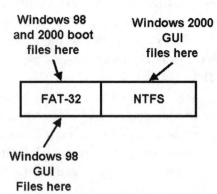

For all these neat tricks, the vast majority of Windows 2000 systems have the boot partition and the system partition share the same big C: partition.

> **NOTE** Windows NT and 2000 consider the initial boot partition (usually the C: partition) as the *system* partition. They see the area that stores the OS's GUI files as the *boot* partition.

## System Partition Boot Files

Both Windows NT and Windows 2000 require these four files in the root directory of the system partition:

- NTLDR (pronounced "NT loader")
- BOOT.INI
- NTDETECT.COM
- NTBOOTDD.SYS (only for SCSI controllers that don't have their own ROM BIOS)

Note that this list does not include IO.SYS, MSDOS.SYS, CONFIG.SYS, COMMAND .COM, or AUTOEXEC.BAT. Windows NT/2000 does not use these files, although you may see them in the root directory of a dual-boot system.

### NTLDR

When the system boots up, the *master boot record* (MBR) on the hard drive starts the NTLDR program. The NTLDR program then launches either Windows NT/2000 or another OS. In order to find the available OSs, the NTLDR program must read the BOOT.INI configuration file. To accomplish this, the NTLDR program loads its own minimal file system, which enables it to read the BOOT.INI file off the system partition.

### BOOT.INI File

The BOOT.INI file is a text file that lists the OSs available to NTLDR, and tells NTLDR where to find the boot partition (where the OS is stored) for each of the OSs. The BOOT.INI file has sections defined by section headings enclosed in brackets. A basic BOOT.INI in Windows 2000 looks like this:

```
[boot loader]
timeout=10
default=multi(0)disk(0)rdisk(0)partition(2)\WINNT
[operating systems]
multi(0)disk(0)rdisk(0)partition(2)\WINNT="Microsoft Windows 2000
Professional" /fastdetect
```

A more complex BOOT.INI may look like this:

```
[boot loader]
timeout=10
default=multi(0)disk(0)rdisk(0)partition(2)\WINNT
[operating systems]
multi(0)disk(0)rdisk(0)partition(2)\WINNT="Microsoft Windows 2000
Professional" /fastdetect
C:\CMDCONS\BOOTSECT.DAT="Microsoft Windows 2000 Recovery Console"/cmdcons
C:\="Previous Operating System on C:"
```

Such a BOOT.INI would result in the boot menu that appears in Figure 11-15.

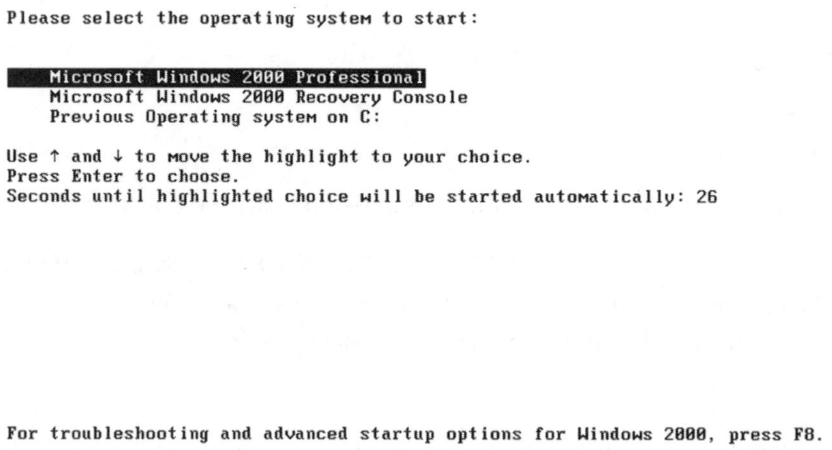

```
Please select the operating system to start:

    Microsoft Windows 2000 Professional
    Microsoft Windows 2000 Recovery Console
    Previous Operating system on C:

Use ↑ and ↓ to move the highlight to your choice.
Press Enter to choose.
Seconds until highlighted choice will be started automatically: 26




For troubleshooting and advanced startup options for Windows 2000, press F8.
```

**Figure 11-15**   Boot loader in Windows 2000 with System Recovery Console

On rare occasions, you might find yourself needing to edit the BOOT.INI file. Any text editor handily edits the BOOT.INI file. However, most of us prefer to edit BOOT.INI via the System Setup dialog box. In Windows 2000, select the System applet from the Control Panel. Click the Advanced tab and then click the Startup and Recovery button. The BOOT.INI options show up at the top (Figure 11-16).

## BOOTSECT.DOS

If the NTLDR detects that you chose to run another OS, such as Windows 9*x*, it reads the BOOTSECT.DOS file to locate the IO.SYS file and then lets the other OS start.

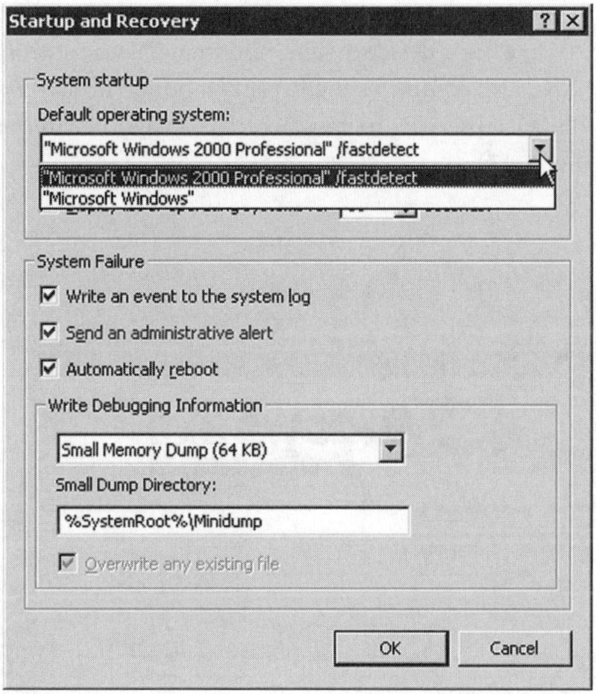

**Figure 11-16**
Choosing which OS
to boot by default

## NTDETECT.COM

If the NTLDR determines that you have chosen to start NT/2000, it boots the system into protected mode and then calls on NTDETECT.COM to detect the installed hardware on the system.

## NTBOOTDD.SYS

If the NTLDR detects that the boot partition resides on a SCSI drive that connects to a host adapter that lacks a ROM chip for BIOS support, it uses the NTBOOTDD.SYS to provide access to the SCSI boot partition. (See Chapter 13 for more information about SCSI drives and host adapters.)

## Critical Files

Naming all of the critical files for NT and 2000 (both OSs share the same core files) is akin to naming every muscle in the human body—completely possible, but time-consuming and without any real use. In the next section, you will see that it takes four floppy disks to boot Windows 2000 from the floppy drive! However, a few of the *most* important files certainly deserve a short notice.

Once NTLDR finishes detections, it loads NTOSKRNL.EXE, HAL.DLL, some of the Registry, and some basic device drivers; and then passes control to the NTOSKRNL.EXE file. NTOSKRNL.EXE completes the Registry loading, initializes all devices drivers, and starts the WINLOGON.EXE program, which displays the famous Windows 2000 logon screen (Figure 11-17).

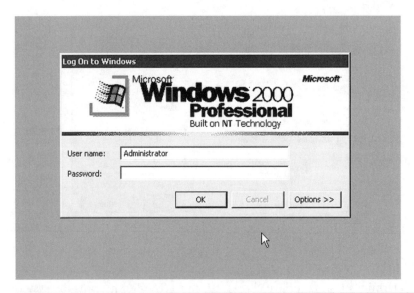

**Figure 11-17** Where do you want to go today?

## Registry

Windows NT and Windows 2000 share very similar registries. The A+ Certification exams do not expect you to memorize every aspect of the Windows 2000 registry. You should, however, understand the basic components of the registry, know how to edit the registry manually, and know the best way to locate a particular setting. Microsoft included a new Registry Editor in Windows 2000 (REGEDT32.EXE), shown in Figure 11-18, although they also left in the older Registry Editor (REGEDIT.EXE). Most techs refer to the two Registry Editor applications by their filenames, Regedt32 and Regedit.

Although Regedt32 has far more power than Regedit, we still use the older Regedit to perform searches because Regedt32's search capabilities are not very good. The best practice: Search with Regedit, but only make changes with Regedt32! Figure 11-19 shows Regedit in action with a typical Windows 2000 system. Note that Windows 2000 dumps the HKEY_DYN_DATA folder seen in Windows 9x, but otherwise, it looks the same.

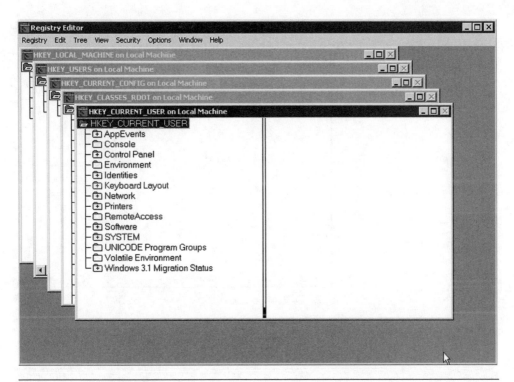

**Figure 11-18**   Regedt32

As you'll recall from Chapter 10, Windows 9x used two binary files to hold the Registry: SYSTEM.DAT and USER.DAT. Windows 2000, in contrast, approaches the Registry files very differently. Windows 2000 uses the term *hives* to describe a group of files that each add something to the Registry. These hive files are located in the \WINNT\SYSTEM32\CONFIG folder and the \WINNT\PROFILES folder. If you want to back up a Registry in Windows 2000, just copy these folders to a safe place.

Take the time to memorize the primary boot files and the boot process for Windows NT/2000. Most boot errors are easily repaired if you know which files are used for boot and in which order they load.

## Versions of Windows NT

Microsoft sold two different versions of Windows NT: Workstation and Server. Windows NT Workstation served as a great alternative to Windows 95 for folks who wanted a powerful and stable OS (Figure 11-20).

Windows NT Server had a number of networking-specific enhancements, especially in *domain-based security*. We'll delve into the concepts of domains and domain-based security in Chapter 20 when we discuss networking in detail.

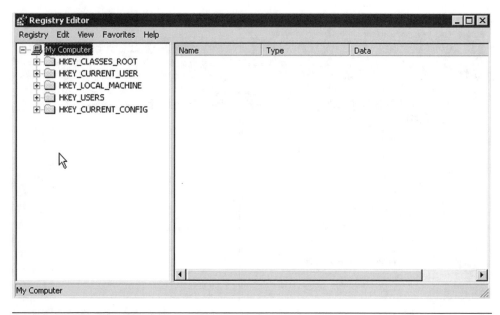

**Figure 11-19** Regedit

**Figure 11-20** NT Workstation

## Service Packs

For all the power of Windows NT, the OS had bugs and a few glaring limitations in the architecture. Microsoft fixed some problems with a number of Service Packs (Microsoft sent out six service packs for Windows NT 4.0). But core limitations meant that Windows NT could not incorporate features that became increasingly in demand as technology improved, such as seamless Internet integration, true Plug and Play, clustering of two or more servers (where if one server failed another would pick up the load without missing a beat), and other high-end server issues. To address the obvious need for a new NT, Microsoft offered the world Windows 2000.

## Windows 2000

As mentioned earlier, Windows 2000 shares much of the same features and power of Windows NT. Many in the industry jokingly call Windows 2000 "NT 5.0." Even the System Information tool (like the one in Windows 98/ME) shows that someone at Microsoft feels the same way (Figure 11-21).

In fact, Windows 2000 combines an improved Windows NT core with many ease-of-use and tech-friendly elements from Windows 9x. Plus, Windows 2000 adds some excellent new features as well, such as the Microsoft Management Console, which creates a central point for the important tools for techs. This section starts with a look at and some discussion about the important new and/or improved features of Windows 2000. It then launches into the specific tasks techs will face: installing and optimizing the OS; installing new hardware; and maintaining the system, including dealing with drives. The chapter finishes with a discussion on troubleshooting Windows 2000. Let's get started!

## Windows 9x Look and Feel

Windows 2000 has a look and feel very similar to Windows 98 (and almost identical to Windows ME). From a user standpoint, all of the aspects of Windows 9x are the same, with the exception of some name changes. Network Neighborhood has become My Network Places, for example, but the Task bar, Start Menu, My Computer, My Documents, Run, and Find (now called Search) are still there (Figure 11-22).

For techs, most of the common tools reside in the same location as on a Windows 9x PC. The Control Panel, for example, contains the important Registry-changing applets, and the tools under Program | Accessories | System Tools handle other chores, such as defragmenting the hard drive.

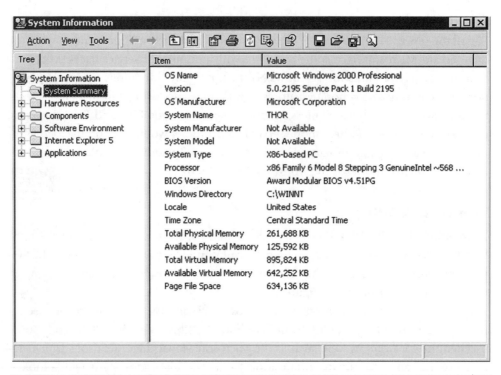

**Figure 11-21**   Hey! It's NT 5.0!

## Plug and Play

Although later service packs of Windows NT provided rudimentary *Plug and Play* (PnP) support, Windows 2000 packs complete PnP support. Windows 2000 now has the Device Manager and the Add New Hardware Wizard, making device installation absolutely identical to the methods described in the previous chapter for Windows 9*x*. Well, Windows 2000 does one thing differently; it doesn't show anything on the screen when installing devices unless there's a problem! I'm not too sure I like that; I miss the old "Windows has found new hardware" message from Windows 9*x*!

## Improvements in NTFS

Windows 2000 comes with a new type of NTFS called NTFS 5.0. (The NTFS that came with NT 4.0 was called NTFS 4.0.) NTFS 5.0 adds four improvements: compression, encryption, drive naming conventions, and dynamic drives.

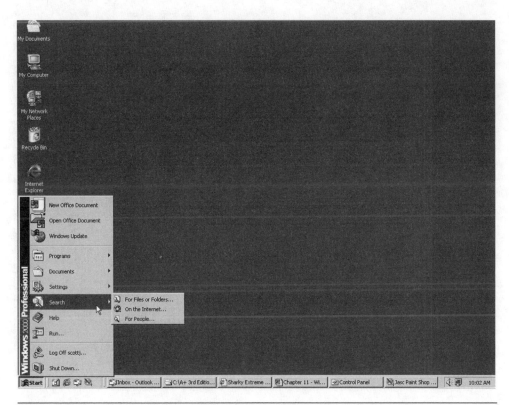

**Figure 11-22** Look familiar?

## Compression

Windows NT had a rudimentary drive compression feature that most of us avoided since it enabled you to compress only an entire drive. Windows 2000 enables you to compress anything—entire drives, folders, even individual files. To compress anything, just select its properties and click the Advanced button on the General tab. Click on the Compress Contents To Save Disk Space check box as shown in Figure 11-23. Compression is safe and powerful.

## Encryption

Windows 2000 NTFS partitions now support on-the-fly encryption. Even if others have access to your file or folder, they won't be able to see it. Only the person who created the encrypted file may see it, although administrators have a method for decrypting files if necessary. If you look at Figure 11-23, you'll notice an option for encryption; just click it, and the file or folder will automatically encrypt itself when saved and decrypt when accessed by the account that encrypted it. No passwords are needed.

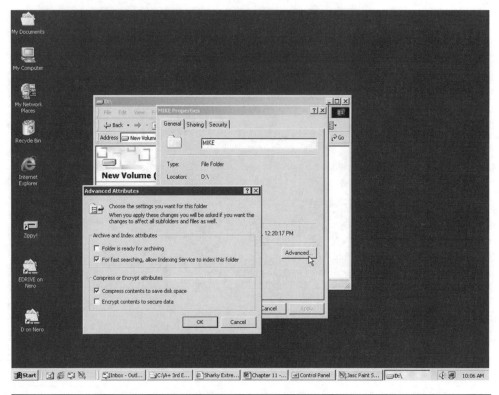

**Figure 11-23**   Compression and encryption

### Volume Naming

Windows 2000 lets you name a volume with either a traditional drive letter or by a directory name on an existing drive. Suppose you add a 30GB drive to your Windows 2000 system. If you wish, you may call that drive C:\BIG DRIVE and it will manifest itself as a folder. Windows 2000 gives the volume a different icon than a normal folder to show that it really is a volume (Figure 11-24).

### Disk Quotas

Disk quotas simply limit the amount of disk space a particular user may use. Virtually every other network OS has had disk quota functions for years, and competitors loved tossing NT's lack of disk quotas in Microsoft's face. Well, they no longer have anything to laugh about. Any NTFS volume supports disk quotas—just go to the drive letter's properties, select the Quota tab, and select the users you want to set quotas for (Figure 11-25).

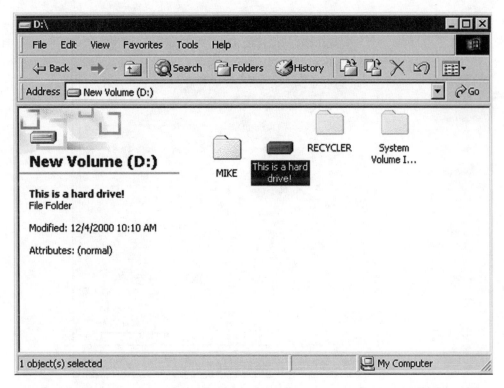

**Figure 11-24** A hard drive you can access like a folder

## Dynamic Drives

Windows 2000 introduces a new drive organization called *dynamic drives*. Dynamic drives throw out the classic MBR and partition paradigm and replace it with a drive that simply supports volumes. A dynamic drive can support an unlimited number of volumes. Dynamic drives can be resized without data loss. Windows 2000 requires the use of dynamic drives when implementing features such as disk striping, spanning, or mirroring (see "Dealing with Drives," later in this chapter). Windows 2000 still completely supports drives using the classic MBR and partition table, calling such drives *basic drives*.

**Figure 11-25**
Is 200KB enough
for you?

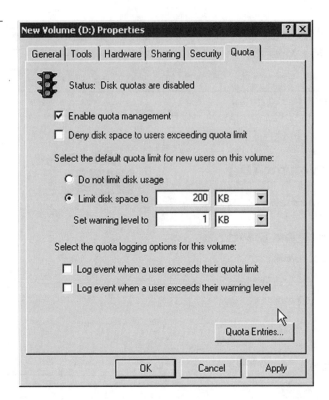

## Boot Menu

Windows 2000 has a boot menu very similar to Windows 9*x* systems, something that Windows NT sadly lacked. Access this menu by holding down F8 at boot. Although most of these settings are identical to Windows 9*x* settings, let's look at these options to appreciate some subtle differences.

### Safe Mode

Selecting the Safe Mode option opens Windows 2000 in a mode that's as close as a high-powered, 32-bit OS can get to a Windows 9*x*-type of Safe Mode. Safe Mode only installs basic drivers for keyboard, mouse, video, and drive access.

### Safe Mode with Networking

This option opens Windows 2000 Safe Mode with very basic network support.

## Safe Mode Command Prompt Only

This option opens Windows in Safe Mode, but with a big command prompt window running (Figure 11-26). You can minimize the command prompt window and use the Task Manager to start Explorer, and you'll see that you're really just in regular Safe Mode.

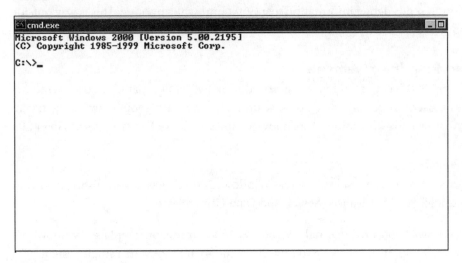

```
cmd.exe                                                    _ □
Microsoft Windows 2000 [Version 5.00.2195]
(C) Copyright 1985-1999 Microsoft Corp.

C:\>_
```

**Figure 11-26**   Safe Mode Command Prompt Only

## Enable Boot Logging

This is very similar to Windows 9x logging. This option logs to a file called NTBT-LOG.TXT.

## Enable VGA Mode

This option tells Windows 2000 to boot normally but with only a standard VGA driver. Use this option for those times when your new super-duper video card decides to cause problems.

## Last Known Good Configuration

Windows 2000 saves a copy of the Registry at every shutdown. The Last Known Good Configuration option provides a great way to recover from bad software installations or other configuration problems. I wish Windows 9x had such a simple method!

### Directory Service Restore Mode

This option is only for Windows 2000 Server; it's meaningless to Windows 2000 Professional.

### Debugging Mode

This option sends debug information to a COM port while booting. This is way outside the scope of A+!

## Networking Improvements

Windows 2000 has tremendously improved in networking capabilities over Windows NT, but most of these will make no sense until after we learn about networking in general! We'll save the discussion of such lovely topics as Active Directory for Chapter 20.

## New Versions

Windows NT had two versions, whereas Windows 2000 comes in four distinct versions: Professional, Server, Advanced Server, and Data Center Server.

- **Windows 2000 Professional**   Windows 2000 Professional replaces Windows NT Workstation. It supports up to two CPUs and 4GB of RAM in a single system.

- **Windows 2000 Server**   Windows 2000 Server replaces Windows NT Server. It contains extra tools and capabilities such as the Internet Information Server and Active Directory and Domain support. It supports up to four CPUs and 4GB of RAM in a single system.

- **Windows 2000 Advanced Server**   This is the same as the Server version, but adds support for eight CPUs and 8GB of RAM in a single system, and two-node clustering. Clustering enables separate systems to act as a single PC.

- **Windows 2000 Data Center Server**   This is the same as the Server version, but has support for 32 CPUs and 64GB of RAM in a single system, and four-node clustering. (Now if I can only get Unreal Tournament to take advantage of all those CPUs . . .)

## Easier Administration

One of the biggest complaints about Windows NT, and to a lesser extent Windows 9x, was the wide dispersal of the many utilities needed for administration and troubleshooting. Despite years of research, Microsoft could never find a place to put all the utilities needed in such a way as to please even a small majority of support people. In a moment of sheer genius, Microsoft determined that the ultimate utility was one that the support person made for himself! This brought on the creation of the amazing Microsoft Management Console.

## Microsoft Management Console (MMC)

The *Microsoft Management Console* (MMC) is simply a shell program that holds individual utilities called *snap-ins*. You can start the MMC by opening the Run option and typing in **MMC** to get a blank MMC console. Blank MMC consoles aren't much to look at (Figure 11-27).

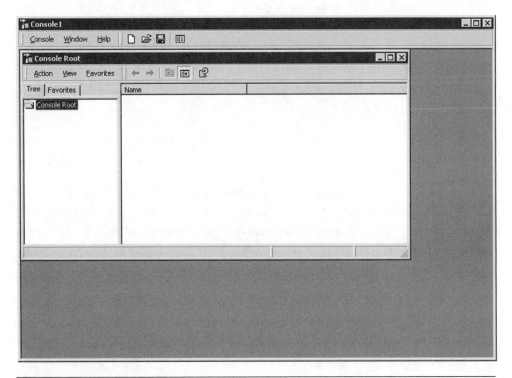

**Figure 11-27** Blank MMC

A blank console is made useful by adding snap-ins. Just click Console | Add/Remove Snap-in, then click the Add button to see a list of available snap-ins (Figure 11-28).

**Figure 11-28**

Available snap-ins

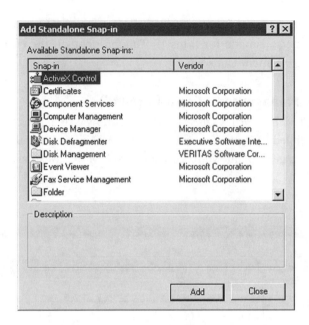

Virtually every traditional tool used by either Windows NT or Windows 9*x* is available as a snap-in. Even good old Device Manager is now a snap-in. Let's add the Device Manager snap-in. Once you click OK, close the Add window and click on the Device Manager. Hey! That looks kind of familiar, doesn't it? (See Figure 11-29.)

You can add as many snap-ins as you'd like, and there are many to choose from. Many companies sell third-party utilities as MMC snap-ins. Once you've added the snap-ins you want, just save the console under any name you want, anywhere you want. I'll save this console as DM (Device Manager) and drop it on my desktop (see Figure 11-30). I'm now just a double-click away from the Device Manager!

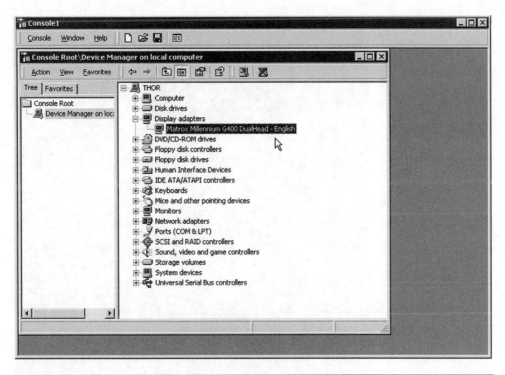

**Figure 11-29** Device Manager as a snap-in

If you want to, you can customize the MMC console. Click Console | Options to change the icons, save it under a different name, or lock it up so it can never be changed, as shown in Figure 11-31.

Be sure to uncheck the Do Not Save Changes to This Console check box. When the console is reopened, notice that the Console, Windows, and Help menu options are gone. This console cannot be changed (Figure 11-32).

**Figure 11-30**
Device Manager on
desktop

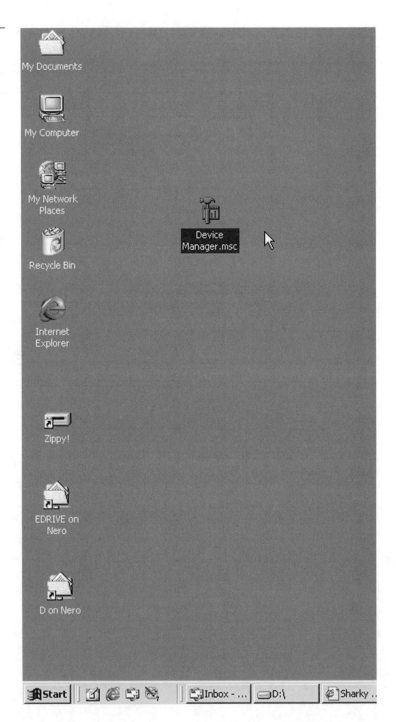

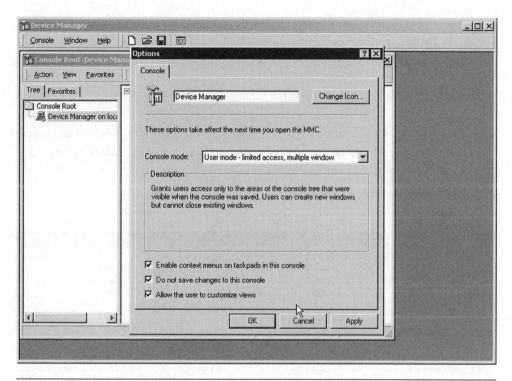

**Figure 11-31**   Lock this up!

**Figure 11-32**
Note the missing
options!

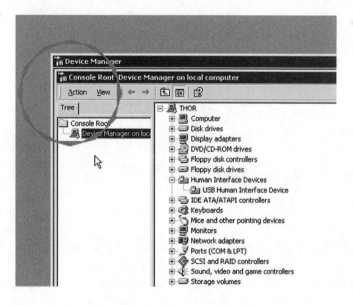

Microsoft knows that some folks like things the old way so they made a bunch of pre-made, locked consoles for you and dropped them in the same places, or at least close to the same places, you'd expect them to be in Windows 9*x*. Open the System Information Utility: Click on Start | Programs | Accessories | System Tools | System Information. It's the good old System Information utility, but notice it has a slightly different look; it's now an MMC snap-in! (Figure 11-33.) If you click on Tools and hold the mouse pointer over the Windows menu, however, you'll notice that the MMC-version has all the same utilities that came with the Windows 9*x* System Information utility. The snap-in versions of the old classics all look a tad different, but they still do the same job; in fact, they usually do it better!

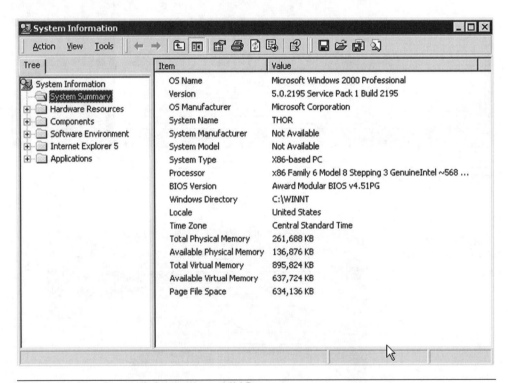

**Figure 11-33**   System Information as MMC

Try opening the Device Manager the old way. Open the properties for My Computer to display the System Properties, as in Figure 11-34.

Hey, wait a minute! New choices are available! Of all those tabs, guess which one you need to click on to see the Device Manager? That's right, Hardware (Figure 11-35)!

**Figure II-34**
System Properties

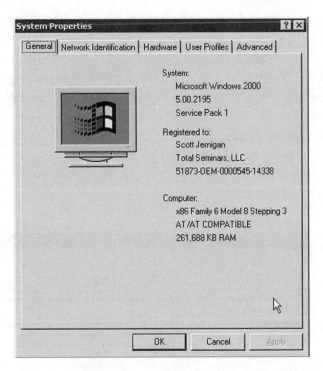

**Figure II-35**
Hardware tab

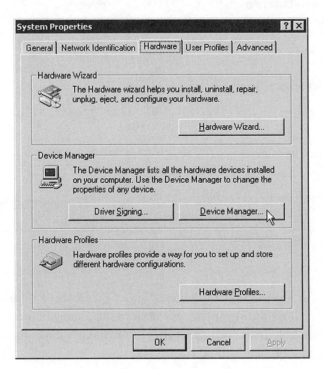

Hey! Where's the Device Manager? See the Device Manager button right in the middle? There you go!

Most techs start off disliking the MMC. But after a little time, they discover the wonderful flexibility of this powerful tool. They quickly start making consoles that contain the utilities they like the best and putting them in a place they find easiest to access!

## Administrative Tools

Windows 2000 has combined almost all of the snap-ins into a new applet in the Control Panel called Administrative Tools. Open the Control Panel and open Administrative Tools (Figure 11-36).

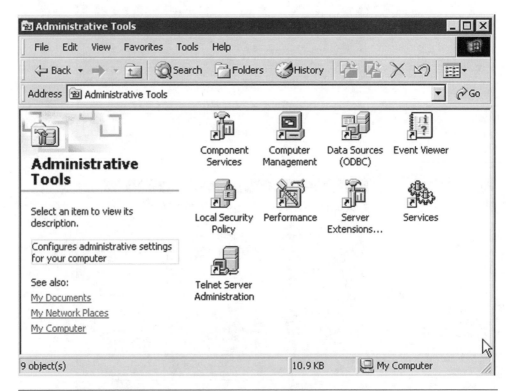

**Figure 11-36**  Administrative Tools

Administrative Tools is really just a folder that stores a number of pre-made consoles. As we poke through these, you'll notice that many of these consoles share some of the same snap-ins—nothing wrong with that. Let's look at some of the most commonly used tools here.

**NOTE** A+ Certification has little interest in many of these snap-ins, so we won't cover them all. If we don't mention it, it's almost certainly not on the test!

## Computer Management

The Computer Management applet is a tech's best new buddy, or at least a place where you'll spend a lot of time when building or maintaining a system. Computer Management is divided into three major headings: System Tools, Storage, and Services and Applications (Figure 11-37). Each of these headings has tools of particular interest to techs.

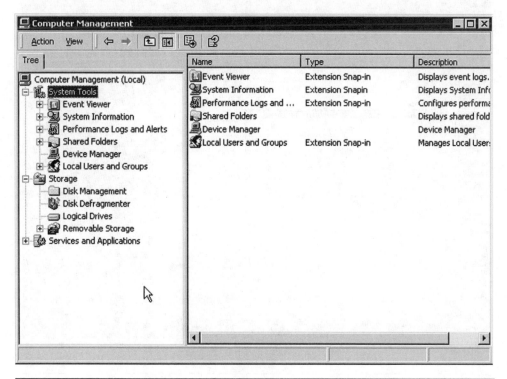

**Figure 11-37** Computer Management applet

**System Tools** System Tools provides a number of handy tools. You might say this is the dumping place for a number of important, but rather unrelated functions. The six default snap-ins are: Event Viewer, System Information, Performance Logs and Alerts, Shared Folders, Device Manager, and Local Users and Groups. Let's look at each one briefly.

*Event Viewer* The Event Viewer keeps three log files of events related to applications (programs starting, stopping), Security (successful/unsuccessful logins), and System (any event that doesn't fit into one of the other functions). An administrator can configure an enormous number of events and can create alarms to warn about any particular event they may want to monitor. Double-clicking on a log event gives details about that event (Figure 11-38).

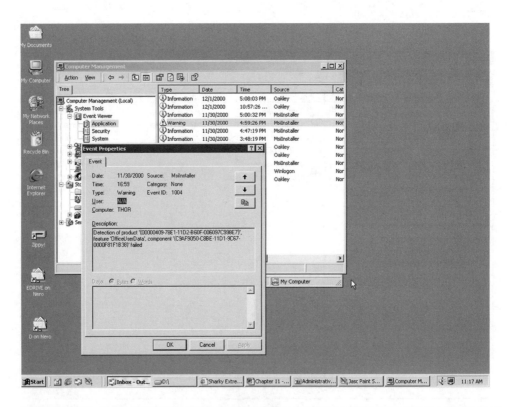

**Figure 11-38** Hmm...*Something* went wrong!

*System Information* System Information is the new System Information tool, very similar to the System Information tool used in Windows 9*x* (Figure 11-39). The Windows 2000 System Information tool provides more information than the version in its cousin OS. The System Information tool even surpasses the Device Manager in terms of raw hardware information but lacks any ability to make changes.

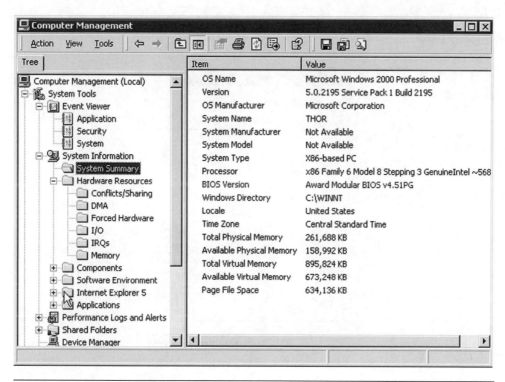

**Figure 11-39** System Information

*Performance Logs and Alerts* This snap-in enables Windows 2000 to create a written record of just about anything that happens on your system. Do you want to know if someone is trying to log onto your system when you're not around? Alternate-click on Counter Logs and select New Log Settings. Give the new setting a name—call it anything you want. Click OK to see a screen similar to the one shown in Figure 11-40.

Here's the process of creating a new log. First, click Add, then select the Use Local Computer Counters radio button. Next, select the Server setting from the Performance Object pull-down menu. Last, highlight Errors Logon so your dialog box looks like Figure 11-41.

Select Add, then Close. Click on Schedule and set up when you want this thing to run—probably from after work till 2:00 A.M.—or the time you most suspect someone is attempting to log into your computer. Click Log Files to see the name of the file and where it's being saved—probably C:\PerfLogs (Figure 11-42). Go back to the General tab, then press OK.

**Figure 11-40**
Building a new
event log

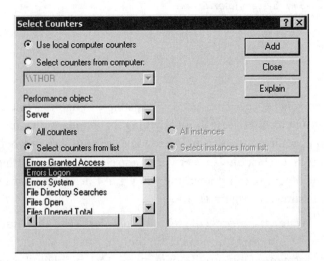

**Figure 11-41**
Proper event log

When you come back in the morning, open the Performance Console in Administrative Tools and click on the System Monitor. Alternate-click anywhere in the graph area and select Properties. Click on the Source tab and use the Browse button to locate your log file. Select the time range you want to see by dragging the small bar to the left. It should look like Figure 11-43.

**Figure 11-42**
Log location?

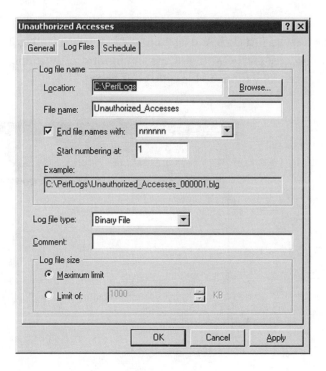

**Figure 11-43**
System Monitor
settings

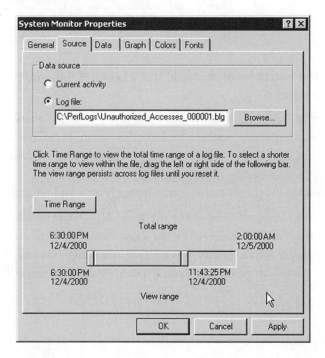

Now, click on the Data tab and select Add. You'll only have one option—your log file—so just click Add again to see it appear as in Figure 11-44.

Now, just click OK. If you see any bumps in the graph, somebody has been unsuccessfully trying to log onto your system!

**Figure 11-44**
Almost ready to go!

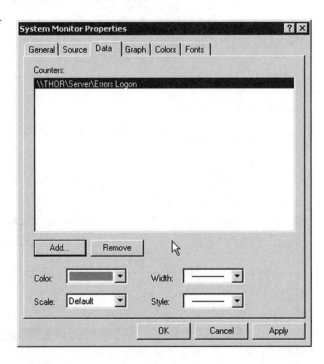

The System Monitor can do more than just this. We'll talk more about it in a moment.

*Shared Folders*   Shared Folders has three sections: Shares, Sessions, and Open Files. Shares shows all the folders your system is sharing on a network. Sessions shows who is accessing your system at this moment, and Open Files shows all the files opened by folks on other systems (Figure 11-45). You can cut people off by stopping shares or sessions, although it's a bad idea to close open files.

*Device Manager*   This is just the good old Device Manager from Windows 9*x*, with a few extra tricks. Click the View button and select Show Hidden Devices. These are all the legacy drivers that Windows 2000 automatically loads. You can disable these drivers if you're positive you don't need them, but the memory

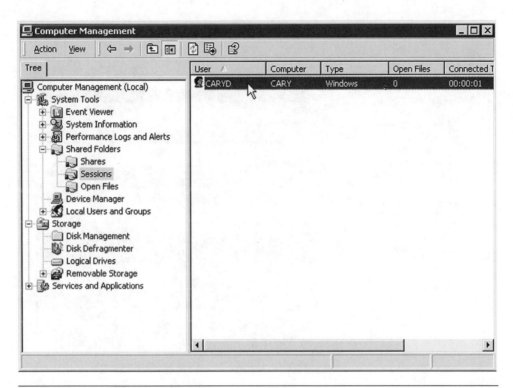

**Figure 11-45**   Shared Folders

savings is so marginal that it's not really worth it. Click View again and see the different ways to sort the devices. Have you noticed anything missing? That's right, you cannot reserve resources for legacy devices in Windows 2000. If you install a legacy device, either try to set it to unused resources or go into your CMOS and reserve the IRQ. Otherwise, the Windows 2000 Device Manager performs exactly like the Windows 9*x* version of the utility.

*Local Users and Groups*   Another place to manage local users and groups.

**Storage**   The Storage tool (Figure 11-46) handles all of the work required for the mass storage devices in the computer. If you need to deal with a hard drive, you do it here. Let's start with the simple ones.

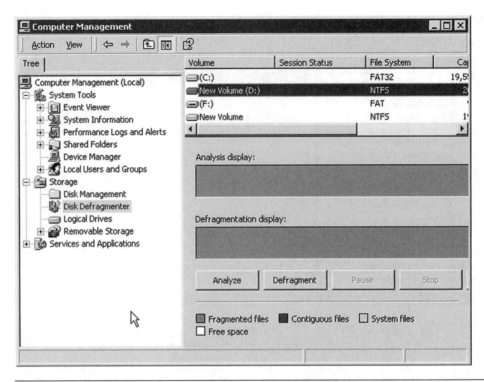

**Figure 11-46**    Storage tool, with Disk Defragmenter selected

*Disk Management*    Disk Management is by far the most important tool under Storage. This is where we deal with all of our mass storage devices. This area is so important that an entire section has been dedicated to the subject later in this chapter, called "Dealing with Drives."

*Disk Defragmenter*    Disk Defragmenter is just good old DEFRAG, although with a much prettier front end. By the way, you may still access Disk Defragmenter from the Programs | Accessories | System Tools | menu, just as in Windows 9*x*.

*Logical Drives*    Logical Drives provides details about each drive. This is identical to alternate-clicking the drive and selecting Properties, except this way displays all the drives in one location.

*Removable Storage*    Removable Storage deals with media pools. A *media pool* is a group of removable media devices that share a common interface, for example, a CD-ROM carousel. Although this is fascinating, A+ Certification does not cover this area.

**Services and Applications**  Services and Applications is another dumping ground for three totally different snap-ins: WMI Control, Services, and Indexing Service.

*WMI Control*  *Windows Management Instrumentation* (WMI) is a method developed by Microsoft to enable third parties to write programs for remote administration of networked systems. For example, somebody may one day come out with a utility that enables you to test a modem or update a BIOS remotely. This is not used very much yet.

*Services*  Windows 2000 runs a large number of separate programs called "services." The best way for a Windows 9*x* person to visualize a service is to think of a TSR—a program that runs, yet is invisible. The Services snap-in enables you to see the status of all services on the system, including services that are not running (Figure 11-47).

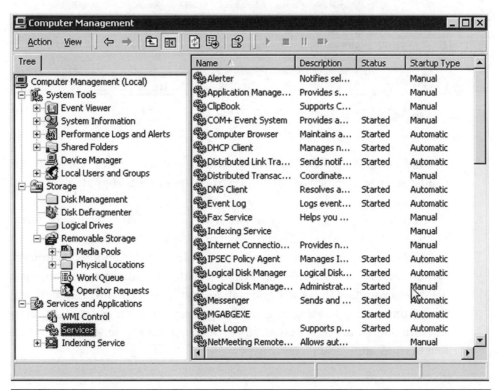

**Figure 11-47**   Services open

Even though you may access the Services snap-in via this console, most techs simply access the Services console under the Administrative tools for the same information but a less cluttered interface (Figure 11-48).

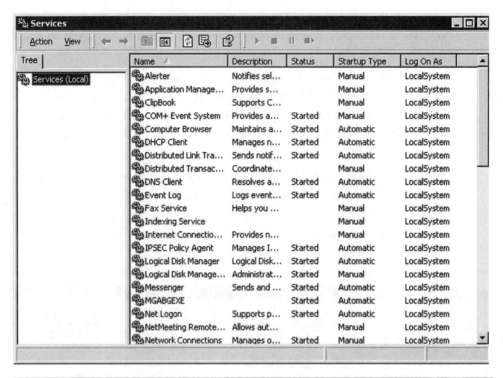

**Figure 11-48**   Services applet

Windows 2000 Professional comes with about 60 services. These services handle a huge number of functions, from application support to network functions.

Select the properties for any service. I chose the Alerter service for Figure 11-49. Notice the four tabs. The General tab is the most interesting tab for us.

See the Startup Type pull-down menu? It shows three options: Automatic, Manual, and Disabled. Automatic means it starts when the system starts; Manual means you have to come to this tab to start it; and Disabled prevents anything from starting it. Make sure you know these three settings and also make sure you understand how to start, stop, pause, and resume services (look at the four buttons underneath Startup Type).

**Figure 11-49**
Alerter Service
Properties

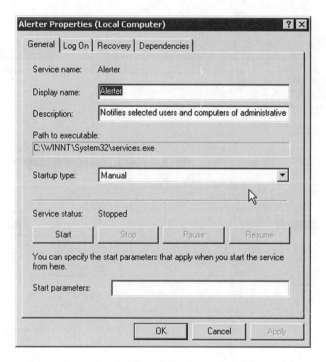

Alerter Properties (Local Computer)

General | Log On | Recovery | Dependencies |

Service name: Alerter

Display name: Alerter

Description: Notifies selected users and computers of administrative

Path to executable:
C:\WINNT\System32\services.exe

Startup type: Manual

Service status: Stopped

Start | Stop | Pause | Resume

You can specify the start parameters that apply when you start the service from here.

Start parameters:

OK | Cancel | Apply

**NOTE** A+ Certification is not interested in having you memorize all of these services—just make sure you can manipulate them!

*Indexing Service* The Indexing Service indexes selected drives and folders, which makes Windows 2000's Search tool much faster. To enable the Indexing Service, open the properties for Indexing Service and select Start. You can also start this service in the Search tool as shown in Figure 11-50. Heavy users of the Search tool should turn the Indexing Service on; it makes searches faster and more thorough.

As you can see, the Computer Management console covers a huge amount of the day-to-day work a technician handles. Administrative Tools has two other snap-ins worth mentioning here because they are useful in many work situations: Performance and Local Security Policy.

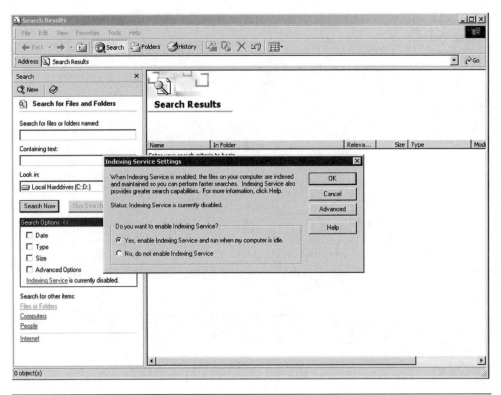

**Figure 11-50**  Enabling the Indexing Service

## Performance

The Performance console consists of two snap-ins: System Monitor and Performance Logs and Alerts. We've already seen both of these earlier for reading logs, but the System Monitor can also monitor real-time data (Figure 11-51).

Suppose you just got a new cable modem and you want to know just how fast you can download data. Click on the plus sign (+) to add a counter. Click Use Local Computer Counters, then locate the Network Interface from the Performance Object pull-down menu. Last, highlight Bytes Received per second. The dialog box should look like Figure 11-52.

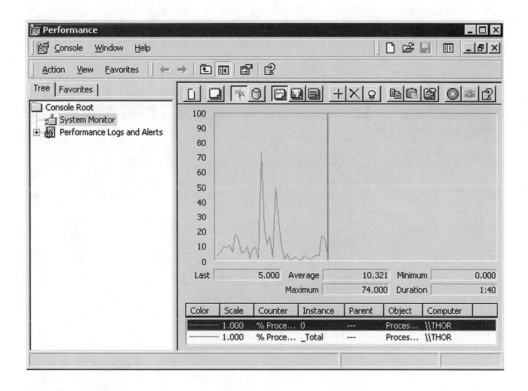

**Figure 11-51** System Monitor in action!

**Figure 11-52**
Setting up a
throughput test

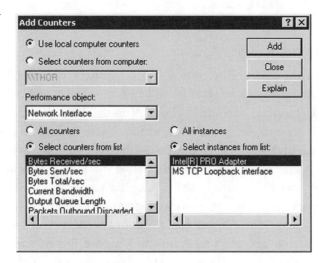

Select Add, then Close—probably not much is happening. Go to a Web site, preferably one where you can select a huge file, and then start downloading. Watch the chart jump; that's the real throughput (Figure 11-53).

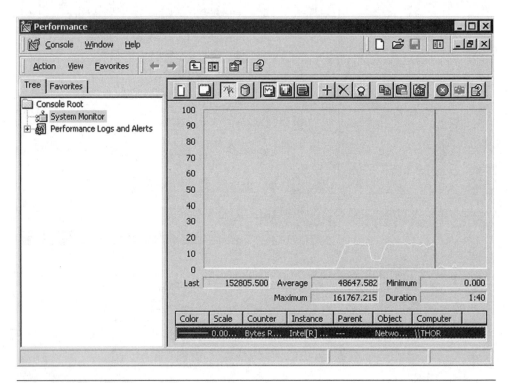

**Figure 11-53**   Blazing speed!

## Local Security Policy

The last of the noteworthy consoles in Administrative Tools, Local Security Policy, enables administrators to set a bewildering number of rights for users and groups. These special settings are called policies. A right, by the way, is not the same thing as a permission. *Permissions*, if you recall, enable you to access and manipulate data on an NTFS-based drive. *Rights*, in contrast, describe what you can do to a system, such as log in or restart the PC. Changing policies enable you to set a bunch of rights all at once.

Let's say you don't want Bob, the late-shift guy, to log onto your system at night because you're running some hairy program and he just plays games, which slows down the process. The program will finish in a week, so you don't want him to delete his account; you just don't want him to log onto the system for a week. Open the Local Security settings and locate the User Rights Assignment under Local Policies (Figure 11-54). Scroll through the policies until you find Deny Logon Locally.

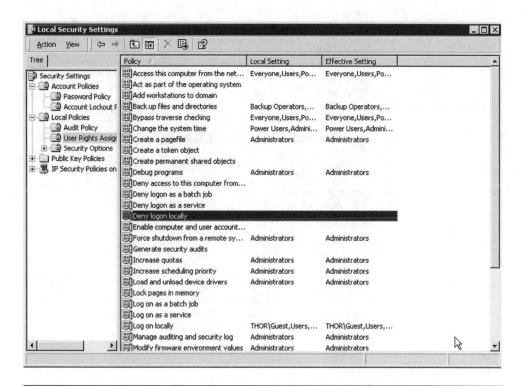

**Figure 11-54** Ready to deny?

Double-click to open it. Click the Add button to add the user Bob. Of course, if you don't have a user called Bob, this won't work! (See Figure 11-55.)

Notice the Local Setting and the Effective Setting. If the Effective Setting is checked, that means that some other policy is overriding yours. For example, if you tried to deny Shut Down the System to Power Users, the Effective Setting for the policy would still show as checked because Power Users always have the right to shut down a system—it's a defined function for that built-in group.

 **EXAM TIP** The A+ Certification exams do not ask you about particular policies. Just understand what policies do and how they can affect you as a tech. Watch out for questions that say, "Why can't you shut down a system?" and be prepared to answer, "Someone has set a policy that prevents me from doing it!"

**Figure 11-55**
Sorry, Bob!

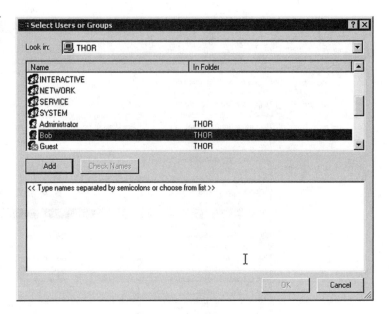

## Control Panel Changes

Most of the applets in the Control Panel function exactly like their equivalents in Windows 9*x*. A few have changed, however, some just a bit and some dramatically. Let's look at the Windows 2000 applets that are significantly different from their Windows 9*x* counterparts.

### Administrative Tools

Windows 2000 adds Administrative Tools to the Control Panel, but many techs like to add Administrative Tools to the Start | Programs menu. Alternate-click on a blank area of the Task bar and select Properties. Click the Advanced button and check the Display Administrative Tools check box as shown in Figure 11-56. The Administrative Tools will now display on the Programs menu—a handy way to access this heavily used tool!

### Add/Remove Hardware

The Add/Remove Hardware Wizard has changed considerably from Windows 9*x*. Although still used to detect legacy devices, it now has a few new jobs. The Add/Remove Hardware Wizard is now accessible from the System Properties applet, so I'll save the new features for that discussion.

**Figure 11-56**
Adding
Administrative
Tools to the
Programs menu

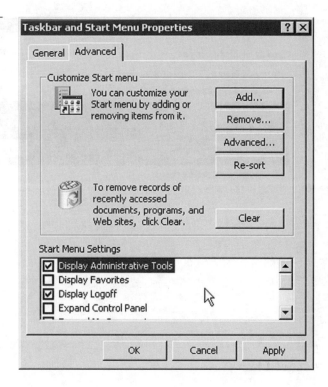

## Add/Remove Programs

Microsoft completely revamped the Add/Remove Programs applet from the Windows 9*x* version, adding a number of handy improvements (Figure 11-57).

In my opinion, adding the size of the application approaches pure genius! So many times people delete programs just to open space on the drives; this really helps the decision-making process. Microsoft also appreciates that a lot of folks install a gazillion programs, so adding the option to sort by name, size, and so on makes my uninstalling life much easier!

The Add/Remove Programs Wizard also has the Add/Remove Windows Components and Add New Programs windows, which function just like their Windows 9*x* counterparts.

The most interesting item is what's not here anymore: the Startup Disk option. Windows 2000 does not have a Startup disk in the sense of Windows 9*x*; it's just too big of an OS. Floppy disks are made for Windows 2000, but they're barely functional. Don't panic, Windows 2000 provides lots of new toys to help in recovery as we'll see in the "Maintaining Windows 2000" section later in this chapter.

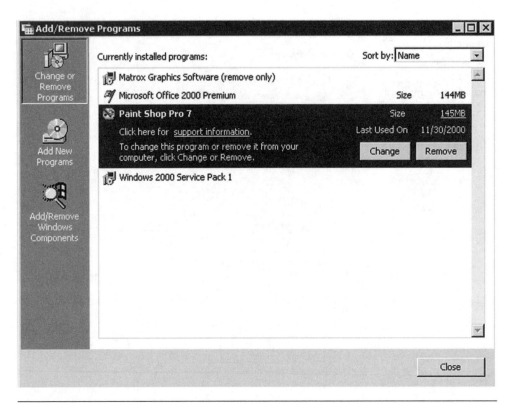

**Figure 11-57**   Add/Remove Programs applet in Windows 2000

### Sound and Multimedia

Not much needs to be said here as we have not yet covered sound or multimedia, but Windows 2000 combines the Windows 9*x* Sound applet and the Multimedia applet into one—no features are lost, just one less applet to try to find.

### System

Do you want to see a big change? OK, let's look at the System properties. The tour begins with a quick trip to the System applet in the Control Panel; open this up. (Yes, you may still alternate-click on My Computer to get here, but it looks very different from the old Device Manager!) Here we see the System Properties dialog box—one of the most important areas to maintain and fix a system (see Figure 11-58).

> **General Tab**   The General tab gives basic information about the PC and mirrors the General tab information on a Windows 9*x* machine. Note that it shows the current service pack, the serial number, and the amount of RAM. It's not good for much else. The Network Identification tab is new to the System applet, but let's save the discussion about this tab for Chapter 20, when we discuss networking in

**Figure 11-58**
System Properties

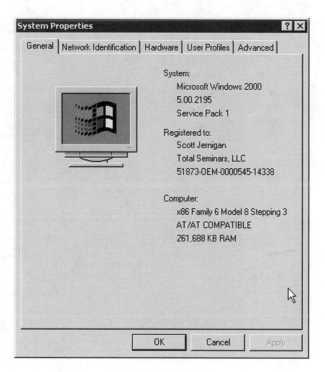

detail. Of all the tabs in System Properties, Hardware tends to be the most heavily used and deserves a more thorough discussion. Figure 11-59 shows the Hardware tab.

**Hardware Tab** The topmost button, the Hardware Wizard, is the same Add/Remove Hardware Wizard that has already been discussed. In today's PnP world, Microsoft expects devices to install automatically. In fact, when you install a device in Windows 2000, you no longer get the famous "Windows has detected new hardware" message. Windows 2000 simply installs the device and only prompts you if it does not have a proper device driver. Microsoft no longer sees the Hardware Wizard as a primary tool for installation. Instead, it sees this as two tools in one. Look at Figure 11-60—note the two radio buttons.

The first, Add/Troubleshoot a Device, works very much like the Windows 9x Wizard but concentrates on PnP devices, enabling you to install or troubleshoot from a list that looks somewhat like the Device Manager. Notice that Microsoft has thoughtfully configured the wizard to place any "problem" devices at the top of the list to bring them to your attention—a very nice touch! (See Figure 11-61.) To add a non-PnP device, you must select Add a New Device, the first option. When you select Add a New Device, you get a slightly updated version of the old Windows 9x Add/Remove Hardware Wizard.

**Figure 11-59**
Hardware tab

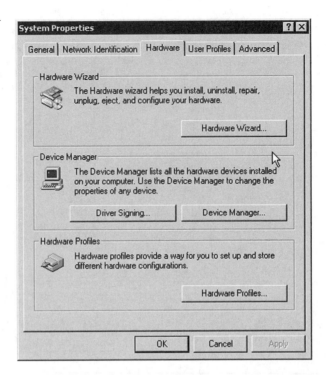

**Figure 11-60**
Hardware Wizard
options

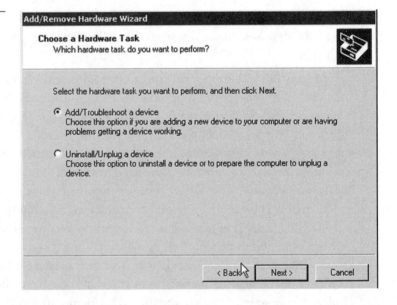

The Uninstall/Unplug a Device radio button is a new feature to the Add/Remove Hardware Wizard. This is really two new features (see Figure 11-62). First, just as Windows 9x added the ability to uninstall applications to deal with

**Figure 11-61**
Add/troubleshoot a
device

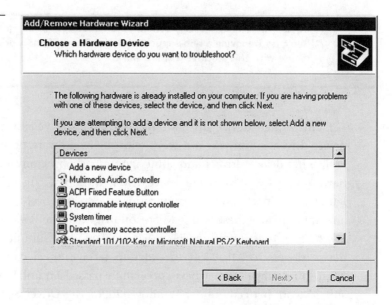

**Figure 11-62**
Uninstall/unplug a
device

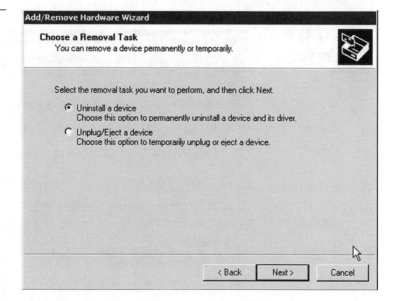

the nightmare of removing complex software installations, Windows 2000 now adds the ability to perform very thorough uninstalls of hardware, cleanly removing all of the unneeded device drivers and other support programs.

Secondly, this option provides support for hot-swappable devices such as FireWire, USB, or any other device designed to unplug or eject without rebooting.

**NOTE** The Unplug/Eject option only works for devices designed to hot swap. Don't try removing a non-supported device like a PCI network card or a PS/2 mouse with this feature! It won't work!

Badly written device drivers have plagued every version of Windows. Some device drivers simply do not work with their hardware properly. Some conflict with other device drivers and some ignore basic programming rules and wreak havoc on the OS itself. Some device drivers work perfectly well but become obsolete as service packs and new applications are created over the life of the OS. In an attempt to reduce these issues, Microsoft instituted the *Windows Hardware Quality Lab* (WHQL) testing center. Hardware makers may submit their hardware and device drivers to Microsoft in order to receive an electronic certificate from Microsoft stating that they have successfully passed a number of rigorous tests and should work perfectly under Windows 2000. The Driver Signing button on the Hardware tab enables you to decide whether or not to allow non-certified device drivers in the system (see Figure 11-63).

**Figure 11-63**
Driver Signing
Options

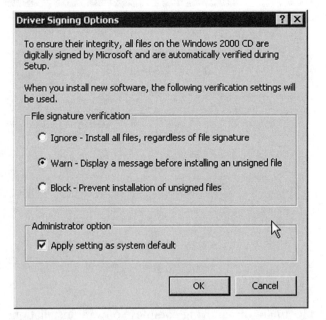

A large percentage of device drivers do not possess a WHQL certificate. In fact, you would find it difficult to find *any* Windows 2000 system that contained nothing but WHQL-certified drivers; as a result, we almost always leave this set to the Warn radio button as shown. The Administrator option simply enables the administrator to set any chosen radio button as the default for all users.

No one knows if driver signing will become standard. Many well-known manufacturers simply ignore WHQL due to the time and cost involved with obtaining the certificate, especially given the fact that most manufacturers update device drivers at least yearly. Other manufacturers separate the WHQL drivers from their latest drivers, giving you the choice between a known safe driver or one that incorporates the latest features. Figure 11-64 shows a part of the driver download page from the very popular Matrox Graphics Web site. Matrox makes a number of great video products—I must admit that I really like Matrox video cards. Note the different driver choices.

**Figure 11-64**
Driver download
page

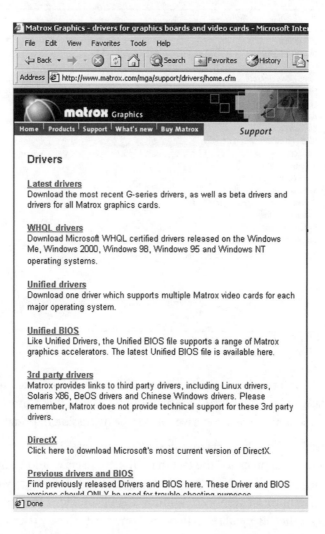

Windows NT did not have the Device Manager. Installing a piece of hardware in NT could challenge even the best of technicians as you needed to access a different Control Panel applet to install or troubleshoot different devices. Many hardware makers would literally install their own Control Panel applets to provide a configuration method for their devices! Microsoft finally ended this insanity by adding the Device Manager to Windows 2000 (Figure 11-65). Note that the Windows 2000 Device Manager is now just another MMC snap-in but works basically the same as the Windows 9*x* Device Manager.

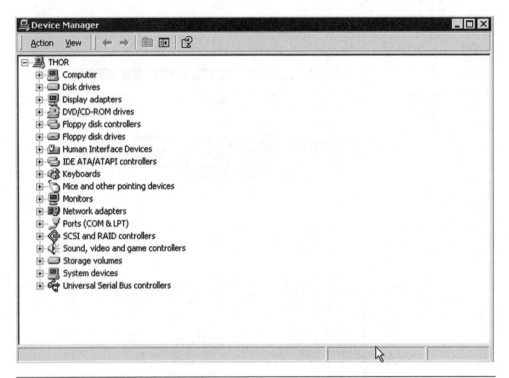

**Figure 11-65**   Device Manager

The last option on the Hardware dialog box, Hardware Profiles, enables you to create different hardware configurations. We use this almost exclusively with laptops, so it makes sense to save this for the discussion of portable PCs in Chapter 18.

**User Profiles Tab**   Having designed Windows 2000 to support multiple users, Microsoft appreciated the fact that different users would want their own desktops, backgrounds, screen savers, and My Documents folders, as well as other personalized settings. In response, Windows 2000 provides for unique user-specific settings, called *user profiles*. When someone creates a new user account on a Windows 2000 system, Windows waits until that user first logs on and creates an entire folder tree. This tree, the user profile, contains all personal settings for that user under the Documents and Settings folder on the boot drive. Figure 11-66 shows a typical folder tree for the user "michaelm." Note the large number of folders; user profiles grow dramatically as the users add files to My Documents, Favorites to Internet Explorer, and many other options.

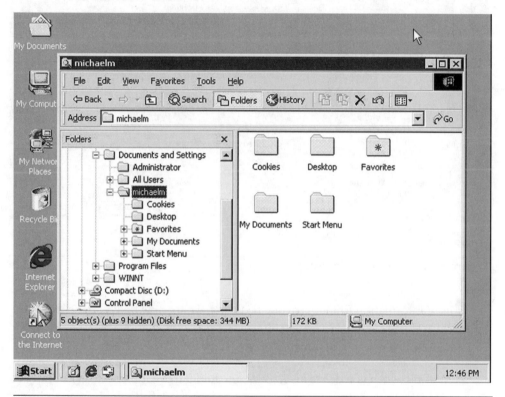

**Figure 11-66**   Documents and Settings

Windows 9x users often like to share their desktops in a network environment. This is common as it provides a handy way for two users to exchange a file. In Windows 9x, you simply share the \WINDOWS\DESKTOP folder. But Windows 2000 may possess many desktops, one for each user. To share a user's desktop, you have to go to the desktop folder under his or her user name and configure sharing on that folder (Figure 11-67).

The User Profiles tab (see Figure 11-68) shows the current profiles on the system. This shows the account name, total size of all personal data, type (we will explain this next), and the date it was last modified. We glean two very important

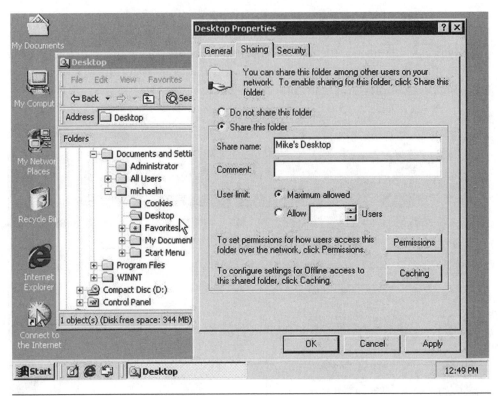

**Figure 11-67**   Sharing an individual desktop

bits of information from this dialog box. First, we see how much drive space a particular user account takes up, enabling us to deal with accounts that may be taking up too much space or that require more.

Second, when you delete an account, the folder tree continues to exist until you remove it. This enables an administrator to go through the folder tree to insure that no important files still exist. After a thorough inspection, he or she can return to the User Profiles dialog box and delete the profile.

Windows 2000 supports two types of profiles: local and roaming. *Local* profiles, as their name implies, only work on that single system. *Roaming* profiles work on *any* system in a network! No matter what system you log onto, you get your desktop, personal settings, and so on, the way you want it! Roaming profiles have some downsides. All systems using roaming profiles must be members of a domain, and lots of large roaming profiles may put a serious strain on the network. (See Chapter 20 for more on domains.) To make a local profile a roaming profile, just click the Change Type button. Very easy!

**Figure 11-68**
User Profiles tab

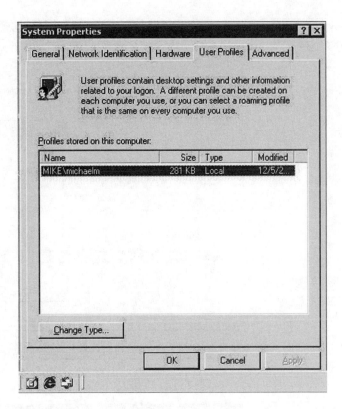

Advanced Tab    The last tab on the System applet, Advanced, comes in a close second to the Hardware tab for the title of most used dialog box for techs (Figure 11-69). Let's skip the first button, Performance Options, until the "Optimizing Windows 2000" section later in this chapter. Just remember where to find it when we look at it again in a moment.

The next button, Environment Variables, provides two items. First is a list of User variables used for backward compatibility with DOS and older Windows applications. We occasionally find a need to add settings here (Figure 11-70). Second is a list of System variables, which are used by Windows 2000 and NT applications to provide system information to any program that may need it. Unlike the User variables, these values rarely change.

The Startup and Recovery button enables editing of the BOOT.INI as well as provides steps to take in the event of system failure (Figure 11-71).

**Figure 11-69**
Advanced tab

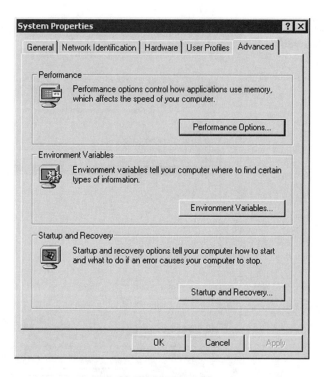

**Figure 11-70**
Environment
Variables

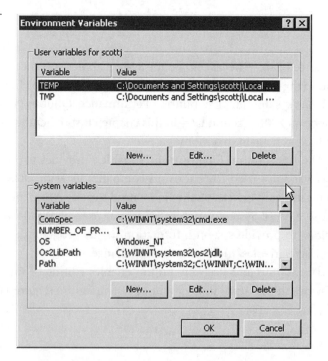

**Figure 11-71**
Startup and
Recovery

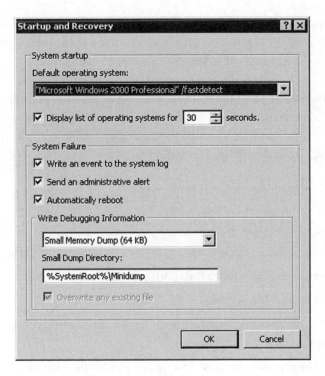

## File Structure

The Windows 2000 directory structure is quite different from Windows 9x. We've already seen most of this structure during earlier discussions, but here's a list of the three most important folders as a review:

- **\WINNT**    Contains all the files and subfolders used by Windows 2000. You'll see many folders and files very similar, if not identical, to Windows 9x.

- **\PROGRAM FILES**    Stores installed programs, just like Windows 9x.

- **\DOCUMENTS AND SETTINGS**    Stores all user-specific information. Note that each user gets his or her own folder. We also see the All Users folder. This includes settings that show up for all users.

## Installing Windows 2000 Professional

On the face of it, installing Windows 2000 Professional seems essentially the same as installing Windows 9x. You insert the CD-ROM, access the setup routine, and go! But that conceptualization does not hold up in practice. Installing Windows 2000 requires you to do many tasks *before* you install, such as making sure that your hardware and applications can handle the new OS.

## Pre-installation Tasks

Working with PCs gives us many "exciting" opportunities for frustrating delays and unproductive side trips! The Windows 2000 installation process holds great potential for lost time. Installing an OS can be a time-consuming task, even when everything goes right. Nothing sets the teeth to grinding as much as an indecipherable error message or "blue screen of death" 55 minutes into an hour-long system installation.

With that in mind, let's look at the tasks you need to complete *before* you insert that CD-ROM. Here's the list, and then discussion follows:

1. Identify your hardware requirements.

2. Verify that your hardware components are on the Windows 2000 *Hardware Compatibility List* (HCL).

3. Decide whether to perform an upgrade or a clean installation.

4. Determine how you want to partition the hard disk.

5. Decide on a file system.

6. Determine your computer's role (standalone, workgroup, or domain membership).

7. Decide on your computer's language and locale settings.

## Hardware Requirements

Microsoft's minimum recommendations for a Windows 2000 Professional installation are as follows:

| COMPONENT | MINIMUM REQUIREMENT |
|-----------|---------------------|
| CPU | Intel Pentium 133 MHz |
| Memory | 64MB |
| Hard disk | 2GB with 650MB of free space |
| Network | None |
| Display | Video adapter and monitor with VGA resolution |
| CD-ROM | 12X (not required if installing over a network) |

The minimum specs represent what Microsoft says you need to install the Windows 2000 Professional OS. Windows 2000 Professional will install and will run on a system with the minimum specifications, but you need to take these numbers and at least double them if you want to be happy with your system's performance!

Here is a more realistic recommendation for a Windows 2000 Professional computer system:

| COMPONENT | RECOMMENDED MINIMUM |
| --- | --- |
| CPU | Intel Pentium II 350 MHz |
| Memory | 128MB |
| Hard disk | 6.4GB hard disk with 2GB of free space |
| Network | Modern PCI network card |
| Display | Video adapter and monitor with SVGA resolution, capable of High Color (16-bit) display |
| CD-ROM | 24X (not required if installing over a network) |
| Floppy Disk Drive | High density |

If your test system(s) exceeds the recommended configuration, all the better! You can never have too fast a processor or too much hard disk space.

## Hardware Compatibility List (HCL)

In addition to meeting the minimal specifications, your hardware also needs to be supported by the Windows 2000 OS. The Hardware Compatibility List is the definitive authority as to whether your component is compatible with the OS. Items on the HCL have been extensively tested with Windows 2000 and are guaranteed by Microsoft to work with your installation.

**NOTE**  If you contact Microsoft's technical support staff, one of the first things they ask is if all of your systems' components are on the HCL.

The HCL is located in the SUPPORT folder on the Windows 2000 CD-ROM (HCL.TXT), but for the most current list, visit the Microsoft Web site (http://www.microsoft.com/hcl). There you can search for a particular component or view the entire HCL.

## Upgrading Issues

Upgrading your computer system from an earlier version of Windows can be a tricky affair, with its own set of pitfalls. It is important to note that you have a somewhat higher risk of running into errors during an upgrade than you normally would by performing a "clean" installation.

Here are some of the issues that you should be aware of before performing an upgrade:

- You can upgrade directly to Windows 2000 Professional from Windows 9x (all versions) and Windows NT Workstation (versions 3.51 and 4.0). To upgrade to Windows 2000 Professional from Windows NT 3.1 or 3.5, you must first upgrade to NT 3.51 or 4.0, then to Windows 2000 Professional.

- Because of Registry and program differences between Windows 9x and Windows 2000, you might need upgrade packs (or migration DLLs) for your Windows 9x applications. Not only does Windows 2000 have hardware issues, it also does not like a lot of Windows 9x software!

- Windows 2000 does not support applications that make use of *Virtual Device Drivers* (VxDs). VxDs enable applications to access hardware directly, bypassing the OS altogether. Many older games and multimedia applications use VxDs, which makes this a potentially very serious issue.

- Third-party disk compression applications are not supported by Windows 2000.

- Third-party power management applications are also likely to cause problems with a Windows 2000 installation.

Obviously, it's worth your time to take a few extra steps before you pop in that CD-ROM! If you plan to upgrade rather than run a clean installation, follow these steps first:

1. First and most importantly, run a compatibility report using the Check Upgrade utility provided with Windows 2000 Professional. The utility generates a detailed list of potentially problematic devices and applications. The compatibility report is generated automatically when performing a "clean" installation of Windows 2000. You can run the utility in two ways:

   - From your current OS, run the WINNT32.EXE program off of the Windows 2000 Professional CD-ROM with the CHECKUPGRADEONLY switch.

   - Download and execute the standalone version of the utility from Microsoft's Web site at the following URL: **http://www.microsoft.com/windows2000/ upgrade/compat/default.asp**.

2. Have an up-to-date backup of your data and configuration files handy.

3. Perform a "spring cleaning" on your system by uninstalling unused or unnecessary applications and deleting old files.

4. Perform a disk scan and a disk defragmentation.

5. Uncompress all files, folders, and partitions.

6. Perform a current virus scan, and then remove or disable all virus-checking software.

7. Disable virus checking in your system CMOS.

8. Lastly, keep in mind that if worse comes to worst, you may have to start over and do a clean installation anyway. This makes step 2 exceedingly important! Back up your data!

## Disk Partition Options

The first thing that the Setup program does is examine your hard disk to determine its existing partition and file system configuration. You then get the option of either installing onto an existing partition (if any) or creating a new partition for installation.

By default, the active partition (typically the C: drive) is where the Windows 2000 system files are copied. The boot partition is where your OS files are located. Typically, this will be C:\WINNT for a clean installation. An upgrade installation will overwrite your current OS files in their current location (that is, \WINNT if upgrading from Windows NT, and \WINDOWS if upgrading from Windows 9x). Microsoft recommends that your boot partition be at least 1GB in size.

**NOTE** You can manage your disk partitions from within Windows 2000 using the Disk Management utility, which will be covered later in this chapter.

## File System Options

At the heart of any OS is the system by which you create and organize your files. Windows 2000 supports FAT16 and FAT32, just like Windows 9x, but also supports its own native NTFS as discussed earlier in this chapter.

**NOTE** Support for FAT32 is a new feature to Windows 2000. Windows NT versions 4.0 and earlier do not support FAT32.

If you choose to format your disk with either version of FAT, the Windows 2000 Setup Wizard will automatically format it with FAT16 if the partition is less than 2GB, and FAT32 if the partition is greater than 2GB.

## NTFS

The NTFS that comes with Windows 2000 (NTFS5) has a few advancements over the older NTFS from Windows NT (NTFS4). Windows 2000 can only create NTFS5 volumes; it cannot make the older NTFS4 volumes. NTFS5 offers the most options for your Windows 2000 OS installation. Using NTFS5, you can do the following new functions that NTFS4 could not do (or did not do as well):

- Compress data on the hard disk to conserve space
- Assign disk quotas to users to limit the amount of hard disk space they can use
- Encrypt files and folders on the hard disk
- Support Windows 2000 Dynamic Disk configurations

Unless you are configuring your system for multiple-boot options, NTFS is the best way to go.

**NOTE** Existing NTFS4 system partitions will be upgraded to Windows 2000 NTFS5 automatically during the installation. If you wish to dual-boot between NT4.0 and 2000, you must first install Service Pack 5 on the NT4.0 machine. This enables NT to read an NTFS5 partition, but the advanced features will not function.

## Networking Options

As with previous versions of Windows NT, the Windows 2000 line is optimized for networking with other computer systems. By default, Windows 2000 installs the client for Microsoft Networks, File and Printer sharing for Microsoft Networks, and Internet Protocol (TCP/IP). You are also given the option of joining either a Workgroup or a Domain.

Your network administrator will supply details for those folks working in a networking environment. For the rest, simply install into a Workgroup and go on with the installation.

 **NOTE** Chapter 20 covers networking terminology and concepts in detail.

### Language and Locale Settings

Windows 2000 can easily be configured to support multiple languages and regional input settings for such things as keyboard layout, currency, time/date display, and numbering.

### Quick Review

This is what you should have resolved so far:

- Your hardware is up to snuff, meaning that it meets the muscle requirements and is on the HCL.
- You've decided on a partition method.
- You've selected your file system(s).
- You know what role your machine is going to play in a network.
- You know what language and locale settings you plan to use.

You should also take a moment to decide on a unique and memorable administrative password. Windows 2000 automatically sets up an administrator's user account during the installation, and you use this account to log on and perform all administrative tasks. Losing or forgetting the password to your administrator account can be very bad news.

After you satisfy all the pre-installation tasks, the actual installation of Windows 2000 is almost a letdown! You simply insert the CD-ROM, answer a couple of questions, kick back, and read a book for an hour or so!

## Optimizing Windows 2000

Like Windows 9x, Windows 2000 comes well optimized out of the box. In fact, Windows 2000's optimization features are substantially less than Windows 9x. For example, there's no obvious way to manipulate the disk cache (I could show you, but I'd have to rename the book, A+ *and Windows 2000 Professional Exam*). Almost every optimization task that techs can perform on a Windows 2000 machine follows basically the same process as in Windows 9x. Windows 2000 has a couple of unique spots where a tech can make a difference: Performance Options and Task Manager.

One of the unique optimization features of Windows 2000 is setting Performance Options, although this has a rather limited utility. To access these options, go to My Computer and select Properties, click the Advanced tab, and select Performance Options. The Performance Options dialog box shows a pair of radio buttons called Applications and Background Services. These radio buttons have nothing to do with virtual memory; they set how processor time is divided between the foreground application and all other background tasks. Set this to Applications if you run applications that need more processor time. Set it to Background Services to give all running programs the same processor usage (Figure 11-72). You can also adjust the size of the swap file—now called a *paging file*—at the Performance Options dialog box.

**Figure 11-72**
Performance
Options

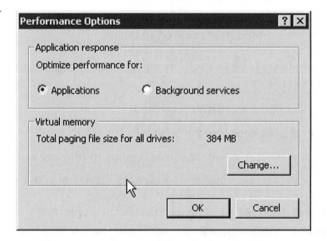

Resource tracking is very important with Windows 2000. Although the System Monitor and logging features are very powerful, most of the time we just want quick, basic information like we got from the Windows 9x System Monitor. Windows 2000 has this, but in a rather strange place: the new Task Manager! Press CTRL-ALT-DEL to bring up the Task Manager and click on the Performance tab (Figure 11-73).

This handy screen provides us with the most commonly used information: CPU usage, available physical memory, the size of the disk cache, commit charge (memory for programs), and kernel memory (memory used by Windows).

One area that confuses folks is the Handles, Threads, and Processes section.

**Figure 11-73**
Performance tab

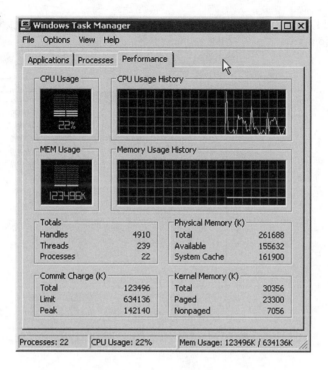

- **Process**   Any running executable program or subsystem (usually a DLL) running on the system. This includes applications and services as well as kernel-based programs.

- **Threads**   Most 32-bit programs break themselves into multiple "mini-programs" called *threads*.

- **Handles**   Opening one program usually involves opening other program or data files. Handles shows all of the interlinks between these programs and the other programs and files they use.

While we are here in the Task Manager, click on the Applications tab (Figure 11-74).

The Applications tab shows all of the currently running applications. In some cases, we must shut down errant applications from this screen. The Windows 9*x* equivalent of this was our last resort for closing programs that locked up.

Windows 2000 enables you to close down applications, but also goes one step further and enables you to shut off processes. The Processes tab (Figure 11-75) is Windows 2000's last resort spot for shutting down locked-up processes in Windows 2000. Shutting down processes is a *very* dangerous thing to do. Don't bother memorizing all these processes because every Windows 2000 shows different ones; just make sure you know how to get to the Task Manager to shut down applications or processes!

**Figure 11-74**
Applications tab

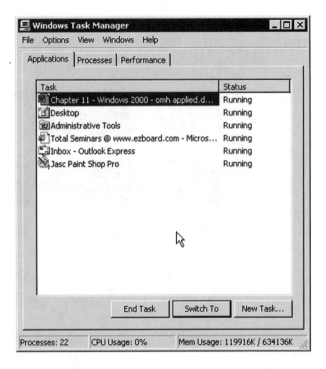

**Figure 11-75**
Processes tab

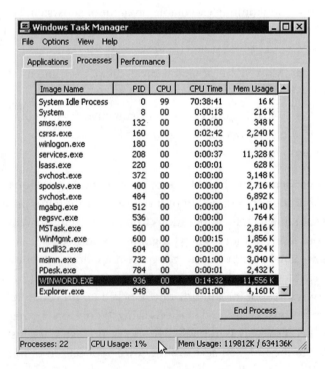

## Installing New Hardware

The processes for installing new hardware are absolutely identical to the procedures you use in Windows 9x, even down to the troubleshooting and backup utilities. Just remember that in the case of a resource conflict, you need to reserve the resource in CMOS! If you know how to install PnP and legacy devices in Windows 9x, you know how to do it in Windows 2000!

## Maintaining Windows 2000

Microsoft has used its close to 15 years of experience with OSs to make Windows 2000 one of the easiest-to-maintain OSs ever invented. Maintenance in Windows 2000 requires you to do several things: keep the system patched; use the typical tools—Disk Defragmenter, ScanDisk, and Disk Cleanup—to keep things running smoothly; and finally, prepare for system crashes with good backups, boot disks, and the Recovery Console.

## Patching

No OS is perfect, and Windows 2000 is no exception. Microsoft had patches written for Windows 2000 before it even hit the store shelves! Part of the job of a tech is to keep systems patched and up to date. Luckily for us, Microsoft has made this job trivially easy with the Windows Update utility.

Make sure to use the Windows Update utility to keep your system up to date on Service Packs, Security updates, and so on. To access the Windows Updater, go to Start | Windows Update. Make sure you're online: The Update utility will take you to Microsoft, and after you select Product Updates from the Web site, scan your system (see Figure 11-76) to show you the files needed. You can then pick and choose which ones you want to download. Figure 11-77 shows the Windows Update utility at work.

**Figure 11-76**
Windows Update
utility scanning

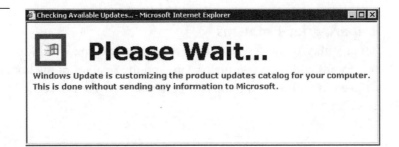

Checking Available Updates... - Microsoft Internet Explorer

# Please Wait...

Windows Update is customizing the product updates catalog for your computer.
This is done without sending any information to Microsoft.

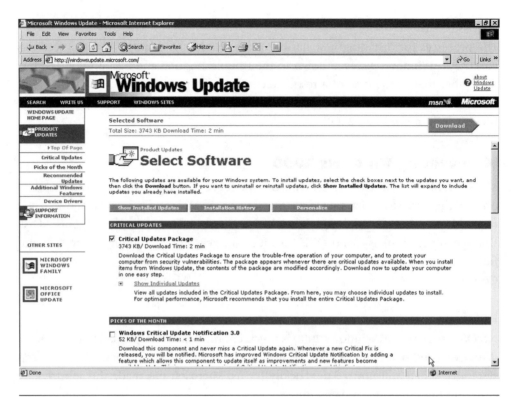

**Figure 11-77**   Windows Update files available for download

## Routine Maintenance

Run the Disk Defragmenter and ScanDisk for system upkeep. You access these tools by selecting the properties of the drive you wish to work with (Figure 11-78).

Don't forget the occasional disk cleanup. Even though you can reach this tool the Windows 9*x* way through the menus, you can also select properties for a drive and click the Disk Cleanup button from the General tab (Figure 11-79).

## Preparing for Problems

Just as with Windows 9*x*, the secret to troubleshooting Windows 2000 is preparation. This means critical system file backup and the creation of the boot disk. Additionally, we need to set up the unique and powerful Recovery Console, a new feature in Windows 2000.

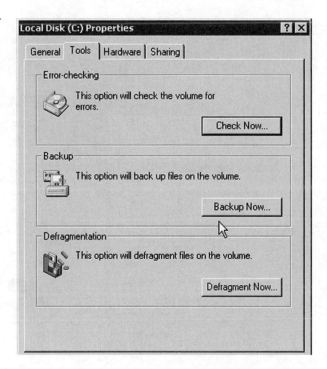

## Backups

Although Windows 9x really needs third-party utilities such as Hyper-Q's Q-Recovery,
Windows 2000 Backup provides almost all the tools we need. Most folks, however, still
turn to third-party utilities to create system, e-mail, browser, and personal data back-
ups. Open Backup by selecting Program Files | Accessories | System Tools | Backup (Fig-
ure 11-80).

Let's first create an *Emergency Repair Disk* (ERD). This disk saves critical boot files
and partition information and is our main tool for fixing boot problems. It is not
a bootable disk, nor does it store very much information; the ERD does not replace a
good system backup! It works with a special folder called \WINNT\REPAIR to store
a copy of your Registry. It's not perfect, but it gets you out of most startup problems. I
always make a new ERD before I install a new device or program.

Click on the ERD button and select the check box as shown in Figure 11-81.

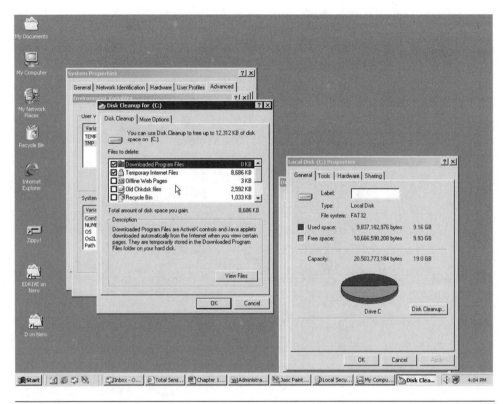

**Figure 11-79**   Disk Cleanup

**Figure 11-80**
Backup

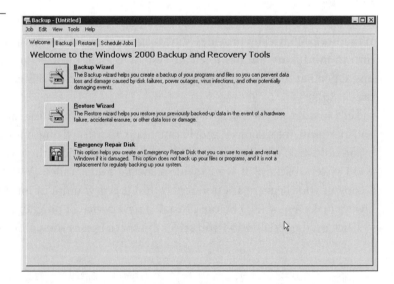

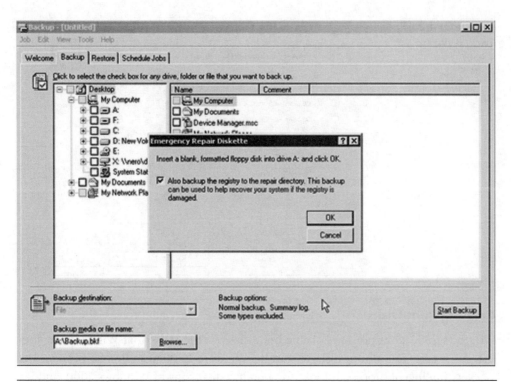

**Figure 11-81**   Creating an ERD

That's it! It's too easy! Your ERD is now ready to save you if you need it. But we're not quite done with Backup. Go back to the Welcome screen and select Backup Wizard. When the wizard starts, click Next to see Figure 11-82.

You have three options here. The first two are fairly self-explanatory: you can back up everything or just system-critical files. The third option needs some explanation. The Only Back Up The System State Data radio button enables you to save "other" system-critical files, but with Windows 2000 Professional, it's not much more than making an ERD with the Registry backup. This option really makes sense for Windows 2000 Server systems because it saves Active Directory information (which your Windows 2000 Professional system does not store) as well as other critical, server-specific functions. (More on these topics in Chapter 20!) But the A+ Certification exams may still expect you to know about it!

**Figure 11-82**
Backup Wizard at
work

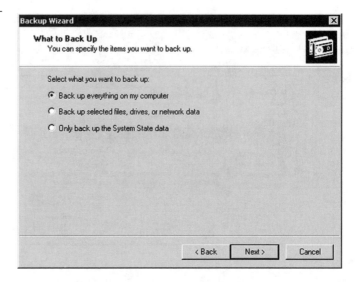

**Creating Boot Disks**

Windows 2000 does not have classic boot disks in the sense that Windows 9x does. Instead, it takes four floppy disks to start the Windows 2000 install/repair process. This is a very intelligent process. It looks for a preinstalled copy of Windows 2000, and if it detects one, it shifts from an install mode into a repair mode. Most Windows 2000 systems come with these four setup disks. If you don't have them, you can make them by following these steps:

1. Go to the \BOOTDISK folder on the CD-ROM. You'll find two .EXE files there: MAKEBOOT.EXE and MAKEBT32.EXE.

2. On a Windows 9x PC, run MAKEBOOT; on a Windows 2000 PC, run MAKEBT32.

3. Follow the onscreen prompts to build the four floppies you need to boot the Windows 2000 installer.

4. Be sure to label your disks!

These setup disks are identical for all copies of Windows 2000; you can use one set to support all Windows 2000 Professional systems.

If you're really geeky, you can make a pseudo-boot floppy. Just copy the following files from the root directory of your system drive to a blank floppy disk:

- NTLDR
- NTDETECT.COM
- BOOT.INI
- NTBOOTDD.SYS (if it's there)

This makes a pseudo-bootable disk. Windows 2000 will boot from this floppy, but it still needs a fully functional Windows 2000 boot partition. I installed Windows 2000 on my D: drive, so for me this was a handy way to boot Windows if my C: drive failed. It's also handy if any of these files become corrupted, even if your system and boot partition are the same. This won't be on the test, but they sure do come in handy!

## Recovery Console

Even though you can't really get Windows 2000 to boot to an A: prompt, you can use something called the Recovery Console. The Recovery Console is as close as Windows 2000 gets to the Windows 95/98 Safe Mode Command Prompt Only feature. First, you need to install it. Log into the system with the administrator account. Grab your Windows 2000 install CD-ROM and drop it in your system. If the Autorun function kicks in, just click the No button. Get to a Windows 2000 command prompt by typing **CMD** into the Start | Run dialog box. (CMD is the 32-bit super command prompt for Windows NT and 2000. It acts exactly like the old COMMAND.COM.) When you get to the command prompt, switch over to the CD-ROM drive letter. (Did you forget how to do this already? Go re-read the DOS chapter!) When you get to the CD-ROM drive letter, type in this command:

```
\i386\winnt32 /cmdcons
```

Just follow the instructions on the screen. From now on, every time the system boots, you will see a boot menu like the one shown in Figure 11-83.

If you don't like looking at this screen, set the BOOT.INI timeout to some smaller number—but not too small! Reboot your system to see the Recovery Console (see Figure 11-84).

The Recovery Console looks like a command prompt and uses many of the commands that worked in DOS as well as some uniquely its own. Here's a list of the most common Recovery Console commands. I've added a description to commands we've not covered previously.

- **ATTRIB**
- **CD**
- **CHKDSK**
- **CLS**   Clears the screen
- **COPY**
- **DEL**
- **DIR**

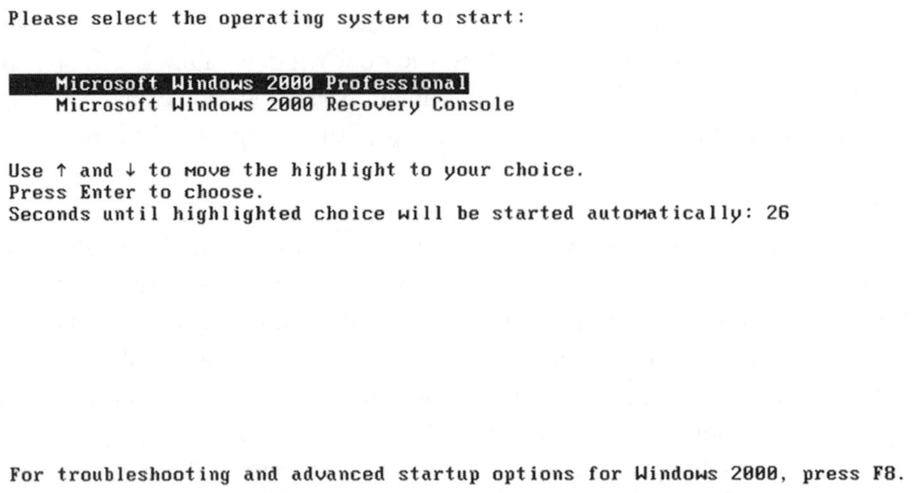

```
Please select the operating system to start:

  Microsoft Windows 2000 Professional
  Microsoft Windows 2000 Recovery Console


Use ↑ and ↓ to move the highlight to your choice.
Press Enter to choose.
Seconds until highlighted choice will be started automatically: 26




For troubleshooting and advanced startup options for Windows 2000, press F8.
```

**Figure 11-83**    Boot menu after installing the Recovery Console

- **DISKPART**    The Windows 2000 equivalent to FDISK

- **EXIT**    Exits the Recovery Console and restarts your computer

- **EXPAND**

- **FIXBOOT**    Writes a new partition table from the backup MST

- **FIXMBR**    The equivalent to FDISK /MBR

- **FORMAT**

- **HELP**    Displays a Help screen

- **LOGON**    Logs on to a Windows 2000 installation

- **MD**

- **REN**

- **RD**

- **SYSTEMROOT**    Sets the current directory to the root of the system directory—usually c:\

```
Microsoft Windows 2000(TM) Recovery Console.

The Recovery Console provides system repair and recovery functionality.

Type EXIT to quit the Recovery Console and restart the computer.


1: C:\WINNT

Which Windows 2000 installation would you like to log onto
<To cancel, press ENTER>? 1
Type the Administrator password: *****
C:\WINNT>_
```

**Figure 11-84**   Recovery Console

The files that make up the Recovery Console reside on the system partition, making the Recovery Console useless for system partition crashes. The Recovery Console shines in the business of manually restoring registries (remember where the ERD put the backup copy of the registry? You better remember!), rebuilding partitions (other than the system partition), or using the EXPAND program to extract copies of corrupted files from a CD-ROM or floppy disk.

## Dealing with Drives—Disk Management

Windows 2000 has completely redefined the concept of drive preparation, maintenance, and repair. First and foremost, Windows 2000 drops FDISK. Windows 2000 handles drive partitioning at install time. For day-to-day partitioning and format duties, Windows 2000 comes with the amazing Disk Management (Figure 11-85).

Disk Management is another MMC snap-in. You can access Disk Management via the Administrative Tools console as described earlier. It provides an attractive, intuitive view of all storage devices on your system. Work with Disk Management for a while and you'll never want to deal with FDISK again!

### Basic vs. Dynamic Disks

When you install an extra drive on a Windows 2000 system, it first manifests itself as a *basic disk*. Basic disks are just good old regular drives with standard partition tables and MBRs. However, Microsoft enables you to upgrade any drive to what's called a *dynamic disk*. Dynamic disks do not use partitions as we've seen in earlier chapters; they use a unique organization that manifests itself as flexible, resizable volumes.

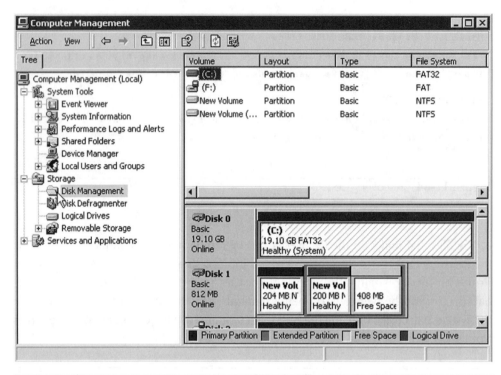

**Figure 11-85**   Disk Management

You should only use dynamic drives if you need features such as:

- **Spanned Volume**   A volume that spans multiple drives
- **Striped Volume**   Two drives that split the data into alternating stripes

With Windows 2000 Server, dynamic drives can be used to make:

- **Mirrored Drives**   Two drives that share identical data
- **RAID 5 Drives**   Three or more drives that provide redundancy in case one drive fails

The bottom line is that in most cases, dynamic drives are not something we use often in Windows 2000 Professional.

To make a basic disk dynamic, just alternate-click on the word "Basic" as shown in Figure 11-86 and select Upgrade to Dynamic Disk. You get a verification screen and then the drive is updated. Your only clue this happens is a lot of grinding noise from the drive and the change of the word "Basic" to "Dynamic."

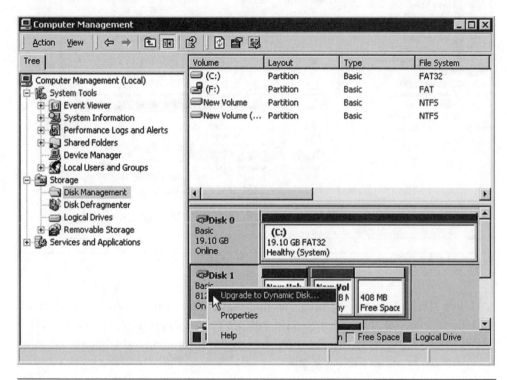

**Figure 11-86** Upgrade to Dynamic Disk

You can take a dynamic disk and revert it back to a basic disk only by first deleting all volumes on the disk. You then alternate-click on the word "Dynamic" and select Revert to Basic Disk.

### Partitioning Basic Disks

Partitioning a basic disk is a trivial matter of alternate-clicking on the disk and selecting Make a Partition. You may choose to make either a primary partition or an extended partition. If you alternate-click on an extended partition, you can make logical drive letters (Figure 11-87).

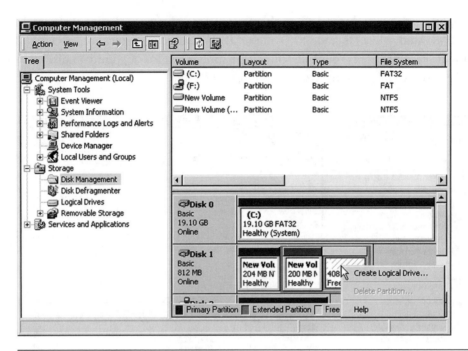

**Figure 11-87** Create logical drive?

Unlike FDISK, Disk Management can make up to four primary partitions to support multiboot scenarios. Just alternate-click on the primary partition you wish to make active and select Make Active Partition. Restart the computer, and whatever OS is on that partition becomes the active one.

### Creating Dynamic Volumes on Dynamic Drives

To make a volume on a dynamic drive, once again alternate-click and select Create Volume. Notice that only simple volume is highlighted. Select the size and format type (Figure 11-88).

### Drive Naming

As we created both basic partitions and dynamic volumes, they were given a default drive letter. This time let's look at that screen in more detail (Figure 11-89).

Note that we can accept the default drive letter, use another (unused) drive letter, or we can mount the drive to an empty folder on another drive. The last option, Do Not Assign This Drive a Letter, is used to hide drives.

**Figure 11-88**
Making a dynamic
drive volume

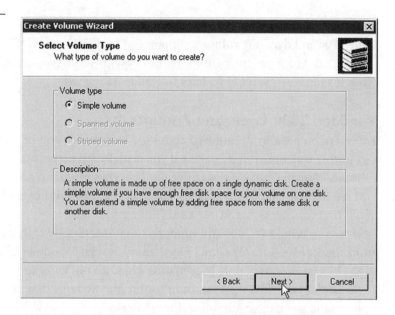

**Figure 11-89**  Changing drive letters

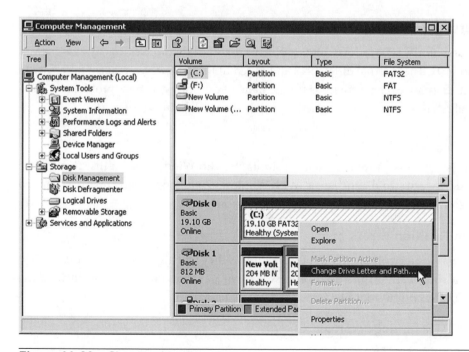

### Formatting

Both basic and dynamic volumes support FAT16, FAT32, or NTFS formats.

The Disk Management snap-in defines how drive management should truly work. Now, do you really want to go back to FDISK? Don't worry, you will!

## Windows 2000 Command Prompts

Folks tend to get a little confused about the command prompt under Windows 2000. The problem stems from the fact that you actually have two totally different command prompts. The first one we saw earlier, CMD, is the command prompt of choice. As you will see in later chapters, Windows 2000 makes heavy use of the command prompt; you'll find yourself doing RUN | CMD quite a bit.

However, Windows 2000 still supports COMMAND.COM. Try running COMMAND from the Run option—it works great! Even though Windows 2000 supports COM-MAND.COM, it is used only in scenarios where an old DOS application needs it.

Be careful here. It is very common to run into systems that deny access to the Run option unless you have Administrator privileges!

## Troubleshooting Windows 2000

The vast majority of Windows 2000 problems manifest themselves exactly as we saw in Windows 9x. The internal differences and different tools, however, make it necessary to look at alternative repair methods for the bane of our industry: boot problems. Otherwise, all repair scenarios work exactly the same as they do in Windows 9x.

## Boot Problems

Windows 2000 boot problems share a similarity with Windows 9x in that they can be divided between two distinct areas. With Windows 2000, boot problems are separated between system partition errors and boot partition errors.

### System Partition Errors

System partition errors stand out quite readily as they will always be text errors or lockups that show early in the boot process. System partition errors tend to include the names of the critical boot files:

- "NTLDR missing or corrupt"
- "Can't find NTDETECT.COM"
- "Unable to read BOOT.INI"

No matter what the error, the fix is always the same. I drop in my homemade boot disk and boot into Windows 2000—that always verifies that I am correct and the problem lies with one of those files. After a quick virus check, I simply copy all of the files off my boot disk into the C:\ drive—that usually fixes the problem. Never use a Windows 9*x* boot disk!

### Boot Partition Errors

Boot partition errors are usually harder to detect. If you're lucky, you'll get an easy error, such as "Registry is corrupt" or the stuck Windows boot screen. When these types of errors show up, first try the Safe Mode boot. Don't do anything, just go into Safe Mode and try restarting normally. If you fail, try restoring the Registry using the Last Known Good Version in the Boot menu. That usually fixes most boot problems. As a very last resort, use the Recovery Console to restore the Registry folders.

If none of these processes work, use the boot diskettes to run the install procedure. When the system asks to install or repair, press **R** to initiate the repair (Figure 11-90).

You have a choice here of manual or fast repair. Both styles essentially reinstall Windows entirely, but differ on what you'll see as an end result. Always use manual repair— fast repair uses an ancient copy of the Registry from when the system was first installed. You'll end up with a working Windows 2000 PC but one without any of your applications, special settings, and so on. With a manual repair, in contrast, everything *but* the Registry is reinstalled. Once the system finishes installing, you can then use a recent backup copy of the Registry and end up with a system similar, if not identical, to the one that crashed!

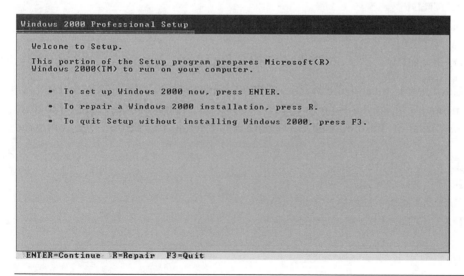

**Figure 11-90** Repairing broken Windows

## Other Problems

Even though Windows 9x and Windows 2000 have vastly different architectures, they share so many common features such as multitasking, swap files, DLLs, and so on—that most of the errors that show in either OS require the same fixes. Review the repair processes from Chapter 10 and the exceptions shown in this chapter to develop a solid understanding of the repair process.

## Review Questions

1. Which of the following is not an advantage of running Windows 2000 on NTFS as opposed to FAT32?
   A. Security
   B. Encryption
   C. Long filenames
   D. Compression

2. John's Windows 2000 system can also boot to Windows 98. What file does the NTFS loader read to know what OS to boot to?
   A. MSDOS.SYS
   B. BOOTLOG.TXT
   C. NTOSKRNL.EXE
   D. BOOT.INI

3. Which of the following files is not necessary for *all* Windows NT/2000 systems?
   A. NTLDR
   B. NTBOOTDD.SYS
   C. NTDETECT.COM
   D. BOOT.INI

4. Lloyd wants to add the Windows 2000 Recovery Console option to his boot menu. He inserts his Windows 2000 Professional installation CD-ROM into drive F:. Which of the following is the correct command to run from the command prompt?
   A. `F:\WINNT32\I386 /cmdcons`
   B. `F:\I386\WINNT /cmdcons`
   C. `F:\I386\WINNT32 /cmdcons`
   D. `F:\WINNT\I386 /cmdcons`

5. Windows 2000 server supports which of the following drive/volume types? (Select all that apply.)
   A. Striped
   B. Mirrored
   C. RAID 5
   D. Spanned

6. Windows 2000 can format a partition with all of the following format types except
   A. FAT16
   B. FAT32
   C. NTFS
   D. HPFS

7. Which of the following commands entered in the Start | RUN dialog box will start the Windows 2000 32-bit command interpreter?
   A. CMD
   B. COMMAND
   C. WINNT32
   D. CMD32

8. Beth boots her Windows 2000 PC and gets a "Registry is corrupt" message. Which of the following should be her first method for repair?
   A. Boot to Safe Mode
   B. Boot to Recovery console
   C. Boot to MS-DOS Mode
   D. Boot to Last Known Good Configuration

9. Mike's Windows 2000 system fails at boot with a "NTLDR missing or corrupt" message. His system has one drive formatted as NTFS. He does not have any boot disks, but his system can boot from a CD-ROM. Which of the following methods will get his system working again?
   A. Boot from a Windows 98 startup disk and copy NTLDR from C:\WINNT to the C:\ drive.
   B. Boot to the Recovery Console and use the Repair utility.
   C. Boot from the CD-ROM and load a new copy of NTLDR.
   D. Boot from the CD-ROM and do a repair installation.

10. Windows 2000 provides a number of ready-made MMC snap-ins stored in the
_____ applet in the Control Panel.
   A. System
   B. Network
   C. Administrative Tools
   D. MMC

## Answers

1. C. Both NTFS and FAT32 support long filenames.

2. D. The BOOT.INI file contains the paths to the different OS boot files.

3. B. NTBOOTDD.SYS is only required for SCSI drives without ROM support on the host adapter.

4. C. F:\I386\WINNT32 /cmdcons is the correct command.

5. A, B, C, D. Windows 2000 server supports all of these drives/volumes.

6. D. Windows 2000 cannot format a drive with HPFS format.

7. A. CMD starts the 32-bit command interpreter in Windows 2000.

8. A. Always first boot to Safe Mode. If that fails, then try Last Known Good Configuration.

9. D. Mike should run the install program off the CD-ROM. When prompted for Install or Repair, he should press **R** to initiate the repair.

10. C. Administrative Tools.

# DOS Memory in a Windows World

In this chapter, you will

• Understand the concept of DOS memory

• Learn how the first megabyte of DOS memory is organized

• Learn how to perform basic DOS memory management

• Understand how to configure DOS applications to run in Windows 9x and Windows 2000

## Why DOS Memory Management?

If you want to make an old tech (someone who's been fixing computers for over five years) scream like a 15-year-old at a Ricky Martin concert, just sneak up behind him or her and whisper "DOS memory management." After coming down from the ceiling, the tech will get you back by droning on for hours with harrowing story after harrowing story. In the days when DOS and Windows 3.x ruled, memory management was an ongoing nightmare that tortured techs on a daily basis. The introduction of Windows 95 substantially reduced the need to understand memory management, but the installed base of DOS applications still thrives. So, until that final *faraway* day when we get to throw out COMMAND.COM for good and load up that next generation "Windows 200X whatever" operating system (OS), the nasty specter of DOS-based memory management still can sneak up on the unprepared PC technician. Good technicians still need to understand memory and the basic principles of memory management.

The A+ Certification exams' memory management questions are fairly simple. They want you to show that you understand how to make DOS programs function inside Windows 9x/2000 systems. Be warned, this chapter goes a bit deeper than required for the A+ Certification exam questions for one very good reason. Windows 95, 98, ME, and 2000 all provide substantial, complex support for the tricky memory needs of DOS programs. Unless you understand how DOS memory works, you will not understand the many detailed settings provided by all versions of Windows to support DOS programs. As long as Microsoft operating systems support DOS memory management, you will want to understand it also.

# Historical/Conceptual

## Hexadecimal

Before going any further, we need to review hexadecimal numbers. This was covered in Chapter 5, but if you're going to perform memory management, you have to know how to talk the dreaded hex! If this section seems familiar, it should. It is very similar to the hex section in the expansion bus chapter, but now we're looking at things from a memory point of view. Let's start by reviewing what we've learned from previous chapters—the address bus and its relation to this thing called "memory."

## Memory in Hex

As you know, the 8086 had a 20-wire address bus. These wires could have either voltage or no voltage on them. A wire with voltage could be represented by a 1, and a wire with no voltage by a 0. With 20 wires, you could generate $2^{20}$ or 1,048,576 different combinations of 1's and 0's, from 00000000000000000000 to 11111111111111111111.

Each combination of charged and uncharged wires represents one memory location. IBM declared that each memory location should be 8 bits long. Because 8 bits = 1 byte, you can address 1,048,576 different one-byte memory locations with an 8086. This number is 1 megabyte (1MB), so the address bus can access 1MB.

Can you imagine what a pain it would be to try to keep track of these locations? Of course the microprocessor would have no problem, but imagine saying something like "Where in memory are you?" or "I'm at location 00101001000101010001110." There has to be an easier way to describe the state of a bunch of wires at any given moment. That is where hexadecimal becomes very useful. You can use hex as a shorthand description of the state of the wires of the 8086 address bus.

So, how does this shorthand work? Pretend you have a computer with a four-wire address bus. How many different patterns can you create with four wires? Here's a list:

| | | | |
|---|---|---|---|
| 0000 | 0100 | 1000 | 1100 |
| 0001 | 0101 | 1001 | 1101 |
| 0010 | 0110 | 1010 | 1110 |
| 0011 | 0111 | 1011 | 1111 |

So, 16 different combinations are possible. No CPU only uses a four-wire address bus, but every processor ever built has an address bus that is a multiple of four wires (8, 16, 20, 24, 32). You can use this fact to create a shorthand notation for four-wire combinations. Let's replace every combination of four 1's and 0's with a single character. Because 16 different combinations are possible, the 16 unique characters of the Base-16 numbering system called hexadecimal are the natural choice. Here are the hex shorthand values for each 4-bit possibility:

| | | | |
|---|---|---|---|
| 0000 = 0 | 0100 = 4 | 1000 = 8 | 1100 = C |
| 0001 = 1 | 0101 = 5 | 1001 = 9 | 1101 = D |
| 0010 = 2 | 0110 = 6 | 1010 = A | 1110 = E |
| 0011 = 3 | 0111 = 7 | 1011 = B | 1111 = F |

So when you talk about a particular memory location, such as 10110110011000101101, you convert it to hexadecimal to make it easier to comprehend. Let's do it!

First, mentally break the 20 digits into five sets of four:

1011 0110 0110 0010 1101

Then give each four-character set its hex shorthand:

1011 = B, 0110 = 6, 0110 = 6, 0010 = 2, and 1101 = D.

Instead of a bunch of 1's and 0's, you'd have something a little bit more palatable: B662D. We can represent any possible address for the 20-bit address bus with a five-digit hex value, starting with all zeros (00000) to all ones (FFFFF).

## Memory Space vs. Memory

Understand that the Intel 8086 CPU can "see" up to 1MB of memory. All these combinations are collectively called the *memory address space.* Just because a CPU has 1MB of memory address space, however, does not mean that it actually uses all of it. To place code at a certain memory location, you need some type of chip at the location that can store the byte of code. You need RAM or ROM chips at every memory location you want to use. Do not confuse the memory address space with the actual memory.

Consider this: When most people first hear the term *memory address,* they hear the word "address" and think in terms of a postal service, visualizing the addresses as physical locations like street addresses. But memory addresses are not physical locations. When you hear "memory address," think of a telephone company instead of a postal service. If one person has the address 515 Main St., Houston, TX 77000 and another person has the address 516 Main St., Houston, TX 77000, you would agree that these two people almost certainly live right across the street from each other, correct? However, if one person has the phone number (713) 555-0784 and another person's phone number is (713) 555-0785, the fact that their phone numbers are sequential has no bearing on whether they live next door to each other. Memory addresses work exactly the same way. Two sequential memory addresses might not be physically next to each other.

## The DOS Memory Map

Continuing the telephone analogy, you must appreciate that not all phone numbers available are always in use. Companies sell special telephone books called "reverse directories." They sort phone numbers not by name, but by phone number. They look something like this:

201-555-0277 SOUTH ORANGE PAVING CO 12 FELDSTONE PL, CALDWELL, NJ

201-555-0278 UNUSED

201-555-0279 RUBIN GOERTZ & CO CPA 101 EISENHOWER PKY, ROSELAND, NJ

201-555-0380 UNUSED

201-555-0381 DEVCO ENGINEERING INC 36 PIER LN, FAIRFIELD, NJ

201-555-0382 GRAND VARIETY 371 BLOOMFIELD AVE, CALDWELL, NJ

201-555-0383 RULLO & GLEESON 127 ROSELAND AVE, CALDWELL, NJ

201-555-0384 UNUSED

201-555-0385 DONALD PLUMBING & HTG 69 DEERFIELD RD, CALDWELL, NJ

It makes sense that certain phone numbers are unused—people move, change numbers, and so on. That same principle applies to memory addresses. To look at the entire range of addressable memory for DOS, you have to make a reverse directory of all the possible memory addresses, from 00000 to FFFFF. We don't know what any of these addresses will be for, so by default let's mark them all unused until we know more:

| | |
|---|---|
| 00000 UNUSED | 00007 UNUSED |
| 00001 UNUSED | 00008 UNUSED |
| 00002 UNUSED | 00009 UNUSED |
| 00003 UNUSED | 0000A UNUSED |
| 00004 UNUSED | 0000B UNUSED |
| 00005 UNUSED | 0000C UNUSED |
| 00006 UNUSED | |

Wait a minute! This list is going to be kind of long, isn't it? You're going to need about 1,048,576 spaces to list every address space. For convenience, let's just represent all the addresses by drawing a bar to represent all the address spaces. We will also start at the bottom of the page and then build the bar up from the bottom. The first eight addresses are shown in Figure 12-1, and the completed *address map* looks like Figure 12-2.

---

**NOTE**  Please do not confuse this memory map—this phone book—with memory chips. This is just a list of different permutations of address bus wires being turned on and off. At this point, there are no chips to correspond to any memory locations.

---

**Figure 12-1**
Addresses

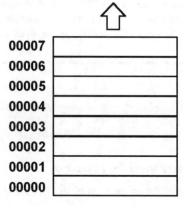

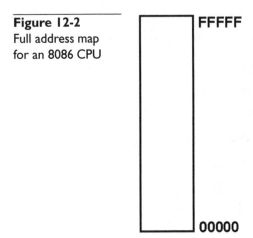

**Figure 12-2**
Full address map
for an 8086 CPU

FFFFF

00000

## Assigning Addresses

When IBM built the PC, the company decided to specify how the memory in the IBM PC was to be used. The PC had an 8086 CPU, so as noted earlier, it had 1MB of address space. The main function of these addresses was for plain old RAM. Other chips, such as the System ROM and optional ROMs on expansion cards, needed addresses as well so that the CPU could access them. To keep things organized, IBM decided to dedicate all the addresses from 00000 to 9FFFF to the exclusive use of regular memory (RAM). IBM reserved the rest of the addresses—from A0000 to FFFFF—for the exclusive use of chips other than regular memory (RAM). Let's look at this in detail.

**NOTE** If you remember from Chapter 9, Microsoft wrote DOS to take advantage of the relative power of the 8086 and 8088 processors. This meant, however, that DOS shared the 20-bit address bus limitation as well. In other words, DOS could only handle a 1MB address space, even on CPUs that exceeded that limit (such as the i386).

## Test Specific

## Conventional and Reserved Memory

The 1MB of memory locations available to a DOS PC breaks down into two distinct areas: conventional and reserved. The area from 0 to 640K (00000h to 9FFFFh) is called *conventional memory* (Figure 12-3).

**Figure 12-3**
Conventional
memory

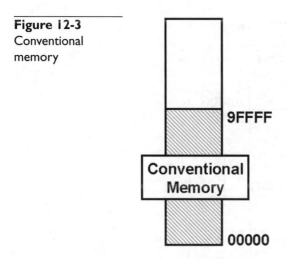

9FFFF

Conventional
Memory

00000

Conventional memory contains all the memory addresses that are set aside for RAM to run programs. All the addresses from A0000 to FFFFF are set aside for other chips that the CPU may need to access, primarily ROMs and specialized RAMs. This memory is called *reserved memory* (Figure 12-4).

**Figure 12-4**
Reserved memory

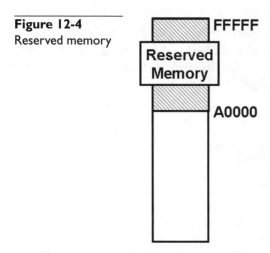

FFFFF

Reserved
Memory

A0000

Conventional memory has 655,360 memory locations (640K), and reserved memory has 393,216 memory locations (384K), for a total of 1,048,576 memory locations (1,024K or 1MB). Figure 12-5 shows a map of the 1MB with both the conventional and reserved area.

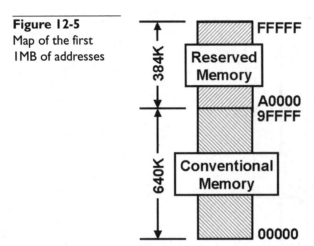

**Figure 12-5**
Map of the first
1MB of addresses

## The Reserved Area

The reserved area is a rather complex compilation of different ROMs and RAMs that use memory. Most of these devices have very distinct memory locations, either determined by IBM long ago or by a *de facto* process of clone makers and device manufacturers "taking over" certain memory locations. All programs take up a range of memory locations. By far the most important device in the reserved area is the System BIOS. Although there can be some variation, it is classically located in the memory locations from F0000 to FFFFF (see Figure 12-6). To clarify this, the starting location is on the left of the chart and the ending location on the right.

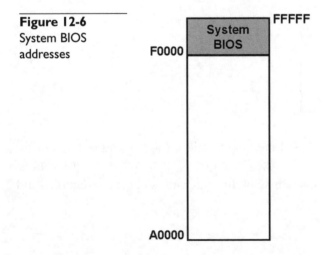

**Figure 12-6**
System BIOS
addresses

Video cards all have RAM that is mapped into the reserved area in three different areas (Figure 12-7). When your video card is in a color text mode (like in DOS), its RAM uses the memory locations from B8000 to BFFFF. When the video card is in graphics mode, its RAM is mapped from A0000 to AFFFF. The first generations of video cards displayed monochrome text. Their video RAM was mapped from B0000 to B7FFF. Most modern video cards have begun to ignore these memory divisions and simply use the entire area from A0000 to BFFFF.

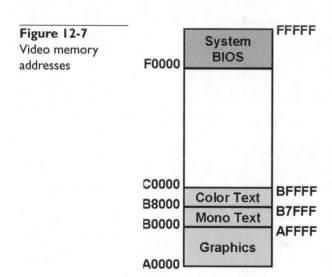

**Figure 12-7**
Video memory addresses

None of the reserved memory addresses from C0000 to EFFFF are dedicated to any particular device. They are for optional ROMs and RAMs that peripheral makers might install on their cards (Figure 12-8). Different types of cards can come with ROMs or RAMs, although no hard and fast rule exists. One device, found in every PC, carries an optional ROM: the video card. The video card's ROM uses the memory range from C0000 to C7FFF (Figure 12-9).

Although all memory addresses from C0000 to EFFFF are theoretically available, every video card has a ROM, and that ROM takes the memory range from C0000 to C7FFF. So this range is not available for optional ROMs.

 **TIP** Take some time to memorize these hex locations for the exam!

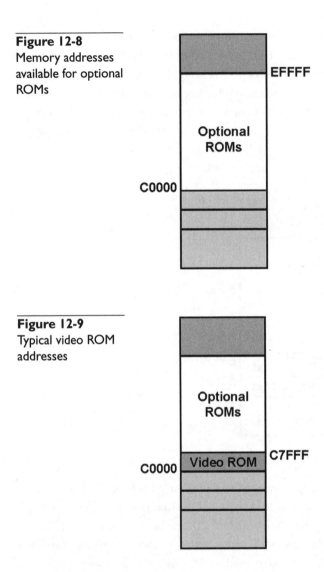

**Figure 12-8**
Memory addresses available for optional ROMs

EFFFF

Optional ROMs

C0000

**Figure 12-9**
Typical video ROM addresses

Optional ROMs

Video ROM   C7FFF

C0000

## The Conventional Area

When IBM was developing the PC in the late 1970s, they felt the 640K maximum of memory addresses was a massive amount of RAM. The maximum amount of memory anybody was using in competing microcomputers was around 64K. IBM also put 64K into the first IBM PC. IBM was confident that they had provided plenty of room for upgrades, but no one anticipated the growth in complexity of DOS and applications.

As users became more sophisticated and more comfortable with PCs, they demanded more powerful applications. Programs like Lotus 1-2-3 were notorious for growing larger as they grew in sophistication to match user demands for more features.

Users also demanded more data—larger spreadsheets and documents. As the size of programs and data grew, users added more RAM chips to computers, which grew from 64K to 128K to 256K to 512K to 640K. As a result, within the first few years of the existence of IBM PCs, 640K of RAM became the standard. 640K of RAM, which was supposed to last until the year 1990, was installed in most PCs by 1984. Even at 640K, however, it became obvious that still more RAM was needed. Unfortunately, 640K was the limit. You could no longer simply add memory chips. See Figure 12-10.

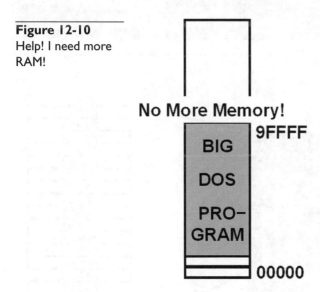

**Figure 12-10**
Help! I need more RAM!

## Expanded Memory

No more memory addresses were available. Of the 1MB of memory addresses, the first 640K of addresses were occupied by RAM chips, and the rest were "reserved" for ROMs and video RAM. If a computer, however, did not have any optional BIOS, relatively large gaps of unused memory addresses were present in the reserved area. Knowing this, an industry group led by Lotus, Intel, and Microsoft got together in 1984 and came up with a way to put more memory into a computer while staying within the 1MB limit. The answer was the *expanded memory specification* (EMS). Expanded memory was originally an expansion card full of RAM chips (Figure 12-11).

The chips on the card were electronically divided into 16K chunks called *pages*. A card could have from 4 to 512 pages. You could even have multiple cards, as long as the total number of pages was 512 or less (512 pages × 16K bytes/page = a maximum of 8 megabytes of memory). Each page was labeled electronically with page numbers (Figure 12-12).

**Figure 12-11** Expanded memory card

**Figure 12-12**
Page numbers

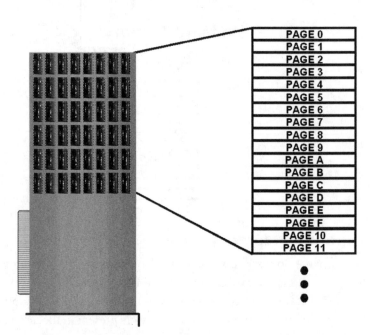

PAGE 0
PAGE 1
PAGE 2
PAGE 3
PAGE 4
PAGE 5
PAGE 6
PAGE 7
PAGE 8
PAGE 9
PAGE A
PAGE B
PAGE C
PAGE D
PAGE E
PAGE F
PAGE 10
PAGE 11

To access this card of RAM chips, you needed two things: a device driver to access the card and applications that knew how to talk to the device driver in order to get work done with the card.

The device driver was called *EMM.SYS*. EMM.SYS electronically readdressed the chips on the expanded memory board. When EMM.SYS initialized, it took the expanded memory card's first four 16K pages and addresses and changed them into one, unused, 64K area in the reserved area. This 64K area was known as the *EMS page frame* (Figure 12-13).

**Figure 12-13**
EMS page frame

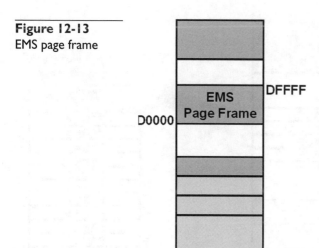

EMM.SYS read jumpers on the card to determine where to put the EMS page frame and, once established, the page frame was immovable. In almost all machines, that address range was from D0000 to DFFFF or from E0000 to EFFFF.

EMM.SYS could swap different pages into and out of this 64K area, so you could load large amounts of data onto the EMS card while using only 64K of memory! For a program to use EMS memory, it had to be specifically written to do so, and virtually every commercial DOS program ever made could utilize EMS. When an EMS-aware program ran, it loaded the first four 16K pages into the 64K page frame. In essence, those first four pages temporarily took the memory addresses (Figure 12-14).

The program would then load its data into those pages instead of using conventional memory. As those pages filled, the program would then tell the EMS card to swap out a filled page for an empty one (Figure 12-15).

Programs only stored data on EMS cards; the programs themselves (that is, the executable part of an application) had to reside in conventional memory. In other words, your spreadsheet file could load in expanded memory, but Lotus itself (the program) had to reside in conventional memory. Also, once a program detected EMM.SYS, it started using EMS memory automatically. You did not have to do anything to make it happen.

**NOTE** Many techs referred to expanded memory as LIM memory, after the LIM 3.2 standard book written collectively by folks from Lotus, Intel, and Microsoft. (Why was the first version 3.2? Actually, earlier versions were made, but 3.2 was the most widely accepted.)

**Figure 12-14**
Paging

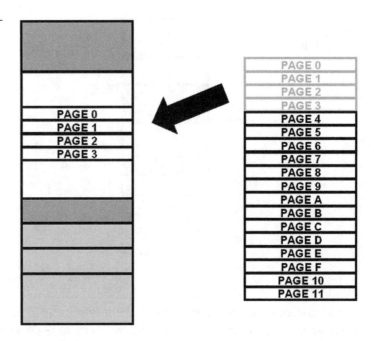

**Figure 12-15**
Swapping a page frame

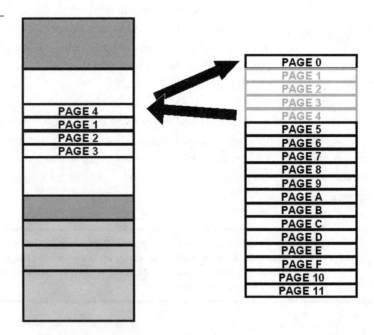

## LIM 3.2 Standard Expanded Memory

EMS was (is) exclusively the domain of DOS programs. Expanded memory enabled programs to use larger pieces of data—bigger spreadsheets, documents, and databases—without breaking the 640K barrier.

- Expanded memory was divided into 16K chunks called *pages.*

- EMM.SYS electronically changed the addresses of the EMS frames to fit within the EMS page frame.

- The EMS page frame was always 64K.

- Applications had to be specially written to use EMS memory.

**NOTE** The terms "LIM," "EMS," and "expanded memory" are interchangeable.

## Shadowing

Another difficulty with IBM's memory setup appeared when motherboard manufacturers started putting more than 640K of RAM onto their motherboards. Potentially, they had both RAM and ROM getting assigned the same addresses. If programs resided in both places, the system would lock up when they were accessed. What could we do with this excess RAM?

One early idea was to mask off the extra 384K of RAM—in essence, turning it off. The idea of masking off this 384K left many motherboard manufacturers unhappy—why waste otherwise perfectly good RAM? They came up with a brilliant idea that is still used on most systems today. They left the RAM at the same memory locations as the reserved area (Figure 12-16) and then rewrote the motherboard BIOS to use it to *shadow* ROM chips. Here's the process.

No two chips can share the same memory location. Having two or more chips with the same memory location is like having telephones with the same phone number in two different houses—when the phones ring, how do you know who should answer? Worse, if the CPU calls one address, code at both locations will be placed on the external data bus and the PC will lock up. So where's the benefit?

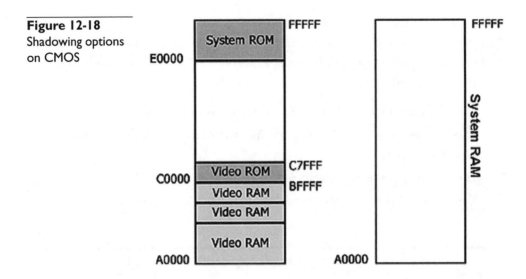

**Figure 12-18**
Shadowing options on CMOS

What is BIOS? BIOS is software stored on ROM so that certain important information is still there when you turn off the computer. But ROM is very slow compared to RAM. Remember that every time you want to talk to the keyboard, the CPU accesses the BIOS routine stored on the ROM chip, a very slow process relative to a RAM access. So, what if you designed the system to copy the BIOS routines from the ROM over to the RAM at the same address, and then turned off the ROM? Then every time the CPU needed a BIOS routine, it could access the routine from RAM, not ROM. This process is called *shadowing*.

Shadowing provides a much faster response from BIOS routines because they are on fast RAM and not slow ROM. Of course, once the PC is turned off or rebooted, all the BIOS routines on RAM are erased. Therefore, shadowing must be redone every time the PC is turned on or rebooted. Figure 12-17 shows shadowing.

Note that the video BIOS is shadowed, but not the video RAM. Video RAM is fast RAM already and would not benefit from shadowing. Every PC made since the late-1980s supports shadowing. You can enable shadowing through the CMOS setup. Figure 12-18 shows a classic CMOS setup screen.

Note that options are available for video BIOS as well as a large number of optional BIOS locations. To shadow, simply enable the address range for whatever you want to shadow. Shadowing is safe and easy. In fact, many modern systems automatically shadow your ROMs. If your CMOS does not give the option for shadowing, don't worry; it shadows automatically.

**Figure 12-17**
Shadowing system
and video BIOS

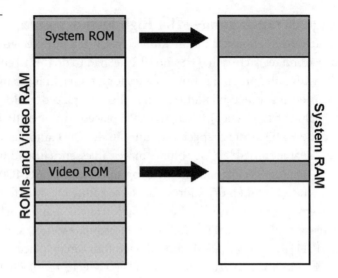

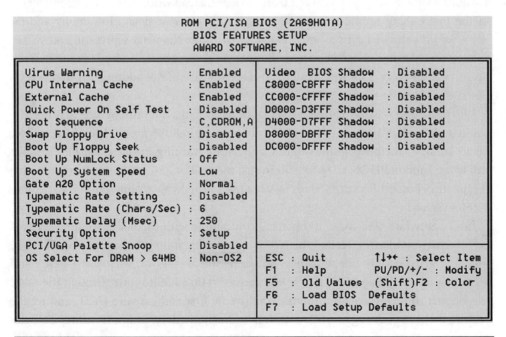

**Figure 12-18**   Shadowing options on CMOS

## The Magic Wrap-Around—The High Memory Area

Even though the 8086 used a 20-bit address bus, it actually created the 20-bit addresses using two 16-bit registers called CS and IP. Intel had to do this to ensure backward compatibility with older programs, but it makes for a rather strange situation: How do two 16-bit registers make a 20-bit address? First, the CPU placed a value in CS. Let's pick the arbitrary value of 124C (hex). Then, the CPU placed a value in IP; let's say 0AE7 (hex). To create the 20-bit address, special circuitry in the CPU automatically did the following: The CS value shifted left four binary places, in essence just adding a zero to the end (124C0). Then, the circuitry added the two values together (124C0 + 0AE8 = 12FA8), giving you the 20-bit memory address. This was a little messy, but it gave the 8086 great backward compatibility. Let's do this calculation again, using much larger numbers.

First, place a value in CS: FFFF (all ones, a legitimate value), and then place the same value in IP: FFFF. The CS value shifts to the left four binary places—FFFF0—and the circuitry again adds the two values together: FFFF0 + FFFF = 10FFEF (trust me on the hex math here), which creates six digits, not just five! But no place was available to store the beginning 1 on a 20-bit address bus. The old 8086 would have a real problem if you accidentally addressed a little too high; the system would immediately crash. The first 1 would simply disappear on an 8086 and would instead write to 0FFEF, or somewhere in the first 64K of memory, a phenomenon called *wrap-around*. How many address wires would you need for six hex characters? Each hex character represents four wires, so 6 × 4 = 24 wires needed to see six hexadecimal characters. Go back to the description of the 286 processor in Chapter 2 and see the size of the address bus that was on the 286—24 bits!

When the 286 was in the final stages of development, Intel discovered that the 286 could address slightly more than 1MB while running in 8086 mode. The 286 could see up to 16MB of memory addresses, but only while running in protected mode. We're still using good old DOS, so we're still in real mode. The 286 could see more than one megabyte because it had extra wires to store the 1. The wrap-around effect didn't cause a 286 to crash.

Intel wanted the 286 to be 100 percent compatible with the 8086, so they "masked off" the twenty-first wire (called the A20 wire), making it invisible to the 286. The 286 therefore acted exactly like an 8086. But someone at Intel or Microsoft (there's still argument on this) discovered that if you ran a certain BIOS routine through the 8042 (keyboard) chip, you could "unmask" the twenty-first address wire (A20) and let the 286 see more memory again. This wasn't that much memory, only 64K minus 16 bytes of memory. This tiny area available only to 286 or better processors is called the *high memory area* (HMA) (Figure 12-19).

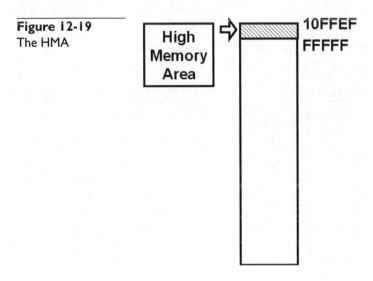

**Figure 12-19**
The HMA

Note that the HMA is simply more memory addresses. In order to use these addresses, RAM chips must populate the addresses above FFFFF. In other words, the system must have physical RAM beyond 1MB, what is called *extended memory.* You must also run the special BIOS routine to unmask the A20 wire, because even the latest Pentium 4 CPUs still mask off the A20 wire for backward compatibility. When the HMA was discovered, the computing industry, still running 8086 processors with only 640K of RAM for the most part, considered the discovery academically fascinating but completely useless. That attitude would soon change.

## Extended Memory

By the late 1980s, IBM began pushing the new graphical operating system OS/2. OS/2 was designed to break the 640K DOS barrier by running in 286 and then 386 protected mode. Once an OS goes into protected mode, it can access more than 1MB of memory. All memory above 1MB is called *extended memory* (XMS) (Figure 12-20). If you have a PC with 128MB of RAM, it has 127MB of extended memory.

DOS cannot directly use extended memory. Because DOS doesn't directly use extended memory, it's not really part of DOS memory management, with the exception of the HMA. But even though the early versions of OS/2 were buggy and slow, IBM told everyone who would listen: "You better buy PCs with at least 2MB of XMS! OS/2 is going to take over, and you'll be sorry if you don't buy PCs now with the memory you'll need later!" When the early versions of OS/2 came out, everyone hated them and no one used them. Therefore, a significant percentage of all machines installed had extended memory but just ran DOS, making the extended memory useless.

**Figure 12-20**
All memory above
1MB is extended
memory.

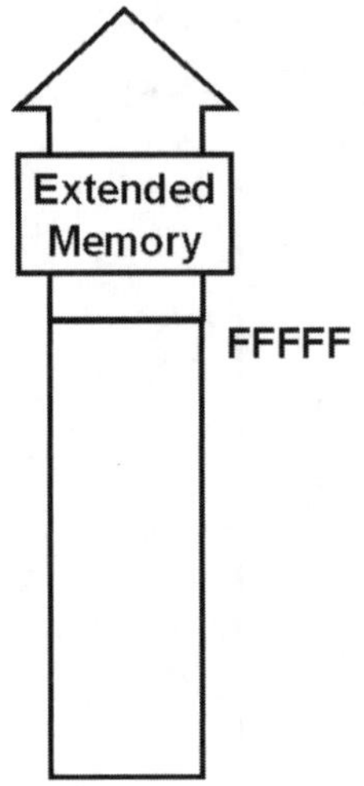

Extended Memory

FFFFF

All this unusable memory drove software developers crazy. Tired of being told to wait for the latest OS/2, they wanted to use extended memory. Companies like Lotus, AutoDesk, and Xerox began developing software applications that would take over some OS functions, particularly XMS access. If they couldn't get an OS to access XMS, they were just going to do it themselves! We started to see DOS programs that went beyond DOS's capabilities and accessed XMS. These were known generically as *DOS extenders.*

In addition, a whole new software cottage industry began selling programs that electronically made XMS act like EMS. These programs were called "limulators" in reference to the LIM standard. Why buy a $700 EMS card when a $40 limulation program could turn unused XMS into EMS? The EMS cards instantly became obsolete.

So around 1989, all this extended memory, ostensibly purchased in anticipation of an OS that never really took off, was invaded by hundreds of different applications and utilities, each accessing extended memory in their own proprietary, incompatible way. Why make your method compatible? No one else was going to use the extended memory, right? Wrong! Windows 3.0 showed up in 1990. In addition, Windows 3.0 wanted extended memory. How could Windows 3.0 exist in extended memory already used by some other program? If any program attempted to use extended memory when another program was already using it, some serious lockups were sure to happen! Plus, remember the HMA? If you had extended memory, you could access the HMA, but no standard method was in place to access it for all PCs. If Microsoft was going to make Windows a success, some kind of standardized "extended memory access method" needed to be hammered out and agreed upon by all the folks using extended memory.

## Microsoft to the Rescue

The solution came from a new device driver Microsoft provided with both Windows and DOS: HIMEM.SYS. This program performed two functions. First, it unmasked the twenty-first address wire (the A20 wire) and created the HMA. Second, it in essence "stood at the gate" of extended memory and forced all applications to sign in, creating a way for applications to know where in extended memory they could and could not go. Any programs that wanted extended memory had to "sign in" with HIMEM.SYS or they would not get any extended memory. Equally, all programs looked for HIMEM.SYS when they ran; if they could not find it, they did not start. HIMEM.SYS quickly became the most common device driver in the world. By the way, any extended memory under the control of HIMEM.SYS is called *XMS memory.*

## Setting HIMEM.SYS

All DOS systems installed HIMEM.SYS the same way. Invariably, the first line of every CONFIG.SYS file looked like one of these two lines, depending on whether you used the HIMEM.SYS that came with DOS or Windows:

```
DEVICE=C:\DOS\HIMEM.SYS
DEVICE=C:\WINDOWS\HIMEM.SYS
```

From this point to today, every computer running Windows 3.*x* or 9*x* still needs HIMEM.SYS, although Windows 9*x* loads it automatically.

## DOS=HIGH

At almost the same time Microsoft introduced HIMEM.SYS, they also introduced a special line to add to the CONFIG.SYS file called *DOS=HIGH*. If you had a DOS system with a 286 or better CPU and some extended memory, you always added the line DOS=HIGH anywhere in your CONFIG.SYS file. This option moves most of the COMMAND.COM file from conventional memory into the HMA.

## Upper Memory Blocks (UMB)

The last type of memory you should be aware of is *upper memory blocks* (UMBs). They are unused memory addresses in the reserved area (Figure 12-21).

In most cases your system will only have one UMB, but in some cases you may have multiple UMBs. For example, what if you install a card that had an onboard ROM that used the memory area of E0000 to E4FFF? That would split the UMB into two pieces.

The UMB, as you are about to see, is the cornerstone of DOS memory management. But what is DOS memory management? Let's answer that question right now!

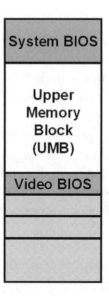

**Figure 12-21**
An upper
memory block

## Reducing Conventional Memory Use

The goal of DOS memory management is to reduce the amount of conventional memory used by anything other than the currently running application. Adding device drivers to CONFIG.SYS and TSRs to AUTOEXEC.BAT eats up conventional memory. During the short reign of the horribly unpopular DOS 4.0, it was common to see systems so loaded with device drivers and TSRs that they couldn't run any programs! This brought a howl from the industry, which demanded some way to open up conventional memory while still enabling systems to keep all of their device drivers and TSRs running.

The secret to reducing conventional memory use is to find some unused memory in which to store programs. Basically, you can move device drivers and TSRs to two places. One is the HMA and the other is a UMB. Special programs, generically called *memory-management* software, can move device drivers and TSRs out of conventional memory and into the HMA and UMBs. This process is called *loading high.*

Our goal in DOS memory management is to reduce the amount of conventional memory used so DOS programs can run. This begs the question, "How much conventional memory do I need?" That depends on what programs you are running. If the only program you use is EDIT, you only need about 350K of conventional memory. But how many people only run EDIT? A good rule to follow is to try to have 600K of conventional memory open, which will enable virtually any DOS program to run comfortably. Let's look at the tools used to move programs out of conventional memory and into the HMA and UMBs.

## UMB Gateways/Memory Managers

By default, UMBs are completely unused and wasted, that is, unless you have a UMB gateway. With a UMB gateway, you can load CONFIG.SYS' device drivers (all those DEVICE= statements) into these UMBs and free up conventional memory. UMB gateways also enable you to load AUTOEXEC.BAT's TSRs (like DOSKEY or MOUSE.COM) into UMBs, again saving precious conventional memory. DOS as well as every version of Windows comes with a UMB gateway called *EMM386.EXE*.

Loading programs into UMBs can be deadly. For example, what if you have an EMS card? The EMS page frame takes up 64K of UMB space! What would happen if you tried to load a device driver into the same addresses as the EMS page frame? Every time you tried to access that driver or EMS memory, the computer would lock up. A good UMB gateway should be able to inspect the entire reserved area and steer clear of ROMs, video RAM, and EMS page frames. Every UMB gateway program is also a memory manager. As a result, nobody uses the term "UMB gateway." Instead, they use the term *memory manager*. EMM386.EXE is Microsoft's memory manager.

Memory managers only prepare the UMB for device drivers and programs. They never do the actual loading into the UMB. The loading is carried out by special commands that are recognized by the memory manager. With EMM386.EXE, there are two different ways to load something high, depending on whether it is a device driver in CONFIG.SYS or a TSR in the AUTOEXEC.BAT. In CONFIG.SYS, you simply change any DEVICE= line to DEVICEHIGH=. For programs in AUTOEXEC.BAT, insert the command LOADHIGH or LH in front of the command you want loaded into the UMB. We'll put this into practice in a moment.

## EMM386.EXE

EMM386 does two jobs in one package: limulation and memory management. EMM386 can perform both functions or just one, depending on how you set it up. You must have a 386SX or better with 1MB of RAM before you can use EMM386.

### Limulation

If you have a 386 or better with extended memory, you can make some or all of the XMS behave identically to EMS. This emulation of the LIM standard, discussed earlier, is known as *limulation*. To limulate, you need a device driver that can access XMS memory and convert it to EMS memory. These programs are known as *limulators*. Limulators are usually expanded memory device drivers that replace EMM.SYS. EMM386.EXE is DOS' built-in limulator. Installing EMM386.EXE into the CONFIG.SYS file automatically turns some or all of your XMS memory into EMS compatible memory. By default, you get a 64K EMS page frame in the UMBs of the reserved area, but EMM386.EXE is highly customizable to take advantage of the more advanced features of LIM. To turn some or all of your XMS into EMS, all you have to do is add the following line to your CONFIG.SYS file (caps are not necessary):

```
DEVICE=C:\DOS\EMM386.EXE
```

The only rule is that you must have the following line before it:

```
DEVICE=C:\DOS\HIMEM.SYS
```

It's that simple. If you have a computer with 4MB of memory, you will now have a computer with 640K of conventional memory, 384K of UMB, and 3,072K (3MB) of EMS. You will have a page frame established in the UMB, and if you run a DOS program that uses EMS memory, such as Lotus 1-2-3, you will be able to make huge spreadsheets before running out of memory.

You can limit the amount of XMS memory that is turned into EMS memory by specifying this with a number. For example:

```
DEVICE=C:\DOS\EMM386.EXE 1024
```

This would convert 1MB (1,024K) of XMS memory into EMS memory, the rest staying as regular extended memory. So on a 4MB system, this command would give you 640K of conventional memory + 386K of UMB + 1,024K of EMS memory + 2,048K of XMS memory = 4MB. Remember, when you limulate, you create a page frame, usually at D000-DFFF.

Starting with DOS 6.0, you never give a value to the amount of EMS memory you want to limulate. By replacing the number with the acronym "RAM" in the EMM386 line, EMM386 will take all the memory and dynamically allocate it as EMS or XMS for programs that need it. Because this provides the most flexibility, the EMM386 line in CONFIG.SYS is often written like this:

```
DEVICE=C:\DOS\EMM386.EXE RAM
```

The capability to change memory on the fly is called *DOS Protected Mode Interface* (DPMI). All versions of Windows include support for DPMI for DOS programs, making the job of getting DOS programs to run under Windows a fairly easy task.

## Preparing to Load High

To let EMM386 know that you want to load high, you must add a few commands. First, add the line DOS=UMB anywhere in the CONFIG.SYS file. This tells DOS that you will be loading high. You can combine the DOS=UMB command with the DOS=HIGH command discussed earlier. All of the following are acceptable: DOS=HIGH,UMB or DOS=UMB,HIGH or DOS=HIGH and DOS=UMB or DOS=UMB and DOS=HIGH.

The next item informs EMM386.EXE what you want to do. Remember that EMM386 enables you both to load high and to limulate. What do you want to do? Say you want to load high, but not limulate. Place the option NOEMS at the end of the EMM386 line:

```
DEVICE=C:\DOS\EMM386.EXE NOEMS
```

The RAM option, in contrast, enables EMM386 to limulate and support loading high:

```
DEVICE=C:\DOS\EMM386.EXE RAM
```

If you don't want to do either, do not use EMM386! Now you're ready to add DEVICEHIGH= statements in CONFIG.SYS as well as LOADHIGH statements in AUTOEXEC.BAT.

## Loading High

After you have prepared everything properly, the last and easiest step is to load your devices into the UMB. I often change all of the DEVICE= statements to DEVICE-HIGH= statements in my CONFIG.SYS, and then add LH to all the TSRs in my AUTOEXEC.BAT. The problem is that only so much UMB space is available. A DOS system with a large number of device drivers and TSRs probably won't load everything high.

Here's a typical DOS system's CONFIG.SYS, loading everything high. Note that HIMEM.SYS and EMM386.EXE never get DEVICEHIGH added.

```
DEVICE=C:\DOS\HIMEM.SYS
DEVICE=C:\DOS\EMM386.EXE RAM
DOS=HIGH,UMB
DEVICEHIGH=C:\SBLABS\SBDRVT.SYS /A:220 /I:5 /D:1,3
DEVICEHIGH=C:\CDROM\OAKCDROM.SYS /D:MSCD001
```

And here's a typical DOS AUTOEXEC.BAT. SMARTDRV is never loaded high because it automatically loads high if the memory management is set up properly.

```
@echo off
prompt $p$g
LH C:\MSMOUSE\MOUSE.COM
LH C:\DOS\MSCDEX.EXE /D:MSCD001
SMARTDRV
```

So how do you know which of these devices loaded high? That's the job of the MEM command!

## The MEM Command

DOS (and every version of Windows) has a very handy command-line program for a quick check of upper memory, called MEM. The MEM program provides great answers to questions like "I just changed my DEVICE= line for my scanner to DEVICEHIGH=; did the scanner device driver actually load into a UMB?"

The MEM command is used in two ways. From a command prompt, type **MEM** without any other switches to determine the amount of conventional and UMB space used and available (Figure 12-22).

```
C:\>mem

Memory Type        Total  =  Used  +  Free
-----------------  -------   -------   -------
Conventional        633K      33K      600K
Upper                75K      63K       12K
Reserved              0K       0K        0K
Extended (XMS)*   15,285K     501K   14,784K
-----------------  -------   -------   -------
Total memory      15,993K     597K   15,396K

Total under 1 MB    708K      96K      612K

Total Expanded (EMS)              15,680 (16,056,320 bytes
Free Expanded (EMS)*              15,024 (15,384,576 bytes

* EMM386 is using XMS memory to simulate EMS memory as needed.
  Free EMS memory may change as free XMS memory changes.

Largest executable program size      599K (613,824 bytes)
Largest free upper memory block        8K   (8,176 bytes)
MS-DOS is resident in the high memory area.

C:\>_
```

**Figure 12-22**  MEM command

The second way MEM is used is with the /C switch. Figure 12-23 shows what you can learn from the MEM /C command. Note that you may need to use the /P command as well (that is, MEM /C /P) so the text does not scroll off the screen faster than you can see it.

Modules using memory below 1 MB:

| Name | Total | | = | Conventional | | + | Upper Memory | |
|------|-------|---|---|--------------|---|---|--------------|---|
| MSDOS | 12,989 | (13K) | | 12,989 | (13K) | | 0 | (0K) |
| HIMEM | 1,168 | (1K) | | 1,168 | (1K) | | 0 | (0K) |
| EMM386 | 3,120 | (3K) | | 3,120 | (3K) | | 0 | (0K) |
| COMMAND | 2,928 | (3K) | | 2,928 | (3K) | | 0 | (0K) |
| JMOUSE | 14,080 | (14K) | | 13,984 | (14K) | | 96 | (0K) |
| OAKCDROM | 36,064 | (35K) | | 0 | (0K) | | 36,064 | (35K) |
| ANSI | 4,256 | (4K) | | 0 | (0K) | | 4,256 | (4K) |
| MSCDEX | 23,824 | (23K) | | 0 | (0K) | | 23,824 | (23K) |
| Free | 626,256 | (612K) | | 613,920 | (600K) | | 12,336 | (12K) |

Memory Summary:

| Type of Memory | Total | = | Used | + | Free |
|----------------|-------|---|------|---|------|
| Conventional | 648,192 | | 34,272 | | 613,920 |
| Upper | 76,576 | | 64,240 | | 12,336 |
| Reserved | 0 | | 0 | | 0 |
| Extended (XMS)* | 15,652,064 | | 513,248 | | 15,138,816 |
| | | | | | |
| Total memory | 16,376,832 | | 611,760 | | 15,765,072 |
| Total under 1 MB | 724,768 | | 98,512 | | 626,256 |
| Total Expanded (EMS) | | | 16,056,320 | (15,680K | |
| Free Expanded (EMS)* | | | 15,384,576 | (15,024K | |

\* EMM386 is using XMS memory to simulate EMS memory as needed.
  Free EMS memory may change as free XMS memory changes.

Largest executable program size        613,824   (599K)
Largest free upper memory block          8,176   (8K)
MS-DOS is resident in the high memory area.

C:\>_

---

**Figure 12-23**   MEM /C

Let's examine each line:

- **MSDOS**   This is the total amount of memory used by the two hidden DOS files, MSDOS.SYS and IO.SYS, as well as the DOS environment space. This is always in conventional memory.

- **HIMEM**   This is HIMEM.SYS and is also always in conventional memory.

- **EMM386**  Notice how little memory (roughly 3K) it uses. EMM386 is actually much larger, but loads mostly into a UMB. If it loads high, why does nothing show up in the Upper Memory column? Beats me; go ask Microsoft.

- **COMMAND**  If you used DOS=HIGH, this is the part of COMMAND.COM that stays in low memory—always in conventional memory.

- **JMOUSE, OAKCDROM, ANSI,** and **MSCDEX**  These are devices in my CONFIG.SYS, as well as TSRs in my AUTOEXEC.BAT. All these devices are loaded high except JMOUSE. These will differ from PC to PC, depending on what drivers are loaded in your CONFIG.SYS.

- **FREE**  This tells us how much free conventional and upper memory is available. In this system, I have 600K conventional and 12K upper memory free.

## MEMORY SUMMARY

This section breaks memory down into four parts with some totals at the bottom:

- **CONVENTIONAL**  Tells you that you have 648,192 (~640K) of conventional memory, of which 34,272 bytes are used, leaving 613,920 bytes free.

- **UPPER**  Tells you that you have 76,576 bytes of UMB space, 64,240 bytes used by devices loaded high, leaving 12,336 bytes free. The total upper memory is determined by the following equation: 393,216 (384K)—all shadowed memory—video memory. In this case, the total available equals 76,576 bytes.

- **RESERVED**  Different machines display the 384K of reserved area memory differently. Often you'll see a number like 393,216 for Total and 0 for Free. In this case, the system simply ignores this useless line.

- **EXTENDED (XMS)**  Shows you have a total of 15,652,064 bytes of extended memory, of which 513,248 bytes are in use by some program (Windows, in this case, and whatever else is running on my system), leaving 15,138,816 bytes free.

The rest of the MEM /C command gives you totals/results for your system's memory usage.

- **TOTAL UNDER 1 MB**  This adds conventional and upper memory.

- **LARGEST EXECUTABLE PROGRAM SIZE**  This is the largest single amount of open conventional memory available. This is almost always slightly smaller than free conventional memory.

- **LARGEST FREE UPPER MEMORY BLOCK**  This is the largest open UMB. If the free upper memory block in Type of Memory is the same as this number, you have only one UMB. As you can see, I have 12,336 bytes of free upper memory, but the largest block is 8,176 bytes. Therefore, I have more than one UMB.

- **MS-DOS IS RESIDENT IN THE HIGH MEMORY AREA**   This tells you that DOS=HIGH is in the CONFIG.SYS file.

The most conventional memory you can free up on a DOS system is about 616K to 620K. You will always have MSDOS, HIMEM, EMM386, and COMMAND in conventional memory. That's okay, because they have actually loaded themselves high, and what you see in conventional memory are small "stubs" that link them to the parts that are loaded high.

You've been given several of tools in this section, but one tool is more important than any other: making sure to take your time with memory management. Be patient. When I'm performing memory management on a DOS PC, I feel lucky if I can do it in 30 minutes and have to reboot the PC only 12 times!

Always make backup copies of CONFIG.SYS and AUTOEXEC.BAT before you start!

## Running DOS Applications in a Windows World

Now that we understand the basics of DOS memory management, let's move forward to the real world of Windows 9*x* and Windows 2000 system support for DOS applications. Depending on the version of Windows, you have a number of methods for running DOS applications in Windows. Let's look at each of these methods and see why Microsoft provides so many ways to what seems to be the same thing—running a DOS program.

---

**NOTE**   Windows 9x and Windows 2000 have many different ways to run DOS applications. Make sure you know which versions of Windows support which methods!

---

DOS programs are  not completely dead, even in a Windows 9*x*/2000 world where almost every application runs in Windows. For some jobs, however, a DOS-based application does the job necessary with less fuss and more efficiency than any GUI-based application. For example, have you wondered where all these CMOS screens come from in this book? You can't do a screen capture of a CMOS setup utility. You can draw them all using a wonderful freeware DOS program called SHMANSI written by Jonathan McPherson (Figure 12-24). It's a powerful program that enables you to draw with the ANSI character set—just one more bit of proof that DOS applications continue to work hard, even on my Windows 2000 system! Thanks, Jonathan!

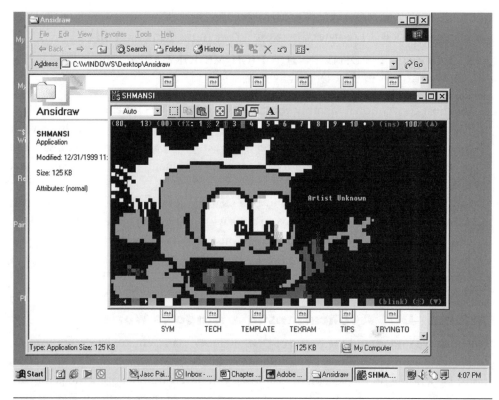

**Figure 12-24**   Having fun with SHMANSI

The most common method of running a DOS application in Windows is via a DOS virtual machine. All versions of Windows use the virtual 8086 function of protected mode to create a virtual 8086 system, complete with whatever type of memory the DOS program requires. The term "running in a DOS box" is often used to reflect this method. Figure 12-25 shows SHMANSI running in a DOS box as I draw another CMOS screen.

If you press the ALT-ENTER key combination, you can make the program run in full-screen mode and even pretend it's 1994. Even though it looks like Windows has disappeared, again pressing ALT-ENTER returns the application to a window. All versions of Windows support DOS virtual machines.

Some DOS programs simply will not run in a virtual machine. In that case, Windows 9x supports a special mode called MS-DOS mode. In MS-DOS mode, the system uses a special CONFIG.SYS and AUTOEXEC.BAT that you create ahead of time and reboots itself into roughly the equivalent of Safe Mode Command Prompt and runs the DOS

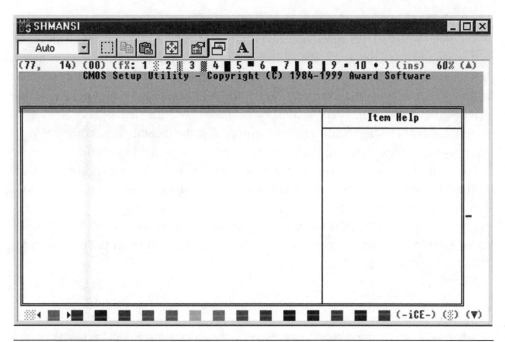

**Figure 12-25**   Building a CMOS screen

program. When you exit the program, Windows 9*x* reboots itself back to normal Windows. MS-DOS mode is slow, given the two reboots required, but it often makes the difference between running and not running a DOS application. Windows NT and 2000 do not provide support for MS-DOS mode.

DOS programs on a Windows system can be run in other ways as well, but these usually just mean avoiding Windows. For example, you can boot off a DOS floppy disk or create a dual-boot system. These methods will not be covered as they really aren't "Running DOS Apps in a  Windows World," but rather "Running DOS Apps by Avoiding Windows." Instead, let's concentrate on virtual machines and MS-DOS mode.

 **NOTE**   A number of subtle differences with command-line programs exist between the DOS examples we've seen and the versions that run in Windows 9*x* and Windows 2000. In most cases, the differences are so subtle that you won't even notice them. But if you do, appreciate that these differences in no way add or take away any functionality. They just display the information in a different way.

## Virtual Machine

If you double-click a DOS application in Windows, Windows immediately creates a virtual machine. The problem is that Windows doesn't know what the program needs. Does it need EMS? Does it need XMS? Does the DOS application use any key combinations that Windows also uses? As a result, Windows makes a default virtual machine that covers every possible need. In most cases, this works quite well, but one in roughly three DOS applications requires special settings that the default virtual machine does not provide. In those cases, you must create a customized virtual machine.

To create a customized virtual machine, just open the properties for the DOS application. You'll see a number of tabs that do not appear in the properties of Windows programs. Let's use good old SHMANSI on a Windows 98 system as a starting example. I copied SHMANSI as well as a number of extra files it needs into a folder called SHMANSI on my Desktop. It looks like Figure 12-26. I select the properties for SHMANSI and see Figure 12-27.

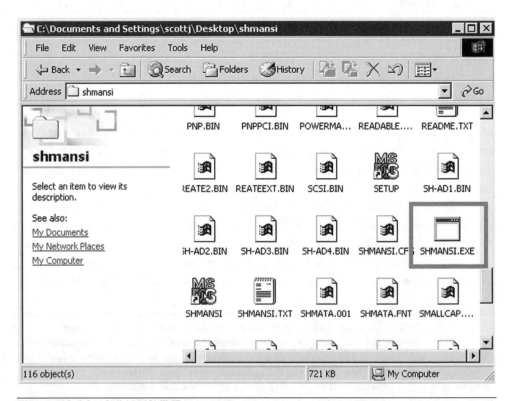

**Figure 12-26**   SHMANSI.EXE

**Figure 12-27**
SHMANSI
properties in
Windows 98,
General tab

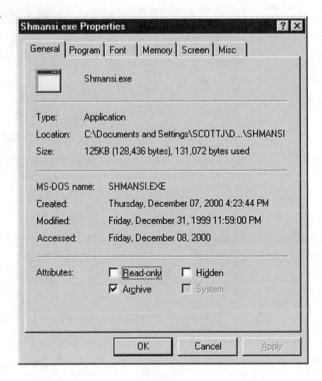

If I were to do the same thing with SHMANSI on a Windows 2000 system, I would see Figure 12-28. Although you will always see many tabs, only five are of interest to you here: Program, Font, Memory, Screen, and Misc. Let's check them out!

**NOTE** With one tiny exception, all of these screens are identical in both Windows 2000 and Windows 98.

If you make any changes to any settings in the DOS application's properties, Windows will create a new file called an "MS-DOS shortcut." These are often referred to as *program information file* (PIF) files and have the extension PIF, although they look like regular Windows shortcuts. The PIF file will be in the same folder as the DOS application, but they can be moved, copied, and deleted just like any other shortcut (Figure 12-29).

**Figure 12-28**
SHMANSI
properties in
Windows 2000,
General tab

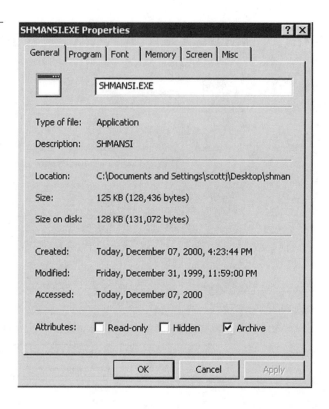

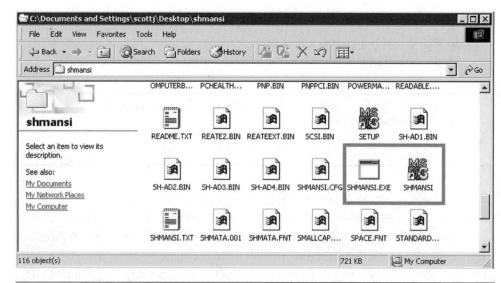

**Figure 12-29**  SHMANSI.EXE icon and its PIF

## Program

The Program tab provides basic information and settings about the DOS application (Figure 12-30). The first line shows the icon for the PIF and the title bar text that shows up when the DOS application runs in a window. You may enter different text and use the Change Icon button to change the icon.

**Figure 12-30**

Program tab

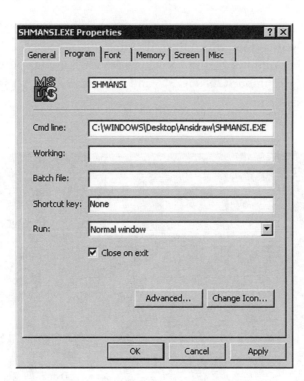

- **Cmd line**   This is what Windows will run to start the program.
- **Working**   This determines the working directory. Most DOS applications look for their data in the working directory, so this enables you to make the program think it started in whatever directory you choose here.
- **Batch file**   You can create a batch file to start any other programs that this program may need.
- **Shortcut key**   This enables you to make a shortcut key to start or switch to the program.

- **Run**  This enables you to choose how this program will run: normal window, minimized, or maximized. Don't confuse maximized with full screen. A maximized DOS program still runs in a window, but you cannot resize the window. Try it.

- **Close on Exit**  If this box is not checked, the window does not close. Instead, it will say "Finished" (Windows 9*x*) or "[Inactive]" (Windows 2000) on the title bar (Figure 12-31). Check this box, unless you like doing the extra step of closing the window.

The Advanced button is the only option that differs between Windows 9*x* and Windows 2000. In Windows 9*x*, this configures MS-DOS mode options, and in Windows 2000, it assigns a unique CONFIG.SYS and AUTOEXEC.BAT. Let's save this for the MS-DOS mode discussion.

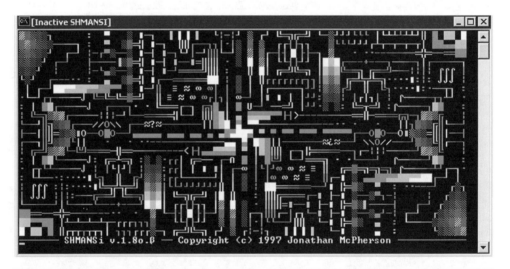

**Figure 12-31**  Oops!

### Font

The Font tab deals with the fonts used by the DOS application (Figure 12-32). The font size determines the size of the window, which is usually just set to Auto. Windows will then use the best font to fit your screen. Some DOS applications have a hard time with Windows TrueType fonts, so you can choose regular bitmap fonts if the fonts look weird.

**Figure 12-32**
Font tab

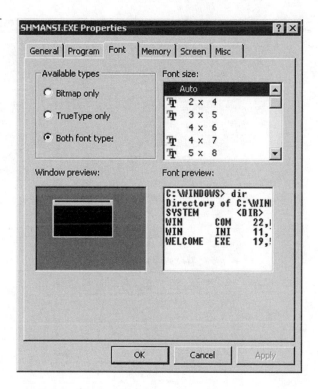

## Memory

The Memory tab defines all the memory needs for the DOS application (Figure 12-33). The chances of you needing to edit anything on this screen are virtually nil. This screen is a throwback from the old Windows 3.x PIF Editor. Back in the Windows 3.x days, we worked hard to keep our virtual machines as small as possible to save RAM. Windows 9x and Windows 2000 offer advanced DPMI functions that automatically provide the DOS application with as much of any type of memory as it might need. In a few cases, we may set a specific value for a type of memory to reduce the amount of memory a particularly memory-hungry application might want to grab.

Note the **Protected** check box. This prevents Windows from moving any memory used by the application into the swap file.

The **Initial environment** sets the DOS environment space. The following are example settings called *environment variables* that may be seen in an AUTOEXEC.BAT:

```
PATH=C:\;C;\DOS;
PROMPT $p$g
SET TEMP=C:\TEMP
SET BLASTER=
```

DOS stores these variables in a special location called the *environment space*. Again, the Auto setting works well.

**Figure 12-33**
Memory tab

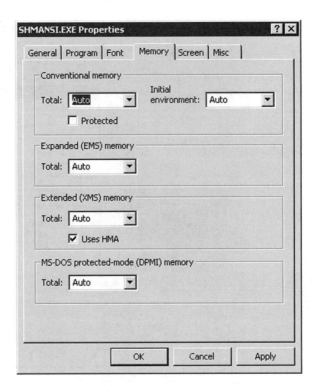

**Screen**

The Screen tab sets a number of display options (Figure 12-34). Go to the **Usage** area of the tab to make the window truly full-screen or windowed. The **Initial size** shows the number of lines on the screen, although most DOS applications will ignore this and default to 24 lines. This can be handy when just running command-line programs, because it shows more lines.

The **Window** area lets you choose whether to see the toolbar. The toolbar is mainly used for cutting and pasting, so unless you intend to cut and paste, don't show the toolbar.

**Restore settings at startup** saves the window's position and restores the program to that state when you start it up again.

The two **Performance** options are also throwbacks from a time when a few DOS programs had problems in Windows 3.*x*. Surprisingly, Microsoft still provides these options. **Fast ROM emulation** enables the Windows video driver to emulate the trivial video calls that most DOS programs need. Keep it checked. Some DOS programs may switch video modes while they run. **Dynamic memory allocation** reserves the entire video area in anticipation of a DOS application switching video modes. This used to be a way to save memory, but the amount of memory saved (usually 64K) means nothing on today's systems. Keep this one checked, too.

**Figure 12-34**
Screen tab

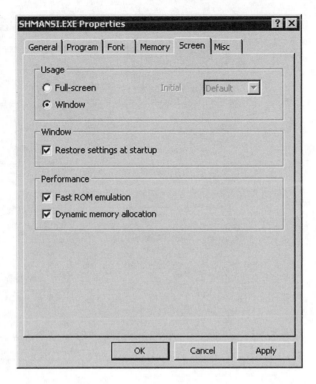

## MISC

Misc stores all the settings that don't fit anywhere else (Figure 12-35):

- **Allow screen saver**   This enables the Windows screen saver to kick in even if the DOS application is in the foreground.

- **Always suspend**   This freezes the DOS application if it's in the background. This is usually not a good idea.

- **Idle sensitivity**   DOS applications get a fairly large timeslice. If Windows notices that a DOS application is idle, it will eventually reduce its timeslice dramatically. Setting this higher just speeds up the process.

- **QuickEdit**   This enables you to cut and paste a DOS application just like a Windows application. If it's not checked, you have to use the Mark and Edit menu settings. If you intend to cut and paste, select this option.

- **Exclusive mode**   This is yet another relic from an earlier time. Exclusive mode permits the mouse to function only in the DOS application.

**Figure 12-35**
Misc tab

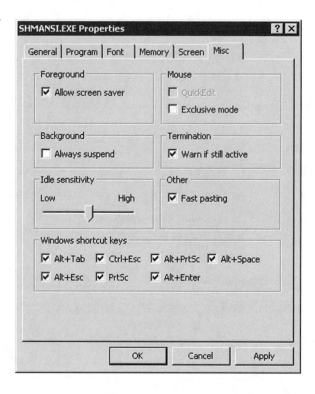

• **Warn if still active** Most DOS programs should be closed through their own close functions, but you can close a DOS window just like any other window if you choose to do so. If you check this option and try to close the DOS program like a regular Windows program, you get the warning shown in Figure 12-36.

**Figure 12-36**
Windows can't end
this program!

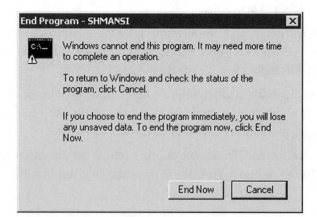

- **Fast pasting**   Some DOS applications can't handle the speed of Windows cut and paste. If you lose characters between DOS applications, turn this off. Windows will add a few milliseconds between characters.

- **Windows shortcut keys**   Certain programs use the same shortcut keys as Windows. You can select any Windows shortcut keys for the exclusive use of the DOS application while it runs.

## Dealing with Problem DOS Programs

As mentioned earlier, some DOS programs just don't like to play in a normal virtual machine. In most cases, this is due to the DOS program requiring special drivers or TSRs, therefore necessitating a unique CONFIG.SYS or AUTOEXEC.BAT file just for that program. Windows 9x and Windows 2000 differ substantially on how they handle this. Windows 9x uses the MS-DOS mode, whereas Windows 2000 simply provides a method to create a unique CONFIG.SYS and AUTOEXEC.BAT.

### Windows 2000's Method

If you click on the Advanced button on the Program tab, you'll see that Windows 2000 brings up Figure 12-37. This screen enables you to select customized CONFIG.SYS and AUTOEXEC.BAT files for the application. Of course, you need to make these files first! I usually just store them in the same folder as the DOS program.

The **Compatible timer hardware emulation** option is just a nice way to say, "slow down the computer!" It is also handy for DOS games.

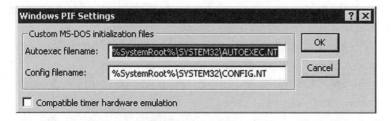

**Figure 12-37**   Windows 2000 PIF settings

### Windows 9x's Method

Windows 2000 may provide custom CONFIG.SYS and AUTOEXEC.BAT files, but many DOS programs need direct access to hardware. Those programs just will not run in Windows 2000; however, Windows 9x provides a clever MS-DOS Mode function that via a reboot removes all but a tiny stub of Windows 9x from memory and creates an environment that most DOS programs find perfectly acceptable. Click the Advanced button in the Program tab to see Figure 12-38.

**Figure 12-38**
MS-DOS mode
options in
Windows 9x

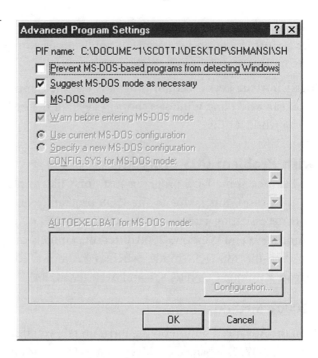

Some DOS programs are very smart and will refuse to run in Windows. **Prevent MS-DOS-based programs from detecting Windows** is supposed to keep that from happening, although the few DOS games still sold have long since learned how to detect Windows anyway.

**Suggest MS-DOS mode as necessary** enables Windows to monitor a DOS program as it loads. If the DOS program attempts to access hardware directly, Windows opens a message recommending that you run in MS-DOS mode and offering to do so.

Checking the **MS-DOS mode** check box forces the program to run in MS-DOS mode. Once you check this check box, a number of other options.appear (Figure 12-39).

**Warn before entering MS-DOS mode** just brings up an Are You Sure? box before starting the reboot process.

From this point on, you may choose to use the existing C:\CONFIG.SYS and C:\AUTOEXEC.BAT or to create your own to make life even easier. You can click the Configuration button to set up EMM386, SMARTDRV, and DOSKEY, and provide direct disk access for the DOS program.

**Figure 12-39**
Make sure the "Specify a new MS-DOS configuration" check box is selected.

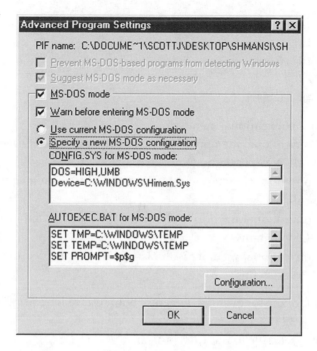

## The End is Near—Not!

DOS has one advantage that Windows will never be able to beat: simplicity. As we add more and more power to Windows, we still see a few classes of programs that use DOS as their OS of choice just to avoid the complexity of Windows. Microsoft recognizes this issue and has made great strides with new technologies such as DirectX to give sophisticated programs the ability to cut through all of the Windows software and get to the system's hardware. Although DOS use is diminishing, software publishers still produce DOS-based applications. As long as DOS applications exist, users will need to know how to make them work under Windows.

## Review Questions

1. DOS was designed to use how much memory?
   A. 64K
   B. 640K
   C. 640MB
   D. 1K

2. How large is the HMA?
   A. 64K
   B. 32K–16 bytes
   C. 32K
   D. 64K–16 bytes

3. What is conventional memory?
   A. Conventional memory is the first 640K of the first megabyte of RAM, needed by all DOS programs.
   B. Conventional memory is the last 640K of the first megabyte of RAM, needed by all DOS programs.
   C. Conventional memory is the first 640K of extended memory, needed by all DOS programs.
   D. Conventional memory is the last 640K of extended memory, needed by all DOS programs.

4. Which of the following statements about reserved memory is incorrect?
   A. It is 384K.
   B. It is set aside to run DOS programs.
   C. Its memory address range is from A0000h to FFFFFh.
   D. Device drivers can sometimes load into reserved memory.

5. Expanded memory enables applications to do what?
   A. Expanded memory enables DOS applications to run in extended memory.
   B. Expanded memory enables DOS applications to run in the reserved area of memory.
   C. Expanded memory enables DOS applications to use more than 640K of RAM.
   D. Expanded memory enables Windows applications to use more than 640K of RAM.

6. What line needs to be in CONFIG.SYS to use expanded memory?
   A. DEVICE=EMS.EXE RAM
   B. DOS=HIGH
   C. DOS=EXPANDED
   D. DEVICE=EMM386.EXE RAM

7. What two lines need to be in CONFIG.SYS to load a portion of DOS into the HMA?

    A. DEVICE=EMM386.EXE HIGH

    B. DEVICE=HIMEM.SYS

    C. DOS=HIGH

    D. DOS=UMB

8. Of the following statements regarding UMBs (upper memory blocks), which ones are true? (Select all that apply.)

    A. A system can have more than one UMB.

    B. A system can have only one UMB.

    C. UMBs are unused memory addresses in the conventional area.

    D. UMBs are unused memory addresses in the reserved area.

9. Which of the following statements is *not* used to load device drivers or TSRs into the upper memory blocks?

    A. DEVICEHIGH=

    B. DH=

    C. LOADHIGH

    D. LH

10. Video ROM classically resides at what memory address?

    A. 00000 to A0000

    B. A0000 to B7FFF

    C. C0000 to C7FFF

    D. D0000 to D7FFF

## Answers

1. **B.** DOS was designed to use 640K of memory.

2. **D.** The HMA is 64K—16 bytes.

3. **A.** Conventional memory is the first 640K of the first megabyte of RAM, needed by all DOS programs.

4. **B.** Reserved memory is NOT set aside to run DOS programs.

5. **C.** Expanded memory enables DOS applications to use more than 640K of RAM.

6. **D.** The RAM switch tells EMM386 to support expanded memory.

7. **B and C.** Both HIMEM.SYS and DOS=HIGH must be loaded in CONFIG.SYS. DOS=UMB, although often combined with DOS=HIGH, is for the upper memory blocks, not the high memory area.

8. **A and D.** UMBs are unused memory addresses in the reserved area. In some cases, a system may have more than one UMB.

9. **B.** There is no command called "DH=".

10. **C.** All video cards use the memory location of C0000 to C7FFF.

# SCSI

## 13

In this chapter, you will

- Learn the appeal of SCSI
- Display SCSI chains, IDs, and terminations
- Discover the different flavors of SCSI
- Learn basic SCSI repair techniques

## Historical/Conceptual

Shugart systems introduced *Small Computer System Interface* (SCSI) in 1979 as a system-independent means of mass storage. SCSI can be best described as a "miniature network" inside your PC. Any type of peripheral can be built as a SCSI device. Common SCSI devices include:

- Hard drives
- Tape backup units
- Removable hard drives
- Scanners
- CD-ROM drives
- Printers

SCSI has gone through a number of changes since its introduction. These different changes are based on a few industry standards such as SCSI-1, SCSI-2, and wide SCSI. Within these industry standards are some manufacturer-specific standards (for example, Western Digital has been trying to push something new, but the industry hasn't yet adopted it) with names like Ultra SCSI. These different types of SCSI are often referred to as "flavors." Using SCSI-2 as a basis, this chapter will address the basic issues involved in implementing SCSI in a PC. Once you have a solid understanding of SCSI-2, the other types of SCSI will be explained so you can understand the differences between them.

SCSI manifests itself through a SCSI chain, which is a series of SCSI devices working together through a host adapter. The host adapter is the device that attaches the SCSI chain to the PC. Figure 13-1 shows a typical PCI host adapter.

**Figure 13-1**
SCSI host adapter

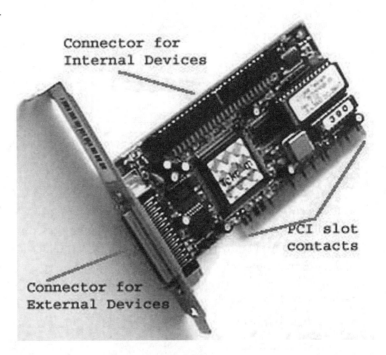

Note that the card has two connections. The first connector, at the left of the figure, is for devices on the outside (external) of the PC. The second connector is at the top of the figure. This connector is for inside (internal) SCSI connections. All SCSI chains connect to the PC through the host adapter. Note that the host adapter in Figure 13-1 is PCI, but you can get SCSI host adapters for just about any expansion bus type. Figure 13-2 shows a 16-bit ISA SCSI host adapter.

**Figure 13-2** ISA host adapter

## Test Specific

### SCSI Chains

All SCSI devices can be divided into two groups: internal and external. External devices stand alone and are hooked to the external connector of the host adapter. Figure 13-3 is an example of an external SCSI device.

Internal SCSI devices are installed inside the PC and connect to the host adapter through the internal connector. Figure 13-4 shows an internal SCSI device, in this case a CD-ROM drive.

All internal devices are connected to the host adapter and each other with a 50-pin ribbon cable. Figure 13-5 shows a common SCSI ribbon cable.

**Figure 13-3**    Back of external SCSI device

**Figure 13-4**    Internal SCSI CD-ROM

Notice that internal 50-pin SCSI cables are very similar to 40-pin IDE cables (Figure 13-6).

Use caution when installing SCSI devices. IDE devices, if they are plugged in wrong, just don't work. SCSI devices, when plugged in incorrectly (such as with the cable backwards), can be damaged! Be careful to install SCSI devices properly the first time. Figure 13-7 illustrates an internal SCSI chain.

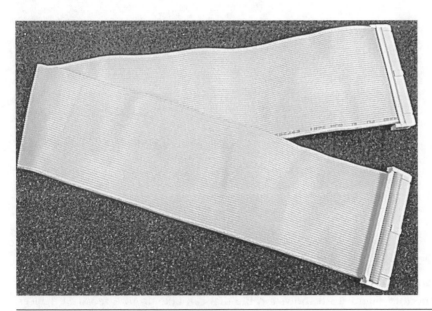

**Figure 13-5**  Typical 50-pin SCSI cable

**Figure 13-6**
SCSI and IDE cables

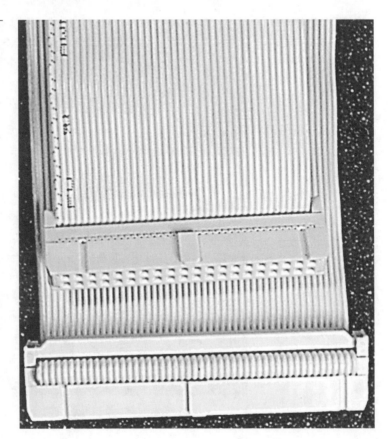

**Figure 13-7**
Internal SCSI chain

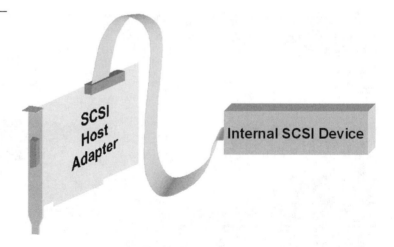

Multiple internal devices can be connected together simply by using a cable with enough connectors. Figure 13-8 shows a cable that can take up to three SCSI devices, including the host adapter. Figure 13-9 shows two internal devices on a SCSI chain.

**Figure 13-8**
SCSI cable with
three connectors

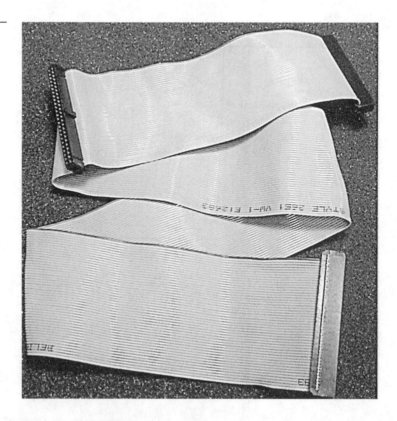

**Figure 13-9**
Internal SCSI chain
with two devices

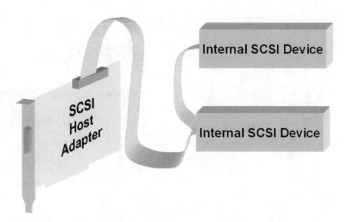

External SCSI devices are a little different. They are connected to the host adapter through the host adapter's special SCSI external connection. Some cheap host adapters do not have external connections, so you cannot put external devices on them. External devices all have two connections in the back, which enable you to daisy-chain multiple external devices together. Figure 13-10 shows a SCSI chain with an external device, and Figure 13-11 shows a SCSI chain with two external devices. SCSI chains can be internal, external, or both (see Figure 13-12). The maximum number of devices you can have on a SCSI chain, including the host adapter, is eight.

**Figure 13-10**
SCSI chain with
external device

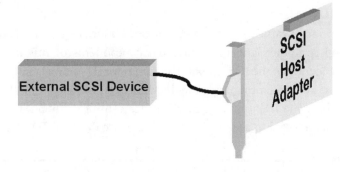

**Figure 13-11**
SCSI chain with two
external devices

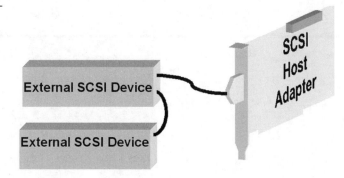

**Figure 13-12**
Internal and exter-
nal devices on one
SCSI chain

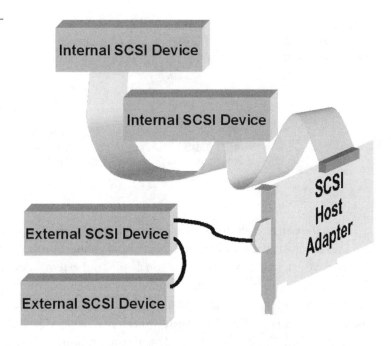

## SCSI IDs

As mentioned earlier, you can view the SCSI interface as a miniature network within a desktop computer, and the individual components of this network each require a unique identifier: the ID number. The values for ID numbers range from 0 to 7. SCSI ID numbers are similar to many other hardware settings in a PC in that no two devices can share the same ID number. A SCSI device can have any SCSI ID, as long as no two devices connected to a single host adapter share the same ID (Figure 13-13).

**EXAM TIP** Make sure you can look at any SCSI device and understand how to set its SCSI ID!

**Figure 13-13**
SCSI IDs

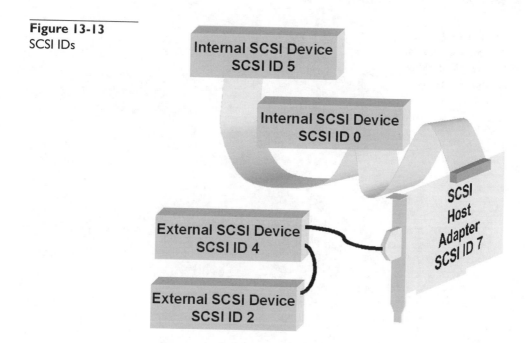

There are some conventions SCSI IDs. Typically, most people set the host adapter to 7. You can usually change this, but you gain nothing by deviating from such a well-established tradition. Note that there is no order for the use of SCSI IDs. It does not matter which device gets which number; you can skip numbers, and any SCSI device can have any SCSI ID (Figure 13-14).

You can set a SCSI ID for a particular device by configuring jumpers or switches on that device. All internal SCSI hard drives, for example, use jumpers to set their SCSI IDs. Figure 13-15 shows typical SCSI hard drive ID jumpers.

Most internal SCSI devices use three jumpers to set the SCSI ID. Unfortunately, these jumpers work about 3 to 4 different ways, and—lucky you—you get to figure them out! The hard drive pictured in Figure 13-15, for example, has three jumpers, numbered (from right to left) 1, 2, and 3. Here's the tricky part, so pay attention. The *value* of the jumper does not necessarily match the *label* on the drive, but on every device, the jumpers follow a set and predictable pattern.

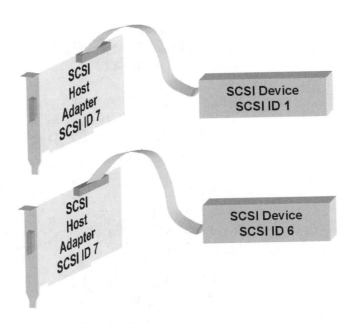

**Figure 13-14**
Any SCSI device can
have any ID as long
as no two match.

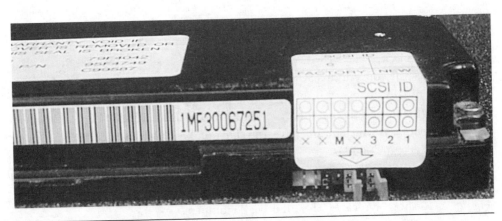

**Figure 13-15** SCSI hard drive jumper settings

Here's how this drive works. The jumper labeled 1 has a *value* of 1; the jumper labeled 2 has a *value* of 2; and the jumper labeled 3 has a *value* of 4. This is known for two reasons. First, it's simply binary math; second, the top of the hard drive said so! In order to set SCSI ID 1, you would put a shunt over jumper 1. In order to get ID 3, you would jumper 1 and 2. In order to get ID 5, you would put shunts over jumpers 1 and 3. Add the value of each jumper and this will make sense (1 + 4 = 5).

Other devices use more or less obvious jumper labeling, so don't get tripped up if a drive has three jumpers labeled 0, 1, 2, or 1, 2, 4. In all three jumper instances when setting SCSI IDs, use the *value* of the three in binary: the first jumper has a value of 1; the second has a value of 2; and the third *always* has a value of 4.

Another convention with SCSI IDs involves bootable SCSI devices. If you want a SCSI drive to be C: (which is required if you want to boot DOS or Windows 9*x* off the drive), you must set that drive to the ID specified by the host adapter as the "bootable" SCSI ID (Figure 13-16). Most manufacturers of host adapters use SCSI ID 0 or 7, although a few older adapters require SCSI ID 6. Read the host adapter information or guess; you will not break anything if you are wrong. Booting SCSI drives is discussed later in this chapter.

**Figure 13-16**
Proper setting of
SCSI IDs for boot
drive

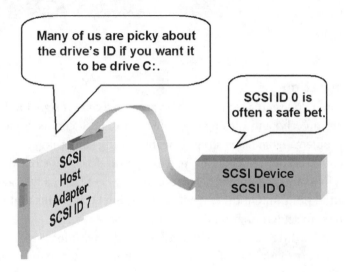

Finally, not all SCSI devices are designed to be set to every SCSI ID. For example, the Iomega ZIP® drive shown in Figure 13-17 can be set only to SCSI ID 5 or 6. Work around it!

## Logical Unit Numbers (LUNs)

SCSI can also support more than one device per ID if you use *Logical Unit Numbers* (LUNs) to provide a unique identifier for up to seven subunits per ID number. These are used primarily in hard-drive arrays, which create one large logical drive out of several smaller physical drives. LUNs are in the realm of network servers running NetWare, Windows NT/2000, and UNIX that require highly specialized software. With the previous exceptions, you can safely ignore LUNs.

**Figure 13-17**
SCSI Zip drive

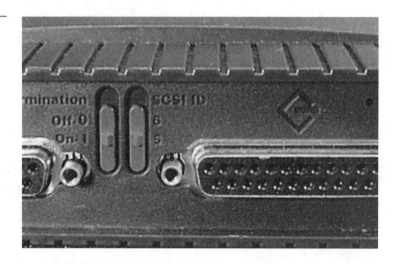

## Termination

Whenever you send a signal down a wire, some of that signal reflects back up the wire, creating an echo and causing electronic chaos. SCSI chains use termination to prevent this problem. *Termination* simply means putting something on the ends of the wire to prevent this echo. Terminators are usually pull-down resistors and can manifest themselves in many different ways. Most of the devices within a PC have the appropriate termination built in. On other devices, including SCSI chains and some network cables, you have to set termination during installation.

The rule with SCSI is that you *must* terminate *only* the ends of the SCSI chain. A SCSI chain refers to a number of devices—including the host adapter—linked by a cable. You have to terminate the ends of the cable, which usually means that you need to terminate the two devices into which the ends of the cable plug. Do *not* terminate devices that are not on the ends of the cable. Figure 13-18 shows some examples of where to terminate SCSI devices.

Because any SCSI device might be on the end of a chain, most manufacturers build SCSI devices that can self-terminate. Some devices will detect that they are on the end of the SCSI chain and will automatically terminate themselves. Most devices, however, require you to set a jumper or switch to enable termination.

The termination can be set in a number of different ways. Figure 13-19 shows a hard drive that is terminated with a jumper setting.

The hard drive in Figure 13-20 has terminating resistors that are inserted. They must be removed to "unterminate" the drive.

The Zip drive in Figure 13-21 has a slide for termination.

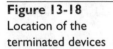

**Figure 13-18**
Location of the
terminated devices

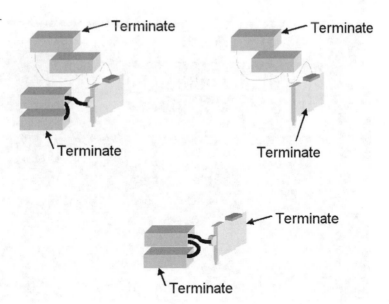

**Figure 13-19**
Setting termination

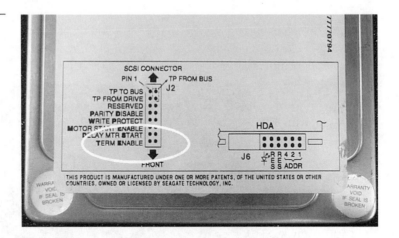

Some host adapters have termination set through software. Figure 13-22 shows a typical host adapter configuration program.

The ancient hard drive in Figure 13-23 is not capable of terminating itself. It needs a separate terminator piece. You can set it up properly by connecting the drive to a connector in the middle of the cable and then adding a terminating resistor to the end of the cable.

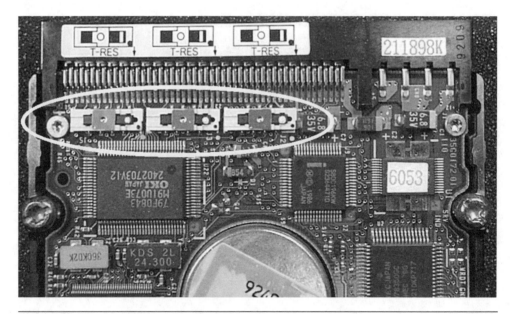

**Figure 13-20**    Hard drive with removable terminating resistors

**Figure 13-21**
Zip drive
termination

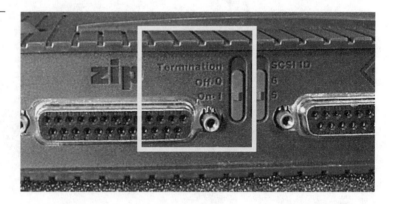

Be careful when you are terminating, because improper termination can cause damage to SCSI hard drives! Unlike setting SCSI IDs, termination can be a little tricky. But before discussing the different types of termination options, you must understand the different types of SCSI.

```
═══════════ Array1000 Family at Bus:Channel 02:A ═══════════
┌─Configuration ─────────────────────────────────────────────┐
│                                                             │
│ SCSI Bus Interface Definition                               │
│   Host Adapter SCSI ID............................... 7      │
│   SCSI Parity Checking............................... Enabled│
│   Host Adapter SCSI Termination...................... Press <Enter>│
│                                                             │
│ Additional Options                                          │
│                                                             │
│   SCSI Device Configuration.......................... Press <Enter>│
│   Array1000 BIOS..................................... Enabled│
│   BIOS Support for Bootable  C-ROM................... Enabled│
│                                                             │
└─────────────────────────────────────────────────────────────┘
        <F6> - Reset to Host Adpater Defaults
```

**Figure 13-22**   Software termination setting

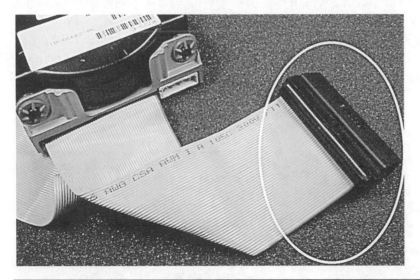

**Figure 13-23**   This old SCSI hard drive requires a separate termination on the cable.

## SCSI Flavors

Way back in 1979, Shugart Associates began work on an interface that would handle data transfers between devices regardless of the type of device. This interface would work at the logical or OS level instead of the device level, creating a stable interface in a world faced with rapid device development. This new interface was called the *Shugart Associates System Interface* (SASI) and was the precursor to SCSI. During 1980 and 1981, various committees from Shugart and the NCR Corporation (a major player in the IT field in those days) met to develop a draft proposal to present to *American National*

*Standards Institute* (ANSI), which facilitates the development of standards in the U.S. In April of 1982, the Accredited Standards Committee X3T9.2 met and drafted a formal proposal for the *Small Computer System Interface* (SCSI), which would be based on SASI. Between 1982 and 1986, the SCSI standard expanded to include more than just hard drives. In June of 1986, the first formal set of standards defining SCSI was approved as ANSI document X3.131-1986. This standard was known as SCSI-1.

## SCSI-1

The SCSI-1 standard defined an 8-bit, 5-MHz bus capable of supporting up to eight SCSI devices, but was very fuzzy in describing many aspects of SCSI. As a result, many manufacturers of SCSI devices had different opinions as to how to implement those standards. So, SCSI-1 was really more of an opinion than a standard. Figure 13-24 shows an early SCSI-1 adapter.

In 1986, SCSI began to appear on IBM-compatible PC machines, and everyone seemed to have a proprietary SCSI device. The key word here is "proprietary" (meaning that only the company that produced, designed, manufactured, and sold the device supported it). SCSI was being used in PCs for stand-alone devices such as hard drives, and each device came with its own host adapter. Makers of SCSI devices had no interest in chaining their particular device with anyone else's, primarily because they assumed (for the most part correctly) that their device was the only SCSI device in the PC. Each SCSI device had its own command set, and no two command sets were the

**Figure 13-24**   Early SCSI-1 adapter

same. Trying to get one vendor's SCSI hard drive to work with another vendor's SCSI adapter card was often impossible.

SCSI-1 devices transferred data only through an 8-bit parallel path, but did support up to seven devices on the chain. For most PCs using SCSI-1 devices, the 8-bit pathway was not much of a bottleneck. Although the devices themselves were not capable of high-speed data transfers, neither were the 80286-based machines of the time. SCSI-1 devices seemed fast in comparison. Plus, the only common hard-drive interface competition was the ST-506 controller, and 8-bit SCSI was far faster!

## SCSI-2

By the time the SCSI-1 standard was adopted, a number of improvements were being adopted by manufacturers. As a result, the SCSI standards committee was put to work creating a new SCSI standard. Their work lasted from July 1986 to February 1989, when they sent their formal proposal (ASC X3T9.2) for SCSI-2 to ANSI. Formal adoption of SCSI-2 was not reached until July 1990.

The SCSI-2 standard was quite detailed and addressed a large number of issues within SCSI. One of the more important parts of the SCSI-2 standard was the definition of 18 commands that have to be supported by any device labeled SCSI-2 compliant. This set of commands, called the *common command set* (CCS), made hooking up devices from various manufacturers less of a nightmare. The CCS also introduced commands to address other devices besides hard drives, including CD-ROM drives, tape drives, and scanners.

SCSI-2 also defined the types of connectors to be used. Before SCSI-2, no true standard for SCSI connectors existed, although a few types became *de facto* standards. The new SCSI-2 connectors ensured that any two SCSI-2 compliant devices could be physically connected. SCSI-2 also more closely defined terminations.

The one area that creates the most confusion with SCSI-2 is the width of the data bus and the speeds. SCSI-2 defined two optional 16-bit and 32-bit buses called *wide* SCSI, and a new, optional 10-MHz speed called *fast* SCSI. SCSI-2 devices could now be 8-bit (narrow), 16-bit (wide), or 32-bit (also called wide), or they could be 5 MHz (slow, the standard) or 10 MHz (fast). This means six "subflavors" of SCSI-2 are available (we'll add SCSI-1 for comparison). See Table 13-1.

**Table 13-1**   Standard SCSI vs. Fast SCSI

| SCSI TYPE/BIT WIDTH | 5 MHz (STANDARD) | 10 MHz (FAST) |
| --- | --- | --- |
| SCSI-1: 8-bit | 5MBps | NA |
| SCSI-2: 8-bit | 5MBps | 10MBps |
| SCSI-2: 16-bit (wide) | 10MBps | 20MBps |
| SCSI-2: 32-bit (wide) | 20MBps | 40MBps |

Even though SCSI-2 defined a 32-bit SCSI bus, it was almost completely ignored by the industry due to its high cost and a lack of demand. In reality, wide SCSI means 16-bits wide.

Fast SCSI-2 transfers data in fast synchronous mode, meaning the SCSI device being talked to (the target) does not have to acknowledge (ack) every individual request (req) for data from the host adapter (initiator). This allows for a doubling of transfer speed, from approximately 5 to 10MBps. However, experience has shown that external fast SCSI devices will rarely provide "fast" performance unless the cable provides proper shielding and electrical impedance or load. Cables that do provide proper shielding and load are generally more expensive but are required to achieve true "fast" performance.

## SE, HVD, and LVD SCSI

SCSI-1 devices were all *single-ended* (SE), meaning they communicated through only one wire per bit of information. This one wire is measured or referenced against the common ground provided by the metal chassis and in turn by the power supply of the system. Noise is usually spread through either the electrical power cables or the data cable, and is called *common-mode noise*. An SE SCSI device is vulnerable to common-mode noise because it has no way of telling the difference between valid data and noise. When noise invades the data stream, the devices must resend the data. The amount of noise generated grows dramatically over the length of a SCSI cable, limiting the total length of an SE SCSI chain to only about six meters, depending on the type of SCSI.

To achieve much longer SCSI chains, SCSI-2 offered an optional solution with *High Voltage Differential* (HVD) SCSI (or what used to be called simply differential SCSI). HVD devices employ two wires per bit of data: one wire for data and one for the inverse of this data. The inverse signal takes the place of the ground wire in the SE cable. By taking the difference of the two signals, the device can reject the common-mode noise in the data stream. This allows for much longer SCSI chains—up to 25 meters.

No obvious difference exists between SE and HVD SCSI devices. The connectors and cabling seem to be identical. This is a bit of a problem because under no circumstances should you try to connect SE and HVD devices on the same SCSI chain. At the very least, you will probably fry the SE device; if the HVD device lacks a security circuit to detect your mistake, you will probably smoke it as well.

Don't panic! Although HVD SCSI devices exist, they are rare and usually found only in aging high-end servers. SE SCSI devices and controllers still reign. The makers of HVD SCSI know the danger and will clearly label their devices.

The problems of cable length versus cost led manufacturers to come up with a second type of differential SCSI called *Low Voltage Differential* (LVD). LVD SCSI requires less power than HVD and is compatible with existing SE SCSI controllers and devices.

LVD devices can sense the type of SCSI and then work accordingly. If you plug an LVD device into an SE chain, it will act as an SE device. If you plug an LVD device into LVD, it will run as LVD. LVD SCSI chains can be up to 12 meters in length. The safety, ease of use, and low cost of LVD has made it quite popular in higher-end PCs and servers.

## SCSI-3

SCSI technology did not stand still with the adoption of SCSI-2. Manufacturers have developed significant improvements in SCSI-2, particularly in increased speeds and easier configuration. The T-10 SCSI committee collected these improvements and created a working set of standards collectively called SCSI-3. SCSI-3 devices have many names and technologies, such as Ultra2 or Wide Ultra. SCSI-3 also includes interfaces for various types of serial SCSI, including the very popular FireWire. Let's take a minute to look at these.

One of the more popular aspects to SCSI-3, and one that has already been widely adopted, is the ability for wide SCSI to control up to 16 devices on one chain. Each device gets a number from 0 to 15, as opposed to just 0 through 7. This ability is often thought to be part of SCSI-2 because wide, 16-device control came out very quickly after the SCSI-2 standard was adopted.

Most manufacturers use the terms Ultra, Ultra2, and Ultra3 to define high-speed SCSI-3 buses—20, 40, and 80 MHz, respectively. You might still run into the older Adaptec-specific terms for the same buses—Fast-20, Fast-40, and Fast-80. The three buses also come in both narrow and wide varieties. Look at the differences in data transfer rates among the buses, listed in Table 13-2.

**Table 13-2**   Narrow SCSI-3 vs. Wide SCSI-3

| SCSI TYPE | BUS SPEED | 8-BIT (NARROW) | 16-BIT (WIDE) |
| --- | --- | --- | --- |
| Ultra SCSI (Fast-20) | 20 MHz | 20MBps | 40MBps |
| Ultra2 SCSI (Fast-40) | 40 MHz | 40MBps | 80MBps |
| Ultra3 SCSI (Fast-80) | 80 MHz | 80MBps | 160MBps |

The SCSI-3 standard also includes optional hot swap capabilities. To *hot swap* means to be able to unplug a drive from the SCSI chain without rebooting or resetting the chain. Hot swapping is extremely helpful in laptops and servers and is already popular for high-end SCSI drives.

With the development of SCSI-3 standards and devices, you might guess that older SCSI-2 devices would go away, but this has not been the case. Manufacturers continue to produce SCSI-2 devices and controllers and put them into the marketplace right alongside the higher-end SCSI-3 devices and controllers. Even worse, they still make both SE and LVD flavors! The SCSI picture as far as techs are concerned is therefore somewhat complex. Table 13-3 shows the current SCSI picture, including the latest and greatest Ultra320 standard and the cabling length considerations for the many flavors.

**Table 13-3**   Current SCSI Picture
(courtesy of the SCSI Trade Association— http://www.scsita.org)

| SCSI TRADE ASSOCIATION TERMS | BUS SPEED (MBps) | BUS WIDTH (BITS) | MAX. BUS LENGTHS, METERS[1] | | | MAX. DEVICE SUPPORT |
|---|---|---|---|---|---|---|
| | | | SE | LVD | HVD | |
| SCSI-1[2] | 5 | 8 | 6 | [3] | 25 | 8 |
| Fast SCSI[2] | 10 | 8 | 3 | [3] | 25 | 8 |
| Fast Wide SCSI | 20 | 16 | 3 | [3] | 25 | 16 |
| Ultra SCSI[2] | 20 | 8 | 1.5 | [3] | 25 | 8 |
| Ultra SCSI[2] | 20 | 8 | 3 | - | - | 4 |
| Wide Ultra SCSI | 40 | 16 | - | [3] | 25 | 16 |
| Wide Ultra SCSI | 40 | 16 | 1.5 | - | - | 8 |
| Wide Ultra SCSI | 40 | 16 | 3 | - | - | 4 |
| Ultra2 SCSI[2,4] | 40 | 8 | [4] | 12 | 25 | 8 |
| Wide Ultra2 SCSI[4] | 80 | 16 | [4] | 12 | 25 | 16 |
| Ultra3 SCSI or Ultra160[6] | 160 | 16 | [4] | 12 | [5] | 16 |
| Ultra320[6] | 320 | 16 | [4] | 12 | [5] | 16 |

[1] The listed maximum bus lengths may be exceeded in Point-to-Point and engineered applications.
[2] Use of the word "narrow" preceding SCSI, Ultra SCSI, or Ultra2 SCSI is optional.
[3] LVD was not defined in the original SCSI standards for this speed. If all devices on the bus support LVD, then 12-meter operation is possible at this speed. However, if any device on the bus is single-ended only, then the entire bus switches to single-ended mode and the distances in the single-ended column apply.
[4] Single-ended is not defined for speeds beyond Ultra.
[5] HVD (Differential) is not defined for speeds beyond Ultra2.
[6] After Ultra2 all new speeds are wide only.

## Serial SCSI

The last and most interesting function under the SCSI-3 standards is serial SCSI. SCSI as we know it is a parallel interface; the SCSI bus consists of 8 or 16 parallel wires passing data. *Serial SCSI* means transferring SCSI commands over a single wire, as in classic serial communications.

There are three main types of serial SCSI cabling: IEEE 1394 (FireWire), fibre channel, and *serial storage architecture* (SSA). These cabling systems are vying for predominance in the SCSI market, with fibre channel currently seeming to be the winner on the high end. Although, IEEE 1394 is also quite popular, especially among the *digital video* (DV) crowd. SSA is not as widely used. These cabling systems offer long cable runs, hot swapping, and a relatively low cost, which has made them quite attractive. Serial cabling systems also enable one SCSI chain to have an amazing number of devices. Table 13-4 shows the serial SCSI standards, listing transfer speeds, device limitations, and maximum bus length.

**Table 13-4**  SCSI-3 Serial Cabling Standards

| CABLING | SPEED | NUMBER OF DEVICES | MAX. BUS LENGTH |
|---------|-------|-------------------|-----------------|
| SSA | Up to 80MBps | 128 | 25 meters |
| IEEE 1394 | Up to 50MBps | 63 | 72 meters |
| Fibre Channel | Up to 400MBps | 126 | 10 kilometers |

## Bus Mastering

Whenever you scan an image or search for a sector on a non-SCSI hard drive (IDE) system, the CPU transfers data for as long as it takes to complete the operation. SCSI devices perform these functions independently by disconnecting through the SCSI bus. This provides other devices an opportunity to perform their tasks faster and with less waiting. When backing up a hard drive to a tape drive in a typical non-SCSI PC, the CPU requests data from the hard drive, loads the data into its registers, and then writes the information to the tape drive, where the data is finally stored. During this entire process, which can last hours, the CPU must still try to handle your requests to run other types of software.

With a SCSI-equipped PC, however, the process is more efficient. A SCSI tape drive and SCSI hard drive connected to the same host adapter can use bus mastering to communicate with each other directly. In such a SCSI bus-mastering situation, the host adapter remains in the circuit only long enough to arbitrate the connection between the hard drive and the tape drive. Once establishing the data transfer, the host adapter drops off and lets the hard drive and tape unit communicate directly with each other while the backup runs. Once the backup is finished, or if the user interrupts the operation, the drives re-establish their presence on the SCSI chain. The great beauty of this lies in the lack of CPU and expansion bus usage. Once the connection is made, the two devices are, for all intents and purposes, no longer on the PC and not consuming any system resources.

## SCSI Cables and Connectors

There are no official SCSI-1, SCSI-2, or Ultra SCSI, cables or connectors, although manufacturers generally follow similar guidelines today. Cable is based on whether the device is internal or external, what types of connectors are available, and the type of SCSI you use.

The most common kind of SCSI cable is type A. It has 50 wires and is used for 8-bit data transfers in both the SCSI-1 and SCSI-2 standards. It is also used for 8-bit fast SCSI-2 (see Figure 13-25).

**Figure 13-25**
SCSI "A" cable

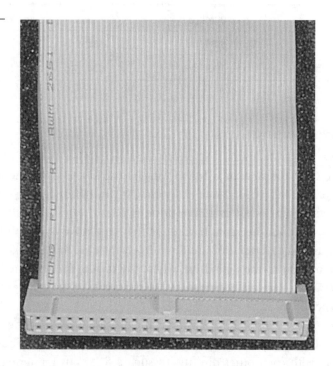

In the earliest days of SCSI-2, 16-bit data transfers required another cable: type B. It had 68 wires and was used in parallel with the 50-wire A cable. Because the industry was so underwhelmed at the dual-cable concept, the B cable quietly and quickly disappeared, to be replaced by the P cable. Like its predecessor, this cable also had 68 wires; unlike the B cable, the P cable can be used alone (see Figure 13-26).

Some of the higher-end SCSI-3 host adapters and drives use an 80-pin cable called a SCA 80. The extra wires enable you to hot swap the drives, but that's about it. The drives will work fine with 68-pin cables and an adapter or with their own 80-pin cable.

**Figure 13-26**
SCSI "P" cable

## Types of External Connectors

All external connectors are female on the devices. The type of external connectors are as follows:

- 50-pin Centronics, an obsolete SCSI-1 connector

- 50-pin HD DB, used for SCSI-2

- 68-pin HD DB, used for wide SCSI-2 and SCSI-3

- 25-pin standard D-type (looks identical to parallel), SCSI-2, most commonly used on Macintoshes and Zip drives

## ASPI

Everything within your computer must have *basic input/output services* (BIOS). BIOS is nothing more than the software that enables the CPU to talk to the rest of the hardware. It can be hard-wired into the motherboard (the system BIOS), hard-wired into the device (for example, a ROM chip built into a video card), or it can be a device driver loaded off of the hard drive. The BIOS for SCSI devices can come from any of these sources.

If all your SCSI devices are hard drives, then the ROM chip on the SCSI host adapter provides all the BIOS you need. A program on the ROM chip runs during the boot process, detecting the SCSI hard drives and initializing the BIOS needed to communicate with them. SCSI devices can be just about anything, however, and not just hard drives. Although the SCSI scan program will detect devices other than hard drives, it does not know how to talk to them. The ROM chips on SCSI host adapters, with rare exceptions, know how to talk only to hard drives. In order to get the BIOS for other SCSI devices, you will most likely need to load device drivers.

Unfortunately, not all device drivers play well together, and their incompatibility plagued early SCSI devices. Sometimes two device drivers simply could not be made to work together. Machines would lock up, reboot spontaneously, or simply give bizarre, seemingly unrelated errors because of incompatible device drivers. To solve this problem, a new standard evolved: *advanced SCSI programmer interface* (ASPI).

ASPI mandates a standard way to write BIOS device drivers for SCSI devices. The beauty of ASPI is that you can install a standardized set of device drivers for all your SCSI devices. Because they are all ASPI drivers, you can be confident that the drivers for a SCSI removable media drive and a SCSI scanner will work well together. Although there have been several "flavors" of ASPI, Adaptec's EZ-SCSI® is an excellent example.

With Adaptec's EZ-SCSI, the host adapter requires its own device driver. Additional devices require additional EZ-SCSI device drivers, although some devices can share a single device's drivers. For example, the EZ-SCSI driver ASPIDSK.SYS supports both removable media drives (for example, an Iomega Zip drive) and traditional SCSI hard drives as long as the ROM chip on the host adapter has been disabled. The ability to use a single device driver for more than one device makes ASPI products such as EZ-SCSI extremely attractive from a memory-management perspective.

Windows 9*x* and Windows 2000 have a complete copy of protected-mode, built-in ASPI drivers. With Windows 9*x* or 2000, as long as the physical connections are all correct, an ASPI-compliant device will automatically be recognized by the system, making the old DOS-based ASPI drivers nearly a dead issue.

Two situations keep the issue of SCSI device drivers alive and necessary for techs to know: startup disks and new technology. If you open the CONFIG.SYS of a Windows 98 startup disk, for example, you will see ASPI drivers for host adapters and CD-ROMs. These drivers enable the startup disk to see a SCSI CD-ROM. Here are some ASPI driver lines from a Windows 98 startup disk. The lines not related to SCSI devices have been removed. The first four lines are for host adapters; the last one is for a SCSI CD-ROM.

```
DEVICE=ASPI2DOS.SYS
DEVICE=ASPI8DOS.SYS
DEVICE=ASPI4DOS.SYS
DEVICE=ASPI8U2.SYS
DEVICE=ASPICD.SYS /D:OEMCD001
```

ASPI drivers also come into play when dealing with new or improved technology and Windows 9*x* or Windows 2000. Even though both operating systems have exhaustive sets of ASPI drivers, many SCSI devices require improved ASPI drivers to reach their full functionality. The Iomega ZIP drive provides a great example. All versions of Windows come with support for Zip drives, but Iomega provides enhanced ASPI drivers that enable you to do neat extras, such as write protection and password protection. Figure 13-27 shows two examples of a SCSI Zip drive in My Computer under Windows 2000. The My Computer on the left shows the default Windows support—not very interesting. The My Computer on the right, in contrast, shows the same drive after installing the special Iomega drivers. Not only do I get a pretty icon, but I also get a lot of extra functions when I alternate-click on the drive! Note the special Iomega features on the system with the enhanced driver; these do not appear with the default Windows drivers.

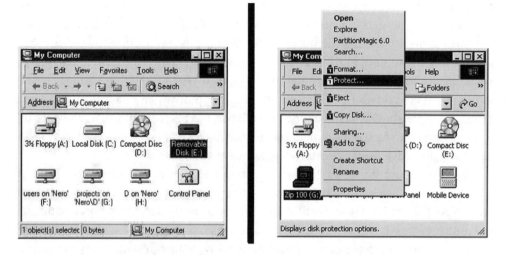

**Figure 13-27** Two views of a SCSI Zip drive with default and special drivers installed

## SCSI Performance

Which can move more cars more quickly—a ten-lane freeway or a four-lane city street? That sums up the effect of the expansion bus on SCSI performance. SCSI is a bus-mastering device; that is, it takes control of the expansion bus to transfer data from one device into memory or from one device to another device not on the SCSI host adapter. This is marvelous because it frees up the CPU to do more important things.

Unfortunately, if you plug a SCSI host adapter into an ISA slot, the best transfer speed you can obtain is approximately 5MBps. Such a transfer rate cannot keep up with modern drives, although slower devices, such as Zip drives or tape backup units, should do fine.

If you really want to see things fly, however, then you need a PCI SCSI host adapter. These buses can support transfers up to 33MBps, the current sustained transfer rates for the fastest hard drives.

## Compatibility Among Flavors of SCSI

Although it might seem unlikely that the various flavors of SCSI would be able to communicate through the same host adapter, that is exactly the case. Each device communicates at the maximum speed supported by that device. Mixing LVD and SE devices, however, provides the biggest exception to this rule. If you add one SE device to an LVD chain, the whole chain slows down to accommodate the slower device.

# Compatibility with IDE

Contrary to a persistent tech myth, you can mix IDE and SCSI hard drives and devices in a single system and the system will work fine. If you have an IDE drive present on your system, it will most probably be the boot drive. Unless the system has a BIOS that enables SCSI drives to boot before the IDE drives, all IDE drives will get a logical drive letter before the SCSI drives. Most current motherboards provide that option.

There are a number of methods of mixing IDE and SCSI. The first is the easiest: don't mix them. Use either IDE or SCSI, not both. The second method is to use the default boot method and let the SCSI drives get their drive letters after the IDE. Last, if the BIOS allows, you can let the SCSI drive(s) boot first. This last method is very system specific. Many motherboards enable you to swap SCSI and EIDE so the former drives get drive letters before the latter drives. If you want to make a SCSI drive the boot drive, you simply make a quick switch in CMOS. Some older motherboards had a "SCSI-first BIOS" that enabled the first SCSI drive to boot as C:, but then assigned drive letters to all IDE drives before getting the rest of the SCSI drives. This could lead to some wacky drive-lettering issues. You might have to play around with a system to get the drive lettering the way you want it.

## Repair and Troubleshooting

SCSI problems can be reduced to certain categories, some of which overlap and not all of which apply to every problem.

## Power and Connectivity

In any PC repair scenario, confirm connectivity and power before going any further. Nothing will work if the devices do not have power and if they cannot access the external data bus and address bus. Fortunately, most SCSI host adapters provide an excellent utility for determining whether or not devices are properly powered and connected: SCSI scan. As the host adapter initializes (provided that the host adapter's BIOS is active), a list of all the devices detected by the host adapter will be displayed on the screen. If one or more of your devices fails to appear, power or connectivity are the most likely problems. If the devices are not properly hooked up, they will not respond to the "identify yourself" commands sent out by the host adapter.

### Power

What kinds of power problems could prevent a device from showing up? It's usually nothing more exotic than forgetting to plug it in. Make sure that both internal and external devices have power. Most SCSI devices, especially external ones, require power in order to provide termination, and all of them require power for operation.

## Connectivity

Make sure that the devices are properly installed. Is the termination set properly (one terminator at each end of the chain and none in between)? Does each device have its own unique SCSI ID? Are the cables seated correctly and firmly? You'll probably need documentation to double-check settings for termination and SCSI IDs.

## Boot Firmware

If you do not see a SCSI scan during the boot process before you see "Starting DOS" or "Starting Windows 98," check to make sure that the ROM BIOS on the host adapter has not been disabled. In addition, other CMOS and SCSI ROM BIOS settings can cause problems. Is the ROM chip on the SCSI host adapter enabled or disabled? What IRQ, DMA, and I/O address is the card using? If you see an "HDD controller failure" or "HDD failure" message, is the CMOS set up to look for an IDE drive that is not present in the system?

## Memory Chips

Problems with memory chips will usually cause problems with all the devices in a PC, not just the SCSI devices. Diagnose problems carefully. Does the symptom, whatever it happens to be, crop up only when using SCSI devices, or does it happen consistently with every device?

## Storage

SCSI hard drives can have the same types of problems as any other hard drive. The partitions and file system—FAT or NTFS—are no different than with IDE drives. In fact, except for the SCSI interface itself, IDE and SCSI drives are virtually identical. For the most part, the same repair and maintenance techniques apply. At a bare minimum, use ScanDisk (Check Disk in Windows 2000) and Defrag on a regular basis. For any error that ends in "Abort, retry, fail" or "Abort, retry, fail, ignore," use a program such as Norton's Disk Doctor or its equivalent. Use the SYS command and the FDISK /MBR command for boot problems. Treat SCSI hard-drive errors the same way you treat IDE hard-drive errors.

## I/O

Certain legacy SCSI host adapters may have resource conflicts with other legacy cards and even a few *Plug and Play* (PnP) cards, although Windows 9x and 2000 do a good job avoiding such problems. IRQ, DMA, and I/O address problems usually manifest themselves fairly quickly. Many legacy SCSI host adapters default to IRQ3, for example, which would cause an IRQ lockup with any device using COM2 (often a modem or mouse). Remember also that many legacy host adapters store resource settings on an onboard chip, so power surges occasionally reset them to their default settings. If a SCSI host adapter suddenly loses its configuration settings, a quick check in Device Manager will always show that the device has a problem. Just rerun the onboard configuration to fix the problem.

This problem is not limited to legacy host adapters! Some PnP SCSI host adapters also store information on an onboard chip. My brand new, ultra wide SCSI host adapter, for example, needs its termination set via its onboard settings. A recent power surge erased all my onboard data, and I had to rerun the setup just to reset the termination.

Proper documentation of these settings for all your legacy devices is the best way to avoid problems. If you don't have it, create your own. Use the F8 key to step through CONFIG.SYS and AUTOEXEC.BAT one line at a time. Many legacy device drivers report their settings as they load. Look at jumper settings. Use a PDI or Discovery card to check for IRQ and DMA usage.

## Device Drivers

If you have SCSI devices other than hard drives, they will require a device driver. Remember that some device drivers do not work well together, especially if you have a mix of legacy and PnP cards in a system. How do you determine if you have a conflict between two device drivers? Try loading only the device drivers for the SCSI devices. Does the symptom still occur? If not, then another device driver is causing the problem. Use the F8 key to determine which one. Once you know which device drivers are incompatible, you have several options. Look in the manuals or readme files of both devices. Your problem might be a known one with a solution. If the device driver is an executable, try running it with the /? option, which will usually show you a variety of command-line switches (for example, MOUSE.EXE /?). Try a variety of switches and see if any of them solve the problem. If not, attempt to find an updated driver for one or both of the devices. If none of those solutions fix the problem, you might be forced to choose between the devices or go to a multiple-boot configuration.

## Cost and Benefits

SCSI is great for the following:

- File servers
- Workstations (both graphical and audio)
- Multitasking systems
- Any system moving large amounts of data among peripheral devices
- Any system with a large number of peripherals
- Any system requiring fault tolerance (mostly file servers)

Because the initial cost of SCSI is higher and the devices themselves are also more expensive, you must answer some questions to determine the need for SCSI:

- Is this a graphics/CAD workstation?

- Is this a network file server?

- Is this a stand-alone machine frequently running multitasking applications?

If the answer to any of the previous questions is "yes," then it will probably be worth the money to invest in SCSI for two reasons. First, a data-intensive application such as CAD/CAM design software will benefit by the increased data throughput available with SCSI devices, especially hard drives and scanners. Second, SCSI is a bus-mastering device. In a multitasking environment, this leaves the CPU free to handle more important things, such as updating an Excel spreadsheet.

## SCSI vs. EIDE

SCSI no longer has as large an advantage over IDE for typical systems as it once did. For many years, SCSI hard drives were the only large hard drives available. Now EIDE drives are pushing into the sizes that once belonged exclusively to SCSI drives. Data throughput for EIDE has also increased to as fast as 100MBps. Although SCSI-3 might support a transfer rate of 360MBps or more, remember that except for the chipset on the disk controller card, IDE and SCSI hard drives are made the same. So the limitation in data transfer speeds comes from the hard-drive assembly, not necessarily the data bus.

Although SCSI's advantages in some areas are not as pronounced as they once were, it still possesses a number of advantages that justify its higher cost. The bus-mastering capability makes SCSI ideal for data-intensive operations. In addition, for external devices that are not hard drives, SCSI remains the high-performance interface of choice. Finally, higher-end parallel SCSI supports up to 15 devices on a single controller, and serial SCSI standards support dramatically more. For servers that need huge data storage capacity, SCSI is the only way to go. For personal systems, in contrast, you can easily and inexpensively add an ATA/100 controller card and attach up to four more hard drives.

## Last Notes on Termination

Termination can be one of four flavors, depending on the type of SCSI chain: passive, active, forced perfect, and LVD termination.

Passive termination is a holdover from the dinosaur days of the ST-506. The termination is nothing more than a network of resistors. The resistors are usually small, black, and shiny, resembling very skinny black caterpillars. This type of termination is typically found only on plain old, 8-bit SCSI devices.

For the quicker fast/wide SCSI, you have to maintain a tighter tolerance on the voltage and impedance of the SCSI chain. To do this, you must use active termination, which uses voltage regulators instead of resistors.

*Forced perfect termination* (FPT) also maintains the correct voltage level on the bus, but does so to a finer tolerance by using *diodes*. These diodes function like a resistor in the passive termination, with one exception: A diode has a lower resistance in one direction, or orientation, than it does in the other. This is called *polarity*. The higher resistance in one direction helps to block current flow backward along the data cable much better than a plain resistor.

LVD SCSI requires its own style of active terminators. This is true even if you have SE devices on the same chain.

# Beyond A+

If you want a peek at some of the upcoming SCSI standards or want to go deeper into issues of high-end SCSI, you can check out the Web sites of the SCSI Trade Association (**http://www.scita.org/**) and the T-10 (SCSI standards umbrella group) (**http://www.t10.org/**). Both sites offer plenty of links to detailed discussions about thrilling subjects, such as 2GBps data transfer rate fibre channel, RAID arrays with SCSI, and cool things like expanders. *Expanders* are devices that enable you to extend the range of a SCSI chain to double or even triple the stated maximum. Another great site with lots of resources available is the Paralan Corporation site (**http://www.paralan.org/**). Definitely check out their SCSI glossary.

## Review Questions

1. Judy is worried that her SCSI chain may be too long to work properly. What is the maximum length for narrow and normal (slow) SCSI-2 chains?

   A. 0.5 meter

   B. 1 meter

   C. 3 meters

   D. 6 meters

2. SCSI devices can be classified into two groups. What are they?

   A. Stand-alone

   B. Internal

   C. External

   D. Variable

3. One of the differences between SCSI and IDE is

   A. SCSI hard drives are much larger and faster.

   B. The red stripe on the SCSI cable always goes toward the Molex power connector.

   C. If a SCSI cable is on the device incorrectly, the device can be damaged. In IDE drives the device, if cabled incorrectly, will not be damaged.

   D. The interface to the computer is the only difference.

4. Which of the following statements are true about SCSI IDs? (Select all that apply.)

   A. They must follow the SCSI chain in sequence.

   B. There is no physical order requirement for the use of SCSI IDs.

   C. The device itself is where the SCSI IDs are set, either by jumpers and shunts or DIP switches.

   D. The host adapter dynamically assigns SCSI IDs for the device when its ROM is enacted on booting the system.

5. Dave wants to boot to his SCSI hard drive. What ID must he use for the drive?

   A. He must set it to the highest possible ID.

   B. He should set it to one ID lower than any EIDE drives in the system.

   C. He needs to set it to whatever the host adapter requires.

   D. It doesn't matter; the system looks for the active partition.

6. It is imperative that SCSI chains

   A. Have at least three devices.

   B. Have terminators at each end of the chain.

   C. Have *Logical Unit Numbers* (LUNs) assigned to the devices.

   D. Have terminators on each individual device.

7. Which of the following is not always a valid SCSI connector?

   A. A 50-pin Centronics

   B. A 50-pin HD D-type

   C. A 68-pin HD D-type

   D. A 25-pin parallel

8. Edwina wants to add a CD-ROM drive to her system. She plugs it into the SCSI host adapter, sets the termination properly, and boots up the system. The host adapter does not recognize the CD-ROM. What did Edwina forget to do?

    A. Install ASPI drivers.

    B. Turn off the host adapter's ROM.

    C. Verify that the CD-ROM has a unique SCSI ID.

    D. Nothing. She just needs to boot two more times for the CD-ROM to kick in.

9. Serial SCSI is part of which SCSI standard?

    A. SCSI-1

    B. SCSI-2

    C. Ultra SCSI

    D. SCSI-3

10. How many devices can narrow SCSI-2 support, including the host adapter?

    A. Six

    B. Seven

    C. Eight

    D. Nine

## Answers

1. **D.** Narrow, slow SCSI has a maximum chain length of 6 meters.

2. **B and C.** All SCSI devices are either internal or external.

3. **C.** Improperly connecting a SCSI device may destroy that device, whereas IDE devices are much more tolerant of poor connections.

4. **B and C.** SCSI IDs may be used in any order and SCSI devices' IDs are set on the device itself.

5. **C.** Most SCSI host adapters reserve ID 0 for bootable devices, but this setting usually can be changed. IBM adapters traditionally reserve ID 6 for bootable devices. The key factor, however, is to match the drive ID to the host adapter setting.

6. **B.** All SCSI chains must be terminated on both ends.

7. **D.** Some SCSI devices use a 25-pin connector that looks exactly like a parallel connector. Don't mix the two!

8. **C.** The CD-ROM and the host adapter are almost certainly using the same SCSI ID.

9. **D.** Serial SCSI is part of the SCSI-3 standard.

10. **C.** Narrow SCSI-2 supports a maximum of eight devices.

# CD Media

In this chapter, you will

- Learn about the different types of CD media
- Learn to install a CD media drive

## Historical/Conceptual

I like to use the term *CD media* as an umbrella term for all the nifty devices that use those shiny, 12-cm wide discs that, if you're a slob like me, collect around your PCs like pizza boxes in a fraternity house. CD stands for *compact disc* and was originally designed over 20 years ago as a replacement for vinyl records. The CD now reigns as the primary method of long-term storage for sound, video, and data. CD media used to be called "CD-ROMs" (Compact Disc-Read-Only Memory), but these little high-capacity beauties now cover a number of new technologies with names such as CD-R, CD-RW, and DVD. Each of these technologies will be discussed in detail in this chapter. But for now, appreciate the fact that although CD media covers a number of different exciting formats, they all basically boil down to the same physical media.

Consider the overall Zen of CD media. Get into a Lotus position, relax, and "find your center." Consider a world without CD media. This technology of high-capacity, tough, easy-to-make discs helped to move the computing world forward by breaking it free from relatively small, floppy-installed applications to the much larger-scale applications available today. It is interesting to speculate on the path of application software if CDs hadn't come along when they did. Would we still be using 1.44MB floppies? Would we need hundreds of floppies to install the software that CDs so beautifully handle with only one disc? At the very least, software complexity would not even approach its current levels without the cheap, large-capacity CD-ROM.

The best way to begin understanding the world of CDs is to sort out the many types of technologies available. Let's begin by looking at the original CD technology: CD-ROMs.

## CD-ROM

As most of us know, CDs didn't begin life in computers. Phillips and Sony developed CDs in the late 1970s and unveiled the technology in 1980 as a replacement for vinyl records. This is the audio CD technology available in all the music stores—still the same today as it was over 20 years ago. Audio compact discs store up to 74 minutes of high-quality sound, and their high data density, random access capability (you can jump to any spot easily), small size, and great sound make them the most popular way to store music today. It didn't take computer folks long to figure out that the same technology that enabled you to listen to the *Best of the Monkees* could be used to store computer data as well. CD-ROM drives soon appeared on the PC.

### How CD-ROMs Work

CD-ROMs store data using microscopic pits burned into a glass master CD-ROM with a powerful laser. Once the CD-ROM producer creates a master, expensive machines create plastic copies made using a very high-tolerance injection molding process. The copies are coated with a reflective metallic coating, and then coated with lacquer for protection. CD-ROMs only store data on one side of the disc—we don't "flip" a CD-ROM as we used to flip vinyl records. The data on a CD-ROM is near the "top" of the CD-ROM, where the label is located (Figure 14-1).

Many people believe that scratching a CD-ROM on the bottom makes it unreadable. This is untrue. If you scratch a CD-ROM on the bottom (the shiny side), polish out the scratches (assuming that they aren't too deep) and re-read the CD. A number of companies sell inexpensive CD-ROM polishing kits. It's the scratches on the top of the disc that wreak havoc on CD-ROMs. Avoid writing on the top with anything other than a soft pen, and certainly don't scratch the top!

CD-ROM drives use a laser and mirrors to read the data off of the CD-ROM. The metallic covering of the CD-ROM makes a highly reflective surface. The pits don't allow reflection, creating binary 1's, and the non-pitted spots make binary 0's. It's actually a little more complicated than this, but you get the idea! These pits are densely packed on the CD-ROM, enabling a vast amount of data to be stored. A CD-ROM can hold 5.2 billion bits or 650 million bytes of data.

**Figure 14-1**
Location of the data

## CD-ROM Formats

CD-ROMs need defined formats for different jobs in the same way hard drives need file formats like FAT16, FAT32, and NTFS. The first CD-ROMs, and all music CD-ROMs, organized the music in a special format called *CD-Digital Audio* (CD-DA), which we usually just call CD-Audio. CD-Audio divides the CD's data into variable length tracks; on music CDs, each songs gets one track. CD-Audio is an excellent way to store music but lacks any error checking, making it a terrible way to store data! Sure, your Rolling Stones CD can miss a few bits and you'd probably never even know it happened. Try copying an EXE file from a CD-ROM that skips a few bits; the system will lock up like a stone the moment you try to run that EXE file.

To store data on a CD-ROM required error checking. This brought forward the next CD-ROM format—ISO-9660. This format is also called "High Sierra" or as many people rather nebulously call it, "CD-ROM" format. The vast majority of data CD-ROMs use this format. If you go to the local software store to purchase a program, the CD in the box uses this format.

Most CD-ROM drives support a number of other formats besides CD-ROM and CD-Audio. Most folks live out their lives blissfully unaware of all these formats until they purchase a new CD-ROM drive and decide to look on the side of the box to see something like Figure 14-2.

Don't panic; with few exceptions, these formats have fallen pretty much by the wayside. Even though most of the formats go unused, three that actually made some inroads deserve quick mention. First is *CD Interactive* (CD-I), developed to enable one CD to store both sound and video and enable simultaneous playback. The idea behind CD-I was to have a machine—a CD-I player—that had all of the necessary electronics to play the CD-ROM. It was a small step to develop PCs with CD-ROM drives that could also play CD-I CD-ROMs.

**Figure 14-2**
What are all these?

## Creative PC-DVD™ 12X drive:

- Maximum transfer rate of 16.2MB/second (12X) for DVD-ROM data** and 6,000KB/second (40X) for CD-ROM data

- Average access times of 110ms (CD) and 130ms (DVD)

- 512KB buffer

- Supports DVD-ROM, CD-Audio, CD-I, CD Extra, CD-ROM, CD-ROM/XA, Photo CD®, CD-R, CD-RW, Video CD, DVD-Video, and Digital Audio Extraction

Second is CD-ROM/XA. CD-ROM/XA is little more than a specialized format that takes most of the interesting aspects of CD-I. Like CD-I, most CD-ROM drives support CD-ROM/XA, even though few CD-ROMs use the format.

Last is Kodak's Photo-CD format, a compressed format that stores many photos on one CD-ROM. Kodak sees the CD-ROM replacing the paper photograph for a broad section of existing computer users. They visualized that a person would purchase a Photo-CD "reader" in the same way one would get a CD-I reader. Most CD-ROM drives can also read Photo-CDs, however, assuming that the proper software is loaded. While CD-I, CD-ROM/XA, and a number of other formats have fallen out of favor, Photo-CD still enjoys a fairly good following. Fortunately, all but the earliest CD-ROM drives easily read all these formats, making the issue of formats for CD-ROMs basically moot (Figure 14-3).

## Test Specific

### MPC

The term "MPC" is used in regard to CD-ROMs. MPC stands for *Multimedia Personal Computer*, and it defines a set of minimum standards for multimedia systems. Established in 1991, MPC has been so far outclassed by current hardware that it no longer really has any meaning in the PC world. MPC3, the last version of MPC, defined the following minimums for a multimedia PC:

**Figure 14-3**
A typical CD-ROM drive can read almost every type of CD format.

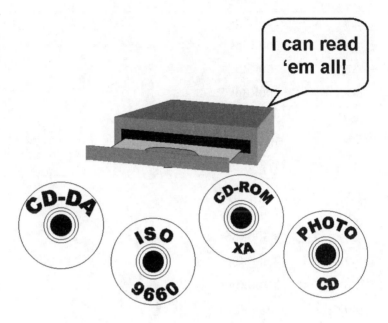

- 8MB RAM

- 540MB disc drive

- 75 MHz Pentium Processor

- 4× CD-ROM

- MPEG support (MPEG is a compression standard for audio and video)

## CD-ROM Speeds

The first CD-ROM drives processed data at roughly 150,000 bytes per second (150KBps), copying the speed from the original CD-Audio format. Although this speed is excellent for listening to music, the CD-ROM industry quickly recognized that installing programs or transferring files off of a CD-ROM at 150KBps was the electronic equivalent of watching paint dry. So, since the day the first CD-ROM drives for PCs hit the market, there has been a desire to speed them up to increase their data throughput. Each increase in speed is measured in multiples of the original 150KBps drives and are given an "×" to show their speed relative to the first (1×) drives. Here's a list of the common CD-ROM speeds, including most of the early speeds that are no longer produced:

| | |
|---|---|
| 1× | 150KBps |
| 2× | 300KBps |
| 3× | 450KBps |
| 4× | 600KBps |
| 6× | 900KBps |
| 8× | 1,200KBps |
| 10× | 1,500KBps |
| 12× | 1,800KBps |
| 16× | 2,400KBps |
| 24× | 3,600KBps |
| 32× | 4,800KBps |
| 36× | 5,400KBps |
| 40× | 6,000KBps |
| 48× | 7,200KBps |
| 52× | 7,800KBps |
| 60× | 9,000KBps |
| 72× | 10,800KBps |

Keep in mind that these speeds are maximums and are rarely met in real-life operation. You can count on a 32× drive reading data faster than an 8× drive. As multipliers continue to increase, however, so many other factors come into play that telling the difference between a 24× and a 32× drive, for example, becomes difficult. However, high-speed CD-ROMs are so inexpensive that we buy them anyway—at least installations will go faster!

## CD-R

The process of making CD-ROMs requires specialized, expensive equipment and substantial expertise, leaving the creation of CD-ROMs to a relatively small number of CD-ROM production companies. Yet, since the day the first CD-ROMs came to market, demand has been terrific for a way that the normal PC user could "burn" his own CD-ROMs. The CD industry made a number of attempts to create a technology that would let users create their own CD-ROMs. For years, a number of different *Write Once Read Many* (WORM) CD technologies appeared and then died, usually because of outrageously high equipment costs.

In the mid-1990s, the CD industry introduced the *CD Recordable* (CD-R) standard, which enables inexpensive CD-R drives, often referred to as *CD burners*, to add data to special CD-R discs. Any CD-ROM drive can then read the data stored on the CD-R, and all CD-R drives can read regular CD-ROMs. CD-R discs come in two varieties: a 74-minute disc that holds approximately 650MB, and an 80-minute variety that holds approximately 700MB (Figure 14-4). A CD-R burner must be specifically designed to support the longer 80-minute CD-R format, something that currently only a minority of CD-R drives do.

**Figure 14-4**
The packaging of 74- and 80-minute CD-Rs clearly displays the capacity of the discs.

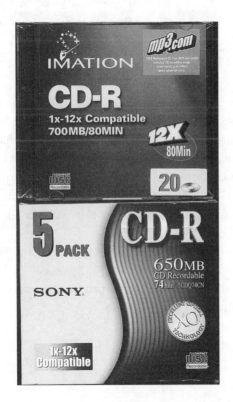

CD-R discs function similarly to regular CD-ROMs, although the chemicals used to make them produce a brightly colored recording side on almost all CD-R discs. CD-ROM discs, in contrast, have a silver recording side.

CD-R drives record data using special organic dyes embedded into the disc. This dye gives the CD-R its distinctive bottom color. CD-R burners have a second "burn" laser, roughly ten times as powerful as the "read" laser that heats the organic dye, causing a change in the reflectivity of the surface, creating the functional equivalent to a CD-ROM's pits (Figure 14-5).

**Figure 14-5**
CD-R vs. CD-ROM

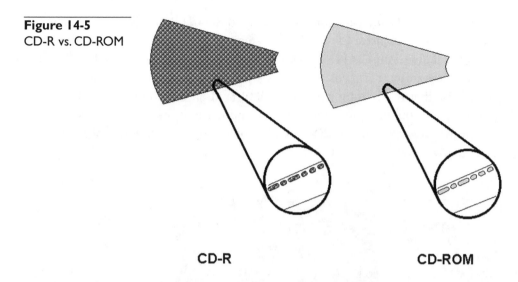

**CD-R**                                    **CD-ROM**

Once the CD-R drive burns data onto a CD-R, the data cannot be erased or changed short of destroying the disc itself. Early CD-R drives required that the entire disc be burned in one burn session, wasting any unused part of the CD-R disc. These are called *single-session drives*. Almost all modern CD-R drives enable you to go back and burn additional data onto the CD-R disc until the disc is full. These are *multisession* drives. Multisession drives also have the ability to "close" a partially-filled CD-R so that no more data may be burned onto that disc.

CD-R drives have two speeds that matter: the record speed and the read speed. These speeds manifest themselves as multiples of the 150KBps speed of the original CD-ROM drives. The record speed, which is always listed first, is always equal to or slower than the read speed. Some common CD-R speeds are

| | |
|---|---|
| $2 \times 2$ | $4 \times 24$ |
| $2 \times 4$ | $8 \times 32$ |
| $4 \times 4$ | $10 \times 32$ |
| $4 \times 8$ | $16 \times 32$ |

A CD-R drive looks exactly like a regular CD-ROM drive in Windows *9x* and Windows NT/2000. Windows displays a CD-R drive in My Computer with the typical CD-ROM icon, for example, and assigns it a drive letter like a CD-ROM drive. If you want to put data onto a CD-R disc, however, you need special *burner* software to burn that data onto the disc. Almost every new CD-R drive comes with some type of burner software, so you rarely need to go out and buy burner software unless you have a special preference for a particular brand. Figure 14-6 shows the opening menu of the popular Adaptec Easy CD Creator burning program.

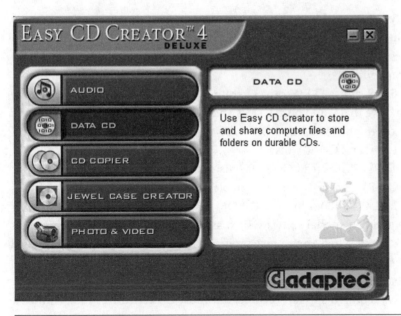

**Figure 14-6**   Adaptec Easy CD Creator CD burning program

For all their power, CD-R drives have virtually disappeared from the market. Notice I did not say CD-R *discs* have disappeared; more CD-R discs get burned now than ever before. Just as CD-R drives could both burn CD-R discs and read CD-ROMs, a new type of drive called CD-RW has appeared. CD-RW reads regular CD-ROMs, burns CD-Rs, and adds something totally new!

## CD-RW

Everyone loves CD-R, but it has some limitations. I generally use CD-R discs for archival storage. When I complete a book, for example, I put the original text and graphics on a couple of CD-R discs for permanent historical reference. But sometimes I want to change the data on my CDs. As I create the contents for the CD that accompanies this book, I may decide to drop an item. That's impossible with a CD-R. However, the new *CD ReWrite* (CD-RW) format takes CD media to the ultimate point of becoming basically a 650MB floppy disk. Once again, CD-RW discs look exactly like CD-ROM discs, with the exception of a colored bottom side.

CD-RW works by utilizing a laser to heat an amorphous (non-crystalline) substance that, when cooled, slowly becomes crystalline. The crystalline areas are reflective, whereas the amorphous areas are not.

The first CD-RW discs could not be read by regular CD-ROM drives, but the CD industry quickly introduced a method called MultiRead that enables CD-ROM drives to read CD-RW discs. All CD-ROM drives manufactured since around January of 2000 have MultiRead capability.

Because both CD-R and CD-RW drives require a powerful laser, it was a simple process to make a drive that could burn CD-Rs and CD-RWs, making plain CD-R drives disappear almost overnight. Why buy a CD-R drive when a comparably priced CD-RW drive could burn CD-R and CD-RW discs?

Even though CD-RW drives read CD-ROM discs, many systems have both a regular CD-ROM and a CD-RW drive. This setup enables them to make fast copies of CD-ROMs. You can place a CD-ROM in the CD-ROM drive and a CD-R or CD-RW disc in the CD-RW drive and run special software such as Adaptec's DiskCopy to create exact replicas of the CD-ROM. When I buy a new program on CD, the first thing I do is make a backup copy, then I stash the original under lock and key. If I break, melt, or otherwise destroy the backup, I quickly create a new one from the original.

The first CD-RWs required special software, but most CD-RW drives today utilize a function called *packet writing* under a special format called *Universal Data Format* (UDF), which gives true drag-and-drop capabilities to CD-RW drives.

CD-RW drive specs have three multiplier values. The first shows the CD-R write speed, the second shows the CD-RW rewrite speed, and the third shows the read speed. Write, rewrite, and read speeds vary tremendously among the various brands of CD-RW drives; here are just a few representative samples:

$2 \times 2 \times 24$

$4 \times 2 \times 20$

$4 \times 4 \times 24$

$8 \times 4 \times 32$

$12 \times 10 \times 32$

CD-RW drives fill functional areas that CD-R drives could not do nearly as well. The best example is backups—not the archival "put it on the disc and stash it in the closet" type backup, but rather the daily/weekly backups that most of us do for our systems. Using CD-R discs for these backups is wasteful; once a disc fills up you throw it away at the next backup. But with CD-RW, you can use the same set of CD-RW discs time and again to perform backups.

## Music CDs

Computers do not hold a monopoly on CD-burning. Many companies offer consumer CD burners that work with your stereo system. These come in a wide variety of formats but usually come as a dual-deck player/recorder combination (Figure 14-7).

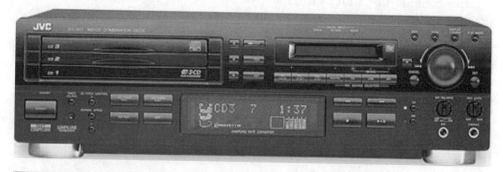

**Figure 14-7**   CD recorder

These recorders do not use regular CD-R or CD-RW discs. Instead, under U.S. law, these home recorders must use a slightly different disc called Music CD-R. Makers of Music CD-Rs pay a small royalty for each CD (and add it to your price). You can record to a Music CD-R, but you cannot record *from* one—the idea being to restrict duplication. If you decide to buy one of these burners, make sure to buy the Music CD-Rs (Figure 14-8).

**Figure 14-8**
Music CD-R

## Installing CD Media Drives

From ten feet away, CD-ROM, CD-R, and CD-RW drives look absolutely identical. Figure 14-9 shows a CD-ROM, CD-R, and CD-RW drive. Can you tell them apart?

In case you were wondering, the CD-R is on the top, the CD-ROM is in the center and the CD-RW is on the bottom. If you look closely at a CD media drive, they usually advertise their function with a small stamp on the front or with text on the label of the CD media's case (Figures 14-10 and 14-11).

**Figure 14-9**
Hey! Which one is
which?

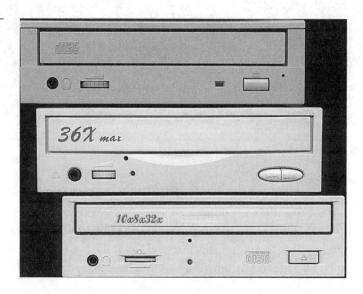

**Figure 14-10**
Stamp on front

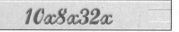

With the exception of some very early CD-ROM drives, all CD media drives come as either ATAPI or SCSI drives, making installation a snap. The following examples use CD-ROM drives, but the installation process applies to all CD media drives.

## Connections

A CD-ROM drive needs to be connected to a PC in order to operate. Since their inception, CD-ROMs in PCs have gone through a fascinating series of controllers and connections, leading to the fast yet simple connections used today. Let's look at these, starting with the first, proprietary connectors.

**Figure 14-11**
Text on label

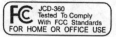

CD-Rewriteable
Model No: CCD-955
10x8x32x

This device complies with Part 15 of the FCC Rules.
Operation is subject to the following two conditions:
(1) this device may not cause harmful interference,
and (2) this device must accept any interference
received, including interference that may cause
undesired operation.

COMPLIES WITH FDA RADIATION PERFORMANCE
STANDARDS. 21 CFR SUBCHAPTER J.

## Proprietary

When the first CD-ROMs began to appear in the early 1990s, no standard connection existed to make them work in a PC. The first CD-ROM makers were compelled to provide their own controllers. The first generation of CD-ROM controllers could be broken down into three groups: Panasonic (also called Creative or MKE), Sony, and Mitsumi. Although these controllers operated acceptably well, the fact that they were proprietary—combined with the fact that they looked extremely similar—made them difficult to use and change. One early adopter of CD-ROM controllers was Creative Labs. Creative Labs saw CD-ROMs as a natural complement to their sound cards. To that end, they began to sell sound cards with CD-ROM controllers built into them. One measure of the frustration of the time was the Creative Labs "Multi-CD" sound card that had three separate CD-ROM controllers—one of each of the popular proprietary types—so this sound card could communicate with any CD-ROM drive you used (Figure 14-12).

## ATAPI

The onset of the ATAPI standard (see the discussion of hard drives in Chapter 8) made virtually all of the proprietary controllers obsolete overnight. Instead of having dedicated connectors and unique drivers, ATAPI treats a CD-ROM exactly as though it were an EIDE drive. ATAPI CD-ROMs have regular 40-pin IDE connectors and master/slave

**Figure 14-12**  Multi-CD sound card

jumpers. You install them the same way you would install any EIDE hard drive. Like any EIDE drive, you must properly jumper an ATAPI CD-ROM in order for it to operate. They act either as master or slave and run on either the primary or secondary controller. Figure 14-13 shows a typical CD-ROM installation with the CD-ROM running as slave with a hard drive on a system's primary IDE controller.

Unlike EIDE drives, ATAPI drives require no CMOS changes as part of the install process. When the industry first introduced ATAPI drives, techs familiar with hard drive installations swamped the CD-ROM makers' service departments, asking how to set up the drives in CMOS. To reduce these calls, BIOS makers added a CD-ROM option in many CMOS setup utilities, just to give the techs something to do! You can find this

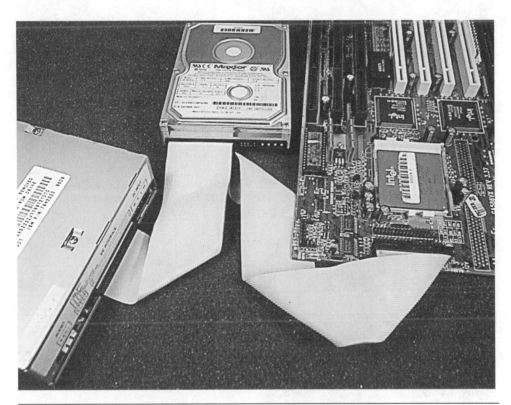

**Figure 14-13**   Typical installation

option (Figure 14-14) in many CMOS setup utilities dated between 1991 and 1996 (with exceptions). This setting actually didn't do anything at all; it just kept users from bothering the CD-ROM makers with silly support calls. Almost no current versions of CMOS provide this option, as the industry assumes that techs now know that they don't need to access CMOS to configure CD-ROM drives. Personally, I wish they had kept it; I still see new techs poking around or running autodetect and wondering why the system doesn't show the CD-ROM drive!

## SCSI

*Small Computer System Interface* (SCSI) (see Chapter 13) predates ATAPI and, although not quite as common, is in many ways a superior way to use CD media, especially CD-ROMs. The SCSI chain enables many CD-ROM drives to be installed on one machine. This is handy for networks that need access to many CD-ROMs. Additionally, the SCSI LUN function makes a SCSI system perfect for CD-ROM "jukeboxes" or "carousels" that store many CD-ROMs and load the requested one as needed (Figure 14-15).

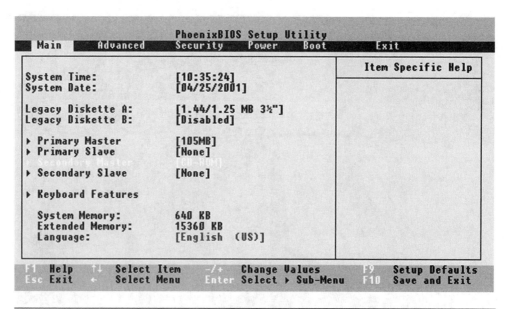

Figure 14-14 Older CMOS showing CD-ROM in drive selection options

**Figure 14-15**
CD-ROM carousel

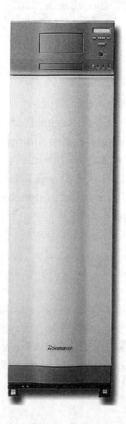

SCSI CD media drives have all the features of any SCSI device. Most SCSI CD media drives use narrow SCSI; the relative speeds of CD media drives and the SCSI bus make wide or fast SCSI overkill. However, some of the newest CD-RWs have moved to wide SCSI.

Like all SCSI devices, SCSI CD media drives need to have a unique SCSI ID and need to be terminated if they are on the end of a SCSI chain. Figure 14-16 shows an internal SCSI CD-ROM with an attached internal cable.

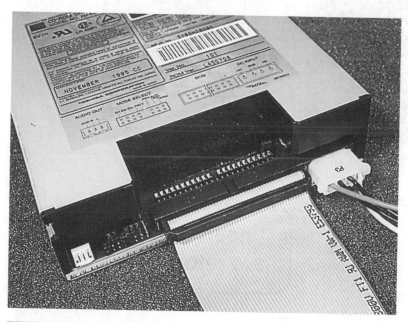

**Figure 14-16**   Internal SCSI

SCSI CD-ROMs are one of the most common external SCSI devices. Figure 14-17 shows the connections for an external SCSI CD-ROM. Note the external terminator.

Once the CD media drive is physically installed, and whatever jumpers the type of connection requires are set correctly, it's time to begin installation of device drivers and support software to make the drive work.

## Device Drivers/Software

CD media drives, like anything else in a PC, need device drivers in order to operate. A CD media drive is a mass storage device like a hard drive. In PCs, the goal is to make the CD media drive look like any other storage device. Basically, the operating system wants to give a CD media drive a drive letter that can be accessed by the OS (Figure 14-18).

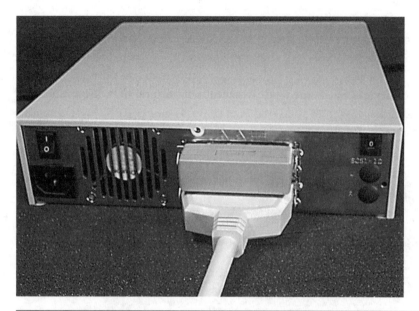

**Figure 14-17**   External SCSI

**Figure 14-18**
I'm recognized!

The process of taking a CD-ROM and turning it into a device visible to the system, with its own drive letter, varies according to the type of CD-ROM connection and the computer's OS. Let's take a look at the device drivers and other programs used by DOS, Windows 9x, and Windows 2000 to make a CD-ROM drive visible to the computer.

## DOS Device Drivers

Although DOS is long gone, it is important to understand how DOS installs device drivers for one huge reason: Windows 9x startup disks still use these tools. A startup disk must recognize the CD drive and provide it a drive letter so that you can load installation or repair CD-ROMs. Windows 98 boot disks configure this automatically, whereas Windows 95 users must specifically set up their startup disk to support the CD-ROM.

I know I used the term "CD-ROM" just now instead of "CD media." Even though you may have a fancy new CD-RW drive, that CD-RW drive still functions perfectly as a CD-ROM drive. In a repair situation, no one cares about burning CDs; they just need a CD-ROM to load files!

**TIP**    Make sure you know how to make a Windows 95 startup disk recognize the CD-ROM!

Microsoft developed a two-step process to install the CD-ROM in DOS. First, a hardware-specific device driver was installed via CONFIG.SYS to create an interface to the CD-ROM. Second, a higher-level, totally hardware non-specific program called MSCDEX was run from the AUTOEXEC.BAT in order to give the CD-ROM a drive letter. The CD-ROM manufacturer provided the CD-ROM's device driver while Microsoft provides a copy of MSCDEX with every version of Windows 9x. Let's look at the configuration steps and files for SCSI and ATAPI drives.

### SCSI DOS Device Drivers

Activating the SCSI CD-ROMs requires two device drivers: the DOS device driver for the host adapter and the DOS ASPI driver for CD-ROMs, ASPICD.SYS. The required /D: option gives the CD-ROMs a system name to which MSCDEX will then assign a drive letter. The name after the /D: has no significance; use /D:CHIMCHIM if you want to— just remember the name! A typical DOS CONFIG.SYS will contain the following at a minimum:

```
DEVICE=C:\DOS\HIMEM.SYS
DEVICE=C:\SCSI\ASPI2DOS.SYS
DEVICE=C:\SCSI\ASPICD.SYS /D:ASPICD
```

A Windows 95 startup disk will already have the HIMEM.SYS line. You will need to locate the ASPI driver for your host adapter and a copy of ASPICD.SYS (every host adapter supplier gives these away), and copy them to the A: drive. A Windows 95 startup disk with support for a SCSI CD-ROM should look like this:

```
DEVICE=A:\HIMEM.SYS
DEVICE=A:\ASPI2DOS.SYS
DEVICE=A:\ASPICD.SYS /D:ASPICD
```

## ATAPI DOS Device Drivers

ATAPI CD-ROMs don't enjoy the high level of standardization of drivers found in SCSI CD-ROMs. But on the flip side, you only need one device driver. Here's a sampling from many different manufacturers. Note that although they may look different from one another, they all still contain the critical /D: option.

```
DEVICE=C:\DEV\ATAPI.SYS /D:SONY_000
DEVICE=C:\NEC_IDE.SYS /D:MSCD001
DEVICE=C:\CDD\WCD.SYS /D:WD_CD-ROM
DEVICE=C:\TSY\TSYCDROM.SYS /D:TSYCD1
DEVICE=C:\DEV\HIT-IDE.SYS /D:MSCD005
DEVICE=C:\MTM\MTMCDAI.SYS /D:MYCD
DEVICE=C:\OAK\OAKCDROM.SYS /D:MSCD001
DEVICE=C:\CDD\WCD.SYS /D:WP_CDROM
```

Many ATAPI device drivers work with virtually any ATAPI CD media device. Search for the popular OAKCDROM.SYS files—numerous Internet locations provide it as a free download. If you have access to a Windows 98 startup disk, copy OAKCDROM.SYS from there. Put the ATAPI CD-ROM driver on the Windows 95 startup disk. A typical Windows 95 startup disk with support for an ATAPI CD-ROM should look like this:

```
DEVICE=A:\HIMEM.SYS
DEVICE=A:\OAKCDROM.SYS /D:MSCD001
```

Assuming that you have copied the files and added the text correctly to the CONFIG.SYS, you should see something like Figure 14-19 during bootup.

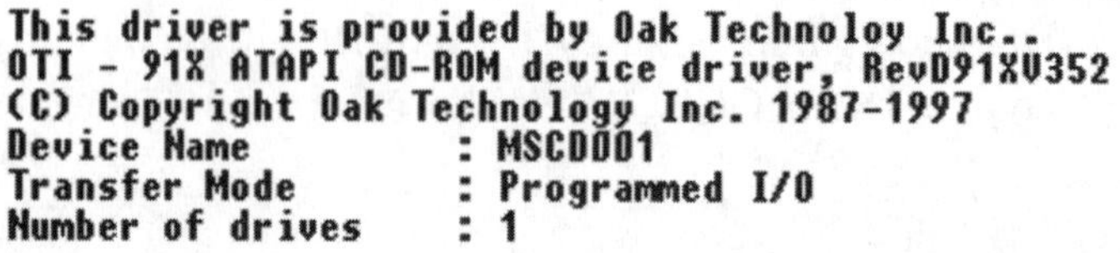

```
This driver is provided by Oak Technoloy Inc..
OTI - 91X ATAPI CD-ROM device driver, RevD91XV352
(C) Copyright Oak Technology Inc. 1987-1997
Device Name        : MSCD001
Transfer Mode      : Programmed I/O
Number of drives   : 1
```

**Figure 14-19** Hey! There's the drive!

## MSCDEX

Once you load the device driver into the CONFIG.SYS file, you then need to place Microsoft's MSCDEX.EXE program into the AUTOEXEC.BAT file. MSCDEX, short for Microsoft CD-ROM Extensions, takes the device name set up in the CD-ROM's device driver line and assigns it a drive letter. Although MSCDEX has many options, the only required one is /D:, to match the /D: name set up in CONFIG.SYS. So, if a device driver line looked like this

```
DEVICE=C:\DEV\HIT-IDE.SYS /D:CHIMCHIM
```

then the MSCDEX line in AUTOEXEC.BAT looks like this:

```
MSCDEX /D:CHIMCHIM
```

Again, there is no significance to the /D: names as long as they match in the driver and MSCDEX. It would work equally well to set up CONFIG.SYS like this:

```
DEVICE=C:\DEV\HIT-IDE.SYS /D:FRED
```

And then set up the MSCDEX line in AUTOEXEC.BAT like this:

```
MSCDEX /D:FRED
```

Make sure to copy the MSCDEX.EXE program from the C:\WINDOWS\COMMAND folder onto the Windows 95 startup disk. Assuming you added the line to the AUTOEXEC.BAT file and remembered to copy the file, you should see what is shown in Figure 14-20.

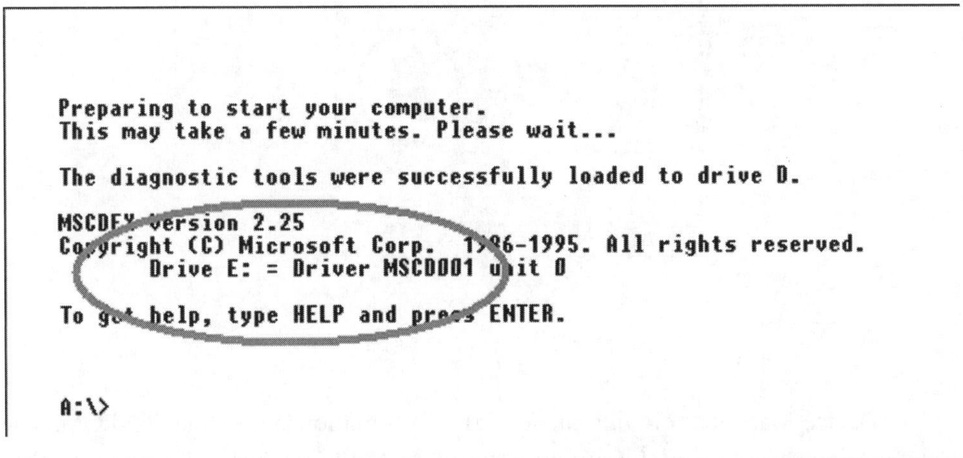

```
Preparing to start your computer.
This may take a few minutes. Please wait...

The diagnostic tools were successfully loaded to drive D.

MSCDEX Version 2.25
Copyright (C) Microsoft Corp.  1986-1995. All rights reserved.
        Drive E: = Driver MSCD001 unit 0

To get help, type HELP and press ENTER.


A:\>
```

**Figure 14-20**   Lovely drive letter!

## Windows 9x and Windows 2000 Device Drivers

Windows 95 has eliminated the inefficiencies of the older DOS/Windows 3.x CD-ROM usage. In particular, MSCDEX has been replaced with the protected-mode *CD File System* (CDFS) driver. Not only is CDFS protected-mode, it is part of the Windows *Installable File System* (IFS) family of cooperative drivers for storage devices. The IFS drivers enable tighter integration of different types of storage devices, resulting in more flexible caching, better cooperation with networked drives, and access to storage from other operating systems. Finally, CDFS, like all protected-mode drivers, don't use conventional memory. Windows also contains built-in drivers for all CD-ROMs. As long as the CD media device has been properly installed, the CD-ROMs are automatically recognized and assigned a drive letter.

## Device Manager

When a new Windows 9*x* system is installed or a new CD-ROM is added to an existing system, the first question to ask is, "Does Windows recognize my CD-ROM?" This can be determined quickly by opening the My Computer icon and verifying if a CD-ROM is present (Figure 14-21).

**Figure 14-21**
CD-ROM drive
letter in My
Computer

The Device Manager contains most of the information about the CD-ROM. The General tab tells you about the current status of the CD-ROM, basically saying whether the device is working properly or not—rather less useful than actually trying the device (Figure 14-22).

Windows 9*x* also has Settings and Driver tabs. The Driver tab enables you to update drivers, which makes a certain sense. Because CD-ROMs use the CDFS, they should not need drivers. This is reflected by the system (Figure 14-23).

The Settings tab contains the bulk of the noteworthy CD-ROM settings. First, this is where the drive letter is determined. You can't directly assign a particular drive letter to a CD-ROM. Instead, Windows selects from a range of reserved drive letters. The trick here is that you can assign a particular drive letter by setting the beginning and ending drive letters to the same value (Figure 14-24).

**Figure 14-22**
General tab

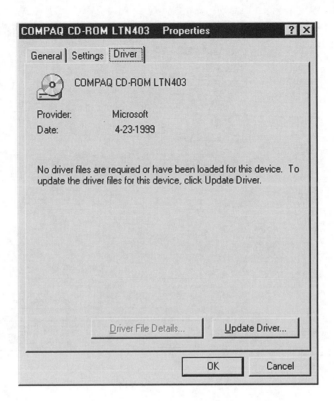

Another setting of note is the Auto Insert Notification option, often referred to as *AutoRun* in Windows 9*x* and *AutoPlay* in Windows 2000. This setting enables Windows to detect automatically the presence of audio or data CD-ROMs when they are placed in the drive. If the CD-ROM is an audio disc, track 1 plays automatically. If the CD-ROM is a data disc, Windows searches the disc's root directory for a special text file called AUTORUN.INF. Although handy, this option can sometimes be annoying and unproductive. In Windows 9*x*, uncheck the Auto Insert Notification option and Windows will no longer automatically run CD-ROMs. Windows 2000 does not provide a simple method to turn off AutoPlay. The only way to turn it off is to use the REGEDT32 version of the Registry Editor. In REGEDT32, access the subkey HKEY_LOCAL_MACHINE\SYSTEM\CurrentControlSet\Services\Cdrom and change Autorun 0 × 1 to 0 × 0. Microsoft must really want you to keep AutoPlay running in Windows 2000!

**Figure 14-23**
Driver tab

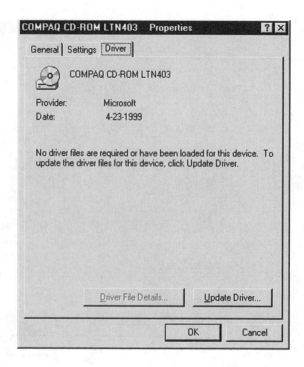

Personally, I like the AutoRun/AutoPlay feature. It's nice to drop in my favorite audio CD and immediately enjoy the music, or to drop in an installation CD and have the install program start without having to search the CD for a setup program. On those rare occasions where I prefer the AutoRun not to start for a certain CD, I just hold down the SHIFT key as I insert the CD.

Windows 2000 provides all the same functions we've just discussed for Windows 9x (with the exception of turning off AutoPlay), but you can find those functions under the Disk Management snap-in. Additionally, Windows 2000 provides the same naming flexibility for CD media drives as for hard drives, including the ability to mount them as folders on existing NTFS drives (Figure 14-25).

**Figure 14-24**
Settings tab

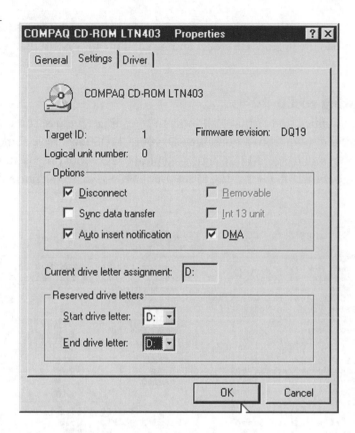

**Figure 14-25**
Change CD drive
letter option in
Disk Management

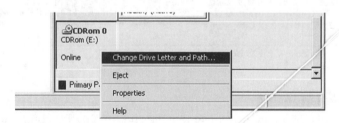

## CD-ROM Applications

A regular CD-ROM drive installation involves no applications. You install it, Windows sees it, and you're done. CD-R and CD-RW drives, in contrast, require applications to enable their burning features. As of this writing, the very popular Roxio (Roxio is a wholly owned subsidiary of Adaptec) Easy CD Creator suite of programs reigns as the most popular CD burning software. One program that comes with Easy CD Creator is DirectCD. DirectCD takes advantage of advanced packet-writing features to make the

CD-R or CD-RW act as a drag-and-drop device. In order to use this tool, you must download the Roxio UDF reader and install it on any system that will need to read that disc.

## Booting to CD-ROMs

Many utilities, and virtually all modern operating systemss, come with bootable CDs. In order to boot from a bootable CD, your CMOS must have some method of setting the boot order. Figure 14-26 shows a typical CMOS boot order setting option. After you boot to the CD-ROM, be sure to set your CMOS back to the normal setting of A:, C:.

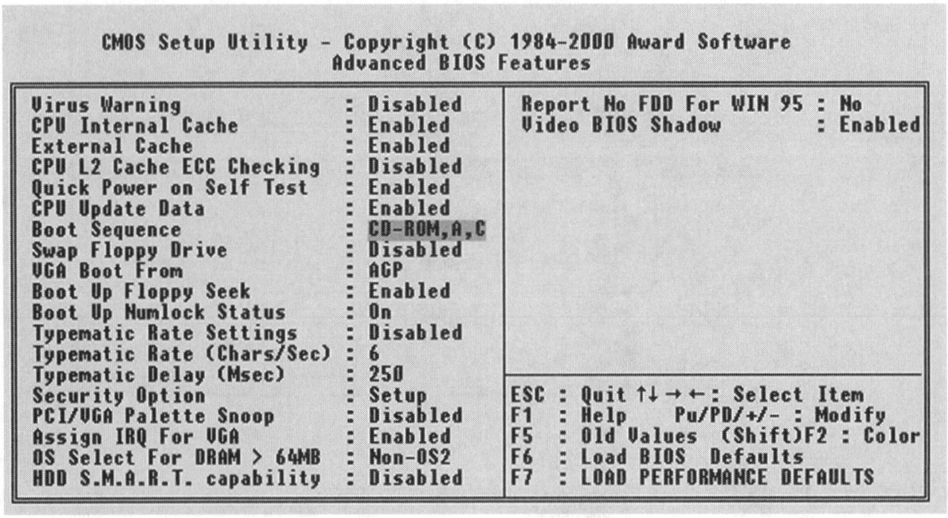

```
       CMOS Setup Utility - Copyright (C) 1984-2000 Award Software
                        Advanced BIOS Features

   Virus Warning               : Disabled   Report No FDD For WIN 95 : No
   CPU Internal Cache          : Enabled    Video BIOS Shadow        : Enabled
   External Cache              : Enabled
   CPU L2 Cache ECC Checking   : Disabled
   Quick Power on Self Test    : Enabled
   CPU Update Data             : Enabled
   Boot Sequence               : CD-ROM,A,C
   Swap Floppy Drive           : Disabled
   VGA Boot From               : AGP
   Boot Up Floppy Seek         : Enabled
   Boot Up Numlock Status      : On
   Typematic Rate Settings     : Disabled
   Typematic Rate (Chars/Sec)  : 6
   Typematic Delay (Msec)      : 250
   Security Option             : Setup      ESC : Quit ↑↓ → ← : Select Item
   PCI/VGA Palette Snoop       : Disabled   F1  : Help    Pu/PD/+/- : Modify
   Assign IRQ For VGA          : Enabled    F5  : Old Values  (Shift)F2 : Color
   OS Select For DRAM > 64MB   : Non-OS2    F6  : Load BIOS  Defaults
   HDD S.M.A.R.T. capability   : Disabled   F7  : LOAD PERFORMANCE DEFAULTS
```

**Figure 14-26** CMOS boot options

## Troubleshooting

CD media drives are extremely reliable and durable PC components. However, there are times when that reliable and durable device decides to turn into an unreliable, non-durable pile of plastic and metal frustration. This section covers a few of the more common problems with CD media drives and how to fix them.

The single biggest problem with CD media drives, especially in a new installation, is the connections—your first guess should be that the drive has not been properly installed in some way. A few of the more common problems are forgetting to plug in a power connector, inserting a cable backwards, and misconfiguring jumpers/ switches. Although you need to know the type of drive (ATAPI or SCSI), the test for an improper physical connection is always the same: using BIOS or DOS-level device drivers to see if the system can see the CD media drive.

The way in which a BIOS detects a CD media drive really depends on the system. Most of the CD media drives used today are the ATAPI type. Knowing this, most BIOS makers have created intelligent BIOS software that can see an installed CD media drive. Here's a modern Award Software, Inc. BIOS recognizing an ATAPI CD-ROM during startup:

```
Award Plug and Play BIOS Extension v1.0A
Copyright (C) 2001, Award Software, Inc.
Found CDROM : TOSHIBA CD-ROM XM-6702B
```

This text tends to move by rather quickly during bootup, so a good eye and/or a fast press on the PAUSE key may be necessary to see this operation. It should be noted that not every BIOS can recognize a CD media drive, nor will even the most advanced BIOS see a SCSI CD media device, with one possible exception. If the system has a SCSI host adapter with onboard BIOS, it will usually display text at boot that says something like this:

```
Press Ctrl-A for SCSI BIOS Selection
```

This will then enable the user to access configuration options. The goal here is to make the host adapter scan the SCSI bus and return a list of devices on the bus. If the SCSI CD-ROM doesn't appear, there is a problem with the hardware. Look for options similar to "Scan SCSI Bus" or "Diagnostic." Different SCSI host adapter makers give the function different names, but in any case, the result is a screen that will look something like this:

```
SCSI ID 0    Seagate ST4302
SCSI ID 1    No Device Detected
SCSI ID 2    No Device Detected
SCSI ID 3    No Device Detected
SCSI ID 4    No Device Detected
SCSI ID 5    IOMEGA ZIP100
SCSI ID 6    HITACHI CD20032
SCSI ID 7    ADAPTEC 2940
```

The fact that the CD-ROM is visible shows that it has a valid SCSI ID, is properly connected and powered, and that the SCSI chain is properly terminated.

If no type of BIOS support is present, the only option is to boot to a DOS-level device driver. This is where a startup disk really comes in handy. Just boot off the startup disk and watch for the CD-ROM device driver:

```
DEVICE=C:\DOS\TRICD.SYS /D:MSCD001
Triones ATAPI CD-ROM Device Driver, Version 3.6
Copyright (c) 1994-1997 Triones Technologies, Inc. All rights reserved.
Secondary/Master: MATSHITA CD-ROM CR-584, Multi-word DMA 1
ATAPI CD-ROM Device Driver installed.
```

Here's the same boot with the data cable intentionally inverted:

```
DEVICE=C:\DOS\TRICD.SYS /D:MSCD001
Triones ATAPI CD-ROM Device Driver, Version 3.6
Copyright (c) 1994-1997 Triones Technologies, Inc. All rights reserved.
Error: No CDROM detected.
```

Of course, you should be sure to have the correct DOS driver for the CD-ROM drive that is being tested! If the device is detected, yet can't read a CD media disc, first try a commercial CD-ROM disc. CD-R and CD-RW discs often have compatibility issues with CD-ROM drives. No CD media drive will read badly scratched discs.

If the drive still does not see a disc, try cleaning the CD media drive. Most modern CD media drives have built-in cleaning mechanisms, but from time to time, you need to use a commercial CD-ROM cleaning kit (Figure 14-27).

**Figure 14-27**
CD media drive
cleaning kit

CD media drives are not cleaned too often, but CD media discs are. Although a number of fine CD-ROM disc cleaning kits are available, most CD media discs can be cleaned quite well with nothing more than a damp soft cloth. Occasionally, a mild detergent can be added. A common "Old Tech's Tale" about cleaning CD media discs is that they can be washed in a dishwasher! Although this may seem laughable, the tale has become so common that it requires a serious response. This is *not true* for two reasons. First, the water in most dishwashers is too hot and can cause the CD media discs to warp. Second, the water pushes the CD media discs around, causing them to hit other objects and get scratched. Don't do it!

# Beyond A+

## Color Books

The term "books" is often referred to in the world of CD media. Books are, well, books! They are standards developed in the industry to describe different media, for example, the Red book describes the original audio CD format. If you have a lot of money—say $3,000 U.S.—you may purchase copies of these books and yes, their covers really match the colors of the standards. You might hear a fellow computer support person using these terms. Instead of saying, "Does your CD-ROM read CD-RWs?" they will say, "Is that CD-ROM of yours Orange book?" Technical specifications also use these terms. I personally don't like the way many people refer to these book colors, but the terms are used enough that you should memorize the meaning of at least three book colors: Red, Yellow, and Orange. Table 14-1 shows a complete list of CD media book colors.

**Table 14-1**   CD Media Book Colors

| APPLICATION | BOOK | SUB-TYPES | |
|---|---|---|---|
| Audio CDs | Red book | N/A | |
| Data CDs | Yellow book | Mode 1 | Original Format |
| | | Mode 2 | Form 1 and Form 2 |
| CD-I | Green book | N/A | |
| Recordable CDs | Orange book | Part I | CD-MO (Magneto-Optical) |
| | | Part II | CD-R, includes PhotoCD |
| | | Part III | CD-RW |
| Video CD | White book | N/A | |
| CD Extra | Blue Book | N/A | |

## Burning Issues

The tremendous growth of the CD-R and CD-RW industry has led to a substantial number of incompatibility issues between discs and drives. Most of these so-called incompatibilities trace back to serious "I.O." (Ignorant Operator) problems; people try to make these discs do jobs they aren't designed to do. But even when people read the manuals and jump through the proper hoops, real problems do arise, many of which you can easily solve with a few checks.

### Know What It Can Do

Most mistakes take place when you purchase. Don't just assume that the device will do this or that. Before I purchase a CD-R or CD-RW drive, I make it a point to get my hands on every technical document provided by the maker to verify exactly the capabilities the drive possesses. I make sure that the drive has a good reputation—just use any search engine and type in **review** and the model number of the drive to get several people's opinions.

### Media Issues

The CD-R and CD-RW Orange book standards committees refused to mandate the types of materials used in the construction of discs. As a result, you see substantial quality differences with CD-R and CD-RW discs. The best recommendation I can give is to find a brand you like and stick with it. Two items come into play here: media speed and inks. Most CD-R and CD-RW media makers certify their CDs to work up to a certain multiplier. A media maker often has two product lines: a quality line guaranteed to work at a certain speed and a generic line where you take your chances. As a rule I buy both. I primarily use cheap discs but always stash five to ten good quality discs in case I run into a problem (Figure 14-28).

**Figure 14-28**
Mike's disc stash—
a stack o' cheapies
plus a few good
ones

As mentioned earlier, CD-R discs use organic inks as part of the burning process. Fellow techs love to talk about which color to use or which color gives the best results. Ignore them—the color itself means nothing. Instead, try a few different brands of CD-R discs when you first get your drive in order to determine what works best for you.

## Buffer Underrun

Every CD burner comes with onboard RAM, called *buffer RAM*—usually just called the *buffer*—that stores the incoming data from the recording source. Buffer underrun, the inability of the source device to keep the burner loaded with data, creates more "coasters" (improperly burned and therefore useless CDs) than any other single problem. Buffer underrun most often occurs when copying from CD-ROM to CD-R or CD-RW. Many factors contribute to buffer underrun, but two stand out as the most important. The first is buffer size. Make sure you purchase CD-RW drives with large buffers—2MB minimum. Unlike with system RAM, you can't get a buffer upgrade. Second is multitasking. Most systems won't enable you to run any other programs while the burner is running. One trick to reducing underrun is using an image file. A CD image file is a bit-by-bit image of the data to be burned on the CD—from one file to an entire CD—stored as a single file on a hard drive. Image files are particularly handy when copying from CD to CD. These huge files take up a lot of drive space. Unlike some CD-ROM drives, however, *any* hard drive can keep up with a CD burner, dramatically reducing your chance of a buffer underrun adding to your coaster collection.

Some current CD-RWs include the new BURN-Proof™ technology developed by Sanyo, which has eliminated the underrun issue. These drives can literally turn off the burning process if the buffer runs out of information and automatically restart as soon as the buffer refills. I love these drives as I can now burn CDs in the background and run other programs without fear of underruns. If you're buying a new CD-RW drive, spend a few extra bucks and get one that has the BURN-proof technology.

## Firmware Updates

Almost all CD media drives come with an upgradeable flash ROM chip. If your drive doesn't read a particular type of media, or if any other non-intermittent reading/writing problems develop, check the manufacturer's Web site to see if they offer a firmware upgrade. Almost every CD media drive seems to get one or two firmware updates during its production cycle.

## DVD

For years the video industry has tried to create a CD media replacement for videotape. The 12-inch diameter laserdisc format originally introduced by Phillips gained some ground in the 1980s and 1990s. But the high cost of both the discs and the players, plus various marketing factors, meant there was never a very large laserdisc market. Although, you still find a few titles and players being produced (Figure 14-29).

*Digital Versatile Disc* (DVD) was developed by a large consortium of electronics and entertainment firms during the early 1990s and released in 1995. With the exception of the DVD logo stamped on all commercial DVD discs (Figure 14-30), DVD discs look exactly like all other CD media; that's pretty much where the similarities end.

**Figure 14-29**
Sample laserdisc

**Figure 14-30**
Typical DVD disc

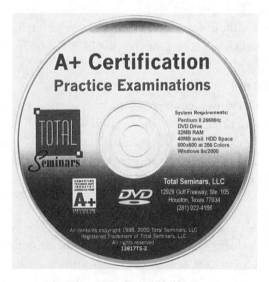

DVD has become the fastest growing media format in history and will almost certainly replace the VHS tape within the next few years for video formats. Additionally, one variant of DVD (the main DVD is called DVD-Video)—DVD-RAM—has enjoyed some success as a mass storage medium.

The single best word to describe DVD is "capacity." All previous CD media stored a maximum of 700MB of data or 80 minutes of video, whereas the lowest capacity DVD disc holds 4.37GB of data or two hours of video, and the highest capacity version DVD discs store roughly 16GB of data or over eight hours of video!

DVD achieves these amazing capacities using a number of technologies, but three are most important. First, DVD uses smaller pits and packs them much more densely than CD media. Second, DVD comes in both *single-sided* (SS) and *dual-sided* (DS) formats. Clearly, a DS disc holds twice the data of a SS disc, but it also requires you to flip the disc to read the other side. Third, DVD discs come in *single-layer* (SL) and *dual-layer* (DL) formats. DL formats use two pitted layers on each side, each with a slightly different reflectivity index. Table 14-2 shows the common DVD disc capacities.

**Table 14-2** DVD Version Capacities

| DVD VERSION | CAPACITY |
| --- | --- |
| DVD-5 (12 cm, SS/SL) | 4.37GB of data, over two hours of video |
| DVD-9 (12 cm, SS/DL) | 7.95GB, about four hours |
| DVD-10 (12 cm, DS/SL) | 8.74GB, about four and a half hours |
| DVD-18 (12 cm, DS/DL) | 15.90GB, over eight hours |

## DVD-Video

The single greatest beauty of DVD-Video lies in its ability to store two hours of video on one side. You drop in a DVD-Video disc and get to watch an entire movie without flipping it over. DVD-Video supports TV-style 4:3 aspect ratio screens as well as 16:9 theatre screens, but it is up to the producer to decide which to use. Many DVD-Video producers distribute DVD movies on double-sided media with a 4:3 ratio on one side and 16:9 ratio on the other.

DVD-Video is simply gorgeous. Nothing short of (possibly) 35mm film compares to the picture quality on a properly configured DVD system. This, however, comes at a price. Even with all the extra capacity, DVD-Video relies on the MPEG-2 standard of video and audio compression to reach the magic of two hours of video per side. *Moving Picture Experts Group* (MPEG) is a group of compression standards for both audio and video. The MPEG-2 standard offers resolutions of up to 1280 × 720 at 60 frames/sec, with full CD-quality audio. All this power creates the need for extra hardware to enjoy the full effect of DVD-Video.

## Decoder

DVD-Videos require some way to uncompress the MPEG data on the fly. These decoders can be either hardware or software. No two people seem to agree which one to use. Personally, I think that software decoders are fine for someone who just wants to play DVDs on their laptop or home computer system as long as that system packs a minimum of a 300 MHz processor with lots of extra RAM. Hardware decoders— usually just an extra PCI card with connections to your monitor and speakers—are a great choice for those who wish to use quality speakers and reduce CPU overhead (Figure 14-31).

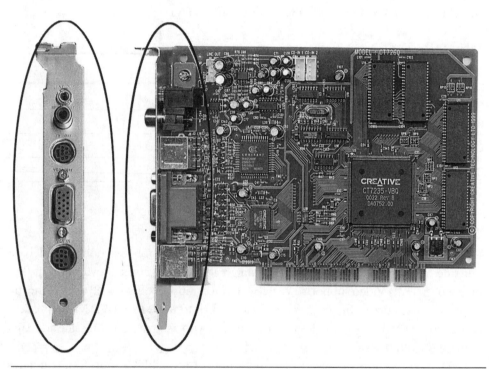

**Figure 14-31**  Typical hardware decoder

## Monitor

DVD-Video requires a monitor that can handle the high-resolution output. Although even an average computer displays DVD-Video quite well, most folks like to output to their television sets. This requires a video card that can output to your country's TV standard (NTSC in the U.S., SECAM or PAL everywhere else in the world), and then the output will not even approach the true quality of DVD. To really see DVD on something other than your PC monitor, you need to purchase a *high-definition television* (HDTV) set—an expensive proposition.

## Speakers

DVD-Video stores up to eight audio tracks. These tracks have many different uses. For example, a DVD producer may store four different languages in stereo. The most common function available with these audio tracks is support for surround sound, using four, five, six, or seven speakers to create amazingly realistic effects. A number of different versions of this are available, which will be mentioned in Chapter 15.

## DVD Players

Many companies sell DVD players for home theatre systems. These systems read DVD-Video discs and are designed for easier connections to digital receivers systems that support surround sound speakers. All DVD players also include video outputs, which usually go to your television (Figure 14-32).

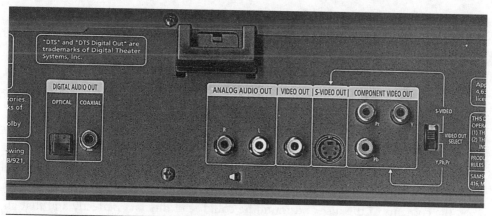

**Figure 14-32**   DVD player connections

## DVD-ROM

DVD-ROM is the DVD-equivalent to the standard CD-ROM data format, except it is capable of storing up to almost 16GB. Almost all DVD-ROM drives also fully support DVD-Video as well as most CD-ROM formats. Most DVD drives sold with PCs are of this type.

## DVD-RAM

DVD-RAM is the DVD equivalent of CD-RW. Although it has gotten off to a bit of a slow start, DVD-RAM holds great promise as a replacement for tape as a backup device. DVD-RAM discs require caddies. The older Type-1 DVD-RAM has the discs permanently installed inside the caddies, whereas the newer Type-2 DVD-RAM discs can be removed from their caddies (Figure 14-33).

**Figure 14-33**
DVD-RAM

## Review Questions

1. Jane has a 4× CD-ROM drive. At what rate does it process data?
   A. 300KBps
   B. 600KBps
   C. 1200KBps
   D. 2400KBps

2. John purchased a new "burnable" CD and put it in his new CD-RW drive. He dumped about 620MB of data on the disc, just to try it. After the burn, he viewed the contents of the disc and found he could read the data perfectly and that all 620MB copied over. When he tried to delete data on the disc, however, he received an error message that said the disc was full or write-protected. What could be the problem? (Choose the best answer.)
   A. The disc must be a 74-minute capacity disc.
   B. The disc must be an 80-minute capacity disc.
   C. He used a CD-RW disc rather than a CD-R disc.
   D. He used a CD-R disc rather than a CD-RW disc.

3. Janet is trying to impress you by referring to her CD-ROM drive as "Red Book-capable." What does this mean?
   A. Her drive can read Audio CDs.
   B. Her drive can read CD-R discs.
   C. Her drive can read CD-RW discs.
   D. Her drive can read DVD discs.

4. Mary found the old CD-ROM that had her favorite casino games on it, but it was scratched on the bottom and her CD-ROM drive failed to read the CD. Cathy told her it was probably ruined. John told her it could still possibly be used. Who is right?

   A. Cathy is right. It is probably ruined.

   B. John is right. Getting a polishing kit and buffing out the scratches can probably salvage the CD.

   C. Neither is right. The CD was formatted for an older operating system.

   D. Neither is right. Older CDs are write-protected.

5. CD-R drives are defined by two speeds: the record speed and the read speed. Which of the following is not a common CD-R speed setting?

   A. $2 \times 4$

   B. $4 \times 4$

   C. $4 \times 32$

   D. $16 \times 4$

6. Which of the following is not a CD-RW drive speed value?

   A. The CD-R write speed

   B. The CD-RW write speed

   C. The CD-RW erase speed

   D. The read speed

7. Which of the following is a common CD-RW speed setting?

   A. $32\times$

   B. $4 \times 12$

   C. $8 \times 4 \times 32$

   D. $4 \times 8 \times 8 \times 32$

8. Bob needs to get his Windows 95 startup disk to read his CD-ROM so that he can install Windows 95 onto a blank hard drive. Which of the following lines in an A:\AUTOEXEC.BAT file would match-up best with this line found in Bob's A:\CONFIG.SYS file?

   ```
   DEVICE=A:\OAKCDROM.SYS /D:MSCD000
   ```

   A. A:\MSCDEX.EXE /D:MSCD001

   B. A:\MSCDEX.EXE \D:MSCD000

   C. A:\MSCDEX.EXE /D:MSCD000

   D. C:\WINDOWS\COMMAND\MSCDEX.COM /D:MSCD000

9. Dana has a CD-ROM in her Windows 2000 machine to which she wants to assign a specific drive letter, but is not quite sure where to do this. You, as a cracker-jack technician ask her why she wants to change the assigned drive letter. The reason she wants to do this is to avoid having application assignments for her programs change if she adds another hard drive later. Good thinking, Dana. Which snap-in under Administrative Tools should she use to change the drive letter?

    **A.** Computer Management

    **B.** Services

    **C.** Device Manager

    **D.** Event Viewer

10. For a CD-ROM to AutoRun/AutoPlay, it must have a file called _____ in its root directory?

    **A.** AUTOEXEC.BAT

    **B.** AUTOEXEC.INF

    **C.** AUTORUN.INF

    **D.** AUTORUN.BAT

## Answers

1. **A.** Because, $4 \times 150\text{KBps} = 600\text{KBps}$.

2. **D.** He used a CD-R disc rather than a CD-RW disk.

3. **A.** By stating the CD-ROM is Red Book capable, she means that it can play Audio CDs.

4. **B.** Buff out those scratches.

5. **D.** The record speed (listed first) is never faster than the read speed.

6. **C.** There is no multiplier called erase speed.

7. **D.** CD-RW drives are defined by three multipliers.

8. **C.** The correct line would most likely be A:\MSCDEX.EXE /D:MSCD000, which matches the CONFIG.SYS settings. Watch out for incorrect back-slashes and mismatched device names.

9. **A.** Computer Management will work here.

10. **D.** The correct name of the file is AUTORUN.INF.

# Sound

In this chapter, you will:

- Learn the different types of sound
- Understand the different components that make sound work
- Learn to install sound cards
- Fix common sound card problems

## Historical/Conceptual

The evolution of PCs has been exciting from the very beginning. It's probably safe to say that since the early 1980s, a two-month period has not gone by without a new technology being unveiled. Granted, most of these technologies have become obsolete (for example, ESDI hard drives) or for one reason or another just didn't catch on (for example, light pens). Although many technologies have been developed, only a few have become milestone—technologies where people speak in terms of "before" and "after" they existed. Certainly, the addition of sound via sound cards is one of those milestones. While sound is now taken for granted, very few techs really understand the processes involved and how they affect the rest of the system. This section will delve into sound and help clarify the many different functions of the average sound card.

## Types of Sound

How can a computer, capable of nothing more than processing a bunch of 1's and 0's, play Handel's *Messiah*? How does a sound card create the dynamic hum of a racecar speeding by at 180 mph? Let's take a moment to understand how a sound card records, stores, and re-creates the sounds that make PCs so much more useful and fun than they were "before."

### WAV

Basically, there are only two ways to make sounds on a PC. The first is to generate waveforms—in essence, a tape recording. You may recall from fourth grade science that sound travels in waves. Higher frequency waves make higher-pitched tones, and lower frequency waves make lower-pitched tones. Visualize sound as a constantly changing series of frequencies entering the ear over time. This can be graphed as a *waveform* (Figure 15-1).

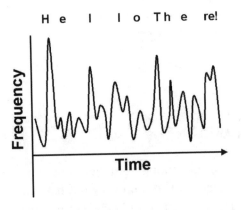

**Figure 15-1**
Typical sound wave-
form

A PC can't save a waveform as such, but rather needs it converted into 1's and 0's. You can turn a waveform into a digital file by taking "samples" at regular intervals. The quality of the recorded sound is based on the number of bits used for each sample and how often the sound is sampled. Furthermore, waveforms get recorded in a number of tracks, which can make a big difference in what you hear (Figure 15-2).

Waveforms are commonly sampled with either 8 or 16 bits per sample. An 8-bit sample stores $2^8$ or 256 different frequencies, which is fine for basic or low quality sounds, such as a telephone conversation. On the other hand, 16-bit samples store $2^{16}$ or 65,536 different frequencies, which covers roughly all of the frequencies the human ear can detect.

The sampling rate for a digital waveform is measured in thousands of times per second, or *kilohertz* (KHz), and usually varies from 11 to about 44 KHz. The more samples per second, naturally, the higher quality of sound you can record. A song that sounds

**Figure 15-2**
Sound being
sampled

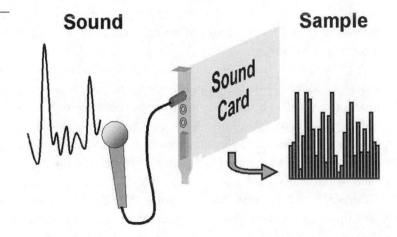

great recorded at 44 KHz and is re-recorded at 11 KHz, for example, would go from crystal clear to hiss-filled and distorted.

Finally, waveforms are sampled in individual tracks. Classically, waveforms would be recorded as monaural or stereo, although a whole new set of 3-D-based sounds uses as many as eight tracks. As you might well imagine, the number of tracks can dramatically change what you hear, as long as you have good enough equipment. FM radio, for example, sounds pretty much the same as AM radio if all you have is a monaural radio receiver, but it's much better through a stereo system. Similarly, you have to have the proper sound card and speakers to appreciate a four- or eight-track waveform recording.

Waveforms are recorded at different bit depths, sample rates, and numbers of tracks for different qualities. As can be imagined, a waveform tends to be a rather large file. A high quality waveform recording, for example, can use over 1MBps!

In the first years of waveforms, when DOS still stood as the primary OS, many types of waveform file formats existed, each requiring its own separate player/recorder application. During the era of Windows 3.*x*, Microsoft adopted a new type of file format, called WAV format for Windows. The WAV format is fairly broad in scope, providing a maximum of 16-bit sampling at 44 KHz on two tracks (stereo). This format is roughly equal to CD-Audio quality. When Microsoft began to add free WAV files and free WAV file applications to later versions of Windows 3.*x*, WAV became the *de facto* waveform standard. Today, WAV files continue to be the most popular waveform format.

## MIDI

*Musical Instrument Digital Interface* (MIDI), is the second most popular type of sound on a PC. MIDI was not designed for the PC; it was designed to enable musicians to create, store, and play a broad cross section of instruments, including instruments that they invent on synthesizers. MIDI starts with a sound card that has built-in recordings of real musical instruments. The number of instruments stored and the quality of the recordings stored for the instruments are what separates cheaper sound cards from more expensive ones.

A MIDI file functions somewhat like traditional sheet music. Each file contains a series of commands that describe what note to play, how long to play it, and which instrument (labeled by number, not type) to use. Each instrument is called a *voice*. The number of different instruments a sound card can play simultaneously is called its *polyphony*. Most sound cards today have at least 32-voice polyphony. Sound cards use one or two methods for storing the musical instruments: *FM synthesis* or *wavetable synthesis*. Wavetable is much higher quality than FM, creating a much more realistic sound.

Because MIDI files store only the notes, they are tiny compared to WAV files; however, this means MIDI is limited only to instruments. You can't save a human voice or the sound of an explosion, but when a game needs a musical soundtrack or a user wants to listen to some classical music, MIDI can't be beat.

### It's All WAV and MIDI

Right now is a very confusing time for sound. Our multimedia world has developed a number of technologies that we equate with sound: 3-D sound, MP3 files, Dolby Digital, DVD, and many others. We'll cover all these terms as we progress through this chapter, but for now, trust me when I tell you that only two types of sound files exist on a PC: waveforms and MIDI.

## Test Specific

### Sound Cards

Waveforms and MIDI are completely different methods of creating and reproducing sounds. A device is needed that can, with the help of a good device driver or two, take these two files as input and generate analog signals to speakers or to a recording device. That device is the sound card. For a sound card to support both waveforms and MIDI, it must have two completely separate sets of components soldered to the card. In essence, a sound card is better thought of as two devices on one card. As the following sections will explain, this usually means providing separate resources (I/O addresses, IRQs, DMAs, drivers) for each type of sound.

### Sound Card Connections

Assuming that the system has the necessary software, the average sound card has the hardware to perform the following functions:

- Record and play waveform files

- Record and play MIDI files

- Enable recording via microphone or auxiliary input (to record from analog CD player, vinyl record, or tape)

- Assist the playing of analog CD-ROMs from the CD-ROM drive

Keep in mind that these are functions of an average sound card! Different sound cards provide different functions. To support these functions, the sound card needs physical connectors to interface with microphones, speakers, and so on. Let's look at the common connections on a sound card and discuss their functions (Figure 15-3).

**Figure 15-3** Typical sound card external connections

## Speakers

The speaker connection enables the sounds to be output to speakers. The classic PC sound card/speaker configuration supports two speakers in a stereo configuration (to support stereo WAV files), but now a new class of 3-D speaker systems offers three, four, five, or more speakers. These more powerful speaker systems will be discussed later in the chapter. For now, let's consider the classic two-speaker system (Figure 15-4).

**Figure 15-4**   Typical two-speaker system

In almost all cases, the classic stereo signal output consists of a single mini audio connector. The first speaker plugs into the connector and the second speaker plugs into the first. Although this connection is quite simple, it is the source of many "I can't hear any sounds!" complaints. The problem is usually the speakers themselves. The sound card has only a minimal amount of amplification, so most speakers come with their own built-in amplifiers. Because these amplifiers need power, speakers tend to need either batteries or an AC adapter (or both) to supply that power. In addition, most speakers will have a power switch and a volume knob. It is important to be sure that the speakers are properly powered, are turned on, and have the volume turned up to ensure that the sound can be heard. Many (if not most) "no sound" problems can be fixed by doing nothing more than pressing an "on" button or replacing dead batteries (Figure 15-5).

Speakers can operate without power. However, if a speaker does not have power, it has no amplification and simply plays the relatively weak signal coming from the sound card. This may be acceptable on a few systems, but unpowered speakers will not provide the louder, better quality, more robust sound that you probably want from your games and other sound applications. If you choose to try to run powered speakers without batteries or AC power, make sure the power switch on the speaker is turned off or the speakers will probably not make any output.

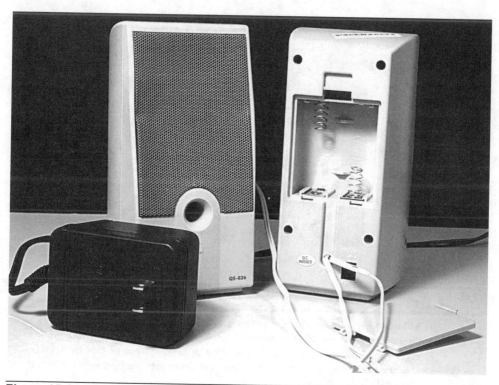

**Figure 15-5**   These speakers use AC or batteries.

### Microphone

Microphones connect to the sound card through a mini audio connector, just like the speakers. You can plug in directly microphones made for the PC, but you need an adapter for full size, traditional microphones.

Problems with microphones generally point to the microphone rather than connections (assuming you plug it into the right socket of course). Microphones often have batteries and these batteries must be good for the microphone to work. Also, better microphones invariably use an on/off switch that must be turned on to enable the microphone to do its job (Figure 15-6). Don't let the simple stuff fool you!

### Line In/Line Out

The Line In and Line Out connectors enable the sound card to send and receive input and output from devices other than a microphone or speaker. Classically, the Line In connector runs to a Line Out or Aux connector on the back of a stereo receiver system. This way, the sound card can take input from an audio CD player, radio, or whatever else is connected to the stereo system. The Line Out is also often connected to a stereo system, primarily to output to big speakers or to enable tape recording.

**Figure 15-6**
Microphone
batteries

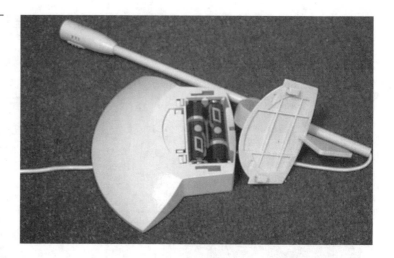

**NOTE**  In my opinion, the hardest part of dealing with these connections is finding the right one for the particular device. Ah, if I only had a dollar for every time I plugged my speaker cable into the Microphone or Line In jacks! This error will not damage anything, but whatever gets plugged into the wrong place definitely will not work!

## CD Media

CD media and sound cards are physically connected in three different ways. Many older sound cards provided support for an ATAPI CD-ROM drive via an onboard 40-pin connection (Figure 15-7). This ATAPI link used a totally separate I/O address and IRQ from the EIDE Primary and Secondary controllers, thereby enabling the system to support a fifth IDE device. This 40-pin connection had nothing to do with sound; it simply provided a place to connect the CD-ROM. This connection requires a separate device driver. Windows 9x and Windows 2000 usually automatically detect these connections and supply a driver, eating badly needed IRQs that other devices may need. Most systems don't need this connection. I usually read the sound card documentation to figure out how to turn off these onboard ATAPI controllers.

The second way to connect CD media and sound cards is using the expansion bus itself. Suppose you put a regular data CD-ROM into your CD media drive. You have stored a sound file on the CD-ROM. In order to play that file, you must run a sound program such as Windows Media Player (Figure 15-8).

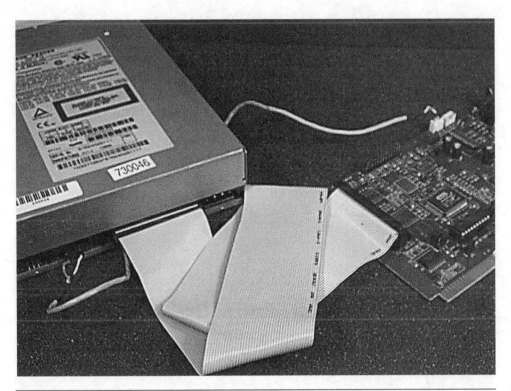

**Figure 15-7**   Sound card with a CD-ROM controller

When you select File | Open from inside Media Player and select a sound file from the CD-ROM, the file loads into RAM via the expansion bus. Then, when you tell Media Player to play the sound file, the program sends the file through the expansion bus again, but this time directly to the sound card. If all goes well, you hear lovely sounds pouring out of your speakers. This connection works as long as each device's resources (I/O addresses, IRQs, and DMAs) are properly configured; most sounds generated on a system work in this fashion.

The third connection option is the CD-ROM connection. The CD-ROM drive can play audio CDs by itself, but to listen you must use the CD-ROM drive's speaker jack. Because most folks don't want to have a second set of speakers, sound cards have a special CD-Audio connector that links the sound card directly to the CD-ROM. CD-ROMs have a corresponding connector, and by adding a special wire between the devices, you can play audio CD-ROMs and output them to the sound card speakers. This connector must be installed to enable Windows 9*x* and Windows 2000 to play audio CD-ROMs (Figure 15-9).

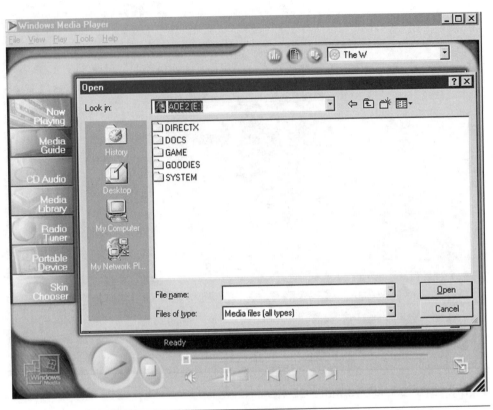

**Figure 15-8**   Select File | Open in Windows Media Player to run a sound program.

### MIDI/Joystick

The beauty of MIDI is the ability to connect to other MIDI devices. For a MIDI-capable sound card to be able to connect to other MIDI devices, it must have a 15-pin, female DB-type connector. This is an excellent MIDI connector but has two drawbacks. First, very few people need or want a MIDI connector because they don't record MIDI files. Second, the connector looks exactly like a game (joystick) port. To make the port more functional and to prevent people from accidentally plugging in their joysticks and calling the sound card manufacturer, the sound card makers did a very smart thing: They made it so that the connector also acts as a game port. Most sound cards autodetect the presence of a joystick and properly configure the port, but some older cards require you to move a jumper or switch to tell the port whether to act as a MIDI or a game port. Figure 15-10 shows a joystick attached to the game port of a sound card.

**Figure 15-9** CD-Audio connection

**Figure 15-10**
Typical joystick in
the game port on a
sound card

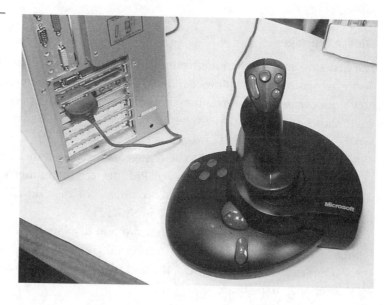

## Device Drivers

Sound cards are notorious for having complicated device drivers, due mainly to their multiple functions of waveform, MIDI, and possibly CD-ROM. The trick to understanding sound card device drivers is to remember this multiple-function aspect and to treat each function as though it were a separate device requiring its own device drivers. Instead of thinking "sound card driver," think "waveform driver," "MIDI driver," "CD-ROM controller driver," and so on, based on what features are contained in the individual sound card. Windows 9x and Windows 2000 *Plug and Play* (PnP) will find just about every sound card ever made, although problems might occur with extra devices such as onboard ATAPI controllers. Installing a sound card normally generates multiple New Hardware Found screens from Windows 9x systems. Watch out for sound cards that add a bunch of applications that you may not want. This is often difficult to determine ahead of time, so be ready to do some uninstalling—unless you want programs like talking parrots that repeat everything you say!

## Windows 9x/2000

PnP in Windows 9x and Windows 2000 has made non-PnP sound cards completely obsolete. Device driver installation has been reduced to inserting a floppy or CD-ROM with the proper INF file—on the rare chance that Windows doesn't already have the necessary sound card. Windows now includes a basic, but complete, set of applications for playing and recording WAV files, and playing MIDI files and CD-ROMs, plus a handy volume control applet that sits on the taskbar. Still, with all the conveniences that Windows 9x and Windows 2000 provide, a good tech should be aware of a few nuances.

### Device Manager

The first stop in understanding sound cards is the Device Manager. It will find any device recognized by Windows 9x/2000. Device Manager demonstrates quite clearly how Windows sees the several functions of the sound card as separate devices. Figure 15-11 shows a sound card as a waveform player and a MIDI player (OPL3 is a type of MIDI device that this sound card emulates).

System resources rarely need to be changed, especially if the sound card is PnP. But as mentioned in earlier chapters, even PnP devices sometimes create unanticipated resource conflicts. You can change the resources for each device simply by selecting properties for that particular device (Figure 15-12).

Once Windows recognizes the sound card and displays the separate devices in the Device Manager without errors, the sound card is ready to go! This assumes that the speaker cables are properly inserted, the speakers are on if necessary, and the volume is set loud enough to be heard.

**Figure 15-11**
Device Manager
sees two devices.

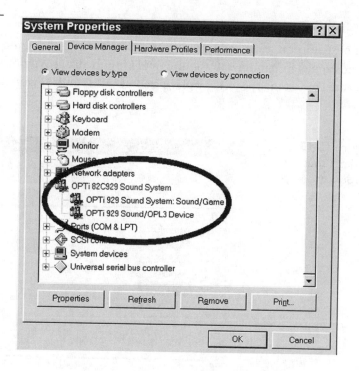

**Figure 15-12**
Resource settings
in Windows 9*x*'s
Device Manager

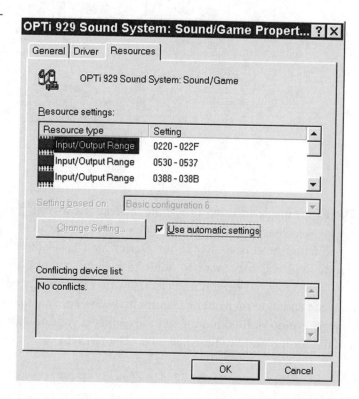

## Control Panel

The next stop on a new sound card install takes us to the Control Panel. I use the Sounds applet in Windows 9*x* (Sounds and Multimedia in Windows 2000) in the Control Panel to test the speakers by playing some test sounds (Figure 15-13).

**Figure 15-13**
Playing a sound in the Sounds applet

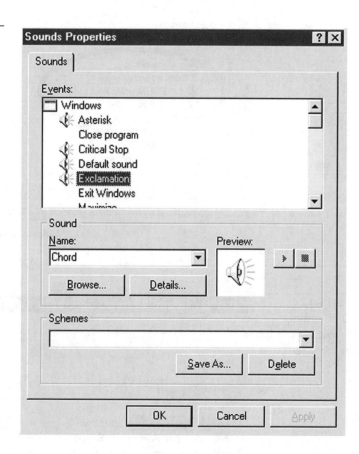

There's no magic in using this applet to test; use anything you want—just make those speakers make some noise! If the Play button in the Sounds applet is grayed out, you had better head back over to the Device Manager—something is wrong! While you're testing, you may want to adjust the sound volume to a level comfortable for you—and for your neighbors. Personally, I set the speaker volume to a mid-range setting and count on the Volume Control in the System Tray for most adjusting duties. Although, Windows 2000 has thoughtfully added a volume slider right in the Sounds tab of the Sounds and Multimedia applet (Figure 15-14).

**Figure 15-14**
Adjusting the
volume in
Windows 2000

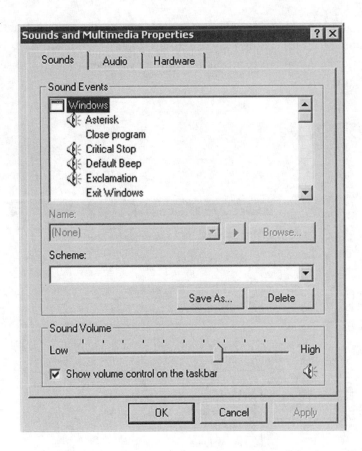

The Volume Control handles volume for both incoming and outgoing sound. Open the Volume Control from the System Tray. One click brings up only the speaker volume—a great way to turn down the volume or mute the sound quickly (Figure 15-15). Alternate-click and select Adjust Audio Properties for a quick trip to the Sounds applet.

**Figure 15-15**
Simple volume
menu

Double-clicking the Volume Control icon on the System Tray brings up the main Volume Control settings. These settings differ by sound card, so be sure to select the Options | Advanced Controls or Options | Properties menu to see all of the devices (Figure 15-16).

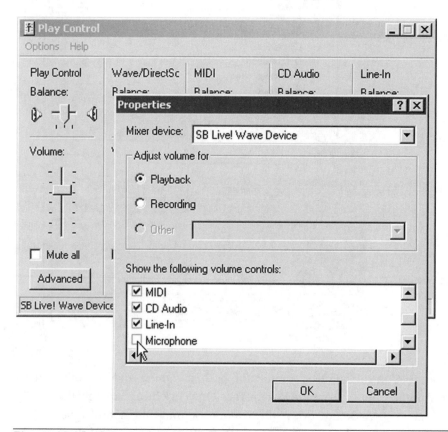

**Figure 15-16**   Selecting which sound devices to display

Going back to the Control Panel you see the Multimedia applet. Windows 2000 combines the Multimedia and the Sound applets. In doing so, Windows 2000 manages to change the positions of a number of settings, hiding the same functions under the Audio and Hardware tabs. Whether you have Windows 9x's Multimedia or Windows 2000 Multimedia and Sound, they share similar functions.

## Multimedia

The Multimedia section in the Control Panel is rarely used but can be a handy tool for determining certain critical information. The Windows 9x Multimedia menu is broken up into five tabs: Audio, Video, MIDI, CD Music, and Advanced (Devices in Windows

98). Windows 2000 just uses the Audio and Hardware tabs. The Audio tab enables you to set playback and recording volumes and set recording quality. As most applications have these settings, this tab goes unused unless you have multiple sound cards and need to select the one you prefer to use at the moment. (Don't laugh—I have two sound cards!) The Video tab is for setting the size of video playback—largely ignored by most video players, as you will see in Chapter 16. The MIDI tab sets the MIDI outputs, which is useless unless you are going to hook up MIDI devices. The CD Music tab (Figure 15-17) displays the drive letter of the CD-ROM the system will use to play audio files, and sets the volume for the audio CD-ROM's output.

The Advanced tab (Windows 2000 uses buttons called Advanced underneath each type of device to do the same thing) handles a number of critical settings, but I'm afraid I'm going to leave you in suspense on these for a moment until we learn a few things about 3-D sound and compression!

**Figure 15-17**
CD Music tab in
Multimedia

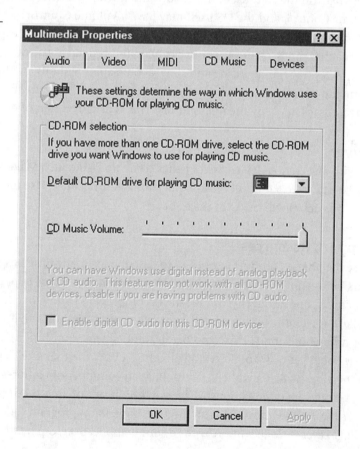

## Troubleshooting Sound

When something goes wrong with your computer's sound, certain factors point to the problem. The trick is to appreciate that all sound problems can be broken down into three groups: physical problems, driver issues, and support resources.

## Physical Problems

Simply stated, something isn't turned on, plugged in, or turned up. Of all problems with sound cards, this is probably the easiest, most common, and also the most overlooked. Fortunately, physical problems are easy to diagnose—the software says everything is great, but no sound comes out (or in the case of a microphone, no sound goes in). A good triple-check is important to verify that all connections are good and to make sure that devices that need power are getting what they need.

Be careful with volume controls. The volume can be changed in up to four different places, and if any of these are turned down, the system will have no sound. Many speakers have a Volume Control, and a few of the older sound cards will have a Volume Control wheel on the card itself. In the software world, individual applications will have a Volume Control, and the OS itself may have a Volume Control.

Finally, remember that speaker and microphone wires are exposed to all of the trauma that shoes, chairs, vacuum cleaners, and general abuse can provide. Most of the time, wires fray on the inside and slowly come apart without anything noticeable happening to the outside jacket. Listen for cracking sounds coming from the speakers and in recordings made by the microphone. This is usually a sign of bad wires.

## Drivers

As with any device, device driver issues come up frequently. Make sure that you install the latest drivers and don't fear a quick uninstall/reinstall. Use the device driver repair methods described earlier in the book.

## Support Resources

I use the phrase "support resources" to describe the many little programs that Windows puts between the device drivers and the applications. These support programs divide into two groups: codecs (compressor/decompressors) and DirectX.

Pure waveform files are huge, near-CD-quality WAV files that average about 10MB per minute of sound. This is no big deal for system sounds like short beeps, but complete songs get really big! Try downloading a WAV file that size—even on a high-speed connection it takes a while. As a result, a large number of compression methodologies exist. Some are quite famous—have you ever heard of an MP3 file? An MP3 is nothing more than a WAV file that uses a special compression program called the Fraunhofer IIS MPEG Layer-3 Codec. In order for a sound application to play the sound file, it needs access to the algorithm that decodes the MP3 format into a waveform. Some applications use their own built-in codecs, whereas Windows provides a broad cross-section of codecs that any sound application may access, leaving the sound application to do other jobs.

Different compression formats meet different needs. Some codecs do a better job of compression, but lose some of the sound quality. Others keep all of the quality, but may not compress as well. Without the proper codec, the sound file, or the sound built into a video file, will not play. If an application refuses to play a particular sound file, or if a video file plays without sound, you need to verify that you have the correct codec installed. Granted, later generation sound and video applications, such as WinAmp or Windows Media Player, will attempt to access the proper codec on their own (Windows Media Player even tries to download the proper one), but they often fail with some type of error that implies an "I don't have the right codec" type of problem (Figure 15-18).

**Figure 15-18**
Unable to download
codec in Windows
Media Player

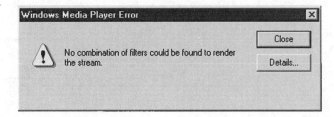

Earlier sound applications usually give no clue other than a useless "Unable to read file" message. When receiving a multimedia file, it is common to ask about both the file format and the codec to ensure you will be able to play the file.

If you're having a problem with a particular audio or video file, check the file's properties. Most, but not all, sound and all video files show their codec in their properties (Figure 15-19).

You can fix most codec problems by downloading the desired codec. All codec installation programs load the codec files and update the Registry—installing codecs is akin to loading a regular application. Figure 15-20 shows the installation of the popular Indeo 5 Codec.

Unfortunately, I've yet to find an established, one-stop Web site for codec downloads. I usually just fire up my Web browser and search on the codec name I want and the word "download."

Folks love to look at all the codecs in their Multimedia settings and try to figure out which codec goes with which type of audio or video file. Who cares? The A+ Certifica-

**Figure 15-19**
AVI file properties

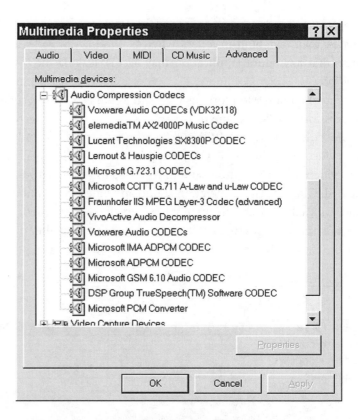

**Figure 15-20**
Installing a codec

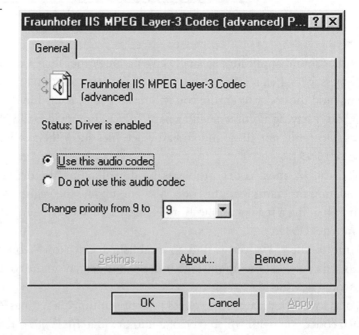

tion exams certainly do not care whether or not you know that the msg723 codec is used for compression of videoconferencing and telephony applications. The A+ exams *do* want you to understand why codecs exist, and that we may need to download one occasionally. The only time I have even the slightest interest in a codec is when I can't get an application to run!

> **EXAM TIP** Don't panic about understanding all the different codecs! Just make sure you know what they do and that you occasionally need to download them!

## DirectX

Windows and games used to have a hard time together. Windows adds so many layers of software between the game and the hardware that real-time gaming on Windows 95 and NT simply did not work. Most of the "cool" games of the mid-1990s such as the classics Quake, Doom, Wing Commander, and Descent, either refused to work with Windows 95, or did not work well (Figure 15-21).

**Figure 15-21**
Many early games did not work well under Windows 95.

Ock! I don't like Windows!

These games had to use DOS because it did not interfere with the powerful 3-D functions and massive, rapid calculations these games needed to run smoothly. Additionally, video cards began to appear that had powerful microprocessors enabling programmers to use commands such as "make fog from here to here," and 3-D standards such as 3dfx's Glide and Sun's OpenGL kept game developers from looking at Windows as a platform for game development.

As you might imagine, Microsoft didn't like this one little bit. As a result, Microsoft came out with a broad family of products lumped together under the name DirectX. DirectX provides applications, primarily games, with virtually complete direct access to hardware.

You install DirectX just like any other application. DirectX has gone through a number of version changes over the last few years and you can bet that plenty more changes are coming. Microsoft must make these changes, because audio and video technologies constantly change. Most applications clearly state on the box or in the documentation the version of DirectX they need to run. If you try to play a game without the proper version of DirectX on your computer, you will quickly know (Figure 15-22).

**Figure 15-22**
Ouch! DirectX
version error

Microsoft gives away DirectX, so most games include the version of DirectX needed along with the game. Windows 9x and Windows 2000 come with DirectX but there's a chance you may need to upgrade, especially if you have Windows 95. Use the DirectX diagnostic tool in the System Information tool to determine your version of DirectX and to test your DirectX functions (Figure 15-23).

Those of you still running Windows 95 do not have a simple way to test for DirectX. If you don't know, you probably don't have DirectX! Just download a copy from the Microsoft Web site. The current Web address is **www.microsoft.com/directx**.

## Application

Any application that uses sounds will have its own set of configuration issues. If I can't get sound to play out of an application, I first double-check using some test sounds in the Control Panel. If I get sound there, I know the problem lies in the application. There are so many items to check here! Look for configuration screens that set sounds.

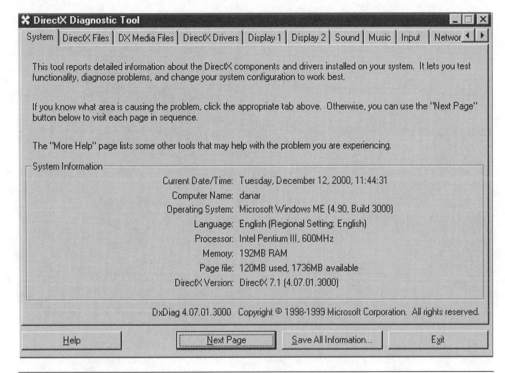

**Figure 15-23**   DirectX diagnostic

For example, Figure 15-24 shows the popular Microsoft Age of Empires game's control screen. Note that it uses three separate volume sliders. If all those are in the down position, you won't get sound.

Other applications may require advanced sound features. Figure 15-25 shows the configuration screen for the popular game Half-Life, showing advanced sound functions. These functions will be discussed in a moment. But at this point, appreciate that if you ask a game to do something the sound cannot do, you will not get sound.

# Beyond A+

Although the A+ Certification exams don't test on some of the more advanced aspects of sound, every tech should have a basic understanding of some of the newer advances in sound technology. Let's look at the most popular of all—3-D sound.

**Figure 15-24** Age of Empires' control screen

**Figure 15-25**
Half-Life's Audio
configuration screen

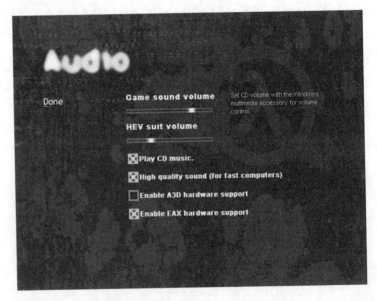

## 3-D Sound

The real fun with sound comes when we break away from that old two-speaker world and jump headlong into the world of 3-D sound. But 3-D sound means two totally different things in the computer world. The first is surround sound, sound designed for music and movies that surrounds the listener with sound. Second is true 3-D sound, primarily used in 3-D games, which enables programmers to make sounds directional. Let's discuss both.

## Surround Sound

Surround sound is exclusively the domain of audio and video recordings. Surround sound uses multiple soundtracks, each track dedicated to one of four or more carefully positioned speakers, to create the fantastic effects similar to what you'd hear in a music hall or a movie theatre. Currently, three types of surround sound predominate: Dolby® Surround, Dolby Digital, and DTS®. In order to use any of these technologies, you must have a device that supports that technology (most DVD players support all of them), enough speakers of the proper configuration, and media that was recorded with this technology. DVD disks will clearly indicate the type of surround sound they support (Figure 15-26).

**Figure 15-26**
Supported surround
sound technologies

## Dolby Surround

Dolby Surround, also known as Dolby Pro Logic, uses four speakers (placed as shown in Figure 15-27) to create surround sound. Dolby Surround is dated and has never received much support from the music world, although it has received extensive support from the video world.

**Figure 15-27**
Dolby Pro Logic
layout

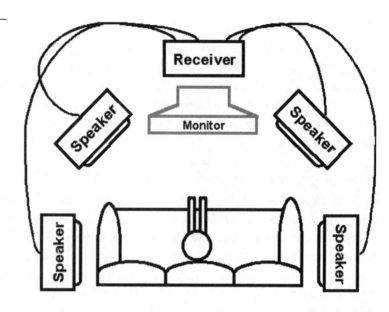

## Dolby Digital

Dolby Digital provides up to six separate channels, each requiring its own speaker. One of these speakers is a subwoofer. The subwoofer makes all those deep sounds that you feel more than you hear. When describing speaker setups, the expression ".1" is used to describe the subwoofer. So, a Dolby Digital 5.1 soundtrack needs four main or *satellite* speakers, a center speaker, and a subwoofer. Figure 15-28 shows a typical layout for a Dolby Digital 5.1 home theatre system.

**Figure 15-28**
Dolby Digital 5.1
layout

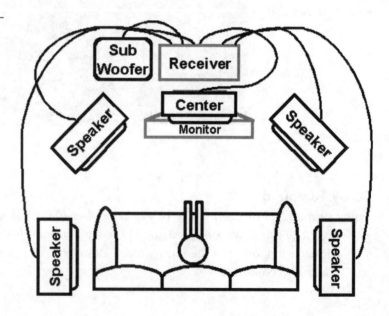

But what if you want to just play a regular stereo audio CD? For stereo output, all players have a built-in, two-channel Dolby Digital decoder that downmixes (squishes) the sound from 5.1 channels to four-channel Dolby Surround.

## DTS

*Digital Theatre Systems* (DTS) is a direct competitor of Dolby Digital. DTS sound uses less compression, requiring more data, but DTS argues that the lower compression ratio makes for a much better sound. I guess they must be right given the large number of DTS encoded systems available today. Other than the compression ratio, DTS and Dolby Digital look identical.

## PCs and Surround Sound

The proliferation of DVD players on PCs encourages users to use their systems as movie players. I feel this is a mistake, unless you're flying from Houston to London and don't feel like watching the bad movies and television shows on the airplane's monitors. True appreciation of DVD titles requires carefully placed speakers, configured home theatre systems, and large (preferably the upcoming *High-Definition Television* (HDTV) standard) monitors. Watching the movie on a 14-inch viewable screen with cheap speakers is like making love in a spacesuit; it just doesn't give you the real experience. Get a DVD for your PC to read DVD-ROM data disks. Get a DVD for your laptop to watch good movies on long trips. Get a home theatre system to enjoy the beauty of surround sound. That's my opinion and I'm sticking to it!

## 3-D Sound on the PC

Today's powerful 3-D graphic systems have always lacked one item: good sound. The beautiful vistas of some of the more modern 3-D games without quality 3-D sound really takes away from the gaming experience. Starting a few years ago, two companies, Aureal and Creative Labs, created competing 3-D sound standards. Aureal's was called A3D and Creative's was called EAX. These sound standards enabled games to use 4.1 speaker systems to create positional sound. Figure 15-29 shows a typical 4.1 speaker setup.

If someone walked up behind your character while you were playing Half-Life, the sound emanated from the back speakers. In MechWarrior you would hear the hiss from front to back as you dodged a salvo of short-range rockets. Distant sounds sounded far away, and if someone whispered, you needed to walk up to them in order to hear. Background music and the subwoofer made outstanding sound effects. It was great!

In 2000, Creative Labs bought the technology from Aureal, which had gone belly up the previous year. Microsoft, in a rare case of fair play, licensed the EAX technology

**Figure 15-29**
Typical 4.1
speaker setup

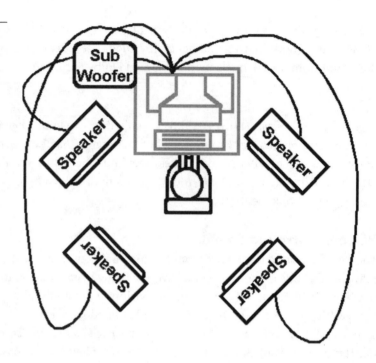

from Creative Labs and added a new piece to DirectX called DirectSound3D. So, as long as you have a sound card that supports DirectSound3D, 4.1 speakers, and an application written to use DirectSound3D, you get all the coolness of 3-D sound—just be careful not to trip over your back speaker wires if you get up to get something to drink!

## Configuring 3-D Sound

One important aspect of 3-D sound is speaker placement. Improperly placed speakers make for some really bizarre sounds, and your immersion in the game combined with weird sound can literally make you sick. Most 3-D cards come with handy applications to help you set up the speakers correctly (Figure 15-30). The Advanced playback button under the Sounds tab of the Windows 2000 Sounds and Media applet even provides a basic setup screen (Figure 15-31), although you'll still want to use the one that comes with your sound card.

## 3-D Sound Issues

Connectivity causes most 3-D sound problems. As of this time, no single method for connecting 3-D sound exists. The majority of earlier 3-D sound cards simply provide a second port on the back of the card for a second pair of speakers and subwoofer. The subwoofer works by grabbing the low-end sounds from the sound stream and amplifying them.

Figure 15-30
Typical 3-D
setup screen for
a SoundBlaster
Live! card

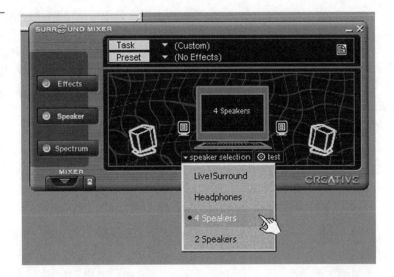

Figure 15-31
Windows 2000
speaker setup

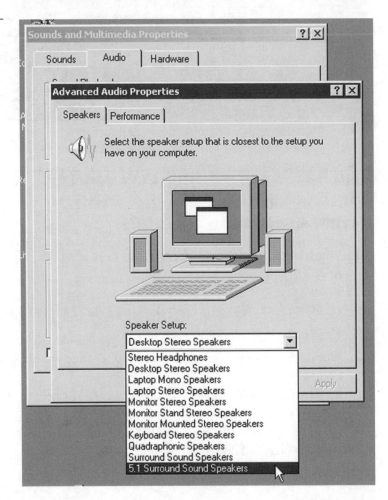

More modern sound cards use a dazzling variety of outputs. Most sound cards provide, at the minimum, a new digital connection that connects to 5.1 speaker systems. This enables either DirectSound3D or DVD, assuming you have a DVD player in the system. Figure 15-32 shows a 5.1 sound card with the connectors labeled. Most sound card manufacturers use the standardized color-coding for connectors as follows (from left to right in reference to Figure 15-32):

| | |
|---|---|
| Digital Out | Orange |
| Line In | Blue |
| Microphone | Pink |
| Output for Front Speakers | Green |
| Output for Rear Speakers | Black |

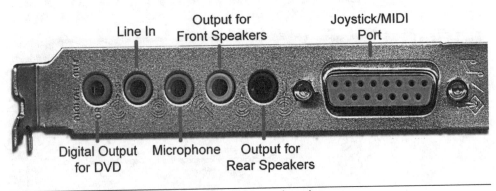

**Figure 15-32**   External connectors on a 5.1 sound card

## Review Questions

1. Which of the following file formats can store a human voice most accurately?
   A. MIDI
   B. WAV
   C. VOICE
   D. FM

2. Why do sound cards sometimes need two separate sets of I/O addresses and DMA channels?
   A. To separate 8-bit and 16-bit sound.
   B. Each set creates different sounds for mixing.
   C. To support both the WAV and MIDI components on a sound card.
   D. No sound card does this.

3. On the back of most sound cards is a 15-pin, female DB connector. This is for what type of peripheral connection? (Choose all that apply.)
   A. A mouse
   B. A joystick
   C. A MIDI controller
   D. A WAV controller

4. In Windows 9x, where would you change the system resources for a sound card?
   A. In the Control Panel, double-click the Multimedia applet and select the Audio and MIDI tabs.
   B. In the Control Panel, alternate-click Multimedia and select Properties.
   C. Select Start | Programs | Accessories | System Tools | System Information.
   D. In the Control Panel, double-click the System applet; select the Device Manager tab; open Sound, video, and game controllers; highlight the sound device; and select Properties | Resource tab.

5. Which of the following is not a tab on the Multimedia control panel applet in Windows 9x?
   A. Audio
   B. Video
   C. MIDI
   D. WAV

6. Which of the following is not a tab in Windows 2000 Sounds and Multimedia control panel applet?
   A. Sounds
   B. Video
   C. Audio
   D. Hardware

7. In the Sounds and Multimedia Properties Audio tab in Windows 2000, which of the following is not one of the options?
   A. Sound Recording
   B. Sound Playback
   C. WAV Music Playback
   D. MIDI Music Playback

8. Which of the following are needed to set up a sound card? (Select all that apply.)
   A. Drivers
   B. I/O Addressing
   C. IRQs
   D. DMAs

9. Which of the following is needed to play audio CD-ROMs through your system's sound card?

   A. A 4-pin cable connecting the sound card and the CD-ROM.

   B. The CD-ROM connected to the sound card with an IDE cable.

   C. Nothing; if both devices are configured properly, it will work.

   D. It cannot be done.

10. When troubleshooting a sound card that was working yesterday but not today, which of the following is least likely to be the problem?

    A. Volume controls

    B. The external wires being broken or frayed

    C. Power

    D. Slot position

## Answers

1. **B.** WAV files are recordings of sound and thus handle voice better than MIDI. VOICE and FM file formats do not exist.

2. **C.** Most sound cards have separate system resources for WAV and MIDI.

3. **B and C.** Most sound cards support both MIDI devices and joysticks through the 15-pin DB connector.

4. **D.** Note the question asked about resources, as in I/O addresses and IRQs. The Device Manager is your first stop in Windows 9*x*. See Windows 2000 for setting resources for hardware.

5. **D.** There is no tab called WAV.

6. **B.** Video uses the Display applet.

7. **C.** The applet does not have an option called WAV music playback.

8. **A, B, C, D.** Windows 9*x* and Windows 2000 will set much of this up with Plug and Play, but a sound card still requires resources and drivers.

9. **A.** The 4-pin cable that runs from the sound card to the CD-ROM enables audio CD-ROMs to play through the sound card.

10. **D.** The slot position is the least likely issue.

# Video

In this chapter, you will

- Understand the different components that make video work
- Learn about refresh rates and how they affect monitors
- Understand how CRT and LCD monitors function
- Learn how to fix basic monitor problems

When the first IBM PC arrived, the choice in monitors was simple. You could choose which color—green or amber—and that was it. Today the choices are not nearly as simple. You need to understand features such as dot pitch, resolution, convergence, refresh, interlaced vs. non-interlaced, pixels, color depth, and energy savings. To add to the confusion, laptop computers no longer have a monopoly on LCD panels. The ongoing price drop of LCD panels has moved them onto enough desktops that we're faced with an entirely new set of issues. Should you buy a traditional monitor or go for an LCD?

In a way, this is two chapters in one. The vast differences between LCD and traditional monitors require two separate "Historical/Conceptual" and "Test Specific" sections. We'll begin with the traditional video card/monitor configuration, covering concepts and test areas, and then repeat the process with LCD. This chapter explains the basics of how video cards and monitors work. So let's get to work, starting with the classic video card and monitor setup.

> **CAUTION** Before we begin, here's a note of warning about the inside of a traditional monitor. I will discuss what can be repaired and what requires a more specialized expertise. Make no mistake—the interior of a monitor might appear similar to the interior of a PC because of the printed circuit boards and related components, but that is precisely where the similarity ends. No PC has voltages exceeding 15,000 to 30,000 volts, but most monitors do. So let's get one thing perfectly clear: Opening up a monitor can be deadly! Even when the power is disconnected, certain components retain a substantial voltage for an extended period of time. You can inadvertently short one of the components and fry yourself—to death. Given this risk, certain aspects of monitor repair lie outside the necessary skill set for a normal PC support person and defiantly outside the A+ test domains! I will show you how to address the problems you can fix safely and make sure you understand the ones you need to hand over to a monitor shop.

# Historical/Conceptual

Video consists of two devices that work as a team to get a picture in front of you: the video card, often called the display adapter, and the monitor (Figure 16-1). The video card in turn has two distinct components: one to take commands from the computer and update its own onboard RAM, and the other to scan RAM and send the data to the monitor.

Let's look at video cards and monitors individually. I'll bring them back together as a team later in the chapter so you can understand the many nuances that make video so challenging. We'll start with the monitor.

**Figure 16-1**
Typical video card
and monitor

Monitor

Video Card
or
Display Adapter

## Video Monitor Components

All monitors have certain components in common, such as a *cathode ray tube* (CRT) and electron guns. To understand monitors, you need a good grasp of each component and how they work together to make a beautiful (or not so beautiful) picture on the screen. Let's take a look.

## CRT

Traditional monitors are called CRT monitors to differentiate them from LCD monitors. All CRT monitors have a CRT, which is a main vacuum tube. One end of this tube is a very slender cylinder that contains three electron guns. The fatter, wide end of the CRT is the display screen. The inside of the screen has a phosphor coating. When power is applied to one or more of the electron guns, a stream of electrons shoots towards the display end of the CRT (Figure 16-2). Along the way, this stream is subjected to magnetic fields generated by a ring of electromagnets called a *yoke* that controls the electron beam's point of impact. When the phosphor coating is struck by the electron beam, it releases its energy as visible light. A picture of the electron gun and magnetic yoke assembly is shown in Figure 16-3.

**Figure 16-2**
Electron stream
in CRT

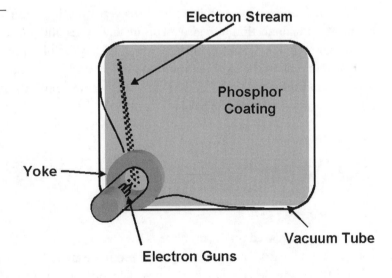

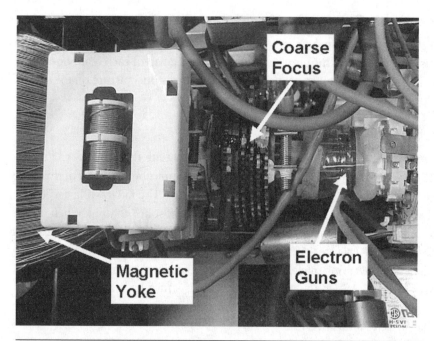

**Figure 16-3** Components of a CRT that generate and direct the electron stream

This phosphorous energy release happens very quickly, too quickly for the human eye and brain connection to register. Fortunately for us, the phosphors on the display screen have a quality called *persistence*, which means the phosphors continue to glow after being struck by the electron beam. Too much persistence and the image is smeary; too little and the image appears to flicker. The perfect combination of beam and persistence creates the illusion of a solid picture.

## Test Specific

### Refresh Rate

Video data is displayed on the monitor as the electron guns make a series of horizontal sweeps across the display, energizing the appropriate areas of the phosphorous coating (Figure 16-4). The sweeps start at the upper-left corner of the monitor and move across and down to the lower-right corner. The screen is "painted" only in one direction, then the electron gun turns and retraces its path across the screen, to be ready for the next sweep. These sweeps are called *raster lines*.

**Figure 16-4**
Screen traces
on monitor

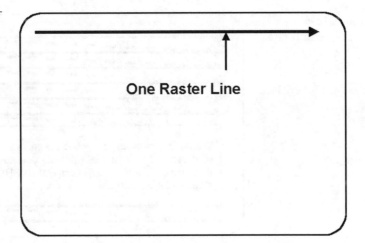

One Raster Line

The speed at which the electron beam moves across the screen is known as the *horizontal refresh rate* (HRR), as shown in Figure 16-5. The monitor draws a number of lines across the screen, eventually covering the screen with glowing phosphors. The number of lines is not fixed, unlike television screens, which all have a fixed number of lines. After the guns reach the lower-right corner of the screen, they all turn off and point back to the upper-left corner. The amount of time it takes to draw the entire screen and get the electron guns back up to the upper-left corner is called the *vertical refresh rate* (VRR), shown in Figure 16-6.

**Figure 16-5**
Horizontal refresh
rate

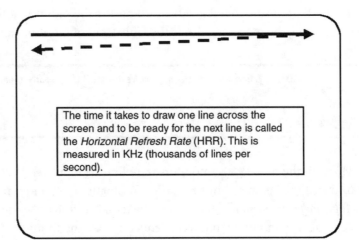

The time it takes to draw one line across the screen and to be ready for the next line is called the *Horizontal Refresh Rate* (HRR). This is measured in KHz (thousands of lines per second).

**Figure 16-6**
Vertical refresh rate

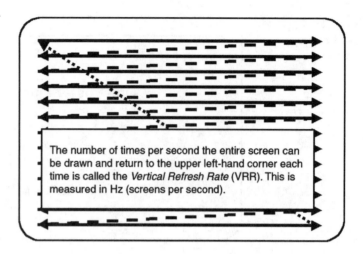

The number of times per second the entire screen can be drawn and return to the upper left-hand corner each time is called the *Vertical Refresh Rate* (VRR). This is measured in Hz (screens per second).

Monitors do not determine the HRR or VRR; video cards "push" the monitor at a certain VRR and then the monitor determines the HRR. If the video card is set to push at too low a VRR, the monitor produces a noticeable flicker, causing eyestrain and headaches for users. Pushing the monitor at too high of a VRR, however, causes a definite distortion of the screen image and will damage the circuitry of the monitor and eventually destroy it. The number one killer of monitors is improper VRR settings, and the number one reason your office is filled with crabby workers is due to the VRR being set too low. All good PC support techs understand this and take substantial time tweaking the VRR to insure that the video card pushes the monitor at the highest VRR without damaging the monitor—this is the Holy Grail of monitor support!

**NOTE** When most techs say "refresh rate," they really mean the VRR!

Up until the mid-1980s, monitors were limited to a fixed VRR. Around 1986, NEC introduced the first monitor to support automatic selection of multiple VRRs, called a *multiple-frequency monitor*. NEC coined the term "MultiSync" to describe its line of multiple-frequency monitors, but techs tended to call any monitor that handled multiple refresh rates a MultiSync monitor. All monitors used on PCs today are MultiSync, so the term has faded from our daily use but pops up enough to at least comment upon.

## Phosphors and Shadow Mask

All CRT monitors contain dots of phosphorous or some other light-sensitive compound that glows red, green, or blue when an electron gun sweeps over them. Each dot is called a *phosphor*. These phosphors are evenly distributed across the front of the monitor (Figure 16-7).

**Figure 16-7**
A monitor is a grid of red, green, and blue phosphors.

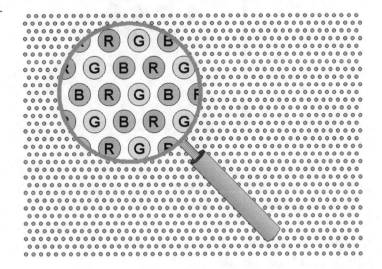

The CRT has three electron guns: one to hit the red phosphors, one for the blue phosphors, and one for the green phosphors. It is important to understand that the electron guns do not fire colored light; they simply fire electrons at different intensities, which then make the phosphors glow. The higher the intensity, the brighter the color. Directly behind the phosphors is the *shadow mask*, a screen that enables only the proper electron gun to light the proper phosphors (Figure 16-8). This prevents, for example, the red electron beam from "bleeding over" and lighting neighboring blue and green dots.

The electron guns sweep across the phosphors as a group, turning rapidly on and off as they move across the screen. When the group reaches the end of the screen, it moves to the next line. It is crucial to understand that turning the guns on and off, combined with moving the guns to new lines, creates a "mosaic" that is the image you see on the screen. The number of times the guns turn on and off, combined with the number of lines drawn on the screen, determines the number of mosaic pieces used to create the image. These individual "pieces" are called *pixels*, from the term "picture elements." You can't hold a pixel in your hand; it's just the area of phosphors lit at one instant when the group of guns is turned on. The size of pixels can change, depending on the number of times the group of guns is turned on and off and the number of lines drawn.

**Figure 16-8**
Shadow mask

Not all monitors use dots. The popular Sony Trinitron line of CRT monitors uses bars of red, green, and blue instead of dots. The holes in the shadow mask have a rectangular shape. Many people feel this makes for a much more crisp, clear monitor. Somebody must agree with them as the Trinitron enjoys tremendous popularity. Even though the phosphors and shadow mask have a different shape, everything you learn here goes for Trinitrons also.

## Resolution

Monitor resolution is always shown as the number of horizontal pixels times the number of vertical pixels. A resolution of 640 × 480, therefore, indicates a horizontal resolution of 640 pixels and a vertical resolution of 480 pixels. If you multiply the values together, you can see how many pixels are on each screen: 640 × 480 = 307,200 pixels per screen. An example of resolution affecting the pixel size is shown in Figure 16-9.

Some common resolutions are 640 × 480, 800 × 600, 1,024 × 768, 1,280 × 1,024, and 1,600 × 1,200. Notice that these resolutions match a 4:3 ratio. This is called the *aspect ratio*. Most monitors are shaped like television screens, with a 4:3 aspect ratio, so most resolutions are designed to match—or at least be close to—that shape.

The last important issue is to determine the maximum possible resolution for a monitor. In other words, how small can one pixel be? Well, the answer lies in the phosphors. A pixel must be made up of at least one red, one green, and one blue phosphor to make any color, so the smallest theoretical pixel would consist of one group of red, green, and blue phosphors, a *triad* (Figure 16-10). Various limitations in screens, controlling electronics, and electron gun technology make the maximum resolution much bigger than one triad.

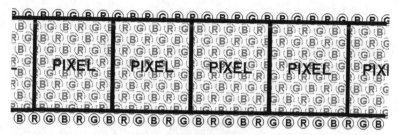

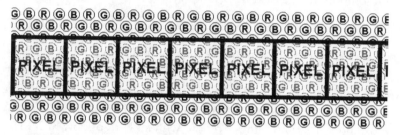

**Lower Resolution**

**Higher Resolution**

**Figure 16-9**    Resolution vs. pixel size

**Figure 16-10**
One triad

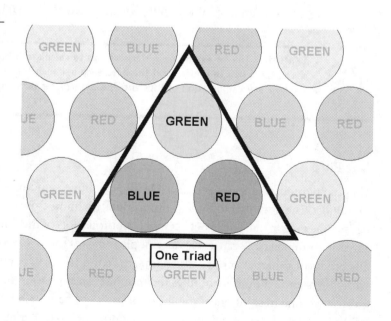

To review: Each discrete dot of phosphorus is called a phosphor dot, each triangle of three phosphors (one red, one green, one blue) is called a triad, and each group of dots painted as the electron beam sweeps across the screen is called a pixel. Higher resolutions sweep a narrower beam with more pixels per row, and lower resolutions sweep a wider beam with fewer pixels per row.

As shown previously, the *horizontal refresh rate* (HRR) defines the speed at which the monitor can draw one line on the screen, while the *vertical refresh rate* (VRR) defines how many times per second the entire screen is redrawn. These values relate to the number of vertical resolution lines, as follows:

$$HRR = (VRR) \times (\text{number of lines}), \text{ so } (\text{number of lines}) = (HRR) \div (VRR)$$

Given the HRR and VRR, you can determine the maximum number of lines of resolution a monitor can support. For example, given an HRR of 31.5 *kilohertz* (KHz = thousands of cycles/second) and a VRR of 72 *Hertz* (Hz), what would be the maximum number of lines on the screen? Could you support 640 × 480? Take 31.5 KHz and divide it by 72 Hz: 31,500 ÷ 72 = 437 lines. So now, with an HRR of only 31.5 KHz, you would have to either reduce the resolution or reduce the VRR and put up with increased screen flicker. By reducing the VRR to 60 Hz, the formula would be 31,500 ÷ 60 = 525 lines. Because 525 > 480, we know your monitor could support 640 × 480 resolution at that HRR and VRR.

Alternately, you could increase the HRR from 31.5 KHz to a value that enables 480 lines at a VRR of 72 Hz. If you used an HRR of 37.9 KHz and divided it by 72, you would have a maximum line value of 526, which would enable a 640 × 480 resolution.

**EXAM TIP** The A+ exam doesn't expect you to calculate HRR and VRR, but it does expect you to understand the difference between the two and to appreciate how any combination of HRR and VRR determines maximum resolution!

### Dot Pitch

The resolution of a monitor is defined by the maximum amount of detail the monitor can render. The dot pitch of the monitor ultimately limits this resolution. The *dot pitch* defines the diagonal distance between phosphorous dots of the same color, and is measured in millimeters. Because a lower dot pitch means more dots on the screen, it usually produces a sharper, more defined image (Figure 16-11). Dot pitch works in tandem with the maximum number of lines the monitor can support in order to determine the greatest working resolution of the monitor. It might be possible to place an image at 1,600 × 1,200 on a 15-inch monitor with a dot pitch of .31 mm, but it would not be very readable.

**Figure 16-11**
Measuring dot pitch

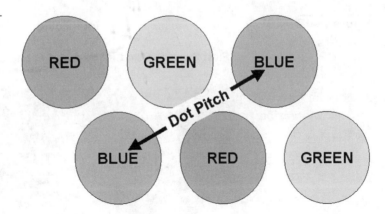

The dot pitch can range from as high as .39 mm to as low as .18 mm. For most Windows-based applications on a 17-inch monitor, most folks find that .28 mm is the maximum usable dot pitch that still produces a clear picture.

**NOTE** When comparing advertised prices, make a note of the monitor's dot pitch in the ad. Watch out for lower-priced monitors with an unacceptably high .39-mm dot pitch. By comparison, a mid-priced television has a dot pitch of approximately .35 mm.

## Interlacing

To keep costs down, some low-end monitors produce interlaced images. This means that the monitor sweeps or refreshes alternate lines of pixels on the display. In other words, it takes two sweeps through the screen to make one image. In its first pass, the monitor covers all the odd lines, and on the next pass it covers the even lines (Figure 16-12). Interlacing enables a low-end monitor to support faster refresh rates by giving it twice as much time to make a screen. But interlacing depends on the ability of the eye and brain to combine the two separate sets of lines into one stable image. Interlacing is another way of creating eyestrain and headaches, and should be avoided.

## Bandwidth

*Bandwidth* defines the maximum number of times the electron gun can be turned on and off per second. Bandwidth is measured in *megahertz* (MHz). In essence, bandwidth tells us how fast the monitor can put an image on the screen. A typical value for a better quality 17-inch color monitor would be around 150 MHz, which means that the electron beam can be turned on and off 150 million times per second. Although most techs ignore the bandwidth, it really is the single most important value you can know

**Figure 16-12**
Interlacing

Interlacing

First Sweep - Odd Lines          Second Sweep - Even Lines

Two Sweeps, One Screen

about a monitor. The value for a monitor's bandwidth will determine the maximum VRR the video card should push the monitor for any given resolution as follows:

$$\text{maximum VRR} = \text{bandwidth} \div \text{pixels per page}$$

For example, what is the maximum VRR that a 17-inch monitor with bandwidth of 100 MHz and a resolution of 1,024 × 768 can support? The answer is:

$$\text{maximum VRR} = 100{,}000{,}000 \div (1{,}024 \times 768) = 127 \text{ Hz}$$

That's a pretty good monitor, as most video cards do not push beyond 120 Hz! At a resolution of 1,200 × 1,024, the vertical refresh would be:

$$100{,}000{,}000 \div (1{,}200 \times 1{,}024) = 81 \text{ Hz}$$

So, we would make sure to set the video card's VRR to 80 Hz or less. If you had a monitor with a bandwidth of only 75 MHz, the maximum VRR at a 1,200 × 1,024 resolution would be only 61 Hz.

Most monitor makers know that people aren't going to take the time to do these calculations. Instead, they do the calculations for you and create tables of refresh rates at certain resolutions to show what a monitor can do. Figure 16-13 shows the sales literature for one of my personal favorite monitors: The ViewSonic GS790. Note the table of resolutions at certain VRRs. That's not to say they're ashamed of advertising the bandwidth, but it's usually tucked into a corner (Figure 16-14).

If you try to calculate the HRR and VRR from these numbers, you won't get quite the same values as shown in the ads. That's due to certain delays inherent to all monitors, but you'll get pretty close!

**Figure 16-13**
Resolution/refresh
rate chart

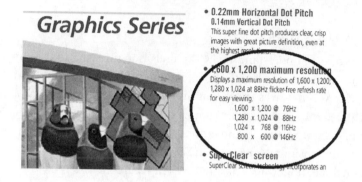

# GS790 Monitor

*Graphics Series*

- **0.22mm Horizontal Dot Pitch**
  0.14mm Vertical Dot Pitch
  This super fine dot pitch produces clear, crisp
  images with great picture definition, even at
  the highest resolutions.

- **1,600 x 1,200 maximum resolution**
  Displays a maximum resolution of 1,600 x 1,200,
  1,280 x 1,024 at 88Hz flicker-free refresh rate
  for easy viewing.
  1,600 x 1,200 @ 76Hz
  1,280 x 1,024 @ 88Hz
  1,024 x 768 @ 116Hz
  800 x 600 @ 146Hz

- **SuperClear screen**
  SuperClear screen technology incorporates an

**Figure 16-14**
Bandwidth listed

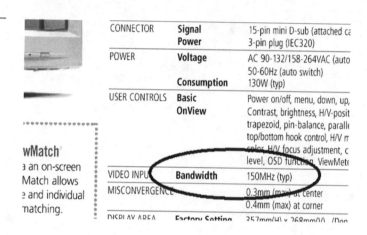

wMatch
a an on-screen
Match allows
e and individual
matching.

| CONNECTOR | Signal | 15-pin mini D-sub (attached ca |
| | Power | 3-pin plug (IEC320) |
| POWER | Voltage | AC 90-132/158-264VAC (auto |
| | | 50-60Hz (auto switch) |
| | Consumption | 130W (typ) |
| USER CONTROLS | Basic | Power on/off, menu, down, up, |
| | OnView | Contrast, brightness, H/V-posit |
| | | trapezoid, pin-balance, paralle |
| | | top/bottom hook control, H/V m |
| | | color, H/V focus adjustment, c |
| | | level, OSD function, ViewMeto |
| VIDEO INPU | Bandwidth | 150MHz (typ) |
| MISCONVERGENCE | | 0.3mm (max) at center |
| | | 0.4mm (max) at corner |
| DISPLAY AREA | Factory Setting | 357mm(H) x 268mm(V) (Dep |

Great! Now that you have the basics of CRT monitors, let's turn to LCD monitors. Although the technology differs dramatically between the monitor types, most of the terms applied to CRTs also apply to nearly identical LCD functions.

## Historical/Conceptual

### LCD

Once reserved only for laptops and people with way too much money, the ongoing price drops of *Liquid Crystal Displays* (LCDs) make them continue to appear on more and more desktops. LCD monitors have many advantages over CRTs: they are thinner and lighter, use much less power, are virtually flicker-free, and don't emit potentially harmful radiation. LCDs come complete with their own family of abbreviations, jargon, and terms that we need to understand in order to install, maintain, and support LCDs.

### How LCDs Work

The secret to understanding LCD panels is to understand the concept of the polarity of light. Anyone who played with a prism in sixth grade or looked at a rainbow knows that light travels in waves (no quantum mechanics here, please!) and the wavelength of the light determines the color. What we don't appreciate is the fact that light waves emanate from a light source in three-dimensions. It's impossible to draw a clear diagram of three-dimensional waves, so instead, let's use an analogy. To visualize this, think of light emanating from a flashlight, as in Figure 16-15.

**Figure 16-15**
Light coming from
a flashlight

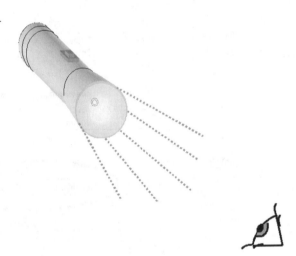

Now think of the light emanating from that flashlight as though someone was shaking a jump rope (Figure 16-16). This is not a rhythmic shaking, back and forth or up and down; it's more as if a person went crazy and was shaking the jump rope all over the place—up, down, left, right, constantly changing the speed.

That's how light really acts. Well, I guess we could take the analogy one step further by saying the person has an infinite number of arms, each holding a jump rope shooting out in every direction to show the "three-dimensionality" of light waves but (a) I can't draw that and (b) one jump rope will suffice to explain LCD panels. The different speeds create wavelengths, from very short to very long. When light comes into our eyes at many different wavelengths, we see white light. If the light came in only one wavelength, we would see only that color. Light flowing through a polarized filter (like sunglasses) is like putting a picket fence between us and the person shaking the rope. We see all of the wavelengths but only the waves of similar orientation (Figure 16-17). We

**Figure 16-16**
Light waves are comparable to someone shaking a jump rope.

**Figure 16-17**
Waves of similar orientation

would still see all of the colors, just less of them because we only see the waves of the same orientation, making the image darker (Figure 16-18). That's why many sunglasses use polarizing filters.

Now, what would happen if we added another picket fence, but put the slats in a horizontal direction, as shown in Figure 16-19? This would effectively cancel out all of the waves. This is what happens when two polarizing filters are combined at a 90-degree angle—no light passes through (Figure 16-20).

**Figure 16-18**
Effect of
polarization

**Regular Image**

**Image viewed
through polarized lens**

**Figure 16-19**
Two sets of slats
at 90 degree angles
enable no waves
to pass.

Now, what would happen if a third fence was added between the two fences with the slats at a 45-degree angle? Well, it would sort of "twist" some of the shakes in the rope so that the waves could then get through (Figure 16-21).

The same thing is true with the polarizing filters. The third filter twists some of the light so that it gets through (Figure 16-22). If you're really feeling scientific, go to any teacher's supply store and pick up three polarizing filters for about $3 U.S. each and try it. It works.

**Figure 16-20**
Two polarizing filters, through which no light passes

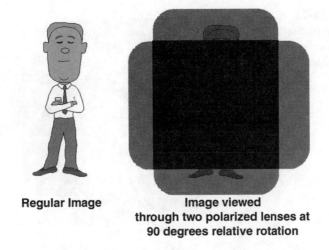

**Regular Image**

**Image viewed through two polarized lenses at 90 degrees relative rotation**

**Figure 16-21**
Three sets of slats, which enable waves to get through

A third set of slats, 45° to the other slats

Liquid crystals take advantage of the property of polarization. Liquid crystals are composed of a specially formulated liquid full of long, thin crystals that always want to orient themselves in the same direction, as shown in Figure 16-23. This substance acts exactly like a liquid polarized filter. If you poured a thin film of this stuff between two sheets of glass, you'd get a darn good pair of sunglasses.

**Figure 16-22**
Three polarizing
filters enable some
light to pass
through.

**Image viewed through two
polarized lenses at 90° relative rotation
with a third 45° lens in between**

**Figure 16-23**
Liquid crystal
molecules

Imagine cutting extremely fine grooves on one side of one of those sheets of glass. When you place this liquid in contact with a finely grooved surface, the molecules naturally line up with the grooves in the surface (Figure 16-24).

If we place another finely grooved surface, with the grooves at a 90-degree orientation to the other surface, opposite of the first one, the molecules in contact with that side will attempt to line up with it. The molecules in between, in trying to line up with both sides, will immediately line up in a nice twist (Figure 16-25).

So if two perpendicular polarizing filters are then placed on either side of the liquid crystal, the liquid crystal will twist the light and enable it to pass (Figure 16-26).

But if we expose the liquid crystal to an electrical potential, the crystals will change their orientation to match the direction of the electrical field. The twist goes away and no light passes through (Figure 16-27).

**Figure 16-24**
Liquid crystal
molecules tend to
line up together.

**Figure 16-25**
Liquid crystal
molecules twisting

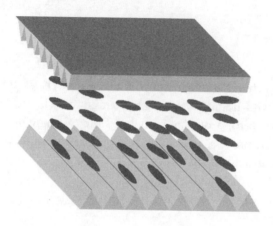

**Figure 16-26**
No charge, enabling
light to pass

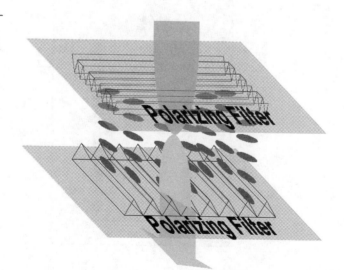

**Figure 16-27**
Electrical charge,
enabling no light
to pass

So, how do you charge the right spot? In the first LCDs, each viewable piece of the screen was filled with liquid crystal. To darken an area, it was charged. Figure 16-28 shows the number zero, a display made possible by charging six areas to make an ellipse of sorts. This process, called *static charging,* is still quite popular in more basic numeric displays such as calculators.

**Figure 16-28**
Single character for
static LCD numeric
display

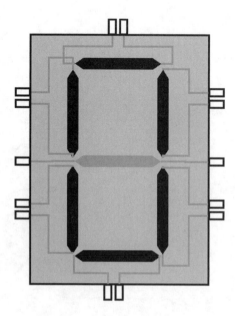

The static method would not work in the PCs due to its inherent inflexibility. Instead, the first generation of PC LCD screens used a matrix of wires (Figure 16-29). The vertical wires, the "Y" wires, would run parallel to each other on one side of the liquid crystal. The horizontal wires, the "X" wires, would run on the other side of the liquid crystal. By lighting any "X" and "Y" wire, a small part of the display received a charge, cutting off light transfer.

**Figure 16-29**
LCD matrix of wires

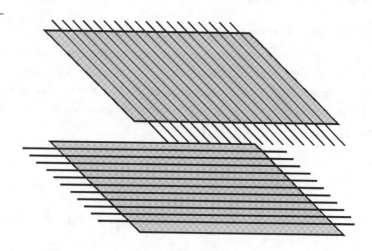

If you want color, you have three matrices. The three matrices intersect very close together. Above the intersections, the glass is covered with tiny red, green, and blue dots. The amount of voltage would enable different levels of red, green, and blue, creating colors (Figure 16-30).

**Figure 16-30**
Color LCD matrix

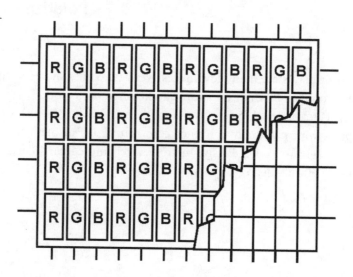

We call this usage of LCD technology *passive matrix*. All LCD displays on PCs used only passive matrix for many years. Unfortunately, passive matrix is slow and tends to create a little overlap between individual pixels. This gives a slightly blurred effect to the image displayed. Manufacturers eventually came up with a speedier method of display, called *dual-scan passive matrix*, where the screen refreshed two lines at a time. Although other LCD technologies have since appeared, dual-scan continues to show up on some lower-end LCD panels.

### Thin Film Transitor (TFT)

A vast improvement over dual scan is called *active matrix* or *thin film transistor* (TFT). Instead of using X, Y wires, one or more tiny transistors control each color dot, providing faster refresh, crisp definition, and much tighter color control. TFT is the LCD of choice today, even though it is much more expensive than passive matrix (Figure 16-31).

**Figure 16-31**
TFT cutaway

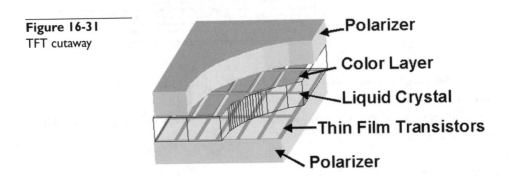

We call this usage

TFT displays have many advantages over passive displays. First, they are brighter with better contrast. Second, they can handle far more colors. Passive LCD's slow speed keeps it at a practical limit of no more than 256 colors (8-bit), whereas the latest TFT displays work at virtually unlimited color. Third, TFT displays have a much wider viewing area (Figure 16-32). Passive matrix is rarely more than 45 degrees, whereas active is closer to 90–100 degrees.

**Figure 16-32**
Viewing angles for
active and passive
matrix LCDs

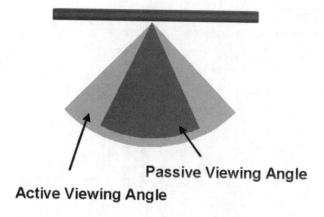

Passive Viewing Angle

Active Viewing Angle

## Test Specific

### LCD Resolution

There is no equivalent to a triad on LCD panels. Each tiny group of three red, green, and blue units on an LCD are called *pixels*. LCD panels come with a fixed number of pixels—always equivalent to a common resolution. No LCD panel can display more than its pixel limitation. If you own an LCD panel with 1,024 × 768 pixels, the best resolution you get is 1,024 × 768. LCD's fixed pixel size creates an issue when trying to use lower resolutions. If you have a 1,024 × 768 fixed pixel LCDs, how do you make the LCD display at 640 × 480, for example? Older LCD simply made the image smaller— only using 640 × 480 of the pixels! Today's LCDs fake lower resolutions by estimating the pixels used with special expansion algorithms. Suppose you have a 1,024 × 768 LCD monitor. At 1,024 × 768, a red, lowercase letter *f* looks like Figure 16-33.

If you lower the resolution to 800 × 600 and want the letter to stay the same physical size, you must make the same letter in the same pixels and use anti-aliasing (subtle color variations) to make the letter "look" as though it had a lower resolution, as Figure 16-34 shows.

**Figure 16-33**
Proper resolution

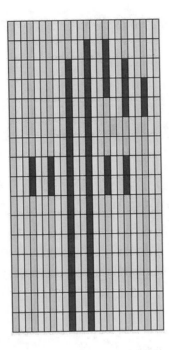

**Figure 16-34**
Same letter at a
lower resolution
using anti-aliasing

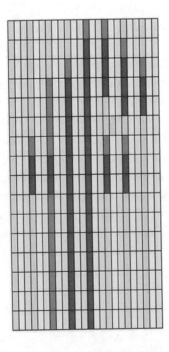

As you can see, anti-aliasing isn't perfect. As a result, the resolution of the LCD monitor is always kept at the true pixel resolution.

### Backlighting

LCD panels need good backlighting to improve visibility. Most LCDs use a type of cold fluorescent light with prisms to spread the light as evenly as possible across the screen. We use the measurement unit *nits* (1 nit = 1 candela/meter$^2$) to quantify the brightness of the backlighting. Backlighting is always a tradeoff. We want as bright a backlight as possible, but brighter backlights consume power. This extra power consumption is trivial on a desktop LCD, but on a laptop LCD, it makes a huge difference in battery life. The LCD's backlight is the number one power eater on a laptop! As a rule, we like to have desktop LCDs with approximately 200 nit backlighting. On laptops, it's more of a personal decision—do you want battery life or a super bright display?

## The Monitor

CRT or LCD, all monitors share a number of characteristics that you need to know for purchase, installation, maintenance, and troubleshooting.

### Size

You need to take care when buying CRT monitors. CRT monitors come in a large number of sizes, all measured in inches (although most metric countries provide the metric equivalent value). All monitors provide two numbers: the monitor size and the actual size of the screen. The monitor size measures from two opposite diagonal corners. The actual screen is measured from one edge of the screen to the opposite diagonal side. This latter measurement is often referred to as the *Viewable Image Size* (VIS) (Figure 16-35). We commonly see a size difference between the two measurements of one to two inches. A 17-inch CRT monitor, for example, might have a 15.5-inch VIS.

LCD monitors dispense with the two values and simply express the VIS value. You must consider this issue when comparing LCDs to CRTs. A 15-inch LCD monitor will have about the same viewing area as a 17-inch CRT.

**Figure 16-35**
Viewable image size
of an LCD

## Connections

CRT monitors for PCs all use the famous 15-pin, 3-row, DB type connector (Figure 16-36) and a power plug. Larger or multipurpose monitors may have a few other connectors, but as far as the CRT is concerned, these are the only two you need for video.

**Figure 16-36**   Traditional CRT connections

### LCD

Not many people use the term "LCD monitor." Instead, we often hear the terms "Flat-panel display" or "LCD panels." I prefer the term LCD monitor, but be prepared to hear it a few different ways.

Unlike the analog SVGA CRTs, LCD monitors need a digital signal. This creates somewhat of an issue. The video information stored on a video card's RAM is clearly digital. All VGA and up video cards include a special chip (or function embedded into a chip that does several other jobs) called the *Random Access Memory Digital-to-Analog Converter* (RAMDAC) As the name implies, RAMDAC takes the digital signal from the video card and turns it into an analog signal for the analog CRT (Figure 16-37). The RAMDAC really defines the bandwidth that the video card outputs.

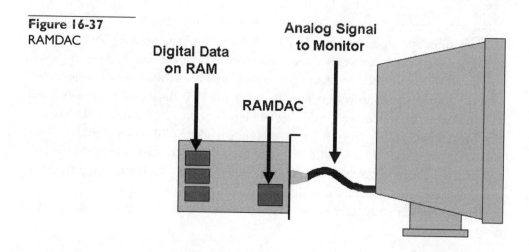

**Figure 16-37**
RAMDAC

Well, RAMDACs certainly make sense for analog CRT monitors. However, if you want to plug your LCD monitor into a regular video card, you need circuitry on the LCD monitor to convert the signal from analog to digital (Figure 16-38).

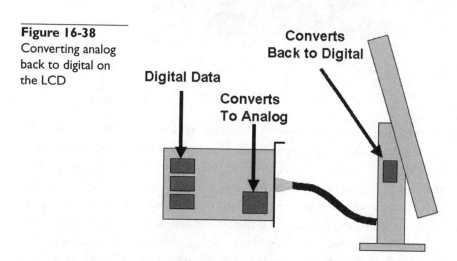

**Figure 16-38**
Converting analog back to digital on the LCD

Many LCD monitors do exactly this process. These are called *analog LCD monitors*. The monitor really isn't analog; it's digital, but it takes a standard SVGA input. These monitors have one advantage: You may use any standard SVGA video card. But these monitors require adjustment of the analog timing signal to the digital clock inside the monitor. This used to be a fairly painful process, but most analog LCD monitors now include intelligent circuitry to make this process either automatic or very easy.

But why convert the signal from digital to analog and then back to digital? Well, many monitor and video card people agree. We now see quite a few digital LCD monitors and digital video cards. They use a completely different connector than the old 15-pin DB connector used on regular video cards and monitors. After a few false starts with connection standards with names like P&D and DFP, the digital LCD world, with a few holdouts, have all moved to the *Digital Video Interface* (DVI) standard. DVI is actually three different connectors that look very much alike: DVI-D is for digital, DVI-A is for analog (for backward compatibility if the monitor maker so desires), and the DVI-A/D or DVI-I (Interchangeable) accepts either a DVI-D or DVI-A (Figure 16-39). DVI-D and DVI-A are keyed so that they will not connect. Just in case you were wondering— no, you cannot use an adapter to convert an analog LCD to use a digital video card or vice versa!

**Figure 16-39**
DVI-A connector

I'm convinced that over time digital will replace analog. Digital makes both the monitor and the video card cheaper, provides a clearer signal because no conversion is necessary, and makes installation trivial. Most digital LCD monitors come with a DVI-D connector, and all analog LCD monitors use the DB-15. Many LCD monitor makers hedge their bets; however, by providing both types of connectors on their monitors, we need to call those monitors analog/digital! Just make sure that when you get an LCD (and you eventually will) that you either get an analog to use with your current video card or purchase a new digital video card if you decide on a digital monitor. Nothing is more embarrassing than handing someone a new LCD monitor that won't connect!

## Adjustments

Most adjustments to the monitor take place at installation, but for now, let's just make sure you know what they are and where they are located. Clearly, all monitors have an On/Off button or switch. Also, see if you can locate the Brightness and Contrast buttons. Beyond that, most monitors (at least the only ones you should buy) have an onboard menu system, enabling a number of adjustments. Every monitor maker provides a different way to access these menus, but they all provide two main functions: physical screen adjustment (bigger, smaller, move to the left, right, up, down, and others) and color adjustment. The color adjustment lets you adjust the red, green, and blue guns to give you the best color tones. All of these settings are a matter of personal taste. Make sure the person who will use the computer understands how to adjust these settings (Figure 16-40).

**Figure 16-40**
Typical menu
controls

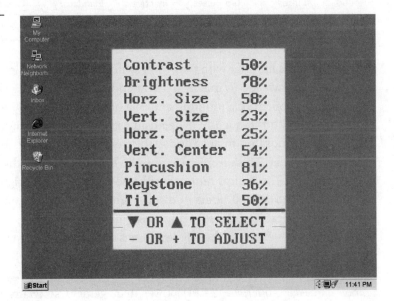

## Power Conservation

Approximately half the power required to run a desktop PC is consumed by the monitor. Monitors that meet the *Video Electronics Standards Association* (VESA) specification for *display power-management signaling* (DPMS) can reduce monitor power consumption by roughly 75 percent. This is accomplished by reducing or eliminating the signals sent by the video card to the monitor during idle periods. By eliminating these pulses, the monitor essentially takes catnaps. The advantage over simply shutting the monitor off is in the time it takes to restore the display. A typical CRT monitor consumes approximately 120 watts. During a catnap or power-down mode, the energy consumption is reduced to below 25 watts, while enabling the screen to return to use in less than 10 seconds. Full shutoff is accomplished by eliminating all clocking pulses to the monitor. While this reduces power consumption to below 15 watts, it also requires anywhere from 15 to 30 seconds to restore a usable display. Table 16-1 shows the various DPMS options.

**Table 16-1**    DPMS Options

| MONITOR STATUS | HORI-ZONTAL SIGNAL | VERTICAL SIGNAL | DISPLAY STATE | DPMS REQUIRE-MENT | POWER SAVINGS | RECOVERY TIME |
|---|---|---|---|---|---|---|
| On | Pulses | Pulses | Active | Mandatory | None | N/A |
| Stand-By | No Pulses | Pulses | Inactive | Optional | Fair | Short |
| Suspend | Pulses | No Pulses | Inactive | Mandatory | Good | Long |
| Off | No Pulses | No Pulses | Inactive | Mandatory | Excellent | Longest |

Turning off the monitor with the power switch is the most basic form of power management. The downside to this is the wear and tear on the CRT. The CRT is the most expensive component of a monitor, and one of the most damaging things to a CRT is to turn it on and off frequently. When using a non-DPMS monitor or video card, it is best to turn the monitor on once during the day, and then turn it off only when you are finished for the day. This on-off cycle must be balanced against the life of the CRT display phosphors. The typical monitor will lose about half its original brightness after roughly 10,000 to 15,000 hours of display time. Leaving the monitor on all the time will bring a noticeable decrease in brightness in just over a year (8,766 hours). The only way around this is enabling the DPMS features of the monitor or taking care to turn the monitor off.

DPMS works with Windows *Advanced Power Management* (APM) or *Advanced Configuration and Power Interface* (ACPI) power management software. We'll go into these specifications in detail in Chapter 18.

## We Have the Basics

We've covered a big piece of ground in this section. Take some time to review the concepts of HRR, VRR, and bandwidth and understand the differences in monitors. We can now move to the second part of the video duo: the video card.

## The Video Card

The video card, or display adapter, handles the video chores within the PC, processing information from the CPU and sending it out to the monitor. The video card is composed of two major pieces: the video RAM and the video processor circuitry. The video RAM stores the video image. On the first video cards, this RAM was good old DRAM, just like the RAM on the motherboard. Today's video cards often have better RAM than your system has! The video processing circuitry takes the information on the video

RAM and shoots it out to the monitor. While early video processing circuitry was little more than an intermediary between the CPU and the video RAM, better video processors are more powerful than a late-generation 486 CPU! It's not at all uncommon to see video cards that need fans to cool their onboard processors (Figure 16-41).

The trick to understanding video cards is to appreciate the beginnings and the evolution of video. Video output to computers was around long before PCs were created. At the time PCs became popular, video was almost exclusively text-based, meaning that the only image the video card could place on the monitor was one of the 256 ASCII characters. These characters were made up of patterns of pixels that were stored in the system BIOS. When a program wanted to make a character, it talked to DOS or to the BIOS, which stored the image of that character onto the video memory. The character then appeared on the screen.

The beauty of text video cards was that they were simple to use and cheap to make. The simplicity was based on the fact that only 256 characters existed, and no color choices were available—just monochrome text (Figure 16-42).

You could, however, choose to make the character bright, dim, normal, underlined, or blinking. It was easy to position the characters, as space on the screen allowed for only 80 characters per line and 24 lines.

Long ago, RAM was very expensive, so video-card makers were interested in using the absolute least amount of RAM possible. Making a monochrome text video card was a great way to keep down RAM costs. Let's consider this for a minute. First, the video RAM is where the contents of the screen are located. You need enough video RAM to hold all the necessary information for a completely full screen. Each ASCII character needs eight bits (by definition), so a monitor with 80 characters/line and 24 lines will need:

80 characters $\times$ 24 lines = 1,920 characters = 15,360 bits or 1,920 bytes

The video card would need less than 2,000 bytes of memory, which isn't much, not even in 1981 when the PC first came out. Now be warned that I'm glossing over a few things—where you store the information about underlines, blinking, and so on. The bottom line is that the tiny amount of necessary RAM kept monochrome text video cards cheap.

Very early on in the life of PCs, a new type of video, called a *graphics video card*, was invented. It was quite similar to a text card. The text card, however, was limited to the 256 ASCII characters, whereas a graphics video card enabled programs to turn any pixel on the screen on or off. It was still monochrome, but programs could access any individual pixel, enabling much more creative control of the screen. Of course, it took more video RAM. The first graphics cards ran at 320 $\times$ 200 pixels. One bit was needed for each pixel (on or off), so:

320 $\times$ 200 = 64,000 bits or 8,000 bytes

**Figure 16-41**
Video card with
cooling fans

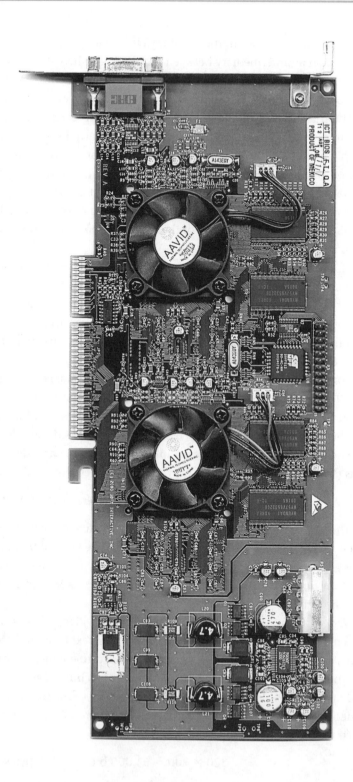

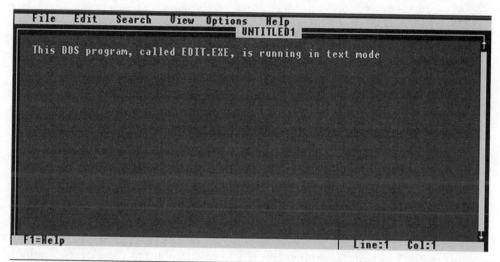

**Figure 16-42**    Text mode

That's a lot more RAM than what was needed for text, but it was still a pretty low amount of RAM—even in the old days. As resolutions increased, however, the amount of video RAM needed to store this information also increased.

Once monochrome video was invented, it was a relatively easy step to move into color for both text and graphics video cards. The only question was how to store color information for each character (text cards) or pixel (graphics cards). This was easy—just set aside a few more bits for each pixel or character. So now the question becomes, "How many bits do you set aside?" Well, that depends on how many colors you want. Basically, the number of colors determines the number of bits. For example, if you wanted four colors, you need two bits (two bits per pixel). Then, you could do something like this:

00 = black

01 = cyan (blue)

10 = magenta (reddish pink)

11 = white

So if you set aside two bits, you could get four colors. If you want 16 colors, set aside four bits, which would make 16 different combinations. Nobody ever invented a text mode that used more than 16 colors, so let's start thinking in terms of only graphics mode and bits-per-pixels. To get 256 colors, each pixel would have to be represented with eight bits. In PCs, the number of colors is always a power of 2: 4, 16, 256, 64K, and so on. Note that as more colors are added, more video RAM is needed to store the information. Here are the most common color depths and the number of bits necessary to store the color information per pixel:

$$2 \text{ colors} = 1 \text{ bit (mono)}$$
$$4 \text{ colors} = 2 \text{ bits}$$
$$16 \text{ colors} = 4 \text{ bits}$$
$$256 \text{ colors} = 8 \text{ bits}$$
$$64K \text{ colors} = 16 \text{ bits}$$
$$16.7M \text{ colors} = 24 \text{ bits}$$
$$4G \text{ colors} = 32 \text{ bits}$$

Most technicians won't say things like "I set my video card to show over 16 million colors." Instead, they'll say, "I set my color depth to 24 bits." Talk in terms of bits, not colors. It is assumed that you know the number of colors for any color depth.

**EXAM TIP**   **Know your color depths both in terms of bits and numbers of colors!**

## Modes

Based on what you know so far, it would seem as though four different types of video cards exist: monochrome text, color text, monochrome graphics, and color graphics. What if a PC wants to do more than one of these? Any PC might want to start with a text mode (at boot) and then switch into color graphics (like when Windows starts). So what are you going to do—keep two video cards in the PC and then switch the cable? Of course not. Instead, today's video cards support all of the previously defined video cards in one card. A modern video card displays text or graphics, monochrome or color, as needed. Each different level of operation is defined as a video mode. First IBM and then the VESA defined specific, uniform video modes for video cards. These video modes are given a hexadecimal value. For example, video mode 06h is defined as monochrome graphics at 640 × 200 pixels. As different types of video cards are discussed in the next few sections, the modes associated with each type will be listed. Let's take a look at video cards from the past into today.

**EXAM TIP** Don't bother memorizing all these different modes' hex values! Do take some time to know the different types of video cards and appreciate how their modes compare to earlier/later video cards.

## MDA

The first video card ever produced with the IBM PC was the text-only *monochrome display adapter* (MDA). An MDA worked well for DOS-based word processing and spreadsheet programs. The MDA had a nine-pin female socket and was found only in the most ancient of PCs—most now fill up landfills. Table 16-2 lists the available MDA modes.

**Table 16-2**   MDA Modes

| MODE | TYPE | COLORS | RESOLUTION/CHARACTERS |
|------|------|--------|------------------------|
| 00h, 01h | Text | Mono | 40 × 25 |
| 07h | Text | Mono | 80 × 25 |

## CGA

The IBM PC offered the first-generation color display adapter, appropriately called the *color graphics adapter* (CGA) card. CGA cards supported colors but did so at the price of resolution. A four-color screen offered only 320 × 200 resolution. It was possible to support 640 × 200 resolution, but the number of available colors dropped to only two. Similar to its less-gifted older sibling, it also used a nine-pin male connector and is now considered a collector's item. Refer to Table 16-3 for CGA modes.

**Table 16-3**   CGA Modes

| MODE | TYPE | COLORS | RESOLUTION/CHARACTERS |
|------|------|--------|------------------------|
| 00h, 01h | Text | 16 | 40 × 25 |
| 02h, 03h | Text | 16 | 80 × 25 |
| 04h, 05h | Graphics | 4 | 320 × 200 |
| 06h | Graphics | 2 | 640 × 200 |

## EGA

The *enhanced graphics adapter* (EGA) was introduced in late 1984 as an improvement on the CGA standard (Table 16-4). It could support resolutions of up to 640 × 350 with 16 colors in text mode, or 640 × 200 and two colors in graphics mode. Unfortunately, problems often occurred with programs not working properly with an EGA card because the EGA standard was not fully backwards-compatible with CGA and MDA. EGA used a nine-pin adapter that had a distinct DIP switch visible from the outside.

**Table 16-4**  EGA Modes

| MODE | TYPE | COLORS | RESOLUTION/CHARACTERS |
|------|------|--------|----------------------|
| 00h, 01h | Text | 16 | 40 × 25 |
| 02h, 03h | Text | 16 | 80 × 25 |
| 07h | Text | Mono | 80 × 25 |
| 0Dh | Graphics | 16 | 320 × 200 |
| 0Eh | Graphics | 16 | 640 × 200 |
| 0Fh | Graphics | 4 | 640 × 350 |
| 10h | Graphics | 16 | 640 × 350 |

## PGA

The *professional graphics adapter* (PGA) card was part of a package developed by IBM. Costing over $4,000 and taking three ISA slots when fully configured, this standard offered 640 × 480 resolution, 3-D rotation, and 60-frame/second animation. It was aimed at the engineering and scientific communities but was dropped by IBM with the introduction of VGA in 1987 (Table 16-5).

**Table 16-5**  PGA Modes

| MODE | TYPE | COLORS | RESOLUTION/CHARACTERS |
|------|------|--------|----------------------|
| 00h, 01h | Text | 16 | 40 × 25 |
| 02h, 03h | Text | 16 | 80 × 25 |
| 04h, 05h | Graphics | 4 | 320 × 200 |
| 06h | Graphics | 2 | 640 × 200 |
| Special PGA only | Graphics | 256 | 640 × 480 |

# VGA

With the introduction of the PS/2, IBM introduced the *video graphics array* (VGA) standard (Table 16-6). This new standard offered 16 colors at a resolution of 640 × 480 pixels. VGA supported more colors by using an analog video signal instead of a digital one, as was the case prior to the VGA standard. A digital signal is either all on or all off. By using an analog signal, the VGA standard can provide 64 distinct levels for the three colors (RGB)—that is, $64^3$ or 262,144 possible colors—although only 16 or 256 can be seen at a time. For most purposes, 640 × 480 and 16 colors defines VGA mode. This is typically the display resolution and color depth referred to on many software packages as a minimum display requirement. True VGA-only cards are very rare.

**Table 16-6** VGA Modes

| MODE | TYPE | COLORS | RESOLUTION/CHARACTERS |
|------|------|--------|------------------------|
| 00h, 01h | Text | 16 | 40 × 25 |
| 02h, 03h | Text | 16 | 80 × 25 |
| 04h, 05h | Graphics | 4 | 320 × 200 |
| 06h | Graphics | 2 | 640 × 200 |
| 07h | Text | Mono | 80 × 25 |
| 0Dh | Graphics | 16 | 320 × 200 |
| 0Eh | Graphics | 16 | 640 × 200 |
| 0Fh | Graphics | 4 | 640 × 350 |
| 10h | Graphics | 16 | 640 × 350 |
| 11h | Graphics | 2 | 640 × 480 |
| 12h | Graphics | 16 | 640 × 480 |
| 13h | Graphics | 256 | 320 × 200 |

# XGA

IBM developed the first standard to break 640 × 480 resolution with the *extended graphics array* (XGA) in 1990. XGA could go up to 1,024 × 768 with 16-bit color. While XGA enjoyed some success, the proliferation of *super video graphics array* (SVGA) standards (see the following section) quickly made XGA obsolete. The last few years has seen a resurgence of the abbreviation XGA on some LCD panels, but this is merely to reflect their maximum of 1,024 × 768 resolution. The terms XGA, SXGA, or one of the many other variants (XGA+, UXGA) don't really have an official meaning as VESA provides equivalent SVGA standards for all these resolutions and color depths—but it sure makes for a good marketing angle for laptop makers. Why call your display SVGA when you can call it XGA!

## SVGA

For years, SVGA was similar to SCSI-1: more opinion than an established standard. Any video-card maker who made a video card with a resolution greater than 640 × 480 and 16 colors called the card SGVA. For many years, the lack of an SVGA standard created serious confusion. One manifestation of this confusion was the emergence of nonstandard modes, in essence, extensions to the VGA modes (Table 16-7). Each video-card maker would define their own modes, even for identical resolution and color depths.

**Table 16-7**  Some Simple Nonstandard SVGA Modes

| MODE | COLORS | RESOLUTION/CHARACTERS | MAKER |
|------|--------|----------------------|-------|
| 2Eh | 256 | 640 × 480 | Tseng |
| 53h | 256 | 640 × 480 | Oak Tech |
| 30h | 256 | 640 × 480 | Everex |
| 5Fh | 256 | 640 × 480 | Paradise |
| 67h | 256 | 640 × 480 | Video 7 |

The VESA established standards for SVGA resolutions, color depth, and video signal timings in the late 1980s. SVGA is an extensible standard, which is a cool way to say, "VESA constantly adds to this list as higher resolutions and deeper color depths develop." The list of VESA SVGA modes would take many pages. Table 16-8 shows the more common ones.

**Table 16-8**  Some Common VESA SVGA Modes

| MODE | TYPE | COLORS | RESOLUTION/CHARACTERS |
|------|------|--------|----------------------|
| 100h | Graphics | 256 | 640 × 400 |
| 101h | Graphics | 256 | 640 × 480 |
| 102h | Graphics | 16 | 800 × 600 |
| 103h | Graphics | 256 | 800 × 600 |
| 104h | Graphics | 16 | 1,024 × 768 |

**Table 16-8**   Some Common VESA SVGA Modes (continued)

| MODE | TYPE | COLORS | RESOLUTION/CHARACTERS |
|------|------|--------|------------------------|
| 105h | Graphics | 256 | 1,024 × 768 |
| 106h | Graphics | 16 | 1,280 × 1,024 |
| 107h | Graphics | 256 | 1,280 × 1,024 |
| 110h | Graphics | 32K | 640 × 480 |
| 111h | Graphics | 64K | 640 × 480 |
| 112h | Graphics | 16.7M | 640 × 480 |
| 113h | Graphics | 32K | 800 × 600 |
| 114h | Graphics | 64K | 800 × 600 |
| 115h | Graphics | 16.7M | 800 × 600 |
| 116h | Graphics | 32K | 1,024 × 768 |
| 117h | Graphics | 64K | 1,024 × 768 |
| 118h | Graphics | 16.7M | 1,024 × 768 |
| 119h | Graphics | 32K | 1,280 × 1,024 |
| 11Ah | Graphics | 64K | 1,280 × 1,024 |
| 11Bh | Graphics | 16.7M | 1,280 × 1,024 |

## Resolution, Color Depth, and Memory Requirements

Different video modes require different amounts of RAM on the video card. To determine the amount of video memory required at a given resolution and color depth, multiply the resolution by the number of bytes of color depth. From the chapter on RAM, you know that memory on a PC is always in byte-sized units, and video memory is no exception. Because bits are used to refer to color depth, you need to convert the color depth bits into bytes. Suppose you have a video card with 1MB of video memory and want to run your video at 800 × 600 with a 24-bit color depth. Does this card have enough memory to do this? Twenty-four bits = 24/8 = three bytes, so you use the equation 800 × 600 × 3 for the memory requirement in bytes. To convert this to megabytes, divide the result by 1,048,576:

$$800 \times 600 = 480,000 \text{ pixels per screen}$$
$$480,000 \times 3 = 1,440,000 \text{ bytes of memory per screen}$$
$$1,440,000 \div 1,048,576 = 1.373 \text{MB per screen}$$

This means that a video card with only 1MB of RAM cannot support that resolution and that color depth. Memory requirements for various resolutions and color depths are shown in Table 16-9.

**Table 16-9**    RAM Requirements for Various Resolutions/Color Depths

| RESOLUTION | NUMBER OF COLORS | | | | |
|---|---|---|---|---|---|
| | 16 | 256 | 64K | 16.7M | 4G |
| 640 × 480 | 0.15MB | 0.29MB | 0.59MB | 0.88MB | 1.17MB |
| 800 × 600 | 0.23MB | 0.46MB | 0.92MB | 1.37MB | 1.83MB |
| 1,024 × 768 | 0.38MB | 0.75MB | 1.50MB | 2.25MB | 3.00MB |
| 1,200 × 1,024 | 0.63MB | 1.25MB | 2.50MB | 3.75MB | 4.69MB |
| 1,600 × 1,200 | 0.92MB | 1.83MB | 3.66MB | 5.49MB | 7.32MB |

## AGP

Using more color depth slows down video functions. Data moving from the video card to the display has to go through the video card's memory chips and the expansion bus, and this can happen only so quickly. The standard PCI slots used in almost all systems are limited to 32-bit transfers at roughly 33 MHz, yielding a maximum bandwidth of 132MBps. It sounds like a lot until you start using higher resolutions, high color depths, and higher refresh rates.

For example, take a typical display at 800 × 600 with a fairly low refresh of 70 Hz. The 70 Hz means the display screen is being redrawn 70 times per second. If you use a low color depth of 256 colors, which is eight bits ($2^8 = 256$), you can multiply all the values together to see how much data per second has to be sent to the display:

$$800 \times 600 \times 1 \text{ byte} \times 70 = 33.6 \text{MBps}$$

If you use the same example at 16 million (24-bit) colors, the figure jumps to 100.8MBps. You might say, "Well, if PCI runs at 132MBps, it can handle that!" That statement would be true if the PCI bus had nothing else to do but tend to the video card, but almost every system has more than one PCI device, each requiring part of that throughput. The PCI bus simply cannot handle the needs of many current systems.

Intel answered the desire for video bandwidth even higher than PCI with the *Advanced Graphics Port* (AGP). AGP is a single, special port, similar to a PCI slot, which is dedicated to video. You will never see a motherboard with two AGP ports. Figure 16-43 shows an early generation AGP port. AGP is derived from the 66-MHz, 32-bit PCI 2.1 specification, and is currently the fastest video available. AGP uses a clock doubling and quadrupling (and soon eight times, "octupling?") function called *strobing* that uses double or quadruple signals from one clock cycle—similar to the 200 MHz and 266 MHz system buses on the Athlon and the 400 MHz with the Pentium 4.

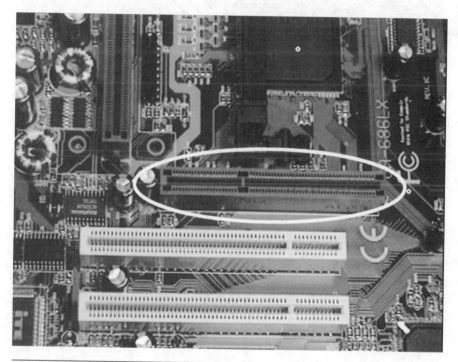

**Figure 16-43**   AGP port

Simply leaving AGP as a faster and wider PCI would seriously misrepresent the power of AGP. AGP has several technological advantages over PCI, including the bus, internal operations, and ability to handle 3-D texturing.

First, AGP currently resides alone on its own personal data bus, connected directly to the northbridge (Figure 16-44). This is very important because more advanced versions of AGP outperform every bus on the system except the frontside bus!

Second, AGP takes advantage of pipelining commands, similar to the way CPUs pipeline. Third, AGP has a feature called *sidebanding*—basically a second data bus that enables the video card to send more commands to the northbridge while receiving other commands at the same time. Further, the upcoming AGP 8× standard will allow for more than one AGP device—assuming the current specification remains unchanged in that regard.

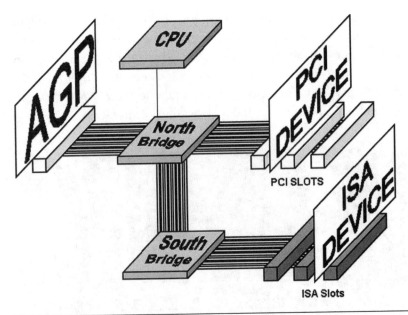

**Figure 16-44**   AGP bus

## Handling 3-D

Computer graphics have changed dramatically in the last couple of years, going from two-dimensional "flat" images to three-dimensional, properly textured pictures. This is especially true in architecture and engineering applications, medical imaging technology, and games. This is discussed further in the "Beyond A+" section later in this chapter, but you need a brief explanation here to understand the last aspect of AGP: handling 3-D textures.

A 3-D image consists of pre-made textures applied to a wireframe drawing, a process called *rendering*. Figure 16-45 shows an ATX power connector I'm building for another project.

Textures are nothing more than bitmap graphics applied to 3-D wireframes like skin over bone and muscle. 3-D applications come with textures appropriate for their wireframes. In this case I'm using the popular 3-D drawing program trueSpace, but I could just as easily be in the middle of one of the many 3-D games that use rendered objects. I select a texture and apply it to the wireframe (Figure 16-46).

Hmm. Very pretty but not much like a real ATX connector. I'll select a texture that more realistically represents a true ATX connector (Figure 16-47).

**Figure 16-45**
Wireframe of ATX
connector

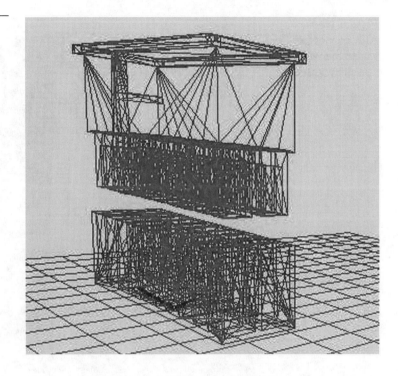

**Figure 16-46**
ATX connector
wireframe with
wacky texture

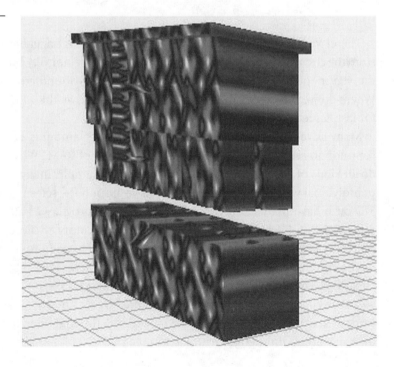

**Figure 16-47**
ATX connector wireframe with realistic texture

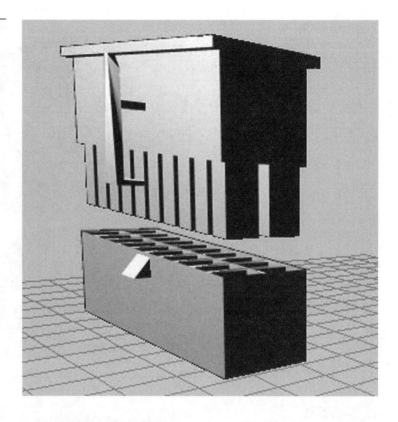

There! Very nice! To use this 3-D object in an animation, game, or whatever, I must store the chosen texture with the program. Textures are not very big, but many games—the very popular Half-Life game, for example—need hundreds of different textures. Where do we put them? They can't go on the hard drive; the CPU needs them in RAM for fast rendering.

Many advanced 3-D video cards come with huge amounts of video RAM. It's very common to see cards with 32, 64, or even 128MB of RAM! Why so much? Well, they do all kinds of neat stuff with this extra RAM; for example, many 3-D cards store copies of individual windows so that they can move around the screen very quickly. But most 3-D cards have all this extra room for textures. AGP provides a pathway so that the AGP card may "steal" chunks of the regular system memory to store video information, especially textures. This is called a *system memory access* and is quite popular.

The current hot AGP is AGP 4×. AGP 4× cards have a 64-bit pathway, requiring a larger slot. These slots are backwardly compatible with earlier AGP video cards but provide the extra pins that AGP 4× cards require (Figure 16-48). Most AGP 4× cards will work with a 32-bit slot as well as the 64-bit slot, although they obviously will not use their maximum throughput with the former.

**Figure 16-48**   AGP 4× slot

AGP has gone through a number of specifications, but the official names tend to be ignored and instead are called AGP 1×, 2×, 4×, and 8×. Table 16-10 shows the four AGP standards and their capabilities.

**Table 16-10**   AGP Types

|  | BUS SPEED | STROBE | WIDTH | THRU-PUT | SIDE BAND | PIPE | SYSTEM MEMORY | MULTIPLE PORTS |
|---|---|---|---|---|---|---|---|---|
| AGP 1× | 66 MHz | 1× | 32-bit | 264MBps | Yes | Yes | No | No |
| AGP 2× | 66 MHz | 2× | 32-bit | 528MBps | Yes | Yes | Yes | No |
| AGP 4× | 66 MHz | 4× | 32-bit* | 1,056MBps | Yes | Yes | Yes | No |
| AGP 4× | 66 MHz | 4× | 64-bit | 2,112MBps | Yes | Yes | Yes | No |
| AGP 8× | 66 MHz | 8× | 64-bit | 4,224MBps | Yes | Yes | Yes | Yes |

*AGP 4× can work at 64 bits, but many installations use only a 32-bit bus.

The only great downside to AGP lies in the close connection tolerances required by the cards themselves. It's very common to snap in a new AGP card and power up just to get a "no video card beep" or a system that doesn't boot. Always take the time to insure that an AGP card is snapped down securely and screwed down before starting the system.

## Video Memory

Video memory is crucial to the operation of a PC. It is probably the hardest-working set of electronics on the PC. Video RAM constantly updates to reflect every change that takes place on the screen. The original video RAM was plain old DRAM, just like the DRAM on the motherboard. Unfortunately, DRAM has some significant limitations. As a result, a number of other types of RAM have been developed especially for video.

Memory produces two bottlenecks for data-access speed and data throughput. Typical low-cost video cards (usually $50 to $100) commonly use DRAM for data storage. A few aspects of DRAM slow it down, making it a less than optimal choice for video RAM. One is the need to refresh DRAM memory approximately 18.5 times per second. During these refresh periods, neither the CPU nor graphics processor can read the memory bits in the video RAM. Another slowdown is the access/response time of DRAM. Even the fastest commonly available DRAM (50 nanoseconds) is too slow to handle the higher resolutions and color depths found on larger monitors. The final bottleneck for DRAM is physical. Its data lines are used both for writing data to the video port and receiving data from the CPU.

Manufacturers have overcome these bottlenecks in two ways: upping the width of the bus between the video RAM and video processor and using specialized RAM that avoids the DRAM issues.

First, manufacturers reorganized the video display memory on cards from the typical 32-bit-wide structure to 64, 128, or even 256 bits wide. This would not be of much benefit—because the system bus is limited to 32 or 64 bits—if it weren't for the fact that most video display cards are really co-processor boards. Most of the graphics rendering and processing is handled on the card by the video processor chip rather than by the CPU. The main system simply provides the input data to the processor on the video card. By making the memory bus on the video card as much as eight times wider than the standard 32-bit pathway (256 bits), data can be manipulated and then sent to the monitor much more quickly.

As well as increasing the width of the bus between video processor and video RAM, manufacturers have come up with quite a few enhanced forms of RAM that help the video significantly. Three of these styles of RAM are specifically for video: VRAM, WRAM, and SGRAM.

The first specialized video RAM option is dual-port memory or *video RAM* (VRAM). VRAM enables data to be written to video memory from the main system over the standard eight data lines in parallel, and provides a serial line for data to the video port. In other words, VRAM can send and receive at the same time. DRAM in contrast can send *or* receive at one time. Although faster, VRAM is more expensive than DRAM, but economies of scale have lowered its price to where it is quite common.

*Windows RAM* (WRAM) is another dual-ported RAM that has experienced success in video cards. WRAM is slightly faster than VRAM and costs about the same. The downside to WRAM is that it has not been as widely manufactured as some of the other specialized video RAMs.

*Synchronous graphics RAM* (SGRAM) is the most popular specialized video RAM available. SGRAM is like SDRAM in that it is synchronized to the system clock. SGRAM is extremely fast and capable of supporting video for the next few years—a veritable lifetime in the PC world!

Although specialized video RAM offers substantial improvements in video speeds, it is also unnecessary in the majority of office applications. Personally, I'm not overly interested in the type of video RAM used by a video card. If I buy a video card, I'm going to get a high-end card, and therefore I know it will use fast RAM—simply because my demands on any video card are high! My primary interests lie in the type of bus (only AGP for me!) and high refresh rates at good resolution and color depths. For example, I really want my video card to refresh at 85Hz at 1,024 × 768 with 16-bit color, but that's just my opinion! Extras that might have some interest for me include issues we haven't yet covered, such as 3-D capabilities and dual-monitor support. Don't panic about the video RAM types; just make sure you know them for the test!

Although I'm not overly concerned with the speed of my video RAM, I'm very interested in the amount of video RAM. I'm not worried if I have enough to handle my resolution and color depths because even the cheapest video cards come with approximately 8MB of RAM. Because I do so much work (and play) with 3-D imagery, I need a video card that handles my high demands. Personally, I wouldn't even consider a video card with less than 32MB of RAM. Now don't try to tell me you don't need RAM for 3-D. I've built too many systems with cheap video cards just to see the customer come back two weeks later, wondering why their son/daughter/wife/brother can't play some cool game they just bought.

Video RAM is only one of many considerations when purchasing a video card, but the other issues are outside the scope of A+. Check out the "Beyond A+" section later in this chapter for more details.

## Video Drivers

Windows 9x and Windows 2000, being graphical operating systems, are extremely interested in video modes. The interest is not based on required modes, as Windows applications will run in any graphical mode from 640 × 480 at 16 colors up to a theoretical maximum of 2,048 × 2,048 at 16.7 million colors. Instead, the interest in modes is based on the users themselves. Different users will have different opinions as to what is the "best" video mode. In order to serve the public, Windows must be able to change the video mode to suit different users. This is accomplished through the Display applet in the Control Panel. You can also access the Display Properties dialog box by alternate-clicking on the Desktop and selecting Properties from the menu that pops up. Once you have opened the Display applet, select the Settings tab to see the resolution and color depth settings (Figure 16-49). This works the same in Windows 9x and Windows 2000.

**Figure 16-49**
Display Properties

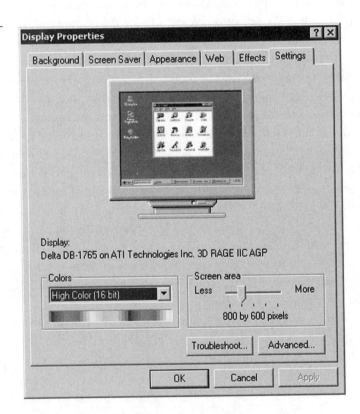

The number of resolutions and color depths that can be chosen is determined by the INF file settings for the video card and the monitor (see the section on INF files in Chapter 10). A good video driver will also provide settings for changing the refresh rate of the video card. Video drivers change all the time. Make a point to browse your video card maker's Web site for updates.

Be careful updating video drivers! Every video card has a quirk of some form that you must address in order to install the new driver correctly. Many driver updates require you to first delete the current video driver before you install the new one. Read the instructions carefully. I've had more than one situation where an otherwise simple video driver upgrade turned into a complete system rebuild!

Unfortunately, although Windows itself can readily change modes, the monitor may have problems with the changes. One of the problems with changing modes, especially in Windows 95, is that the amount of black space surrounding the screen will change. All CRTs have some amount of black space where the screen is not being used (Figure 16-50).

Although some black space is normal, changing modes or refresh rates will often make the black space unacceptably large, preventing the screen view from being as large as it could be. Plus, changing a video mode or refresh rate may cause the screen to shift up, down, left, or right. The screen may also take on a pincushion or trapezoidal shape. In some cases, the screen may tilt in one direction or another. These changes are annoying and counter-productive.

**Figure 16-50**
Unused black space

**Black Area**

A number of methods can be used for adjusting the screen to optimize the screen size. First, use the external controls on the monitor if possible to adjust the screen manually. Many monitors enable users to set a video mode optimized for a particular resolution and refresh rate. When the monitor has been adjusted, the settings are stored in the monitor itself. From then on, when the monitor detects a change in video mode or refresh rate, it retrieves these settings and readjusts itself. It is a common procedure when combining a video card and a monitor to take a few moments to adjust the screen. Second, most video cards provide software to adjust the screen position. You usually access these settings by clicking an icon installed in the System Tray or through the Advanced button on the Settings tab of the Display Properties screen. My Matrox video card adds a large number of options—and it took a good bit of reading to understand what it all did (Figure 16-51)!

**Figure 16-51**
Matrox display
adapter settings

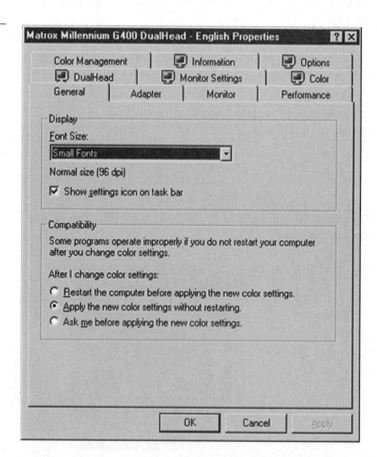

Finally, adjust your software to get the highest refresh rates possible for each resolution that your monitor can handle (Figure 16-52). Setting the refresh rate substantially higher reduces eyestrain. Most people prefer a refresh rate of at least 72 Hz, although even higher (85 Hz or so) will make the screen much easier on the eyes. The downside to higher refresh rates is that it may limit the resolution and/or color depth. Although a monitor may be able to handle easily an 800 × 600 at 64K color mode at 72 Hz, it may only be able to handle 1024 × 768 at 64K color at a refresh rate of 60 Hz. The choice is really up to the user.

**Figure 16-52**
Typical refresh settings

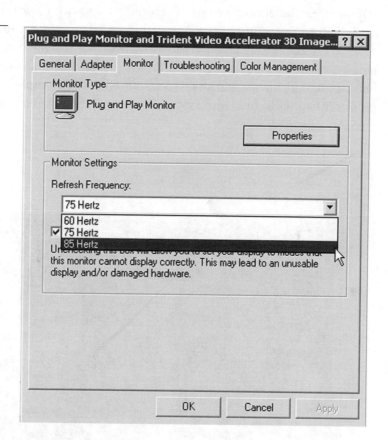

## When Video Cards Go Bad

Fortunately, video cards rarely break. The majority of problems in video can be attributed to improper drivers, poor connections, and bad monitors. Unfortunately, when they do break, invariably the only option is to throw them away. One area for possible repair is the video RAM. On the rare occasion where the video card is the problem, the usual culprit is the video RAM. Many video cards today have video RAM that is mounted in sockets, as opposed to being soldered directly to the video card. Video cards come with sockets so that one video card can be sold with varying amounts of RAM. However, sockets also enable you to replace the video RAM when necessary (Figure 16-53).

The trick is to recognize the classic signs of bad video RAM. The first is fixed speckles or spots on the screen. These spots can be any color, but are usually black. The important point to note here is that the speckles don't move; they are fixed in one location, although they might turn on and off a few times an hour. This is not always true with LCD monitors as almost every LCD monitor comes with a few bad pixels—there's no fix for bad pixels on LCD monitors. The second symptom is funny colors in Windows. We're not talking about a bad Windows color scheme here! This looks like a monitor covered with a colored film. The color is almost always complex. It won't be blue or red, but rather a "bluish-green with maybe a little purple" type of color. If you get this "filmy" look, boot into Safe Mode. If the filmy look is still present, the RAM is probably bad.

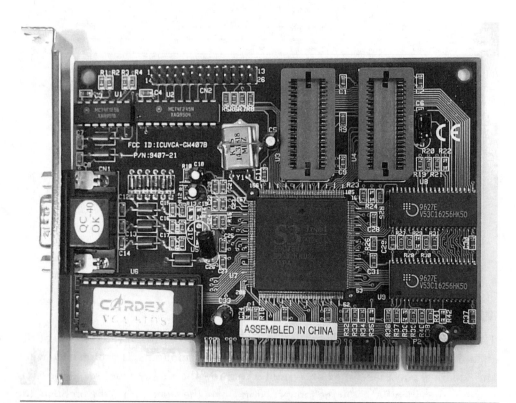

**Figure 16-53**  Video card with sockets for replacing video RAM

The last and the most common symptom of this uncommon problem is what I call *screen decay*. Have you ever seen a movie where the film inside the projector suddenly melts? It usually starts with a small hole in the film and then quickly spreads throughout the film. Bad video RAM can cause this type of look. This is most common on video cards that have been upgraded and haven't been properly inserted into the sockets. The machine runs fine for a moment or two until the cards heat up, disconnecting the improperly inserted RAM and causing this rather cool-looking, but also very disturbing screen decay.

## Troubleshooting Monitors

Because of the inherent dangers of the high-frequency and high-voltage power required by monitors, and because proper adjustment requires specialized training, this section will concentrate on giving a support person the information necessary to decide whether a trouble call is warranted. Virtually no monitor manufacturers make schematics of their monitors available to the public because of liability issues regarding possible electrocution. To simplify troubleshooting, look at the process as two separate parts: external and internal adjustments.

## External Adjustments

Monitor adjustments range from the simplest—brightness and contrast—to the more sophisticated—pincushioning and trapezoidal adjustments. The external controls provide users with the opportunity to fine-tune the monitor's image. Many monitors have controls for changing the tint and saturation of color, although plenty of monitors put those controls inside the monitor. Better monitors enable you to square up the visible portion of the screen with the monitor housing.

Finally, most monitors have the ability to *degauss* themselves with the push of a button. Over time, the shadow mask picks up a weak magnetic charge that interferes with the focus of the electron beams. This magnetic field makes the image look slightly fuzzy and streaked. Most monitors have a special built-in circuit called a *degaussing coil* to eliminate this magnetic buildup. When the degaussing circuit is used, an alternating current is sent through a coil of wire surrounding the CRT, and this current generates an alternating magnetic field that demagnetizes the shadow mask. The degaussing coil is activated using the Degauss button or menu selection on the monitor. Degaussing usually makes a rather nasty "thunk" sound and the screen goes crazy for a moment—don't worry, that's normal. Whenever a user calls me with a "fuzzy monitor" problem, I always have them degauss first.

## Internal Adjustments

As shipped, most monitors do not produce an image out to the limits of the screen because of poor convergence at the outer display edges. *Convergence* defines how closely the three colors can meet at a single point on the display. At the point of convergence, the three colors will combine to form a single white dot. With misconvergence, a noticeable halo of one or more colors will appear around the outside of the white point. The farther away the colors are from the center of the screen, the more likely the chance for misconvergence (Figure 16-54). Low-end monitors are especially susceptible to this problem. Even though adjusting the convergence of a monitor is not difficult, it does require getting inside the monitor case and having a copy of the schematic, which shows the location of the variable resistors. For this reason, it is a good idea to leave this adjustment to a trained specialist.

**Figure 16-54**
Example of misconvergence halo effect

I don't like opening a CRT monitor. I avoid doing this for two reasons: (1) I know very little about electronic circuits and (2) I once almost electrocuted myself. At any rate, the A+ exams expect you to have a passing understanding of adjustments you might need to perform inside a monitor. Before we go any further, let me remind you about a little issue with CRT monitors (Figure 16-55).

**Figure 16-55**
Hey! That's 25,000 volts! BE CAREFUL!

265V ⏦   This product includes critical mechanical and electrical parts which are essential for x-radiation safety. For continued safety replace critical components indicated in the service manual only with exact replacement parts given in the parts list. Operating high voltage for this product is 25kV at minimum brightness. Refer to service manual for measurement procedures and proper service adjustments.

Inside every CRT monitor is a piece of equipment called the *high-voltage anode*, as shown in Figure 16-56. If you lift that suction cup, you will almost certainly get seriously electrocuted. Underneath that cup is a wire—the actual high-voltage anode. On the other side of that wire leading into the high-voltage anode is the flyback transformer. Don't worry about what they do; just worry about what they can do to *you*! There's a big capacitor that holds upwards of 25,000 volts. The capacitor will hold that charge if the monitor is turned off. It will hold the charge if the monitor is unplugged. That capacitor (depending on the system) can hold a charge days, weeks, months, or even years. Knowing this, you should learn how to discharge a CRT.

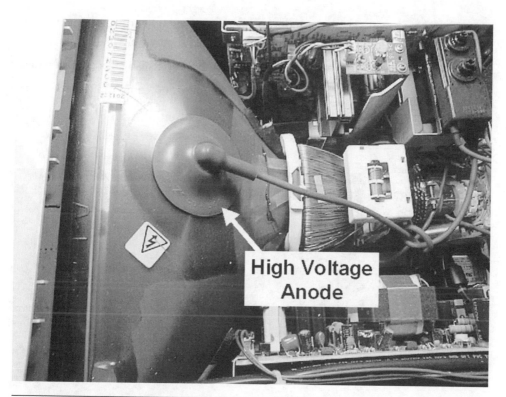

**Figure 16-56**   High-voltage anode

## Discharging a CRT

There are 75,000 opinions on how to properly discharge a CRT. Although my procedure may not follow the steps outlined in someone's official handbook or electrical code, I know this works. Read the rules and then look at Figure 16-57.

1. Make sure everything is unplugged.

2. If possible, let the monitor sit for a couple of days. Most good monitors will discharge themselves in two to three days, maximum.

3. Get a heavy, well-insulated, flat-bladed screwdriver.

4. Get a heavy gauge wire with alligator clips on each end.

5. Do not let yourself be grounded in any way. Wear rubber-soled shoes, and no rings or watches.

6. Wear safety goggles to protect yourself in the very rare chance the CRT implodes.

7. Remove the monitor's case. Remember where the screw went in.

8. Clip one alligator clip to an unpainted part of the metal frame of the monitor.

9. Clip the other end to the metal shaft of the screwdriver.

10. Slide the screwdriver blade under the suction cup. Make triple-sure neither you nor the screwdriver is in any incidental contact with anything metal.

11. Slide the blade under until you hear a loud pop—you'll also see a nice blue flash.

12. If anyone is in the building, they will hear the pop and come running. Tell them everything's OK.

13. Wait about 15 minutes and repeat.

**Figure 16-57**
Discharging a CRT

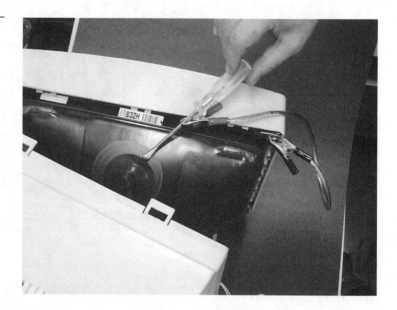

The main controls that require you to remove the monitor case to make adjustments include those for convergence, gain for each of the color guns, and sometimes the focus control. A technician with either informal or formal training in component-level repair can usually figure out which controls do what. Balance the cost of repairing the monitor against the cost of death or serious injury—is it worth it? Finally, before making adjustments to the display image, especially with the internal controls, give the monitor at least 15 to 30 minutes of warm-up time. This is necessary for both the components on the printed circuit boards and for the CRT itself.

## Cleaning Monitors

Cleaning monitors is easy. Always use antistatic monitor wipes or at least a general antistatic cloth. Some LCD monitors may require special cleaning equipment. Never use window cleaners or any liquid because the danger of liquid getting into the monitor may create a shocking experience! Many commercial cleaning solutions will also melt an LCD screen—never a good thing!

# Common Monitor Problems

Although I'm not super comfortable diving into the guts of a CRT, you can fix a substantial percentage of monitor problems yourself. The following list describes the most common monitor problems and tells you what to do—even when that means sending it to someone else.

- Almost all CRT and LCD monitors have replaceable controls. If the Brightness knob or Degauss button stops working or seems loose, check with the manufacturer for replacement controls. They usually come as a complete package.

- For problems with ghosting, streaking, and/or fuzzy vertical edges, check the cable connections and the cable itself. These problems rarely apply to monitors; more commonly, they point to the video card.

- If one color is missing, check cables for breaks or bent pins. Check the front controls for that color. If the color adjustment is already maxed out, the monitor will require internal service.

- As monitors age, they lose brightness. If the brightness control is turned all the way up and the picture seems dim, the monitor will require internal adjustment. This is a good argument for power-management functions. Don't leave the monitor on with a picture on it, as this will reduce monitor life significantly. Do use the power-management options in Windows or use the power switch.

- If your LCD monitor cracks, it is not repairable.

- Almost everything else wrong with an LCD Panel *can* be fixed! Never pay to replace an LCD panel that is not broken. Search for a specialty LCD repair company. Hundreds of these companies exist all over the world.

# Common Problems Specific to CRTs

The complexity of CRTs compared to LCDs requires us to look at a number of monitor problems unique to CRTs. Most of these problems require opening the monitor, so be careful! When in doubt, take it to a repair shop.

- You can fix most out of focus monitors. Focus adjustments are usually on the inside somewhere close to the flyback transformer. This is the transformer that provides power to the high-voltage anode. A picture of a typical flyback transformer is shown in Figure 16-58.

- Hissing or sparking sounds are often indicative of an insulation rupture on the flyback transformer. This sound is usually accompanied by the smell of ozone. If your monitor has these symptoms, it definitely needs a qualified technician. Having replaced a flyback transformer once myself, I can say it is not worth the hassle and potential loss of life and limb.

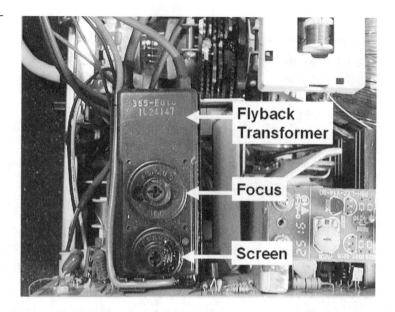

**Figure 16-58**
Typical flyback transformer and controls

Flyback Transformer

Focus

Screen

- Big color blotches are present on the display. This is an easy and cheap repair. Find the Degauss button and use it. If your monitor doesn't have a Degauss button, you can purchase a special tool called a degaussing coil at any electronics store.

- Bird-like chirping sounds occurring at regular intervals usually indicate a problem with the monitor power supply.

- Suppose you got a good deal on a used 17-inch monitor, but the display is kind of dark, even though you have the brightness turned up all the way. This points to a dying CRT. So, how about replacing the CRT? Forget it. Even if the monitor was free, it just isn't worth it, as a replacement tube runs in the hundreds of dollars. Nobody ever sold a monitor because it was too bright and too sharp. Save your money and buy a new monitor.

- The monitor displays only a single horizontal or vertical line. This is probably a problem between the main circuit board and the yoke, or a blown yoke coil. This definitely requires a service call.

- A single white dot on an otherwise black screen means the high-voltage flyback transformer is most likely shot. Take it in to the repair shop.

The only time I'll open a monitor is to replace a control knob or switch or to try to adjust the focus. These tips are great to know for the A+ Certification exams, but I'm just way too chicken to do most of these myself. Here is a list of a few last dos and don'ts that I abide by to keep my monitors happy:

- Do keep the screen clean.

- Do keep the cables tightened.

- Do use quality cabling.

- Do use power-management features if available.

- Don't block the ventilation slots on the monitor.

- Don't use a refresh rate higher than recommended by the manufacturer.

- Don't leave the monitor on all the time, even with a screen saver.

- Don't place magnetic objects such as unshielded speakers close to the monitor. (This can cause color problems at best and could permanently magnetize the shadow mask at worst.)

- Be careful about disposing of a dead monitor. Many local governments have laws regarding safe disposal of monitors. Be sure to check with your local waste disposal entity or your company to verify proper disposal methods.

## Beyond A+

### Video and CMOS

I'm always impressed by the number of video options provided in CMOS, especially in some of the more advanced CMOS options. I'm equally impressed by the amount of disinformation provided on these settings. In this section, I'll touch on some of the most common CMOS settings that deal with video. You may notice that no power-management video options have been included. Those are discussed in Chapter 18.

### Video

Every standard CMOS setup shows an option for video support. The default setting is invariably EGA/VGA. Many years ago, this setting told the BIOS what type of card was installed on the system, enabling it to know how to talk to that card. Today, this setting has no meaning. No matter what you put there, it will be ignored and the system will boot normally.

### Init Display First

This CMOS setting usually resides in an advanced options or BIOS options screen. In multimonitor systems, Init Display First enables you to decide between AGP and PCI as to which monitor initializes at boot. This will also determine the initial primary monitor for Windows 9x and Windows 2000.

## Assign IRQ for VGA

Many video cards do not need an IRQ. This option gives you the ability to choose whether your video card gets an IRQ. In general, lower-end cards that do not provide input to the system do not need an IRQ. Most advanced cards will need one; try it both ways. If you need it, your system will freeze up if you do not assign an IRQ. If you don't need an IRQ, you get an extra IRQ.

## VGA Palette Snoop

True VGA devices only show 16 out of a possible 262,000 colors at a time. The 16 current colors are called the *palette*. VGA Palette Snoop opens a PCI video card's palette to other devices that may need to read or temporarily change the palette. I am unaware of any device made today that still needs this option.

## Video Shadowing Enabled

As mentioned in previous chapters, this setting enables you to shadow the Video ROM. In most cases, this option is ignored as today's video cards perform their own automatic shadowing. A few cards require this setting to be off, so I generally leave it off now after years of leaving it on.

## 3-D Graphics

No other area of the PC world reflects the amazing acceleration of technological improvements more than 3-D video, in particular, 3-D gaming. We are spectators to an amazing new world where software and hardware race to produce new levels of realism and complexity displayed on the computer screen. Powered by the wallets of tens of millions of PC gamers always demanding more and better, the video industry constantly introduces new video cards and new software titles that make today's games so incredibly realistic and fun. Although the gaming world certainly leads the PC industry in 3-D technologies, many other PC applications such as *Computer Aided Design* (CAD) programs quickly snatch up these technologies, making 3-D more useful in many ways other than just games. In this section, we'll add to the many bits and pieces of 3-D video encountered over previous chapters in the book and put together an understanding of the function and configuration of 3-D graphics.

Before the early 1990s, PCs did not mix well with 3-D graphics. Certainly, many 3-D applications existed, primarily 3-D design programs such as AutoCAD and Intergraph, but these applications used proprietary methods to generate 3-D graphics and often required the users to purchase complete systems as opposed to simply dropping an install disk into their desktop system. Even though these systems worked extremely well, their high cost and steep learning curves kept them hidden inside organizations such as design firms and government entities that needed them. UNIX systems enjoyed

3-D graphics very early on, but even the most powerful UNIX workstations of the early 1980s relegated almost all 3-D functions to CAD applications.

The big change took place in 1992 when a small company called id Software created a new game called Wolfenstein 3D that launched an entirely new genre of games now called *first-person shooters* (FPS) (Figure 16-59). In these games, the player looks out into a 3-D world, interacting with walls, doors, and items, and shoots whatever bad guys the game provides.

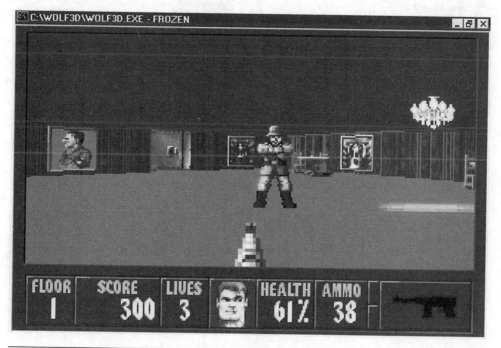

**Figure 16-59**  Wolfenstein 3D

Wolfenstein 3D shook the PC gaming world to its foundations. An upstart little company suddenly appears with this new format, making Wolfenstein 3D and id Software overnight sensations; id Software knew that their 3-D game required substantial RAM and CPU strength for the time. They gambled that enough systems existed to handle the massive calculations required to keep track of the position of objects, keyboard inputs, and most importantly, the incredibly complex process of placing the 3-D world on the screen. The gamble paid off, making John Carmack and John Romero, the creators of id Software, the fathers of 3-D gaming.

Early 3-D games used fixed 3-D images called *sprites* to create the 3-D world. A sprite is nothing more than a bitmapped graphic like a BMP file. These early first-person shooters would calculate the position of an object from the player's perspective and place a sprite to represent the object. Any single object would only have a fixed number of sprites—if you walked around an object, you noticed an obvious "jerk" as the game replaced the current sprite with a new one to represent the new position. Figure 16-60 shows different sprites for the same bad guy in Wolfenstein 3D. Sprites weren't pretty, but they worked without seriously taxing the 486s and early Pentiums of the time.

**Figure 16-60**
Each figure has a limited number of sprites.

The second generation of 3-D began to replace sprites with true 3-D objects. True 3-D objects are not sprites. True 3-D objects are drastically more complex than a sprite. A true 3-D object is composed of a group of points called *vertices*. Each vertice has a defined X, Y, and Z position in a 3-D world. Figure 16-61 shows the vertices for an airplane in a 3-D world.

**Figure 16-61**
Vertices for a 3-D airplane

The computer must track all of the vertices of all of the objects in the 3-D world, including the ones you cannot currently see. Keep in mind that objects may be motionless in the 3-D world (like a wall), may have animation (like a door opening and closing), or may be moving (like bad monsters trying to spray you with evil alien goo). This calculation process is called *transformation* and, as you might imagine, is extremely taxing to most CPUs. Intel's SIMD and AMD's 3DNow! processor extensions were expressly designed to perform transformations.

Once the CPU has determined the positions of all vertices, the system then begins to fill in the 3-D object. The process begins by drawing lines (the 3-D term is *edges*) between vertices to build the 3-D object into many triangles. Why triangles? Well, mainly by consensus of game developers, any shape works, but triangles make the most sense from a mathematical standpoint. I could go into more depth here but that would require talking about trigonometry, and I'm gambling you'd rather not read that detailed of a description! All 3-D games use triangles to connect vertices. The 3-D process then groups triangles together into various shapes called *polygons*. Figure 16-62 shows the same model shown previously, now showing all of the vertices connected to create a large number of polygons.

**Figure 16-62**
Vertices connected
forming polygons
on 3-D airplane

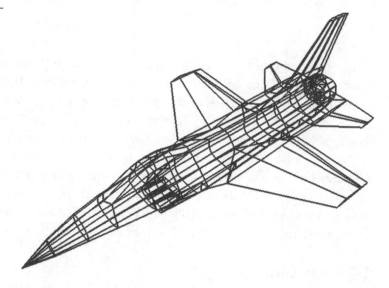

Originally, the CPU handled these calculations to create triangles, but now special 3-D video cards do the job, greatly speeding up the process.

The last step in second generation games was texturing. Every 3-D game stores a number of bitmaps called *textures*. The program wraps textures around the object to give it a surface. Textures work well as they provide dramatic detail without the need to use a lot of triangles. A single object may take one texture or many textures applied to single triangles or groups of triangles (polygons). Figure 16-63 shows the finished airplane.

**Figure 16-63**
3-D airplane with textures added

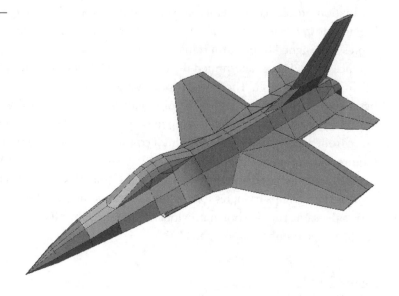

These second-generation games made a much more realistic environment, but the heavy demands of true 3-D often forced game designers to use both 3-D and sprites in the same game. Figure 16-64 shows the famous game Doom. Note that the walls, floors, doors, and such were 3-D images, whereas the bad guys continued to manifest as sprites. Notice how pixilated the bad guy looks compared to the rest of the scene.

True 3-D, more often referred to as "rendered" objects, immediately created the need for massively powerful video cards and much wider data buses. Intel's primary motivation for creating AGP was to provide a big enough pipe for massive data pumping between the video card and the CPU. Intel gave AGP the ability to read system RAM to support textures. If it weren't for 3-D games, AGP would almost certainly not exist.

## 3-D Video Cards

No CPU of the mid-1990s could ever hope to handle the massive processes required to render 3-D worlds. Keep in mind that in order to create realistic movement, the 3-D world must refresh at least 24 times per second. That means that this entire process from transformation to texturing must repeat once every 1/24$^{th}$ of a second! Furthermore, while the game re-creates each screen, it must also keep score, track the number of bullets, provide some type of intelligence to the bad guys, and so on. Something had to happen to take workload off of the CPU. The answer came from the video cards.

**Figure 16-64** A mix of 3-D objects and sprites

The first generation of 3-D video cards are better named as 3-D rendering cards. These cards did not perform any transformation functions—that was the CPU's job. Instead, they helped the CPU by taking over some, and eventually all, the rendering duties. 3-D cards have massive amounts of RAM to store textures, as well as powerful processors to deal with the creation of triangles and the placement of textures at incredibly high speeds.

But a problem exists with this setup: How do we talk to these cards? This is done by means of a device driver, of course, but wouldn't it be great if we could create standard commands to speed up the process? The best thing to do would be to create a standardized set of instructions that any 3-D program could send to a 3-D card to do all the basic work, such as "make a cone" or "lay texture 237 on the cone you just made." These standards manifested themselves originally with the popular OpenGL standards, initially created for UNIX systems but quickly ported over to Windows NT and Windows 95 in the mid-1990s. Additionally, a small company called 3Dfx began to market a powerful, but proprietary standard called Glide, at roughly the same time. Although Microsoft Windows supported both OpenGL and Glide on Windows 9x and Windows NT systems, the DirectX standard dominates the current market.

## DirectX and Video Cards

In earlier chapters, we discussed how DirectX provides a closer link between the 3-D application and the hardware. The primary impetus for DirectX was to build a series of products to enable Windows to run 3-D games. When we say DirectX, we really mean a broad set of programming standards for multiple devices on the PC. These include the following:

- **DirectDraw** supports direct access to the hardware for 2-D graphics.

- **Direct3D** supports direct access to the hardware for 3-D graphics—the most important part of DirectX.

- **DirectInput** supports direct access to the hardware for joysticks and other game controllers.

- **DirectSound** supports direct access to the hardware for waveforms.

- **DirectMusic** supports direct access to the hardware for MIDI devices.

- **DirectPlay** supports direct access to network devices for multiplayer games.

- **DirectShow** supports direct access to video and presentation devices.

Microsoft constantly adds and tweaks this list. As almost all games need DirectX and all video cards have drivers to support DirectX, you need to verify that DirectX is installed and working properly on your system. To do this, use the DirectX diagnostic tool in the System Information program. After you open System Information (it usually lives in the Accessories | System Tools area of the Start menu), click on the Tools menu and select DirectX Diagnostic Tool (Figure 16-65).

The System tab gives the version of DirectX. The system pictured in Figure 16-65 runs DirectX 8.0. You may then test the separate DirectX functions by running through the other tabs and running the tests.

So, what does DirectX do for video cards? Well, video card makers must find ways to make their video cards better than other video cards. To do this, the chip and card makers constantly add a number of interesting features and then push Microsoft to add it to their DirectX tools. This has led to major upgrades of DirectX at a minimum of twice a year as new fascinating tools are introduced. Some of these functions work completely within the video card, and the makers are more than glad to expound on features that make their card better than others. Literally thousands of extra functions have been touted by different makers, making them impossible to list. But the bottom line is that

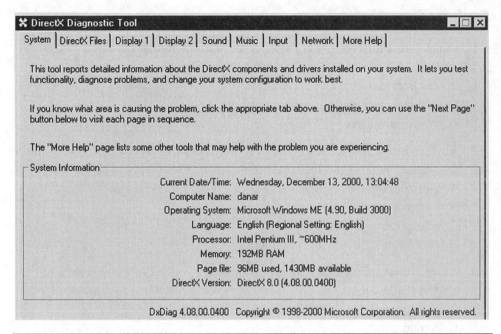

**Figure 16-65** DirectX Diagnostic Tool

once a maker touts a new function, other video card makers add that function or a suitable equivalent very quickly. Trying to decide what video card to buy gives me the shakes—too many options! One good rule to help in a buying decision is to see what video chipset is "hot" at the moment. I make a point to check out these Web sites whenever I'm getting ready to buy in order to see what everyone says is the best:

www.arstechnica.com

www.tomshardware.com

www.sharkyextreme.com

## Review Questions

1. Which of the following is not a physical component of a *cathode ray tube* (CRT)?
   A. Yoke
   B. Electron guns
   C. Display screen with phosphor coating
   D. Phase transducer

2. Some tech by the water cooler kept speaking about "raster lines" and "painting the screen." What could she have been referring to?
   A. Horizontal refresh rates
   B. Video drivers
   C. Phosphors
   D. An art project involving an old door

3. A set of three phosphors—red, green, and blue—on the monitor is called
   A. The shadow mask
   B. Resolution
   C. A triad
   D. A phosphor dot

4. The definition of dot pitch is
   A. The diagonal distance between the holes of the shadow mask
   B. The physical size of the pixels
   C. The size of a triad
   D. The diagonal distance between phosphorous dots of the same color

5. Bandwidth is known as
   A. The length of time it takes to complete HRR
   B. The length of time it takes to complete VRR
   C. The crossover speed at which interlacing takes over for noninterlacing monitors
   D. The number of times the electron gun must be turned on and off in a period of time

6. Which of the following types of video cards are capable of supporting 640 × 480 resolution at 16 colors? (Choose all that apply.)
   A. CGA
   B. EGA
   C. VGA
   D. SVGA

7. Raphael wants to run his new 19-inch monitor at 1,280 × 1,024 with true color (24 bits, 16.7 million colors). He has an older 1MB ATI video card. What do you say to him?

   A. Sorry, 19-inch monitors cannot display that high of a resolution.

   B. Give it up, Raphael! You need a video card with a lot more RAM.

   C. Cool! Invite me to your cubicle for Quake III!

   D. It's not going to work—no monitor can do that resolution!

8. Monitor resolution is shown as the number of

   A. Horizontal triads times the number of vertical triads

   B. Horizontal pixels times the number of vertical pixels

   C. Horizontal phosphor dots times the number of vertical phosphor dots

   D. Horizontal refresh lines times the number of vertical refresh lines

9. The area of a monitor that holds the most voltage is

   A. The anode

   B. The electron guns

   C. The magnetic yoke

   D. The vacuum tube

10. Which of the following are some of the adjustments you can make to a modern monitor?

   A. Pincushioning

   B. Brightness

   C. Contrast

   D. All of the above

## Answers

1. **D.** A phase transducer is something out of a science fiction story. The other three are components common to all CRTs.

2. **A.** Although an argument could be made for the other three choices, "horizontal refresh rates" makes the most sense.

3. **C.** A triad.

4. **D.** Technically, you measure on the diagonal, although you have to be careful with the marketing descriptions of some monitors.

5. **D.** The number of times the electron gun must be turned on and off in a period of time defines the bandwidth.

6. **C and D.** Both VGA and SVGA adapters can display "VGA mode," that is, 640 × 480 at 16 colors.

7. **B.** Some 19-inch monitors cannot go to 1,280 × 1,024 presumably, but clearly the minimal video RAM on the card is the bottleneck.

8. **B.** Resolution describes the pixels displayed.

9. **A.** The anode, even when the monitor is unplugged, can hold up to 30,000 volts of electricity. Remember, messing around inside the monitor can kill you! Be very careful.

10. **D.** Older monitors generally had brightness and contrast controls, but little else. Newer monitors have dozens of options for users to adjust.

# Modems

**17**

In this chapter, you will

- Understand the difference between analog and serial communication
- Understand the function of modems and UARTs
- See examples of synchronous and asynchronous communication
- Be able to define different speed, error correction, and data compression standards
- Look at the AT commands for modems
- Clarify IRQ and I/O issues concerning modems

While so many other technologies continue to improve and grow, the world of modems (those little devices that enable your PC to use the telephone to talk to other computers) has had no serious technological changes in almost five years. That doesn't make modems unimportant—more people use modems rather than any other method to access the Internet—but it does make them a bit less interesting to the A+ Certification exams. As a result, most of this chapter fits under the Historical/Conceptual banner. Don't let that fool you! The A+ exams still expect you to install and configure a modem, so be prepared for a few modem questions; although, you'll find them pretty basic.

## Historical/Conceptual

The term "modem" is an abbreviation of modulator/demodulator. Modems are used in PCs primarily to enable computers to talk to each other via standard commercial telephone lines. Telephone wires transfer data via analog signals, that is, continuously changing voltages on a wire. Figure 17-1 is a diagram of an analog signal.

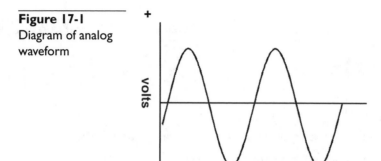

**Figure 17-1**
Diagram of analog waveform

Computers hate analog signals. Computers need digital signals, voltages that are on or off, meaning the wire has voltage present or it does not. Computers, being binary by nature, use only two states of voltage: zero volts and positive volts. Figure 17-2 is a diagram of a digital signal.

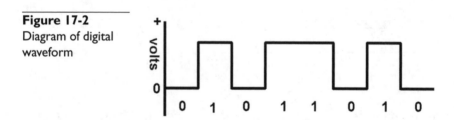

**Figure 17-2**
Diagram of digital waveform

Modems take analog signals from telephone lines and turn them into digital signals that your PC's COM ports can understand (Figure 17-3). Modems also take digital signals from the PC's COM ports and convert them into analog signals for the outgoing telephone line.

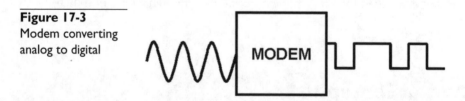

**Figure 17-3**
Modem converting analog to digital

Modems convert signals from analog to digital and back to analog. This data is just a series of 1's and 0's, which is why it's called *serial communication*; however, your CPU needs to access data in discrete 8-bit chunks (Figure 17-4).

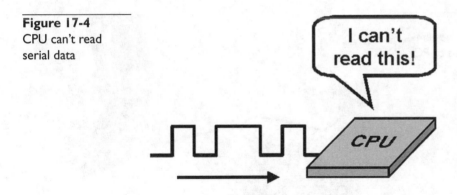

**Figure 17-4**
CPU can't read
serial data

The serial bits of data are converted into 8-bit "bytes" of data via the UART, which stands for *Universal Asynchronous Receiver/Transmitter*. The UART chip converts the serial bits of analog data into 8-bit bytes that the PC can understand (Figure 17-5).

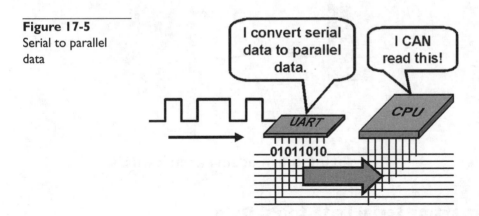

**Figure 17-5**
Serial to parallel
data

All COM ports are really little more than UARTs. A mouse is a serial device; it sends its data as a series of bits down one wire (the other wires are used for things other than sending data). If you have a mouse hooked to a COM port, the UART converts the serial information into the 8-bit-wide data that the external data bus can understand. There are many types of UARTs, each with different functions.

External modems only convert analog to digital and back, because they are connected to COM ports that handle the job of converting the serial data bits into the 8-bit-wide data the CPU needs (Figure 17-6). Internal modems come with their own COM port that handles the whole process (Figure 17-7).

**Figure 17-6**
External modem
connected to PC

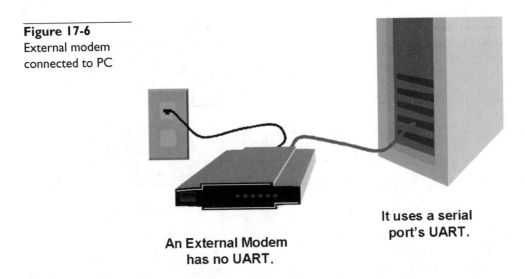

An External Modem
has no UART.

It uses a serial
port's UART.

**Figure 17-7**
Internal modem

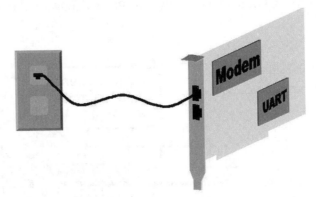

An internal modem has its own UART.

## Converting Serial Data to PC Data

A problem still exists with this scenario. How does a port know which of the serial bits are the actual data? Even assuming the data is 8 bits wide, which is not always the case, how does the port decide where one 8-bit burst stops and the next one starts? There has to be a system that enables the port to "chop up" the incoming signal and "package" the outgoing signal (Figure 17-8). There are two ways of organizing serial transmissions: asynchronous and synchronous.

## Asynchronous Organization

Asynchronous data transfers are the primary way in which two serial ports communicate. With this type of transfer, the data is chopped up into 7- or 8-bit packets. These are the bits that actually carry the data (Figure 17-9).

**Figure 17-8**
Unorganized data

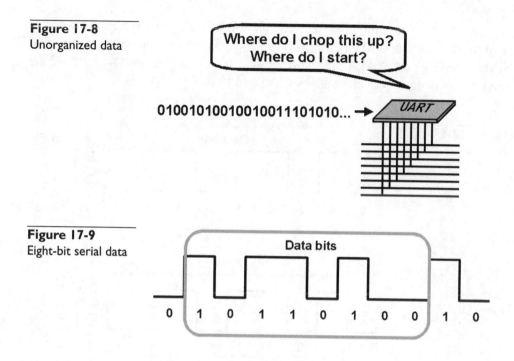

**Figure 17-9**
Eight-bit serial data

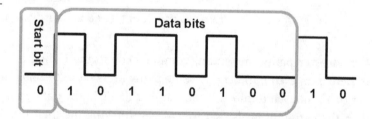

Eight-bit data is the most common, although 7-bit data is still used occasionally. Each packet begins with a start bit to tell the receiving modem that it is the beginning of a piece of data (Figure 17-10). The start bit is always 0.

Each data packet ends with a *stop bit,* to tell the receiver that the packet is over (Figure 17-11).

**Figure 17-10**
Start bit inserted
at the beginning of
the byte

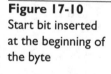

**Figure 17-11**
Stop bit added to
the end of the byte

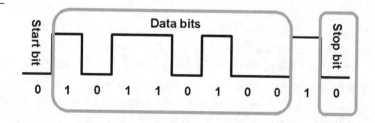

Asynchronous communication packets may also have an optional *parity bit*, which is used for error detection. The parity bit is generated by the sending port and then used by the receiving port to determine whether the data is good (Figure 17-12). There are two types of parity bit calculations: even and odd (Figure 17-13).

**Figure 17-12**
Parity bit

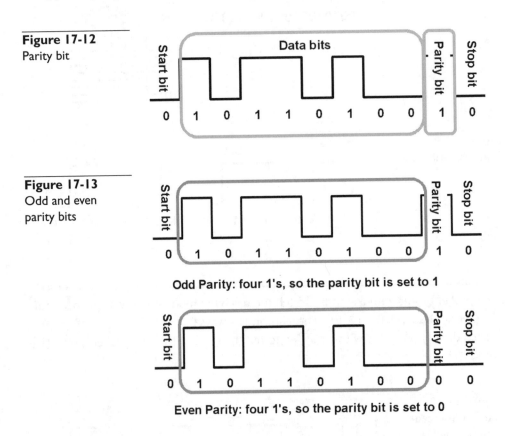

**Figure 17-13**
Odd and even parity bits

Odd Parity: four 1's, so the parity bit is set to 1

Even Parity: four 1's, so the parity bit is set to 0

To do even parity, the sending computer counts the 1's in the data part of the packet. If there is an even number of 1's, the parity bit is set to 0, which leaves the total number of 1's an even number. If the number of 1's in the data part of the packet is odd, then the parity bit is also set to 1—again making the total number of 1's even. The receiving port counts the data bits and compares its answer to the parity bit. Odd parity works in exactly the same way, except that the total number of bits is odd.

Parity bits are optional! In fact, almost no one uses parity bits anymore because newer modems are really good about reading data. It's usually no big deal if a character or two gets a little screwed up every now and then.

Asynchronous packet settings are described in a particular order: data bits, parity type, then stop bits. So if a system uses 8 data bits, no parity, and 1 stop bit, you'd say 8-N-1. If a system uses 7 data bits, even parity, and 1 stop bit, you'd say 7-E-1. Virtually everything uses 8-N-1 or 7-E-1 today.

## Synchronous Organization

There is a time, however, when there can be no errors in data, such as when you're uploading or downloading a program to or from your computer. Even one incorrect bit in an EXE or COM file will probably make the file unusable. So, when transferring files, you'll engage a completely different type of communication: *synchronous communication* (SC).

Although there are many types or *protocols* of synchronous communication, with names like Xmodem, Ymodem, and Zmodem, they all work in basically the same way. When a modem is about to send data via SC, it sends a series of standardized bytes called *sync* bytes. The port on the other end receives the sync bytes, which tell the receiving port that it is about to receive SC data, enabling it to synchronize with the incoming data (see Figure 17-14).

**Figure 17-14**
Synchronized
handshaking

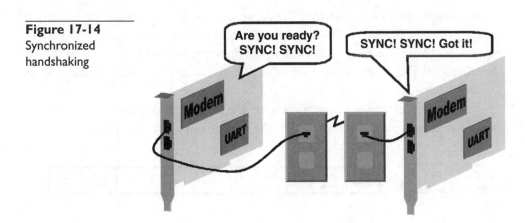

Okay, reality check. Protocols are not programs; they don't "do" anything. They are sets of definitions used by communication programs, so that both computers are speaking the same "language." When transferring a file between systems, both sender and receiver must use the same protocol, which will usually have to be set manually on both the sending and receiving sides. Figure 17-15 shows the protocol selection screen of an older Windows communication program.

After the sync bytes, the sending modem adds an STX, or *start-of-text* marker. Then the data bytes are sent. The data in a synchronous transmission is processed in *packets* or "blocks" of a fixed length, which varies depending upon the protocol used. For a synchronous data transfer to occur, the incoming modem must know the protocol. That's why the protocols have to be set when the file transfer is initiated.

**Figure 17-15**
Protocol selection
screen

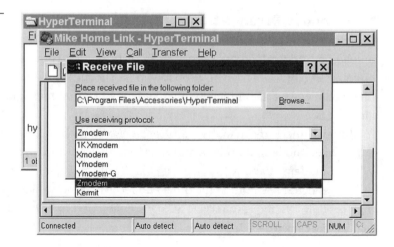

After the data has been transferred, the packet ends with an *end-of-text* (ETX) marker and *error-checking characters* (ECCs). These characters use a clever algorithm to check the accuracy of the incoming data. The receiver then responds with an "ack" (acknowledge character) if the data is good, or a "nack" (no acknowledge) if there is an error (Figure 17-16).

Note that in asynchronous communication, the receiving modem does not respond; it just reads the data and acts on it. In SC, the receiving modem must respond.

**Figure 17-16**
Synchronous data
packet

| Sync byte | Sync byte | STX byte | Data Packet | ETX byte | ECC |
|---|---|---|---|---|---|

## File Transfer Protocols

In the PC world, many commonly used FTPs enable you to exchange files with mainframes, minis, or other PCs. They should be included in the software package that comes with your modem. Once you have established communication with a host, you can usually ask the host what type of protocol it uses, and select yours accordingly before transferring files.

- **ASCII**  This transfer protocol transmits each character as if it had come off the keyboard. This is not a good protocol for transferring program files. It has no error-checking features or compression.

- **XMODEM**  This protocol uses an error-detection method for transferring files. It transfers 128-byte blocks of data and one checksum character. The receiving computer calculates a new checksum and compares the two. If they are the same, it will reply with an "ack." If they are different, it will send back a "nack," and the transmitting computer will retransmit the problematic data block.

- **YMODEM**  Ymodem transfers in 1,024-byte blocks. Larger blocks mean less time spent verifying data with acks and nacks. If you make an error-free connection, meaning both modems are error correcting, choose Ymodem.

- **ZMODEM**  Use this protocol whenever possible, because it includes all the features of Xmodem and Ymodem, and adds a few new features, including crash recovery, automatic downloading, and a "streaming" file-transfer method.

- **KERMIT**  This was the first synchronous protocol used for uploading and downloading from a mainframe. Although the early versions of Kermit are virtually unused today, Kermit has kept up with the times, and later versions enjoy widespread use in specialized communication scenarios.

## Baud Rate

The baud rate is the basic cycle of time that a modem uses as its carrier frequency. For instance, a modem that is working at 300 baud means that the basic carrier frequency has 300 cycles per second. On a dial-up phone line, you can go up to 2,400 cycles, known as a *"baud rate* of 2,400" (Figure 17-17).

Theoretically, if each cycle is one bit, then the fastest data rate at which you could transmit would be 2,400 bits per second; however, through different types of modulation you can "chop up" the cycles to produce more than one bit per cycle (Figure 17-18).

**Figure 17-17**
One cycle: one baud and one bit

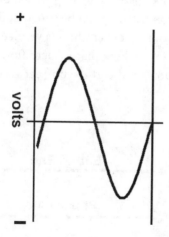

1 Cycle = 1 Baud

**Figure 17-18**
Two bits for each baud

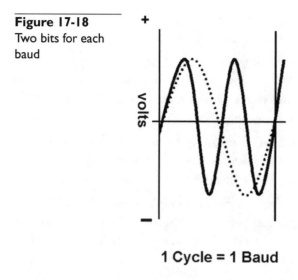

1 Cycle = 1 Baud

This is where you get the actual modem *speed*, measured in *bits per second* (bps). If your 2,400-baud modem modulates one bit for each baud cycle, then your modem *speed* is 2,400 bps. If your 2,400-baud modem modulates two bits for one cycle of time, your modem is said to have a speed of 4,800 bps, not a baud rate of 4,800. If four bits are modulated with one cycle time, then you have a modem speed of 9,600 bps. Don't make the mistake of confusing bps with baud rate.

## Flow Control (Handshaking)

Flow control, also known as *handshaking,* is the process by which two serial devices verify a conversation. Imagine people talking on a CB radio. When one finishes speaking, he will say "over." That way the person listening can be sure that the sender is finished speaking before he starts. Each side of the conversation is verified. During a file transfer, there are two distinct conversations taking place where flow control is required: local (between modem and COM port) and end-to-end (between modems). See Figure 17-19.

**Figure 17-19**
Example of local and end-to-end flow control

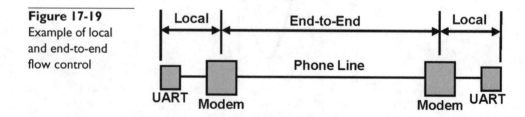

The modems themselves handle flow control between them; you have no control over this. However, local flow control between the modem and COM port is very much within your control. PCs can do local flow control in two ways: hardware and software. A PC with hardware flow control employs some of the extra wires in the serial connection between its modem and COM port to let one device tell the other that it is ready to send or receive data. These extra wires are called *ready to send* (RTS) and *clear to send* (CTS), so hardware handshaking is often called RTS/CTS. Software flow control uses a special character called XON to signal that data is beginning, and another special character called XOFF is used to signal that data transmission is finished; therefore, software handshaking is often called XON/XOFF. XON/XOFF is very rarely used in modems anymore, because software handshaking is slower and not as dependable as hardware handshaking. Only some very old modems still use software handshaking. When in doubt, always use hardware flow control. See Figure 17-20.

**Figure 17-20**
Flow control
selection window

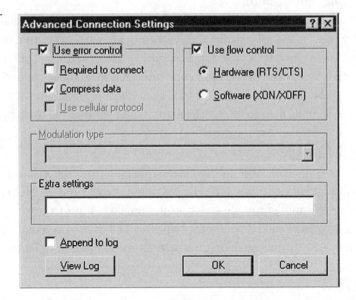

### Error Detection

End-to-end error detection is usually the realm of the synchronous protocol software being used; however, some modems can perform hardware-based error detection that is blindingly fast and invisible to the software itself. Note that both modems must be able to perform this function in order to take advantage of error detection in a file transmission.

## Data Compression

Some modems can perform on-the-fly data compression. These data compression algorithms are virtually identical to the ones used in ZIP files and can significantly enhance the amount of data sent between modems. Of course, each modem must be able to understand the other's compression standard. The modem maker Micron Data started compression under their proprietary MNP5 standard. There are now industry standards for data compression.

## Communication Standards

In the early days of modem communication, computers were restricted to using the same type of modems on each side of the connection. For example, an XYZ modem would have to talk to another identical XYZ modem. Most of the time, depending on the computer and modem, a technician would have to set up the operation using jumpers and specific cables. Compatibility was a great concern, and proprietary modems were the norm.

These incompatibilities created a desperate need for industry standardization. There had to be a standard way for modems to query each other to determine each other's speed, error correction, and data compression. This standardization has come through two developments. First, certain companies released aspects of their modem functions to the public domain, and other modem makers copied them. Second, standards committees were formed to create standards, which all modem makers adopted.

### Bell 212A/103

The first really common modem standard came from the Bell 212A/103. This modem could send data at either 1,200 or 300 baud, depending on programming. The popularity of this modem made other modem makers want to copy the way the Bell 212A spoke to other Bell 212As. In other words, a Bell 212A could dial up a modem that was not a Bell 212A and speak to it because the other modem *emulated* a Bell 212A.

### CCITT

After the Bell 212A, modem standards came under the control of a United Nations agency, the *Consultative Committee on International Telephony and Telegraphy/Comité Consultatif International Téléphonique et Télégraphique* (CCITT). This committee established what are known as V standards—each standard is specified by the letter *V* followed by a number. These standards include modem speed, data compression, error correction, and fax. They have equivalents in the Bell standards. The CCITT is now known as the *International Telecommunication Union Telecommunication Standardization Sector* (ITU-T).

## MNP

The Microcom Company has released a series of standards for error detection and data compression to the public domain. These standards are known as the *Microcom Network Protocols* (MNP) standards. Although still supported by most modem makers, they have been superseded by the ITU-T standards.

## Speed

Speed standards for modems are listed in Table 17-1.

**Table 17-1**    Speed Standards

| STANDARD | BAUD | BPS | COMMENT |
|---|---|---|---|
| Bell 103 | 300 | 300 | U.S. and Canada standard |
| Bell 212A | 600 | 1,200 | U.S. and Canada standard |
| V.21 | 300 | 300 | Similar to Bell 103 |
| V.22 | 600 | 1,200 | Incompatible with 212A |
| V.22bis | 600 | 2,400 | Worldwide compatibility |
| V.23 | 1,200 | 1,200 | |
| V.32 | 2,400 | 9,600 | |
| V.32bis | 2,400 | 14,400 | |
| V.32terbo | 2,400 | 19,200 | |
| V.34 | 2,400 | 28,800<br>33,600 | |
| X2 | 2,400 | 56K | US Robotics (3Com)<br>Incompatible with Kflex |
| Kflex56 | 2,400 | 56K | Lucent/Motorola<br>Incompatible with X2 |
| V.90 | 2,400 | 56K | |

## Error Detection and Data Compression

Error detection and data compression protocols are listed in Table 17-2.

**Table 17-2**   Other Standards

| STANDARD | BAUD | BPS | TYPE | COMMENTS |
|----------|------|-----|------|----------|
| V.42 | 2,400 | 2,400 and up | Error correction | |
| MNP 14 | 2,400 | 2,400 and up | Error correction | |
| V.42BIS | 2,400 | 9,600/38.4K | Data compression | V.42 Must be present |
| MNP 5 | n/a | n/a | Both | |

## Modem Commands

Modems have many functions, and there must be a way to speak to a modem to tell it which function to perform (answer the phone, perform data compression, and so on). These commands are known collectively as the *modem command set*. You'd think that there would be a standard for modem commands, but there isn't. Modem commands vary from manufacturer to manufacturer, although a few front-runners tend to control things. The No. 1 name in modem command sets is certainly Hayes. Hayes developed the famous AT command set in the early 80s and released it to the public. All modem manufacturers follow the majority of these commands. AT commands are entered through the keyboard into the modem. Before you can use these commands, however, you have to make sure the communication software is loaded and that you are either in terminal mode or at a terminal screen. Unless your modem is set up to auto-connect, which is the online mode, it should be in command mode, which is where you use the AT commands. Although there are hundreds of these commands, Table 17-3 lists only the ones that technicians actually use.

**Table 17-3**   Common AT Commands

| AT COMMAND | FUNCTION |
|------------|----------|
| AT | Your modem should respond with an OK, letting you know that your modem is plugged in and turned on. |
| ATE1 | This echos your command on the screen. |
| ATE0 | This turns off the echo to the screen. Some modems will not run correctly with the echo on, so make sure you turn it off when done with it. |

**Table 17-3**   Common AT Commands

**Table 17-3** Common AT Commands (continued)

| AT COMMAND | FUNCTION |
|---|---|
| ATH1 | This is taking the phone off the hook. You should get a reply of OK or 0 back from the modem, a dial tone, and an OH indicator on the modem if it's an external modem. |
| ATL0 | ATL commands set the speaker volume level. ATL0 is the lowest; ATL1 is the default; ATL2 is medium end; and ATL3 is high. |
| ATM1 | This turns the speaker on; this is for the dial tone. |
| ATM0 | This turns the speaker off. |
| ATD | This command will take the phone off the hook as ATH1 did. It will also dial a number if you include it with your command, that is, ATDT2222222. The T is for tone. Put a P in its place for a pulse phone. If you include a W (ATDTW), it will wait for a dial tone before dialing. If you include a (,) anywhere after the command, it will pause before continuing to dial. For instance, you may need a 9 for an outside line. |
| ATQ0 | This enables result codes. This aids in troubleshooting problems. If you typed an ATV1 before this command, you will get back verbose result codes (OKBUSYCONNECT 2400,9600COMPRESSION:V.42bis). If you type ATV or ATV0, then you will get number or short codes: that is, 0, 12,10. |
| ATQ1 | This disables result codes. |
| ATH,ATH0 | This makes the modem hang up. |
| ATZ | This resets your modem to a predefined state. You can reconfigure your own profile for the modem for resetting. If it wasn't set previously, then it will reset to the factory's setting. |

## RS-232 Connector

To make a physical connection through a serial port from an external modem to a PC, you use a cable that meets *Electronic Industries Associations* (EIA) standard RS-232. RS stands for *Recommended Standards*, and RS-232 is the revision that applies to serial ports. This standard is defined in Europe as V.24. RS-232 describes only the signals, not the physical plug, but RS-232 revision D specifies a 25-pin D-type connector. This 25-pin connector was mostly used for synchronous communications. The data transfer between serial ports and modems in PCs is always asynchronous. Asynchronous communication can be handled with far fewer than 25 pins. Therefore, starting with the 286-based AT, IBM began using an IBM-developed proprietary 9-pin connector. See Figure 17-21.

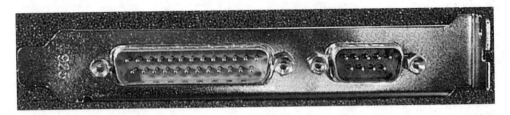

**Figure 17-21** Serial connectors: 25-pin and 9-pin

## Talking to Serial Ports

Serial-port gurus often use the terms DCE and DTE. DCE stands for *Data Communication Equipment* and DTE stands for *Data Terminal Equipment*. The DCE is the device that *sends* data, and the DTE is the device that *receives* data. The connection between the DCE and the DTE is what we call the *handshake*. It ensures that the DCE and the DTE are in sync with each other when passing data that must be transmitted correctly and not lost. The signal ground and data signal rates are missing from the 9-pin norm. The signal names, direction, and purpose are listed in Table 17-4.

**Table 17-4** RS-232 Pinouts

| 25-PIN | 9-PIN | SIGNAL | DIRECTION | DESCRIPTION |
| --- | --- | --- | --- | --- |
| 1 | | | | Protective ground |
| 2 | 3 | TD | DTE-DCE | Transmitted data |
| 3 | 2 | RD | DCE-DTE | Received data |
| 4 | 7 | RTS | DTE-DCE | Request to send |
| 5 | 8 | CTS | DCE-DTE | Clear to send |
| 6 | 6 | DSR | DCE-DTE | Data set ready |
| 7 | 5 | | | Signal ground (common) |
| 8 | 1 | DCD | DCE-DTE | Data carrier detect |
| 20 | 4 | DTR | DTE-DCE | Data terminal ready |
| 22 | 9 | RI | DCE-DTE | Ring indicator |
| 23 | | DSRD | DCE-DTE | Data signal rate detector |

## Telephone Lines

The good old phone line you use to talk to your mother every Sunday is an analog line. The basic analog phone line is guaranteed to handle speeds only up to 2,400 baud. (Telephone companies think in terms of baud, not bps.) These lines were designed for voice communication, not to transfer data, and are notorious for providing poor-quality transmissions. The problem is that your line is connected to the telephone company's main switch via a series of connections at smaller distribution switches. Each subswitch can cause degradation of phone quality by creating "noise" on the line. See Figure 17-22.

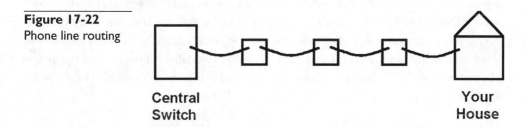

**Figure 17-22**
Phone line routing

**Central Switch**

**Your House**

A common trick to verify that you are getting the best quality is to call the phone company. Complain that you have a high-speed modem and the highest baud rate you can get is 1,200 baud. If you complain that your 28,800-bps modem is working at only 14,400 bps, the phone company will tell you that you're getting 2,400 baud, and they won't do anything. However, if you complain that you're getting only 1,200 baud, the phone company has to fix the line. Most phone companies guarantee a minimum of 2,400 baud telephone lines.

To improve your telephone lines, the phone company will first create a direct line between your line and the local switch. Then, they will check your line to see if you have too much of a voltage drop. A phone line should run at approximately 48 volts. If the phone company feels that the voltage drop is too much (there's no definite number here, it's up to them), they will *condition* the line. Conditioning simply means adding a little voltage to the line to compensate for the voltage drop. See Figure 17-23.

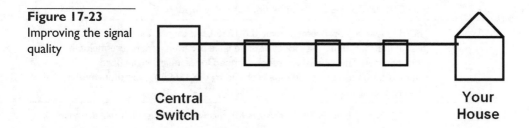

**Figure 17-23**
Improving the signal quality

**Central Switch**

**Your House**

## Test Specific

Yeah, I know I said most of this chapter is Historical/Conceptual, but for some reason the A+ Certification exams are interested in versions of UART chips (see the following section), as well as a few other aspects of modem data transfer. Make sure you know your UARTs!

### Universal Asynchronous Receiver/Transmitter Chips (UARTs)

The UART is the heart of many serial ports used in PCs and other computer applications. UARTs take the parallel information off data buses and turn it into serial information to be sent out to a modem or to another serial device. They can also receive serial information and turn it into parallel information to be put back on data buses for a computer's use, and they provide control signals for flow control to the serial devices. Table 17-5 shows the most popular and viable chips that are used for serial communications.

**Table 17-5**   UARTs

| CHIP | DESCRIPTION |
| --- | --- |
| 8250 | This is the original chip selected by IBM for use in the PC. It had several bugs built into it, but IBM worked around them with built-in routines written in the PC and XT ROM BIOS. |
| 8250A | This chip was developed to fix the bugs in the 8250, but in doing so, it would not work properly with the PC and XT BIOS. This chip would work with the AT BIOS. This chip does not work adequately at 9,600 bps or above. |
| 8250B | This chip was developed to fix the bugs in the previous chips and also designed with the interrupt enable bug that was in the 8250 chip. This made it compatible with the PC/XT BIOS, and it may work with the AT BIOS. However, it still has problems with bps rates above 9,600. |
| 16450 | This chip was initially picked by IBM for their AT systems. In fact, it is a bare minimum for their OS/2 systems, or the serial ports will not function properly. This chip has a higher throughput than the previous chips and has an added scratch register to aid in speed. The only drawback is that it cannot be used with the PC/XT BIOS due to the interrupt bug being fixed. |
| 16550 | This chip was an improvement over the 16450, but cannot be used for FIFO (first in first out) buffering modes. It did enable programmers to use multiple DMA channels. This chip is not recommended for standard high-speed communication use and should be replaced by the 16550A, even though it has a higher throughput. |
| 16550A | This chip has 16 built-in FIFO registers for receive and transmit. It will increase your throughput without losing characters at higher rates of speed, due to the added registers. This is the only UART installed on today's systems. |

It's important to know what type of UART is in your COM ports. To ensure quality data communication at 9,600 bps or better, you need a 16550A. You can easily determine the type of UART by checking the Diagnostics tab | More Info button under the Modems applet in the Control Panel under Windows 9*x*. In Windows 2000, use the Phone and Modem Options applet. Figure 17-24 shows a typical modem's UART information.

**Figure 17-24**
More Info in
Windows 9*x*
showing UART

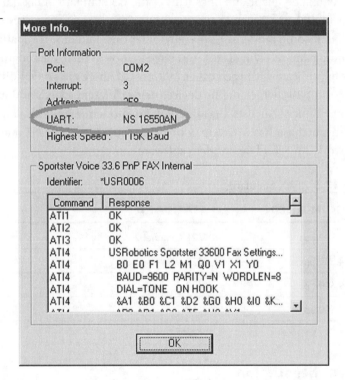

## Fax Modems

An inventor named Alexander Bain developed the technology for faxes in 1842. He invented an electromechanical device that could translate wire-based signals into marks on paper. The technology has certainly evolved over the years! In fact, so many different facsimile standards had proliferated by the early 1970s that the CCITT stepped in and came up with international standards for the transmission of facsimile data for both computer modems and fax machines.

Modems work differently when transmitting data and facsimiles. Modems transmit computer data in packets that get reassembled by a receiving modem, but transmit facsimiles as single dots (bits of data), which are then converted into text. Computers store images as a collection of dots as well, which means facsimiles can quite easily be converted into an image format, such as bitmap (*.BMP).

Four different classes or groups of fax standards are found in the PC environment. The first CCITT standards—Groups 1 (1974) and 2 (1976)—were analog standards for fax modems operating at 300-baud communication rates, basically an advanced extension of the Hayes modem command standards. Although these standards are still supported by fax modems, they are old, slow, and obsolete, and thus rarely used. In 1980 CCITT introduced the *Group 3* (G3) standard for digital facsimile devices to communicate over analog telephone lines. Under the G3 standard, a fax transmission can be as fast as 14,400 bps, whereas the maximum data mode speed is only 2,400 bps. This means that some modems (especially older ones) are not compatible with each other for sending and receiving faxes. You have to look at their V standards to make sure they can communicate with each other. Within G3, there are several different classes (such as V17 and V29), which define devices using different speeds and methods of communicating. Table 17-6 lists the different fax-modem standards. Ensure that your fax-modem purchase has a Group 3 or G3 fax-modem standard marked on the box or paperwork. Any good fax-modem software can run G3.

**Table 17-6** FAX Standards

| MAXIMUM SPEED | STANDARD |
| --- | --- |
| 300 bps | V.21 Channel 2 |
| 4,800 bps | V.27 |
| 9,600 bps | V.29 |
| 14,400 bps | V.17 |

## Modem Negotiations

Have you wondered about all the noise that you hear when your modem calls another modem? Those different tones—jokingly referred to as the "mating call" of modems—are actually a very standardized series of queries and responses between the two modems so they can determine optimal speeds, data compression, error detection, and so on. Two examples of a modem performing a mating call are "V.22bis modem calling a V.22bis modem" (Table 17-7) and "V.32 modem calling a V.32 modem" (Table 17-8). As you can see, these procedures are quite complicated, and you do not need to know them to operate or troubleshoot a modem. I just wanted to give you an idea of what you might hear when a connection is being established.

**Table 17-7** V.22 Calling V.22

| MODEM 1 (TRANSMITTER) | MODEM 2 (RECEIVER) |
|---|---|
| (1) Initiates call (dialing number). | |
| | (2) Detects a ring, goes off hook, waits 2 seconds for billing purposes. |
| | (3) Transmits an answer tone of 2,100 Hz for 3.3 ± 7 sec to inform the originator that it has reached a modem and can go to data mode. This also disables echo suppressors so that transmission can be done in both directions. |
| | (4) Goes silent for 75 ± 20 msec (this separates the answer tone from the signals that follow). |
| | (5) Transmits unscrambled binary 1's at 1,200 bps (USB1). This is done at 2,250 Hz and 2,550 Hz. |
| (6) Detects the USB1 signal in 155 ± 10 ms. Goes silent for 456 ± 3 ms. | (6) Still transmitting (USB1). |
| (7) Transmits double-digit 00s and 11s @ 1,200 bits (S1) for 100 ± 3 ms. If this is a 1,200 or V.22 modem, it won't transmit this signal. | (7) Still transmitting (USB1). If it detects the (S1), it will then send 100 ms of (S1) signal to the caller to let it know that it is capable of going to 2,400 bps. |
| (8) Transmits scrambled 1's and 0's (SB1) @ 1,200 bits to even out the bandwidth. This is known as White noise. | (8) Switches to sending SB1 for 500 ms. |
| | (9) Switches to sending scrambled 1's at 2,400 bps for 200 ms. Now it's ready to pass data. |
| (10) 600 ms after detecting SB1, it will transmit scrambled 1's for 200 ms; then it's ready to pass data. | |

**Table 17-8** V.32 Calling V.32

| MODEM 1 (TRANSMITTER) | MODEM 2 (RECEIVER) |
|---|---|
| (1) Dials up number to receiver. | (2) Detects ring, goes off hook, waits 2 seconds, then transmits a V.25 answer tone, but the signal is phase reversed every 450 ms, which sounds like a clicking noise. This is done to let the network know that the modems will do the echo cancellation themselves and to disable the network echo cancellors. |
| (3) After 1 second of the answer tone, it transmits an 1,800 Hz tone. This is known as "AA" in V.32 lingo. This lets the answering modem know that it is talking to another V.32 modem. | (4) If this modem hears the AA signal before the end of the answer tone (3.3 sec), it will try to connect as a V.32 modem immediately. If it doesn't hear the AA, it will send a USB1 for 3 seconds to see if it can hook up as a V.22bis modem. |
| | (5) If there is no response to the USB1 signal, it will try to reconnect as a V.32 modem by transmitting a 600-Hz signal with a 3,000-Hz signal together for 1/2400 sec (64 symbol intervals). This signal is AC. It then reverses phase to send the signal CA. |
| (6) When this modem detects the phase reversal from the receiving modem, it reverses its phase, which changes its AA to CC. | (7) When this modem detects the phase reversal, it reverses its signal to AC. Both modems are able to check the propagation time and round-trip delays to cancel signal echos. |
| | (8) Both modems then go into half-duplex to exchange training signals, to train the adaptive equalizers, test the quality of the phone lines, and agree on the data rate to be used. This modem transmits first, from 650 ms to 3,525 ms, then goes silent. |
| (9) This modem responds with a similar signal and leaves on the signal. | (10) This modem responds one more time, establishing their data rate. |
| (11) Both modems respond by sending scrambled binary 1's for at least 128 symbol intervals, and then are ready to pass data. | (11) Both modems respond by sending scrambled binary 1's for at least 128 symbol intervals, and then are ready. to pass data |

# TAPI

To enable a program to perform telephone functions such as dialing numbers or receiving calls, the program must know how to "talk" like a telephone through the modem. For example, if a program wants to use the modem to call a particular number, it must be able to discern a dial tone before a call is made and react properly if a dial tone is not present. Early communication software handled this directly, as no support for telephone functions was built into DOS or Windows 3.x. This changed with Microsoft's introduction of *Telephony Application Programmers Interface* (TAPI). TAPI is a set of *dynamic link libraries* (DLLs) that enables Windows 3.*x* and Windows 9*x* to perform telephone functions.

When a modem is installed, a good TAPI installation (the Modems applet in the Control Panel is a good example) will configure the modem type, I/O address and IRQ, local phone number, long-distance dialing codes, plus all of the other details needed by TAPI to enable it to use the modem (Figure 17-25).

**Figure 17-25**
Modem settings in
Windows

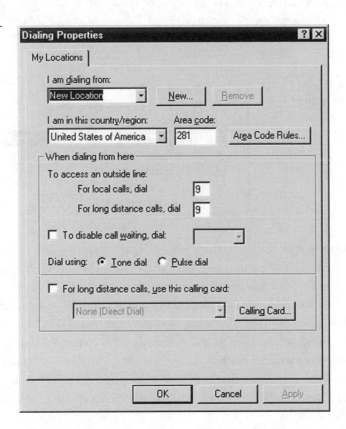

Once TAPI is aware of the modem, any program can use the TAPI DLL to handle telephone functions. Yet TAPI goes far beyond simply making telephone calls. Answering machines are a common TAPI implementation. A TAPI answering machine can link with the existing multimedia functions of Windows 3.*x* or Windows 9*x* and enable recording and playback of announcements and messages in standard WAV format. TAPI can enable voice mailboxes and even voice recognition. Finally, TAPI provides the ability to handle faxing, call forwarding, caller ID, and paging.

## Installation and Troubleshooting

Modems are extremely robust devices. The chance of a modem failing at the hardware level is quite small. The majority of the time, modem problems are actually problems with COM ports or with the way the communication software talks to the modem.

### Set Up and Verify the COM Ports

Even in today's Plug and Play world, the No. 1 reason that modems do not work is COM port and IRQ conflicts. Make sure you install nonconflicting I/O addresses and interrupts. Always check the modem in Device Manager to verify the modem is in proper working order (Figure 17-26).

**Figure 17-26**
Modem in good working order—no errors shown

If by any chance you're stuck with a legacy modem, don't forget that COM3 and COM4 on most older modems were preset to IRQ4 and IRQ3, respectively. If COM1 and COM2 are already in use, then they are almost certainly using IRQ3 and IRQ4. Be sure to set the modem's IRQ to something other than IRQ3 or 4. Use IRQ5, 7, or whatever the legacy modem allows you to use (Figure 17-27).

The ability of Windows 9x and Windows 2000 to handle PnP modems makes most installations a true no-brainer—as long as the modem is configured for PnP. Most PnP modems have a jumper that turns the PnP option on or off. If the modem is not PnP, the Add New Hardware Wizard will usually do an excellent job finding your modem (Figure 17-28).

Unfortunately, the Add New Hardware Wizard in Windows 9x will sometimes have trouble with uncommon IRQs. After running the Install Wizard, verify the port settings through the Device Manager. If the settings are incorrect, manually change them and reboot.

### Verify the Modem's BIOS

Modern modems all have onboard BIOS. The term "BIOS" is actually a bit of a misnomer. A better term might be "command set"—the ability to handle different commands from modem drivers or from other modems. This "BIOS" doesn't occupy any DOS memory addresses, thus avoiding memory-management problems. It usually

**Figure 17-27**
Jumper settings for
port and IRQ

| COM | IRQ | ON |
|-----|-----|------|
| 1 | 4 | 1,2,5 |
| 2 | 3 | 2,4 |
| 3 | 4 | 1,5 |
| 3 | 5 | 1,6 |
| 4 | 3 | 4 |
| 4 | 2 | 3 |

manifests as a flash ROM on the modem, making it upgradable through software. Upgradability is very convenient, because as anticipated new technologies arise (the latest one being the 56K V.90 standard) modem makers can easily upgrade modems, giving customers confidence to purchase modems in the face of ongoing improvements. Upgrading is quite simple: Download a program from the Internet, AOL, CompuServe, a BBS, or whatever, and then run the program from a DOS prompt (the actual upgrade process depends on the maker of the modem). The downside is that the BIOS can be corrupted quite easily, usually by something as simple as removing and reinserting the modem. Many upgrades can be made to the BIOS, so making sure you have the right version is important. Contact the modem's manufacturer to verify the current version.

**Figure 17-28**
Windows 9x Add
New Hardware
Wizard

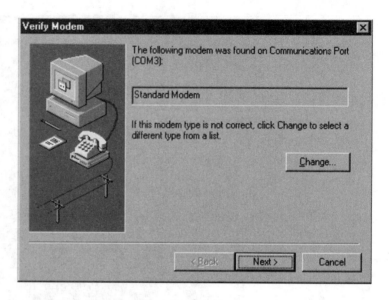

## Set Up the Correct Command Set

Now that the modem's COM port is correct, you must make sure that the communication software knows the type of modem you have, so it will know how to give the correct AT commands.

### Communication Programs

Windows communication programs do not need to know what type of modem you have installed; this information is handled by the Windows operating system. Just make sure that you have the latest INF file for your modem and version of Windows to ensure seamless operation. The INF files that come with Windows 9x are almost certainly unacceptable. As a rule, always take a quick trip to the manufacturer's Web site to grab the latest INF file before you install.

Given the low level of changes in modem technology, the modem drivers that come with Windows 2000 are often superb. The biggest problem with Windows 2000 is finding drivers for older modems, not worrying if the built-in Windows 2000 driver is the latest version.

On the rare occasions where Windows has difficulty recognizing your modem, try installing another brand of driver instead. Try Hayes Compatible or Standard settings, if available. Try modems that sound like your modem. Look at your modem and see if you have a chipset name, and then look for an option based on the chipset rather than the modem type. If you can't determine a chipset, try "Rockwell." It's a very common and fairly generic type. You *can* find one that will work—just keep trying!

## Windows 2000

To configure dialing rules and settings for a modem in Windows 2000, use the "Phone and Modem Options" tool in the Control Panel. As with many "tech" features of Windows 2000, you need to be logged on as an administrator or a member of the Administrators group to be able to change some settings in the Phone and Modem Options applet. Windows 2000 will do a lot of work for you, but it will not detect certain internal modems, requiring you to do a manual installation through the Control Panel. Also, you may have to adjust the mode settings of modems supported by Network and Dial-up Connections to make them work with other modems on the Microsoft Windows Hardware Compatibility List. You may have to experiment with the settings a little bit, but in general, Windows 2000 is great at installing and configuring modems. Finally, it may be useful to check the Microsoft Web site (**www.microsoft.com/**) for service packs and updates that might include additional modem support and fixes.

## When Modems Break

A broken modem is probably the most frustrating repair problem in the PC world. But by following these steps, you can make the problem much easier (I didn't say easy, just easier) to repair.

## Is the Modem Using a Non-Conflicting COM Port and IRQ?

To find out, I turn to a very powerful shareware program called Modem Doctor, made by Hank Volpe. This program is supplied with the accompanying CD-ROM and will query all your COM ports, looking for a modem (Figure 17-29).

Modem Doctor does an excellent job detecting COM ports and determining whether there is a modem at a particular COM port.

**Figure 17-29**
Modem Doctor looking for a modem

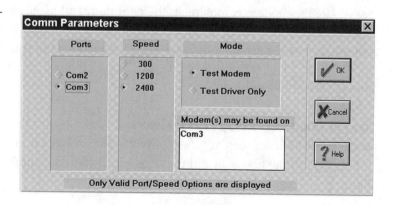

Many technicians make the mistake of not considering a COM port or IRQ conflict unless the modem or some other hardware has just been installed. Do not do that! Many different cards can be changed by software or corrupted files. Assume nothing!

Modem Doctor does far more than just verify COM ports. Many times a technician wants to know if the modem is still good. That is where Modem Doctor shines. Modem Doctor will test your modem thoroughly and give you a complete description of its quality. The one nice thing about modems is that they never get sick; they just die. Modem Doctor will let you know without a doubt if your modem is alive or dead (Figure 17-30 shows a modem passing with flying colors).

**Figure 17-30**
A diagnostic display
of Modem Doctor

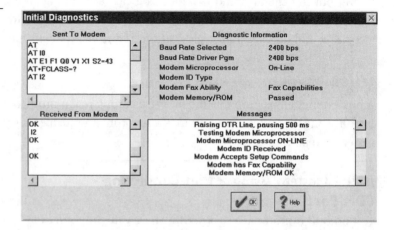

If Modem Doctor says your modem is okay, then it's time to look at the software. At this point, you need to focus on the type of problem.

## The Software Says There's No Modem

Make sure the modem is looking at the right port, and make sure there's no conflict with another device. Reinstall the modem software and reconfigure to make sure you haven't corrupted a driver. If the modem is Plug and Play and you're using Windows 9x or Windows 2000, make sure the Device Manager shows the modem and that the modem is working properly.

## The Modem Works Sporadically

Make sure you have the right modem installed or try another modem type. Check the phone lines in the house, or call the phone company and complain about the phone lines.

# Review Questions

1. What is the primary function of a modem (modulator/demodulator)?
   A. To turn AC voltage into DC voltage and back again
   B. To convert bits of data into viable, byte-wide data
   C. To turn analog signals into digital signals and back again
   D. To connect to the Internet

2. Choose all that apply. A modem is a(n)
   A. Serial device
   B. Parallel device
   C. Synchronous device
   D. Asynchronous device

3. Which of the following modem commands will take the phone off the hook?
   A. ATQ
   B. ATD
   C. ATM0
   D. ATH0

4. Which of the following has a Universal Asynchronous Receiver/Transmitter (UART)? (Select all that apply.)
   A. Internal modem
   B. External modem
   C. Serial port
   D. Parallel port

5. Joey has an older system that should work well as an Internet station. He plugs a new 56K external modem into his second serial port and sets up the software in Windows 98. The modem works great but seems limited to 9,600 bps data transfer rates. What most likely is the problem?
   A. The serial port is disabled in CMOS.
   B. The serial port is disabled in Windows.
   C. The serial port has a 16550A UART.
   D. The serial port has a substandard UART.

6. The serial port has a 8250A UART. What are the main reasons why a modem might not work? (Select all that apply.)
   A. I/O address conflict
   B. IRQ conflict
   C. DMA conflict
   D. PnP jumper off while running PnP BIOS

7. When setting up a new non-PnP modem in your Windows 9x system, what is mandatory to ensure seamless operation?

   A. You need the latest INF file for the modem.

   B. You need the newest "patches" for Windows.

   C. Make sure that the legacy jumpers are set to correct I/O addresses and IRQs.

   D. Make sure to set the "UART enabled" option in the Modems applet to "on."

8. What settings can you use as last resorts if your Windows 9x system has difficulty recognizing a newly installed modem? (Select all that apply.)

   A. Use a setting that refers to the type of chipset your new modem has.

   B. Use a Hayes-compatible modem setting.

   C. Use the Standard settings for the modem.

   D. None—you need to get a modem that is compatible with your system.

9. Where would you configure the dialing rules and settings for a modem on a Windows 2000 system?

   A. Control Panel | Modem and Dialing Options applet

   B. Control Panel | Phone and Modem Options applet

   C. Control Panel | Dial-up Operations

   D. Device Manager | Modem properties

10. To change the dialing rules and settings for a modem in a Windows 2000 system, what do you need?

   A. You must have User rights to the system.

   B. The permissions must be set properly so you can make changes.

   C. You must be logged into that system as the Administrator or part of the Admin group.

   D. Nothing special. Simply open the appropriate applet and configure things.

# Answers

1. **C.** Modems convert from analog to digital, and vice versa.

2. **A, C, and D.** Depending on the type of connection, modems can communicate asynchronously or synchronously. Modems are serial devices.

3. **B.** Think "D" for dial or dial tone.

4. **A and C.** Internal modems and serial ports have their own UARTs.

5. **D.** The serial port clearly has a substandard UART.

6. **A and B.** Incorrect Plug and Play settings may cause configuration problems, but such problems boil down to good old-fashioned I/O address and IRQ conflicts.

7. **A.** The latest INF files are needed to ensure seamless operation.

8. **A, B, and C.** You can use any of the following as last resorts: using the modems' chipset, Hayes Compatible, or the Standard settings.

9. **B.** You would configure in Control Panel | Phone and Modem Options.

10. **C.** You must be logged in as the Administrator, or have rights to the Admin group.

# Portable PCs

In this chapter, you will

- Appreciate the issues that separate portable PCs from desktop PCs
- Understand the different types of batteries used
- Discover power management

From the moment that PCs first began to appear in the early 1980s, people wanted to be able to move a PC from one location to another. The ability of a PC to hold and process data drove a strong market impetus to come up with a way to transform the static desktop PC into a mobile device to serve an increasingly mobile business environment. The upside to the mobile PC was the promise of increased efficiency and profitability. The downside to making the PC a mobile device was that the desktop PC, as envisioned by IBM, was an absolute nightmare to make mobile for a number of reasons (Figure 18-1).

## Historical/Conceptual

The biggest problem was power. The first desktop PCs used standard 120-volt AC current, using big power supplies to convert to multiple voltages of DC current. At least the low DC current demands of PCs made batteries, and therefore truly mobile PCs, possible. One interesting note: Early on, IBM pushed for voltages higher than 12 volts for

**Figure 18-1**
Getting a PC to "go mobile" was a daunting task.

some aspects of the PC. If that effort had been successful, development of the mobile PC might have been substantially delayed. But even running at 12 volts or less, a first-generation PC with a hard drive quickly would have drained any of the small, inexpensive batteries available in the early 1980s. The first generation of mobile computers got around the power problem quite elegantly—they didn't have batteries. If you wanted to move the PC, you turned it off, unplugged it, lugged it (the first ones were heavy) to the next location, plugged it back in, and turned it back on to start using it again.

This was fine for a person moving from office to office, but what about the person working in a car, plane, or some other place where a power outlet wasn't available? Batteries, and the power they provided, quickly became very important to mobile computing.

This simultaneous demand for more battery power and for PC components that use less power has created an entire family of PC products that are functionally identical to their desktop equivalents but that use much less power. Low-power monitors, CPUs, chipsets, hard drives, and CD-ROMs are now the *de facto* standards on laptops. Many of these low-power components, or at least the technologies that make them low power, have made strong inroads back into the desktop market.

The second big challenge was to ensure reliability. Desktop hard drives and floppy drives were never designed to be used in the back of a bouncing pickup truck or in a turbulent coach seat. Their read/write heads would bounce around, never accessing the data properly, or worse, destroying it. New methods of drive design compensated for missed data and helped to prevent the heads from crashing into the drive. These technologies have become standard even on desktop PCs. In addition, the entire PC needed to be more robust. Many first-generation mobile PCs actually had small shock absorbers to help compensate for shocks and to make the PC generally more robust than its desktop equivalent.

The last challenge was functionality. Mobile PCs needed to be able to mimic the functions of their desktop brothers within the constraints of a smaller, lighter form-factor. A great example is the mouse. Even though the first mobile PCs could support a mouse, the standard desktop rodent would hardly serve a businessperson packed into the middle seat of a 737, or a busy duty nurse making his or her rounds in a ward. The demand for a mobile mouse spawned a series of new, innovative pointing devices, from trackballs to touchpads.

The problems of power, reliability, and functionality still challenge mobile computing. We continue to demand longer running, more reliable PCs while we expect the same convenience, firepower, and speed that we enjoy on our desktops. Unfortunately, the ability to conquer one challenge usually creates new problems in another. As improvements in batteries and power management continue to increase the availability of power to a mobile PC, new features and devices continue to be developed that demand even more of that power, and new demands on reliability begin to surface. The cycle is unending (Figure 18-2).

**Figure 18-2**
The demand for
more functionality

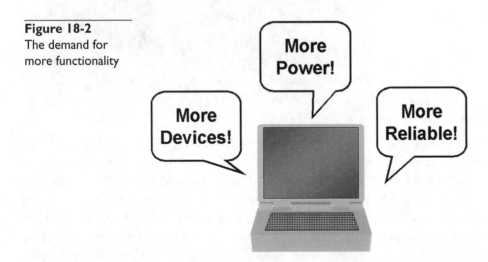

## History

Trying to identify the first mobile computer is guaranteed to produce fisticuffs between any two computer historians. Rather than start a fight, it may be easier simply to zero in on the first computers that were widely marketed and available to the public. This crown arguably belongs to the famous Osborne One from the late 1970s. Although not truly a PC (it didn't use IBM's BIOS or have any parts interchangeable with the PC) the

Osborne One defined a series of technologies that helped to define *how* the first generation of portable computers would look and operate. In particular, the Osborne defined the concept of the "suitcase luggable." The Osborne One was equipped with a small screen, 5.25-inch floppy drives, and a keyboard that acted as a cover during transport (Figure 18-3).

**Figure 18-3**
The Osborne One
(Photo courtesy of
Obsolete Computer
Museum)

Due to its proprietary design, the Osborne cannot be officially listed as the first mobile PC clone. (Remember, only IBM can make a PC; everyone else makes clones. It's just that the term "PC" now encompasses all IBMs and IBM clones.) That distinction goes to the mobile PCs developed by Compaq in the early 1980s (Figure 18-4). Not only were these the first mobile PC clones, Compaqs were the first PC clones of any type. Before Compaq, only IBM made PCs; it was Compaq that started the entire clone concept. Compaq's portables were quickly followed by a succession of similar machines, including a genuine IBM luggable version of the PC.

Luggables were all AC powered, so no battery problems occurred. They ran on 8086 or equivalent CPUs, with the same DOS as their desktop cousins. Therefore, they could easily exchange data and programs with those machines. These mobile PC-compatible computers had a tremendous impact on many industries, substantially changing the way they did business. But of all the industries affected by the advent of portable PCs, the public accounting business was probably the most significantly affected.

**Figure 18-4**
The Compaq
portable (Photo
courtesy of
Obsolete
Computer
Museum)

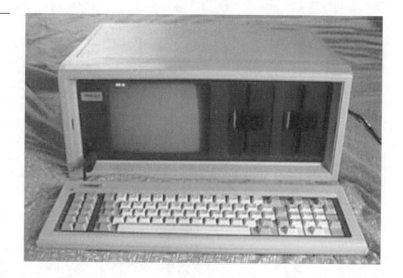

First-generation luggables, combined with the early spreadsheet programs, such as Lotus 1-2-3, transformed the way the big (and not so big) accounting firms conducted their day-to-day business.

Public accounting firms like Coopers & Lybrand or Arthur Andersen are hired by companies to do their auditing. As any new CPA will tell you, the life of a young auditor is a highly mobile affair—flying from one client's location to another, diving through records, and running around collecting financial information for the audit. The combination of luggables and spreadsheets was a perfect fit; public accounting firms were major purchasers of early mobile computers. They also gave rise to the ancient tech support joke, "What do you get when you cross an accountant with a spreadsheet? One heckuva big spreadsheet!" Well, we thought it was funny back in the old days!

The first generation of suitcase luggable PCs, although highly functional, was seriously limited. First, they were very heavy. Some systems weighed in excess of 40 lbs., which made the system's mobility a function of brawn more than convenience. Second, they had tiny screens due to their limited front panel area. Third, they were bulky. They needed to be placed on a stout platform in order to work safely. You would never even consider placing them on a flimsy table, cardboard box, or, heaven forbid, a person's lap! See Figure 18-5.

## Laptops

As 286 CPUs began to dominate the desktop market, two separate technologies simultaneously came to fruition, or at least became cheap enough that PCs could at last become truly portable. First was the portable battery. Obviously, batteries have been

**Figure 18-5**
A luggable isn't a
laptop.

around for quite a while, but regular batteries, like the D cells in a common flashlight, are unacceptable for use in PCs. The problem is the voltage. Think about those D batteries in a flashlight for a moment. When a new set of batteries is put in a flashlight, the light is quite bright. But over time, the batteries begin to wear down, and the light dims and eventually goes out (Figure 18-6).

**Figure 18-6**
Flashlights can
go dim.

**Flashlights can run on lower voltages; they just get dimmer.**

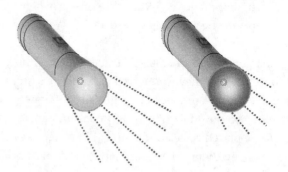

The reason is simple. As regular batteries begin to lose power, their voltage output drops correspondingly. Although this is no big deal with a flashlight, it is absolutely unacceptable in a computer. PCs need continuous, steady voltage to operate properly; without it, they will lock up (Figure 18-7).

**Figure 18-7**
PCs need constant
voltage.

## If a PC's voltage gets too low, it locks up.

This need for continuous voltage led to the invention of the *Nickel-Cadmium* (Ni-Cd) battery. Ni-Cd batteries were the first of a series of battery technologies that provided the necessary constant voltage that mobile PCs need to operate.

The second technology that enabled PCs to develop from luggable to truly mobile was the *Liquid Crystal Display* (LCD). The *cathode ray tube* (CRT) displays in the first-generation mobile PCs were usually very small—no bigger than 4″ to 6″ measured diagonally. They couldn't be any larger and still fit inside the luggable. Plus, the extra weight of a larger tube would make the already overweight portable even heavier. Clearly, there was a need for a lighter and larger display. Enter the LCD. By the time PC makers considered them, LCDs had been around for some time. They had been heavily used in watches and calculators since the early 1970s. These early LCDs, however, were too slow to keep up with constantly changing PC screens. Then came a new technology called *super twist nematic* (STN) that became the cornerstone of all LCD displays. The technology of LCDs continues to improve.

## Laptop/Notebook

It was Zenith (some folks say it was Data General) who first combined a Ni-Cd battery and LCD display with a mobile computer, massively reducing the overall size and turning a heavy, awkward, marginally mobile device into the prototypical mobile device we know today. These new mobile PCs could run anywhere, thanks to their improved batteries and relatively low weight. In fact, the most common place for these new mobile PCs to operate was on the user's lap, hence the name "laptop." The first laptops did away with the old suitcase concept and instead converted mobile PCs into the basic shape still used today: a clamshell, keyboard-on-the-bottom and LCD-screen-at-the-top design that is now considered "the shape" of mobile PCs (Figure 18-8).

**Figure 18-8**   Zenith laptops (Photo courtesy of Obsolete Computer Museum)

As mobile computing, led by laptop PCs, continued to grow as a percentage of all PCs, users began to demand something even smaller and lighter. The problem with laptops was that they were still large enough to demand their own carrying case, and even the lightest laptops approached 15 lbs., making cross-town and cross-country trips still a rather daunting task for all but the most hearty laptop-hauling users. The dream now was to reduce the size of the laptop so that it could fit in a briefcase. The laptop would then have to reduce its size to the size of a notebook, somewhere in the 8 1/2 × 11-inch range. Thus, the term "notebook" was given to all mobile PCs in the new, small size (Figure 18-9).

Most mobile PCs today are still in notebook size. It seems that notebook size is the optimal size for a mobile computer. Although the technology exists to build much smaller PCs, human factors such as keyboard and display size keep the notebook form the standard today. Interestingly, mobile PCs may actually be getting larger instead of smaller, for a number of reasons. First, the concept of throwing your PC into your briefcase hasn't really come to pass. Today's notebooks usually travel in their own specialized travel cases, so a little extra size no longer bothers most users. Second, the extra size is used to provide larger screens and keyboards—two areas that have always been too small for most people. Third, the extra size no longer includes significant extra weight and provides users with virtually all of the amenities and peripherals that they can get on their desktops—the holy grail of mobile computing.

**Figure 18-9**
A notebook PC

## Personal Digital Assistant (PDA)

Yet even since the earliest mobile computers, there has been a demand for very small, reduced-function PCs. These devices might or might not use the same *operating systems* (OSs) as their desktop brethren, but they would be able to interface with them. Such devices wouldn't have all of the firepower of bigger machines, but they would be able to handle the demands of on-the-go executive/sales types. The devices could at the very least store names, addresses, and phone numbers; track appointments and meetings; and provide to-do lists. Preferably, they could handle faxes and e-mail, maybe even pagers and Internet access! Generically, these devices have been called "palmtops" or *personal digital assistants* (PDAs). PDAs are definitely niche players, but they have been around since the first of the mobile computers and continue to grow in popularity. Figure 18-10 shows one of the first PDAs—the Poqet PC. The Poqet had 640K RAM and an 8086 CPU. It ran DOS and all of the popular DOS programs of the day. It even had the first type of PC Card! (See "PC Cards," later in this chapter.)

The goal of a PDA is to fit into a shirt or pants pocket and to weigh as little as possible. With this in mind, PDAs over the years have made great strides in removing superfluous equipment, particularly the keyboard. Many of today's PDAs use handwriting recognition combined with modified mouse functions, usually in the form of a pen-like stylus to make a new type of input called *pen-based computing*. One example of a modern PDA is the popular Palm Pilot series of PDAs from 3Com (Figure 18-11).

**Figure 18-10**
A Poqet PC

**Figure 18-11**
3Com Palm Pilot

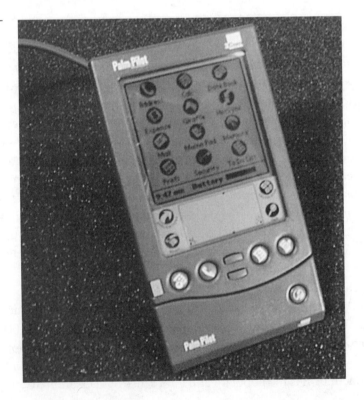

As usual, when Microsoft sees a good thing, it tries to copy it. Microsoft developed a cut-down version of its Windows OS for PDAs called Windows CE; however, it wasn't good enough to make serious inroads against the dominant Palm OS. Microsoft then went back to the drawing board and redeveloped Windows CE into the far better Pocket PC OS. This OS, combined with a new series of very powerful CPUs designed exclusively for the PDA market, has enabled Pocket PC PDAs to gain some momentum. I use the new Compaq iPAQ PDA—I call it my right arm (Figure 18-12).

**Figure 18-12**
My Compaq iPAQ
3650 Pocket PC

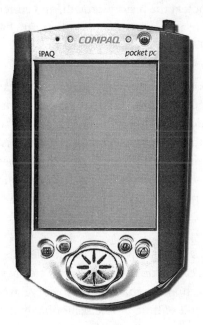

Let's take a moment to clear up a common misunderstanding about the names for the different mobile PC layouts. These range from "suitcase" and "laptop" to "notebook" and "palmtop." The broad use of these terms implies a clear definition for each layout. There is no such definition; they are marketing terms that have moved into mainstream usage. As a result, many devices may fit in more than one category. For example, an extra-large notebook might just as easily be described as a small laptop. A more full-featured PDA might qualify in some eyes as a small notebook. This overlap, this gray area, is perfectly acceptable and understood.

# Test Specific

## Mobile Technologies

Now that you understand the different layouts of mobile computing, let's delve into some of the technologies of mobile computing in detail. This will include visits with some technologies discussed previously, such as batteries and LCDs, as well as a tour of a few not yet covered. We'll look at the history, growth, and current usage of each technology, so that you can provide at least basic support for virtually any mobile PC.

## Batteries

Of all the many technologies unique to mobile PCs, batteries are probably the most obvious, most frustrating, and yet most easily supported component. The secret to understanding batteries is understanding the different types of batteries used by mobile PCs and appreciating each of their special needs/quirks. Once this is clear, battery problems are *usually* easy to spot and fix. To begin with, only three types of batteries are commonly used in mobile PCs: *Nickel-Cadmium* (Ni-Cd), *Nickel-Metal Hydride* (Ni-MH), and *Lithium-Ion* (Li-Ion) batteries. Let's investigate each of these types.

### Nickel-Cadmium

Ni-Cds were the first batteries commonly used in mobile PCs. As previously mentioned, PCs, unlike flashlights or Walkmans, must have a steady voltage. Before Ni-Cd, there wasn't a cheap battery technology that could provide that steady voltage. Ni-Cd, being the first of its type, was full of little problems. Probably most irritating was a little thing called *battery memory*, the tendency of a Ni-Cd battery to lose a significant amount of its rechargeability if it was charged repeatedly without being totally discharged. A battery that originally kept a laptop running for two hours would eventually only keep that same laptop going for 30 minutes or less.

To prevent memory problems, a Ni-Cd battery had to be discharged completely before each recharging. Recharging was tricky as well, because Ni-Cd batteries disliked being overcharged. Unfortunately, there was no way to verify when a battery was fully charged without an expensive charging machine, which none of us had. As a result, most Ni-Cd batteries lasted an extremely short time and had to be replaced. A quick fix was to purchase a *conditioning charger*. These chargers would first totally discharge the Ni-Cd battery, then generate a special "reverse" current that, in a way, "cleaned" internal parts of the battery so that it could be recharged more often and would run longer on each recharge (Figure 18-13).

**Figure 18-13**
Ni-Cd battery

Ni-Cd batteries would at best last for 1,000 charges, and far fewer with poor treatment. Ni-Cds were extremely susceptible to heat and would self-discharge over time if not used. Leaving a Ni-Cd in the car in the summer was like throwing it in the garbage. But Ni-Cd batteries didn't stop causing trouble after they died. The highly toxic metals inside the battery made it unacceptable simply to throw them in the trash. Ni-Cd batteries should be disposed of via specialized disposal companies. This is very important! Even though Ni-Cd batteries aren't used in PCs very often anymore, many devices, such as cellular and cordless phones, still use Ni-Cds. Don't trash the environment by tossing Ni-Cds in a landfill. Turn them into the closest special disposal site; most recycling centers are glad to take them. Also, many battery manufacturers/distributors will take them. The environment you help preserve just might be yours—or your kids'!

### Nickel Metal Hydride

Ni-MH batteries were the next generation of mobile PC batteries and are still quite common today. Basically, Ni-MH batteries are Ni-Cd batteries without most of the headaches. Ni-MH batteries are much less susceptible to memory problems, can better tolerate overcharging, can take more recharging, and last longer between rechargings. Like Ni-Cds, Ni-MH batteries are still susceptible to heat, but at least they are considered nontoxic to the environment. It's still a good idea to do a special disposal. Unlike a Ni-Cd, it's usually better to recharge a Ni-MH with shallow recharges as opposed to a complete discharge/recharge. Ni-MH is a popular replacement battery for Ni-Cd systems (Figure 18-14).

### Lithium Ion

The most common type battery used today is Li-Ion. Li-Ion batteries are very powerful, completely immune to memory problems, and last at least twice as long as comparable Ni-MH batteries on one charge. Sadly, they can't handle as many charges as Ni-MHs,

**Figure 18-14**
Ni-MH battery

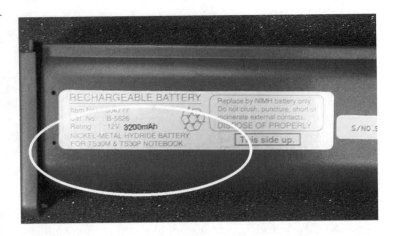

but today's users are usually more than glad to give up total battery lifespan in return for longer periods between charges. Li-Ion batteries simply cannot be overcharged; otherwise, they will explode. So all Li-Ion batteries sold with PCs have built-in circuitry to prevent accidental overcharging. Lithium batteries can only be used on systems designed to use them. They can't be used as replacement batteries (Figure 18-15).

**Figure 18-15**
Li-Ion battery

## Smart Batteries

In an attempt to provide better maintenance for laptop batteries, manufacturers have developed a new type of battery called the *smart battery*. Smart batteries tell the computer when they need to be charged, conditioned, or replaced.

## The Care and Feeding of Batteries

In general, keep in mind the following basics. First, always store batteries in a cool place. Although a freezer is in concept an excellent storage place, moisture, metal racks, and food make it a bad idea. Second, condition your Ni-Cd and Ni-MH batteries; they'll last longer. Third, keep battery contacts clean with a little alcohol or just a dry cloth. Fourth, *never* handle a battery that has ruptured or broken; battery chemicals are very dangerous. Finally, always recycle old batteries.

## PC Cards

PC Cards, still commonly known by their older name, PCMCIA (Personal Computer Memory Card International Association), are as standard on today's mobile computers as the hard drive. PC Cards are credit-card sized, hot-swappable devices that can, and do, perform virtually every PC function. Although originally visualized as memory cards, today PC Cards hold hard drives, modems, network cards, sound cards, SCSI host adapters—the list can continue indefinitely. PC Cards are easy to use, inexpensive, and convenient (Figure 18-16).

**Figure 18-16**  PC Card

Unfortunately, it is this same convenience and ease of use that can make PC Cards a real challenge to configure and troubleshoot. As with so many other parts of the PC, the secret is to understand the individual components of PC Cards so you can recognize symptoms when they happen. The place to start with PC Cards is to recognize that they come in three different physical sizes, as determined by the PCMCIA committee. They are called Type I, Type II, and Type III. Although PCMCIA doesn't require that certain sizes perform certain functions, most PC Cards follow their recommendations.

**Table 18-1**  PC Card Types and Their Typical Uses

| TYPE | LENGTH | WIDTH | THICKNESS | RECOMMENDED USE |
| --- | --- | --- | --- | --- |
| **Type I** | 85.6 mm | 54.0 mm | 3.3 mm | Flash memory |
| **Type II** | 85.6 mm | 54.0 mm | 5.0 mm | I/O (Modem, LAN, etc.) |
| **Type III** | 85.6 mm | 54.0 mm | 10.5 mm | Hard drives |

The only difference between these three types is the thickness of the card. All PC Cards share the same 68-pin interface. As long as the slot that accepts the card is high enough, any PC card will work in that slot. Type II cards are by far the most common of PC Cards. Therefore, most laptops will have two Type II slots, one above the other, to enable the computer to accept two Type I or II cards or one Type III card (Figure 18-17).

**Figure 18-17**
PC Card slots

The PCMCIA standard defines two levels of software drivers to support PC Cards. The first, lower level is known as *socket services*. Socket services are device drivers that support the PC card socket, enabling the system to detect when a PC Card has been inserted or removed, and providing the necessary I/O to the device. The second, higher level is known as *card services*. The card services level recognizes the function of a particular PC Card and provides the specialized drivers necessary to make the card work.

The early days of PCMCIA put most of the responsibility of making PC Cards work in the hands of the individual laptop manufacturers. This meant that if you wanted to be sure a PC Card worked, you purchased the PC Card from the same place you got the laptop. This problem continued until Windows 95 and modern laptop chipsets arrived on the scene. In today's laptops, the socket services are standardized and are handled by the system BIOS. Windows itself handles all card services and has a large preinstalled base of PC Card device drivers, although most PC Cards come with their own drivers. The Windows Card Services can be accessed via the PCMCIA option in the Control Panel. Figure 18-18 shows the card services applet in a Windows 2000 system.

**Figure 18-18**
Windows 2000
Card Services
applet

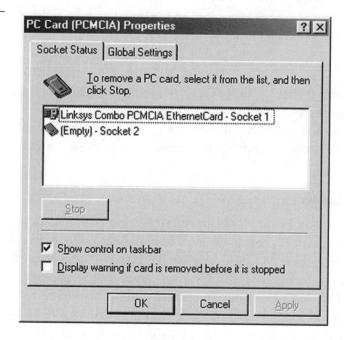

Many PC Card makers advertise a Type IV slot. This slot is not part of the PCMCIA standard. It is used to describe any PC Card thicker than the Type III.

The newest type of PC Card is called CardBus. A CardBus card is nothing more than a special 32-bit PC Card with a special slot. CardBus cards have some major advantages over regular PC cards. First, a 32-bit card beats a regular 16-bit card. Second, CardBus can handle PCI bus mastering (CardBus is really an extension of PCI). Finally, a single CardBus card can perform up to eight functions, whereas regular PC cards have a maximum of two functions. An example of a two-function PC card would be a modem/network card. Don't be surprised if soon you can purchase a modem/network/ISDN/sound/SCSI card! A CardBus PC Card uses the same Types and has the same pinout as a regular PC Card. This enables a regular PC Card to work in a CardBus slot.

Unfortunately, a CardBus card will not work in a regular PC Card socket. In fact, CardBus uses 3.3-volt power instead of the regular 5-volt PC Card power, so a CardBus card has special keying that prevents you from accidentally plugging it into a regular PC Card socket. Finally, in order for CardBus to operate, the laptop should be running Windows 95 OSR2 or later. CardBus has become the PC Card of the future and is standard equipment on most new laptops.

## USB

USB ports belong on all systems, not just portables, but the heavy use of USB on laptops makes them a nice fit for this chapter. We've already seen what USB connectors look like and understand the concept of USB hubs. Now I want to discuss USB in more depth, to help you appreciate the power and problems of USB—not just for laptops, but with any USB system.

### USB Limits

In theory, up to 127 devices may use a single USB port. In reality, USB's maximum throughput of 12 Mb/s limits most USB sharing to three or four devices, depending on their functions. USB ports also supply power to connected devices, but too many devices on a single USB chain will overtax its power capabilities.

USB devices run at one of two speeds: a low speed of 1.5 Mb/s and a high speed of 12 Mb/s. Some low-speed devices will not get along with high-speed devices. Fortunately, most systems that support USB also provide more than one USB port, so you can put one of the devices on the other port to get around this issue.

Watch the cable lengths with USB. USB allows for a maximum cable length of 5 meters, although you may add a powered USB hub every 5 meters to extend this distance. Although most USB devices never get near this maximum, many devices such as digital cameras try to use very long (5-meter) cables. Pushing USB to these maximum lengths might cause problems. Because USB is a two-way (bi-directional) connection, as the cable grows longer, even a standard, well-shielded, 20-gauge, twisted-pair USB cable begins to suffer from electrical interference. I stick to around 2 meters maximum.

## USB Configuration

Improper USB CMOS and driver configuration will make your USB installations nightmarish. Always make sure to follow these steps:

1. Be sure that the CMOS provides an IRQ for the USB ports. Look for a setting similar to Figure 18-19.

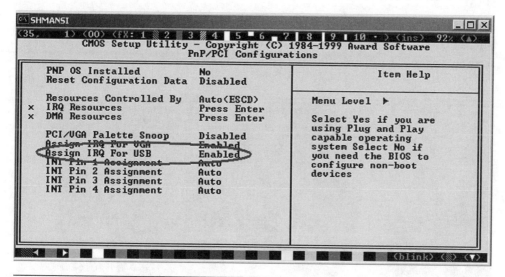

**Figure 18-19** IRQ for USB in CMOS

2. Ensure that your operating system supports USB. This is a no-brainer in Windows because USB is supported by every version, with the exception of Windows 95A. If you have Windows 95A, just download the USB supplement from the Microsoft Web site.

3. Always install the device driver for a new USB device *before* you plug it in. Once you've installed the device and you know the ports are active (running properly in Device Manager), feel free to hot swap to your heart's content. USB really makes device installation a breeze once the drivers are installed—just plug it in!

Windows 2000 has a large number of built-in drivers for USB devices. You can count on Windows 2000 to recognize keyboards, mice, and other basic devices with its built-in drivers. Just be aware that if your new mouse or keyboard has some extras, the default USB drivers will probably not support them. I always install the driver that comes with the device.

## The Modular Laptop

For years, portable PC makers required completely proprietary components for each system model they developed. For the most part, this proprietary attitude still prevails, but we're starting to see some modularity in today's portable PCs, enabling us to make basic replacements and upgrades without going back to the manufacturer for expensive, proprietary components. You need to surf the Web for companies that sell the components, because very few storefronts stock them. Here are the most common ones:

### RAM

Every decent laptop has upgradable RAM slots. These slots all use either 72-pin or 144-pin SO-DIMMs. Be sure to check with the manufacturer of the laptop for any special features required, such as PC100, ECC, and so on (Figure 18-20).

**Figure 18-20**   Good laptops have upgradable RAM slots.

## Hard Drives

ATA drives in the 2.5-inch drive format now rule in all laptops. Although much smaller than regular ATA drives, they still use all the features and configurations. Again, some manufacturers may use strange settings such as requiring the drive to use a "cable select" setting as opposed to master or slave, so check with the laptop maker for any special issues. Otherwise, no difference exists between 2.5-inch drives and their larger 3.25-inch brethren (Figure 18-21).

## Modular CPUs

Both Intel and AMD long have sold specialized, modular CPUs for laptops, yet only now are folks realizing that they can easily upgrade many systems by removing the old module and replacing it with a new one. Be very careful to follow manufacturer's specifications! See Figure 18-22.

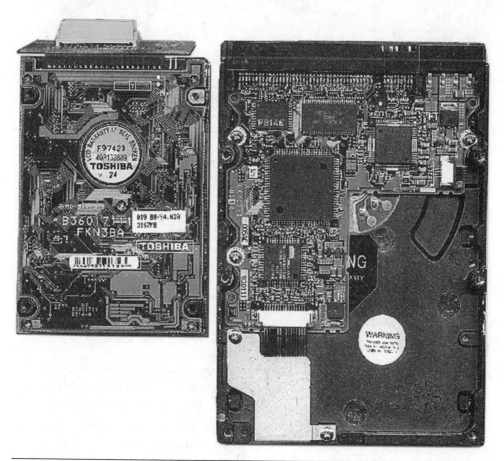

**Figure 18-21**   The 2.5-inch and 3.25-inch drives are mostly the same.

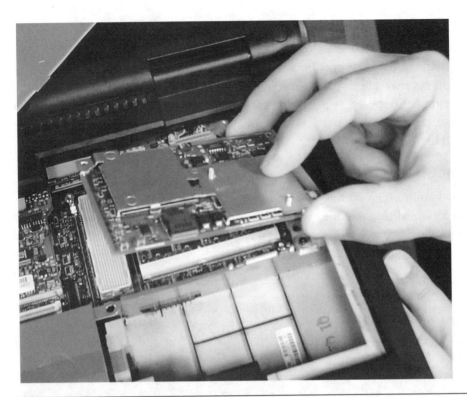

**Figure 18-22**  Modular CPU

### Video Cards

Video card makers have quickly begun to join the modular laptop component arena. Although no single standard works in all systems, a quick phone call to the tech support department of the laptop maker often reveals upgrade options. Modular video cards are the least standardized of all modular components, but as manufacturers adopt more industry-wide standards, we'll be able to replace video cards in laptops more readily (Figure 18-23).

## Power Management

Many different parts are included in the typical laptop, and each part uses power. The problem with early laptops was that every one of these parts used power continuously, whether the system needed that device at that time. For example, the hard drive would continue to spin whether or not it was being accessed, and the LCD panel would continue to display, even when the user walked away from the machine.

The optimal situation would be a system where the user could instruct the PC to shut down unused devices selectively, preferably by defining a maximum period of inactivity which, when reached, would trigger the PC to shut down the inactive device. Longer

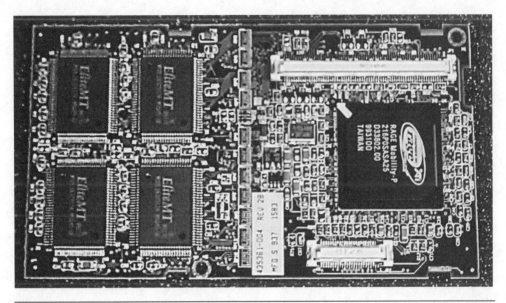

**Figure 18-23**   Modular video card

periods of inactivity would eventually enable the entire system to shut itself down, leaving critical information loaded in RAM, ready to restart if a wake-up event (such as moving the mouse or pressing a key) would tell the system to restart. The system would have to be sensitive to potential hazards such as shutting down in the middle of writing to a drive, and so on. Also, this feature could not add significantly to the cost of the PC. Clearly, a machine that could perform these functions would need specialized hardware, BIOS, and operating system, to operate properly. This process of cooperation between the hardware, the BIOS, and the OS to reduce power use is known generically as *power management*.

## SMM

Intel began the process of power management with a series of new features built into the 386SX CPU. These new features enabled the CPU to slow down or stop its clock without erasing the register information, as well as having a number of features that enabled power saving in peripherals. These features were collectively called *System Management Mode* (SMM). From its humble beginnings in the 386SX, SMM slowly started to show up in more PC CPUs and is now a common addition. Although a power-saving CPU was okay, power management was relegated to special "sleep" or "doze" buttons that would stop the CPU and all of the peripherals on the laptop. To take real advantage of SMM, the system needed a specialized BIOS and OS to go with the SMM CPU. To this end, Intel put forward the *Advanced Power Management* (APM) specification in 1992 and the *Advanced Configuration and Power Interface* (ACPI) standard in 1996.

## Requirements for APM/ACPI

APM and ACPI require a number of items in order to function fully. First is an SMM-capable CPU. As virtually all CPUs are SMM capable, this is easy. Second is an APM-compliant BIOS, which enables the CPU to shut off the peripherals when desired. The third requirement is devices that will accept being shut off. These devices are usually called "Energy Star" devices, which signals their compliance with the EPA's Energy Star standard. To be an Energy Star device, a peripheral must have the ability to shut down without actually turning off. Last, the system's OS must know how to request that a particular device be shut down, and the CPU's clock must be slowed down or stopped.

ACPI goes beyond the APM standard by supplying support for hot-swappable devices—always a huge problem with APM. This feature aside, it is a challenge to tell the difference between an APM system and an ACPI system at first glance.

## APM/ACPI Levels

APM defines five different power-usage operating levels for a system. These levels are intentionally fuzzy to give manufacturers considerable leeway in their use; the only real difference among them is the amount of time each takes to return to normal usage. These levels are as follows:

### Full On

Everything in the system running at full power. There is no power management.

### APM Enabled

CPU and RAM are running at full power. Power management is enabled. An unused device may or may not be shut down.

### APM Standby

CPU is stopped. RAM still stores all programs. All peripherals are shut down, although configuration options are still stored. (In other words, to get back to APM Enabled, you won't have to reinitialize the devices.)

### APM Suspend

Everything in the PC is shut down or at its lowest power-consumption setting. Many systems use a special type of Suspend called *hibernation*, where critical configuration information is written to the hard drive. Upon a wake-up event, the system is reinitialized the data is read from the drive to return the system to the APM Enabled mode. Clearly, the recovery time between Suspend and Enabled will be much longer than the time between Standby and Enabled.

ACPI handles all of these levels plus a few more, such as "soft power on/off," which enables you to define the function of the power button.

## Configuration of APM/ACPI

We configure APM/ACPI via CMOS settings or through Windows. Windows settings will override CMOS settings. Even though the APM/ACPI standards enable a great deal of flexibility, and therefore some confusion among different implementations, certain settings apply generally to CMOS configuration. First is the ability to initialize power management; this enables the system to enter the APM Enabled mode. Often CMOS will then present time frames for entering Standby and Suspend mode, as well as settings to determine which events take place in each of these modes. Also, many CMOS versions will present settings to determine wake-up events, such as directing the system to monitor a modem or a particular IRQ (Figure 18-24).

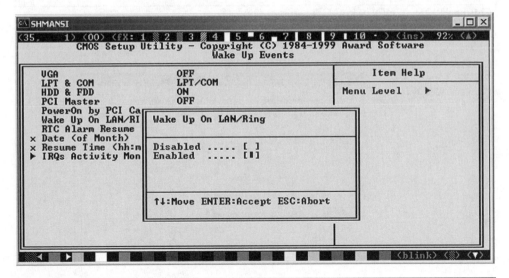

**Figure 18-24** Setting a wake-up event in CMOS

A true ACPI-compliant CMOS provides an ACPI setup option. Figure 18-25 shows a typical modern BIOS that provides this setting.

APM/ACPI settings can be found in one of two areas in Windows. The first place is the Display applet in the Control Panel. Because the monitor is one of the biggest power users on a computer, this is a great place to start the power management configuration process (Figure 18-26).

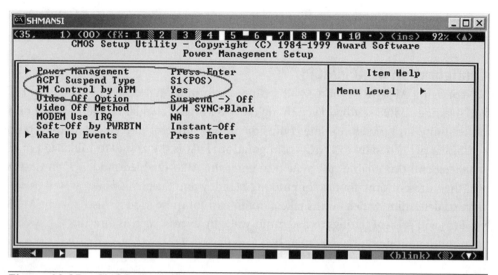

**Figure 18-25** CMOS with ACPI setup option

**Figure 18-26**
Monitor settings

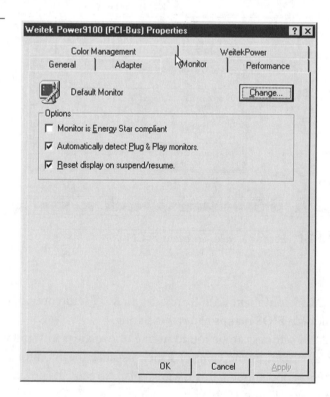

With the exception of adding the Suspend option to the Start button, Windows 95/98 hides the APM/ACPI concepts of Standby and Suspend. Instead, Windows provides you individual control for the big power eaters—monitors, PC Cards, and hard drives—and makes its own assumptions for everything else in the PC. These controls can be found in the Power Management applet of the Control Panel (Figure 18-27).

Windows 2000 calls the applet Power Options and indeed gives you a few configuration options in addition to those in Windows 9x. One feature, Hibernate mode, takes everything in active memory and stores it on the hard drive just before the system powers down. When the PC comes out of hibernation, Windows reloads all the files and applications into RAM. Figure 18-28 shows the Hibernate tab in the Power Options Properties applet in Windows 2000.

**Figure 18-27**
Power Management controls

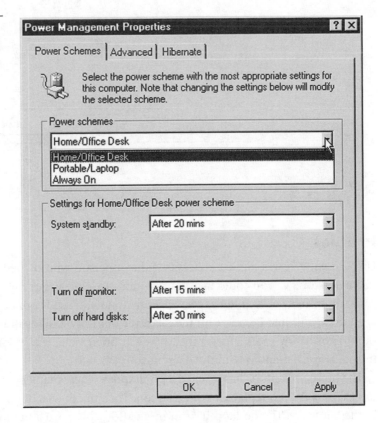

**Figure 18-28**
Hibernate tab

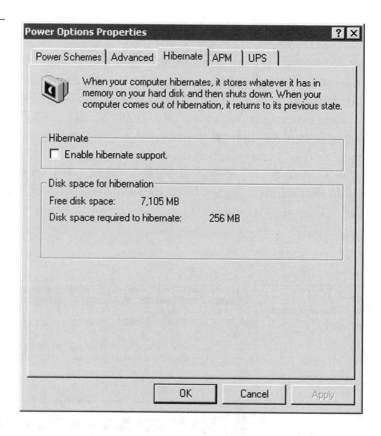

Power Options Properties

Power Schemes | Advanced | Hibernate | APM | UPS

When your computer hibernates, it stores whatever it has in memory on your hard disk and then shuts down. When your computer comes out of hibernation, it returns to its previous state.

Hibernate
☐ Enable hibernate support.

Disk space for hibernation
Free disk space:          7,105 MB
Disk space required to hibernate:          256 MB

OK          Cancel          Apply

# Beyond A+

## Profiles

Until recently, it was almost always true that a person who owned a portable PC also had a desktop PC. You could take your portable to a job site or on a trip—and that was cool—but when you wanted to get real work done, you used your desktop computer. To keep these multiple-PC users on the near side of sanity, Microsoft has long provided a number of handy tools such as the Microsoft briefcase to assist you in synchronizing the data on your laptop with the data on your PC.

The power of laptops has reached a point today where many people forego the desktop PC entirely and replace it with a laptop. The only downside to this arrangement is in the hardware. The desktop PC can more affordably have a big monitor, big storage devices, and extra groovy features such as a CD-RW drive. Recognizing this problem, manufacturers of portable PCs provide (for a price) a docking station that gives the laptop access to big monitors, full-sized mice, network connections, secondary mass storage, and so on. Figure 18-29 shows a typical laptop connected to a docking station.

Docking stations provide fantastic convenience, but there's a catch: If the laptop is connected to a docking station, it must have some method of knowing what hardware is available on the docking station and be able to use that equipment. Equally, if the laptop is disconnected, it must know what hardware is not available. Windows handles this problem via hardware profiles.

**Figure 18-29**
Laptop in a docking station

A *hardware profile* is a list of devices that Windows automatically enables or disables in the Device Manager, depending on what devices the system detects. Alternatively, the user can manually choose a profile from a list at bootup. The manual method has become less prominent because smarter laptops can detect their current state and easily choose the proper profile via the PnP process.

Both Windows 9*x* and Windows 2000 configure their hardware profiles in the System Properties window on the Hardware Profiles tab. Figure 18-30 shows the hardware profiles for a laptop running Windows 98. One profile is for what this user calls Stand-alone—not connected to the docking station. The other hardware profile is used when the laptop is connected to the docking station.

**Figure 18-30**
Hardware profiles

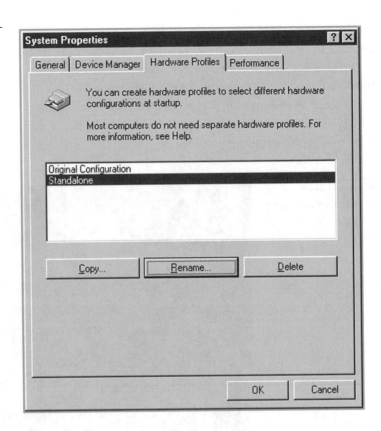

In theory, you can create hardware profiles for any system, but in reality, hardware profiles are for laptops. In fact, the hardware profile features in Windows 2000 simply assume that if you use hardware profiles, you are using a laptop (Figure 18-31). The only trick to hardware profiles is that a good tech needs to appreciate that some devices will show as disabled in the Device Manager, depending on which profile is active. Don't panic if you see a red "x" on a device in Device Manager on a laptop—it just might mean that a particular device isn't being used by the current profile!

**Figure 18-31**
Hardware profile
settings in Windows
2000

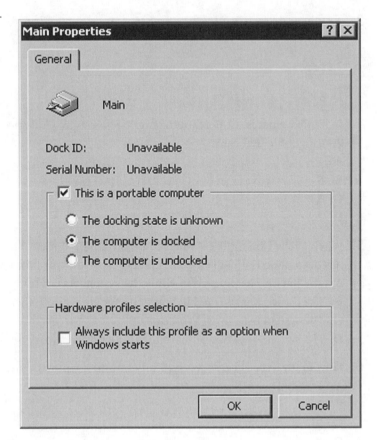

## Review Questions

1. Which of the following is not true about PCMCIA (PC cards)?
   A. Socket Services need to be set to detect whether a card is installed.
   B. PCMCIA Services must be setup in CMOS.
   C. Card Services need to be set up to detect the function of the card installed.
   D. PC Cards are hot-swappable.

2. How many Type III cards can typically fit into a laptop at one time?
   A.  1
   B.  2
   C.  3
   D.  4

3. A Universal Serial Bus (USB) port can support _____ devices?
   A. 1
   B. 16
   C. 32
   D. 127

4. In meters, what is the maximum length between two full-speed USB devices using 20-gauge shielded cables?
   A. 6
   B. 5
   C. 3
   D. 2

5. When a new USB mouse is plugged in, the laptop does not recognize that a device has been added. What is the most likely cause for this problem?
   A. The device was plugged in while the system was running.
   B. The device was plugged in while the system was off, then booted.
   C. The system is running Windows 98.
   D. The system does not yet have the proper drivers loaded.

6. How many Type II cards can typically fit into a laptop at one time?
   A. 1
   B. 2
   C. 3
   D. 4

7. Which of the following is typically not possible?
   A. Having two Type II cards in a laptop at one time
   B. Having a Type I and a Type II card in a laptop at one time
   C. Having two Type I cards in a laptop at one time
   D. Having a Type II and a Type III card in a laptop at one time

8. If the USB port is active and Windows 2000 includes a driver for the peripheral, what is the minimum number of steps it takes to install the peripheral?
   A. Shut the system down, plug the device in, start the system, run Add/Remove Hardware Wizard, select the device, load the driver, and then restart the system.
   B. Plug in the device, start the system, run Add/Remove Hardware Wizard, select the device. The device will be recognized by Windows 2000 automatically. Windows will install the drivers and initialize the device.

C. Turn off the system, plug in the device, and start the system. The device will be recognized by Windows 2000 automatically. Windows will install the drivers and initialize the device.

D. Plug the device into a running system. The device will be recognized by Windows 2000 automatically. Windows will install the drivers and initialize the device.

9. Which of the following are good ideas when it comes to smart batteries? (Choose all that apply.)

A. Keep the contacts clean by using alcohol and a soft cloth.

B. Store them in the freezer if they will not be used for a long period of time.

C. Toss them in the garbage when they wear out.

D. Store them in a cool, dry place.

10. How many pins do PC Cards have?

A. 30

B. 40

C. 68

D. 168

## Answers

1. **B.** PCMCIA Services are not set up in CMOS.

2. **A.** Due to their thickness, only one Type III PCMCIA card can fit into the slots at a time.

3. **D.** A USB port can support up to 127 devices.

4. **B.** The maximum length between two full-speed USB devices using 20-gauge shielded cables is 5 meters. However, you should keep the length less than the maximum.

5. **D.** You must have the proper drivers installed.

6. **B.** Two Type II cards can be installed at the same time.

7. **D.** If you use a Type III card, you cannot fit another card into the socket.

8. **D.** Installing USB devices in a Windows 2000 PC is easy.

9. **A and D.** Keeping a battery in the freezer is a good idea theoretically, but not practically. All batteries contain toxic chemicals. **Never** treat them like regular trash.

10. **C.** There are 68 pins on PC Cards and sockets.

## CHAPTER 19

# Printers

In this chapter, you will

- Understand the different types of printers used today
- Take a detailed tour through laser printers
- Observe and repair basic printer errors

Despite all of the talk about the "paperless office," printers continue to be a vital part of the typical office. In many cases, PCs are used exclusively for the purpose of producing paper documents. Many people simply prefer dealing with a "hard copy." Programmers cater to this preference by using metaphors such as page, workbook, and binder in their applications. The A+ Certification strongly stresses the area of printing and expects a high degree of technical knowledge of the function, components, maintenance, and repair of all types of printers. This chapter does not include a "conceptual" section!

## Test Specific

### Impact Printers

Largely obsolete in today's office environment, impact printers leave an image on paper by physically striking an inked ribbon against the surface of the paper. Daisy-wheel printers (essentially an electric typewriter attached to the PC instead of directly to a keyboard) and dot-matrix printers are the two prominent types of impact printers. Once the dominant printing technology, impact printers have largely disappeared from store shelves because of their inability to combine high quality and flexibility at a low cost. They still retain a niche market for two reasons: they have a large installed base, and they can be used for multipart forms because they actually strike the paper. Impact printers tend to be relatively slow and noisy, but when speed, flexibility, and print quality are not critical, they provide acceptable results. PCs used for printing multipart forms (such as *Point of Sale* (POS) machines that need to print receipts with multiple copies) represent the major market for new impact printers, although many older dot-matrix and daisy-wheel printers remain in use.

Daisy-wheel printers, while producing acceptable text quality, lack flexibility: You can only print in the single font on the daisy wheel, and only in one size. Daisy-wheel printers are completely obsolete today, although they are still employed in some situations where only a single font is needed or for multipart forms.

Dot-matrix printers offer far more flexibility than daisy-wheel printers, although the quality of their character printing tends to be inferior to that of daisy-wheel printers. Dot-matrix printers use an array of pins, also known as *printwires*, to strike an inked printer ribbon and produce images on paper. Using either 9 or 24 pins, dot-matrix printers treat each page as a picture broken up into a raster image. The BIOS for the printer (either built into the printer or a printer driver) interprets the raster image in the same way that a monitor does, "painting" the image as individual dots. Naturally, the more pins the higher the resolution. Figure 19-1 illustrates the components common to dot-matrix printers.

**Figure 19-1**
Inside a dot-matrix printer

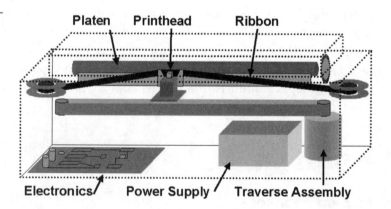

Platen     Printhead     Ribbon

Electronics     Power Supply     Traverse Assembly

## Troubleshooting Dot-Matrix Printer Problems

One downside to dot matrix is the need for ongoing maintenance. Keep the platen (the roller or plate on which the pins impact) and the printhead clean with denatured alcohol. Be sure to lubricate gears and pulleys according to the manufacturer's specifications. Never lubricate the printhead, however, because the lubricant will smear and stain the paper. Figure 19-2 illustrates a typical printhead.

**Figure 19-2**
The dot-matrix printhead

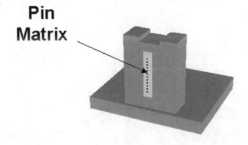

### White Bars on Text

White bars going through the text point to a dirty or damaged printhead. Try cleaning the printhead with a little denatured alcohol. If the problem persists, replace the printhead. Printheads for most printers are readily available from the manufacturer.

### Chopped Text

If the characters look chopped off at the top or bottom, the printhead probably needs to be adjusted. Refer to the manufacturer's instructions for proper adjustment.

### Pepper-Look

If the paper is covered with dots and small smudges—the "pepper look"—the platen is dirty. Clean the platen with denatured alcohol.

### Faded Image

If the image is faded, and you know the ribbon is good, try adjusting the printhead closer to the platen.

### Light to Dark

If the image is okay on one side of the paper but fades as you move to the other, the platen is out of adjustment. Platens are generally difficult to adjust, so your best plan is to send it to the manufacturer's local warranty/repair center. The $30-50 you'll spend is far cheaper than the frustration of trying to do it yourself!

## Ink-Jet Printers

Ink-jet printers work by ejecting ink through tiny tubes. Most ink-jet printers use heat to move the ink. The ink is heated by tiny resistors or electroconductive plates at the end of each tube. These resistors or plates literally boil the ink, creating a tiny air bubble that ejects a droplet of ink onto the paper, thus creating portions of the image (Figure 19-3). Recent Epson printers, in contrast, use a mechanical method rather than heat for achieving the same results—ink on paper.

**Figure 19-3**
Detail of the ink-jet printhead

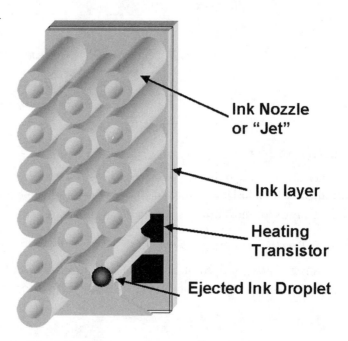

Ink Nozzle or "Jet"

Ink layer

Heating Transistor

Ejected Ink Droplet

Ink-jet printers are relatively simple devices, consisting of the printhead mechanism; support electronics; a transfer mechanism to move the printhead back and forth; and a paper feed component to drag, move, and eject paper (Figure 19-4).

A common problem with ink-jet printers is the tendency for the ink inside the jets to dry out when not used even for a relatively short time. To counter this problem, all ink-jet printers move the printhead to a special position that keeps the ink from drying. This area has many names, the most common being the "park," "cleaning," or "maintenance" area.

Figure 19-4
Inside an ink jet

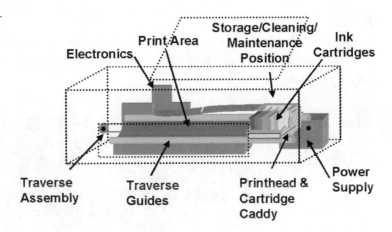

**Figure 19-4**
Inside an ink jet

Electronics  Print Area  Storage/Cleaning/ Maintenance Position  Ink Cartridges

Traverse Assembly  Traverse Guides  Printhead & Cartridge Caddy  Power Supply

## Laser Printers

Laser printers have become the printer of choice in most applications. They produce high-quality and high-speed output of both text and graphics. Figure 19-5 shows a typical laser printer. Although they remain more expensive than ink-jet or impact printers, laser printer prices have declined steadily in recent years.

Laser printers rely on the photoconductive properties of certain organic compounds. *Photoconductive* means that particles of these compounds, when exposed to light (that's the "photo" part), will *conduct* electricity. Laser printers use lasers as a light source because of their precision.

**Figure 19-5**
Typical laser printer

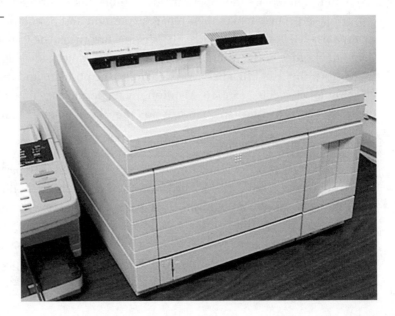

## Parts

In order to reduce maintenance costs, many of the laser printer parts, including those that suffer the most wear and tear, have been incorporated into the toner cartridge (Figure 19-6).

**Figure 19-6**
Laser printer's toner cartridge

Although this makes replacement of individual parts nearly impossible, it greatly reduces the need for replacement; those parts that are most likely to break are replaced every time you replace the toner cartridge. Unlike ink-jet printers, the relatively higher cost of laser printers makes their repair a common and popular option. A number of companies sell laser printer parts. My personal favorite is The Printer Works. They are a large mail-order outfit with salespeople who are quite knowledgeable. Like an auto parts store, they can often help you determine the problem and then sell you the part. Their number is 800-225-6116. Mention my name and they'll bend over backwards to help you (heck, mention my name or not, they'll still be more than glad to help!).

### The Photosensitive Drum

The photosensitive drum is an aluminum cylinder coated with particles of photosensitive compounds (Figure 19-7). The drum itself is grounded to the power supply, but the coating is not. When light hits these particles, whatever electrical charge they may have had drains out through the grounded cylinder. The drum, usually contained in the toner cartridge, can be wiped clean if it becomes dirty. *Exercise extreme caution here!!* If the drum becomes scratched, the scratch will appear on every page printed from that point on. The only repair in the event of a scratch is to replace the toner cartridge.

**Figure 19-7**
Toner cartridge
with photosensitive
drum exposed

## Erase Lamp

The erase lamp exposes the entire surface of the photosensitive drum to light, making the photosensitive coating conductive. Any electrical charge present in the particles bleeds away into the grounded drum, leaving the surface particles electrically neutral.

## Primary Corona

The primary corona wire, located close to the photosensitive drum, never touches the drum. When charged with an extremely high voltage, an electric field (or corona) forms, enabling voltage to pass to the drum and charge the photosensitive particles on its surface. The *primary grid* regulates the transfer of voltage, ensuring that the surface of the drum receives a uniform negative voltage of between ~600 and ~1,000 volts.

## Laser

The laser acts as the writing mechanism of the printer. Any particle on the drum struck by the laser becomes conductive, enabling its charge to be drained away into the grounded core of the drum. The entire surface of the drum has a uniform negative charge of between ~600 and ~1,000 volts following its charging by the primary corona wire. When particles are struck by the laser, they are discharged and left with a ~100 volt negative charge. Using the laser, we can "write" an image onto the drum. Note that the laser writes a positive image to the drum.

## Toner

The toner in a laser printer is a fine powder made up of plastic particles bonded to iron particles. The *toner cylinder* charges the toner with a negative charge of between ~200 and ~500 volts. Because that charge falls between the original uniform negative charge of the photosensitive drum (~600 to ~1,000 volts) and the charge of the particles on the drum's surface hit by the laser (~100 volts), particles of toner are attracted to the areas of the photosensitive drum that have been hit by the laser (that is, areas that have a *relatively* positive charge with reference to the toner particles).

## Transfer Corona

To transfer the image from the photosensitive drum to the paper, the paper must be given a charge that will attract the toner particles off of the drum and onto the paper. The transfer corona applies a positive charge to the paper, drawing the negatively charged toner particles to the paper. The paper, with its positive charge, is also attracted to the negatively charged drum. To prevent the paper from wrapping around the drum, a *static charge eliminator* removes the charge from the paper.

## Fuser

The toner is merely resting on top of the paper after the static charge eliminator has removed the paper's static charge. The toner must be permanently attached to the paper to make the image permanent. Two rollers, a pressure roller and a heated roller, are used to fuse the toner to the paper. The pressure roller presses against the bottom of the page while the heated roller presses down on the top of the page, melting the toner into the paper. The heated roller has a nonstick coating such as Teflon to prevent the toner from sticking to the heated roller.

## The Printing Process—The Physical Side

Let's put these steps together to see how a typical laser printer performs these steps. Keep in mind that some brands of laser printers may depart from this exact process, although most work in exactly this order. The printing process takes six steps in this order:

1. Clean
2. Charge
3. Write
4. Develop
5. Transfer
6. Fuse

**EXAM TIP**  Know the order of a laser printer's printing process!

## Clean the Drum

The printing process begins with the physical and electrical cleaning of the photosensitive drum (Figure 19-8). Before printing each new page, the drum must be returned to a clean, fresh condition. All residual toner left over from printing the previous page must be removed, usually by scraping the surface of the drum with a rubber cleaning blade. If residual particles remain on the drum, they will appear as random black spots and streaks on the next page. The physical cleaning mechanism either deposits the residual toner in a debris cavity or recycles it by returning it to the toner supply in the toner cartridge. The physical cleaning must be done carefully. Damage to the drum will cause a permanent mark to be printed on every page.

**Figure 19-8**
Cleaning and erasing
the drum

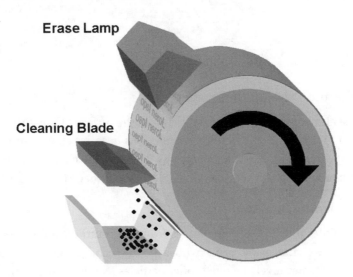

The printer must also be electrically cleaned. One or more erase lamps bombard the surface of the drum with the appropriate wavelengths of light, causing the surface particles to completely discharge into the grounded drum. After the cleaning process, the drum should be completely free of toner and have a neutral charge.

### Charge the Drum

To make the drum receptive to new images, it must be charged (Figure 19-9). Using the primary corona wire, a uniform negative charge is applied to the entire surface of the drum (usually between ~600 and ~1,000 volts).

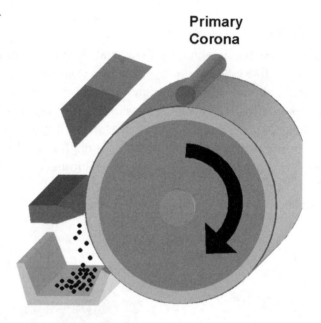

**Figure 19-9**
Charging the drum
with a uniform
negative charge

**Primary
Corona**

### Write and Develop the Image

A laser is used to write a positive image on the surface of the drum. Every particle on the drum hit by the laser will release most of its negative charge into the drum. Those particles with a lesser negative charge will be positively charged relative to the toner particles and will attract them, creating a developed image (Figure 19-10).

### Transfer the Image

The printer must transfer the image from the drum onto the paper. Using the transfer corona, we charge the paper with a positive charge. Once the paper has a positive charge, the negatively charged toner particles leap from the drum to the paper. At this point the particles are merely resting on the paper. They must still be permanently affixed to the paper.

### Fuse the Image

The particles must be fused to the paper. They have been attracted to the paper because of the positive charge given to the paper by the transfer corona, but if the process stopped there, the toner particles would fall off the page as soon as the page was lifted.

**Figure 19-10**
Writing the image
and applying the
toner

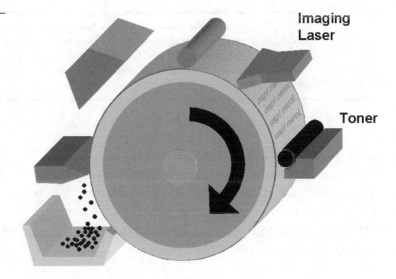

The toner particles are mostly composed of plastic, so they can be melted to the page.
Two rollers, a heated roller coated in a nonstick material and a pressure roller, melt the
toner to the paper, permanently affixing it. Finally, static charge eliminator removes the
paper's positive charge (Figure 19-11). Once the page is complete, the printer ejects the
printed copy and the process begins again with the physical and electrical cleaning of
the printer.

**Figure 19-11**
Transferring the
image to the paper
and fusing the final
image

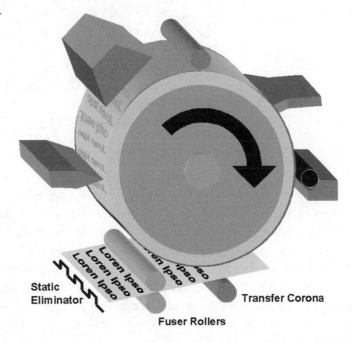

> **NOTE** The heated roller produces enough heat to melt some types of plastic media, particularly overhead transparency materials. *Never use transparencies in a laser printer unless they are specifically designed for use in laser printers.* Use of nonapproved materials can seriously damage your laser printer and void your warranty.

## And Now, the Rest of the Laser Printer

Although the majority of the printing activity takes place within the toner cartridge, many other parts of the laser printer are hard at work outside the cartridge (Figure 19-12). In order to appreciate these "other" components and their functions, we need to take a look at a regular print job and the many steps that are necessary to make the page appear on the paper.

**Figure 19-12**
Components inside a laser printer

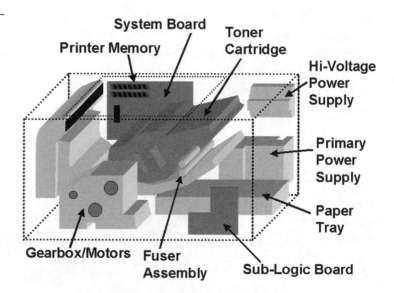

### Power Supplies

All laser printers are distinguished by at least two separate power supplies. The first power supply is called the "primary power supply" or sometimes just the "power supply." This power supply, which may actually be more than one power supply, provides power to the motors that move the paper, the system electronics, the laser, and the transfer corona. The high-voltage power supply usually only provides power to the primary corona. The extremely high voltage of the high-voltage power supply makes it one of the most dangerous devices in the world of PCs! In addition to inserting a new toner cartridge, it is imperative that you *always turn off* a laser printer before you open it up!

## Turning Gears

A laser printer has many mechanical functions. First, the paper must be picked up, printed upon, and kicked out of the printer. Next, the photosensitive roller must be turned and the laser, or a mirror, must be moved from left to right. Finally, the toner must be evenly distributed, and the fuser assembly must squish the toner into the paper. All of these functions are served by complex gear systems. In most laser printers, these gear systems are packed together in discrete units generically called *gear packs* or *gearboxes*. Most laser printers will have two or three gearboxes that are relatively easy to remove in the rare case when one of them fails. Most gearboxes will also have their own motor or solenoid to move the gears.

## Fusing

The fuser assembly is almost always separate from the toner cartridge. It is usually quite easy to locate as it will be close to the bottom of the toner cartridge and will usually have two rollers to fuse the toner. Sometimes the fuser is relatively enclosed and is difficult to recognize, because the rollers are hidden from view. To help you determine the location of the fuser, think about the data path of the paper and the fact that fusing is the final step of printing. In some laser printers, the transfer corona may also be outside the toner cartridge. This is a thin wire, usually protected by other thin wires. The transfer corona is a particularly difficult part as it is prone to dirt build-up and must be cleaned, yet it is also quite fragile. Most printers with an exposed transfer corona will provide a special tool to clean it.

## System Board

Every laser printer will contain at least one electronic board. On this board is the main processor, the printer's ROM, and RAM used to store the image before it is printed. Many printers will divide these functions among two or three boards dispersed around the printer. The printer may also have an extra ROM chip and/or a special slot where you can install an extra ROM chip, usually for special functions such as PostScript (see the "PostScript" section later in this chapter).

Of particular importance is the printer's RAM. When the printer doesn't have enough RAM to store the image before it prints, you get a memory overflow problem. Also, some printers will store other information in the RAM, including fonts or special commands. Adding RAM is usually a very simple job—just snapping in a SIMM stick or two—but getting the *right* RAM is important. Call the printer manufacturer and ask what type of RAM you need. Although most printer companies will happily sell you their expensive RAM, most printers can use generic DRAM like the kind you use in your PC.

### Ozone Filter

The coronas inside laser printers generate ozone ($O_3$). While not harmful to humans, high concentrations of ozone will cause damage to printer components. To counter this problem, most laser printers have a special ozone filter that needs to be vacuumed or replaced periodically.

### Sensors and Switches

Every laser printer has a large number of sensors and switches spread throughout the machine. The sensors are used to detect a broad range of conditions such as paper jams, empty paper trays, or low toner levels. Many of these sensors are really tiny switches that detect open doors and so on. Most of the time these sensors/switches work reliably. Yet occasionally, they can become dirty or broken, sending a false signal to the printer. Simple inspection is usually sufficient to determine if a problem is real or just the result of a faulty sensor/switch.

## The Printing Process—The Electronic Side

Now that we have looked at the many parts of a laser printer and discussed their basic functions, let's delve into some of the electronic functions of laser printing.

### Raster Images

Impact printers transfer data to the printer one character or one line at a time, whereas laser printers transfer entire pages at a time to the printer. Laser printers generate a raster image of the page representing what the final product should look like. A raster image is merely a pattern of dots. Laser printers use a device (the laser) to "paint" a raster image on the photosensitive drum. Because laser printers have to "paint" the entire surface of the photosensitive drum before they can begin to transfer the image to paper, they have to process the image one page at a time.

Laser printers use a chip called the *Raster Image Processor* (RIP) to translate the raster image sent to the printer into commands to the laser. The RIP needs memory (RAM) in order to store the data that it must process. A laser printer must have enough memory to process an entire page. Some images that require high resolutions require more memory. Insufficient memory to process the image will usually be indicated by a memory overflow ("MEM OVERFLOW") error. The solution to a memory overflow error is simply to add more RAM to the laser printer.

Do not assume that every error with the word "memory" in it can be fixed by simply adding more RAM to the printer. Just as adding more RAM chips will not solve every conventional PC memory problem, adding more RAM will not solve every laser printer memory problem. For example, on an HP LaserJet, the message "21 ERROR" indicates that "the printer is unable to process very complex data fast enough for the print engine." This means that the data is simply too complex for the RIP to handle. Adding more memory would *not* solve this problem; it would only make your wallet lighter. The only answer in that case is to reduce the complexity of the page image (that is, fewer fonts, less formatting, reduced graphics resolution, and so on).

## Resolution

Laser printers can print at different resolutions, just as monitors can display different resolutions. The maximum resolution that a laser printer can handle is determined by its physical characteristics. Laser printer resolution is expressed in *dots per inch* (dpi). Common resolutions are 300 dpi × 300 dpi or 600 dpi × 600 dpi. The first number, the horizontal resolution, is determined by how fine a focus can be achieved by the laser. The second number is determined by the smallest increment by which the drum can be turned. Higher resolutions produce higher quality output, but keep in mind that higher resolutions also require more memory. In some instances, complex images can only be printed at lower resolutions because of their high memory demands. Even printing at 300 dpi, laser printers produce far better quality than dot-matrix printers because of *Resolution Enhancement Technology* (RET).

Laser printers achieve high quality printing not merely by printing at high resolutions, but also by employing RET. RET enables the printer to insert smaller dots among the characters, smoothing out the jagged curves that are typical of printers that do not use RET (Figure 19-13).

**Figure 19-13**
RET fills in gaps with smaller dots in order to smooth out jagged characters.

 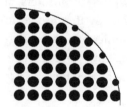

## Printer Languages

How do you tell a printer to make a letter "A" or to print a picture of your pet iguana? Printers are designed to accept predefined printer languages that handle both characters and graphics. Your software must use the proper language when communicating with your printer, so that your printer can output your documents onto a piece of paper. Let's look at the more common printer languages.

### American Standard Code for Information Interchange (ASCII)

We usually think of ASCII as nothing more than a standard set of characters, the basic alphabet in upper and lower case with a few strange symbols thrown in. ASCII actually contains a variety of control codes for transferring data, some of which can be used to control printers. For example, ASCII code 10 (or 0A in hex) means "Line Feed," and ASCII code 12 (0C) means "Form Feed." These commands have been standard since before the creation of IBM PCs, and all printers respond to them. If they did not, the PRINT SCREEN key would not work with every printer. Being highly standardized has advantages, but the control codes are extremely limited. Utilizing high-end graphics and a wide variety of fonts requires more advanced languages.

### Hewlett Packard Printer Control Language (PCL)

Hewlett Packard developed PCL as a more advanced printer language. PCL features a greatly expanded set of printer commands. Hewlett Packard designed PCL with text-based output in mind. It does not support advanced graphical functions. The most recent version of PCL, PCL6, features scalable fonts and additional line drawing commands; however, unlike PostScript (see the following section), PCL is dependent on the printer hardware. It is not a true page description language in the sense that it uses a series of commands to define the characters on the page; its commands must be supported by the individual printer, and do not define the page as a single raster image.

### PostScript

Adobe systems developed PostScript *Page Description Language* (PDL) in the early 1980s as a device-independent printer language capable of high-resolution graphics and scalable fonts. PostScript interpreters are embedded in the printing device. Because PostScript is understood by printers at a hardware level, the majority of the image processing is done by the printer and not the PC's CPU, so PostScript printers print faster. PostScript files are extremely portable; they can be created on one machine or platform and reliably printed out on another machine or platform (including, for example, high-end typesetters).

### Windows GDI

Windows *9x* and Windows 2000 use the *Graphical Device Interface* (GDI) component of the operating system to handle print functions. Although you *can* use an external printer language such as PostScript, most users simply install printer drivers and let Windows do all the work.

The GDI uses the CPU rather than the printer to process a print job and then sends the completed job to the printer. When you print a letter with a TrueType font in Windows, for example, the GDI processes the print job and then sends bitmapped images of each page to the printer. The printer sees a page of TrueType text, therefore, as a picture, not as text. As long as the printer has a capable enough RIP and plenty of RAM, you don't need to worry about the printer language at all in most situations. We'll revisit printing in Windows in more detail later in this chapter.

## Laser Printer Maintenance and Troubleshooting

Unlike with PCs, laser printer maintenance and troubleshooting follows a fairly well established procedure. Follow these steps to insure a long, healthy life for your system.

### Switch Boxes

If you want to use multiple printers hooked into the same parallel port, you have to use a switch box. Laser printers should never be used with mechanical switch boxes. Mechanical switch boxes create power surges that can damage your printer. If you must use a switch box, use a box that switches between printers electronically and has built-in surge protection.

### Reverse Power Up

Both laser printers and PCs require more power during their initial power up (the POST on a PC and the Warm Up on a laser printer) than once they are running. Hewlett Packard recommends a *reverse power up*. Turn on the laser printer first and allow it to finish its warm up before turning on the PC. This avoids having two devices drawing their peak loads simultaneously.

### Keeping It Clean

Laser printers are quite robust as a rule. A good cleaning every time you replace the toner cartridge, however, will help that printer last for many years. There are many examples of original HP LaserJet I printers continuing to run perfectly after 10-12 years of operation. The secret is that they were kept immaculately clean.

There are generally only two ways to get your laser printer dirty. First is excess toner. Toner is hard to see due to its black color, but it will slowly coat the entire printer. Second is paper dust, sometimes called *paper dander*. This tends to build up where the paper is bent around rollers or where pickup rollers grab paper. Unlike toner, paper dust is easy to see and is usually a good indicator that a printer needs to be cleaned. Without being printer-specific, usually a thorough cleaning using a can of de-ionized, pressurized air to blow out the printer is the best cleaning you can do for that printer. It's best to do this outdoors or you may end up looking like one of those chimney sweeps from *Mary Poppins*! If you must clean a printer indoors, use a special low-static vacuum designed especially for electronic components (Figure 19-14).

Every laser printer has its own unique cleaning method, but one little area tends to be skipped in the cleaning instructions that come with laser printers. Every laser printer has a number of rubber guide rollers through which the paper is run during the print process. These little rollers tend to pick up dirt and paper dust over time, making them slip and jam paper. They are easily cleaned with a little general purpose cleaner such as

**Figure 19-14**
Low static vacuum

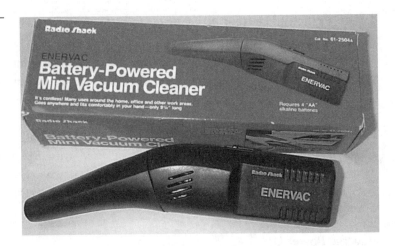

Formula 409 or even just a little water. Also, remember to clean the corona wires if specified by the manufacturer. Most of these wires are quite fragile and require a special tool or a delicate touch, so be careful!

If you're ready to get specific, get the printer's service manual. Almost every printer manufacturer sells these; they are a key source for information on how to keep a printer clean and running. Sadly, not all printer manufacturers provide these, but most do. Call The Printer Works to get most service manuals. While you're at it, see if the manufacturer has a Quick Reference Guide; these can be very handy for most printer problems!

Finally, be aware that Hewlett Packard sells maintenance kits for most of their laser printers. These are sets of replacement parts for the parts most likely to wear out on each particular type of HP LaserJet. Although their use is not required to maintain warranty coverage, using these kits when prescribed by HP helps to assure the continuing reliability of your LaserJet.

### Periodic Maintenance

Although keeping the printer clean is critical to its health and well being, every laser printer has certain components that will need to be replaced periodically. Even though these parts vary among different models, certain parts are commonly replaced. Here's a quick list of possible parts:

- Ozone filter
- Fuser assembly
- Transfer corona
- Paper guides/rollers
- Thermal fuse (used to keep the fuser from overheating)

Of course, your ultimate source for determining the parts that need to be replaced (and when to replace them) is the printer manufacturer. Following the manufacturer's maintenance guidelines will help to ensure years of trouble-free, dependable printing from your laser printer.

## Determining Laser Problems

Laser printers usually manifest problems by creating poor output. One of the most important tests you can do on any printer, not just a laser printer, is called a *diagnostic print page* or an *engine test page*. This is usually done by holding down the On Line button as the printer is started (Figure 19-15). The following is a list of the most common problems and where to look to fix them.

**Figure 19-15**
Creating a diagnostic print page by holding down the On Line button during startup

### Blank Paper

Blank sheets of paper usually mean the printer is out of toner. If the printer does have toner and nothing prints, print a diagnostic print page. If that is also blank, remove the toner cartridge and look at the imaging drum inside. If the image is still there, you know the transfer corona or the high-voltage power supply has failed. Check the printer's maintenance guide to see how to focus on the bad part and replace it.

### Ghosting

Ghost images sometimes appear at regular intervals on the printed page. This can be caused either because the imaging drum has not fully discharged (and is picking up toner from a previous image) or because a previous image has used up so much toner that either the supply of charged toner is insufficient or the toner has not been adequately charged.

### Light Ghosting vs. Dark Ghosting

A variety of problems can cause both light and dark ghosting, but the most common source of light ghosting is "developer starvation." If you ask a laser printer to print an extremely dark or complex image, it can use up so much toner that the toner cartridge will not be able to charge enough toner to print the next image. The proper solution is to use less toner (a.k.a. "don't do that anymore!") by:

- Lowering the resolution of the page (print at 300 dpi instead of 600 dpi)
- Using a different pattern
- Avoiding 50-percent grayscale and "dot-on/dot-off patterns"
- Changing the layout so that grayscale patterns do not follow black areas
- Making dark patterns lighter and light patterns darker
- Printing in landscape orientation
- Adjusting print density and RET settings
- Printing a completely black page immediately prior to the page with the ghosting image, and as part of the same print job

Low temperature and low humidity can aggravate ghosting problems. Check your users' manual for environmental recommendations.

Dark ghosting can sometimes be caused by a damaged drum. It may be fixed by replacing the toner cartridge. Light ghosting would *not* be solved in this way. Switching other components will not usually affect ghosting problems because they are a side effect of the entire printing process.

### Vertical White Lines

Vertical white lines are usually due to clogged toner preventing the proper dispersion of toner on the drum. Try shaking the toner cartridge to dislodge the clog. If that doesn't work, replace the toner cartridge.

### Blotchy Print

This is most commonly due to uneven dispersion of toner, especially if the toner is low. Try shaking the toner from side to side and then try to print. Also be sure that the printer is level. Finally, make sure the paper is not wet in spots. If the blotches are in a regular order, check the fusing rollers and the photosensitive drum for any foreign objects.

## Spotty Print

If the spots appear at regular intervals, the drum may be damaged or some toner is stuck to the fuser rollers. Try wiping off the fuser rollers. Check the drum for damage. If the drum is damaged, get a new toner cartridge.

## Embossed Effect

If your prints are getting an embossed effect (like putting a penny under a piece of paper and rubbing it with a lead pencil), there is almost certainly a foreign object on a roller. Use Formula 409 or regular water with a soft cloth to try to remove it. If the foreign object is on the photosensitive drum, you're going to have to use a new toner cartridge.

## Incomplete Characters

Incompletely printed characters on laser-printed transparencies can sometimes be corrected by adjusting the print density. Be extremely careful to use only materials approved for use in laser printers.

## Creased Pages

Laser printers have up to four rollers. In addition to the heat and pressure rollers of the fusing assembly, other rollers move the paper from the source tray to the output tray. These rollers crease the paper in order to avoid curling that would cause paper jams in the printer. If the creases are noticeable, try using a different paper type. Cotton bond paper is usually more susceptible to noticeable creasing than other bonds. You might also try sending the output to the face up tray, which avoids one roller. There is no hardware solution to this problem. It is simply a side effect of the process.

## Warped, Overprinted, or Poorly Formed Characters

Poorly formed characters can indicate either a problem with the paper (or other media), or a problem with the hardware. Let's look at both.

Incorrect media causes a number of these types of problems. Avoid paper that is too rough or too smooth. Paper that is too rough interferes with the fusing of characters and their initial definition. If the paper is too smooth (like some coated papers, for example), it may feed improperly, causing distorted or overwritten characters. Even though you can purchase laser printer-specific paper, all laser printers will run acceptably on standard photocopy paper. Try to keep the paper from becoming too wet. Don't open a ream of paper until it is loaded into the printer. Always fan the paper before loading it into the printer, especially if the paper has been left out for more than just a few days.

The durability of a well-maintained laser printer makes hardware a much more rare source of character printing problems, but you should be aware of the possibility. Fortunately, it is fairly easy to check the hardware. Most laser printers have a self-test function—often combined with a diagnostic printout, but sometimes as a separate process. This self-test shows whether the laser printer can properly develop an image without having to actually send print commands from the PC. The self-test is quite handy to verify the question "Is it the printer or is it the computer?" Run the self-test to check for connectivity and configuration problems. Possible solutions are as follows:

- Replace the toner cartridge, especially if you hear popping noises.
- Check the cabling.
- Replace the data cable, especially if there are bends, crimps, or objects resting on the cable.
- If you have a Front Menu Panel, turn off Advanced Functions and High Speed Settings to determine if the advanced functions are either not working properly or not supported by your current software configuration (check your manuals for configuration information).
- If you are using Windows 3.x, go into the Control Panel, select Printers, and choose Connect. Change the port settings to LPT1 and remove the X from the Fast Printing Direct to Port check box.

If these solutions do not work, the problem may not be user serviceable. Contact an authorized service center.

## Dealing with Consumables

All printers tend to generate a lot of trash in the form of what we call *consumables*. Impact printers use paper and ribbons, ink-jet printers use paper and ink cartridges, and laser printers use paper and toner cartridges. In today's environmentally sensitive world, many laws regulate proper disposal of most printer components. Be sure to check with the local sanitation department or disposal services company before throwing away any component. Of course, you should never throw away toner cartridges—certain companies will *pay* for used cartridges!

When in doubt about what to do with a component, check with the manufacturer for a *Material Safety Data Sheet* (MSDS). These standardized forms provide detailed information about the potential environmental hazards associated with different components and proper disposal methods. For example, Hewlett Packard provides an MSDS for almost every part and consumable they manufacture. Check out **http://www.hp.com/hpinfo/community/environment/msds_laserjet.htm** for the latest MSDS for any Hewlett Packard toner cartridge.

Most PC components have associated MSDSs—monitors, hard drives, laptop batteries, and so on. When in doubt about how to get rid of any PC component, check with the manufacturer for an MSDS.

## Parallel Communication

The parallel port was included in the original IBM PC as a faster alternative to serial communication. The IBM engineers considered serial communication, limited to one bit at a time, to be too slow for the "high-speed" devices of the day (for example, dot-matrix printers). Parallel is far faster than serial. Like so much of the technology used in PCs today, the standard parallel port (sometimes referred to as the Centronics standard) has been kept around for backward compatibility despite several obvious weaknesses.

Speed is the major concern with parallel ports. The speed of the standard parallel port has remained the same despite speed improvements in almost every other part of the PC. The maximum data transfer rate of a standard parallel port, for example, is still only approximately 150 *kilobytes per second* (KBps). Standard parallel communication on the PC also relies heavily on software, eating up a considerable amount of CPU time that could be better used.

The second problem with the "standard" parallel port is that no standard exists. Although the phrase "Centronics standard" is widely used, there is no such animal. This lack of standardization remains a source of incompatibility problems for some parallel devices, although a very loose set of "standards" adopted by manufacturers has reduced the number of incompatible parallel devices on the market. The lack of standards also applies to the parallel cables. Because no standards exist for electromagnetic shielding on the cables, parallel cables longer than six feet are rare.

A lack of true bi-directional capability has also become a problem. While one-way communication was acceptable for simple line printers and dot-matrix printers, parallel communication also became popular for a wide range of external devices that required two-way communication. Although it is possible to get two-way communication out of a standard parallel port (see the "Nibble Mode" section later in this chapter), the performance is not impressive. A new standard was needed.

**NOTE** Many techs confuse the concept of "duplex" printing—a process that requires special printers capable of printing on both sides of a sheet of paper—with bi-directional printing. They have nothing to do with each other!

## IEEE 1284 Standard

The IEEE 1284 standard attempts to deal with both problems (poor performance and a lack of standardization) while maintaining backward compatibility. In 1991, a group of printer manufacturers proposed to the *Institute of Electrical and Electronics Engineers* (IEEE) that a committee be formed to propose a standard for a backward-compatible, high-speed, bi-directional parallel port for the PC. The committee was the IEEE 1284 committee (hence the name of the standard).

The IEEE 1284 standard requires

- Support for all five modes of operation (Compatibility, Nibble Mode, Byte Mode, EPP, and ECP)

- A standard method of negotiation for determining which modes are supported both by the host PC and by the peripheral device.

- A standard physical interface (that is, the cables and connectors).

- A standard electrical interface (that is, termination, impedance, and so on)

Because there is only one set of data wires, all data transfer modes included in the IEEE 1284 standard are half-duplex: Data is transferred in only one direction at a time.

### Compatibility Mode/Centronics Mode

The standard parallel port used in the original IBM PC is often referred to as a *Centronics* port. This connection normally manifests itself as a female DB25 (25-pin) connector on the PC and as a corresponding male connector on the cable.

Eight wires are used as grounds, four for control signals, five for status signals, and eight for data signals going from the PC to the device. The control wires are used for control and handshaking signals going from the PC to the printer. The status wires are used for handshaking signals from the printer (or other peripheral device) to the PC, and for standardized signals from the printer to the PC such as "out of paper," "busy," and "offline." Only eight wires are used for passing data, and that data travels in only one direction: from the PC to the peripheral device. All of the IEEE 1284 transfer modes use this 25-pin cable for backward compatibility reasons, although other types of connections are included in the standard.

The advantage to Centronics mode is backward compatibility, but its disadvantages are clear. Data passes in only one direction, from the PC to the peripheral device (a.k.a. "forward" direction only). In addition, the CPU must constantly poll the status wires for error messages and handshaking signals, using up significant numbers of CPU clock cycles. Standard/Centronics mode transfers are limited to approximately 150KBps.

Some manufacturers have included an enhanced form of Centronics mode that is not a part of the IEEE 1284 standard. Devices that support this alternative mode, referred to as "Fast Centronics" or "Parallel Port FIFO Mode," add a hard-wired

*First In First Out* (FIFO) buffer to the parallel port. Once the data reaches the buffer, the software that had been handling the data transfer assumes that the data has reached the printer and relinquishes control of the CPU to other programs. Once the data is in the buffer, the buffer handles any further handshaking. By having the buffer emulate the handshaking normally done by the software, Fast Centronics mode works on legacy peripheral devices that operate in the old Centronics mode. Using this non-standard mode, some systems can achieve data transfer rates of up to 500KBps, a significant improvement. Remember that IEEE 1284 does *not* require support for this Fast Centronics mode. With legacy devices (such as older dot-matrix and laser printers) that do not support the ECP or EPP modes, however, a Fast Centronics parallel port will actually provide superior performance compared to an IEEE 1284 parallel port without that mode. If possible, look for parallel ports that support both Fast Centronics mode and the IEEE 1284 standard.

## Nibble Mode

Nibble mode is the simplest way to transfer data in "reverse direction," from the peripheral device to the PC. Nibble mode requires no special hardware, and can normally be used with any "standard" parallel port (that is, it does not require an IEEE 1284 parallel port). All parallel ports have five status wires that are designed to send signals from the peripheral to the PC. Using four of these wires at a time, we can transfer a byte (8 bits) of data in two pieces, one nibble (4 bits) at time. Nibble mode is even more software intensive than compatibility/Centronics mode, eating up many CPU clock cycles. This intensive use of CPU time, combined with the limitation of passing data one nibble at a time, limits nibble mode data transfers to approximately 50KBps. Nibble mode will work on any PC parallel port, however, and when used in concert with compatibility/Centronics mode provides a very limited form of bi-directional communication.

## Byte Mode/Enhanced Bi-Directional Port

Although a combination of compatible/Centronics and nibble mode transfers can produce two-way communications, the resulting speed is not very satisfactory. As higher-performance external peripherals came to market, people saw a need for a more powerful means of two-way parallel communication. A number of manufacturers (including IBM on their PS/2 parallel port) began to add a new data transfer mode to their parallel ports: byte mode. Byte mode enables reverse direction (peripheral to PC) parallel communication using all eight data wires. To accomplish this, extra hardware is added that handles the negotiation between the PC and the peripheral. (Remember, the original standard only allowed the data wires to be used for forward communication, from the PC to the peripheral.) By using byte mode in conjunction with Centronics mode, two-way communication that uses eight bits in each direction is possible.

With byte mode, two-way communication can achieve speeds approaching the speed of the one-way Centronics data transfers, approximately 150KBps. Parallel ports capable of byte mode transfers are sometimes referred to as "enhanced bi-directional ports." This terminology has led to some confusion between these early bi-directional ports and the more advanced parallel ports. The enhanced bi-directional port is far less capable, but byte mode is often supported by parallel ports and devices that do not support the entire IEEE 1284 standard.

### Enhanced Parallel Port (EPP)

For peripherals that require constant two-way communication with the PC, the *Enhanced Parallel Port* (EPP) protocol offers high-speed, two-way data transfers with relatively little software overhead. Hardware handles the handshaking and synchronization between the peripheral device and the PC. By removing the CPU from the handshaking process, an EPP port enables the CPU to transfer data to and from the port with a single command, saving a significant number of clock cycles.

Unlike ECP (see the following section), the EPP protocol calls for a close "coupling" between the program running the parallel port and the peripheral device; that way the program can monitor and control the flow of data at all times. This enables the program to change the direction of the communication easily, making EPP the ideal protocol for devices that frequently change from input to output and back again (external hard drives, tape backup units, and so on).

Because control of the handshaking and synchronization process is dependent on the hardware, manufacturers have considerable flexibility with regard to performance enhancements. As long as the device responds properly to the standardized EPP signals, manufacturers are free to implement any performance improvements they wish without violating the EPP standard. The end result is that data transfers using the EPP protocol can approach the speed of an ISA bus, transferring between 500KBps and 2MBps.

The Enhanced Parallel Port was developed before the creation of the IEEE 1284 committee. As a result, the early EPP protocol has a minor difference from the version adopted by the IEEE 1284 committee. Because of this difference, IEEE 1284 EPP parallel ports can fail to recognize that a pre-IEEE 1284 device is not ready to receive or send data. In that case, the device may fail to work properly. IEEE 1284 peripherals, however, work just fine with the pre-IEEE 1284 parallel ports. These pre-IEEE 1284 ports and devices are sometimes called EPP 1.7 devices, referring to an earlier proposed standard.

### Extended Capability Port (ECP)

Microsoft and Hewlett Packard proposed the *Extended Capability Port* (ECP) protocol in response to the need for high-performance parallel communication for printers and scanners. ECP is considered the fastest of all the parallel standards. ECP data transfers are *loosely* "coupled," meaning that once the data transfer has begun, the software that initiated the transfer (for example, a printer driver) cannot monitor the progress of the transfer. The software must wait for a signal that shows that the transfer has been completed. Even more than with EPP, this reduces the number of clock cycles used by the transfer to a bare minimum. Although it also reduces the amount of control that the software has over the process, not much control is needed. ECP is designed for operations that involve moving large chunks of data (for example, a print job going out to a printer, or an image coming in from a scanner). These types of data transfers do not require much monitoring.

ECP ports use a data compression method called *Run Length Encoding* (RLE). With RLE, data can be compressed by a ratio of up to 64:1. This enhances performance significantly, because printers and scanners deal with raster images, which tend to compress well. For RLE to work, both the device and the parallel port must support it. Note that RLE compression is not actually part of the IEEE 1284 standard, but is instead part of Microsoft's standard for implementing the ECP protocol.

The ECP standard provides the same degree of flexibility to hardware manufacturers as EPP. As long as the parallel port and devices respond to the standardized ECP commands, manufacturers can enhance performance any way that they wish. Because data transfers that use ECP do not require manipulation of the data, many manufacturers have added special capabilities to the ports, especially *Direct Memory Access* (DMA) channels, something never seen on any other form of parallel port. The capabilities of the port (or lack thereof) depend on the manufacturer.

## Support for the Standard

Also remember that manufacturers do not always embrace the entire standard. On the peripheral side, this is not much of a problem. Some modes are more appropriate for some types of devices than for others. ECP excels at handling large blocks of data via DMA channels, making it ideal for printers and scanners, but not so attractive for devices such as external CD-ROMs. External devices that must frequently switch back and forth between read and write operations are better served by EPP's ability to change the direction of the data flow without additional handshaking and overhead.

Many peripheral manufacturers will not support all five modes because it would be wasteful; however, on the parallel port side, support for all five modes is vital. Because Centronics mode and nibble mode are controlled through software, any parallel port ever made for an IBM PC can do both. However, control for byte mode, ECP, and EPP resides in the hardware. Without the appropriate hardware support, expensive devices capable of high-speed communication must slow down to the speed of the parallel port. Check your parallel port settings in CMOS to verify that the port is set to the appropriate mode (Figure 19-16).

```
                    ROM PCI/ISA BIOS (2A69KS21)
                      INTEGRATED PERIPHERALS
                       AWARD SOFTWARE, INC.

    IDE HDD Block Mode        : Enabled    Onboard Parallel Port : 378/IRQ7
    IDE Primary Master P10    : Auto       Parallel Port Mode    :  SPP
    IDE Primary Slave  P10    : Auto
    IDE Secondary Master P10  : Auto
    IDE Secondary Slave  P10  : Auto
    IDE Primary Master UDMA   : Auto
    IDE Primary Slave  UDMA   : Auto
    IDE Secondary Master UDMA : Auto
    IDE Secondary Slave  UDMA : Auto
    On-Chip Primary   PCI IDE : Enabled
    On-Chip Secondary PCI IDE : Enabled
    USB Keyboard Support      : Disabled
    Init Display First        : PCI Slot

    Onboard FDC Controller    : Enabled    ESC :  Quit    ↑↓ → ← : Select Item
    Onboard Serial Port 1     : Disabled   F1  :  Help       PU/PD/+/-  :Modify
    Onboard Serial Port 2     : 2F8/IRQ3   F5  :  Old Values (Shift)F2:Color
    UR2 Mode                  : Standard   F7  :  Load Setup Defaults
```

**Figure 19-16**   Parallel port settings in CMOS

## Connections, Cabling, and Electricity

Although no true standard exists, "standard parallel cable" usually refers to a printer cable with a male DB25 connector on one end and a 36-pin Centronics connector on the other (Figures 19-17 and 19-18). The shielding (or lack thereof) of the internal wiring and other electrical characteristics are largely undefined except by custom. In practice, these standard cables are acceptable for transferring data at 10KBps, and for distances under six feet, but would be dangerously unreliable for ECP or EPP operations.

**Figure 19-17**
36-pin Centronics
connector

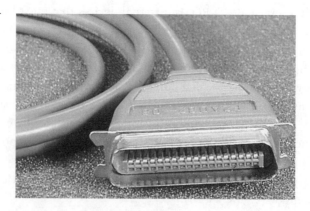

**Figure 19-18**
DB25 connector

Some new printers now use USB connections, especially in legacy-free or legacy-reduced systems. Because USB provides far faster throughput than any parallel interface, these printers tend to run quite fast. Again, make sure that the CMOS assigns an IRQ to the USB port or the printer will not work.

## Printing in Windows

Although printing looks the same in Windows 9x and Windows 2000, the two operating systems use very different printing methodologies. Let's take a moment to understand how Windows 9x and Windows 2000 do printing, and then see how to install, configure, and troubleshoot printers in each OS.

## Windows 9x Printing

Windows 9x systems take a fairly simple approach to printing. The print mechanism is divided into three distinct parts: the printer, the print driver, and the print spooler (Figure 19-19).

**Figure 19-19**
Windows 9x:
printer, print driver,
and print spooler

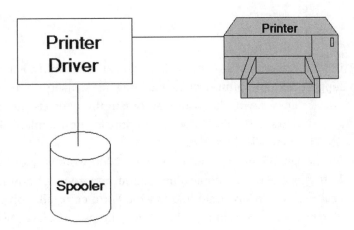

When you send out a print job (that is, when you click Print), the application sends the print job to the print spooler. The print spooler, working with the print driver, formats the print job in a language that the printer can understand and stores it as a temporary file on the hard drive. Once the print job has been "spooled" to the hard drive, the print job is then sent to the printer (to speed things up, you can also have the computer send the beginning of the print job to the printer *before* the entire print job has spooled).

Windows 2000 uses a dramatically more complex method. First, to Windows, a "printer" is not a physical device; it is a *program* that controls one or more physical printers. The *physical* printer is called a "print device." Printer drivers and a spooler are still present, but in Windows 2000 they are integrated into the "printer" itself (Figure 19-20).

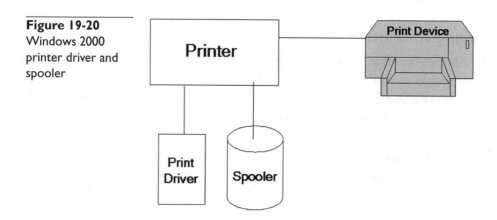

**Figure 19-20**
Windows 2000
printer driver and
spooler

This arrangement gives Windows 2000 amazing flexibility. For example, one printer can support multiple print devices, enabling a system to act as a print server. If one print device goes down, the printer automatically redirects the output to a working printer. Windows 2000 also provides support for nonstandard ports, enabling extra functions for networked printers.

Even though Windows 9*x* and Windows 2000 work very differently "beneath the hood," the general installation, configuration, and troubleshooting issues are basically identical. Let's watch a typical Windows 2000 printer installation. I'll mention the trivial differences between Windows 2000 and Windows 9*x* as we see the process.

## Setting Up Printers

Setting up a printer is so easy that it's almost scary. Most printers are Plug and Play, so installing a printer is reduced to simply plugging it in and loading the driver if needed. If the system does not detect the printer or if the printer is not PnP, click Start | Settings | Printers to open the Printers applet. The icon for this applet can also be found in the Control Panel. Figure 19-21 shows a Printer applet with no printers installed. Note the only icon: Add Printer.

**Figure 19-21**
Empty Printer applet

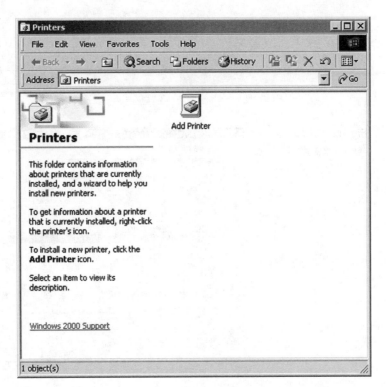

As you might guess, a new printer is installed by starting the Add Printer applet. This starts the Add Printer Wizard. After a pleasant intro screen, the screen shown in Figure 19-22 appears.

You may choose to install a printer plugged directly into your system or a network printer. Windows 2000 also adds the Automatically Detect and Install My PnP Printer option—a nice extra touch. If you choose a local printer (networked printers will be discussed in Chapter 20), Windows 2000 asks you to select a port; pick the one where you installed the new printer (Figure 19-23).

**Figure 19-22**
Local or network
printer?

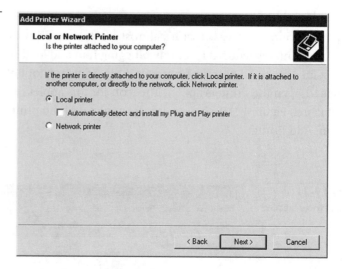

**Figure 19-23**
Selecting a port

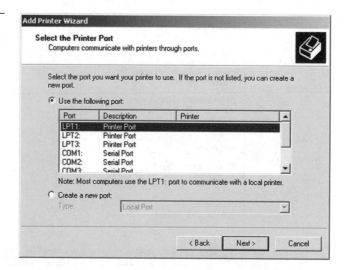

Once you select the port, Windows 2000 then asks for the type of printer. Select the type from the list or use the Have Disk option just as you would for any other device (Figure 19-24). Note the handy Windows Update option to pull the latest printer driver from the Internet.

Windows 2000 then installs the printer. (Windows 9x reverses the port and printer type selection screens but otherwise works the same way.) Figure 19-25 shows a typical printer applet with one printer installed. Note the small check mark in the corner; this shows that the device is the default printer. If you have multiple printers, you can change the default printer by selecting the printer's properties and checking Make Default Printer.

**Figure 19-24**
Choosing your
printer

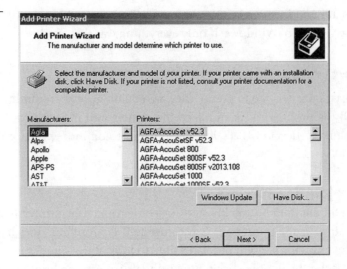

**Figure 19-25**
Default printer,
properly installed

Installing printers in Windows 9x and Windows 2000 is one of the easiest processes in any version of Windows. If only everything was this easy!

## Printer Problems

As easy as printers are to set up, they are equally robust at running, assuming that you install the proper drivers and keep the printer well maintained. But printer errors do occasionally develop. Let's look at the most common print problems in Windows 9x/2000.

## Print Job Never Prints

If you hit the Print button but nothing comes out of the printer, first check all the obvious things. Is the printer on? Is it connected? Is it online? Does it have paper? Assuming the printer is in good order, it's time to look at the spooler. You can see the spooler status either by double-clicking the printer's icon in the Printers applet, or by clicking the tiny printer icon in the System Tray, if it's present. If you're having a problem it will almost always be there (Figure 19-26).

**Figure 19-26**
Printer icon in
System Tray

Print spoolers can easily overflow or become corrupt due to a lack of disk space, too many print jobs, or one of a thousand other factors. This window shows all of the pending print jobs and enables you to delete, start, or pause print jobs. I usually just delete the print jobs and try again.

## Strange Sizes

A print job that comes out a strange size usually points to a user mistake in setting up the print job. All applications have a Print command and a Page Setup. The Page Setup enables you to define a number of print options, which vary from application to application. Figure 19-27 shows the Page Setup options for Microsoft Word. Make sure the user is setting up the page properly.

**Figure 19-27**
Page setup options

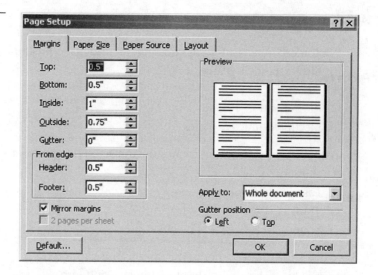

If you know the page is set up correctly, recheck the printer drivers. If necessary, uninstall and reinstall the printer drivers. If the problem persists, you may have a serious problem with the printer's print engine, but that only comes up as a likely answer when you continually get the same strangely-sized printouts using a number of different applications.

## Misaligned or Garbage Prints

Misaligned or garbage printouts invariably point to a corrupted or incorrect driver. Make sure you're using the right driver (it's hard to mess this up but not impossible) and then uninstall and reinstall the printer driver. If the problem persists, you may be asking the printer to do something it cannot do. For example, you may be printing to a PostScript printer with a PCL driver. Check the printer type to verify that you haven't installed the wrong type of driver for that printer!

## Review Questions

1. What mechanism is used by most ink-jet printers to push ink onto the paper?
   A. Electrostatic discharge
   B. Gravity
   C. Air pressure
   D. Electro-conductive plates

2. With a laser printer, what creates the image on the photosensitive drum?
   A. Primary corona
   B. Laser imaging unit
   C. Transfer corona
   D. Toner

3. What is the proper order of the laser printing process?
   A. Clean, charge, write, develop, transfer, and fuse
   B. Charge, write, transfer, fuse, develop, and clean
   C. Clean, write, develop, transfer, fuse, and charge
   D. Clean, charge, write, develop, fuse, and transfer

4. Which of the following has the highest throughput?
   A. ECP
   B. EPP
   C. SPP
   D. IEEE 1284, Fast Centronics

5. On a dot-matrix printer, what physically strikes the ribbon to form an image?
   A. Electromagnets
   B. Printwires
   C. Character wheel
   D. Print hammers

6. Which of these items are considered to be dot-matrix printer consumables? (Select all that apply.)
   A. Drive motor
   B. Paper
   C. Flywheel
   D. Ribbon

7. What part must be vacuumed or replaced periodically to prevent damage as a result of the action of the corona?
   A. The rubber rollers
   B. The ozone filter
   C. The transfer filter
   D. The cleaning blade

8. What is the most common cause of "light-ghosting" problems?
   A. Misaligned laser
   B. "Developer starvation"
   C. A damaged drum
   D. Low temperature and humidity

9. What is the newest type of printer interface?
   A. Parallel
   B. USB
   C. Infrared
   D. RS-232

10. A stand-alone printer will print a test page just fine, but it makes gobbledy-gook out of your term paper. What's probably wrong?
    A. Out of toner
    B. Fuser error
    C. Printer interface
    D. Faulty software configuration

## Answers

1. **D.** Most ink-jet printers use electroconductive plates to push the ink onto the paper.

2. **B.** The laser imaging unit creates an image on the photosensitive drum.

3. **A.** Clean, charge, write, develop, transfer, and fuse is the proper process.

4. **A.** ECP has the best throughput of those listed.

5. **B.** Printwires physically strike the ribbon in dot-matrix printers.

6. **B. and D.** Both paper and ribbons are considered dot-matrix printer consumables.

7. **B.** The ozone filter should be periodically vacuumed or changed.

8. **B.** The *most* common cause is developer starvation. Humidity and temperature can sometimes have an effect as well.

9. **B.** USB is the newest type of printer interface.

10. **D.** The application (software) that is trying to print is probably configured incorrectly.

## CHAPTER 20

# Networks

In this chapter, you will

- Learn the basics of network cabling
- See how to install a network card
- Understand how Windows 9x and Windows 2000 use networking
- Perform basic network troubleshooting

## Historical/Conceptual

Early on in the life of PCs, it became obvious that individual PCs needed to share data and peripherals with other PCs. Certainly, any PC can read another PC's data off of floppy disks, but that requires time to copy the data to a floppy, take the floppy to the other machine (a.k.a. "SneakerNet"), insert the floppy, and access the data. This works, but it is a very slow process, and for certain types of data, completely useless. In particular, the PC world likes to have one database that many users can access simultaneously. The data stored in databases includes customer lists, product inventories, student enrollment—examples of this type of data are endless. Next, there is a great demand for sharing devices. Why buy everyone in the company a laser printer when a single laser printer, accessible to everyone, would suffice?

Clearly, there was a strong motivation to create a grouping of PCs, a network, that could enable users to share data and peripherals. So the big question was: *How?* It's easy to say, "Well, just run a wire between them!" Although most networks do manifest themselves via some type of cable, this barely touches the thousands of questions that come into play here. Here are a few of the *big* questions.

- How will each computer be identified? If two or more computers want to talk at the same time, how do you ensure all conversations are understood?

- What kind of wire? What gauge? How many wires in the cable? Which wires do which things? How long can the cable be? What type of connectors?

- If more than one PC is accessing the same file, how can they be prevented from destroying each other's changes to that file?

- How can access to data and peripherals be controlled?

Clearly, making a network entails a lot more than just stringing up some cable! I have a rather unique way of looking at computer networks that I humbly call "Mike's Four-Layer Model." You won't see this term on the A+ exams, but you will find it a great way to understand networks so that you *can* answer the questions on the A+ exams!

I break all networks into four major areas: Hardware, Protocols, Network, and Shared Resources. This chapter, for the most part, follows these four categories and discusses each one in great detail. Let's take a quick look at these categories so you know what to expect.

## Hardware

Hardware is probably the most self-explanatory of the four categories. This section will cover the many different ways data can be moved from one PC to another. Here we discuss the different types of cabling. This section also explains how network cards are installed and tested. Plus, the Hardware category hits on all of those interesting boxes, such as hubs, switches, or repeaters, among which all of the wires in the network run. Finally, this section will explain all of those hardware terms like "Ethernet," "10BASE-T," and "topology."

## Protocols

This section should really be called "Network Protocols," but it may be confused with the next one. Protocols are the languages of networks. These languages have interesting names such as NetBEUI, IPX/SPX, and the ever-popular TCP/IP. A protocol is a highly standardized language that handles most of the "invisible" functions on a network, like determining which computer is SERVER1, or disassembling/reassembling data passed over the network. In early computer networks, only one protocol existed. Today it is common for the same network to run more than one protocol, primarily to enable that network to connect to other networks. This section will cover the most common protocols used today and will show how they are installed, configured, and repaired.

## Network

Once the hardware is installed and the protocol determined, the next step is to decide which systems will share resources. Then we need to come up with some way to name the systems so that they can "see" each other. In this section, the concepts of "client/server," "peer-to-peer," and "domain-based" will be clarified. This section describes in detail how networks make resources available and how they control access to those resources.

## Shared Resources

Once all the systems have names, we need to identify the resources they will share, like files, folders, and printers. If a drive, directory, or file is to be shared, there must be a way to identify it as available for sharing. The rules for naming shared resources are called *naming conventions*. A great example would be a system that offers its D:\FRED directory for sharing. This D:\FRED directory needs a network name such as SERVE_FRED. It is this network name that is displayed to all of the devices on the network. The process of creating shared resource names will be covered in this section.

A network also needs to control access to resources. A laser printer, for example, might be available for sharing but might best be used solely by the accounting department, excluding other departments. Individual systems need to be able to access the shared resources. There needs to be a process where a PC can look out on the network and see what is available. Having found those available resources, the PC then needs to make them look and act as though they were local resources. For example, suppose another computer has offered a shared resource called SERVE_FRED. The local machine may want to create a phony drive called "H:" that is really the SERVE_FRED resource. The process of taking network resources and making them perform like local resources is popularly called *redirecting*.

Let's begin with the most fun of all four: the hardware.

## Test Specific

## Hardware

The most obvious item, which is shared by all networks, is the need for hardware. There must be some way to get the bits of data between computers. For the overwhelming majority of networks, this means all of the PCs are linked together through some type of cabling. Invariably, all of the cables from all of the PCs come together in some mysterious box called a *hub*. Even though most networks share the same basic look and feel, the way the data moves around inside those wires may be quite different from one network to the next. The term *topology* is used to describe these different configurations of the cabling between computers.

## Packets/Frames

Before we dive into the concept of topology, we need to understand that data is moved from one PC to another in discrete chunks called *packets* or *frames*. The terms packet and frame are interchangeable. Every network card (commonly called a "NIC," for network interface card) in the world has a built-in identifier called a *Media Access Control* (MAC) address. This address is a binary address that is unique for every network card. Yes, that's right! Every network card in the world has a unique MAC address. The MAC address is 48 bits long, giving over 281 *trillion* MAC addresses, so there are plenty of MAC addresses to go around (Figure 20-1).

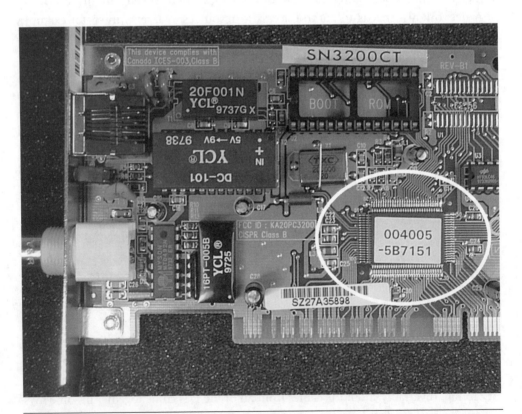

**Figure 20-1**   MAC address

All the many varieties of frames share certain common features (Figure 20-2). First, packets contain the MAC address of the network card to which the data is being sent. Second, they have the MAC address of the network card that sent the data. Third, is the data itself (at this point, we have no idea what the data is—certain software handles that question), which can vary in size depending on the type of frame. Finally, some type of data check is performed to enable the receiving network card to verify if the data was received in good order.

**Figure 20-2**
Generic frame

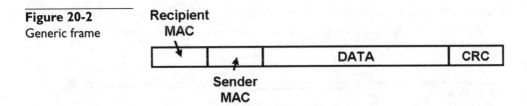

## Topology

Since the first networks were invented over 30 years ago, many types of topologies have been invented. However, only two types of topologies are commonly used in today's networks: *bus* topology and *ring* topology. Each of these topologies has advantages and disadvantages. The best topology for a specific situation depends on a variety of factors, including cost, speed, ease of installation, the physical position of the PCs, and the number of PCs in the network.

### Bus Topology

The first type of topology was bus topology. Bus topology means that all the PCs are connected via a single cable that runs to all the PCs. Although bus topologies actually look something like Figure 20-3, we draw them like Figure 20-4 for simplicity.

**Figure 20-3**
Real bus topology

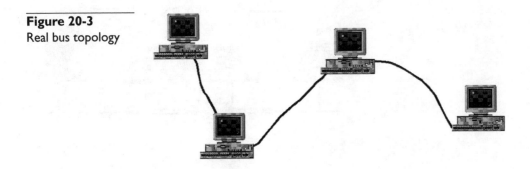

**Figure 20-4**
Simplified bus
topology diagram

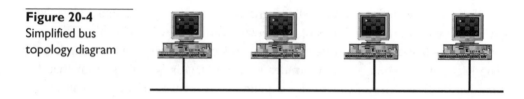

Bus topology works like a big telephone party line; all devices must first listen to see if anyone else is sending packets before they can send a packet (Figure 20-5). If the cable is not being used, the device sends its packet on the line. Every network card on the bus sees and reads the packet! This is called *Carrier Sense Multiple Access/Collision Detection* (CSMA/CD).

**Figure 20-5**
CSMA/CD

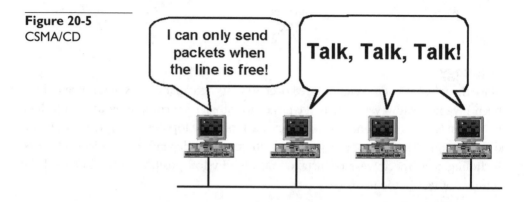

Sometimes two cards do talk at the same time. This is called a *collision,* and the cards themselves arbitrate to see who gets to resend their frames first (Figure 20-6).

**Figure 20-6**
Collision

## Reflection and Termination

The ends of the bus topology present a bit of a problem for the signal moving along the wire. Anytime a device sends voltage along a wire, some voltage bounces back or "reflects" when it reaches the end of the wire (Figure 20-7).

**Figure 20-7**
Reflection

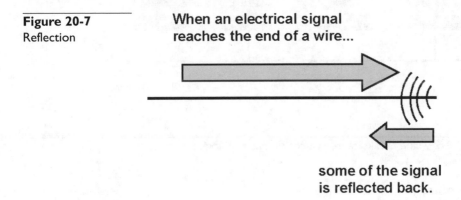

When an electrical signal reaches the end of a wire...

some of the signal is reflected back.

Network cables are no exception. Based on what we know so far, the packets uselessly reflect back and forth, making the cards that want to send data wait for no reason. We call this a *packet storm*. After a short while, the bus is so full of reflecting packets that no other card can send data. To prevent the packets from being reflected, a device called a *terminator* must be plugged into the end of the bus cable. A terminator is nothing more than a resistor that absorbs the signal, thus preventing reflection (Figure 20-8).

**Figure 20-8**
Terminator

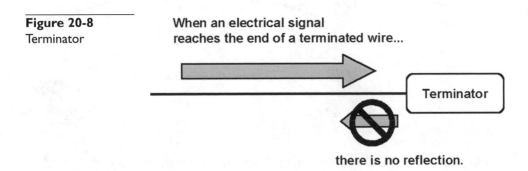

When an electrical signal reaches the end of a terminated wire...

Terminator

there is no reflection.

This need for termination is a weak spot in bus topology. If the cable breaks anywhere, a packet storm is instantly created and no device can send data, even if the break is not between the devices exchanging data (Figure 20-9).

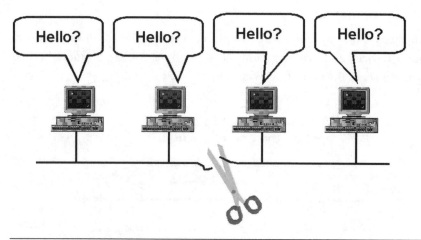

**Figure 20-9**   Line breaks cause failures on bus topologies.

## Ring Topology

Ring topology is more recent than bus topology (although that does not make it more popular). A ring topology connects all the PCs together on a single cable much like bus topology. However, as the name implies, this bus is shaped like a ring (Figure 20-10).

**Figure 20-10**
Ring topology

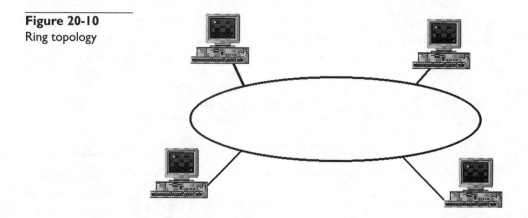

Ring topologies use a transmission method called *token passing*. In token passing, a mini packet called a *token* constantly passes from one card to the next in one direction (Figure 20-11). If one PC wants to talk to another, it must wait until it gets the token. The PC's NIC then attaches data to the token and sends the packet back out the ring. If another PC wants to send data, it must wait until a free token (one that doesn't have an attached packet) comes around.

**Figure 20-11**
Token passing

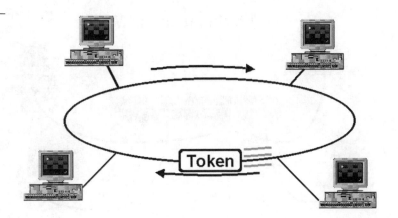

Because ring topologies use token passing, the term *token ring* is often used when describing ring networks. There were a few exceptions where a ring topology used features other than token passing, but they were few and are long gone. All current ring networks use an IBM-trademarked version of token passing, appropriately called *Token Ring*. So if it is a ring topology, it is Token Ring.

## Star Ring

Token Ring topology was, if not invented, perfected and packaged by IBM. Token Ring actually uses a topology called *star ring*. Instead of running a ring of cable all around the LAN, as shown in Figure 20-12, the ring is stored inside a special box called *Multi-Station Access Unit* (MSAU). It is often just called an MAU or "hub," although any "in-the-know" Token Ring techs would have a heart attack if you said it in earshot of them! Although Token Ring is a ring, it looks more like a star (Figure 20-13).

**Figure 20-12**
Regular ring

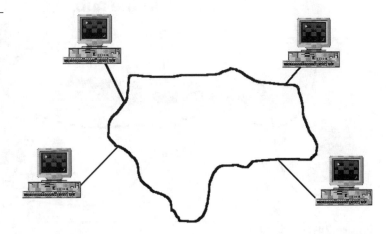

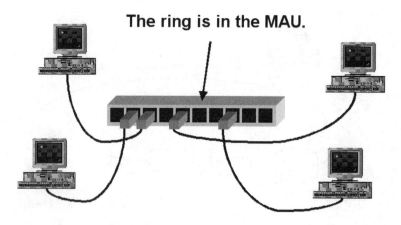

**Figure 20-13**   Star ring

Token Ring is slowly losing market share to bus-type topologies due to its cost and the fact it was proprietary IBM technology. However, it is still heavily used in hundreds of thousands of networks. Because Token Ring normally uses a more robust type of cabling, it is also still very popular in areas where a lot of electrical interference occurs.

### Star Bus

The star configuration used in Token Ring made it very dependable and easy to expand. This led to a variation of the bus topology called *star bus* topology. Both the star and the bus topologies have significant advantages and disadvantages. Imagine if we were to take a bus network and shrink the bus down so it would fit inside a hub (Figure 20-14).

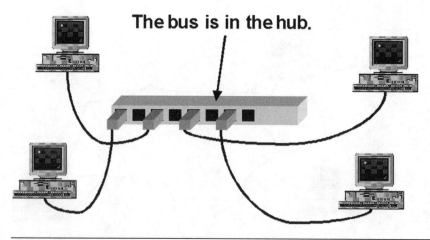

**Figure 20-14**   Star bus

The bus topology would sure look a lot like a star, wouldn't it? This type of star bus topology is the single most popular topology today. Cheap and centralized, a star bus network does not go down if a cable breaks. True, the network would go down if the hub itself failed, but that is very rare. Even if a hub fails, replacing a hub in a closet is much easier than tracing a bus running through walls and ceilings trying to find a break!

## Hardware Protocols

Now that you have the concept of topologies, the next big question is "What are the different types of frames?" The problem in answering this question is that it encompasses so many items. When the first networks were created, *everything* from the frames to the connectors to the type of cable had to be invented from scratch. A consortium of companies centered on Digital Equipment, Intel, and Xerox invented the first network in the mid-1970s. More than just creating a network, they wrote a series of standards that defined everything necessary to get data from one computer to another. This series of standards was called *Ethernet*, and it is the dominant standard for today's networks.

### Ethernet

The Ethernet standard is quite broad and is based on CSMA/CD bus topology. The Ethernet standard was released to the *Institute of Electrical and Electronics Engineers* (IEEE) standards body, which still controls it today. The IEEE committee, designated to handle the Ethernet standard, was formed in February 1980 and was given the name "802." The 802 committee is still the primary body in charge of changes and enhancements to the Ethernet standard, as well as to other network standards.

#### Coaxial Cable

Coaxial cable is the oldest of all types of network cable. It is still widely used and supported. Coaxial cable ("coax") is the only cable type used in bus topologies, with a few exceptions (most notably, star bus). By definition, coaxial cable is a cable within a cable—two cables that share the same center or axis. Coax consists of a center cable (core) surrounded by insulation. This in turn is covered with a *shield* of braided cable. The inner core actually carries the signal. The shield effectively eliminates outside interference. The entire cable is then surrounded by a protective insulating cover.

#### Thick Ethernet—10BASE-5

The original Xerox Ethernet specification defined a very specific type of cabling for the first Ethernet networks. This type of cable is called *Thick Ethernet*. Thick Ethernet, also known as *Thicknet*, is a very thick (about half an inch in diameter) coaxial cable that is manufactured under the Belden 9580 standard. (Belden is a *big* cable manufacturer, and their internal part number (9580) for Thick Ethernet is a very popular way to define Thicknet.)

The cable to which a PC is connected is called the *segment*. Thicknet supports up to 100 devices hooked to one segment. The maximum length of one segment is 500 meters (Figure 20-15).

**Figure 20-15**
10BASE-5

# 10BASE-5

Max 100 PCs on one segment.

←—Max segment length is 500 meters.—→

Thicknet is clearly marked every 2.5 meters. These marks show where to connect devices to the cable. All devices on a Thicknet must be connected at these marks. This assures that all devices are some multiple of 2.5 meters apart. This spacing is required to reduce noise due to oscillations in the signal (Figure 20-16).

**Figure 20-16**
Connection mark

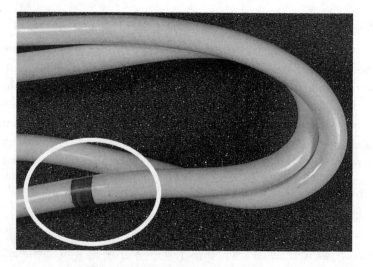

Devices connect to Thicknet by means of a *vampire connector*. The vampire connector pierces the cable, creating the connection. The vampire connector is also a transceiver, a device that both receives and sends data. The transceiver is the device that enables connections between devices and the common cable. Transceivers also detect when collisions take place. Actually, all networks use transceivers, but Thicknet uses an external transceiver. The cable from the vampire connector/transceiver to the device must be no more than 50 meters (Figure 20-17).

**Figure 20-17**
10BASE-5
transceiver

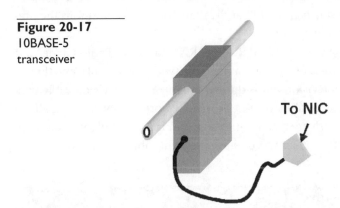

To NIC

Thick Ethernet uses a bus topology; therefore, it needs terminators. A very specific terminator is made just for Thicknet. It is a 50-ohm terminator and must be placed on each end of the segment. Thicknet connects to a PC's network card via a 15-pin male connector. This connector is called the AUI or sometimes the *Digital, Intel, Xerox* (DIX) connector (Figure 20-18).

**Figure 20-18**  DIX connector

Thick Ethernet is on the way out. Bus topology is always risky because one break on the cable will cause the entire network to fail. In addition, Thicknet is expensive and hard to work with. The cable, transceivers, and terminators cost far more than those in any other network. Nevertheless, there is a massive installed base, and it is still actively used, especially where longer distances or heavy shielding are needed.

### Thin Ethernet—10BASE-2

Thin Ethernet, also known as *Thinnet* or *Cheapernet*, was invented as a cheap alternative to Thicknet. Thinnet cable is much easier to handle than Thicknet cable and is the preferred type of cabling for small networks.

Thinnet uses a specific type of coax called RG-58. "RG" stands for Radio Grade, and it is an industry standard for measuring coax cables. This type of coax looks exactly like the coax used by your cable television but is quite different. Your television cable uses RG-6. If you attempt to use RG-6 cable, your network will work poorly or not at all.

The RG rating should be clearly marked on the cable. If it is not, it will say something like "Thinnet" or "802.3" to let you know you have the right cable (Figure 20-19).

**Figure 20-19**
Cable markings

Although thin Ethernet also runs at 10 Mbps, it has several big limitations that Thick Ethernet does not share. Thin Ethernet supports only 30 devices per segment, and each segment can be no more than 185 meters long (Figure 20-20).

**Figure 20-20**
10BASE-2

# 10BASE-2

Max 30 PCs on one segment.

Max segment length is 185 meters.

On the plus side, cabling with Thinnet is a snap compared with Thicknet. The cable is much thinner and more flexible than Thicknet. In addition, the transceiver is built into the Thinnet network card, so Thinnet does not require an external transceiver. Each Thinnet network card is simply connected to the bus cable with a T connector (Figure 20-21).

The Thinnet cable has twist-on connectors, called *BNC connectors,* that attach to the T connector, forming the network. Termination is handled by twisting small, specialized terminators onto the unused end of the T connector on the machines at the ends of the chain.

**Figure 20-21**
T connector

When installing Thinnet, it is important that one of the terminators be grounded. Special terminators can be grounded to the case of the PC. Just be sure the PC is also grounded! You *must* use a T connector! Connecting the cable as shown in Figure 20-22 does not work. Figure 20-23 shows some examples of complete Thinnet networks.

To add another PC to the network, simply remove the terminator from the last PC, add another piece of cable with another T connector, and add the terminator on the new end. It is also very easy to add a PC between two systems by unhooking one side of a T connector and adding another PC and cable in between.

Thinnet still enjoys popularity for *small office home office* (SOHO) networks; however, its relatively short maximum segment lengths and small number of devices per segment make Thinnet totally unacceptable for larger networks.

**Figure 20-22**
Incorrect use of
10BASE-2

**Figure 20-23**
Typical Thinnet
networks

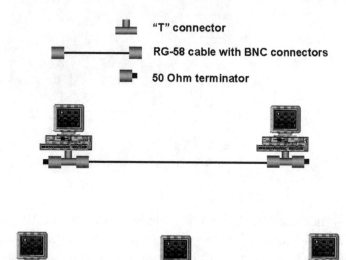

"T" connector

RG-58 cable with BNC connectors

50 Ohm terminator

## 10BASE-T

Probably the most popular of all networks today is Ethernet 10BASE-T. This standard defines Ethernet running on *unshielded twisted pair* (UTP), at 10 Mbps, in a star bus topology. Unlike the other Ethernet flavors, 10BASE-T does not use coaxial cable. Instead, 10BASE-T is designed to work with unshielded twisted pair cable.

**Unshielded Twisted Pair**   UTP cabling is the defined cabling for 10BASE-T and is the predominant cabling system used today. Many different types of twisted pair cabling are available to choose from, depending on the needs of the network. Twisted pair cabling consists of AWG 22-26-gauge wire twisted together into color-coded pairs. These pairs are loosely encased in a common insulated jacket (Figure 20-24).

**Figure 20-24**
Typical UTP cable

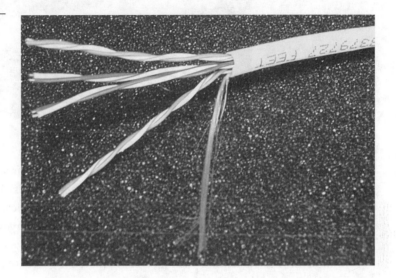

**CAT Levels**   UTP cables come in categories that define the maximum speed at which data can be transferred (also called *bandwidth*). The five major categories (CATs) are

- **CAT1**   Standard phone line
- **CAT2**   Data speeds up to 4 Mbps (ISDN and T1 lines)
- **CAT3**   Data speeds up to 16 Mbps
- **CAT4**   Data speeds up to 20 Mbps
- **CAT5**   Data speeds up to 100 Mbps

The CAT level should be clearly marked on the cable, as Figure 20-25 shows.

These categories are established by the *Telecommunication Industry Association/Electronics Industry Association* (TIA/EIA) and are under the EIA-568 specification. Currently, most installers use CAT5 cable if they can afford it (CAT5 is about 30 percent more expensive than CAT3). Although most networks run at 10 Mbps, the industry standard is currently shifting to fast networks designed to run at 100 Mbps. Because only CAT5 handles these speeds, just about everyone is installing CAT5, even if they are running at speeds that CAT3 or CAT4 would do. Consequently, it is becoming harder to get anything but CAT5 cable.

**Figure 20-25**
Cable markings
for CAT level

There can also be different numbers of pairs. Currently, two- and four-pair cable are the most popular choices. Virtually everyone is buying four-pair UTP. The reason for this is simple: fear of the future. No one knows what network speeds will be common in the future or how many pairs they will need, so just about everyone is playing it safe and installing four-pair, CAT5 UTP. You should, too!

A number of wire makers are pushing UTP with even higher ratings. A good example is Belden Wire and Cable's DataTwist™ 350 cable, designated to run as fast as 350 Mbps. These new cables tend to get names like "CAT6," "CAT6a," and "CAT7," but as of now there are no official CAT levels above CAT5.

### Back to 10BASE-T

The 10BASE-T cabling standard requires two pairs of wires, a pair for sending and a pair for receiving. 10BASE-T runs on CAT3, CAT4, or CAT5 cable.

These cables use a special connector called RJ-45. The "RJ" designation was invented by Ma Bell years ago and is still used today. Currently, only two types of RJ connectors are used: RJ-11 and RJ-45 (Figure 20-26).

RJ-11 is the connector that hooks your telephone to the telephone jack. It supports up to two pairs of wires, though most phone lines only use one pair. The other pair is used to support a second phone line. RJ-11 connectors are not used in any common network installation, although a few weird (and out of business) "network in a box"-type companies used them. RJ-45 is the standard for UTP connectors. RJ-45 has connections for up to four pairs and is visibly much wider than RJ-11.

Use Figure 20-27 to determine the #1 pin on an RJ-45 jack.

**Figure 20-26**
RJ-11 and RJ-45

**Figure 20-27**
RJ-45 pin numbers

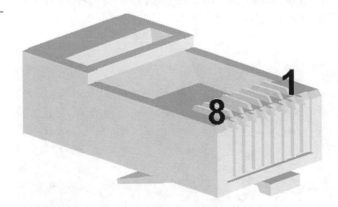

The *Electronics Industry Association/Telecommunication Industry Association* (EIA/TIA) has two standards: the EIA/TIA 568A and the EIA/TIA 568B. Both are acceptable. You do not have to follow any standard as long as you use the same pairings on each end of the cable; however, you will make your life simpler if you choose a standard. Make sure that all of your cabling uses the same standard and you will save a great deal of work in the end. Most importantly, *keep records!*

Like all wires, the wires in UTP are numbered. However, a number does not appear on each wire. Instead, each wire has a standardized color. Table 20-1 shows the official EIA/TIA Standard Color Chart for UTP.

**Table 20-1** UTP Cabling Color Chart

| PIN # | 568A | 568B |
|-------|------|------|
| 1 | White/Green | White/Orange |
| 2 | Green | Orange |
| 3 | White/Orange | White/Green |
| 4 | Blue | Blue |
| 5 | White/Blue | White/Blue |
| 6 | Orange | Green |
| 7 | White/Brown | White/Brown |
| 8 | Brown | Brown |

## Combo cards

Because 10BASE-T uses the same language as 10BASE-2 or 10BASE-5, you can find Ethernet combo network cards that support two or even three different types of connections (Figure 20-28).

**Figure 20-28** Ethernet combo cards

## Hubs

In a 10BASE-T network, each PC is connected to a 10BASE-T hub. These hubs have multiple connections called ports, one per connected device. To add a device to the network, simply plug another cable into the hub (Figure 20-29).

**Figure 20-29**   Typical rack-mounted hub

Remember that 10BASE-T uses the star bus topology. The hub holds the actual bus and allows access to the bus through the ports. By using a star bus topology, we create a robust network; the failure of a single node will not bring down the entire network (Figure 20-30).

**Figure 20-30**
10BASE-T

# 10BASE-T

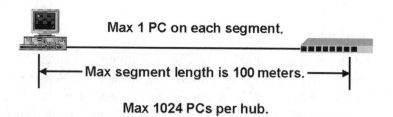

Max 1 PC on each segment.

Max segment length is 100 meters.

Max 1024 PCs per hub.

The maximum distance from the hub to any device is 100 meters. No more than one PC can be hooked to each segment, and the maximum number of PCs that may be hooked to any one hub is 1,024; although, you will be hard pressed to find a hub with that many connectors. Most hubs come with 4, 8, 16, 32, or 64 ports. 10BASE-T hubs act as repeaters, amplifying the signals between devices hooked into the network. They need power to provide this amplification, so make sure that the hubs are plugged into a good power source.

You can actually hook two 10BASE-T network cards together without a hub; just connect the two PCs together with a crossover cable! Crossover cables work great as a quick way to network two PCs. You can make a crossover cable by making one end TIA586A and the other TIA568B.

## Combining Different Types of Ethernet

Many 10BASE-T hubs have a Thinnet BNC connector or a Thicknet AUI connector in the back. The hubs can be connected directly to either a Thinnet or Thicknet backbone. These connectors are not only great for connecting to an existing Thicknet or Thinnet network but also for connecting multiple hubs together (Figure 20-31).

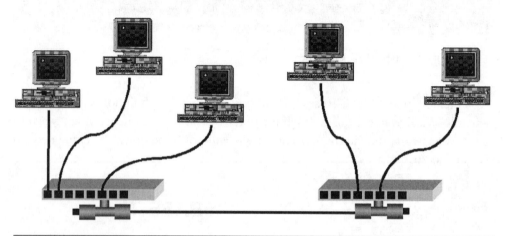

**Figure 20-31**    Mixed Ethernet media network

### Repeaters

When discussing 10BASE-T hubs, we brought up the concept of a repeater. A *repeater* is an electronic device that amplifies the signal on a line. Repeaters are used to extend the useful length of a cable segment beyond its specified maximum. Networks use two different types of repeaters. The first type is a dedicated box that takes input from one segment, amplifies it, and then passes it to another segment. Figure 20-32 shows a photo of a common repeater for 10BASE-2.

Using a repeater as shown in Figure 20-33, we can link together two 10BASE-2 segments. This would enable us to get past the 185-meter maximum length.

The second type of repeater is the 10BASE-T hub. As mentioned earlier, hubs are also repeaters, enabling a maximum separation of 200 meters between PCs on a 10BASE-T network (Figure 20-34).

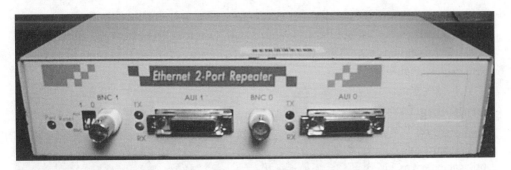

**Figure 20-32**  Repeater

**Figure 20-33**
Using a repeater

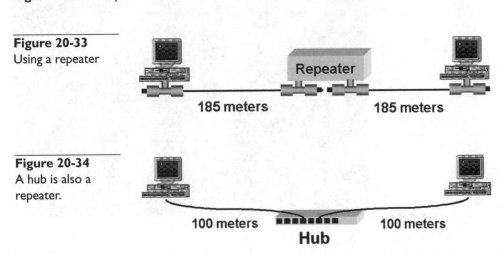

**Figure 20-34**
A hub is also a
repeater.

## Fast Ethernet

A strong move toward even faster Ethernet networks is evident today. The biggest push is toward 100 Mbps or "100BASE-T" Ethernet. Unfortunately, no 100BASE-T standard exists. The two most common types of 100BASE-T are called 100BASE-T4 and 100BASE-TX. 100BASE-T4 requires four-pair CAT3 or better UTP, whereas 100BASE-TX requires only two-pair CAT5. In either case, these high-speed Ethernets need their own 100BASE-T4 or 100BASE-TX network cards and hubs. They are incompatible with each other, although most 100BASE hubs and cards will support 10BASE-T.

## Fiber Optic Ethernet

Fiber optic cable is a very attractive way to transmit network packets. First, because it uses light instead of electricity, fiber optic cable is immune to electrical problems like lightning, short circuits, and static. Second, fiber optic signals travel much farther, usually 2,000 meters (compared with 100 meters for 10BASE-T or 100BASE-T). There are two standards for using fiber optic cable with Ethernet. In either case, the cabling is the same. It is called "62.5/125 multimode" fiber optic. All fiber Ethernets need two of these cables (Figure 20-35).

**Figure 20-35**
Typical fiber optic cables with connectors

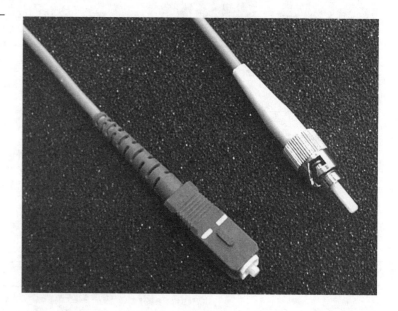

The two fiber optic standards are called 10BASE-FL and 100BASE-FX. As you can guess by the names, the only real difference is the speed of the network (there are some important differences in the way hubs are interconnected, and so on). Unfortunately, fiber optic cabling is delicate, expensive, and difficult to use, so it is usually relegated to backbone-type situations. A backbone would be the main piece of Ethernet to which all other hubs are connected. Figure 20-36 shows an example.

## Token Ring

"Token Ring" is a confusing term. The problem is that Token Ring refers to two related but different things. First, Token Ring is a topology. Second, Token Ring is a set of network standards developed by IBM that define a complete network system. Token Ring is completely incompatible with Ethernet and is considered a competitor to Ethernet. Token Ring runs at either 4 Mbps or 16 Mbps, depending on the type of Token Ring network cards you buy. Token Ring was originally based around the IBM Type 1 cable. Type 1 cable is a two-pair, *shielded twisted pair* (STP, see "STP Types," next section) cable designed to handle speeds up to 20 Mbps (Figure 20-37). Today, Token Ring can use either STP or UTP.

**Figure 20-36**
Fiber optic
backbone

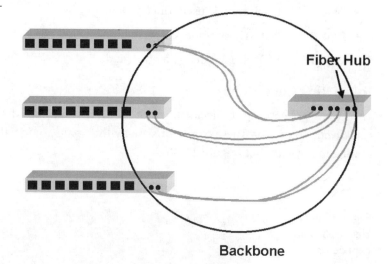

Fiber Hub

Backbone

**Figure 20-37**
Type 1 STP Token
Ring cable

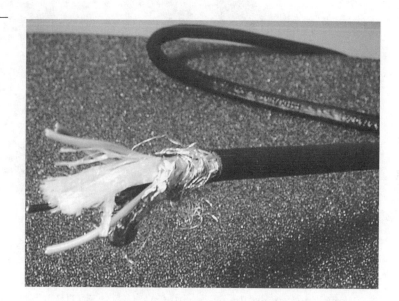

## STP Types

STP cables also have certain categories. These are called types and are defined by IBM.
The most common types are

- **Type 1**      Standard STP with two pairs—the most common STP cable
- **Type 2**      Standard STP plus two pairs of voice wires
- **Type 3**      Standard STP with four pairs

- **Type 6**    Patch cable—used for connecting hubs
- **Type 8**    Flat STP for under carpets
- **Type 9**    STP with 2 pairs—Plenum grade

### Token Ring Connectors

The Type 1 Token Ring connectors are not RJ-45. Instead, IBM designed a unique *hermaphroditic* connector. These connectors are neither male nor female; they are designed to plug into each other (Figure 20-38).

**Figure 20-38**
Hermaphroditic
connector

Token Ring network cards use a nine-pin female connector. A standard Token Ring cable has a hermaphroditic connector on one end and a nine-pin connector on the other.

Token Ring can also be used with CAT 3, 4, or 5 UTP. When combined with UTP, Token Ring uses an RJ-45 connector, so from a cabling standpoint, Token Ring UTP and Ethernet UTP look the same. Many Token Ring network cards are combo cards, which means they come with both a nine-pin connection for STP and an RJ-45 connection for UTP.

As discussed earlier, Token Ring uses a star ring topology; therefore, it also uses a hub. A Token Ring hub is *not* interchangeable with an Ethernet hub. IBM has a special name for its hubs. They are called either MAUs or *multi-station access units* (MSAUs). Unfortunately, they are also sometimes just called hubs (usually by Ethernet people who do not know any better). See Figure 20-39.

- Token Ring can support up to 260 PCs using STP and up to 72 PCs using UTP.

- Using UTP, the maximum distance from any MAU to a PC is 45 meters.

- Using STP, the maximum distance from any MAU to a PC is 100 meters.

**Figure 20-39**
Token Ring

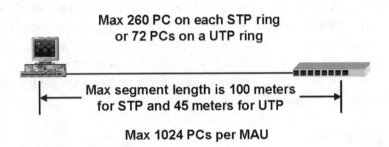

# Token Ring

**Max 260 PC on each STP ring
or 72 PCs on a UTP ring**

**Max segment length is 100 meters
for STP and 45 meters for UTP**

**Max 1024 PCs per MAU**

Token Ring also uses repeaters. Token Ring repeaters can only be used between MAUs. With a repeater, the functional distance between two MAUs increases to 360 meters (with UTP) and 720 meters (with STP).

## Network Protocols

Simply moving data from one machine to another is hardly sufficient to make a complete network; many other functions need to be handled. For example, if a file is being copied from one machine to another, something must keep track of all the packets so that the file can be properly reassembled. If many machines are talking to the same machine at once, that machine must somehow keep track of which packets should be sent to or received from each of the other PCs. Another issue arises if one of the machines in the network has its network card replaced. Up to this point, the only way to distinguish one machine from another was by the MAC address on the network card. To solve this, each machine must have a name, an identifier for the network, which is "above" the MAC address. Each machine, or at least one of them, needs to keep a list of all of the MAC addresses on the network, and the names of the machines, so that packets and names can be correlated. That way, if a network card is replaced, the network, after some special queries, will update the list to associate the new network card's MAC address with the name of that PC.

The protocol software takes data from the network card, keeps it organized, sends it to the correct program that needs the data, and then hands data to the card to be sent out. All networks have a protocol. Although many different protocols exist, the top three—IPX/SPX from Novell, NetBEUI from Microsoft, and TCP/IP from UNIX/Internet—hold a virtual lock on all networks.

## IPX/SPX

Novell invented the *Internetwork Packet Exchange/Sequenced Packet Exchange protocol* (IPX/SPX) and built all versions of NetWare around it. The IPX/SPX protocol is speedy, works well with routers, and takes up relatively little RAM when loaded.

## NetBEUI

During the 1980s, IBM developed *NetBIOS Extended User Interface* (NetBEUI), the default protocol for Windows for Workgroups, LANtastic, and Windows 95. NetBEUI offers small size and a relatively high speed but cannot be used for routing. Its inability to handle routing limits NetBEUI to networks smaller than approximately 200 nodes. A *node* is any device that has a network connection—usually a PC, although other devices can be nodes. For example, many printers now connect directly to a network and can therefore be thought of as nodes.

## TCP/IP

*Terminal Control Protocol/Internet Protocol* (TCP/IP) was originally developed for the Internet's progenitor, the *Advanced Research Projects Agency Network* (ARPANET) of the U.S. Department of Defense. In 1983, TCP/IP became the built-in protocol for the popular BSD UNIX, and other flavors of UNIX quickly adopted it as well. TCP/IP is becoming a preferred protocol for larger (>200 nodes) networks. The biggest network of all, the Internet, uses TCP/IP as its default protocol. Windows NT also uses TCP/IP as its default protocol. TCP/IP lacks speed and takes up a large amount of memory when loaded (especially in real mode), but it is robust, well understood, and universally supported.

## AppleTalk

AppleTalk is the proprietary Apple protocol. Similar to IPX, it is small and relatively fast. The only reason to use an AppleTalk protocol is to communicate with Apple computers on a network.

## Network Operating Systems

A *network operating system* (NOS) is the program that makes a network function. All NOSs can be broken into three basic organizational groups: peer-to-peer, client/server, and domain-based. To appreciate these three groups, let's first look at the needs of a typical network.

We want to share resources across a network. How do we make that happen? Can everyone share his or her hard drives with everyone else? Should we place limits on sharing? If everyone needs access to a particular file, where will it be stored? What about security? Can anyone access the file? What if someone erases it accidentally? How are backups to be handled? Different NOSs answer these questions differently.

## Client/Server

Take one machine and dedicate it as a resource to be shared over the network. This machine will have a dedicated NOS optimized for sharing files. This special OS includes powerful caching software that enables high-speed file access. It will have extremely high levels of protection and an organization that permits extensive control of the data. This machine is called a *dedicated* server. All of the other machines that use the data are called *clients* or *workstations.*

This system is called client/server. Client/server means to dedicate one machine to act as a "server." Its only function is to serve up resources to the other machines on the network. These servers do not run DOS or Windows 9x. They use highly sophisticated and expensive NOSs that are optimized for the sharing and administration of network resources. Currently, only one NOS fits the client/server concept: the popular Novell NetWare.

A NetWare server is not used directly by anyone. It does not run Windows; it only runs Novell NetWare. NetWare has its own commands and requires substantial training to use, but in return, you get an amazingly powerful NOS! Novell NetWare just *serves* shared resources; it does not run programs like Excel or CorelDraw. Many network administrators will even remove the keyboard and monitor from a Novell NetWare server to keep people from trying to use it.

Client/server NOSs such as Novell NetWare provide powerful security for shared resources. Do you remember the powerful NTFS permissions used by Windows 2000 Professional? Many people feel that Microsoft copied many of the aspects of NTFS permissions from Novell NetWare, because they are very similar.

## Peer-to-Peer

Some NOSs do not require dedicated servers. In these networks, every computer can act as both a server and a client. Peer-to-peer networks are much cheaper than client/server networks, because the software costs less and does not require a high-end machine to be the dedicated server. The most popular peer-to-peer NOSs today are Windows 9x and Windows 2000 Professional. A peer-to-peer network enables any or all of the machines on the network to act as a server. As long as the total number of machines on the network stays relatively low, no problem occurs. As the number of machines begins to go past 20–30, the entire network begins to slow down. If one file is being shared heavily, even five or six machines can bring the entire system to a crawl.

Security is the other big weakness of peer-to-peer networks. Each system on a peer-to-peer network maintains its own security (this is called *distributed security*). Microsoft has really poor network security. When a Windows 9*x* system shares a resource like a folder or printer, it only has three levels of network rights from which to choose:

- Read-Only
- Full Access
- Depends On Password

Microsoft does this on purpose. If you want real security, you need to buy Windows 2000. But even a network composed only of Windows 2000 machines requires that you place a local account on every system. So, even though you get better security in a Windows 2000 Professional peer-to-peer network, system administration entails a lot of running around to individual systems to create and delete local users every time someone joins or leaves the network.

Windows peer-to-peer networks organize the networked systems into *workgroups*, which is little more than a method for organizing systems in a pretty way so that navigating through Network Neighborhood is a little easier (Figure 20-40). In reality, workgroups have no security value.

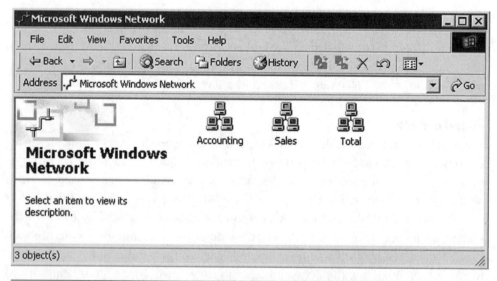

**Figure 20-40**   Multiple workgroups in a network

Peer-to-peer remains very popular, however, because the price (usually free because it comes with Windows 9x and 2000 Professional) combined with its tremendous ease of use make peer-to-peer the NOS of choice for smaller networks that do not need the high level of protection and the high speed provided by client/server network operating systems.

Many people feel that part of the definition of a peer-to-peer network includes the use of the TCP/IP protocol. This is not true; you can run a peer-to-peer network composed of all Windows 2000 Professional systems using only the NetBEUI protocol if you desire. Windows 9x and Windows 2000 always assume you want to use TCP/IP and automatically install it—I guess that's where the idea came from.

## Domain-Based

Client/server networks, especially NetWare, dominated networking for many years. In order to access a NetWare server, you must have an account created on that system, and then go through a logon process. Each serving system stores a database of accounts and passwords. If you want to access a server, you must log on. When only one server exists, the logon process takes only a second and works very well. The trouble comes when your network contains multiple servers. In that case, every time you access a different server, you must repeat the logon process (Figure 20-41). In larger networks containing many servers, this becomes a time-consuming nightmare, not only for the user but also for the network administrator. Imagine if Tom Smith decides to quit the company. The network administrator must walk up to each server and delete the account—a major hassle.

**Figure 20-41**
Peer-to-peer

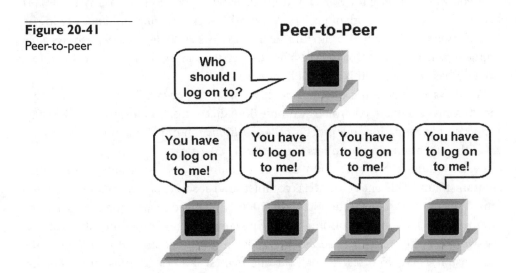

A domain-based NOS uses a different concept. In a domain-based environment, one server holds the security database for all systems. This one database holds a single list of all users and passwords. When you log on to your computer or to any computer, the logon request goes to this single system, called the *Primary Domain Controller* (PDC) in Windows NT, to verify the account and password (Figure 20-42). Obviously, the PDC is a very important system, so Microsoft enables other systems to act as *Backup Domain Controllers* (BDCs) that can take over in case the PDC goes down. Domain-based security saves time and effort.

**Figure 20-42**
Just log on to me!

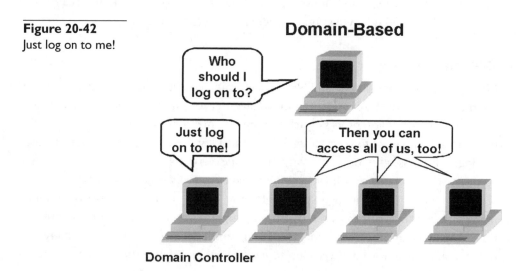

Domain Controller

If you wanted to use the power of domains, you needed to purchase Windows NT Server. If you had a network of just NT Workstation systems, you would need to log on to each system separately. This is still true in Windows 2000. Figure 20-43 shows what happens when you attempt to access another system; it requires you to log on. In a domain-based network, this will not happen.

Windows 2000 does not use the PDC/BDC. Instead, any Windows 2000 Server system becomes a domain controller. Multiple domain controllers all automatically share the security information in a process called *replication*. If one domain controller fails, all of the other domain controllers automatically take over.

Every Windows NT and 2000 system contains a very special account called "administrator." This one account has complete and absolute power over the entire system. When you install Windows NT or 2000, you must create a password for the administrator account. As you might imagine, anyone who knows the administrator password has the ability to read any file and run any program. You should keep the administrator password secret to all but the highest level of administrators. Equally important, losing the administrator password usually requires completely reinstalling Windows NT or 2000—so don't lose it!

**Figure 20-43**
Trying to access
another Windows
2000 system
without a domain

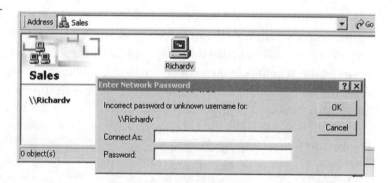

NOTE  Some third-party "find the administrator account" packages and services are available, but they are all difficult to use and expensive.

Any Windows 9x system may also become a member of a domain, although Windows 9x's use of non-NTFS file systems makes its sharing security much weaker than Windows NT or Windows 2000 systems. We usually add Windows 9x systems to a domain simply as clients. To make or change a Windows 9x system's workgroup membership, use the Identification tab in the Network Neighborhood properties (Figure 20-44).

**Figure 20-44**
Changing the
workgroup in
Windows 98

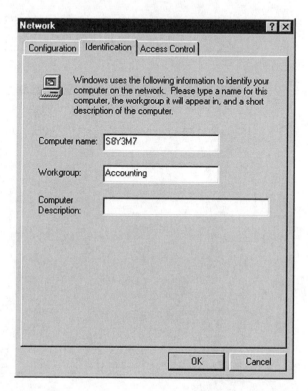

Making or changing a domain membership takes a little more effort. Click on the properties for Client for Microsoft Networks, check Log on to Windows NT domain (even if it is a Windows 2000 domain), and then enter the domain name as shown in Figure 20-45. Windows 2000, as usual, makes the process a little easier. Open the properties for My Computer, and select the Network Identification tab, as shown in Figure 20-46. This shows your current selection.

**Figure 20-45**
Entering a domain name in Windows 98

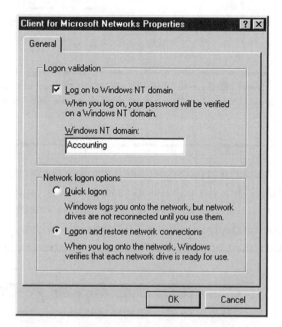

**Figure 20-46**
Network Identification tab

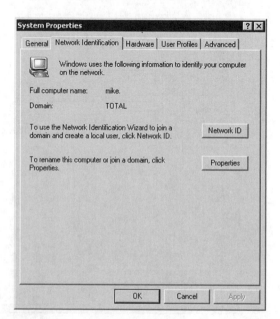

Clicking the Network ID button opens the Network Identification Wizard, but most techs just use the Properties button (Figure 20-47). They both do the same thing, but the wizard does a lot of explaining that you don't need if you know what you want to do. Make sure you have a good domain account when logging into a domain, or you won't be able to log in.

**Figure 20-47**
Network
Properties
button

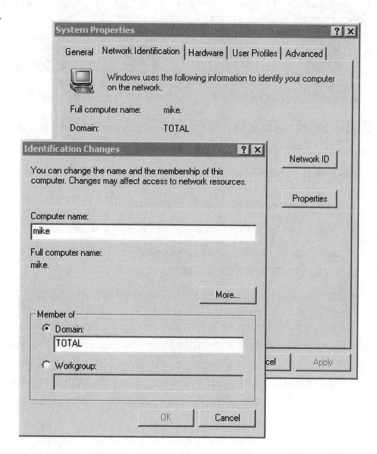

## Local Groups and Global Groups

Domain-based networks create a problem. Imagine a network of only Windows 2000 Professional systems. Each of these systems uses NTFS permissions. As we know from Chapter 11, each of these systems has local user accounts and local groups (Figure 20-48).

So what happens when we add a Windows 2000 Server system and create a domain? Do the local user accounts and local groups disappear? No! Windows domain-based networks create a second layer of accounts and groups called domain accounts. For a user to log in to a domain, he or she must have a domain account on the domain controller. How do we deal with two sets of users and two sets of domains?

# Local Users and Groups

**Figure 20-48**   How do you deal with multiple sets of users and groups?

Easy, we use them in a very special way. Here are the rules as stipulated by Microsoft:

- Individual people get a global user account.

- Global user accounts become members of global groups.

- Each system (Server or Professional) creates local groups. Each local group gets NTFS permissions on that local system.

- Domain-based networks should not use local accounts.

The beauty of this setup lies in the flexibility. An administrator may create domain accounts and domain groups from any Windows 2000 Server system. (You cannot create domain accounts or groups on Windows 2000 Professional.) The only time they still need to run around is if they need to change a local group on a remote system, and Windows 2000 provides remote manipulation of local groups! Lazy people really like Windows 2000!

Windows 2000 domains add another layer of complexity that did not exist in Windows NT: the Active Directory. The Active Directory is a common organizational database of all that is in the network, even when a network uses multiple domains! By creating this one storage area for every user account, every shared folder, every printer, everything that is the network, applications can oversee powerful administration functions. Active Directory is not required in a Windows 2000 domain-based network, but it makes a lot of tasks easier for administrators.

> **EXAM TIP**   Don't panic about domains and domain groups and all that stuff; just understand that a domain provides a centralized security function and that you must have at least one copy of Windows NT Server or Windows 2000 Server to have a domain. The rest was added just for completeness. If you really want to get into networks, take the Network+ certification and then go for the *Microsoft Certified Systems Engineer* (MCSE) certification!

Enough of this conceptual talk! The A+ Certification exams assume you know how to configure a Windows 9*x* or Windows 2000 Professional system to work on either a Windows peer-to-peer or Windows domain-based network. Fortunately, the process follows Mike's Four-Layer Model that we discussed at the beginning of this chapter:

1. **Hardware**   Cabling, installing NICs

2. **Protocol**   Choosing the network protocol to use

3. **Network**   Enabling sharing, naming the system

4. **Resource Sharing**   Providing resources to share and accessing those shared resources

All four layers work great for explaining all kinds of networks, and especially well for Windows networks! Let's march through the four-layer process of installing a Windows 9*x* or Windows 2000 machine on a network!

## Installing NICs

We've already covered most of the hardware issues. At this point, we assume that you have all the network cabling installed and you are getting ready to set up a system for networking. The first step is to install NIC. Installing NIC into any version of Windows is usually a no-brainer, as most NICs today are completely Plug and Play. For the most part, it is simply a matter of turning off the PC, installing the card, and turning the system back on. The only trick is to remember that you should use the disk that comes with the NIC, even if Windows offers to use its own drivers. All of the issues discussed with respect to installing devices also hold true for NICs—just because they are network cards doesn't mean anything else special needs to happen. If the NIC shows up in the Device Manager, you're done with this step. If it doesn't, go back to any of the previous chapters and review what it takes to install a device! Figure 20-49 shows a typical NIC, nicely installed in Windows 2000 Device Manager.

**Figure 20-49**
Windows 2000
showing a NIC
installed

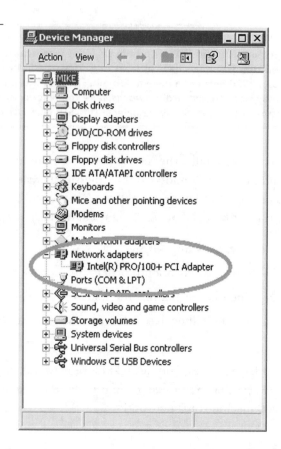

A few legacy NICs survive out there, so you still may need to install a NIC manually. As with all cards in the PC, NICs will use an I/O address and IRQ. Some will even use memory locations or DMA channels. It is important to remember that with legacy NICs, the card first needs to be configured using its setup program, which usually means first booting to Safe Mode Command Prompt Only to run the configuration program that came with the NIC. After setting up the NIC's I/O address, IRQ, and so on, you restart Windows, install the NIC's driver, and manually set the system resources for the NIC in the Device Manager. Although some cards still use jumpers, most NICs use software-based resource setting manifested by a setup/install program on an accompanying floppy disk. Figure 20-50 shows a screen shot from such a program.

These programs should only be run from Safe Mode Command Prompt Only or from a bootable floppy, because Windows will invariably interfere with them if you try to install them in Windows. After you set up the NIC, be sure to save the information on the card (some do this automatically). Then, write down the information so that you don't have to try to remember it when you need to set up the system resources

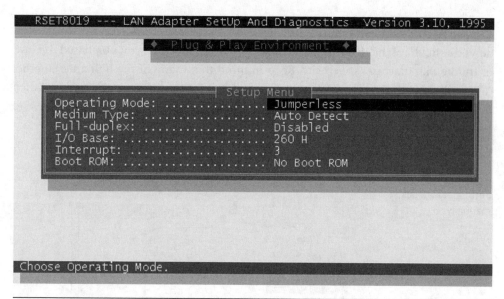

**Figure 20-50** DOS setup program for a NIC

manually. If you forget, you'll just get to run that setup program again. After the card has been installed, you can then install the drivers manually. Click the Install New Hardware icon in the Control Panel. Although Windows will often find a legacy card automatically, it's usually faster to do the install manually. Select Network Adapters and then click the Have Disk button to tell Windows where to locate the driver (Figure 20-51).

**Figure 20-51**
Have Disk button

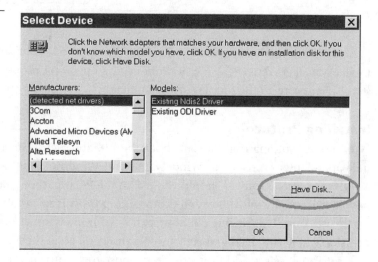

If the NIC did not come with a diskette, check to see if Windows has a driver. If Windows doesn't have the driver, contact the company from which you purchased the card or try the manufacturer's Web site. Keep in mind that many of the no-name Ethernet cards will use a driver called NE2000 compatible. Most of the time, the card will then install itself with a series of preset, and always incorrect, resources that you'll have to correct manually (Figure 20-52).

**Figure 20-52**
Setting resources manually

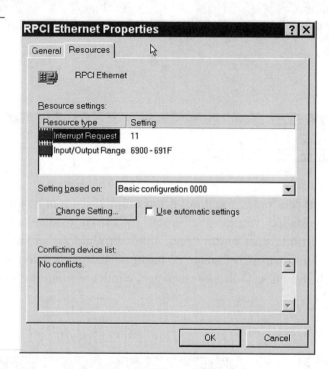

After setting the proper resources, restart Windows one more time and reopen the Device Manager. Verify that the network card is operating properly. Congratulations, step 1, Hardware, of the four layers is complete!

## Installing Protocols

Windows 95 automatically installs both the IPX and NetBEUI protocols whenever a network adapter is installed. Windows 98 and Windows 2000 automatically install TCP/IP. So which protocol should you use? If the PC is part of a network, the network people will usually tell you which protocol or protocols to install. Virtually the entire world uses only TCP/IP, but Windows comes with many other protocols. On the rare occasion where you need to install another protocol, go to the Network window in the Control Panel, select Add Protocol, and choose the protocol you wish to install (Figure 20-53).

**Figure 20-53**
Adding a network
protocol

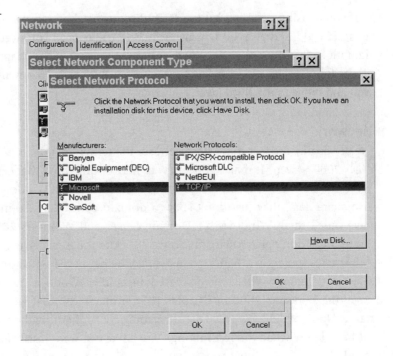

In many networks, it is common to have a number of protocols installed in order to support different NOSs. Figure 20-54 shows a system with both the NetBEUI and the TCP/IP protocols loaded.

**Figure 20-54**
Two protocols
installed

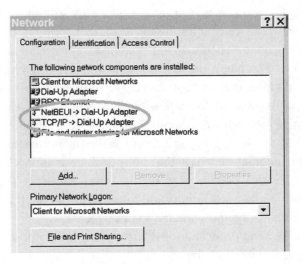

If you're using anything *but* the TCP/IP protocol, that's all you need to do. If you're using TCP/IP (and everybody is using TCP/IP these days) you need to do a lot of configuration! I've given TCP/IP its own section at the end of the chapter just to talk about all the fun configuration work you need to do! But for the moment, we'll assume all is well and move to the third layer: Network.

## Network

I really dislike the fact that Microsoft uses the terms "Windows NT Server" and "Windows 2000 Server." It makes folks new to networking think that only these versions of Windows share data. We now know that Windows 9*x* and Windows 2000 Professional also share data; they just don't share a domain controller! I think Microsoft should have called them Windows NT Domain Server and Windows 2000 Active Directory Server, but I don't own Microsoft, so we'll stick to the terms given.

Every computer on a Windows network, whether peer-to-peer or domain-based, gets a network name. When we discussed installing Windows 9*x* in Chapter 10 and installing Windows 2000 in Chapter 11, you may recall that we gave the computer a name. Now you know why we did this. You were configuring the system for a network. I'll bet I know what you're thinking: "But Mike, we were just installing the system as stand-alone in those chapters. What good is a computer name in a stand-alone system?" You're right! Computer names in stand-alone systems *are* meaningless; Microsoft just wants you to name it in case you decide to install it on a network later.

So, the first part of the network layer, the computer's name, is handled at install. The second part, setting the system as sharing or not sharing, varies between Windows 9*x* and Windows 2000.

With Windows 9*x*, any PC can be a server or a workstation. By default, all machines are workstations. To make a PC a server, some extra software, called a *service,* must be added. A special service enables the PC to share its printers, its hard drives, or both. Once again, open the Network applet. A second way to get to the Network applet is by alternate-clicking on Network Neighborhood and selecting Properties (Figure 20-55). This also works for Windows 2000, but the screen is very different!

Click on Add again, and this time select Services | Locate File | Print Sharing. You can choose to share files, printers, or both (Figure 20-56).

Windows 2000 doesn't give you a choice, as file and printer sharing are automatically installed. You automatically have the ability to share anything. To see this, select Properties under My Network Places to see the screen shown in Figure 20-57. Select the properties for your network connection to see Figure 20-58. It looks just like the Windows 9*x* one. Remember how you got to this screen!

Note that File and Printer Sharing is already installed. If for some reason you wanted to *stop* sharing, just uncheck the box.

**Figure 20-55**
Much faster than
going to the
Control Panel!

**Figure 20-56**
File and
Print sharing
options in
Windows 9x

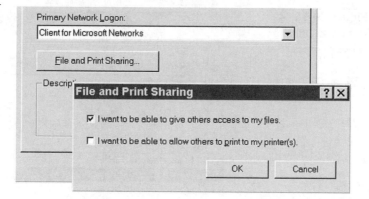

**EXAM TIP** Only systems that have File and Printer Sharing enabled are
visible in Network Neighborhood!

Super! The system has a name and we've set up the machine so that it can share
resources. But installing File and Printer Sharing simply gives the machine the *ability* to
share. To start actually sharing requires the last layer of my Four-Layer Model: Sharing
Resources.

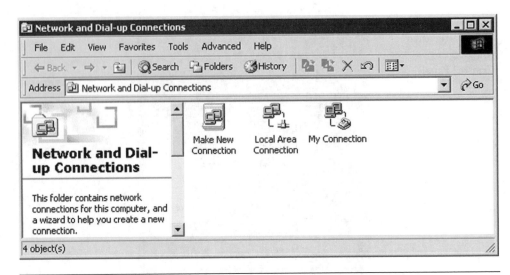

**Figure 20-57** Network and Dial-up Connections

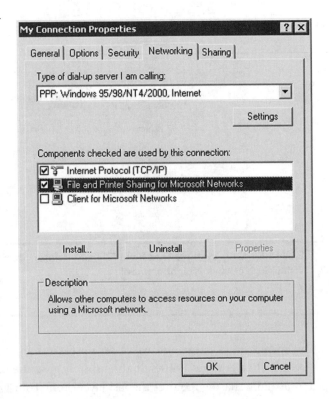

**Figure 20-58**
Windows 2000
network properties

## Sharing Resources

Windows systems can share all kinds of resources: files, folders, entire drives, printers, faxes, Internet connections, and much more. Conveniently for you, the A+ Certification exams limit their interests to folders, printers, and Internet connections. Let's see how to share folders and printers now; we'll save Internet connection sharing for the TCP/IP section.

## Sharing Drives and Folders

All versions of Windows share drives and folders in basically the same manner. Simply alternate-click on any drive or folder and select Sharing. If you don't see the Sharing option, that means you have not enabled File sharing on the system. In Windows 9*x*, the following menu appears (Figure 20-59).

**Figure 20-59**
Sharing window

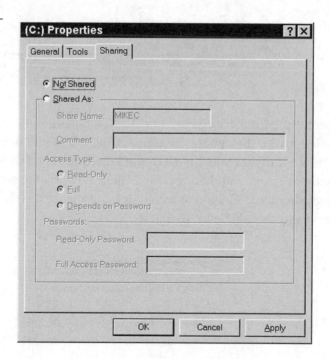

By clicking on the Shared As radio button, you can add a share name. This is the name that the other workstations will see when they are looking for resources to access. The trick here is to give it a name that clearly describes the resource. For example, if the goal is to share a C: drive, sharing that drive as "C:" could confuse this C: drive with other C: drives being shared around the network. Instead, try a more detailed name like FREDC or SALES3C. As a rule, try to keep the name short and without spaces (Figure 20-60).

**Figure 20-60**
Sharing the folder

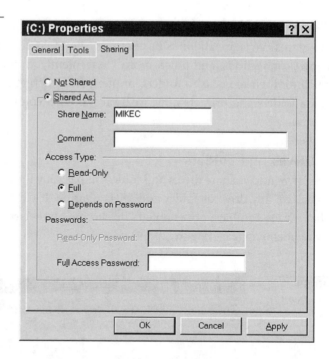

After establishing the share name, note that you can determine *how* it is to be shared. Under Windows 9*x*, the options are simple: Full, Read-Only, and Depends On Password. This is one of the major limitations of Windows 9*x* networks. We'll do Windows 2000 next to see some real sharing power! After you select the network name and the access level, click the OK button to see a little hand appear; this shows that the network resource is being shared (Figure 20-61).

**Figure 20-61**
Shared drive

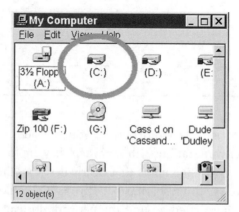

Windows 2000 folder shares are created the same way, with a little added complexity due to Windows 2000's use of NTFS. When you select the properties for a folder in Windows 2000 and select the Sharing tab, you see Figure 20-62. Select Share this folder, add a Comment and a User limit if you wish (they're not required), and click Permissions to see Figure 20-63.

**Figure 20-62**
Windows Sharing
tab on NTFS volume

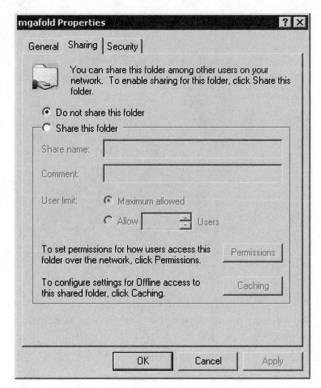

Hey! Doesn't NTFS have all those wild permissions like Read, Execute, Take Ownership, and all that? Yes it does, but NTFS permissions and network permissions are totally separate beasties. Microsoft wanted Windows 2000 to support many different types of partitions, old and new (NTFS, FAT16, FAT32, HPFS); Bill Gates wants everyone's business! Network permissions are Bill's way of enabling you to administer file sharing on any type of partition supported by Windows, no matter how ancient. Sure, your options will be pretty limited if you are working with an older partition type, but you *can* do it. The beauty of Windows 2000 is that it gives you another tool—NTFS permissions—that can do much more. NTFS is where the power lies, but power always comes with a price: You have to configure two separate sets of permissions. If you are sharing a folder on an NTFS drive, as you normally are these days, you must set *both* the network permissions and the NTFS permissions to let others access your shared resources.

**Figure 20-63**
Network
permissions

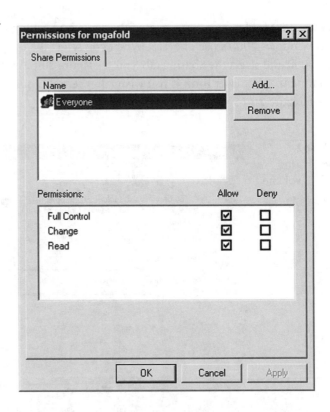

Some good news: This is actually no big deal! Just set the network permissions to give everyone full control, and then use the NTFS permissions to exercise more precise control over *who* accesses the shared resources and *how* they access them. Click the Security tab to set the NTFS permissions.

 **NOTE** Windows 2000 has two types of sharing: Network permissions and NTFS permissions. Windows 9x has only Network permissions.

## Accessing Shared Drives/Directories

Once you have set up a drive or directory to be shared, the final step is to access that shared drive or directory from another machine. In Windows 9x, you access the shared devices through the Network Neighborhood (Figure 20-64). Windows 2000 uses My Network Places, although you'll need to do a little clicking to get to the shared resources (Figure 20-65).

**Figure 20-64**
Shared resources
in Network
Neighborhood

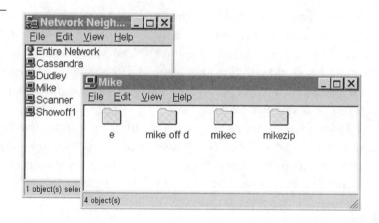

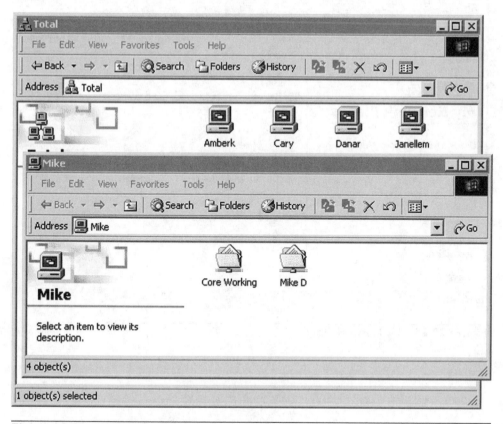

**Figure 20-65**   Shared resources in My Network Places

Network resources can also be "mapped" to a local resource name. For example, the FREDC share can be mapped to be a local hard drive such as E: or F:. This can be done in Windows 9*x* from Windows Explorer or by alternate-clicking on a share in Network Neighborhood and selecting Map Network Drive. Mapping is usually done when you want a permanent connection, or to support older programs that might have trouble accessing a drive called FREDC.

Windows 2000 supports Map Network Drive, but it adds a handy Add Network Place icon in My Network Places. This lets you add network locations you frequently access without using up drive letters (Figure 20-66). Here's my Windows 2000 system. Notice the "3rd Edition" network place? I've been going there a lot lately!

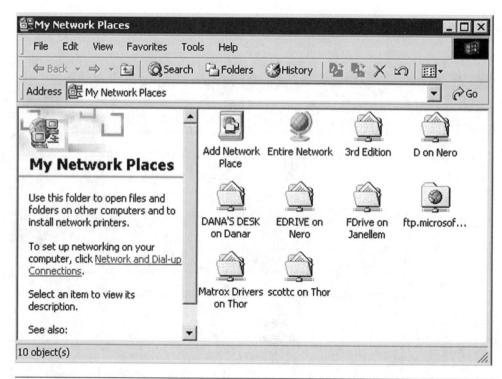

**Figure 20-66**   My Network Places

## UNC

All computers that share must have a network name, and all of the resources they share must also have a network name. Any resource on the network can be described by combining the names of the sharing system and the resource being shared. If a machine called SERVER1 is sharing its C: drive as FREDC, the complete name would be described like this:

```
\\SERVER1\FREDC
```

This is called the *Universal Naming Convention* (UNC). The UNC is distinguished by its use of double backslashes in front of the sharing system name, and a single backslash in front of the shared resource name.

## Sharing Printers

Sharing printers in Windows is just as easy as sharing drives and directories. Assuming that the system has printer sharing services loaded, just go to the Printers folder in the Control Panel and alternate-click the printer you wish to share. Select properties, go to the Sharing tab, click Shared As, and give it a name (Figure 20-67).

**Figure 20-67**

Giving a name to a shared printer

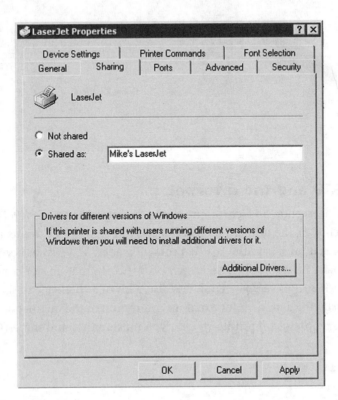

To access a shared printer in any version of Windows, simply click the Add Printer icon in the Printers folder. When asked if the printer is Local or Network, select Network; browse the network for the printer you wish to access, and Windows takes care of the rest! In almost all cases, Windows will copy the printer driver from the sharing machine. In the rare case where it doesn't, it will prompt you for the drivers.

Before Windows 95, most network printing was done via the redirection of an LPT port. A printer would be installed and an unused LPT port, like LPT2 or LPT3, would then take all of the print information. This redirected LPT would then send the print job over the network to the proper network printer. Although this is unnecessary in most cases today, all versions of Windows still provide this option to support older applications (Figure 20-68).

**Figure 20-68**
Capturing a printer port

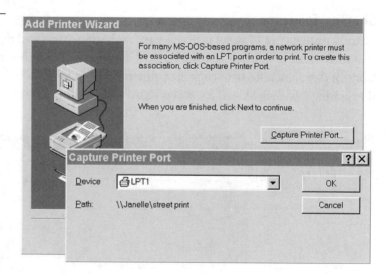

## TCP/IP and the Internet

This final section on Networking covers the Internet and TCP/IP. TCP/IP, or to be more correct, IP, is the primary protocol of the Internet. If a PC wants to have access to the Internet, it must have the TCP/IP protocol loaded. TCP/IP has become so predominant that most network folks use it even on networks that do not connect to the Internet. While TCP/IP is very powerful, it is also a bit of a challenge to set up. So whether you are installing a modem for a dial-up connection to the Internet or setting up 500 computers on their own private *intranet*, you must understand some TCP/IP basics.

## TCP/IP Basics

In a TCP/IP network, the systems don't have names. Instead, they use four sets of eight binary numbers (octets) separated by a period. This is called *dotted-octet notation.* So, instead of a computer being called SERVER1, it gets a name like

```
202.34.16.11
```

Remember, there are $2^8 = 256$ different permutations that an eight-bit binary number can have, from eight 0's (00000000) to eight 1's (11111111). So instead of writing an address like

```
11110010.00000101.00000000.00001010
```

the TCP/IP folks decided to write the decimal equivalents:

```
00000000 = 0
00000001 = 1
00000010 = 2
. . .
11111111 = 255
```

This method enables a total of 256 different octets. So, in theory, you have all the IP addresses from 0.0.0.0 to 255.255.255.255. Unfortunately, certain rules in the TCP/IP world make many IP addresses unusable. For example, no address may use all 0's or all 1's, making addresses such as 207.255.43.167 illegal (255 is 11111111 in binary and is not allowed). This significant reduction in IP addresses, combined with the explosion of new systems on the Internet, has actually placed a serious strain on the number of available IP addresses. This shortage of IP addresses has led to the creation of a method that enables systems to share IP addresses (see "DHCP/WINS," later in this chapter).

TCP/IP is a very different type of protocol. Although it certainly supports file and printer sharing, it adds a number of special sharing functions unique only to TCP/IP. These are lumped together under the umbrella term of *TCP/IP services.* The most famous TCP/IP service is called *HyperText Transfer Protocol* (HTTP), the language of the World Wide Web. If you want to surf the Internet, you must have TCP/IP. But TCP/IP supplies many other services beyond just HTTP. You can access a remote system as though you were actually in front of that machine; this service is called TELNET. Another example is a handy utility called PING. PING enables one machine to check whether it can communicate with another machine. Figure 20-69 shows an example of PING running on a Windows 2000 system. Isn't it interesting that many TCP/IP services run from a command prompt! Good thing you know how to access one!

```
C:\WINNT\System32\cmd.exe                                              _ □ X

C:\>ping 192.168.4.253

Pinging 192.168.4.253 with 32 bytes of data:

Reply from 192.168.4.253: bytes=32 time<10ms TTL=128
Reply from 192.168.4.253: bytes=32 time<10ms TTL=128
Reply from 192.168.4.253: bytes=32 time<10ms TTL=128
Reply from 192.168.4.253: bytes=32 time<10ms TTL=128

Ping statistics for 192.168.4.253:
    Packets: Sent = 4, Received = 4, Lost = 0 (0% loss),
Approximate round trip times in milli-seconds:
    Minimum = 0ms, Maximum =  0ms, Average =  0ms

C:\>
```

**Figure 20-69**   Successful PING in action

There are plenty more services that I'll show you in a moment. The goal of TCP/IP is to link together multiple networks (which we'll call *local area networks* or LANs) to make an entire *wide area network* (WAN). LANs are usually linked together via some type of telephone service, ranging from basic dial-ups to dedicated, high-speed (and expensive) data lines (Figure 20-70).

**Figure 20-70**
WAN concept

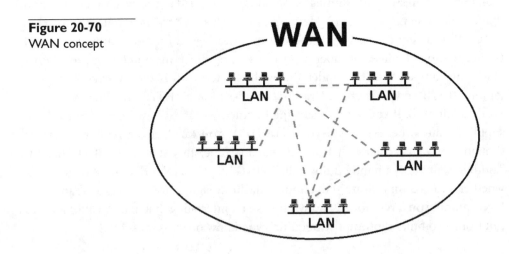

The goal is to make a WAN that uses the expensive links for as little traffic as possible. The machines that connect the phone lines to each LAN are specialized computers called *routers* (Figure 20-71). To reduce traffic, each router decides which packets on the LAN should go out to the WAN. The router makes these decisions based on the packets' IP addresses.

**Figure 20-71**   Typical router

Routers are most commonly used in TCP/IP networks, but other protocols also use them, especially IPX/SPX. There are even special routers called *brouters* (bridging routers) that translate between different protocols, although the translation process makes them relatively slow compared with regular routers.

## TCP/IP Settings

TCP/IP has a number of unique settings that you must set up correctly for proper network functionality. Unfortunately, these settings can be quite confusing, and quite a few of them exist. Not all settings are used for every type of TCP/IP network, and it's not always obvious where you go to set them. The two primary locations for TCP/IP settings are: one for dial-up connections (modems) and one for direct (NIC) connections. When using Windows 9x computers that use a modem to access the Internet, start in My Computer and click the Dial-up Networking icon. Alternate-click on the connections whose TCP/IP properties you wish to set, and select Properties | Server Type | TCP/IP Settings (Figure 20-72). The place to configure TCP/IP settings for direct connections is the Control Panel. Select Networks | TCP/IP, and click the Properties button (Figure 20-73).

Windows 2000 makes this a lot easier by letting you configure both dial-up and network connections using the My Network Places properties (Figure 20-74). Simply select the connection you wish to configure, and then set its TCP/IP properties.

**Figure 20-72**
TCP/IP settings
for dial-up in
Windows 95

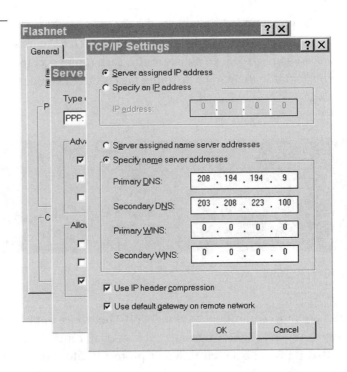

**Figure 20-73**
TCP/IP properties
in a Windows 95
system

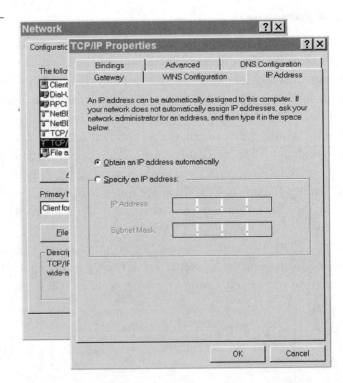

**Figure 20-74**
My Network Places
showing a dial-up
and a network
connection

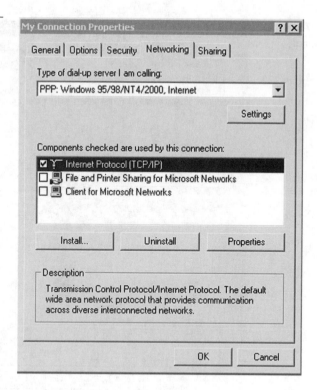

The A+ Certification exams assume that someone else, such as a tech support person or some network guru, will tell you the correct TCP/IP settings for the network. Your only job is to understand roughly what they do and to know where to enter these numbers so the system works. Let's discuss some of the more common TCP/IP settings.

 **EXAM TIP** The A+ Certification exams have a rather strange view of what you should know about networking. Take a lot of time practicing how to get to certain network configuration screens. Be ready for questions that ask "which of the following steps will enable you to change" a particular value.

## Default Gateway

A computer that wants to send data to another machine outside its LAN is not expected to know all the IP addresses of all the computers on the Internet. Instead, all IP machines know the name of one computer, to which they pass all the data they need to send outside the LAN. This machine is called the *default gateway*, and it is usually just the local router (Figure 20-75).

**Figure 20-75**
Setting a default gateway

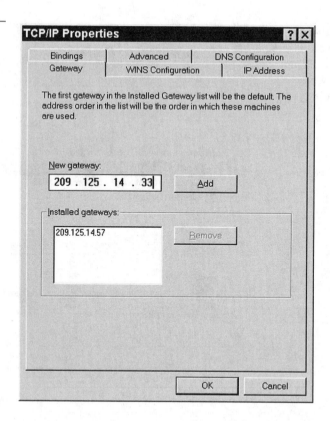

**Domain Name Service**

Knowing that users were not going to be able to handle raw IP addresses, early Internet pioneers came up with a way to correlate those numbers with more human-friendly computer designations. Special computers, called *Domain Name Service* (DNS) servers, keep databases of IP addresses and their corresponding names. For example, a machine called TOTAL.SEMINAR1 will be listed in a DNS directory with a corresponding IP address, such as 209.34.45.163. So instead of accessing the \\209.34.45.163\FREDC directory to copy a file, you can ask to see \\TOTAL.SEMINAR1\FREDC. Your system will then query the DNS server to get TOTALSEMINAR1's IP address, and use that to find the right machine. Virtually all TCP/IP networks require you to set up DNS server names (Figure 20-76).

The Internet has very regulated domain names. If you want a domain name that others can access on the Internet, you must register your domain name and pay a small yearly fee. In most cases, your Internet service provider can handle this for you. Originally, DNS names all ended with one of the following seven domain name qualifiers:

.com    General business

.org    Nonprofit organizations

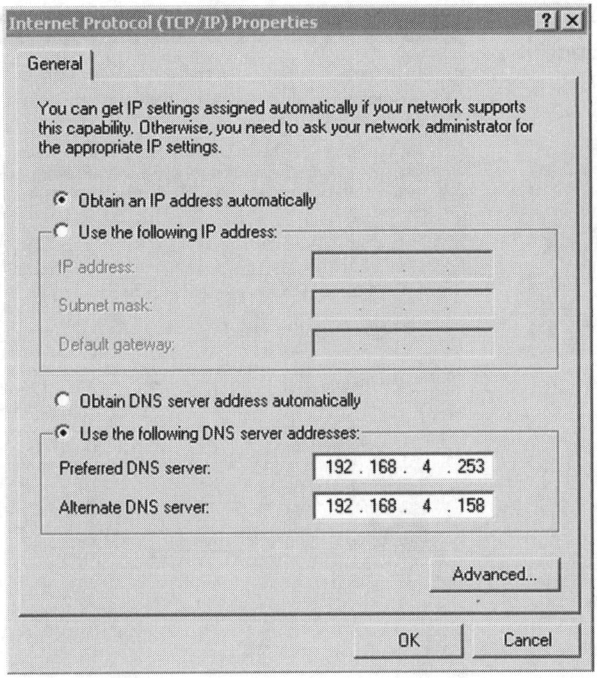

**Figure 20-76**

Adding two
DNS servers in
Windows 2000

.edu       Educational organizations

.gov       Government organizations

.mil        Military organizations

.net        Internet organizations

.int        International

As more and more countries joined the Internet, an entire new level of domains was added to reflect the country, although the original seven are still supported. It's very common to see DNS names such as **www.where.to** or **www.who.do**. Recently, the *Internet Corporation for Assigned Names and Numbers* (ICANN) announced the creation of several new domains, and given the explosive growth of the Internet, they are unlikely to be the last ones.

## DHCP/WINS

The last items that most TCP/IP networks require are *Dynamic Host Configuration Protocol* (DHCP) and *Windows Internet Name Service* (WINS). To understand DHCP, we must first remember that every machine must have an IP address. In many systems this is manually added to each machine in the TCP/IP properties menu. A permanent IP address assigned to a machine is known as a *static* IP address (Figure 20-77).

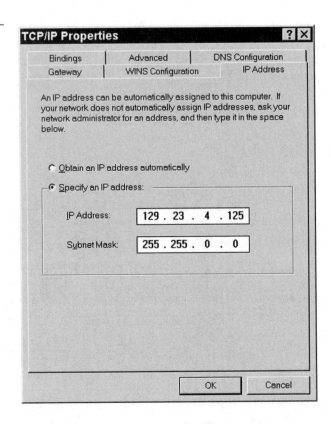

**Figure 20-77**
Setting a static IP
address

DHCP enables you to create a pool of IP addresses, which are given to machines when they need them and taken away when they are no longer needed. DHCP is especially handy for networks that have a lot of dial-in systems. Why give a machine that is only on for a few minutes a day a static IP address? For that reason, DHCP is quite popular. If you add a NIC to a Windows 2000 or Windows 98 system, the TCP/IP settings are set to use DHCP. When you accept those automatic settings, you're really telling the machine to use DHCP (Figure 20-78).

WINS enables Windows network names like SERVER1 to be correlated to IP addresses, like DNS does; except we're talking about *Windows* network names, not Internet names. All you have to do to set up WINS is either type in the IP address for the WINS server, or let DHCP handle it for you (Figure 20-79). Windows 2000 doesn't use WINS; it uses an improved "dynamic" DNS that supports both Internet names and Windows names.

**Figure 20-78**
Automatically use
IP address

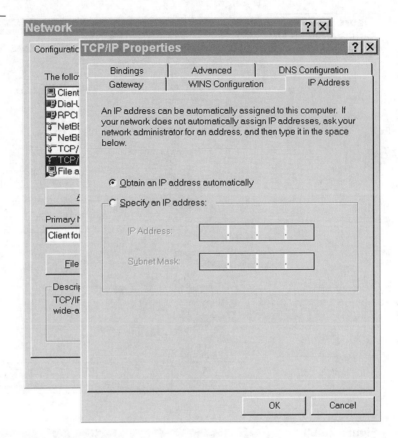

## TCP/IP Tools

All versions of Windows come with handy tools to test TCP/IP. We've already seen
PING—a really great way to see if you can talk to another system. Windows 9*x* provides
the handy WINIPCFG program. Type in **WINIPCFG** from the Run menu option to see
Figure 20-80.

Click the More Info button to see all your TCP/IP options (Figure 20-81). The Release
and Renew buttons let you get new TCP/IP information from a DHCP server.

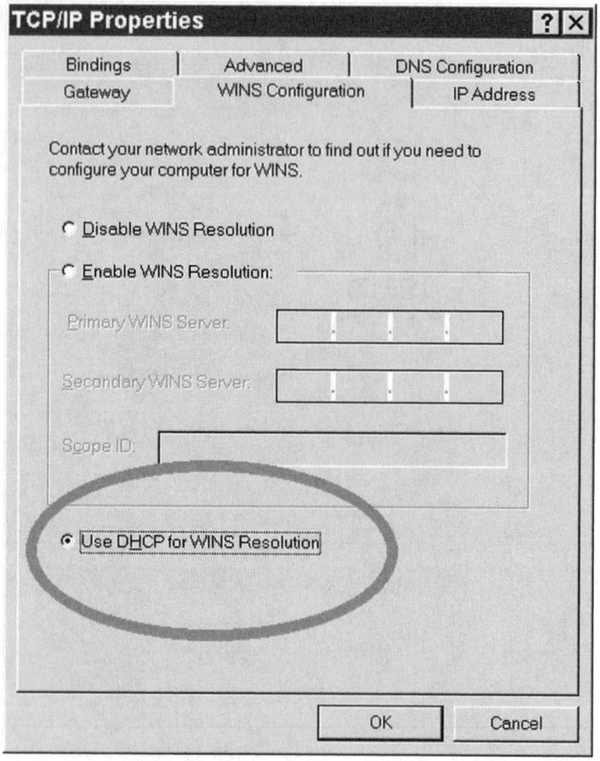

**Figure 20-79**
Setting up WINS to
use DHCP

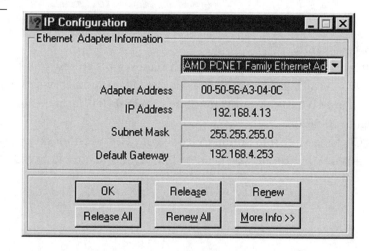

**Figure 20-80**
WINIPCFG
in action on a
Windows 98
system

**Figure 20-81**
Advanced
WINIPCFG on
Windows 98

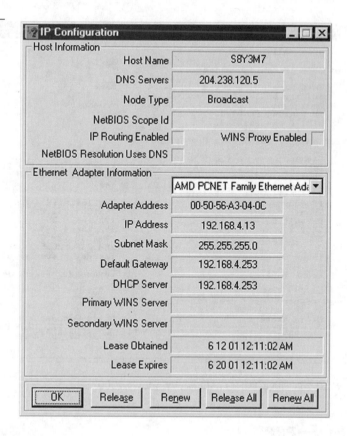

Windows 2000 does not use WINIPCFG. Instead, you once again must go to a command prompt and run IPCONFIG. You can type **IPCONFIG /ALL** to see all of your TCP/IP settings (Figure 20-82).

**EXAM TIP**   Make sure you know that Windows 9x uses WINIPCFG and Windows NT/2000 uses IPCONFIG.

```
C:\WINNT\System32\cmd.exe                                                    _ □ ✕

C:\>ipconfig /all

Windows 2000 IP Configuration

        Host Name . . . . . . . . . . . . : mike
        Primary DNS Suffix  . . . . . . . :
        Node Type . . . . . . . . . . . . : Broadcast
        IP Routing Enabled. . . . . . . . : No
        WINS Proxy Enabled. . . . . . . . : No

Ethernet adapter Local Area Connection:

        Connection-specific DNS Suffix  . :
        Description . . . . . . . . . . . : Intel(R) PRO/100+ PCI Adapter
        Physical Address. . . . . . . . . : 00-A0-C9-98-9A-40
        DHCP Enabled. . . . . . . . . . . : Yes
        Autoconfiguration Enabled . . . . : Yes
        IP Address. . . . . . . . . . . . : 192.168.4.12
        Subnet Mask . . . . . . . . . . . : 255.255.255.0
        Default Gateway . . . . . . . . . : 192.168.4.253
        DHCP Server . . . . . . . . . . . : 192.168.4.253
        DNS Servers . . . . . . . . . . . : 204.238.120.5
                                            204.238.120.5
        Lease Obtained. . . . . . . . . . : Tuesday, December 12, 2000 1:45:14 A
M
        Lease Expires . . . . . . . . . . : Wednesday, December 20, 2000 1:45:14
  AM

Ethernet adapter Local Area Connection 2:

        Media State . . . . . . . . . . . : Cable Disconnected
        Description . . . . . . . . . . . : Intel(R) PRO/100+ PCI Adapter #2
        Physical Address. . . . . . . . . : 00-A0-C9-98-12-F4

C:\>_
```

**Figure 20-82**   IPCONFIG /ALL on Windows 2000

## Dial-up—PPP

Dial-up links to the Internet have their own special hardware protocol called *Point-to-Point Protocol* (PPP). PPP is a streaming protocol developed especially for dial-up Internet access. To Windows, a modem is nothing more than a special type of network adapter. Modems will have their own configuration in the Networks settings (Figure 20-83).

As mentioned earlier, modems also have a second set of settings in the Dial-Up Networking Settings/Properties on Windows 9*x* systems. These properties are broken into three windows: the main Properties window as shown earlier, the Server Types window (Figure 20-84), and the TCP/IP Settings window shown earlier and repeated in Figure 20-85.

**Figure 20-83**
Main Window in
dial-up

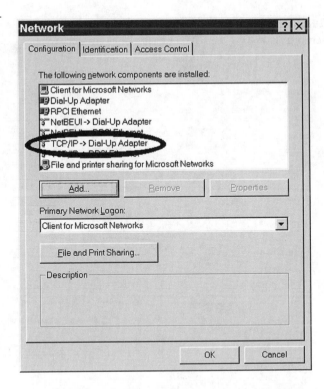

**Figure 20-84**
Server Types
window

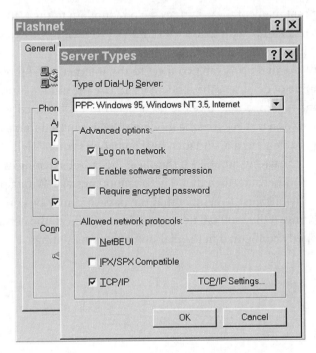

**Figure 20-85**
TCP/IP Settings

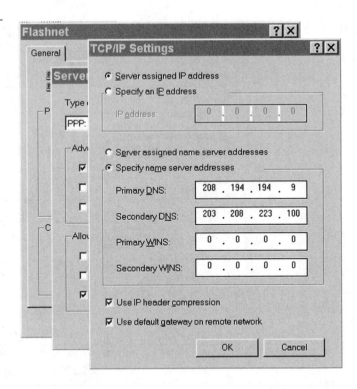

Notice that many of these settings seem redundant to the Network Settings window. The TCP/IP dial-up settings override the TCP/IP settings to enable multiple dial-up options—handy when traveling with a laptop.

Most of the dial-up "I can't connect to the Internet"-type problems are user errors. Your first line of defense is the modem itself. Use the modem's properties to make sure the volume is turned up. Have the users listen to the connection. Do they hear a dial tone? If they don't, check that the modem's line is plugged into a good phone jack. Do they hear the modem dial and then hear someone saying, "Hello? Hello?" If so, I'll bet they dialed the wrong number! If they hear the famous mating call as the modem connects on the other side, then they'll get a failure message. Wrong password failure messages are obvious; just remember that the password may be correct but the username may be wrong. If they still fail to connect, it's time to call the network folks to see what is not properly configured in the dial-up networking settings.

## Setting Up TCP/IP Services

TCP/IP offers the following commonly used services:

- World Wide Web

- E-mail

- Newsgroups

- FTP

Each of these services (sometimes referred to by the overused term of "TCP/IP proto-cols") requires a special application, and each of those applications has special settings. Let's look at all four of the services and see how to configure them.

### World Wide Web

To use the *World Wide Web* (WWW), you need a Web browser. The two most common Web browsers are Microsoft's Internet Explorer and AOL's Netscape Navigator. While the WWW is the most popular part of the Internet, setting up a Web browser takes almost no effort. As long as the Internet connection is working and WINIPCFG shows good settings, Web browsers work automatically. This is not to say that there aren't plenty of settings, but the default browser settings work almost every time. If you type in a Web address and it doesn't work, check the line, make sure the DNS server is up (PING works great for this!), and you'll know where the problem is! Browsers are trivial as far as troubleshooting is concerned.

---

**NOTE** PING may be your best friend for diagnosing TCP/IP errors. PING always works; you don't need to log on to a server or even log on to a system. You can type in either DNS names or IP addresses. You can even PING yourself—just type PING 127.0.0.1 (127.0.0.1 is known as the loopback address). If you get the famous "Request timed out" message, the device you are trying to ping is not available. When using PING on the Internet, however, "Request timed out" messages are fairly common.

---

### E-Mail

You need an e-mail program to access e-mail. The two most popular are Microsoft's Outlook Express and Netscape's Messenger. E-mail clients need a little more setup. First, you must provide your e-mail address and password. All e-mail addresses come in the now-famous **accountname@Internet domain** format. Figure 20-86 shows me adding my e-mail information to Outlook Express.

**Figure 20-86**
Adding an e-mail
account to Outlook
Express

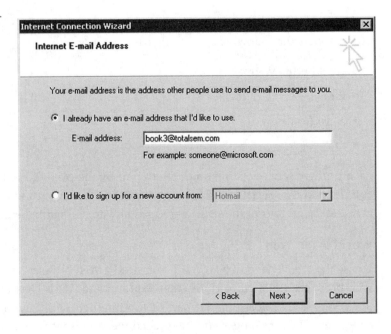

The second item that you must add is the *Post Office Protocol version 3* (POP3) server and the *Simple Mail Transfer Protocol* (SMTP) server names. The *Post Office Protocol version 3* (POP3) server is the name of the computer that handles outgoing e-mail. The SMTP server provides you with your incoming e-mail. These two systems may often have the same, or close to the same name, as shown in Figure 20-87. All of these settings should be provided to you by your Internet service. If they are not, you should be comfortable knowing what to ask for. If either one is incorrect, you will either not get your e-mail or not be able to send e-mail. If an e-mail setup that has been working well for a while suddenly gives you errors, either the POP3 or SMTP server is down, or the DNS server has quit working.

When I'm given the name of a POP3 or SMTP server, I use PING to determine the IP address for the device, as shown in Figure 20-88. I make a point to write this down.

If I ever have a problem getting mail, I'll go into my SMTP or POP3 settings and type in the IP address (Figure 20-89). If my mail starts to work, I know the DNS server is not working.

**Figure 20-87**
Adding POP3 and
SMTP information in
Outlook Express

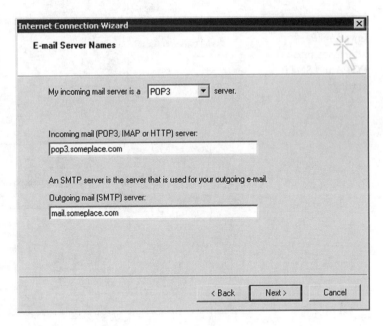

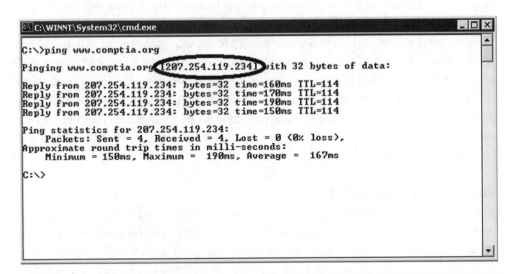

**Figure 20-88**   Using PING to determine the IP address

**Figure 20-89**
Entering IP addresses into POP3 and SMTP settings

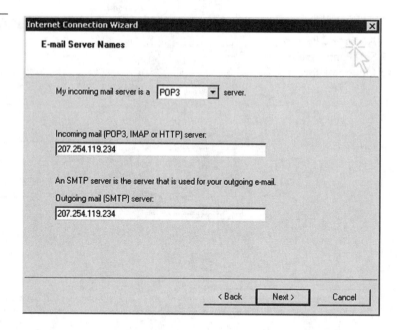

## Newsgroups

Newsgroups are one of the oldest services of the Internet. To access a newsgroup, you must use a newsreader program. A number of third-party newsreaders exist, such as the popular Forté Free Agent included on the CD-ROM that comes with this book, but Microsoft's Outlook Express is the most common of all newsreaders, given the fact it comes for free with most versions of Windows. To access a newsgroup, you must know the name of a news server. *News servers* run the *Network News Transfer Protocol* (NNTP), and you must have access to the news server. There are public news servers, but they are extremely slow. Your Internet service provider will tell you the name of the server and will provide you a username and password if necessary (Figure 20-90).

## File Transfer Protocol (FTP)

FTP is used to access systems that we would otherwise not be able to access, such as a Macintosh system. FTP is also a great way to share files, but you need an FTP server. To access an FTP site, you must use an FTP client such as WS_FTP, although later versions of Internet Explorer and other Web browsers provide support for FTP. You just type in the name of the FTP site. Figure 20-91 shows Internet Explorer accessing **ftp.microsoft.com**.

Even though you can use a Web browser, all FTP sites require you to log on. Web browsers only know the most common method, using the username "anonymous" and then your e-mail address for a password. This is called an anonymous logon and works

**Figure 20-90**
Configuring
Outlook Express
for a news server

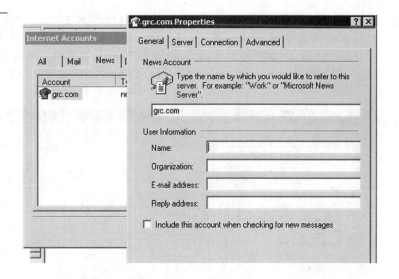

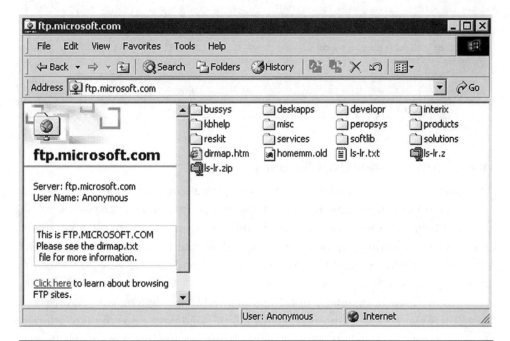

**Figure 20-91** Accessing an FTP site in Internet Explorer

fine for most public FTP sites. However, if you need to access a site that requires a special username and password, third-party programs are preferred, because they store these settings to enable you to access the FTP site later more easily than a Web browser. Figure 20-92 shows my personal favorite FTP application, WS_FTP.

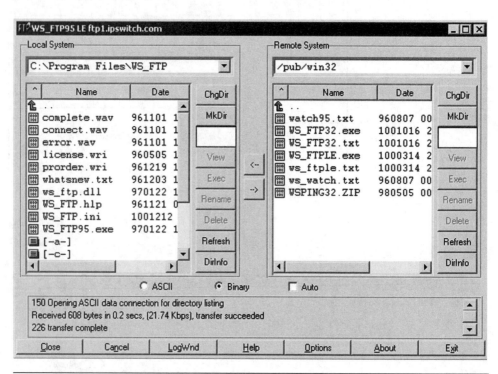

**Figure 20-92** WS_FTP

## Internet Connection Sharing

Windows 98 SE came out with a number of improvements over Windows 98, but one of the most popular was the inclusion of the very popular *Internet Connection Sharing* (ICS). ICS enables one system to share its Internet connection with other systems on the network, providing a quick and easy method for multiple systems to use one Internet connection. Windows 2000 also provides this handy tool. Figure 20-93 shows a typical setup for ICS.

Windows 98 SE does not install ICS automatically. Most systems will require you to install ICS via the Add/Remove Programs tab in Windows Setup. The ICS is located under Internet Tools options. ICS turns the sharing system into a mini-DHCP server, but there are a few minor restrictions on setup. Windows 2000, yet one more time, makes this even easier. Open the properties for My Network Places, and then open to the properties of the connection you wish to share. Click the Sharing tab, and select Enable Internet Connection Sharing For This Connection (Figure 20-94).

**Figure 20-93**
Typical ICS setup

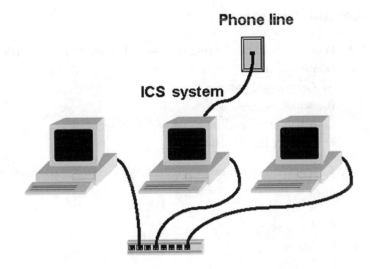

**Figure 20-94**
ICS in Windows
2000

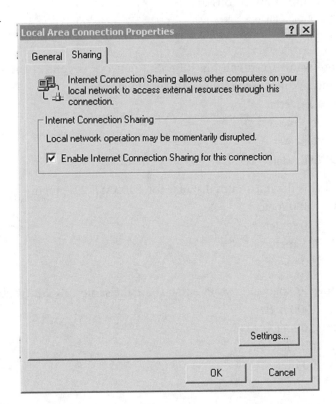

## Review Questions

1. Pick two of the following that would describe basic characteristics of a peer-to-peer network.
   A. Centralized security
   B. Bridge
   C. A relatively small number of computers
   D. Security that is distributed

2. To provide a computer a physical and electronic connection to a network, what must be installed?
   A. A hub
   B. A router
   C. A NIC
   D. A bridge

3. Which of the following is needed to configure a Plug and Play NIC in a Windows 2000 system?
   A. CMOS
   B. Configuration software
   C. Device Driver
   D. DMA

4. Jose wants to extend his 10BASE-2 network beyond its maximum segment distance. Which of the following does he need?
   A. Converter
   B. Expander
   C. Repeater
   D. Extender

5. What is the maximum distance for a 10BASE-2 segment?
   A. 1,000 meters
   B. 330 meters
   C. 185 meters
   D. 100 meters

6. How far apart can two PCs that share the same 10BASE-T hub be placed?
   A. 1,000 meters
   B. 330 meters
   C. 200 meters
   D. 100 meters

7. Everything worked fine on your 10BASE-T network yesterday, but today no one can connect to the server. The server seems to be in good running order. Which of the following is the most likely problem?

    A. A malfunctioning hub.

    B. Someone changed all the passwords for server access.

    C. Someone's "T" connector has come loose on the bus.

    D. The server's cable is wired as EIA/TIA 568A and all the others are wired as EIA/TIA 568B.

8. What is the minimum specification of cable types for 100BASE-TX networks?

    A. Category 2

    B. Category 3

    C. Category 4

    D. Category 5

9. What does it mean if a network administrator can ping a resource server using its IP address but not its Internet name?

    A. The computer is not configured to use WINS.

    B. The computer is not configured to use ARP.

    C. The computer is not configured to use DHCP.

    D. The computer is not configured to use DNS.

10. Where do you go to join a Domain or Workgroup in Windows 2000?

    A. Control Panel |Network and Dial-up Connections | Network Identification tab

    B. Control Panel | System | System Properties | Network Identification tab

    C. Administrative Tools | Membership Manager | Domain tab

    D. Device Manager | Network Interface Card Properties | Identification tab

## Answers

1. **C and D.** Peer-to-peer networks have decentralized (distributed) security and can only support a relatively small number of computers.

2. **C.** A system must have a network interface card to participate in any type of network.

3. **C.** PnP only requires the proper driver.

4. **C.** Jose needs a repeater.

5. **C.** 10BASE-2 has a maximum distance of 185 meters.

6. **C.** As each system can be 100 meters from the hub, any two systems can be up to 200 meters apart.

7. **A.** Although someone might have changed all the passwords or the cables during the night, the bad hub is the most probable answer.

8. **D.** 100BASE-TX requires CAT5 rated cabling.

9. **D.** A system must have DNS configure in order to access systems by their Internet name.

10. **B.** Control Panel | System | System Properties | Network Identification tab

# INDEX

## X-Z

# INTERNATIONAL CONTACT INFORMATION

**AUSTRALIA**
McGraw-Hill Book Company Australia Pty. Ltd.
TEL +61-2-9417-9899
FAX +61-2-9417-5687
http://www.mcgraw-hill.com.au
books-it_sydney@mcgraw-hill.com

**CANADA**
McGraw-Hill Ryerson Ltd.
TEL +905-430-5000
FAX +905-430-5020
http://www.mcgrawhill.ca

**GREECE, MIDDLE EAST,**
**NORTHERN AFRICA**
McGraw-Hill Hellas
TEL +30-1-656-0990-3-4
FAX +30-1-654-5525

**MEXICO (Also serving Latin America)**
McGraw-Hill Interamericana Editores S.A. de C.V.
TEL +525-117-1583
FAX +525-117-1589
http://www.mcgraw-hill.com.mx
fernando_castellanos@mcgraw-hill.com

**SINGAPORE (Serving Asia)**
McGraw-Hill Book Company
TEL +65-863-1580
FAX +65-862-3354
http://www.mcgraw-hill.com.sg
mghasia@mcgraw-hill.com

**SOUTH AFRICA**
McGraw-Hill South Africa
TEL +27-11-622-7512
FAX +27-11-622-9045
robyn_swanepoel@mcgraw-hill.com

**UNITED KINGDOM & EUROPE**
**(Excluding Southern Europe)**
McGraw-Hill Publishing Company
TEL +44-1-628-502500
FAX +44-1-628-770224
http://www.mcgraw-hill.co.uk
computing_neurope@mcgraw-hill.com

**ALL OTHER INQUIRIES Contact:**
Osborne/McGraw-Hill
TEL +1-510-549-6600
FAX +1-510-883-7600
http://www.osborne.com
omg_international@mcgraw-hill.com